The Oxford Handbook of Work Engagement, Motivation, and Self-Determination Theory

OXFORD LIBRARY OF PSYCHOLOGY

EDITOR-IN-CHIEF

Peter E. Nathan

AREA EDITORS:

Clinical Psychology
David H. Barlow

Cognitive Neuroscience
Kevin N. Ochsner and Stephen M. Kosslyn

Cognitive Psychology
Daniel Reisberg

Counseling Psychology
Elizabeth M. Altmaier and Jo-Ida C. Hansen

Developmental Psychology
Philip David Zelazo

Health Psychology
Howard S. Friedman

History of Psychology
David B. Baker

Methods and Measurement
Todd D. Little

Neuropsychology
Kenneth M. Adams

Organizational Psychology
Steve W. J. Kozlowski

Personality and Social Psychology
Kay Deaux and Mark Snyder

OXFORD LIBRARY OF PSYCHOLOGY

Editor in Chief PETER E. NATHAN

The Oxford Handbook of Work Engagement, Motivation, and Self-Determination Theory

Edited by
Marylène Gagné

Oxford University Press is a department of the University of
Oxford. It furthers the University's objective of excellence in research,
scholarship, and education by publishing worldwide.

Oxford   New York
Auckland   Cape Town   Dar es Salaam   Hong Kong   Karachi
Kuala Lumpur   Madrid   Melbourne   Mexico City   Nairobi
New Delhi   Shanghai   Taipei   Toronto

With offices in
Argentina   Austria   Brazil   Chile   Czech Republic   France   Greece
Guatemala   Hungary   Italy   Japan   Poland   Portugal   Singapore
South Korea   Switzerland   Thailand   Turkey   Ukraine   Vietnam

Oxford is a registered trademark of Oxford University Press
in the UK and certain other countries.

Published in the United States of America by
Oxford University Press
198 Madison Avenue, New York, NY 10016

© Oxford University Press 2014

First issued as an Oxford University Press paperback, 2015

All rights reserved. No part of this publication may be reproduced, stored in
a retrieval system, or transmitted, in any form or by any means, without the prior
permission in writing of Oxford University Press, or as expressly permitted by law,
by license, or under terms agreed with the appropriate reproduction rights organization.
Inquiries concerning reproduction outside the scope of the above should be sent to the
Rights Department, Oxford University Press, at the address above.

You must not circulate this work in any other form
and you must impose this same condition on any acquirer.

Library of Congress Cataloging-in-Publication Data
The Oxford handbook of work engagement, motivation, and self-determination theory / edited by Marylene Gagne.
    pages cm.—(Oxford library of psychology)
Includes bibliographical references and index.
ISBN 978–0–19–979491–1 (hardcover); 978–0–19–027699–7 (paperback)
1. Employee motivation.   2. Autonomy (Psychology)   3. Organizational behavior.   4. Psychology, Industrial.
I. Gagne, Marylene.
HF5549.5.M63O92 2014
158.7—dc23
2014010913

9 8 7 6 5 4 3 2 1
Printed in the United States of America
on acid-free paper

SHORT CONTENTS

Oxford Library of Psychology   vii

About the Editor   ix

Contributors   xi

Table of Contents   xv

Chapters   1-432

Index   433

OXFORD LIBRARY OF PSYCHOLOGY

The *Oxford Library of Psychology,* a landmark series of handbooks, is published by Oxford University Press, one of the world's oldest and most highly respected publishers, with a tradition of publishing significant books in psychology. The ambitious goal of the *Oxford Library of Psychology* is nothing less than to span a vibrant, wide-ranging field and, in so doing, to fill a clear market need.

Encompassing a comprehensive set of handbooks, organized hierarchically, the *Library* incorporates volumes at different levels, each designed to meet a distinct need. At one level are a set of handbooks designed broadly to survey the major subfields of psychology; at another are numerous handbooks that cover important current focal research and scholarly areas of psychology in depth and detail. Planned as a reflection of the dynamism of psychology, the *Library* will grow and expand as psychology itself develops, thereby highlighting significant new research that will impact on the field. Adding to its accessibility and ease of use, the *Library* will be published in print and, later on, electronically.

The *Library* surveys psychology's principal subfields with a set of handbooks that capture the current status and future prospects of those major subdisciplines. This initial set includes handbooks of social and personality psychology, clinical psychology, counseling psychology, school psychology, educational psychology, industrial and organizational psychology, cognitive psychology, cognitive neuroscience, methods and measurements, history, neuropsychology, personality assessment, developmental psychology, and more. Each handbook undertakes to review one of psychology's major subdisciplines with breadth, comprehensiveness, and exemplary scholarship. In addition to these broadly-conceived volumes, the *Library* also includes a large number of handbooks designed to explore in depth more specialized areas of scholarship and research, such as stress, health and coping, anxiety and related disorders, cognitive development, or child and adolescent assessment. In contrast to the broad coverage of the subfield handbooks, each of these latter volumes focuses on an especially productive, more highly focused line of scholarship and research. Whether at the broadest or most specific level, however, all of the *Library* handbooks offer synthetic coverage that reviews and evaluates the relevant past and present research and anticipates research in the future. Each handbook in the *Library* includes introductory and concluding chapters written by its editor to provide a roadmap to the handbook's table of contents and to offer informed anticipations of significant future developments in that field.

An undertaking of this scope calls for handbook editors and chapter authors who are established scholars in the areas about which they write. Many of the nation's and world's most productive and best-respected psychologists have agreed to edit *Library* handbooks or write authoritative chapters in their areas of expertise.

For whom has the *Oxford Library of Psychology* been written? Because of its breadth, depth, and accessibility, the *Library* serves a diverse audience, including graduate students in psychology and their faculty mentors, scholars, researchers, and practitioners in psychology and related fields. Each will find in the *Library*

vii

the information they seek on the subfield or focal area of psychology in which they work or are interested.

Befitting its commitment to accessibility, each handbook includes a comprehensive index, as well as extensive references to help guide research. And because the *Library* was designed from its inception as an online as well as a print resource, its structure and contents will be readily and rationally searchable online. Further, once the *Library* is released online, the handbooks will be regularly and thoroughly updated.

In summary, the *Oxford Library of Psychology* will grow organically to provide a thoroughly informed perspective on the field of psychology, one that reflects both psychology's dynamism and its increasing interdisciplinarity. Once published electronically, the *Library* is also destined to become a uniquely valuable interactive tool, with extended search and browsing capabilities. As you begin to consult this handbook, we sincerely hope you will share our enthusiasm for the more than 500-year tradition of Oxford University Press for excellence, innovation, and quality, as exemplified by the *Oxford Library of Psychology*.

Peter E. Nathan
Editor-in-Chief
Oxford Library of Psychology

ABOUT THE EDITOR

Marylène Gagné, Ph.D.
Marylène Gagné is professor of industrial and organizational psychology at the University of Western Australia and was previously the Royal Bank of Canada Distinguished Professor in Work Motivation at the John Molson School of Business, Concordia University. She researches organizational and personal factors that affect worker motivation, and how this motivation affects worker performance and well-being.

CONTRIBUTORS

Nicole M. Aitken
School of Psychology
University of Ottawa
Ottawa, ON, Canada

Stéphanie Austin
Département des Sciences de la Gestion
Université du Québec à Trois-Rivières
Trois-Rivières, QC, Canada

Geneviève Beaulieu
Department of Psychology
Université de Montréal
Montréal, QC, Canada

Jacqueline Carpenter
Department of Psychology
University of Akron
Akron, OH, USA

Michel Cossette
Department of Human Resources Management
HEC Montréal
Montreal, QC, Canada

François Courcy
Département de Psychologie
Université de Sherbrooke
Sherbrooke, QC, Canada

Véronique Dagenais-Desmarais
Département de Psychologie
Université de Montréal
Montréal, QC, Canada

Edward L. Deci
Department of Clinical and Social Sciences in
Psychology
University of Rochester
Rochester, NY, USA

James M. Diefendorff
Department of Industrial/Organizational
Psychology
University of Akron
Akron, OH, USA

Anders Dysvik
Department of Leadership and Organizational
Behavior
BI Norwegian Business School
Oslo, Norway

Amar Fall
Département de Management des Ressources
Humaines
Université de Pau et des Pays de l'Adour
PAU, France

Claude Fernet
Département des Sciences de la Gestion
Université du Québec à Trois-Rivières
Trois-Rivières, QC, Canada

D. Lance Ferris
Department of Management and Organization
The Pennsylvania State University
University Park, PA, USA

Mark Fleming
Department of Psychology
Saint Mary's University
Halifax, NS, Canada

Jacques Forest
Département d'Organisation et Ressources
Humaines
UQAM School of Management Science
Montréal, QC, Canada

Marylène Gagné
School of Psychology
University of Western Australia
Crawley, Western Australia, Australia

Marie-Hélène Gilbert
Department of Management
Université Laval
Québec City, QC, Canada

Stephanie L. Gilbert
Department of Psychology
Saint Mary's University
Halifax, NS, Canada

Maynor G. González
Department of Counseling and Human
Development
University of Rochester
Rochester, NY, USA

Gary J. Greguras
Lee Kong Chian School of Business
Singapore Management University
Singapore

Frederick M. E. Grouzet
Department of Psychology
University of Victoria
Victoria, BC, Canada

Nora Hope
Department of Psychology
McGill University
Montreal, QC, Canada

Nathalie Houlfort
Département de Psychologie
Université du Québec à Montréal
Montréal, QC, Canada

E. Kevin Kelloway
Department of Psychology
Saint Mary's University
Halifax, NS, Canada

Richard Koestner
Department of Psychology
McGill University
Montreal, QC, Canada

Bård Kuvaas
Department of Leadership and Organizational
Behavior
BI Norwegian Business School
Oslo, Norway

Philippe LeBrock
Department of Psychology
Université de Montréal
Montréal, QC, Canada

John P. Meyer
Department of Psychology
The University of Western Ontario
London, ON, Canada

Mario Mikulincer
School of Psychology
Interdisciplinary Center (IDC)
Herzliya, Israel

Sigalit Ronen
Department of Management
College of Business and Economics
California State University
Northridge, CA, USA

Christopher P. Niemiec
Department of Psychology
University of Rochester
Rochester, NY, USA

Margit Osterloh
Center for Research in Economics,
Management and the Arts
Zurich, Switzerland

Alexandra Panaccio
John Molson School of Business
Concordia University
Montréal, QC, Canada

Sharon K. Parker
UWA Business School
University of Western Australia
Crawley, Western Australia, Australia

Luc G. Pelletier
School of Psychology
University of Ottawa
Ottawa, ON, Canada

Christine Porath
McDonough School of Business
Georgetown University
Washington, DC, USA

Johnmarshall Reeve
Department of Education
Korea University
Seoul, South Korea

Patrice Roussel
Département Management des Ressources
Humaines
Centre de Recherche en Management
Toulouse, France

Richard M. Ryan
Department of Clinical and Social Sciences
in Psychology
University of Rochester
Rochester, NY, USA

Natasha Scott
Department of Psychology
Saint Mary's University
Halifax, NS, Canada

Gretchen M. Spreitzer
Ross School of Business
University of Michigan
Ann Arbor, MI, USA

Dan Stone
Von Allmen School of Accountancy
University of Kentucky
Lexington, KY, USA

Karoline Strauss
Warwick Business School
University of Warwick
Coventry, UK

Yu-Lan Su
College of Education
University of Iowa
Iowa City, IA, USA

Christian Tröster
Department of Management and Economics
Kuehne Logistic University
Hamburg, Germany

Robert J. Vallerand
Department of Educational and Counselling
Psychology
Université du Québec à Montréal
Montréal, QC, Canada

Antoinette Weibel
Institute for Leadership and Human Resource
Management
University of St. Gallen
St. Gallen, Switzerland

Meike Wiemann
Institute for Leadership and Human Resource
Management
University of St. Gallen
St. Gallen, Switzerland

Geoffrey C. Williams
Healthy Living Center
Departments of Medicine, Psychiatry,
and Psychology
University of Rochester
Rochester, NY, USA

CONTENTS

1. The History of Self-Determination Theory in Psychology and Management   1
   Marylène Gagné and *Edward L. Deci*

Part One • Conceptual Issues

2. The Importance of Universal Psychological Needs for Understanding
   Motivation in the Workplace   13
   Edward L. Deci and *Richard M. Ryan*
3. Employee Commitment, Motivation, and Engagement: Exploring the Links   33
   John P. Meyer
4. Effective and Sustained Proactivity in the Workplace: A Self-Determination
   Theory Perspective   50
   Karoline Strauss and *Sharon K. Parker*
5. A Behavioral Economics Perspective on the Overjustification
   Effect: Crowding-In and Crowding-Out of Intrinsic Motivation   72
   Antoinette Weibel, Meike Wiemann, and *Margit Osterloh*
6. Passion for Work: Determinants and Outcomes   85
   Robert J. Vallerand, Nathalie Houlfort, and *Jacques Forest*

Part Two • Individual Considerations

7. The Foundation of Autonomous Motivation in the Workplace:
   An Attachment Perspective   109
   Sigalit Ronen and *Mario Mikulincer*
8. Contingent Self-Esteem: A Review and Applications to
   Organizational Research   127
   D. Lance Ferris
9. Person-Environment Fit and Self-Determination Theory   143
   Gary J. Greguras, James M. Diefendorff, Jacqueline Carpenter,
   and *Christian Tröster*

Part Three • Organizational and Contextual Considerations

10. The Motivational Power of Job Design   165
    Marylène Gagné and *Alexandra Panaccio*
11. Leadership   181
    Stephanie L. Gilbert and *E. Kevin Kelloway*
12. Compensation and Work Motivation: Self-Determination Theory
    and the Paradigm of Motivation through Incentives   199
    Amar Fall and *Patrice Roussel*

13. Self-Determination Theory and Workplace Training and Development   218
    Anders Dysvik and *Bård Kuvaas*

Part Four   •   Outcomes of Work Motivation

14. Self-Determination and Job Stress   231
    Claude Fernet and *Stéphanie Austin*

15. Self-Determination as a Nutriment for Thriving: Building an Integrative
    Model of Human Growth at Work   245
    Gretchen M. Spreitzer and *Christine Porath*

16. Emotional Labor through the Lens of Self-Determination Theory   259
    Michel Cossette

17. Understanding Why Employees Behave Safely from a Self-Determination
    Theory Perspective   276
    Natasha Scott, Mark Fleming, and *E. Kevin Kelloway*

18. Understanding Workplace Violence: The Contribution of
    Self-Determination Theory   295
    Véronique Dagenais-Desmarais and *François Courcy*

19. Encouraging Environmental Actions in Employees and in the Working
    Environment: A Self-Determination Theory Perspective   314
    Luc G. Pelletier and *Nicole M. Aitken*

20. Translating Research Results in Economic Terms: An Application of
    Economic Utility Analysis Using SDT-Based Interventions   335
    Jacques Forest, Marie-Hélène Gilbert, Geneviève Beaulieu,
    Philippe LeBrock, and *Marylène Gagné*

Part Five   •   Domains of Application

21. Teacher Motivation   349
    Johnmarshall Reeve and *Yu-Lan Su*

22. At the Interface of Work and Health: A Consideration of the Health
    Gradient using Self-Determination Theory   363
    Maynor G. González, Christopher P. Niemiec, and *Geoffrey C. Williams*

23. What is a Functional Relationship to Money and Possessions?   374
    Dan Stone

24. Development, Changes and Consolidation of Values and Goals in Business
    and Law Schools: The Dual Valuing Process Model   386
    Frederick M. E. Grouzet

25. A Self-Determination Theory Approach to Goals   400
    Richard Koestner and *Nora Hope*

26. Self-Determination Theory in the Work Domain: This is Just
    the Beginning   414
    Marylène Gagné

Index   433

CHAPTER

1

The History of Self-Determination Theory in Psychology and Management

Marylène Gagné *and* Edward L. Deci

Abstract

Self-determination theory is a theory of human motivation that has the potential to provide voluminous new knowledge to the field of organizational psychology. In this book, renowned self-determination theory researchers as well as renowned organizational psychology researchers have come together to present what they have been doing with the theory and what could be done with it in the future. This chapter presents a historical overview of the theory as it has been developed and used in general and organizational psychology over the past 40 years.

Key Words: self-determination theory, history, management, work motivation, psychology

---

The Beginnings

Self-determination theory (SDT) has developed gradually over the last 40 years to become a major theory of human motivation. It was initially developed by Edward L. Deci and Richard M. Ryan and has been elaborated and refined with the help of many other scholars from around the world. The theory was born out of an interest in the study of intrinsic motivation, defined as doing something for its own sake, out of interest and enjoyment. Accounts of seemingly intrinsically motivated behavior was provided by scholars studying the behavior of monkeys and other animals, whose behavior was not explainable using behavioristic, drive-theory principles (Berlyne, 1950, 1955; Dashiell, 1925; Harlow, 1950; Montgomery, 1952; Nissen, 1930; Premack, 1959; Welker, 1956). Hull's (1943) drive theory was dominant at the time, so researchers often described their observations of intrinsically motivated behaviors as being energized by an exploratory drive. However, the behavioral patterns associated with the so-called exploration drive did not fit the description of behaviors energized

through drives. First, exploratory behaviors did not lead to anxiety reduction so they could not be motivated by the drive to avoid pain; indeed, exploration seemed to be accompanied by excitement (Harlow, 1953). Furthermore, exploratory behaviors did not decrease following "consumption"; that is, they did not evidence the homeostatic cycle associated with drives, so the motivation underlying exploration did not align with the definition of drive. Thus, accepting the idea of an exploratory drive would have required a whole new definition of the drive.

White (1959) wrote a compelling article arguing against the use of the drive approach to describe what he labeled effectance motivation, suggesting that competence-promoting behavior "satisfies an intrinsic need to deal with the environment" (p. 318). Other motivation theorists provided other explanations for the exploratory behaviors; for example, Hebb (1955) considered them to be energized by a central nervous system need for optimal arousal. Still, White's approach gradually took hold and de Charms (1968) subsequently added that intrinsically motivated behavior resulted from a need to feel personal causation, an idea that Deci (1971) combined with a need for competence (effectance) to craft his first study on intrinsic motivation.

Amid the behaviorist movement, Deci was curious to know what happened when people were rewarded for doing something they were quite willing to do in the absence of rewards—that they were intrinsically motivated to do (Deci, 1995). Would rewards increase the enjoyment they already felt when they were engaged in interesting activities, such as a sport, a game, or a hobby? He tested this by giving a group of students a monetary reward for completing enjoyable SOMA puzzles (while a control group did the same puzzles but got no reward), and the results showed that students' intrinsic motivation and enjoyment dropped after being rewarded (Deci, 1971) relative to those who were not rewarded. In other words, their focus seemed to change from the intrinsically motivating properties of the activity to the monetary reward. Using de Charms's (1968) distinction between internal and external perceived locus of causality (not to be confused with locus of control), Deci suggested that the rewards prompted a shift in perceived locus of causality for the behavior from internal (i.e., feeling like an origin with respect to the behavior) to external (i.e., feeling like a puppet or pawn). That is, the rewards diminished people's feelings of autonomy and in so doing turned play into work (Lepper & Greene, 1975) and turned origins into pawns. Based on this hypothesis, other factors were examined and found to decrease intrinsic motivation, because they also diminished how autonomous people feel: threats, deadlines, imposed goals, surveillance, evaluations, and competition (Amabile, DeJong, & Lepper, 1976; Deci, 1972; Deci, Bentley, Kahle, Abrams, & Porac, 1981; Enzle & Anderson, 1993; Lepper & Greene, 1975; Mossholder, 1980). On the other hand, giving people choices, which allowed them to feel more autonomous, enhanced their intrinsic motivation (Zuckerman, Porac, Lathin, Smith, & Deci, 1978). Cognitive evaluation theory was born.

Refinements

In addition to showing how feelings of autonomy (locus of causality) influence intrinsic motivation, research has found that intrinsic motivation flourishes only when people feel like they are mastering their environment, which yields a feeling of competence (Vallerand & Reid, 1984; White, 1959). Competence is necessary but insufficient for being intrinsically motivated. In fact, competence is necessary for any kind of motivation, whether it be extrinsic or intrinsic; otherwise, one is likely to feel helpless and amotivated. Recent research has indeed shown that people need to feel both competent and autonomous in order to experience intrinsic motivation (Dysvik, Kuvaas, & Gagné, 2013). Although subsequent refinements concerning the effects of rewards have increased our understanding of when rewards would be experienced as controlling, thus undermining intrinsic motivation and when they would be experienced as an affirmation of competence (Ryan, Mims, & Koestner, 1983), and despite the fact that such research has led to heated debates among motivation researchers, meta-analytic findings provide strong support for cognitive evaluation theory (Deci, Koestner, & Ryan, 1999).

Ryan, Koestner, and Deci (1991) reported that sometimes, people engage in seemingly intrinsically motivated behaviors when they are in fact ego-involved. Ego-involvement is an internal type of motivation in which people's feelings of worth are dependent on what they do or how they do it, so people feel pressured or controlled to do what would make them feel worthy. This issue arose because intrinsic motivation was often measured with the so-called free-choice period in which people have various interesting activities to choose from, including a target activity. The idea was that the higher their intrinsic motivation for the target activity, the more time they would devote to it in the free-choice period; however, it turned out that if they were ego-involved with respect to the target activity, they would also spend time on it without any external prods after they had received negative performance feedback. Without examining accompanying affect, this ego-involved persistence could be wrongly labeled as being intrinsic motivation. When people are intrinsically motivated their affect is positive, but when they are ego-involved positive affect is absent and there may even be feelings of pressure or tension.

These findings have led researchers to be careful when using free-choice behavioral measures of intrinsic motivation, using some means to be sure it is accompanied by interest, enjoyment, or positive affect. Moreover, these results, and earlier ones on ego-involvement (Plant & Ryan, 1985), showed that there may be more than two types of motivation. In addition to extrinsic and intrinsic motivation, there seems to be an ego-involved type of motivation. This ego-based motivation is not prodded by outside factors, such as rewards and punishments, and although it is internally driven, it is not the same as intrinsic motivation. This has led to complementing cognitive evaluation theory with a theory of organismic integration, both of which are now under the umbrella of SDT, along with four other mini-theories: (1) causality orientations theory, (2) basic psychological needs theory, (3) goal contents theory, and (4) relationships motivation theory. Organismic integration theory relies heavily on the concept of internalization, defined as taking in values, behaviors, and beliefs and making them one's own (Ryan, 1995).

Being social animals, human beings must learn to sometimes relinquish their personal urges to do behaviors they do not find enjoyable but are presumably for their own good and are also for the good of the collective. In developmental psychology, the process of learning the norms and behaviors necessary to coexistence is called internalization. SDT, being an organismic theory, assumes that socialization is not something "done" to people, but instead is what the organism does naturally by using environmental supports and nourishments (Deci, 1995). Without such supports, the internalization functions less effectively. As Deci (1995, p. 98) put it " if you put an avocado pit in a pot of earth it will probably grow into a tree, because it is in the nature of avocados to do that . . . [But for that to occur] they need sun; they need water; and they need the right temperatures. Those elements do not make trees grow, but they are the nutriments that the developing avocados need, that are necessary in order for the avocados to do what they do naturally." In the same vein, human beings transform the values and behaviors they absorb from the environment into internal tools to regulate themselves—they internalize them—but only if they have adequate nutriments or supports for doing so.

There are two ways in which internalization can happen. If the context is pressuring and controlling, people are likely to introject a value or regulation and use it to measure their own worth (which is ego-involvement). On the other hand, if the context in which the nourishment is given makes people feel autonomous and agentic, they are likely to identify with its personal value for themselves and then integrate it into their core self-regulatory system, which in SDT is labeled the "self." What this means is that extrinsic motivation—the doing of an action that is not interesting and enjoyable to get a separate consequence—can be internalized to differing degrees resulting in different types of extrinsic motivation that, when enacted, would vary in their degree of autonomy. Ryan and Connell (1989) examined these processes in schoolchildren who,

for example, may not be intrinsically motivated to do their homework, but are asked to do it anyway. In addition to finding that children sometimes do their homework purely out of intrinsic motivation or the classic instance of extrinsic motivations, to get rewards or avoid punishments, they also found evidence for two other types of motivations: introjection (i.e., a partial internalization that involves doing something for ego reasons, to feel worthy or avoid shame) and identification (i.e., a fuller internalization that involves doing something out of personal values or self-selected goals). Introjection, like classic extrinsic motivation through rewards and punishments (which they relabeled *external regulation*), has an external perceived locus of causality, even though introjection is a motivation that is internal to the person, but is external to one's own integrated sense of self. Identification, like intrinsic motivation, has an internal perceived locus of causality because it has been more fully internalized into one's self. In order to empirically verify the consequences of these different regulatory styles, Ryan and Connell constructed the first scale that asked people to rate different reasons for doing an activity, which reflected the different regulatory styles.

This measure has led to the development of similar measures in many applied areas of psychology, such as education (e.g., Vallerand et al., 1992; Williams & Deci, 1996), sports (Pelletier, Vallerand, & Sarrazin, 2007), exercise and gymnastics (Gagné, Ryan, & Bargmann, 2003; Mullan, Markland, & Ingledew, 1997), religion (Ryan, Rigby, & King, 1993), prosocial behavior (Ryan & Connell, 1989), psychotherapy (Pelletier, Tuson, & Haddad, 1997), relationships (Blais, Sabourin, Richer, & Vallerand, 1990), health care (Williams, Grow, Freedman, Ryan, & Deci, 1996), politics (Koestner, Losier, Vallerand, & Carducci, 1996), environmental behavior (Pelletier, Tuson, Green-Demers, Noels, & Beaton, 1998), personal goals (Sheldon & Elliot, 1998), and work (Gagné, Forest, Vansteenkiste, Crevier-Braud, Van den Broeck, et al., 2014), that have become more psychometrically refined over time. This proliferation of scales consequently led to a voluminous amount of empirical research on the antecedents and consequences of these different forms of motivational regulations. For example, one recent meta-analysis of studies in the health domain used 184 different data sets (Ng, Ntoumanis, Thørgersen-Ntoumani, Deci, Ryan, Duda, & Williams, 2012). In terms of the consequences of different regulatory styles, the body of research shows that autonomous types of motivation (intrinsic motivation and identified regulation) yield more positive behavioral and affective outcomes than controlled types of motivation (external and introjected regulation) (see Deci & Ryan, 2000, 2008 for reviews).

In terms of their antecedents, the question that was raised was how to promote internalization and intrinsic motivation. Cognitive evaluation theory proposed that when people feel competent and autonomous, they are more likely to be intrinsically motivated. So, researchers examined whether the same factors would also promote internalization, and indeed they do (e.g., Deci, Eghrari, Patrick, & Leone, 1994). However, feeling related to others was also found to be important facilitator of internalization, along with competence and autonomy (e.g., Baard, Deci, & Ryan, 2004), which led to the assertion that there are three basic psychological needs that are universal necessities and that represent the essential nutriments for autonomous motivation—that is, for maintaining intrinsic motivation and promoting internalization of extrinsic motivation (e.g., Deci & Ryan, 2000; Ryan & Deci, 2000).

Various theories in psychology have emphasized the importance of competence and relatedness for human behavior and wellness, whether or not they have referred to them as universal needs. However, SDT is the only theory that has emphasized the essential nature of autonomy for well-being, and indeed the concept of a need for autonomy has been the most controversial. In their discussions of autonomy, Deci and Ryan (e.g., 1985, 2000) have clearly indicated that autonomy is not the same as independence, individualism, defiance, or detachment, that it means volition and endorsement of one's behaviors. Still, many people criticized SDT's assertion that autonomy is a universal psychological need, either confusing autonomy with the number of behavioral options available to one (Iyengar & DeVoe, 2003) or confusing it with independence (Markus & Kitayama, 2003). Their arguments were made primarily in terms of cultures, asserting that autonomy is a concept central to North American and Western European countries where independence and individualism are valued, but that it is not relevant in East Asian collectivistic cultures, where interdependence and deference are valued.

Chirkov, Ryan, Kaplan, and Kim (2003) responded that although the values are different in these parts of the world, people can enact both individualistic and collectivistic values in an autonomous way, or they can enact the values in a controlled way. Thus, autonomy versus control is conceptually orthogonal to individualism, as it is to collectivism. These researchers then did a study in which they found that the degree to which people enacted either collectivist or individualist behaviors in an autonomous way was significantly related to people's psychological health and well-being, and that this relation was not moderated by culture. In other words, regardless of which culture it was, and of the values that were emphasized within it, the greater the degree to which people in the culture behaved autonomously when enacting the behaviors their culture valued or the behaviors valued by different cultures, the greater psychological health the individuals displayed. Numerous studies have now shown that all three are universally necessary and sufficient for well-being in collectivistic as well as individualistic cultures (Bao & Lam, 2008; Vansteenkiste, Lens, Soenens, & Luycks, 2006; Vansteenkiste, Zhou, Lens, & Soenens, 2005; Zhou, Ma, & Deci, 2009).

As already mentioned, in the mid-1980s, when the third basic need (relatedness) was introduced, initially because it was important for internalization, it received considerable attention. There is much evidence in the psychology literature for the importance of relatedness for optimal development and well-being (see Ainsworth, 1979; Baumeister & Leary, 1995). Bringing relatedness into the picture, and showing how autonomy and relatedness are not inherently antagonistic, or opposite ends of a continuum, helped clarify the complementarity of the two needs (Deci & Ryan, 2000). But adding the third need also led people to question how many basic psychological needs there might be. Different candidate needs have been suggested (see Andersen, Chen, & Carter, 2000; Reis, Sheldon, Gable, Roscoe, & Ryan, 2000; Sheldon, Elliot, Kim, & Kasser, 2001), but there has not yet been a convincing case made that any other need is necessary to explain the empirical phenomena that have emerged in this literature. As such, the basic psychological needs for competence, autonomy, and relatedness are currently considered necessary and sufficient to promote human growth and functioning (Deci & Ryan, 2000; Sheldon & Filak, 2008). In other words, competence, autonomy, and relatedness act for human psychological functioning like water, sun, and soil do for avocados.

Much research has examined outcomes associated with the satisfaction versus thwarting of the three psychological needs. Autonomy-supportive contexts, in which people use perspective taking, provide meaningful rationales, and give choice, were thoroughly studied and found to facilitate internalization and promote intrinsic motivation across many life domains (see Deci & Ryan, 2008, for a review). SDT-driven research has also examined reward structures, task structures, and interaction quality with key people in various contexts and has shown that they do influence the adoption of certain motivational styles. Translated to the work context, performance management and compensation systems, job design, and management/leadership should influence the quality of employees' work motivation.

SDT in the Work Domain

Various aspects of SDT have received considerable attention in the management literature through the years. In the mid-1970s, following the initial research on reward effects on intrinsic motivation, there was considerable discussion and debate about this research and its meaning for management (e.g., Calder & Staw, 1975; Deci, 1976; Deci, Cascio, & Krusell, 1975; Scott, 1975). In fact, the amount of attention that cognitive evaluation theory, which was used to interpret the intrinsic motivation research results (Deci & Ryan, 1980), received at that time led Ambrose and Kulik (1999) to refer to it as one of the seven traditional theories of work motivation in organizations. Subsequently, Gagné and Deci (2005) presented a concept discussion of SDT with regard to management and organizations. It has generated sufficient interest to become one of the most frequently downloaded and highly cited articles published in the *Journal of Organizational Behavior*. Management applications of SDT have included the examination of such topics as the effect of need satisfaction not only on the adoption of different types of motivation in the workplace, but also on work outcomes, such as performance evaluation and workplace adjustment, and how individual differences concepts, such as causality orientations (Deci & Ryan, 1985), also influence performance and wellness variables in work organizations.

Applied SDT research has been most voluminous in the psychological study of education, sport, exercise, and health, although it has also appeared in several other applied areas, including the work domain. Research examining SDT as a theory of work motivation has been growing in the last several years. This book was written to present various discussions concerned with that SDT research in the work domain. Such studies have included Deci, Connell, and Ryan (1989); Kasser, Davey, and Ryan (1992); Ilardi, Leone, Kasser, and Ryan (1993); Richer and Vallerand (1995); Gagné, Senécal, and Koestner (1997); Gagné, Koestner, and Zuckerman (2000); Deci et al. (2001); Richer, Blanchard, and Vallerand (2002); Bono and Judge (2003); Fernet, Guay, and Senécal (2004); Vansteenkiste, Lens, Dewitte, De Witte, and Deci (2004); Baard et al. (2004); Lynch, Plant, and Ryan (2005); Otis and Pelletier (2005); Spreitzer, Sutcliffe, Dutton, Sonenshein, and Grant (2005). More recent works include, among others, Vansteenkiste et al. (2007); Grant (2008); Gagné, Chemolli, Forest, and Koestner (2008); Roca and Gagné (2008); Van den Broeck, Vansteenkiste, De Witte, and Lens (2008); Gagné (2009); Greguras and Diefendorff (2009); Burstyn, Jonasi, and Wild (2010); Fernet, Gagné, and Austin (2010); Parker, Jimmieson, and Amiot (2010); Van den Broeck, Vansteenkiste, De Witte, Soenens, and Lens (2010); Fernet (2011); Grant and Berry (2011); Grant, Normohamed, Ashford, and Dekas (2011); Ten Brummelhuis, Ter Hoeven, Bakker, and Peper (2011); Van den Broeck et al. (2011); Van den Broeck, Van Ruysseveldt, Smulders, and De Witte (2011); Mitchell, Gagné, Beaudry, and Dyer (2012); Porath, Spreitzer, Gibson, and Garnett (2012); Wang and Gagné (2013); Marescaux, De Winne, and Sels (2013); Dysvik et al. (2013); Fernet, Austin Trépanier, and Dussault (2013); Fernet, Austin, and Vallerand (2012); Gillet, Fouquereau, Forest, Brunault, and Colombat (2012); Gillet, Gagné, Sauvagère, and Fouquereau (2013).

The Current Volume

This Handbook is a forum that not only discusses past research on SDT and work but also provides researchers with a clear agenda for the future. It is organized into five sections. The first section is devoted to current conceptual issues in work motivation. Edward Deci and Richard Ryan [Chapter 2] start by presenting an in-depth analysis of the issue of basic psychological needs as it applies to the work domain. John Meyer [Chapter 3] explores conceptual links between work motivation, employee engagement, and commitment. Karoline Strauss and Sharon Parker [Chapter 4] then explore the motivational underpinnings of proactive work behavior, and Antoinette Weibel, Meike Wieman, and Margit Osterloh [Chapter 5] provide a behavioral economics perspective on work motivation that is based on principles drawn from SDT. Lastly, Robert Vallerand, Nathalie Houlfort, and Jacques Forest [Chapter 6] present the dual model of passion, which is a recent extension of SDT, and explain how it applies to the work domain.

The second section is devoted to the issue of individual factors likely to affect work motivation. Sigalit Ronen and Mario Mikulincer [Chapter 7] present attachment styles as a foundation of work motivation, and Lance Ferris [Chapter 8] discusses the role that contingent self-esteem plays in affecting work motivation and work-related well-being. Finally, Gary Greguras, James Diefendorff, Jacqueline Carpenter, and Christian Tröster [Chapter 9] discuss person-environment fit issues in organizations and how they can be studied using SDT.

The third section is devoted to organizational factors that affect work motivation. Marylène Gagné and Alexandra Panaccio [Chapter 10] discuss job design theories from the point of view of SDT. Stephanie Gilbert and Kevin Kelloway [Chapter 11] explore the motivational aspect of leadership using SDT. Amar Fall and Patrice Roussel [Chapter 12] analyze how compensation systems are likely to influence work motivation from the point of view of SDT. Finally, Anders Dysvik and Bård Kuvaas [Chapter 13] explore how SDT can contribute to the practice of training and development to ensure positive effects on work motivation and outcomes.

The fourth section is devoted to work-related outcomes that are likely to be affected by need satisfaction and work motivation. Claude Fernet and Stephanie Austin [Chapter 14] start off by presenting an SDT-based model of job stress, followed by Gretchen Spreitzer and Christine Porath [Chapter 15], who present a new model of human thriving at work. Michel Cossette [Chapter 16] continues with a treaty on the role of motivation in the process of emotional regulation. Natasha Scott, Mark Fleming, and Kevin Kelloway [Chapter 17] discuss how motivation affects workplace safety behaviors, and present a new safety motivation scale. Véronique Dagenais-Desmarais and François Courcy [Chapter 18] explore how workplace violence is affected by, and affects, work motivation. Luc Pelletier and Nicole Aitken [Chapter 19] then discuss how organizations can promote sustainable employee behaviors. Finally, Jacques Forest, Marie-Hélène Gilbert, Geneviève Beaulieu, Philippe LeBrock, and Marylène Gagné [Chapter 20] present a method that allows for the evaluation of the economic impact of interventions that aim to improve employee well-being.

The fifth section is devoted to research on specific work-related applications of SDT. Johnmarshall Reeve and Yu-Lan Su [Chapter 21] start off with a discussion of what can affect teacher motivation and of the effects of such motivation on pupils, followed by Maynor Gonzalez, Christopher Niemiec, and Geoffrey Williams [Chapter 22], who discuss psychosocial mechanisms, based on SDT, that affect the occupational health gradient. Dan Stone [Chapter 23] continues with a description of what a functional relationship with money and possessions would look like when using SDT as a framework. Frederick Grouzet [Chapter 24] discusses how professional values and training can influence personal values, and how these can affect well-being. To conclude this section, Richard Koestner and Nora Hope [Chapter 25] present a SDT approach to goals. The last chapter [Chapter 26] of the book attempts to integrate some of the ideas presented in the chapters, but also concentrates on offering information about what is not covered in the Handbook but could have been as well as what could (and hopefully would) be in the Handbook in 10 or 20 years from now.

The chapters of this Handbook provide a wide array of work-related applications of SDT, and our sincere hope is that this Handbook inspires researchers in management and organizational psychology to conduct more research and develop more organizational interventions and practices based on the premises of SDT.

References

Ainsworth, M. D. S. (1979). Infant-mother attachment. *American Psychologist, 34*, 932–937.

Amabile, T. M., DeJong, W., & Lepper, M. R. (1976). Effects of externally imposed deadlines on subsequent intrinsic motivation. *Journal of Personality and Social Psychology, 34*, 92–98.

Ambrose, M. L., & Kulik, C. T. (1999). Old friends, new faces: Motivation research in the 1990s. *Journal of Management, 25*, 231–292.

Andersen, S. M., Chen, S., & Carter, C. (2000). Fundamental human needs: Making social cognition relevant. *Psychological Inquiry, 11*, 269–275.

Baard, P. P., Deci, E. L., & Ryan, R. M. (2004). Intrinsic need satisfaction: A motivational basis of performance and well-being in two work settings. *Journal of Applied Social Psychology, 34*, 2045–2068.

Bao, X., & Lam, S. (2008). Who makes the choice? Rethinking the role of autonomy and relatedness in Chinese children's motivation. *Child Development, 79*, 269–283.

Baumeister, R., & Leary, M. R. (1995). The need to belong: Desire for interpersonal attachments as a fundamental human motivation. *Psychological Bulletin, 117*, 497–529.

Berlyne, D. E. (1950). Novelty and curiosity as determinants of exploratory behavior. *British Journal of Psychology, 41*, 68–80.

Berlyne, D. E. (1955). The arousal and satiation of perceptual curiosity in the rat. *Journal of Comparative and Physiological Psychology, 48*, 238–246.

Blais, M. R., Sabourin, S., Boucher, C., & Vallerand, R. J. (1990). Toward a motivational model of couple happiness. *Journal of Personality and Social Psychology, 59*, 1021–1031.

Bono, J. E., & Judge, T. A. (2003). Self-concordance at work: Toward understanding the motivational effects of transformational leaders. *Academy of Management Journal, 46*(5), 554–571.

Burstyn, I., Jonasi, L., & Wild, C. (2010). Obtaining compliance with occupational health and safety regulations: A multilevel study using self-determination theory. *International Journal of Environmental Health Research, 20*, 271–287.

Calder, B. J., & Staw, B. M. (1975). The interaction of intrinsic and extrinsic motivation: Some methodological notes. *Journal of Personality and Social Psychology, 31*, 76–80.

Chirkov, V. I., Ryan, R. M., Kim, Y., & Kaplan, U. (2003). Differentiating autonomy from individualism and independence: A self-determination theory perspective on internalization of cultural orientations and well-being. *Journal of Personality and Social Psychology, 84*, 97–110.

Dashiell, J. F. (1925). A quantitative demonstration of animal drive. *Journal of Comparative Psychology, 5*, 205–208.

de Charms, R. (1968). *Personal causation: The internal affective determinants of behavior.* New York: Academic Press.

Deci, E. L. (1971). Effects of externally mediated rewards on intrinsic motivation. *Journal of Personality and Social Psychology, 18*, 105–115.

Deci, E. L. (1972). Effects of contingent and non-contingent rewards and controls on intrinsic motivation. *Organizational Behavior and Human Performance, 8*, 217–229.

Deci, E. L. (1976). Notes on the theory and metatheory of intrinsic motivation. *Organizational Behavior and Human Performance, 15*, 130–145.

Deci, E. L. (with Richard Flaste) (1995). *Why we do what we do: The dynamics of personal autonomy.* New York: Grosset/ Putnam.

Deci, E. L., Betley, G., Kahle, J., Abrams, L., & Porac, J. (1981). When trying to win: Competition and intrinsic motivation. *Personality and Social Psychology Bulletin, 7*, 29–83.

Deci, E. L., Cascio, W. F., & Krusell, J. (1975). Cognitive evaluation theory and some comments on the Calder and Staw critique. *Journal of Personality and Social Psychology, 31*, 81–85.

Deci, E. L., Connell, J. P., & Ryan, R. M. (1989). Self-determination in a work organization. *Journal of Applied Psychology, 74*, 580–590.

Deci, E. L., Eghrari, H., Patrick, B. C., & Leone, D. R. (1994). Facilitating internalization: The self-determination theory perspective. *Journal of Personality, 62*, 119–142.

Deci, E. L., Koestner, R., & Ryan, R. M. (1999). A meta-analytic review of experiments examining the effects of extrinsic rewards on intrinsic motivation. *Psychological Bulletin, 125*, 627–668.

Deci, E. L., & Ryan, R. M. (1980). The empirical exploration of intrinsic motivational processes. In L. Berkowitz (Ed.), *Advances in experimental social psychology,* 13 (pp. 39–80). New York: Academic Press.

Deci, E. L., & Ryan, R. M. (1985). *Intrinsic motivation and self-determination in human behavior.* New York: Plenum.

Deci, E. L., & Ryan, R. M. (2000). The "what" and "why" of goal pursuits: Human needs and the self-determination of behavior. *Psychological Inquiry, 11*, 227–268.

Deci, E. L., & Ryan, R. M. (2008). Facilitating optimal motivation and psychological well-being across life's domains. *Canadian Psychology, 49*, 14–23.

Deci, E. L., Ryan, R. M., Gagné, M., Leone, D., Usunov, J., & Kornazheva, B. P. (2001). Need satisfaction, motivation, and well-being in the work organizations of a former Eastern Bloc country. *Personality and Social Psychology Bulletin, 27*, 930–942.

Dysvik, A., Kuvaas, B., & Gagné, M. (2013). An investigation of the unique relations between basic psychological needs and intrinsic motivation. *Journal of Applied Social Psychology, 43*, 1050–1064.

Enzle, M. E., & Anderson, S. C. (1993). Surveillant intentions and intrinsic motivation. *Journal of Personality and Social Psychology, 64*, 257–266.

Fernet, C. (2011). Development and validation of the Work Role Motivation Scale for School Principals (WRMS-SP). *Educational Administration Quarterly, 47*(2), 307–331.

Fernet, C., Austin, S., Trépanier, S. G., & Dussault, M. (2013). How do job characteristics contribute to burnout? Examining the distinct mediating role of perceived autonomy, competence, and relatedness. *European Journal of Work and Organizational Psychology, 22*, 123–137.

Fernet, C., Austin, S., & Vallerand, R. J. (2012). The effects of work motivation on employee exhaustion and commitment: An extension of the JD-R model. *Work & Stress, 26*, 213–219.

Fernet, C., Gagné, M., & Austin, S. (2010). When does quality of relationships with coworkers predict burnout over time? The moderating role of work motivation. *Journal of Organizational Behavior, 31*(8), 1163–1180.

Fernet, C., Guay, F., Senecal, C. (2004). Adjusting to job demands: The role of work, self-determination and job control in predicting burnout. *Journal of Vocational Behavior, 65*, 39–56.

Gagné, M. (2009). A model of knowledge sharing motivation. *Human Resource Management, 48*, 571–589.

Gagné, M., Chemolli, E., Forest, J., & Koestner, R. (2008). The temporal relations between work motivation and organizational commitment. *Psychologica Belgica, 48*, 219–241.

Gagné, M., & Deci, E. L. (2005). Self-determination theory as a new framework for understanding organizational behavior. *Journal of Organizational Behavior, 26*, 331–362.

Gagné, M., Forest, J., Vansteenkiste, M., Crevier-Braud, L., Van den Broeck, A.,… & Westbye, C. (2014). The Multidimensional Work Motivation Scale: Validation evidence in seven languages and nine countries. *European Journal of Work and Organizational Psychology.* Advance Online Publication.

Gagné, M., Koestner, R., & Zuckerman, M. (2000). Facilitating acceptance of organizational change: The importance of self-determination. *Journal of Applied Social Psychology, 30*, 1843–1852.

Gagné, M., Ryan, R. M., & Bargmann, K. (2003) The effects of parent and coach autonomy support on need satisfaction and well being of gymnasts. *Journal of Applied Sport Psychology, 15*, 372–390.

Gagné, M., Senécal, C., & Koestner, R. (1997). Proximal job characteristics, feelings of empowerment, and intrinsic motivation: A multidimensional model. *Journal of Applied Social Psychology, 27*, 1222–1240.

Gillet, N., Fouquereau, E., Forest, J., Brunault, P., & Colombat, P. (2012). The impact of organizational factors on psychological needs and their relations with hedonic and eudaimonic well-being. *Journal of Business and Psychology, 27*, 437–450.

Gillet, N., Gagné, M, Sauvagère, S., & Fouquereau, E. (2013). Predicting employees' satisfaction and turnover intentions using self-determination theory. *European Journal of Work and Organizational Psychology, 22*, 450–460.

Grant, A. M. (2008). Does intrinsic motivation fuel the pro-social fire? Motivational synergy predicting persistence, performance, and productivity. *Journal of Applied Psychology*, *93*(1), 48–58.

Grant, A. M., & Berry, J. W. (2011). The necessity of others is the mother of invention: Intrinsic and prosocial motivations, perspective-taking, and creativity. *Academy of Management Journal*, *54*, 73–96.

Grant, A. M., Nurmohamed, S., Ashford, S. J., & Dekas, K. (2011). The performance implications of ambivalent initiative: The interplay of autonomous and controlled motivations. *Organizational Behavior and Human Decision Processes*, *116*(2), 241–251.

Greguras, G. J., & Diefendorff, J. M. (2009). Different fits satisfy different needs: Linking person-environment fit to employee commitment and performance using self-determination theory. *Journal of Applied Psychology*, *94*(2), 465–477.

Harlow, H. F. (1950). Learning and satiation of response in intrinsically motivated complex puzzle performance in monkeys. *Journal of Comparative and Physiological Psychology*, *43*, 289–294.

Harlow, H. F. (1953). Motivation as a factor in the acquisition of new responses. In M. R. Jones (Ed.), *Current theory and research on motivation* (pp. 24–49). Lincoln, NE: University of Nebraska Press.

Hebb, D. O. (1955). Drives and the CNS (conceptual nervous system). *Psychological Review*, *62*, 243–254.

Hull, C. L. (1943). *Principles of behavior: An introduction to behavior theory.* New York: Appleton-Century-Crofts.

Ilardi, B. C., Leone, D. R., Kasser, T., & Ryan, R. M. (1993). Employee and supervisor ratings of motivation: Main effects and discrepancies associated with job satisfaction and adjustment in a factory setting. *Journal of Applied Social Psychology*, *23*, 1789–1805.

Iyengar, S. S., & DeVoe, S. E. (2003). Rethinking the value of choice: Considering cultural mediators of intrinsic motivation. In V. Murphy-Berman & J. J. Berman (Eds.), *Nebraska symposium on motivation: Cross-cultural differences in perspectives on self* (Vol. 49, pp. 129–174). Lincoln, NE: University of Nebraska Press.

Kasser, T., Davey, J., & Ryan, R. M. (1992). Motivation and employee-supervisor discrepancies in a psychiatric vocational rehabilitation setting. *Rehabilitation Psychology*, *37*, 175–187.

Koestner, R., Losier, G. F., Vallerand, R. J., & Carducci, D. (1996). Identified and introjected forms of political internalization: Extending self-determination theory. *Journal of Personality and Social Psychology*, *70*, 1025–1036.

Lepper, M. R., & Greene, D. (1975). Turning play into work: Effects of adult surveillance and extrinsic rewards on children's intrinsic motivation. *Journal of Personality and Social Psychology*, *31*, 479–486.

Lynch, M. F., Plant, R., & Ryan, R. M. (2005). Psychological need satisfaction, motivation, attitudes and well being among psychiatric hospital staff and patients. *Professional Psychology*, *36*, 415–425.

Marescaux, E., De Winne, S., & Sels, L. (2013). HR practices and HRM outcomes: The role of basic need satisfaction. *Personnel Review*, *42*(1), 4–27.

Markus, H. R., & Kitayama, S. K. (2003). Models of agency: Sociocultural diversity in the construction of action. In V. Murphy-Berman & J. J. Berman (Eds.), *Nebraska symposium on motivation: Cross-cultural differences in perspectives on self* (Vol. 49, pp. 1–57). Lincoln, NE: University of Nebraska Press.

Mitchell, J. I., Gagné, M., Beaudry, A., Dyer, L. (2012). The moderating effect of motivation on the relationship between attitude and IT usage. *Computers in Human Behavior*, *28*, 729–738.

Montgomery, K. C. (1952). A test of two explanations of spontaneous alternation. *Journal of Comparative and Physiological Psychology*, *45*, 287–293.

Mossholder, K. W. (1980). Effects of externally mediated goal setting on intrinsic motivation: A laboratory experiment. *Journal of Applied Psychology*, *65*, 202–210.

Mullan, E., Markland, D. A., & Ingledew, D. K. (1997). A graded conceptualisation of self-determination in the regulation of exercise behaviour: Development of a measure using confirmatory factor analytic procedures. *Personality and Individual Differences*, *23*, 745–752.

Ng, Y., Ntoumanis, N., Thørgersen-Ntoumani, C., Deci, E. L., Ryan, R. M., Duda, J. L., & Williams, G. C. (2012). Self-determination theory applied to health contexts: A meta-analysis. *Perspectives on Psychological Science*, *7*, 325–340.

Nissen, H. W. (1930). A study of exploratory behavior in the white rat by means of the obstruction method. *Journal of Genetic Psychology*, *37*, 361–376.

Otis, N., & Pelletier, L. G. (2005). A motivational model of daily hassles, physical symptoms, and future work intentions among police officers. *Journal of Applied Social Psychology*, *35*, 2193–2214.

Parker, S. L., Jimmieson, N. L., & Amiot, C. E. (2010). Self-determination as a moderator of demands and control: Implications for employee strain and engagement. *Journal of Vocational Behavior*, *76*(1), 52–67.

Pelletier, L. G., Tuson, K. M., Green-Demers, I., Noels, K., & Beaton, A. M. (1998). Why are you doing things for the environment? The motivation towards the environment scale [MTES]. *Journal of Applied Social Psychology*, *28*, 437–468.

Pelletier, L. G., Tuson, K. M., & Haddad, N. K. (1997). Client motivation for therapy scale: A measure of intrinsic motivation, extrinsic motivation, and amotivation for therapy. *Journal of Personality Assessment*, *68*, 414–435.

Pelletier, L. G., Vallerand, R. J., Sarrazin, P. (2007). The revised six-factor sport motivation scale (Mallett, Kawabata, Newcombe, Otero-Forero, & Jackson, 2007): Something old, something new, and something borrowed. *Psychology of Sport and Exercise*, *8*, 615–621.

Plant, R., & Ryan, R. M. (1985). Intrinsic motivation and the effects of self-consciousness, self-awareness, and ego-involvement: An investigation of internally controlling styles. *Journal of Personality*, *53*, 435–449.

Porath, C., Spreitzer, G., Gibson, C., & Garnett, F. (2012). Thriving at work: Toward its measurement, construct validation, and theoretical refinement. *Journal of Organizational Behavior*, *33*, 250–271.

Premack, D. (1959). Toward empirical behavior laws: Part 1. Positive reinforcement. *Psychological Review*, *66*, 219–233.

Reis, H. T., Sheldon, K. M., Gable, S. L., Roscoe, J., & Ryan, R. M. (2000). Daily well being: The role of autonomy, competence, and relatedness. *Personality and Social Psychology Bulletin*, *26*, 419–435.

Richer, S., Blanchard, C. M., Vallerand, R. J. (2002). A motivational model of work turnover. *Journal of Applied Social Psychology*, *32*, 2089–2113.

Richer, S. F., & Vallerand, R. J. (1995). Supervisors' interactional styles and subordinates' intrinsic and extrinsic motivation. *Journal of Social Psychology, 135*, 707–722.

Roca, J. C., & Gagné, M. (2008). Understanding e-learning continuance intention in the workplace: A self-determination theory perspective. *Computers in human behavior, 24*, 1585–1604.

Ryan, R. M. (1995). Psychological needs and the facilitation of integrative processes. *Journal of Personality, 63*, 397–427.

Ryan, R. M., & Connell, J. P. (1989). Perceived locus of causality and internalization: Examining reasons for acting in two domains. *Journal of Personality and Social Psychology, 57*, 749–761.

Ryan, R. M., & Deci, E. L. (2000). Self-determination theory and the facilitation of intrinsic motivation, social development, and well-being. *American Psychologist, 55*, 68–78.

Ryan, R. M., Koestner, R., & Deci, E. L. (1991). Ego-involved persistence: When free-choice behavior is not intrinsically motivated. *Motivation and Emotion, 15*, 185–205.

Ryan, R. M., Mims, V., & Koestner, R. (1983). Relation of reward contingency and interpersonal context to intrinsic motivation: A review and test using cognitive evaluation theory. *Journal of Personality and Social Psychology, 45*, 736–750.

Ryan, R. M., Rigby, S., King, K. (1993). Two types of religious internalization and their relations to religious orientation and mental health. *Journal of Personality and Social Psychology, 65*, 586–596.

Scott, W. E., Jr. (1975). The effects of extrinsic rewards on "intrinsic motivation": A critique. *Organizational Behavior and Human Performance, 14*, 117–129.

Sheldon, K. M., & Elliot, A. J. (1998). Not all personal goals are personal: Comparing autonomous and controlled reasons as predictors of effort and attainment. *Personality and Social Psychology Bulletin, 24*, 546–557.

Sheldon, K. M., Elliot, A. J., Kim, Y., Kasser, T. (2001). What is satisfying about satisfying events? Testing 10 candidate psychological needs. *Journal of Personality and Social Psychology, 89*, 325–339.

Sheldon, K. M., & Filak, V. (2008). Manipulating autonomy, competence and relatedness support in a game-learning context: New evidence that all three needs matter. *British Journal of Social Psychology, 47*, 267–283.

Spreitzer, G., Sutcliffe, K., Dutton, J., Sonenshein, S., & Grant, A. (2005). A socially embedded model of thriving at work. *Organization Science, 16*(5), 537–549.

Ten Brummelhuis, L. L., Ter Hoeven, C. L., Bakker, A. B., & Peper, B. (2011). Breaking through the loss cycle of burnout: The role of motivation. *Journal of Occupational and Organizational Psychology, 84*, 268–287

Vallerand, R. J., Pelletier, L. G., Blais, M. R., Briere, N. M., Senecal, C., & Vallieres, E. F. (1992). The academic motivation scale: A measure of intrinsic, extrinsic, and amotivation in education. *Educational and Psychological Measurement, 52*, 1003–1019.

Vallerand, R. J., & Reid, G. (1984). On the causal effects of perceived competence on intrinsic motivation: A test of cognitive evaluation theory. *Journal of Sport Psychology, 6*, 94–102.

Van den Broeck, A., Schreurs, B., De Witte, H., Vansteenkiste, M., Germeys, F., & Schaufeli, W. B. (2011). Understanding workaholics' motivations: A self-determination perspective. *Applied Psychology: An International Review, 60*(4), 600–621.

Van den Broeck, A., Van Ruysseveldt, J., Smulders, P., & De Witte, H. (2011). Does an intrinsic work value orientation strengthen the impact of job resources? A perspective from the Job Demands–Resources Model. *European Journal of Work and Organizational Psychology, 20*(5), 581–609.

Van den Broeck, A., Vansteenkiste, M., De Witte, H., & Lens, W. (2008). Explaining the relationships between job characteristics, burnout, and engagement: The role of basic psychological need satisfaction. *Work & Stress, 22*(3), 277–294.

Van den Broeck, A., Vansteenkiste, M., De Witte, H., Soenens, B., & Lens, W. (2010). Capturing autonomy, competence, and relatedness at work: Construction and initial validation of the Work-Related Basic Need Satisfaction Scale. *Journal of Occupational and Organizational Psychology, 83*(4), 981–1002.

Vansteenkiste, M., Lens, W., Dewitte, S., De Witte, H., & Deci, E. L. (2004). The "why" and "why not" of job search behavior: Their relation to searching, unemployment experience, and well-being. *European Journal of Social Psychology, 34*, 345–363.

Vansteenkiste, M., Lens, W., Soenens, B., Luyckx, K. (2006). Autonomy and relatedness among Chinese sojourners and applicants: Conflictual or independent predictors of well-being and adjustment? *Motivation and Emotion, 30*, 273–282.

Vansteenkiste, M., Neyrinck, B., Niemiec, C. P., Soenens, B., de Witte, H., & Van den Broeck, A. (2007). On the relations among work value orientations, psychological need satisfaction, and job outcomes: A self-determination theory approach. *Journal of Occupational and Organizational Psychology, 80*, 251–277.

Vansteenkiste, M., Zhou, M., Lens, W., Soenens, B. (2005). Experiences of autonomy and control among Chinese learners: Vitalizing or immobilizing? *Journal of Educational Psychology, 97*, 468–483.

Wang, Z., & Gagné, M. (2013). A Chinese-Canadian cross-cultural investigation of transformational leadership, autonomous motivation and collectivistic value. *Journal of Leadership and Organization Studies, 20*, 134–142.

Welker, W. L. (1956). Some determinants of play and exploration in chimpanzees. *Journal of Comparative and Physiological Psychology, 49*, 84–89.

White, R. W. (1959). Motivation reconsidered: The concept of competence. *Psychological Review, 66*, 297–333.

Williams, G. C., & Deci, E. L. (1996). Internalization of biopsychosocial values by medical students: A test of self-determination theory. *Journal of Personality and Social Psychology, 70*, 767–779.

Williams, G. C., Grow, V. M., Freedman, Z. R., Ryan, R. M., & Deci, E. L. (1996). Motivational predictors of weight loss and weight-loss maintenance. *Journal of Personality and Social Psychology, 70*, 115–126.

Zhou, M., Ma, W. J., Deci, E. L. (2009). The importance of autonomy for rural Chinese children's motivation for learning. *Learning and Individual Differences, 19*, 492–498.

Zuckerman, M., Porac, J., Lathin, D., Smith, R., & Deci, E. L. (1978). On the importance of self-determination for intrinsically motivated behavior. *Personality and Social Psychology Bulletin, 4*, 443–446.

PART 1

Conceptual Issues

CHAPTER

2

The Importance of Universal Psychological Needs for Understanding Motivation in the Workplace

Edward L. Deci *and* Richard M. Ryan

Abstract

One of the key propositions of self-determination theory is that human beings have deeply evolved psychological needs to be competent, autonomous, and related to others, such that in contexts where these needs are satisfied people evidence more volitional, high-quality motivation and greater well-being, and when these psychological needs are thwarted people display various forms of diminished motivation and more symptoms of ill-being. This chapter addresses how the self-determination-theory concept of basic psychological needs differs from the needs concepts in other psychological and management theories; provides empirical evidence for the validity of our approach; relates need satisfaction to autonomous motivation and controlled motivation; explains how need satisfaction versus thwarting affects engagement and effective performance; examines how social environments, personality characteristics, and people's long-term goals affect satisfaction versus thwarting of their basic psychological needs; and discusses the relevance of these issues for management.

Key Words: psychological needs, autonomy, work adjustment, productivity, autonomous motivation, life goals

---

Introduction

Substantial portions of the lives of hundreds of millions of adults around the world are spent in workplaces. Whether in executive offices, on farms, in boutiques, or at filling stations, most people are accountable to authorities within their work organizations. Strategies to motivate such employees have long been a matter of interest to leaders within organizations, as well as to researchers, because motivation has appropriately been recognized to be an important antecedent of productivity. In this chapter we discuss factors within the employees and the work environments, particularly in relation to employees' basic psychological need satisfactions, that have been taken into account when analyzing individuals' work motivation and workplace wellness (e.g., Gagné & Deci, 2005; Grant & Shin, 2012).

From the perspective of self-determination theory (SDT; Deci & Ryan, 2000), although productivity is a critical dependent variable for such analyses, we maintain that the psychological health and well-being of employees is also extremely important as a workplace outcome not only from an ethical perspective but also as a central indicator of longer-term organizational health. Indeed, our theoretical viewpoint and empirical findings indicate that the very conditions that nurture and support employee wellness are also those most conducive to and supportive of productivity, commitment, creativity, and other characteristics of highly effective employees. As such, we focus both on particular motivational variables and phenomena that predict wellness and productivity at work, and on factors in the workplace that either support or undermine those motivational dynamics.

Two Types of Psychological Needs Theories

One of the more commonly used concepts in research on work motivation has been that of *psychological needs*. Numerous psychologists have assessed needs with questionnaire, projective, or implicit measures and have used those variables, either as main effects or in interaction with environmental variables, to predict performance and/or job satisfaction. Much of that research has assessed the strength of particular needs, in the tradition of Murray's (1938) personality theory. More specifically, much of the research has involved assessing the strength of a person's need for some psychological state or experience, such as dominance, acquisitiveness, or achievement, and using that value to predict the person's behaviors that were expected to lead to those experiences. In other words, *need strength* has been viewed as an individual difference variable that resulted from development (i.e., was learned) and was considered a primary predictor of behavior. Need strength was essentially a reflection of what people desired, with the implication being that the more they desired a general outcome (e.g., affiliation, or achievement), the harder they would work to attain it—that is, the more motivated they would be for behaviors they believed would lead to the desired outcome.

Such need strengths (also called desires or motives) were theorized to be a function of the developmental histories people had during the years when they were growing up (e.g., whether their parents were supportive and/or whether they held high standards for the children), so the children were thought to develop different need strengths for particular kinds of experiences (e.g., being dominant over others, or being affiliated with others). Within this tradition, need strength was used to predict outcomes, such as managers' effectiveness or employees' efficiency on the job, because it was believed that people would perform appropriately to attain outcomes that would provide satisfaction of their strongly held needs. Working in this tradition, McClelland and colleagues examined the strength of the needs for achievement, power, and affiliation as predictors of work-related behaviors and effectiveness (e.g., McClelland, 1985), finding for example that a strong need for power was an important predictor of successful leadership (McClelland & Boyatzis, 1982).

An alternative approach to the study of psychological needs has focused not on the strength of needs but rather on the degree to which needs that are evolved and universal have been satisfied versus thwarted. Self-determination theory (SDT) is a comprehensive and widely studied motivational theory that views psychological needs as human universals, defined as essential psychological nutrients. As such, they must be satisfied for ongoing, high-quality performance and for psychological health; to the degree that they are not satisfied there will be negative consequences. The theory specifies that people have three *basic psychological needs* that are evolved rather than learned: the needs for competence, autonomy, and relatedness (e.g., Deci & Ryan, 2000). This conceptualization of basic or fundamental needs for making predictions or interpretations can be applied at the specific-task level (e.g., making a strategic plan), the domain level (e.g., at work), or the global level (i.e., one's personality). Then, whatever the level of analysis, one can use the degree of satisfaction or thwarting of the basic needs to predict outcomes at the corresponding level.

One reason to distinguish needs as individual differences in the strength of learned desires from needs as evolved necessities for wellness that can be satisfied to differing degrees is that some things people may learn to strongly desire can have negative consequences for performance and well-being. Stated differently, not all strong motives are good for individuals or for their organizations (e.g., "needs" for dominance; "needs" for abasement). In contrast, the SDT approach specifies how the attainment of any learned desire impacts satisfaction of evolved needs, thereby explaining how even success at strong desires or motives can sometimes produce negative outcomes. Indeed, some of the phenomena that SDT researchers have examined, and which are reviewed in this chapter, are ones in which people's strongly held desires or goals, even when attained, actually diminish rather than enhance their workplace adjustment and effective work behavior.

Maslow's Theory

Perhaps the best known of all needs theories is Maslow's needs hierarchy theory (1943, 1970), which has been studied in terms of both the need-strength and need-satisfaction conceptualizations. Maslow specified five categories of human needs, including the physiological and the psychological needs and the deficit and growth needs. The five categories within Maslow's theory were then organized in a hierarchical format. He argued that the lowest order needs (e.g., for oxygen, food, drink, and sex) are very powerful, physiological, deficit-oriented motivators when they have not been well satisfied.

When they have been well satisfied, however, the person moves on to the next higher level, at which such needs as safety and security become centrally salient. The levels then proceed through the affiliative needs to esteem needs and finally to the need for self-actualization, which caps the hierarchy. A less-well-known hierarchical theory that has only three levels was presented by Alderfer (1972).

Maslow maintained that the needs in his hierarchy are evolved, and indeed there can be no doubt that some of them are (certainly the lowest level physiological needs are inherent aspects of being human). However, little or no research using the Maslow framework has attempted to determine whether the various needs are indeed innate or may instead either be learned or emerge when evolved needs are unsatisfied. In general, there has been relatively little research using this framework, and much of what has been done has examined whether, when needs at one level are fairly well satisfied, it is then and only then that needs at the next higher level become strong, salient motivators (e.g., Diener, Horowitz, & Emmons, 1985). There has been little evidence supporting that central proposition of the theory (e.g., Hagerty, 1999).

Accepting the general idea of a hierarchy, many organizational psychologists have argued that because the lower-order needs are generally well satisfied among residents of the United States, Canada, and Western Europe, it is primarily the higher-order needs that are the strong motivators in these locales. For example, one of the earliest theorists to make this point was McGregor (1960) in this Theory Y approach to management. In essence, he suggested that, because most people have their lower-order needs satisfied, it is their higher-order needs that are the most operative and important in the workplace. As such, he suggested, people tend to be motivated primarily to achieve, accomplish, and master their environments, so managers should focus on these intrinsic motivators that are linked primarily to the higher-order needs.

Research with Higher- and Lower-order Needs

In line with this thinking, it has been common in research on work motivation to collapse the five levels of needs from Maslow's framework into two categories—the lower-order and the higher-order needs—with the higher-order ones including the needs for esteem, accomplishment, and actualization. Hackman and colleagues (e.g., Hackman & Lawler, 1971; Hackman & Oldham, 1976) were

among the researchers who did so, using the two concepts as individual differences and arguing that for some people the higher-order needs are stronger, whereas for others the lower-order needs are stronger. Their research then revealed that people who had strong higher-order needs performed better and felt more satisfied if they had jobs with enriched job characteristics, such as feedback, independence, and variety, whereas those who were focused more on the lower-order needs were less motivated by enriched jobs.

SDT and Maslow's Theory

The SDT perspective differs from Maslow's in three important ways. First, although both theories suggest that there are universal psychological and physiological needs, SDT does not consider all of the needs in Maslow's hierarchy to be basic (i.e., evolved) needs, instead suggesting that some of them, such as the needs for security and self-esteem, are not actually basic needs but are *need substitutes* that result from thwarting of the basic needs (Deci & Ryan, 2000). For example, when people continually experience satisfaction of their needs for competence, autonomy, and relatedness, they do not think about and try to build self-esteem (Ryan & Brown, 2003). The search for self-esteem becomes important to people mainly when they are not experiencing satisfaction of the basic psychological needs, so the desire to feel worthy becomes more salient (Deci & Ryan, 1995). In short, people do not inherently work to experience self-esteem; self-esteem accrues as they get their basic psychological needs satisfied. When, however, needs are thwarted and insecurities mount, self-esteem becomes a "need," in the sense of a strong motive or desire.

Second, SDT does not organize the needs in a hierarchical fashion, maintaining instead that the basic psychological needs as well as the basic drives (i.e., physiological needs) are operative across the life span. As such, it is not necessary to have the so-called lower-order needs consistently well satisfied before the higher-order needs emerge. Indeed, people often pursue higher-order needs to the neglect of lower-order ones. Moreover, although evidence for hierarchical ordering has not been compelling, what is clear is that the basic psychological needs for autonomy, competence, and relatedness, which are growth-oriented (i.e., higher order), as opposed to deficit (i.e., lower order) needs, are of ongoing functional import. They are operative from birth onward. Infants, for example, need strong relatedness with their primary caregivers from the time they are born, and they also begin quickly to use their capacities (e.g., moving their fingers and touching objects), which lead toward mastering their bodies and environments and yield experiences of competence and autonomy. Later these same needs to exercise capacities, master environments, and connect with others are operative in schools, sport fields, and the workplace. In short, the basic psychological needs function as important motivators for people across the lifespan and domains of activity, and through periods when the drives are being less-versus-more satisfied.

Third, SDT focuses on the degree to which psychological needs are satisfied, rather than the strength of the needs, as a primary predictor of outcomes. Thus, for example, we would not use the strength of the higher-order needs as our central focus, but rather the degree to which these needs were satisfied on the job, to predict high-quality performance, work satisfaction, and other important employee outcomes. This does not mean that we are arguing that there are no differences in the strength of basic psychological needs for different individuals. Rather, our point is that need satisfaction versus thwarting is more important in cutting variance in important outcomes than is need strength. Furthermore, focusing on the satisfaction versus thwarting of basic needs gives important information about how to structure workplaces so people experience greater satisfaction of the basic needs and in turn evidence greater well-being and effective performance. Finally, it is noteworthy that what appear to be differences in need strength may indeed be compensations for prior thwarting of the needs. For example, Baumeister and Leary (1995) argued that there is a universal need for belongingness (which is essentially the same as relatedness), yet they also examined individual differences in the need to belong (Leary, Kelly, Cottrell, & Schreindorfer, 2007). Importantly, however, many of the items on the scale imply that the participants' need for belongingness has been thwarted or that the individuals are fearful that it will be—such as, "I try hard not to do things that will make other people avoid or reject me." That item does not reflect a growth-oriented need to belong but rather suggests insecurity that comes from having had the basic need thwarted.

Self-Determination Theory

SDT is a macro-theory of personality, development, and well-being in social contexts that has used motivational concepts to hypothesize, organize, and predict phenomena across various areas of psychology and across numerous applied domains (Deci & Ryan, 1985b), including the domain of motivation in the workplace (Gagné & Deci, 2005). It was founded upon an organismic meta-theory, which assumes an active organism inherently oriented toward mastering the environment and assimilating experiences into a unified set of inner processes and structures, referred to as *self*, that promotes autonomous motivation and behavior.

SDT has posited, based on many years of research, that there are three evolved psychological needs (the needs for competence, autonomy, and relatedness), which are considered universal necessities for wellness. The theory is thus a dialectical theory that examines human beings (i.e., proactive organisms) as they function to get their basic psychological needs satisfied within a social context that can either support or thwart need satisfaction. It is the outcome of this dialectic that is the basis for SDT predictions. In general, to the degree that the basic needs are more satisfied, more positive outcomes are predicted, and to the degree that the needs are more thwarted, more negative outcomes are predicted.

Basic Psychological Needs and Work-related Outcomes

Various studies have indicated that when people experience satisfaction of the basic psychological needs, they are more *autonomously motivated*, which means that they behave with a full sense of volition, willingness, and choice, as opposed to being either *controlled*, which refers to behaving with a sense of pressure and obligation (e.g., Lynch, Plant, & Ryan, 2005), or *amotivated*, which means having a lack of intention and motivation with respect to work (e.g., Pelletier, Dion, Tuson, & Green-Demers, 1999). Autonomous motivation comprises both intrinsic motivation, which means doing an activity out of interest and enjoyment, and fully internalized extrinsic motivation, which means doing the activity volitionally because of its personal value and importance. Satisfaction of the basic psychological needs promotes both types of autonomous motivation (see Deci & Ryan, 2000).

Furthermore, numerous studies have related basic need satisfaction to psychological health and well-being (e.g., Nix, Ryan, Manly, & Deci, 1999; Reis, Sheldon, Gable, Roscoe, & Ryan, 2000). For example, Niemiec, Ryan, and Deci (2009) found that increases in well-being and decreases in ill-being over a 1-year period for postcollege, early career adults was explained by changes in basic psychological need satisfaction. Need satisfaction has also been found to predict more effective performance (e.g., Baard, Deci, & Ryan, 2004). The research relating need satisfaction to well-being and high-quality performance has also been done in many domains (e.g., Deci & Ryan, 2008) in addition to the motivation-at-work domain. These include education (Ryan & Deci, 2009), parenting (Soenens & Vansteenkiste, 2010), health care (Ryan, Patrick, Deci, & Williams, 2008), virtual worlds (Ryan, Rigby, & Przybylski, 2006), psychotherapy (Ryan & Deci, 2008), and close relationships (La Guardia & Patrick, 2008), among others.

THE THREE NEEDS, WORK READINESS, AND JOB SATISFACTION

Many studies have been accomplished using the SDT framework examining the relations of need satisfaction to workplace well-being and performance. In what follows we present some illustrative findings rather than providing a comprehensive review.

One early study using the concept of satisfaction of the three basic psychological needs in the workplace was conducted in a sheltered workshop affiliated with a state psychiatric hospital (Kasser, Davey, & Ryan, 1992). Participants received job training, employment, and pay in the program, which was intended to help them move toward employment in regular settings. Kasser and colleagues examined whether employees' experiencing satisfaction of the three basic psychological needs at work would predict their potential for employment. Indeed, employees' need satisfaction was significantly related to the number of hours these employees spent at their current workshop jobs; to managers' ratings of the employees' adjustment in those jobs; and, importantly, to managers' ratings of the employees' readiness for standard employment. Although this was not a typical work setting because of the study population and the conditions of work, it is important to note that, even in this nonconventional setting, employees' feelings of basic need satisfaction predicted managers' ratings of the employees' work performance.

In a subsequent study, basic psychological needs satisfaction was assessed in workers and supervisors employed in a manufacturing setting (Ilardi, Leone, Kasser, & Ryan, 1993). More than 100 employees participated, reporting on both extrinsic satisfactions at work and basic psychological need satisfactions. Regression analyses confirmed that employees who reported greater need satisfaction when at work also reported greater job satisfaction in general, higher feelings of self-esteem, and lower levels of psychosomatic symptoms, after controlling for job status and pay. Furthermore, when their managers rated the employees' feelings of need satisfaction, those ratings also predicted the same work outcomes that had been predicted by the employees' ratings of basic need satisfaction, thus indicating that the relations were not just a function of method variance.

Hofer and Busch (2011) did a study in which they found strong relations between satisfaction of the competence need and job satisfaction in the workplace. In addition, they had used an implicit measure of the strength of the achievement motive and found a moderator effect such that people who were high in the achievement motive had stronger relations between competence need satisfaction than did people low in the implicit achievement motive. In other words, there was a main effect of need satisfaction on job satisfaction in this study as in many other studies, but in addition these researchers found that people learning to value achievement more strongly showed the relation of the competence need to job satisfaction to be even stronger.

NEED SATISFACTION AMONG HIGHLY EDUCATED PROFESSIONALS

In a study of business school alumni from a Canadian university who worked in both the public and private sectors, Richer, Blanchard, and Vallerand (2002) reasoned that for working adults to experience autonomy in the workplace, they would need to experience satisfaction of the competence and relatedness needs, because these needs are essential for individuals to be motivated rather than amotivated. The researchers thus assessed satisfaction of the competence and relatedness needs, as well as the individuals' autonomous motivation for work, and then used structural equation modeling to test whether satisfaction of the competence and relatedness needs are essential antecedents of autonomous motivation. Also included in the model were a positive link from autonomous motivation to job satisfaction and a negative link from autonomous motivation to emotional exhaustion (i.e., burnout). Finally, job satisfaction was negatively predictive of intentions to leave their jobs and emotional exhaustion was positively predictive of those intentions. The researchers further collected follow-up data a year later to determine whether the participants were still in the jobs they had had a year earlier, hypothesizing that turnover intentions would predict actual turnover. Analyses of the results indicated that their proposed model was in fact supported by the data, with a significant path coefficient for each path specified above. In short then, feelings of competence, relatedness, and autonomy at work were found to positively predict job satisfaction and negatively predict emotional exhaustion, which in turn explained variance in the employees' turnover intentions and then their actual turnover a year later.

In another study, Roca and Gagné (2008) surveyed employees of four international agencies affiliated with the United Nations. The participants were all involved in e-learning courses focused on professional and analytic skills that were being offered for employees in their agencies. Focus of the study was on participants' experiences of competence, relatedness, and autonomy need satisfactions with regard to their e-learning courses, and how those experiences related to their satisfaction and enjoyment of the courses and their intentions to take further ones. Analyses of the data indicated that satisfaction of all three needs in the e-learning courses predicted the participants' enjoyment of the learning, that satisfaction of the needs for competence and autonomy predicted usefulness of the course material, and that satisfaction of the need for competence alone predicted their experience of being able to easily put the material to use. In turn, enjoyment, usefulness, and easily putting the material to use all predicted the participants' intentions to take additional e-learning courses in the future.

NEED SATISFACTION WHEN WORKING AND NOT WORKING

Ryan, Bernstein, and Brown (2010) recently did a study in which full-time working adults from a variety of employment settings reported on the degree to which they were experiencing satisfaction of their autonomy, competence, and relatedness needs at randomized intervals over a 21-day period. They also reported on their positive and negative mood, sense of vitality, and physical well-being. Multilevel modeling analyses indicated that on weekdays the individuals experienced less positive mood, more negative mood, less vitality, and more physical symptoms than on weekends. In other words, people in general felt better on weekends than during the week, and the relation between weekdays versus weekends and well-being outcomes was mediated by need satisfaction. On weekdays people felt less satisfaction of the autonomy and

relatedness needs than on weekends, and it is this lower level of need satisfaction during the week that explained why people's general well-being was lower on weekdays.

The researchers reasoned that the difference in need satisfaction and well-being in the two different parts of the week was likely a function of the fact that people are generally at work during the week but not on weekends. Accordingly, they did the analyses on the basis of days that people worked or did not work and found results quite similar to those based on weekdays versus weekends. Their discussion of results suggested that many workplaces are structured in ways that interfere with people's fundamental need satisfaction, which results in people evidencing poorer mental and physical health. From the SDT perspective, as seen in the next sections, making the workplace more need satisfying for employees can in fact have a quite positive effect for the employees as well as for the customers they serve, and thus fewer employees will find themselves "waiting for the weekend."

From the previously reviewed studies as well as many others that are more or less directly linked to work organizations, we can conclude that when people experience greater satisfaction of the basic psychological needs for competence, relatedness, and autonomy in the workplace, they are more autonomously motivated and more engaged in their work, and display better adjustment and well-being.

Basic Psychological Needs and the Social Environment

One of the most important functions of the concept of psychological needs, when defined as necessities for effective functioning and psychological health in the workplace, is the clear implications for predicting how the work environment will affect people's performance and adjustment in that setting. Simply stated, SDT proposes that environments supportive of people's needs for competence, autonomy, and relatedness promote better work performance and better adjustment at work.

The idea of a basic need for autonomy emerged from early research on the effects of external factors on intrinsic motivation (see Deci, 1975). In general, the research showed that tangible rewards, evaluations, threats of punishment, and deadlines tended to undermine intrinsic motivation, whereas choice and having one's perspectives and feelings acknowledged tended to enhance intrinsic motivation. The idea of a need for autonomy that would be thwarted as people became dependent on rewards and other controlling factors, thus resulting in an external perceived locus of causality (de Charms, 1968; Heider, 1958), but that would be supported by choice and by having their internal perspectives acknowledged by others, leading to a more internal perceived locus of causality, provided a meaningful way to synthesize the various results (e.g., Deci, Eghrari, Patrick, & Leone, 1994; Deci, Koestner, & Ryan, 1999). Furthermore, the idea of a need for competence, which had been proposed by White (1959), allowed for an interpretation of the findings that positive feedback enhanced intrinsic motivation, whereas negative feedback diminished it (e.g., Ryan, 1982). Finally, the idea of a need for relatedness was important for providing an account of the internalization of values, attitudes, mores, and extrinsic motivations within a social environment (e.g., Ryan, 1995). That is, it became clear that people internalize values and extrinsic regulations in part to be related to people who endorse those values.

AN ORGANIZATION DEVELOPMENT INTERVENTION

Other research has focused not on specific external, social-contextual factors, such as rewards and choice, but instead on the general social climate or ambience being either supportive of autonomy or controlling of behaviors. For example, research examining an organization development intervention assessed the degree to which managers in branch offices of a Fortune 500 company were autonomy supportive versus controlling and found that those who were more autonomy supportive had employees who were more satisfied with their jobs and were more trusting of the top management, thus indicating that managerial styles of immediate supervisors affect how their subordinates experience not only their jobs but even the company's top-level managers (Deci, Connell, & Ryan, 1989). The intervention spanned about 8 weeks during which the managers were supported to become more autonomy supportive with their employees. Each manager in each intervention branch worked with the change agent for about 3.5 days during the intervention period, and the results of the study indicated that the managers did become more autonomy supportive and that, even more importantly, the positive change in the managers radiated to more positive experiences for their subordinates. The employees of the trained managers reported greater work satisfaction and more trust in the company. In short, employees in intervention locations showed increased positive attitudes toward both their work and their organization relative to control locations.

Research has further shown that when managers were autonomy supportive, their employees reported more satisfaction not only of the need for autonomy, but also of the needs for competence and relatedness. Presumably, when managers were autonomy supportive, they also were supportive of the other two basic needs, and it is also likely that when managers were autonomy supportive, employees felt free to find ways to get satisfaction of their other two needs as well. On the other hand, when managers were controlling, employees typically felt constrained from getting any of their needs satisfied. In turn, need satisfactions predicted both workplace wellness and performance (e.g., Baard et al., 2004), whereas need deprivation predicted more negative outcomes.

EMPLOYEES IN A PSYCHIATRIC FACILITY

Another study of employees' motivation examined the work lives of caregivers at a psychiatric inpatient facility for adolescents. The facility had been having trouble with staff members being very controlling and constraining of the patients, leading to resistance from the patients and generally unpleasant attitudes and interactions between the staff and patients. The director of the facility engaged a group of SDT researchers to work with the staff to facilitate meaningful change in the orientations of the staff and their interactions with the patients. Of concern were the degree to which these employees experienced not only basic need satisfaction on the job, but also threat to their safety, and how these factors would relate to their job satisfaction, well-being at work, attitudes toward the patients, and buy-in to a training program being implemented at the hospital that trained the employees to treat patients in a less controlling and constraining way (Lynch et al., 2005). As well, the researchers explored the need satisfaction of patients in the facility and the relation of their need satisfaction to their autonomous motivation for being in treatment.

First, employees who were found to experience more basic need satisfaction in the facility displayed more positive attitudes toward the patients and greater buy-in to the program. It seems that the more the senior management could create a climate that supported need satisfaction of the employees, the more the employees would take a positive orientation toward the patients and the more willing they would be to try dealing with the patients in a less constraining way. Furthermore, the staff members' experiences of psychological need satisfaction also predicted their job satisfaction and sense of well-being at the facility. Of course, the degree to which the staff felt that the patients threatened their safety negatively predicted their feelings of well-being, and it also positively predicted the staffs' controlling attitudes toward the patients.

Data collected from the patients a year after the intervention had been completed indicated that the patients' feelings of need satisfaction in the hospital setting predicted the degree to which they had internalized the motivation for treatment and thus engaged in therapy in a more autonomous way. That is, the relation between need satisfaction and autonomous motivation was strong among the adolescents, thus paralleling the results between need satisfaction and autonomous motivation among the staff. It seems that, as the staff felt greater need satisfaction, they were able to interact with the patients in a way that left the patients feeling greater need satisfaction, thus having a positive impact on the patients' motivation for participating in therapy.

NEED SATISFACTION IN A NOT-FOR-PROFIT ORGANIZATION

Research by Gagné (2003) conducted in a nonprofit animal shelter examined the antecedents and consequences of psychological need satisfaction of volunteers working in that setting. She examined not only the participants' perceptions of the degree to which their supervisors were autonomy supportive, as an assessment of the work climate, but also the participants' own autonomous causality orientations (Deci & Ryan, 1985a).

Causality orientations are a set of general, individual differences in people's motivational orientations. There are three orientations: (1) the autonomy orientation, the (2) controlled orientation, and (3) the impersonal orientation. The *autonomy orientation* indexes the degree to which individuals orient toward the environment as a source of information for making effective choices, and are motivated autonomously (i.e., by intrinsic and well-internalized extrinsic motivation) across situations and domains. The *controlled orientation* reflects people's tendency to orient toward the environment as if it were pressuring them to think, feel, and behave in particular ways, and to be controllingly motivated by external contingencies and contingencies that have been introjected (i.e., partially internalized but not accepted as

their own). The *impersonal orientation* represents the degrees to which people orient to the environment as if it were an indicator that they are incompetent and unlovable, and to which they lack intentions to behave (i.e., are amotivated) in relation to activities and tasks across settings. Research has indicated that the autonomy orientation is related to self-esteem, ego-development, integration in personality, and positive social relations (e.g., Hodgins, Koestner, & Duncan, 1996; Weinstein, Deci, & Ryan, 2011); that the controlled orientation is related to public self-consciousness, the Type A personality, road rage, and inconsistency among attitudes, traits, and behaviors (e.g., Koestner, Bernieri, & Zuckerman, 1992; Neighbors, Vietor, & Knee, 2002); and that the impersonal orientation is related to self-derogation and depressive symptoms (Deci & Ryan, 1985a).

According to SDT, each person has each causality orientation to some degree, so researchers can use one, two, or all three of the orientations when making predictions, depending on which one or more seems theoretically relevant. Gagné (2003) used participants' autonomy orientations as well as their perceptions of the supervisors' autonomy support in her study at the animal shelter. This allowed her not only to examine how people's own motivational orientations affected their need satisfaction and work-relevant outcomes, but also to remove variance attributed to the participants' personalities from that associated with their perceptions of the supervisors. Outcomes in this study were the number of hours voluntarily worked and self-reports of engagement with their work at the shelter.

Gagné used structural equation modeling to test whether individuals' autonomy orientations and their experienced autonomy support would explain independent variance in the degree to which they felt satisfaction of all three psychological needs, and whether in turn need satisfaction predicted more hours worked and greater feelings of engagement. Results indicated that each of these predicted paths was significant, suggesting that both personality and environmental factors affected need satisfaction and involvement with the voluntary work. Analyses also indicated, however, that there was a direct path from autonomy orientation to work engagement, suggesting that individuals high in the autonomy orientation were most likely to be engaged in this volunteer work for the nonprofit organization.

NEED SATISFACTION AND WORK PERFORMANCE IN BANKING

Employees from two large banking organizations in the New York City area participated in research examining people's need satisfaction, wellness, and work performance (Baard et al., 2004). In the primary study, more than 500 first-line employees of an investment-banking firm participated by completing questionnaires. These jobs are frequently quite stressful, so being able to deal with the pressuring demands while both performing well and also maintaining a sense of wellness can be somewhat challenging. Of interest was, first, whether basic need satisfaction would explain the degree to which the employees were able to both achieve success at work and also feel good about themselves, and, second, whether social-contextual and personality factors would predict need satisfaction.

Analyses revealed that autonomy support and the autonomous causality orientation were significantly correlated with each other, but that each accounted for independent variance in predicting satisfaction of the competence and relatedness needs, with autonomy support being the primary predictor of satisfaction of the autonomy need. In turn, each of the need satisfactions was related to adjustment in the workplace, and satisfaction of the relatedness need was the strongest predictor of work performance (i.e., performance evaluations done by supervisors). Then, in the model where autonomy support and autonomy orientation each predicted overall need satisfaction, with need satisfaction predicting both performance evaluations and workplace well-being, the model fit the data very well.

One interesting result from the Baard et al. (2004) research was a set of findings that men perceived the work climate to be more autonomy supportive than did women, that men displayed better adjustment than women, and that men received higher performance evaluations than did women. Of course, the fact of greater adjustment and better performance being associated with higher perceived autonomy support makes good sense and is what would be predicted by SDT. The puzzling thing is why men would be higher than women in perceptions of autonomy support from the managers. Might the managers have treated women differently, less supportively; might women have perceived the managers as less supportive even if they did not treat the genders differently; or might the differences be attributable to a difference in socialization in workplaces such that men were more accustomed to the way in which people relate to each other in settings such as these? We have no clear answer to this puzzle, but there is some indication that the third option may be part of the answer because men also had a tendency to experience higher relatedness need satisfaction in that work setting. Understanding this more fully will take replication of the results and more research focused on its causes, but the data show the importance of looking at the need satisfaction differences in subsets of employees to identify where issues in the workplace may be occurring.

Basic Needs and People's Life Goals

Other research has examined how people's long-term goals can affect the degree to which they experience satisfaction of the basic psychological needs (e.g., Ryan, Sheldon, Kasser, & Deci, 1996). That is, the goals that people take with them to the workplace or adopt while there can be either need-congruent or need-incongruent. Accordingly, these life goals affect the need satisfaction employees experience while working, just as the work environment and the employees' causality orientations affect need satisfaction. In turn, of course, if the employees experience greater need satisfaction, they typically perform better at their jobs and experience greater wellness at work. In contrast, if people's long-term goals interfere with need satisfaction, greater ill-being is likely to result.

GOALS, WELL-BEING, AND PERFORMANCE

Research by Kasser and Ryan (1993, 1996) that used factor analyses indicated that the life goals or aspirations people hold tend to fall into at least two broad categories: one that the researchers referred to as *extrinsic aspirations*, which included amassing wealth, becoming famous, and presenting an attractive and trendy image; and another called *intrinsic aspirations*, which included developing personally, building meaningful relationships, contributing to one's community, and being physically fit. A team of researchers working in 15 cultures (Grouzet et al., 2005) found that this distinction between intrinsic and extrinsic aspiration held up across the cultures.

Kasser and Ryan found (1996) that people who held stronger extrinsic life goals, relative to intrinsic goals, displayed poorer mental health indexed, for example, by lower self-actualization and self-esteem, and by higher anxiety, depression, and narcissism. Analyses also indicated that the poorer well-being associated with extrinsic aspirations was not a function of people lacking confidence about being able to attain these extrinsic goals relative to the intrinsic ones. In other words, this was an issue of goal contents, not relative efficacy. Additionally, research showed that when people attained their intrinsic goals they also showed increases in well-being and decreases in ill-being, but when they attained their extrinsic goals, doing so did not contribute to well-being but it did contribute to greater ill-being (Niemiec et al., 2009). Importantly, the Niemiec et al. study further showed that the relations between goal content and well-being and ill-being were mediated by psychological need satisfaction. That is, the pursuit and attainment of intrinsic aspirations led to greater need satisfaction and in turn, to more well-being and less ill-being. As well, the relations of extrinsic aspirations to outcomes were likely also a function of needs—in this case, need thwarting.

A further study (Sheldon, Ryan, Deci, & Kasser, 2004) examined both controlled motivation and extrinsic life goals as predictors of well-being, and the study revealed that each of the two motivational concepts accounted for independent variance in the prediction of well-being outcomes. This study thus confirmed that the negative relations of the strong extrinsic goals of wealth, fame, and image to well-being resulted not just from the fact that people often pursue extrinsic goals in a controlled way, as had been suggested by Carver and Baird (1998) and Srivastava, Locke, and Bartol (2001), but rather that the content of the extrinsic life goals explained independent variance in the lower well-being, beyond that accounted for by the controlled motive for pursuing the goals. This too was theorized to be a function of need satisfaction versus thwarting.

The previously mentioned studies concerned aspirations or life goals that were conceptualized as individual-difference variables resulting from developmental experiences, and they used well-being as the primary outcome. In contrast, other research has manipulated people's goal contents by framing activities in terms of either an intrinsic or an extrinsic goal and has also used learning as the primary outcome. The studies found, for example, that when the activity in a martial arts class was framed in terms of the extrinsic goal of being thin and attractive, people learned the activity less well and performed it less well than when the learning was framed in terms of the intrinsic goal of becoming more healthy (Vansteenkiste, Simons, Lens, Sheldon, & Deci, 2004). As another example, when business school students' learning of communication skills was framed in terms of the extrinsic goal of making more money, they learned less well than

when the activities were framed in terms of the intrinsic goal of developing themselves.

GOALS AND NEED SATISFACTION IN THE WORKPLACE

In a large study of Belgian workers, Vansteenkiste et al. (2007) found that, after controlling for demographics, employees who held strong extrinsic, relative to intrinsic, work aspirations were less satisfied with their jobs and less happy in their lives. When income was examined, it was found that people who made more money at their jobs were more satisfied with the jobs and happier, but income did not moderate the relation between aspirations and satisfaction. Thus, regardless of how much money individuals made, if their aspirations were strongly oriented toward the extrinsic aspirations, they were still less satisfied and happy than those who were comparably remunerated and oriented toward the intrinsic aspirations.

A study of extrinsic relative to intrinsic work values by Van den Broeck, Vansteenkiste, Lens, and De Witte (2009) complementarily found that holding intrinsic work values was positively associated with flexibility on the job, whereas holding extrinsic work values was negatively associated with flexibility. Finally, another study by Vansteenkiste et al. (2007) reported that higher scores on extrinsic relative to intrinsic work aspirations related to greater work-family conflict, emotional exhaustion, and turnover intentions. Furthermore, and importantly, satisfaction of the competence, autonomy, and relatedness needs mediated the relations between relative importance of the extrinsic versus intrinsic work aspirations and each of the well-being outcomes. In sum, satisfaction of the basic psychological needs played an important role in explaining the impact of people's work aspirations on psychological well-being and work engagement, as did their motivational (i.e., causality) orientations and the need supportiveness of the work environment.

Basic Psychological Needs as Universal Necessities

The SDT proposition that the three basic psychological needs are universal necessities for all people's healthy development, engagement, and well-being has been tested in cross-cultural research in diverse cultures, especially ones in which one or another of the needs is not valued by the culture.

Generally speaking, the idea of a universal need for relatedness is, in principle, noncontroversial among psychologists (even those who do not use the concept of needs in their own research or theorizing) because most psychologists readily accept the evidence that relationships are fundamentally important for people (e.g., Baumeister & Leary, 1995; Harlow, 1958). Furthermore, most cultures (including individualistic Western cultures) value collectives and endorse the idea of members of families and other groups providing support and involvement to one another. Thus, although studying the need for relatedness in various cultures is important, it does not represent the most critical test of the key SDT proposition that satisfaction of all three needs are important for integrity and wellness. Similarly, the idea that competence is universally important has caused little controversy. For example, self-efficacy theory (Bandura, 1996) has proposed and research has confirmed that people having the expectation of being competent at an activity is a primary ingredient in their being motivated for the activity. Thus, although that and related theories do not propose a human need for competence, the importance of people feeling competent is generally accepted within Western psychology. Furthermore, the idea that competence is important for people would seem to be recognized in most cultures, as education and training are not only valued in North American and Western European cultures, but are also robustly emphasized in East Asian cultures, such as South Korea and Japan, which place strong cultural importance on children studying hard and achieving well in school for the honor of their families and the advancement of their cultures.

Of the three SDT basic psychological needs, the one that has been by far the most controversial is the need for autonomy. In placing strong emphasis on the collective, ranging from their families to the society, East Asian and other collectivist cultures proclaim that individuals should put collectives ahead of themselves and do what the collectives value rather than what the individuals believe is important for themselves. Accordingly, various cross-cultural psychologists who take a cultural-relativist perspective (e.g., Markus, Kitayama, & Heiman, 1996) have argued that, because people's needs, like their values and beliefs, are learned from their cultures, and because autonomy or personal choice is not valued in collectivist cultures, the need for autonomy is not relevant for the people in those cultures.

We have pointed out elsewhere (e.g., Deci & Ryan, 2000) that such cross-cultural psychologist have tended to define autonomy differently from the way it is defined within SDT and then criticized SDT based on their different definition

(e.g., Iyengar & DeVoe, 2003). Specifically, SDT defines autonomy as behaving with a sense of volition, endorsement, willingness, and choice, yet it is defined either implicitly or explicitly by others, such as Markus and Kitayama (1991), as independence rather than volition. We agree that people can have too much "independence" and that it can be detrimental for their well-being, but we do not agree that they can have too much "volition." Indeed, being independent of loved ones is not necessarily healthy, as some amount of volitional dependence is important for people feeling satisfied and well (Ryan, La Guardia, Solky-Butzel, Chirkov, & Kim, 2005). Stated differently, people can be autonomously dependent just as they can be autonomously independent. For example, most people quite freely depend on their spouses, partners, best friends, or next-door neighbors. As well, children volitionally depend on their parents, and adults autonomously rely on their physicians when they have a medical problem. So the issue of dependence versus independence is conceptually orthogonal to the issue of controlled versus autonomous.

In spite of the criticism of "autonomy" as a cross-culture concept, many studies have now shown the importance of autonomy and volition for well-being in collectivist cultures as well as in more individualistic ones. For example, recent research by Miller, Das, and Chakravarthy (2011) showed that, in both India and the United States, even when people were behaving to meet the expectations of others, they could experience autonomy while doing so, and to the extent that they did positive outcomes were likely to follow. Further, Chirkov, Ryan, Kim, and Kaplan (2003) did a study in four cultures (Turkey, Korea, Russia, and the United States) that varied in their degree of collectivism versus individualism (see Triandis, 1995). These researchers found that college students from each of these cultures who felt more rather than less autonomous when behaving in accord with cultural values also reported greater well-being. After ensuring comparability of the constructs across cultures (Little, 1997), Chirkov and colleagues showed that the degree of autonomy for enacting individualistic values as well as collectivistic values was a significant predictor of a composite measure of psychological well-being, and these relations were not moderated by country. That is, the same results appeared for residents of each of the four countries.

In the domain of work, Deci et al. (2001) did a study in Bulgarian and American organizations. Participants from America were corporate employees, whereas those from Bulgaria worked for state-owned organizations that operated largely by central-planning principles. Results of the study confirmed that satisfaction of the needs for autonomy, competence, and relatedness in both cultures was associated with well-being. Employees who reported the most need satisfaction on the job also showed the highest level of psychological health. Furthermore, in this study, when the managers of the employees in both Bulgaria and America were more supportive of autonomy, the employees experienced greater need satisfaction, which, as mentioned, led to better work outcomes. In short, in these and other studies, considerable cross-cultural evidence has accumulated indicating that when people experience satisfaction of their autonomy need, as well as their competence and relatedness needs, they experience greater engagement and wellness, regardless of the values endorsed by their cultures (Chirkov, Ryan, & Sheldon, 2010).

Rewards, Need Satisfaction, Motivation, and Management

Viewing needs as basic necessities for healthy development, engagement, and well-being has led us to devote considerable attention to examining the conditions that diminish versus promote need satisfaction and thus its positive sequelae, and then to ask the question: what are the implications of our findings for management? With respect to management, we are particularly interested in the issue of reward effects because salaries and other payments are an integral aspect of the workplace, although, as mentioned, feedback and choice are also very important external factors to consider regarding work motivation.

THE REWARD FINDINGS: UNDERMINING INTRINSIC MOTIVATION?

The earliest studies in the SDT tradition that investigated the effects of social-contextual factors on motivation were the experiments that explored the effects of tangible rewards and positive feedback on intrinsic motivation (e.g., Deci, 1971, 1972). The initial findings showed that tangible rewards undermined intrinsic motivation for college students (Deci, 1971), high school students (Kruglanski, Friedman, & Zeevi, 1971), and nursery school students (Lepper, Greene, & Nisbett, 1973). Furthermore, positive feedback was found, on average, to increase intrinsic motivation (Deci, 1971). This set of studies was the basis for our initial proposal that the concept of satisfaction versus

thwarting of basic psychological needs for autonomy and competence by factors in the social environment would provide a meaningful and effective way of explaining the experimental results (Deci & Ryan, 1980). That is, the undermining of intrinsic motivation was theorized to have occurred because becoming dependent on the rewards thwarted people's feelings of autonomy, whereas the enhancement of intrinsic motivation by feedback was theorized to result from its supporting satisfaction of the competence need. These two findings also had immediate relevance to management because rewards and feedback are widely discussed as important motivators in the workplace.

The findings of undermining of intrinsic motivation by tangible rewards (especially money) were extremely controversial at the time in terms of both basic principles and their applications and implication for life domains, such as education (Ryan & Deci, 2000a) and work (Deci, 1972; Gagné & Deci, 2005). In terms of basic principles, the idea of rewards having any negative effects was anathema to operant behaviorists (e.g., Cameron & Pierce, 1994; Reiss & Sushinsky, 1975), and concerning the workplace the idea of money decreasing intrinsic motivation was problematic given that money is considered by many to be the primary motivator of work performance (e.g., Scott, 1975) and because at least some psychologists believed that intrinsic and extrinsic motivation were positively additive (Eisenberger & Cameron, 1996; Porter & Lawler, 1968). In spite of the controversy, however, a meta-analysis of 128 experiments confirmed that tangible extrinsic rewards, on average, significantly decreased intrinsic motivation for the rewarded activity (Deci et al., 1999), as had other meta-analyses (e.g., Tang & Hall, 1995; Wiersma, 1992). Furthermore, a meta-analysis of positive feedback studies confirmed that positive feedback enhanced intrinsic motivation (Henderlong & Lepper, 2002).

The key findings from the reward experiments were that tangible rewards—both concrete (e.g., money) and symbolic (e.g., good player awards)—decreased intrinsic motivation for the target activity, particularly if the rewards were contingent on doing the activity, expected when doing it, and salient. Furthermore, studies showed that the undermining of intrinsic motivation by these short manipulations in a laboratory setting remained significant for up to 2 weeks (see Deci et al., 1999).

Rewards that were given to participants simply for showing up for an experiment and thus did not require them to do the target activity to get the rewards did not undermine intrinsic motivation for the activity (Deci, 1972). Rewards that were unexpected and were given after participants completed the task as a kind of unexpected bonus also did not undermine intrinsic motivation. Finally, rewards that were kept nonsalient also were not detrimental to intrinsic motivation. These studies are particularly important, because although on average tangible rewards diminish intrinsic motivation, these studies make clear the conditions within which rewards are less likely to be detrimental.

Interestingly, a study by Ryan, Mims, and Koestner (1983) showed that when monetary rewards were made performance-contingent (i.e., were given to signify excellent performance on the activity) and were administered with an autonomy-supportive interpersonal style, the subsequent level of intrinsic motivation was higher than that for participants who had gotten no performance-contingent rewards and no positive feedback, thus having received nothing to indicate that their performance was excellent. So, it seems that receiving rewards that carry the message that one had performed extremely well are not detrimental for intrinsic motivation relative to no rewards and no feedback. However, it is worth noting that the study by Ryan and colleagues also revealed that participants who were told, with an autonomy-supportive style, that their performance was excellent but did not receive the monetary rewards displayed a level of intrinsic motivation that was significantly higher than the level for the people who got the performance contingent rewards conveying that they had done excellently. Simply stated, the presence of the monetary reward itself, independent of the positive feedback it conveyed, did in fact decrease intrinsic motivation, although the positive feedback, whether or not it was accompanied by rewards, had a positive effect on intrinsic motivation as other studies had previously shown (e.g., Boggiano & Ruble, 1979). Thus, the positive feedback and the monetary reward had opposite effects on intrinsic motivation, with the feedback increasing it and the tangible rewards decreasing it, so the overall effect depended on whether the control group used for making the comparisons did or did not include positive feedback.

The two most important implications of all the studies of reward effects on intrinsic motivation are that it is important to keep rewards relatively nonsalient, and that, when given, they should convey a sense of acknowledgment for performance well done. Of course in work organizations people are virtually always paid, and most people would not be in their jobs if they were not being paid. So, any argument that claims that the primary implication of the rewards literature is that employers should stop paying their employees (or should pay them much less) is obviously absurd. Fortunately, that argument is also not an accurate interpretation of the findings, for the research shows that noncontrolling (e.g., unexpected, noncontingent, and nonsalient) rewards are unlikely to have negative effects, and rewards that acknowledge excellent performance tend to be positive relative to those that do not acknowledge effectiveness. Thus, the more appropriate conclusion is that rewards should typically not be used explicitly and deliberately to try to motivate employees to do work tasks because it is likely that if they are the employees will experience the reward contingencies as controlling and thwarting of their autonomy and will thus tend to lose intrinsic motivation.

Three other findings within the intrinsic and extrinsic motivation literature have extremely important implications for management. First, studies have shown that competition undermines intrinsic motivation (Deci, Betley, Kahle, Abrams, & Porac, 1981), especially if there is pressure to win within the social context (Reeve & Deci, 1996) or if people are competing to earn monetary rewards (Pritchard, Campbell, & Campbell, 1977). We interpret these findings in terms of people becoming dependent on the outcome of winning the competition itself or the rewards that it yields and thus losing a sense of autonomy with respect to the target activity, and we emphasize the importance of the findings because many work environments administer rewards based on the outcome of competitions among their employees, whether individually or as groups.

The second important finding is that providing people with choice about how to do the activities they were engaged with led to increased intrinsic motivation for the activities (e.g., Zuckerman, Porac, Lathin, Smith, & Deci, 1978), and a subsequent meta-analysis confirmed this across numerous experiments (Patall, Cooper, & Robinson, 2008). Whereas rewards and competition have tended to thwart satisfaction of the autonomy need and promote an external perceived locus of causality, choice has tended to support autonomy, prompt a more internal perceived locus of causality, and enhance intrinsic motivation. Importantly, the autonomy job characteristic, which encompasses choice, has been found meta-analytically to facilitate job satisfaction, internal work motivation, well-being, and objective work performance (Humphrey, Nahrgang, & Morgeson, 2007).

Third, research has also shown that when authorities acknowledge the feelings and perspectives of their subordinates, those subordinates evidence greater intrinsic motivation (Koestner, Ryan, Bernieri, & Holt, 1984) as well as fuller internalization and integration of regulations for activities that are not inherently interesting and thus not intrinsically motivated (Deci et al., 1994). Indeed, the concept of autonomy support has the element of individuals (e.g., authorities) taking the others' (e.g., subordinates') perspective or internal frame of reference as its foundational element (e.g., Ryan & Deci, 2000b). It is thus extremely important in the workplace as well as many other life domains, including even close personal relationships (Deci, La Guardia, Moller, Scheiner, & Ryan, 2006).

We turn now to a discussion of applying the results of the motivation research that have been reviewed thus far to the domain of management.

MOTIVATION AND MANAGEMENT

Many writing about management and motivation have explicated approaches to management based on whether the authors assume that the most important motivators are intrinsic or extrinsic. Typically, they have detailed managerial orientations, policies, and practices that tend to facilitate one or the other type of motivation, or both (e.g., Vroom & Deci, 1992).

Within SDT, we do not focus primarily on intrinsic motivation and extrinsic motivation when discussing the bases for different management approaches, but instead we build our comments about management around the concepts of autonomous motivation and controlled motivation (Gagné & Deci, 2005). Because theories other than SDT have failed to differentiate types of extrinsic motivation, they have not recognized that the outcomes associated with well-internalized extrinsic motivation have more similarities to the outcomes associated with intrinsic motivation than they do to those associated with the controlled forms of extrinsic motivation. Accordingly, within SDT, we emphasize the importance of promoting full internalization of extrinsic motivation as well as maintaining or enhancing intrinsic motivation in order to facilitate optimal motivation. We then propose ways to organize social environments so they support basic need satisfaction and thus autonomous motivation, rather than thwarting the basic needs

and yielding external and introjected forms of controlled motivation, or even amotivation.

As the research reviewed in this chapter has made clear, the conditions that promote autonomous motivation are those that support satisfaction of the basic psychological needs for autonomy, competence, and relatedness. Furthermore, we maintain that all managerial functions, including for example making decisions, setting goals, and evaluating performance can be done in ways that are consistent with either autonomous motivation or controlled motivation. For the past half-century, various management theories have recognized this important point and have proposed approaches to management that are relatively consistent with the idea of autonomous motivation being the key to effective workplace behavior and performance and have described management accordingly. Argyris (1957) and McGregor (1960) were among the earliest to describe approaches to management that were generally consistent with the idea of promoting autonomous motivation. Other more recent ones include Lawler's (1986) high involvement management. Some such as Herzberg (1968) have used the concept of intrinsic motivation as the route to effective management. However, as already mentioned, none of the theorists used the concept of autonomous motivation.

The SDT Contributions

The primary contributions made by SDT that supplement other theories of work motivation and management such as those just mentioned involve the clarification of specific factors from the social context (i.e., the work environment) that support (versus thwart) the basic psychological needs and facilitate autonomous (versus controlled) motivation as well as the positive work-related outcomes that follow from it. Organizational psychologists and management theorists have increasingly used this empirical evidence from the SDT literature to make more precise propositions, prescriptions, and predictions about motivation, effective performance, and psychological well-being in the workplace.

First, consider the issue of rewards. In the literature reviewed we pointed out that rewards are a necessary aspect of work situations and made clear that managers who use rewards in less-salient and noncontrolling ways, rather than emphasizing them as a way to motivate employees, are more effective at maintaining autonomous motivation in their employees. As well, we explained that raises and bonuses are most effective when used to acknowledge a job well done and when accompanied by specific positive feedback. Finally, we saw that it is important that reward structures not require people to compete for rewards, because competing for rewards is highly detrimental to autonomous motivation and to organizational health.

Indeed, research has shown that when employees get focused on rewards, their tendency is to take the shortest path to the outcome (e.g., Shapira, 1976), which can easily be manifest as cheating, gaming the system, and sacrificing the long-term best interests of the company in service of short-term goals. This contamination effect (e.g., Deci & Ryan, 2012; Ryan & Brown, 2005) is readily apparent in the corporate world, perhaps most infamously in the Enron saga.

There is another point about rewards that is very important in the workplace, although it has received very little attention in the SDT literature. It is that employees need to feel equitably paid in order to be optimally motivated. When all things are considered, such as level of one's education and training, the ongoing effectiveness of one's performance on the job, and the level of pay being received by others doing the same job with the same seniority, employees who feel that their pay is relatively equitable will be more optimally motivated than those who feel it is inequitable, especially if it is inequitably low (Adams, 1963; Carrell & Dittrich, 1978; Messick & Cook, 1983; Spector, 2008). In short, compensation structures and other workplace rewards will be most effective and least detrimental when they are relatively nonsalient, reflective of good performance, noncompetitive, and equitable.

SDT research and both the Patall et al. (2008) and the Humphrey et al. (2007) meta-analyses have confirmed that integrating as much choice as is reasonable into workplace activities is an important factor in promoting optimal motivation. The idea of choice as discussed in SDT concerns people experiencing a sense of choice while engaging in their work. Making decisions either individually or as members of groups facilitates the experience of choice so long as the nature and number of options are appropriate for the situation (e.g., Moller, Deci, & Ryan, 2006). Within management, choice has been discussed as part of both participative management (e.g., Marrow, Bowers, & Seashore, 1967) and participative leadership (e.g., Yukl, 2010), and the Vroom and Jago (1988) approach to leadership and decision making has detailed the conditions in which using participative decision-making is most effective.

Within SDT we have highlighted facilitation of autonomous motivation by implementing individual and group decision-making as frequently as possible within the managerial process. For example, we endorse Vroom and Jago's discussion of managerial decision-making and further suggest that the idea of facilitating the experience of choice for employees entails having them involved in the goal-setting process both with respect to goals for their individual jobs and for the work group more broadly, and to participate actively in problem solving as part of the performance evaluation process.

The SDT literature has also highlighted the importance of managers or supervisors acknowledging the feelings and perspectives of subordinates in any interactions with them. As reviewed earlier, this has been shown to be a critical factor in autonomy support and thus in facilitating autonomous motivation. In terms of management, this points to the importance of managers using an interpersonal style that is respectful and acknowledging of their employees as a starting place in all interactions.

Deci et al. (1989), in a study described previously, did an organization development intervention in a division of a large corporation in which the focus of the intervention was exactly the factors outlined in this section. By teaching, modeling, and facilitating the factors of taking the others' perspectives and acknowledging their feelings, offering choice, using effective feedback, minimizing control, and using rewards and recognition in less salient, more informative ways, the change agent was able to facilitate the managers becoming more need-supportive of their employees, which resulted in the employees experiencing greater satisfaction and engagement.

Conclusion

SDT, which has gained prominence in organizational psychology and management during recent years, proposes that all people have evolved psychological needs for competence, autonomy, and relatedness; and that it is important to differentiate types of motivation, the most important distinction being between autonomous and controlled motivation, when making predictions about effective performance and workplace adjustment. As such, it provides yet another theory of work motivation that is based in needs. This might lead one to ask, "What is new about this theory of needs and why do we need another theory of needs when we have already had several that did not work very well?" The answer to this question is (1) that it is the first empirically derived motivation theory that specifies a small number of evolved, universal, growth-oriented psychological needs; (2) that it specifically focuses on the satisfaction versus thwarting of these psychological needs (rather than their strength) as the basis for making predictions; and (3) that its primary aim has been to use satisfaction versus thwarting of the basic psychological needs to predict whether employees' primary motivation will be autonomous or controlled and whether they will in turn persist at their work, perform it effectively, and evidence psychological well-being when doing it.

The theory explicates the idea that extrinsic motivation can vary in the degree to which it is autonomous or self-determined, depending on the degree to which the values and regulations contained within extrinsic motivations have been fully internalized. As such, the theory has not focused on intrinsic versus extrinsic motivation as many prior theories have done, but instead has addressed autonomous versus controlled motivation. Autonomous motivation encompasses intrinsic motivation and well-internalized extrinsic motivation and has been found to lead to greater psychological well-being and more effective performance (especially on heuristic tasks) than has controlled motivation, which comprises external control and control by introjects, the latter being partially internalized demands and contingencies.

In sum, the theory postulates that when people's basic psychological needs are satisfied in the workplace they are more autonomously motivated to work, and when their basic needs are thwarted they are controlled or amotivated when at work. Autonomous motivation, which recruits the whole-hearted efforts of employees, has payoffs in terms of productivity, creativity, and lower burnout and turnover. Substantial research in the psychological laboratory and in work organizations has supported this viewpoint, and managers who have adopted orientations and procedures that support rather than thwart their subordinates' basic needs have been shown to be more effective.

Future Directions

Cognitive evaluation theory (CET) is one of six mini-theories that make up SDT. CET was formulated to provide an account of the effects of social-contextual factors, such as rewards and feedback on intrinsic motivation (e.g., Deci, 1975;

Deci & Ryan, 1980). It became sufficiently prominent in organizational psychology during the 1980s and 1990s that Ambrose and Kulik (1999) referred to CET as one of seven traditional theories of motivation in organizations. However, the application of CET to work organizations was largely concerned with the use of rewards and their relations to intrinsic motivation. Only more recently have organizational researchers begun to consider the importance of well-internalized extrinsic motivation in addition to intrinsic motivation as the more effective type of motivation, and only during that time have they recognized the importance of people's basic psychological need satisfaction on the job as the basis of effectiveness and wellness. This has allowed practitioners to use SDT research to guide prescriptions about effective managerial and leadership behaviors.

The important future directions concern the thoughtful use of SDT (rather than just CET) to address a wide range of questions in work-organization research. For example, more specific exploration of how managers can carry out their various functions, such as goal setting, performance evaluation, and decision-making, in ways that are need supportive rather than thwarting would be very useful. Research on how SDT interacts with transformational leadership, in terms of both developing visions and motivating others to help carry them out, seems like fertile ground for examination. Specific studies of change in organizations would be extremely useful. This could include studies of how to restructure organizations—which are all too often structured in ways that are depriving rather than supportive of basic psychological need satisfaction. As well, it could include research on how, within an organizational unit, managers who see the necessity of making some change could work with their employees to plan and implement the change in ways that are need satisfying for the employees, some of whom may initially have opposed the change, while ensuring that the needed change does occur. These are but a few instances of possible future directions. It is noteworthy that the necessary concepts all exist within SDT for addressing these issues. For example, the concept of internalizing extrinsic motivation is clearly central to issues of change within organizations, and there is now prolific research on promoting individual change that persists over time within various domains although it has only begun to make its way into the field of work motivation.

Research in applied domains, such as education (Ryan & Deci, 2009), health care (Sheldon,

Williams, & Joiner, 2003), and physical activity (Hagger & Chatzisarantis, 2007), has used the broader theory (i.e., SDT) extensively in making predictions and interpreting results, and it seems appropriate for organizational researcher to follow in that same path.

References

Adams, J. S. (1963). Toward an understanding of inequity. *Journal of Abnormal and Social Psychology, 67,* 422–436. doi: 10.1037/h0040968

Alderfer, C. P. (1972). *Existence, relatedness, and growth.* New York: Free Press.

Ambrose, M. L., & Kulik, C. T. (1999). Old friends, new faces: Motivation research in the 1990s. *Journal of Management, 25,* 231–292. doi: 10.1177/014920639902500302

Argyris, C. (1957). *Personality and organization.* New York: Harper.

Baard, P. P., Deci, E. L., & Ryan, R. M. (2004). Intrinsic need satisfaction: A motivational basis of performance and well-being in two work settings. *Journal of Applied Social Psychology, 34,* 2045–2068. doi: 10.1111/j.1559-1816.2004.tb02690.x

Bandura, A. (1996). *Self-efficacy: The exercise of control.* New York: Freeman.

Baumeister, R., & Leary, M. R. (1995). The need to belong: Desire for interpersonal attachments as a fundamental human motivation. *Psychological Bulletin, 117,* 497–529. doi: 10.1037/0033-2909.117.3.497

Boggiano, A. K., & Ruble, D. N. (1979). Competence and the overjustification effect: A developmental study. *Journal of Personality and Social Psychology, 37,* 1462–1468. doi: 10.1037/0022-3514.37.9.1462

Cameron, J., & Pierce, W. D. (1994). Reinforcement, reward, and intrinsic motivation: A meta-analysis. *Review of Educational Research, 64,* 363–423. doi: 10.3102/00346543064003363

Carrell, M. R., and Dittrich, J. E. (1978). Equity theory: The recent literature, methodological considerations, and new directions. *The Academy of Management Review, 3,* 202–210.

Carver, C. S., & Baird, E. (1998). The American dream revisited: Is it what you want or why you want it that matters? *Psychological Science, 9,* 289–292. doi: 10.1111/1467-9280.00057

Chirkov, V., Ryan, R. M., Kim, Y., & Kaplan, U. (2003). Differentiating autonomy from individualism and independence: A self-determination theory perspective on internalization of cultural orientations and well-being. *Journal of Personality and Social Psychology, 84,* 97–110.

Chirkov, V. I., Ryan, R. M., & Sheldon, K. M. (Eds.) (2010). *Human autonomy in cross-cultural context: Perspectives on the psychology of agency, freedom, and well-being.* New York: Springer.

de Charms, R. (1968). *Personal causation: The internal affective determinants of behavior.* New York: Academic Press.

Deci, E. L. (1971). Effects of externally mediated rewards on intrinsic motivation. *Journal of Personality and Social Psychology, 18,* 105–115.

Deci, E. L. (1972). Effects of contingent and non-contingent rewards and controls on intrinsic motivation. *Organizational Behavior and Human Performance, 8,* 217–229. doi: 10.1016/0030-5073(72)90047-5

Deci, E. L. (1975). *Intrinsic motivation.* New York: Plenum.

Deci, E. L., Betley, G., Kahle, J., Abrams, L., & Porac, J. (1981). When trying to win: Competition and intrinsic motivation. *Personality and Social Psychology Bulletin, 7,* 79–83. doi: 10.1177/014616728171012

Deci, E. L., Connell, J. P., & Ryan, R. M. (1989). Self-determination in a work organization. *Journal of Applied Psychology, 74,* 580–590. doi: 10.1037/0021-9010.74.4.580

Deci, E. L., Eghrari, H., Patrick, B. C., & Leone, D. R. (1994). Facilitating internalization: The self-determination theory perspective. *Journal of Personality, 62,* 119–142. doi: 10.1111/j.1467-6494.1994.tb00797.x

Deci, E. L., Koestner, R., & Ryan, R. M. (1999). A meta-analytic review of experiments examining the effects of extrinsic rewards on intrinsic motivation. *Psychological Bulletin, 125,* 627–668. doi: 10.1037/0033-2909.125.6.627

Deci, E. L., La Guardia, J. G., Moller, A. C., Scheiner, M. J., & Ryan, R. M. (2006). On the benefits of giving as well as receiving autonomy support: Mutuality in close friendships. *Personality and Social Psychology Bulletin, 32,* 313–327. doi: 10.1177/0146167205282148

Deci, E. L., & Ryan, R. M. (1980). The empirical exploration of intrinsic motivational processes. In L. Berkowitz (Ed.), *Advances in experimental social psychology* (Vol. 13, pp. 39–80). New York: Academic Press.

Deci, E. L., & Ryan, R. M. (1985a). The General Causality Orientations Scale: Self-determination in personality. *Journal of Research in Personality, 19,* 109–134. doi: 10.1016/0092-6566(85)90023-6

Deci, E. L., & Ryan, R. M. (1985b). *Intrinsic motivation and self-determination in human behavior.* New York: Plenum.

Deci, E. L., & Ryan, R. M. (1995). Human autonomy: The basis for true self-esteem. In M. Kernis (Ed.), *Agency, efficacy, and self-esteem* (pp. 31–49). New York: Plenum.

Deci, E. L., & Ryan, R. M. (2000). The "what" and "why" of goal pursuits: Human needs and the self-determination of behavior. *Psychological Inquiry, 11,* 227–268. doi:10.1207/S15327965PLI1104_01

Deci, E. L., & Ryan, R. M. (2008). Facilitating optimal motivation and psychological well-being across life's domains. *Canadian Psychology, 49,* 14–23. doi: 10.1037/0708-5591.49.1.14

Deci, E. L., & Ryan, R. M. (2012). Motivation, personality, and development within embedded social contexts: An overview of self-determination theory. In R. M. Ryan (Ed.), *The Oxford handbook of motivation* (pp. 85–107). New York: Oxford University Press.

Deci, E. L., Ryan, R. M., Gagné, M., Leone, D. R., Usunov, J., & Kornazheva, B. P. (2001). Need satisfaction, motivation, and well-being in the work organizations of a former Eastern Bloc country. *Personality and Social Psychology Bulletin, 27,* 930–942. doi: 10.1177/0146167201278002

Diener, E., Horowitz, J., & Emmons, R. A. (1985). Happiness of the very wealthy. *Social Indicators Research, 16,* 263–274.

Eisenberger, R., & Cameron, J. (1996). Detrimental effects of reward: Reality or myth? *American Psychologist, 51,* 1153–1166. doi: 10.1037/0003-066X.51.11.1153

Gagné, M. (2003). The role of autonomy support and autonomy orientation in the engagement of prosocial behavior. *Motivation and Emotion, 27,* 199–223. doi: 10.1023/A:1025007614869

Gagné, M., & Deci, E. L. (2005). Self-determination theory and work motivation. *Journal of Organizational Behavior, 26,* 331–362. doi: 10.1002/job.322

Grant, A. M., & Shin, J. (2012). Work motivation: Directing, energizing, and maintaining research. In R. M. Ryan

(Ed.), *The Oxford handbook of motivation* (pp. 505–519). New York: Oxford University Press.

Grouzet, F. M., Kasser, T., Ahuvia, A., Dols, J. M., Kim, Y., Lau, S.,...Sheldon, K. M. (2005). The structure of goals across 15 cultures. *Journal of Personality and Social Psychology, 89*, 800–816. doi: 10.1037/0022-3514.89.5.800

Hackman, J. R., & Lawler, E. E. (1971). Employee reactions to job characteristics. *Journal of Applied Psychology, 55*, 259–286. doi: 10.1037/h0031152

Hackman, J. R., & Oldham, G. R. (1976). Motivation through the design of work: Test of a theory. *Organizational Behavior and Human Performance, 16*, 250–279. doi: 10.1016/0 030-5073(76)90016-7

Hagerty, M. R. (1999). Testing Maslow's hierarchy of needs: National quality-of-life across time. *Social Indicators Research, 46*, 249–271.

Hagger, M. S., & Chatzisarantis, N. L. (2007). *Intrinsic motivation and self-determination in exercise and sport.* Champagne, IL: Human Kinetics.

Harlow, H. F. (1958). The nature of love. *American Psychologist, 13*, 673–685.

Heider, F. (1958). *The psychology of interpersonal relations.* New York: Wiley.

Henderlong, J., & Lepper, M. R. (2002). The effects of praise on children's intrinsic motivation: A review and synthesis. *Psychological Bulletin, 128*, 774–795. doi: 10.1037/0033-29 09.128.5.774

Herzberg, F. (1968). One more time: How do you motivate employees? *Harvard Business Review, 46*, 53–62.

Hodgins, H. S., Koestner, R., & Duncan, N. (1996). On the compatibility of autonomy and relatedness. *Personality and Social Psychology Bulletin, 22*, 227–237. doi: 10.1177/ 0146167296223001

Hofer, J., & Busch, H. (2011). Satisfying one's needs for competence and relatedness: Consequent domain-specific well-being depends on strength of implicit motives. *Personality and Social Psychology Bulletin, 37*, 1147–1158. doi: 10.1177/0146167211408329

Humphrey, S. E., Nahrgang, J. D., & Morgeson, F. P. (2007). Integrating motivational, social, and contextual work design features: A meta-analytic summary and theoretical extension of the work design literature. *Journal of Applied Psychology, 92*, 1332–1356. doi: 10.1037/0021-9010.92.5. 1332

Ilardi, B. C., Leone, D., Kasser, T., & Ryan, R. M. (1993). Employee and supervisor ratings of motivation: Main effects and discrepancies associated with job satisfaction and adjustment in a factory setting. *Journal of Applied Social Psychology, 23*, 1789–1805. doi: 10.1111/j.1559-1816.1993.tb01066.x

Iyengar, S. S., & DeVoe, S. E. (2003). Rethinking the value of choice: Considering cultural mediators of intrinsic motivation. In V. Murphy-Berman & J. J. Berman (Eds.), Nebraska symposium on motivation: Cross-cultural differences in perspectives on self (Vol. 49, pp. 129–174). Lincoln, NE: University of Nebraska Press.

Kasser, T., Davey, J., & Ryan, R. M. (1992). Motivation and employee-supervisor discrepancies in a psychiatric vocational rehabilitation setting. *Rehabilitation Psychology, 37*, 175–187. doi: 10.1037/h0079104

Kasser, T., & Ryan, R. M. (1993). A dark side of the American dream: Correlates of financial success as a central life aspiration. *Journal of Personality and Social Psychology, 65*, 410–422. doi: 10.1037/0022-3514.65.2.410

Kasser, T., & Ryan, R. M. (1996). Further examining the American dream: Differential correlates of intrinsic and extrinsic goals. *Personality and Social Psychology Bulletin, 22*, 280–287. doi: 10.1177/0146167296223006

Koestner, R., Bernieri, F., & Zuckerman, M. (1992). Self-determination and consistency between attitudes, traits, and behaviors. *Personality and Social Psychology Bulletin, 18*, 52–59. doi:10.1177/0146167292181008

Koestner, R., Ryan, R. M., Bernieri, F., & Holt, K. (1984). Setting limits on children's behavior: The differential effects of controlling versus informational styles on intrinsic motivation and creativity. *Journal of Personality, 52*, 233–248. doi: 10.1111/j.1467-6494.1984.tb00879.x

Kruglanski, A. W., Friedman, I., & Zeevi, G. (1971). The Effects of extrinsic incentive on some qualitative aspects of task performance. *Journal of Personality, 39*, 606–617. doi: 10.1111/ j.1467-6494.1971.tb00066.x

La Guardia, J. G., & Patrick, H. (2008). Self-determination theory as a fundamental theory of close relationships. *Canadian Psychology, 49*, 201–209. doi: 10.1037/a0012760

Lawler, E. E. (1986). *High involvement management.* San Francisco: Jossey-Bass.

Leary, M. R., Kelly, K. M., Cottrell, C. A., & Schreindorfer, L. S. (2007). *Individual differences in the need to belong: Mapping the nomological network.* Unpublished manuscript, Duke University.

Lepper, M. R., Greene, D., & Nisbett, R. E. (1973). Undermining children's intrinsic interest with extrinsic rewards: A test of the "overjustification" hypothesis. *Journal of Personality and Social Psychology, 28*, 129–137. doi: 10.1037/h0035519

Little, T. D. (1997). Mean and covariance structure (MACS) analysis of cross-cultural data: Practical and theoretical issues. *Multivariate Behavioral Research, 32*, 53–76. doi: 10.1207/ s15327906mbr3201_3

Lynch, M. F., Plant, R. & Ryan, R. M. (2005). Psychological need satisfaction, motivation, attitudes and well being among psychiatric hospital staff and patients. *Professional Psychology, 36*, 415–425. doi: 10.1037/0735-7028.36.4.415

Markus, H. R., & Kitayama, S. (1991). Culture and the self: Implications for cognition, emotion, and motivation. *Psychological Review, 92*, 224–253. doi: 10.1037/0033-295X. 98.2.224

Markus, H. R., Kitayama, S., & Heiman, R. J. (1996). Culture and basic psychological principles. In E. T. Higgins & A. W. Kruglanski (Eds.), *Social psychology: Handbook of basic principles* (pp. 857–913). New York: Guilford.

Marrow, A. J., Bowers, D. G., & Seashore, S. E. (1967). *Management by participation.* New York: Harper and Row.

Maslow, A. H. (1943). A theory of human motivation. *Psychological Review, 50*, 370–396. doi: 10.1037/h0054346

Maslow, A. H. (1970). *Motivation and personality* (2nd ed.). New York: Harper and Row.

McClelland, D. C. (1985). *Human motivation.* Glenview, IL: Scott, Foresman.

McClelland, D. C., & Boyatzis, R. E. (1982). The leadership motive pattern and long term success in management. *Journal of Applied Psychology, 67*, 737–743. doi: 10.1037/0021-9010. 67.6.737

McGregor, D. (1960). *The human side of enterprise.* New York: McGraw-Hill.

Messick, D., & Cook, K. (1983). *Equity theory: psychological and sociological perspectives.* Westport, CT: Praeger.

Miller, J. G., Das, R., & Chakravarthy, S. (2011). Culture and the role of choice in agency. *Journal of Personality and Social Psychology, 101,* 46–61. doi: 10.1037/a0023330

Moller, A. C., Deci, E. L., & Ryan, R. M. (2006). Choice and ego-depletion: The moderating role of autonomy. *Personality and Social Psychology Bulletin, 32,* 1024–1036. doi: 10.1177/0146167206288008

Murray, H. A. (1938). *Explorations in personality.* New York: Oxford University Press.

Neighbors, C., Vietor, N. A., & Knee, C. R. (2002). A motivational model of driving anger and aggression. *Personality and Social Psychology Bulletin, 28,* 324–335. doi: 10.1177/0146167202286004

Niemiec, C. P., Ryan, R. M., & Deci, E. L. (2009). The path taken: Consequences of attaining intrinsic and extrinsic aspirations in post-college life. *Journal of Research in Personality, 43,* 291–306. doi: 10.1016/j.jrp.2008.09.001

Nix, G., Ryan, R. M., Manly, J. B., & Deci, E. L. (1999). Revitalization through self-regulation: The effects of autonomous and controlled motivation on happiness and vitality. *Journal of Experimental Social Psychology, 35,* 266–284. doi: 10.1016/j.jrp.2008.09.001

Patall, E. A., Cooper, H., & Robinson, J. C. (2008). The effects of choice on intrinsic motivation and related outcomes: A meta-analysis of research findings. *Psychological Bulletin, 134,* 270–300. doi: 10.1037/0033-2909.134.2.270

Pelletier, L. G., Dion, S., Tuson, K. M., & Green-Demers, I. (1999). Why do people fail to adopt environmental behaviors? Towards a taxonomy of environmental amotivation. *Journal of Applied Social Psychology, 29,* 2481–2504.

Porter, L. W., & Lawler, E. E. (1968). *Managerial attitudes and performance.* Homewood, IL: Irwin-Dorsey.

Pritchard, R. D., Campbell, K. M., & Campbell, D. J. (1977). Effects of extrinsic financial rewards on intrinsic motivation. *Journal of Applied Psychology, 62,* 9–15. doi: 10.1037/0021-9010.62.1.9

Reeve, J., & Deci, E. L. (1996). Elements within the competitive situation that affect intrinsic motivation. *Personality and Social Psychology Bulletin, 22,* 24–33. doi: 10.1177/0146167296221003

Reis, H. T., Sheldon, K. M., Gable, S. L., Roscoe, J., & Ryan, R. M. (2000). Daily well-being: The role of autonomy, competence, and relatedness. *Personality and Social Psychology Bulletin, 26,* 419–435. doi: 10.1177/0146167200266002

Reiss, S., & Sushinsky, L. W. (1975). Overjustification, competing responses, and the acquisition of intrinsic interest. *Journal of Personality and Social Psychology, 31,* 1116–1125. doi: 10.1037/h0076936

Richer, S. F., Blanchard, C., & Vallerand, R. J. (2002). A motivational model of work turnover. *Journal of Applied Social Psychology, 32,* 2089–2113. doi: 10.1111/j.1559-1816.2002.tb02065.x

Roca, J. C., & Gagné, M. (2008). Understanding e-learning continuance intention in the workplace: A self-determination theory perspective. *Computers in Human Behavior, 24,* 1585–1604. doi: 10.1016/j.chb.2007.06.001

Ryan, R. M. (1982). Control and information in the intrapersonal sphere: An extension of cognitive evaluation theory. *Journal of Personality and Social Psychology, 43,* 450–461. doi: 10.1037/0022-3514.43.3.450

Ryan, R. M. (1995). Psychological needs and the facilitation of integrative processes. *Journal of Personality, 63,* 397–427. doi: 10.1111/j.1467-6494.1995.tb00501.x

Ryan, R. M., Bernstein, J. H., & Brown, K. W. (2010). Weekends, work, and well-being: Psychological need satisfactions and day of the week effects on mood, vitality, and physical symptoms. *Journal of Social and Clinical Psychology, 29,* 95–122. doi: 10.1521/jscp.2010.29.1.95

Ryan, R. M., & Brown, K. W. (2003). Why we don't need self-esteem: Basic needs, mindfulness, and the authentic self. *Psychological Inquiry, 14,* 71–76.

Ryan, R. M., & Brown, K. W. (2005). Legislating competence: The motivational impact of high stakes testing as an educational reform. In A. J. Elliot & C. S. Dweck (Eds.) *Handbook of competence* (pp. 354–374). New York: Guilford Press.

Ryan, R. M., & Deci, E. L. (2000a). Intrinsic and extrinsic motivations: Classic definitions and new directions. *Contemporary Educational Psychology, 25,* 54–67. doi: 10.1006/ceps.1999.1020

Ryan, R. M., & Deci, E. L. (2000b). Self-determination theory and the facilitation of intrinsic motivation, social development, and well-being. *American Psychologist, 55,* 68–78. doi: 10.1037/0003-066X.55.1.68

Ryan, R. M., & Deci, E. L. (2008). A self-determination approach to psychotherapy: The motivational basis for effective change. *Canadian Psychology, 49,* 186–193. doi: 10.1037/a0012753

Ryan, R. M., & Deci, E. L. (2009). Promoting self-determined school engagement: Motivation, learning, and well-being. In K. R. Wentzel & A. Wigfield (Eds.), *Handbook on Motivation at School* (pp. 171–195). New York: Routledge (Taylor and Francis Group).

Ryan, R. M., La Guardia, J. G., Solky-Butzel, J., Chirkov, V., & Kim, Y. (2005). On the interpersonal regulation of emotions: Emotional reliance across gender, relationships, and cultures. *Personal Relationships, 12,* 145–163. doi: 10.1111/j.1350-4126.2005.00106.x

Ryan, R. M., Mims, V., & Koestner, R. (1983). Relation of reward contingency and interpersonal context to intrinsic motivation: A review and test using cognitive evaluation theory. *Journal of Personality and Social Psychology, 45,* 736–750. doi: 10.1037/0022-3514.45.4.736

Ryan, R. M., Patrick, H., Deci, E. L., & Williams, G. C. (2008). Facilitating health behavior change and its maintenance: Interventions based on self-determination theory. *The European Health Psychologist, 10,* 2–5.

Ryan, R. M., Rigby, C. S., & Przybylski, A. (2006). The motivational pull of video games: A self-determination theory approach. *Motivation and Emotion, 30,* 347–364. doi: 10.1007/s11031-006-9051-8

Ryan, R. M., Sheldon, K. M., Kasser, T., & Deci, E. L. (1996). All goals are not created equal: An organismic perspective on the nature of goals and their regulation. In P. M. Gollwitzer & J. A. Bargh (Eds.), *The psychology of action: Linking cognition and motivation to behavior* (pp. 7–26). New York: Guilford.

Scott, W. E. (1975). The effects of extrinsic rewards on "intrinsic motivation": A critique. *Organizational Behavior and Human Performance, 14,* 117–129. doi: 10.1016/0030-5073(76)90032-5

Shapira, Z. (1976). Expectancy determinants of intrinsically motivated behavior. *Journal of Personality and Social Psychology, 34,* 1235–1244. doi: 10.1037/0022-3514.34.6.1235

Sheldon, K. M., Ryan, R. M., Deci, E. L., & Kasser, T. (2004). The independent effects of goal contents and motives on well-being: It's both what you pursue and why you pursue it. *Personality and Social Psychology Bulletin, 30*, 475–486. doi: 10.1177/0146167203261883

Sheldon, K. M., Williams, G. C., & Joiner, T. (2003). *Self-determination theory in the clinic: Motivating physical and mental health*. New Haven, CT: Yale University Press.

Soenens, B., & Vansteenkiste, M. (2010). A theoretical upgrade of the concept of parental psychological control: Proposing new insights on the basis of self-determination theory. *Developmental Review, 30*, 74–99. doi: 10.1016/j.dr.2009.11.001

Spector, P. E. (2008). *Industrial and organizational behavior* (5th ed.). Wiley: Hoboken, NJ.

Srivastava, A., Locke, E. A., & Bartol, K. M. (2001). Money and subjective well-being: It's not the money, it's the motive. *Journal of Personality and Social Psychology, 80*, 959–971. doi: 10.1016/j.dr.2009.11.001

Tang, S.-H., & Hall, V. C. (1995). The overjustification effect: A meta-analysis. *Applied Cognitive Psychology, 9*, 365–404. doi: 10.1002/acp.2350090502

Triandis, H. C. (1995). *Individualism and collectivism*. Boulder, CO: Westview Press.

Van den Broeck, A., Vansteenkiste, M., Lens, W., & De Witte, H. (2009). Unemployed individuals' work values and job flexibility: An explanation from expectancy-value theory and self-determination theory. *Applied Psychology: An International Review, 59*, 296–317. doi: 10.1111/j.1464-0597.2009.00391.x

Vansteenkiste, M., Neyrinck, B., Niemiec, C. P., Soenens, B., de Witte, H., & Van den Broeck, A. (2007). On the relations among work value orientations, psychological need satisfaction, and job outcomes: A self-determination theory approach. *Journal of Occupational and Organizational Psychology, 80*, 251–277. doi: 10.1348/096317906X111024

Vansteenkiste, M., Simons, J., Lens, W., Sheldon, K. M., & Deci, E. L. (2004). Motivating learning, performance, and persistence: The synergistic effects of intrinsic goal contents and autonomy-supportive contexts. *Journal of Personality and Social Psychology, 87*, 246–260. doi: 10.1037/0022-3514.87.2.246

Vroom, V. H., & Deci, E. L. (Eds.). (1992). *Management and motivation* (2nd ed.). London and Baltimore: Penguin.

Vroom, V. H., & Jago, A. G. (1988). *The new leadership: Managing participation in organizations*. Englewood Cliffs, NJ: Prentice Hall.

Weinstein, N., Deci, E. L., & Ryan, R. M. (2011). Motivational determinants of integrating positive and negative past identities. *Journal of Personality and Social Psychology, 100*, 527–544. doi: 10.1037/a0022150

White, R. W. (1959). Motivation reconsidered: The concept of competence. *Psychological Review, 66*, 297–333. doi: 10.1037/h0040934

Wiersma, U. J. (1992). The effects of extrinsic rewards in intrinsic motivation: A meta-analysis. *Journal of Occupational and Organizational Psychology, 65*, 101–114. doi: 10.1111/j.2044-8325.1992.tb00488.x

Yukl, G. A. (2010). *Leadership in organizations* (7th ed.). Prentice Hall.

Zuckerman, M., Porac, J., Lathin, D., Smith, R., & Deci, E. L. (1978). On the importance of self-determination for intrinsically motivated behavior. *Personality and Social Psychology Bulletin, 4*, 443–446. doi: 10.1177/014616727800400317

CHAPTER

3

Employee Commitment, Motivation, and Engagement: Exploring the Links

John P. Meyer

Abstract

Commitments in the workplace can take different forms and be directed at different targets (e.g., organization, teams, goals). As a force that binds individuals to a course of action of relevance to the target, commitment has motivational properties, but it is only recently that theories of commitment and motivation have been integrated. This chapter traces the development of the three-component model of commitment and highlights the important role played by self-determination theory in its integration into the work motivation literature. It also describes how the three-component model and self-determination theory have been combined to serve as the basis for an evidence-based model of employee engagement. The chapter concludes by identifying directions for future research.

Key Words: commitment, motivation, engagement, three-component model, self-determination theory

---

Introduction

Although there is considerable agreement that organizations stand to benefit from having a committed workforce, there has been much less consensus among organizational scientists with regard to the meaning of commitment (Klein, Malloy, & Cooper, 2009; Becker, Klein, & Meyer, 2009). Scientific interest in commitment was stimulated initially by concerns over declining loyalty and increasing rates of turnover in the 1960s and 1970s (Mowday, Porter, & Steers, 1982). Employee commitment (organizational commitment) was studied alongside job satisfaction as a potential contributor to employees' decision to stay with or leave an organization. It is perhaps because of this pairing with job satisfaction that commitment gained prominence as an important *work attitude*. Indeed, most textbooks in industrial and organizational psychology feature commitment prominently in the work attitudes chapter. Some theorists agree with this categorization and suggest that our understanding of the construct might be enhanced by tying it even

more closely with mainstream attitude theory (e.g. Solinger, van Olffen, & Roe, 2008). Others argue that commitment is much more than an attitude, and that it has strong motivational properties (e.g., Meyer & Herscovitch, 2001). This is the position I take in this chapter. Moreover, in line with the theme of the Handbook, I illustrate how our understanding of commitment can be advanced by linking it to theories of motivation, most notably Deci and Ryan's (1985, 2000) self-determination theory (SDT).

Although acknowledging the lack of consensus on the meaning of commitment, for present purposes I focus discussion on a well-established theoretical framework, the three-component model (TCM) developed by Meyer and colleagues (Allen & Meyer, 1990; Meyer & Allen, 1991, 1997; Meyer & Herscovitch, 2001). In the initial formulation of the TCM, attention was focused primarily on employee commitment to the organization and commitment was conceptualized within the *attitudinal tradition* (Mowday et al., 1982;

Salancik, 1977). However, as the theory evolved, it expanded to include commitment to other work-relevant foci, including one's occupation, supervisor, work team, and customers (e.g., Meyer, Allen, & Smith, 1993; O'Shea, Goodwin, Driskell, Salas, & Ardison, 2009; Stinglhamber, Bentein, & Vandenberghe, 2002). Ultimately, it developed into a general model purported to apply to any and all commitments (Meyer & Herscovitch, 2001). With this evolution came recognition of the motivational properties inherent in commitment and efforts to link the TCM to theories of work motivation (Meyer, Becker, & Vandenberghe, 2004). This endeavor was greatly facilitated by inclusion of SDT—a theory that was only beginning to be acknowledged within the work motivation literature (see Gagné & Deci, 2005).

My objectives in this chapter are to provide a brief overview of theory and research on employee commitment, describe its evolution as a motivational construct within the TCM (Meyer & Allen, 1991; Meyer & Herscovitch, 2001), and illustrate how this evolution was facilitated by establishing links with SDT (Meyer et al., 2004). I also elaborate on recent developments in commitment theory (e.g., Meyer, Becker, & Van Dick, 2006; Meyer & Maltin, 2010; Meyer & Parfyonova, 2010) and research (e.g., Gellatly, Meyer, & Luchak, 2006; Meyer, Stanley, & Parfyonova, 2012; Somers, 2009; 2010; Wasti, 2005) to demonstrate how the integration of the TCM and SDT has helped to advance understanding of the nature, development, and consequences of commitment. Finally, I describe how SDT in combination with the TCM was applied recently to the development of a theoretical framework to guide research and practice pertaining to employee engagement (Meyer & Gagné, 2008; Meyer, Gagné, & Parfyonova, 2010). I conclude by offering an agenda for future research.

The TCM of Organizational Commitment

Meyer and Allen (1991, 1997; Allen & Meyer, 1990) developed the TCM of organizational commitment to address observed similarities and differences in existing unidimensional conceptualizations of the construct (e.g., Becker, 1960; Mowday et al., 1982; Wiener, 1982). Common to all was the belief that commitment binds an individual to an organization and reduces the likelihood of turnover. The main differences were in the psychological state, or mindset, presumed to characterize the commitment. These mindsets reflected three distinguishable

themes: (1) affective attachment to the organization, (2) obligation to remain, and (3) perceived cost of leaving. To distinguish among these mindsets, Meyer and Allen used the labels *affective commitment*, *normative commitment*, and *continuance commitment*, respectively. They referred to affective, normative, and continuance commitment as *components* rather than *types* of commitment to acknowledge that employees can experience all three to varying degrees. For example, one employee might have a strong desire to remain, feel obligated to do so, and recognize that there would be modest costs associated with leaving. Another might have little desire to remain and feel only a moderate sense of obligation to do so, but see the costs of leaving as very high (e.g., reduced salary, disruption associated with relocation).

One of the most important reasons for distinguishing among the components of commitment was that they can have different implications for behavior. Although all three relate negatively to turnover, their relations with on-the-job work behaviors can be quite different (see Meyer, Stanley, Herscovitch, & Topolnytsky, 2002). Indeed, research shows that affective commitment has the strongest positive correlation with job performance, organizational citizenship behavior, and attendance, followed by normative commitment. Continuance commitment tends to be unrelated, or negatively related, to these behaviors. Although Meyer and Allen argued that the nature of employees' commitment and its implications can be best understood by considering the three components together, they did not elaborate on how the components might combine, how the combinations would be experienced, and how they might influence behavior. Consequently, most research focused primarily on relations involving individual components, with only a few investigators exploring interactions (e.g., Jaros, 1997; Randall, Fedor, & Longenecker, 1990; Somers, 1995). This is an issue I address in more detail later.

Toward a General Model of Commitment

Another major development in commitment theory in the 1980s and 1990s was recognition that employees develop commitments to targets, or foci, other than the organization (e.g., Becker, 1992; Morrow, 1983; Reichers, 1985). In many cases, as researchers shifted their attention to these other foci (e.g., occupation, union, team), they simply adapted a measure of organizational commitment and changed the referent to the target of interest. In some cases, commitment was treated as a unidimensional construct (e.g., Bishop & Scott, 2000; Vandenberg, & Scarpello, 1994). In other cases, a multidimensional framework was applied (e.g., Becker, Billings, Eveleth, & Gilbert, 1996), including the TCM (e.g., Meyer et al., 1993; Stinglhamber et al., 2002). In still other cases, most notably union commitment (Gordon, Philpot, Burt, Thompson, & Spiller, 1980), quite extensive modifications were made to the models and accompanying measures. Thus, the shift in attention to other targets provided a major stimulus for commitment research, but the adoption of different conceptualizations and measures created confusion and served as an obstacle to communication and integration of research findings.

Meyer and Herscovitch (2001) argued that the essence of the commitment construct should remain the same regardless of the target and therefore attempted to develop a unifying theoretical framework. In so doing, they identified five key issues that needed to be resolved. First, a choice had to be made among the existing conceptualizations as the basis for a unifying definition of commitment. Second, it was necessary to determine whether a unidimensional or multidimensional conceptualization was optimal. Third, it was important to make a clear distinction between commitment and related constructs (e.g., attitudes, motivation). Fourth, it was necessary to conceptualize the outcomes of commitment in such a way that the model could be used to guide hypothesis development regardless of the focus of the commitment. Finally, the potential antecedents of commitment had to be described in such a way that similar principles could be applied to explain the development of commitment to any target. Together, the links to antecedent and consequence variables formed the nomological network (Cronbach & Meehl, 1955) used to validate measures, test theory, and direct practice.

Given the emerging consensus that commitment could take different forms, the large overlap among existing multidimensional conceptualizations (e.g., Jaros, Jermier, Koehler, & Sincich, 1993; Mayer & Schoorman, 1998; Meyer & Allen, 1991; Penley & Gould, 1988), and the relative dominance of the TCM within the organization commitment literature, Meyer and Herscovitch (2001) addressed issues one and two above by adopting the TCM as the basis for their general model. That is, they proposed that regardless of the target, commitment could be characterized by at least three distinct mindsets: (1) desire (affective), (2) obligation (normative), and (3) perceived cost (continuance). Moreover, following Meyer and Allen (1991), they argued that each of these mindsets could be experienced to varying degrees and that the consequences of commitment would vary as a function of the relative strength of all three. Unlike Meyer and Allen, however, Meyer and Herscovitch developed a set of propositions with regard to how the components might combine to influence behavior. I discuss these propositions in more detail below. First, it is important to consider how Meyer and Herscovitch addressed the issues of providing a unifying definition of commitment and linking it to other variables across diverse contexts.

Defining Commitment

Unfortunately, adapting the TCM as a guiding framework did not provide the general definition needed to establish the *core essence* of the construct and to distinguish commitment from related constructs (e.g., motive, attitudes). Meyer and Herscovitch (2001) considered such a distinction to be particularly important because, without it commitment loses its value as an explanatory concept. That is, "[i]f commitment is nothing more than a state of mind that exists when an individual experiences a positive exchange relationship with some entity, it contributes nothing beyond exchange theories of motivation (e.g., expectancy, equity) to our understanding of organizational behavior. Similarly, if commitment is viewed simply as a positive attitude, there is little to be gained by continuing to study it outside the confines of more general attitude research" (p. 301).

Earlier scholars (e.g., Brickman, 1987; Brown, 1996; Oliver, 1990; Scholl, 1981) had similarly sought to define commitment in such a way that distinguished it from other motives or attitudes. Meyer and Herscovitch (2001, p. 301) found that common among these definitions was the notion that commitment was a "stabilizing or obliging force" that "gives direction to behavior (i.e., restricts freedom, binds the person to a course of action)." Therefore, this notion of commitment as a stabilizing force served as one key element in the development of a unifying conceptualization.

Another challenge in the development of a general definition was the diversity of potential targets. More specifically, some researchers were interested in studying commitment to other individuals (e.g., marital partner, supervisor) or collectives (e.g., organization, union, team), whereas others were interested in commitments to a course of action (e.g., exercise routine, performance improvement), or a stimulus to action (e.g., goal, program, change initiative). This raised the question as to whether commitment is to an entity, an action, or both, and whether it is possible to define commitment in such a way that it applies in all cases. Although seemingly similar, this issue is different from the long-standing distinction between attitudinal and behavioral commitment (see Mowday et al., 1982; Salancik, 1977). The latter distinction relates more to the process by which commitment develops than to the target of commitment per se.[1] To address the target issue, Meyer and Herscovitch (2001) noted that the distinction between commitment to an entity and commitment to behavior might be largely a function of emphasis. That is, most commitments involve both an entity and a course of action. For example, a commitment to an organization typically includes a set of explicit or implied *terms* (Brown, 1996), such as staying for a particular period of time and/or performing at some accepted level. Similarly, there is often an entity implied in a commitment to a course of action. For instance, the entity implied in commitment to goal-directed behavior is the objective or beneficiary of the goal. Thus, Meyer and Herscovitch argued that there may be advantages to including both the entity and behavior in the definition of commitment. Combining this with the notion of commitment as a stabilizing force accompanied by different mindsets, they offered the following general definition: "Commitment is a mind-set that can take different forms and binds an individual to a course of action that is relevant to a particular target" (p. 310).

Developing a Context-free Nomological Network

Because commitment can be directed at different foci, the factors contributing to its development differ, as do the relevant behavioral consequences. For example, the conditions that contribute to the development of commitment to an organization are different from those involved in the development of commitment to a specific project. The behavioral manifestations of these commitments also are different (e.g., staying with the organization vs. working overtime to meet a project deadline). Therefore, a general model requires specification of classes of variables within a nomological network that can be used to guide the selection of relevant variables

across varying contexts. For present purposes, and in the interests of space, I focus here on how Meyer and Herscovitch (2001) addressed this problem with regard to the consequences of commitment.

According to the general model, commitment has similar implications for those behaviors specified within the terms of the commitment regardless of the accompanying mindset. However, the *quality* of this behavior, and/or the probability of related behaviors, varies as a function of the mindset. Meyer and Herscovitch (2001) referred to the behaviors stated or implied within the terms of the commitment as *focal* behaviors. In the case of organizational commitment, the focal behavior typically involves staying (Mowday et al., 1982), whereas in commitment to a change initiative the focal behavior is compliance with the requirements for change (Herscovitch & Meyer, 2002). Meyer and Herscovitch described behaviors that fall outside the explicit or implied terms of a commitment as *discretionary*. They argued that, in most cases, the entity affected by a commitment (e.g., organization, change initiative) also benefits from behaviors not clearly specified within the terms of a commitment. For example, an organization is better off if employees not only stay but perform at a level beyond the minimum requirements. Similarly, a change initiative is more likely to be successful when employees go beyond what is required (e.g., promoting the change to others, finding innovative solutions to problems). Although, theoretically, it is possible to include these latter behaviors within the terms of the commitment (in which case they become focal), in practice it is difficult to anticipate all of the activities that might be required to achieve a desired objective (e.g., a successful change initiative). According to the general model, it is the potential for discretionary activity that makes distinctions among the mindsets important.

Behavioral Implications of Commitment

Having distinguished the two general forms of commitment-relevant behavior—focal and discretionary—Meyer and Herscovitch (2001) offered a set of propositions regarding how these behaviors vary as a function of the commitment mindsets. Consistent with the original TCM, they predicted that affective commitment would have the strongest positive correlation with both types of behavior, followed by normative commitment and continuance commitment. Continuance commitment was expected to relate positively with focal behavior, but to be unrelated or negatively related to discretionary behavior. More importantly, Meyer and Herscovitch (2001) developed hypotheses concerning the combined effects of the three components. They argued that each individual has a *commitment profile* reflecting the relative strength of affective, normative, and continuance to any particular target (e.g., organization). To illustrate, they identified eight potential profile groups, each characterized by a combination of high or low scores on the three components. They argued that the optimal profile for both focal and discretionary behavior would be one with strong affective commitment combined with weak normative and continuance commitment. Hereinafter, I refer to this as an affective-dominant profile, and use the term *dominant* similarly in other profile labels to identify the strongest (i.e., dominant) components in the profile.

Because continuance commitment (perceived cost) and normative commitment (obligation) both involve constraints on behavior, Meyer and Herscovitch (2001) proposed that high scores on these components would have a mitigating effect on the impact of strong affective commitment. Thus, although the probability of staying and performing effectively should be relatively high for employees with fully committed (i.e., strong affective, normative, and continuance commitment), affective/normative-dominant, and affective/continuance-dominant profiles, it was expected to be lower than for employees with an affective-dominant profile. Employees with continuance-dominant, normative-dominant, or continuance/normative-dominant profiles were expected to have a greater likelihood of staying than uncommitted employees (i.e., those with low scores on all three components), but were not expected to do more than required in terms of performance.

Meyer and Herscovitch's (2001) general model stimulated considerable research, which I discuss in more detail below, but also led to further advances in theory. Most notably, it served as the basis for the integration of commitment theory with theories of work motivation (Meyer et al., 2004). As noted in the next section, this integration was greatly facilitated by the incorporation of SDT into the general framework.

Commitment and Motivation: Toward an Integrative Model

Like commitment, motivation is a complex construct that is difficult to capture in a simple definition. Because of this complexity, motivation has been examined from a variety of perspectives—both in general and in a work context. In an effort to capture the complexity of the construct and reflect the diversity in theoretical perspectives, Pinder (1998, p. 11) provided the following definition of work motivation: "Work motivation is a set of energetic forces that originates both within as well as beyond an individual's being, to initiate work-related behavior, and to determine its form, direction, intensity, and duration." Meyer et al. (2004) noted that, although distinguishable, there are several similarities between commitment and motivation. Most notably, both have been described as energizing forces with implications for behavior. Motivation was described by Pinder (1998) as a *set* of energizing forces, and commitment was described by Meyer and Herscovitch (2001) as a force that *binds* an individual to a course of action. Putting these together, Meyer et al. suggested that motivation is a broader concept than commitment and that commitment might best be considered one in the set of energizing forces contributing to motivated (intentional) behavior. Importantly, however, they noted that the binding nature of commitment makes it unique among the many forces. Indeed, this is reflected in the everyday use of the terms, where *commitment* is generally reserved for important actions or decisions that have relatively long-term implications (e.g., commitment to a relationship, commitment to environmental protection). By contrast, people describe themselves or others as being *motivated* even in cases that have relatively trivial and shorter-term implications (e.g., motivation to organize one's office). Thus, Meyer et al. concluded that commitment can serve as a particularly powerful source of motivation and can often lead to persistence in a course of action even in the face of opposing forces, such as outcome contingencies or fairness concerns (cf. Brickman, 1987; Scholl, 1981).

As another point of comparison, Meyer et al. (2004) noted that general interests in motivation and commitment both stem from a desire to understand, predict, and influence a wide range of behaviors. However, when applied to work, theories of motivation have typically focused on job performance as an outcome, whereas the dominant outcome in organizational commitment research was retention. Meyer et al. argued that theories of work motivation and commitment can both be expanded to explain any form of intentional behavior (e.g., attendance, turnover, in-role performance, organizational citizenship). This argument raises the possibility that theories of work motivation and commitment might be integrated to a common end, but also increases the importance of clarifying the distinction between the constructs.

As a starting point for the development of their integrative model of motivation and commitment, Meyer et al. (2004) adapted Locke's (1997) general model of work motivation. This model incorporates mainstream theories of work motivation (e.g., need, expectancy, and goal-setting theories) to explain the mechanisms underlying employees' motivation to perform on the job. However, the model required some revision to accommodate the integration of commitment theory. Specifically, adjustments were required to address differences in the structure (dimensionality) and behavioral consequences of the key constructs.

Dimensionality of Motivation and Commitment

Locke's (1997) general model, and the theories it incorporates, treat motivation as a unitary concept. That is, although they recognize variation in the degree of motivation, they generally do not acknowledge differences in the psychological states, or mindsets, which can accompany this motivation. This was problematic for the integration of a model of commitment where the nature of the accompanying mindset is important. To address this problem, Meyer et al. (2004) drew from motivation theories outside the mainstream work motivation literature, most notably SDT (Deci & Ryan, 1985, 2000) and regulatory focus theory (Higgins, 1997, 1998). Both theories acknowledge the multidimensionality of motivation and, in particular, the fact that motivation can be accompanied by different mindsets. For present purposes, I focus primarily on SDT. Meyer et al. noted that there were strong similarities between the mindsets described in SDT and those identified in the TCM of commitment—consequently it played a central role in the development of their integrative model.

A detailed description of SDT is provided by Gagné and Deci [Chapter 1]. Therefore, for present purposes I focus here on a few key distinctions regarding the nature of motivation. First, individuals can have little or no motivation for goal-directed activities (amotivation), they can be motivated by interest in the task itself (intrinsic motivation), or they can be motivated to attain outcomes linked to task engagement and/or performance (extrinsic motivation). Moreover, the motivational state accompanying extrinsic motivation can vary depending on the nature of the outcome and contingency. When an individual is motivated to attain rewards or avoid punishments controlled by others, he or she experiences *external regulation*. When the motive comes from a desire to evaluate oneself positively or avoid feelings of guilt or shame, he or she experiences *introjected regulation*. Finally, when the motive is to be self-expressive and/or to achieve outcomes consistent with personal values, he or she experiences *identified regulation* (sometimes described as *integrated regulation*).

Meyer et al. (2004) proposed that employees with a strong affective commitment to their organization would be most likely to experience intrinsic motivation or identified regulation—both are considered to be *autonomous* forms of regulation within SDT and are compatible with the *want to* mindset characterizing affective commitment. In contrast, individuals who have a strong continuance commitment and feel trapped in the organization due to lack of alternatives or other potential costs of leaving are more likely to experience external regulation; both continuance commitment and external regulation involve a high degree of perceived outside control. Finally, Meyer et al. proposed that employees who have a strong normative commitment would be likely to experience introjected regulation in their day-to-day tasks. That is, employees who have a strong sense of obligation to remain with the organization may judge themselves by the degree to which they live up to their own expectations and/or the expectations of others. As discussed below, these propositions have since been modified in light of evidence suggesting that a particular component of commitment can be experienced differently depending on how it combines with other components. For now, however, I turn to the second modification to Locke's (1997) model: the behavioral consequences of motivation.

Behavioral Consequences of Motivation

In Locke's (1997) model, the key outcome of motivation is task performance. For the most part, task performance involves a fairly circumscribed outcome that can be measured against an explicit or implied goal. Although important, it fails to take into account the possibility that employees might, under some circumstances, modify or expand the goal. Recall that Meyer and Herscovitch (2001) distinguished between focal and discretionary behavior and described them as qualitatively distinct. Moreover, they argued that the differences in commitment mindsets would be reflected most clearly in discretionary behaviors. For example, they proposed that employees with strong affective commitment are more likely to engage in discretionary behaviors that fall outside the terms of the commitment than are employees with strong continuance commitment (Meyer et al., 2002). Meyer et al. (2004) argued that the same might be the case with motivated behavior, but this possibility was not readily apparent from Locke's model. Interestingly, however, research addressing the behavioral consequences of the motivational states in SDT provides evidence for a pattern similar to that observed for the components of commitment. That is, although controlled motivation can contribute to effective performance on mundane tasks, more autonomous forms of motivation (i.e., intrinsic motivation and identified regulation) have been found to lead to greater performance on difficult and complex tasks requiring flexibility, creativity, and heuristic problem solving (see Gagné & Deci, 2005). Thus, inclusion of SDT into the integrative model also helped to justify the expansion of the outcomes of motivation to include both nondiscretionary (focal) and discretionary behaviors.

The Issue of Causality

As a final note on the integrative model, it is important to consider briefly the issue of causality. Meyer et al. (2004) proposed that the nature of an employee's organizational commitment would have important implications for the motivational state experienced during task performance. Therefore, their emphasis was on the causal effects of commitment mindsets on motivational mindsets. However, they acknowledged that, over time, the intrinsic and extrinsic consequences of performance would have implications for commitment—potentially strengthening or weakening the various mindsets. For example, an employee who regularly experiences autonomy at work is likely to develop a stronger affective attachment to the organization. In contrast, an employee whose activities are more highly controlled might become less affectively committed to the organization, but develop a stronger continuance commitment if the source of control (e.g., performance-based pay) would make it costly to leave. Thus, the causal connection between commitment and motivational states might best be considered reciprocal.

Tests of and Refinements to the Integrative Model

Given its complexity, it is impossible to test Meyer and colleagues' (2004) model in its entirety.

Consequently, the focus has been on some of the more novel elements, including the hypothesized relations between the commitment and motivational mindsets. These relations have now been examined in a few recent studies with mixed support (e.g., Gagné, Chemolli, Forest, & Koestner, 2008; Gagné et al., 2010; Meyer et al., 2012). Gagné et al. (2008) examined correlations within and across time in an Italian organization undergoing a merger. As expected, they found that affective commitment correlated most strongly with autonomous regulation, followed by introjected regulation. Interestingly, normative commitment correlated significantly, and at approximately the same magnitude, with autonomous and introjected regulation. Both affective and normative commitment correlated significantly, albeit less strongly, with external regulation prior to the merger, but did not correlate significantly postmerger. Separate correlations were computed for two facets of continuance commitment: high sacrifice and low alternatives. Only the low-alternatives facet correlated more strongly and positively with external regulation than with autonomous motivation as predicted; the high-sacrifice facet correlated moderately in a positive direction with all three of the motivation variables.

More recently, Gagné et al. (2010) also found that affective commitment correlated positively with more autonomous forms of motivation (intrinsic motivation and identified regulation), somewhat less so with introjected regulation, and negatively with external regulation. Continuance commitment correlated positively with external and introjected regulation, but did not correlate significantly with identified regulation or intrinsic motivation. Again, normative commitment correlated positively with both autonomous motivation and introjected regulation; however, it correlated negatively with external regulation in this study. Finally, Meyer et al. (2012) correlated the commitment components with a measure reflecting the relative strength of autonomous versus controlled regulation and found that both affective and normative commitment correlated positively and continuance commitment correlated negatively.

Thus, initial tests of the relations between the commitment and motivational mindsets generally support the predicted relations with affective and continuance commitment (particularly the low-alternatives facet). Normative commitment correlated positively with introjected regulation as expected, but it also correlated positively with more autonomous forms of motivation, and its correlations with external regulation varied in both magnitude and sign across studies. Interestingly, although the latter findings did not support the original predictions, they are consistent with some recent developments in theory and research pertaining to normative commitment (Gellatly et al., 2006; Meyer & Parfyonova, 2010). These and other new developments regarding profiles of commitment have broader implications for Meyer and colleague's (2004) integrative model, and in particular for the link between SDT and the TCM, and therefore warrant further discussion.

Commitment Profiles and Their Implications

Recall that Meyer and Herscovitch (2001) offered a set of propositions concerning how the three components of commitment combine to influence behavior. Early tests of these propositions (e.g., Gellatly et al., 2006; Somers, 2009, 2010; Wasti, 2005) provided some support, but also yielded some unexpected results that led to further refinements to the theory. For example, Gellatly et al. (2006) measured affective, normative, and continuance commitment and used a median-split approach to create the eight profile groups discussed by Meyer and Herscovitch (2001). The profile groups were then compared with regard to mean scores on self-report measures of intention to stay and organizational citizenship behavior. Contrary to expectation, employees with an affective/continuance-dominant profile did not differ from the affective-dominant group in terms of intention to remain or citizenship behavior. Moreover, intention to stay and citizenship behavior were *greater* for employees with an affective/normative-dominant profile than for those with an affective-dominant profile.[2]

Gellatly et al. (2006) also conducted moderated regression analyses and found three-way interactions for both intention to stay and organizational citizenship behavior. Follow-up simple slopes analyses involving citizenship behavior revealed a particularly interesting finding. Specifically, normative commitment related positively to citizenship behavior when it was combined with strong affective commitment. However, when combined with strong continuance commitment and weak affective commitment, normative commitment correlated *negatively* with citizenship behavior. Based on these findings, Gellatly et al. argued that the other components in a profile might provide a *context* that has implications for how a particular component is experienced. Most notably, when normative commitment (obligation) is combined with strong affective commitment (desire) it might be experienced as a "moral imperative" (i.e., a desire to do the right thing). However, when combined with strong continuance commitment (perceived cost) in the absence of affective commitment, normative commitment may be experienced as an "indebted obligation" (i.e., a need to do what is expected). Therefore, it appears that normative commitment is positively related to organizational citizenship behavior when experienced as a moral imperative, but is negatively related when experienced as an indebted obligation.

Although not specifically conducted to test for context effects, several other profile studies have provided relevant findings. For example, studies using k-means cluster analysis or latent profile analysis to identify naturally occurring profile groups have consistently demonstrated the lowest levels of turnover intention among employees with fully committed, affective/normative-dominant, and affective-dominant profiles (Somers, 2009; Stanley, Vandenberg, Vandenberghe, & Bentein, 2009; Wasti, 2005). Turnover intentions were found to be significantly greater for employees with uncommitted, continuance-dominant, and continuance/normative-dominant profiles. Somers (2010) compared profile groups in terms of actual turnover and found the lowest rates in the fully committed and affective/normative-dominant groups, although only the former differed significantly from the other groups.

A similar pattern of findings was obtained in comparisons involving job performance and organizational citizenship behavior. For example, Wasti (2005) found that citizenship behavior was greatest among employees with a fully committed profile, followed by those with affective-dominant and affective/normative-dominant profiles. In a study focusing on affective and continuance commitment only, Sinclair, Tucker, Wright, and Cullen (2005) found that supervisor-rated performance and organizational citizenship behavior were lowest among employees with moderate continuance commitment and low affective commitment. Performance and citizenship behavior for employees with moderate affective and continuance commitment did not differ from those with moderate affective and low continuance commitment (no profile group demonstrated strong scores on affective or continuance commitment). Thus, the negative impact of continuance commitment for performance may be

40 | EMPLOYEE COMMITMENT, MOTIVATION, AND ENGAGEMENT

restricted to conditions where it is combined with weak affective commitment.

One implication of these findings is that correlations between individual components of commitment and other variables, including motivational states, can be misleading. In one recent study, Meyer et al. (2012) developed and tested hypotheses pertaining to motivational states associated with different profiles. They found that autonomous regulation was greatest among employees with fully committed and affective/normative-dominant profiles, and lowest among those with uncommitted and continuance-dominant profiles. Of particular interest here is the observation that continuance commitment was associated with more controlled (less autonomous) regulation when it dominated the profile; it was actually associated with high autonomous regulation when part of a fully committed profile. Again, this is consistent with the notion that continuance might be experienced differently depending on the context created by the other components in the profile (Gellatly et al., 2006).

Commitment and Employee Well-being

Another recent development in the TCM was the inclusion of employee well-being as a potential outcome of commitment (Meyer & Maltin, 2010). This development was also facilitated by establishing links between the TCM and SDT. According to SDT, satisfaction of the needs for autonomy, competence, and relatedness are essential for psychological health (Deci & Ryan [Chapter 2]; Ryan & Deci, 2001; Ryan, Huta, & Deci, 2008). The need for autonomy is satisfied when, at a deep level of reflection, individuals believe that what they are doing is freely chosen and consistent with their core values. The need for competence is satisfied when people believe they have the capability and resources needed to accomplish their tasks and achieve their objectives. Finally, the need for relatedness is satisfied when they feel valued and appreciated by others. Satisfaction of these needs is a prerequisite for the experience of autonomous regulation. When one or more of the needs is thwarted, particularly the need for autonomy, a person is more likely to experience amotivation or a form of controlled regulation.

Meyer and Maltin (2010) reasoned that satisfaction of the core needs is also likely to be associated with the nature of an employee's commitment mindset. For example, employees working in a context where their needs are satisfied are likely to want to remain and therefore have a strong affective commitment. It is unlikely that they will feel that they are staying only to meet obligations (normative commitment) or avoid economic costs (continuance commitment). In contrast, when their needs are not being met, social obligations and/or perceived costs may be the only thing that holds them in the organization. However, these hypotheses focus on the individual components of commitment. In light of the theory and research pertaining to commitment profiles described above, Meyer and Maltin argued that the links between commitment and both need satisfaction and well-being might be best understood by considering commitment profiles rather than the individual components themselves.

Only a few studies have addressed the relations between commitment profiles and employee well-being (e.g., Markovits, Davis, & van Dick, 2007; Somers, 2009; Wasti, 2005), and only one has done so within the context of SDT (Meyer et al., 2012). Wasti found that Turkish employees with affective-dominant and affective/normative-dominant profiles experienced less job stress than those with a continuance-dominant profile. In a second study, she found that fully committed employees experienced less stress than all other profile groups. Somers found that US nurses with an affective/normative-dominant profile were among the lowest of any profile group in job stress, and *the* lowest in carry-over stress (i.e., work-related stress that persists outside the workplace). Finally, in a study of employees from three Canadian human service organizations, Meyer et al. (2012) found the highest levels of need satisfaction, autonomous regulation, and well-being for those with fully committed and affective/normative-dominant profiles; the lowest levels of both were observed among employees with uncommitted and continuance-dominant profiles. Thus, as was the case for turnover and job performance, relations between the commitment components, particularly continuance and normative commitment, and employee well-being appear to depend on the strength of the other components in the profile.

Profiles of Motivation

Before concluding this section, it is worth noting that there is a small body of SDT research that has also examined profiles, in this case motivational profiles (e.g., Bioché, Sarrazin, Grouzet, Pelletier, & Chanal, 2008; Ratelle, Guay, Vallerand, Larose, & Senécal, 2007; Stephan, Bioché, & Le Scanff, 2010). The premise underlying this research is that the motivational states identified in SDT are not mutually exclusive. Indeed, even the more externally regulated forms of motivation are not necessarily incompatible with autonomous regulation. For example, Ratelle et al. found that some students had academic motivational profiles reflecting high levels of both autonomous and controlled regulation. As has been the case in commitment research, profiles involving controlled forms of regulation in combination with more autonomous forms were found in some cases to be associated with high levels of achievement. Extrapolating to a work context, it seems reasonable for an employee to feel fully autonomous in his/her work activities while recognizing that effective performance in these activities is essential for the attainment of desired external rewards such as a performance bonus or promotion. Moreover, recognition that there are extrinsic rewards associated with the attainment of valued work goals might lead to even greater persistence and higher levels of performance than autonomous regulation alone. I address the integration of profile studies pertaining to motivation and commitment in greater detail later as a direction for future research.

Toward an Evidence-based Model of Employee Engagement

Meyer et al. (2004) argued that, in addition to the implications for commitment and motivation theories themselves, integration of the theories might have benefits for related literatures (e.g., leadership, identification). Indeed, Meyer et al. (2006) used the integrative model to help clarify the links between organizational identification and commitment. For present purposes, I focus on another recent application that takes particular advantage of the integration of the TCM and SDT: the development of an evidence-based model of employee engagement.

In a recent essay, Macey and Schneider (2008) noted that interest in employee engagement is relatively new and originated in the business world rather than from academic research. Indeed, they argued that "[a]cademic researchers are now slowly joining the fray" (p. 3). However, Meyer and colleagues (Meyer & Gagné, 2008; Meyer et al., 2010) argued that, although the term has indeed been popularized by management and human resources consultants, it has solid roots in academic theory and scientific research. Thus, rather than slowly joining the fray, academics can draw on a large body of scientific research to serve as the basis

for understanding the nature, development, and consequences of employee engagement. To illustrate their point, Meyer et al. (2010) provided a model of employee engagement based on SDT and the TCM. Before describing the model, it is important to take a closer look at the meaning of engagement.

Defining Engagement

Although there is no clear consensus to date on the meaning of engagement, examination of some of the more popular definitions can help to identify its core elements. In one of the earliest definitions, Kahn (1990, p. 694) described engagement "as the harnessing of organizational members' selves to their work roles; in engagement, people employ and express themselves physically, cognitively, and emotionally during role performances." In contrast, he described disengagement as "the uncoupling of selves from work roles; in disengagement, people withdraw and defend themselves physically, cognitively, and emotionally during role performances." What is particularly salient in this definition is the involvement of self in the work role.

Schaufeli and his colleagues (Schaufeli, Salanova, Gonzalez-Roma, & Bakker, 2002, p. 74) defined engagement as "a positive, fulfilling, work-related state of mind that is characterized by vigor, dedication, and absorption." More recently, Saks (2006) adopted the Kahn and Schaufeli et al. definitions but expanded the construct to include job and organizational engagement. Masson, Royal, Agnew, and Fine (2008, p. 57) also acknowledged that, while academic research often focuses on engagement with work and job roles, in applied settings there is also an interest in "engagement with the organization." Thus, engagement must be conceptualized in such a way that it applies to multiple targets.

In an effort to synthesize the existing theory and research, Macey and Schneider (2008) argued that engagement can be conceptualized as a trait, a state, and a behavioral tendency. They proposed that "engagement as a state has a strong affective tone, connoting, at a minimum, high levels of involvement (passion and absorption) in the work and the organization (pride and identity) as well as affective energy (enthusiasm and alertness) and a sense of self-presence at work" (p. 14). This is largely consistent with the definitions offered by Kahn (1990) and Schaufeli et al. (2002). They defined *behavioral engagement* as "adaptive behavior intended to serve an organizational purpose, whether to defend and protect the status quo in response to actual or anticipated threats or to change and/or promote change in response to actual or anticipated events" (p. 18). This definition focuses on the visible manifestations of employee engagement and helps to illustrate its importance for organizations. Finally, Macey and Schneider proposed that engagement can also have more stable dispositional qualities and defined *trait engagement* as "the [dispositional] tendency to experience work in positive, active, and energetic ways and to behave adaptively" (p. 21). The treatment of engagement as a stable individual difference raises the possibility that organizations might be able to select for characteristics that predispose employees to be engaged.

Considering these various descriptions of the facets and foci of engagement together, Meyer et al. (2010, p. 64) offered the following working definition: "Engagement is experienced as enthusiasm and self-involvement with a task or collective (e.g., organization), is fostered by a corresponding dispositional orientation and facilitating climate, and manifests itself in proactive value-directed behavior."

The Engagement Model

With the foregoing definition as a guide, Meyer et al. (2010) devised a theoretical framework based on SDT and the TCM. This framework, which is reproduced in Figure 3.1, allowed them to describe the mechanisms involved in the development of engagement, identify dispositions and situational factors that trigger these mechanisms, and explain the benefits that derive from engagement.

LEVELS AND CATEGORIES OF ENGAGEMENT

The model makes a basic distinction between *activity engagement* (based on SDT) and *organizational engagement* (based on the TCM). This is consistent with the argument that employees can be engaged at both the task and organizational level (Masson et al., 2008; Saks, 2006). However, Meyer et al. (2010) noted that there are likely to be other forms of engagement (e.g., engagement in teams, projects, and change initiatives). These can be accommodated by the extension of the TCM to other commitment foci as described previously (see Meyer & Herscovitch, 2001) and applications of SDT at different levels of abstraction (see Vallerand, 1997).

For both the activity and organizational foci, the model makes distinctions between three categories of engagement: (1) disengagement, (2) contingent engagement, and (3) full engagement. Employees who are disengaged are expected to experience what is referred to in SDT as *amotivation*: the absence of intentional regulation or goal-directed activity. At the organization level, they have little commitment of any form and therefore can be expected to leave at their convenience. By contrast,

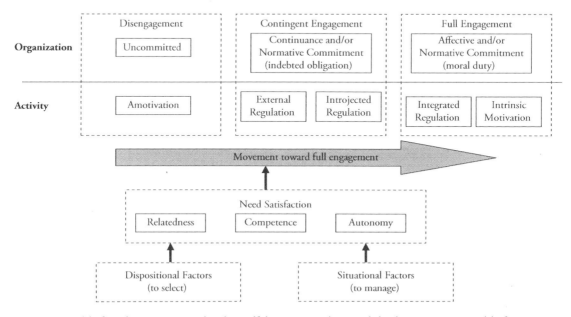

Fig. 3.1. A model of employee engagement based on self-determination theory and the three-component model of commitment (Reprinted from Meyer, J. P., Gagné, M., & Parfyonova, N. M. (2010). Toward an evidence-based model of engagement: What we can learn from motivation and commitment research. In S. Albrecht (Ed.), *The handbook of employee engagement: Perspectives, issues, research and practice* (pp. 62–73). Cheltenham, UK: Edward Elgar Publishing. With permission from Edward Elgar Publishing.)

fully engaged employees are autonomously regulated. This can be experienced as intrinsic motivation, where performance of task-relevant activities is enjoyable, or as identified regulation, where the work is not intrinsically interesting but is valued and meaningful. At the organizational level, fully engaged employees are likely to have a strong affective commitment, perhaps accompanied by strong normative commitment reflecting a sense of moral duty to remain and contribute to the success of the organization (Gellatly et al., 2006; Meyer & Parfyonova, 2010).

Meyer et al. (2010) included a third category of engagement in their model—contingent engagement—to acknowledge that many employees fall somewhere between the two extremes. These employees recognize that performance of their tasks is a necessity and is linked to continued employment, compensation, and benefits. In SDT terminology, they experience a sense of controlled regulation—they do not enjoy their job or see it as particularly meaningful, but rather as a means to attain desired outcomes largely controlled by others. At the organizational level, these employees are likely to experience high levels of continuance commitment, perhaps based on a lack of alternative employment opportunities or concerns over the potential loss of status, benefits, or other perks that depend on their continued employment in the organization (Powell & Meyer, 2004). If this is the case, based on research findings reviewed previously, employees who are contingently engaged are likely to stay and perform for the organization, but their efforts may be restricted to meeting minimum performance requirements. At a time when jobs were well defined and performance standards clearly articulated, the use of contingent rewards and sanctions could be quite effective. However, in the highly competitive and ever-changing business environment of today where employees are expected to continually adapt and find innovative and creative ways to contribute to organizational success, contingent engagement may not be enough. Therefore, organizations must find ways to get employees more fully engaged.

DEVELOPMENT OF ENGAGEMENT

According to the model proposed by Meyer and colleagues (2010), the key to moving employees along the continuum toward full engagement is the satisfaction of employees' basic psychological needs. This can be achieved, in part, by selecting employees who are predisposed to engagement, but ultimately depends on the creation of a work climate

that affords the opportunities for need satisfaction. Again, one of the advantages of basing a model of engagement on established theory is that it is possible to draw on a large body of existing research to identify personal and situational variables that are likely to relate to engagement (Meyer, 2013). In the absence of research regarding a specific variable (e.g., human resource management practice), the theory provides a set of principles that can be used to anticipate its effects.

According to SDT, one of the dispositional factors related to need satisfaction and autonomous regulation, and therefore likely to contribute to engagement, is *general causality orientation*—a stable tendency to self-regulate and seek out situations that are value-congruent and support self-initiation. Although much of the research on general causality orientation has been conducted outside of a work context (see Ryan & Deci, 2000), Baard, Deci, and Ryan (2004) found that it related positively to perceived need satisfaction and, through need satisfaction, to job performance and psychological adjustment in a sample of investment bank employees. Thus, general causality orientation might be a factor for organizations to consider in the selection process as part of a general strategy to promote higher levels of employee engagement.

It is unlikely that high levels of state and behavioral engagement can be achieved and maintained through selection practices alone. Therefore, it is important for organizations to create a *climate for engagement*. Arguably, it is here that the extensive research generated by SDT and the TCM makes its greatest contribution. According to SDT, job design, management practices, and reward systems play important roles in satisfying employee needs and promoting autonomous regulation (Gagné & Deci, 2005). When jobs are designed to be more stimulating and meaningful, they are associated with employee need satisfaction (Gagné, Sénécal, & Koestner, 1997). Similarly, managers can satisfy employees' needs and increase autonomous regulation by using a variety of autonomy-supportive behaviors, including acknowledging employees' perspective, providing relevant information in a noncontrolling manner, offering choice, and encouraging initiative (e.g., Baard et al., 2004; Deci, Connell, & Ryan, 1989; Deci et al., 2001; Parfyonova, 2009). Finally, when rewards and recognition are given to acknowledge employee competence, rather than to control their behavior, they can increase autonomous motivation (Gagné & Forest, 2008).

Research pertaining to the TCM has also led to the identification of several workplace factors instrumental in the development of a strong affective and normative commitment to organizations, including organizational support (Rhoades & Eisenberger, 2002), organizational justice (Colquitt, Conlon, Wesson, Porter, & Ng, 2001), transformational leadership (Meyer et al., 2002), and person-organization fit (Kristof-Brown, Zimmerman, & Johnson, 2005). Many of these factors are similar to those identified by the research on SDT, and are likely to contribute to need satisfaction and autonomous motivation. Each of the factors has been subjected to considerable research in its own right, and therefore there is a large body of evidence to draw on to identify specific management policies and practices. Thus, even if one argues that there is more to engagement than what is reflected in this SDT/TCM-based model, the integration of these two theories goes a long way to explaining the nature, development, and consequences of employee engagement, and can serve as a useful guide for research and management practice.

Conclusions

Meyer et al. (2004) laid the groundwork for the integration of commitment and motivation theories. The inclusion of SDT as a linchpin between a multidimensional conceptualization of commitment and traditional work motivation theories proved to be a particularly important contribution, and stimulated further theoretical developments (Meyer et al., 2006; Meyer et al., 2010; Meyer & Maltin, 2010; Meyer & Parfyonova, 2010) and research (e.g., Gagné et al., 2008; Gagné et al., 2010; Meyer et al., 2012). Among other implications, the integration of SDT and the TCM recently served as the basis for the development of a model of employee engagement. This model should allow both researchers and practitioners to draw on a large body of existing research to guide future research and practice pertaining to this "new" phenomenon. Although many of the links between variables identified in the integrative model are based on well-established findings, others derive largely from theory. Moreover, recent research findings, most notably those pertaining to profiles of commitment (e.g., Gellatly et al., 2006; Meyer et al., 2012; Somers, 2009, 2010; Wasti, 2005) and motivation (e.g., Bioché et al., 2008; Ratelle et al., 2007; Stephan et al., 2010), suggest the need to revisit some of the original propositions. Therefore, to conclude this chapter, I identify some of the issues that warrant further research.

Future Directions

A key to the integration of the TCM and SDT was the correspondence between the commitment and motivational mindsets. Although the connections initially proposed by Meyer et al. (2004) have received some empirical support (e.g., Gagné et al., 2008; Gagné et al., 2010; Meyer et al., 2012), there was some variability across studies in the strength and direction of relations, particularly those involving normative commitment. This may have been caused in part by the use of different samples and measures. As discussed below, it might also be caused by the fact that normative commitment can be experienced both as a moral imperative and an indebted obligation (Gellatly et al., 2006; Meyer & Parfyonova, 2010). However, the inconsistency in findings suggests the need for additional research to examine how the motivational states and commitment mindsets relate to one another, and why these relations might vary across conditions.

A second related issue has to do with the direction of causality between commitment to a social entity (e.g., organization, professional association, team) and goal regulation (motivation) as it pertains to behaviors of relevance to that commitment. Recall that Meyer et al. (2004) proposed a causal path between the commitment mindsets and goal regulation, suggesting that the nature of an employee's commitment to the organization would have a bearing on how they regulate task behavior on a day-to-day basis. However, they also proposed a feedback loop suggesting that goal regulation might influence commitment over time through its impact on performance and the consequences of that performance. To date, only one study has examined relations between commitment mindsets and motivational states over time (Gagné et al., 2008), and this study provided more evidence for the motivation to commitment link than vice versa. However, more research is needed, ideally using analytic procedures, such as latent growth modeling, that address the issue of how changes in one variable relate to changes in another (see Vandenberg & Stanley [2009] for a discussion of the analytic strategy; see Bentein, Vandenberg, Vandenberghe, & Stinglhamber [2005] and Vandenberghe, Panaccio, Bentein, Mignonac, & Roussel [2011] for applications in commitment research).

Third, as noted earlier, one of the major contributions of SDT to commitment theory is the introduction of need satisfaction as a potential basis for the development of commitment. Indeed, it has been proposed that need satisfaction may mediate the impact of many of the major antecedents of commitment such as perceived organizational support, organizational justice, transformational leadership, and person-organization fit (see Meyer & Maltin, 2010; Meyer et al., 2010). Although there is now some research linking need satisfaction to the commitment mindsets (e.g., Greguras & Diefendorff, 2009; Meyer et al., 2012), research has yet to examine its mediating role. Establishing need satisfaction as a proximal determinant of commitment that can explain the impact of environmental conditions is important because it could then serve as a basic principle to guide management initiatives designed to foster commitment. That is, for any initiative under consideration, management might begin with the thought experiment: "What impact is this likely to have on the satisfaction of employees' needs for autonomy, competence, and/or relatedness?"

Fourth, recent research has confirmed initial beliefs (e.g., Meyer & Allen, 1991) that the components of commitment combine to influence behavior (e.g., Gellatly et al., 2006; Somers, 2009, 2010; Wasti, 2005). Moreover, theory and research has expanded to include employee well-being as a consequence of the combined mindsets (e.g., Meyer & Maltin, 2010; Meyer et al., 2012). Interestingly, as noted previously, there is also research demonstrating that motivational states can combine differently among subgroups and have different implications for behavior (e.g., Bioché et al., 2008; Ratelle et al., 2007; Stephan et al., 2010). Findings such as this raise the possibility that there may be correspondence between varying configurations, or profiles, of motivation and commitment. It also suggests that more controlled forms of motivation and commitment can have positive outcomes under certain conditions. However, research to date is limited and motivational profiles have yet to be studied in a work context, so there is a need for more research on motivation and commitment profiles, both individually and in combination.

Finally, both SDT and the TCM were developed in North America and, although they have been tested in other cultures, there have been questions raised about whether such theories apply and/or fully capture the relevant constructs in all cultures (e.g., Boyacigiller & Adler, 1991; Gelfand, Erez, & Aycan, 2007). Recent meta-analytic investigations of TCM research (e.g., Fischer & Mansell, 2009; Stanley et al., 2007) have provided evidence for both similarities and differences across cultures. For example, although affective and normative commitment have been found to relate to turnover intentions, job performance, and organizational citizenship behavior across cultures, the strength of the relation varies somewhat, particularly in the case of normative commitment. Some of this variability can be explained by cultural values, such as individualism/collectivism and power distance (Hofstede, 1980; 2001). Moreover, some researchers (e.g., Lee, Allen, Meyer, & Rhee, 2001; Wasti, 2002) found that it was helpful to modify the commitment measures slightly to make them more culture relevant. Wasti and Önder (2009) argued that, despite the apparent empirical support for the TCM across cultures, it is still not clear that the way commitments are experienced in other cultures is fully understood. SDT has also been tested with some success in other non-Western cultures (e.g., Chirkov, Ryan, Kim, & Kaplan, 2003; Deci et al., 2001), but systematic cross-cultural comparison in a work context is limited and therefore more research is warranted.

These are admittedly only a few of the many research questions that stem from efforts to integrate the TCM and SDT. The implications of this integration appear to be wide ranging and it is hoped will serve as a catalyst for integration with other theories and as a guide to policy and practice as they pertain to employee engagement and management in general.

Notes

1. In the behavioral tradition, commitment is operationalized as persistence in a course of action and develops under conditions where the initial action was freely chosen (volitional), public, important, and irrevocable.

2. This information was not reported in the article but was obtained from the authors

References

Allen, N. J., & Meyer, J. P. (1990). The measurement and antecedents of affective, continuance, and normative commitment to the organization. *Journal of Occupational Psychology*, *63*, 1–18.

Baard, P. P., Deci, E. L., & Ryan, R. R. (2004). Intrinsic need satisfaction: A motivational basis of performance and well-being in two work settings. *Journal of Applied Social Psychology*, *34*, 2045–2068.

Becker, H. S. (1960). Notes on the concept of commitment. *American Journal of Sociology*, *66*, 32–40.

Becker, T. E. (1992). Foci and bases of commitment: Are these distinctions worth making? *Academy of Management Journal*, *35*, 232–244.

Becker, T. E., Billings, R. S., Eveleth, D. M., & Gilbert, N. W. (1996). Foci and bases of commitment: Implications for performance. *Academy of Management Journal*, *39*, 464–482.

Becker, T. E., Kline, H. J., & Meyer, J. P. (2009). Commitment in organizations: Accumulated wisdom and new directions. In H. J. Klein, T. E., Becker, & J. P. Meyer (Eds.),

Commitment in organizations: Accumulated wisdom and new directions (pp. 419–452). Florence, KY: Routledge/Taylor and Francis Group.

Bentein, K., Vandenberg, R., Vandenberghe, C., & Stinglhamber, F. (2005). The role of change in the relationship between commitment and turnover: A latent growth modeling approach. *Journal of Applied Psychology, 90*, 468–482.

Bishop, J. W., & Scott, K. D. (2000). An examination of organizational and team commitment in a self-directed team environment. *Journal of Applied Psychology, 85*, 439–450.

Boiché, J. C. S., Sarrazin, P. G., Grouzet, F. M. E., Pelletier, L. G., & Chanal, J. P. (2008). Students' motivational profiles and achievement outcomes in physical education: A self-determination perspective. *Journal of Educational Psychology, 100*, 688–701.

Boyacigiller, N. A., & Adler, N. J. (1991). The parochial dinosaur: Organizational science in a global context. *Academy of Management Review, 16*, 262–290.

Brickman, P. (1987). Commitment. In B. Wortman & R. Sorrentino (Eds.), *Commitment, conflict, and caring* (pp. 1–18). Englewood Cliffs, NJ: Prentice-Hall.

Brown, R. B. (1996). Organizational commitment: Clarifying the construct and simplifying the existing construct typology. *Journal of Vocational Behavior, 49*, 230–251.

Chirkov, V., Ryan, R. M., Kim, Y., & Kaplan, U. (2003). Differentiating autonomy from individualism and independence: A self-determination theory perspective on internalization of cultural orientations and well-being. *Journal of Personality and Social Psychology, 84*, 97–118.

Colquitt, J. A., Conlon, D. E., Wesson, M. J., Porter, C. O. L. H., & Ng, K. Y. (2001). Justice at the millennium: A meta-analytic review of 25 years of organizational justice research. *Journal of Applied Psychology, 86*, 425–445.

Cronbach, J. L., & Meehl, P. E. (1955). Construct validity in psychological tests. *Psychological Bulletin, 52*, 281–302.

Deci, E. L., Connell, J. P., & Ryan, R. M. (1989). Self-determination theory in a work organization. *Journal of Applied Psychology, 74*, 580–590.

Deci, E. L., & Ryan, R. M. (1985). *Intrinsic motivation and self-determination in human behavior.* New York: Plenum.

Deci, E. L., & Ryan, R. M. (2000). The "what" and "why" of goal pursuits: Human needs and the self-determination of behavior. *Psychological Inquiry, 11*, 227–268.

Deci, E. L., Ryan, R. M., Gagné, M., Leone, D. R., Usunov, J., & Kornazheva, B. P. (2001). Need satisfaction, motivation, and well-being in the work organizations of a former Eastern Bloc country: A cross-cultural study of self-determination. *Personality and Social Psychology Bulletin, 27*, 930–942.

Fischer, R., & Mansell, A. (2009). Commitment across cultures: A meta-analytical approach. *Journal of International Business Studies, 40*, 1339–1358.

Gagné, M., Chemolli, E., Forest, J., & Koestner, R. (2008). A temporal analysis of the relation between organisational commitment and work motivation. *Psychologica Belgica, 48*, 219–241.

Gagné, M., & Deci, E. L. (2005). Self-determination theory and work motivation. *Journal of Organizational Behavior, 26*, 331–362.

Gagné, M., & Forest, J. (2008). The study of compensation systems through the lens of self-determination theory: Reconciling 35 years of debate. *Canadian Psychology, 49*, 225–232.

Gagné, M., Forest, J., Gilbert, M.-H., Aubé, C., Morin, E., & Malorni, A. (2010). The motivation at work scale: Validation

evidence in two languages. *Educational and Psychological Measurement, 70*, 628–646.

Gagné, M., Senécal, C., & Koestner, R. (1997). Proximal job characteristics, feelings of empowerment, and intrinsic motivation: A multidimensional model. *Journal of Applied Social Psychology, 27*, 1222–1240.

Gelfand, M. J., Erez, M., & Aycan, Z. (2007). Cross-cultural organizational behavior. *Annual Review of Psychology, 58*, 479–514.

Gellatly, I. R., Meyer, J. P., & Luchak, A. A. (2006). Combined effects of the three commitment components on focal and discretionary behaviors: A test of Meyer and Herscovitch's propositions. *Journal of Vocational Behavior, 69*, 331–345.

Gordon, M. E., Philpot, J. W., Burt, R. E., Thompson, C. A., & Spiller, W. E. (1980). Commitment to the union: Development of a measure and an examination of its correlates. *Journal of Applied Psychology, 65*, 479–499.

Greguras, G. J., & Diefendorff, J. M. (2009). Different fits satisfy different needs: Linking person-environment fit to employee commitment and performance using self-determination theory. *Journal of Applied Psychology, 94*, 465–477.

Herscovitch, L., & Meyer, J. P. (2002). Commitment to organizational change: Extension of a three-component model. *Journal of Applied Psychology, 87*, 474–487.

Higgins, E. T. (1997). Beyond pleasure and pain. *American Psychologist, 52*, 1280–1300.

Higgins, E. T. (1998). Promotion and prevention: Regulatory focus as a motivational principle. In M. P. Zanna (Ed.), *Advances in experimental social psychology* (Vol. 30, pp. 1–46). New York: Academic Press.

Hofstede, G. (1980). *Cultures consequences: International differences in work-related values.* London: Sage Publications.

Hofstede, G. (2001). *Cultures consequences: Comparing values, behaviors, institutions, and organizations Across Nations* (2nd Ed.). London: Sage Publications.

Jaros, S. J. (1997). An assessment of Meyer and Allen's (1991) three-component model of organizational commitment and turnover intentions. *Journal of Vocational Behavior, 51*, 319–337.

Jaros, S. J., Jermier, J. M., Koehler, J. W., & Sincich, T. (1993). Effects of continuance, affective, and moral commitment on the withdrawal process: An evaluation of eight structural equation models. *Academy of Management Journal, 36*, 951–995.

Kahn, W. A. (1990). Psychological conditions of personal engagement and disengagement at work. *Academy of Management Journal, 33*, 692–724.

Klein, H. J., Molloy, J. C., & Cooper, J. T. (2009). Conceptual foundations: Construct definition and theoretical representations of workplace commitments. In H. J. Klein, T. E. Becker, & J. P. Meyer (Eds.), *Commitment in organizations: Accumulated wisdom and new directions* (pp. 3–36). Florence, KY: Routledge/Taylor and Francis Group.

Kristof-Brown, A. L., Zimmerman, R. D., & Johnson, E. C. (2005). Consequences of individual's fit at work: A meta-analysis of person-job, person-organziation, person-group, and person-supervisor fit. *Personnel Psychology, 58*, 281–342.

Lee, K., Allen, N. J., Meyer, J. P., & Rhee, K. Y. (2001). The three-component model of organizational commitment: An application to South Korea. *Applied Psychology: An International Review, 50*, 596–614.

Locke, E. A. (1997). The motivation to work: What we know. *Advances in Motivation and Achievement, 10*, 375–412.

Macey, W. H., & Schneider, B. (2008). The meaning of employee engagement. *Industrial and Organizational Psychology*, *1*, 3–30.

Markovits, Y., Davis, A., J., & van Dick, R. (2007). Organizational commitment profiles and job satisfaction among Greek private and public sector employees. *International Journal of Cross-cultural Management*, *7*, 77–99.

Masson, R. C., Royal, M. A., Agnew, T. G., & Fine, S. (2008). Leveraging employee engagement: The practical implications. *Industrial and Organizational Psychology: Perspectives on Science and Practice*, *1*, 56–59.

Mayer, R. C., & Schoorman, F. D. (1998). Differentiating antecedents of organizational commitment: A test of March and Simon's model. *Journal of Organizational Behavior*, *19*, 15–28.

Meyer, J. P. (2013). The science-practice gap and employee engagement: It's a matter of principle. *Canadian Psychology*, *54*, 235–245.

Meyer, J. P., & Allen, N. J. (1991). A three-component conceptualization of organizational commitment. *Human Resource Management Review*, *1*, 64–89.

Meyer, J. P., & Allen, N. J. (1997). *Commitment in the workplace: Theory, research, and application*. Thousand Oaks, CA: Sage.

Meyer, J. P., Allen, N. J., & Smith, C. A. (1993). Commitment to organizations and occupations: Extension and test of a three-component conceptualization. *Journal of Applied Psychology*, *78*, 538–551.

Meyer, J. P., Becker, T. E., & Vandenberghe, C. (2004). Employee commitment and motivation: A conceptual analysis and integrative model. *Journal of Applied Psychology*, *89*, 991–1007.

Meyer, J. P., Becker, T. E., & Van Dick, R. (2006). Social identities and commitment at work: Toward an integrative model. *Journal of Organizational Behavior*, *27*, 665–683.

Meyer, J. P., & Gagné, M. (2008). Employee engagement from a self-determination theory perspective. *Industrial and Organizational Psychology: Perspectives on Science and Practice*, *1*, 60–63.

Meyer, J. P., Gagné, M., & Parfyonova, N. M. (2010). Toward an evidence-based model of engagement: What we can learn from motivation and commitment research. In S. Albrecht (Ed.), *The handbook of employee engagement: Perspectives, issues, research and practice* (pp. 62–73). Cheltenham, UK: Edward Elgar Publishing.

Meyer, J. P., & Herscovitch, L. (2001). Commitment in the workplace: Toward the general model. *Human Resource Management Review*, *11*, 299–326.

Meyer, J. P., & Maltin, E. R. (2010). Employee commitment and well-being: A critical review, theoretical framework, and research agenda. *Journal of Vocational Behavior*, *77*, 323–337.

Meyer, J. P., & Parfyonova, N. M. (2010). Normative commitment in the workplace: A theoretical analysis and re-conceptualization. *Human Resource Management Review*, *20*, 283–294.

Meyer, J. P., Stanley, D. J., Herscovitch, L., & Topolnytsky, L. (2002). Affective, continuance, and normative commitment to the organization: A meta-analysis of antecedents, correlates, and consequences. *Journal of Vocational Behavior*, *61*, 20–52.

Meyer, J. P., Stanley, L. J., & Parfyonova, N. M. (2012). Employee commitment in context: The nature and implications of commitment profiles. *Journal of Vocational Behavior*, *80*, 225–245.

Morrow, P. C. (1983). Concept redundancy in organizational research: The case of work commitment. *Academy of Management Review*, *8*, 486–500.

Mowday, R. T., Porter, L. W., & Steers, R. M. (1982). *Employee-organization linkages: The psychology of commitment, absenteeism, and turnover*. New York: Academic Press.

Oliver, N. (1990). Rewards, investments, alternatives and organizational commitment: Empirical evidence and theoretical development. *Journal of Occupational Psychology*, *63*, 19–31.

O'Shea, P. G., Goodwin, G. F., Driskell, J. E., Salas, E., & Ardison, S. (2009). The many faces of commitment: Facet-level links to performance in a military context. *Military Psychology*, *21*, 5–23.

Parfyonova, N. (2009). *Employee motivation, performance, and well-being: The role of managerial support for autonomy, competence and relatedness needs* (Unpublished doctoral dissertation). Department of Psychology, The University of Western Ontario, Canada.

Penley, L. E., & Gould, S. (1988). Etzioni's model of organizational involvement: a perspective for understanding commitment to organizations. *Journal of Organizational Behavior*, *9*, 43–59.

Pinder, C. C. (1998). *Work motivation in organizational behavior*. Saddle River, NJ: Prentice Hall.

Powell, D. M., & Meyer, J. P. (2004). Side-bet theory and the three-component model of organizational commitment. *Journal of Vocational Behavior*, *65*, 157–177.

Randall, D. M., Fedor, D. B., & Longenecker, C. O. (1990). The behavioral expression of organizational commitment. *Journal of Vocational Behavior*, *36*, 210–224.

Ratelle, C. F., Guay, F., Vallerand, R. J., Laorse, S., & Senécal, C. (2007). Autonomous, controlled, and amotivated types of academic motivation: A person-oriented analysis. *Journal of Educational Psychology*, *99*, 734–746.

Reichers, A. E. (1985). A review and reconceptualization of organizational commitment. *Academy of Management Review*, *10*, 465–476.

Rhoades, L., & Eisenberger, R. (2002). Perceived organizational support: A review of the literature. *Journal of Applied Psychology*, *87*, 698–714.

Ryan, R. M., & Deci, E. L. (2000). Self-determination theory and the facilitation of intrinsic motivation, social development, and well-being. *American Psychologist*, *55*, 68–78.

Ryan, R. M., & Deci, E. L. (2001). On happiness and human potentials: A review of research on hedonic and eudaemonic well-being. *Annual Review of Psychology*, *52*, 141–166.

Ryan, R. M., Huta, V., & Deci, E. L. (2008). Living well: A self-determination theory perspective on eudaimonia. *Journal of Happiness Studies*, *9*, 139–170.

Saks, A. M. (2006). Antecedents and consequences of employee engagement. *Journal of Managerial Psychology*, *21*, 600–619.

Salancik, G. R. (1977). Commitment and the control of organizational behavior and belief. In B. M. Staw and G. R. Salancik (Eds.), *New directions in organizational behavior* (pp. 1–54). Chicago: St. Clair Press.

Schaufeli, W. B., Salanova, M., Gonzalez-Roma, V., & Bakker, A. B. (2002). The measurement of engagement and burnout: A two sample confirmatory factor analytic approach. *Journal of Happiness Studies*, *3*, 71–92.

Scholl, R. W. (1981). Differentiating commitment form expectancy as a motivating force. *Academy of Management Review*, *6*, 589–599.

Sinclair, R. R., Tucker, J. S., Wright, C., & Cullen, J. C. (2005). Performance differences among four organizational commitment profiles. *Journal of Applied Psychology, 90,* 1280–1287.

Solinger, O. N., van Olffen, W., & Roe, R. A. (2008). Beyond the three-component model of organizational commitment. *Journal of Applied Psychology, 93,* 70–83.

Somers, M. J. (1995). Organizational commitment, turnover and absenteeism: An examination of direct and interaction effects. *Journal of Organizational Behavior, 16,* 49–58.

Somers, M. J. (2009). The combined influence of affective, continuance, and normative commitment on employee withdrawal. *Journal of Vocational Behavior, 74,* 75–81.

Somers, M. J. (2010). Patterns of attachment to organizations: Commitment profiles and work outcomes. *Journal of Occupational and Organizational Psychology, 83,* 443–453.

Stanley, D. J., Meyer, J. P., Jackson, T. A., Maltin, E. R., McInnis, K. J., Kumsar, Y., & Sheppard, L. (2007, April). *Cross-cultural generalizibility of the three-component model of commitment.* Paper presented at the annual meeting of the Society for Industrial and Organizational Psychology, New York, NY.

Stanley, L. J., Vandenberg, R. J., Vandenberghe, C., & Bentein, K. (2009, April). *Commitment profiles and turnover intentions.* Paper presented at the annual meeting of the Society for Industrial and Organizational Psychology, New Orleans, LA.

Stephan, Y., Boiché, J., & Le Scanff, C. (2010). Motivation and physical activity behaviors among older women: A self-determination perspective. *Psychology of Women Quarterly, 34,* 339–348.

Stinglhamber, F., Bentein, K., & Vandenberghe, C. (2002). Extension of the three-component model of commitment to five foci: Development of measures and substantive test. *European Journal of Psychological Assessment, 18,* 123–138.

Vallerand, R. J. (1997). Toward a hierarchical model of intrinsic and extrinsic motivation. In M. P. Zanna (Ed.), *Advances in experimental social psychology* (Vol. 29, pp. 271–360). San Diego, CA: Academic Press.

Vandenberg, R. J., & Scarpello, R. J. (1994). A longitudinal assessment of the determinant relationship between employee commitments to the occupation and organization. *Journal of Organizational Behavior, 15,* 535–547.

Vandenberg, R. J., & Stanley, L. J. (2009). Statistical and methodological challenges for commitment researchers: Issues of invariance, change across time, and profile differences. In H. J. Klein, T. E. Becker, & J. P. Meyer (Eds.), *Commitment in organizations: Accumulated wisdom and new directions* (pp. 383–416). Florence, KY: Routledge/Taylor and Francis Group.

Vandenberghe, C., Panaccio, A., Bentein, K., Mignonac, K., & Roussel, P. (2011). Assessing longitudinal change of and dynamic relationships among role stressors, job attitudes, turnover intention, and well-being in neophyte newcomers. *Journal of Organizational Behavior, 32,* 652–671.

Wasti, S. A. (2002). Affective and continuance commitment to the organization: Test of an integrated model in the Turkish context. *International Journal of Intercultural Relations, 26,* 525–550.

Wasti, S. A. (2005). Commitment profiles: Combinations of organizational commitment forms and job outcomes. *Journal of Vocational Behavior, 67,* 290–308.

Wasti, S. A., & Önder Ç. (2009). Commitment across cultures: Progress, pitfalls and propositions. In H. J. Klein, T. E. Becker, & J. P. Meyer (Eds.), *Commitment in organizations: Accumulated wisdom and new directions* (pp. 309–343). Florence, KY: Routledge/Taylor and Francis Group.

Weiner, Y. (1982). Commitment in organizations: A normative view. *Academy of Management Review, 7,* 418–428.

CHAPTER

4

Effective and Sustained Proactivity in the Workplace: A Self-Determination Theory Perspective

Karoline Strauss *and* Sharon K. Parker

Abstract

Proactivity involves self-starting and future-focused action that aims to bring about change, either in the self or in one's work environment. In this chapter, drawing particularly on self-determination theory, we outline and develop current conceptualizations of how proactivity is motivated, and how to promote proactivity that is effective in bringing about change. We propose that autonomous regulation increases the likelihood that proactivity results in positive change for both individuals and organizations, and introduce a dynamic model that represents the positive upward spiral of autonomously regulated proactivity. Autonomously regulated proactivity involves a more complete goal regulation process and a greater sense of ownership and involvement of the self, thus making it more likely for proactive goals to be achieved. Via the satisfaction of psychological needs, autonomously regulated proactivity enables high levels of individual proactivity that are sustained over time, and stimulates proactivity that is in line with organizational goals. We outline how organizations can encourage autonomously regulated individual proactivity that enhances employees' well-being and personal growth, and contributes to organizational effectiveness.

Key Words: proactivity, self-determination, psychological need satisfaction, autonomous regulation, goal regulation

Introduction

Over the last few decades researchers have increasingly acknowledged that individuals in organizations are not merely "passive, reactive respondents to their context" (Parker, Bindl, & Strauss, 2010, p. 828) but they play an active role in shaping their roles, careers, work environment, social context, and organizations. Individuals "create visualized futures that act on the present; construct, evaluate and modify alternative causes of action to secure valued outcomes; and override environmental influences" (Bandura, 2006, p. 164). The concept of proactivity at work most strongly expresses this view of organizations as environments of and for human agency. Proactivity involves challenging the current situation and working toward what "could be." Specifically, being proactive reflects self-starting

and future-focused action that aims to bring about change, either in the self or in one's work environment (Parker et al., 2010). This conceptualization of behavior in organizations emphasizes intentionality and forethought, and acknowledges that individuals are not always merely motivated by tangible reward contingencies. Proactivity makes room for individual goals that are not tied to external rewards but are pursued because they are interesting, highly valued, or reflect authentic interests. Correspondingly, proactive individuals experience a greater sense of self-determination in their lives (Greguras & Diefendorff, 2010; Seibert, Crant, & Kraimer, 1999).

Research has found that proactivity is associated with a range of positive outcomes (Fuller & Marler, 2009), including job performance (Crant,

1995; Thompson, 2005), career success (Seibert, Kraimer, & Crant, 2001), life satisfaction (Greguras & Diefendorff, 2010), and innovation (Kickul & Gundy, 2002). Proactive individuals are proposed to contribute to organizational effectiveness in dynamic and uncertain environments because in these contexts, for example, it is not possible to anticipate and prespecify all that is required of employees; instead, employees need to use their initiative and actively take charge of their environments (Griffin, Neal, & Parker, 2007).

Nevertheless, although there is good reason to expect positive benefits of proactivity, as well as supporting evidence, scholars have increasingly called for an acknowledgement of the potential downsides of proactivity. Not all proactive behavior predicts supervisors' judgments of overall job performance (Chan, 2006; Fuller, Marler, & Hester, 2012; Grant, Parker, & Collins, 2009). There can also be costs of proactivity, both to individuals and organizations (Belschak, Den Hartog, & Fay, 2010; Bolino, Valcea, & Harvey, 2010). In considering proactivity, we therefore need to consider not only how to motivate this type of behavior in organizations but also how to promote proactivity that is effective for organizations and not so costly for individuals that it cannot be sustained over time.

In this chapter, drawing particularly on self-determination theory, we outline and develop current conceptualizations of how proactivity is motivated, as well as how to promote proactivity that is effective in bringing about change. Self-determination theory provides a particularly fruitful theoretical lens for explaining how proactivity is motivated. The first part of the chapter reviews how different types of motivation influence the instigation of proactivity. For example, we argue that identifying with important outcomes (identified regulation) is more likely to stimulate proactivity than payment or other external rewards (extrinsic regulation). The second part of the chapter draws on self-determination theory to propose ways to enhance the likelihood that proactivity is effective, both for the individual (e.g., preserving their resources over time) and/or for the organization (e.g., having a positive effect on job performance). The third part of the chapter brings the previous arguments together to propose a virtuous circle by which autonomous motivation promotes effective proactivity which, through a number of mechanisms, contributes to further proactivity, resulting in a positive upward spiral. Finally, we elaborate on how organizations can support and encourage proactivity without undermining its self-determined nature. Prior to our focus on the motivation of effective proactivity, we begin by briefly reviewing the history of the concept of proactivity and the various conceptual approaches that have emerged.

Proactivity in the Workplace: Disposition, Behavior, or Process?

Echoing developments in psychological theorizing about the nature of human behavior (Bandura, 1989, 2001, 2006), research on vocational and organizational behavior has over the last few decades increasingly adopted a more agentic view of individuals. This shift reflects structural changes affecting organizations as well as individual careers. Because organizations increasingly need to respond flexibly to rapidly shifting market conditions, managing people in organizations is no longer about ensuring that clearly defined jobs are carried out effectively by enforcing rules and using controls. Instead, it becomes about articulating a vision and empowering an increasingly self-reliant workforce to work toward it (Cascio, 1995; cf. Griffin et al., 2010). In uncertain and unpredictable environments, work performance is no longer about fulfilling a prescribed job role, but involves taking "self-directed action to anticipate or initiate change in the work system or work roles" (Griffin et al., 2007, p. 329). At the same time, individual careers become increasingly independent from traditional organizational career arrangements. Concepts such as the protean career (Hall, 1976) or the boundary-less career (Arthur & Rousseau, 1996) acknowledge the increasing mobility between roles, jobs, organizations, or occupations, and emphasize developmental progression and a holistic perspective (Hall, 1996).

As job roles and career paths have become less predictable, scholars have moved beyond traditional theories of work motivation that primarily focus on assigned goals and have begun to explore "the creative ways in which employees deliberately plan and act to influence, change, and alter their environments" (Grant & Ashford, 2008, p. 6). Several originally isolated streams of research have explored different forms of proactive behavior in organizations: individuals in organizations voice suggestions (LePine & Van Dyne, 1998), implement ideas (Parker, Williams, & Turner, 2006), and thus contribute to change and innovation (Howell & Higgins, 1990; Scott & Bruce, 1994); they shape (Tims & Bakker, 2010; Wrzesniewski & Dutton, 2001), expand (Nicholson, 1984), and negotiate their tasks and roles (Ashford & Black, 1996); they actively build networks and relationships (Morrison, 2002); they seek out information to improve their job performance (Ashford, Blatt, & VandeWalle, 2003); and they develop their skills and shape their careers (Claes & Ruiz-Quintanilla, 1998; Seibert et al., 2001; Tharenou & Terry, 1998).

Research on these different forms of proactive behaviors has grown rapidly, but has largely been phenomenon-driven (Grant & Ashford, 2008; Parker et al., 2010). Since the turn of the century, researchers have increasingly called for an integration of these different types of proactive behaviors (Crant, 2000; Parker, 2000). In an effort to empirically integrate different proactive behaviors, Parker and Collins (2010) identified three higher-order categories: (1) proactive work behavior, (2) proactive strategic behavior, and (3) proactive person-environment fit behavior. Proactive work behavior is aimed at bringing about change within the organization, such as by improving work methods, voicing ideas or concerns, and taking action to prevent problems from reoccurring. Proactive strategic behavior concerns enhancing an organization's effectiveness and fit with the external environment, for example by identifying opportunities or threats or by bringing issues to the attention of top management in an effort to influence strategy. Through proactive person-environment fit behavior individuals improve the compatibility between their needs and abilities on one hand, and the opportunities and demands in the work environment on the other hand (cf. Edwards, 1996). It can involve proactively developing skills to meet anticipated demands, seeking feedback, or shaping one's job or role to better fit with one's needs or preferences.

Parallel to this phenomenon-driven focus on distinct proactive behaviors, researchers have investigated broader concepts of proactivity. Bateman and Crant (1993) identified proactive personality, the dispositional tendency to initiate change in one's environment, as a driver of proactive behavior across different domains. Evidence from a meta-analysis supports the role that proactive personality plays for job performance as well as a range of different proactive behaviors, and shows a positive relationship between proactive personality and career success (Fuller & Marler, 2009). Frese and colleagues (Frese & Fay, 2001; Frese, Fay, Hilburger, Leng, & Tag, 1997; Frese et al., 2002; Frese, Kring, Soose, & Zempel, 1996) identified the concept of personal initiative, an "active performance concept" (Frese & Fay, 2001, p. 133) that captures a constellation of work behaviors defined as self-starting, proactive, and persistent in the face of obstacles. By definition, these behaviors are aligned with organizational goals. In a recent meta-analysis, Thomas, Whitman, and Viswesvaran (2010) showed that personal initiative is positively associated with performance.

More recently, scholars have adapted a process view of proactive behavior. Frese and Fay (2001) drew on action theory (Hacker, 1998) to describe a sequential model of personal initiative. In a personal initiative action sequence, individuals first develop goals, then collect information and make prognoses about the future; they develop plans and execute them before they finally monitor the execution of their plan and gather feedback on whether their actions have been successful or need to be adjusted. Grant and Ashford (2008) distinguished between three phases of the proactive behavior process. In the anticipation phase, individuals envision possible future outcomes. They imagine possible futures (cf. Strauss, Griffin, & Parker, 2012) and the potential costs of pursuing these various possible futures. They then generate plans of how to implement their ideas. They transform the anticipated future into an implementation guide that specifies how it will be promoted or achieved (Gollwitzer, 1999). This can involve the development of alternative strategies and backup plans. Finally, individuals engage in "action directed toward future impact" (Grant & Ashford, 2008, p. 18). In a combination of the Frese and Fay model and the Grant and Ashford model, Bindl and colleagues (Bindl, Parker, Totterdell, & Hagger-Johnson, 2012) proposed and tested a model of proactive goal regulation. They identified four phases of a proactive goal regulation process. In the envisioning phase, individuals identify opportunities for change and imagine a future that is different from the status quo. In the planning phase they prepare for bringing this future about by mentally simulating different scenarios of how to bring about the envisioned change and by identifying different pathways. The enacting phase involves engaging in proactive behavior. Finally, in the reflecting phase individuals reflect on the consequences of their behavior and gather information that will inform future proactive goal regulation. The authors showed these phases are distinct from each other, and differentially predicted by affect.

Parker and colleagues (2010) similarly conceptualize proactivity as a goal-driven process. Following more general self-regulation theory (Kanfer & Ackerman, 1989), they distinguish between proactive goal generation, which corresponds with the envisioning and planning phases of Bindl et al.'s model and involves the anticipation of desired future states and outcomes, and the development of strategies to bring these states about. Goal striving captures the enacting and reflecting phases of the Bindl et al. model and involves "the behavioral and psychological mechanisms by which individuals purposively seek to accomplish proactive goals" (Parker et al., 2010, p. 832). According to this conceptualization, for a goal-driven process to reflect proactivity, it needs to involve both processes of proactive goal generation and proactive goal striving. For example, this definition excludes instances where individuals envision a proactive goal (generation) but then do not follow through with action (striving).

In the present chapter we define proactivity as a goal-driven process aimed at bringing about a different future that involves goal-generation and goal-striving elements. Conceptualizing proactivity as goal-oriented process has important implications for the understanding of how proactive behavior is motivated, as we elaborate next.

What Motivates Proactivity in the Workplace? Insights from Self-Determination Theory

Antecedents of proactivity, including individual differences in the tendency to engage in proactive behavior, have received extensive attention in the literature. Individual differences investigated in previous research include demographics, knowledge and abilities, as well as personality (including proactive personality, as discussed previously). Critical situational factors include job design, leadership, and climate (see Bindl & Parker, 2011b, for a detailed review). Scholars have argued that individual differences and contextual variables influence proactivity indirectly by proactive motivational states (Frese & Fay, 2001; Parker et al., 2010; Parker et al., 2006). Drawing on existing perspectives on motivation, Parker and colleagues (2010) identified three different groups of proximal motivational states through which more distal variables influence proactivity: (1) reason to motivation, (2) can do motivation, and (3) energized to motivation. Individuals will set and pursue proactive goals

1. If they have a compelling *reason to* engage in proactivity (Vroom, 1964), for example because it relates to their current or future goals (Eccles et al., 1983)
2. If they believe they *can* (i.e., that they have an impact on significant outcomes; outcome

expectations, Bandura, 1977; Frese & Fay, 2001), and that they can be successful in being proactive and dealing with the consequences of their proactive behavior (efficacy expectations, Bandura, 1997; Parker, 2000)
3. If they feel *energized* through the experience of high-activation positive affect (Bindl et al., 2012).

Self-determination theory can contribute to the understanding of each of these states and thus provides insights into how proactivity is motivated, as outlined below. In self-determination theory, a continuum of autonomous to controlled motivation is proposed, with different underlying processes and consequences for the individual of the types of motivation (Deci & Ryan, 2000; Ryan & Deci, 2000). At one end of this continuum is intrinsic motivation, which involves the engagement in a behavior for its own sake, such as for enjoyment or a sense of challenge, independent of its contingencies. At the other end of the continuum lies external motivation, which involves the initiation and maintainance of behavior by consequences external to the person (external contingencies, such as payment). In between these extremes are integrated, identified, and introjected motivation, which are experienced as more autonomous than external motivation, even though they are not intrinsic. The sense of autonomy derives from a process of internalization, in which people take in attitudes, values, and regulatory structures (Ryan, Connell, & Deci, 1985).

These different forms of motivation can be translated into *reasons to* engage in proactivity (Parker et al., 2010). The arguments are straightforward in relation to intrinsic motivation, the most autonomously regulated form in which behaviors are engaged in "out of interest without the necessity of separable consequences" (Deci & Ryan, 2000, p. 233). Parker et al. (2010) argued that, because of its emphasis on change-oriented behavior, being proactive increases challenge, thereby fulfilling individuals' basic needs for competence and autonomy. They gave the example of individuals who voluntarily, often in their own time, engage in the development of new open-source software because they find it intellectually stimulating (Lakhani & Wolf, 2003). Likewise, feelings of flow arise from engaging in challenging activities (Massimini & Carli, 1988), so the desire for flow can therefore prompt proactive efforts. Finally, some types of proactivity (e.g., individual innovation) involve creative processes, which are inherently enjoyable for some individuals.

However, individuals also pursue proactive goals if the tasks involved are not especially enjoyable or intrinsically motivating. In regard to integrated motivation, individuals "take in" and internalize values and regulations into their own identity. Thus, as with intrinsic motivation, Parker et al. (2010) argued that integrated motivation is likely to be a strong driving force for proactivity. That is, individuals will set and strive to achieve proactive goals to fulfill important life goals or express values that are central to the self. For example, individuals engage in proactive behavior to bring about their Future Work Self, a representation of the self in the future that captures their hopes and aspirations in relation to work (Strauss et al., 2012).

Identified regulation occurs when "an individual consciously values the behavioral goal or regulation such that the action is accepted or owned as personally important," similar to the utility judgment in expectancy theory. Identified regulation can also therefore prompt proactivity because individuals "recognize that change toward the envisioned future outcome is important, for themselves and/or for others" (Parker et al., 2010, p. 838). For example, if feedback is seen as useful to achieving goals, then an individual is more likely to engage in feedback seeking (Ashford et al., 2003). Likewise, the concept of flexible role orientation (Parker, Wall, & Jackson, 1997) relates to identified regulation because this refers to the breadth of ownership and responsibility that an individual has internalized into their construction of their role (Parker & Ohly, 2008). Evidence suggests individuals with a flexible role orientation are indeed more likely to engage in proactive work behavior (Parker et al., 2006). Related concepts, such as felt responsibility for change (Fuller, Marler, & Hester, 2006; Morrison & Phelps, 1999) and perceived job breadth (McAllister, Kamdar, Morrison, & Turban, 2007), also reflect employees' internalization of values and, as such, can predict proactive work behavior (Fuller et al., 2006).

Regarding which of intrinsic, integrated, and identified forms provide the strongest reason to be proactive, drawing on research showing intrinsic motivation is best for interesting tasks but that identified and integrated were best for important yet uninteresting tasks, Parker et al. (2010, p. 848) suggested that having more than one reason to, or multiple motivation forms, might provide a flexible motivation base sufficient to stimulate proactive goals and to see them through: "Evidence from education suggests the combination of intrinsic regulation with identified or integrated regulation might be the most powerful: Intrinsic motivation promotes a focus on the task and results in feelings such as excitement, whereas identification facilitates a focus on the long-term significance of the action and promotes persistence" (Deci & Ryan, 2000, p. 848).

Whether proactivity is regulated by more controlled forms of motivation is less clear. Parker and colleagues (2010) have argued that proactivity by definition involves a sense of volition and is thus autonomously regulated to at least some degree. Raub and Robert (2010) also argued that proactive behavior is less likely to be regulated by controlled forms of motivation than in-role behaviors and affiliative extra-role behaviors, such as helping. They propose that in-role behaviors are likely to be motivated mostly by external motivation as not performing them is likely to lead to punishments, whereas performing them is linked to contractual rewards. According to Raub and Robert, affiliative behaviors are likely to be regulated by introjected regulation, "based on social norms for appropriate interpersonal behavior" (p. 1747). Individuals would engage in affiliative behaviors, such as helping, because they experience a sense of pride when engaging in these behaviors, or because they would feel guilty otherwise. The authors propose that proactive behavior is expected to be controversial, however, and may even go against norms (cf. Morrison, 2006), and argue that proactivity is thus likely to be perceived as self-expressive and to be motivated by more autonomous forms of regulation.

Other authors have argued that there are increasing external pressures on individuals to display proactive behavior (Bolino et al., 2010; Erdogan & Bauer, 2005). This implies that proactive behavior may also be driven by controlled motivation. In regard to introjected regulation of proactive behavior, Campbell (2000) observes that job descriptions increasingly mention proactive behavior. Employees may thus feel guilty when they are not engaging in proactive behavior. This is an example of introjected regulation where proactive goals have been taken in by the person but have not been accepted as their own. Introjected regulation occurs when behavior is regulated by internal pressures, such as guilt, anxiety, and self-esteem maintenance (Rigby, Deci, Patrick, & Ryan, 1992). As with external regulation, behavior is not self-determined, but is contingent on its consequences. However, in the case of introjected regulation these contingent consequences are administered by individuals themselves.

In regard to introjected motivation, Parker et al. (2010) suggested that achieving positive self-evaluation might prompt proactivity more so than avoiding negative self-evaluations. The desire to feel better about oneself might prompt individuals to gain useful information on their performance and seek feedback (Ashford et al., 2003). Nevertheless, although it is possible for proactive behavior to be motivated by introjected regulation, this form of motivation is unlikely to lead to proactivity that can be sustained over time, as outlined in the next section of the chapter. It might also in some cases suppress proactivity. For example, Parker and Collins (2010) showed that a strong performance goal orientation (in which individuals have a strong emphasis on approval) is negatively linked to proactive work behaviors, which they suggested is because these individuals do not want to "risk" being seen as incompetent when engaging in new or challenging behaviors.

Extrinsic regulation occurs when behavior is maintained by consequences external to the person, such as financial rewards. Marinova and colleagues (Marinova, Moon, & Van Dyne, 2010) found that employees see proactive behavior as instrumental in leading to rewards, such as bonuses, promotion, or salary increases. Proactive behavior may also be used as an impression management tactic (Bolino, 1999; Hui, Lam, & Law, 2000). For example, individuals may try to enhance their positive image by seeking favorable feedback by asking for additional feedback after a positive performance review (Morrison & Bies, 1991).

Whether all proactive behavior that leads to external rewards represents extrinsic regulation, however, is unclear, because it could be that individuals see proactivity as leading to important outcomes for themselves, yet is still freely chosen, and thus driven by identified regulation. It could also be the case that outcomes that can be seen as external rewards are instrumental to individuals' authentic goals. For example, a person's Future Work Self (i.e., the representation of his or her hopes and aspirations in relation to work; Strauss et al., 2012) may involve working in a job with more responsibility; career progression is then instrumental to the individual's life goals, and engaging in proactivity to achieve a promotion may thus be driven by integrated regulation. However, it might be that individuals see their salary or job security as entirely contingent on proactivity, giving them little or no choice. In this case, they would feel under pressure to engage in proactive behavior, which would then be driven by extrinsic regulation. Proactive behavior may thus also be regulated by extrinsic contingencies, although we elaborate next why we believe such behavior is likely to be relatively less effective for individuals and organizations.

Importance of Autonomous Regulation for Effective Proactivity

So far, we have argued that all types of regulation can potentially prompt proactive goal generation and striving, but that autonomously motivated forms, relative to controlled forms, are the most likely reasons to be proactive. However, Parker et al. (2010) argued that not all proactive goal setting and striving results in actual change in the self or situation. They suggested that whether actual change occurs depends in part on the quality of the goal processes, and factors that affect these processes (e.g., goal regulation). Drawing on this perspective, in this section we argue that autonomous forms of motivation are not only more likely to prompt proactive action in the first place, but they are more likely to stimulate proactive behavior that is effective in bringing about change for individuals and organizations. From an individual perspective, effectively bringing about change means doing so in a way that protects or even enhances individual resources and well-being, thereby increasing the likelihood the individual will continue to engage in proactivity beyond a specific episode. From an organizational perspective, effectively bringing about change means making a positive difference to the individual, team, or organization, such as might be reflected in positive judgments of overall job performance from supervisors.

The idea that autonomously regulated proactivity is more effective is not new. Grant and colleagues (Grant, Nurmohamed, Ashford, & Dekas, 2011) provided preliminary empirical support for the idea that proactivity is more effective when it is autonomously regulated. In a sample of 106 job seekers, they found that personal initiative was only strongly associated with the number of job offers individuals received if their job search was highly autonomously motivated and low in controlled motivation. In a sample of 219 call center workers, the number of calls (used as a measure of initiative) was only related to the amount of hourly revenue generated by a call center worker if their motivation to "invest effort in their job" was high in autonomous and low in controlled motivation. These authors explained their findings in terms of individuals' energy and willpower. They proposed that proactivity that is intrinsically motivated will be pursued with more energy and passion, in other words, it will be associated with enhanced goal striving.

In addition, proactive behavior often requires self-control. Self-control refers to efforts to inhibit impulses, emotions, or behaviors that would interfere with one's goal-directed behavior (e.g., Kanfer & Karoly, 1972). It is a psychological resource that is limited and once used is temporarily depleted (Muraven, Rosman, & Gagné, 2007). Under conditions of controlled motivation, self-control depletes more strongly. For example, Muraven et al. (2007) showed in a series of experiments that individuals in a controlling situation involving performance contingent rewards performed worse on a subsequent test of self-control than individuals in an autonomy-supportive condition. The authors found that the differences in self-control depletion did not result from differences in negative mood or motivation; instead, autonomously motivated individuals experienced greater feelings of vitality, a "positive sense of aliveness and energy" (Ryan & Fredrick, 1997, p. 530). These results were replicated in a series of experiments that used a sense of pressure rather than contingent rewards to elicit the experience of controlled motivation (Muraven, Gagné, & Rosman, 2008). Proactivity that is driven by controlled motivation is thus likely to result in greater resource depletion, and will consequently be less effective and potentially detrimental to individuals' well-being.

Supporting this argument, Bolino and colleagues (2010) argued that proactive behavior is associated with negative well-being outcomes when individuals who lack resources engage in proactive behavior, for example, because the organization expects them to. This is in line with Chan's (2006) finding that proactive behavior is only associated with positive performance and well-being outcomes when individuals possess resources that enable them to make effective judgments about how and when to be proactive. Hahn and colleagues (Hahn, Frese, Binnewies, & Schmitt, 2012) also suggested that personal initiative involves a range of effortful behaviors that require psychological resources that are likely to deplete over time. According to Grant et al., proactivity that is driven by controlled regulation is associated with an additional sense of pressure, which contributes to the depletion of self-control, thus making it difficult for individuals to focus their energy on their proactive behavior, making it ultimately less effective.

We propose more specifically that, because autonomously regulated individual proactivity consumes less psychological resources, individuals have more resources to successfully bring about change within a proactive goal episode, and more resources to sustain high levels of proactivity over time. Autonomously regulated proactivity will be more effective by making it more likely that a single proactive goal will be achieved, and that individuals will continuously set and pursue proactive goals, and thus be successful in bringing about a different future for themselves and/or their organization.

We also propose additional processes by which autonomous forms of motivation promote more effective and sustained proactivity. Specifically, we argue the following:

1. Autonomously motivated individual proactivity tends to involve a more complete self-regulatory goal process, including greater likelihood of each of envisioning, planning, and reflecting, as well as more sustained forms of enacting (persistence, recovery from setbacks, and so forth). It is therefore more effective in bringing about change than individual proactivity regulated by controlled motivation.

2. Autonomously motivated individual proactivity engages the "self" and involves stronger ownership of the intended outcome, thereby enhancing individuals' commitment toward the proactive goal.

3. Autonomously motivated individual proactivity enables the satisfaction of psychological needs, which in turn:

 a. contributes to the effectiveness of proactivity by facilitating the internalization of organizational goals, thus enhancing the benefits of individual proactivity for the organization, and

 b. enables sustained proactivity, via its effect on the proactive goal regulation process and its contribution to personal growth.

We elaborate each of these arguments next.

Completeness of the Self-Regulatory Goal Process

We suggest that controlled regulation is likely to result in an emphasis on the enactment of proactive behavior, whereas the phases of envisioning, planning, and reflecting are neglected. When individuals are concerned with being "seen" to be proactive or feel guilty if they do not engage in proactive behavior, they likely emphasize the enactment phase, but spend less time and energy on the phases of the proactivity process that cannot easily be observed. Although this has yet to be tested empirically, Bindl and colleagues (2012) argued that proactive goals can only be achieved if individuals successfully engage in each of the phases of proactive goal regulation. Where proactive behavior is regulated by external or internal pressures, the associated envisioning does involve outcome simulations of achieving rewards for proactivity, rather than process simulations of how to successfully achieve a proactive goal. Process simulations are more effective in regulating behavior (Taylor, Pham, Rivkin, & Armor, 1998). They encourage planning and other problem-focused activities, and may prevent the intrusion of irrelevant thoughts (Taylor & Schneider, 1989). Outcome simulations in contrast are concerned with the anticipation of positive emotions and involve the enjoyment of success without providing a basis for achievement (Oettingen, 1999; Oettingen & Mayer, 2002). Without effective envisioning, planning how to achieve the proactive goal and overcome obstacles is impaired.

Individuals who engage in proactive behavior for the sake of being seen to do so also have little incentive to engage in reflection. Their goal is not about successfully bringing about change, but about the rewards associated with having shown initiative. A lack of reflection reduces the effectiveness of subsequent proactivity episodes because the individual fails to extract lessons learned. Reflection generates information that serves as a basis of future envisioning, planning, and enacting. Through reflection, individuals gain and consolidate the strategic, relational, and normative knowledge about how to achieve proactive goals in their organizational context, which is critical for the successful implementation of change (Dutton, Ashford, O'Neill, & Lawrence, 2001). Reflection is likely to result in more accurate judgments about how and when to strive for proactive goals, thus making proactivity more effective (Chan, 2006).

In addition, we propose that autonomously regulated proactivity is associated with sustained enacting. According to self-concordance theory (Sheldon & Elliot, 1999), goals consistent with individuals' core values and interests are associated with enhanced goal striving. Thus, proactivity driven by integrated and identified forms of motivation is associated with sustained efforts of bringing about the proactive goal. However, enacting based on controlled motivation is unlikely to be sustained over time because individuals are less likely to recover from setbacks and to persist in the face of obstacles. Having engaged in less planning, they have fewer contingency plans for when things go wrong and give up more readily. They also are less motivated to achieve their ultimate proactive goal and may be satisfied by having engaged in proactive behavior, regardless of whether they have successfully brought about change. Hui et al. (2000) provide support for this argument in relation to discretionary work behaviors. In a sample of 293 bank tellers, they found that when organizational citizenship behavior is extrinsically motivated (i.e., performed for the instrumental purpose of getting promoted) it is not sustained after this purpose has been attained. Grant (2008) similarly found that individuals who feel pressured cannot persist at their efforts over time.

To summarize, we propose:

> Proposition 1: Autonomously regulated individual proactivity is likely to be more effective in achieving proactive goals than proactivity that is regulated by controlled motivation because it involves more envisioning, planning, and reflecting, as well as more persistent and sustained enacting. A complete self-regulatory goal process makes future proactive goal episodes more effective, resulting in a sustained high level of individual proactivity.

Engagement of the Self

Autonomously regulated proactivity by definition involves greater engagement of the "self" because individuals behave in this way for reasons that are core to their identity, values, and interests. Because nobody is directing the individual to be proactive, and the impetus for action is coming from within, individuals have strong feelings of ownership over the proactive goal (Parker et al., 1997). In essence, there is no one else to blame if the proactive efforts are not successful because autonomously regulated proactivity is self-initiated.

Drawing on the self-concordance model (Sheldon & Elliot, 1999), we suggest this greater investment of the self in autonomously regulated proactive action enhances an individual's determination to see their project through successfully. Proactive goals representing a person's authentic interests and values are integrated with the self, and are perceived as resulting from self-made choices. Because these interests and values are enduring facets of a person's personality, autonomous proactive goals are likely to be pursued with sustained effort over time (Sheldon & Elliot, 1999). Proactive goals driven by controlled motivation are less likely to be linked to enduring interests and values; they thus tend to be abandoned when obstacles are encountered.

It is important to note that we do not suggest autonomously motivated people's self-esteem is more dependent on achieving the proactive goal as that would impact a rather unstable sense of self-esteem (Kernis, Cornell, Sun, Berry, & Harlow, 1993). Rather, we suggest that autonomously motivated individuals care a lot about achieving their proactive goal because it arises out of their own interests and values, and so persist accordingly. For example, if an academic decides to implement a new ethics course because she or he believes strongly that students need to be more ethical, this academic is likely to persist more in the face of colleagues' resistance than an individual who set out to introduce the course to boost their next performance appraisal score. In the face of resistance, the latter individual might opt to find an easier way to get a better appraisal.

Our proposition is:

> Proposition 2: Autonomously regulated individual proactivity is likely to be more effective in achieving proactive goals than proactivity that is regulated by controlled motivation because it involves greater ownership and engagement of the self, thereby increasing individual's efforts to achieving a successful outcome.

Autonomously Motivated Proactivity and Psychological Need Satisfaction

Self-determination theory proposes that individuals' well-being depends on the satisfaction of the three psychological needs of competence, autonomy, and relatedness (Tharenou & Terry, 1998). Individuals have the inherent need to feel that they are able to produce desired outcomes (White, 1955), to feel that they are the causal agent of their actions (Crant, 1995), and to feel connected to others (Baumeister & Leary, 1995). Satisfaction of these needs is a requirement for well-being and psychological growth (Deci & Ryan, 2000). We propose that autonomously regulated proactivity is likely to result in higher psychological need satisfaction, which, as we elaborate next, in turn contributes to further episodes of proactivity, resulting in individual proactivity that is sustained over long periods of time.

Autonomous proactivity enables the satisfaction of the three basic psychological needs of competence, autonomy, and relatedness in two different ways. First, it enables satisfaction of psychological needs directly. Proactive goals are often challenging and can create opportunities to experience competence. When individuals feel that they freely choose to engage in proactivity, they are likely to feel agentic and self-directed, satisfying their need for autonomy (deCharms, 1968). Finally, despite its occasional portrayal as self-centered and individualistic (e.g., Hirschfeld, Thomas, & Bernerth, 2011) proactivity often focuses on social processes (Grant & Ashford, 2008). For example, during organizational socialization, newcomers seek to build relationships with their new boss and colleagues (Ashford & Black, 1996; Ashforth, Sluss, & Saks, 2007). Prosocial forms of proactive behavior may also allow individuals to feel connected to others at work. Through these forms of socially oriented proactivity, individuals are likely to satisfy their desire to be connected with others.

Second, employees engaging in autonomous proactivity are also more likely to find themselves in work environments that are conducive to the satisfaction of their psychological needs. They actively seek out environments that match their values and interests (Parker & Collins, 2010) or shape their environment according to their needs and preferences (Bakker, 2010; Tims & Bakker, 2010; Wrzesniewski & Dutton, 2001). These environments afford individuals with the opportunity to fulfill their needs (Arthur, Bell, Villado, & Doverspike, 2006). In a study involving 163 full-time employees in Singapore, Greguras and Diefendorff (2009) found that fit between the individual's and the organization's values was positively related to psychological need satisfaction assessed 3 weeks later. Individuals proactively shape their job to optimize their job characteristics and maximize their job resources (Tims & Bakker, 2010). They set proactive goals to create conditions that allow the satisfaction of psychological needs, for example by "crafting" their job so that it provides an optimal level of challenge and involves enjoyable activities, or affords the possibility of flow (Csikszentmihalyi, 1988). In line with this argument, Bakker and colleagues (Bakker, Albrecht, & Leiter, 2011) suggested that engaged employees attempt to sustain their state of engagement through proactive behavior. Manzoni and Barsoux (2009) suggested a more indirect mechanism through which proactivity leads to more favorable work environments. More proactive employees may be seen as stronger performers by their leader, and as a consequence, receive more developmental and supportive supervision, and greater autonomy.

Our proposition is as follows:

Proposition 3: Autonomously regulated individual proactivity is likely to lead to satisfaction of psychological needs both directly, and by creating contexts in which one can fulfill one's needs.

The satisfaction of psychological needs in turn facilitates effective and sustained proactivity. First, it contributes to beneficial outcomes of proactivity for the organization, through its contribution to higher job performance, and by enabling the internalization of organizational goals, which enhances pro-organizational proactivity. Second, it contributes to sustained proactivity and enables individuals to act as agents of continuous positive change by enhancing the proactive goal regulation process, and by contributing to personal growth and progressive expectations, which result in the continuous setting of proactive goals. We elaborate these proposed pathways next.

Psychological Need Satisfaction Enhances the Benefits of Proactivity for the Organization

Psychological need satisfaction is likely to enhance the positive effects of proactivity for the organization. First, the greater opportunity for psychological needs satisfaction created by autonomously motivated proactivity may be a mechanism for the well-established relationship between proactivity and job performance (Fuller & Marler, 2009). Greguras and Diefendorff (2010) found that employees high in proactive personality were more likely to pursue and attain autonomous goals, which in turn predicted psychological need satisfaction. Baard and colleagues (Baard, Deci, & Ryan, 2004) found that greater need satisfaction on the job was associated with higher supervisor-rated performance in a sample 528 employees of an investment banking firm. Taken together, these findings suggest that autonomously regulated proactivity is likely to lead to satisfaction of psychological needs (via the setting and pursuit of proactive goals that are self-concordant, that is, that are in line with individuals' values and interests [Sheldon & Elliot, 1999]), which in turn leads to higher job performance.

Second, through the process of internalization, psychological need satisfaction also encourages the setting of proactive goals in line with organizational aims, and thus enables proactivity that is likely to have positive outcomes for the organization.

Psychological need satisfaction facilitates the internalization of values and regulatory processes (Ryan, 1995). When coupled with a strong commitment to the organization, need satisfaction is likely to lead to individuals' internalizing organizational aims, and setting proactive goals in accordance with them. In other words, when an individual's needs are fulfilled, and they also care about and want to belong to the organization, employee proactivity is more likely to be "pro-organizational" (Belschak & Den Hartog, 2010, p. 475) and is aimed at contributing to organizational effectiveness. The pro-organizational focus of autonomously motivated proactivity is further supported by the positive effect of autonomous motivation on affective organizational commitment (Gagné, Chemolli, Forest, & Koestner, 2008). Previous research has linked affective commitment to proactivity (Den Hartog & Belschak, 2007; Griffin et al., 2007; Rank, Carsten, Unger, & Spector, 2007; Strauss, Griffin, & Rafferty, 2009), and self-determination theory suggests that through internalization processes, proactivity associated with high levels of organizational commitment is likely to be more beneficial for the organization. Autonomously regulated proactivity is thus more likely to have positive outcomes for the organization than controlled proactivity that is driven by, for example, feelings of guilt, obligation, or impression management motives.

To summarize, we propose:

Proposition 4: Psychological need satisfaction enhances the benefits of individual proactivity for the organization by contributing to job performance and, when coupled with organizational commitment, facilitates the internalization of organizational aims and thus the setting of proactive goals in accordance with these aims.

Psychological Need Satisfaction Contributes to Sustained Proactivity

This far we have outlined how autonomously regulated proactivity can contribute to the satisfaction of psychological needs, which results in positive outcomes for the organization. Opportunities to satisfy psychological needs are also likely to in turn lead to autonomous motivation of proactivity (Gagné, 2009) and, by contributing to proactive goal regulation and proactive motivational states, facilitate proactivity that is sustained over time as we elaborate next.

Satisfaction of the need for autonomy is not only likely to be a key outcome of proactivity; it also further contributes to self-starting and self-directed behavior. Autonomy involves "acting with a sense of volition and having the experience of choice" (Gagné & Deci, 2005, p. 333), which is likely to contribute to the setting of and striving for proactive goals. In line with this argument, there is empirical support for the positive relationship between the experience of autonomy of work, and proactivity (Hornung, Rousseau, & Glaser, 2008; Parker et al., 2006).

Satisfaction of the need for competence reflects a sense of self-efficacy, a key component of *can do* motivation, which has consistently been linked to proactivity (e.g., Axtell, Holman, Unsworth, Wall, & Waterson, 2000; Frese, Garst, & Fay, 2007; Kanfer, Wanberg, & Kantrowitz, 2001; Morrison & Phelps, 1999; Parker et al., 2006). Because proactivity involves intentionality and forethought, individuals make a conscious decision whether or not to set and pursue a proactive goal (Bindl et al., 2012; Morrison & Phelps, 1999; Parker et al., 2006). Proactivity can involve risks for one's ego or image, because its self-started nature implies that it cannot easily be blamed on external circumstances (Grant & Ashford, 2008). It may also be met with resistance by others and create interpersonal problems (Bateman & Crant, 1999; Bolino et al., 2010). It is therefore important that individuals believe they can be successful in being proactive and dealing with the consequences of their proactive behavior, which is likely to be enabled by their sense of competence.

Satisfaction of the need for relatedness finally provides a sense of security, which is likely to make proactivity seem less risky and reduce its perceived interpersonal costs, thus also contributing to *can do* motivation. This is consistent with findings that proactive behavior is more likely to occur in social environments characterized by trust and support (Parker et al., 2006), and psychological safety (Detert & Burris, 2007).

Deci and Ryan (2000) have argued that satisfaction of the psychological needs for competence, autonomy, and relatedness is essential for personal growth and psychological well-being. There is also empirical support for the relationship between satisfaction of psychological needs at work and well-being (Baard et al., 2004; Deci et al., 2001). Through its contribution to personal growth, psychological need satisfaction encourages the continuous setting of proactive goals and thus contributes to sustained proactivity. Without personal growth, individuals would have no reason to set and pursue

further proactive goals after they have achieved satisfactory fit with their environment (Greguras & Diefendorff, 2009), or have "crafted" their job so that it provides sufficient resources for the satisfaction of psychological needs (Tims & Bakker, 2010). However, individuals often continue to be proactive after they have achieved their goals as evidenced by many longitudinal studies that find positive relationships between past and future proactivity (e.g., Frese et al., 2007; Griffin et al., 2010). Individuals whose psychological needs are satisfied are likely to set increasingly higher standards for themselves and their organizations. Even though they reach their proactive goals, their raising standards give them new reasons to engage in proactive behavior. For example, employees increasing the demands of their job to make it more challenging in order to satisfy their need for competence subsequently develop their skills and become more confident in their ability. In order to experience optimal levels of demands at work, they need to seek out additional challenges in their job. Support for the idea that individuals raise their levels of aspiration in response to favorable work environment comes from Bruggeman and colleagues' (Bruggeman, Groskurth, & Ulich, 1975; see Buessing, 2002; Buessing & Bissels, 1998) work on different forms of job satisfaction. The authors propose that different forms of job satisfaction result from a comparison of a person's expectations and the actual work situation, and their level of aspiration. We propose that satisfaction of psychological needs associated with autonomously regulated proactivity results in progressive job satisfaction. Progressive job satisfaction occurs when a person finds his or her original expectations met by the organizational environment, and consequently raises his or her expectations. Individuals are then likely to continuously set and pursue proactive goals, resulting in high levels of proactivity that are sustained over long periods of time.

Psychological need satisfaction also plays an important role for the *energized to* motivational path of proactivity. To successfully engage in the process of proactive goal regulation, individuals need to harness and maintain their psychological resources as they persist in working toward their proactive goal. Autonomous regulation of proactivity is likely to be associated with higher vitality, a person's "positive sense of aliveness and energy" (Ryan & Fredrick, 1997, p. 530), via the satisfaction of psychological needs (Weinstein & Ryan, 2010). Reis and colleagues (Reis, Sheldon, Gable, Roscoe, & Ryan, 2000) found that day-level satisfaction of psychological needs led to day-level experiences of energy. When people are autonomously regulated they do not experience their efforts as draining and may even feel that they have more energy available to the self (Nix, Ryan, Manly, & Deci, 1999; Sheldon & Kasser, 1995; Weinstein & Ryan, 2010). This is in line with Grant and colleague's (2011) argument that autonomous motivation makes it easier for individuals to focus their attention on their proactive goal and maintain high levels of energy and enthusiasm. Individuals engaging in autonomously regulated proactivity thus have more energy available to themselves, which enables a more effective and sustained proactive goal-regulation process. A high degree of activation leads to increased effort (Brehm, 1999) and will increase striving toward proactive goals, thus enabling persistent proactivity that is more likely to be successful and have positive outcomes. Satisfaction of the psychological needs for competence, autonomy, and relatedness thus result in higher levels of energy available to the individual; this is likely to facilitate a more effective self-regulation and engagement in all four phases of the proactive goal-regulation process.

Positive activated states, such as vitality or engagement, not only make proactivity more effective by reducing its resource requirements and contributing to persistence, they also contribute to the proactive goal-regulation process both directly and indirectly (Parker et al., 2010).

First, as Bindl and Parker (2011a) argued, experiences of positive activated states, such as vitality and engagement, influence proactivity directly through three different mechanisms: (1) they facilitate the complex cognitive processes involved in proactivity by encouraging openness and flexibility (Fredrickson, 1998), (2) they promote future-oriented thinking (Foo, Uy, & Baron, 2009), and (3) they promote the setting of more challenging goals (Ilies & Judge, 2005). In line with these arguments Bindl and colleagues (2012) showed that high-activation positive mood, encompassing enthusiasm, excitement, inspiration, and joy, was positively associated with all four phases of proactive goal regulation. Support for the positive effect of energy and enthusiasm on proactive behavior also comes from research on work engagement, a "positive, fulfilling, work-related state of mind that is characterized by vigor, dedication, and absorption" (Schaufeli, Salanova, Gonzalez-Roma, & Bakker, 2002, p. 74). Work engagement has been found to be positively associated with self-reported personal initiative (Salanova & Schaufeli, 2008), and

was positively associated with later personal initiative in a longitudinal study over 3 years (Hakanen, Perhoniemi, & Toppinen-Tanner, 2008). Hahn and colleagues (2012) similarly found that vigor was related to later personal initiative in a longitudinal study of entrepreneurs.

Second, positive activated states also contribute to sustained proactivity indirectly, by influencing *can do* and *reason to* motivational states (Seo, Barrett, & Bartunek, 2004; Seo, Bartunek, & Barrett, 2010). Individuals experiencing positive affective states more easily recall positive material in memory (Isen, Clark, Shalker, & Karp, 1977). They are thus more likely to focus on successful past episodes of proactivity and experience enhanced *can do* motivation. They generate higher expectancy judgments for the outcomes of proactivity (Wegener & Petty, 1996) and experience higher self-efficacy (Tsai, Chen, & Liu, 2007). They also feel that they have made more progress toward their goals (Johnson & Tversky, 1983), which is likely to have a positive reinforcing effect, further facilitating persistence and goal striving. Positive affective states also influence *reason to* motivation. They facilitate the experience of intrinsic motivation, and make the internalization of regulation more likely (Isen & Reeve, 2005), thus enabling the identified and integrated regulation of proactive behavior.

In summary, we propose:

> Proposition 5: Psychological need satisfaction facilitates sustained individual proactivity by contributing to proactive motivational states and proactive goal regulation.

The Positive Upward Spiral of Autonomously Regulated Proactivity

Thus far we have proposed that autonomously regulated proactivity results in stronger reasons to initiate proactivity and increases the likelihood that proactivity results in positive change for individuals and organizations. In this current section we bring together the arguments discussed previously in a dynamic model that outlines what we call the positive upward spiral of autonomously regulated proactivity.

Autonomously regulated proactivity makes it more likely that proactive goals are achieved because it involves a more complete self-regulatory process and thus more effective goal regulation. Effective goal regulation also enhances individuals' resources that enable the achievement of future proactive goals, such as by generating knowledge and facilitating better planning through reflection.

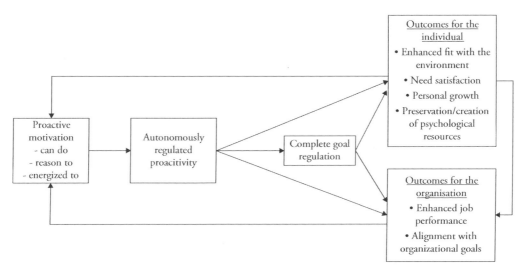

Fig. 4.1. The upward spiral of autonomously regulated proactivity.

We propose that autonomously regulated proactivity has positive effects on individuals' well-being and introduce psychological need satisfaction as a key outcome of autonomously regulated proactivity. Engaging in individual proactivity can directly contribute to the satisfaction of the three psychological needs of autonomy, competence, and relatedness. In addition, it contributes to need satisfaction indirectly. Through proactive behaviors, such as job crafting, individuals create environments that provide a good fit with their values and needs and afford further opportunities for the satisfaction of psychological needs.

Need satisfaction in turn plays a key role for sustaining high levels of individual proactivity by influencing proactive motivation, and the continuous setting of proactive goals. Individuals who find their psychological needs are met experience personal growth and consequently raise their expectations for themselves, and for their jobs. Their expectations provide a new *reason to* set and pursue proactive goals. As a consequence they continue to work toward positive change.

The concept of need satisfaction also adds to the understanding of the role of psychological resources in the regulation of proactive behavior. Grant and colleagues (2011) suggested that autonomously regulated proactivity requires less self-regulatory resources and is thus more effective. We propose that autonomously regulated proactivity may even be associated with an increase in the psychological resources available to the individual because psychological need satisfaction is likely to be accompanied by feelings of vitality and aliveness (Ryan & Fredrick, 1997).

The satisfaction of psychological resources also plays a key role in explaining the relationship between autonomously regulated proactivity and beneficial outcomes for the organization. Psychological need satisfaction is associated with higher job performance, and facilitates the internalization of organizational norms and goals, enhancing pro-organizational forms of proactivity.

In a positive upward spiral, the outcomes of autonomously regulated proactivity for the individual and for the organization contribute in turn to the can do, reason to, and energized to processes of proactive motivation and stimulate the setting of further proactive goals and thus future episodes of individual proactivity (Figure 4.1).

Implications: Encouraging Effective and Sustained Proactivity in Organizations

Organizations can encourage proactivity by creating work climates that enable the satisfaction of psychological needs. These work climates enhance the autonomous regulation of proactivity and, as we have outlined previously, facilitate internalization of proactive goals to encourage proactivity in line with organizational goals (Gagné & Deci, 2005).

Designing Jobs that Facilitate Effective and Sustained Proactivity

A number of studies have investigated the link between job characteristics and proactivity, highlighting the importance of such variables as job autonomy (e.g., Frese et al., 2007; Parker et al., 2006), leadership support (e.g., Den Hartog &

Belschak, 2012; Morrison & Phelps, 1999; Rank et al., 2007), and a positive work climate (e.g, Griffin et al., 2007; LePine & Van Dyne, 1998). This research has been extensively reviewed elsewhere (see e.g., Bindl & Parker, 2011b) and we do not repeat this work here, but rather identify different mechanisms through which these positive effects of work design might occur. To date, it has been argued that these work variables can promote the motivational states of can do, reason to, and energized to motivation, which in turn shape proactivity (see Parker et al., 2010). We additionally suggest that job characteristics not only potentially motivate proactivity per se, but are more likely to motivate *autonomously regulated* proactivity, such as via a process of psychological need satisfaction.

Thomas and Velthouse (1990) provide a theoretical framework for this link and propose that autonomous motivation at work is based on employees' experiencing feelings of impact, competence, meaningfulness, and choice. Impact refers to the assessment that one's behavior is "making a difference" toward accomplishing the intended purpose. Thomas and Velthouse equate this construct with Hackman and Oldham's (1976) "knowledge of results." In Bandura's (1977) terms, it captures outcome expectations, rather than efficacy expectations, which are reflected in the assessment of one's competence. Meaningfulness reflects the value of the goal in relation to a person's ideals or standards. Choice finally reflects a person's assessment of his or her autonomy and sense of volition. In a sample of 199 employees of a Canadian telephone company, Gagné, Senécal, and Koestner (1997) showed that autonomy support (a composite score of skill variety, task significance and task identity, feedback on one's performance obtained from supervisors or coworkers, and feedback on one's performance obtained from job activities) was significantly related to employees' assessments of impact, competence, meaningfulness, and choice, which in turn explained significant variance in intrinsic motivation.

In a sample of 124 volunteers at a community clinic, Millette and Gagné (2008) found that Hackman and Oldham's (1976) Motivational Potential Score, a multiplication of core job characteristics intended to reflect their impact on critical psychological states, was positively related to volunteers' autonomous motivation. Specifically, it was significantly related to their intrinsic motivation and, marginally, to their identified motivation.

Job-demands resources theory also proposes that job characteristics translate into autonomous motivation by allowing the satisfaction of psychological needs (e.g., Bakker & Demerouti, 2007). For example, feedback is proposed to foster learning and satisfy the need for competence. In line with this argument, Kelloway and Barling (1991) found that skill variety, autonomy support, and feedback from the job significantly predicted employees' perceived competence. Parker (1998) found that increased job autonomy predicted the development of role-breath self-efficacy (which is similar to the experience of competence) over time. Decision latitude or job control is likely to enable the satisfaction of individuals' need for autonomy, and social support is likely to satisfy their need for relatedness (Bakker & Demerouti, 2007).

Van den Broeck and colleagues (Van den Broeck, Vansteenkiste, De Witte, & Lens, 2008) provided empirical support for the link between job demands and resources and psychological need satisfaction. In a sample of 745 employees across 17 Belgian organizations, need satisfaction was positively related to the job resources of task autonomy, skill utilization, and positive feedback. A latent job demand factor encompassing workload, emotional and physical demands, and work-home interference showed a small negative relationship with need satisfaction. The zero-order correlation between workload and need satisfaction was, however, positive. The effect of workload on autonomous motivation is likely to depend on individuals' assessments of autonomy (Marinova et al., 2010). Under conditions of high autonomy, increasing job demands were accompanied by an increase in intrinsic motivation in a sample of 555 nurses (Van Yperen & Hagedoorn, 2003).

In sum, we extend existing arguments that job characteristics can influence proactivity via their effect on individuals' can do, reason to, and energized to motivational states by also suggesting that these job characteristics result in psychological need satisfaction, which encourages autonomous motivation of proactivity. As we have argued already, autonomously motivated proactivity is more likely to be successful, for individuals and organizations, than controlled proactivity.

Providing Autonomy Support

Autonomy has long been identified as crucial for intrinsic motivation at work (e.g., Hackman & Oldham, 1976), and autonomy support is the most important social-contextual variable that predicts autonomous forms of motivation (Deci, Egharri, Patrick, & Leone, 1994; Nicholson, 1984;

Williams & Deci, 1996; Williams, Freedman, & Deci, 1998; Williams, Gagné, Ryan, & Deci, 2002). Deci, Connell, and Ryan (1989) argue that autonomy support in organizations is primarily provided by the supervisor. Baard and colleagues even more explicitly state that autonomy support is the "interpersonal climate created by the manager in relating to subordinates" (Baard et al., 2004, p. 2048). Supervisor behavior can be seen as either informational (i.e., promoting competence and supporting autonomy) or controlling (i.e., pressuring employees to think, feel, or behave in specified ways) (Deci & Ryan, 1985). A controlling supervisory style has been found to have a detrimental effect on subordinates' intrinsic motivation (Richer & Vallerand, 1995). Supervisors who try to restrict and control employees' behavior rather than supporting their autonomy are thus likely to undermine autonomous motivation of proactivity. Autonomy supportive supervision, however, encourages autonomous forms of motivation.

Facilitating Alignment of Proactive Goals through Internalization

As outlined previously, when individuals' proactive goals are based on their internalization of organizational values, they are in line with organizational aims and contribute to organizational effectiveness. The social-contextual factors outlined so far that enhance and maintain autononomous forms of motivation also enable the internalization of behavioral standards. Autonomy support contributes to autonomous motivation of proactivity, but it can also promote the alignment of employees' proactive goals with organizational aims through internalization. In a field study, Parker et al. (1997) showed that the internalization of organizational goals (as measured by flexible role orientation) occurred as a result of the introduction of autonomous work groups. In a laboratory experiment, Deci et al. (1994) found that internalization was facilitated by acknowledgement of the participants' perspective, by providing a rationale for the respective behavior that highlights its personal utility for the participant, and by providing opportunities for choice. By highlighting the value of proactivity for the organization, by acknowledging the costs and risks, but also the opportunities it may involve for the employee, and by providing autonomy and choice, supervisors can encourage the setting and pursuit of proactive goals that benefit the organization without undermining employees' sense of volition. Autonomy support not only encourages

the internalization of proactive goals, it also ensures that this internalization is integrated (i.e., that it becomes an integral part of a person's work-related identity) rather than being introjected (i.e., engaged in out of a sense of obligation), thus contributing to its sustainability.

In addition to these factors, Gagné and Deci (2005) note two factors that uniquely contribute to internalization but are not important for intrinsic motivation. First, internalization depends on the presence of structures and contingencies that can be internalized. Second, internalization is facilitated by the endorsement of the respective behavior by significant others.

In the case of effective proactivity, organizations can facilitate the internalization of proactive goals by creating a clear vision of the future the organization is trying to achieve (Griffin et al., 2010). A successful vision of the organizational future also allows employees to imagine themselves as part of this future (Levin, 2000) and to work toward their Future Work Self, a representation of an individual's hopes and aspirations in relation to work that can serve as a further source of proactive goals (Strauss et al., 2012). Providing visions of the future thus provides essential guidance for proactivity, which can be internalized and stimulate proactive behavior in alignment with organizational goals.

Organizations can further enhance proactivity by encouraging the internalization of a sense of responsibility for bringing this future about (Parker, 2000; Strauss, Griffin, & Parker, 2009). In a sample of 115 employees of a not-for-profit utility company in the United States, Fuller et al. (2006) found that access to resources was a critical determinant of employees' felt responsibility for constructive change in the organization (see also Spreitzer, 1996). Autonomy to use resources signals the organization's support for proactivity (Scott & Bruce, 1994) and trust that the resources will be used responsibly. Access to resources to pursue proactive goals also communicates to employees the organization's endorsement of proactivity.

Leaders and managers can also facilitate the internalization of proactive goals in line with organizational aims by signaling their endorsement and approval of employee proactivity. They may communicate their endorsement by demonstrating proactive behavior and acting as role models. They can also contribute to the internalization of proactive goals through autonomy support, as outlined previously, and by shaping the work environment accordingly. Formal and informal organizational practices and procedures can guide and support proactivity at work. By creating a "climate for initiative," organizations can encourage high levels of proactivity in the workforce (Baer & Frese, 2003, p. 48). This is likely to facilitate the internalization of proactive ways of behaving.

Rewarding Proactive Behavior

The unpredictable nature of proactivity makes it difficult to introduce clear reward-behavior contingencies (Parker et al., 2010). In addition, despite some controversy over the undermining effect of rewards on intrinsic motivation, there is meta-analytical evidence that contingent tangible rewards undermine intrinsic motivation (Deci, Koestner, & Ryan, 1999). Attempts to monitor, assess, and reward proactivity are thus likely to undermine its autonomous motivation (Harackiewicz, Manderlink, & Sansone, 1984; Lepper & Greene, 1975), and encourage a focus on proactive behavior rather than full engagement in the proactive goal-regulation process. Making proactivity part of performance appraisal systems and compensation contingent on employees having displayed proactive behavior can thus be problematic. However, rewards may have a positive effect on autonomous proactivity when they function as positive feedback. Meta-analytical evidence of laboratory studies suggests that positive feedback may have a positive effect on the autonomous regulation of proactivity (Deci et al., 1999). Providing positive feedback for desirable forms of proactivity is likely to contribute to sustaining proactivity, because it may enhance feelings of competence (Gagné & Forest, 2008), which in turn is likely to feed into future can do motivational states. Importantly, this positive feedback has to be informational rather than controlling. Controlling positive feedback that emphasizes the pressure for employees to maintain their high level of proactivity is likely to lead to lower levels of autonomous motivation than informational positive feedback (Pittman, Davey, Alafat, Wetherill, & Kramer, 1980; Ryan, 1982). These ideas have yet to be tested.

Practical Recommendations

In summary, these findings highlight the crucial role of supervisors in enabling and maintaining autonomously regulated proactivity and have implications for leaders aiming to enhance proactivity in the workplace. As discussed, employees are increasingly expected to be proactive (Bolino et al., 2010; Erdogan & Bauer, 2005). How these expectations are communicated determines whether employees engage in proactive behavior that is driven by controlled motivation and unlikely to be sustained or effective, or whether they engage in autonomously regulated, effective proactivity. When expectations about proactive behavior at work are communicated in a controlling or pressuring way this is likely to impair internalization and integration of proactive goals (Deci et al., 1994). Instead, organizations can encourage the internalization of proactive goals in line with organizational aims and values by providing autonomy support, by increasing job autonomy, by communicating a compelling vision of the future that can guide proactivity, and by instilling a sense of responsibility for bringing this future about, for example, by making relevant resources available. To encourage effective proactivity, organizations need to provide jobs that facilitate the satisfaction of psychological needs and provide positive feedback on desirable forms of proactivity without creating a sense of pressure and undermining employees' sense of volition. Under these circumstances, employees will fully engage in the proactive goal regulation process, making the achievement of their proactive goals more likely. They will experience personal growth and continuous learning, and proactivity will contribute to organizational effectiveness and individual thriving.

Conclusion

Conceptualizing proactivity as a goal-driven process and drawing on self-determination theory, we have investigated the consequences of different motivations for individual proactivity. We propose that proactivity is most effective when it is autonomously motivated. Proactivity that is driven by autonomous motivation is likely to result in a positive upward spiral. It enables enhanced fit between the individual and their environment, and contributes directly to the satisfaction of psychological needs. By facilitating psychological need satisfaction, enhancing psychological resources, and contributing to personal growth, it is likely to be sustained over time, and contribute to individual well-being, as well as positive outcomes for the organization. The proposed differential outcomes of proactive behavior, depending on how it is motivated, have important practical implications for organizations aiming to enhance the proactivity of their workforce.

Future Directions

Although there is preliminary support for the idea that autonomously regulated proactivity is more effective (Grant et al., 2011), our propositions have yet to be tested empirically. In particular, further research is needed to explore whether effective proactivity does indeed require full engagement in the proactive goal-regulation process, and whether this is facilitated by autonomous motivation, and potentially impaired by controlled motivation.

Future research may also explore whether individual proactivity makes a unique contribution to the satisfaction of psychological needs at work, and focus on the well-being outcomes of proactivity. To date, there is surprisingly little empirical research exploring the consequences of proactivity for individuals' work-related well-being. The proposed positive effect of autonomously motivated proactivity on psychological need satisfaction makes positive well-being outcomes likely, for example, because autonomously regulated proactivity may require less self-regulatory resources. These mechanisms have yet to be tested.

Further research is also needed to explore the potential negative consequences of failing to achieve an autonomous proactive goal. We argued that autonomously motivated proactivity is likely to be positive for individuals' well-being, such as through a process of need satisfaction. Nevertheless, it is important to recognize that failed proactive efforts might jeopardize employees' well-being more strongly if these are autonomously motivated than if their proactivity is controlled. We argued that the greater engagement of the self means that autonomously motivated proactivity is more likely to involve persistence than controlled proactivity. As well as this upside, however, we also suspect that autonomous proactivity that is ultimately thwarted or goes awry is more threatening to an individual's well-being than thwarted controlled proactivity. Some evidence supports this. Sheldon and Kasser (1998) found that goal attainment is only associated with enhanced well-being for autonomous goals, not for controlled goals, and that not achieving goals is associated with lowered well-being for autonomous but not controlled goals (see also Ryan et al., 1999). In other words, autonomously motivated proactivity might be positive for well-being when the proactive goal is achieved, but might also be quite damaging to well-being when the goal is not achieved. Although the exact role of affect in relation to thwarted proactivity needs further investigation, one potentially significant implication of this reasoning is that individuals might need additional support from their work environment when their autonomous proactive efforts are not

successful. Supervisors and leaders might thus need to be particularly strongly attuned to addressing the emotional consequences of unsuccessful autonomous proactivity. Such a possibility needs to be further investigated.

Finally, we have focused our arguments here on proactivity. Whether similar processes apply to related outcomes, such as creativity, needs to be investigated. If innovation includes both creativity (novel idea generation) and proactivity (implementation of these ideas) as others have suggested (e.g., West, 2002), then our discussion also likely has implications for stimulating innovation in organizations.

References

Arthur, M. B., & Rousseau, D. M. (1996). *The boundaryless career: A new employment principle for a new organizational era.* New York: Oxford University Press.

Arthur, W. J., Bell, S. T., Villado, A. J., & Doverspike, D. (2006). The use of person-organization fit in employment decision making: An assessment of its criterion-related validity. *Journal of Applied Psychology, 91*(4), 786–801. doi: 10.1037/0021-9010.91.4.786

Ashford, S. J., & Black, J. S. (1996). Proactivity during organizational entry: The role of desire for control. *Journal of Applied Psychology, 81*(2), 199–214. doi: 10.1037/0021-9010.81.2.199

Ashford, S. J., Blatt, R., & VandeWalle, D. (2003). Reflections on the looking glass: A review of research on feedback-seeking behavior in organization. *Journal of Management, 29*(6), 773–799. doi: 10.1016/S0149-2063(03)00079-5

Ashforth, B. E., Sluss, D. M., & Saks, A. M. (2007). Socialization tactics, proactive behavior, and newcomer learning: Integrating socialization models. *Journal of Vocational Behavior, 70,* 447–462. doi: 10.1016/j.jvb.2007.02.001

Axtell, C. M., Holman, D. J., Unsworth, K. L., Wall, T. D., & Waterson, P. E. (2000). Shop floor innovation: Facilitating the suggestion and implementation of ideas. *Journal of Occupational and Organizational Psychology, 73*(3), 265–285. doi: 10.1348/096317900167029

Baard, P. P., Deci, E. L., & Ryan, R. (2004). Intrinsic need satisfaction: A motivational basis of performance and well-being in two work settings. *Journal of Applied Social Psychology, 34*(10), 2045–2068. doi: 10.1111/j.1559-1816.2004.tb02690.x

Baer, M., & Frese, M. (2003). Innovation is not enough: Climates for initiative and psychological safety, process innovations, and firm performance. *Journal of Organizational Behavior, 24*(1), 45–68. doi: 10.1002/job.179

Bakker, A. B. (2010). Engagement and "job crafting": Engaged employees create their own great place to work. In S. L. Albrecht (Ed.), *Handbook of employee engagement: Perspectives, issues, research and practice* (pp. 229–244). Glos, UK: Edward Elgar.

Bakker, A. B., Albrecht, S. L., & Leiter, M. P. (2011). Key questions regarding work engagement. *European Journal of Work and Organizational Psychology, 20*(1), 4–28. doi: 10.1080/13 59432x.2010.485352

Bakker, A. B., & Demerouti, E. (2007). The job demands-resources model: State of the art. *Journal of Managerial Psychology, 22*(3), 309–328. doi: 10.1108/02683940710733115

Bandura, A. (1977). Self-efficacy: Toward a unifying theory of behavioral change. *Psychological Review, 84*(2), 191–215. doi:10.1037//0033-295X.84.2.191

Bandura, A. (1989). Human agency in social cognitive theory. *American Psychologist, 44*(9), 1175–1184. doi: 10.1037/0003-066X.44.9.1175

Bandura, A. (1997). *Self-efficacy: The exercise of control.* New York: Freeman.

Bandura, A. (2001). Social cognitive theory: An agentic perspective. *Annual Review of Psychology, 52*, 1–26. doi: 10.1146/annurev.psych.52.1.1

Bandura, A. (2006). Toward a psychology of human agency. *Perspectives on Psychological Science, 1*(2), 164–180. doi: 10.1111/j.1745-6916.2006.00011.x

Bateman, T. S., & Crant, J. M. (1993). The proactive component of organizational-behavior: A measure and correlates. *Journal of Organizational Behavior, 14*(2), 103–118. doi: 10.1002/job.4030140202

Bateman, T. S., & Crant, J. M. (1999). Proactive behavior: Meaning, impact, recommendations. *Business Horizons, 42*(3), 63–70. doi: 10.1016/S0007-6813(99)80023-8

Baumeister, R. F., & Leary, M. R. (1995). The need to belong: Desire for interpersonal attachments as a fundamental human motivation. *Psychological Bulletin, 117*(3), 497–529. doi: 10.1037/0033-2909.117.3.497

Belschak, F. D., & Den Hartog, D. N. (2010). Pro-self, pro-social, and pro-organizational foci of proactive behavior: Differential antecedents and consequences. *Journal of Occupational and Organizational Psychology, 83*(2), 475–498. doi: 10.1348/096317909X439208

Belschak, F. D., Den Hartog, D. N., & Fay, D. (2010). Exploring positive, negative and context-dependent aspects of proactive behaviours at work. *Journal of Occupational and Organizational Psychology, 83*(2), 267–273. doi: 10.1348/096317910X501143

Bindl, U. K., & Parker, S. K. (2011a). Feeling good and performing well? Psychological engagement and positive behaviors at work. In S. Albert (Ed.), *Handbook of employee engagement: Perspectives, issues, research and practice* (pp. 385–398). Cheltenham: Edward-Elgar Publishing.

Bindl, U. K., & Parker, S. K. (2011b). Proactive work behavior: Forward-thinking and changeoriented action in organizations. In S. Zedeck (Ed.), *APA handbook of industrial and organizational psychology* (Vol. 2, pp. 567–598). Washington, DC: American Psychological Association.

Bindl, U. K., Parker, S. K., Totterdell, P., & Hagger-Johnson, G. (2012). Fuel of the self-starter: How mood relates to proactive goal regulation. *Journal of Applied Psychology, 97*(1), 134–150. doi: 10.1037/a0024368

Bolino, M. C. (1999). Citizenship and impression management: Good soldiers or good actors? *Academy of Management Review, 24*(1), 82–98. doi: 10.2307/259038

Bolino, M. C., Valcea, S., & Harvey, J. (2010). Employee, manage thyself: The potentially negative implications of expecting employees to behave proactively. *Journal of Occupational and Organizational Psychology, 83*(2), 325–345. doi: 10.1348/096317910X493134

Brehm, J. W. (1999). The intensity of emotion. *Personality and Social Psychology Review, 3*(1), 2–22. doi: 10.1207/s15327957pspr0301_1

Bruggeman, A., Groskurth, P., & Ulich, E. (1975). *Arbeitszufriedenheit.* Bern: Huber.

Buessing, A. (2002). Motivation and satisfaction. In A. Sorge (Ed.), *Organization* (pp. 371–387). London: Thomson Learning.

Buessing, A., & Bissels, T. (1998). Different forms of work satisfaction: Concept and qualitative research. *European Psychologist, 3*, 209–218. doi: 10.1027/1016-9040.3.3.209

Campbell, D. J. (2000). The proactive employee: Managing workplace initiative. *Academy of Management Executive, 14*(3), 52–66.

Cascio, W. F. (1995). Whither industrial and organizational psychology in a changing world of work. *American Psychologist, 50*(11), 928–939. doi: 10.1037//0003-066X.50.11.928

Chan, D. (2006). Interactive effects of situational judgement effectiveness and proactive personality on work perceptions and work outcomes. *Journal of Applied Psychology, 91*(2), 475–481. doi: 10.1037/0021-9010.91.2.475

Claes, R., & Ruiz-Quintanilla, S. A. (1998). Influences of early career experiences, occupational group, and national culture on proactive career behavior. *Journal of Vocational Behavior, 52*, 357–378. doi: 10.1006/jvbe.1997.1626

Crant, J. M. (1995). The proactive personality scale and objective job performance among real estate agents. *Journal of Applied Psychology, 80*(4), 532–537. doi: 10.1037/0021-9010.80.4.532

Crant, J. M. (2000). Proactive behavior in organizations. *Journal of Management, 26*(3), 435–462. doi: 10.1177/014920630002600304

Csikszentmihalyi, M. (1988). The flow experience and its significance for human psychology. In M. Csikszentmihalyi & I. S. Csikszentmihalyi (Eds.), *Optimal experience: Psychological studies of flow in consciousness* (pp. 15–35). Cambridge: Cambridge University Press.

deCharms, R. (1968). *Personal causation.* New York: Academic Press.

Deci, E. L., Connell, J. P., & Ryan, R. M. (1989). Self-determination in a work organization. *Journal of Applied Psychology, 74*(4), 580–590. doi: 10.1037//0021-9010.74.4.580

Deci, E. L., Egharri, H., Patrick, B. C., & Leone, D. R. (1994). Facilitating internalization: The self-determination theory perspective. *Journal of Personality, 62*(1), 119–142. doi: 10.1111/j.1467-6494.1994.tb00797.x

Deci, E. L., Koestner, R., & Ryan, R. M. (1999). A meta-analytic review of experiments examining the effects of extrinsic rewards on intrinsic motivation. *Psychological Bulletin, 125*(6), 627–668. doi: 10.1037/0033-2909.125.6.627

Deci, E. L., & Ryan, R. M. (1985). *Intrinsic motivation and self-determination in human behavior.* New York: Plenum.

Deci, E. L., & Ryan, R. M. (2000). The "what" and "why" of goal pursuits: Human needs and the self-determination of behavior. *Psychological Inquiry, 11*(4), 227–268. doi: 10.1207/S15327965PLI1104_01

Deci, E. L., Ryan, R. M., Gagné, M., Leone, D. R., Usunov, J., & Kornazheva, B. P. (2001). Need satisfaction, motivation, and well-being in the work organizations of a former eastern bloc country: A cross-cultural study of self-determination *Personality and Social Psychology Bulletin, 27*(8), 930–942. doi: 10.1177/0146167201278002

Den Hartog, D. N., & Belschak, F. D. (2007). Personal initiative, commitment and affect at work. *Journal of Occupational and Organizational Psychology, 80*(4), 601–622. doi: 10.1348/096317906X171442

Den Hartog, D. N., & Belschak, F. D. (2012). When does transformational leadership enhance employee proactive behavior? The role of autonomy and role breadth self-efficacy.

Journal of Applied Psychology, 97(1), 194–202. doi: 10.1037/a0024903

Detert, J. R., & Burris, E. R. (2007). Leadership behavior and employee voice: Is the door really open? *Academy of Management Journal, 50*(4), 869–884. doi: 10.5465/AMJ.2007.26279183

Dutton, J. E., Ashford, S. J., O'Neill, R. M., & Lawrence, K. A. (2001). Moves that matter: Issue selling and organizational change. *Academy of Management Journal, 44*(4), 716–736. doi: 10.2307/3069412

Eccles, J. S., Adler, T. F., Futterman, R., Goff, S. B., Kaczala, C. M., Meece, J. L., & Midgley, C. (1983). Expectancies, values, and academic behaviors. In J. T. Spence (Ed.); *Achievement and achievement motivation.* San Francisco: Freeman.

Edwards, J. R. (1996). An examination of competing versions of the person-environment fit approach to stress. *Academy of Management Journal, 39*(2), 292–339. doi: 10.2307/256782

Erdogan, B., & Bauer, T. N. (2005). Enhancing career benefits of employee proactive personality: The role of fit with jobs and organizations. *Personnel Psychology, 58*, 859–891. doi: 10.1111/j.1744-6570.2005.00772.x

Foo, M.-D., Uy, M. A., & Baron, R. A. (2009). How do feelings influence effort? An empirical study of entrepreneurs' affect and venture effort. *Journal of Applied Psychology, 94*(4), 1086–1094. doi: 10.1037/a0015599

Fredrickson, B. L. (1998). What good are positive emotions? *Review of General Psychology, 2*(3), 300–319. doi: 10.1037/1089-2680.2.3.300

Frese, M., & Fay, D. (2001). Personal initiative: An active performance concept for work in the 21st century. *Research in Organizational Behavior, 23*, 133–187. doi: 10.1016/S0191-3085(01)23005-6

Frese, M., Fay, D., Hilburger, T., Leng, K., & Tag, A. (1997). The concept of personal initiative: Operationalization, reliability and validity in two German samples. *Journal of Occupational and Organizational Psychology, 70*, 139–161. doi: 10.1111/j.2044-8325.1997.tb00639.x

Frese, M., Garman, G., Garmeister, K., Halemba, K., Hortig, A., Pulwitt, T., & Schildbach, S. (2002). Training zur Erhoehung der Eigeninitiative bei Arbeitslosen: Bericht ueber einen Pilotversuch (Training to increase personal initiative in unemployed: A pilot study). *Zeitschrift fuer Arbeits—und Organisationspsychologie, 46*(2), 89–97. doi: 10.1026//0932-4089.46.2.89

Frese, M., Garst, H., & Fay, D. (2007). Making things happen: Reciprocal relationships between work characteristics and personal initiatice in a four-wave longitudinal structural equation model. *Journal of Applied Psychology, 92*(4), 1084–1102. doi: 10.1037/0021-9010.92.4.1084

Frese, M., Kring, W., Soose, A., & Zempel, J. (1996). Personal initiative at work: Differences between East and West Germany. *Academy of Management Journal, 39*(1), 37–63. doi: 10.2307/256630

Fuller, J. B., & Marler, L. E. (2009). Change driven by nature: A meta-analytic review of the proactive personality literature. *Journal of Vocational Behavior, 75*(3), 329–345. doi: 10.1016/j.jvb.2009.05.008

Fuller, J. B., Marler, L. E., & Hester, K. (2006). Promoting felt responsibility for constructive change and proactive behavior: Exploring aspects of an elaborated model of work design. *Journal of Organizational Behavior, 21*, 1089–1120. doi: 10.1002/job.408

Fuller, J. B., Marler, L. E., & Hester, K. (2012). Bridge building within the province of proactivity. *Journal of Organizational Behavior, 33*(8), 1053–1070. doi: 10.1002/job.1780

Gagné, M. (2009). A model of knowledge-sharing motivation. *Human Resource Management, 48*(4), 571–589. doi: 10.1002/hrm.20298

Gagné, M., Chemolli, E., Forest, J., & Koestner, R. (2008). A temporal analysis of the relation between organisational commitment and work motivation. *Psychologica Belgica, 48*(2–3), 219–241.

Gagné, M., & Deci, E. L. (2005). Self-determination theory and work motivation. *Journal of Organizational Behavior, 26*(4), 331–362. doi: 10.1002/job.322

Gagné, M., & Forest, J. (2008). The study of compensation systems through the lens of self-determination theory: Reconciling 35 years of debate. *Canadian Psychology/Psychologie canadienne, 49*(3), 225–232. doi: 10.1037/a0012757

Gagné, M., Senécal, C. B., & Koestner, R. (1997). Proximal job characteristics, feelings of empowerment, and intrinsic motivation: A multidimensional model. *Journal of Applied Social Psychology, 27*(14), 1222–1240. doi: 10.1111/j.1559-1816.1997.tb01803.x

Gollwitzer, P. M. (1999). Implementation intentions: Strong effects of simple plans. *American Psychologist, 54*(7), 493–503. doi: 10.1037//0003-066X.54.7.493

Grant, A. M. (2008). Does intrinsic motivation fuel the prosocial fire? Motivational synergy predicting persistence, performance, and productivity. *Journal of Applied Psychology, 93*(1), 48–58. doi: 10.1037/0021-9010.93.1.48

Grant, A. M., & Ashford, S. J. (2008). The dynamics of proactivity at work. *Research in Organizational Behavior, 28*, 3–34. doi: 10.1016/j.riob.2008.04.002

Grant, A. M., Nurmohamed, S.; Ashford, S. J., & Dekas, K. (2011). The performance implications of ambivalent initiative: The interplay of autonomous and controlled motivations. *Organizational Behavior and Human Decision Processes, 116*(2), 241–251. doi: 10.1016/j.obhdp.2011.03.004

Grant, A. M., Parker, S. K., & Collins, C. G. (2009). Getting credit for proactive behavior: Supervisor reactions depend on what you value and how you feel. *Personnel Psychology, 62*(1), 31–55. doi: 10.1111/j.1744-6570.2008.01128.x

Greguras, G. J., & Diefendorff, J. M. (2009). Different fits satisfy different needs: Linking person-environment fit to employee commitment and performance using self-determination theory. *Journal of Applied Psychology, 94*(2), 465–477. doi: 10.1037/a0014068

Greguras, G. J., & Diefendorff, J. M. (2010). Why does proactive personality predict employee life satisfaction and work behaviors? A field investigation of the mediating role of the self-concordance model. *Personnel Psychology, 63*(3), 539–560. doi: 10.1111/j.1744-6570.2010.01180.x

Griffin, M. A., Neal, A., & Parker, S. K. (2007). A new model of work role performance: Positive behavior in uncertain and interdependent contexts. *Academy of Management Journal, 50*(2), 327–347. doi: 10.5465/AMJ.2007.24634438

Griffin, M. A., Parker, S. K., & Mason, C. M. (2010). Leader vision and the development of adaptive and proactive performance: A longitudinal study. *Journal of Applied Psychology, 95*(1), 174–182. doi: 10.1037/a0017263

Hacker, W. (1998). *Allgemeine arbeitspsychologie.* Bern: Huber.

Hackman, J. R., & Oldham, G. R. (1976). Motivation through the design of work: Test of a theory. *Organizational Behavior and Human Decision Processes, 16,* 250–279. doi: 10.1016/0 030-5073(76)90016-7

Hahn, V. C., Frese, M., Binnewies, C., & Schmitt, A. (2012). The role of hedonic and eudaimonic well-being in business owners' personal initiative. *Entrepreneurship: Theory & Practice, 36*(1), 97–114. doi: 10.1111/j.1540-6520.2011.0 0490.x

Hakanen, J. J., Perhoniemi, R., & Toppinen-Tanner, S. (2008). Positive gain spirals at work: From job resources to work engagement, personal initiative and work-unit innovativeness. *Journal of Vocational Behavior, 73*(1), 78–91. doi: 10.1016/j.jvb.2008.01.003

Hall, D. T. (1976). *Careers in organizations.* Glenview, IL: Scott, Foresman.

Hall, D. T. (1996). Protean careers of the 21st century. *Academy of Management Executive, 10*(1), 8–16.

Harackiewicz, J. M., Manderlink, G., & Sansone, C. (1984). Rewarding pinball wizardry—Effects of evaluation and cue value on intrinsic interest. *Journal of Personality and Social Psychology, 47*(2), 287–300. doi: 10.1037//0022-3514.47.2 .287

Hirschfeld, R. R., Thomas, C. H., & Bernerth, J. B. (2011). Consequences of autonomous and team-oriented forms of dispositional proactivity for demonstrating advancement potential. *Journal of Vocational Behavior, 78,* 237–247. doi: 10.1016/j.jvb.2010.09.001

Hornung, S., Rousseau, D. M., & Glaser, J. (2008). Creating flexible work arrangements through idiosyncratic deals. *Journal of Applied Psychology, 93*(3), 655–664. doi: 10.1037/ 0021-9010.93.3.65

Howell, J. M., & Higgins, C. A. (1990). Champions of technological innovation. *Administrative Science Quarterly, 35*(2), 317–341. doi: 10.2307/2393393

Hui, C., Lam, S. S. K., & Law, K. K. S. (2000). Instrumental values of organizational citizenship behavior for promotion: A field quasi-experiment. *Journal of Applied Psychology, 85*(5), 822–828. doi: 10.1037/0021-9010.85.5.822

Ilies, R., & Judge, T. A. (2005). Goal regulation across time: The effects of feedback and affect. *Journal of Applied Psychology, 90*(3), 453–467. doi: 10.1037/0021-9010.90.3.453

Isen, A. M., Clark, M., Shalker, T. E., & Karp, L. (1977). Affect, accessibility of material in memory, and behavior: A cognitive loop? *Journal of Personality and Social Psychology, 36*(1), 1–12. doi: 10.1037/0022-3514.36.1.1

Isen, A. M., & Reeve, J. (2005). The influence of positive affect on intrinsic and extrinsic motivation: Facilitating enjoyment of play, responsible work behavior, and self-control. *Motivation and Emotion, 2*(4), 295–323. doi: 10.1007/ s11031-006-9019-8

Johnson, E. J., & Tversky, A. (1983). Affect, generalization, and the perception of risk. *Journal of Personality and Social Psychology, 45*(1), 20–31. doi: 10.1037/0022-3514.45.1.20

Kanfer, F. H., & Karoly, P. (1972). Self-control: A behavioristic excursion into the lion's den. *Behavior Therapy, 3*(3), 398–416. doi: 10.1016/S0005-7894(72)80140-0

Kanfer, R., & Ackerman, P. L. (1989). Motivation and cognitive abilities: An integrative/aptitude-treatment interaction approach to skill acquisition. *Journal of Applied Psychology, 74*(4), 657–690. doi: 10.1037/0021-9010.74.4.657

Kanfer, R., Wanberg, C. R., & Kantrowitz, T. M. (2001). Job search and employment: A personality-motivational analysis and meta-analytic review. *Journal of Applied Psychology, 86*(5), 837–855. doi: 10.1037//0021-9010.86.5.837

Kelloway, E. K., & Barling, J. (1991). Job characteristics, role stress, and mental health. *Journal of Occupational Psychology, 64*(4), 291–304. doi: 10.1111/j.2044-8325.1991.tb00561.x

Kernis, M. H., Cornell, D. P., Sun, C.-R., Berry, A., & Harlow, T. (1993). There's more to self-esteem than whether it is high or low: The importance of stability of self-esteem. *Journal of Personality and Social Psychology, 65*(6), 1190–1204. doi: 10. 1037/0022-3514.65.6.1190

Kickul, J., & Gundy, L. K. (2002). Prospecting for strategic advantage: The proactive entrepreneurial personality and small firm innovation. *Journal of Small Business Management, 40*(2), 85–97. doi: 10.1111/1540-627X.00042

Lakhani, K. B., & Wolf, R. G. (2003). Why hackers do what they do: Understanding motivation and effort in free/open source software projects. In J. Feller, B. Fitzgerald, S. Hissam, & K. Lakhani (Eds.), *Perspectives on free and open source software* (pp. 3–22). Boston, MA: MIT Press.

LePine, J. A., & Van Dyne, L. (1998). Predicting voice behavior in work groups. *Journal of Applied Psychology, 83*(6), 853–868. doi: 10.1037/0021-9010.83.6.853

Lepper, M. R., & Greene, D. (1975). Turning play into work: Effects of adult surveillance and extrinsic rewards on children's intrinsic motivation. *Journal of Personality and Social Psychology, 31*(3), 479–486. doi: 10.1037/h0076484

Levin, I. M. (2000). Vision revisited: Telling the story of the future. *Journal of Applied Behavioral Science, 36*(1), 91–107. doi: 10.1177/0021886300361005

Manzoni, J.-F., & Barsoux, J.-L. (2009). The interpersonal side of taking charge. *Organization Dynamics, 38*(2), 106–116. doi: 10.1016/j.orgdyn.2009.02.005

Marinova, S. V., Moon, H., & Van Dyne, L. (2010). Are all good soldier behaviors the same? Supporting multidimensionality of organizational citizenship behaviors based on rewards and roles. *Human Relations, 63*(10), 1463–1485. doi: 10.1177/0018726709359432

Massimini, F., & Carli, M. (1988). The systematic assessment of flow in daily life. In M. Csikszentmihalyi & I. S. Csikszentmihalyi (Eds.), *Optimal experience: Psychological studies of flow in consciousness* (pp. 266–287). New York: Cambridge University Press.

McAllister, D. J., Kamdar, D., Morrison, E. W., & Turban, D. B. (2007). Disentangling role perceptions: How perceived role breath, discretion, instrumentality, and efficacy relate to helping and taking charge. *Journal of Applied Psychology, 92*(5), 1200–1211. doi: 10.1037/0021-9010.92.5.1200

Millette, V., & Gagné, M. (2008). Designing volunteers' tasks to maximize motivation, satisfaction and performance: The impact of job characteristics on volunteer engagement. *Motivation and Emotion, 32*(1), 11–22. doi: 10.1007/ s11031-007-9079-4

Morrison, E. W. (2002). Newcomers' relationships: The role of social network ties during socialization. *Academy of Management Journal, 45*(6), 1149–1160. doi: 10.2307/3069430

Morrison, E. W. (2006). Doing the job well: An investigation of pro-social rule breaking. *Journal of Management, 32*(1), 5–28. doi: 10.1177/0149206305277790

Morrison, E. W., & Bies, R. J. (1991). Impression management in the feedback-seeking process: A literature review and research agenda. *Academy of Management Review, 16*(3), 522–541. doi: 10.2307/258916

Morrison, E. W., & Phelps, C. C. (1999). Taking charge at work: Extrarole efforts to initiate workplace change. *Academy of Management Journal, 42*(4), 403–419. doi: 10.2307/257011

Muraven, M., Gagné, M., & Rosman, H. (2008). Helpful self-control: Autonomy support, vitality, and depletion. *Journal of Experimental Social Psychology*, *44*(3), 573–585. doi: 10.1016/j.jesp.2007.10.008

Muraven, M., Rosman, H., & Gagné, M. (2007). Lack of autonomy and self-control: Performance contingent rewards lead to greater depletion. *Motivation and Emotion*, *31*, 322–330. doi: 10.1007/s11031-007-9073-x

Nicholson, N. (1984). A theory of work role transitions. *Administrative Science Quarterly*, *29*(2), 172–191. doi: 10.2307/2393172

Nix, G. A., Ryan, R. M., Manly, J. B., & Deci, E. L. (1999). Revitalization through self-regulation: The effects of autonomous and controlled motivation on happiness and vitality. *Journal of Experimental Social Psychology*, *35*(3), 266–284. doi: 10.1006/jesp.1999.1382

Oettingen, G. (1999). Free fantasies about the future and the emergence of developmental goals. In J. Brandstädter & R. M. Lerner (Eds.), *Action and self-development: Theory and research through the life span* (pp. 315–342). Thousand Oaks: Sage.

Oettingen, G., & Mayer, D. (2002). The motivating function of thinking about the future: Expectations versus fantasies. *Journal of Personality and Social Psychology*, *83*(5), 1198–1212. doi: 10.1037//0022-3514.83.5.1198

Parker, S. K. (1998). Enhancing role breadth self-efficacy: The roles of job enrichment and other organizational interventions. *Journal of Applied Psychology*, *83*(6), 835–852. doi: 10.1037/0021-9010.83.6.835

Parker, S. K. (2000). From passive to proactive motivation: The importance of flexible role orientations and role breadth self-efficacy. *Applied Psychology: An International Review*, *49*(3), 447–469. doi: 10.1111/1464-0597.00025

Parker, S. K., Bindl, U. K., & Strauss, K. (2010). Making things happen: A model of proactive motivation *Journal of Management*, *36*(4), 827–856. doi: 10.1177/0149206310363732

Parker, S. K., & Collins, C. G. (2010). Taking stock: Integrating and differentiating multiple proactive behaviors. *Journal of Management*, *36*(3), 633–662. doi: 10.1177/0149206308321554

Parker, S. K., & Ohly, S. (2008). Designing motivating jobs. In R. C. Kanfer & R. Pritchard (Eds.), *Work motivation: Past, present, and future* (pp. 233–384). New York: Routledge.

Parker, S. K., Wall, T. D., & Jackson, P. R. (1997). "That's not my job": Developing flexible employee work orientations. *Academy of Management Journal*, *40*(4), 899–929. doi: 10.2307/256952

Parker, S. K., Williams, H. M., & Turner, N. (2006). Modeling the antecedents of proactive behavior at work. *Journal of Applied Psychology*, *91*(3), 636–652. doi: 10.1037/0021-9010.91.3.636

Pittman, T. S., Davey, M. E., Alafat, K. A., Wetherill, K. V., & Kramer, N. A. (1980). Informational versus controlling verbal rewards. *Personality and Social Psychology Bulletin*, *6*(2), 228–233. doi: 10.1177/014616728062007

Rank, J., Carsten, J. M., Unger, J. M., & Spector, P. E. (2007). Proactive customer service performance: Relationships with individual, task, and leadership variables. *Human Performance*, *20*(4), 363–390. doi: 10.1080/08959280701522056

Raub, S., & Robert, C. (2010). Differential effects of empowering leadership on in-role and extra-role employee behaviors: Exploring the role of psychological empowerment and power values. *Human Relations*, *63*(11), 1743–1770. doi: 10.1177/0018726710365092

Reis, H. T., Sheldon, K. M., Gable, S. L., Roscoe, J., & Ryan, R. M. (2000). Daily well-being: The role of autonomy, competence, and relatedness. *Personality and Social Psychology Bulletin*, *26*(4), 419–435. doi: 10.1177/0146167200266002

Richer, S. F., & Vallerand, R. J. (1995). Supervisors' interactional styles and subordinates' intrinsic and extrinsic motivation. *Journal of Social Psychology*, *135*(6), 707–722. doi: 10.1080/00224545.1995.9713974

Rigby, C. S., Deci, E. L., Patrick, B. C., & Ryan, R. M. (1992). Beyond the intrinsic-extrinsic dichotomy: Self-determination in motivation and learning. *Motivation and Emotion*, *16*(3), 165–185. doi: 10.1007/BF00991650

Ryan, R. M. (1982). Control and information in the intrapersonal sphere: An extension of cognitive evaluation theory. *Journal of Personality and Social Psychology*, *43*(3), 450–461. doi: 10.1037//0022-3514.43.3.450

Ryan, R. M. (1995). Psychological needs and the facilitation of integrative processes. *Journal of Personality*, *63*(3), 397–427. doi: 10.1111/j.1467-6494.1995.tb00501.x

Ryan, R. M., Chirkov, V. I., Little, T. D., Sheldon, K. M., Timoshina, E., & Deci, E. L. (1999). The American dream in Russia: Extrinsic aspirations and well-being in two cultures. *Personality and Social Psychology Bulletin*, *25*(12), 1509–1524. doi: 10.1177/01461672992510007

Ryan, R. M., Connell, J. P., & Deci, E. L. (1985). A motivational analysis of self-determination and self-regulation in education. In C. Ames & R. E. Ames (Eds.), *Research on motivation in education: The classroom milieu* (pp. 13–51). New York: Academic Press.

Ryan, R. M., & Deci, E. L. (2000). Self-determination theory and the facilitation of intrinsic motivation, social development, and well-being. *American Psychologist*, *55*(1), 68–78. doi: 10.1037//0003-066X.55.1.68

Ryan, R. M., & Fredrick, C. M. (1997). On energy, personality and health: Subjective vitality as a dynamic reflection of well-being. *Journal of Personality*, *65*(3), 529–565. doi: 10.1111/j.1467-6494.1997.tb00326.x

Salanova, M., & Schaufeli, W. B. (2008). A cross-national study of work engagement as a mediator between job resources and proactive behaviour. *International Journal of Human Resource Management*, *19*(1), 116–131. doi: 10.1080/09585190701763982

Schaufeli, W. B., Salanova, M., Gonzalez-Roma, V., & Bakker, A. B. (2002). The measurement of burnout and engagement: A two-sample confirmatory factor analytic approach. *Journal of Happiness Studies*, *3*(1), 71–92. doi: 10.1023/A:1015630930326

Scott, S. G., & Bruce, R. A. (1994). Determinants of innovative behavior: A path model of individual innovation in the workplace. *Academy of Management Journal*, *37*(3), 580–607. doi: 10.2307/256701

Seibert, S. E., Crant, J. M., & Kraimer, M. L. (1999). Proactive personality and career success. *Journal of Applied Psychology*, *84*(3), 416–427. doi: 10.1037//0021-9010.84.3.416

Seibert, S. E., Kraimer, M. L., & Crant, J. M. (2001). What do proactive people do? A longitudinal model linking proactive personality and career success. *Personnel Psychology*, *54*(2), 845–874. doi: 10.1111/j.1744-6570.2001.tb00234.x

Seo, M.-G., Barrett, L. F., & Bartunek, J. M. (2004). The role of affective experience in work motivation. *Academy of Management Review*, *29*(3), 423–439. doi: 10.2307/20159052

Seo, M.-G., Bartunek, J. M., & Barrett, L. F. (2010). The role of affective experience in work motivation: Test of a conceptual model. *Journal of Organizational Behavior, 31*(7), 951–968. doi: 10.1002/job.655

Sheldon, K. M., & Elliot, A. J. (1999). Goal striving, need satisfaction, and longitudinal well-being: The self-concordance model. *Journal of Personality and Social Psychology, 76*(3), 482–497. doi: 10.1037//0022-3514.76.3.482

Sheldon, K. M., & Kasser, T. (1995). Coherence and congruence: Two aspects of personality integration. *Journal of Personality and Social Psychology, 68*(3), 531–543. doi: 10.1037//0022-3514.68.3.531

Sheldon, K. M., & Kasser, T. (1998). Pursuing personal goals: Skills enable progress, but not all progress is beneficial. *Personality and Social Psychology Review, 24*(12), 1319–1331. doi: 10.1177/01461672982412006

Spreitzer, G. M. (1996). Social structural characteristics of psychological empowerment. *Academy of Management Journal, 39*(2), 483–504. doi: 10.2307/256789

Strauss, K., Griffin, M. A., & Parker, S. K. (2009). *Solving the Initiative Paradox: Leader vision and the collective future self.* Paper presented at the 14th European Congress of Work and Organizational Psychology, Santiago de Compostela, Spain.

Strauss, K., Griffin, M. A., & Parker, S. K. (2012). Future Work Selves: How salient hoped-for identities motivate proactive career behaviors. *Journal of Applied Psychology, 97*(3), 580–598. doi: 10.1037/a0026423

Strauss, K., Griffin, M. A., & Rafferty, A. E. (2009). Proactivity directed toward the team and organization: The role of leadership, commitment, and role-breadth self-efficacy. *British Journal of Management, 20*(3), 279–291. doi: 10.1111/j.1467-8551.2008.00590.x

Taylor, S. E., Pham, L. B., Rivkin, I. D., & Armor, D. A. (1998). Harnessing the imagination: Mental simulation, self-regulation, and coping. *American Psychologist, 53*(4), 429–439. doi: 10.1037//0003-066X.53.4.429

Taylor, S. E., & Schneider, S. K. (1989). Coping and the simulation of events. *Social Cognition, 7*(2), 174–194. doi: 10.1521/soco.1989.7.2.174

Tharenou, P., & Terry, D. J. (1998). Reliability and validity of scores on scales to measure managerial aspirations. *Educational and Psychological Measurement, 58*(3), 475–492. doi: 10.1177/0013164498058003008

Thomas, J. P., Whitman, D. S., & Viswesvaran, C. (2010). Employee proactivity in organizations: A comparative meta-analysis of emergent proactive constructs. *Journal of Occupational and Organizational Psychology, 83*(2), 275–300. doi: 10.1348/096317910X502359

Thomas, K. W., & Velthouse, B. A. (1990). Cognitive elements of empowerment: An "interpretive" model of intrinsic task motivation. *Academy of Management Review, 15*(4), 666–681. doi: 10.2307/258687

Thompson, J. A. (2005). Proactive personality and job performance: A social capital perspective. *Journal of Applied Psychology, 90*(5), 1011–1017. doi: 10.1037/0021-9010.90.5.1011

Tims, M., & Bakker, A. B. (2010). Job crafting: Towards a new model of individual job redesign. *South African Journal of Industrial Psychology, 36*, 1–9.

Tsai, W. C., Chen, C. C., & Liu, H. L. (2007). Test of a model linking employee positive moods and task performance. *Journal of Applied Psychology, 92*(6), 1570–1583. doi: 10.1037/0021-9010.92.6.1570

Van den Broeck, A., Vansteenkiste, M., De Witte, H., & Lens, W. (2008). Explaining the relationships between job characteristics, burnout, and engagement: The role of basic psychological need satisfaction. *Work & Stress, 22*(3), 277–294. doi: 10.1080/02678370802393672

Van Yperen, N. W., & Hagedoorn, M. (2003). Do high job demands increase intrinsic motivation or fatigue or both? The role of job control and job social support. *Academy of Management Journal, 46*(3), 339–348. doi: 10.2307/30040627

Vroom, V. (1964). *Work and motivation.* New York: Wiley.

Wegener, D. T., & Petty, R. E. (1996). Effects of mood on persuasion processes: Enhancing, reducing, and biasing scrutiny of attitude-relevant information. In L. L. Martin & A. Tesser (Eds.), *Striving and feeling: Interactions among goals, affect, and self-regulation* (pp. 329–362). Mahwah, NJ: Lawrence Erlbaum.

Weinstein, N., & Ryan, R. M. (2010). When helping helps: Autonomous motivation for prosocial behavior and its influence on the well-being for the helper and the recipient. *Journal of Personality and Social Psychology, 98*(2), 222–244. doi: 10.1037/a0016984

West, M. A. (2002). Sparkling fountains or stagnant ponds: An integrative model of creativity and innovation implementation in work groups. *Applied Psychology, 51*(3), 355–387. doi: 10.1111/1464-0597.00951

White, R. W. (1955). Motivation reconsidered: The concept of competence. *Psychological Review, 66*(5), 297–333. doi: 10.1037/h0040934

Williams, G. C., & Deci, E. L. (1996). Internalization of biopsychosocial values by medical students: A test of self-determination theory. *Journal of Personality and Social Psychology, 70*(4), 767–779. doi: 10.1037//0022-3514.70.4.767

Williams, G. C., Freedman, Z. R., & Deci, E. L. (1998). Supporting autonomy to motivate patients with diabetes for glucose control. *Diabetes Care, 21*(10), 1644–1651. doi: 10.2337/diacare.21.10.1644

Williams, G. C., Gagné, M., Ryan, R. M., & Deci, E. L. (2002). Facilitating autonomous motivation for smoking cessation. *Health Psychology, 21*(1), 40–50. doi: 10.1037//0278-6133.21.1.40

Wrzesniewski, A., & Dutton, J. E. (2001). Crafting a job: Revisioning employees as active crafters of their work. *Academy of Management Review, 26*(2), 179–201. doi: 10.2307/259118

CHAPTER

5

A Behavioral Economics Perspective on the Overjustification Effect: Crowding-In and Crowding-Out of Intrinsic Motivation

Antoinette Weibel, Meike Wiemann, *and* Margit Osterloh

Abstract

In the last two decades, economic motivation research has undergone a paradigm shift when it comes to the effect of incentive schemes on individual performance and motivation. Inspired by self-determination theory, a new branch in economics evolved called behavioral economics. Especially by evidencing the negative effect of "pay-for-performance" on intrinsic motivation, called the "crowding-out" or "overjustification" effect, it challenges the economic paradigm of the relative price-effect and its inherent belief in incentives as universal remedy for motivation and individual performance. This article reviews the findings of behavioral economics on motivation. Drawing on these results we discuss which institutional conditions strengthen rather than weaken intrinsic motivation. We demonstrate that fairness, participation, market-driven wages, and normatively affected decision-making contexts have a positive effect on intrinsic motivation.

Key Words: intrinsic motivation, extrinsic motivation, pay-for-performance, crowding-out effect, overjustification effect, behavioral economics, institutional conditions

Cognitive[1] evaluation and self-determination theory (SDT) inspired one of the most dramatic changes in economic theory. When Bruno Frey demonstrated in the 1990s (Frey, 1992, 1997a, 1997b) that the so-called relative price-effect (i.e., the performance-enhancing effect of incentives), in certain cases is counterbalanced, even outruled by a negative effect on individual performance termed "crowding-out effect," many economic theories needed to be rewritten. Bruno Frey was one of the pioneers of behavioral economics whose proponents started to test the behavioral assumptions of economic theory rigorously by means of a bold empirical "invasion" (Camerer, Loewenstein, & Rabin, 2004). This article summarizes the findings of behavioral economics on the negative and positive effects of incentives on intrinsic motivation and individual performance.

At the core of behavioral approaches to economics lies the idea that social communities

cannot flourish without voluntary, intrinsically motivated contributions to public goods (Ostrom, 2000). We show, from this behavioral economics view, which institutional conditions inhibit or boost intrinsic motivation. In particular, variable "pay-for-performance" schemes, which are commonly used by practitioners, can have a negative effect on employees' intrinsic motivation. A positive effect on intrinsic motivation, however, can be achieved through mechanisms of participation, fairness, normatively affected decision contexts, and market-driven salaries.

Is "Pay-for-Performance" Recommendable? A Taste of Heated Discussion in the Field of Economics

In many companies, incentive pay has caught on as the embodiment of modern management methods. Such pay-for-performance schemes focus on the relative price-effect, which states that behavior depends on relative prices and assumes that for employees low engagement becomes more costly when they are paid for their performance; hence with pay-for-performance less "idling" is expected. Standard economic theory assumes that the promise of higher payment tied to measurable performance always leads to increased performance. Empirically, such a positive effect has been confirmed particularly for piece-rate wages paid for simple jobs (Stajkovic & Luthans, 1997). A much quoted example is the field experiment of the personnel economist Lazear (2000) on the US company *Safelite Glass*: after changing from fixed hourly wages to piece rate, the productivity increased by an astounding 36% (incentive effect, 20%; selection effect, 16%), whereas the labor costs only rose by 9%. Those human resource management scholars that rely strongly on economic theories have also welcomed these insights. For instance Barry Gerhart and Sara L. Rynes (2003) in their comprehensive review on compensation—particularly on the effect of pay-for-performance on individual performance—clearly seem to recommend the use of incentive pay because it "can produce substantial increases in productivity" (p. 195) and will assist companies in "getting rid of the poor performers through turnover" (p. 195). Hence the universal recommendation for human resource managers is to install what has been termed "high performance work practices," which always entail some form of individual incentive pay (Becker & Huselid, 1998; Huselid, 1995). As a consequence, the principle of piece-rate wages has been increasingly transferred to all employment forms, for example to companies' middle and upper management (e.g., Bebchuk & Grinstein, 2005), government agencies (e.g., Bertelli, 2006; Schneider, 2007), and even to the public sector (i.e., the new W-salary levels in German universities; Osterloh & Frey, 2002). However, in contrast to typical piece-rate work, these occupations are characterized by a large scope of action, complexity, and are intrinsically interesting. They are difficult to control, and therefore call for much more personal initiative (Osterloh, 2006; Osterloh & Frey, 2000).

Psychological theories have questioned the universal validity of the relative price-effect for a long time, particularly for tasks that call for more personal initiative. They show that, under certain conditions, variable performance-related payment lessens performance (Deci & Ryan, 1985). This is referred to as the "hidden costs of rewards" (Deci, 1976), the "overjustification effect" (Lepper & Greene, 1978), or the "corruption effect" (Kruglanski, 1975). Bruno Frey (1992, 1997b) introduced this effect to economics as the so-called crowding-out effect, which states that extrinsic and intrinsic motivation are related in such a way that external interventions (aimed to strengthen extrinsic motivation) can diminish intrinsic motivation. He thereby fructified one of the fundamental new orientations called for by behavioral economics. By now, a sizeable number of experiments and field studies from behavioral economics have demonstrated such a crowding-out effect caused by pay-for-performance in a variety of sectors. Coincidentally and more recently, the findings that examined the crowding-out effect have been supplemented with a number of findings on the crowding-in effect, dealing with institutional conditions that strengthen intrinsic motivation. In addition, behavioral economics has provided a number of theoretical explanations for these effects, which nicely complement the self-determination framework.

What is "Behavioral Economics"?

For more than 30 years standard economic theory has dominated business school research and economic research in dealing with human motivation (Gintis & Khurana, 2008). Standard economic theory has been highly valuable in its capacity to explain competitive markets and it has been successful in permeating managerial practice through prominent subtheories, such as the principal-agency theory and transaction cost economics. For example, nowadays it seems to be common wisdom to view CEOs as agents, who are knowledgeable "contractors" steering companies for their owners, which are in turn seen as principals. In addition, one theoretical assumption of the standard-economic principal-agent model has been taken for granted in the business press and elsewhere, namely that CEOs are often portrayed as employees with their own hidden agenda, who mainly use their formidable inside knowledge of the company to satisfy their own interest (Jensen & Murphy, 1990).

However, standard economic theories use a behavioral model that disregards psychological factors almost completely (Frey & Benz, 2004). The Homo Economicus model treats individuals as utility maximizers, who are rational (cognitive limitations resulting in systematically suboptimal decisions are disregarded), self-controlled (self-control problems and emotions are not considered), and self-interested (the Homo Economicus does not have prosocial preferences) (Camerer & Loewenstein, 2003; for a recent account see Tomer, 2007). Each of these key assumptions is now systematically challenged by findings in behavioral economics, which suggest that "humans are dumber, nicer, and weaker than the Homo Oeconomicus" (Thaler, 1996, p. 227). Yet, the challenge of the motivational characteristics of the Homo Economicus, namely the assumption that individuals on average are "nicer" than assumed so far, entices by far the most heated discussion between standard and behavioral economists (Osterloh & Frost, 2009).

The underlying motivational assumptions of standard economic theory can be typified by the following three assumptions (e.g., Frey, 1990; Kirchgässner, 1991):

1. There is a strict division between preferences (i.e., needs, values, and utilities, which underlie motivation) and restrictions (i.e., external incentives and limitations of one's freedom of action).

2. The individual's preferences are fixed and relatively enduring (Stigler & Becker, 1977). As a consequence, changes in individual behavior are mainly a result of changes in restrictions.

3. Individuals only know self-serving preferences. Other person's preferences are not included in one's own preference function.

In addition, standard economic theory often adapts an even narrower version of the self-interested human being than the "traditional" Homo Economicus model: individuals are assumed to maximize their own tangible interests, that is, their own monetary or goods payoff (Camerer, 2005) and are depicted to be solely extrinsically motivated by tangible rewards or avoidance of punishment. Preferences, and thus, intrinsic motivation, cannot be influenced in the short term and are therefore excluded from the analysis.

Behavioral economics rigorously tests these assumptions and usually proceeds as follows (Camerer & Loewenstein, 2003):

1. Identification of an assumption within the standard economic model

2. Identification of deviations from this assumption

3. Use of these deviations in order to generate an alternative hypothesis to the standard economic model

4. Construction of a behavioral economic model out of the alternative hypothesis

5. Testing of this model

6. Development of new implications

The aim of behavioral economics is to stepwise modify conventional assumptions of standard economics in order to set up a more realistic psychological-empirical foundation of (usually mathematical) models, keeping the standard economic model at the same time as a reference (Camerer, 2005; Frey & Benz, 2004; Rabin, 2002). This proceeding explains behavioral economics' preference for laboratory experiments because they allow the isolation of individual variables and their modification under controlled conditions (Camerer & Fehr, 2006). In addition, adhering to the skepticism of economics toward survey data, observable facts, such as a change in the quantity or quality of performing a task, are taken as *explanandum* and in a reverse engineering process the *explanans* is concluded (Camerer & Loewenstein, 2003). Despite the preference for laboratory experiments, field experiments (e.g., Gneezy & Rustichini, 2000) and experimental survey studies, such as vignettes, recently have complemented the behavioral economist's toolkit. These latter studies often also incorporate actors' subjective interpretation (i.e., they seek to measure motivation as well as changes in motivation; Weibel, Rost, & Osterloh, 2007).

The Motivational Perspective of Behavioral Economics

In contrast to standard economics, behavioral economics has developed a much richer understanding of the motivational characteristics of human beings. Particularly, it is proposed that an empirically grounded Homo Economicus is typified by the following:

1. Proself and prosocial preferences (Meier, 2006)

2. Heterogeneous preferences (Andreoni, 1990; Fischbacher, Fehr, & Gächter, 2001)

3. Preferences, which are plastic and systematically susceptible to the design of institutions, working conditions, and the quality of human interactions (Ostrom, 2000)

4. Preferences, which are often not known to the individuals (Ariely, Loewenstein, & Prelec, 2006) or are falsely interpreted by them (Stutzer & Frey, 2007)

The most ubiquitous finding of behavioral economics is that prosocial behavior is much more prevalent than standard economic theory suggests (Meier, 2006), a fact that cannot be explained assuming individuals to be solely self-interested and extrinsically motivated. For instance, a large body of research has been accumulated on whether, when, and why individuals contribute to (the) commons. Large-scale survey studies show that individuals contribute substantial amounts of money and time to public goods. In the United States almost 70% of all households make charitable contributions, exceeding 1% of the Gross Domestic Product (Andreoni, Gale, & Scholz, 1996). Volunteer work in Europe is estimated to amount to 4.5 million full-time equivalent volunteers for 10 European countries studied (Anheier & Salamon, 1998). Similar "selfless" behavior is observed in laboratory experiments, where behavioral economists have studied participants' behavior in social dilemma situations. In this situation, standard economic theory assumes that for a self-interested individual, the unique dominant strategy would be to defect, for example to free-ride on others' contributions. In contrast to this gloomy prediction, experiments of behavioral economists (and social psychologists) show that people cooperate quite often. For example, it has been demonstrated that participants in such experiments invest up to between 40% and 60% of their endowments in public goods (Fehr & Gächter, 1998). Henrich et al. (2001, p. 77) conducted a series of ultimatum games in 15 societies around the world and came to the conclusion that "the canonical model of the self-interested material pay-off—maximizing actor is systematically violated."

The most popular explanation of these "anomalies" is the introduction of motivational propensities to economic theory. Next to the standard assumption of "egoism", two further "intrinsic motivation propensities" have been introduced, namely altruism (i.e., unconditional prosocial motivation) and strong reciprocity (i.e., conditional prosocial motivation). Altruism depicts the tendency of an individual to pay a personal cost to provide benefits to others in general (Fowler & Kam, 2007). Strong reciprocity is understood as a tendency to reciprocate kind intentions of the interaction partner because of a moral obligation. Thus, reciprocists' moral obligation is conditioned by the intentions and the behavior of others (i.e., uncooperative and proself-oriented behavior is met by a change in ones' own behavior; Nyborg, 2010). In laboratory experiments, different types of motivational tendencies are found: overall about 50% of the test persons can be characterized as reciprocitists, 20% as altruists, and 30% as egoists (Andreoni & Miller, 2002; Fischbacher, et al., 2001). Field studies show a smaller proportion of altruists (Frey & Meier, 2004).

A second way to explain this high amount of prosocial behavior is to introduce different types of motivation to economic theory. *Extrinsic motivation* is directed by external incentives for the individual (awards or penalties). These make mediated satisfaction possible, especially by the means of money. In the situations studied by behavioral economics, extrinsic motivation cannot explain prosocial behavior completely. *Intrinsic motivation* is understood as the direct satisfaction of needs (i.e., activities that are performed for their own sake). Intrinsic motivation can, on the one hand, be seen as a *hedonistic preference*, self-serving for one's own fulfillment or well-being. On the other hand, intrinsic motivation can be directed to the well-being of others as a *prosocial preference*. This is included in one's own preference function and imparts a "warm glow" (Andreoni, 1990). In this case, motivation is derived from internalized social norms (Lindenberg, 2001). Both types of intrinsic motivation have been used to explain the high proportion of prosocial behavior in the studies mentioned previously and both types of intrinsic motivation are seen as plastic, and, hence, are influenced systematically by institutions.

Thus, behavioral economics, just like SDT, seeks to differentiate different qualities of motivation but it is done so in slightly different ways. Intrinsic motivation in the economic understanding means autonomous motivation in SDT language. Hence although economists do not care to differentiate different forms of extrinsic motivation it is still apparent that their understanding of intrinsic motivation includes what SDT views as identified—or integrated extrinsic motivation *and* as pure intrinsic motivation. Furthermore, behavioral economics concurs with the SDT distinction of intrinsic motivation as the desire to fulfill a task, because it is inherently interesting, and prosocial motivation as the desire to serve others (e.g., Grant & Berry, 2011). Nevertheless, behavioral economists rather concentrate on analyzing whether both types of preferences are governed by the same set of mechanisms (like both being control-independent, autonomous forms of motivation), than on targeting their separate underlying psychological processes.

Managing Intrinsic Motivation: Crowding-Out and Crowding-In

Behavioral economics states that extrinsic and intrinsic motivation cannot be seen as additive phenomena. Rather both forms of motivation interact in a predictable way (Frey, 1997b). The *crowding-out effect* states that intrinsic motivation for an activity can be repressed by extrinsic rewards (or punishments) and by certain forms of control. The *crowding-in effect* states that specific institutional conditions might increase intrinsic motivation for an activity (e.g., Andreoni, 1990; Frey & Osterloh, 2002). There are different theories used to explain the two effects (see Bolle & Otto, 2010; Frey, 1997b; Sliwka, 2003). In this section we synthesize the literature on crowding effects, assigning the crowding-out of intrinsic motivation to effects of pay-for-performance as well as to the exertion of control, and the crowding-in effect to participation, procedural fairness, priming, and market-driven wages. At the end, we conclude how crowding effects are conditioned and what implications researchers and practitioners can derive from these findings.

The Crowding-Out Effect
CROWDING-OUT THROUGH PAY-FOR-PERFORMANCE

There are many different explanations for why, and through which mechanisms, performance-related compensation leads to a crowding-out of intrinsic motivation. The most famous theory, imported to behavioral economics in order to explain the crowding-out effect, is the psychological theory of *cognitive evaluation* (Deci, 1980; Frey, 1997b), which also constitutes the basis for SDT (Deci, Connell, & Ryan, 1989; Deci & Ryan, 1985). Cognitive evaluation theory draws on unobservable cognitive processes to explain the negative effects of rewards on motivation. One of those governing processes is depicted by the concept of "locus of causality" (De Charms, 1968), which provides a systematic explanation for the transition from intrinsic to extrinsic motivation, because it accounts for why and under which conditions external incentives lead to a shift in motivation. The so-called perceived locus of causality pictures a person's attribution concerning a certain behavior, whereby holding an internal locus of causality means to attribute an activity to one's own initiative and endorsement, and holding an external locus of causality means to ascribe one's own behavior to external constraints (De Charms, 1968). According

to Deci et al. (1989), an internal locus of causality results in intrinsic motivation, relative to an external locus of causality, which is linked to extrinsic motivation.

External conditions are proposed to foster an internal locus of causality, and hence intrinsic motivation, if they provide informational feedback and thereby enable individuals to learn and to feel self-determined (Ryan, 1982). Incentive pay, however, is perceived as controlling feedback, which reduces the perception of self-determination (Deci, Koestner, & Ryan, 1999a, 1999b). Individuals feel like "puppets on strings", experience a strong external locus of causality, which thwarts their intrinsic motivation (Deci, 1971), and, as a consequence, motivation shifts to be predominantly extrinsic. Bruno Frey has "imported" this explanation to behavioral economics: monetary incentives and tight, punishment-oriented regulations crowd-out intrinsic motivation if these are perceived to be controlling and hence do not offer acknowledgement of voluntary engagement (Frey & Benz, 2004).

Another cognitive explanation of the phenomenon of crowding-out has been developed by Lindenberg (2006). In his *goal-framing theory* he assumes that all behavior is goal-oriented and that these goals affect the orientation of motivation. At any time, there are a number of goals competing for an individuals' attention. The goal that eventually wins this competition acts as a dominant frame, which steers attention processes (Lindenberg, 2001). The so-called hedonic frame enables intrinsic motivation, the normative frame prosocial motivation and the gain frame extrinsic motivation. In this view, tangible, contingent rewards strengthen the gain frame and let the hedonic and/or normative frame fade to the background of the individual's attention. As a consequence, an activity, formerly framed as enjoyable or appropriate, looks less enjoyable and appropriate if a strong gain frame is induced by external incentives (Lindenberg, 2001). Lindenberg and Steg (2007) exemplarily show how to apply framing theory to the policy question of how to encourage proenvironmental behavior. They conclude that the normative frame is central to the issue of environmentally friendly behavior, because this type of behavior is often framed in a normative way as a behavior that is "good and right." In contrast, a prominent gain or hedonic frame would work in the opposite direction, because "environmental protection" is often associated with high expenditures, thus reducing individual rewards, and a lot of personal constraints thereby lowering individual comfort and pleasure. Therefore effective institutional interventions would have to actively increase individuals' moral obligation while at the same time, the competing gain and hedonic frame need to be de-emphasized, for instance by creating low-cost possibilities to engage in environmental friendly behavior.

Other authors hold "the information aspect of extrinsic incentives" responsible for their crowding-out effect on intrinsic motivation. Extrinsic incentives are proposed to signal to the agent that the principal does not trust in him or her or that the principal considers a certain task to be either not attractive, generally difficult to achieve, or particularly difficult to achieve for the agent (Bénabou & Tirole, 2003). Thus, contingent rewards signal which tasks are not enjoyable, and hence cannot create any intrinsic motivation (e.g., Gneezy, Meier, & Rey-Biel, 2011). Bolle and Otto (2010) extend this view by demonstrating that such a signaling effect of prices can have persistent effects. The authors argue that rewards attach values to activities, which can be problematic, particularly in situations where no "official price tag" to an activity is available. For instance, blood donation is a voluntary act in many countries; introducing rewards in return for a blood donation implies an economic valuation. Those clearly defined prices have been found to often have a negative effect on the amount of blood donation in a country. Bolle and Otto (2010) argue that such crowding-out takes place because individuals previously attached a higher, symbolic price to their contribution to this public good, and that such a crowding-out effect is persistent once the prices are officially defined. Finally Bénabou and Tirole (2006) extend their argument on the signaling effect of prices: rewards also inform individuals about their intentions. The authors claim that individuals are not clear about their preferences and thus about their real "goodness." As a consequence, individuals experience a warm glow in observing themselves behaving prosocially, because it confirms their self-serving assumption to be intrinsically "good." However, as soon as fines or rewards are linked to these "good deeds" people face the possibility that their contributions are rather motivated by extrinsic incentives than by high moral values as originally assumed. As a consequence, individuals tend to stop contributing to such deeds voluntarily and in the absence of rewards.

Irrespectively of the different mechanisms underlying the crowding-out effect, Frey and Jegen (2001) identify three *conditions*, under which variable, performance-related compensation leads to a reduction in effort at work:

1. The activity was originally intrinsically motivated.

2. The reward is interpreted as a monitoring device.

3. And the extrinsic motivation generated by reward does not counterbalance the loss of intrinsic motivation.

By now, there are a large number of *laboratory experiments* as well as *meta-analyses of these experiments* that studied influencing factors of the crowding-out effect in detail. The effect is stronger with expected rewards than with unexpected ones, and stronger with pecuniary incentives than with symbolic ones (Deci, et al., 1999a; Heckhausen, 2006). Moreover, there is a stronger crowding-out effect with interesting activities than with less interesting, monotonous jobs (Weibel, Rost, & Osterloh, 2010). Jenkins, Gupta, Mitra, and Shaw (1998), although not finding a negative effect of rewards, still provided evidence that these rewards are ineffective when it comes down to performance quality rather than quantity. Furthermore, crowding-out was found to effect contributions to public goods that are delivered in public, but not always to privately delivered public goods (Ariely, Bracha, & Meier, 2009).

In addition, a number of field experiments have supported the existence of a crowding-out effect (e.g., Ariely, Gneezy, Loewenstein, & Mazar, 2009; Frey, Eichenberger, & Oberholzer-Gee, 1996; Frey & Götte, 1999; Holmas, Kjerstad, Luras, & Straume, 2010). Holmas and colleagues (2010), for example, show in a unique natural experiment that monetary punishment strongly crowds out prosocial behavior. A long-standing problem in the Norwegian heathcare system is the transfer of elderly patients that need specialist care from the treatment hospital to the care facility in the patients' home municipalities. This transfer has to be arranged by the local facilities but is often delayed for a number of reasons. In order to speed-up this transfer some municipalities started to fine their long-term providers for transfer delays, whereas other municipalities were at the same time abolishing their already existing fining system. Holmas et al. (2010) demonstrated that the implementation of these monetary punishments results in a "bed-blocking behavior" from the owners of long-term care institutions. Thus, fines seemed to prolong rather than to shorten patient stays in state hospitals. In contrast, where fines had been formerly in place and were suddenly abolished, patients' length of stay was significantly shortened. Hence, in this case contingent punishments diminished performance, whereas the abolishment of fines had a positive effect on performance. Another recent study reveals how salient rewards negatively influence performance (Ariely, Gneezy, Loewenstein, & Mazar, 2009). The authors conducted a set of experiments in India and the United States to look at how rewards influence respondents' performance on different tasks. In India, respondents showed lower performance across different types of tasks when performance-contingent rewards were high in comparison with a situation where rewards were rather low. Thus, it could be argued that only salient contingent rewards crowd-out intrinsic motivation. In the United States, the effect of rewards on performance was moderated by the task at hand. On tasks that require motor skills, performance significantly increased with high rewards (in the experiment the high reward condition offered 10 times the rewards of the low reward condition). However, performance decreased when rewards were tied to cognitive or creative tasks.

Some experiments conducted by behavioral economists also show how both crowding-out and the price-effect operate in conjunction. Gneezy and Rustichini (2000), for instance, demonstrated how crowding-out and the price effect operate in opposite directions: the authors investigated the influence of financial incentives on the voluntary fundraising behavior of 180 students. These were divided into three groups. The first group received no financial bonus, the second received 1%, and the third 10% of the fundraising. The group with the 1% bonus fundraised considerably less than the group that received nothing. The third group fundraised more than the second group, but still fell short of the achievement of the first group. Thus, the price and crowding-out effect work in opposite directions (Frey & Osterloh, 2002): according to the price effect, the increased bonus boosts work effort (Figure 5.1). Without a bonus (i.e., being intrinsically motivated) the children engage at the A1 level. As long as there is no crowding-out effect, intrinsic motivation stays constant, so the addition of a bonus B raises work effort from A1 to A2.

According to the crowding-out effect, a bonus decreases work efforts as soon as it is being perceived as autonomy-thwarting. The supply curve moves from S to S' (Figure 5.2), indicating that intrinsic motivation decreases. As a result, work effort

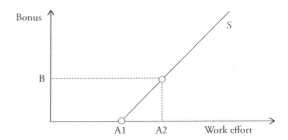

Fig. 5.1. The price effect.

drops to A3. If the crowding-out effect is weaker, that is, the intrinsic motivation is not reduced to zero, a lesser decline or even a slight but expensive rise in work effort can result. For this reason, the authors Gneezy and Rustichini (2000, p. 791) entitled their article: "Pay enough or don't pay at all." This trade-off has recently been substantiated by Pouliakas (2010, p. 618), who finds, that "monetary incentives may have a positive effect on workers' utility and performance as long as they are large enough."

Summarizing the vast evidence about the effects of performance-pay on performance and intrinsic motivation, pay-for-performance is clearly shown to have a negative effect on individual-level performance for interesting and more challenging tasks as well as for complex tasks. The crowding-out effect tends to be stronger for tangible and salient incentives, although current research has yet to unravel what drives the "salience" of rewards in a company context. However, it is safe to say that the current omnipresent use of individual-level pay-for-performance does not reflect scientific evidence: the effect of pay-for-performance on knowledge-based work and higher level managerial work is dubious and cannot be recommended based on current evidence from behavioral economics. These findings are also in accordance with research from psychology as a recent review of Gagné and Forest (2008) shows.

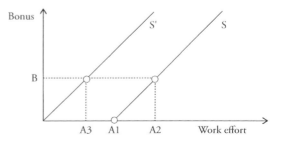

Fig. 5.2. The net effect of the price effect and the crowding-out effect.

CROWDING-OUT THROUGH FORMAL CONTROL

The second institutional mechanism, which is closely linked to crowding-out, is formal control. Here we define control as the purposive influence on the regulation of an individual's behavior through hierarchical authority, which leads to the attainment of institutional goals (see Fayol & Urwick, 1963; Gulati, 1998; Snell, 1992). Thus, formal control is firmly built on influencing extrinsic motivation: common goals are defined, goal attainment is monitored by supervisors, and individuals are rewarded or sanctioned depending on their compliance. The negative effect of formal control on intrinsic motivation is still a matter of debate, but by now, many authors suggest that formal control undermines intrinsic motivation if certain conditions are met (Weibel, 2010). Two arguments are advanced to explain the possible negative effects of formal control on intrinsic motivation. First, formal control, almost by definition, is seen as a form of externally devised influence on the work context as well as the work process of employees, and is thus naturally "at odds" with the need for autonomy (Argyris, 1957; Walton, 1985). Second, formal control is often portrayed to interrupt social relations (Bijlsma-Frankema & Costa, 2005; Fox, 1974), it signals suspicion (Falk & Kosfeld, 2006; Kramer, 1999; McGregor, 1960; Sitkin & Stickel, 1996), and exacerbates the hierarchical distance between the controller and the controlled (Weibel, 2007).

A number of empirical studies show that formal control crowds-out intrinsic motivation. For example, Barkema (1995), in an econometric study, demonstrates that managers in Dutch companies are more willing to do overtime when they are less monitored by their supervisors. The crowding-out effect of formal control is particularly strong if the controller holds a "controlling," that is, a suspicious intention. In this spirit, current empirical studies of behavioral economists supports McGregor's (1960) conceptual model of the negative effect of monitored working relations on intrinsic work engagement under the condition that the controller initiates control with a "theory X" in mind, that is, a suspicious and negative view of employees' work morale. For example, Falk and Kosfeld (2006) tested the effect of managerial monitoring in a two-stage principal agent game. The principal could choose to monitor the agents' effort either lightly, moderately, severely, or not at all. The experiment showed that principals who chose to trust, that is, not to monitor their agents at all, fared best. To put a figure on it, agents who were trusted showed twice the effort of agents who were lightly controlled. In an effort to understand the underlying reason for the performance reduction, the authors designed two games with different types of control: in the first case monitoring was chosen by the principal, whereas in the second case control was exogenously given. Agents reduced their efforts only in the first case, which means that agents seemed to react negatively to the principal's suspicious mind-set, and not the monitoring per se (see also Strickland, 1958). These findings from behavioral economics are corroborated by findings from SDT research, which similarly show that a nonsuspicious and supporting managerial style has a positive effect on autonomous motivation (Deci, et al., 1989).

In addition, Sliwka (2007) proposed that formal and suspicion-based control affects above all individuals with a specific motivation propensity, which he dubbed "conformist." He argues that four types of motivation propensity should be distinguished: (1) altruists, (2) reciprocitists, (3) egoists, and (4) conformists. Conformists are proposed to behave in the way that is perceived to be the most prevalent in their environment: conformists behave in a prosocial way if their environment is seen to be prosocially oriented and in an egoistic way if their environment is seen to be egoistically oriented. Thus, if a supervisor signals trust, even when enacting formal control, the controlled is much more likely to act in a trustworthy way in response, as prosocial behavior is framed as "prevalent" in this environment.

The Crowding-In Effect

The crowding-in effect has been investigated to a much lesser extent than the crowding-out effect. Still, many findings show that certain institutional measures can have a positive impact on intrinsic motivation and job performance in the long run.

CROWDING-IN THROUGH PARTICIPATION AND THROUGH ORGANIZATIONAL FAIRNESS

Participation, that is, codetermination at work (Frey & Osterloh, 2002), increases employees' intrinsically motivated efforts. Participation can also buffer against the crowding-out effect caused by variable performance-related compensation: It has been shown that at the same income level, self-employed persons obtain higher intrinsic benefit from their work than salaried employees (Benz & Frey, 2008). Further support for the crowding-in-through-participation effect is provided by Feld and Frey (2002) and Frey and

Torgler (2007), who show that participation in political decision-making processes increases tax morale. Tax morale can be understood as an individual's willingness to pay taxes out of moral obligation. A number of laboratory experiments conducted in different countries show that such an intrinsic motivation to pay taxes differs across countries. Alm and Torgler (2006) speculate that countries with direct-democratic elements in their political system consistently feature higher tax morale than countries with fewer political participation possibilities. Alm and Torgler (2006) argue that such an offer for active political participation signals a trusting stance and thereby fosters citizens' identification and loyalty toward their country, which translates into their higher willingness to pay taxes.

Participation is strongly linked to organizational fairness perceptions, which have also been found to be positively related to intrinsic motivation. Tyler and Blader (2000) showed that *procedural fairness* has a positive effect on employees' prosocial behavior and on their intrinsic motivation. Procedures are perceived to be fair if these allow for participation, that is, codetermination, neutrality, impartiality, respect, and appreciative treatment. This positive relationship between procedural justice and intrinsic motivation was also demonstrated by justice researchers (Zapata-Phelan, Colquitt, Scott, & Livingston, 2009). In a laboratory experiment, Fehr and Rockenbach (2003) provided further evidence for the importance of impartiality: principals who imposed sanctions out of self-interest received less support within the team than principals who imposed sanctions for the team's interests.

The evidence is less conclusive as to whether distributive fairness, which refers to the perceived justice of decision outcomes, also fosters intrinsic motivation. Gagné and Forest (2008) reviewed studies demonstrating that both forms of fairness contribute to psychological need satisfaction, and thereby to intrinsic motivation. Other authors, however, link distributive fairness to instrumental expectations, and thus to extrinsic motivation (Tyler, 1999; Tyler & Blader, 2003). A study by Maier, Streicher, Jonas, and Frey (2007) adds an interesting facet to this debate. The authors found that an inherent personal need for procedural justice was positively related to intrinsic motivation, whereas an inherent personal need for distributive justice was negatively related to intrinsic motivation. They argued that individuals who are intrinsically motivated and strive for autonomy, competence, and relatedness also acquire appropriate procedural justice conditions (for themselves and others) that allow for the satisfaction of those needs. In contrast, individuals who are naturally oriented toward distributive justice are highly susceptible to extrinsic incentives and in turn generally experience less intrinsic motivation.

CROWDING-IN THROUGH NORMATIVELY SHAPED DECISION-MAKING FRAMES

Individuals contribute more to public goods if the *decision-making frame* signals unambiguously that prosocial behavior is expected (Lindenberg, 2006). Such a strong signaling effect has been demonstrated very vividly in a public goods game[2]: cooperation in two identical test arrangements differed highly depending on whether the public goods game was labeled as a "Community Game" or as a "Wall-Street-Game." In the first case, about 70% of the respondents contributed to the public goods, whereas in the second case only about 30% did so (Liberman, Samuels, & Ross, 2004). A recent experimental test by Reeson and Tisdell (2008) showed that people's behavioral choices depend on whether or not a normative frame is signaled. Participants were also playing public goods games. Results demonstrated a significant increase in public contribution every time after participants were reminded that they should contribute (i.e., a normative frame was signaled), and a significant decrease following-up the regulation treatment that exercised a certain kind of institutional control (consistent with the findings presented earlier). Ariely, Bracha and Meier (2009) provided an explanation for people's strong response to the signaling of social norms. Next to intrinsic and extrinsic motivation, the authors identified *image motivation* as a determinant of people's decision to act prosocially. In other words, individuals wanted to be considered "good" by others and by themselves (consistent with Bénabou & Tirole, 2006). In a laboratory and a field experiment the authors showed that if a certain public goods is socially considered "good" and the contribution to that public goods is visible (e.g., blood donations), image motivation is crowded-in, adding an "image value" to the contribution; and that monetary incentives crowd out such publicly visible contributions, because they decrease the image value, signaling to others (or oneself) that one's contribution could also be motivated by opportunistic motives.

CROWDING-IN THROUGH MARKET-DRIVEN WAGES

Wages can reinforce employees' intrinsic motivation if they are perceived as a *signal* for the company's *goodwill* and as *appreciation* of the employee's performance (Akerlof, 1982). Field studies (Kuvaas, 2006) and laboratory experiments (Irlenbusch & Sliwka, 2005) show that a principal's offering of high fixed wages is recompensed by high voluntary cooperation of the agents. More recently, a number of behavioral economists have demonstrated that fixed pay, particularly "generous" fixed pay, is positively related to self-esteem and to non-extrinsic motivation (Bénabou & Tirole, 2003; Ellingsen & Johannesson, 2008). Moreover, fixed pay has been shown to strengthen trust and thereby leads to higher intrinsic motivation. Sliwka (2007), for instance, demonstrated that the choice of pay, namely the decision to either introduce incentive pay or to stick with fixed pay, sends strong signals to employees: fixed pay is taken as a strong signal of trust, and, as a consequence, employees that are receptive to social norms show much higher individual performance under fixed pay than under variable pay schemes.

Conclusion

Behavioral economics shows that prosocial behavior is more common than assumed in standard economics. This finding concurs with the imposing evidence on the prevalence of prosocial, citizenship, and contextual performance behavior studied in the field of organizational behavior (Penner, Dovidio, Piliavin, & Schroeder, 2005). In addition, behavioral economics has clearly shown that preferences are plastic, that is, subject to systematic influences, and thus contingent on institutional mechanisms. Like SDT, behavioral economics expects performance-contingent rewards and control to have a detrimental effect on intrinsic motivation under certain conditions: if intrinsic engagement was present before rewards were introduced; if these rewards are tangible, contingent, and salient; and if the controls are authoritative and mistrusting (Deci, et al., 1999a; Weibel, et al., 2010). In addition, such a crowding-out effect is expected to reduce individual performance if it is stronger than a possible price-effect exerted by rewards or controls. Overall these findings are quite similar to findings in the field of psychology; however, these additional findings should be seen as producing more robustness for the field because these results were produced using different methods than those used in psychology. Finally, small but growing evidence shows that participation, fairness, normative framing, and fair market-oriented fixed wages strengthen intrinsic motivation.

In addition, findings from the field of behavioral economics have clear practical implications. First, companies should refrain from using pay-for-performance schemes for challenging, creative, and complex work. Second, generous fixed pay, participation, procedural fairness, and clear normative signals to behave prosocially are robust drivers of intrinsic motivation. In addition, several aspects merit further investigation. At present it is unclear what drives the salience of incentive pay and hence its negative effect on intrinsic motivation. Although it seems clear that a high fraction of variable pay in the overall pay mix and frequent performance evaluations drive salience perceptions, we still do not know what "high" and "frequent" means in practical terms. Further research is also needed to unravel the conditions under which formal control can have a positive effect on intrinsic motivation—such a crowding-in effect has been partially shown in research in the field of organizational behavior but findings are still fragile and scattered. Finally, it is unclear whether distributive fairness crowds-in or crowds-out intrinsic motivation. To conclude, behavioral economics clearly shows that the universal application of pay-for-performance as practiced today is not warranted by scientific facts.

Notes

1. This chapter is an extended and refreshed version of a German journal article: Osterloh, M., & Weibel, A. (2008). Managing Motivation—Verdrängung und Verstärkung der intrinsischen Motivation aus Sicht der psychologischen Ökonomik. *WIST, 37*, 406–411.
2. In a public goods game participants are asked to choose how many of their *private* tokens they contribute to a shared pool. The tokens in the shared pool are multiplied by a factor and this "*public goods*" payoff is then evenly shared among all participants. In addition, all subjects also keep the tokens they do not contribute.

References

Akerlof, G. A. (1982). Labor contracts as partial gift exchange. *Quarterly Journal of Economics, 97*, 543–569.

Alm, J., & Torgler, B. (2006). Culture differences and tax morale in the United States and Europe. *Journal of Economic Psychology, 27*, 224–246.

Andreoni, J. (1990). Impure altruism and donations to public goods: A theory of warm-glow giving *Economic Journal, 100*(401), 464–477.

Andreoni, J., Gale, W. G. & Scholz, J. K. (1996). Charitable contributions of time and money. *University of Wisconsin–Madison Working Paper.*

Andreoni, J., & Miller, J. (2002). Giving according to Garp: An experimental test of the consistency of preferences for altruism. *Econometrica, 70*, 737–753.

Anheier, H. K., & Salamon, L. M. (1998). Nonprofit institutions and the household sector. In United Nations Statistics Division (Ed.), *The household sector*. New York: United Nations.

Argyris, C. (1957). Individual and organization: Some problems of mutual adjustment. *Administrative Science Quarterly, 2*(1), 1–24.

Ariely, D., Bracha, A., & Meier, S. (2009). Doing good or doing well? Image motivation and monetary incentives in behaving prosocially. *The American Economic Review, 99*(1), 544–555.

Ariely, D., Gneezy, U., Loewenstein, G., & Mazar, N. (2009). Large stakes and big mistakes. *Review of Economic Studies, 76*(2), 451–469.

Ariely, D., Loewenstein, G., & Prelec, D. (2006). Tom Sawyer and the construction of value. *Journal of Economic Behavior & Organization, 60*, 1–10.

Barkema, H. G. (1995). Do top managers work harder when they are monitored? *Kyklos, 48*(1), 19–42.

Bebchuk, L., & Grinstein, Y. (2005). The growth of executive pay. *Oxford Review of Economic Policy, 21*(2), 283–303.

Becker, B. E., & Huselid, M. A. (1998). High performance work systems and firm performance: A synthesis of research and managerial implications. In G. R. Ferris (Ed.), *Research in personnel and human resources* (Vol. 16, pp. 53–101). Stanford, CA: JAI Press.

Bénabou, R., & Tirole, J. (2003). Intrinsic and extrinsic motivation. *Review of Economic Studies, 70*, 489–520.

Bénabou, R., & Tirole, J. (2006). Incentives and prosocial behavior. *American Economic Review, 96*(5), 1652–1678.

Benz, M., & Frey, B. S. (2008). Being independent is a great thing: Subjective evaluations of self-employment and hierarchy. *Economica, 75*(298), 362–383.

Bertelli, A. M. (2006). Motivation crowding and the federal civil servant: Evidence from the U.S. Internal Revenue Service. *International Public Management Journal, 9*(1), 3–23.

Bijlsma-Frankema, K., & Costa, A. C. (2005). Understanding the trust-control nexus. *International Sociology, 20*(3), 259–282.

Bolle, F., & Otto, P. (2010). A price is a signal: On intrinsic motivation, crowding-out and crowding-in. *Kyklos, 63*(1), 9–22.

Camerer, C. F. (2005). Behavioral economics. In *World Congress of the Econometric Society*, 18–24 August 2005, London.

Camerer, C. F., & Fehr, E. (2006). Does "economic man" dominate social behavior? *Science, 311*, 47–52.

Camerer, C. F., & Loewenstein, G. (2003). Behavioral economics: Past, present future. In C. F. Camerer, G. Loewenstein & M. Rabin (Eds.), *Advances in behavioral economics* (pp. 3–51). Princeton, NJ: Princeton University Press.

Camerer, C. F., Loewenstein, G., & Rabin, M. (2004). *Advances in behavioral economics*. Princeton, NJ: Princeton University Press.

De Charms, R. (1968). *Personal causation: The internal affective determinants of behavior*. New York: Academic Press.

Deci, E. L. (1971). Effects of externally mediated rewards on intrinsic motivaiton. *Journal of Personality and Social Psychology, 18*, 105–115.

Deci, E. L. (1976). The hidden costs of rewards. *Organizational Dynamics, 4*(3), 61–72.

Deci, E. L. (1980). *The psychology of self-determination*. Lexington, MA: D. C. Heath: Lexington Books.

Deci, E. L., Connell, J. P., & Ryan, R. M. (1989). Self-determination in a work organization. *Journal of Applied Psychology, 74*(4), 580–590.

Deci, E. L., Koestner, R., & Ryan, R. M. (1999a). A meta-analytic review of experiments examining the effects of extrinsic rewards on intrinsic motivation. *Psychological Bulletin, 125*(6), 627–668.

Deci, E. L., Koestner, R., & Ryan, R. M. (1999b). The undermining effect is a reality after all—extrinsic rewards, task interest, and self-determination: Reply to Eisenberger, Pierce, and Cameron (1999) and Lepper, Henderlong, and Gingras (1999). *Psychological Bulletin, 125*, 692–700.

Deci, E. L., & Ryan, R. M. (1985). *Intrinsic motivation and self-determination in human behavior*. New York: Plenum Publishing Co.

Ellingsen, T., & Johannesson, M. (2008). Pride and prejudice: The human side of incentive theory. *The American Economic Review, 98*(3), 990–1008.

Falk, A., & Kosfeld, M. (2006). The hidden costs of control. *American Economic Review, 96*(5), 1611–1630.

Fayol, H., & Urwick, L. F. (1963). *General and industrial management*. London: Pitman.

Fehr, E., & Gächter, S. (1998). Reciprocity and economics: The economic implications of homo reciprocans. *European Economic Review, 42*, 845–859.

Fehr, E., & Rockenbach, B. (2003). Detrimental effects of sanctions on human altruism. *Nature, 422*, 137–140.

Feld, L., & Frey, B. S. (2002). Trust breeds trust. *Economics and Governance, 3*, 87–99.

Fischbacher, U., Fehr, E., & Gächter, S. (2001). Are people conditionally cooperative? Evidence from public good experiments. *Economic Letters, 71*, 397–404.

Fowler, J. H., & Kam, C. D. (2007). Beyond the self: Social identity, altruism, and political participation. *Journal of Politics, 69*(3), 811–825.

Fox, A. (1974). *Beyond contract: Work, power and trust relations*. London: Faber and Faber.

Frey, B. S. (1990). *Ökonomie ist Sozialwissenschaft. Die Anwendung der Ökonomie auf neue Gebiete*. München: Vahlen.

Frey, B. S. (1992). Tertium datur: Pricing, regulating and intrinsic motivation. *Kyklos, 45*(2), 161–184.

Frey, B. S. (1997a). A constitution for knaves crowds out civic virtues. *Economic Journal, 107*(July), 1043–1053.

Frey, B. S. (1997b). *Not just for the money. An economic theory of personal motivation*. Cheltenham: Edward Elgar.

Frey, B. S., & Benz, M. (2004). From imperialism to inspiration: A survey of economics and psychology. In J. B. Davis, A. Marciano, & J. Runde (Eds.), *The Elgar companion to economics and philosophy* (pp. 61–84). Cornwall, UK: Edward Elgar.

Frey, B. S., Eichenberger, R., & Oberholzer-Gee, F. (1996). The old lady visits your backyard: A tale of morals and markets. *Journal of Political Economy, 104*, 193–209.

Frey, B. S., & Götte, L. (1999). Does pay motivate volunteers? Unpublished. Institute for Empirical Research in Economics.

Frey, B. S., & Jegen, R. (2001). Motivation crowding theory: A survey of empirical evidence. *Journal of Economic Surveys, 15*(5), 589–611.

Frey, B. S., & Meier, S. (2004). Social comparisons and pro-social behavior: Testing "conditional cooperation" in a field experiment. *American Economic Review, 94*, 1717–1722.

Frey, B. S., & Osterloh, M. (2002). *Successful management by motivation. Balancing intrinsic and extrinsic incentives*. Heidelberg: Springer.

Frey, B. S., & Torgler, B. (2007). Tax morale and conditional cooperation. *Journal of Comparative Economics, 35*, 136–159.

Gagné, M., & Forest, J. (2008). The study of compensation systems through the lens of self-determination theory: Reconciling 35 years of debate. *Canadian Psychology/ Psychologie Canadienne, 49*(3), 225–232.

Gerhart, B., & Rynes, S. L. (2003). *Compensation. Theory, evidence, and strategic implications.* Thousand Oaks, CA: Sage.

Gintis, H., & Khurana, R. (2008). Corporate honesty and business education: A behavior model. In P. J. Zak (Ed.), *Moral Markets: The Critical Role of Values in the Economy* (pp. 300–327). Princeton, NJ: Princeton University Press.

Gneezy, U., Meier, S., & Rey-Biel, P. (2011). When and why incentives (don't) work to modify behavior. *Journal of Economic Perspectives, 265*(4), 191–210.

Gneezy, U., & Rustichini, A. (2000). Pay enough or don't pay at all. *Quarterly Journal of Economics, 115*(3), 791–810.

Grant, A. M., & Berry, J. W. (2011). The necessity of others is the mother of invention: Intrinsic and prosocial motivations, perspective taking, and creativity. *The Academy of Management Journal, 54*(1), 73–96.

Gulati, R. (1998). Alliances and networks. *Strategic Management Journal, 19,* 293–317.

Heckhausen, J. (2006). *Motivation und Handeln.* Berlin: Springer.

Henrich, J., Boyd, R., Bowles, S., Camerer, C., Fehr, E., Gintis, H., & McElreath, R. (2001). In search of Homo Economicus: Behavioral experiments in 15 small-scale societies. *The American Economic Review, 91*(2), 73–78.

Holmas, H., Kjerstad, E., Luras, H., & Straume, O. R. (2010). Does monetary punishment crowd out pro-social motivation? A natural experiment on hospital length of stay. *Journal of Economic Behavior & Organization, 75,* 261–267.

Huselid, M. A. (1995). The impact of human resource management practices on turnover, productivity, and corporate financial performance. *Academy of Management Journal, 38*(3), 635–672.

Irlenbusch, B., & Sliwka, D. (2005). Incentives, decision frames and motivation crowding out—an experimental investigation. IZA Discussion Paper No. 1758.

Jenkins, D. G., Gupta, N., Mitra, A., & Shaw, J. D. (1998). Are financial incentives related to performance? A meta-analytic review of empirical research. *Journal of Applied Psychology, 83*(5), 777–787.

Jensen, M. C., & Murphy, K. J. (1990). CEO incentives—its not how much you pay, but how. *Harvard Business Review, 68*(3), 138–149.

Kirchgässner, G. (1991). *Homo Oeconomicus.* Tübingen: Mohr.

Kramer, R. M. (1999). Trust and distrust in organizations: Emerging perspectives, enduring questions. *Annual Review of Psychology, 50*(1), 569–598.

Kruglanski, A. W. (1975). Endogenous exogenous partition in attribution theory. *Psychological Review, 82,* 387–406.

Kuvaas, B. (2006). Work performance, affective commitment, and work motivation: The roles of pay administration and pay level. *Journal of Organizational Behavior, 27*(3), 365–385.

Lazear, E. P. (2000). Performance pay and productivity. *The American Economic Review, 90*(5), 1346–1361.

Lepper, M. R., & Greene, D. (1978). *The hidden costs of reward: New perspectives on the psychology of human motivation.* Hillsdale, NJ: Lawrence Erlbaum Associates.

Liberman, V., Samuels, S. M., & Ross, L. (2004). The name of game: Predictive power of reputations versus situational labels in determining prisoner's dilemma game moves. *Personality and Social Psychology Bulletin, 30,* 1175–1185.

Lindenberg, S. (2001). Intrinsic motivation in a new light. *Kyklos, 54*(2/3), 317–342.

Lindenberg, S. (2006). Prosocial behavior, solidarity, and framing processes. In D. Fetchenhauer, A. Flache, B. Buunk & S. Lindenberg (Eds.), *Solidarity and prosocial behavior* (pp. 23–44). Springer US.

Lindenberg, S., & Steg, L. (2007). Normative, gain, and hedonic goal-frames guiding environmental behavior. *Journal of Social Issues, 63*(1), 117–137.

Maier, G. W., Streicher, B., Jonas, E., & Frey, D. (2007). Bedürfnisse nach organisationaler Gerechtigkeit und Bereitschaft zu innovativem Handeln. *Wirtschaftspsychologie, 9*(2), 43–54.

McGregor, D. (1960). *The human side of enterprise.* New York: McGraw Hill.

Meier, S. (2006). *The economics of non-selfish behaviour: Decisions to contribute money to public goods.* Cheltenham, UK: Mass.

Nyborg, K. (2010). Will green taxes undermine moral motivation? *Public Finance and Management, 10*(2), 331–351.

Osterloh, M. (2006). Human resources management and knowledge creation. In I. Nonaka & I. Kazuo (Eds.), *Handbook of knowledge creation* (pp. 158–175). Oxford: Oxford University Press.

Osterloh, M., & Frey, B. S. (2000). Motivation, knowledge transfer, and organizational forms. *Organization Science, 11,* 538–550.

Osterloh, M., & Frey, B. S. (2002). Does pay for perfomance really motivate employees? In A. D. Neely (Ed.), *Business performance measurement: theory and practice* (pp. 107–122). Cambridge University Press.

Osterloh, M., & Frost, J. (2009). Bad for practice—good for practice. From economic imperialism to multidisciplinary mapping. *Journal of International Business Ethics, 2*(1), 36–45.

Ostrom, E. (2000). Crowding out citizenship. *Scandinavian Political Studies, 23,* 3–16.

Penner, L. A., Dovidio, J. F., Piliavin, J. A., & Schroeder, D. A. (2005). Prosocial behavior: Multilevel perspectives. *Annual Review of Psychology, 56,* 365–392.

Pouliakas, K. (2010). Pay enough, don't pay too much or don't pay at All? The impact of bonus intensity on job satisfaction. *Kyklos, 63*(4), 597–626.

Rabin, M. (2002). A perspective on psychology and economics. *European Economic Review, 46,* 657–685.

Reeson, A. F., & Tisdell, J. G. (2008). Institutions, motivations and public goods: An experimental test of motivational crowding. *Journal of Economic Behavior & Organization, 68*(1), 273–281.

Ryan, R. M. (1982). Control and information in the intrapersonal sphere—an extension of cognitive evaluation theory. *Journal of Personality and Social Psychology, 43*(3), 450–461.

Schneider, M. (2007). Zielvorgaben und Organisationskultur. Eine Fallstudie. *Die Betriebswirtschaft, 67*(6), 619–637.

Sitkin, S. B., & Stickel, D. (1996). The road to hell: The dynamics of distrust in an era of quality. In R. M. Kramer & T. R. Tyler (Eds.), *Trust in organizations: Frontiers of theory and research* (pp. 196–215). Thousand Oaks, CA: Sage Publications.

Sliwka, D. (2003). Anreize, Motivationsverdrängung und Prinzipal-Agenten-Theorie. *Die Betriebswirtschaft, 63*(3), 293–308.

Sliwka, D. (2007). Trust as a signal of a social norm and the hidden costs of incentive schemes. *The American Economic Review, 97*(3), 999–1012.

Snell, S. A. (1992). Control-theory in strategic human-resource management—the mediating effect of administrative information. *Academy of Management Journal, 35*(2), 292–327.

Stajkovic, A., & Luthans, F. (1997). A meta-analysis of the effects of organizational behavior modification on task performance. *Academy of Management Journal, 40*, 1122–1149.

Stigler, G. J., & Becker, G. S. (1977). De gustibus non est disputandum. *American Economic Review, 67*, 76–90.

Strickland, L. H. (1958). Surveillance and trust. *Journal of Personality, 26*(2), 200–215.

Stutzer, A., & Frey, B. S. (2007). What happiness research can tell us about self-control problems and utility misprediction. In A. Stutzer & B. S. Frey (Eds.), *Economics and psychology. A promising new cross-disciplinary field* (pp. 169–195). Cambridge, MA: MIT Press.

Thaler, R. H. (1996). Doing economics without Homo Economicus. In S. G. Medema & W. G. Samuels (Eds.), *Foundations of research in economics: How do economists do economics?* Cheltenham, UK: Edward Elgar.

Tomer, J. F. (2007). What is behavioral economics. *Journal of Socio-Economics, 36*(6), 463–479.

Tyler, T. R. (1999). Why people cooperate with organizations: An identity-based perspective. In R. I. Sutton & B. M. Staw (Eds.), *Research in organizational behavior* (Vol. 21). Stamford, CT: Jai Press Inc.

Tyler, T. R., & Blader, S. L. (2000). *Cooperation in groups: Procedural justice, social identity, and behavioral engagement.* Philadelphia: Psychology Press.

Tyler, T. R., & Blader, S. L. (2003). The group engagement model: Procedural justice, social identity, and cooperative behavior. *Personality and Social Psychology Review, 7*(4), 349–361.

Walton, R. E. (1985). From control to commitment in the workplace. *Harvard Business Review, 63*(2), 77–84.

Weibel, A. (2007). Formal control and trustworthiness—never the twain shall meet? *Group & Organization Management, 32*(4), 500–517.

Weibel, A. (2010). Managerial objectives of formal control: High motivation control mechanisms. In S. B. Sitkin, L. B. Cardinal & K. Bijlsma-Frankema (Eds.), *Control in organizations: New directions in theory and research* (pp. 434–462). Cambridge, UK: Cambridge University Press.

Weibel, A., Rost, K., & Osterloh, M. (2007). Disziplinierung der Agenten oder Crowding-Out?—Gewollte und ungewollte Anreizwirkungen von variablen Löhnen. *Zeitschrift für betriebswirtschaftliche Forschung, 59*(12), 1029–1054.

Weibel, A., Rost, K., & Osterloh, M. (2010). Pay for performance in the public sector—benefits and (hidden) costs. *Journal of Public Administration Research & Theory, 20*(2), 387–412.

Zapata-Phelan, C. P., Colquitt, J. A., Scott, B. A., & Livingston, B. (2009). Procedural justice, interactional justice, and task performance: The mediating role of intrinsic motivation. *Organizational Behavior and Human Decision Processes, 108*(1), 93–105.

CHAPTER
6

Passion for Work: Determinants and Outcomes

Robert J. Vallerand, Nathalie Houlfort, *and* Jacques Forest

Abstract

Passion can be uplifting and energizing; it can also be destructive and obsessive. The work realm represents a fertile ground to observe this duality of passion. This chapter provides a 10-year overview of the research on passion for work. The initial work on passion and its conceptualization is followed by a more focused presentation of the studies conducted in the workplace. First, various studies are presented that validate the concept of passion for work, distinguishing between harmonious passion and obsessive passion. Second, research that has examined the convergent and divergent validity of these two types of passion for work and their consequences on cognitive processes, psychological well-being, interpersonal relationships, and performance is discussed. Third, we present research on the determinants of passion, specifically the individual and social factors involved in the early and on-going development of passion for work. Finally, future research directions are proposed to stimulate new and exciting research in this growing field.

Key Words: passion, work, cognitive processes, psychological well-being, interpersonal relationships, performance, harmonious passion, determinants of passion

---

"Nothing is as important as passion. No matter what you do with your life, be passionate"

(Jon Bon Jovi)

The above quote from famous rock star Jon Bon Jovi underscores one major point: If you want to succeed in your field of endeavor, be passionate! And Bon Jovi is not the only one to believe so. For instance, the late Steve Jobs, founder and former CEO of Apple, underscored the role of passion in persisting and reaching one's business goals, and business mogul Donald Trump believes in the energy that passion provides while working toward one's goals. Even the famous philosopher Hegel (1770–1831) suggested that "Nothing great in this world has ever been accomplished without passion." But is it the case? Does passion matter

with respect to performance? What about other outcomes, such as the quality of relationships that one develops and maintains at work and one's psychological well-being? Does passion for one's work matter as well?

Until recently, it was difficult to answer these questions because little to no psychological research was conducted on passion, let alone passion for work. However, roughly 10 years ago, psychologists started to empirically study passion, largely using the dualistic model of passion (DMP; Vallerand et al., 2003) as a basic structure. Since then, an increasing amount of research has been conducted in a variety of areas including the workplace (e.g., Vallerand & Houlfort, 2003). This chapter reviews such research. The first section describes the concept of passion, the DMP (Vallerand, 2008, 2010), and initial research on elements of the model. The second section reviews research dealing with the role of passion in different outcomes relevant for the workplace. The third section reviews research on the determinants of passion, again with an emphasis on research conducted in the workplace. Finally, the last section offers suggestions for future research as well as some conclusions.

On the Psychology of Passion
The Concept of Passion

Passion has generated a lot of attention from philosophers, especially from an emotional perspective. Two positions have emerged (see Rony, 1990). The first posits that passion entails a loss of reason and control (see Plato, 429–347 BC and Spinoza, 1632–1677). In line with the etymology of the word passion (from the Latin "passio" for suffering) people afflicted with passion are seen as experiencing a kind of suffering, as if they were slaves to their passion, because it comes to control them. The second perspective portrays passion in a more positive light. For instance, Descartes (1596–1650) sees passions as strong emotions with inherent behavioral tendencies that can be positive as long as reason underlies the behavior. Similarly, as seen previously, Hegel (1770–1831) argues that passions are necessary to reach the highest levels of achievement. Thus, this second view of passion portrays passion in a more positive light because some adaptive outcomes may be experienced when individuals are in control of their passion. Taken together, these two positions highlight the duality of passion, where "good" and "bad" outcomes can result from passion.

Very little has been written on the psychology of passion up until recently. The few psychologists who have looked at the concept have underscored its motivational aspect. For instance, some authors have proposed that people spend large amounts of time and effort in order to reach their passionate goals (see Frijda, Mesquita, Sonemans, & Van Goozen, 1991) or working on the activity that they love (Baum & Locke, 2004). Nearly all empirical work on passion has been conducted in the area of passionate love (e.g., Hatfield & Walster, 1978). Although such research is important, it does not deal with the main topic at hand, namely passion toward activities.

There has been some research on passion in the workplace. Such research has basically focused on passion as love for one's work. For instance, Baum and colleagues (Baum & Locke, 2004; Baum, Locke, & Smith, 2001), Cardon (2008; Cardon et al., 2005, 2009), and Lam and Pertulla (2008)

define passion as simply love for one's work. Although we agree that one's love for the activity (and in the present case, work) is an important feature of passion, it is not the only one. As seen below, other features are important to consider as pertains to passion. Also of importance is the fact that it is crucial to distinguish between different types of passion so as to account for the duality inherent in passion underscored by philosophers.

A Dualistic Model of Passion

In line with self-determination theory (SDT; Deci & Ryan, 2000), we propose that people engage in various activities throughout life in order to grow as individuals. After a period of trial and error that seems to start in early adolescence (Erikson, 1968), most people eventually start to show preference for some activities, especially those that are perceived as particularly enjoyable and important, and that have some resonance with how they see themselves. They engage on a regular basis in some of these activities and only a few turn into passionate activities. In line with the above, Vallerand et al. (2003) define passion as a strong inclination toward a self-defining activity that one loves, finds important and meaningful, and in which one invests a significant amount of time and energy. These activities come to be so self-defining that they represent central features of one's identity. Clearly, work is central to our lives. We spend more than half our waking life at work (Vallerand & Houlfort, 2003). We come to value it deeply and at some point, work becomes part of our identity. Thus, when asked what they do, people may typically say "I *am* a teacher," "I *am* a nurse," or "I *am* a salesperson." To the extent that we love what we do, that we value it and find it meaningful, our work is part of our identity and we are likely to develop a passion for it.

Past research has shown that values and regulations can be internalized in either a controlled or an autonomous fashion (see Deci et al., 1994; Sheldon, 2002; Vallerand, Fortier, & Guay, 1997). Similarly, the DMP posits that activities that people like (or love) will also be internalized in the person's identity and self to the extent that these are highly valued and meaningful for the person (Aron, Aron, & Smolan, 1992; Csikszentmihalyi, Rathunde, & Whalen, 1993). Furthermore, it is proposed that there are two types of passion, obsessive and harmonious, that can be distinguished in terms of how the passionate activity has been internalized.

Obsessive passion results from a controlled internalization of the activity into one's identity and self. A controlled internalization originates from intrapersonal and/or interpersonal pressure typically because certain contingencies are attached to the activity, such as feelings of social acceptance or self-esteem (Lafrenière, Bélanger, Vallerand, & Sedikides, 2011; Mageau, Carpentier, & Vallerand, 2011), or because the sense of excitement derived from activity engagement is uncontrollable. Such an internalization process leads the activity representation to be part of the person's identity. Furthermore, it also leads to values and regulations associated with the activity to be at best partially internalized in the self, and at worse to be internalized in the person's identity but completely outside the integrating self (Deci & Ryan, 2000). People with an obsessive passion can thus find themselves in the position of experiencing an uncontrollable urge to partake in the activity they view as important and enjoyable. They cannot help but to engage in the passionate activity. The passion must run its course as it controls the person. Consequently, the person risks experiencing conflicts and other negative affective, cognitive, and behavioral consequences during and after activity engagement. For instance, if a university professor has an obsessive passion for his academic work, he might not be able to stop working on an important paper knowing that he will come late at home for dinner and family activities. But it is as if he cannot resist the urge to pursue the writing. While writing, however, he might feel upset with himself for writing instead of being home. He might therefore have difficulties concentrating on the task at hand (writing) and he may not experience as much positive affect and flow as he could while writing. It is thus proposed that with obsessive passion individuals come to display a rigid persistence toward the activity, as oftentimes they cannot help but to engage in the passionate activity. This is so because ego-invested rather than integrative self processes (Hodgins & Knee, 2002) are at play with obsessive passion leading the person to eventually become dependent on the activity. Although such persistence may lead to some benefits (e.g., high levels of performance, such as more papers published for the professor in the preceding example), it may also come at a cost for the individual, potentially leading to lower levels of functioning both within the confines of the passionate activity (e.g., being less happy at work) and in other aspects of life because of the conflict it can create (e.g., work-family problems). Obsessive passion can also lead to frustration and rumination about work when prevented from engaging in it. Thus, if the

professor somehow manages to leave on time for dinner with the family, he still may end up suffering because he may have difficulties forgetting about the lost opportunity to write the ever-important scientific paper.

Conversely, harmonious passion results from an autonomous internalization of the activity into the person's identity and self. Such internalization occurs when individuals have freely accepted the activity as important for them without any contingencies attached to it. This type of internalization emanates from the intrinsic and integrative tendencies of the self (Deci & Ryan, 2000; Ryan & Deci, 2003) and produces a motivational force to engage in the activity willingly and engenders a sense of volition and personal endorsement about pursuing the activity. When harmonious passion is at play, individuals freely choose to engage in the beloved activity. With this type of passion, the activity occupies a significant but not overpowering space in the person's identity and is in harmony with other aspects of the person's life. In other words, with harmonious passion the authentic integrating self (Deci & Ryan, 2000) is at play allowing the person to fully partake in the passionate activity with a flexible and mindful (Brown, Ryan, & Creswell, 2007), open manner that is conducive to positive experiences (Hodgins & Knee, 2002). Consequently, people with a harmonious passion should be able to fully focus on the task at hand and experience positive outcomes both during task engagement (e.g., positive affect, concentration, flow, and so forth) and after task engagement (general positive affect, satisfaction, and so forth). Thus, there should be little or no conflict between the person's passionate activity and his or her other life activities. Furthermore, when prevented from engaging in their passionate activity, people with a harmonious passion should be able to adapt well to the situation and focus their attention and energy on other tasks that need to be done. Finally, with harmonious passion, the person is in control of the activity and can decide when and when not to engage in the activity. Thus, when confronted with the possibility of writing the scientific paper or going home for dinner and family activities, the professor with a harmonious passion can readily go home without thinking about the missed opportunity to write some more. Thus, behavioral engagement in the passionate activity can be seen as flexible.

It is important to underscore that both types of passionate involvement reflect an equal level of passion. Thus, people with a predominant harmonious passion toward work are no less passionate for work than people with a predominant obsessive passion. The difference between the two types of passion does not lie in the level of one's passion but rather in its quality. The two types of passion are qualitatively different with harmonious passion leading one to experience a more autonomous form and obsessive passion a more controlled form of passionate involvement. In fact, research by Bélanger, Lafrenière, Vallerand, and Kruglanski (2013a) has indeed shown that statistically controlling for the passion criteria (or the passion level) does not change the effects of harmonious and obsessive passion on outcomes.

Passion is often discussed in relation to intrinsic and extrinsic motivation. Intrinsic motivation shares some conceptual similarity with passion, because both involve interest and liking (or loving) for the activity. However, intrinsically motivated activities are typically not seen as being internalized in the person's identity and are best seen as emerging at the short-term level (Koestner & Losier, 2002). Furthermore, intrinsic motivation does not address the duality of passion where both adaptive and maladaptive outcomes can result from one's love for an activity. Intrinsic motivation is hypothesized to lead to only adaptive outcomes (Deci & Ryan, 2000). On the other hand, extrinsic motivation does not entail performing the activity out of enjoyment, but for reasons other than for the activity itself, such as external or internal pressure. Therefore, although some forms of extrinsic motivation, such as identified and integrated regulation, entail some internalization of an activity that one does not like in the self, a fundamental difference between extrinsic motivation and passion is the relative lack of liking (or loving) for the activity that is present with extrinsic motivation.

The difference between integrated regulation and harmonious passion deserves additional attention. The two concepts are very different because of the fundamental teleological distinction between them. The goal that is sought with the two constructs is completely different. With passion one engages in the activity out of love. With integrated regulation, one does not engage in the activity out of love but rather out of extrinsic motivation even if there is a high level of autonomy involved. Thus, although there is internalization in both constructs the basis of such internalization differs. In one case, it is based solely in a profound love for the activity; in the other in an autonomous valuing of an activity that one does not intrinsically love.

Research empirically supports these distinctions between passion and intrinsic and the different types of extrinsic motivation (external, introjected, and identified regulation) and even shows that controlling for intrinsic and extrinsic motivation does not change the role of harmonious and obsessive passion in the prediction of positive and negative affect (Gousse-Lessard, Vallerand, Carbonneau, & Lafrenière, 2013; Houlfort, Philippe, Vallerand, & Ménard, 2014; Vallerand et al., 2003, Study 2).

Initial Research on the Concept of Passion

There were several purposes to the initial work on passion (Vallerand et al., 2003), including three mentioned here: (1) to determine the prevalence of passion for an activity in one's life, (2) to develop the Passion Scale, and (3) to test the validity of some of the elements of the passion constructs. In the initial study, we (Vallerand et al., 2003, Study 1) had over 500 university students complete the Passion Scale with respect to an activity that they loved, that they valued, and in which they invested time and energy (i.e., the passion definition criteria), as well as other scales allowing us to test predictions derived from the DMP. A large variety of passionate activities were reported ranging from physical activity and sports to watching movies, playing a musical instrument, and reading. Participants reported engaging in one specific passionate activity for an average of 8.5 hours per week and had been engaging in that activity for almost 6 years. Thus, clearly passionate activities are meaningful to people and are long-lasting in nature. Of importance regarding the first purpose of this research, 84% of participants indicated that they had at least a moderate level of passion for a given activity in their lives (they scored at least 4 out of 7 on a question asking them if their favorite activity was a "passion" for them). In a similar vein, a subsequent study (Philippe, Vallerand, & Lavigne, 2009) with over 750 participants ranging in age from 18 to 100 years using a more stringent criterion of having a mean of 5 out of 7 on the criteria of passion seen previously revealed that 75% of participants had a high level of passion for an activity in their life. It would thus appear that the prevalence of passion is rather high and not the exclusivity of the happy few, at least in the Province of Québec, Canada (see also Liu, Chen, & Yao, 2011; Stenseng, 2008 for similar results in other countries).

Second, as pertains to the development of the Passion Scale, Vallerand et al. (2003, Study 1) conducted exploratory and confirmatory factor analyses that supported the presence of two factors corresponding to the two types of passion. These findings on the factor validity of the Passion Scale have been replicated in a number of studies with respect to a variety of activities (e.g., Carbonneau, Vallerand, Fernet, & Guay, 2008; Castelda et al., 2007; Rousseau, Vallerand, Ratelle, Mageau, & Provencher, 2002; Vallerand & Houlfort, 2003; Vallerand, Rousseau, Grouzet, Dumais, & Grenier, 2006, Studies 1, 2, and 3). The Passion Scale consists of two subscales of six items each reflecting obsessive (e.g., "I almost have an obsessive feeling toward this activity") and harmonious passion (e.g., "This activity is in harmony with other activities in my life"). Furthermore, internal consistency analyses have shown that both subscales are reliable (typically 0.75 and above). Finally, test-retest correlations over periods ranging from 4 to 6 weeks revealed moderately high stability values (in the range of 0.80; Rousseau et al., 2002). More recently, using archival data of more than 3,500 participants, Marsh et al. (2013) have shown that the Passion Scale is invariant over gender, language (English and French), and five types of activities (leisure, sport, social, work, and education). Thus, overall, the factorial validity and reliability of the scale is well established.

With respect to the third purpose, a series of critical findings with partial correlations (controlling for the correlation between the two types of passion) revealed that both harmonious and obsessive passions were positively associated with the passion criteria thereby providing support for the definition of passion. These findings were replicated in the Marsh et al. (2013) study. These findings support the view that both harmonious and obsessive passions are indeed a "passion" because each one reflects the definition of the passion construct. In addition, both types of passion were found to relate to one's identity and obsessive passion was found to more strongly relate to a measure of conflict with other life activities than harmonious passion. Furthermore, research provided support for the hypotheses dealing with affect, where harmonious passion positively predicted positive affect during and after engagement in the passionate activity, whereas obsessive passion was unrelated to positive affect but positively related to negative affect especially after task engagement and while prevented from engaging in the activity. Finally, other studies in this initial research (Vallerand et al., 2003) have also shown that obsessive (but not harmonious) passion correlated to rigid persistence in ill-advised activities (Vallerand et al., 2003, Studies 3 and 4).

Initial Research in the Workplace

Interestingly, initial research in the workplace has yielded findings highly similar to the initial research reported previously. First, with samples of workers as diverse as teachers, managers, and technicians, Vallerand and Houlfort (2003) found that 77% displayed at least a moderate level of passion. Subsequent research found percentages that varied from over 90% with teachers (Carbonneau et al., 2008) to 78% with managers, professionals, and white collar workers (Houlfort & Vallerand, 2013). Thus, although there seems to be some variation in the level of passion displayed by workers, presumably as a function of the type of work, the percentages of passionate workers are typically quite high. Thus, passion for work (at least at the moderate level) is not a feature of the happy few but rather seems to be firmly anchored in the workplace. Second, the Passion Scale has been fully validated as pertains to work. For instance, Vallerand and Houlfort (2003) reported results that replicated those of Vallerand et al. (2003) with respect to the two-factor solution of the scale, as well as to the internal consistency of the scale. These findings have been replicated in several studies involving workers in different areas including teaching (Carbonneau et al., 2008) and public service (Lavigne, Forest, & Crevier-Braud [2012], Study 1). Finally, Vallerand and Houlfort (2003) showed that both harmonious and obsessive passion positively correlated with the definitional elements of passion (liking one's work, valuing it, and spending time and energy in it), thereby providing support for the construct validity of the passion construct.

In sum, initial research provided support for the concept of harmonious and obsessive passion as well as for the validation of the Passion Scale. Furthermore, passion seems to be prevalent in most realms of activities, including work. Since the initial research (Vallerand et al., 2003; Vallerand & Houlfort, 2003), more than 100 studies have been conducted on the role of passion in a host of cognitive, affective, behavioral, relational, and performance outcomes experienced within the realms of hundreds of passionate activities conducted in both our own as well as other laboratories (see Vallerand, 2010). In the present chapter, we focus on passion research conducted in the workplace, and now turn to this issue.

Passion and Outcomes

In this section, we review research on the role of passion in outcomes that would appear to matter for the work domain. Specifically, we address the role of passion for work in cognitive processes, psychological well-being, interpersonal relationships, and performance.

Passion and Cognitive Processes

Based on the DMP, harmonious passion should facilitate adaptive cognitive processes while obsessive passion should not, or at least less so. This is so because with harmonious passion, integrative self-processes are at play leading the person to fully partake in the passion activity with an openness that is conducive to mindful attention, concentration, and flow in the process. The situation is different when obsessive passion is at play because ego-invested processes are involved (Hodgins & Knee, 2002). Such processes lead individuals to have an eye on the task, but another on external elements, such as the outcomes and other participants, with a defensive orientation that only permits a partial investment in the activity. Thus, less than full attention, concentration, and flow should be experienced in the process.

Research provides support for the above hypothesis. For instance, in the Vallerand et al. (2003, Study 1) study, participants were asked to complete the Passion Scale as well as indicate to what extent they typically experience high levels of concentration while they engage in the passionate activity. The results revealed that harmonious passion predicted significantly higher levels of concentration in the passionate activity than obsessive passion. The results from Vallerand et al. (2003, Study 1) were replicated in several studies outside the workplace (e.g., Mageau, Vallerand, Rousseau, Ratelle, & Provencher, 2005; Philippe et al., 2009) as well as in the workplace. For instance, with workers from a large service company (Forest, Mageau, Sarrazin, & Morin, 2011) and an insurance company (Ho, Wong, & Lee, 2011) in two different countries (Canada and China), it was found that harmonious passion facilitated the experience of concentration and attention, whereas obsessive passion was either unrelated or negatively related to it.

Another cognitive concept that deserves attention is flow (Csikszentmihalyi, 1978; Csikszentmihalyi et al., 1993). Flow refers to a desirable state that people experience when they feel completely immersed in the activity (e.g., "I have a feeling of total control"). Because harmonious passion allows the person to fully partake in the passionate activity with a secure sense of

self-esteem, flexibility, and an openness to experience the world in a nondefensive, mindful manner, it should be conducive to focusing on the task at hand and consequently to experiencing flow. Conversely, with obsessive passion, internally controlling rather than integrative self-processes are at play leading the person to engage in the activity with a fragile and contingent sense of self-esteem (e.g., Crocker, 2002; Kernis, 2003; Lafrenière et al., 2011), and eventually becoming defensive rather than open to experience. Such a state should not be conducive to the experience of flow.

Much research supports these hypotheses in activities other than work where harmonious passion has been found to positively predict flow, whereas obsessive passion has not (e.g., Philippe et al., 2009, Study 2; Vallerand et al., 2003, Study 1). These findings have been replicated in several studies in the workplace (e.g., Forest et al., 2011; Houlfort et al., 2011, Study 1; Lavigne et al. 2012, Studies 1 and 2). Of importance, Lavigne et al. (2012, Study 2) conducted a longitudinal study wherein both types of passion and flow were assessed twice over a 6-month interval. Because Lavigne et al. had assessed passion and flow at both points in time, they were in a position to conduct cross-lagged panel design analyses and determine if outcomes (e.g., flow) predict changes in passion or if the opposite takes place. Two important findings were obtained. First, passion was found to predict *changes* in flow that took place at work over the 6-month period, with harmonious passion significantly predicting increases in flow and obsessive passion being weakly related ($p < .10$) to flow. Thus, Lavigne et al. replicated past findings on the role of passion in flow. Second, Lavigne et al. also found that flow at Time 1 did not predict changes in passion from Time 1 to Time 2. Although an experimental design was not used in this study, these last results suggest that passion is involved in some ways in causing changes in outcomes, such as flow, whereas the reverse did not take place. Interestingly, using the same type of analyses, Carbonneau et al. (2008) also found that harmonious (but not obsessive) passion predicted increases in positive outcomes (work satisfaction), whereas the reverse was not true.

Passion and Psychological Well-Being

Recently, Vallerand (2012) proposed that engaging in a passionate activity on a regular basis has the potential to not only provide a boost in psychological well-being but also to lead to sustainable gains in well-being. In a nutshell, the rationale behind this hypothesis rests on three elements. First, passion for the activity is important because it is the motivational force that leads the person to engage in the activity on a regular basis. This is the sustainable part. Passion for a given activity leads the person to return to the activity regularly. Second, the type of effects that will be experienced during activity engagement depends on the type of passion. Much research in a variety of life domains, including work, reveals that harmonious passion leads the person to experience a number of positive affective experiences (e.g., positive emotions, task satisfaction) during task engagement and may even serve to protect against negative task experiences. Typically, obsessive passion induces little positive experiences and may even facilitate negative experiences (e.g., Mageau & Vallerand, 2007; Vallerand et al., 2003, Studies 1 and 2; Vallerand et al., 2006, Studies 2 and 3; see also Vallerand, 2008, 2010 for reviews). This is the quality part of the equation. Finally, in line with the Broaden-and-Build theory (Fredrickson, 2001), much research reveals that such positive affective experiences facilitate psychological well-being because they expand the self and broaden one's repertoire of skills. This is the function part of the equation. Thus, overall, it is proposed that the high quality of affective experiences that one derives from having a harmonious passion for an activity serves a purpose because it facilitates one's psychological well-being at the short-term level. Furthermore, because one's passion for the activity leads us to re-engage in the activity on a regular basis, these short-term gains in well-being do not disappear as they are experienced regularly and thus are sustained over time at the long-term level.

The research reviewed by Vallerand (2012) provided support for the role of passion in psychological well-being. Specifically, a harmonious passion for (nonwork) activities has been found to lead to psychological well-being (e.g., Rousseau & Vallerand, 2003; Vallerand et al., 2007, Studies 1 and 2; Vallerand, Mageau et al., 2008, Study 2), whereas obsessive passion for the same activities was either negatively related (Houlfort et al., 2011; Vallerand et al., 2007, Study 2) or unrelated (Vallerand et al., 2007, Study 1; Vallerand, Mageau et al., 2008, Study 2) to well-being. Furthermore, harmonious passion has been found to protect against psychological ill-being, such as anxiety and depression, whereas obsessive passion has been found to be positively related to it (Houlfort et al.,

2011; Rousseau & Vallerand, 2003). Of additional interest, research by Philippe et al. (2009, Study 1) showed that people with a harmonious passion toward a given activity displayed higher levels of psychological well-being than those with an obsessive passion or those without passionate activities in their life. In addition, people with a harmonious passion displayed an *increase* in psychological well-being over a 1-year interval, whereas both those with an obsessive passion and those without a passionate activity experienced a *decrease* in well-being (Philippe et al., 2009, Study 2). Finally, research by Rousseau and Vallerand (2008) provided support for the hypothesized mediating processes. Specifically, using a prospective design and structural equation modeling analyses, these authors found that a harmonious passion for exercise leads to situational positive emotions experienced during exercise that, in turn, over time, lead to an *increase* in psychological well-being. Obsessive passion was found to directly and negatively affect psychological well-being but was unrelated to positive emotions.

The above findings were obtained with respect to passion for nonwork activities. However, there are some important differences between work and nonwork activities. Among other things, leisure (or nonwork) activities contain mostly positive task features, whereas work may contain a number of less attractive features in addition to the most enjoyable ones. Also, people typically engage in passionate nonwork activities for an average of 8.5 weekly hours (see Vallerand et al., 2003, Study 1), whereas they typically engage in work for 35 weekly hours and sometimes much more. Can the less enjoyable features and the long hours at work erode the positive effects of harmonious passion on psychological well-being? Do the positive affective experiences at work also account for the positive effects of harmonious passion for work on psychological well-being?

Research conducted in the realm of work led to results similar to those obtained with nonwork activities. First, harmonious passion for work has been found to positively predict psychological well-being and to be negatively related to ill-being, whereas obsessive passion for work has been found to be either unrelated or negatively related to psychological well-being and to be positively related to ill-being (e.g., Carbonneau et al., 2008; Forest et al., 2011; Houlfort et al., 2014; Houlfort et al., 2011, Studies 1–3; Lavigne et al., 2012, Studies 1 and 2). It thus appears that research in the workplace provides support for the major hypothesis regarding the promotion of psychological well-being and the prevention of ill-being of harmonious passion for work, and the less adaptive role of obsessive passion. Second, it seems that the same mediating processes come into play in the workplace, because positive work experiences mediate the positive effects of harmonious passion on psychological well-being. For instance, in a study with workers from different public and private organizations, Houlfort et al. (2011, Study 3) showed that harmonious passion for work predicted positive affect experienced at work that, in turn, predicted increases in psychological well-being that took place over a 6-month period.

Another significant contribution of the Houlfort et al. (2011, Study 3) study is that it was found that the impact of obsessive passion on psychological well-being and ill-being was mediated by the experience of positive emotions at work (partial and full mediation, respectively). Hence, obsessive passion for work seems to increase ill-being and reduce well-being by preventing workers from experiencing positive emotions. These findings are intriguing because they differ from those of Rousseau and Vallerand (2008) who found that positive affect experienced during an exercise session did not mediate the negative effects of obsessive passion on psychological well-being. Clearly, future research is needed to understand why affect would play different roles when engaged in work and leisure activities.

Forest et al. (2011) studied the role of another mediating factor in the passion-psychological well-being relationship. In a study with over 400 employees from a large service company, Forest et al. (2011) found that positive experiences of competence, autonomy, and relatedness (i.e., need satisfaction in SDT) mediated the positive effects of harmonious passion on psychological well-being. These findings provide support for SDT on the role of need satisfaction in the workplace in psychological well-being as well as the role of harmonious passion in the experience of need satisfaction.

The above research provides support for the role of harmonious passion in leading to positive affective experiences and the role of the latter in promoting psychological well-being. However, such research did not address the role of the psychological mediators in the second role of harmonious passion, namely the protective role these mediating processes may play in psychological ill-being. If harmonious passion protects one from experiencing psychological ill-being, then are positive work experiences the mediating processes involved in the process? In a longitudinal study on burnout with bureaucrats from the Provincial government, Lavigne et al. (2012, Study 2) showed that harmonious passion for work predicted increases in flow over time that, in turn, predicted decreases in burnout over time. Obsessive passion was only found to directly predict increases in emotional exhaustion. It would thus appear that positive work experiences do mediate the protective effects of harmonious passion on ill-being.

It is important to note that research discussed so far has shown that obsessive passion is negatively related to psychological well-being (Lavigne et al., 2012; Rousseau & Vallerand, 2008). Furthermore, Houlfort et al. (2011, Study 3) found that affective experiences mediate the obsessive passion–psychological well-being or ill-being relationship. Vallerand, Paquet, Philippe, and Charest (2010) reasoned that another likely mediator of the contributive effect that obsessive passion should have on ill-being may be the psychological conflict experienced between the passionate activity (work) and other life activities (e.g., family activities). Past research has highlighted the role of obsessive (but not harmonious) passion in conflict between the passionate activity and other life activities (see Vallerand et al., 2003, Study 1; Vallerand, Ntoumanis, et al., 2008, Studies 1 and 3), including conflict between work and other life activities (see Caudroit, Boiché, Stephan, Le Scanff, & Trouilloud, 2011). Because with obsessive passion one experiences an uncontrollable urge to engage in the passionate activity, it becomes very difficult for the person to fully disengage from thoughts about the activity (or from disengaging in the activity altogether), leading to conflict with other activities in the person's life. Such conflict can prevent the person from replenishing himself or herself in other life pursuits. The person thus remains mentally stale, which over time may contribute to ill-being (Garland et al., 2010). In addition, because obsessive passion is typically unrelated or negatively related to positive affective experiences both during task engagement in the passionate activity (work) and in other life pursuits outside of it, obsessive passion does not trigger the protective function against ill-being like harmonious passion does. Conversely, with harmonious passion, the person can let go of the passionate activity after task engagement and fully immerse in other life pursuits without experiencing conflict between the two (see Carpentier, Mageau, & Vallerand, 2012). Thus, harmonious passion should allow the person to experience affective rewards both during task engagement in the passionate activity as well as in other life pursuits, thereby protecting the person against ill-being.

The above reasoning was tested with respect to psychological burnout in two studies with professional nurses from two cultures (France and Canada; Vallerand et al., 2010, Studies 1 and 2). In Study 1, 100 nurses from France completed scales assessing passion, psychological conflict, work satisfaction, and burnout. The results from structural equation modeling analyses supported the model, even when controlling for the weekly number of hours worked. Specifically, obsessive passion facilitated the experience of burnout through the psychological conflict it induced between work and other life activities. There was also an absence of relationship between obsessive passion and work satisfaction. However, harmonious passion prevented the experience of conflict and contributed to the experience of work satisfaction that, in turn, negatively predicted burnout. Through its effects on work satisfaction and conflict, harmonious passion was able to protect the person from experiencing burnout. These findings were replicated in a second study using a prospective design with nurses from the Province of Québec (Vallerand et al., 2010, Study 2), allowing researchers to predict changes in burnout over a 6-month period.

In sum, it seems that harmonious passion promotes psychological well-being and prevents ill-being, largely because it leads the person to experience some affective rewards during task engagement and allows the person to fully disengage from the passionate activity when not engaging in it (see Carpentier et al., 2012). Conversely, it seems that obsessive passion may not promote psychological well-being because it is unrelated or negatively related to positive work experiences during task engagement. In addition, obsessive passion may facilitate negative states of ill-being, such as burnout, because of the rigid persistence it entails and the conflict it creates with other aspects of one's life.

Passion and Interpersonal Relationships

Passionate individuals are typically seen as highly engaging and full of energy. As such they should be highly popular and able to make friends easily. Is it the case? And if it is the case, what is the process through which they make friends? In line with the reasoning presented thus far, the DMP posits that the passion that one holds toward work should have an impact on the quality of relationships that one develops and maintains at work. As has been shown previously, harmonious passion is conducive to positive affect much more than obsessive passion, whereas the latter has been found to lead to negative affect (see Vallerand, 2010). Of importance, the work of Waugh and Fredrickson (2006) has shown that positive affect is important for relationships. Specifically, positive affect opens up people's thought-action repertoires and self, leading one to experience the environment and surroundings more fully, thereby facilitating smiles, positive sharing of the activity, and connection and openness toward others that are conducive to positive relationships. The reverse is true for negative emotions. It thus follows that harmonious passion for work should lead to better relationships at work than obsessive passion through their differential effects on positive and negative emotions.

A series of studies conducted in a variety of settings, including the sport and work domains (Lafrenière, Jowett, Vallerand, Donahue, & Lorimer, 2008, Studies 1 and 2; Philippe, Vallerand, Houlfort, Lavigne, & Donahue, 2010, Studies 1 to 4), provides support for the previous hypotheses. In all six studies, harmonious passion was positively correlated with the quality of relationships experienced within the purview of the passionate activity, whereas obsessive passion was not. Of particular interest are two studies conducted in work-related settings (Philippe et al., 2010, Studies 1 and 4). In the first study (Philippe et al., 2010, Study 1), close to 200 teachers and managers completed the Passion Scale for work, positive emotions experienced at work, as well as a scale assessing the quality of relationships with one's workmates. As expected, results revealed that harmonious passion predicted positive emotions that, in turn, positively predicted better relationships. Obsessive passion was unrelated to relationships or positive affect. In a subsequent study, Philippe et al. (2010, Study 4), sought to replicate the findings of the first study while incorporating negative emotions in the model. Furthermore, this study was conducted with management students working in teams on various projects over an entire semester and only students who had never met before participated in the study. Thus, the present study focused on the *development* of new friendships. Results from structural equation modeling analyses revealed that harmonious passion positively predicted positive affect, but negatively predicted negative affect, whereas obsessive passion only positively predicted negative affect. In turn, positive and negative affect experienced over the semester positively and negatively predicted relationship quality, respectively. Of additional interest, Philippe et al. (2010) also had workmates assess the relationship quality that they had with each other. The same results were obtained for both self and other assessments of relationship quality. Overall, these two studies underscore the role of harmonious passion in the development of new relationships (Philippe et al., 2010, Study 4) and the maintenance of existing relationships (Philippe et al., 2010, Study 1) in work-related settings.

Finally, other research has revealed that the positive effects of harmonious passion on the quality relationships also applies to relationships where one is a supervisor and the other a subordinate, as assessed by people in both positions (Lafrenière et al., 2008, Studies 1 and 2). Specifically, it was found that both coaches and players with a harmonious passion for their sport enjoyed a better relationship with each other than those with an obsessive passion. Similarly, it appears that positive emotions also mediate the quality of such relationships (Lafrenière et al., 2008, Study 2). However, these latter findings were obtained in the sport domain (with coaches and athletes) with already existing relationships. Future research is needed to replicate these findings in the workplace with both new and existing one-up relationships.

There is a second process through which passion for work can affect relationships. Specifically, passion for work can negatively influence relationships in other areas of our lives through the conflict it might create. This negative effect should result from obsessive passion as people typically have difficulties disengaging physically and mentally from work and thus may experience conflict between work and relationships in other spheres of one's life, especially family and love relationships. Such should not be the case for harmonious passion. No research to date has tested these hypotheses directly with respect to passion for work. However, research in other fields lends credence to these hypotheses. For instance, Vallerand et al. (2003, Study 1) have shown that obsessive (but not harmonious) passion for a nonwork activity was positively associated with experiencing conflict between activity engagement and other aspects of one's life. Caudroit et al. (2011) have shown that nurses with an obsessive passion experienced conflict between their work and engaging in leisure physical activity. Finally, other research has shown that having a passion for the Internet (Séguin-Lévesque, Laliberté, Pelletier, Blanchard, & Vallerand, 2003) and for being a soccer fan (in Europe; Vallerand, Ntoumanis et al.,

2008, Study 3), conflicted with the quality of the relationship with one's spouse. Because these findings were obtained with respect to an obsessive passion for nonwork activities, future research should attempt to replicate them with respect to passion for work.

Passion and Performance

So far, we have seen that passion, and especially harmonious passion, can contribute to several positive work outcomes. But what about performance at work? Does passion matter? Over the years, several authors have suggested that it does. Years ago, the philosopher Hegel (1770–1831) suggested that passion was essential for high levels of achievement to take place. Thus, according to Hegel and others (as discussed in the Introduction section), passion is essential to high levels of performance. Is it the case?

One approach we took (Vallerand, 2014, Study 1) in order to test the above question was to compare individuals who had been selected by a provincial committee as "Personalities of the Week" for their major contributions to Québec society in a variety of areas (business, music and arts, sports, and so forth) over the past 10 years with regular workers. Results revealed that the Personalities of the Week were significantly more passionate than regular workers. Indeed, using a stringent average score of 5 out of 7 on the passion criteria, 96% of the Personalities indicated being highly passionate for their activity, whereas only 33% of the regular workers did so. Furthermore, the Personalities of the Week displayed higher levels of both harmonious and obsessive passion than the regular workers. Finally, the Personalities of the Week reported working 9 hours more per week than regular workers (47 vs. 38 hours). Interestingly, when statistically controlling for the number hours worked, the differences in passion remained. Thus, passion seems to be involved in high-level performance at work.

So, if passion is involved in high-level performance, what is the process through which it affects performance? There seems to be two key dimensions of performance that need to be distinguished: short-term and long-term performance. With respect to short-term performance, it would appear that one needs to take into account the factors involved in facilitating high performance at a given moment. It seems that the positive situational factors (e.g., positive affect, flow) that harmonious passion allows one to experience at work may be conducive to high performance. Results from two studies by Liu et al. (2011) provide some support for this hypothesis. Using a total of over 1,000 employees from a manufacturing firm (Study 1) and a large commercial bank (Study 2) in China, the authors found in the two studies that harmonious passion positively predicted individual performance (in this case creativity) as assessed by the supervisor. These findings held up even after controlling for a number of variables, such as participants' age, gender, level of education, tenure, technical positions, and work unit.

Obsessive passion and the potential mediating role of experiential factors were not assessed in the Liu et al. (2011) studies. However, the role of these variables was tested in a study by Ho et al. (2011). These authors measured both types of passion, levels of absorption in their work (a construct similar to flow), and performance as assessed by supervisors in over 500 employees from an insurance company. Results from a path analysis revealed that harmonious passion positively predicted levels of absorption that, in turn, positively predicted objective performance. Obsessive passion was unrelated to absorption or performance. These findings thus provide some support for the positive role of harmonious (but not obsessive) passion in short-term performance.

With respect to long-term performance, research reveals that to reach high-level performance in any given field one needs to spend several years (specifically 10 years and 10,000 hours; Ericsson & Charness, 1994) of considerable engagement in one specific type of task engagement called deliberate practice. Deliberate practice entails engaging in the activity with clear goals of improving on certain task components. For instance, an economist has to go through formal university training and several years of internship and coaching before being in a position to make educated decisions regarding the economy. We believe that passion represents the underlying motivational force that leads individuals to remain engaged in the activity and to spend so much time in perfecting their skills in the long-term. Indeed, if one is to engage in the activity for long hours over several years and sometimes a lifetime, one must love the activity dearly and have the desire to persist in the activity especially when times are rough. Thus, the two types of passion (harmonious and obsessive) should lead to engagement in deliberate practice that, in turn, should lead to improved performance.

The above model was tested in research with elite basketball players (Vallerand, Mageau et al., 2008, Study 1) and among the best dramatic arts students in the Province of Québec (Vallerand et al., 2007, Study 1). The results of these two studies were essentially the same. The dramatic arts study is particularly relevant, as the participants will become professionals working in a variety of areas in dramatic arts in the Province of Québec. In this study, a prospective design was used where students completed scales assessing their passion for dramatic arts as well as deliberate practice (based on Ericsson & Charness, 1994) early in the term. Teachers independently rated the students' performance at the end of the term. Results from a path analysis revealed that both types of passion led to engagement in deliberate practice that, in turn, led to high levels of objective performance.

Initial research by Baum and Locke (2004; see also Baum et al., 2001), had shown that the CEO's passion for entrepreneurship predicted the company's growth (or performance) through the mediating role of different factors, including goals. However, such research did not assess the two types of passion. Subsequent research on passion and performance did. Such research conducted with athletes (Vallerand, Mageau, et al., 2008, Study 2) and classical musicians (including professional world-class musicians; Bonneville-Roussy, Lavigne, & Vallerand, 2011) found support for a more elaborate model wherein one adaptive type of achievement goals (Elliot & Church, 1997) termed mastery goals (having the goal to improve at the task) mediates the impact of both types of passion on deliberate practice, whereas a maladaptive type of goals, performance-avoidance goals (having the goal to not do worse than others), mediates the negative impact of obsessive passion on performance. It seems that whereas harmonious passion facilitates only the use of adaptive goals, obsessive passion leads to the adoption of both adaptive (mastery) and dysfunctional (performance-approach) goals as pertains to performance.

Also of interest is the finding that in several of the passion-performance studies (Bonneville-Roussy et al., 2011; Vallerand et al., 2007, Study 1; Vallerand, Mageau, et al., 2008, Study 2), psychological well-being was also assessed. Results revealed that harmonious passion was positively and significantly related to psychological well-being, whereas obsessive passion was either negatively related or unrelated to it. This is in line with research reported previously on passion and psychological well-being. It thus appears that both types of passion can positively contribute to long-term performance. However, with harmonious passion, there is a bonus as one may reach high levels of performance while "having a life" (i.e., being happy). Such does not seem to be the case for obsessive passion.

Clearly additional research is needed regarding the role of passion in performance at work. However, the present findings highlight the fact that there seem to be two roads to high performance: the harmonious and the obsessive roads. The harmonious road is characterized by the sole goal of wanting to improve (i.e., mastery goal), which leads to deliberate practice and high levels of performance over time. In addition, through the experience of positive experiential factors (i.e., absorption), harmonious passion seems to be conducive to high-level short-term, performance. Of additional interest is that the harmonious road to excellence seems to be paved with psychological well-being. Thus, high-levels of short-term and long-term performance need not be obtained at the expense of happiness. On the other hand, the obsessive path to excellence is paved with both adaptive (i.e., mastery) and maladaptive (i.e. performance-avoidance) goals and a less intense level of absorption that is not conducive to performance or psychological well-being. Thus, although passion is necessary to reach excellence, harmonious passion seems more adaptive than obsessive passion.

In sum, research reviewed in this section reveals that passion for work is involved in a number of outcomes. Furthermore, the type of passion makes a difference. Specifically, having a harmonious passion for one's work is positively associated with better cognitive functioning, affective experiences, psychological well-being (and the absence of ill-being), positive relationship development and maintenance, and performance. Although obsessive passion has been positively related to some positive outcomes (e.g., performance), it is typically either unrelated or negatively related to outcomes reviewed in this chapter. The fact that obsessive passion may at times lead to some positive outcomes needs to be further studied. For instance, not giving up in the face of obstacles is certainly a consequence that should follow from obsessive passion because of the rigid persistence it creates, and perhaps more so than from harmonious passion. Thus, depending on whether giving up at some point is adaptive or not, there may be situations where obsessive passion may lead to better outcomes than harmonious passion. Future research on this issue is important.

Perhaps one caveat is in order. In this section, we have been using the term "outcomes." One is reminded that the reviewed research mostly used correlational designs. Thus, we cannot firmly conclude that passion "causes" outcomes. However, two important sets of studies need to be considered. First, the results of two studies conducted in the workplace using a cross-lagged panel design revealed that although passion predicts changes in outcomes, outcomes do not predict changes in passion (Carbonneau et al., 2008; Lavigne et al., 2012, Study 2). Second, recent laboratory research reveals that experimentally inducing harmonious passion leads to better situational outcomes (more adaptive cognitive processes, less energy depletion, and so forth) than inducing obsessive passion (Bélanger, Lafrenière, Vallerand, & Kruglanski, 2013b). This is basically done by having people write extensively about a recent engagement in the passionate activity that was either harmonious or obsessive in content (see Bélanger et al., 2013b). Clearly, additional research on the causality issue between passion and outcomes is necessary before one can firmly conclude that passion *causes* outcomes, and especially in the workplace. However, the previous research suggests that it may indeed be the case.

On the Determinants of Passion
Initial Development of Passion

How does one become passionate for one's work? And if one becomes passionate, how does he or she develop a harmonious rather than an obsessive passion? In light of the important role that passion plays in a variety of work outcomes, these questions become of major interest. The DMP posits that three processes are particularly important: activity selection, activity valuation, and the internalization of the activity in identity (Mageau et al., 2009; Vallerand, 2008, 2010). Activity selection refers to the person's preference for the activity over other activities. In line with SDT (Deci & Ryan, 2000), we believe that people explore their environment in order to grow as individuals. In so doing, they engage in a variety of activities. At some point, people start to show preference for some activities, especially those that are enjoyable and allow them the satisfaction of the needs for competence, autonomy, and relatedness. Of these activities, a limited few are perceived as particularly enjoyable and to have some resonance with how people see themselves. Of course, this is all subjective and an activity that is perceived as enjoyable and as related to identity by someone may not be perceived as such by another person. To the extent that the person feels that a specific activity reflects true choice and interests and is consonant with his or her identity, the person may start to value this activity greatly. Activity valuation (or the subjective importance given to the activity by the person) represents the second process in the development of passion. It is expected to play a key role in the internalization of the activity in identity. Indeed, theory and research underscores the fact that behavior (Kelman, 1968), regulations (Deci et al., 1994; Sheldon, 2002; Vallerand, 1997), groups we belong to (Tajfel & Turner, 1986), as well as the people we love (Aron et al., 1992) can be internalized in identity and self. Thus, what was once outside in the environment is now part of us. If what we highly value is an enjoyable activity (or its representation) that is consonant with our identity, then the activity will be internalized in the self, and a passion for the activity is likely to develop.

In line with SDT (Deci & Ryan, 1985, 2000), the DMP posits that such an internalization process is much more than an inside versus outside process. Specifically, what has been internalized inside of us can be more or less aligned with one's sense of self, depending on the type of internalization that takes place. The more aligned with the self is the internalized representation, the more the latter is in line with our values, regulations, and under our control. In other words, what has been internalized can be of different quality depending on the type of internalization that has taken place. SDT posits the existence of two main types of internalization process, the autonomous internalization process and the controlled internalization process, each leading to either harmonious or to obsessive passion. Obsessive passion results from a controlled internalization of the activity into one's identity. A controlled internalization originates from intrapersonal and/or interpersonal pressure typically because certain contingencies are attached to the activity, such as feelings of social acceptance or self-esteem (see Mageau et al., 2011), or because the sense of excitement derived from activity engagement is uncontrollable. Conversely, harmonious passion results from an autonomous internalization of the activity representation into the person's identity. An autonomous internalization occurs when individuals have freely accepted the activity as important to them without any or little contingencies attached to it. This type of internalization emanates from the intrinsic and integrative tendencies of the self (Deci & Ryan, 2000; Ryan & Deci, 2003).

The DMP further posits that the type of internalization process that occurs depends on at least two types of variables: the social environment and one's personality. To the extent that one's social environment (e.g., parents, teachers, coaches) is autonomy-supportive, an autonomous internalization is likely to take place, leading to harmonious passion. Conversely, to the extent that one's social environment is controlling, a controlled internalization takes place, leading to obsessive passion. Similarly, if an individual has a type of personality that fosters one's autonomy, such as an autonomous personality (as indexed by the Global Motivation Scale; Guay, Mageau, & Vallerand, 2003), then, the autonomous internalization process should take place, leading to harmonious passion. However, when one's personality is more of the controlled type (generally doing things out of internal or external pressure), the controlled internalization process should be in operation, leading to obsessive passion.

These hypotheses were tested in two series of studies (Mageau et al., 2009; Vallerand et al., 2006; Studies 1 and 3). In a first series of studies (Mageau et al., 2009, Study 3), the role of the autonomy-supportive social environment as well as that of activity selection and valuation and identity processes in the development of passion were assessed. First-year high school students who had *never* played a musical instrument before and who were taking their first music class completed a series of questionnaires early in the term assessing activity selection (i.e., preference for music over other activities) and valuation (perceived parental activity valuation and perceived parental and child activity specialization), autonomy support from parents and music teachers, as well as identity processes. The authors sought to determine who would develop a passion for music by the end of the semester, and among these passionate students, which type of passion they would display (i.e., harmonious or obsessive passion). Results from discriminant analyses revealed that the students who ended up being moderately passionate for music (36% of the sample) at the end of the term had, earlier in the term, reported higher levels of activity valuation and specialization, identity processes, and parental and teacher autonomy support than those students who did not develop a passion. Thus, these variables (activity selection, activity valuation, identity processes, and autonomy support from the environment) seem to represent the key variables in the development of a passion for an activity, such as music, as hypothesized.

Subsequent analyses focused on the 36% of passionate novice musicians and compared those who had developed a harmonious passion with those who had developed an obsessive passion. It was found that high perceived autonomy support from close adults (parents and music teachers) and children's activity valuation were conducive to the development of harmonious passion. High levels of parental perceived valuation for music and lack of autonomy support were found to predict the development of obsessive passion. Results of two other studies dealing with sports and music revealed that both *perceived* (Mageau et al., 2009, Study 1) and *actual* autonomy support (as reported by the parents themselves; Mageau et al., 2009, Study 2) were conducive to harmonious passion. In sum, the results of the Mageau et al. (2009) studies demonstrate the role of activity valuation and autonomy support (and control) from significant adults in the development of a passion in general, and harmonious (obsessive) passion in particular.

In the second series of studies, Vallerand et al. (2006, Studies 1 and 3) tested the role of activity valuation and personality variables in the occurrence of the two types of passion among athletes. In the first study (Vallerand et al., 2006, Study 1), results from a path analysis revealed that activity valuation coupled with an autonomous personality (as assessed by the Global Motivation Scale; Guay et al. 2003) predicted harmonious passion. Obsessive passion resulted from activity valuation coupled with a controlled personality. These findings were replicated in a second study (Vallerand et al., 2006, Study 3) using a short longitudinal design. Thus, overall, in addition to social factors, personality factors also appear to play a role in the development of both types of passion.

The On-Going Development of Passion

The DMP further posits that once a passion for a given activity has initially developed, its development continues as it is on-going. Thus, increases and decreases in activity valuation lead to similar modulation in the intensity of passion. Furthermore, the presence or absence of social and personal factors that pertain to the autonomous versus controlled internalization process influence the on-going development of passion in a corresponding fashion (e.g., more harmonious than obsessive passion). It should be noted that the internalization process is not an all or none process. Thus, elements referring to both types of passion may have been internalized to different degrees leading both types of passion to be present within the individual to different degrees. One important consequence of this state of affairs is that it should be possible to facilitate one or

the other type of passion by making salient certain social or personal factors. In other words, although a predominant type of passion is usually in operation for a given individual toward a specific activity, it is possible to further reinforce the predominant passion or to make the other type of passion operative depending on which type of social or personal factors is made salient. Recently, research conducted in the workplace has looked at the role of both personal and social factors as determinants of the two types of passion.

PERSONAL FACTORS

We have seen in the previous section that individuals with an autonomous personality (e.g., Guay et al., 2003) are more likely to internalize an activity in their self in a more autonomous way and thus to develop a harmonious passion for a given activity, whereas individuals with a controlled personality are more likely to internalize things in a more controlled fashion and to develop an obsessive passion (Vallerand et al., 2006). Recent research conducted in the workplace has also underscored the role of two other individual differences in the development of passion for work. A first one pertains to emotional intelligence. Emotional intelligence refers to a group of abilities that allows one to work efficiently with one's emotions and those of others at the intrapersonal and interpersonal levels (Brackett & Mayer, 2003; Salovey & Mayer, 1990). Managers that have a high level of emotional intelligence are more in tune with their strengths and weaknesses; show more empathy; know what impact they have on others; and are more competent at coping, managing, and making good use of their emotions as well as that of others (Salovey & Mayer, 1990). The opposite is believed to be true for managers with a low level of emotional intelligence.

Workers with high emotional intelligence thus should be able to behave and think in a more autonomous way—act out of choice and in congruence with their personal emotion and values—a condition that should facilitate the emergence of harmonious passion. In a recent study, Houlfort and Rinfret (2010) tested this hypothesis with the chief executives of 55 health and social services centers from the Province of Québec. The Bar-On Emotional Quotient Inventory was used to assess the presence and level of emotional intelligence. Results from a path analysis found that high level of emotional intelligence within chief executives was positively and significantly related with harmonious passion for work. Unfortunately, obsessive passion was not assessed in this study, and thus we cannot confirm that the absence or lack of emotional intelligence predicts obsessive passion for work. However, we hypothesize that because individuals with little emotional intelligence are less in-tune with their authentic self, when passionate for work, they should develop an obsessive passion. Future research is needed to determine the role of emotional intelligence (or lack of) in obsessive passion.

Another important personality variable refers to signature strengths use. Strengths are considered as "pre-existing capacity for a particular way of behaving, thinking, or feeling that is authentic and energizing to the user, and enables functioning, development and performance" (Linley, 2008). It has been shown that people use their strengths to different degrees and that those who use their strengths more seem to experience positive outcomes to a larger degree than those who use their strengths less. For instance, workers who use their strengths in their everyday job perform at higher levels (Buckingham & Clifton, 2001; Clifton & Harter, 2003; Harter, Schmidt, & Hayes, 2002), have higher levels of well-being (Berman, 2008; Govindji & Linley, 2007; Park, Peterson, & Seligman, 2004), and remain longer in their organization (Asplund, Lopez, Hodges, & Harter, 2007). Because using one's strengths allows one to have access to the authentic self, it should also make operative harmonious passion.

Recently, Forest et al. (2012) have tested the above hypothesis. Seligman, Steen, Park, and Peterson's (2005) intervention program was adapted to the workplace, wherein participants in the experimental condition (n = 186) identified their signature strengths and were trained to visualize and describe themselves at their personal best and to use their strengths in their current job for a period of 2 weeks. The experiment also involved a control group (n = 36) and both groups participated in a follow-up 2 months after the intervention. Harmonious and obsessive passions for work were measured before and after the intervention. Three key findings were obtained. First, the experimental program was successful in increasing strengths use. Second, increases in the use of signature strengths from Time 1 to Time 2 predicted increases in harmonious passion for work between Time 1 and Time 2. Finally, results also showed that harmonious passion mediated the relationship between strengths' use and positive outcomes. No significant relationship was found between strengths' use and obsessive passion. Hence, workers who were aware of their signature strengths and who could enact them at work were more likely to have an increase in harmonious passion than workers who did not know their strengths or could not use them. As hypothesized, it appears that the use of one's signature strengths allows workers to behave and think in an autonomous way that, in turn, facilitates the experience of harmonious passion for one's work.

In sum, developing a harmonious or an obsessive passion is partly in workers' hands. Indeed, both emotional intelligence and signature strengths use are coachable and can be increased as was shown in the Forest et al. (2012) study. By increasing one's emotional intelligence and identifying and using one's signature strengths more often, workers can facilitate the emergence of a harmonious passion for work and the positive outcomes that follow.

SOCIAL FACTORS

It was seen previously that significant adults (e.g., parents, coaches, teachers; Mageau et al., 2009) who provide children with autonomy support, that is who provide room for choices and active involvement, foster harmonious passion while those who are more controlling are more likely to either fail to promote passion or to facilitate obsessive passion. Similarly, it is proposed that organizational contexts that are autonomy supportive should promote the development of a harmonious passion for work. In opposition, a controlling working environment would lead to a more obsessive passion.

Houlfort and Vallerand (2013) have examined how two key organizational factors, namely leadership style and organizational culture, can affect passion for work. Leaders are expected to have a great impact on their followers and can become significant figures for workers. Leaders color the vision, mission, and values of organizations, have a say in who gets hired, and what policies will be implemented. On top of this, leaders also influence how these activities are carried out. Thus, leaders determine how much autonomy support will take place in the workplace. Two important types of leadership are transformational and transactional leaderships. Transformational leadership takes place when the leader acts toward "the follower beyond immediate self-interests through idealized influence (charisma), inspiration, intellectual stimulation, or individual consideration" (Bass, 1999, p. 11). Transformational leaders act in a way that supports workers' autonomy and values behaviors and thinking that promote autonomy. Conversely, transactional leadership characterizes the leader-follower relationship when gratification of self-interest is at the center of the relationship (Bass, 1999). Leaders with a transactional style use monitoring and corrective actions to manage and act in a more controlled way. Transformational leadership has repeatedly been shown to have more positive consequences than transactional leadership (DeGroot, Kiker, & Cross, 2000; Dumdum, Low, & Avolio, 2002; Judge & Piccolo, 2004; Wang, Oh, Courtwright, & Colbert, 2011).

Two studies by Houlfort and Vallerand (2013) examined the relationship between leadership style and passion for work. Participants were teachers (Study 1, $n = 1,059$) and white collars, managers, and professionals of an important public organization (Study 2, $n = 147$). The authors used the Multifactor Leadership Questionnaire (Avolio, Bass, & Jung, 1999) to assess participants' perception of the leadership style adopted by their immediate supervisor and tested whether leadership, transformational and transactional leadership could predict harmonious and obsessive passion, respectively. Correlational and path analyses supported the hypothesized predictions. Specifically, transformational leadership positively predicted harmonious passion, whereas transactional leadership positively predicted obsessive passion. Hence, leaders, just as parents in Mageau et al.'s (2009) research, can promote an autonomous internalization of work within the self by supporting workers' autonomy. Conversely, when leaders pressure workers to pursue a task or to engage in it a certain way, passionate workers are more likely to develop an obsessive passion.

Another important social factor to consider is that of organizational culture. Organizational culture represents "how things are done around here," and thus reflects the formal and informal organizational structures and processes, values (strategies, goals, and philosophies), and underlying assumptions (unconscious, taken for granted beliefs, perceptions, and thoughts) (Schein, 2009). An organizational culture brings a particular flavor to workers' experiences because it influences how everyone should behave and think. As such, it can have multiple effects on organizational outcomes. For instance, organizational culture has been found to influence performance (Lee & Yu, 2004), creativity and innovation (Martins & Terblanche, 2003), and knowledge management (Alavi, Kayworth, & Leidner, 2005), just to name a few outcomes. Each culture thus creates a specific working environment with nutrients that can possibly nourish or hinder the development of a harmonious or an obsessive passion for work. Two types of cultures proposed by Cameron and Quinn (2006) were of particular importance in the Houlfort and Vallerand's (2013, Study 2) study. The clan culture is based on collaboration, commitment, development, and communication that take place within an organization. Leaders are seen as mentors and team builders and such an organization identifies with innovativeness, vision, and new resources as key ingredients to organization effectiveness (Cameron & Quinn, 2006). Because of its emphasis on worker support and human values, it was hypothesized that a clan culture would lead to harmonious passion for work. Conversely, a market culture focuses on competition, goal achievement, and profitability. Leaders who endorse such a culture are seen as hard driving, highly competitive, and focused on productivity. Because of its aggressive nature and the lack of consideration of workers as individuals with psychological needs, a market culture seems to entail a more controlled environment, and thus it was hypothesized to foster obsessive passion for work.

The above hypotheses were confirmed. Indeed, Houlfort and Vallerand (2013, Study 2) found that the clan culture is positively related to harmonious passion for work. A clan culture promotes autonomy support (i.e., facilitate employees' participation in decision making, team work, competence feedback, and so forth) and thus fosters the development of a harmonious passion because it allows for an autonomous internalization of work within the self. Conversely, a market culture endorses control and competition and puts forward tangible rewards while minimizing employees' participation. Unsurprisingly, it was found to nurture the development of an obsessive passion among their passionate workers. Indeed, such environments are thought to promote a controlled type of internalization of work, such that the value of work is, at best, partially integrated within the self (Deci & Ryan, 2000). Sometimes, however, a leader has to command and dictate what and how work needs to be done. SDT, and specifically research on informational interpersonal contexts, suggests that this can still be done in an autonomy supportive fashion. By using a noncontrolling language, acknowledging workers' feelings, and giving a rationale for the imposed rules and structures, leaders can command and dictate without affecting workers' autonomy (see Deci et al., 1994). This interpersonal style creates a work environment favorable for the development of harmonious passion.

In sum, these findings on the determinants of passion highlight the importance of activity selection, activity valuation, and internalization of the activity within identity and self in the initial development of passion. Once the potential for passion is present and well anchored, personal characteristics, such as emotional intelligence and signature strengths, as well as the interpersonal style adopted by leaders and managers, can affect the on-going development of passion for work. In other words, the worker's idiosyncratic interface with the passionate activity and the organizational environment in which he or she works contribute in determining if the passion is harmonious or obsessive. Additional research is needed to increase the understanding of the development of passion. In this light, both personal and social factors as well as their interaction should be further scrutinized.

Conclusions

In the present paper, research on passion for work was reviewed using the DMP as an organizing structure. The DMP posits the existence of two types of passion, harmonious and obsessive, which can be differentiated in terms of how the representation of the passionate activity has been internalized into one's identity. Harmonious passion originates from an autonomous internalization of the activity into one's identity and promotes a mindful and open form of activity engagement that should facilitate a number of positive work outcomes. Conversely, obsessive passion takes origin in a controlled internalization and is hypothesized to instill a more rigid and conflicted form of task engagement and thus lead to less adaptive outcomes. In addition, the DMP posits that both personal and social factors represent important determinants of passion. Research conducted in the workplace provides strong support for the DMP.

Several directions for future research can be proposed. A first deals with the mediating role of different types of positive work experiences in several outcomes (e.g., psychological well-being, relationships). Specifically, do different types of work experiences (e.g., positive emotions, flow, need satisfaction) have the same impact on outcomes? Which one contributes the most? What is the role of passion in these various work experiences? A second research direction that seems important deals with the fact that harmonious passion typically leads to positive effects with respect to most if not all outcomes. However, is it always the case? For instance, Amiot, Vallerand, and Blanchard (2006) found that obsessively passionate hockey players were found to be happier than harmoniously passionate players in highly competitive hockey leagues, whereas the reverse was true in less competitive leagues. Does the same situation apply to the workplace? Can harmonious passion sometimes lead to less adaptive outcomes than obsessive passion? And if so, under what type of situation does this take place? Research is needed on this issue. A third potential research area deals with deviant behavior. Research in sports and leisure activities reveals that obsessive passion leads to deviant and immoral behavior, whereas harmonious passion does not (Bureau, Vallerand, Ntoumanis, & Lafrenière, 2013). In light of some of the deviant behavior that took place in the banking system in recent years, such research in the work domain seems important. A fourth research direction pertains to individuals who are nonpassionate for their work. Most of the research reviewed compared harmonious with obsessive passion for work. Thus, very little is known about nonpassionate workers. How do they fare relative to those who have a predominant harmonious or obsessive passion with respect to work outcomes? The only available research reveals that nonpassionate people display lower levels of psychological well-being than people who are harmoniously passionate for a given activity (Philippe et al., 2009) but do not differ from those who display an obsessive passion. Would this pattern of results hold up with respect to passion for work? Research is needed to shed some light on this issue.

Finally, a last research avenue pertains to the determinants of passion. Such research should attempt to identify how best to promote the development of a harmonious passion (and prevent an obsessive passion) for work, thereby leading to optimal outcomes. How can we best promote the transference of passion (see Cardon, 2008), and especially harmonious passion in organizations? Already we know that both encouraging the use of personal strengths (e.g., Forest et al., 2012) and fostering autonomy-supportive environments through transformational leadership and choice (e.g., Houlfort & Vallerand, 2013; Liu et al., 2011) facilitates harmonious passion. However, do these practices work for all workers, including those who may have already developed an obsessive passion for work? Research is needed in order to develop best practices that would take into account individual differences in one's passion at entry point to facilitate a harmonious passion and associated benefits in a specific work environment.

In sum, research reviewed in this chapter underscores the fact that passion for work does matter. However, the type of passion also matters. Specifically, harmonious passion for work generally leads to the experience of positive work outcomes, whereas obsessive passion, although ensuring heavy work engagement, does not lead to optimal outcomes and may even lead to some deleterious effects. In this light, attention should be given to determinants that promote a harmonious passion for work. Future research on some of the issues raised above therefore appears rather promising.

References

Alavi, M., Kayworth, T. R., & Leidner, D. E. (2005–2006). An empirical examination of the influence of organizational culture on knowledge management practices. *Journal of Management Information System, 22*, 191–224. doi: 10.2753/MIS0742-1222220307

Amiot, C., Vallerand, R. J., & Blanchard, C. (2006). Passion and psychological adjustment: A test of the person-environment fit hypothesis. *Personality and Social Psychology Bulletin, 32*, 220–229. doi: 10.1177/0146167205280250

Aron, A., Aron, E. N., & Smollan, D. (1992). Inclusion of other in the self scale and the structure of interpersonal closeness. *Journal of Personality and Social Psychology, 63*, 596–612.

Asplund, J., Lopez, S., Hodges, T., & Harter, J. K. (2007). *The Clifton Strengths Finder technical report: Development and validation*. Gallup: Gallup Technical Report.

Avolio, B. J., Bass, B. M., & Jung, D. I. (1999). Re-examining the components of transformational and transactional leadership using the Multifactor Leadership Questionnaire. *Journal of Occupational and Organizational Psychology, 72*, 441–462. doi: 10.1348/096317999166789

Bass, B. M. (1999). Two decades of research and development in transformational leadership. *European Journal of Work and Organizational Psychology, 8*, 9–32. doi: 10.1080/135943299398410

Baum, J. R., & Locke, E. A. (2004). The relationship of entrepreneurial traits, skill, and motivation to subsequent venture growth. *Journal of Applied Psychology, 89*, 587–598.

Baum, J. R., Locke, E. A., & Smith, K. G. (2001). A multi-dimensional model of venture growth. *Academy of Management Journal, 44*, 292–303. doi: 10.2307/3069456

Bélanger, J., Lafrenière, M.-A., Vallerand, R. J., Kruglanski, A. W. (2013a). Driven by fear: The role of failure in passionate individuals' performance. *Journal of Personality and Social Psychology, 104*, 180–195.

Bélanger, J., Lafrenière, M.-A., Vallerand, R. J. & Kruglanski, A. W. (2013b). When passion makes the heart grow colder: The role of passion in alternative goal suppression. *Journal of Personality and Social Psychology, 104*, 126–147.

Berman, J. (2008). *The relationship between one's character strengths and psychological well—being*. Unpublished doctoral thesis, University of California.

Bonneville-Roussy, A., Lavigne, G. L. & Vallerand, R. J. (2011). When passion leads to excellence: The case of musicians. *Psychology of Music, 39*, 123–138. doi: 10.1177/0305735609352441

Brackett, M. A., & Mayer, J. D. (2003). Convergent, discriminant, and incremental validity of competing measures of emotional intelligence. *Personality and Social Psychology Bulletin, 29*, 1147–1158.

Brown, K. W., Ryan, R. M., Creswell, J. D. (2007). Mindfulness: Theoretical foundations and evidence for its salutary effects. *Psychological Inquiry, 18*, 211–237.

Buckingham, M., & Clifton, D. O. (2001). *Now, discover your strengths*. New York: Free Press.

Bureau, J., Vallerand, R. J., Ntoumanis, N., & Lafrenière, M.-A. (2013). On passion and moral behavior in achievement settings: The mediating role of pride. *Motivation and Emotion, 37*, 121–133.

Cameron, K. S., & Quinn, R. E. (2006). *Diagnosing and changing organizational culture*. San Francisco, CA: Jossey-Bass.

Carbonneau, N., Vallerand, R. J., Fernet, C., & Guay, F. (2008). The role of passion for teaching in intrapersonal and interpersonal consequences. *Journal of Educational Psychology, 4*, 977–987. doi: 10.1037/a0012545

Cardon, M. S. (2008). Is passion contagious? The transference of entrepreneurial passion to employees. *Human Resource Management Review, 18*, 77–86.

Cardon, M. S., Wincent, J., Singh, J., & Drnovsek, M. (2009). The nature and experience of entrepreneurial passion. *Academy of Management Review, 34*, 511–532.

Cardon, M. S., Zietsma, C., Saparito, P., Matherne, B. P., & Davis, C. (2005). A tale of passion: New insights into entrepreneurship from a parenthood perspective. *Journal of Business Venturing, 20*, 53–45.

Carpentier, J., Mageau, G. A., & Vallerand, R. J. (2012). Ruminations and flow: Why do people with a more harmonious passion experience higher well-being? *Journal of Happiness Studies, 13*, 501–518. doi 10.1007/s10902-011-9276-4

Castelda, B. A., Mattson, R. E., MacKillop, J. E, Anderson, E. J., Burright, R., & Donovick, P. J. (2007). Psychometric validation of the gambling passion scale (GPS). *International Gambling Studies, 7*, 173–182. doi: 10.1080/14459790701387485

Caudroit, J., Boiché, J., Stephan, Y., Le Scanff, C., & Trouilloud, D. (2011). Predictors of work/family interference and leisure-time physical activity among teachers: The role of passion towards work. *European Journal of Work and Organizational Psychology, 20*, 326–344. doi: 10.1080/13594320903507124

Clifton, D. O., & Harter, J. K. (2003). Investing in strengths. In K. S. Cameron, J. Dutton, & R. Quinn (Eds.), *Positive organisational scholarship* (pp. 111–121). San Francisco: Berrett-Koehler.

Crocker, J. (2002). The costs of seeking self-esteem. *Journal of Social Issues, 58*, 597–615.

Csikszentmihalyi, M. (1978). Intrinsic rewards and emergent motivation. In M. R. Lepper, & D. Greene (Eds.), *The hidden costs of reward: New perspectives on the psychology of human motivation* (pp. 205–216). Hillsdale, NY: Erlbaum.

Csikszentmihalyi, M., Rathunde, K., & Whalen, S. (1993). *Talented teenagers: The roots of success and failure*. New York: Cambridge University Press.

Deci, E. L., Eghrari, H., Patrick, B. C., & Leone, D. R. (1994). Facilitating internalization: The self-determination perspective. *Journal of Personality, 62*, 119–142. doi: 10.1111/j.1467-6494.1994.tb00797.x

Deci, E. L., & Ryan, R. M. (1985). *Intrinsic motivation and self-determination in human behavior*. New York: Plenum Press.

Deci, E. L., & Ryan, R. M. (2000). The "what" and "why" of goal pursuits: Human needs and the self-determination of behavior. *Psychological Inquiry, 11*, 227–268.

DeGroot, T., Kiker, D. S., & Cross, T. C. (2000). A meta-analytic review of organizational outcomes related to charismatic leadership. *Canadian Journal of Administrative Sciences, 17*, 356–371. doi: 10.1111/j.1936-4490.2000.tb00234.x

Dumdum, U. R., Low, K. B., & Avolio, B. J. (2002). A meta-analysis of transformational and transactional leadership correlates of effectiveness and satisfaction: An update and extension. In B. J. Avolio, & F. Yammarino (Eds.). *Transformational and charismatic leadership: The road ahead* (Vol. 2 of Monographs in Leadership and management, pp. 35–66). St. Louis: Elsevier.

Elliot, A. J., & Church, M. A. (1997). A hierarchical model of approach and avoidance achievement motivation. *Journal of Personality and Social Psychology, 72*, 218–232.

Ericsson, K. A., & Charness, N. (1994). Expert performance. *American Psychologist, 49*, 725–747. doi: 10.1037/0022-3514.72.1.218

Erikson, E. H. (1968). *Identity: Youth and crisis.* New York: W.W. Norton.

Forest, J., Mageau, G. A., Crevier-Braud, L., Dubreuil, P., Bergeron, E., & Lavigne, G. L. (2012). Harmonious passion as a mediator of the relation between signature strengths' use and optimal functioning at work: Test of an intervention program. *Human Relations, 65*, 1233–1252.

Forest, J., Mageau, G. A., Sarrazin, C., & Morin, E. M. (2011). "Work is my passion": The different affective, behavioural, and cognitive consequences of harmonious and obsessive passion toward work. *Canadian Journal of Administrative Sciences, 28*, 17–30. doi: 10.1002/CJAS.170

Fredrickson, B. L. (2001). The role of positive emotions in positive psychology: The broaden-and-build theory of positive emotions. *American Psychologist, 56*, 218–226. doi: 10.1037//0003-066X.56.3.218

Frijda, N. H., Mesquita, B., Sonnemans, J., & Van Goozen, S. (1991). The duration of affective phenomena or emotions, sentiments and passions. In K. T. Strongman (Ed.), *International review of studies on emotion* (Vol. 1, pp. 187–225). New York: Wiley.

Garland, E. L., Fredrickson, B., Kring, A., Johnson, D. P., Meyer, P. S., & Penn, D. L. (2010). Upward spirals of positive emotions counter downwoard spirals of negativity: Insights from the Broaden-and-Build theory and affective neurosicnece on the treatment of emotion dysfunctions and deficits in psychopathology. *Clinical Psychology Review, 30*, 849–864. doi: 10.1016/j.cpr.2010.03.002

Gousse-Lessard, A-S., Vallerand, R. J., Carbonneau, N., & Lafrenière, M.-A. K. (2013). The Role of Passion in Mainstream and Radical Behaviors: A Look at Environmental Activism. *Journal of Environmental Psychology, 35*, 18–29.

Govindji, R., & Linley, P. A. (2007). Strengths use, self-concordance and well-being: Implications for strengths coaching and coaching psychologists. *International Coaching Psychology Review, 2*, 143–153.

Guay, F., Mageau, G., & Vallerand, R. J. (2003). On the hierarchical structure of self-determined motivation: A test of top-down and bottom-up effects. Personality and Social Psychology Bulletin, *29*, 992–1004.

Harter, J. K., Schmidt, F. L., & Hayes, T. L. (2002). Business-unit-level relationships between employee satisfaction, employee engagement, and business outcomes

A meta-analysis. *Journal of Applied Psychology, 87*, 268–279. doi: 10.1037/0021-9010.87.2.268

Hatfield, E., & Walster, G. W. (1978). *A new look at love.* Reading, MA: Addison-Wesley.

Ho, V. T., Wong, S.-S., & Lee, C. H. (2011). A tale of passion: Linking job passion and cognitive engagement to employee work performance. *Journal of Management Studies, 48*, 26–47. doi: 10.1111/j.1467-6486.2009.00878.x

Hodgins, H. S., & Knee, R. (2002). The integrating self and conscious experience. In Deci, E. L., & Ryan, R. M. (Eds.). (2002). *Handbook on self-determination research: Theoretical and applied issues* (pp. 87–100). Rochester, NY: University of Rochester Press.

Houlfort, N., Philippe, F., Vallerand, R. J., & Ménard, J. (2014). On passion as heavy work investment and its consequences. *Journal of Managerial Psychology, 29*(1), 25–45.

Houlfort, N., & Rinfret, N. (2010). Favoriser la satisfaction au travail des directeurs généraux du réseau de la santé et des services sociaux: Impact du style de leadership adopté et de la passion envers le travail. (To facilitate the work satisfaction of general managers of health and social services: The impact of leadership style and passion for work). In D. B. Raveleau, & F. B. Hassel (Eds). *Management humain des organisations: grandeurs et misères de la fonction de dirigeant (Human management in organizations: The ups and downs of the manager position).* Paris: Éditions L'Harmattan.

Houlfort, N., Vallerand, R. J., Lavigne, G. L., Koestner, R., Forest, J., Benabou, C., & Crevier-Braud, L. (2011). *On the role of passion for work in psychological well-being.* Manuscript submitted for publication.

Houlfort, N., & Vallerand, R. J. (2013). *Leadership and organizational culture as determinants of passion for work.* Manuscript submitted for publication.

Judge, T. A., & Piccolo, R. (2004). Transformational and transactional leadership: A meta-analytic test of their relative validity. *Journal of Applied Psychology, 89*, 755–768.

Kelman, H. C. (1968). *A time to speak: On human values and social research.* San Francisco, CA: Jossey-Bass.

Kernis, M. H. (2003). Toward a conceptualization of optimal self-esteem. *Psychological Inquiry, 14*, 1–26.

Koestner, R. & Losier, G. (2002). Distinguishing among three types of highly motivated individuals. In E. L. Deci, & R. M. Ryan (Eds.), *Handbook of self-determination research* (pp. 101–121). Rochester, NY: University of Rochester Press.

Lafrenière, M.-A., Jowett, S., Vallerand, R. J., Donahue, E. G., & Lorimer, R. (2008). Passion in sport: On the quality of the coach-player relationship. *Journal of Sport and Exercise Psychology, 30*, 541–560.

Lafrenière, M.-A. K., Bélanger, J. J., Sedikides, C., & Vallerand, R. J. (2011). Self-esteem and passion for activities. *Personality and Individual Differences, 51*, 541–544.

Lam, C. F., & Pertulla K. (2008). *Work is my passion: Toward a conceptualization of passion for one's work.* Paper presented at the annual meeting of the Academy of Management, Anaheim, CA.

Lavigne, G. L., Forest, J., & Crevier-Braud, L. (2012). Passion at work and burnout: A two-study test of the mediating role of flow experiences. *European Journal of Work and Organizational Psychology, 21*(4), 518–546.

Lee, S. K. J., Yu, K. (2004). Corporate culture and organizational performance. *Journal of managerial Psychology, 19*, 340–359. doi: 10.1108/02683940410537927

Linley, A. (2008). *Average to A+: Realizing Strengths in yourself and others.* Coventry: CAPP Press.

Liu, D., Chen, X.-P., Yao, X. (2011). From autonomy to creativity: A multilevel investigation of the mediating role of harmonious passion. *Journal of Applied Psychology*, *96*, 295–309. doi: 10.1037/a0021294

Mageau, G., Carpentier, J., & Vallerand, R. J. (2011). The role of self-esteem contingencies in the distinction between obsessive and harmonious passion. *European Journal of Social Psychology*, *51*, 541–544.

Mageau, G., & Vallerand, R. J. (2007). The moderating effect of passion on the relation between activity engagement and positive affect. *Motivation and Emotion*, *31*, 312–321. doi 10.1007/s11031-007-9071-z

Mageau, G. A., Vallerand, R. J., Charest, J., Salvy, S.-J., Lacaille, N., Bouffard. T., & Koestner, R. (2009). On the development of harmonious and obsessive passion: The role of autonomy support, activity valuation, and identity processes. *Journal of Personality*, *77*, 601–645. doi: 10.1111/j.1467-6494.2009.00559.x

Mageau, G. A., Vallerand, R. J., Rousseau, F. L, Ratelle, C. F., & Provencher, P. J. (2005). Passion and gambling: Investigating the divergent affective and cognitive consequences of gambling. *Journal of Applied Social Psychology*, *35*, 100–118. doi: 10.1111/j.1559-1816.2005.tb02095.x

Marsh, H. W., Vallerand, R. J., Lafrenière, M.-A. K., Parker, P., Morin, A. J. S., Carbonneau, N... Paquet, Y. (2013). Passion: Does one scale fit all? Construct validity of two-factor passion scale and psychometric invariance over different activities and languages. *Psychological Assessment*, *25*, 796–809.

Martins, E. C., & Terblanche, F. (2003). Building organizational culture that stimulates creativity and innovation. *European Journal of Innovation Management*, *6*, 64–74. doi: 10.1108/14601060310456337

Park, N., Peterson, C., & Seligman, M. E. P. (2004). Strengths of character and well-being. *Journal of Social and Clinical Psychology*, *23*, 603–619. doi: 10.1521/jscp.23.5.603.50748

Philippe, F. L., Vallerand, R. J., Houlfort, N., Lavigne, G. L., & Donahue, E. G. (2010). Passion for an activity and quality of interpersonal relationships: The mediating role of emotions. *Journal of Personality and Social Psychology*, *98*, 917–932. doi: 10.1037/a0018017

Philippe, F., Vallerand, R. J., Lavigne, G. (2009). Passion does make a difference in people's lives: A look at well-being in passionate and non-passionate individuals. *Applied Psychology: Health and Well-Being*, *1*, 3–22. doi: 10.1111/j.1758-0854.2008.01003.x

Rony, J.-A. (1990). *Les passions (The passions)*. Paris: Presses universitaires de France.

Rousseau, F. L., & Vallerand, R. J. (2003). Le rôle de la passion dans le bien-être subjectif des aînés [The role of passion in the subjective well-being of the elderly]. *Revue Québécoise de Psychologie*, *24*, 197–211.

Rousseau, F. L., & Vallerand, R. J. (2008). An examination of the relationship between passion and subjective well-being in older adults. *International Journal of Aging and Human Development*, *66*, 195–211.

Rousseau, F. L., Vallerand, R. J., Ratelle, C. F., Mageau, G. A., & Provencher, P. J. (2002). Passion and gambling: On the validation of the Gambling Passion Scale (GPS). *Journal of Gambling Studies*, *18*, 45–66.

Ryan, R. M., & Deci, E. L. (2003). On assimilating identities of the self: A Self-Determination Theory perspective on internalization and integrity within cultures. In M. R. Leary, & J. P. Tangney (Eds.), *Handbook of self and identity* (pp. 253–272). New York: Guilford.

Salovey, P., & Mayer, J. D. (1990). Emotional intelligence. *Imagination, Cognition and Personality*, *9*, 185–211.

Schein, E. H. (2009). *Organizational psychology (3rd edition)*. Englewood Cliffs, NJ: Prentice Hall.

Séguin-Lévesque, C., Laliberté, M.-L., Pelletier, L. G., Blanchard, C., & Vallerand, R. J. (2003). Harmonious and obsessive passion for the internet: Their associations with the couple's relationships. *Journal of Applied Social Psychology*, *33*, 197–221. doi: 10.1111/j.1559-1816.2003.tb02079.x

Seligman, M. E. P., Steen, T. A., Park, N., & Peterson, C. (2005). Positive psychology progress: Empirical validation of interventions. *American Psychologist*, *60*, 410–421. doi: 10.1037/0003-066X.60.5.410

Sheldon, K. M. (2002). The Self-Concordance Model of healthy goal-striving: When personal goals correctly represent the person. In E. L. Deci, & R. M. Ryan (Eds.), *Handbook of self-determination research* (pp. 65–86). Rochester, NY: The University of Rochester Press.

Stenseng, F. (2008). The two faces of leisure activity engagement: Harmonious and obsessive passion in relation to intrapersonal conflict and life domain outcomes. *Leisure Sciences*, *30*, 465–481. doi: 10.1080/01490400802353224

Tajfel, H., & Turner, J. C. (1986). The social identity theory of inter-group behavior. In S. Worchel, & L. W. Austin (Eds.), *Psychology of intergroup relations* (pp. 7–24). Chicago: Nelson-Hall.

Vallerand, R. J. (1997). Toward a hierarchical model of intrinsic and extrinsic motivation. *Advances in Experimental and Social Psychology*, *29*, 271–360.

Vallerand, R. J. (2008). On the psychology of passion: In search of what makes people's lives most worth living. *Canadian Psychology*, *49*, 1–13. doi: 10.1037/0708-5591.49.1.1

Vallerand, R. J. (2010). On passion for life activities: The dualistic model of passion. In M. P. Zanna (Ed.), *Advances in experimental social psychology* (Vol. 42, pp. 97–193). New York: Academic Press.

Vallerand, R. J. (2012). The role of passion in sustainable psychological well-being. *Psychological Well-Being: Theory, Research, and Practice*, *2*, 1–21.

Vallerand, R. J. (2014). *On contributing to society*. Manuscript in preparation.

Vallerand, R. J., Blanchard, C. M., Mageau, G. A., Koestner, R., Ratelle, C., Léonard, M., Gagné, M., & Marsolais, J. (2003). Les passions de l'âme: On obsessive and harmonious passion. *Journal of Personality and Social Psychology*, *85*, 756–767. doi: 10.1037/0022-3514.85.4.756

Vallerand, R. J., Fortier, M. S., Guay, F. (1997). Self-determination and persistence in a real-life setting: Toward a motivational model of high school dropout. *Journal of Personality and Social Psychology*, *72*, 1161–1176.

Vallerand, R. J., & Houlfort, N. (2003). Passion at work: Toward a new conceptualization. In S. W. Gilliland, D. D. Steiner, & D. P. Skarlicki (Eds.), *Emerging perspectives on values in organizations* (pp. 175–204). Greenwich, CT: Information Age Publishing.

Vallerand, R. J., Mageau, G. A., Elliot, A., Dumais, A., Demers, M.-A., & Rousseau, F. L. (2008). Passion and performance attainment in sport. *Psychology of Sport & Exercise*, *9*, 373–392. doi: 10.1016/j.psychsport.2007.05.003

Vallerand, R. J., Ntoumanis, N., Philippe, F., Lavigne, G. L., Carbonneau, C., Bonneville, A., Lagacé-Labonté, C., & Maliha, G. (2008). On passion and sports fans: A look at football. *Journal of Sport Sciences, 26,* 1279–1293. doi: 10.1080/02640410802123185

Vallerand, R. J., Paquet, Y., Philippe, F. L., & Charest, J. (2010). On the role of passion in burnout: A process model. *Journal of Personality, 78,* 289–312. doi: 10.1111/j.1467-6494.2009.00616.x

Vallerand, R. J., Rousseau, F. L., Grouzet, F. M. E., Dumais, A., & Grenier, S. (2006). Passion in sport: A look at determinants and affective experiences. *Journal of Sport & Exercise Psychology, 28,* 454–478.

Vallerand, R. J., Salvy, S.-J., Mageau, G. A., Elliot, A. J., Denis, P., Grouzet, F. M. E., & Blanchard, C. B. (2007). On the role of passion in performance. *Journal of Personality, 75,* 505–534. doi: 10.1111/j.1467-6494.2007.00447.x

Wang, G., Oh, I., Courtwright, S., & Colbert, A. (2011). Transformational leadership and performance across criteria and levels: A meta-analytic review of 25 years of research. *Group & Organization Management, 36,* 223–270. doi: 10.1177/1059601111401017

Waugh, C. E., & Fredrickson, B. L. (2006). Nice to know you: Positive emotions, self-other overlap, and complex understanding in the formation of new relationship. *Journal of Positive Psychology, 1,* 93–106.

PART 2

Individual Considerations

CHAPTER 7

The Foundation of Autonomous Motivation in the Workplace: An Attachment Perspective

Sigalit Ronen *and* Mario Mikulincer

Abstract

Drawing on attachment theory, we propose the constructs of *secure home base* and *secure work base* as two psychological mechanisms that shape autonomous motivation in the workplace. Secure home base is a sense of security that develops from satisfactory interactions with available, sensitive, responsive, and supportive close relationship partners. People with a secure home base feel they receive unconditional positive regard from their close relationship partners, and they can rely on them for support and protection while autonomously dealing with life challenges. Secure work base is a context-specific sense of security that develops from interactions with the organization or its members where employees feel that support is available when needed, that their capabilities and efforts are being affirmed and appreciated, and where their acts and initiatives are not being interfered with or interrupted. A secure home base promotes effective stress regulation and supports the development of an integrated goal system. A secure work base facilitates autonomous task engagement.

Key Words: secure home base, secure work base, motivation, attachment, attachment theory, self-determination theory

Introduction

In the last decade, evidence has accumulated that autonomous motivation is a powerful mode of motivation that is associated with a high level of individual performance (Koestner & Losier, 2002; Shirom et al., 1999). Self-determination theory (SDT; Deci & Ryan, 1980, 1985a, 2000; Ryan & Deci, 2000) has indicated that the degree to which people are proactive and autonomously motivated is largely a result of the sociopsychological conditions in which they grow and function. The theory, however, has paid limited attention to underlying psychological processes and mechanisms through which people become more (or less) autonomously motivated. Knowledge about these processes might be useful in attempting to understand the development of stable orientations toward initiation and regulation of behaviors (i.e., *general causality*

orientations). Furthermore, such knowledge may be used as a guiding tool for promoting autonomous motivation and for extenuating controlled behaviors at the workplace.

We draw on attachment theory (Bowlby, 1973, 1982), which was originally developed to explain how early relationships with parents establish a motivational mechanism through which people regulate their behaviors. We also draw on recent developments in adult attachment research (e.g., Feeney & Thrush, 2010), which elucidate the role that *secure base* plays in autonomous behavior (vis., explorative behavior). On this basis, we attempt to describe the attachment-related mechanisms that underlie the development of general causality orientations, and suggest ways by which this knowledge can be applied to support autonomous motivation in the work context. The goal of this chapter is twofold. First, we explain how a person's past and current experience in close relationships affects his or her orientation toward the initiation and regulation of behaviors; and second, we describe how social interactions at the workplace can facilitate employees' context-specific autonomous behavior.

In the following pages, we review the SDT and attachment literatures. First, we explain how autonomous or controlled orientations toward task engagement develop and are maintained. After presenting basic theoretical concepts that are relevant to our work, we discuss two major psychological mechanisms that can shape the development of general causality orientations and context-specific autonomous motivation, which we refer to as *secure home base* and *secure work base*, respectively.

Basic Concepts in Self Determination Theory and Research

SDT (Deci & Ryan, 1980, 1985a, 2000; Ryan & Deci, 2000) provides a normative and a descriptive perspective on the development of autonomous motivation and healthy functioning. In the following, we focus on both perspectives interchangeably and highlight SDT's emphasis on the role that need satisfaction plays in the development of autonomous motivation.

Autonomous and Controlled Motivation

SDT describes a motivational continuum that ranges from amotivation (lack of motivation) to intrinsic motivation (an entirely self-determined motivation), and focuses mainly on the distinction between autonomous motivation and controlled motivation (Deci & Ryan, 1985a). Controlled motivation refers to a sense of being compelled or forced to engage with an activity, without an inner sense of choice, and in order to achieve something that is not directly related to the activity itself. Autonomous motivation refers to acting volitionally and with a sense of choice and willingness. Intrinsic motivation, which refers to engaging with a task because it is enjoyable and interesting (a state that Albert Einstein called "the enjoyment of seeing and searching"), represents the highest level of autonomous motivation or self-determination. Recent studies have shown that autonomous motivation (either intrinsic or extrinsic) is associated with higher levels of performance than controlled motivation in various work tasks (e.g., Gagné & Deci, 2005).

Because the lion's share of most people's jobs is considered as not typically enjoyable or highly interesting, productive engagement with work tasks requires individuals to set in motion regulatory capacities, such as self-control, orderliness, perseverance in the face of difficulties, self-discipline, and restraint. Following this reasoning, Deci and Ryan (2000) suggested that people's work behavior is regulated by *internalization processes* that facilitate engagement with tasks that are not typically intrinsically motivating. These internalization processes, they argue, link between individuals' activities or behaviors and some vicarious consequences or rewards that result from these behaviors, and explain people's motivation to engage with their work activities. Such internalization processes can explain, for example, nurses' willingness to treat their patients, soldiers' motivation to serve their country, and athletes' drive to exert effort toward achievements.

Deci and Ryan (2000) identify four types of internalization processes that underlie four corresponding types of motivations (controlled motivation, moderately controlled motivation, moderately autonomous motivation, and autonomous motivation): (1) external regulation, (2) introjected regulation, (3) identified regulation, and (4) integrated regulation. External regulation refers to the process by which a person is motivated to behave in a certain way, because the behavior can potentially bring about desirable outcomes, such as tangible rewards, or prevent nondesired consequences, such as punishments. This regulation is prototypical of controlled motivation. Introjected regulation refers to an internalization process that is not entirely external to the person but the person does not accept the motivation to behave in a specific manner as part of his or her own identity. Contingent self-esteem and ego-involvement, which lead people to behave in order to feel worthy or to boost their frail egos, are examples of this regulation (DeCharms, 1968; Ryan, 1982). Introjected regulation is prototypical of moderately controlled motivation. Identified regulation underlies behavior that is more congruent with a person's inner goals and identity. This regulation is prototypical of moderately autonomous motivation, because the behavior reflects an aspect of a person's values and beliefs. Integrated regulation represents the fullest type of internalization, which renders motivation truly autonomous or volitional. An integrated behavior is perceived as an integral part of one's own self and thus as self-determined. However, integrated regulation does not necessarily underlie intrinsic motivation, because one might not find the activity enjoyable or highly interesting (Gagné & Deci, 2005).

Overall, Deci and Ryan (2000) suggest that while autonomous motivation that involves integration results from internalizing the significance and values that are associated with a behavior, controlled motivation is the outcome of more fragmented or imperfect internalization. According to Deci and Ryan (2000), being controlled refers to engaging with tasks or activities not because one has accepted their values as one's own but rather to gain desired external goals or outcomes, such as winning others' approval, boosting a sense of self-worth, or avoiding criticism, punishment, or other types of aversive states.

General Causality Orientations

Deci and Ryan (1985b) also describe individual differences in stable orientations toward the initiation and regulation of behaviors, which they call *general causality orientations.* These orientations are assumed to develop from social contexts that support or thwart a person's basic needs (Deci & Ryan, 2000). SDT describes three types of orientations: (1) autonomy, (2) control, and (3) impersonal orientations. The *autonomy orientation* refers to a general inclination toward internal regulation, such as identification and integration, and describes a tendency to approach activities with a sense of volition, freedom, and choice. The *control orientation* refers to a general inclination toward external regulation, such as introjection, and describes a tendency to approach activities with a sense of being coerced and pressured to act. Finally, the *impersonal orientation* refers to a general inclination toward experiencing lack of motivation. Studies had shown that the autonomous orientation is related to self-actualization, self-esteem, and satisfying interpersonal relationships. The control orientation was found to be associated with type-A behavior pattern; defensive functioning; and placing emphasis on extrinsic motivators, such as pay. Amotivation was found to be associated with depression and an external locus of control (Deci & Ryan, 1985b; Hodgins, Koestner, & Duncan, 1996; see Gagné & Deci, 2005, for a review).

Basic Psychological Needs

Beyond differentiating the content of people's desired outcomes and the regulatory processes by which these outcomes are pursued, SDT uses the concept of *basic psychological needs* to explain the conditions under which positive (and negative) psychological consequences, such as well-being and growth (or ill-being), accrue. Needs are defined

in the theory as "innate psychological nutriments that are essential for ongoing psychological growth, integrity, and well-being" (Deci & Ryan, 2000, p. 229), and it is suggested that healthy human development requires nutriments in the form of support from the social environment. Specifically, SDT focuses on three fundamental psychological needs of relatedness, competence, and autonomy, and argues that satisfaction of these needs is necessary for healthy functioning and personal growth.

Satisfying these needs in social contexts, according to the theory, is said to facilitate the internalization processes that are involved in the development of autonomous motivation (Deci & Ryan, 2000). In other words, SDT argues that to the extent that individuals receive support for experiencing a sense of relatedness, competence, and autonomy, they internalize the significance and values that are associated with their behaviors, and can then develop an autonomy orientation. Whereas substantial need support is required to promote internalization of the significance and values that are associated with behaviors, and thus to facilitate autonomous motivation, thwarted need support can impede the internalization process and lead to either controlled motivation or amotivation, depending on whether a partial or a total lack of internalization took place.

In sum, SDT postulates that need satisfaction facilitates internalization processes that build a stable autonomy orientation toward growth and well-being (Deci & Ryan, 2000). The theory, however, does not elaborate much on the mechanisms by which need satisfaction enhances internalization processes. Moreover, SDT does not relate to alternative or additive paths of influence that link need satisfaction with autonomous motivation. Finally, whereas SDT emphasizes the significance of need satisfaction to autonomous motivation, it does not explain how the nature of the social conditions within which needs are being satisfied or thwarted (e.g., quality of close relationships) affect a person's development and functioning.

To broaden current understanding of the ways by which need satisfaction contributes to healthy functioning and psychological growth, we build on attachment theory and relate to secure home base and secure work base as two main psychological mechanisms that can explain individual differences in both general autonomy orientations and autonomous behavior in the workplace. We first discuss the contribution of secure home base to the development of causality orientations, and highlight two main paths by which secure home base may affect motivation: promotion of effective stress regulation that enables better functioning of the exploration system, and development of an integrated goal system that facilitates the internalization of the significance and value of one's behavior. After discussing the contribution of secure home base to the development of causality orientations, we explain our notion of secure work base, how it is different from secure home base, and how it can facilitate autonomous task engagement in the workplace (Figure 7.1). Throughout this chapter, we develop propositions that can be used to guide future studies on the mechanisms that promote autonomous task engagement.

Attachment Theory and Research

Attachment theory (Bowlby, 1982, 1973) is a motivational theory that was originally formulated to explain how early relationships with parents shape children's regulation of their interpersonal behaviors and autonomous explorative endeavors. Being influenced by control systems theory, cognitive developmental theory, and ethology, Bowlby (1982) suggested that individuals' behavior at all ages is regulated by coordinated operations of a few goal-directed *behavioral systems*, such as the *attachment* and the *exploration systems*, that have evolved through evolution because they serve particular functions that are critical for survival and reproduction. The establishment of an inner sense of protection or security (phrased "felt security" by Sroufe & Waters, 1977) was viewed by Bowlby (1982) as the main goal of the attachment system, and he considered proximity maintenance to available, sensitive, responsive, and supportive parents or other relationship partners in times of need ("attachment figures") as the main avenue through which this goal is obtained. Bowlby (1973) further suggested that repeated and prolonged experiences of felt security within close relationships ("secure attachment") not only help sustain relationship quality and satisfaction, but also provide the psychological foundation for healthy functioning and psychological growth in all life domains. These ideas were supported in numerous studies indicating that a secure attachment orientation in close relationship is a strong predictor of a healthy approach to work and relationships, as well as of psychological well-being and mental health in adulthood (see Mikulincer and Shaver, 2007, for a review).

Secure attachment in close relationships, according to the theory, is developed when a caregiver or a relationship partner is reliably available, attentive, and supportive to one's cues of distress and one's needs for exploration, autonomy, and personal growth. Bowlby (1973) coined the terms *safe haven* and *secure base* to metaphorically describe two distinct types of support that promote secure attachment. Safe haven refers to the provision of support, comfort, and reassurance in stressful times with the

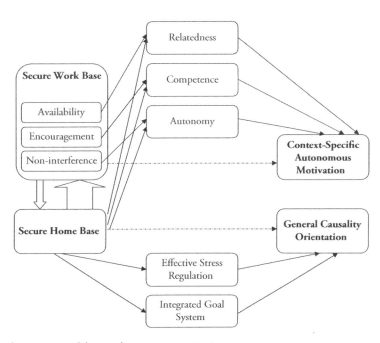

Fig. 7.1. Secure home base, secure work base, and autonomous motivation.

aim of soothing a person's fears, pain, and distress and assisting him or her in restoring emotional equanimity and returning to other activities in a relaxed manner. Secure base refers to the support of a person's goal striving, exploration, and personal growth, and the provision of a dependable base from which he or she can engage with nonattachment activities, take risks and challenges, and autonomously pursue his or her goals, while feeling confident that he or she can return to this base in times of need. In the words of Feeney and Thrush (2010), a safe haven functions to support a relationship partner coming into the relationship, whereas a secure base functions to support a relationship partner going out from the relationship. We mainly focus here on the secure base function of close relationships and the ways in which the provision of a secure base assists a relationship partner in developing his or her own personal identity, independence, and sense of autonomy outside the relationship, including in the workplace.

As mentioned, we focus on two distinct types of secure base provisions: secure home base and secure work base. We define secure home base as a general and relatively stable sense of security that develops from satisfactory interactions with available, sensitive, responsive, and supportive close relationship partners (e.g., parents, romantic partners, close friends, close family members, therapists). People with a secure home base feel that they receive unconditional positive regard from their close relationship partners, and that they can rely on them for support and protection while dealing autonomously with life challenges.

Next, we suggest two ways by which a secure home base can contribute to the development of autonomous orientation: by the facilitation of effective stress regulation, and by establishing a well-integrated goal system.

Secure Home Base and the Facilitation of Stress Regulation and Exploratory Activities

In this section we explain how secure home base can facilitate stress regulation and allow for a smoother operation of the exploration system that in turn increases autonomous work motivation. We then discuss the implications of such a process for people's ability to function in leadership roles in the workplace.

The ability to handle stress effectively is important for almost any type of activity with which a person engages. This idea has been supported in numerous studies indicating that stress can have detrimental effects on people's functioning, mainly when it is perceived as overwhelming and uncontrollable (Lazarus, 1993; Lazarus & Folkman, 1984). In fact, one of the problems with stress is that it narrows one's ability to think clearly and freely because under the effect of stress, the brain operates on a threat mode that gives precedence to "fight or flight" reactions rather than to mundane activities. Indeed, research has indicated that perceptions of stress harm the quality of the decisions people make (e.g., Keinan, 1987; Svenson & Maule, 1993), the ability to think perspicaciously on problems and to behave in an innovative and creative manner (e.g., Bunce & West, 1996).

Similar ideas are expressed in attachment theory, which describes how stress activates the attachment system and inhibits the operation of other behavioral systems that might hinder a person's survival chances under threat conditions. Relying on a biological survival perspective, Bowlby (1982) suggested that the attachment system protects infants from harm by assuring that they will seek proximity to caregivers who can provide them with protection and safety. Given the high importance of ensuring a person's safety in times of threat, proximity-seeking behaviors become highly activated under threatening conditions, and other behavioral systems, such as the exploration system, which drives people to learn about their environment and master it (Ainsworth, Blehar, Waters, & Wall, 1978; Bowlby, 1982), are inhibited until felt security is restored. Indeed, research has indicated that when people feel stressed, they tend to seek proximity to attachment figures, and these proximity-seeking behaviors persist until protection and security are attained (e.g., Ainsworth et al., 1978). Furthermore, there is evidence that when people are stressed and lack a sense of attachment security, both the quality and frequency of their explorative behaviors are reduced (e.g., Mikulincer, 1997). Thus, a sense of attachment security and consequent effective stress regulation seem essential for optimal functioning of the exploration system, which is responsible for goal striving and work behavior in adulthood (Hazan & Shaver, 1990).

Bowlby (1973) referred to *attachment working models* as the main mechanism through which interactions with attachment figures affect stress regulation. Working models are mental residues or representations of experiences with attachment figures, and they are said to have a strong influence on the way the attachment system functions. Working models that are based on relationships with parents and other close relationship partners tend to be chronically accessible in a person's mind; resistant to change; and affect the way the person views himself or herself, other people he or she engages with, and the world. Adults who, early on, had experienced their attachment figures as available, sensitive, responsive, and supportive (i.e., providing them with a secure home base) accumulate positive memories of themselves as valued and worthy of being cared for, and of others as reliable, warm, and dependable. The accumulation of episodic memories, where one's basic need for security has been fundamentally supported by close relationship partners, develops into neural molds that positively bias the way adults view themselves and others. That is, people with a history of positive interactions with available, sensitive, responsive, and supportive attachment figures tend to hold positive working models of themselves and others and to perceive themselves and others with whom they interact more favorably. Over time, people with chronic positive working models become securely attached and people with negative working models (that result from negative experiences with attachment figures) become insecurely attached.

Most of the research examining individual differences in attachment-system functioning in adults has focused on the systematic pattern of relational expectations, emotions, and behavior that results from one's attachment history, what Hazan and Shaver (1987) called *attachment style*. Research clearly indicates that attachment styles can be measured in terms of two independent dimensions: attachment-related anxiety and avoidance (Brennan, Clark, & Shaver, 1998). A person's position on the anxiety dimension indicates the degree to which he or she worries that a partner will not be available and responsive in times of need. A person's position on the avoidance dimension indicates the extent to which he or she distrusts relationship partners' goodwill and strives to maintain behavioral independence, self-reliance, and emotional distance. The two dimensions can be measured with reliable and valid self-report scales (e.g., Brennan et al., 1998), and they are associated in theoretically predictable ways with relationship quality and adjustment (see Mikulincer & Shaver, 2007, for an extensive review).

Mikulincer and Shaver (2007) proposed that a person's location on the two-dimensional conceptual space, defined by attachment anxiety and avoidance, reflects both the person's sense of attachment security and the ways in which he or she deals with threats and distress. People who score low on these dimensions are generally secure and tend to use constructive and effective affect-regulation strategies. Those who score high on either the attachment anxiety or the avoidance dimension (or both) suffer from insecurity and tend to rely on what Cassidy and Kobak (1988) called secondary attachment strategies, either deactivating or hyperactivating their attachment system to cope with threats.

According to Mikulincer and Shaver (2007), people scoring high on avoidant attachment tend to rely on deactivating strategies—trying not to seek proximity, denying attachment needs, and avoiding closeness and interdependence in relationships. These strategies develop in relationships with attachment figures who disapprove of, and punish, closeness and expressions of need or vulnerability (Ainsworth et al., 1978). In contrast, people scoring high on attachment anxiety tend to rely on hyperactivating strategies—energetic attempts to achieve proximity, support, and love, combined with lack of confidence that these resources will be provided and with resentment and anger when they are not provided (Cassidy & Kobak, 1988). These reactions occur in relationships in which an attachment figure is sometimes responsive but unreliably so, placing the needy person on a partial reinforcement schedule that rewards persistence in proximity-seeking attempts because they sometimes succeed (Ainsworth et al., 1978).

Because attachment styles reflect the most chronically accessible working models a person possesses, they indicate a person's typical functioning of the attachment system in times of stress. Recent studies have shown that securely attached individuals are more likely than insecure individuals (either anxious or avoidant) to regulate their stress by approaching relationship partners for support and by activating memories of interactions with supportive figures (e.g., Mikulincer, Florian, & Weller, 1993; Mikulincer & Shaver, 2004). These studies also show that, whereas secure people are able to use these proximity-seeking techniques quite effectively to regulate their negative emotions, insecure people cannot rely on either real or imagined proximity seeking to soothe themselves because their attachment history has left them with mental imprints that portray proximity seeking as either completely futile (in the case of avoidant people) or partially effective (in the case of anxiously attached people) in restoring emotional equanimity. Accordingly, adult attachment studies have shown that these problems in emotion regulation are directly manifested in a person's approach to exploration, and learning of new skills and perspectives, leading more insecure people to be less curious, less tolerant of ambiguity, and less open to new information, and more prone to rely on dogmatic and stereotypic thinking (e.g., Mikulincer, 1997; Mikulincer & Arad, 1999).

ATTACHMENT ANXIETY, EXPLORATION, AND AUTONOMOUS MOTIVATION

Anxiously attached people who tend to hyperactivate their attachment system are constantly preoccupied with attachment-related concerns (Shaver & Hazan, 1993). They feel that their basic relatedness needs are not being supported in close relationships, and they are highly sensitive to signals of social disapproval, criticism, or rejection (Ronen & Baldwin, 2010). This pattern of focusing attention on disruptive rather than on positive aspects of social experience takes its toll in drawing mental resources that could have otherwise been used for exploration, goal striving, and personal growth. In addition, anxious individuals' tendency to intensify distress and worries (Cassidy & Berlin, 1994) can interfere with and overwhelm the calm and steady state of mind necessary for open, curious exploration of novel stimuli and conditions. Moreover, their chronic sense of insecurity and their belief that forceful attempts to get attention and care from a nonresponsive partner may succeed not only in keeping anxiously attached people fixated on these attempts, but also in rendering nonattachment activities, such as exploration, as interfering with the pursuit of others' love (Mikulincer, 1997). A recent longitudinal study provides strong evidence of the harmful effect of focusing on, and worrying about, social rejection at the workplace among anxiously attached employees (Ronen & Baldwin, 2010). This study shows that hypersensitivity to social rejection leads anxiously attached people to experience more stress and burnout, even after controlling for initial levels of perceived stress and burnout.

We propose that, being preoccupied with attachment-related concerns, anxiously attached people tend to refrain from pursuing autonomous goals at the workplace. Their motivation is controlled by the desire to obtain other people's acceptance and protection, and by fear of being rejected, disapproved of, or criticized by others. Therefore, at work, their behavior tends to be driven more by attempts to please others and less by the need to pursue autonomous goals (Hazan & Shaver, 1990).

We further propose that, being controlled by fears of rejection and relational concerns, anxious people are less willing and less able to occupy leadership positions at the workplace. First, leadership roles entail being independent, exposed to criticism by others, and isolated from others—probably the most undesirable outcomes for anxiously attached individuals. Second, being controlled by relational concerns may make it hard for anxious people to become effective in leadership positions that require considerable amounts of stability, self-discipline, and restraint to carryout carefully planned organizational objectives. Indeed, anxious people's extreme sensitivity to social threats makes them more erratic and prone to mood swings that harm their ability to behave in an orderly and coherent manner. Third, anxious people's excessive preoccupation with their unlovability and lack of felt security makes it hard for them to adopt leadership styles that entail being sensitive to followers' needs and acting as mentors or coaches who listen to followers' concerns (i.e., transformational and charismatic leadership style; see Bass, 1985; Burns, 1978 for a review). Indeed, a recent study that examined the contribution of leaders' attachment styles to their motivation to lead found that anxiously attached leaders endorse self-enhancing motives as opposed to prosocial and task-oriented motives (Davidovitz, Mikulincer, Shaver, Ijzak, & Popper, 2007). That is, anxiously attached people's motivation to lead seems to be controlled by the desire to gain social approval and admiration from followers. Another indication to the ineffective leadership of anxiously attached people comes from a recent study that looked at the relationship between managers' attachment styles and subordinates' work outcomes in 85 work groups from a variety of job roles. Findings showed that attachment anxiety of managers predicted higher burnout and lower work engagement of their subordinates, and that the ineffective caring orientation of the managers mediated these links (Ronen & Mikulincer, 2011).

ATTACHMENT AVOIDANCE, EXPLORATION, AND AUTONOMOUS MOTIVATION

Avoidant people tend to deactivate their attachment system and stay away from situations that may require them to cope with stress. Due to their typical insecure home base where their proximity-seeking attempts have been consistently ignored or rejected, their attachment system is not geared for resolving stress effectively by using other people's support. Moreover, stressful situations may bring to the surface painful memories of being rejected on attempting to seek support from one's caregivers. As means of protecting themselves from re-experiencing such pain and anxiety, avoidant people adopt a compulsive self-reliance stance and they draw away from challenges and risks that may put their coping abilities into test (Mikulincer & Shaver, 2003). As a result, the activity of their exploration system is bounded to experiences that do not jeopardize their ostensibly cool state of mind and sense of mastery. We propose that, although avoidant people are more motivated to pursue autonomy as means of becoming less dependent on others and more self-reliant, their motivation is still likely to become controlled because autonomous motivation entails acting with a sense of freedom from contingencies, such as risk aversion and fear of closeness. In other words, we suggest that avoidant people's fear of being close to and dependent on others obstruct their motivation from becoming autonomous. This is reminiscent of recent research on the dependency paradox (Feeney, 2007) and of other research findings (e.g., Allen & Land, 1999; Moore, 1987; Noom, Dekovic, & Meeus, 1999) that show that independence is most easily established not at the expense of close relationships with attachment figures, but against a backdrop of secure relationships where people feel that they can depend on their attachment figures for care and support when needed.

We further propose that avoidant people are less likely to perform well in challenging work activities and especially in leadership roles that require, among other things, perseverance in face of difficulties. Indeed, recent findings show that avoidant individuals are less likely to endorse mastery goals due to their tendency to avoid the excitement and challenge of achievement activities (Elliot & Reis, 2003). In addition, avoidant people's motivation to lead others seems to be controlled by the desire to evade close relationships and to remain self-reliant. Recent research findings showed that more avoidant army leaders endorsed more self-reliance motives to lead and less prosocially oriented motives (Davidovitz et al., 2007). That is, they were less interested in leading as a way to promote followers' well-being and growth and more as a way to achieve a sense of self-control. That is, avoidant people who defensively distance themselves from involvement in interpersonal relationships are less likely to adopt leadership styles that emphasize empowering followers (e.g., transformational and charismatic leadership styles).

ATTACHMENT SECURITY, EXPLORATION, AND AUTONOMOUS MOTIVATION

Securely attached people, who owe their effective stress regulation abilities to their secure home base, enjoy a relatively steady sense of security that allows them to "make sorties into the outside world" (Bowlby, 1988, p. 11), being confident in their self-worth and abilities, and trusting that support will come their way whenever they would need it. Being treated by caregivers who had consistently supported their basic needs of relatedness, competence, and autonomy (by being unconditionally supportive, warm and available, encouraging, and noninterfering), secure people tend to be less preoccupied with concerns over their interpersonal relationships or over their abilities to cope with threats and challenges they may encounter at work. As a result, their prolific mental resources are readily available to be invested in challenging and interesting work activities. On this basis, we propose that securely attached individuals experience high levels of autonomous motivation when engaging with work tasks. That is, they report acting with a sense of free will when carrying out their job responsibilities and their functioning at work tends to suffer less from relational concerns. This proposition has received support in research findings indicating that, as compared to less secure individuals, secure individuals report higher levels of job satisfaction, less interpersonal problems inside or outside of the workplace, higher work-related self-efficacy, and more trust in peers and supervisors (e.g., Hazan & Shaver, 1990; Ronen & Mikulincer, 2009).

We further propose that securely attached people are more successful than insecure people in mastery positions that require a considerable amount of self confidence in one's abilities and trust in others to lead followers effectively in executing organizational goals. Moreover, we think that given their fully developed prosocial tendencies, securely attached people have better chances to become effective leaders in their organization. Indeed, a few studies have found important links between leaders' secure attachment and effective leadership (e.g., Mikulincer & Florian, 1995; Popper, Amit, Gal, Mishkal-Sinai, & Lisak, 2004; Popper, Mayseless, & Castelnovo, 2000).

In sum, secure home base facilitates stress regulation that deactivates the attachment system and allows for a smoother operation of the exploration system that can render people's work motivation more autonomous. In contrast, insecure home base introduces more stress into people's life. Being overwhelmed with fears of rejection or being intimidated by the anxiety and pain that such rejection may inflict, insecure individuals' attention and energy is directed at lowering their anxiety level. As a result, their motivation to explore the environment and to engage in challenging and interesting activities are controlled by such relational concerns and attempts to achieve solace rather than by the genuine interest and joy that is inherent in exploration, goal pursuit, and task engagement.

Secure Home Base and the Promotion of Internalization Processes

In our view, secure home base contributes to the development of an integrated goal system that facilitates internalization processes and the resulting autonomous motivation. SDT views internalization as the highway to autonomous motivation. The theory suggests that the more a behavior is integrated with or stems from inner values and personal goals that are coherent with one another, the more autonomous the motivation to enact the behavior will become (Deci & Ryan, 2000). For example, if Dan strongly believes in the importance and significance of helping others in need and if he sees himself as a caring and a sensitive person, showing care and concern for others will become a second nature to him because there is a considerable amount of fit between his authentic self and his behavior. Using SDT terminology, we would say that Dan's caring behavior is well integrated with other aspects of his identity (e.g., values, self views, and goals) that are coherent with one another. This type of regulation process (i.e., integrated regulation) reflects the highest level of internalization and it underlies autonomous motivation. Moreover, because the behavior stems from a person's inner self, it is expected to be more durable, less superficial, and more coordinated with external demands than a behavior that has its origin in outer contingencies. Using another example, if showing care and concern for others is not rooted in David's goal system, SDT would argue that David's caring behavior is externally regulated or that the motivation that underlies it is controlled by external contingencies, such as the need to create a good impression or the sense of having to display expected emotions (e.g., emotional labor that is typically experienced by service agents during service encounters).

As mentioned previously, SDT argues that need satisfaction facilitates internalization processes but it does not elaborate much on the process by which need satisfaction leads to internalization. For example, it is not very clear why supporting Dan's needs of relatedness, competence, and autonomy should make his caring behaviors more congruent with his inner goals and values, or how need support is said

to influence internalization processes in people with an incoherent or fragmented set of personal goals. Furthermore, SDT does not specify the type of relationship wherein need satisfaction should yield robust versus frail effects on internalization processes. Building on attachment theory, we propose that the provision of a secure home base in close relationships sets the foundation for building an integrated goal system. We propose that people with a secure home base, and especially with a history of attachment security in their close relationships, hold goals that are related to, and harmonious with, but yet distinct from, one another. Such a relatively consolidated but flexible goal structure facilitates the internalization processes that underlie autonomous motivation.

INDIVIDUAL DIFFERENCES IN GOAL-SYSTEM ORGANIZATION

Theory and research on personal goals have indicated that people are different in the way they organize their goals and in the extent to which their goals are coherent with one another (e.g., Cantor & Langston, 1989; Emmons, 1986, 1997). In his work on motives and goals, Emmons (1997) suggests that there are three dimensions along which people vary when organizing their strivings within a goal system. The first dimension, level of intergoal conflict, refers to the degree to which people believe that the pursuit or attainment of one goal interferes with the pursuit or attainment of another goal. The second dimension, goal differentiation, refers to the degree to which people perceive their goals as distinct, dissimilar, and unrelated to one another. The third dimension, goal integration, refers to the degree that people possess superordinate goal categories that connect different subordinate goals without eliminating their uniqueness and contradictions. Whereas highly integrated people possess sets of differentiated goals that are part of higher level goal categories, less integrated people have fragmented goal systems in which different goals are not coherently linked to an overarching, unifying goal or set of goals. Research findings indicate that a high degree of goal integration predicts higher commitment to, and success in, personal striving (Sheldon & Emmons, 1995), and that high levels of intergoal conflict hinder goal engagement and elicit negative affect (e.g., Emmons, 1986, 1992; Emmons & King, 1988).

Recently, Mikulincer and Shaver (2008) investigated how variations in attachment-system functioning affect the way people construe and organize their personal strivings. They suggested that anxious people, who rely on hyperactivating strategies, may perceive more conflict between goals (especially between the goal of achieving others' love and other nonattachment goals), which may interfere with the formation of an integrated and coherent goal system. They further suggested that avoidant people's deactivating strategies that promote segregation of attachment-related goals from other kinds of goals in their goal system can also interfere with the formation of an integrated and coherent superordinate system. Indeed, their research findings showed that attachment anxiety and avoidance were associated with lower ratings of goal integration and failure to integrate goals into superordinate meaning structures. Attachment anxiety was further associated with higher ratings of intergoal conflict and lower ratings of success in goal pursuit (Mikulincer & Shaver, 2008).

In sum, secure home base seems to contribute to the development of an integrated goal system that can facilitate internalization processes and the resulting autonomous motivation. Internalization is most easily established against a backdrop of an integrated goal system where new goals can be assimilated into a solid set of coherent personal goals and values. On this basis, we suggest that the provision of secure home base can be viewed as one explanatory mechanism by which need support in close relationships contributes to integrated internalization and autonomous motivation.

Secure Work Base

In this chapter we present secure home base and secure work base as two different sources of felt security that are important for the development and maintenance of autonomous motivation in the workplace. Whereas secure home base refers to a general and relatively stable sense of security, secure work base is regarded as a context-based sense of security that promotes employees' confidence in themselves as valuable, competent, and autonomous members of a working group.

We define secure work base as a sense of security that develops from daily interactions with the organization or any of its members, where employees feel that support is available when needed, that their capabilities and efforts are being affirmed and appreciated, and where their acts and initiatives are not being interfered with or interrupted. This definition is based on Feeney and Thrush's (2010) view of secure base provision as involving three

elements: (1) being available to fulfill a person's need in comfort and assistance, (2) encouraging a person to pursue his or her personal goals, and (3) not interfering with a person's initiatives and activities. Recently, Ronen and Lane (manuscript in preparation) developed and validated a secure work base measure that includes three subscales: (1) availability, (2) encouragement, and (3) reduced interference. Sample items include: "At work, I am usually willing to take risks and try new things because I know that others will be available to help and comfort me if things don't turn out well" (availability); "At work, others are complimenting my efforts" (encouragement); "At work, others are too dominating in their support attempts" (reduced interference—reversed item).

Interestingly, these three secure work base elements seem to match the three basic psychological needs identified by Deci and Ryan (1985a). To wit, whereas availability mainly supports the need for relatedness, encouragement mainly supports the need for competence, and noninterference mainly supports the need for autonomy. On this basis, we argue that secure work base can support a person's basic needs and thus promote autonomous motivation in the context of the workplace.

RELATEDNESS SUPPORT IN THE WORKPLACE

Attachment theory does not explicitly discuss relatedness as a major human need. Nevertheless, it argues that proximity seeking and proximity maintenance are essential for healthy psychological development and autonomous functioning (Ainsworth et al., 1978; Bowlby, 1988). Indeed, extensive findings have pointed to the negative consequences of not being able to establish close connections with others (e.g., DeWall, Baumeister, & Vohs, 2008). These theoretical assertions and empirical evidence are consistent with SDT's notion of relatedness support as an essential nutriment for people's well-being and growth.

According to attachment theory, being available to respond to a relationship partner's proximity bids in times of need is an important predictor of exploratory behavior (Bowlby, 1988). Availability of a caregiver or a close relationship partner is one of the main sources of people's "felt security," which allows them to explore most effectively and peacefully (Ainsworth et al., 1978; Bowlby, 1988). That is, when people are confident that a relationship partner is available to comfort and assist them should things go wrong, it is much easier for them to get involved in explorative activities away from their relationship partners, and to accept challenges, take risks, and try new things (Mikulincer & Shaver, 2007). Indeed, the few studies that have looked at the outcomes of a relationships partner's availability during exploration have shown that it is a good predictor of the other partner's autonomous functioning. For example, Ryan, Stiller, and Lynch (1994) assessed perceived availability of parents and teachers among middle-school children and found that children who perceived parents and teachers as more available in times of need felt better about themselves, coped more positively with instances of academic failures, were more autonomous in regulating their behaviors at school, and were more engaged with their learning activities. Other studies indicated that children who experienced their teachers as warm and caring showed greater intrinsic motivation (Ryan & Grolnick, 1986; Ryan et al., 1994). In addition, Feeney and Thrush (2010) found that when partners were more available to each other during an exploration activity, they persevered longer at the activity and were less stressed or anxious. These results are consistent with previous findings showing that the ability to depend on a relationship partner in times of need allows people to function more autonomously (Feeney, 2007).

These studies looked at how a relationship partner's availability supports people's exploratory behavior by making them feel more related to and supported by the partner. SDT does not specifically state which work environment features or events may be associated with a sense of relatedness among employees. However, clues are available from existing research on that subject. For example, a study that looked at how participation in daily activities at the workplace promotes individuals' sense of relatedness showed that performing a meaningful talk with an interaction partner, feeling understood and appreciated by him or her, and participating in shared and enjoyable activities, contribute to a sense of relatedness and elevated well-being (e.g., Reis, Sheldon, Gable, Roscoe, & Ryan, 2000). Other studies have explored the effects of a number of social-contextual factors on relatedness support, mainly among athletes and students, and found that support exhibited by coaches and teachers had a significant effect on need support (e.g., Hagger & Chatzisarantis, 2007).

These preliminary findings lead us to think that three factors may be relevant to relatedness satisfaction in the workplace: (1) group cohesion, (2) leader-member exchange (LMX), and (3) supervisors' prosocial behavior. These factors represent different sources of support where availability to respond to one's peers' or subordinates' needs is a key to the relationship and to work engagement.

From each group member's perspective, appraisal of work group cohesion refers to a person's evaluation of the level of care, cooperation, and support he or she feels in his or her group (Hogg, 1992; Levine & Moreland, 1990). From a group perspective, group cohesion reflects the tendency of a group to stick together and remain united in the pursuit of the group's goals (Carron & Brawley, 2000). Because the need for relatedness is fulfilled by feeling that one is close and connected to others (Deci & Ryan, 1985a), it makes sense that the more the group is cohesive, the more a person feels related to his or her peers and feel more confident that they will provide him or her with instrumental or emotional support when needed. Indeed, Rom and Mikulincer (2003) found that more cohesive groups facilitated the formation of a more secure attachment to the group and buffered the detrimental effects of a group member's attachment anxiety on his or her task performance within the group. On this basis, we propose that group cohesion can contribute to group members' sense of secure work base and satisfy their need for relatedness, which, in turn, enhances their autonomous motivation.

Another variable that may explain individual differences in relatedness satisfaction at the workplace is the prosocial behavior exhibited by managers and supervisors in the organization. Descriptions of leaders in the literature suggest that effective leadership behavior depends fundamentally on leaders' relational competencies or social capabilities. These capabilities entail guiding and supporting followers, attending to followers' needs, acting as mentors or coaches, and listening to followers' concerns (e.g., House & Howell, 1992; Mumford, Zaccaro, Harding, Jacobs, & Fleishman, 2000; Shamir, House, & Arthur, 1993). Recent adult attachment studies have shown that managers' ineffective provision of care, comfort, and support to subordinates predicts job burnout and job dissatisfaction among them (Ronen & Mikulincer, 2011), and that it harms subordinates' socioemotional functioning and mental health (Davidovitz et al., 2007). On this basis, we propose that leaders' prosocial behavior contributes to subordinates' sense of secure work base and supports their need for relatedness, which, in turn, enhances their autonomous motivation at the workplace.

Another stream of research that may be relevant is LMX, which shows that the quality of exchange relationship and trust that develops between employees and supervisors greatly affects followers' behavior and attitudes (Gerstner & Day, 1997). Followers who have high LMX relationships were shown to engage in citizenship behavior (e.g., Deluga, 1994), report higher levels of affective commitment (e.g., Liden, Wayne, & Sparrowe, 2000), higher levels of performance and job satisfaction, and less absenteeism and turnover (e.g., Cogliser, Schriesheim, Scandura, & Gardner, 2009). These positive effects are often attributed to the emotional attachment that followers develop toward the supervisors with whom they have high exchange relationships (e.g., Klein, Becker, & Meyer, 2009). On this basis we propose that high LMX relationships support followers' relatedness needs, which then enhance autonomous motivation.

COMPETENCE SUPPORT IN THE WORKPLACE

The need for competence fits the description of effectance motivation, a term that was coined by White (1959) to describe people's basic motivation to be effective and competent in their social environment. Effectance motivation entails a desire for understanding and mastering one's surrounding, which causes people to experience pleasure by being effective. This energizing force, which is prototypically manifested in intrinsically motivated activity, is believed to be one of the sources of healthy human development (White, 1959). According to SDT, the need for competence is fulfilled by the experience that one can effectively bring about desired effects and outcomes (Deci & Moller, 2005; Deci & Ryan, 2000).

The ways by which the need for competence is supported in the workplace have not been well studied. However, there is some knowledge on the conditions that support or thwart competence in other social contexts. For example, Danner and Lonky (1981) showed that optimal challenges within a classroom contribute to a child's sense of competence. Optimally challenging activities, Deci (1975) argues, provide people the opportunity to experience a sense of competence by overcoming the challenges. Other studies have found that positive feedback has a similar effect on perceived competence. For example, a laboratory experiment indicated that the provision of positive feedback on performance at a puzzle-solving activity (as compared with no feedback) led students to heighten their subsequent engagement with the activity (Deci, 1971). In addition, Vallerand and Reid (1984) found that felt competence mediated the

effects of positive feedback on intrinsic motivation. These effects of positive feedback seem to be maximized when it contains information about how to perform a task autonomously (e.g., Deci, 1975; Ryan, 1982). In contrast, negative feedback, particularly if it is critical and evaluative or administered in a controlling manner, tends to diminish perceived competence (e.g., Deci, Ryan, & Williams, 1996).

According to Feeney and Thrush (2010), relationship partners' encouragement and acceptance of a person's exploration and autonomy needs is an important component of secure base support and it motivates people to take on challenges, pursue personal goals, and learn and discover new skills and perspectives. Feeney and Thrush (2010) suggest that encouragement is expected to facilitate exploration and make it pleasurable because it conveys a positive message of excitement regarding exploration and also because it conveys confidence in the performer's abilities to explore effectively. In their study with married couples, they found that when spouses exhibited encouragement during an exploration activity, their partners performed better and expressed greater enthusiasm while exploring. Moreover, after the activity, their mood was more positive, they felt more knowledgeable and smart, and perceived their spouses as being more helpful and supportive. The authors suggested that encouragement was the only component of secure base support, among the three they explored, that served an important emotional, and hence motivating, function. They concluded that encouragement plays a key role in making people feel more competent at, and positive about, what they do.

It seems that optimal challenges, positive feedback, and relationship partners' encouragement support peoples' need for competence. Because there has been no research on the conditions that support competence in the workplace, more detailed empirical examination of these issues seems warranted. Deci and Ryan (2000) contend that "competence motivation is not a content-specific mechanism, but rather is a relatively nonspecific tendency of humans, for whom a curious, assimilative nature is a defining feature" (p. 253). Although we tend to agree with that, we also think that competence motivation can be contextually enhanced. Based on our review, we propose that encouragement can be viewed as a component of secure work base and can include, among other things, the administration of optimal challenges and the provision of positive feedback to employees, and messages that convey confidence in their ability to deal effectively with work tasks and challenges.

AUTONOMY SUPPORT IN THE WORKPLACE

Feeney and Thrush (2010) identified noninterference as another important component of secure base provision. They suggest that interfering with a partner's explorative endeavors is antithetical to sensitive and responsive support provision. Moreover, interfering may be perceived by the explorer as a sign that he or she is not qualified or capable of engaging in independent acts, and that he or she cannot be trusted to carry out explorative tasks successfully. This may undermine the explorer's self-confidence, which may in turn hinder his or her performance. Moreover, the person may develop negative attitudes toward exploration and the interest and joy that is typically inherent in the exploration process may be blocked.

Interference can thwart people's need for autonomy, because it interrupts the natural flow of activities that are authentically endorsed by them. In other words, interference may thwart people's need for autonomy because it deprives them from determining how to do things and how much effort to exert to accomplish their tasks. Such an obstruction can be costly for both their motivation and performance. Indeed, research on autonomy support in schools has shown that teachers' controlling approach and interference with students' learning has detrimental effect on students' competence, motivation, and self-esteem (e.g., Chirkov & Ryan, 2001; Vansteenkiste, Simons, Soenens, & Lens, 2004). For example, Deci et al. (1981) found that autonomy-supportive teachers who adopted a noninterfering and noncontrolling approach to teaching (by promoting students' initiatives and allowing students to learn from their own experiences, rather than by relying on teacher's instructions) had more intrinsically motivated students who felt more competent at schoolwork and showed more autonomy, curiosity, and preference for a challenging learning environment. Similar findings were obtained in studies that examined the relationship between parents' autonomy-supportive behaviors and children's motivation, psychological health, learning attitudes, and school performance (e.g., Grolnick & Ryan, 1989; Williams, Cox, Hedberg, & Deci, 2000). A similar pattern of finding was detected in studies that examined the importance of autonomy support in other kinds of relationships. For example, autonomy support provided by physicians has been found to positively affect patients' motivation to adopt a healthier lifestyle (e.g., Williams, Grow, Freedman, Ryan, & Deci, 1996; Williams et al., 2006; Williams, Rodin, Ryan, Grolnick, & Deci, 1998). In addition, coaches' autonomy support was found to promote athletes' autonomous motivation to engage in sport activities (e.g., Hagger, Chatzisarantis, Culverhouse, & Biddle, 2003; Pelletier, Fortier, Vallerand, & Brie`re, 2001). Close relationship partners' autonomy support was also found to increase the relationship quality and the general well-being of their spouses (e.g., Blais, Sabourin, Boucher, & Vallerand, 1990; Patrick, Knee, Canevello, & Lonsary, 2007). Moreover, managers' autonomy support was found to predict employees' satisfaction with the job and with various aspects of the work setting (Deci et al., 1989), and to contribute to work engagement, subjective well-being, and task performance among employees (Baard, Deci, & Ryan, 2004).

In many of these studies, a person or an environment are considered less autonomy supportive or more controlling if they (1) do not allow enough choice about behavioral enactments, (2) do not provide a meaningful rationale for doing a task, and (3) do not acknowledge that people might not find activities interesting or enjoyable. To our knowledge, no research has examined the extent to which intrusive and interfering behavior impairs autonomy support and autonomous motivation at the workplace. Although not allowing enough choice may have common qualities with interfering behavior, these two concepts are by no means synonymous. It is possible that a context or a person will not allow much choice but will not interfere with another person's activities. Moreover, a context or a person may allow more choice but may also interfere with a person's activities. In addition, in many work contexts, where the choice offered to employees is limited, interfering behaviors can have more pervasive effects on employees' motivation and functioning than merely having less choice.

In two studies, Feeney (2004) and Feeney and Thrush (2010) have shown the negative effects intrusive behavior can have on a relationship partner's exploration. Feeney (2004) showed that more intrusive partner's behavior during a couple's goal-related discussion led to less individualized thinking, and that this behavior was perceived by partners more negatively. Moreover, partners' negative views of interfering behavior predicted a decrease in their self-esteem and positive mood after an exploration activity (Feeney, 2004). Recently, Feeney and Thrush (2010) found that spouses' interferences during the exploration activity of their partner had a negative effect on their partner's performance, persistence at the activity, enthusiasm for the activity, and attitudes toward the spouse. Additionally, after the activity, the partner experienced a decrease in self-esteem and perceived his or her spouse as being less helpful and less supportive (Feeney & Thrush, 2010). To the best of our knowledge, with the exception of these two studies, no research heretofore had examined the effects of intrusive, interfering behavior on exploration in adulthood. Although these two studies examined these effects among married couples, we believe that the findings can be generalized to other types of relationships and settings, including those in the workplace.

Interfering behavior, based on the items Feeney and Thrush (2010) used to assess this variable, refers to interference with a relationship partner's activities (when he or she is exploring or performing a challenging activity or task), trying to get involved and do the task for the partner, or interfering with the partner's ability to accomplish his or her personal goals. We suggest that such interfering behaviors in the workplace might undermine a person's sense of secure work base and thwart his or her need for autonomy as well as his or her autonomous motivation.

Future Directions

One question that could be raised regarding the constructs of secure work base and secure home base concerns the interactive effect of secure home base and secure work base on work motivation. We believe that attachment security (that is associated with secure home base) influences not only stable orientations toward initiation and regulation of behaviors (i.e., general causality orientations), but also the ability to satisfy the needs for relatedness, competence, and autonomy in the work context. For example, it is more likely that secure individuals (high secure home base) will benefit more from their managers' prosocial behavior (high secure work base) and would become more autonomously motivated as a result, compared with insecure individuals (low secure home base) who lack important emotional resources and social skills. Secure work base can therefore play the role of a moderator and a mediator in the relationship between secure home base and motivation. That is, the positive relationship between secure home base and autonomous motivation can become stronger in situations where people perceive higher levels of secure work base. Additionally, the perception and experience of higher levels of secure work base depend not only on contextual factors, but also on the level of attachment security a person possesses. In a related manner, it would be interesting to know who benefits more from higher levels of secure work base—secure employees, who tend to be less stressed out and who are also more confident and satisfied, or insecure employees, who have difficulties trusting others but who also crave more needed support.

Another interesting topic for future research is the prediction of different work outcomes based on the interaction between high or low secure work base and secure home base. It seems likely that high levels of job performance and job satisfaction can be observed in work contexts that are higher in secure work base and where the employees are more securely attached. In contrast, work contexts that are characterized by low levels of secure work base might lead to higher turnover rates, and the combination of lower secure work base and lower secure home base might predict low performance and more exploitation of employees.

Finally, it will be interesting to know whether a strong and stable sense of higher or lower secure work base can affect people's attachment styles over time. In light of the predictions presented in this chapter, these and other models need to be tested.

Practical Implications

This chapter views work motivation as being affected by both dispositional attachment security (secure home base) and by contextual factors at the workplace that support people's basic needs (secure work base). Although turning insecure people into securely attached people is beyond the ability and the scope of work organizations, designing the work context to address important employee needs should be an important task of every organization. We suggest that relatedness, competence, and autonomy are three important needs that can be supported in the workplace and that enhance employees' autonomous motivation. We also explain how each of these needs can be fulfilled in the work context. Based on a review of the literature, we conclude that group cohesion, LMX, and supervisors' prosocial behavior are relevant to relatedness satisfaction in the workplace; that optimal challenges, positive feedback, and encouragement can help support people's need for competence; and that noninterfering behaviors can contribute to people's sense of autonomy in the work context. We believe that each of these factors can affect autonomous motivation and job performance. However, although we provided theoretical and empirical rationales to support our predictions, it is important that future research examines and confirms these and other predictions before any practical application is to take place.

Summary and Concluding Remarks

In this chapter, we have drawn on attachment theory to describe and illustrate two psychological mechanisms that may shape the development of a person's general causality orientations and context-specific autonomous motivation: secure home base and secure work base. We define secure home base as a sense of security that develops from satisfactory interactions with available, sensitive, responsive, and supportive close relationship partners (e.g., parents, romantic partners, close friends, close family members, therapists), and explain that people with secure home base believe that they receive unconditional positive regard from their close relationship partners, and can rely on them for support and protection while autonomously dealing with life challenges. We define secure work base as a context-specific sense of security that develops from interactions with the organization, or any of its members, where employees believe that support is available when needed, that their capabilities and efforts are being affirmed and appreciated, and where their acts and initiatives are not being interfered with or interrupted.

We suggest that secure home base affects motivation by promoting effective stress regulation and the smooth functioning of the exploration system, which, in turn, contributes to autonomous behavior in adulthood. We further suggest that secure home base contributes to autonomous motivation through the development of an integrated goal system that facilitates integration of behavior with one's values and identity. We discuss ways in which secure work base may facilitate autonomous task engagement in the workplace. Specifically, we identify group cohesion, LMX, and supervisors' prosocial behavior as relevant factors to relatedness satisfaction in the workplace; optimal challenges, positive feedback, and encouragement as supporting people's need for competence; and noninterfering behaviors as contributing to people's sense of autonomy in the work context.

This application of attachment theory to the motivation field encourages us to think that the psychosocial conditions within which people develop and operate have a fundamental effect on their motivation and performance. Whereas nurturing conditions facilitate the development of autonomous motivation and yield behaviors that are more self-determined, conditions of insecurity impede people's healthy development and force the use of defenses that render their behaviors more controlled by external contingencies.

It is hoped that the ideas and findings presented in this chapter stimulate scholars to apply Bowlby's attachment theory to the study of human motivation. Throughout this review, we have developed propositions that can be used to guide future studies on the mechanisms that promote autonomous task engagement. We believe that exploring these propositions would yield a much broader conception of autonomous motivation in the workplace.

References

Ainsworth, M. D. S., Blehar, M. C., Waters, E., & Wall, S. (1978). *Patterns of attachment: Assessed in the strange situation and at home*. Hillsdale, NJ: Erlbaum.

Allen, J. P., & Land, D. (1999). Attachment in adolescence. In J. Cassidy, & P. R. Shaver (Eds.), *Handbook of attachment: Theory, research, and clinical applications* (pp. 319–335). New York: Guilford Press.

Baard, P. P., Deci, E. L., Ryan, R. M. (2004). Intrinsic need satisfaction: A motivational basis of performance and well-being in two work settings. *Journal of Applied Social Psychology, 34,* 2045–2068.

Bass, B. M. (1985). *Leadership and performance beyond expectations*. New York: Free Press.

Blais, M. R., Sabourin, S., Boucher, C., & Vallerand, R. (1990). Toward a motivational model of couple happiness. *Journal of Personality and Social Psychology, 59,* 1021–1031.

Bowlby, J. (1973). *Attachment and loss: Separation, anxiety and anger*. New York: Basic Books.

Bowlby, J. (1982). *Attachment and loss: Vol. 1. Attachment (2nd ed.)*. New York: Basic Books. (Original ed. 1969)

Bowlby, J. (1988). *A secure base: Clinical applications of attachment theory*. London: Routledge.

Brennan, K. A., Clark, C. L., & Shaver, P. R. (1998). Self-report measurement of adult attachment: An integrative overview. In J. A. Simpson, & W. S. Rholes (Eds.), *Attachment theory and close relationships* (pp. 46–76). New York: Guilford Press.

Bunce, D., & West, M. A. (1996). Stress management and innovation at work. *Human Relations, 49,* 219–232.

Burns, J. M. (1978). *Leadership*. New York: Harper & Row.

Cantor, N., & Langston, C. A. (1989). Ups and downs of life tasks in a life transition. In L. A. Pervin (Ed.), *Goal concepts in personality and social psychology* (pp. 87–126). Hillsdale, NJ: Erlbaum.

Carron, A. V., & Brawley, L. R. (2000). Cohesion: Conceptual and measurement issues. *Small Group Research, 31,* 89–106.

Cassidy, J., & Berlin, L. J. (1994). The insecure/ambivalent pattern of attachment: Theory and research. *Child Development, 65,* 971–991.

Cassidy, J., & Kobak, R. R. (1988). Avoidance and its relation to other defensive processes. In J. Belsky, & T. Nezworski (Eds.), *Clinical implications of attachment* (pp. 300–323). Hillsdale, NJ: Erlbaum.

Chirkov, V. I., & Ryan, R. M. (2001). Parent and teacher autonomy-support in Russian and U.S. adolescents:

Common effects on well-being and academic motivation. *Journal of Cross Cultural Psychology, 32,* 618–635.

Cogliser, C. C., Schriesheim, C. A., Scandura, T. A., & Gardner, W. L. (2009). Balance in leader and follower perceptions of leader-member exchange: Relationships with performance and work attitudes. *The Leadership Quarterly, 20,* 452–465.

Danner, F. W., & Lonky. E. (1981). A cognitive-developmental approach to the effects of rewards on intrinsic motivation. *Child Development, 52,* 1043–1052.

Davidovitz, R., Mikulincer, M., Shaver, P. R., Ijzak, R., & Popper, M. (2007). Leaders as attachment figures: Their attachment orientations predict leadership-related mental representations and followers' performance and mental health. *Journal of Personality and Social Psychology, 93,* 632–650.

deCharms, R. (1968). *Personal causation: The internal affective determinants of behavior.* New York: Academic Press.

Deci, E. L. (1971). Effects of externally mediated rewards on intrinsic motivation. *Journal of Personality and Social Psychology, 18,* 105–115.

Deci, E. L. (1975). *Intrinsic motivation.* New York: Plenum.

Deci, E. L., Betley, G., Kahle, J., Abrams, L., & Porac, J. (1981). When trying to win: Competition and intrinsic motivation. *Personality and Social Psychology Bulletin, 7,* 79–83.

Deci, E. L., Connell, J. P., & Ryan, R. M. (1989). Self-determination in a work organization. *Journal of Applied Psychology, 74,* 580–590.

Deci, E. L., & Moller, A. C. (2005). The concept of competence: A starting place for understanding intrinsic motivation and self determined extrinsic motivation. In A. J. Elliot, & C. S. Dweck (Eds.), *Handbook of competence and motivation* (pp. 579–597). New York: Guilford.

Deci, E. L., & Ryan, R. M. (1980). The empirical exploration of intrinsic motivational processes. In L. Berkowitz (Ed.), *Advances in experimental social psychology* (Vol. 13, pp. 39–80). New York: Academic Press.

Deci, E. L., & Ryan, R. M. (1985a). *Intrinsic motivation and self determination in human behavior.* New York: Plenum.

Deci, E. L., & Ryan, R. M. (1985b). The general causality orientations scale: Self-determination in personality. *Journal of Research in Personality, 19,* 109–134.

Deci, E. L., & Ryan, R. M. (2000). The "what" and "why" of goal pursuits: Human needs and the self-determination of behavior. *Psychological Inquiry, 11,* 227–268.

Deci, E. L., Ryan, R. M., & Williams, G. C. (1996). Need satisfaction and the self-regulation of learning. *Learning and Individual Differences, 8,* 165–183.

Deluga, R. J. (1994). Supervisor trust building, leader-member exchange and organizational citizenship behavior. *Journal of Occupational and Organizational Psychology, 67,* 315–326.

DeWall, C. N., Baumeister, R. F., & Vohs, K. D. (2008). Satiated with belongingness? Effects of acceptance, rejection, and task framing on self-regulatory performance. *Journal of Personality and Social Psychology, 95,* 1367–1382.

Elliot, A. J., & Reis, H. T. (2003). Attachment and exploration in adulthood. *Journal of Personality and Social Psychology, 85,* 317–331.

Emmons, R. A. (1986). Personal strivings: An approach to personality and subjective well-being. *Journal of Personality and Social Psychology, 51,* 1058–1068.

Emmons, R. A. (1992). Abstract versus concrete goals: Personal striving level, physical illness, and psychological well-being. *Journal of Personality and Social Psychology, 62,* 292–300.

Emmons, R. A. (1997). Motives and goals. In R. Hogan, J. Johnson, & S. Briggs (Eds.), *Handbook of personality psychology* (pp. 485–512). New York: Academic Press.

Emmons, R. A., & King, L. (1988). Conflict among personal strivings: Immediate and long-term implications for psychological and physical well-being. *Journal of Personality and Social Psychology, 54,* 1040–1048.

Feeney, B. C. (2004). A secure base: Responsive support of goal strivings and exploration in adult intimate relationships. *Journal of Personality and Social Psychology, 87,* 631–648.

Feeney, B. C. (2007). The dependency paradox in close relationships: Accepting dependence promotes independence. *Journal of Personality and Social Psychology, 92,* 268–285.

Feeney, B. C., & Thrush, R. L. (2010). Relationship influences on exploration in adulthood: The characteristics and functions of a secure base. *Journal of Personality and Social Psychology, 98,* 57–76.

Gagné, M., & Deci, E. L. (2005). Self-determination theory and work motivation. *Journal of Organizational Behavior, 26,* 331–362.

Gerstner, C. R., & Day, D. V. (1997). Meta-analytic review of leader-member exchange theory: Correlates and construct issues. *Journal of Applied Psychology, 82,* 827–844.

Grolnick, W. S., & Ryan, R. M. (1989). Parent styles associated with children's self-regulation and competence in school. *Journal of Educational Psychology, 81,* 143–154.

Hagger, M. S., & Chatzisarantis, N. L. D. (Eds.). (2007). *Intrinsic motivation and self determination in exercise and sport.* Champaign, IL: Human Kinetics.

Hagger, M. S., Chatzisarantis, N. L. D., Culverhouse, T., & Biddle, S. J. H. (2003). The process by which perceived autonomy support in physical education promotes leisure-time physical activity intentions and behavior: A trans-contextual model. *Journal of Educational Psychology, 95,* 784–795.

Hazan, C., & Shaver, P. R. (1987). Romantic love conceptualized as an attachment process. *Journal of Personality and Social Psychology, 52,* 511–524.

Hazan, C., & Shaver, P. R. (1990). Love and work: An attachment-theoretical perspective. *Journal of Personality and Social Psychology, 59,* 270–280.

Hodgins, H. S., Koestner, R., & Duncan, N. (1996). On the compatibility of autonomy and relatedness. *Personality and Social Psychology Bulletin, 22,* 227–237.

Hogg, M. A. (1992). *The social psychology of group cohesiveness: From attraction to social identity.* Hemel Hempstead, UK: Harvester Wheatsheaf.

House, R. J., & Howell, J. M. (1992). Personality and charismatic leadership. *Leadership Quarterly, 3,* 81–108.

Keinan, G. (1987). Decision making under stress: Scanning of alternatives under controllable and uncontrollable threats. *Journal of Personality and Social Psychology, 52,* 639–644.

Klein, H. J., Becker, T. E., & Meyer, J. P. (2009). *Commitment in organizations: Accumulated wisdom and new directions.* New York, NY: Taylor & Francis.

Koestner, R., & Losier, G. F. (2002). Distinguishing three ways of being internally motivated: a closer look at introjection, identification, and intrinsic motivation. In E. L. Deci, & R. M. Ryan (Eds.), *Handbook of self-determination research* (pp. 101–121). Rochester, NY: University of Rochester Press.

Lazarus, R. S. (1993). Coping theory and research: Past, present, and future. *Psychosomatic Medicine, 55,* 234–247.

Lazarus, R. S., & Folkman, S. (1984). *Stress, appraisal and coping.* New York: Springer.

Levine, J. M., & Moreland, R. L. (1990). Progress in small group research. *Annual Review of Psychology, 41,* 585–634.

Liden, R. C., Wayne, S. J., & Sparrowe, R. T. (2000). An examination of the mediating role of psychological empowerment on the relations between the job, interpersonal relationships, and work outcomes. *Journal of Applied Psychology, 85,* 407–416.

Mikulincer, M. (1997). Adult attachment style and information processing: Individual differences in curiosity and cognitive closure. *Journal of Personality and Social Psychology, 72,* 1217–1230.

Mikulincer, M., & Arad, D. (1999). Attachment, working models, and cognitive openness in close relationships: A test of chronic and temporary accessibility effects. *Journal of Personality and Social Psychology, 77,* 710–725.

Mikulincer, M., & Florian, V. (1995). Appraisal and coping with real-life stressful situation: The contribution of attachment styles. *Personality and Social Psychology Bulletin, 21,* 408–416.

Mikulincer, M., Florian, V., & Weller, A. (1993). Attachment styles, coping strategies, and posttraumatic psychological distress: The impact of the Gulf war in Israel. *Journal of Personality and Social Psychology, 64,* 817–826.

Mikulincer, M., & Shaver, P. R. (2003). The attachment behavioral system in adulthood: Activation, psychodynamics, and interpersonal processes. In M. P. Zanna (Ed.), *Advances in experimental social psychology* (Vol. 35, pp. 53–152). San Diego, CA: Academic Press.

Mikulincer, M., & Shaver, P. R. (2004). Security-based self representations in adulthood: Contents and processes. In W. S. Rholes, & J. A. Simpson (Eds.), *Adult attachment: Theory, research, and clinical implications* (pp. 159–195). New York: Guilford Press.

Mikulincer, M., & Shaver, P. R. (2007). *Attachment in adulthood: Structure, dynamics, and change.* New York: Guilford Press.

Mikulincer, M., & Shaver, P. R. (2008). Contribution of attachment theory and research to motivational science. In J. Y. Shah, & W. L. Gardner (Eds.), *Handbook of motivation science* (pp. 201–216). New York: Guilford Press.

Moore, D. (1987). Parent–adolescent separation: The construction of adulthood by late adolescents. *Developmental Psychology, 23,* 298–307.

Mumford, M. D., Zaccaro, S. J., Harding, F. D., Jacobs, T. O., & Fleishman, E. A. (2000). Leadership skills for a changing world. *Leadership Quarterly, 11,* 11–35.

Noom, M. M., Dekovic, M., & Meeus, W. H. J. (1999). Autonomy, attachment and psychosocial adjustment during adolescence: A double edged sword? *Journal of Adolescence, 22,* 771–783.

Patrick, H., Knee, C. R., Canevello, A., & Lonsbary, C. (2007). The role of need fulfillment in relationship functioning and well-being: A self determination theory perspective. *Journal of Personality and Social Psychology, 92,* 434–457.

Pelletier, L. G., Fortier, M. S., Vallerand, R. J., & Brie`re, N. M. (2001). Associations among perceived autonomy support, forms of self regulation, and persistence: A prospective study. *Motivation and Emotion, 25,* 279–306.

Popper, M., Amit, K., Gal, R., Mishkal-Sinai, M., & Lisak, A. (2004). The capacity to lead: Major psychological differences between leaders and non-leaders. *Military Psychology, 16,* 245–263.

Popper, M., Mayseless, O., & Castelnovo, O. (2000). Transformational leadership and attachment. *Leadership Quarterly, 11,* 267–289.

Reis, H. T., Sheldon, K. M., Gable, S. L., Roscoe, J., & Ryan, R. M. (2000). Daily well being: The role of autonomy, competence, and relatedness. *Personality and Social Psychology Bulletin, 26,* 419–435.

Rom, E., & Mikulincer, M. (2003). Attachment theory and group processes: The association between attachment style and group-related representations, goals, memories, and functioning. *Journal of Personality and Social Psychology, 84,* 1220–1235.

Ronen, S., & Baldwin, M. W. (2010). Hypersensitivity to social rejection and perceived stress as mediators between attachment anxiety and future burnout: A prospective analysis. *Applied Psychology: An International Review, 58,* 1–24.7.

Ronen, S., & Lane, S. T. (2014). *The Secure Work Base scale: Development of a measure.* A manuscript in preparation.

Ronen, S., & Mikulincer, M. (2009). Attachment orientations and job burnout: The mediating role of team cohesion and organizational fairness. *Journal of Social and Personal Relationships, 26,* 549–567.

Ronen, S., & Mikulincer, M. (2011). Predicting employees' satisfaction and burnout from managers' attachment and caregiving orientations. *European Journal of Work and Organizational Psychology, 1,* 1–22.

Ryan, R. M. (1982). Control and information in the intrapersonal sphere: An extension of cognitive evaluation theory. *Journal of Personality and Social Psychology, 43,* 450–461.

Ryan, R. M., & Deci, E. L. (2000). Self-determination theory and the facilitation of intrinsic motivation, social development, and well-being. *American Psychologist, 55,* 68–78.

Ryan, R. M., & Grolnick, W. S. (1986). Origins and pawns in the classroom: Self-report and projective assessments of individual differences in children's perceptions. *Journal of Personality and Social Psychology, 50,* 550–558.

Ryan, R. M., Stiller, J., & Lynch, J. H. (1994). Representations of relationships to teachers, parents, and friends as predictors of academic motivation and self-esteem. *Journal of Early Adolescence, 14,* 226–249.

Shamir, B., House, R. J., & Arthur, M. B. (1993). The motivational effects of charismatic leadership: A self-concept based theory. *Organization Science, 4,* 1–17.

Shaver, P. R., & Hazan, C. (1993). Adult romantic attachment: Theory and evidence. In D. Perlman, & W. Jones (Eds.), *Advances in personal relationships* (Vol. 4, pp. 29–70). London: Jessica Kingsley.

Sheldon, K. M., & Emmons, R. A. (1995). Comparing differentiation and integration within personal goal systems. *Personality and Individual Differences, 18,* 39–46.

Shirom, A., Westman, M., & Melamed, S. (1999). The effects of pay systems on blue-collar employees' emotional distress: the mediating effects of objective and subjective work monotony. *Human Relations, 52,* 1077–1097.

Sroufe, L. A., & Waters, E. (1977). Attachment as an organizational construct. *Child Development, 48,* 1184–1199.

Svenson, O., & Maule, A. J. (Eds.). (1993). *Time pressure and stress in human judgment and decision making.* New York: Plenum Press.

White, R. W. (1959). Motivation reconsidered: The concept of competence. *Psychological Review, 66,* 297–331.

Williams, G. C., Cox, E. M., Hedberg, V., & Deci, E. L. (2000). Extrinsic life goals and health risk behaviors in adolescents. *Journal of Applied Social Psychology, 30,* 1756–1771.

Williams, G. C., Grow, V. M., Freedman, Z., Ryan, R. M., & Deci, E. L. (1996). Motivational predictors of weight loss and weight-loss maintenance. *Journal of Personality and Social Psychology, 70*, 115–126.

Williams, G. C., McGregor, H. A., Sharp, D., Kouides, R. W., Levesque, C., Ryan, R. M., & Deci, E. L. (2006). A self-determination multiple risk intervention trial to improve smokers' health. *Journal of General Internal Medicine, 21*, 1288–1294.

Williams, G. C., Rodin, G. C., Ryan, R. M., Grolnick, W. S., & Deci, E. L. (1998). Autonomous regulation and long-term medication adherence in adult outpatients. *Health Psychology, 17*, 269–276.

Vallerand, R. J., & Reid, G. (1984). On the causal effects of perceived competence on intrinsic motivation: a test of cognitive evaluation theory. *Journal of Sport Psychology, 6*, 94–102.

Vansteenkiste, M., Simons, J., Soenens, B., & Lens, W. (2004). How to become a persevering exerciser? Providing a clear, future intrinsic goal in an autonomy supportive way. *Journal of Sport & Exercise Psychology, 26*, 232–249.

CHAPTER

8

Contingent Self-Esteem: A Review and Applications to Organizational Research

D. Lance Ferris

Abstract

Contingent self-esteem, or the extent to which one's self-esteem is contingent on success and failures in certain life domains, has major implications for an individual's well-being and performance. To date, however, most research done on contingent self-esteem has been in nonorganizational contexts. The aim of this chapter is to introduce the contingent self-esteem construct to organizational audiences through a review of the extant social psychological literature on contingent self-esteem. Subsequently, applications to organizational research are covered, including validity concerns specific to organizational research. Finally, a review of the limited organizational contingent self-esteem research to date is provided, as well as areas for future organizational contingent self-esteem research.

Key Words: self-esteem, contingent self-esteem, performance contingent self-esteem, job performance, motivation

As anyone who has experienced failures knows, some losses sting more acutely than others. Although I may accept my early exit from a poker tournament with equanimity, or laugh off comments about the quality of my cooking, I may become despondent or feel validated depending on if I solve the daily newspaper's Sudoku puzzle, or experience depression or a surge of self-worth when a manuscript submitted for publication is rejected or accepted. However, I need only turn on the latest cooking reality show to see that not everyone feels the same way; indeed, for some people, whether or not their sorbets are frozen provokes tears (yet I strongly suspect these same individuals would care little about receiving rejection letters from academic journals).

What determines how we react to success and failures in different life domains? In the past decade, a new field of research has emerged dealing with the construct of *contingent self-esteem*. Contingent self-esteem is characterized as "a domain or category of outcomes on which a person has staked his/her

self-esteem, so that person's view of his/her value or worth depends on perceived successes or failures or adherence to self-standards in that domain" (Crocker & Wolfe, 2001, p. 594). In other words, contingent self-esteem represents ego-involvement in specific domains (Deci & Ryan, 1995), which in turn influences our actions in a domain and the reactions we experience in response to failures and successes in that domain. In the pages that follow, I introduce and review theory and research on the contingent self-esteem construct for organizational audiences, and discuss possible future areas for organizational research on contingent self-esteem.[1]

Contingent Self-Esteem

Contingent self-esteem represents the extent to which an individual's sense of self-worth is contingent on outcomes in a particular life domain. When individuals succeed in domains on which they have staked their self-esteem, their self-esteem may increase; however, should individuals fail in domains on which they have staked their self-esteem, their self-esteem decreases (Crocker & Wolfe, 2001). In this sense, contingencies of self-esteem potentiate the outcomes in a domain to influence one's state self-esteem: in contingent domains, success makes one feel great about oneself and is eagerly sought after, whereas failure makes one feel terrible about oneself and is anxiously avoided; over the long run, continued success or failure in contingent domains can influence one's trait level of self-esteem (Crocker & Wolfe, 2001). In contrast, in noncontingent domains, both success and failure hold little implication for how an individual feels about himself or herself, and success or failure in noncontingent domains are hence neither pursued nor avoided with any great zeal. Contingencies differ from domain to domain and from individual to individual: whereas one individual's self-esteem may be contingent on outcomes in the publishing domain yet be unaffected by outcomes in the kitchen, for other individuals the reverse may be true. Moreover, individuals may have multiple contingencies: an individual may base their self-worth not only on their cooking abilities, but also on their attractiveness or the approval of their circle of friends.

Aside from the implication that state self-esteem should rise and fall in accordance with success and failure in contingent domains, a more profound implication is that through its ability to influence how outcomes in a domain make one feel about oneself, contingent self-esteem represents a potent motivational force (Crocker, Brook, Niiya, & Villacorta, 2006). In particular, it has been argued that individuals pursue increases (or try to avoid decreases) in state self-esteem (Crocker & Park, 2004). As a result, individuals tend to invest effort in domains on which their self-esteem is contingent. For example, studies have found that individuals spent more time engaging in activities congruent with their contingencies: Crocker, Luhtanen, and colleagues (2003) found those with appearance-contingent self-esteem spent more time grooming and shopping, whereas Wilson, Allen, Strahan, and Ethier (2008) found that those who base their self-esteem on being virtuous are more likely to express behavioral intentions to volunteer. Yet at the same time, contingent self-esteem represents vulnerability for individuals, in that failure in contingent domains can make individuals feel worthless and depressed. As such, individuals may abandon tasks or self-handicap where failure is likely (Crocker et al., 2006) or engage in other defensive techniques to deny failure in contingent

domains (Crocker & Park, 2004). Moreover, when failure does occur and is acknowledged, individuals experience a variety of maladaptive outcomes, ranging from the aforementioned lowered self-esteem to depression to anxiety to behavioral disorders (as reviewed below).

Given the plethora of negative outcomes possible, why might individuals develop contingent self-esteem? Although little research has addressed this question, contingent self-esteem is thought to develop through interactions with caregivers and exposure to cultural norms and values at a young age (Crocker & Wolfe, 2001). In particular, children learn what actions cause individuals to be accepted and valued (or rejected and denigrated). For example, some parents may focus on proficiency in the classroom or on the sports field, whereas certain cultures may focus on appearance more so than others. Individuals internalize such information and begin to stake their self-esteem to domains valued by social groups, which facilitates navigating social situations and reduces the likelihood of an individual being excluded by others (vanDellen, Hoy, Fernandez, & Hoyle, 2011).

Contingent Self-Esteem and Self-Determination Theory

Self-determination theory has been influential in the development and understanding of the contingent self-esteem literature. A 1995 chapter by Deci and Ryan provided an initial treatise on the drawbacks of contingent self-esteem, and subsequent contingent self-esteem research has conceptualized the pursuit of self-esteem as negatively impacting basic psychological needs for autonomy, competence, and relatedness (Crocker, Luhtanen, & Sommers, 2004; Crocker & Park, 2004). With respect to autonomy, pursuing self-esteem represents a more extrinsic form of motivation, in that it involves engaging in behavior to avoid shame and guilt (Deci & Ryan, 2000). As Deci, Eghrari, Patrick, and Leone (1994, p. 121) note, contingent self-esteem "is an example of internally controlling regulation that results from introjection. One is behaving because one feels one has to and not because one wants to, and this regulation is accompanied by the experience of pressure and tension." Consistent with this, Crocker and colleagues (2006) review a series of studies that show contingent self-esteem is related to less intrinsic motivation. Pursuing self-esteem also undermines satisfaction of the need for competence. When pursuing self-esteem, individuals tend to be more concerned with performance than learning, or as Crocker and Park (2004, p. 399) put it, "learning becomes a means to desired performance outcomes that validate the self, instead of performance outcomes becoming opportunities for learning." Moreover, individuals also react defensively to failure in contingent domains (Crocker & Park, 2004; Kernis, Lakey, & Heppner, 2008), limiting opportunities to learn and ultimately feel more competent. Finally, pursuing self-esteem negatively impacts an individual's ability to form and maintain nurturing relationships (as summarized below), which ultimately thwarts an individual's relatedness needs.

Given its negative impact on basic psychological needs and intrinsic motivation, contingent self-esteem is typically hypothesized to have negative effects on a variety of different outcomes. In the sections below, extant research findings from the contingent self-esteem literature are reviewed. To begin, issues with the measurement of contingent self-esteem are discussed; subsequently, I review the various areas where the effects of contingent self-esteem have been examined.

Review of Contingent Self-Esteem Research
Contingent Self-Esteem Measurement

Modern measures of contingent self-esteem have typically taken one of two approaches: assessing contingent self-esteem in particular domains (e.g., self-esteem contingent on how competent or attractive one is), or assessing contingent self-esteem as an overall latent factor (i.e., one tends to have contingent or noncontingent self-esteem, leading to contingent or noncontingent self-esteem across all domains). A third approach, more rarely used, has been to split domain-contingent self-esteem measures into two groups: those reflecting internal contingencies (i.e., contingent domains that are less dependent on others, such as one's sense of virtue or God's love) and external contingencies (i.e., contingent domains that are more dependent on others, such as other's approval or one's attractiveness to others). Each of these approaches is reviewed below.

MEASURES OF DOMAIN-SPECIFIC CONTINGENT SELF-ESTEEM

The first approach, assessing contingent self-esteem in particular domains, best represents how James (1890) originally conceptualized contingent self-esteem. In particular, James noted how his proficiency as a psychologist was what he staked his self-esteem on, and not his proficiency in Greek. In other words, James' self-esteem is influenced by outcomes in one domain (proficiency as a psychologist) and not another (proficiency in Greek). Mirroring this approach, Crocker, Luhtanen, and colleagues (2003) developed a measure assessing the extent to which university student's self-esteem is contingent on different domains. Their measure, which is the most frequently used measure in contingent self-esteem research, assesses the extent to which self-esteem is contingent on seven different domains: (1) other's approval, (2) appearance, (3) competing with (and beating) others, (4) academic competence, (5) support from one's family, (6) being a virtuous person, and (7) God's love.

Although the Crocker, Luhtanen, et al. (2003) measure outlined seven different domains on which self-esteem can be made contingent, the authors note that other domains likely exist (an earlier version of the scale assessed self-worth contingent on power, social identities, and self-reliance; Crocker, Sommers, & Luhtanen, 2002). Moreover, whereas their measure focuses more on student-relevant contingencies (e.g., academic competence), according to contingent self-esteem theory the specific context is less important than the overarching contingency (e.g., of "competency"; Crocker & Park, 2004; Crocker & Wolfe, 2001). In other words, as one moves from a student role to a work role, one does not simply abandon one's contingencies. Rather, they transfer from one domain (e.g., academic competence) to a new domain (i.e., workplace competence). As such, the contextual wording in the original scales should be readily adaptable to new domains (see Ferris Lian, Brown, Pang, & Keeping, 2010, for an example). In this sense, the measure is flexible with respect to its specific target domain while still assessing the underlying contingency of competence. This feature is shared with other established measures of organizational constructs, such as Colquitt's (2001) measure of procedural justice, which allows the target referenced in the scale items to be changed while still assessing procedural justice.

Consistent with this approach, numerous studies have either modified Crocker, Luhtanen, et al.'s (2003) measures to assess different contexts, or developed measures assessing contingent self-esteem in domains not originally examined by Crocker, Luhtanen, et al. (2003). New measures have been developed assessing the extent to which self-esteem is contingent on one's body weight (Clabaugh, Karpinski, & Griffin, 2008), exercise (Arndt et al., 2009), being an environmentalist (Vess & Arndt, 2008), voting in elections (Britt et al., 2010), the social abilities of one's child (Grolnick, Price, Beiswenger, & Sauck, 2007), one's intelligence (Lemay & Clark, 2008), one's performance in sports (McArdle, 2010), one's friendships (Cambron, Acitelli, & Steinberg, 2010), whether or not one is in a romantic relationship (Sanchez & Kwang, 2007), and whether or not one's romantic relationship is operating smoothly (Knee, Canvello, Bush, & Cook, 2008). Aside from these new domains, researchers have developed alternate measures of existing domains, such as competence and other's approval (Johnson & Blom, 2007), or of existing domains but for specific populations, such as adolescents (Burwell & Shirk, 2006). In terms of cross-cultural research, Hu, Yang, Wang, and Liu (2008) developed a measure of contingent self-esteem for use in Chinese populations, assessing contingent self-esteem in the domains of ability, behavioral style, appearance, social status, nationality, and family. Finally, perhaps of more relevance to organizational researchers, measures have been developed assessing the extent to which self-esteem is contingent on workplace performance (Ferris, Brown, Lian, & Keeping, 2009; Ferris et al., 2010; Innstrand, Langballe, Espnes, Aasland, & Falkum, 2010); these are discussed in greater detail next.

MEASURES OF OVERALL CONTINGENT SELF-ESTEEM

The second approach to contingent self-esteem measurement is to assess contingent self-esteem as an overall construct—that is, an individual either does or does not have contingent self-esteem, regardless of domains. This approach is best exemplified in the work of Kernis (2003; Kernis & Goldman, 2006) and parallels early writings on contingent self-esteem (Deci & Ryan, 1995), which did not entertain the notion of domain-specific contingencies (discussed previously). Notwithstanding the conceptualization of contingent self-esteem as something individuals tend to have or not have, the Kernis and Goldman (2006) measure nonetheless appears to tap into different domains of self-esteem contingencies. For example, such items as "My overall feelings about myself are heavily influenced by how much other people like and accept me" taps into other's approval, whereas such items as "An important measure of my worth is how physically attractive I am" taps into appearance-contingent self-esteem. Similarly, researchers have used subsets of items from the Kernis and Goldman (2006)

scale to assess specific domains, such as competence (Hill, Hall, & Appleton, 2011).

Although measures of overall contingent self-esteem has been used successfully in past research (e.g., Neighbors, Larimer, Geisner, & Knee, 2004; Patrick, Neighbors, & Knee, 2004), domain-specific measures of contingent self-esteem seem preferable for conceptual, empirical, and practical reasons. Conceptually, it seems it would be rare to find an individual whose self-esteem is contingent on virtually every domain; similarly, it seems difficult to call to mind an individual whose self-esteem is not contingent on any domain. Such individuals would be either so affected (or unaffected) by everyday events that it would be difficult for them to successfully navigate the social aspects of living. Although such individuals may exist, one presumes they would be extremely rare and such a conceptualization would mitigate the relevance of contingent self-esteem to everyday audiences.

Empirical research similarly supports the notion that overall contingent self-esteem does not exist. Crocker, Luhtanen, and colleagues (2003) used confirmatory factor analysis to compare whether a single factor model where all their domain-contingent scale items loaded on a single latent factor, versus a seven-factor model where each domain-contingent scale item only loaded on its relevant domain-specific latent factor, provided a better fit for the data. This comparison tests whether or not contingent self-esteem is best represented as a single overall factor (consistent with the measure used by Kernis & Goldman, 2006) or as being domain-specific. Their data indicated domain-specific contingencies provided a better fit to the data than a single overall factor.

Finally, from a purely practical point of view, researchers are more likely to find effects when using measures that conceptually align with their constructs of interest. This maxim has existed for a long time in psychological research (see Swann, Chang-Schenider, & McClarty, 2007 for a recent discussion) and simply reflects the fact that the extent to which a measure captures irrelevant variance in addition to one's construct of interest, the measure will be less likely to support one's hypotheses. Put simply, if one wants to see how people react when told they are ugly, one should use a measure assessing their appearance-contingent self-esteem, not a measure assessing the extent to which self-esteem is contingent on appearance, other's approval, and competence. The latter measure may still work, but it seems like one would be stacking the odds against oneself with such a measure.

MEASURES OF INTERNAL VERSUS EXTERNAL CONTINGENCIES

Finally, researchers have also grouped domain-specific contingent self-esteem measures into two classes: internal and external contingencies, or the extent to which one's self-esteem is contingent on internal aspects of the self or external validation from others (see, e.g., Sanchez & Crocker, 2005; Sargent, Crocker, & Luhtanen, 2006). This approach, however, retains all of the problems inherent in measures of overall contingencies discussed previously. Moreover, it has been criticized for confounding internal and external conceptualizations with more or less abstract contingencies (Updegraff, Emanuel, Suh, & Gallagher, 2010). That is, contingencies usually conceptualized as "internal" tend to be quite abstract (e.g., being virtuous, having God's love) and hence allow for more defenses to be marshaled to discount negative feedback; "external" contingencies, however, tend to be quite concrete (e.g., looking good, doing well at school, beating others in competitions), and hence more objective and susceptible to negative feedback. This is particularly problematic, because Updegraff and colleagues (2010) found that it was the abstractness of one's contingencies, not whether they were internal or external, that moderated the effect of negative events on one's state self-esteem. This, taken in conjunction with the problems associated with measures of overall contingencies, suggests that the use of internal and external contingencies cannot be condoned.

SELF- VERSUS OTHER-REPORTS OF CONTINGENT SELF-ESTEEM

Aside from the varied measures used to assess contingent self-esteem, a different topic in the literature deals with who should provide ratings of self-esteem contingencies: that is, whether or not contingent self-esteem scales should be completed by the focal individual, or by another individual (e.g., a work peer, friend, significant other, or spouse). The debate has focused on whether or not contingent self-esteem operates at a conscious or unconscious level (and hence whether or not it is better assessed using self-reports or other-reports). As Crocker, Sommers, and Luhtanen (2002, p. 1285) state, "some contingencies of self-worth may operate outside of conscious awareness and, hence, outside the ability of our [self-report] measures to detect them." Expanding on this, Anthony, Holmes, and Wood (2007) have noted that in general, people can be inaccurate with self-reports on their own psychology (Nisbett & Wilson, 1977) and in particular, individuals are also reluctant to admit that feedback (e.g., within a particular domain) influences how they feel about themselves (Wood, 1996). These concerns may have particular relevance for self-report measures of contingent self-esteem. For example, one study found that even though individuals stated that their self-esteem was not contingent on other individuals' feedback, under experimental conditions, their self-esteem level *was* shown to fluctuate in response to feedback (Leary et al., 2003).

As this suggests, it is possible that self-reports of contingencies of self-esteem are not always accurate. Indeed, although self-reports have often been used by researchers assessing contingent self-esteem, this practice has just as frequently been noted as a limitation (Anthony et al., 2007; Crocker et al., 2006; Crocker & Luhtanen, 2003; Crocker, Luhtanen, et al., 2003; Crocker et al., 2002; Park, Crocker, & Kiefer, 2007; Sanchez & Crocker, 2005). Moreover, some evidence exists that suggests self-report measures of contingent self-esteem may relate (albeit weakly) to social desirability (Crocker, Luhtanen, et al, 2003). Yet at the same time, there is no denying that self-reports of contingent self-esteem are useful, given the intriguing and theoretically consistent findings that have accumulated thus far on the topic. Notably, and contrary to the Leary et al. (2003) finding, such research frequently does find that state self-esteem levels do not vary according to negative feedback or events in domains that one has self-reported as unimportant to one's self-esteem level (e.g., Park & Crocker, 2008).

Given these contradictory findings, and given that research on contingent self-esteem is still in a fairly early stage, issues such as who (self or other) is best suited to report on an individual's contingencies of self-esteem remain to be settled. Notably, one paper (Ferris et al., 2010) presented the results of two studies, each using either self-ratings or peer-ratings of workplace-contingent self-esteem. Across the two studies, results were similar regardless of whether self-ratings or peer-ratings were used. Although this paper does not resolve the debate regarding who is the most valid source of ratings of contingent self-esteem, it provides preliminary evidence that both self-ratings and peer-ratings of workplace-contingent self-esteem operate similarly.

Contingent Self-Esteem Research Findings

A remarkable amount of research has been amassed in the decade since Crocker and Wolfe's

(2001) paper reintroduced contingent self-esteem to researchers. Below, I briefly review and categorize general themes and domains on which this work has focused; this categorization scheme is not meant to be definitive or theoretically derived, but rather to be descriptive and provide some preliminary structure for understanding the different contexts and variables on which contingent self-esteem research has focused. Organizational contingent self-esteem research is discussed separately in the subsequent section.

APPEARANCE AND BODY CONCERNS

Several studies have examined the effects of contingent self-esteem on variables associated with concern over one's appearance. In general, these studies argue that individuals with contingent self-esteem (typically measured with scales assessing appearance-contingent self-esteem, body weight–contingent self-esteem, external contingencies, or overall measures of contingent self-esteem) can have several negative consequences. Such contingencies have been argued to develop due to internalization of societal or gender norms for attractiveness (Sanchez & Crocker, 2005; Strathan et al., 2008), although others have argued instead that internalization of societal standards is a result of, not a cause of, contingent self-esteem (Vartanian, 2009).

A review of the published studies indicates that those with contingent self-esteem tend to be more concerned with their weight (particularly women) and musculature (particularly men; Grossbard, Lee, Neighbors, & Larimer, 2009), and tend to be more depressed and anxious, less satisfied with life, and more likely to exhibit behaviors consistent with eating disorders (Clabaugh et al., 2008). One study examining relationship-contingent self-esteem also found that those whose self-esteem was contingent on relationships were more likely to be ashamed of their bodies, exhibit bulimic symptoms, and have low self-esteem (Sanchez & Kwang, 2007).

Consistent with contingent self-esteem theory, studies have shown that perceiving oneself to be unattractive is especially devastating for those with contingent self-esteem. Contingent self-esteem has been shown to moderate the effects of comparisons with attractive people, engendering more negative (and less positive) affect for those high in contingent self-esteem (Patrick et al., 2004), and also rendering individuals more likely to diet, display eating disorders (Bergstrom, Neighbors, & Lewis, 2004), or have unstable self-esteem (Clabaugh et al., 2008) when they perceived themselves to be overweight.

EDUCATION

A number of studies, almost all of which use variations on Crocker, Luhtanen, et al.'s (2003) measure of academic competence–contingent self-esteem, have looked at contingent self-esteem as a moderator of reactions to negative scholastic events. The results indicate that individuals with highly contingent self-esteem exhibit more negative affect, decreased self-esteem, and less identification with their major on days in which they received bad grades (Crocker, Karpinski, Quinn, & Chase, 2003) or received word their applications to graduate schools were rejected (Crocker et al., 2002). Subsequent studies have focused on moderators of these interactions (i.e., three-way interactions), demonstrating that those high in self-esteem level (Park et al., 2007) or those with incremental theories of intelligence (Niiya, Crocker, & Bartmess, 2004; see also Lawrence & Crocker, 2009) tend not to exhibit such negative reactions to adverse academic events, even with highly contingent self-esteem.

RELATIONSHIPS

Numerous studies have examined contingent self-esteem and relationships (both romantic relationships and general relationships with others). Individuals with self-esteem contingent on one's appearance or being in a relationship tend to show greater desire to be in relationships and greater desire for their significant others to be physically attractive (Sanchez, Good, Kwang, & Saltzman, 2008). Interestingly, however, once in a relationship, contingent self-esteem tends to undermine the relationship. For example, basing one's self-esteem on other's approval has been shown to lead to a lowered sense of sexual autonomy and pleasure (Sanchez, Crocker, & Boike, 2005). Lemay and Clark (2008) argued that contingent self-esteem undermines relationship satisfaction because individuals with contingent self-esteem constantly seek positive feedback from their partners. Consequently, partners provide inauthentic feedback, which leaves both individuals unsatisfied—the partner for having provided inauthentic feedback, and the contingent individual because of doubts about the veracity of the feedback (see also Cambron & Acitelli, 2010; Cambron et al., 2010). Park and Crocker (2005) outline another way in which contingent self-esteem undermines relationships: by rendering individuals unresponsive to the needs of others. They found that following negative feedback in a contingent domain, high self-esteem participants who interacted with a novel relationship partner who described a personal problem were rated by the partner as less supportive and likable (presumably because they were preoccupied with the negative feedback).

Studies have also examined contingent self-esteem as a moderator of reactions to negative relationship events. Results indicate that those whose self-esteem is contingent on relationships, friendships, or other's approval in general tend to be more depressed and have lower self-esteem and more negative emotions following negative relationship events (Cambron et al., 2010; Knee et al., 2008; Park & Crocker, 2008).

Finally, the relation of domain-specific contingencies of self-esteem to attachment and interpersonal styles in general has also been examined (Park, Crocker, & Mickelson, 2004; Zeigler-Hill, 2006); appearance-contingent, competition-contingent, and academic competence–contingent self-esteem tended to be related to more detrimental styles (e.g., preoccupied or fearful attachment styles and hostile interpersonal styles), whereas self-esteem contingent on family support, God's love, or other's approval led to more positive styles (e.g., supportive or non-dismissive attachment styles and nurturing interpersonal styles). However, such relations might vary depending on culture (Cheng & Kwang, 2008).

DRINKING BEHAVIOR

It has been argued that if drinking alcohol is motivated by a desire to fit in or to cope with threats to one's self-esteem, then individuals with contingent self-esteem should be more likely to drink more and/or engage in binge drinking. Two studies (Luhtanen & Crocker, 2005; Neighbors et al., 2004) found support for this prediction. However, Luhtanen and Crocker found that what self-esteem was contingent on mattered: basing one's self-worth on appearance was related to more drinking, whereas basing one's self-worth on virtue, God's love, or academic competence was related to less drinking. Neighbors et al. (2004) used an overall measure of contingent self-esteem; such distinctions consequently cannot be examined. Neighbors et al. (2004) also argued contingent self-esteem generally develops out of feeling pressured by the environment (i.e., a controlled orientation), and that contingent self-esteem mediates the relation of external pressure on drinking behavior.

WELL-BEING

Although some of the studies reviewed above have focused on well-being as an outcome arising from a specific context (e.g., increased negative affect and decreased self-esteem in reaction to bad grades; Crocker, Karpinski, et al., 2003), other studies have focused exclusively on the relation between contingent self-esteem and well-being, regardless of context. For example, contingent self-esteem was found to relate to greater depression, anxiety, eating disorders, and disruptive behavior among a sample of adolescents (Bos, Huijding, Muris, Vogel, & Biesheuvel, 2011); the same study also found that contingent self-esteem moderated the relation of self-esteem level to many of these outcomes, such that decreased self-esteem level only produced detrimental effects when combined with highly contingent self-esteem. Numerous other studies have also looked at the relation between contingent self-esteem and well-being–related outcomes, such as depression (Burwell & Shirk, 2006; Sargent et al., 2006); self-esteem level (Lemay & Ashmore, 2006; Zeigler-Hill, 2007); health (Johnson, 2011); and social, financial, and academic problems (Crocker & Luhtanen, 2003). These studies generally find a negative effect of contingencies on well-being, although one study found that having contingent self-esteem could lead to an increase in well-being, so long as one self-perceived they were doing well in the particular domain (i.e., having self-esteem contingent on appearance and believing oneself to be attractive; Breines, Crocker, & Garcia, 2008).

PERFECTIONISM

Studies have examined the relation between contingent self-esteem and perfectionism, generally suggesting that domain-specific contingencies lead to domain-specific perfectionism. For example, McArdle (2010) found that self-esteem contingent upon sports or academics correspondingly predicted perfectionism in sports or school work; Hill et al. (2011) found that demanding perfection from oneself was related to basing self-esteem on one's competence or outperforming others, while perceiving that others demand perfection of oneself was related to basing self-esteem on the approval of others and outperforming others.

NARCISSISM

As with perfectionism, domain-specific contingencies have been suggested to lead to different forms of narcissism: vulnerable or covert narcissism (characterized by seeking the approval of others) and grandiose narcissism (characterized by a disregard for others). Zeigler-Hill, Clark, and Pickard (2008) found that vulnerable narcissism related positively to all contingent domains in Crocker, Luhtanen, et al.'s (2003) scale except God's love; grandiose narcissism was found to relate positively to competition-contingent self-esteem, and negatively to other's approval, family support, and appearance-based contingencies of self-esteem. Relatedly, individuals with contingent self-esteem were found to exhibit narcissistic behaviors (being more verbally defensive when describing a personal fault; Kernis et al., 2008).

SOCIAL MOTIVATION AND COGNITION

Separate streams of research provide converging evidence that contingent self-esteem influences social motivation and attention to social information. In general, these studies have shown that contingent self-esteem acts as an indicator of how others expect the individual to act. For example, Arndt and colleagues (2009) found that following a threat to one's mortality, individuals engaged in (or evaluated positively) activities in their contingent domain (e.g., tanning, exercising, smoking), presumably as a way of seeking social approval and mitigating the mortality threat (see also Vess & Arndt, 2008). Park and Maner (2009) argued that the social activities individuals engage in following threat differs depending on self-esteem level, with high self-esteem individuals engaging in more direct activities (e.g., seeking out others directly) and low self-esteem individuals engaging in more indirect activities (e.g., engaging in activities to increase one's attractiveness to others). Horberg and Chen (2010) also found that priming significant others led to individuals staking their self-esteem to domains the significant other considered important, again presumably to seek social approval. Finally, it has been argued that individuals pay particular attention to events in contingent domains because failure to do so could result in social exclusion. Supporting this idea, it has been shown that individuals more readily associate and access words from contingent domains with or after exclusion (vanDellen et al., 2011; vanDellen, Hoy, & Hoyle, 2009).

Contingent Self-Esteem Research in Organizations

Although more limited in scope in comparison with the broader social and personality psychology literature on the topic, contingent self-esteem has also been applied to organizational settings. Although organizations have a variety of domains on which one might stake one's self-esteem, extant research has focused on self-esteem that is contingent on workplace performance.

Before reviewing this research, a short diversion into nomenclature is necessary to deal with issues specific to contingent self-esteem research in organizational domains. In particular, the question arises as to what we should label self-esteem that is contingent on workplace performance. In an earlier paper (Ferris, Brown, Lian, & Keeping, 2009) my colleagues and I used the term "workplace-contingent self-esteem" to capture this construct, but in retrospect that initial wording was unfortunate for two reasons. First, it does not clarify which part or aspect of the workplace one's self-esteem is contingent on (i.e., performance); and second, and perhaps most importantly, "workplace-contingent self-esteem" sounds quite similar to "organization-based self-esteem," a term in use since the late 1980s to refer to one's self-esteem *level* (i.e., high or low) in the organizational domain (Pierce, Gardner, Cummings, & Dunham, 1989; Pierce & Gardner, 2004). In a subsequent paper (Ferris et al., 2010) we used the term "importance of performance to self-esteem" (IPSE) to refer to having one's self-esteem contingent on workplace performance. The IPSE term is not necessarily ideal—one surmises that it should denote "workplace performance" or "job performance" and not simply performance (see also Innstrand et al., 2010)—but it strikes a balance between being succinct and not overlapping with other organizational terminology for constructs.

One unfortunate consequence of this name changes is that although it avoids overlap with organization-based self-esteem terminology, it also runs the risk of isolating organizational contingent self-esteem research from the broader literature by omitting a key term (contingencies or contingent). In order to avoid this, my coauthors and I use the term "contingent self-esteem" when discussing the general concept, and IPSE when discussing the specific example of having self-esteem contingent on workplace performance; this approach is followed next when discussing organizational contingent self-esteem research.

Research on Discriminant Validity

When introducing any new organizational construct it is important to differentiate it from pre-existing organizational constructs. For the IPSE, its relation vis-à-vis measures of the importance of work to an individual (including work centrality and work involvement) and measures of self-worth frequently used in organizational research (including the aforementioned organization-based self-esteem and core self-evaluations) seem particularly relevant. With respect to measures of workplace importance, both work centrality (Paullay, Alliger, & Stone-Romero, 1994) and work involvement (Kanungo, 1982) tap into the extent to which work is viewed as important to the individual. Although these constructs doubtlessly do tap into the notion that one's self-esteem is based on workplace performance, other sources of variance are also assessed by these measures (Innstrand et al., 2010). For example, "[t]he most important things that happen in life involve my present job," from Kanungo's (1982, p. 342) work involvement scale, may reflect self-esteem contingencies or it may reflect an individual's boring social life. At a theoretical level, a distinction can also be made between importance and self-esteem contingencies by contrasting the self-relevant implications of success and failure in contingent domains with merely important domains: although one may consider it to be important to maintain good dental care, one does not necessary experience a burst of self-esteem or joy each time he or she successfully deploys his or her toothbrush. However, if one's self-esteem is contingent on good dental care, this is what one would expect. Consistent with the above arguments, empirical research indicates that the IPSE is separate from more general measures of workplace importance. Ferris and colleagues (2010), for example, found that IPSE correlated moderately with work centrality ($r = .48$) and work involvement ($r = .34$).

With respect to measures of self-worth frequently used in organizational research, organization-based self-esteem represents a form of domain-specific self-esteem level—one's self-esteem level in the workplace. Core self-evaluations similarly represent a fundamental self-appraisal that is posited to be the latent factor accounting for the relation between four narrower self-appraisals: (1) self-estee m, (2) generalized self-efficacy, (3) neuroticism, and (4) locus of control (Chang, Ferris, Johnson, Rosen, & Tan, 2012; Judge, Erez, Bono, & Thoresen, 2003). Although not organizational in focus, core self-evaluations research has primarily occurred in organizational settings and hence its relation to self-esteem contingencies may be questioned.

Given contingent self-esteem and self-esteem level are thought to be orthogonal (with contingent self-esteem typically accounting for unique variance in outcomes; Crocker, Luhtanen, et al., 2003; Kernis, 2003), one would a priori expect similar findings to research examining the relation between organizational self-esteem contingencies and organizational measures of self-worth. Indeed, the correlation between the IPSE and organization-based self-esteem has been observed to be low ($r = .26$; Ferris et al., 2010). Although no published data have been presented on the relation of the IPSE and core self-evaluations (or its components), my colleagues and I have examined its relation to both direct and indirect measures of core self-evaluations. We assessed the IPSE using the measure reported by Ferris et al. (2010); a 12-item direct measure (Judge et al., 2003) was used to directly assess core self-evaluations. We also assessed each of the four core self-evaluation traits individually with measures of trait self-esteem (Rosenberg, 1965), generalized self-efficacy (Chen, Gully, & Eden, 2001), locus of control (Levenson, 1981), and neuroticism (Goldberg, 1992). We collected data from 127 participants (see p. 575 of Ferris et al., 2010, for more information on procedures and demographics); the results are presented in Table 8.1.

As can be seen in Table 8.1, IPSE was not significantly related to self-esteem level, locus of control, neuroticism, or the 12-item core self-evaluations scale. In fact, IPSE was only significantly correlated with generalized self-efficacy ($r = .27$; $p < .01$), although the magnitude of the correlation was small, with approximately 93% of the variance between IPSE and generalized self-efficacy being unique. These results provide further support for the notion that measures of self-esteem contingencies are separate from organizational measures of self-worth.

Negative Consequences of IPSE

Concerns over discriminant validity aside, organizational contingent self-esteem research has, consistent with the broader contingent self-esteem literature, viewed self-esteem contingent on job performance as leading to negative consequences. In particular, the IPSE has been argued to represent a type of vulnerability that can lead to burnout. Drawing from the work of Hallsten (1993), who positioned IPSE as an antecedent of burnout, studies (Innstrand et al., 2010; Innstrand, Langballe, & Falkum, 2011; Langballe, Innstrand, Aasland, & Falkum, 2011) have correlated the importance of performance to self-esteem to higher burnout levels, as well as increased levels of work-family conflict and family-work conflict. Similar findings were also reported in a sample of Swedish medical students (Dahlin, Joneborg, & Runeson, 2007). These studies have used different measures

Table 8.1 Correlation of IPSE and core self-evaluation measures.

	Mean	SD	1	2	3	4	5	6	7	8	9
1. Age	35.25	9.59	—								
2. Gender	.45	.50	.21*	—							
3. Tenure	69.02	86.42	.62**	.16	—						
4. Importance of performance to self-esteem	5.00	.97	.01	.06	.01	**.78**					
5. Self-esteem level	3.82	.73	.03	−.07	.17	.11	**.91**				
6. Locus of control	4.59	.69	−.02	.03	.09	.00	.54**	**.84**			
7. Neuroticism	2.65	.89	−.07	.28**	−.13	.05	−.70**	−.54**	**.90**		
8. Self-efficacy	4.00	.55	.01	−.06	.05	.27**	.73**	.59**	−.52**	**.90**	
9. Core-self evaluations	3.56	.70	.02	−.10	.17	.05	.85**	.66**	−.76**	.78**	**.90**

Note. Alphas are on the diagonal in bold.
*$p < .05$; **$p < .01$.

developed for the purpose of the studies, including a four-item Swedish measure (Dahlin et al., 2007) and a three-item Norwegian measure (for an English translation, see Innstrand et al., 2010). One item from the three-item measure, however, seems to tap into concerns with the perceptions of others ("If I don't do a really good job, I will lose the respect of others") and caution should accordingly be exercised.

Positive Consequences of IPSE

A second theme of organizational contingent self-esteem research has primarily focused on using contingent self-esteem as a moderator of self-esteem's relation to job performance (job performance being broadly defined as encompassing in-role performance, workplace deviance, and organizational citizenship behaviors; Rotundo & Sackett, 2002). These studies (Ferris, Brown, Lian, & Keeping, 2009; Ferris et al., 2010, 2011) have measured IPSE by adapting Crocker, Luhtanen, et al.'s (2003) five-item measure of competence-contingent self-esteem to the workplace (see Ferris et al., 2010, for the items). Interestingly, this work stands in contrast to most contingent self-esteem research in that it suggests that IPSE may not represent vulnerability. In particular, it has found that IPSE actually *mitigates* the relation between low self-esteem level (as well as high role conflict levels) and job performance. That is, when one's self-esteem is contingent on one's job performance, individuals maintain a high level of job performance—regardless of such factors as low self-esteem or high role conflict.

This work has primarily set out to contribute not just to the contingent self-esteem literature, but to the broader motivation literature as a whole. In particular, it positions contingent self-esteem as a boundary condition for self-consistency and behavioral plasticity theory predictions. Self-consistency (Korman, 1970, 1976) or self-verification (Swann, 1992, 2011) perspectives suggest that individuals act in a manner consistent with their self-perceptions. As such, individuals with low self-esteem should, on average, perform more poorly at work than their high self-esteem counterparts (Korman, 1970, 1976; see also Ferris, Brown, & Heller, 2009). Similarly, from a behavioral plasticity theory perspective, individuals with low self-esteem should be more negatively affected by negative events at work (including role stressors; Brockner, 1988). Given that self-esteem acts as a buffer that individuals can draw on in times of strain (Hobfoll, 1989), high self-esteem individuals are theoretically better equipped to deal with stressful situations and self-esteem levels should moderate the impact of workplace stressors. Unfortunately, the empirical support for self-consistency/self-verification and behavioral plasticity theory predictions is decidedly mixed. For example, narrative (Baumeister, Smart, & Boden, 1996; Baumeister, Campbell, Kreuger, & Vohs, 2003) and meta-analytic (Judge & Bono, 2001) reviews suggest that the main effect of self-esteem on performance outcomes is highly variable and subject to moderation; similarly, self-esteem's moderating effect appears to be, at best, inconsistent (Grandey & Cropanzano, 1999; Jex & Elacqua, 1999; Mossholder, Bedeian, & Armenakis, 1981, 1982; Pierce, Gardner, Dunham, & Cummings, 1993).

To reconcile the mixed support for self-consistency/self-verification theory predictions, the IPSE has been positioned as a moderator of self-esteem level's main effect on counterproductive (Ferris, Brown, Lian, & Keeping, 2009), in-role (Ferris et al., 2010), and citizenship behaviors (Ferris et al., 2011). Similarly, the IPSE has been argued to moderate the moderating effect of self-esteem level on role stressors (i.e., a three-way interaction) in the prediction of counterproductive and in-role performance (Ferris, Brown, Lian, & Keeping, 2009; Ferris et al., 2010). These papers have argued that because poor job performance is a threat to the individual's sense of self when self-esteem is contingent on workplace performance, such individuals are less likely to lower their job performance even in the face of lowered self-esteem or role stressors. In other words, individuals only act consistent with their self-esteem (i.e., perform poorly when one has low self-esteem) or succumb to the combination of low self-esteem and workplace stressors when their self-esteem is *not* contingent on job performance. Across multiple different samples, using different sources as ratings for contingent self-esteem and workplace behaviors, Ferris and colleagues (Ferris, Brown, Lian, & Keeping, 2009; Ferris et al., 2010, 2011) have found support for their predictions.

This work positions contingent self-esteem prominently within a motivational framework, in that it suggests contingent self-esteem moderates our desire to self-verify or exhibit behavioral plasticity. In so doing it contributes to the broader debate on if or when self-esteem does, or does not, predict outcomes (Baumeister et al., 2003; Swann et al., 2007, 2008). Finally, it also presents a more positive view of contingent self-esteem, in that it outlines situations where highly contingent self-esteem is associated with positive outcomes: high job performance. Although high levels of job performance may be viewed as primarily beneficial to the organization (increasing organizational performance, for example; Johnson, 2003; Motowidlo, Borman, & Schmit, 1997), it also plays an important part in determining the employee's pay, promotion, assignments, and workplace recognition (Cleveland, Murphy, & Williams, 1989) and hence is also beneficial to employees.

Lest managers view this as a call to develop workforces with contingent self-esteem, it should be noted organizational contingent self-esteem research is still in its infancy (and hence represents an area where enterprising researchers or doctoral students can yet make a mark). As a result, future findings may outline more negative effects associated with the IPSE, consistent with the work reviewed in the prior section and the broader contingent self-esteem literature. For example, it is entirely possible that whereas individuals with high IPSE maintain levels of performance, the extrinsic nature of IPSE motivation may undermine creativity (Amabile, Conti, Coon, Lazenby, & Herron, 1996).[2]

Future Directions in Organizational Contingent Self-Esteem Research
On the Relation between IPSE and Job Performance

To date, work by my colleagues and I (Ferris, Brown, Lian, & Keeping, 2009; Ferris et al., 2010, 2011) stands out in that it demonstrates how a form of contingent self-esteem (IPSE) can have positive consequences: not only does it buffer an individuals' performance against the negative effects of personal (low self-esteem level) and situational (stressors) variables, it also tends to have a positive main effect on performance. These results are noteworthy because they seem to contradict contingent self-esteem theorizing (and unpublished findings from experimental settings; see Crocker et al., 2006). In particular, as a form of introjected motivation that negatively impacts basic psychological needs (Crocker & Park, 2004), contingent self-esteem should have a negative effect on motivation. Clearly, untangling this paradox represents an important area for future research.

One possibility is, as noted above, to examine alternate forms of performance, such as creativity. Although such work would provide an interesting counterpoint to the positive findings found (Ferris et al., 2010, 2011), it would not in and of itself explain the positive effect of contingent self-esteem on other forms of performance. Another possibility is to look at performance over time: it has been suggested that contingent self-esteem can provide a powerful motivational force but that, over the long term, it ultimately undermines performance by engendering anxiety and drains self-regulatory capacity necessary for maintaining performance (Crocker et al., 2006). With that being said, one study (Ferris, Brown, Lian, & Keeping, 2009) used a 6-month time lag between the assessment of the

IPSE and employee performance, suggesting that the positive relation between contingent self-esteem and performance remains robust over at least a 6-month period.

Alternately, it is possible that these results point to a need to reconsider contingent self-esteem theorizing. It is possible that having self-esteem contingent on performance simply does not negatively affect performance. It may, however, negatively affect outcomes in other domains, as discussed next.

Cross-Domain Behavioral Effects of Contingent Self-Esteem

Most contingent self-esteem research has focused on the effects of contingent self-esteem in the domain of the contingency. For example, the effects of the IPSE are examined with respect to job performance (Ferris et al., 2010); the effects of appearance-contingent self-esteem are examined with respect to dieting attitudes and behavior (Berstrom et al., 2004). Although this is logical (and entirely consistent with theory), a fruitful area for future research may lie in examining the effects of domain-contingent self-esteem on outcomes in other domains. For example, an individual who feels highly stressed at work yet views performance as important to self-esteem will not engage in deviant behavior (Ferris, Brown, Lian, & Keeping, 2009), but at the end of the day the individual still feels stressed. It seems likely that such individuals are especially likely to, say, kick the dog (or worse) when they return home as a way of venting frustration. In other words, when an individual cannot engage in negative behavior in one domain, in the face of frustrating events, spillover effects to other (noncontingent) domains may be observed. Spillover effects are frequently invoked as explanations in organizational research (Lian, Ferris, & Brown, 2012); contingent self-esteem research may help us to understand which individuals are particularly likely to exhibit spillover effects. Moreover, such research may help paint a more complete understanding of the IPSE: although it may have positive effects on performance, it may ultimately result in negative effects in other domains.

Contingent Self-Esteem and Attitudinal and Well-Being Outcomes

As this review indicates, most research has examined the negative effects of contingent self-esteem on attitudinal and well-being outcomes. Although some research has examined the relation of contingent self-esteem to burnout (e.g., Innstrand et al.,

2010), other attitudinal and well-being outcomes remain to be examined. As with cross-domain behavioral effects, demonstrating any negative effects of the IPSE on attitudinal or well-being outcomes can help paint a better picture of its positive and negative effects.

What Other Organizational Contingencies Exist?

To date, organizational contingent self-esteem research has focused exclusively on the IPSE. However, the organizational realm undoubtedly has other domains on which one might stake one's self-esteem. Using Crocker, Luhtanen, et al.'s (2003) domains as a starting point, one can imagine staking one's self-esteem on competing with other firms (or fellow employees), on the approval of one's peers, on the approval of one's supervisor, or on upholding ethical business practices. Alternately, new contingencies specific to the organizational realm may be relevant, such as staking self-esteem to a profession (e.g., human resources, information technology specialist), corporate policies (e.g., corporate social responsibility policies), or the performance of one's subordinates or mentees. Although such work should clearly be theory driven and relevant to a pressing organizational issue rather than exploratory, uncovering what specific aspects of organizations individuals stake their self-esteem to represents one way organizational researchers can contribute both to the larger contingent self-esteem literature as well as organizational research in general.

Development of Contingencies in Organizations

Finally, another area where organizational researchers can contribute to both organizational contingent self-esteem research while addressing a fundamental unanswered question in the contingent self-esteem literature is regarding the development of contingent self-esteem. Although contingent self-esteem is thought to develop largely in childhood through internalization of important societal values and norms from significant others (Crocker & Wolfe, 2001), no studies have examined this proposition. Although employed individuals are clearly not children, organizations do represent novel environments where individuals can be exposed to new expectations and values, and also represent areas where membership is typically desired (versus being fired). As such, organizational researchers could fruitfully examine the development of contingencies in new employees over time (or expatriate workers in new cultures) in response to organizational variables, such as organizational culture or leader values. Given that few studies examine contingent self-esteem as a dependent variable, such research would be of value both to understanding employee socialization as well as to the broader contingent self-esteem literature.

Conclusion

Contingent self-esteem research has only become a topic of active research in the past decade and, in many ways, is still in its infancy. This description is even more accurate with respect to organizational contingent self-esteem research, where studies have been infrequent. As such, many questions and areas of organizational contingent self-esteem research remain open to enterprising researchers. As the present chapter indicates, contingent self-esteem plays an important motivational role for individuals, and has the ability to influence actions, attitudes, and well-being. It is my belief, and hope, that researchers can begin examining ways that contingent self-esteem can fruitfully contribute to different organizational research areas.

Notes

1. I thank G. Russ Gott for his helpful comments on earlier versions of this chapter.
2. I thank Edward Deci and Richard Ryan for this suggestion.

References

Amabile, T. M., Conti, R., Coon, H., Lazenby, J., & Herron, M. (1996). Assessing the work environment for creativity. *Academy of Management Journal, 28*, 1154–1184. doi:10.2307/256995

Anthony, D. B., Holmes, J. G., & Wood, J. V. (2007). Social acceptance and self-esteem: Tuning the sociometer to interpersonal value. *Journal of Personality and Social Psychology, 92*, 1024–1039. doi:10.1037/0022-3514.92.6.1024

Arndt, J., Cox, C. R., Goldenberg, J. L., Vess, M., Routledge, C., Cooper, D. P., & Cohen, F. (2009). Blowing in the (social) wind: Implications of extrinsic esteem contingencies for terror management and health. *Journal of Personality and Social Psychology, 96*, 1191–1205. doi:10.1037/a0015182

Baumeister, R. F., Campbell, J. D., Krueger, J. I., & Vohs, K. D. (2003). Does high self-esteem cause better performance, interpersonal success, happiness, or healthier lifestyles? *Psychological Science in the Public Interest, 4*, 1–44. doi:10.1111/1529-1006.01431

Baumeister, R. F., Smart, L., & Boden, J. M. (1996). Relation of threatened egotism to violence and aggression: The dark side of high self-esteem. *Psychological Review, 103*, 5–33. doi:10.1037//0033-295X.103.1.5

Bergstrom, R. L., Neighbors, C., & Lewis, M. A. (2004). Do men find "bony" women attractive? Consequences of misperceiving opposite sex perceptions of attractive body image. *Body Image, 1*, 183–191. doi:10.1016/S1740-1445(03)00025-1

Bos, A. E. R., Huijding, J., Muris, P., Vogel, L. R. R., & Biesheuvel, J. (2011). Global, contingent and implicit self-esteem and psychopathological symptoms in adolescents. *Personality and Individual Differences, 48*, 311–316. doi:10.1016/j.paid.2009.10.025

Breines, J. G., Crocker, J., & Garcia, J. A. (2008). Self-objectification and well-being in women's daily lives. *Personality and Social Psychology Bulletin, 34*, 583–598. doi:10.1177/0146167207313727

Britt, T. W., McKibben, E. S., Greene-Shortridge, T. M., Beeco, A., Bodine, A., Calcaterra, J.,…West, A. (2010). Self-engagement as a predictor of performance and emotional reactions to performance outcomes. *British Journal of Social Psychology, 49*, 237–257. doi:10.1348/014466609X438090

Brockner, J. (1988). *Self-esteem at work: Research, theory and practice.* Lexington, MA: D.C. Heath & Co.

Burwell, R. A., & Shirk, S. R. (2006). Self processes in adolescent depression: The role of self-worth contingencies. *Journal of Research on Adolescence, 16*, 479–490. doi:10.1111/j.1532-7795.2006.00503.x

Cambron, M. J., & Acitelli, L. K. (2010). Examining the link between friendship-contingent self-esteem and the self-propagating cycle of depression. *Journal of Social and Clinical Psychology, 29*, 701–726. doi:10.1521/jscp.2010.29.6.701

Cambron, M. J., Acitelli, L. K., & Steinberg, L. (2010). When friends make you blue: The role of friendship-contingent self-esteem in predicting self-esteem and depressive symptoms. *Personality and Social Psychology Bulletin, 36*, 384–397. doi:10.1177/0146167209351593

Chang, C.-H., Ferris, D. L., Johnson, R. E., Rosen, C. C., & Tan, J. A. (2012). Core self-evaluations: A review and evaluation of the literature. *Journal of Management, 38*, 81–128. doi:10.1177/0149206311419661

Chen, G., Gully, S. M., & Eden, D. (2001). Validation of a new general self-efficacy scale. *Organizational Research Methods, 4*, 62–83. doi:10.1177/109442810141004

Cheng, S.-T., & Kwang, K. W. K. (2008). Attachment dimensions and contingencies of self-worth: The moderating role of culture. *Personality and Individual Differences, 45*, 509–514. doi:10.1016/j.paid.2008.06.003

Clabaugh, A., Karpinski, A., & Griffin, K. (2008). Body weight contingency of self-worth. *Self and Identity, 7*, 337–359. doi:10.1080/15298860701665032

Cleveland, J. N., Murphy, K. R., & Williams, R. E. (1989). Multiple uses of performance appraisal: Prevalence and correlates. *Journal of Applied Psychology, 74*, 130–135. doi:10.1037//0021-9010.74.1.130

Colquitt, J. A. (2001). On the dimensionality of organizational justice: A construct validation of a measure. *Journal of Applied Psychology, 86*, 386–400. doi:10.1037//0021-9010.86.3.386

Crocker, J., Brook, A. T., Niiya, Y., & Villacorta, M. (2006). The pursuit of self-esteem: Contingencies of self-worth and self-regulation. *Journal of Personality, 74*, 1749–1771. doi:10.1111/j.1467-6494.2006.00427.x

Crocker, J., Karpinski, A., Quinn, D. M., & Chase, S. K. (2003). When grades determine self-worth: Consequences of contingent self-worth for male and female engineering and psychology majors. *Journal of Personality and Social Psychology, 85*, 507–516. doi:10.1037/0022-3514.85.3.507

Crocker, J., & Luhtanen, R. K. (2003). Level of self-esteem and contingencies of self-worth: Unique effects on academic, social and financial problems in college students.

Personality and Social Psychology Bulletin, 29, 701–712. doi:10.1177/0146167203029006003

Crocker, J., Luhtanen, R. K., Cooper, M. L., & Bouvrette, A. (2003). Contingencies of self-worth in college students: Theory and measurement. *Journal of Personality and Social Psychology, 85*, 894–908. doi:10.1037/0022-3514.85.5.894

Crocker, J., Luhtanen, R. K., & Sommers, S. R. (2004). Contingencies of self-worth: Progress and prospects. *European Review of Social Psychology, 15*, 133–181. doi:10.1080/10463280440000017

Crocker, J., & Park, L. E. (2004). The costly pursuit of self-esteem. *Psychological Bulletin, 130*, 392–414. doi:10.1037/0033-2909.130.3.392

Crocker, J., Sommers, S. R., & Luhtanen, R. K. (2002). Hopes dashed and dreams fulfilled: Contingencies of self-worth and graduate school admissions. *Personality and Social Psychology Bulletin, 28*, 1275–1286. doi:10.1177/01461672022812012

Crocker, J., & Wolfe, C. T. (2001). Contingencies of self-worth. *Psychological Review, 108*, 593–623. doi:10.1037//0033-295X.108.3.593

Dahlin, M., Joneborg, N., & Runeson, B. (2007). Performance-based self-esteem and burnout in a cross-sectional study of medical students. *Medical Teacher, 29*, 43–48. doi:10.1080/01421590601175309

Deci, E. L., Eghrari, H., Patrick, B. C., & Leone, D. (1994). Facilitating internalization: The self-determination theory perspective. *Journal of Personality, 62*, 119–142. doi:10.1111/j.1467-6494.1994.tb00797.x

Deci, E. L., & Ryan, R. M. (1995). Human agency: The basis for true self-esteem. In M. H. Kernis (Ed.), *Efficacy, agency, and self-esteem* (pp. 31–50). New York: Plenum Press.

Deci, E. L., & Ryan, R. M. (2000). The "what" and "why" of goal pursuits: Human needs and the self-determination of behavior. *Psychological Inquiry, 11*, 227–268. doi:10.1207/S15327965PLI1104_01

Ferris, D. L., Brown, D. J., & Heller, D. (2009). Organizational supports and organizational deviance: The mediating role of organization-based self-esteem. *Organizational Behavior and Human Decision Processes, 108*, 279–286. doi:10.1016/j.obhdp.2008.09.001

Ferris, D. L., Brown, D. J., Lian, H., & Keeping, L. M. (2009). When does self-esteem relate to deviant behavior? The role of contingencies of self-worth. *Journal of Applied Psychology, 63*, 1345–1353. doi:10.1037/a0016115

Ferris, D. L., Lian, H., & Brown, D. J. (2011). Ostracism and job performance: A moderated mediation model. Manuscript submitted for publication.

Ferris, D. L., Lian, H., Brown, D. J., Pang, F. X. J., & Keeping, L. M. (2010). Self-esteem level and job performance: The moderating role of self-esteem contingencies. *Personnel Psychology, 63*, 561–593. doi:10.1111/j.1744-6570.2010.01181.x

Goldberg, L. R. (1992). The development of markers for the big-five factor structure. *Psychological Assessment, 4*, 26–42. doi:10.1037//1040-3590.4.1.26

Grandey, A. A., & Cropanzano, R. (1999). The conservation of resources model applied to work-family conflict and strain. *Journal of Vocational Behavior, 54*, 350–370. doi:10.1006/jvbe.1998.1666

Grolnick, W. S., Price, C. E., Beiswenger, K. L., & Sauck, C. C. (2007). Evaluative pressure in mothers: Effects of situation, maternal, and child characteristics on autonomy supportive versus controlling behavior. *Developmental Psychology, 43*, 991–1002. doi:10.1037/0012-1649.43.4.991

Grossbard, J. R., Lee, C. M., Neighbors, C., & Larimer, M. E. (2009). Body image concerns and contingent self-esteem in male and female college students. *Sex Roles, 60*, 198–207. doi:10.1007/s11199-008-9535-y

Hallsten, L. (1993). Burning out: A framework. In W. Schaufeli, C. Maslach, & T. Marek (Eds.), *Professional burnout: Recent developments in theory and research* (pp. 95–113). Washington: Taylor & Francis.

Hill, A. P., Hall, H. K., & Appleton, P. R. (2011). The relationship between multidimensional perfectionism and contingencies of self-worth. *Personality and Individual Differences, 50*, 238–242. doi:10.1016/j.paid.2010.09.036

Hobfoll, S. E. (1989). Conservation of resources: A new attempt at conceptualizing stress. *American Psychologist, 44*, 513–524. doi:10.1037//0003-066X.44.3.513

Horberg, E. J., & Chen, S. (2010). Significant others and contingencies of self-worth: Activation and consequences of relationship-specific contingencies of self-worth. *Journal of Personality and Social Psychology, 98*, 77–91. doi:10.1037/a0016428

Hu, J., Yang, Y., Wang, D., & Liu, Y. (2008). Contingency as a moderator of the effect of domain self-esteem on global self-esteem. *Social Behavior and Personality, 36*, 851–864. doi:10.2224/sbp.2008.36.6.851

Innstrand, S. T., Langballe, E. M., Espnes, G. A., Aasland, O. G., & Falkum, E. (2010). Personal vulnerability and work-home interaction: The effect of job performance-based self-esteem on work/home conflict and facilitation. *Scandinavian Journal of Psychology, 51*, 480–487. doi:10.1111/j.1467-9450.2010.00816.x

Innstrand, S. T., Langballe, E. M., & Falkum, E. (2011). The longitudinal effects of individual vulnerability, organizational factors, and work-home interaction on burnout among male church ministers in Norway. *Mental Health, Religion & Culture, 14*, 241–257. doi:10.1080/13674670903470621

James, W. (1890). *The principles of psychology (Vol. 1)*. Cambridge, MA: Harvard University Press.

Jex, S. M., & Elacqua, T. C. (1999). Self-esteem as a moderator: A comparison of global and organization-based measures. *Journal of Occupational and Organizational Psychology, 72*, 71–81. doi:10.1348/096317999166509

Johnson, J. W. (2003). Toward a better understanding of the relationship between personality and individual job performance. In M. Barrick, & A. M. Ryan (Eds.), *Personality and work* (pp. 83–120). San Francisco: Jossey-Bass.

Johnson, M. (2011). Active and passive maladaptive behavior patterns mediate the relationship between contingent self-esteem and health. *Personality and Individual Differences, 51*, 178–182. doi:10.1016/j.paid.2011.03.039

Johnson, M., & Blom, V. (2007). Development and validation of two measures of contingent self-esteem. *Individual Differences Research, 5*, 300–328.

Judge, T. A., & Bono, J. E. (2001). Relationship of core self-evaluations traits—self-esteem, generalized self-efficacy, locus of control, and emotional stability—with job satisfaction and job performance: A meta-analysis. *Journal of Applied Psychology, 86*, 80–92. doi:10.1037//0021-9010.86.1.80

Judge, T. A., Erez, A., Bono, J. E., & Thoresen, C. J. (2003). The Core Self-Evaluations Scale: Development of a measure. *Personnel Psychology, 56*, 303–331. doi:10.1111/j.1744-6570.2003.tb00152.x

Kanungo, R. N. (1982). Measurement of job and work involvement. *Journal of Applied Psychology, 67*, 341–349. doi:10.1037//0021-9010.67.3.341

Kernis, M. H. (2003). Toward a conceptualization of optimal self-esteem. *Psychological Inquiry, 14*, 1–26. doi:10.1207/S15327965PLI1401_01

Kernis, M. H., & Goldman, B. G. (2006). Assessing stability of self-esteem and contingent self-esteem. In M. H. Kernis (Ed.), *Self-esteem issues and answers: A sourcebook of current perspectives* (pp. 77–85). New York: Psychology Press.

Kernis, M. H., Lakey, C. E., & Heppner, W. L. (2008). Secure versus fragile high self-esteem as a predictor of verbal defensiveness: Converging findings across three different markers. *Journal of Personality, 76*, 477–512. doi:10.1111/j.1467-6494.2008.00493.x

Knee, C. R., Canvello, A., Bush, A. L., & Cook, A. (2008). Relationship-contingent self-esteem and the ups and downs of romantic relationships. *Journal of Personality and Social Psychology, 95*, 608–627. doi:10.1037/0022-3514.95.3.608

Korman, A. K. (1970). Toward an hypothesis of work behavior. *Journal of Applied Psychology, 54*, 31–41. doi:10.1037/h0028656

Korman, A. K. (1976). Hypothesis of work behavior revisited and an extension. *Academy of Management Review, 1*, 50–63. doi:10.2307/257359

Langballe, E. M., Innstrand, S. T., Aasland, O. G., & Falkum, E. (2011). The predictive value of individual factors, work-related factors, and work-home interaction on burnout in female and male physicians: A longitudinal study. *Stress and Health: Journal of the International Society for the Investigation of Stress, 27*, 73–85. doi:10.1002/smi.1321

Lawrence, J. S., & Crocker, J. (2009). Academic contingencies of self-worth impair positively—and negatively-stereotyped students' performance in performance goal settings. *Journal of Research in Personality, 43*, 868–874. doi:10.1016/j.jrp.2009.05.002

Leary, M. R., Gallagher, B., Fors, E., Buttermore, N., Baldwin, E., Kennedy, K., & Mills, A. (2003). The invalidity of disclaimers about the effects of social feedback on self-esteem. *Personality and Social Psychology Bulletin, 29*, 623–636. doi:10.1177/0146167203029005007

Lemay, E. P., Jr., & Ashmore, R. D. (2006). The relationship of social approval contingency to trait self-esteem: Cause, consequence, or moderator? *Journal of Research in Personality, 40*, 121–139. doi:10.1016/j.jrp.2004.09.012

Lemay, E. P., Jr., & Clark, M. S. (2008). "You're just saying that." Contingencies of self-worth, suspicion, and authenticity in the interpersonal affirmation process. *Journal of Experimental Social Psychology, 44*, 1376–1382. doi:10.1016/j.jesp.2008.05.001

Levenson, H. (1981). Differentiating among internality, powerful others, and chance. In H. M. Lefcourt (Ed.), *Research with the locus of control construct* (pp. 15–63). New York: Academic Press.

Lian, H., Ferris, D. L., & Brown, D. J. (2012). Does power distance exacerbate or mitigate the effects of abusive supervision? It depends on the outcome. *Journal of Applied Psychology, 97*, 107–123. doi:10.1037/a0024610

Luhtanen, R. K., & Crocker, J. (2005). Alcohol use in college students: Effects of level of self-esteem, narcissism, and contingencies of self-worth. *Psychology of Addictive Behaviors, 19*, 99–103. doi:10.1037/0893-164X.19.1.99

McArdle, S. (2010). Exploring domain-specific perfectionism. *Journal of Personality, 78*, 493–508. doi:10.1111/j.1467-6494.2010.00624.x

Mossholder, K. W., Bedeian, A. G., & Armenakis, A. A. (1981). Role perceptions, satisfaction, and performance: Moderating effects of self-esteem and organizational level. *Organizational Behavior and Human Performance, 28*, 224–234. doi:10.1016/0030-5073(81)90023-4

Mossholder, K. W., Bedeian, A. G., & Armenakis, A. A. (1982). Group process-work outcome relationships: A note on the moderating impact of self-esteem. *Academy of Management Journal, 25*, 575–585. doi:10.2307/256081

Motowidlo, S. J., Borman, W. C., & Schmit, M. J. (1997). A theory of individual differences in task and contextual performance. *Human Performance, 10*, 71–83. doi:10.1207/s15327043hup1002_1

Neighbors, C., Larimer, M. E., Geisner, I. M., & Knee, C. R. (2004). Feeling controlled and drinking motives among college students: Contingent self-esteem as a mediator. *Self and Identity, 3*, 207–224. doi:10.1080/13576500444000029

Niiya, Y., Crocker, J., & Bartmess, E. N. (2004). From vulnerability to resilience: Learning orientations buffer contingent self-esteem from failure. *Psychological Science, 15*, 801–805. doi:10.1111/j.0956-7976.2004.00759.x

Nisbett, R. E., & Wilson, T. D. (1977). Telling more than we can know: Verbal reports on mental processes. *Psychological Review, 84*, 231–259. doi:10.1037//0033-295X.84.3.231

Park, L. E., & Crocker, J. (2005). Interpersonal consequences of seeking self-esteem. *Personality and Social Psychology Bulletin, 31*, 1587–1598. doi:10.1177/0146167205277206

Park, L. E., & Crocker, J. (2008). Contingencies of self-worth and responses to negative interpersonal feedback. *Self and Identity, 7*, 184–203. doi:10.1080/15298860701398808

Park, L. E., Crocker, J., & Kiefer, A. K. (2007). Contingencies of self-worth, academic failure, and goal pursuit. *Personality and Social Psychology Bulletin, 33*, 1503–1517. doi:10.1177/0146167207305538

Park, L. E., Crocker, J., & Mickelson, K. D. (2004). Attachment styles and contingencies of self-worth. *Personality and Social Psychology Bulletin, 30*, 1243–1254. doi:10.1177/0146167204264000

Park, L. E., & Maner, J. K. (2009). Does self-threat promote social connection? The role of self-esteem and contingencies of self-worth. *Journal of Personality and Social Psychology, 96*, 203–217. doi:10.1037/a0013933

Patrick, H., Neighbors, C., & Knee, C. R. (2004). Appearance related social comparisons: The role of contingent self-esteem and self—perceptions of attractiveness. *Personality and Social Psychology Bulletin, 30*, 501–514. doi:10.1177/0146167203261891

Paullay, I. M., Alliger, G. M., & Stone-Romero, E. F. (1994). Construct validation of two instruments designed to measure job involvement and work centrality. *Journal of Applied Psychology, 29*, 224–228. doi:10.1037//0021-9010.79.2.224

Pierce, J. L., & Gardner, D. G. (2004). Self-esteem within the work and organizational context: A review of the organization-based self-esteem literature. *Journal of Management, 30*, 591–622. doi:10.1016/j.jm.2003.10.001

Pierce, J. L., Gardner, D. G., Cummings, L. L., & Dunham, R. B. (1989). Organization-based self-esteem: Construct definition, measurement, and validation. *Academy of Management Journal, 32*, 622–645. doi:10.2307/256437

Pierce, J. L., Gardner, D. G., Dunham, R. B., & Cummings, L. L. (1993). Moderation by organization-based self-esteem of role condition—employee response relationships. *Academy of Management Journal, 36*, 271–288. doi:10.2307/256523

Rosenberg, M. (1965). *Society and the adolescent self-image.* Princeton, NJ: Princeton University Press.

Rotundo, M., & Sackett, P. R. (2002). The relative importance of task, citizenship, and counterproductive performance to global ratings of job performance: A policy-capturing approach. *Journal of Applied Psychology, 87*, 66–80. doi:10.1037//0021-9010.87.1.66

Sanchez, D. T., & Crocker, J. (2005). How investment in gender ideals affects well-being: The role of external contingencies of self-worth. *Psychology of Women Quarterly, 29*, 63–77. doi:10.1111/j.1471-6402.2005.00169.x

Sanchez, D. T., Crocker, J., & Boike, K. R. (2005). Doing gender in the bedroom: Investing in gender norms and the sexual experience. *Personality and Social Psychology Bulletin, 31*, 1445–1455. doi:10.1177/0146167205277333

Sanchez, D. T., Good, J. J., Kwang, T., & Saltzman, E. (2008). When finding a mate feels urgent: Why relationship contingency predicts men's and women's body shame. *Social Psychology, 39*, 90–102. doi:10.1027/1864-9335.39.2.90

Sanchez, D. T., & Kwang, T. (2007). When the relationship becomes her: Revisiting women's body concerns from a relationship contingency perspective. *Psychology of Women Quarterly, 31*, 401–414. doi:10.1111/j.1471-6402.2007.00389.x

Sargent, J. T., Crocker, J., & Luhtanen, R. (2006). Contingencies of self-worth and depressive symptoms in college students. *Journal of Social and Clinical Psychology, 25*, 628–646. doi:10.1521/jscp.2006.25.6.628

Strahan, E. J., Lafrance, A., Wilson, A. E., Ethier, N., Spencer, S. J., & Zanna, M. P. (2008). Victoria's dirty secret: How sociocultural norms influence adolescent girls and women. *Personality and Social Psychology Bulletin, 34*, 288–301. doi:10.1177/0146167207310457

Swann, W. B., Jr. (1992). Seeking "truth," finding despair: Some unhappy consequences of a negative self-concept. *Current Directions in Psychological Science, 1*, 15–18. doi:10.1111/1467-8721.ep10767800

Swann, W. B., Jr. (2011). Self-verification theory. In P. Van Lang, A. Kruglanski, & E. T. Higgins (Eds.), *Handbook of theories of social psychology* (pp. 23–42). London: Sage.

Swann, W. B., Jr., Chang-Schneider, C., & McClarty, K. L. (2007). Do people's self-views matter? *American Psychologist, 62*, 84–94. doi:10.1037/0003-066X.62.2.84

Swann, W. B., Jr., Chang-Schneider, C., & McClarty, K. L. (2008). Yes, cavalier attitudes can have pernicious consequences. *American Psychologist, 63*, 65–66. doi:10.1037/0003-066X.63.1.65

Updegraff, J. A., Emanuel, A. S., Suh, E. M., & Gallagher, K. M. (2010). Sheltering the self from the storm: Self-construal abstractness and the stability of self-esteem. *Personality and Social Psychology Bulletin, 36*, 97–108. doi:10.1177/0146167209353331

vanDellen, M. R., Hoy, M. B., Fernandez, K., & Hoyle, R. H. (2011). Academic-contingent self-worth and the social monitoring system. *Personality and Individual Differences, 50*, 59–63. doi:10.1016/j.paid.2010.08.022

vanDellen, M. R., Hoy, M. B., & Hoyle, R. H. (2009). Contingent self-worth and social information processing: Cognitive associations between domain performance and social relations. *Social Cognition, 27*, 847–866. doi:10.1521/soco.2009.27.6.847

Vartanian, L. R. (2009). When the body defines the self: Self-concept clarity, internalization, and body image. *Journal of Social and Clinical Psychology, 28*, 94–126. doi:10.1521/jscp.2009.28.1.94

Vess, M., & Arndt, J. (2008). The nature of death and the death of nature: The impact of mortality salience on environmental concern. *Journal of Research in Personality, 42*, 1376–1380. doi:10.1016/j.jrp.2008.04.007

Wilson, A. E., Allen, J. W., Strahan, E. J., & Ethier, N. (2008). Getting involved: Testing the effectiveness of a volunteering intervention on young adolescents' future intentions. *Journal of Community and Applied Social Psychology, 18*, 630–637. doi:10.1002/casp.970

Wood, J. V. (1996). What is social comparison and how should we study it? *Personality and Social Psychology Bulletin, 22*, 520–537. doi:10.1177/0146167296225009

Zeigler-Hill, V. (2006). Contingent self-esteem and the interpersonal circumplex: The interpersonal pursuit of self-esteem. *Personality and Individual Differences, 40*, 713–723. doi:10.1016/j.paid.2005.08.009

Zeigler-Hill, V. (2007). Contingent self-esteem and race: Implications for the black self-esteem advantage. *Journal of Black Psychology, 33*, 51–74. doi:10.1177/0095798406295096

Zeigler-Hill, V., Clark, C. B., & Pickard, J. D. (2008). Narcissistic subtypes and contingent self-esteem: Do all narcissists base their self-esteem on the same domains? *Journal of Personality, 76*, 753–774. doi:10.1111/j.1467-6494.2008.00503.x

CHAPTER
9

Person-Environment Fit and Self-Determination Theory

Gary J. Greguras, James M. Diefendorff, Jacqueline Carpenter, *and* Christian Tröster

---

Abstract

Despite self-determination and person-environment fit theories being comprised of several common key components, rarely have these theoretical frameworks been integrated. Both self-determination and person-environment fit theories highlight the importance of individuals' need satisfactions and motivations. For example, self-determination theory highlights the importance of the reasons for goal pursuit in predicting individual well-being. Similarly, in person-environment fit theories, employee-environment value congruence is important because values influence outcomes through goals (motivation). We begin by discussing the similarities and differences between these two theoretical frameworks and then devote attention to integrating these frameworks and presenting an agenda for future research. We also discuss social network theory and research and highlight the potential usefulness of integrating these lines of research. A main premise of our analysis is that self-determination theory is likely a useful framework for better understanding the processes through which person-environment fit influences employee outcomes.

Key Words: person-environment fit, self-determination theory, value congruence, motivation, social network theory

---

Introduction

Self-determination theory (SDT) posits that a requirement for individual well-being and thriving is that individuals satisfy their basic psychological needs (Deci & Ryan, 2000). Such need satisfaction is more likely to occur when the environment within which a person resides provides opportunities and the appropriate "nutriments" to do so (Deci & Ryan, 2000). Although SDT argues that what is needed is universal (i.e., all people have the same needs), the particular ways in which needs are satisfied vary as a function of a person's unique constellation of characteristics. As such, the level of need satisfaction (and therefore well-being) is the result of personal attributes, the environmental context, and the match between them. Although the idea that the fit between the person and environment is important

seems inherent to many of the propositions of SDT, and indeed much SDT research has focused on both individual and contextual factors (Sheldon & Gunz, 2009), this notion of person-environment (PE) fit rarely has received explicit attention in SDT research (Greguras & Diefendorff, 2009).

PE fit research focuses explicitly on the match or congruence between individuals and their environments as a key determinant of well-being and effectiveness (Kristof-Brown, Zimmerman, & Johnson, 2005). Recognizing the importance of this congruency, Arthur, Bell, Doverspike, and Villado (2006) noted that "Theoretically, the relation between fit and attitudes is predicated on the reasoning that when there is fit, the environment affords individuals the opportunity to fulfill their needs" (p. 787). Thus, both SDT and PE fit research emphasize the importance of understanding the person-in-context and assume that whether a person thrives depends on the degree of correspondence between personal attributes and contextual factors.

In the following sections, we first briefly review the general theories and research of both SDT and PE fit. Next, we discuss various theories and research that help to integrate these two frameworks. In doing so, we argue that SDT provides explanatory mechanisms for the effects of PE fit on well-being, effectiveness, and other favorable employee outcomes. We next discuss social networks theory and research and the potential usefulness of integrating these literatures. Finally, we highlight opportunities for future research aimed at integrating these literatures.

Self-Determination Theory
Need Satisfaction
Deci and Ryan (2000) developed a model of human functioning that focuses on how individuals interface with their environments as a key determinant of whether they experience ill-being and stunted psychological growth, or well-being and thriving. In SDT, the primary determinant of psychological health is whether individuals can satisfy their basic psychological needs of autonomy, competence, and relatedness. The need for autonomy pertains to the sense that one is in control of one's actions; in short, it is the extent to which one feels self-determined versus other-determined in the pursuit of activities. The need for competence pertains to the belief that one can positively impact one's outcomes and surroundings. The need for relatedness pertains to the extent to which one feels connected to and close with others. According to Deci and Ryan (1985, 2000), need satisfaction is associated with experiencing actions as more intrinsically motivating and less extrinsically motivating. Interestingly, different researchers adopt different causal orders for need satisfaction and motivation, with Deci and Ryan (2000) suggesting that need satisfaction is a precursor to intrinsic motivation, and Sheldon and Elliot (1999) arguing that the reasons (i.e., motivations) for pursuing activities can determine the level of need satisfaction. Indeed, research exploring the causal relation between intrinsic motivation and psychological need satisfaction has been equivocal (e.g., Grouzet, Vallerand, Thill, & Provencher, 2004; Guay, Boggiano, & Vallerand, 2001). This equivocal research suggests what we and others have speculated, namely that the causal direction is likely reciprocal. Although likely reciprocal,

we expect that at the level of tasks or events much of the direction goes from motivations (i.e., the reasons for doing something) to need satisfactions given that ultimately it is the satisfaction of our psychological needs that brings about well-being.

Forms of Motivated Action
The pursuit of intrinsically derived goals has been associated with better subjective well-being, more positive affect, less negative physical symptoms, and less negative affect (e.g. Ryan, Sheldon, Kasser, & Deci, 1996; Sheldon & Elliot, 1999). In contrast, the pursuit and attainment of extrinsic goals may thwart psychological need satisfaction and lead to lower well-being (Sheldon & Elliot, 1999). Deci and Ryan (2000) argued that task characteristics that consistently thwart one's needs because they are experienced as controlling lead to low levels of well-being (Deci & Ryan, 2000). As such, a major contribution of SDT is that it describes how different motivations for action can contribute to psychological need satisfaction and well-being (Deci & Ryan, 2000; Gagne & Deci, 2005).

Deci and Ryan (1985, 2000) argue that any action can be categorized as either motivated or amotivated. Amotivation occurs when individuals lack intentionality with regard to a task and are not sure why they engage in the action (Gagné & Deci, 2005). In contrast, motivated behavior is experienced as purposefully and deliberately enacted. The reasons for goal pursuit fall into two categories: intrinsic (i.e., because the task is inherently interesting or enjoyable) and extrinsic (i.e., because of the influence of an external pressure). Intrinsically motivating tasks are always experienced as autonomous (i.e., originating from the self), whereas extrinsically motivating tasks can be experienced as either autonomous or controlled (i.e., originating from outside the self).

Whether an extrinsically motivating task is experienced as autonomous or controlling depends on the extent to which the reasons for pursuing the task have been internalized by the individual (Gagné & Deci, 2005). The idea that external tasks can be internalized and integrated with the self is a key contribution of SDT (Deci & Ryan 1985, 2000). The process of internalization involves the individual "taking in" and identifying with some aspect of the activity (i.e., the underlying values, regulatory structures), which eliminates the need for a purely external force. As a result of this process, individuals can experience more or less autonomous forms of extrinsic motivation.

The least internalized type of extrinsic motivation is external regulation, which is when external contingencies guide actions. An example is when an employee only performs an activity because of the promise of compensation or the threat of punishment (e.g., pay for performance, performance monitoring). Representing a more internalized form of extrinsic motivation, introjected regulation occurs when the person has come to self-administer rewards or punishments associated with the activity. As such, the person has not internalized the underlying reasons for the activity and does not think it is important or valuable, but rather only does it to avoid feeling shame or guilt if it is not performed (Deci & Ryan, 2000). With both external and introjected motivations, the individual experiences tasks as controlling, which make them less likely to result in psychological need satisfaction, and therefore, well-being.

Another form of extrinsic motivation that is more internalized is identified regulation. In this circumstance, the individual identifies with the underlying value of the behavior and experiences the activity as being one's own (Deci & Ryan, 1985). However, the person has not fully internalized the reasons for the doing the tasks, although the person understands the tasks and sees them as somewhat valuable. Here, the activity is experienced as being moderately autonomous (and moderately controlling). The most complete form of internalization is integrated regulation, in which the person believes that the task aligns with an important aspect of the self (Deci & Ryan, 1985, 2000). As such, the person sees the task as being aligned with one's true, valued self and pursues it independently, even though it has not achieved the status of being intrinsically motivating (i.e., it is still not inherently enjoyable).

Gagné and Deci (2005) reviewed research on these different forms of motivation and reported that more autonomous forms of motivation (i.e., intrinsic, identified, integrated) are linked to higher performance on complex or interesting tasks than controlled forms of motivation (i.e., external, introjected). However, researchers observed that these differences were not present for boring or mundane tasks (e.g., Koestner & Losier, 2002). Further, more autonomous forms of motivation are linked to higher job satisfaction, organizational commitment, and well-being than are more controlled forms of motivation (e.g., Baard, Deci, & Ryan, 2004; Gagné, Koestner, & Zuckerman, 2000). These findings are consistent with SDT such that those behaviors that are more self-determined (and therefore more autonomously motivated) result in positive outcomes for the individual.

To focus on task-specific motivation and to consolidate the reasons for goal pursuit into one construct, Sheldon and colleagues (Sheldon & Elliot, 1998; Sheldon & Houser-Marko, 2001) developed the self-concordance model. This model is grounded in SDT and delineates the processes by which motivation for specific activities relates to well-being, need satisfaction, and other outcomes. The model begins when people adopt a goal and addresses the longitudinal process from initial goal adoption to effort allocation and to goal attainment, need satisfaction, and other positive outcomes. As implied by the name of the model, it is the degree of self-concordance (i.e., the extent to which it is concordant with the true self) of the goal pursuit that is important. Self-concordance is often operationalized by creating an overall autonomous motivation score and an overall controlled motivation score for a goal and then subtracting controlled motivation from autonomous motivation.

Propositions of the self-concordance model have been largely supportive, although the model has not been widely applied to organizational contexts (for exceptions, see Bono & Judge, 2003; Greguras & Diefendorff, 2010; Judge, Bono, Erez, & Locke, 2005); instead many investigations have used student samples in an academic context (e.g., Sheldon, Ryan, Deci, & Kasser, 2004; Sheldon & Elliot, 1998, 1999; Sheldon & Houser-Marko, 2001). In field samples of employees, personality traits (Greguras & Diefendorff, 2010; Judge et al., 2005) and transformational leadership (Bono & Judge, 2003) are among the few antecedents associated with setting and pursuing self-concordant goals in organizational contexts. Specifically, individuals with a positive self-regard, measured in terms of core self evaluations, were more likely to pursue self-concordant goals (Judge et al., 2005) as were those who score higher in proactive personality (Greguras & Diefendorff, 2010). The self-concordance model also was specified as a mechanism through which transformational leaders affect performance and well-being of their followers. It seems apparent from the existing literature on self-concordance that there may be other, broad precursors to autonomous goal pursuit. PE fit is a concept that warrants investigation as an antecedent to the established self-concordant goals.

The Process of Internalization

An important process in SDT is the internalization of extrinsically motivating tasks or goals. Given that psychological need satisfaction is influenced by the pursuit of more autonomous tasks, it is important to understand what organizations can do to better ensure that work tasks are internalized by their employees. Although SDT argues that the natural tendency of human beings is to internalize the external, socially constructed reasons for doing tasks, the theory also describes aspects of the person (e.g., autonomous orientation vs. controlled orientation) and context (e.g., autonomy supportive context) that can facilitate this process. The degree to which individuals come to naturally value and pursue tasks that important others value, can greatly affect acceptance into social groups and the development of social networks. Thus, the more individuals internalize the socially constructed values underlying activities, the more they will feel accepted by others (satisfying the need for relatedness), experience the work as being autonomously derived (satisfying the need for autonomy), and perceive that one is in control of the outcomes of one's actions (satisfying the need for competence).

In addition to the internalization of goals being a natural tendency, organizations can attempt to facilitate or quicken this process by designing work tasks so that individuals have more discretion, tasks are more challenging and less routine, and work has a greater positive impact on other people (Deci & Ryan, 2000; Humphrey, Nahrgang, & Morgeson, 2007). In sum, the work demands need to align with personal values and employee strengths to better ensure that the person cares about the work and feels fully utilized on the job. Furthermore, changing the way leaders interact with their employees can enhance the internalization process. Specifically, leaders who provide a meaningful rationale for tasks, acknowledge that tasks may not be interesting, and provide choices in pursuing activities can lead individuals to feel more autonomous in the pursuit of goals and tasks (Baard et al., 2004; Deci, Eghrari, Patrick, & Leone, 1994). We argue in subsequent sections that different aspects of PE fit can influence psychological need satisfaction by either directly creating opportunities to experience more autonomous motivation or through the process of greater internalization of external activities.

PE Fit

The match or congruence between a person and an environment is a widely used framework for understanding the attitudes and behavior of organizational actors (Kristof-Brown et al., 2005). The general idea of fit, often referred to as PE fit, is defined as "the congruence, match, similarity, or correspondence between the person and the environment" (Edwards & Shipp, 2007, p. 211). The basic premise of PE fit theory is that this alignment is a desired state resulting in positive outcomes for individuals, and thus organizations (Ostroff & Shulte, 2007). Although research is scarce regarding the mechanisms accounting for why PE fit results in favorable outcomes, as we discuss throughout the remainder of the chapter, several theoretical explanations for these relationships suggest a connection with SDT and need satisfaction.

PE fit is the overarching framework encompassing distinct types of fit and different environmental foci. PE fit includes complementary and supplementary types of fit (Cable & Edwards, 2004; Edwards & Shipp, 2007; Kristof, 1996). Complementary fit occurs when a "weakness or need of the environment is offset by the strength of the individual, and vice versa" (Muchinsky & Monahan, 1987, p. 271). Thus, complementary fit refers to instances when fulfillment of the demands of a task or job requires certain skills and abilities, referred to as demands-abilities (DA) fit, or when the wants and needs of an individual are provided and fulfilled by the environment, referred to as needs-supplies (NS) fit (Cable & DeRue, 2002; Cable & Edwards, 2004). Supplementary fit exists when a person possesses similar or matching characteristics to the environment and is most often represented by examining value congruence (Kristof, 1996). Value congruence frequently is used to operationalize fit because values are seen as enduring and guiding principles that " . . . organize people's attitudes, emotions, and behaviors, and typically endure across time and situations" (Kasser, 2002, p. 123).

These types of fit (DA fit, NS fit, and value congruence) can be conceptualized at different environmental levels or foci. For example, person-organization (PO) fit refers to the degree to which an individual fits with the organization. PO fit is most often conceptualized in terms of value congruence (Chatman, 1991; Kristof, 1996), a supplementary fit approach, but it has also been studied with the complementary approach in research investigating how organizational characteristics, such as reward structures, meet employee needs (Cable & Edwards, 2004; Kristof-Brown & Jansen, 2007). Aside from the organizational level, complementary and supplementary fit have been investigated at the group, job, and individual level. Person-group (PG) fit, person-job (PJ) fit, and person-supervisor (PS) fit are common designations for the various conceptualizations at these levels, respectively (Kristof-Brown et al., 2005; Verquer, Beehr, & Wagner, 2003).

Several meta-analytic reviews of the fit literature indicate that the varying operationalizations of the construct have resulted in differential relationships with antecedents and outcomes (Hoffman & Woehr, 2006; Kristof-Brown et al., 2005; Verquer et al., 2003). For example, PJ fit operationalized in terms of NS fit had stronger associations with attidudinal outcomes than PJ fit operationalized in terms of DA fit (Kristof-Brown et al., 2005). Similarly, value fit (PO fit defined in terms of values) had stronger meta-analytic correlations with outcomes than other PO fit operationalizations (Hoffman & Woehr, 2006). Meta-analyzed correlations in Kristof-Brown et al. (2005) indicate that different types of fit are moderately correlated, ranging from .30 (PG-PS fit) to .58 (PO-PJ fit). Although the different types of fit are correlated, most studies that measure multiple types of fit observe that each type differentially predicts various outcomes (Kristof-Brown et al., 2005).

In addition to multiple operational definitions, there are various techniques for measuring fit and analyzing fit data. Terminology with regard to fit measurement varies among different authors, but in general three main approaches to operationalizing fit can be identified in the literature: (1) objective, (2) indirect, and (3) direct (Edwards, Cable, Williamson, Lambert, & Shipp, 2006; Ostroff, Shin, Kinicki, 2005). *Objective fit* approaches compare an individual's perception or rating of themselves (P) on some attribute with independently gathered assessments of the focal other (E) on the same attribute. These independent assessments can come from a variety of sources, including the supervisor, workgroup (Vancouver & Schmitt, 1991), or company records of the organization (OReilly, Chatman, & Caldwell, 1991). *Indirect fit* approaches require the employee to rate both the self (P) and a focal other (E) on some dimensions of interest. As such, the objective and indirect methods primarily differ on from where the information on the focal other (E) come: the employee themselves (indirect) or some other source (objective). Both the objective and indirect approaches require mathematical comparison of the person and environment to determine fit. The most appropriate method for calculating and representing these mathematical comparisons has been the subject of some debate in the literature (Edwards, 2001).

In contrast to the first two approaches, the *direct fit* approach elicits a summary judgment from individuals regarding how well they fit the environment on a particular dimension or dimensions. This measurement strategy has been used most often to assess fit (Edwards et al., 2006; Kristof-Brown et al., 2005). As discussed by Edwards and colleagues (2006), the direct approach to assessing fit may involve either the discrepancy that a person perceives between the self and environment (e.g., asking whether the environment has or provides more or less of a given resource or attribute than is desired or held, reflecting the nature of any misfit) or obtaining an overall evaluation of how well one fits with the environment concerning a particular dimension (in which the direction of misfit is ignored). Direct measures of fit based on subjective perceptions have been widely used because perceptions of fit or misfit are believed to affect employee attitudes and behaviors more strongly than objective or indirect fit that relies on researcher calculations (e.g., Cable & Judge, 1996; Endler & Magnusson, 1976). However, Edwards et al. (2006) argue that the direct approach to fit measurement is saturated with positive affect. As such, researchers should remain cognizant of the implications associated with various approaches to fit measurement.

Several meta-analytic reviews of the fit literature indicate that the degree to which PE fit is associated with behavioral and attitudinal outcomes varies depending on type of fit conceptualization, environmental foci, and measurement method (for detailed reviews see Hoffman & Woehr, 2006; Kristof-Brown et al., 2005; Verquer et al., 2003). Although research is sparse concerning antecedents of fit (Edwards, et al., 2006), PE fit, and its various dimensions, have been associated with a myriad of outcomes at the task, individual, and organization levels including organizational attraction, job choice, job satisfaction, organizational commitment, task performance, contextual performance, trust in managers, turnover intentions, and psychological well-being (Arthur et al., 2006; Cable & Judge, 1996; Kristof, 1996; Kristof-Brown et al., 2005).

Despite the application of this PE fit framework to many organizational phenomena, little is known about the psychological mechanisms and processes through which PE fit relates to outcomes. Greguras and Diefendorff (2009) argued that SDT may be a useful framework for examining how PE fit relates to outcomes. Specifically, they argued that PE fit may facilitate the satisfaction of employees' needs and this need satisfaction subsequently predicts well-being and favorable outcomes. Although need satisfaction or fulfillment is a central aspect of both self-determination and PE fit theories, the conceptualization of needs differs between these theoretical frameworks. Because the needs are conceptualized differently, we first discuss these differences before discussing how PE fit may satisfy employee needs.

The Concept of Needs

Central to both the PE fit and the SDT literatures is the concept of needs. However, as discussed in Greguras and Diefendorff (2009), needs are conceptualized differently in these two literatures thereby requiring a few words of clarification. In the PE fit literature, and indeed in most organizational research, needs are often equated with desires (Baard et al., 2004). For example, if an employee desires a higher degree of work-family balance, the PE fit literature would identify this desire for more balance as a need. Similarly, if an employee wants a higher salary, salary would be considered a need in the PE fit literature. However, a better work-family balance and a higher salary would be considered desires or wants, but not needs, by SDT. According to SDT, needs are considered to be "innate, essential, and universal" (Ryan & Deci, 2000, p. 74). As such, a better work-life balance would not be considered innate, essential, or universal, and therefore, would not be considered a need. As discussed previously, SDT focuses on individuals' psychological needs and proposes that human beings' needs for autonomy, competence, and relatedness meet the criteria of being innate, essential, and universal.

In the PE fit literature, the difference between what an employee wants or desires and what the employee actually receives (NS fit) represents the amount of misfit. Theoretically, the amount of fit or misfit is predicted to affect one's motivation, attitudes, and behaviors. In contrast, in SDT, it is not the satisfaction of desires that leads to favorable outcomes per se, but rather it is the satisfaction of our psychological needs that lead to favorable outcomes. Only to the degree that satisfying desires also satisfies our psychological needs (e.g., obtaining more work-life balance may help an individual to spend more time with his friends and thereby satisfy relatedness needs) would such satisfaction of desires lead to favorable outcomes. Indeed, satisfying desires that do not lead to the satisfaction of psychological needs

may lead to positive or negative outcomes (e.g., Kasser & Ryan, 1996; Sheldon & Kasser, 1998). In contrast, SDT argues that the satisfaction of a psychological need always leads to favorable outcomes because the satisfaction of a need that is essential cannot logically lead to unfavorable outcomes (Deci & Ryan, 2000). It is important to note that, although all humans have the same psychological needs, ones' ability to satisfy these needs differs between individuals. When one's needs are not satisfied and one perceives insufficient autonomy, relatedness, or competence need satisfaction, one desires and strives to have these needs satisfied (Sheldon & Gunz, 2009). A basic premise of this chapter is that PE fit (misfit) is one factor that facilitates (thwarts) the satisfaction of these innate psychological needs, and therefore leads to favorable (unfavorable) outcomes. PE fit also can shape the reasons for goal pursuit by directly impacting the level of autonomous-controlled motivation experienced and by indirectly shaping autonomous-controlled motivation through the process of internalization. In the next section, we consider how PE fit may impact psychological need satisfaction and employee motivation.

PE Fit and Direct Links to Psychological Need Satisfaction

As noted previously, a fundamental tenet of SDT is that individuals strive to satisfy their psychological needs for autonomy, relatedness, and competence. To do so, individuals seek environments in which they are able satisfy their needs while attempting to avoid environments that might limit their ability to satisfy these needs. One such factor is PE fit given that fit theoretically relates to favorable employee outcomes through the satisfaction of employee needs (e.g., Arthur et al., 2006). Although very little research has directly linked PE fit with SDT (for exceptions see Amiot, Vallerand, & Blanchard, 2006; O'Connor & Vallerand, 1994) or the satisfaction of one's psychological needs (an exception discussed later is Greguras & Diefendorff, 2009), next we discuss theoretically why various types of fit might be expected to relate to need satisfaction and review research that has linked PE fit to related constructs. Consistent with Kristof-Brown et al. (2005), we focus on the primary types of fit: PO, PS, PJ, and PG fit.

PO Fit

PO fit refers to the degree of congruence between the organization and an employee. Typically, PO fit is operationalized by looking at the degree to which employee values match those of the organization

(Kristoff, 1996). PO fit perhaps has received the most research attention out of the various PE fit components. Meta-analyses reveal that PO fit relates to a variety of favorable employee outcomes including increased job satisfaction and organizational commitment (Kristof-Brown et al., 2005; Verquer et al., 2003).

Several theoretical frameworks and associated literatures provide guidance for linking PO fit with the satisfaction of psychological needs. For example, Schneider and colleagues' (Schneider, 1987; Schneider, Goldstein, & Smith, 1995) attraction–selection-attrition model posits that individuals are attracted to, join, and remain in organizations where they "fit." Fit within the attraction–selection-attrition model has been operationalized, for example, as value congruence, personality congruence, or NS fit. The theory of work adjustment similarly argues that employees that fit better with their organization are better able to satisfy their needs, thereby resulting in greater employee satisfaction and less turnover. According to theory of work adjustment, when the needs of the employee or the organization are not met, one or both parties engage in adjustment behaviors aimed at satisfying the unmet needs (Dawis & Lofquist, 1984). Fit is important in both models because fit allows employees to attain their goals, and presumably satisfy their needs. We suggest that one's increased adjustment (fit) over time may result as a function of employees increasingly internalizing organizational goals and values, and this internalization results in greater autonomous goal striving thereby resulting in greater need satisfaction and well-being.

The community psychology literature provides another framework for expecting PO fit to relate to need satisfaction. This literature argues that a sense of community is derived when individuals feel that they belong, matter, and can fulfill their needs by being a part of a community (McMillan & Chavis, 1986). Extending this to an organizational context, Masterson and Stamper (2003) argued that individuals with greater PO fit also are better able to satisfy their needs, and therefore should report a greater sense of membership and community in the organization thereby resulting in more favorable outcomes. Taken together, these theoretical frameworks suggest that, over time, employees will attempt to adjust their fit with the organization and that only employees who "fit" and develop a sense of belonging with the organization (PO fit) will remain. This resultant fit leads to more favorable employee outcomes via the satisfaction of one's needs perhaps either directly or because of a greater internalization of the organization's goals and values.

PS Fit

The fit between supervisors and subordinates also has received significant attention in the literature. Similar to other types of fit, PS fit may be operationalized in many different ways including attitudinal similarity, demographic similarity, or value congruence. PS fit relates to a variety of outcomes including job satisfaction, perceived performance (Kristof-Brown et al., 2005), and organizational commitment (Meglino, Ravlin, & Adkins, 1989). Research also has observed that the quality of the work relationship between a supervisor and subordinate influences their attitudes and behaviors toward one another (Judge & Ferris, 1993). As with PO fit, PS fit often is operationalized based on value congruency between a supervisor and a subordinate. Given that values determine what is personally beneficial (Locke, 1991), and given that supervisors shape employees' work environments (Lord & Brown, 2001), it is likely that PS fit based on value congruency would allow employees to satisfy their needs and lead to favorable outcomes.

Several theories highlight the importance of the congruence (fit) between the supervisor and the subordinate. Drawing from the leadership literature, leader-member exchange (LMX) theory proposes that leaders develop unique exchange relationships with each follower. These relationships may be differentiated based on the degree to which they range from being based exclusively on the employment contract (low LMX relationships) to those that involve a reciprocal exchange of valued currencies (e.g., affect, respect) between the leader and follower (high LMX relationships; Liden & Maslyn, 1998). As such, LMX represents the quality (fit) of the supervisor-subordinate relationship (Graen & Cashman, 1975; Graen, Novak, & Sommerkamp, 1982). Based on role theory, (Kahn, Wolfe, Quinn, Snoek, & Rosenthal, 1964), LMX theory would suggest that higher-quality relationships are those based on currency exchanges (e.g., professional respect) that allow each other to satisfy one's needs. For example, the degree to which subordinates comply with supervisors' role expectations influences the supervisors' willingness to reciprocate by providing work-related resources, challenging work assignments, and by increasing a subordinate's autonomy (Graen & Scandura, 1987). That is, based on exchange theory, it could be argued that when there is greater fit, both the subordinate and the supervisor are more likely to help the other satisfy one's needs by supplying what that person needs.

As yet another example of a related but relevant literature, consider the literature on abusive supervision (e.g., Tepper, 2007). Situations in which supervisors are abusive toward their employees would likely represent poor fit for the subordinate. Indeed, Tepper, Moss, and Duffy's (2011) model of abusive supervision hypothesizes that perceived dissimilarity in attitudes or values with the subordinate leads to abusive supervision. These abusive supervisors control resources and influence the employee's environment. Abusive supervision has been associated with a variety of negative subordinate outcomes including decreased well-being (e.g., psychological distress; Tepper, 2000). SDT would argue that this decreased well-being is a likely result of the employees not being able to satisfy their needs (Deci & Ryan, 2000). Interestingly, Tepper's (2000) items measuring abusive supervision directly suggest that such supervision likely would decrease employee need satisfaction. For example, two items nicely demonstrate this point: "Does not allow me to interact with my coworkers," which would be expected to influence relatedness need satisfaction; and "Tells me I'm incompetent," which would be expected to impact competence need satisfaction.

Although we only present a few examples of theories addressing the supervisor-subordinate working relationship, these theories and others regarding supervisor-subordinate relationships or fit suggest that higher fit leads to favorable outcomes and greater well-being for the subordinate. We suggest, according to SDT, that this occurs because greater PS fit results in employees better being able to satisfy their psychological needs and/or enhanced internalization of shared values. That is, when PS fit is higher, supervisors and subordinates are likely to share similar values, goals, and perspectives thereby resulting in higher levels of subordinate autonomous motivation. One stream of SDT research that explicitly investigates how a supervisor treats a subordinate might influence need satisfaction is the literature examining supervisory autonomy support.

The extensive literature on controlling versus autonomy-supportive environments clearly demonstrates that controlling environments decrease intrinsic motivation and one's self-determination, whereas autonomy-supportive environments increase intrinsic motivation and one's self-determination

(for a review see Deci, Koestner, & Ryan, 1999). Controlling environments include those that, for example, focus on external rewards, provide little flexibility regarding one's job, or allow little discretion regarding how employees complete their work. Autonomous environments include those environments, for example, that allow employees flexibility, freedom, and participatory decision making.

Several studies have investigated the degree to which supervisors support an autonomous or controlled work environment affects outcomes. For example, Pelletier, Fortier, Vallerand, and Brière (2002) observed that athletes who perceived their coaches as being more autonomy-supportive were more self-determined and persistent in their goal-related behaviors. Similarly, Guay et al. (2001) found that students whose teachers who were autonomy-supportive reported feeling more competent in their academic work than students with less autonomy-supportive teachers. Numerous other studies have shown that subordinates with supervisors who are more autonomously-supportive report a host of positive outcomes, such as higher performance, increased well-being, increased intrinsic motivation, and more favorable work attitudes (e.g., Baard et al., 2004; Deci, Connell, & Ryan, 1989). Research further indicates that an autonomy-supportive environment relates to favorable outcomes through the satisfaction of one's psychological needs (e.g., Deci et al., 2001). The good news also is that research suggests supervisors can be trained to be more autonomy-supportive of their subordinates (Deci et al., 1989; Hardré & Reeve, 2009) and that teachers can be trained to be more autonomy-supportive of their students (Reeve, Hyungshim, Carrell, Soohyun, & Barch, 2004). It is important to recall, however, that individuals likely prefer different ways or options for satisfying their needs for autonomy. In order for supervisors to facilitate autonomy need satisfaction, they should provide numerous opportunities for employees to satisfy this need. Some ideas include providing the subordinate with options (e.g., flexible benefits, options on how to finish one's work, scheduling flexibility, participative decision making) and encouraging employees to do things on their own (Deci & Ryan, 1985). It should also be noted that managers who provide various options and opportunities for employees to satisfy their needs for autonomy may be doing so through increasing fit. That is, tailoring options to the desires of subordinates may increase PE fit, and in doing so, help employees to satisfy their needs.

PG Fit

PG fit refers to the congruency between an employee and ones' coworkers. In contrast to PO or PJ fit, considerably less research has focused on PG fit. Meta-analytic results indicate that PG fit relates to a variety of positive employee behaviors and attitudes including employee job satisfaction, coworker satisfaction, overall performance, and contextual performance (Kristof-Brown et al., 2005). As with other types of fit, PG fit has been operationalized in a variety of ways, including demographic similarity, attitudinal similarity, and value congruence. Although demographic similarity is important, Harrison, Price, and Bell (1998) argue that "deep-level" attributes (e.g., value congruence) is especially important in influencing individual-level outcomes. Next we discuss why PG fit, especially when based on "deep-level" attributes, likely leads to favorable employee outcomes.

The similarity-attraction hypothesis (Byrne, 1971) posits that individuals are attracted to individuals who are similar to themselves, communicate more frequently with similar others, and as a result develop more cohesive work relationships. This value congruence and resulting cohesiveness translates into less experienced role ambiguity and role conflict because sharing similar values allows coworkers to better coordinate and understand others' actions (Meglino et al., 1989). In addition to being more attracted to similar others because of the reduced role conflict and ambiguity, individuals who share similar values are likely to share similar goals, and therefore perceive their coworkers as facilitating goal attainment (Kristof-Brown & Stevens, 2001). Furthermore, individuals may prefer to interact with similar others because such interactions serve to self-validate their own beliefs, attitudes, and preferences (e.g., Swann, SteiNSeroussi, & Giesler, 1992).

The previous discussion suggests that PG fit facilitates the satisfaction of psychological needs. For example, the similarity-attraction hypothesis suggests that we like people who are similar to ourselves. Indeed, Kristof-Brown et al.'s (2005) meta-analysis indicated that PG fit most strongly correlated with coworker satisfaction. We would expect this coworker satisfaction to help to satisfy one's relatedness needs. Similarly, because less role conflict and ambiguity would be expected to facilitate goal attainment, we would expect such goal attainment to increase one's competence need satisfaction (or psychological need satisfaction in general). Finally, because employees who are attracted to a group (PG fit) often feel that they have some influence over its members (McMillian & Chavis, 1986), we would expect that PG fit would positively relate to autonomy need satisfaction.

PJ Fit

Unlike the previous types of PE fit discussed, PJ is not operationalized by value congruence. Rather, either objective measures or perceptions of DA fit or NS fit typically are used (Cable & DeRue, 2002). DA fit refers to whether the individual has the abilities to meet the demands of the job. NS fit refers to whether the job supplies what the employee wants. Most research has relied on employee perceptions to measure these types of PJ fit. Overall, PJ fit positively relates to employee job satisfaction, organizational commitment, organizational identification, and strain (Kristof-Brown et al., 2005). Moderator analyses in Kristof-Brown et al.'s (2005) meta-analysis indicated that when predicting attitudinal outcomes, overall PJ fit was the best predictor, followed by NS fit, followed by DA fit. Interestingly, NS fit also predicted job performance than did DA fit, suggesting that need fulfillment may be more important for employee performance and attitudes than DA fit. As with the other types of PE fit discussed previously, several theoretical frameworks exist that may be used to link PJ fit with need satisfaction.

One of the earliest interests of organizational scientists was investigating how to best match the person to a job in order to increase proficiency. Recognizing that these earlier approaches often resulted in unfavorable employee outcomes (e.g., decreased satisfaction, increased turnover), subsequent efforts to design jobs focused more on employee well-being factors, such as employee motivation (Humphrey et al., 2007). One such framework is Hackman and Oldham's (1976) job characteristics model. Hackman and Oldham's model argues that core job characteristics (e.g., autonomy) lead to critical psychological states (e.g., experienced meaningfulness of the work), which lead to favorable outcomes (e.g., internal work motivation). Their model subsequently has been expanded by researchers to include additional motivational (e.g., job specialization), social (e.g., social support), and work context (e.g., physical demands) characteristics (e.g., Humphrey et al., 2007). Other related work design approaches include, for example, job enrichment, job enlargement, and autonomous teams.

Linking PJ fit to psychological need satisfaction seems intuitive. That is, if one has the ability to meet the demands of the job, we would expect that person to experience competence need satisfaction. If the job provides one with what one needs, we expect that the job allows for the satisfaction of each of the three innate needs discussed previously. Indeed, recently developed measures assessing job design include items measuring such constructs as social support and work methods autonomy (Morgeson & Humphrey, 2006), which might be expected to relate to relatedness and autonomy need satisfaction, respectively. However, what happens if a person is overqualified for a job? Will this person still experience need satisfaction and increased motivation, or will this person become bored, feel unchallenged, and therefore not experience need satisfaction? As hypothesized by Feldman (1996), underemployment (lack of DA fit) likely results in a variety of negative employee outcomes including decreased motivation, well-being, and job performance. Interestingly, in a seminal piece on underemployment, Bashshur, Hernández, and Peiró (2011) suggest that the negative effects of underemployment on employee performance may be through different channels. Specifically, these authors argue that *objective* overqualification may affect task performance through increased procedural and declarative knowledge but that *perceived* overqualification might simultaneously decrease motivation, thereby negating the benefits of the increased knowledge. This suggests that the exact nature of the fit is important to consider and may affect one's needs differently.

Mediating Role of Psychological Need Satisfaction

Previously we suggested that SDT might be a useful framework for examining the processes through which PE fit relates to favorable employee outcomes. We also noted the virtual lack of research integrating SDT and PE fit frameworks. One exception is a study by Greguras and Diefendorff (2009). They hypothesized that various types of fit would be associated with different types of employee psychological need satisfaction. Furthermore, they hypothesized that psychological need satisfaction would mediate the relations between PE fit and employee outcomes (i.e., job performance and affective commitment). Consistent with their hypotheses, results indicated that PO fit positively related to the satisfaction of all three needs, PG fit predicted employees' relatedness need satisfaction, and PJ fit (operationalized as DA fit) was associated with greater competence need satisfaction. In addition to

these direct effects, results indicated that PO, PG, and PJ fit significantly predicted affective commitment indirectly through their associated relations with the psychological needs discussed previously. PJ fit also indirectly affected job performance through employee competence need satisfaction. Furthermore, both PO and PJ fit directly related to affective commitment. Taken together, this study suggests that SDT is a useful framework for explicating some of the processes through which PE fit relates to employee outcomes, mainly through the satisfaction of employees' psychological needs. Throughout this chapter we have argued that PE fit may influence both psychological need satisfaction and one's motivation. Next we discuss the relations between PE fit and employee motivation.

PE Fit and Autonomous-Controlled Motivation

As previously articulated, within SDT an important consideration is the extent to which work is experienced as autonomous or controlling (Deci & Ryan, 2000; Gagné & Deci, 2005). Perhaps it goes without saying that need satisfaction is most likely to occur when individuals pursue tasks for intrinsically motivating reasons—these individuals simply enjoy their tasks and find the tasks interesting, which make them feel autonomous and competent. However, it may also go without saying that the experience of pure intrinsic motivation at work is probably relatively rare, and when it does occur, it is probably not sustained over time. As such, the goal of many employees (and their organizations) may be to try to maximize the extent to which work is experienced as autonomous (i.e., as being important and aligned with one's values). Thus, job characteristics and social contexts that can facilitate the internalization process better enable employees to experience work as more autonomous (i.e., internalized and identified forms of motivation) and less controlling (i.e., introjected and extrinsic forms of motivation), which results in greater psychological need satisfaction.

As discussed, autonomous motivation is achieved when individuals pursue tasks for purely intrinsic reasons (i.e., the tasks are enjoyable) or because they have internalized the reasons for pursuing the tasks (i.e., they value the tasks). This process of internalization reflects the ways in which individuals learn to "take in" the external reasons for working on something. Organizations and their members clearly specify most work goals and tasks. As such, the process of internalization is likely to be easier and more complete when the reasons for pursuing the task naturally align with (i.e., fit) how the employee views the task (i.e., they naturally see it as valuable). We argue that PE fit plays an integral role in shaping the level of autonomous motivation experienced by employees, with some aspects of fit operating directly by creating contexts that match existing values and already established intrinsic motivators, and other aspects of fit operating indirectly by facilitating the internalization process by helping to align external reasons for performing an activity with existing employee values. In the following sections we discuss how PE fit may relate to, or influence, the reasons for one's goal pursuit.

Complementary Fit and Autonomous Motivation

Fit theory argues that environments can vary along several dimensions that correspond to personal attributes, desires, values, or motives of individuals. As such, an environment characteristic that allows the natural expression of one's attributes should enable individuals to experience greater levels of intrinsic motivation. The notion of complementary fit is that the environment requires something that the person possesses, or vice versa. We contend that this type of fit is likely to facilitate autonomous motivation by providing an environmental context that naturally aligns with existing employee attributes (e.g., values, skills, abilities). Perhaps the most obvious example of complementary fit is that of PJ fit, in which the person has abilities that are demanded of the job.

High levels of PJ fit indicate that the person's capabilities are not less than or greater than what is needed to do the job well; rather the skills and abilities just match what the job requires. This circumstance is likely to lead to high levels of effort and engagement on the part of employees because they are sufficiently challenged by the work, but not so much so that they become exhausted or overwhelmed. This circumstance is reminiscent of the antecedents of flow (Csikszentmihalyi, 1990), which is characterized by absorption, enjoyment, and intrinsic motivation (Bakker, 2008). Bakker (2008) argued that "the occurrence of flow is most likely when people perceive a balance between the challenge of a situation and their own skills to deal with this challenge" and that "employees should particularly experience flow when their job demands match their professional skills" (p. 401). Similarly, Vancouver, More, and Yoder (2008) showed that individuals are most likely to exert high effort when there is a good match between challenge and ability, with effort decreasing when there is a mismatch in either direction. Thus, it seems that PJ fit may lead to need satisfaction because it engages the more autonomous forms of motivation on the part of employees. When PJ fit is high, employees are working on tasks that are challenging, absorbing, and enjoyable.

However, there are likely some exceptions to the ability of PJ fit to lead to enhanced autonomous motivation. Consider situations in which the personal attributes needed to perform the job are themselves maladaptive for well-being or need satisfaction. For instance, bill collectors are often required to show negative emotions to delinquent customers to get them to comply with requests to pay their bills (Sutton, 1991). In this situation, high PJ fit may be achieved when the person is high in negative affectivity, trait anger, hostility, or neuroticism. However, these traits may directly harm well-being (Elfenbein, 2007), despite high PJ fit occurring. Similarly, Williams, Grow, Freedman, Ryan, and Deci (1996) showed that individuals high in a controlled causality orientation (i.e., dispositional orientation to experience environments as more controlling) did not fare better when placed in controlling contexts; rather both high controlled orientation and high autonomy orientation individuals were better off when placed in autonomous contexts suggesting that the fit hypothesis was not supported (Gagné & Deci, 2005). Similarly, Baard et al. (2004) found that autonomy support and autonomy orientation both exhibited main effects on need satisfaction, rather than an interaction effect that might conform to the fit hypothesis (e.g., that low autonomy orientation might be better in a low autonomy-supportive context). Although these studies are suggestive about the potential for PJ fit to not always lead to better employee outcomes, no research directly examining the impact of fit on autonomy-controlled aspects of the person and environment has been conducted.

Supplementary Fit and Autonomous Motivation

As previously articulated, supplementary fit occurs when the person matches the environment on some characteristic. The most commonly discussed type of supplementary fit is that of value congruence, which can occur between the person and a variety of social targets (i.e., the organization, supervisor, group, coworkers). We argue that value congruence forms of PE fit largely operate on autonomous motivation indirectly through the process of internalization described previously. In particular, fit dimensions that emphasize the congruence of values between the employee and others in the work environment likely lead to higher levels of autonomous motivation and need satisfaction through the process of individuals internalizing the reasons for performing the work. That is, value congruence (e.g., PO fit, PG fit, PS fit) means that the employee and other important social entities at work agree on underlying values, which can be thought of as goals that exist toward the top of an organizational goal hierarchy and shape the goals that exist at lower levels of the goal hierarchy (Diefendorff & Chandler, 2010). As such, the behavioral goals that are pursued on a day-to-day basis serve as the means by which the higher level goals (i.e., values) are achieved. Furthermore, the higher-level goals give meaning to and serve as the basis for pursuing the day-to-day activities. As such, the existence of high value congruence can infuse more meaning into behavioral goals pursued by employees. However, value congruence may come about as a result of socialization practices and the internalization process described by SDT. The internalization process outlined by SDT explicitly invokes the idea that individuals have come to accept external reasons for performing an activity as one's own; that they have come to value the reasons for doing tasks and see the tasks as important in their own right. This notion is similar to participative goal setting in which the person assigning the goals explains the reasons and importance for the goal as a way to help the employee understand and buy into the underlying value guiding the goal (Sue-Chan & Ong, 2002). Achieving value congruence means that an employee agrees with the organization's guiding principles. This value congruence provides an interpretive frame for the establishment of mid- and lower-level goals pertaining to work that needs to be done on a shorter-term basis. With an important underlying value supporting these goals, the person is more likely to experience the work as being autonomously derived, which should enhance the likelihood of need satisfaction on the job. This circumstance is in contrast to one in which employees experience low value congruence. Here, the person does not value the underlying reasons for performing work activities and the only organizational mechanisms that influence employee action involve the performance management system (i.e., performance appraisal, compensation, discipline practices). Thus, the work is experienced

as controlling (i.e., extrinsic, introjected) and the performance of the work may actually thwart psychological need satisfaction.

As described by Sheldon and Elliot (1999), "Identified activity . . . fits with the person's superordinate values and deeper beliefs" (p. 547). Koestner and Losier (2002) purport that "the extent to which individuals have consciously integrated the value of domain-relevant activities into their personal goals and values will be more important [for investment and persistence] than their intrinsic interest in the domain" (p. 114). So, for one to pursue a goal with identified motivation, one must be able to internalize the importance of the goal and make connections between one's own beliefs and values. Fit via value congruence assumes a similar awareness of one's values and an ability to connect the experiences in one's environment with one's personal values. Thus, it is likely that those who perceive a match between their own values and those espoused and exemplified in their environment and among social others in their environment are better able to identify with and internalize the value of their goal pursuits within that environment. In contrast, it could be argued that whether value congruence relates to intrinsic motivation depends on what is actually valued. For example, if the employee and organization both value making money, this extrinsic value may not relate to autonomous motivation. We maintain, however, that value congruence (which is typically measured generally) most likely predicts autonomous work motivation because a fundamental value of human beings is to satisfy their psychological needs (Deci & Ryan, 2000).

In addition to the theoretical link between the concept of value congruence and identified intrinsic motivation, there is overlap in recently tested models of the relationship between both fit perceptions and self-concordance model outcomes. Notably, many of the outcomes associated with PE fit overlap with those identified as outcomes of the self-concordance model. This parallel research suggests the relevance of goal self-concordance as a potential explanatory mechanism for the bivariate relationships observed in the PE fit literature. The connection between PE fit and the self-concordance model also was mentioned by Judge and Kristof-Brown (2004) as a promising avenue for future fit research. Additionally, need satisfaction has appeared as a proximal influence on employee well-being and performance outcomes in both the PE fit literature (Cable & Edwards, 2004; Greguras & Diefendorff, 2010) and investigations expanding the understanding of the self-concordance model in organizations (Greguras & Diefendorff, 2009). Although not typically considered within the PE fit literature, we believe one's social network is directly relevant to PE and self-determination theories.

Social Networks, PE Fit, and SDT

Social network analysis deals with the web of relationships that connects persons in an organization (Borgatti & Foster, 2003; Scott, 2000). Although interpersonal dyads are the building blocks of social network analysis, the added value of the social network approach is that it goes beyond the dyad and considers indirect relationships through which people are connected (Brass, 2011). These direct and indirect relationships are the channels through which resources flow, identities form, and opportunities are constrained or provided. Thus, the unit of analysis is an individual's position within the social network. Social network theory views peoples' behavior, attitudes, and cognitions as outcomes of social structure (Mayhew, 1980). Although Brass (forthcoming) recently reviewed various individual outcomes of social networks (e.g., turnover, task performance, creativity), need satisfaction and motivation were missing from this list. We believe that social network theory offers a unique opportunity for integrating itself with PE fit and SDT research. Specifically, social networks likely provide the channels leading to PE fit, and thereby, the satisfaction of psychological need satisfaction and the degree of autonomous-controlled motivation experienced by employees.

Social Networks as PE Fit Formation

We argue in this section that one's social network presents individuals with different opportunities (e.g., opportunities to work for different organizations) and choices (e.g., choice between which group to join) that ultimately affect their PE fit. For example, recruiters may select individuals from their own social networks because they perceive doing so to reduce the risk of uncertainty. Indeed, Leung (2003) observed that founders of start-up companies used their social networks to find new employees. Similarly, once individuals enter the organization, their networks may influence the tasks for which they are responsible (PJ fit), the groups to which they join (PG fit), or the supervisor to which they are assigned (PS fit).

Social network theory can also inform theories about the role of organizational socialization initiatives aimed at increasing PE fit. In contrast to the PE fit literature that has mainly focused on different kinds of socialization tactics (e.g., institutionalized vs. socialized), the social network literature has focused on newcomers' socialization through their interactions with experienced organizational members. Morrison (2002) proposed that newcomers' network diversity should facilitate organizational learning about norms, goals, policies, history, and politics—all of which facilitate both PE fit and the internalization of organizational goals. Diverse networks, the degree to which people are connected to people from different groups, provide access to broad organizational knowledge because people from the same group are likely to share knowledge that is already known by its members and because they are less receptive of new information (Stasser & Titus, 1985, 1987).

Based on the network diversity argument, Morrison proposed a number of network characteristics that improve socialization through the acquisition of organizational knowledge. First, network size (i.e., the number of contacts) should increase the chance that contacts have different organizational backgrounds and thus possess diverse knowledge. Second, newcomers' number of contacts into different organizational units (i.e., network range) should provide access to diverse organizational knowledge (Reagans & McEvily, 2003). Finally, some of these network contacts might also be connected to each other. Mutually connected contacts are likely to share information with each other and therefore provide redundant knowledge (Burt, 1992). Missing ties among employees' contacts (i.e., low network density) therefore increase the access to diverse information and broader organizational knowledge. Thus, large networks of unrelated contacts in different organizational units should increase access to diverse organizational knowledge and therefore PO fit.

Social Networks and DA Fit

Although diverse network contacts are useful when newcomers search for broad and diverse knowledge, their benefits are limited when employees need to develop job competencies. The knowledge to perform a job (task mastery) and knowing the responsibilities and constraints associated with it (task clarity) require the transfer of complex knowledge (Morrison, 2002). Job-related knowledge is often not fully documented or expressed in writing and includes tacit knowledge. Moreover, tasks in the organization might be related through interdependencies, which further increase the complexity of task-related knowledge. However, ties into diverse and distal parts of the organization are often infrequent and of low emotional intensity (i.e., the notion of weak ties; Granovetter, 1973). Ideally, newcomers or employees who want to increase their understanding of their jobs seek out contacts that are motivated to provide this complex information, are motivated to invest time and effort in explaining the matter, and are familiar with the recipients' information needs (Borgatti & Cross, 2003). Employees are less likely to find this motivation and understanding in contacts to which they are only loosely linked through infrequent interactions. Instead, complex knowledge transfer requires strong ties where people frequently exchange information with each other and feel emotionally close (Hansen, 1999). Strong ties have greater motivation to assist and be available (Granovetter, 1973). This gives employees the opportunity to try, err, and seek instructions and feedback from strongly tied organizational members (Hansen, 1999). Moreover, strong ties might have developed communication styles that support the transfer of complex knowledge (Uzzi, 1997). Strong ties should therefore promote task mastery and role clarity and help newcomers align their abilities with the job demands (i.e., DA fit).

Social Networks and PG Fit

A frequent finding in social networks is that people who have friends in common but do not yet know each other sooner or later meet and find similarities that bring them closer to each other. Thus, friendship works as an integrative force in social networks that brings together otherwise unfamiliar people and supports the development of strong interpersonal connections. These strong ties are important for the fit with the group because they confer strong normative expectations (Coleman, 1988) and help newcomers to internalize a clear and consistent set of values (Podolny & Baron, 1997). For example, Rentsch (1990) found that the interactions between organizational members increased their similarity in the interpretation of organizational events, and Burkhardt (1994) showed that communication frequency increased similarity in task-related beliefs. Moreover, it requires time and energy to maintain close and interconnected relationships, which limit the size of dense and cohesive networks (Burt, 1992). PG fit is defined as the congruency between an employee and her or his coworkers. We propose that small networks of

strong and cohesive ties foster integration into the group and PG fit.

Direct Effects of Social Networks on Need Satisfaction

Of course, networks might also have a direct effect on need satisfaction and thus motivation. The most obvious relationship is probably the one between relatedness need satisfaction and networks. Small and dense networks of strong ties should be an important source of relatedness need satisfaction. In these networks, the intimacy and connectedness among its members are the greatest. Network members in these networks are emotionally closely linked and reciprocally connected. Cohesive networks therefore form a source of mutual support for tangible (e.g., money) but also social resources (i.e., help) (Colemann, 1988; Wellman & Wortley, 1990). Thus, we propose a direct effect of small and dense networks of strong ties on its members' relatedness need satisfaction.

Another possible direct link between social networks and need satisfaction is the link of networks and competence. Job-related complex knowledge should come from strongly connected network contacts in similar job positions, which have the motivation and the expertise to transfer complex and often job-related knowledge (cf. Borgatti & Cross, 2003). The second network correlate of need competence satisfaction comes from the employee's ability to creatively solve job-related tasks and anticipate and proactively engage with task-related challenges. Specifically, employees with large and fragmented networks of loosely connected individuals have access to more diverse and nonredundant information and are aware of more alternative ways of thinking and behaving, which increase their ability to foresee problems and make better decisions (Burt, 1992). Moreover, these networks allow them to communicate ideas across a broader range of issues and reach a broader audience, which, in turn, increases their influence and potential to elicit support for their enterprises (Cohen and Levinthal, 1990; Reagans & McEvily, 2003). Thus, large and fragmented networks of weak ties should increase competence need satisfaction through employee's experience of their efficacy.

Finally, simmelian ties—strong ties that reciprocally connect at least three individuals (Krackhardt, 1999)—might reduce autonomy because once a group of this nature is formed, group norms develop by which each member must play (Schein, 1965). Simmelian ties become even more restraining when they associate the individual with more than one group. In this case, a person has even less choice of permissible behaviors because he or she has to conform to the norms of at least two groups (Krackhardt, 1999). Thus, autonomy may likely decrease with the number of groups to which an individual is connected.

PE Fit and Social Network Formation

We have argued that weak ties in large uncoupled networks and strong ties in intimate and cohesive networks promote employees' fit with their organization because it helps them to find out "how to fit in here." This might be particularly true for newcomers because they face a reality shock when they enter a new organization, which should increase the importance of social networks for the development of their fit with the organization. However, it might also be possible that employees' fit with their organization affects the development of their social networks. First, PG fit measures the perceived value similarity to coworkers. Following the similarity-attraction paradigm (Byrne, 1971) perceived similarity should increase attraction to and liking of other employees. Consequently, employees high in PG fit might initiate more friendly interactions, which should increase the strength of their relationships to their coworkers. Finally, people with high DA fit are more time efficient in their role and might use the saved time to build relationships at work (Anderson, Spataro, & Flynn, 2008).

PE Fit and Social Networks: A Summary

The relationship between social networks and motivation has received surprisingly little attention. We proposed that PE fit serves as a viable mechanism for linking both concepts. PO fit is established through the transfer of broad, organizational knowledge about cultural norms and values. According to the social network perspective this is best accomplished through large, low-density network of weak ties that reach into diverse social units of the organization. Although weak ties might suffice to acquire broad organizational knowledge, strong ties are necessary to transfer complex job-related knowledge (DA fit). Moreover, small, dense networks of strong ties foster integration into work groups (PG fit). Interestingly, strong ties therefore might also directly increase motivation and competence need satisfaction and relatedness need satisfaction.

Finally, it might be that PE fit facilitates the formation of new relationships.

In sum, social networks, PE fit, and SDT share many common themes. We also believe that research and theorizing in each area can help inform the other. With this discussion, we hope to encourage research that integrates themes and findings from these different research areas to facilitate a better understanding of social networks, PE fit, motivation, and the satisfaction of psychological needs.

Future Directions

Our review and integration highlights several directions for future research. We discuss these next.

• The complex interplay between fit and intrinsic motivation has yet to be directly tested. Given the myriad of environmental foci, and operationalizations of fit, research on the relationship between fit with autonomous motivation, controlled motivation, and goal self-concordance seems to be a promising avenue for exploration. Future research may examine the extent to which greater autonomous motivation (and less controlled motivation) flows from the experience of different types of fit, and whether the level of autonomy-control experienced mediates the links of fit perceptions with employee outcomes. Future research could test the proposition that complementary forms of PE fit relate to autonomous motivation directly (i.e., by activating already established values, skills, interest), whereas supplementary forms of PE fit relate to autonomous motivation indirectly by facilitating the process of internalization (i.e., by having the person come to adopt the values underlying organizational activities). That is, socialization processes and the amount of time on the job may be important for observing the effects of supplementary fit, whereas the effects of complementary fit may occur more rapidly and without the need for internalization processes.

• The directionality and causal ordering of the fit, motivation, and need satisfaction relationships could be examined. Although we reviewed the literature assuming fit may be an antecedent to intrinsic motivation and subsequent goal pursuit, need satisfaction, and attitude and behavioral outcomes, it could be argued that experiencing intrinsic motivation precludes the experience of fit with one's environment. The experience of need satisfaction could similarly be conceived as a possible antecedent to fit. Research is needed to determine whether experiencing intrinsic motivation and/or need satisfaction influences an individual's evaluations of their fit with different environmental foci or, measuring fit another way, whether need satisfaction may motivate one to alter oneself or the environment to achieve a better fit. Longitudinal research designs aimed at isolating the causal direction by including the lagged independent variable *and* lagged dependent variable as predictors of the dependent variable—and then switching which variable is the dependent variable—could be useful for determining the relative strength of the causal direction of effects.

• Specification of the mechanism by which the established relationships between fit and desirable workplace outcomes function could provide clarity and opportunity for managers regarding ways to leverage or ameliorate the effects of fit on well-being. Establishment of a more specific mechanism of fit's influence on attitudinal and behavioral outcomes also bolsters the argument that fit is an important entry criteria (Kristof, 1996). Linking the two concepts also addresses a general lack of research incorporating PO fit and organizational identification with motivation concepts (Diefendorff & Chandler, 2010).

• Existing theoretical frameworks and empirical research suggest that intrinsic motivation is optimal while extrinsic motivation is suboptimal. We encourage research that looks at the interplay among intrinsic and extrinsic motivation. Polynomial regression that seeks to understand the levels at which intrinsic and extrinsic motivation combine for optimal performance or well-being might be especially useful in better understanding the effects of motivation on employee outcomes.

• Surprisingly little is known about the relationship between social networks and motivation. We think that fit provides an interesting mechanism through which both can be linked. We have provided arguments for different aspects of social networks and how they can be linked to different kinds of fit. We also argue that fit can affect the development of social networks. Future research will have to test whether these propositions hold.

Conclusion

Although PE fit, SDT, and social network theory historically have represented parallel streams of theorizing and research, we argue that there are many commonalities and that these bodies of work can complement and inform each other. As such, future research aimed at integrating these areas of research is needed. We propose that PE fit and social networks directly and indirectly (via the internalization of goals) affect psychological need satisfaction, and ultimately individual well-being. Because PE fit represents fit between individuals and their environments, numerous existing theoretical frameworks (e.g., LMX theory, social networks theory) also have the potential to guide research aimed at understanding the complex interplay between PE fit, SDT, and employee well-being.

References

Amiot, C. E., Vallerand, R. J., & Blanchard, C. M. (2006). Passion and psychological adjustment: A test of the person-environment fit hypothesis. *Personality and Social Psychology Bulletin, 32*, 220–229.

Anderson, C., Spataro, S. E., & Flynn, F. J. (2008). Personality and organizational culture as determinants of influence. *Journal of Applied Psychology, 93*, 702–710.

Arthur, W. A. Jr., Bell, S. T., Doverspike, D., & Villado, A. J. (2006). The use of person-organization fit in employment decision making: An assessment of its criterion-related validity. *Journal of Applied Psychology, 91*(4), 786–801.

Baard, P. P., Deci, E. L., & Ryan, R. M. (2004). Intrinsic need satisfaction: A motivational basis of performance and well-being in two work settings. *Journal of Applied Social Psychology, 34*, 2045–2068.

Bakker, A. B. (2008). The work-related flow inventory: Construction and initial validation of the WOLF. *Journal of Vocational Behavior, 72*, 400–414.

Bashshur, M. R., Hernández, A., & Peiró, J. M. (2011). The impact of underemployment on individual and team performance. In D. C. Maynard, & D. C. Feldman (Eds.), *Underemployment: Psychological, economic, and social challenges* (pp. 187–213). New York: Springer.

Bono, J. E., & Judge, T. A. (2003). Self-concordance at work: Toward understanding the motivational effects of transformational leaders. *Academy of Management Journal, 46*(5), 554–571.

Borgatti, S. P., & Cross, R. (2003). A relational view of information seeking and learning in social networks. *Management Science, 49*, 432–445.

Borgatti, S. P., & Foster, P. C. (2003). The network paradigm in organizational research: A review and typology. *Journal of Management, 29*, 991–1013.

Brass, D. J. (2011). A social network perspective on industrial/organizational psychology. In S. W. J. Kozlowski (Ed.), *The Oxford handbook of organizational psychology* (pp. 135–169). New York: Oxford University Press.

Burkhardt, M. E. (1994). Social interaction effects following a technological change: A longitudinal investigation. *Academy of Management Journal, 37*, 898.

Burt, R. S. (1992). *Structural holes: The social structure of competition.* Cambridge, MA: Harvard University Press.

Byrne, D. (1971). *The attraction paradigm.* New York: Academic Press.

Cable, D. M., & DeRue, D. S. (2002). The convergent and discriminant validity of subjective fit perceptions. *Journal of Applied Psychology, 87*(5), 875–884.

Cable, D. M., & Edwards, J. R. (2004). Complementary and supplementary fit: A theoretical and empirical integration. *Journal of Applied Psychology, 89*(5), 822–834.

Cable, D. M., & Judge, T. A. (1996). Person-organization fit, job choice decisions, and organizational entry. *Organizational Behavior and Human Decision Processes*, *67*(3), 294–311.

Chatman, J. A. (1991). Matching people and organizations: Selection and socialization in public accounting firms. *Administrative Science Quarterly*, *36*, 459–484.

Cohen, W. M., & Levinthal, D. A. (1990). Absorptive capacity: A new perspective on learning and innovation. *Administrative Science Quarterly*, *35*, 128–152.

Coleman, J. S. (1988). Social capital in the creation of human capital. *American Journal of Sociology*, *94*, 95–120.

Csikszentmihalyi, M. (1990). *Flow: The psychology of optimal experience*. New York: Harper & Row.

Dawis, R. V., & Lofquist, L. H. (1984). *A psychological theory of work adjustment*. Minneapolis: University of Minnesota Press.

Deci, E. L., Connell, J. P., & Ryan, R. M. (1989). Self-determination in a work organization. *Journal of Applied Psychology*, *74*, 580–590.

Deci, E. L., Eghrari, H., Patrick, B. C., & Leone, D. R. (1994). Facilitating internalization: The self-determination theory perspective. *Journal of Personality*, *62*, 119–1142.

Deci, E. L., Koestner, R., & Ryan, R. M. (1999). A meta-analytic review of experiments examining the effects of extrinsic rewards on intrinsic motivation. *Psychological Bulletin*, *125*, 627–668.

Deci, E. L., & Ryan, R. M. (1985). *Intrinsic motivation and self-determination in human behavior*. New York: Plenum.

Deci, E. L., & Ryan, R. M (2000). The "what" and "why" of goal pursuits: Human needs and the self-determination of behavior. *Psychological Inquiry*, *11*, 227–268.

Deci, E. L., Ryan, R. M., Gagné M., Leone, D. R., Usunov, J., & Kornazheva, B. P. (2001). Need satisfaction, motivation, and well-being in the work organizations of a former Eastern bloc country: A cross-cultural study of self-determination. *Personality and Social Psychology Bulletin*, *27*, 930–942.

Diefendorff, J. M., & Chandler, M. M. (2010). Motivating employees. In S. Zedeck (Ed.), *Handbook of industrial and organizational psychology* (pp. 65–135). Washington, DC: American Psychological Association.

Edwards, J. R. (2001). Ten difference score myths. *Organizational Research Methods*, *4*(3), 265–287.

Edwards, J. R., Cable, D. M., Williamson, I. O., Lambert, L. S., & Shipp, A. J. (2006). The phenomenology of fit: Linking the person and environment to the subjective experience of person-environment fit. *Journal of Applied Psychology*, *91*(4), 802–827.

Edwards, J. R., & Shipp, A. J. (2007). The relationship between person-environment fit and outcomes: An integrative theoretical framework. In C. Ostroff, & T. A. Judge (Eds.), *Perspectives on organizational fit* (pp. 209–258). Mahwah, NJ: Lawrence Erlbaum Associates Publishers.

Elfenbein, H. A. (2007). Emotion in organizations: A review and theoretical integration in stages. *Academy of Management Annals*, *1*, 315–386.

Endler, N. S., & Magnusson, D. (1976). Toward and interactional psychology of personality. *Psychological Bulletin*, *83*(5), 956–974.

Feldman, D. C. (1996). The nature, antecedents, and consequences of underemployment. *Journal of Management*, *22*, 385–407.

Gagné, M., & Deci, E. L. (2005). Self-determination theory and work motivation. *Journal of Organizational Behavior*, *26*, 331–362.

Gagné, M., Koestner, R., & Zuckerman, M. (2000). Facilitating acceptance of organizational change: The importance of self-determination. *Journal of Applied Social Psychology*, *30*(9), 1843–1852.

Graen, G., & Cashman, J. F. (1975). A role making model in formal organizations: A developmental approach. In J. G. Hunt, & L. L. Larson (Eds.), *Leadership frontiers* (pp. 143–165). Kent, OH: Kent State Press.

Graen, G. B., Novak, M. A., & Sommerkamp, P. (1982). The effects of leader-member exchange and job design on productivity and satisfaction: Testing a dual attachment model. *Organizational Behavior and Human Performance*, *30*, 109–131.

Graen, G. B., & Scandura, T. A. (1987). Toward a psychology of dyadic organizing. In L. L. Cummings, & B. M. Staw (Eds.), *Research in organizational behavior*, *9*, 175–208.

Granovetter, M. S. (1973). The strength of weak ties. *American Journal of Sociology*, *78*, 1360–1380.

Greguras, G. J., & Diefendorff, J. M. (2009). Different fits satisfy different needs: Linking person-environment fit to employee commitment and performance using self-determination theory. *Journal of Applied Psychology*, *94*, 465–477.

Greguras, G. J., & Diefendorff, J. M. (2010). Why does proactive personality predict employee life satisfaction and work behaviors? A field investigation of the mediating role of the self-concordance model. *Personnel Psychology*, *63*, 539–560.

Grouzet, F. M. E., Vallerand, R. J., Thill, E. E., & Provencher, P. J. (2004). From environmental factors to outcomes: A test of an integrated motivational sequence. *Motivation and Emotion*, *28*, 331–346.

Guay, F., Boggiano, A. K., & Vallerand, R. J. (2001). Autonomy support, intrinsic motivation, and perceived competence: Conceptual and empirical linkages. *Personality and Social Psychology Bulletin*, *27*, 643–650.

Hackman, J. R., & Oldham, G. R. (1976). Motivation through the design of work: Test of a theory. *Organizational Behavior and Human Performance*, *16*, 250–279.

Hansen, M. T. (1999). The search-transfer problem: The role of weak ties in sharing knowledge across organization subunits. *Administrative Science Quarterly*, *44*, 82.

Hardé, P. L., & Reeve, J. (2009). Training corporate managers to adopt a more autonomy-supportive motivating style toward employees: An intervention study. *International Journal of Training and Development*, *13*, 165–184.

Harrison, D. A., Price, K. H., & Bell, M. P. (1998). Beyond relational demography: Time and the effects of surface—and deep-level diversity on work group cohesion. *Academy of Management Journal*, *41*, 96–107.

Hoffman, B. J., & Woehr, D. J. (2006). A quantitative review of the relationship between person-organization fit and behavioral outcomes. *Journal of Vocational Behavior*, *68*, 389–399.

Humphrey, S. E., Nahrgang, J. D., & Morgeson, F. P. (2007). Integrating motivational, social, and contextual work design features: A meta-analytic summary and theoretical extension of the work design literature. *Journal of Applied Psychology*, *92*, 1332–1356.

Judge, T. A., Bono, J. E., Erez, A., & Locke, E. A. (2005). Core self-evaluations and job and life satisfaction: The role of self-concordance and goal attainment. *Journal of Applied Psychology*, *9*(2), 257–268.

Judge, T. A., & Ferris, G. R. (1993). Social context of performance evaluation decisions. *Academy of Management Journal*, *36*, 80–105.

Judge, T. A., & Kristoff-Brown, A. (2004). Personality, interactional psychology, and person-organization fit. In B. Schneider, & D. Brent Smith (Eds.), *Personality in organizations* (pp. 87–109). London: Lawrence Erlbaum Associates.

Kahn, R. L., Wolfe, D. M., Quinn, R. P., Snoek, J. D., & Rosenthal, R. A. (1964). *Organizational stress: Studies in role conflict and ambiguity.* New York: Wiley.

Kasser, T. (2002). Sketches for a self-determination theory of values. In E. L. Deci, & R. M. Ryan (Eds.), *Handbook of self-determination research* (pp. 123–140). Rochester, NY: University of Rochester Press.

Kasser, T., & Ryan, R. M. (1996). Further examining the American dream: Differential correlates of intrinsic and extrinsic goals. *Journal of Personality and Social Psychology, 65,* 410–422.

Koestner, R., & Losier, G. F. (2002). Distinguishing three ways of being internally motivated: A closer look at introjections, identification, and intrinsic motivation. In E. L. Deci & R. M. Ryan (Eds.), *Handbook of self-determination research* (pp. 101–121). Rochester, NY: University of Rochester Press.

Krackhardt, D. (1999). The ties that torture: Simmelian tie analysis in organizations. *Research in the Sociology of Organizations, 16,* 183–210.

Kristof, A. L. (1996). Person-organization fit: An integrative review of its conceptualizations, measurement, and implications. *Personnel Psychology, 49,* 1–49.

Kristof-Brown, A. M., & Jansen, K. J. (2007). Issues in person-organization fit. In C. Ostroff, & T. A. Judge (Eds.), *Perspectives on organizational fit* (pp.123–154). Mahwah, NJ: Lawrence Erlbaum Associates Publishers.

Kristof-Brown, A. L., & Stevens, C. K. (2001). Goal congruence in project teams: Does the fit between members' personal mastery and performance goals matter? *Journal of Applied Psychology, 86,* 1083–1095.

Kristof-Brown, A. L., Zimmerman, R. D., & Johnson, E. C. (2005). Consequences of individual's fit at work: A meta-analysis of person-job, person-organization, person-group, and perso-upervisor fit. *Personnel Psychology, 58,* 281–342.

Leung, A. (2003). Different ties for different needs: Recruitment practices of entrepreneurial firms at different developmental phases. *Human Resource Management, 42,* 303–320.

Liden, R. C., & Maslyn, J. M. (1998). Multidimensionality of leader-member exchange: An empirical assessment through scale development. *Journal of Management, 24,* 43–72.

Locke E. A. (1991). The motivation sequence, the motivation hub, and the motivation core. *Organizational Behavior and Human Decision Processes, 50,* 288–299.

Lord, R. G., & Brown, D. J. (2001). Leadership, values, and subordinate self-concepts. *Leadership Quarterly, 12,* 1–21.

Matterson, S. S., & Stamper, C. L. (2003). Perceived organizational membership: An aggregate framework representing the employee-organization relationship. *Journal of Organizational Behavior, 24*(5), 473–490.

Mayhew, B. H. (1980). Structuralism versus individualism: Part 1, shadowboxing in the dark. *Social Forces, 59,* 335–375.

McMillan, D. W., & Chavis, D. M. (1986). Sense of community: A definition and theory. *Journal of Community Psychology, 14,* 6–23.

Meglino, B. M., Ravlin, E. C., & Adkins, C. L. (1989). A work values approach to corporate culture: A field test of the value congruence process and its relationship to individual outcomes. *Journal of Applied Psychology, 74,* 424–432.

Morgeson, F. P., & Humphrey, S. E. (2006). The work design questionnaire (WDQ): Developing and validating a comprehensive measure for assessing job design and the nature of work. *Journal of Applied Psychology, 91,* 1321–1339.

Morrison, E. W. (2002). Newcomers' relationships: The role of social network ties during socialization. *Academy of Management Journal, 45,* 1149–1160.

Muchinski, P. M., & Moynihan, C. J. (1987). What is person-environment congruence? Supplementary versus complementary models of fit. *Journal of Vocational Behavior, 31,* 268–277.

O'Connor, B. P., & Vallerand, R. J. (1994). Motivation, self-determination, and person-environment fit as predictors of psychological adjustment among nursing home residents. *Psychology and Aging, 9,* 189–194.

O'Reilly, C. A., Chatman, J., & Caldwell, D. F. (1991). People and organizational culture: A profile comparison approach to assessing person-organization fit. *Academy of Management Journal, 34*(3), 487–516.

Ostroff, C., Shin, Y., & Kinicki, A. J. (2005). Multiple perspectives of congruence: Relationships between value congruence and employee attitudes. *Journal of Organizational Behavior, 26,* 591–623.

Ostroff, C., & Shulte, M. (2007). Multiple perspectives of fit in organizations across levels of analysis. In C. Ostroff, & T. A. Judge (Eds.), *Perspectives on organizational fit* (pp.123–154). Mahwah, NJ: Lawrence Erlbaum Associates Publishers.

Pelletier, L. G., Fortier, M. S., Vallerand, R. J., & Brière, N. M. (2002). Associations among perceived autonomy support, forms of self-regulation, and persistence: A prospective study. *Motivation and Emotion, 25,* 279–306.

Podolny, J. M., & Baron, J. N. (1997). Resources and relationships: Social networks and mobility in the workplace. *American Sociological Review, 62,* 673–693.

Reagans, R., & McEvily, B. (2003). Network structure and knowledge transfer: The effects of cohesion and range. *Administrative Science Quarterly, 48,* 240–267.

Reeve, J., Hyungshim, J., Carrell, D., Soohyun, J., & Barch, J. (2004). Enhancing students' engagement by increasing teachers' autonomy support. *Motivation and Emotion, 28,* 147–169.

Rentsch, J. R. (1990). Climate and culture: Interaction and qualitative differences in organizational meanings. *Journal of Applied Psychology, 75,* 668–681.

Ryan, R. M., & Deci, E. L. (2000). Self-determination theory and the facilitation of intrinsic motivation, social development, and well-being. *American Psychologist, 55,* 68–78.

Ryan, R. M., Sheldon, K. M., Kasser, T., & Deci, E. L. (1996). All goals are not created equal: An organismic perspective on the nature of goals and their regulation. In P. M. Gollwitzer, & J. A. Baugh (Eds.), *The psychology of action: Linking cognition and motivation to behavior* (pp. 7–26). New York: Guilford.

Schein, E. H. (1965). *Organizational psychology.* Englewood Cliffs, NJ: Prentice Hall.

Schneider, B. (1987). The people make the place. *Personnel Psychology, 40,* 437–453.

Schneider, B., Goldstein, H. W., & Smith, D. B. (1995). The ASA framework: An update. *Personnel Psychology, 48,* 747–773.

Scott, J. (2000). *Social network analysis: A handbook (2nd ed.).* Thousands Oaks, CA: Sage.

Sheldon, K. M., & Elliot, A. J. (1998). Not all personal goals are personal: Comparing autonomous and controlled reasons for goals as predictors of effort and attainment. *Personality and Social Psychology Bulletin, 24*, 546–557.

Sheldon, K. M., & Elliot, A. J. (1999). Goal striving, need satisfaction, and longitudinal well-being: The self-concordance model. *Journal of Personality and Social Psychology, 76*, 482–497.

Sheldon, K. M., & Gunz, A. (2009). Psychological needs as basic motives, not just experiential requirements. *Journal of Personality, 77*, 1467–1492.

Sheldon, K. M., & Houser-Marko, L. (2001). Self-concordance, goal attainment and the pursuit of happiness: Can there be an upward spiral? *Journal of Personality and Social Psychology, 80*, 152–165.

Sheldon, K. M., & Kasser, T. (1998). Pursuing personal goals: Skills enable progress but not all progress is beneficial. *Personality and Social Psychology Bulletin, 24*, 1319–1331.

Sheldon, K. M., Ryan, R. M., Deci, E. L. & Kasser, T. (2004). The independent effects of goal contents and motives on well-being: It's both what you pursue and why you pursue it. *Personality and Social Psychology Bulletin, 30*, 475–486.

Stasser, G., & Titus, W. (1985). Pooling of unshared information in group decision making: Biased information sampling during discussion. *Journal of Personality and Social Psychology, 48*, 1467–1478.

Stasser, G., & Titus, W. (1987). Effects of information load and percentage of shared information on the dissemination of unshared information during group discussion. *Journal of Personality and Social Psychology, 53*, 81–93.

Sue-Chan, C., & Ong, M. (2002). Goal assignment and performance: Assessing the mediating roles of goal commitment and self-efficacy and the moderating role of power distance. *Organizational Behavior and Human Decision Processes, 89*(2), 1140–1161.

Sutton, R. I. (1991). Maintaining norms about expressed emotions: The case of bill collectors. *Administrative Science Quarterly, 36*, 245–268.

Swann, W. B., Steinseroussi, A., & Giesler, R. B. (1992). Why people self-verify? *Journal of Personality and Social Psychology, 62*, 392–401.

Tepper, B. J. (2000). Consequences of abusive supervision. *Academy of Management Journal, 43*, 178–190.

Tepper, B. J. (2007). Abusive supervision in work organizations: Review, synthesis, and directions for future research. *Journal of Management, 33*, 261–289.

Tepper, B. J., Moss, S. E., & Duffy, M. K. (2011). Predictors of abusive supervision: Supervisor perceptions of deep-level dissimilarity, relationship conflict, and subordinate performance. *Academy of Management Journal, 54*, 279–294.

Uzzi, B. (1997). Social structure and competition in interfirm networks: The paradox of embeddedness. *Administrative Science Quarterly, 42*, 35.

Vancouver, J. B., More, J. M., & Yoder, R. J. (2008). Self-efficacy and resource allocation: Support for a nonmonotonic discontinuous model. *Journal of Applied Psychology, 93*(1), 35–47.

Vancouver, J. B., & Schmitt, N. W. (1991). An exploratory examination of person-organization fit: Organizational goal congruence. *Personnel Psychology, 44*, 333–354.

Verquer, M. L., Beehr, T. A., & Wagner, S. H. (2003). A meta-analysis of relations between person-organization fit and work attitudes. *Journal of Vocational Behavior, 63*, 473–489.

Wellman, B., & Wortley, S. (1990). Different strokes from different folks: Community ties and social support. *American Journal of Sociology, 96*, 558–588.

Williams, G. C., Grow, V. M., Freedman, Z. R., Ryan, R. M., & Deci, E. L. (1996). Motivational predictors of weight loss and weight-loss maintenance. *Journal of Personality and Social Psychology, 70*, 115–126.

PART 3

Organizational and Contextual Considerations

CHAPTER 10

The Motivational Power of Job Design

Marylène Gagné *and* Alexandra Panaccio

Abstract

As technology and the globalization of the economy change the way we work nowadays, the design of our jobs remains an important source of motivation. Much of what constitutes the body of job design research assumes that motivation is a major explanatory mechanism in the effect that job design has on the worker. However, motivation is rarely assessed in job design research, and we consequently argue that assessing autonomous and controlled motivation, and assessing the satisfaction of psychological needs, would be useful to advance job design research. In this chapter, we propose that autonomous motivation is more likely to be promoted if the design of the job satisfies basic needs for autonomy, competence, and relatedness. The chapter also discusses two recent phenomena of interest: proactive work behavior and job crafting.

Key Words: self-determination theory, job design, work motivation, proactive work behavior, job crafting

---

Introduction

Job design is as important today as it was in the early 1900s, when scientists began to pay attention to the design of jobs during the early industrial revolution. Job design has for a long time been defined as "the set of opportunities and constraints structured into assigned tasks and responsibilities that affect how an employee accomplishes and experiences work" (Grant, Fried, & Juillerat, 2010, p. 418). As technology and globalization of the economy changes the way we work nowadays, the design of our jobs remains as important a source of motivation, but we now define it more broadly as "encapsulating the processes and outcomes of how work is structured, organized, experienced, and enacted" (Grant et al., 2010, p. 418). This definition takes into consideration not only how organizations divide labor and coordinate the work to be done, but also how the individual influences the process of designing his or her own job, as well as his or her reactions to it.

It is not the goal of this chapter to provide a review of the job design literature. The reader can find excellent recent reviews of this large and complex literature (e.g., Grant, Fried, & Juillerat, 2010; Parker & Ohly, 2008, 2009). Instead, we revisit this literature from the point of view of self-determination theory (SDT). Using the concepts offered by SDT, such as the different types of regulations and the three psychological needs, we explain how and why job design influences the motivation, performance, and attitudes of workers. As is shown throughout this literature review, much of what constitutes the body of job design research assumes that motivation is a major explanatory mechanism in the effect of job design on the worker. However, motivation is rarely assessed in job design research, and we consequently argue that assessing autonomous and controlled motivation, and assessing the satisfaction of psychological needs, are useful to advance job design research. Using SDT (Deci & Ryan, 1985), we argue that autonomous motivation is more likely to be promoted if the design of jobs satisfies basic needs for autonomy, competence, and relatedness. We therefore orient this review of the job design literature toward examination of this issue.

We start by discussing early approaches to job design, such as Taylorism and the Human Relations Movement. We continue with the multimethod job design model, which reconciles these two early views, followed by the most popular model, namely the job characteristics model (JCM) and its recent extensions. We then discuss the sociotechnical systems model and the job demands/job resource models. We end by touching on two recent phenomena of interest, namely proactive work behavior and job crafting.

Early Approaches

Early approaches to job design stemmed from economics and engineering (Babbage, 1835; Smith, 1776; Taylor, 1911). These approaches emphasized cost cutting and efficiency, but did not consider the experiences of the worker doing the job. In other words, the psychological effects of job design were not taken into consideration. Examples of what was considered adequate design included breaking down jobs into simple tasks, so that people could "specialize" in particular tasks and waste less time during task rotations. Scientific management emerged during this period, and advocated job specialization and standardization, and the use of performance-contingent pay systems (Taylor, 1911).

Evaluating these job design methods from the point of view of SDT, we can expect that breaking down a job into several tasks to be done by different workers is likely to make the tasks less enjoyable, challenging, and interesting, and this is likely to decrease the intrinsic motivation of workers. Intrinsic motivation requires matching task difficulty with the actor's current level of competence, such that task difficulty slightly exceeds current competence level. This provides the optimal stimulation required to feel aroused during task engagement (Csikszentmihalyi, 1990). However, it is possible that for minimally educated or minimally skilled workers, such tasks may still provide them with some challenge, though perhaps only for a short period. This challenge could increase their feeling of competence, but most likely not maximally and not for the long term. Breaking down tasks is also likely to not only make the job less interesting, but less meaningful. It is likely to make the outcomes of

a job well done less obvious to workers, who do not have access to the "big picture" or to the impact that their work has on stakeholders. Because job specialization also involved determining how each job task is most efficiently done, thereby standardizing how it is to be accomplished, such a design also necessarily involves taking away a lot of decision-making power. This is likely to make people feel less autonomous, because internalization of the value of work tasks is diluted through job specialization. Finally, job specialization was often done using an assembly line design at the time, which is likely to decrease contact between workers, thereby reducing the satisfaction of the need for relatedness.

Scientific management also involves the use of piece-rate pay systems, and such compensation systems are still a matter of debate today. SDT has contributed greatly to feeding this debate. Although piece-rate systems can offer some form of performance feedback that can enhance feelings of competence, they can also make people switch from an internal to an external locus of causality (Deci & Ryan, 1985), thereby decreasing feelings of autonomy. Although this has been shown quite clearly in the laboratory (Deci, Koestner, & Ryan, 1999), the overall effect of such pay systems is quite complex (Gagné & Forest, 2008) and should be studied systematically in the field. Moreover, individual performance-contingent pay systems are known to decrease cooperative behavior and group cohesion (Baker, Jensen, & Murphy, 1988), and we argue that they are likely to decrease feelings of relatedness (Gagné & Forest, 2008). Overall, the Tayloristic approach is unlikely to yield high autonomous work motivation because of its potentially negative effects on the satisfaction of the three psychological needs (see also Fay & Kamps, 2006).

The Human Relations Movement closely followed Taylorism. Because Taylorism was found to create monotonous jobs where people could not exercise any discretion, felt dissatisfied and alienated (Fay & Kamps, 2006), the Human Relations Movement was an attempt to rectify this situation by considering the psychological needs of workers. The famous Hawthorne studies (Roethlisberger & Dickson, 1939), conducted in the 1920s, were one of the instigators of this movement, where researchers found that, no matter what manipulation was introduced to test different work conditions, workers increased their productivity. This was interpreted as a reaction to the attention they were getting from the researchers during the study. Dubbed the Hawthorne effect, this iatrogenic phenomenon has become a matter of concern in the design of psychology experiments (Adair, 1984). Although measurements of attitudes were not taken in the Hawthorne studies, and some of the conclusions drawn from them have since been questioned quite critically (Adair, 1984; Sonnenfeld, 1985; Yorks & Whitsett, 1985), we can, in a post hoc fashion, guess that whatever positive outcome was obtained from the attention given by the researchers increased feelings of relatedness in the employees, which in turn fostered a more autonomous form of motivation in them.

Approximately 40 studies subsequently attempted to clarify and explain the Hawthorne effect (Adair, 1984), although none of them directly measured motivation or need satisfaction. Many of these studies failed to replicate the Hawthorne effect, which led researchers to question its very existence. One possible moderator that could explain the variability found in the results is the research participants' baseline levels of need satisfaction. Hawthorne participants were blue-collar workers in the 1920s and 1930s, who worked in what we could consider today to be dire work conditions. Manufacturing work in those years was physically taxing, and the work contract involved long work hours (often more than 60 hours per week), poor job security, and authoritarian management. Participants in later experiments were most often children in schools or college students, who were more likely to experience higher daily need satisfaction. It could therefore be argued that participants in the Hawthorne studies started out so low in terms of need satisfaction, compared with participants in subsequent studies, that the presence of the researchers was enough to significantly increase their need satisfaction and consequently their productivity.

We could possibly test this hypothesis today by comparing plants in developing countries with plants in developed countries. If the hypothesis is supported, we could conclude that the Hawthorne effect is something specific to people who start out disadvantaged. One study actually provides preliminary support for this hypothesis. Rosen and Sales (1966) detected a Hawthorne effect only for older workers, nonunionized workers, and workers who came from a rural background. In short, the Hawthorne studies have served to alert researchers and practitioners to the importance of psychological needs in motivating workers, and subsequently led to the development of many management theories that take them into consideration.

Likert's (1967) four management systems serve to categorize management styles from exploitative to participative, arguing that participative styles yield better outcomes for the organization, because they respect the needs of the workers. Examining the features of exploitative versus participative management styles, one can observe that participative styles are likely to yield greater need satisfaction through the use of team work, group decision-making, and the setting of challenging goals. McGregor (1960) similarly discussed differences between Theory X versus Theory Y management styles, which resemble Likert's typology. McGregor argued that managers' own beliefs about their workers' motivation could lead to self-fulfilling prophecies, such that when a manager believes that workers are unmotivated (Theory X), he or she ends up having to control their behavior through coercive measures to get anything out of them, whereas when a manager believes that workers are self-motivated (Theory Y), he or she can give them autonomy as they seem to be self-driven.

Herzberg's hygiene versus motivators framework (Herzberg, 1966; Herzberg, Mausner, & Snyderman, 1959), considered a classic theory of motivation, is relevant to job design because it introduced the notion of job enrichment to organizational behavior and applied psychology (Grant et al., 2010). In essence, this "dual factor" theory proposes that job satisfaction and job dissatisfaction are different states that result from different forces. Job satisfaction was proposed to derive from "motivators" (i.e., characteristics related to the nature and content of the job itself, such as opportunities to achieve, recognition, interesting work, responsibility, and the possibility to grow and advance within the organization). By contrast, job dissatisfaction was thought to result from "hygiene" factors (i.e., characteristics related to the context of the job, such as policy and administration, supervision, interpersonal relations, working conditions, salary, status, and security). Enhancing the motivators was proposed to be a key to enriching a job (i.e., increasing its motivational power).

Herzberg's theory has been criticized on various grounds, including the confusion between motivation and job satisfaction (cf. House & Wigdor, 1967), and the fact that it has received little empirical support (House & Wigdor, 1967; Locke, 1969; Parker & Ohly, 2009). Unsurprisingly, this theory is rarely used in contemporary motivation research. However, the two-factor theory provides interesting insights into the role that need satisfaction may play in eliciting motivation. Indeed, making a parallel with other classic needs theories of motivation, such as Maslow's (1943, 1954) and Alderfer's

(1972), the hygiene factors in Herzberg's theory fulfill lower-order needs, such as physiological and safety needs, whereas motivators contribute to satisfying higher-order needs, such as achievement and self-actualization. The idea that motivators (i.e., positive characteristics related to the nature of the job) contribute to intrinsic motivation through the fulfillment of the basic needs is consistent with SDT, because this theory emphasizes psychological versus physiological needs. In Herzberg's theory, motivators would fall within the category of "social circumstances and task characteristics" that contribute to satisfying psychological needs.

The difference between these early need theories and SDT is that SDT has been more careful and systematic in crafting testable propositions and basing them on empirical research, yielding a well-validated account of what constitutes a need and providing evidence for the importance of each of them for growth and well-being (Deci & Ryan, 2000; Sheldon, Elliot, Kim, & Kasser, 2001; Sheldon & Filak, 2008). Like Maslow and Alderfer, Herzberg viewed the structure of need as being relatively universally distributed (Salancik & Pfeffer, 1977). This is also consistent with evidence amassed by SDT researchers that the basic needs for autonomy, competence, and relatedness as universally held needs (Deci & Ryan, 2000; Ryan, Sheldon, Kasser, & Deci, 1996). In sum, Herzberg's two-factor theory is conceptually linked with SDT because it highlights the importance of providing work conditions that contribute to fulfilling "higher-order needs," such as the basic needs for autonomy, competence, and relatedness, which occupy a central role within SDT.

We can conclude from the human relations era that it has brought to the forefront two important considerations. First, human beings must have a certain level of autonomy in their job in order to be fully engaged. Second, human beings are social beings, a fact that cannot be ignored when designing jobs. These two points touch on two of the psychological needs postulated in SDT: autonomy and relatedness.

The Multimethod Job Design Model

A contemporary approach that attempts to integrate scientific management and the human relations movement into a unique model, and allows the examination of the benefits and drawbacks of each, as well as their interaction, is Campion and Thayer's (1985) multimethod job design model. This model includes motivational, mechanistic, biological, and perceptual/motor subcomponents of job design. The motivational approach borrows from the JCM (discussed at length later), whereas the mechanistic approach draws from engineering and scientific management. The biological approach borrows from medicine, which emphasizes physical comfort and health, whereas the perceptual/motor approach draws from ergonomics and cognitive sciences, which emphasize the reduction of information processing and physical requirements through the use of technology and monitoring.

Campion (1988) showed that motivational designs are linked to satisfaction outcomes, whereas mechanical designs are linked to efficiency outcomes, biological designs are linked to health outcomes, and perceptual/motor designs are linked to reliability outcomes. Campion and McClelland (1991, 1993) showed a tradeoff between the motivational and mechanistic approaches, whereby an increase in the motivational characteristics often results in a decline in mechanistic characteristics and vice versa, with associated consequences. Some research has shown that it is not easy to have a design that is motivationally *and* mechanically sound (Campion, 1988). Indeed, the introduction of just-in-time methods, for example (a mechanistic approach), has been shown to decrease individual autonomy (Klein, 1991). Similarly, the introduction of lean production practices (lean teams, assembly lines, and workflow formalization) is associated with decreased perceptions of job characteristics, such as job autonomy and skill utilization, which in turn is associated with reduced organizational commitment, self-efficacy, and depression (Parker, 2003; Parker, Wall, & Jackson, 1997).

However, more recent research shows that there are ways to design jobs to make them sound both motivationally and mechanically (Morgeson & Campion, 2002), by increasing specialization without decreasing motivational characteristics. Using task clusters, defined as the smallest collection of logically related tasks performed by a single person to form naturally designed jobs where the person performs a whole identifiable piece of work, Morgeson and Campion examined how to combine interdependent task clusters to form the most mechanistically and motivationally sound jobs. Task clusters were evaluated in terms of job characteristics (e.g., simplicity, autonomy, impact, feedback) and then combined in a way to maximize both the mechanistic and motivational potential of the overall job. This approach ultimately results in breaking down several jobs into task clusters and recombining them differently to form new jobs constituting a new organizational structure, which is quite involving for an organization. However, it may be the most efficient way to maximize gains from such an intervention.

What has not been evaluated within the multimethod job design model is the impact of redesigning jobs on motivational mechanisms, such as need satisfaction and work motivation. We argue that the results obtained in research, such as the one conducted by Morgeson and Campion (2002), could be explained by examining how each approach affects the satisfaction of psychological needs. Although a mechanistic approach may make the person feel more competent in their job tasks (as long as the person is still challenged), it may decrease feelings of autonomy and relatedness. In contrast, a motivational approach may foster autonomy and relatedness at the expense of feelings of efficiency. Morgeson and Campion (2002) found a good tradeoff by increasing specialization without making the job too simple and repetitive, thereby maintaining the challenge, and increasing or maintain motivational characteristics all the same, thereby maintaining feelings of autonomy and relatedness.

Parker et al. (1997) were also able to demonstrate that one can introduce lean production practices by combining them with the use of autonomous work groups, and reap the benefits of both: reducing production costs, while maintaining and even enhancing employee engagement. These researchers undertook a rigorous study comparing three types of work groups: (1) work groups that were not redesigned, (2) work groups where just-in-time and total-quality-management methods were introduced, and (3) work groups where just-in-time and total-quality-management methods were introduced in conjunction with establishing autonomous work groups. The authors observed that the latter group cognitively redefined their role in the organization more than the other two groups, such that employees in this group developed a more strategic orientation (i.e., endorsing the organization's key strategies) and a broader role orientation (i.e., changing their views of their work responsibilities). Parker et al. argued that it was the addition of job autonomy in the third group that made the difference. These results concur with other research showing that increasing task variety without increasing autonomy can have detrimental long-term effects on how people perceive their organizational role, and on their productivity (Axtell & Parker, 2003). We could interpret these results as showing that

increasing feelings of competence (e.g., through increasing variety) is a necessary but insufficient condition for increasing autonomous work motivation: autonomy is also necessary for autonomous work motivation to increase. This is supported by research showing that feelings of competence are related to intrinsic motivation only when feelings of autonomy are also high (Dysvik, Kuvaas, & Gagné, 2013).

The Job Characteristics Model
The Original JCM

Arguably the best known and influential model in job design, the JCM was developed decades ago by Hackman and Oldham (1975, 1976, 1980). This model focuses on five "core characteristics," which were thought to reflect objective properties of jobs: (1) task significance, (2) task identity, (3) skill variety, (4) feedback, and (5) autonomy. Task significance refers to the extent to which the job has a substantial impact on the lives or work of others, whether in the immediate organization or in the external environment; task identity, the extent to which it requires completion of a whole and identifiable piece of work; and skill variety, the extent to which it entails a variety of different activities that demand the use of a number of different skills and talents. Feedback reflects the extent to which carrying out the work activities required by the job results in the individual being given direct and clear information about the effectiveness of his or her performance. Lastly, autonomy is the extent to which it provides freedom, independence, and discretion to the individual in scheduling the work and in determining the procedures to be used in carrying it out. Enhancing these five characteristics results in "job enrichment." Although the model suggests these core characteristics are objective properties of jobs, it emphasizes the importance of employee perceptions in regards to these characteristics, because employee reactions are influenced primarily by their perceptions (Hackman & Lawler, 1971).

The JCM proposes that enhancing the five core job characteristics (in a way that is perceived by employees) leads employees to experience three critical psychological states. The first of these states, meaningfulness of the work, is experienced when the individual perceives his or her work as important, valuable, and worthwhile. The second state, responsibility for the outcomes of the work, is experienced when the individual feels accountable for the results of the work. Lastly, knowledge of results of work activities is experienced when the individual has an understanding, on a regular basis, of the effectiveness of his or her performance. Specifically, the JCM contends that variety, identity, and significance lead to experienced meaningfulness; autonomy fosters responsibility; and feedback provides knowledge of results. In turn, these positive psychological states are thought to result in increased internal work motivation, a form of motivation that, within the terms of SDT, can be considered to include both intrinsic and autonomous motivation (Gagné & Deci, 2005), and other positive employee and organizational outcomes, such as enhanced job satisfaction and performance, and lower absenteeism and turnover. Furthermore, the JCM suggests that because the strength of higher-order needs varies among individuals, the same job characteristics may have different motivational implications for different employees. The notion of "growth need strength" was proposed to capture this individual difference, and is proposed to moderate the relationships between the core characteristics and the psychological states, and between the psychological states and the attitudinal and behavioral outcomes.

The JCM draws from classic need theories of motivation, such as Maslow's (1943, 1954) and Alderfer's (1972) theories. In essence, it is based on the idea that enhancing a job's core characteristics contributes to fulfilling employee higher-order needs, such as accomplishment and growth, which in turn elicits internal motivation and other positive outcomes (Hackman & Lawler, 1971; Parker & Ohly, 2008). The motivating power of conditions that satisfy higher-order needs is due to the fact that these needs are not necessarily easily satisfied in contemporary society. By contrast, because lower-order needs can be satisfied relatively easily, they are generally void of motivating power. Although the JCM does not specifically draw from SDT, the two are aligned because SDT also views enhancing the core job characteristics as a means of fostering autonomous motivation (Gagné & Deci, 2005). The two approaches diverge, however, with regards to the proposed underlying mechanisms: SDT contends that satisfaction of the basic needs for autonomy, competence, and relatedness mediate relationships between work characteristics and motivation, whereas the JCM proposes the three psychological states of meaningfulness, responsibility, and knowledge of results as mediating mechanisms. Another difference is that the JCM emphasizes the role of individual differences in higher-order need strength (Hackman & Oldham, 1975), whereas SDT focuses on individual differences in need satisfaction (Deci

& Ryan, 2000). However, whereas SDT views needs as universal, innate, and essential for well-being, it does not contend that there are no differences in need strength (Deci & Ryan, 2000), just that it focuses more on the level of satisfaction than on the level of need as a source of optimal functioning. This difference between the two approaches is thus more apparent than real.

Although meta-analytic results generally support the validity of the JCM, in particular with regards to the positive relationship between the core job characteristics and internal motivation (e.g., Fried & Ferris, 1987; Humphrey, Nahrgang, & Morgeson, 2007), they also reveal how broadly this internal motivation has been defined. In contrast, SDT offers a more differentiated and complete view of the range of motivation types that can be studied. As Gagné and Deci (2005) suggest, it is often useful in the work domain to look beyond the study of intrinsic motivation, defined as doing something out of enjoyment, to include identified regulation, defined as doing something out of personal values. Studies looking specifically at autonomous motivation using the SDT framework have indeed found significant relationships between the core job characteristic and this type of motivation (e.g., Derous & Ryan, 2008; Gagné, Senécal, & Koestner, 1997; Millette & Gagné, 2008). Research thus generally supports the contention that the five core job characteristics lead to internal (intrinsic and autonomous) motivation.

In addition, relatively few studies have directly examined the mechanisms underlying these relationships. Specifically, empirical studies examining the mediating role of the three psychological states are surprisingly rare. Notable exceptions are studies by Johns, Xie, and Fang, (1992) and Renn and Vandenberg (1995). Johns and colleagues' (1992) study suggested that meaningfulness is a "particularly encompassing psychological state" (p. 667), because it mediated relationships between each of the five core job characteristics and some outcomes at least partially. Recent meta-analytic results indicate a similar pattern (Humphrey et al., 2007). Renn and Vandenberg (1995) found that psychological states only partially mediated the relationships between job characteristics and motivation. In other words, empirical evidence does not entirely support Hackman and Oldham's propositions concerning the mediating role of the three psychological states, and their contention that different job characteristics would foster different psychological states. This suggests that further theoretical and empirical work is needed on the mediating processes underlying the relationships between job characteristics and motivation and other outcomes, and the use of the concept of need satisfaction may be useful in such an endeavor.

In an attempt to shed light on the mediating processes linking job characteristics with motivation and other outcomes, some scholars have integrated other theoretical advances into the JCM, and examined potential mediators other than the three psychological states proposed by Hackman and Oldham. For instance, Gagné and colleagues (1997) examined the four dimensions of psychological empowerment (autonomy, competence, meaning, and impact; Spreitzer, 1995) as potential mediators between job characteristics and intrinsic motivation. The empowerment framework is a logical choice, because three of its dimensions closely resemble the psychological states of meaningfulness, knowledge of results, and responsibility within the JCM (Gibson, Gibbs, Stanko, Tesluk, & Cohen, 2011), but also two of the three psychological needs in SDT. Gagné et al. found meaning to partially mediate the relationship between significance and motivation, autonomy to mediate the relationship between feedback and motivation, and competence and autonomy to mediate the relationship between job autonomy and motivation. Interestingly, however, the relationships between job autonomy and competence, and competence and motivation were negative. Although the other findings were in line with SDT, the negative relationship obtained with the competence dimension of empowerment is somewhat puzzling, especially as prior research has shown perceived competence to contribute positively to intrinsic motivation (Vallerand & Reid, 1984). A potential explanation is that the participants in the Gagné et al. (1997) study (technicians and sales representatives) were not accustomed to having job autonomy, which resulted in threatened feelings of competence. This suggests initial reactions to enhanced job autonomy may not always be positive, especially when employees are not accustomed to, or do not expect high levels of autonomy. Alternatively, the authors did not examine potential interactions between the four components of empowerment. Dysvik et al. (2013) found that competence was only positively related to intrinsic motivation when feelings of autonomy were high. Perhaps this could explain why competence was negatively related to intrinsic motivation in the Gagné et al. (1997) study.

One fruitful approach may be to integrate SDT within the JCM and, consistent with the view put forward by Deci & Ryan (2000), propose satisfaction of the basic needs for autonomy, competence, and relatedness as the key mediators between job characteristics and motivation. Conceptually, there appear to be close connections between these theories. First, the core characteristic of job autonomy, which is the extent to which the job provides freedom, independence, and discretion to the individual in scheduling the work and in determining the procedures to be used, is conceptually very close to SDT's psychological need for autonomy, which is a desire to experience ownership of one's behavior and to act with a sense of volition (Deci & Ryan, 2000). It thus seems logical to assume that enhancing autonomy within the job would contribute to fulfilling the need for autonomy.

Increasing task identity, that is, enhancing the extent to which the job requires completion of a whole and identifiable piece of work, should contribute to fulfilling employees' need for competence, the desire to feel capable of mastering the environment and bring about desired outcomes (Deci & Ryan, 2000; White, 1959). This is consistent with Hackman and Lawler's (1971) view that task identity should be associated with feelings of worth. Task feedback may also contribute to fulfilling the need for competence, because felt competence has been shown to mediate the impact of feedback on intrinsic motivation (Vallerand & Reid, 1984).

Indeed, receiving direct and clear information about the effectiveness of one's performance should either convey a message that one is competent (if the feedback is positive) or provide some guidance for employees to improve their performance (if the feedback is negative), which over time may lead to higher performance. Consistent with this view, meta-analytic results suggest feedback often results in improved performance (Kluger & DeNisi, 1996; although this meta-analysis and subsequent studies suggest that several variables moderate this relationship). Increasing variety may also contribute to feelings of competence, because it may result in the employee developing a broader skill set. Lastly, enhancing significance, the extent to which the employee through his or her job has an impact on the lives or work of others, should contribute to fulfilling the need for relatedness, which is a desire to feel connected to others (Deci & Ryan, 2000). This last proposition is not only supported by recent research (Grant, 2008), but is an important addition to the JCM, which has left out social aspects of job design (Grant & Parker, 2009). Moreover, replacing the critical psychological states with the satisfaction of basic needs is consistent with the foundations of the JCM given that early work on job design (e.g., Hackman & Lawler, 1971; Lawler & Hall, 1970), which led to the development of the JCM, clearly emphasized the role of need satisfaction.

Extensions of the JCM

Despite its undeniable influence on job design research, the JCM and traditional job design theories have been criticized on several grounds. For instance, they offer few useful insights on the mediating mechanisms or processes through which work characteristics impact outcomes, and the contingencies that may moderate those links (Parker, Wall, & Cordery, 2001). Furthermore, recent changes in the work context, such as the prevalence of service and knowledge work, the increased use of teams and flexible forms of work, and the trend towards leaner, more integrated organizations have brought on new challenges for which traditional job design theories are inadequate. To remedy these shortcomings, Parker and colleagues (2001) proposed an elaborated model of work design that includes antecedents to work characteristics at the organizational level (external and internal) and at the individual level. It expands work characteristics to include individual-level characteristics, such as control, variety, and feedback, but also cognitive, physical, and emotional demands, group-level characteristics, such as team autonomy, team feedback and team interdependence, and interactions between work characteristics at the individual and the group level. Motivation is proposed as a mediating mechanism, along with quick response, learning and development, and interaction processes. The range of outcomes is broadened to individual and group outcomes, such as job performance, affective reactions, safe working, and creativity, as well as organizational outcomes, such as productivity, customer satisfaction, and innovation. Lastly, organizational, group, and individual factors are proposed as moderating factors (contingencies). These include interdependence and uncertainty (organizational level); norms; size and skill composition (group level); and growth need strength, ability, and context satisfaction (individual level).

Traditional work design theories, such as the JCM, have also been criticized for adopting a narrow conceptualization of job design, and more specifically for omitting to take into account contextual variables (cf. Grant, Fried, & Juillerat, 2010). To remedy this flaw, Morgeson and Humphrey (2006) recently proposed a conceptual extension of Hackman and Oldham's original model to include knowledge-related characteristics, such as level of complexity and problem solving, social characteristics, such as social support, interdependence and feedback from others, and work context characteristics, such as physical demands and work conditions, in addition to the JCM's five task-related characteristics. Parker and colleagues' and Morgeson and Humphrey's models have yet to be tested extensively; however, meta-analytic results already provide some evidence that knowledge, support, and context characteristics help explain additional variance in a variety of outcomes (Humphrey et al., 2007).

In terms of mediating processes, Morgeson and Humphrey did not specifically propose variables other than Hackman and Oldham's three critical psychological states. However, in line with the proposed view that basic need satisfaction may mediate relationships between work characteristics and motivation and other outcomes, Deci and Ryan (2000) suggested that relationships observed between work characteristics, such as deadlines (Amabile, DeJong, & Lepper, 1976) and choice (Zuckerman, Porac, Lathin, Smith, and Deci, 1978) were linked to intrinsic motivation through their impact on employee's locus of causality, a concept closely related to the degree of experienced autonomy. Similarly, Parker and colleagues' (2001) do not propose specific mediating mechanisms between work characteristics and motivation. However, Parker and Ohly (2008, 2009) emphasize the role of experienced meaningfulness, self-efficacy, psychological empowerment (of which the meaning component is akin to meaningfulness, the competence component corresponds to self-efficacy, and the choice component represents self-determination), and internalization, that is, the process by which employees adopt values, attitudes, and regulatory structures such that a behavior becomes internally regulated (Gagné & Deci, 2005), as potential important mediating processes. These mediators are conceptually close to the basic needs for competence and autonomy within SDT.

Furthermore, Grant and Parker (2009) argue that the relational side of job design has been neglected following the rise of the JCM, which focused mostly on task characteristics, leaving aside social characteristics. Grant (2008) focused on task significance as a characteristic particularly likely to foster feelings of relatedness, which he has shown fosters meaning-based (identified) work motivation (which he calls prosocial motivation). Task significance is argued to be a relational job characteristic, linking the worker to a beneficiary (Grant, 2007). Increasing contact between workers and beneficiaries may have an effect on the workers' identification processes (which could be explained through social identity theory) and possibly the workers' feelings of relatedness (which could be explained through SDT). Grant and Parker (2009) also argue for the triggering of empathy, which may be affected by both identification and relatedness satisfaction. The other side of the coin is when contact with beneficiaries leads to increased distress, due to the fact that one's job necessarily requires to harm the beneficiary in order to bring positive outcomes in the long-term (Grant & Campbell, 2007; Margolis & Molinsky, 2008). Examples include medical professions that require inflicting physical pain during medical procedures. Grant and Campbell (2007) found in two studies that perceiving such work as having a positive impact on beneficiaries attenuates the fact that the tasks involve harming them, helps preserve job satisfaction, and buffer against burnout. It would be extremely interesting to see how workers deal with these issues from the point of view of need satisfaction. Does inflicting pain for good reasons increase or decrease feelings of competence, autonomy, and relatedness? Does experiencing high relatedness to beneficiaries enhance feelings of distress resulting from such task requirements? Since Fernet, Gagné, and Austin (2010) have shown that the autonomous motivation of teachers does buffer against burnout, would it also buffer against distress caused by doing harm?

The Sociotechnical Systems Approach

Another stream of research on job design, called the sociotechnical systems approach, focuses on the interaction between people, technology, and organizational structure (Cherns, 1976; Rousseau, 1977). Developed at the Tavistock Institute in London, pioneers Trist and Bamford (1951) observed in a study that despite improved technology, productivity remained stagnant, and that increased pay did not make a difference. They found, however, that the use of autonomous work groups improved things considerably, especially when workers were given management autonomy. Autonomous work groups typically do the following things (e.g., Kemp, Wall, Clegg, & Cordery, 1983): they distribute work among team members, strive to reach production targets and quality standards, solve production problems, make maintenance calls, record production data, organize schedules, order materials, manage a budget, and participate in the selection and training of new recruits. Most interesting is that these groups are not managed by supervisors, but are self-managed and report to a general manager instead.

Research supports the superiority of autonomous work groups over conventional plant designs in manufacturing organizations in terms of increased productivity. Wall, Corbett, Martin, Clegg, and Jackson (1990) found that giving machine operators control over maintenance and programming (in addition to loading, monitoring, and unloading tasks) improved their productivity and their job satisfaction, and lowered perceived job pressure. Kemp and colleagues (1983) found that employees working in autonomous work groups reported higher job satisfaction and perceived greater work role complexity compared with workers in another industrial organization using traditional design. Other research demonstrates that the positive effects of autonomous work groups are long-lasting, especially on intrinsic work motivation (Wall, Kemp, Jackson, & Clegg, 1986).

Autonomous work groups arguably enrich the design of tasks (Campion, Medsker, & Higgs, 1993; Campion, Papper, & Medsker, 1996; Griffin, Patterson, & West, 2001). The tasks accomplished by autonomous work group are enriched from the point of view of Morgeson and Humphrey's work design model. Not only do members of these autonomous work groups have more task and skill variety, task identity, and significance, but the responsibilities they have increase their levels of autonomy, and they have more sources of feedback. Moreover, the task interdependence in these groups is enhanced, and so is the level of knowledge. Indeed, some researchers have integrated notions from team and job design research to develop, for example, a team characteristics model (Strubler & York, 2007). Cohen, Ledford, and Spreitzer (1996) demonstrated that autonomous work groups demonstrated better group management, such as clear norms, better coordination, and more expertise and innovation, because of the enriched design this form of work organization creates, that they performed better (in terms of quality, productivity, costs, and safety) and that they were less absent. Like in the previous section on the JCM, the fact that motivational characteristics are enhanced in autonomous work groups may be the cause of these positive results, and as argued in the previous section, need satisfaction is likely to be an important mediator in these effects.

As discussed earlier, Parker and colleagues (1997) showed how the introduction of autonomous work groups in manufacturing plants can change the way people view their organizational roles and responsibilities, thereby increasing efficiency and productivity. We argue that this happens through a process of internalization, which in SDT is essential to the development of autonomous work motivation (Ryan, 1995). Internalization has also been shown to be promoted by the satisfaction of the three psychological needs for autonomy, competence, and relatedness, and it is very possible that when work is organized through autonomous work groups, the satisfaction of these needs is enhanced from within the teams—although this remains to be tested. The use of teams has been related to feeling autonomous (Meier, 1984) and to reports of more motivating task design, higher-quality relationships among team members, decreased work load, and increased well-being (van Mierlo, Rutte, Seinen, & Kompier, 2000).

The Job Demands/Job Resources Models

A different way to conceptualize job design is found in work on job demands, control, support, and resources by Karasek and colleagues (Karasek, 1979; Karasek & Theorell, 1990) and, more recently, by other scholars (e.g., Demerouti, Bakker, Nachreiner, & Schaufeli, 2001; Schaufeli & Bakker, 2004). Known as the job demands-control-support and the job demands-resources (JD-R) model, respectively, these frameworks were developed with the goal of understanding how characteristics of the work could impact workplace stress and well-being. Unlike "narrow" models, such as Hackman and Oldham's JCM, these models seek to consider a broad array of work-related variables, including contextual variables.

The initial job demands-control (later expanded to include support) model proposed that job demands exerted a direct, negative effect on workplace well-being, whereas control (i.e., autonomy) and support moderate that effect such that, under conditions of high control or high support, the negative impact of demands on well-being was weaker. This model, and specifically, the proposed interactive effect, has received mixed empirical support (e.g., de Lange, Taris, Kompier, Houtman, & Bongers, 2003; Taris & Kompier, 2005; van Yperen & Hagedoorn, 2003).

The JD-R model, a revised version of the framework, has received more empirical support (e.g.,

Demerouti et al., 2001). This model proposes independent main effects for demands and resources on different facets of workplace well-being. Specifically, it contends that job demands, defined as features of the work context that tax employees' personal capacities (Bakker, Demerouti, Taris, Schaufeli, & Schreurs, 2003; de Jonge & Dormann, 2006), are negatively related to burnout through an energetic process, whereas job resources, "those physical, psychological, social, or organizational aspects of the work context that either/or (1) reduce job demands and the associated physiological and psychological costs; (2) are functional in achieving work goals, and (3) stimulate personal growth, development, and learning" (Schaufeli & Bakker, 2004, p. 296) are positively related to job engagement through a motivational process (Van den Broeck, Vansteenkiste, De Witte, & Lens, 2008). Central to these processes is the satisfaction of basic needs, such as the needs for autonomy, competence, and relatedness (Schaufeli & Bakker, 2004; Van den Broeck et al., 2008).

The JD-R presents clear conceptual links with SDT because both theories view the satisfaction of basic needs as important motivational mechanisms (Deci & Ryan, 2000; Schaufeli & Bakker, 2004). Recently, scholars have begun integrating these theories (e.g., Boudrias et al., 2011; Fernet, Guay, & Sénécal, 2004; Van Beek, Hu, Schaufeli, Taris, & Schreurs, 2012; Van den Broeck et al., 2008). Indeed, both theories recognize that work-context characteristics—demands and resources, among others—can influence the fulfillment of basic needs, and as was recently pointed out, both theories have implications for occupational health (Van den Broeck et al., 2008). In line with this, Van den Broeck and colleagues (2008) found job demands to be negatively and job resources positively related to overall basic needs fulfillment. However, subsequent research only found a positive relationship between job resources and need satisfaction, failing to find a significant negative relationship between job demands and need satisfaction (Boudrias et al., 2011). Further research bridging SDT and the JD-R is thus needed to determine whether need satisfaction is mainly influenced by job resources, as Schaufeli and Bakker (2004) originally suggested, or if job demands can also influence (reduce) need satisfaction, as suggested for instance by Van den Broeck and colleagues (2008). The distinction between challenging versus hindering job demands (cf. Podsakoff, LePine, & LePine, 2007) may also be relevant in explaining their impact on need satisfaction.

Looking Ahead: Proactive Work Behavior and Job Crafting

Proactive work behavior is defined as behavior that is meant to initiate change, is self-starting, and is future oriented (Griffin, Neal, & Parker, 2007; Parker, Bindl, & Strauss, 2010). The motivation of such behavior, according to Parker et al. (2010), depends on three factors: (1) whether the person believes he or she can do it, (2) the reasons for wanting to do it, and (3) where the energy to do it comes from (affect is proposed to bring this energy about). The first factor depends heavily on feelings of competence, whereas the second depends heavily on feelings of autonomy. Reasons for engaging in proactive behavior can be evaluated using measures of autonomous and controlled motivation, though according to Parker et al. (2010), proactive behavior is by definition autonomously regulated. However, we leave further discussion of proactive work behavior to Strauss and Parker [Chapter 4].

We will focus instead on the issue of job crafting, a particular type of proactive work behavior that involves redesigning one's own job. Wrzesniewski and Dutton (2001) more formally developed the concept of job crafting to describe the process through which employees proactively alter the boundaries of their own tasks and relationships to enhance meaning and identity in the workplace. Employees can change physical task boundaries by altering the number or type of tasks that they complete, and they can change relational boundaries by altering with whom and how they interact and communicate at work. Job crafting usually involves attempting to achieve a better fit between one's own skills and knowledge, and those of the work environment, including job tasks, through negotiation with the employer (Parker et al., 2010).

When thinking about job crafting more deeply, it becomes obvious that we must stop thinking about jobs, and think instead of roles that workers play in an organization (Ilgen & Hollenbeck, 1991). A role is defined as a combination of formal and informal task elements, and employees, to different degrees, initiate the incorporation or transformation of new task elements to make the role fit their aspirations and their skills (Grant, Fried, & Juillerat, 2010). Parker et al. (1997) capture this phenomenon very well through the concept of role orientation, and have found that both competence and autonomy are essential for its development (see also Morgeson, Delaney-Klinger, & Hemingway, 2005; Parker, 1998), which fits SDT's postulates very well. Wrzesniewski and Dutton (2001) similarly argue that people attempt to satisfy three needs when crafting their job: (1) the need for control and meaning, (2) the need for a positive self-image, and (3) the need for connecting with others. These three needs overlap in great part with the needs for autonomy, competence, and relatedness postulated in SDT.

Essentially, job crafting involves enhancing the motivational potential of one's job through one's own redesign, rather than top-down work redesign. So not only can it be promoted through need satisfaction, as mentioned previously, but it is likely, and has been shown, to lead to subsequently higher need satisfaction (Frese, Garst, & Fay, 2007). Because challenge needs to be relatively high in order for flow to be possible (Massimini & Carli, 1988), individuals need increasingly greater challenge to remain intrinsically motivated. Job crafting is a good way to obtain more challenging and stimulating work. Furthermore, job crafting may be both an indicator of internalization and a mechanism to bring about internalization, because in order for the job to have greater meaning to the employee, it must become more consistent with his or her goals and values. Through job crafting, employees would thus themselves make the job more autonomously motivating. In short, recent views of job design move away from viewing job design as a static construct toward viewing it as a dynamic and constantly changing construct (Clegg & Spencer, 2007), which is exciting for the development of future job design theories.

The Changing Work Environment

From the time early theories of job design were developed to the ones used today, many changes have occurred in the world of work. These changes include a shift from a manufacturing to a service-oriented economy, the rise of the knowledge worker, an increase in the use of teams (which leads to an increase in task interdependence), a globalization of the economy and consequently of migration patterns of the workforce, leading to increased ethnic and cultural diversity within organizations, as well as transformed psychological contracts. In addition, we are dealing with an ageing population, and an ever complexifying technology, which is partly responsible for more and more creative work arrangements, such as virtual work (Grant, Fried, Parker, & Frese, 2010). These factors are bound to transform our theories of job design, or at least force us to revisit them in light of this changing work environment.

Telecommuting, for example, has been argued to increase job autonomy (Feldman & Gainey, 1997; Hill, Ferris, & Martinson, 2003), and to require that employees be more self-regulated in their work behavior (Raghuram, Wiesenfeld, & Garud, 2003). It has also been thought to isolate workers by separating them from their social network (Kurland & Bailey, 1999). Although the use of telecommuting has been positively related to firm performance (Sanchez, Perez, de Luis Carnicer, & Jimenez, 2007), very little research actually tests whether telecommuting increases job autonomy and requires more self-regulation than traditional jobs, or to what extent it creates a feeling of isolation among telecommuters. No research, to our knowledge, has ever looked at the design characteristics of telecommuting jobs. Research on telecommuting should compare the design of these types of jobs with the design of more traditional and equivalent work arrangements (i.e., the same job done on organizational premises). Job autonomy and feelings of isolation may actually vary across different telecommuting jobs, depending on the rules that are established for these workers, the technology they need to use, and the type of work that is accomplished.

Another recent trend in work organizations is the use of depersonalized work design. Workplace decor can be analyzed in terms of physical identity markers that help individual employees forge their identity as organizational members (Elsbach, 2004). The formation of social identities relies on a process of internalization that may function similarly to the motivational one proposed in SDT (Tajfel, 1982; Ryan, 1995). As mentioned previously, internalization depends on the satisfaction of the psychological needs, and in the case of social identity, we argue that the needs for relatedness and autonomy may be particularly important. What is really interesting in Kim Elsbach's research is the finding that when organizations use nonterritorial work environments, where employees must book their workspace daily and evacuate completely at the end of each day, people report feeling that their identity is threatened and go to great lengths to reaffirm their identity in the organization (Elsbach, 2003).

Although these arrangements are financially attractive to employers, for whom space is expensive (Turner & Myerson, 1998), and may be perceived as a good arrangement for employees who travel a lot as part of their job (e.g., consultants, salespeople) and for telecommuters, the cost of the potential decrease in employee morale and productivity is not taken into consideration (Donald, 1994). Having dedicated office space is one of the important factors that forge organizational identity (Elsbach, 2003), which is an important factor for retention (Ashforth & Mael, 1989). Some noted reactions to nonterritorial workplaces include the loss of valued employees, conflict over the choice of workstations between employees, squatting, more idiosyncratic behavior and dress to attract attention to themselves, and leaving marks on the desktop of workstation computers (Donald, 1994; Elsbach, 2003). This may be happening because employees feel less valued by the organization, are less able to forge relationships at work with other employees because of the constant migration that occurs, and because employees feel this standardization is a threat to their autonomy. It was also observed that people take a long time to "set up" their space when they arrive, a setup that often includes portable artifacts (Elsbach, 2003), which leaves less time for productive work, which in turn could affect their feelings of competence. It would be very interesting to explore these ideas in future research, along with an examination of the impact of such work arrangements on work motivation.

By providing a theoretical framework explaining why and how specific work characteristics enhance motivation, that is, satisfaction of the three basic needs, SDT provides direction for organizations to shape these new work arrangements in a manner that is conducive to greater autonomous motivation. For instance, organizations that use telecommuting may implement and encourage employees to use in-house social networks, and organize regular social events to ensure employees' need for relatedness is fulfilled despite the lack of regular face-to-face interaction with coworkers and supervisors. Employers using depersonalized work spaces may provide employees with opportunities to choose their work stations and personalize their work spaces in a way that does not preclude others from using it, to avoid thwarting their need for autonomy.

Conclusion

We argue for the use of SDT (Deci & Ryan, 1985) to better understand the explanatory mechanisms underlying job design effects on employee outcomes. The satisfaction of psychological needs for competence, autonomy, and relatedness seems particularly helpful in understanding these effects. They are useful inasmuch as they help us analyze and predict how a particular work environment is likely to affect worker motivation, and they can serve as useful guides in determining optimal job design. But the effect of need satisfaction may be a bit more complex. Job autonomy, for example, may have more than just a motivational function. Job autonomy has for effect not only to increase the satisfaction of the need for autonomy, but also to allow the employee to exercise more skills and learn new things, which is likely to lead to increased knowledge as well as increased competence satisfaction (Grant & Parker, 2009; Wall, Jackson, & Mullarkey, 1995). Other such examples may exist as well.

SDT can contribute to our understanding of why certain job designs have their effects on employee outcomes. It provides some of the necessary psychological mediators that help explain the effects of job characteristics on employee outcomes. Internalization, for example, has not been considered as an explanatory mechanism through which job characteristics may lead to increased worker motivation and commitment, but may be at the core of the matter (Parker & Ohly, 2008). SDT can also be used to better our understanding of how certain job characteristics interact with other organizational factors, such as organizational structure, leadership style, and technologies (Parker et al., 2001).

What is striking when reading the recent literature is to see that although the way jobs are designed has evolved, it varies tremendously. Some research argues that some new job designs are as "Tayloristic" as they were 100 years ago, dubbing contemporary job designs as "electronic sweat-shops" (Davis, 2010). Other research focuses on job crafting (Berg, Wrzesniewski, & Dutton, 2010). On the one hand, this can been seen as exciting, because the view of job design that we have today is much broader than it was 100 years ago. On the other hand, this can be seen as discouraging, because some of the so-called progress seems to simply be a masquerade of technology with no improvement to the human experience. What this really illustrates is that job design research is still needed, and that SDT may help forge new grounds in this exciting field of research.

References

Adair, J. G. (1984). The Hawthorne effect: A reconsideration of the methodological artifact. *Journal of Applied Psychology*, *69*(2), 334–345. doi: 10.1037/0021-9010.69.2.334

Alderfer, C. P. (1972). *Existence, relatedness, and growth*. New York: Free Press.

Amabile, T. M., DeJong, W., & Lepper, M. R. (1976). Effects of externally imposed deadlines on subsequent intrinsic motivation. *Journal of Personality and Social Psychology*, *34*, 92–98. doi: 10.1037/0022-3514.34.1.92

Ashforth, B. E., & Mael, F. (1989). Social identity theory and the organization. *Academy of Management Review*, *14*, 20–39.

Axtell, C. M., & Parker, S. K. (2003). Promoting role breadth self-efficacy through involvement, work redesign and training. *Human Relations*, *56*(1), 112–131. doi:10.1177/0018726703056001452

Babbage, C. (1835). *On the economy of machinery and manufactures*. London: Charles Knight.

Baker, G., Jensen, M. C., & Murphy, K. J. (1988). Compensation and incentives: Practice vs. theory. *Journal of Finance*, *43*, 593–616.

Bakker, A. B., Demerouti, E., Taris, T., Schaufeli, W., & Schreurs, P. (2003). A multigroup analysis of the job demands-resources model in four home care organizations. *International Journal of Stress Management*, *10*, 16–38. doi: 10.1037/1072-5245.10.1.16

Berg, J. M., Wrzesniewski, A., & Dutton, J. E. (2010). Perceiving and responding to challenges in job crafting at different ranks: When proactivity requires adaptivity. *Journal of Organizational Behavior*, *31*(2), 158–186. doi: 10.1002/job.645

Boudrias, J., Desrumaux, P., Gaudreau, P., Nelson, K., Brunet, L., & Savoie, A. (2011). Modeling the experience of psychological health at work: The role of personal resources, social-organizational resources, and job demands. *International Journal of Stress Management*, *18*(4), 372–395. doi: 10.1037/a0025353

Campion, M. A. (1988). Interdisciplinary approaches to job design: A constructive replication with extensions. *Journal of Applied Psychology*, *73*, 467–481.

Campion, M. A., & McClelland, C. L. (1991). Interdisciplinary examination of the costs and benefits of enlarged jobs: A job design quasi-experiment. *Journal of Applied Psychology*, *76*(2), 186–198. doi:10.1037/0021-9010.76.2.186

Campion, M. A., & McClelland, C. L. (1993). Follow-up and extension of the interdisciplinary costs and benefits of enlarged jobs. *Journal of Applied Psychology*, *78*(3), 339–351. doi:10.1037/0021-9010.78.3.339

Campion, M. A., Medsker, G. J., & Higgs, A. C. (1993). Relations between work group characteristics and effectiveness: Implications for designing effective work groups. *Personnel Psychology*, *46*, 823–823.

Campion, M. A., Papper, E. M., & Medsker, G. J. (1996). Relations between work team characteristics and effectiveness: A replication and extension. *Personnel Psychology*, *49*, 429–452.

Campion, M. A., & Thayer, P. W. (1985). Development and field evaluation of an interdisciplinary measure of job design. *Journal of Applied Psychology*, *70*, 29–43. doi: 10.1037/0021-9010.70.1.29.

Cherns, A. (1976). The principles of sociotechnical design. *Human Relations*, *29*, 783–792. doi:10.1177/001872677602900806

Clegg, C., & Spencer, C. (2007). A circular and dynamic model of the process of job design. *Journal of Occupational and Organizational Psychology*, *80*(2), 321–339. doi:10.1348/096317906X113211

Cohen, S. G., Ledford, G. E., & Spreitzer, G. M. (1996). A predictive model of self-managing work team effectiveness. *Human Relations*, *49*, 643–676. doi: 10.1177/001872679604900506.

Csikszentmihalyi, M. (1990). *Flow: The psychology of optimal experience*. New York: Harper and Row.

Davis, G. F. (2010). Job design meets organizational sociology. *Journal of Organizational Behavior, 31,* 302–308. doi: 10.1002/job.604

De Jonge, J., & Dormann, C. (2006). Stressors, resources and strain at work: A longitudinal test of the triple match principle. *Journal of Applied Psychology, 91,* 1359–1379. doi: 10.1037/0021-9010.91.5.1359

de Lange, A. H., Taris, T. W., Kompier, M. A. J., Houtman, I. L. D., & Bongers, P. M. (2003). The very best of the millenium: Longitudinal research and the demand-control-(support) model. *Journal of Occupational Health Psychology, 8,* 282–305. doi: 10.1037/ 1076-8998.8.4.282

Deci, E. L., Koestner, R., & Ryan, R. M. (1999). A meta-analytic review of experiments examining the effects of extrinsic rewards on intrinsic motivation. *Psychological Bulletin, 125*(6), 627–668. doi:10.1037/0033-2909.125.6.627

Deci, E. L., & Ryan, R. M. (1985). *Intrinsic motivation and self-determination in human behavior.* New York, NY: Plenum Publishing Co.

Deci, E. L., & Ryan, R. M. (2000). The "what" and "why" of goal pursuits: Human needs and the self-determination of behavior. *Psychological Inquiry, 11,* 227–268.

Demerouti, E., Bakker, A. B., Nachreiner, F., & Schaufeli, W. B. (2001). The job demands-resources model of burnout. *Journal of Applied Psychology, 86,* 499–512. doi: 10.1037//0021.9010.86.3.499

Derous, E., & Ryan, A. M. (2008). When earning is beneficial for learning: The relation of employment and leisure activities to academic outcomes. *Journal of Vocational Behavior, 73,* 118–131. doi:10.1016/j.jvb.2008.02.003

Donald, I. (1994). Management and change in office environments. *Journal of Environmental Psychology, 14,* 21–30.

Dysvik, A., Kuvaas, B., & Gagné, M. (2013). An investigation of the unique, synergistic and balanced relationships between basic psychological needs and intrinsic motivation. *Journal of Applied Social Psychology, 43,* 1050–1064. doi: 10.1111/jasp.12068

Elsbach, K. D. (2003). Relating physical environment to self—categorizations: Identity threat and affirmation in a non-territorial office space. *Administrative Science Quarterly, 48*(4), 622–654. doi:10.2307/3556639

Elsbach, K. D. (2004). Interpreting workplace identities: The role of office décor. *Journal of Organizational Behavior, 25*(1), 99–128. doi:10.1002/job.233

Fay, D., & Kamps, A. (2006). Work characteristics and the emergence of a sustainable workforce: Do job design principles matter? *Gedrag & Organisatie, 19,* 184–203.

Feldman, D. C., & Gainey, T. W. (1997). Patterns of telecommuting and their consequences: Framing the research agenda. *Human Resource Management Review, 7,* 369–388. doi: 10.1016/S1053-4822(97)90025-5.

Fernet, C., Gagné, M., & Austin, S. (2010). When does quality of relationships with coworkers predict burnout over time? the moderating role of work motivation. *Journal of Organizational Behavior, 31*(8), 1163–1180. doi:10.1002/job.673

Fernet, C., Guay, F., & Senécal, C. (2004). Adjusting to job demands: The role of work self-determination and job control in predicting burnout. *Journal of Vocational Behavior, 65,* 39–56. doi: 10.1016/S0001-8791(03)00098-8.

Frese, M., Garst, H., & Fay, D. (2007). Making things happen: Reciprocal relationships between work characteristics and personal initiative in a four-wave longitudinal structural

equation model. *Journal of Applied Psychology, 92*(4), 1084–1102. doi:10.1037/0021-9010.92.4.1084

Fried, Y., & Ferris, G. R. (1987). The validity of the job characteristics model: A review and meta-analysis. *Personnel Psychology, 40,* 287–322. doi: 10.1111/j.1744-6570.1987.tb00605.x

Gagné, M., & Deci, E. L. (2005). Self-determination theory and work motivation. *Journal of Organizational Behavior, 26,* 331–362. doi: 10.1002/job.322

Gagné, M., & Forest, J. (2008). The study of compensation systems through the lens of self-determination theory: Reconciling 35 years of debate. *Canadian Psychology/Psychologie Canadienne, 49*(3), 225–232. doi:10.1037/a0012757

Gagné, M., Senécal, C. B., & Koestner, R. (1997). Proximal job characteristics, feelings of empowerment, and intrinsic motivation: A multidimentional model. *Journal of Applied Social Psychology, 27,* 1222–1240.

Gibson, C. B., Gibbs, J. L., Stanko, T. L., Tesluk, P., & Cohen, S. G. (2011). Including the "I" in virtuality and modern job design: Extending the job characteristics model to include the moderating effectof individual experiences f electronic dependence and copresence. *Organization Science, 22,* 1481–1499. doi: 10.1287/orsc.1100.0586

Grant, A. M. (2007). Relational job design and the motivation to make a prosocial difference. *Academy of Management Review, 32,* 393–417.

Grant, A. M. (2008). The significance of task significance: Job performance effects, relational mechanisms, and boundary conditions. *Journal of Applied Psychology, 93*(1), 108–124. doi:10.1037/0021-9010.93.1.108

Grant, A. M., & Campbell, E. M. (2007). Doing good, doing harm, being well and burning out: The interactions of perceived prosocial and antisocial impact in service work. *Journal of Occupational and Organizational Psychology, 80,* 665–691. doi: 10.1348/096317906X169553

Grant, A. M., Fried, Y., & Juillerat, T. (2010). Work matters: Job design in classic and contemporary perspectives. In S. Zedeck (Eds.), *APA handbook of industrial and organizational psychology* (Vol. 1, pp. 417–453). Washington, DC: American Psychological Association.

Grant, A. M., Fried, Y., Parker, S. K., & Frese, M. (2010). Putting job design in context: Introduction to the special issue. *Journal of Organizational Behavior, 31*(2–3), 145–157. doi:10.1002/job.679

Grant, A. M., & Parker, S. K. (2009). 7 redesigning work design theories: The rise of relational and proactive perspectives. *Academy of Management Annals, 3*(1), 317–375. doi:10.1080/19416520903047327

Griffin, M. A., Neal, A., & Parker, S. K. (2007). A new model of work role performance: Positive behavior in uncertain and interdependent contexts. *Academy of Management Journal, 50*(2), 327–347. doi:10.5465/AMJ.2007.24634438

Griffin, M. A., Patterson, M. G., & West, M. A. (2001). Job satisfaction and teamwork: The role of supervisor support. *Journal of Organizational Behavior, 22,* 537–550. doi: 10.1002/job.101

Hackman, R., & Lawler, E. E. (1971). Employee reactions to job characteristics. *Journal of Applied Psychology, 55,* 259–286. doi: 10.1037/h0031152

Hackman, J. R., & Oldham, G. R. (1975). Development of the job diagnostic survey. *Journal of Applied Psychology, 60,* 159–170. doi: 10.1037/h0076546.

Hackman, J. R., & Oldham, G. R. (1976). Motivation through the design of work: Test of a theory. *Organizational Behavior and Human Performance, 16,* 250–279. doi: 10.1016/0030-5073(76)90016-7

Hackman, J. R., & Oldham, G. R. (1980). *Work redesign.* Reading, MA: Addison-Wesley.

Herzberg, F. (1966). *Work and the nature of man.* New York: Thomas Y. Crowell.

Herzberg, F., Mausner, B., & Snyderman, B. (1959). *The motivation to work.* New York: Wiley.

Hill, E. J., Ferris, M., & Martinson, V. (2003). Does it matter where you work? A comparison of how three work venues (traditional office, virtual office, and home office) influence aspects of work and personal/family life. *Journal of Vocational Behavior, 63,* 220–241. doi: 10.1016/s0001.8791(03)00042-3

House, R. J., & Wigdor, L. A. (1967). Herzberg's dual-factor theory of job satisfaction and motivation: A review of the evidence and a criticism. *Personnel Psychology, 20,* 369–390. doi: 10.1111/j.1744-6570.1967.tb02440.x

Humphrey, S. E., Nahrgang, J. D., & Morgeson, F. P. (2007). Integrating motivational, social, and contextual work design features: A meta-analytic summary and theoretical extension of the work design literature. *Journal of Applied Psychology, 92,* 1332–1356. doi: 10.1037/0021-9010.92.5.1332.

Ilgen, D. R., & Hollenbeck, J. R. (1991). The structure of work: Job design and roles. In M. D. Dunnette, L. M. Hough, M. D. Dunnette, & L. M. Hough (Eds.), *Handbook of industrial and organizational psychology* (Vol. 2, 2nd ed., pp. 165–207). Palo Alto, CA: Consulting Psychologists Press.

Johns, G., Xie, L., & Fang, Y. (1992). Mediating and moderating effects in job design. *Journal of Management, 18,* 657–676. doi: 10.1177/014920639201800404

Karasek, R. A. (1979). Job demands, job decision latitude, and mental strain: Implications for job design. *Administrative Science Quarterly, 24,* 285–308.

Karasek, R. A., & Theorell, T. (1990). *Healthy work.* New York: Basic Books.

Kemp, N. J., Wall, T. D., Clegg, C. W., & Cordery, J. L. (1983). Autonomous work groups in a greenfield site: A comparative study. *Journal of Occupational Psychology, 56,* 271–288. doi: 10.1111/j.2044-8325.1983.tb00134.x

Klein, J. A. (1991). A reexamination of autonomy in light of new manufacturing practices. *Human Relations, 44,* 21–38. doi: 10.1177/001872679104400102.

Kluger, A. N., & DeNisi, A. (1996). Effects of feedback intervention on performance: A historical review, a meta-analysis, and a preliminary feedback intervention theory. *Psychological Bulletin, 119,* 254–284. doi: 10.1037/0033-2909.119.2.254

Kurland, N. B., & Bailey, D. E. (1999). Telework: The advantages and challenges of working here, there, anywhere, and anytime. *Organizational Dynamics, 28,* 53–68.

Lawler, E. E., & Hall, D. T. (1970). Relationship of job characteristics to job involvement, satisfaction, and intrinsic motivation. *Journal of Applied Psychology, 54,* 305–312. doi: 10.1037/h0029692

Likert, R. (1967). *The human organization: Its management and value.* New York: McGraw-Hill.

Locke, E. (1969). What is job satisfaction? *Organizational Behavior and Human Performance, 4,* 309–336. doi: 10.1016/0030-5073(69)90013-0

Margolis, D., & Molinsky, A. L. (2008). Navigating the bind of necessary evils: Psychological engagement and the production of interpersonally sensitive behavior. *Academy of Management Journal, 51,* 847–872.

Maslow, A. (1943). A theory of human motivation. *Psychological Review, 50,* 370–396.

Maslow, A. (1954). *Motivation and personality.* New York: Harper & Row.

Massimini, F., & Carli, M. (1988). The systematic assessment of flow in daily experience. In M. I. S. Csikszentmihalyi, M. Csikszentmihalyi, & I. S. Csikszentmihalyi (Eds.), *Optimal experience: Psychological studies of flow in consciousness* (pp. 266–287). New York, NY: Cambridge University Press.

McGregor, D. (1960). *The human side of the enterprise.* New York: McGraw-Hill.

Meier, R. B. (1984). The impact of the structural organization of public welfare offices on the psychosocial work and the treatment environments. *Journal of Social Service Research, 7,* 1–18. doi:10.1300/J079v07n02_01

Millette, V., & Gagné, M. (2008). Designing volunteers' tasks to maximize motivation, satisfaction and performance: The impact of job characteristics on volunteer engagement. *Motivation and Emotion, 32,* 11–22. doi: 10.1007/s11031-007-9079-4

Morgeson, F. P., & Campion, M. A. (2002). Minimizing tradeoffs when redesigning work: Evidence from a longitudinal quasi-experiment. *Personnel Psychology, 55,* 589–612.

Morgeson, F. P., Delaney-Klinger, K., & Hemingway, M. A. (2005). The importance of job autonomy, cognitive ability, and job-related skill for predicting role breadth and job performance. *Journal of Applied Psychology, 90,* 399–406. doi: 10.1037/0021-9010.90.2.399.

Morgeson, F. P., & Humphrey, S. E. (2006). The Work Design Questionnaire (WDQ): Developing and validating a comprehensive measure for assessing job design and the nature of work. *Journal of Applied Psychology, 91,* 1321–1339. doi: 10.1037/0021-9010.91.6.1321.

Parker, S. K. (1998). Enhancing role breadth self-efficacy: The roles of job enrichment and other organizational interventions. *Journal of Applied Psychology, 83*(6), 835–852.

Parker, S. K. (2003). Longitudinal effects of lean production on employee outcomes and the mediating role of work characteristics. *Journal of Applied Psychology, 88,* 620–634. doi: 10.1037/0021-9010.88.4.620.

Parker, S. K., Bindl, U. K., & Strauss, K. (2010). Making things happen: A model of proactive motivation. *Journal of Management, 36*(4), 827–856. doi: 10.1177/ 0149206310363732

Parker, S. K., & Ohly, S. (2008). Designing motivating jobs. In R. Kanfer, G. Chen, & R. Pritchard (Eds.), *Work motivation: Past, present, and future* (pp. 233–284). New York, NY: Psychology Press.

Parker, S. K., & Ohly, S. (2009). Extending the reach of job design theory: Going beyond the job characteristics model. In A. Wilkinson, N. Bacon, T. Redman, & S. Snell (Eds.), *The Sage handbook of human resource management* (pp. 269–285). Sage, London.

Parker, S. K., Wall, T. D., & Cordery, J. L. (2001). Future work design research and practice: Towards an elaborated model of work design. *Journal of Occupational & Organizational Psychology, 74*(4), 413. doi: 10.1348/096317901167460

Parker, S. K., Wall, T. D., & Jackson, P. R. (1997). "That's not my job": Developing flexible employee work orientations. *Academy of Management Journal, 40,* 899–929.

Podsakoff, N. P., LePine, J. A., & LePine, M. A. (2007). Differential challenge stressor-hindrance stressor relationships with job attitudes, turnover intentions, turnover, and withdrawal behavior: A meta-analysis. *Journal of Applied Psychology*, *92*, 438–454. doi: 10.1037/0021-9010.92.2.438

Raghuram, S., Wiesenfeld, B., Garud, R. (2003). Technology enabled work: The role of self-efficacy in determining telecommuter adjustment and structuring behavior. *Journal of Vocational Behavior*, *63*, 180–198. doi: 10.1016/S0001-8791(03)00040-X.

Renn, R. W., & Vandenberg, R. J. (1995). The critical psychological states: An underrepresented component in job characteristics model research. *Journal of Management*, *21*, 279–303. doi: 10.1177/014920639502100206

Roethlisberger, F. J., & Dickson, W. J. (1939). *Management and the worker*. New York: Wiley.

Rosen, N. A., & Sales, S. M. (1966). Behavior in a nonexperiment: The effects of behavioral field research on the work performance of factory employees. *Journal of Applied Psychology*, *50*(2), 165–171.

Rousseau, D. M. (1977). Technological differences in job characteristics, employee satisfaction, and motivation: A synthesis of job design research and sociotechnical systems theory. *Organizational Behavior and Human Performance*, *19*, 18–42. doi: 10.1016/0030-5073(77)90052-6.

Ryan, R. M. (1995). Psychological needs and the facilitation of integrative processes. *Journal of Personality*, *63*(3), 397–427. doi:10.1111/j.1467-6494.1995.tb00501.x

Ryan, R. M., Sheldon, K. M., Kasser, T., & Deci, E. L. (1996). All goals were not created equal: an organismic perspective on the nature of goals and their regulation. In P. M. Gollwitzer, & J. A. Bargh (Eds.), *The psychology of action: Linking cognition and motivation to behavior* (pp. 7–26). New York: Guilford.

Salancik, G. R., & Pfeffer, J. (1977). An examination of need-satisfaction models of job attitudes. *Administrative Science Quarterly*, *22*, 427–456.

Sánchez, A. M., Pérez, M. P., de Luis Carnicer, P., & Jiménez, M. J. (2007). Teleworking and workplace flexibility: A study of impact on firm performance. *Personnel Review*, *36*, 42–64. doi: 10.1108/00483480710716713

Schaufeli, W. B., & Bakker, A. B. (2004). Job demands, job resources, and their relationship with burnout and engagement: A multi-sample study. *Journal of Organizational Behavior*, *25*, 293–315. doi: 10.1002/job.248

Sheldon, K. M., Elliot, A. J., Kim, Y., Kasser, T. (2001). What is satisfying about satisfying events? Testing 10 candidate psychological needs. *Journal of Personality and Social Psychology*, *89*, 325–339. doi: 10.1037//O022-3514.80.2.325

Sheldon, K. M., & Filak, V. (2008). Manipulating autonomy, competence and relatedness support in a game-learning context: New evidence that all three needs matter. *British Journal of Social Psychology*, *47*, 267–283. doi:10.1348/014466607X238797

Smith, A. (1776). *An inquiry into the nature and causes of the wealth of nations*. Chicago, IL: University of Chicago Press.

Sonnenfeld, J. (1985). Shedding light on the Hawthorne studies. *Journal of Occupational Behavior*, *6*(2), 111–130. doi: 10.1002/job.4030060203

Spreitzer, G. M. (1995). Psychological empowerment in the workplace: Dimensions, measurement, and validation. *Academy of Management Journal*, *38*, 1442–1465.

Strubler, D. C., & York, K. M. (2007). An exploratory study of the team characteristics model using organizational teams. *Small Group Research*, *38*, 670–695. doi: 10.1177/1046496407304338.

Tajfel, H. (1982). The social psychology of intergroup relations. *Annual Review of Psychology*, *33*, 1–39. doi: 10.1146/annurev.ps.33.020182.000245

Taris, T. W., & Kompier, M. A. J. (2005). Job demands, job control, strain and learning behavior: Review and research agenda. In A. S. G. Antoniou, & C. L. Cooper (Eds.), *Research companion to organizational health psychology* (Vol. 17, pp. 132–150). Northampton, MA: Edward Elgar Publishing.

Taylor, F. W. (1911). *The principles of scientific management*. New York, NY: Harper Bros.

Trist, E., & Bamforth, K. (1951). Some social and psychological consequences of the longwall method of coal getting in. *Human Relations*, *4*, 3–38. doi: 10.1177/001872675100400101

Turner, G., & Myerson, J. (1998). *New work space, new culture: Office design as a catalyst for change*. Brookfield, VA: Gower.

Vallerand, R. J., & Reid, G. (1984). On the causal effects of perceived competence on intrinsic motivation: A test of cognitive evaluation theory. *Journal of Sport Psychology*, *6*, 94–102.

Van Beek, I., Hu, Q., Schaufeli, W. B., Taris, T. W., & Schreurs, B. H. J. (2012). For fun, love, or money: What drives workaholic, engaged, and burned-out employees at work? *Applied Psychology-an International Review—Psychologie Appliquee-Revue Internationale*, *61*(1), 30–55. doi: 10.1111/j.1464-0597.2011.00454.x

Van den Broeck, A., Vansteenkiste, M., De Witte, H., & Lens, W. (2008). Explaining the relationships between job characteristics, burnout, and engagement: The role of basic psychological need satisfaction. *Work and Stress*, *22*, 277–294. doi: 10.1080/02678370802393672

van Mierlo, H., Rutte, C., Seinen, B., & Kompier, D. (2000). Autonomous team work, individual task characteristics and psychological well-being: A pilot study. *Gedrag en Gezondheid*, *28*, 259–171.

Van Yperen, N. W., & Hagedoorn, M. (2003). Do high job demands increase intrinsic motivation or fatigue or both? The role of job control and job social support. *Academy of Management Journal*, *46*, 339–348.

Wall, T. D., Corbett, J. M., Martin, R., Clegg, C. W., & Jackson, P. R. (1990). Advanced manufacturing technology, work design, and performance: A change study. *Journal of Applied Psychology*, *75*, 691–697. doi:10.1037/0021-9010.75.6.691

Wall, T. D., Jackson, P. R., & Mullarkey, S. (1995). Further evidence on some new measures of job control, cognitive demand and production responsibility. *Journal of Organizational Behavior*, *16*(5), 431–455. doi: 10.1002/job.4030160505

Wall, T. D., Kemp, N. J., Jackson, P. R., & Clegg, C. W. (1986). Outcomes of autonomous workgroups: A long-term field experiment. *Academy of Management Journal*, *29*, 280–304.

White, R. W. (1959). Motivation reconsidered: The concept of competence. *Psychological Review*, *66*, 297–333. doi: 10.1037/h0040934

Wrzesniewski, A., & Dutton, J. E. (2001). Crafting a job: Revisioning employees as active crafters of their work. *Academy of Management Review*, *26*(2), 179–201. doi:10.5465/AMR.2001.4378011

Yorks, L., & Whitsett, D. A. (1985). Hawthorne, Topeka, and the issue of science versus advocacy in organizational behavior. *Academy of Management Review*, *10*(1), 21–30. doi:10.5465/AMR.1985.4277329

Zuckerman, M., Porac, J., Lathin, D., Smith, R., & Deci, E. L. (1978). On the importance of self-determination for intrinsically motivated behavior. *Personality and Social Psychology Bulletin*, *4*, 443–446. doi: 10.1177/014616727800400317

CHAPTER
11
Leadership

Stephanie L. Gilbert *and* E. Kevin Kelloway

Abstract

This chapter addresses the motivational aspects of leadership within the context of self-determination theory. We first review the three basic psychological needs and discuss previous work on autonomy support and employee outcomes. Next, we review five prominent leadership theories in the management literature and how each theory is related to self-determination theory. We also discuss how specific leader behaviors can promote followers' intrinsic need satisfaction (relatedness, autonomy, and competence) and how each leadership theory addresses these three needs. We finish with a discussion of leaders' own motivations by linking transformational leadership theory with self-determination theory. Here, we propose a new program of research on motivation to lead, which examines what motivates individuals to behave as leaders.

Key Words: leadership, motivation, transformational leadership theory, charismatic leadership, authentic leadership, behavioral leadership

---

Introduction

For many, organizational leadership is synonymous with motivation. The role of organizational leaders is largely described in terms of motivating the behaviors of others, and there is an extensive body of literature that considers how leadership in organizations affects organizational behaviors and attitudes, such as motivation (for a review, see Barling, Christie, & Hoption, 2010). A central research question in the organizational leadership literature has been: what can managers do to promote or maintain the motivation of employees to be efficient and productive workers? Despite the importance of this research question, there has been little empirical research directly linking motivation to leadership styles and various leadership theories. This chapter addresses this gap in the literature in the context of formal leadership positions within organizations, including managers and supervisors.

Diefendorff and Chandler (2011) describe leadership as a proximal external influence on motivation, meaning that leaders can provide employees with external motivation driven primarily by social influence, but also by manipulating job characteristics, policies, assigned goals, rewards, and perceived equity and fairness. Specifically, the control that managers wield over these aspects of the workplace gives them considerable influence over how employees perceive the work environment to be controlling versus autonomous, which can in turn impact employees' sense of self-determination. This major influence that leaders can exert on followers highlights the importance of understanding how leader behavior can either motivate or demotivate employees to work productively in organizations.

This chapter addresses the question of how leaders motivate followers within the context of self-determination theory. We first review the three psychological needs followed by the literature on manager autonomy support and how it influences employee outcomes. Here we also provide practical suggestions for increasing autonomy support. Second, we briefly describe five prominent leadership theories in the management literature: (1) transformational leadership theory, (2) charismatic leadership theory, (3) leader-member exchange (LMX), (4) behavioral leadership theory, and (5) authentic leadership. We go into detail about what each theory says about motivating employees, and through what specific mechanisms each leadership style may motivate followers. We also describe how each of the five leadership theories covered in this chapter addresses each of the three intrinsic psychological needs. Finally, we discuss a new program of research on motivation to lead, which examines what motivates individuals to be leaders.

The Effects of Leadership Behavior on Need Satisfaction

Leader behaviors that promote the satisfaction of the basic psychological needs of employees are likely to produce positive outcomes like motivation, whereas behaviors that prevent need satisfaction will likely lead to negative outcomes (Baard, Deci, & Ryan, 2004). According to self-determination theory, these basic psychological needs are autonomy, relatedness, and competence. Autonomy means choosing to engage in behavior that is compatible with one's values, out of personal interest or expression of the self (Ryan & Deci, 2002). Relatedness means feeling connected with others, feeling interdependent with others, and feeling a sense of belonging to a group or with other individuals (Ryan & Deci, 2002). Finally, competence refers to the need for a sense of proficiency and feelings of effectiveness in one's work (Deci, 1975; Ryan & Deci, 2002). By satisfying employees' basic psychological needs, managers are creating an environment where all employees can perform optimally and are more likely to enjoy participating in work activities (Baard, 2002). This enjoyment may promote intrinsic satisfaction of engaging in work tasks. When leaders or managers take specific action to attempt to satisfy these basic needs in employees, they make the workplace more conducive to the growth and well-being of employees (Ryan & Deci, 2002), and the result may be more highly motivated and better functioning employees.

Overall intrinsic need satisfaction scale scores as measured by a 23-item intrinsic need satisfaction scale were positively related to work engagement, job satisfaction, and psychological adjustment (Leone,

1995), as well as work performance as assessed by employees' most recent performance appraisals (Baard et al., 2004). Thus, employees who have their needs for autonomy, relatedness, and competence satisfied on the job are more likely to have more positive work attitudes and are more likely to receive better performance reviews by their managers. The intrinsic need satisfaction scale has high internal consistency, as shown by Cronbach's alpha values of .87 (Baard et al., 2004) and .90 (Leone, 1995).

The extent to which employees feel that their intrinsic needs are satisfied in their jobs may be influenced by their autonomy orientation (see Deci & Ryan, 1985). Autonomy orientation influences the extent to which individuals perceive leader behaviors to be autonomy-supportive versus controlling and it is related to how people regulate their behavior and what they attend to in their environment (Deci & Ryan, 1987). Those with a high autonomy orientation are more likely to take initiative on their own, more likely to view their managers as supportive, and more likely to seek out aspects of the work environment that support their self-regulation (Baard et al., 2004). Autonomy orientation is related to sustained behavior change (Williams, Grow, Freedman, Ryan, & Deci, 1996) as well as the satisfaction of all three intrinsic needs (Baard et al., 2004). Satisfaction of all three psychological needs was predicted independently by both autonomy support and autonomous causality orientation (Baard et al., 2004).

Baard et al. (2004) found overall support for a model in which perceived manager autonomy support and autonomous causality orientation predicted intrinsic need satisfaction, which in turn predicted performance evaluation and psychological adjustment. These findings reinforce the importance of leader behaviors on work motivation, suggesting that when leaders promote autonomy in employees, their needs will be met, and they may in turn be motivated to work more efficiently and productively, resulting in more favorable performance reviews. In sum, it is important for managers to keep in mind the needs of their subordinates and support those needs to promote a healthy and productive workplace. First, let us review the three psychological needs and look at the effects of leaders' efforts to promote autonomy.

Autonomy

Need for autonomy refers to initiating a behavior out of personal interest or expression of the self, meaning that the individual chooses to engage in a behavior because it is compatible with his or her values (Ryan & Deci, 2002). Autonomy must be distinguished from independence such that an autonomous behavior can still be influenced by outside sources, as long as the behavior is still personally valued by the individual, whereas independence refers to not relying on external influences at all (Ryan & Deci, 2002). For example, an employee may still autonomously complete a task that has been assigned by a supervisor as long as the employee believes that the nature of the task is inherently interesting and congruent with his or her values. An independent employee would not have a supervisor who would delegate tasks to them, and would choose tasks without external influence. However, employees may act in the absence of autonomy or independence, as in when an employee complies with direction from others without experiencing choice or enacting the values associated with the assigned task. Satisfying employees' need for autonomy encourages the employee to view their work from an internal locus of causality, and is therefore likely to promote intrinsic motivation (Ryan & Deci, 2002).

Leader behaviors that support autonomy include manager autonomy support (Baard et al., 2004), where managers give employees influence over their workplace. This sharing of responsibility and power by the manager is commonly known as empowerment. Baard (2002) provides many suggestions for managerial behaviors that are supportive of autonomy, including sharing control and influence with employee about how the work gets done, allowing employees to choose their tasks, allowing for the possibility of failure, providing feedback in a noncontrolling way, communicating assertively rather than aggressively, using incentives to reward good work, trying to understand the subordinates' perspective, and eliminating excessive rules.

Relatedness

Relatedness means feeling connected with others, feeling interdependent with others, and feeling a sense of belonging to a group or with other individuals (Ryan & Deci, 2002). Although relatedness does seem to promote intrinsic motivation, this relationship is less straightforward than the relationship between both competence and autonomy and intrinsic motivation (Ryan & Deci, 2002). More empirical evidence is needed to explain the relationships between relatedness

and intrinsic motivation. Autonomous causality orientation is also predictive of relatedness need satisfaction (Baard et al., 2004). In Baard et al.'s (2004) study, relatedness was the psychological need most highly related to performance appraisal ratings.

Leader behaviors that support relatedness are those that foster teamwork, mutual respect, reliance on other team-members, and shared group goals. Some examples of opportunities for managers to support employees' need for relatedness include holding regular meetings, encouraging cooperation and discouraging competition, speaking only favorably about others in the workplace that are not present, communicating effectively and sharing information, and conducting team-building activities (Baard, 2002).

Competence

The need for competence is the third innate psychological need, which refers to the need for a sense of proficiency and feelings of effectiveness in one's work (Deci, 1975; Ryan & Deci, 2002). Employees are likely to feel more competent when they have the opportunity to engage in challenging tasks that allow them to use, and to build on, their unique existing skills and abilities (Ryan & Deci, 2002).

Leaders can satisfy the need for competence by delegating tasks that fit well with an individual employee's skills and abilities. Baard (2002) suggests the following managerial behaviors as supportive of the need for competence: properly training and supporting subordinates, discussing and agreeing on achievable goals with subordinates, delegating interesting tasks that develop new skills, providing regular feedback, and removing barriers to efficient performance. By attempting to satisfy the need for competence, managers may promote well-being in employees. When employees' need for competence is satisfied, they are more likely to experience intrinsic motivation (Ryan & Deci, 2002). Baard et al. (2004) found that satisfaction of need for competence was negatively related to an index of anxiety and depression and was also related to autonomous causality orientation.

Self-Determination Theory–Based Work on Manager Autonomy Support and Employee Outcomes

One way in which leaders can affect employee motivation is by providing autonomy support— promoting intrinsic motivation by providing employees with choices and flexibility in determining their own behavior so that they may express themselves through their work (Deci & Ryan, 1987). By choosing their own behavior, they are self-regulating and such behavior is referred to as self-determined (Deci & Ryan, 1987). In an autonomy-supportive climate, employees are likely to feel like they are initiating their own behavior and deciding for themselves how to achieve desired outcomes (Deci & Ryan, 1987). Autonomy, however, is not to be confused with independence where an individual acts alone and does not rely on others (Deci & Ryan, 2008). One can still be autonomous and be a member of an interdependent team or be dependent on another employee for certain components of their work. The opposite of an autonomy-supportive management style is a controlling management style, whereby the manager demands certain behaviors from employees without providing flexibility in choice or developing creative solutions to problems.

Manager autonomy support can be described as a social-contextual factor in the workplace pertaining to the general interpersonal orientation of the manager (Deci, Connell, & Ryan, 1989). More specifically, autonomy support refers to the interpersonal style of the manager regarding how they interact with subordinates and how they carry out their leadership duties (Baard et al., 2004).

Gagné, Koestner, and Zuckerman (2000) argue that managers can support autonomy in a given task in three ways: (1) by providing a rationale for the task they ask the employee to do, (2) offering employees a choice about how to do the task, and (3) acknowledging employees' feelings about the task. In illustrating each of these components, we use the example of having to complete an employee timesheet, which is a common organizational practice where employees must account for all of the time they spend at work and document what tasks they complete during that time. Filling out a timesheet is often a daunting task that distracts the employee from their work, and is therefore viewed negatively by employees. By providing a rationale for the task, managers can convey to the employee that the task is meaningful and has personal utility for them. In the above example, the manager may explain to the employee that the timesheet can be a useful log of tasks completed that the employee can consult at any time. It may also indicate whether time is being spent efficiently across important tasks, which may help the employee evaluate their time management skills to become even more efficient.

By offering employees with choices about how to do the task, managers encourage personal initiative and the work can become a form of self-expression for the employee, making it more interesting to them. In the above example, employees could be allowed some flexibility and choice involving when to complete the timesheet to satisfy personal preference (e.g., right after completing each task or at the end of the day) and controlling language by the manager (e.g., "must," "have to") should be avoided. By understanding and acknowledging employees' feelings about the task, managers can facilitate a trusting relationship and show empathy towards the employee. In the above example, conveying understanding to employees that filling out a timesheet may be distracting may acknowledge the legitimacy of the employees' feelings toward the task and reduce tension around that task. Through these three critical sociocontextual managerial behaviors that support self-determination, employees may come to internalize the value of the tasks they engage in at work.

Previous research has supported the effectiveness of these managerial behaviors for promoting employee internalization of tasks. Deci, Eghrari, Patrick, and Leone (1994) conducted a laboratory study looking at how participants internalized a boring task when support for self-determination was manipulated. Participants who were offered a rationale for the task, choice about whether they would do the task, and acknowledgement of their feelings about doing the task were much more likely to continue to engage in a boring task (representing integrated internalization) during a free activity period after the completion of the study than participants who did not receive these supportive behaviors.

Managerial autonomy support is similar to the concepts of participative management and vertical job enlargement. The primary difference between these concepts and manager autonomy support is that the latter emphasizes the interpersonal orientation of the manager, whereas the former emphasize job design or decision-making processes (Deci et al., 1989).

Managerial autonomy support can be measured using two different scales, which were both developed by Deci et al. (1989): the Problems at Work Scale and the Work Climate Survey. The Problems at Work scale (Deci et al., 1989) presents eight problem situations that managers may encounter and four different ways of responding to each of the eight situations. This scale may be adapted to either ask managers to rate themselves (e.g., Deci et al., 1989) or to ask employees to rate their manager (e.g., Baard et al., 2004). The participant is asked to rate on a seven-point scale the extent to which each of the four manager responses to the problem is characteristic of their own manager or their own managerial style. The four possible responses to each vignette represent highly controlling, moderately controlling, moderately autonomy-supportive, and highly autonomy-supportive managerial leadership styles. Highly controlling responses are characterized by the manager specifying a solution to the problem and demanding that employees follow that solution, sometimes involving threat of punishment for noncompliance or promise of reward for compliance with their solution. Rewards and punishment play a controlling role in motivating behavior because they pressure employees to act in certain ways, which undermines intrinsic motivation (Deci & Ryan, 1987). Moderately controlling responses involve the manager deciding on a solution to a problem and encouraging the employee to follow that choice. Moderately autonomy-supportive responses refer to a situation where the manager encourages an employee to develop their own plan for addressing the problem based on their observation of how others in the organization have addressed similar problems in the past or other workplace norms. Finally, highly autonomy-supportive responses involve the manager listening to and acknowledging employees' perspectives on the problem, and encouraging employees to devise their own creative plan for addressing the problem, while providing feedback, if necessary, in a supportive way. By focusing on what a manager *would do* rather than asking questions about how managers actually behave in the workplace, this scale assesses a more abstract conceptualization of autonomy support.

In addition to the Problems at Work Scale, autonomy support may also be measured using the Work Climate Survey (Deci et al., 1989). This survey was developed based on Hackman and Oldham's (1975) Job Diagnostic Survey and consists of three sections assessing subordinate reactions to management, the workplace, and the organization. The first section asks employees to respond to questions about aspects of their work climate, such as quality of supervision. In the second section, 11 words or phrases are presented, such as "under the gun" or "relaxed." The employee is asked to indicate how applicable each word or phrase is to his or her work environment or feelings about the work environment. The third section of the survey presents 10 job characteristics, such as job security and work atmosphere, and asks the employee to rate how satisfied they are with each characteristic in their workplace. An eleventh item asks how satisfied the subordinate is with his or her job overall. This scale assesses the extent to which the work climate itself allows for satisfaction of intrinsic needs, from the subordinates' point of view. In contrast to the Problems at Work Scale, which asks how a manager is most likely to respond to a hypothetical situation, the work climate survey asks subordinates about how their managers actually behave at work. This type of measure provides a more concrete measure of enacted manager autonomy-supportive behavior and autonomy-supportive aspects of the work environment.

The impact of autonomy support on various outcomes has been examined in many work settings. Gagné et al. (2000) found that, in an organization undergoing organizational change, the degree to which managers supported autonomy by explaining the reasons for the change, acknowledging employee feelings about the change, and providing employees with some degree of control or choice in the change process, predicted change acceptance 1 year later. In an educational setting, teacher's autonomy support for students promoted student engagement in learning (Jang, Reeve, & Deci, 2010). Further work has been done on leader autonomy support in nonwork settings. Williams et al. (2006) found that when patients were provided with autonomy support from a smoking cessation counselor who discussed with them their attitudes toward smoking, helped them devise their own smoking cessation plan, and provided them with information about the consequences of smoking on their health, they were significantly more likely to remain abstinent from smoking after 6 months than individuals who did not have the support of the counselor. Those in the counselor treatment condition were also more likely to use smoking cessation medications to help them remain abstinent from smoking.

Autonomy support is related to employee outcomes, such as trust in the organization (Deci, Connell, & Ryan, 1989), job satisfaction (Blais & Brière, 1992; Deci et al., 1989), self-motivation (Deci et al., 1981), less absenteeism (Blais & Brière, 1992), and better physical and psychological well-being (Blais & Brière, 1992). Manager autonomy support as measured by the Problems at Work scale was also significantly related to employee performance evaluation ratings and to psychological adjustment characterized by vitality, somatization, and anxiety (Baard et al., 2004). As the aforementioned evidence suggests, by promoting employee autonomy, managers may also promote both employee well-being as well as organizational outcomes, such as productivity and lower absenteeism.

There is evidence that managerial autonomy support can be developed in managers through interventions. After implementing an intervention directed at improving manager autonomy support, Deci et al. (1989) saw a significant increase in manager autonomy support in the intervention group compared with a control group as measured by the managers' self-reports on the Problems at Work scale. Also, subordinates of the managers in the intervention group had significantly higher trust in the organization and satisfaction with potential for advancement, suggesting that the intervention also had effects on subordinates' perceptions. The intervention included activities and discussion with the managers around how to provide positive and supportive feedback to subordinates, how to promote employee initiative-taking, and how to recognize and acknowledge employees' needs and feelings. In a similar study, Hardré and Reeve (2009) trained an intervention group of managers on autonomy-supportive leader behaviors and found that they displayed a significantly more autonomy-supportive managerial style than did managers in a control group who were not trained. Furthermore, the employees of the managers in the intervention group showed significantly more autonomous motivation and work engagement 5 weeks after the intervention than did employees of the managers in the control group. Both of these studies suggest that managerial style is malleable, and more importantly, that autonomy-supportive style can be developed in leaders in order to promote internalization and self-regulation by employees.

Parallels with Leadership Theories in Management

Over the past several decades, many leadership theories have emerged in the management literature, and many of these theories share considerable overlap in their conceptualization. This section deals with five of the most popular leadership theories in the literature, what each theory says about motivating subordinates, and how they can be distinguished from one another with respect to self-determination theory and need satisfaction. We begin with one of the most widely researched leadership theories, transformational leadership theory, followed by charismatic, authentic, LMX, and behavioral leadership theories.

Transformational Leadership Theory

The most extensively researched (Barling et al., 2010) of all the theories of leadership is Bass's (1990) transformational leadership theory. Transformational leadership has been defined as superior leadership performance that occurs when leaders "broaden and elevate the interests of their employees, when they generate awareness and acceptance of the purposes and mission of the group, and when they stir their employees to look beyond their own self-interest for the good of the group" (Bass, 1985, p. 21). Bass (1985) suggested that the transformational leadership style comprises four dimensions: (1) idealized influence, (2) inspirational motivation, (3) intellectual stimulation, and (4) individualized consideration. Idealized influence occurs when leaders engender the trust and respect of their followers by doing the right thing, thereby serving as a role model. Leaders who engage in inspirational motivation "raise the bar" for their employees, encouraging them to achieve levels of performance beyond their own expectations. Intellectual stimulation involves engaging the rationality of subordinates, getting them to challenge their assumptions and to think about old problems in new ways. Lastly, individualized consideration deals with treating employees as individuals and helping them to meet their needs.

Bass (1985) also defined less effective styles of leadership, including laissez-faire, active and passive management by exception, and contingent-reward leadership. Taken together, Bass referred to these four leadership styles as "transactional leadership." Laissez-faire leadership occurs when a leader is simply not involved in the tasks of leadership. Leaders who rely on the laissez-faire style avoid decision making and the responsibilities associated with their position (Bass, 1985; Hater & Bass, 1988). Management-by-exception occurs when leaders only intervene when there is a problem, and this style may be either active or passive. Active management by exception (Bass, 1985) is characterized by leaders who actively monitor employees to ensure that there are no deviations in performance. Leaders engaging in the passive management by exception style do not intervene until problems are either brought to their attention or become serious enough to demand action (Bass, 1985). Finally, contingent reward is seen as a more positive form of transactional leadership in which leaders actively engage in goal setting and the provision of task-contingent feedback to employees, both positive and negative.

Empirical data largely support the effectiveness of transformational leadership behaviors. For example, leaders' display of these behaviors is associated with subordinates' satisfaction (Hater & Bass, 1988; Koh, Steers, & Terborg, 1995), commitment to the organization (Barling, Weber, & Kelloway, 1996; Bycio, Hacket, & Allen, 1995; Koh et al., 1995), trust in management (Barling et al., 1996), and organizational citizenship behaviors (Koh et al., 1995). Laboratory-based experimental investigations show that transformational leadership styles result in higher task performance (e.g., Howell & Frost, 1989; Kirkpatrick & Locke, 1996; Sosik, Avolio, & Kahai, 1997). Field studies also support the positive performance impact of transformational leadership. In longitudinal studies, for example, Howell and Avolio (1993) linked transformational leadership to better unit financial performance. Similarly, Barling et al. (1996) showed that subordinates' perceptions of supervisors' transformational leadership led to enhanced affective commitment to the organization and, through this effect on affective commitment, to enhanced group performance.

Importantly, the available data also suggest that leadership development interventions (e.g., training and coaching) are effective in enhancing leaders' enactment of transformational leadership theory (Barling et al., 1996; Kelloway, Barling, & Helleur, 2000; McKee, Driscoll, Kelloway, & Kelley, 2009; Mullen & Kelloway, 2009). Moreover, when leaders enhance their transformational leadership, both personal (e.g., psychological well-being, McKee et al., 2009; workplace safety, Mullen & Kelloway, 2009; work attitudes, Barling et al., 1996) and organizational (e.g., financial performance, Barling et al., 1996) outcomes are enhanced. Because this body of literature supporting leadership development interventions is still quite small due to difficulties in measuring the effectiveness of intervention outcomes, more research is needed in this area (Kelloway & Barling, 2010).

By engaging in transformational leadership behaviors, leaders can motivate employees by inspiring them to achieve a certain vision (Bass, 1998). By communicating a vision, transformational leaders may convey their own values to employees, which may come to be shared and internalized by employees (Jung & Avolio, 2000; Bono & Ilies, 2006). By aligning their values with those of employees', transformational leaders may contribute to employees' intrinsic motivation to strive toward achieving a shared vision. In support of this idea, value congruence between leaders and followers has been found to be positively related to follower performance (Jung & Avolio, 2000). Sharing a clear vision may also make work seem more meaningful to employees. Piccolo and Colquitt (2006) found that followers of transformational leaders found more meaning in their work, and in turn, experienced more intrinsic motivation. Followers of transformational leaders also tend to be more likely to choose more autonomous and intrinsic goals rather than controlled and extrinsic goals (Bono & Judge, 2003), supporting a strong link between transformational leadership and self-determined behavior of subordinates. Through inspirational motivation from their leader, which encourages employees to strive for more than they originally thought was possible, employees may find satisfaction from performing beyond their own expectations, resulting in higher intrinsic motivation.

Another mechanism through which this leadership style may influence employees is through emotional processes, whereby the positive emotions of the leader spread to employees (Rubin, Munz, & Bommer, 2005). When employees associate positive and optimistic feelings with their leader, employees may be more likely to show higher performance and to act in congruence with their leaders' wishes. Followers tend to have more positive perceptions of transformational leaders, which may serve as another motivational mechanism. Transformational leader behaviors, particularly those related to idealized influence, such as empowering and respecting followers, making sacrifices for the good of the group, and involving followers in decision-making, are likely to encourage positive perceptions and trust (Barling et al., 2010). As a result of their positive perceptions of the leader, employees may be more likely to exert effort in their work due to greater commitment to the leader (Barling et al., 2010), representing a form of external motivation. There are many empirical studies showing links between transformational leadership and employee performance (e.g., Pillai, Schriesheim, & Williams, 1999; Piccolo & Colquitt, 2006). Through intellectual stimulation, transformational leaders empower their followers to become involved in decision-making and encourage them to voice their opinions (Barling et al., 2010), which may foster a sense of ownership over the groups' success. Empowering leadership behaviors have been linked to intrinsic motivation (Srivatava, Bartol, & Locke, 2006). Finally, transformational leaders may be more likely to promote identification with both the leader and the group (Kark, Shamir, & Chen, 2003), which may be motivational such that the employee becomes committed to the group and its overall success, and may therefore be more willing to exert effort toward the groups' goals.

NEED SATISFACTION BY TRANSFORMATIONAL LEADERS

Each of the leadership theories described in this chapter play a role in promoting the three intrinsic psychological needs. Table 11.1 provides a summary of the intrinsic needs that each theory explicitly addresses. A checkmark indicates that a particular need is addressed by the theory, and if one particular component of the leadership theory addresses a need, the name of the component is given. Here, we address how transformational leadership theory satisfies employees' intrinsic needs. Transformational leaders promote autonomy through intellectual stimulation, whereby leaders encourage employees to think for themselves and develop their own strategies for approaching their work (Barling et al., 2010). Transformational leaders may satisfy employees' need for relatedness through individualized consideration, where leaders develop positive relationships with employees that are characterized by respect, support, and caring. Idealized influence may also promote relatedness by communicating a shared vision, which may foster a sense of togetherness among workers. Inspirational motivation by leaders may help to satisfy subordinate needs for competence by encouraging challenging, but achievable goals, and overcoming obstacles to high performance. When employees remove barriers in their way to achieving high goals, they may be more effective at reaching those goals, resulting in feelings of competence, resilience, and efficacy.

Charismatic Leadership Theory

The word charisma is Greek for divinely inspired gift (Barling et al., 2010). Generally, charisma is associated with extraordinary individuals who are likeable, articulate, and who inspire others. A charismatic leader is likely to exhibit unconventional behaviors related to changing the status quo, articulating a clear vision of the future, transforming followers to share their vision, and taking risks or self-sacrificing to achieve goals (Conger & Kanungo, 1987). Two theories of charismatic leadership have been proposed: the attribution theory (Conger & Kanungo, 1987) and the self-concept theory (House, 1977). Both theories overlap considerably, with very similar measurement tools, and share only minor differences (Barling et al., 2010; Conger & Kanungo, 1998; House & Podsakoff, 1994).

Conger and Kanungo's (1987) attributional model of charismatic leadership views charisma as an attribution made by followers based on certain behaviors exhibited by the leader. In contrast to the attributional model of charismatic leadership, House's (1977) self-concept model focuses on the actual leadership behaviors exhibited by leaders rather than attributions made by followers. This is the key difference between the attributional and self-concept theories.

There are several mechanisms through which charismatic leaders may motivate followers. These mechanisms highlight the similarities between charismatic and transformational leadership theories, as Shamir, House, and Arthur (1993) referred to three posited effects of charismatic leadership as the "transformational effects of charismatic leadership." These effects involve the leaders' ability to elevate the followers' need satisfaction levels to higher levels in Maslow's hierarchy, raise followers' morality to higher levels of judgment, and motivate followers' to transcend their own personal interests for the sake of the group's interests. The authors further theorize

Table 11.1 Leadership theories addressing intrinsic needs.

Intrinsic needs	Transformational leadership	Leadership Theories			
		Authentic leadership	Behavioral leadership	Leader-member exchange	Charismatic leadership
Autonomy	√ (intellectual stimulation)	√		√	√
Relatedness	√ (individualized consideration and idealized influence)	√	√ (consideration)	√	√
Competence	√ (inspirational motivation)	√	√ Initiating structure	√	√

√ Theory addresses this need.

that charismatic leadership behaviors de-emphasize extrinsic rewards while encouraging the idea that putting effort into work is a reward in and of itself, enhancing the intrinsic value of work. That is, putting effort into work represents important values and makes a moral statement. Charismatic leaders also emphasize goal attainment as a group effort, which may enhance meaning in work because the follower identifies with the group, and this identification may further motivate employees. The most important mechanism through which charismatic leaders can motivate employees is by articulating a clear vision to followers. When followers perceive that the goals set forth by leaders are consistent with their own values, this may increase intrinsic motivation to strive toward achieving those goals. Furthermore, setting goals can give followers the sense of hope that their work makes an impact toward a better future, which may increase meaningfulness of the work and promote intrinsic motivation. Transformational leadership shares these same motivational mechanisms in common with charismatic leadership and both leadership styles satisfy all three basic psychological needs of followers.

NEED SATISFACTION BY CHARISMATIC LEADERS

Charismatic leaders promote autonomy by presenting goals to followers in terms of the values they represent. Associating important values with a task may increase its meaningfulness because the follower can identify with the work and, thus, it may contribute positively to their self-concept (Shamir et al., 1993). That is, when followers believe that work goals are compatible with their own values, they are more likely to engage in self-regulated behavior. Charismatic leaders promote collective identity of followers with the group by emphasizing shared goals (Shamir et al., 1993), which promotes relatedness among group members. Charismatic leaders also are sensitive to the needs of followers (Barling et al., 2010), which may promote positive relationships between the leader and each follower. According to self-concept charismatic leadership theory, when leaders are charismatic, they show high expectations of followers, coupled with strong confidence that followers can accomplish the goals set out for them to achieve, which may promote self-efficacy and competence (Shamir et al., 1993).

Authentic Leadership

Another leadership theory that parallels autonomy supportive management is authentic leadership, which has emerged out of the literature on positive organizational scholarship. In their integration of the body of literature in this area, Walumbwa, Avolio, Gardner, Wernsing, and Peterson (2008) defined authentic leadership as "a pattern of leader behavior that draws upon and promotes both positive psychological capacities and a positive ethical climate, to foster greater self-awareness, an internalized moral perspective, balanced processing of information, and relational transparency on the part of leaders working with followers, fostering positive self-development" (p. 94). According to this definition, authentic leadership is conceptualized as comprising four components: (1) self-awareness, (2) relational transparency, (3) balanced processing of information, and (4) positive moral perspective. Self-awareness refers to the way a leader views himself or herself and his or her knowledge of strengths and weaknesses. Relational transparency involves sharing one's true self in a transparent manner with others. Balanced processing of information involves assessing all relevant information before arriving at a decision, and soliciting information that is inconsistent with one's views. Internalized moral perspective refers to self-regulation that is guided by moral values. An authentic individual is more likely to have higher, more stable, levels of self-esteem and be less sensitive to biases of others, and therefore more comfortable developing open and transparent relationships and behaving in a manner that is consistent with their values (Walumbwa et al., 2008).

Many leadership theories share considerable conceptual overlap, so Walumbwa et al. (2008) compared authentic leadership theory with transformational leadership theory and ethical leadership to highlight their similarities and differences. Whereas both authentic and ethical leadership theories describe the leader as a moral person who also models ethical behavior, ethical leadership contains a transactional component that is not contained in authentic leadership whereby the leader uses rewards and discipline to encourage ethical behavior among followers. A second difference is that the self-awareness, relational transparency, and balanced processing are all components of authentic leadership that are not included in the definition of ethical leadership. Authentic and transformational leadership theories also share considerable overlap; however, authentic leadership does not include aspects of inspirational motivation, intellectual stimulation, or individualized consideration in its conceptualization. Both theories, however, share an idealized influence component, as well as all components comprising authentic and ethical leadership. Avolio and Gardner (2005) argued that to be transformational, one has to be authentic, but being an authentic leader does not necessarily mean that the leader is transformational.

Although there has been little empirical research on testing proposed models of authentic leadership, studies have linked this leadership style to organizational outcomes, such as follower job satisfaction, organizational citizenship behavior, supervisor ratings of follower job performance (Walumbwa et al., 2008), and work engagement (Walumbwa, Wang, Wang, Schaubroeck, & Avolio, 2010).

Authentic leaders may motivate employees by serving as role models for followers to themselves exhibit authentic leader behavior, which is characterized by self-regulated behavior (Ilies, Morgeson, & Nahrgang, 2005). This idea is in line with social learning theory, whereby individuals change their behavior based on observation. Thus, by watching an authentic leader in everyday work, a follower may learn to become more authentic as well, and in turn, to be more intrinsically motivated. Ilies et al. (2005) argued that authentic leaders promote follower identification with the leader due to the transparent nature of their relationship. This personal identification may further translate into organizational identification, because leaders represent the values of the organization. This identification with both the leader and the organization may contribute to the followers' sense of meaning at work if there is high value congruency between the leader or organization and the follower. An enhanced sense of meaningfulness at work may then translate into greater internalization.

NEED SATISFACTION BY AUTHENTIC LEADERS

Authentic leaders may promote autonomy through modeling authenticity in and of itself, which may promote authenticity among followers and, in turn, promote self-expression by followers. This effect is in line with research that supports the idea that authenticity is characterized by intrinsic motivation and, particularly, self-expression (Ilies et al., 2005). Authentic leaders facilitate relatedness because they strive toward open, trusting, and cooperative relationships with followers. Ilies et al. (2005) also argued that authentic leaders promote follower identification with both the leader and the organization, because the leader represents the values and interests of the organization. This identification may promote a sense of belonging within

the organization. Finally, authentic leadership may promote competence in followers because the trusting and cooperative relationship developed between leader and follower promotes a free exchange of information and knowledge that may facilitate performance (Ilies et al., 2005; Jones & George, 1998) and provides followers with more opportunity to learn and develop new skills (Walumbwa, Luthans, Avey, & Oke, 2011).

Leader-Member Exchange

Originally proposed by Dansereau, Graen, and Haga (1975), LMX theory focuses on the interactions between leaders and subordinates, which are called exchanges. The relationship between the leader and a single follower is referred to as a dyad, and leaders have a unique dyadic relationship with each follower. Within the dyad, each member (either the supervisor or the subordinate) can contribute valuable outcomes that can influence the others' behavior. The manager can provide the subordinate with job latitude, information, support, and involvement in decision-making, whereas the subordinate can reciprocate with greater commitment, higher productivity, or taking on greater responsibility (Dansereau et al., 1975). The nature of this exchange relationship means that the leader must recognize that they are somewhat dependent on their subordinate and should not use his or her authority against the subordinate (Dansereau et al., 1975). Central to this theory is the idea that supervisors develop unique relationships with every subordinate, such that every dyadic relationship within the work unit is different in quality (Dansereau et al., 1975). High-quality relationships are characterized by high mutual respect, trust, and obligation, whereas low-quality relationships are characterized by distrust, disrespect, and low obligation (Graen & Uhl-Bien, 1995). In a meta-analysis, Gerstner and Day (1997) found that, across multiple studies, high-quality LMX relationships were consistently related to higher job performance, satisfaction and commitment, and lower role conflict and turnover intentions. High-quality LMX is positively associated with transformational leadership behaviors (Graen & Uhl-Bien, 1995; Howell & Hall-Merenda, 1999) suggesting that transformational leaders are likely to also have high-quality dyadic relationships with followers.

LMX influences employee motivations primarily through direct social influence (Diefendorff & Chandler, 2011). When a relationship is characterized by positive interactions, each member of the dyad may be more likely to reciprocate positive behaviors, as in social exchange theory. Wang, Law, Hackett, Wang, and Chen (2005) found that transformational leadership behaviors were related to greater subordinate perceptions of high-quality LMX relationships with their leader, which in turn led to greater follower performance. Thus, employees may work more efficiently and productively when they have positive perceptions of their relationship with their leader. Also, because the exchange relationship is characterized by mutual influence, both the leader and the follower are empowered by high-quality LMX relationships to move beyond their formal work roles and partner with one another to achieve more.

NEED SATISFACTION BY HIGH-QUALITY LMX

LMX theory addresses followers' need for autonomy, in that, when dyadic relationships are of high quality, followers are empowered to take on greater responsibility in partnership with their leader, who trusts the follower to manage their own work (Graen & Uhl-Bien, 1995). That is, in high-quality LMX relationships, followers are likely to be entrusted by leaders with greater responsibility, freedom, and choice at work. High-quality LMX relationships may also promote relatedness because they are characterized by respectful and trusting partnerships between the leader and follower. High LMX relationships also encourage individuals to transcend their own self-interests in favor of those of the group (Howell & Hall-Merenda, 1999), which may promote relatedness among group members. Likewise, high LMX relationships may promote competence because the supportive partnership between the leader and follower facilitates goal accomplishment and because followers are often entrusted with more responsibility (Graen & Uhl-Bien, 1995).

Behavioral Leadership Theory

The Ohio Leadership Studies lead by Stogdill (1950) set out to identify the smallest number of dimensions that would accurately describe effective leadership behaviors. In factor analyses, a total of 150 examples of leadership behaviors consistently fell into two main categories of effective leadership behaviors: initiating structure and consideration. These categories represent more task-focused and person-focused behaviors, respectively (Barling, et al, 2010). Initiating structure refers to the extent to which a leader actively organizes his or her role, as well as the roles of subordinates, in order to accomplish goals (Fleishman & Peters, 1962). Those high in initiating structure would be more active in planning, scheduling, delegating, and communication. Specifically, behaviors consistent with this category of leader behavior may include providing constructive criticism for poor work, delegating tasks to subordinates and supervising the work, encouraging efficiency and good time management, and offering new approaches to problems. Consideration is the second major category of effective leader behavior and involves relationships between the leader and followers that are characterized by mutual respect, trust, and consideration for the others' feelings (Fleishman & Peters, 1962). Highly considerate leaders would develop a good rapport with subordinates and engage in frequent two-way communication with them. Consideration is reflected in leader behaviors, such as consulting the group before making decisions, acting friendly and approachable, treating group members like equals, and doing personal favors for group members. During early research on this theory, researchers hypothesized that high levels of both initiating structure and consideration would generate the most positive follower and organizational outcomes (see Kerr, Schreisheim, Murphy, & Stogdill, 1974), but there has been conflicting evidence in the literature regarding whether both behaviors tend to co-occur in the same leader. Some studies found negative relationships between the two categories of leader behavior (see Judge, Piccolo, & Ilies, 2004) and there were inconsistent relationships between the leader behaviors and employee outcomes across studies (see Kerr et al., 1974).

As the leadership literature evolved, however, the content validity and measurement of this behavioral theory of leadership was criticized, and the theory was quickly replaced with newer theories. Particularly, measures were criticized for having little predictive validity for outcome variables like subordinate satisfaction and the theory in general was criticized for ignoring the effects of context on subordinates' perceptions (e.g., Korman, 1966). Future theories evolved to take into consideration the effects of the situation on leadership behaviors and the outcomes of those behaviors. However, in their recent meta-analysis, Judge et al. (2004) found support for the predictive validity of consideration and initiating structure and advocate for the utility of the theory such that it should not be abandoned in leadership research.

Consideration and initiating structure might motivate employees by providing them with specific and challenging goals to achieve while also providing necessary support to achieve goals (Barling et al., 2010). By setting challenging goals, leaders may inspire followers and create meaning in the work. Interestingly, Judge et al. (2004) found that, although both behaviors were related to motivation, consideration was more highly related to motivation than was initiating structure and initiating structure was more highly related to follower performance.

Judge et al. (2004) suggest that organizational justice may be a mediational mechanism through which initiating structure and consideration influence motivation and performance. There are three types of organizational justice: (1) distributive, (2) interactional, and (3) procedural. Distributive justice refers to the perceived fairness of reward allocation (Cropanzano & Greenberg, 1997) and perceptions of distributive justice are thought to be based on equity. Procedural justice refers to the fairness of the procedures through which outcomes are determined (Greenberg, 1987). Procedures that are unbiased, ethical, accurate, subject to appeal, consistently implemented, and representative of all relevant parties are viewed as more fair than those that are not (Leventhal, Karuza, & Fry, 1980; Thibaut & Walker, 1975). Interactional justice refers to being treated fairly in social interactions (Bies & Moag, 1986; Cropanzano, Byrne, Bobocel, & Rupp, 2001). Leaders high in initiating structure are likely to set rules regarding standards of performance and to determine consequences of goal attainment, which may foster perceptions of distributive justice. Leaders high in consideration should foster interactional justice because they are concerned for the welfare of subordinates and treat them with respect. Consideration and initiating structure may both promote procedural justice because employees are involved in decision-making, and employees have clear expectations laid out by the leader for their work. However, Judge et al. (2004) emphasized that high initiating structure may also lead to lower perceptions of justice because of lower autonomy and involvement in decision-making due to strict expectations.

NEED SATISFACTION BY BEHAVIORAL LEADERS

Behavioral leadership theory does not explicitly promote autonomy in employees, but may do so implicitly by providing the structure and support required to achieve goals, which may be a form of empowerment for followers. Leaders high in consideration, which is one component of behavioral leadership theory, may promote satisfaction of the need for relatedness because they develop positive social relationships with employees. However, consideration promotes relatedness with only the manager and falls short of promoting a sense of belonging and community among the group of workers. Similarly, the initiating structure component of behavioral leadership theory may satisfy the need for competence by clarifying the process through which work should be done by giving clear expectations and guidelines, thereby facilitating the achievement of goals. Leaders high in initiating structure set challenging goals that, when achieved with the leaders' support, can contribute to employees' feelings of competence and self-efficacy. However, although this behavior may facilitate the achievement of goals, the goals to be met will not necessarily be challenging, because initiating structure is also characterized by uniform procedures, which may not allow employees to continue to develop their skills by conducting their work in innovative ways.

Motivation to Lead

Our discussion of leadership thus far has been on the motivational influences that leaders can have on subordinates. But what about leaders' *own* motivations? There are two avenues of research in this area: one relating to leader emergence or role occupancy and one relating to leader performance. First, what makes a follower motivated to occupy a leadership role? Second, what makes a leader, once in a formal leadership role, motivated to perform well as a leader? The discussion next addresses leaders' motivation to take on a leadership role and to perform well in that role by integrating transformational leadership theory and self-determination theory.

Although a great deal of research supports the basic propositions of transformational leadership theory (see Judge & Piccolo, 2004), comparatively little attention has been focused on the question of why leaders might choose to engage in transformational, or transactional, leadership behaviors. What motivates individuals to occupy leadership roles? Once in a leadership role, what actually motivates individuals to *behave* as good leaders? It is these questions that provide the basis for our new program of study on motivation to lead, which we describe next.

This new program of study seeks to extend transformational leadership theory (Bass, 1985; 1998)—the single most researched of all leadership theories

192 | LEADERSHIP

(Barling et al., 2010; Judge & Piccolo, 2004)—in two ways. First, much of the existing leadership research is based on the assumption that individuals in formal leadership positions in organizations are motivated to be leaders. Empirical evidence (e.g., Chan & Drasgow, 2001) suggests that individuals vary in the extent to which they wish to assume a formal leadership role. The motivation to lead study considers individual motivations to enact transformational leadership behaviors and examines how such motivations to lead might be reflected in leadership behaviors and outcomes. Thus, this new research links transformational leadership theory to self-determination theory—a widely researched motivation theory (e.g., Gagné & Deci, 2005). Second, most research on transformational leadership views leadership as a "style"—a relatively consistent attribute of the leaders' behavior. In contrast, this new theory proposes an interactional perspective on transformational leadership. This approach builds on previous research suggesting that transformational leadership varies over time (e.g., daily; Hoption, Barling, & Kelloway, 2010) and suggests the need to understand the nature of specific leader-subordinate interactions in order to understand how leaders enact transformational leadership.

Full-Range Leadership Motivation

Given that individuals from all walks of life define good and poor leadership in similar terms (Kelloway & Barling, 2000), the question arises as to why individuals would not consistently choose to engage in positive, and eschew negative, leadership behaviors. Unfortunately, the empirical literature does not provide a clear answer to this question. Indeed, most contemporary models of leadership behavior begin with leadership style as the predictor variable and ignore the factors that might predict leaders' behavior.

According to transformational leadership theory, effective leaders are those who intend to elevate followers and do so by enacting four key behaviors: (1) initiating structure, (2) individualized consideration, (3) inspirational motivation, and (4) intellectual stimulation (Bass, 1985). The proposed research is predicated on the assumption that not all leaders are equally motivated to engage in these effective leadership behaviors. Individuals assume a leadership position in an organization for a variety of reasons (e.g., career advancement, salary, prestige) and it is not at all clear that incumbents in such positions are equally motivated to engage in effective leadership behaviors.

Leadership researchers commonly distinguish between leadership role occupancy and leaders' behaviors as two distinct lines of research (Barling et al., 2010). A focus on role occupancy involves examining the factors that lead an individual to assume a formal leadership position in an organization. Previous accounts of leader motivation have focused on an individual's motivation to hold a leadership position (Chan & Drasgow, 2001). In contrast, the proposed research focuses on individual motivation to engage in transformational leadership behaviors.

This research is situated within the context of self-determination theory (Deci & Ryan, 1985; 2000), which posits that both the level and the type of motivation influence behavior. Self-determination theorists distinguish between three basic types of motivation. Intrinsic motivation occurs when the behavior itself is seen as enjoyable and satisfying. For individuals who are intrinsically motivated, the behavior is its own reward. For example, a leader who is intrinsically motivated to behave as a good leader may choose to do so because he or she finds it enjoyable, fun, or interesting.

Extrinsic motivation applies to behaviors, such as job search, that are primarily instrumental—being governed by the prospect of reward and punishment. Self-determination theory further suggests that there are different types of extrinsic motivation that range along a continuum of self-determination (see Gagné & Deci, 2005). For example, a leader could be motivated through external regulation, where the environment provides rewards and punishments for being a good leader. Here, an individual may put effort into being a good leader in order to glean greater job security, a promotion, or to avoid losing their job. Extrinsically motivated individuals may be likely to accept a formal leadership role for the sake of the perks and rewards associated with the role. Introjected regulation is when the individual internalizes control over behavior. Self-esteem becomes a source of reward and feelings of anxiety and guilt at not performing the behavior become a source of punishment (Gagné & Deci, 2005). Specifically, leaders motivated by introjected regulation may behave as a good leader because they feel guilty if they do not, or because they feel it is their duty to be a good leader. In identified regulation, the individual sees their behavior as more congruent with their personal goals and interests, and thus feels more autonomous in choosing the behavior (Gagné & Deci, 2005). Leaders who are motivated by identified regulation are likely to enact effective leadership because they personally value the importance of effective leadership behavior for achieving goals and promoting the well-being of themselves and followers. Finally, integrated regulation occurs when the behavior has been fully integrated into the individual's self-definition. A leader motivated by integrated regulation is likely to feel that being a good leader is a part of who they are, that it fits with their life goals, and is a means through which to reach self-actualization.

Self-determination theory also recognizes the possibility of amotivation—the state that exists when an individual experiences a lack of intentional regulation of his or her behavior (Gagné & Deci, 2005). Amotivated leadership behaviors are mechanical and not typically sustained over a long period of time because the leader feels that good leadership is not a priority. Amotivated individuals are least likely to emerge as leaders, and if they do occupy leadership roles, they may be likely to leave the position or to be dismissed by their organizations after a short period of time. However, amotivated individuals who remain in leadership roles may be extremely detrimental to the well-being of followers and organizational functioning. In order to avoid this situation, organizations should screen out leader candidates who are unmotivated to enact effective leadership.

One can think of the types of motivation listed previously as comprising two basic classes: autonomous and controlled motivation (Deci & Ryan, 2000). Autonomous motivation comprises intrinsic motivation, integrated and identified regulation, and occurs when an individual chooses to engage in a behavior under his or her own volition. In contrast, controlled motivation comprises extrinsic and introjected regulation and occurs when an individual believes he or she has little or no choice but engage in a behavior due to external contingencies.

Motivation to Lead Scale

No scale exists in the leadership literature that measures motivation to lead as we conceptualize it in this theory. Chan and Drasgow (2001) had developed a measure of motivation to lead; however, it measures an individual's attitude toward taking on a *leadership role* in a more formal sense rather than attitude toward *behaving* as an effective leader. In an initial study of motivation to lead, we developed a scale adapted from the self-determined safety behaviors scale (Scott, Fleming, & Kelloway, forthcoming) which addresses each level of internalization. The scale begins with the question stem "I put

effort into being a good leader. . ." and responses are scored on a scale from 1 (strongly disagree) to 7 (strongly agree). Items address each type of motivation, including external regulation (e.g., "Because I risk losing my job if I don't"), introjected regulation (e.g., "Because it makes me feel proud of myself"), identified regulation (e.g., "Because I personally value leadership"), integrated regulation (e.g., "Because being a leader allows me to express my personal values"), and intrinsic motivation (e.g., "Because being a leader makes me happy"). To measure amotivation, we changed the question stem to "Please rate the extent to which you agree or disagree on how you feel about being a good leader" (e.g., "I just don't care about being a good leader"). This scale has yet to be validated, so future research should determine the validity and reliability of this scale and how motivation to lead is related to follower outcomes and perceptions.

In the context of full range (Bass and Avolio, 1994) transformational leadership theory, we hypothesize that these three basic classes of motivation will correspond to the dimensions of leadership behavior. Specifically, individuals who are amotivated will be more likely to engage in laissez-faire or passive (Kelloway, Mullen, & Francis, 2006; Mullen, Kelloway, & Teed, 2011) leadership behaviors. Extrinsic or controlled motivation, including external and introjected regulation, is hypothesized to result in transactional leadership behaviors, such as contingent reward and management by exception. Finally, autonomous motivation, including identified and integrated regulation and intrinsic motivation, is hypothesized to result in leaders engaging in transformational leadership behaviors. In terms of leader emergence, we hypothesize that individuals who are amotivated will be unlikely to emerge as leaders. Individuals motivated extrinsically will be likely to emerge as leaders for the sake of the rewards that come with the role, whereas autonomously motivated individuals will emerge as leaders for intrinsic reasons.

Practical Implications

Given this discussion about the importance of leader behavior in motivating employees, it seems fitting here to provide some practical recommendations for managers and organizations. Managers may be able to best motivate employees by exhibiting leadership behavior that satisfies employees' basic psychological needs. Baard (2002) provides helpful strategies for managers to promote each need, which are summarized here. Managers may satisfy employees' need for competence by properly training and supporting subordinates, discussing and agreeing on achievable goals with subordinates, delegating interesting tasks that develop new skills, providing regular feedback, and removing barriers to efficient performance. Behaviors that satisfy employees' need for relatedness may include fostering a culture of teamwork, mutual respect, reliance on other team members, and developing shared group goals. Managers may also support employees' need for relatedness by holding regular meetings, encouraging cooperation and discouraging competition, speaking only favorably about others in the workplace that are not present, communicating effectively and sharing information, and conducting team-building activities. Finally, behaviors that satisfy employees' need for autonomy may include sharing control and influence with employees about how the work gets done, allowing employees to choose their tasks, allowing for the possibility of failure, providing feedback in a noncontrolling way, communicating assertively rather than aggressively, using incentives to reward good work, trying to understand the subordinates' perspective, and eliminating excessive rules.

As shown in Table 11.1, transformational leadership addresses all three intrinsic needs in employees and has been widely supported in the literature as an effective form of leadership to enact in the workplace (Barling et al., 2010; Judge & Piccolo, 2004). Transformational leadership theory can also be translated easily into practical strategies for leaders to implement in their work, according to the four behaviors of transformational leaders. Intellectual stimulation involves encouraging employees to think for themselves and develop their own strategies for approaching their work (Barling et al., 2010), which may promote autonomy. Individualized consideration involves developing respectful, supportive, and caring relationships with employees, which may promote relatedness. Idealized influence involves communicating a shared vision, which may also satisfy need for relatedness by promoting cohesiveness among workers. Finally, inspirational motivation may satisfy the need for competence because it involves encouraging followers to set challenging, but achievable goals, and to overcome obstacles to high performance. When employees remove barriers in their way to achieving high goals, they may be more effective at reaching those goals, resulting in feelings of competence, resilience, and efficacy.

Organizations must also play a role in supporting its leaders in effectively motivating employees. First, organizations should recognize that motivating employees is a basic leadership function. As such, leaders should be provided with enough time to effectively enact the behaviors described above that are likely to satisfy employees' basic psychological needs. Rather than leaving this aspect of leadership until the leader has some "spare time," flexibility should be built into leaders' schedules so that they may regularly satisfy employees' needs. By supporting and recognizing the role of leader as motivator, organizations may foster a culture of need satisfaction. Second, organizations should carefully consider how leaders are selected, and include candidates' own motivation as a factor in decision-making. Candidates who are intrinsically motivated to take on a leadership role may make more effective leaders than those who are extrinsically motivated. Finally, organizations could consider training leaders on the satisfaction of employees' basic psychological needs. Hardré and Reeve (2009) and Deci et al. (1989) found that an autonomy-supportive managerial style could be developed in leaders through training, and that the training positively impacted employee outcomes. Similar results may be found for training leaders to support competence and relatedness. Thus, training leaders in supporting employee autonomy, competence, and relatedness may prove beneficial for organizational and employee outcomes and promote more effective leadership.

Conclusion

It is easy to see how self-determination theory is generalizable to so many life domains including the workplace, and in particular, the effects of leadership on followers' motivation. This chapter reviews literature on how leaders can motivate followers to engage in self-determined behavior at work. First, the three intrinsic needs of employees that leaders may aim to address are reviewed. Second, leader autonomy support in the workplace and related outcomes for followers are examined. Third, five main leadership theories that are prominent in the literature are reviewed, describing how each theory proposes to motivate followers, and how each theory addresses each of the three intrinsic needs. Finally, a new line of research is proposed examining leaders' own motivations to lead within the context of both transformational leadership theory and self-determination theory.

Future Directions

Our suggestions for future research in the area of leadership and motivation are threefold. First, we suggest that researchers integrate leadership theories and motivation theories by exploring the mechanisms through which leadership style is linked to motivation. Second, we suggest that future research examine whether certain types of motivation may serve as a substitute for leadership. For example, perhaps intrinsic or autonomously motivated employees require less leadership in order to be effective, because they internally regulate their behavior. Conversely, perhaps extrinsically regulated employees require leadership more, because their behavior is regulated largely by external contingencies. Similarly, research could examine whether effective leadership has more of an impact on individuals at different levels of internalization. Finally, future research should examine leaders' own motivation to lead and how it is related to effectiveness of leadership. Different levels and types of motivation may lead to different leadership styles. Motivation to enact effective leadership may also be examined with respect to other leadership theories besides transformational leadership, including the theories discussed in this chapter or other theories, such as servant leadership.

References

Avolio, B. J., & Gardner, W. L. (2005). Authentic leadership development: Getting to the root of positive forms of leadership. *The Leadership Quarterly, 16*, 315–338. doi:10.1016/j.leaqua.2005.03.001

Baard, P. P. (2002). Intrinsic need satisfaction in organizations: A motivational basis of success in for-profit and not-for-profit settings. In E. L. Deci & R. M. Ryan (Eds.), *Handbook of self-determination research* (pp. 255–275). Rochester, NY: University of Rochester Press.

Baard, P. P., Deci, E. L., & Ryan, R. M. (2004). Intrinsic need satisfaction: A motivational basis of performance and well-being in two work settings. *Journal of Applied Social Psychology, 34*(10), 2045–2068. doi:10.1111/j.1559-1816.2004.tb02690.x

Barling, J., Christie, A., & Hoption, C. (2010). Leadership. In S. Zedeck (Ed.), *Handbook of Industrial and Organizational Psychology* (pp. 183–240). Washington, DC: American Psychological Association.

Barling, J., Weber, T., & Kelloway, E. K. (1996). Effects of transformational leadership training on attitudinal and financial outcomes: A field experiment. *Journal of Applied Psychology, 81*, 827–883. doi:10.1037/0021-9010.81.6.827

Bass, B. (1985). *Leadership and performance beyond expectations.* New York: Free Press.

Bass, B. (1990). From transactional to transformational leadership: Learning to share the vision. *Organizational Dynamics, 18*(3), 19–36. doi:10.1016/0090-2616(90)90061-S

Bass, B. M. (1998). *Transformational leadership: Industrial, military, and educational impact.* Lahwah, NJ: Lawrence Erlbaum Associates.

Bass, B. M., & Avolio, B. J. (1994). *Improving organizational effectiveness through transformational leadership.* Sage/Thousand Oaks.

Bies, R. J., & Moag, J. F. (1986). Interactional justice: Communication criteria of fairness. In R. J. Lewicki, B. H. Sheppard, & M. H. Bazerman (Eds.), *Research on negotiations in organizations* (Vol. 1, pp. 43–55). Greenwich, CT: JAI Press

Blais, M. R., & Brière, N. M. (1992). *On the mediational role of feelings of self-determination in the workplace: Further evidence and generalization.* Unpublished manuscript, University of Quebec at Montreal.

Bono, J. E., & Ilies, R. (2006). Charisma, positive emotions, and mood contagion. *The Leadership Quarterly, 17*, 317–334. doi:10.1016/j.leaqua.2006.04.008

Bono, J. E., & Judge, T. A. (2003). Self-concordance at work: Toward understanding the motivational effects of transformational leaders. *Academy of Management Journal, 46*, 554–571. doi:10.2307/30040649

Bycio, P., Hackett, R. D., & Allen, J. S. (1995). Further assessments of Bass's (1985) conceptualization of transactional and transformational leadership. *Journal of Applied Psychology, 80*, 468–478. doi:10.1037/0021-9010.80.4.468

Chan, K., & Drasgow, F. (2001). Toward a theory of individual differences and leadership: Understanding the motivation to lead. *Journal of Applied Psychology, 86*(3), 481–498. doi:10.1037/0021-9010.86.3.481

Conger, J. A., & Kanungo, R. N. (1987). Towards a behavioural theory of charismatic leadership in organizational settings. *Academy of Management Review, 12*(4), 637–647. doi:10.2307/258069

Conger, J. A., & Kanungo, R. N. (1998). *Charismatic leadership in organizations.* Thousand Oaks, CA: Sage.

Cropanzano, R., Byrne, Z. S., Bobocel, D. R., & Rupp, D. E. (2001). Moral virtues, fairness heuristics, social entities, and other denizens of organizational justice. *Journal of Vocational Behavior, 58*, 164–209. doi:10.1006/jvbe.2001.1791

Cropanzano, R., & Greenberg, J. (1997). Progress in organizational justice: Tunneling through the maze. In C. L. Cooper, & I. T. Robertson (Eds.), *International review of industrial and organizational psychology* (Vol. 12, pp. 317–372). London: Wiley.

Dansereau, F., Graen, G., & Haga, W. J. (1975). A vertical dyad linkage approach to leadership with formal organizations: A longitudinal investigation of the role making process. *Organizational Behaviour and Human Performance, 13*, 46–78. doi:10.1016/0030-5073(75)90005-7

Deci, E. L. (1975). *Intrinsic motivation.* New York: Plenum.

Deci, E. L., Connell, J. P., & Ryan, R. M. (1989). Self-determination in a work organization. *Journal of Applied Psychology, 74*(4), 580–590. doi:10.1037/0021-9010.74.4.580

Deci, E. L., Eghrari, H., Patrick, B. C., & Leone, D. R. (1994). Facilitating internalization: The self-determination theory perspective. *Journal of Personality, 62*(1), 119–142. doi:10.1111/j.1467-6494.1994.tb00797.x

Deci, E. L., Nezlek, J., & Sheinman, L. (1981). Characteristics of the rewarder and intrinsic motivation of the rewardee. *Journal of Personality and Social Psychology, 40*, 1–10. doi:10.1037/0022-3514.40.1.1

Deci, E. L., & Ryan, R. M. (1985). *Intrinsic motivation and self-determination in human behavior.* New York: Plenum.

Deci, E. L., & Ryan, R. M. (1987). The support of autonomy and the control of behaviour. *The Journal of Personality and Social Psychology, 53*(6), 1024–1037. doi:10.1037/0022-3514.53.6.1024

Deci, E. L., & Ryan, R. M. (2000). The "What" and "Why" of goal pursuits: Human needs and the self-determination of behavior. *Psychological Inquiry, 11*, 227–268. doi:10.1207/S15327965PLI1104_01

Deci, E. L., & Ryan, R. M. (2008). Facilitating optimal motivation and psychological well-being across life's domains. *Canadian Psychology*, *49*(1), 14–23. doi:10.1037/0708-5591.49.1.14

Diefendorff, J. M., & Chandler, M. M. (2011). Motivating employees. In S. Zedeck (Ed.), APA handbook of industrial and organizational psychology: Maintaining, expanding, and contracting the organization (Vol. 3, pp. 65–135). Washington, DC: APA Books.

Fleishman, E. A., & Peters, D. R. (1962). Interpersonal values, leadership attitudes, and managerial success. *Personnel Psychology*, *15*, 127–143. doi:10.1111/j.1744-6570.1962.tb01855.x

Gagné, M., & Deci, E. L. (2005). Self-determination theory and work motivation. *Journal of Organizational Behaviour*, *26*, 331–362. doi:10.1002/job.322

Gagné, M., Koestner, R., & Zuckerman, M. (2000). Facilitating acceptance of organizational change: The importance of self-determination. *Journal of Applied Social Psychology*, *30*(9), 1843–1852. doi:10.1111/j.1559-1816.2000.tb02471.x

Gerstner, C. R., & Day, D. V. (1997). Meta-analytic review of leader-member exchange theory: Correlates and construct issues. *Journal of Applied Psychology*, *82*(6), 827–844. doi:10.1037/0021-9010.82.6.827

Graen, G. B., & Uhl-Bien, M. (1995). Relationship-based approach to leadership: Development of a leader-member exchange (LMX) theory of leadership over 25 years: Applying a multi-level multi-domain perspective. *Leadership Quarterly*, *6*, 219–247.

Greenberg, J. (1987). A taxonomy of organizational justice theories. *Academy of Management Review*, *12*(1), 9–22. doi:10.2307/257990

Hackman J. R., & Oldham, G. R. (1975). Development of the Job Diagnostic Survey. *Journal of Applied Psychology*, *60*, 159–170. doi:10.1037/h0076546

Hardré, P. L., & Reeve, J. R. (2009). Training corporate managers to adopt a more autonomy-supportive motivating style toward employees: An intervention study. *International Journal of Training and Development*, *13*(3), 165–184. doi:10.1111/j.1468-2419.2009.00325.x

Hater, J. J., & Bass, B. M. (1988). Superiors' evaluations and subordinates' perceptions of transformational and transactional leadership. *Journal of Applied Psychology*, *73*, 695–702. doi:10.1037/0021-9010.73.4.695

Hoption, C., Barling, J., & Kelloway, E. K. (2010). *Daily transformational leadership*. Manuscript submitted for publication.

House, R. J. (1977). A 1976 theory of charismatic leadership. In J. G. Hunt, & L. L. Larsen (Eds.), *Leadership: The cutting edge* (pp. 189–207). Carbondale, IL: Southern Illinois University Press.

House, R. J., & Podsakoff, P. M. (1994). Leadership effectiveness: Past perspectives and future directions for research. In J. Greenberg (Ed.), *Organizational behaviour: The state of the science* (pp. 45–82). Hilldale, NJ: Erlbaum.

Howell, J. M., & Avolio, B. J. (1993). Transformational leadership, transactional leadership, locus of control and support for innovation: Key predictors of consolidated-business-unit performance. *Journal of Applied Psychology*, *78*, 891–902. doi:10.1037/0021-9010.78.6.891

Howell, J. M., & Frost, P. J. (1989). A laboratory study of charismatic leadership. *Organizational Behavior and Human Decision Processes*, *43*, 243–269. doi:10.1016/0749-5978(89)90052-6

Howell, J. M., & Hall-Merenda, K. E. (1999). The ties that bind: The impact of leader-member exchange, transformational, and transactional leadership, and distance on predicting follower performance. *Journal of Applied Psychology*, *84*(5), 680–694. doi:10.1037/0021-9010.84.5.680

Ilies, R., Morgeson, F. P., & Nahrgang, J. D. (2005). Authentic leadership and eudaemonic well-being: Understanding leader-follower outcomes. *The Leadership Quarterly*, *16*, 373–394. doi:10.1016/j.leaqua.2005.03.002

Jang, H., Reeve, J., & Deci, E. L. (2010). Engaging students in learning activities: It is not autonomy support or structure but autonomy support and structure. *Journal of Educational Psychology*, *102*(3), 588–600. doi:10.1037/a0019682

Jones, G. R., & George, J. M. (1998). The experience and evolution of trust: Implications for cooperation and teamwork. *Academy of Management Review*, *23*, 531–546. doi:10.2307/259293

Judge, T. A., Piccolo, R. F. (2004). Transformational and transactional leadership: A meta-analytic test of their relative validity. *Journal of Applied Psychology*, *89*(5), 755–768. doi:10.1037/0021-9010.89.5.755

Judge, T. A., Piccolo, R. F., & Ilies, R. (2004). The forgotten ones? The validity of consideration and initiating structure in leadership research. *Journal of Applied Psychology*, *89*(1), 36–51. doi:10.1037/0021-9010.89.1.36

Jung, D. I., & Avolio, B. J. (2000). Effects of leadership style and followers' cultural orientation on performance in groups and individual task conditions. *Academy of Management Journal*, *47*, 208–218.

Kark, R., Shamir, B., & Chen, G. (2003). The two faces of transformational leadership: Empowerment and dependency. *Journal of Applied Psychology*, *88*, 246–255. doi:10.1037/0021-9010.88.2.246

Kelloway, E. K., & Barling, J. (2000). What we've learned about developing transformational leaders. *The Leadership and Organization Development Journal*, *21*, 157–161. doi:10.1108/01437730010377908

Kelloway, E. K., & Barling, J. (2010). Leadership development as an intervention in occupational health psychology. *Work and Stress 24*(3), 260–279. doi:10.1080/02678373.2010.518441

Kelloway, E. K., Barling, J., & Helleur, J. (2000). Enhancing transformational leadership: The roles of training and feedback. *The Leadership and Organizational Development Journal*, *21*, 145–149. doi:10.1108/01437730010325022

Kelloway, E. K., Mullen, J., & Francis, L. (2006). Divergent effects of passive and transformational leadership on safety outcomes. *Journal of Occupational Health Psychology*, *11*, 76–86. doi:10.1037/1076-8998.11.1.76

Kerr, S., Schreisheim, C. A., Murphy, C. J., & Stogdill, R. M. (1974). Toward a contingency theory of leadership based upon the consideration and initiating structure literature. *Organizational Behaviour and Human Performance*, *12*, 62–82. doi:10.1016/0030-5073(74)90037-3

Kirkpatrick, S. A., & Locke, E. A. (1996). Direct and indirect effects of three core charismatic leadership components on performance and attitudes. *Journal of Applied Psychology*, *81*, 36–51. doi:10.1037/0021-9010.81.1.36

Koh, W. L., Steers, R. M., & Terborg, J. R. (1995). The effects of transformational leadership on teacher attitudes and student performance in Singapore. *Journal of Organizational Behavior*, *16*, 319–333. doi:10.1002/job.4030160404

Korman, A. K. (1966). "Consideration," "initiating structure" and organizational criteria—A review. *Personnel Psychology*, *19*, 349–361. doi:10.1111/j.1744-6570.1966.tb00310.x

Leone, D. (1995). *The relation of work climate, higher-order need satisfaction, need salience, and causality orientations to work engagement, psychological adjustment, and job satisfaction*. Unpublished doctoral dissertation, University of Rochester.

Leventhal, G. S., Karuza, J., & Fry, W. R. (1980). Beyond fairness: A theory of allocation preferences. In G. Mikula (Ed.), *Justice and social interaction* (pp. 167–218). New York: Springer-Verlag.

McKee, M., Driscoll, C., Kelloway, E. K., & Kelley, E. (2009). *Leading to wellbeing*. Paper presented at the annual meeting of the European Academy of Work and Organizational Psychology, Santiago de Compostella, Spain.

Mullen, J., & Kelloway, E. K. (2009). Safety leadership: A longitudinal study of the effects of transformational leadership on safety outcomes. *Journal of Occupational and Organizational Psychology*, *20*, 253–272. doi:10.1348/096317908X325313

Mullen, J., Kelloway E. K., & Teed, M. (2011). Inconsistent leadership as a predictor of safety behavior. *Work & Stress*, *25*(1), 41–54. doi:10.1080/02678373.2011.569200

Piccolo, R. F., & Colquitt, J. A. (2006). Transformational leadership and job behaviours: The mediating role of core job characteristics. *Academy of Management Journal*, *49*, 327–340. doi:10.5465/AMJ.2006.20786079

Pillai, R., Schriesheim, C. A., & Williams, E. S. (1999). Fairness perceptions and trust as mediators for transformational and transactional leadership: A two-sample study. *Journal of Management*, *25*, 897–933. doi:10.1177/014920639902500606

Rubin, R. S., Munz, D. C., & Bommer, W. H. (2005). Leading from within: The effects of emotion recognition and personality on transformational leadership. *Academy of Management Journal*, *48*, 845–858. doi:10.5465/AMJ.2005.18803926

Ryan, R. M., & Deci, E. L. (2002). Overview of self-determination theory: An organismic dialectical perspective. In E. L. Deci, & R. M. Ryan (Eds.), *Handbook of self-determination research* (pp. 3–33). Rochester, NY: University of Rochester Press.

Scott, N., Fleming, M., & Kelloway, E. K. (forthcoming). Understanding why employees behave safely from a self-determination theory perspective. In M. Gagné (Ed.) *The Oxford Handbook of Work Engagement, Motivation, and Self-Determination Theory*. Oxford University Press.

Shamir, B., House, R. J., & Arthur, M. B. (1993). The motivational effects of charismatic leadership: A self-concept based

theory. *Organization Science*, *4*(4), 577–594. doi:10.1287/orsc.4.4.577

Sosik, J., Avolio, B., & Kahai, S. (1997). Effects of leadership style and anonymity on group potency and effectiveness in a group decision support system environment. *The Journal of Applied Psychology*, *82*(1), 89–103. doi:10.1037/0021-9010.82.1.89

Srivatava, A., Bartol, K. M., & Locke, E. A. (2006). Empowering leadership in management teams: Effects on knowledge sharing, efficacy, and performance. *Academy of Management Journal*, *49*, 1239–1251. doi:10.5465/AMJ.2006.23478718

Stogdill, R. M. (1950). Leadership, membership and organization. *Psychological Bulletin*, *47*, 1–14.

Thibault, J., & Walker, L. (1975). *Procedural justice: A psychological analysis*. Hillsdale, NJ: Erlbaum.

Walumbwa, F. O., Avolio, B. J., Gardner, W. L., Wernsing, T. S., & Peterson, S. J. (2008). Authentic leadership: Development and validation of a theory based measure. *Journal of Management*, *34*(1), 89–126. doi:10.1177/0149206307308913

Walumbwa, F. O., Luthans, F., Avey, J. B., & Oke, A. (2011). Authentically leading groups: The mediating role of collective psychological capital and trust. *Journal of Organizational Behaviour*, *32*, 4–24. doi:10.1002/job.653

Walumbwa, F. O., Wang, P., Wang, H., Schaubroeck, J., & Avolio, B. J. (2010). Psychological processes linking authentic leadership to follower behaviours. *The Leadership Quarterly*, *21*, 901–914. doi:10.1016/j.leaqua.2010.07.015

Wang, H., Law, K. S., Hackett, R. D., Wang, D., & Chen, Z. X. (2005). Leader-member exchange as a mediator of the relationship between transformational leadership and followers' performance and organizational citizenship behaviour. *Academy of Management*, *48*, 420–432. doi:10.5465/AMJ.2005.17407908

Williams, G. C., Grow, V. M., Freedman, Z. R., Ryan, R. M., & Deci, E. L. (1996). Motivational predictors of weight loss and weight-loss maintenance. *Journal of Personality and Social Psychology*, *70*, 115–126. doi:10.1037/0022-3514.70.1.115

Williams, G. C., McGregor, H. A., Sharp, D., Levesque, C., Kouides, R. W., Ryan, R. M., & Deci, E. L. (2006). Testing a self-determination theory intervention for motivating tobacco cessation: Supporting autonomy and competence in a clinical trial. *Health Psychology*, *25*(1), 91–101. doi:10.1037/0278-6133.25.1.91

CHAPTER 12

Compensation and Work Motivation: Self-Determination Theory and the Paradigm of Motivation through Incentives

Amar Fall *and* Patrice Roussel

Abstract

The predominant theories of motivation at work in management practice consider compensation as an important factor of motivation toward effort and performance. Several theories in psychology and economics converge to support this general hypothesis, to the point where they form a paradigm: that of work motivation through incentives. Another stream of research, consisting of the theories of intrinsic motivation, has long contradicted the former theoretical position. The latest developments in intrinsic motivation research, along with the contributions of self-determination theory, make it possible to take a new look at the question of the motivational power of compensation. This chapter aims to show that self-determination theory offers a promising theoretical perspective for understanding the relationships between compensation and motivation. The chapter concludes with a set of theoretical propositions drawing together research in psychology, economics, and management.

Key Words: motivation, effort, incentive, rewards, bonuses

Introduction

Since the works of Frederic W. Taylor and throughout the 20th century, a dominant paradigm widely accepted in the context of organizations has been that based on the virtues of compensation as an incentive. This paradigm considers compensation to be an influential factor in motivation at work, and has been supported by policies of human resources management in companies and in some public administrations. Built up by the dominant theories of management, economics, and organizational psychology, a paradigm of motivation through incentive has gradually become dominant; this supports the general hypothesis that making compensation contingent on performance incites employees to give of their best. This paradigm is rooted in the earliest works on the concept of motivation; from the 1930s to the 1950s these studied the link between work motivation and individual performance (e.g., Lewin, Peak, Rotter, and Tolman). From that time

on, a set of theoretical and empirical work has come to light on seeking factors of motivation that could act on effort and subsequently affect performance at work (e.g., Maslow, Herzberg, and Alderfer). In this context, theoretical and empirical research on the question of the relationship between compensation and work motivation really took off. The outcome of this reflexion on the processes activating motivation then generated highly specific theories on the influential role of compensation on work motivation. Equity theory (Adams, 1963, 1965), and especially expectancy theory (Nadler & Lawler, 1977; Porter & Lawler, 1968; Vroom, 1964), proposed highly convincing theoretical perspectives, to the point of dominating the academic literature as well as organizational psychology and management research. The development of these theories resulted in the influential goal-setting theory (Locke, 1968; Locke, Shaw, Saari, & Latham, 1981) and organizational justice theory (Bies & Moag, 1986; Greenberg, 1987).

In economics, agency theory is included in this paradigm, devoting the dominant functionalist ideas to the potentially positive effects of compensation on work motivation (Jensen & Meckling, 1976). The efficiency wage theory (Solow, 1979), Akerlof and Yellen's fair wage model (1988, 1990), and tournament theory (Lazear & Rosen, 1981) made particular contributions to the consolidation of the dominant theoretical basis in economics. In the first part of the chapter, we shall return to the respective contributions of these fields of research with an analysis of the contributions and limitations of the dominant paradigm of motivation through incentive.

However, a certain number of research fields have countered this paradigm of motivation through incentives. For the last 10 years, "mainstream" economists have joined the theoretical perspective devoted to intrinsic and extrinsic motivation (Bénabou & Tirole, 2002, 2003), often contested during the previous 40 years. This theoretical perspective was initiated in the work of Herzberg in the late 1950s and developed by the psychologists Deci and Ryan during the 1970s. Its theoretical positioning meant that for many years it was sidelined into the fields of management and organizational psychology, for it placed intrinsic and extrinsic motivation in a dual opposition. First it considered that only intrinsic motivation could have a lasting influence on both an individual's well-being and his or her performance at work. Second, it proposed that compensation could not act positively on intrinsic motivation. The influence of this theoretical perspective was long restricted by the lack of empirical studies in the organizational setting (Gomez-Mejia & Balkin, 1992; Pinder, 1984; Staw, 1977). Conversely, the dominant economic trend, particularly in the light of agency theory, showed that incentive systems for performance were efficient (e.g., Gupta & Mitra, 1998; Lazear, 2000) and made it possible to satisfy stakeholders' expectations by reconciling the interests of the company, the shareholders, and the employees. However, with the evolution of Deci and Ryan's thinking, self-determination theory (SDT) gradually achieved recognition as an influential theoretical framework in the organizational field (Gagné & Deci, 2005; Kohn, 1993). One of the strengths of this theoretical framework is to suggest a coherent and synergistic explanation of job performance and well-being at work through autonomous and intrinsic motivation. This growing concern of modern economies (Gagné & Forest, 2009) probably led

economists and managers to become more interested in SDT.

Following on from the work of Gagné and Deci (2005) and Gagné and Forest (2008), the second part of this chapter examines the contribution of this theory to the field of compensation management. The literature review attempts to show the convergence of research in psychology, economics, and management toward the central question of the motivational power of compensation according to SDT. We formulate a set of theoretical propositions and discuss the distinctive conditions explaining the effects of compensation on autonomous motivation and controlled motivation.

The Paradigm of Motivation through Incentives: Contributions and Limits of the Dominant Theories of Work Motivation

The paradigm of motivation through incentives was gradually built up around the viewpoints of two complementary and mutually enriching disciplines: psychology and economics. In organizational psychology, the equity and organizational justice theories (Adams, 1963, 1965; Greenberg, 1987), expectancy theory (Nadler & Lawler, 1977; Porter & Lawler, 1968; Vroom, 1964), and goal-setting theory (Locke, 1968; Locke et al., 1981) long dominated the literature and research relative to the influence of compensation on work motivation. In economics, agency theory (Jensen & Meckling, 1976) influenced thought about companies' compensation policies throughout the 1980s. This theory encouraged fields of research that consolidated the thinking about the efficiency of compensation systems and their incentive power. This is particularly the case with efficiency wage theory (Solow, 1979), tournament theory (Lazear & Rosen, 1981), or even the fair wage model (Akerlof & Yellen, 1988, 1990). This set of research fields completed and enriched the analysis of psychologists. Exploring the problem of incentive through compensation from different perspectives, it attempted to explain the conditions under which practices intending to encourage effort at work were effective.

The Contribution of Theories of Organizational Psychology

Theories of organizational psychology highlight the stimulating role of performance objectives when these are linked to compensation. These theories postulate that individuals are rational. In this sense, they make reasoned choices about activating efforts at work as well as the direction and intensity of those efforts and how long they will be maintained. The theories also suppose that individuals are hedonistic when they make choices, that they decide among several possible behaviors in such a way as to try to maximize the positive affect and minimize the negative affect by adopting behaviors directed toward obtaining the results with the greatest perceived value or overall usefulness (Kanfer, 1990). These theories also suppose that the choices individuals make are subject to principles of bounded rationality (Simon, 1957). The premises of these theoretical bases were laid down between 1930 and 1950 (Lewin, 1938; Peak, 1955; Rotter, 1955; Tolman, 1959) and were particularly influential in guiding the development of expectancy theory (Nadler & Lawler, 1977; Porter & Lawler, 1968; Vroom, 1964), equity theory (Adams, 1963, 1965), and goal-setting theory (Locke, 1968). Each of these research fields contributes a complementary perspective for understanding the relationship between compensation and work motivation. Each of them has influenced managerial thinking and companies' compensation policies (e.g., Gerhart & Milkovich, 1992; Gerhart & Rynes, 2003; Gomez-Mejia & Balkin, 1992; Heneman, 1992; Lawler, 1981, 1990).

THE CONTRIBUTIONS OF EXPECTANCY THEORY

Since Vroom's work (1964), expectancy theory (or valence-instrumentality-expectation theory) has been frequently used in the literature as an analytical framework for understanding how a compensation system can turn out to be motivating or not (e.g., Igalens & Roussel, 1999; Lawler, 1981; Mitchell, 1974). Further enhanced by the models of Porter and Lawler (1968), Lawler (1971), and Nadler and Lawler (1977), this theory explains how compensation can generate positive effects on work motivation. Expectancy theory presents compensation as a potentially powerful lever of motivation (Lawler, 1971, 1981, 1990). It explains that the choices individuals make are guided by their perceptions of the probable consequences of the various alternatives being evaluated. These perceptions are conceived of as expectancies of events whose probability of being realized are weighed up by the individual concerned. Work motivation is thus determined by several expectancies: (1) expectancies that providing a given level of effort will result in a desired level of performance (expectation), (2) expectancies that reaching a given level of performance will result in a given reward (instrumentality), and (3) the affective value of the reward obtained (valence).

According to this perspective, three conditions must thus be fulfilled if compensation is to incite individuals to increase their efforts at work. The first is that the person perceives that he or she is capable of achieving the performance goals thanks to his or her efforts. The second condition is that the person perceives that the achievement of these goals will generate rewards (wage increase and/or performance bonus). The third and final condition is that the person perceives the reward to be obtained positively; more precisely, this particular reward must be desirable. For example, is a holiday offered as a reward for good sales performances more highly appreciated than a monetary bonus of similar value? The answer to this question is eminently subjective and thus depends on the individual.

This conceptualization of the motivational process and the influential role of compensation have dominated managerial thinking since the 1960s. Company executives, human resources specialists, and compensation experts all receive training in line with this theoretical framework (e.g., Gomez-Mejia, Balkin, & Cardy, 2001; Milkovich & Newman, 2008; Saint-Onge & Thériault, 2006). The works of Porter and Lawler (1968), Lawler (1971), and Nadler and Lawler (1977) have contributed to enriching this analytical framework. The theoretical models they propose offer complete systems for comprehending the determinants and consequences of the work motivation process. Among their theoretical propositions, one is particularly relevant to compensation. This is the feedback loop that links job satisfaction to work motivation. These three theoretical models have in common that each proposes a causal chain between motivation, performance, and job satisfaction. What distinguishes the models from each other is their reference to different theoretical moderating and mediating variables that influence the causal process. Concerning the influential role of compensation on motivation, it turns out that once the three basic conditions of the motivational process described previously (expectation, instrumentality, and valence) have been met, individual effort increases. If the work context is favorable and if the individual has the necessary resources, especially in terms of competence, clear distribution of tasks and missions, problem solving methods, and so forththen an increased effort should generate the expected performance. From their experience at work, individuals observe the intrinsic and extrinsic rewards that they stand to receive according to their performance. If these are judged to be fair, the individual is satisfied by the job experience. This feeling of satisfaction or dissatisfaction then acts retroactively on future perceptions as to the probable effects of efforts on future performance as well as on the valence of the rewards individuals might receive in return for performance. Thus, the compensation (wage increase and/or bonus) plays a positive or a negative role in strengthening motivation at work depending on the level of satisfaction or dissatisfaction the individual has experienced from previous efforts made and rewards obtained.

During the period from 1960 to 1980 a great many empirical studies tested the different hypotheses put forward by this theory and largely supported it (see: state of the art by Pinder, 1984). For this reason, this theoretical perspective contributed greatly to spreading the idea that performance contingent pay was an efficient way to motivate employees (Heneman, 1992; Igalens & Roussel, 1999; Lawler, 1990).

THE CONTRIBUTIONS OF EQUITY THEORY AND ORGANIZATIONAL JUSTICE THEORY

Equity theory (Adams, 1963, 1965) had a profound influence on expectancy theory (e.g., Porter & Lawler, 1968) and compensation management (e.g., Milkovich & Newman, 2008). Equity theory is based on the hypothesis that each individual compares the advantages derived from his or her job (outcomes) and the contributions that he or she makes to it (input). This comparison takes the form of a confrontation of two types of ratio that individuals develop according to their own perceptions of the situation and professional context. Individuals compare their personal "advantages/contributions" ratio with the "advantage/contributions" ratio of others who they take as references. According to equity theory, motivation relies on individuals' disposition to compare their personal situation with that of others taken as references, either within the company (internal equity) or outside it (external equity). The discrepancy between what individuals perceive as their lot and what they desire is a source of psychological tension. This leads them to behave in such a way as to reduce both the tension and the discrepancy. They compare their own situation with that of others: if they are dissatisfied, the perceived unfairness creates tension that they seek to reduce. This tension triggers individuals into behavior aimed at a goal, (the behavior in this case being to make the necessary effort, and the goal to reduce the feeling of unfairness), thus they are motivated. If the individuals are satisfied with their comparisons with others, they are motivated to maintain this situation of psychological equilibrium.

This explanation of the motivational process also influences thinking on compensation management (e.g., Milkovich & Newman, 2008; Saint-Onge & Thériault, 2006). Specifically, research on internal equity was the guide behind the elaboration of company base-pay scales (job descriptions, analysis and evaluation of jobs, job classification, and so forth), whereas research on external equity guided the benchmarking of salaries among companies on the market (fixing wage levels and salary bands).

According to equity theory, compensation is one of the main outputs that individuals analyze in their evaluation of whether they are fairly or unfairly treated in their organization. Greenberg (1987, 1990) proposes using the concept of distributive justice to designate the feeling of equity toward levels of reward. A second proposal aims to show that the level of compensation is not, on its own, enough to explain the feeling of fairness or unfairness. The individual also observes the procedures used to manage these outputs, notably decision processes in terms of allocating rewards and compensation, as well as individuals' annual appraisal processes.

Greenberg proposes considering procedural justice in analyzing organizational justice. Procedural justice is high when decision-making concerning rewards and recognition is based on procedures that are fair, transparent, and relevant, and when management facilitates information and explanation, listens to grievances, and is open to revizing decisions. This approach is particularly relevant to the analysis of personnel assessment systems as well as decision-making processes concerning wage increases based on merit and performance bonuses (e.g., Folger & Konovsky, 1989).

Bies and Moag (1986) specified that another form of justice, interactional justice, also has an important role. Interactional justice results from the perceived behavior of middle or top management. According to Greenberg (1993), interactional justice first corresponds to informational justice. This is fulfilled when management communicates information fairly in terms of quality, quantity, and transparency. It also corresponds to interpersonal justice, this being fulfilled when managers respect the dignity of their collaborators, listen to them, and treat them courteously. This theoretical perspective suggests that compensation management is not only about fixing base pay levels and procedures governing decisions about wages. It also depends on the art of managing collaborators—that means making decisions about wage increases and bonuses and being able to explain them (e.g., Colquitt,

Conlon, Wesson, Porter, & Ng, 2001; Shaw, Wild & Colquitt, 2003; Skarlicki & Folger, 1997).

THE CONTRIBUTIONS OF GOAL-SETTING THEORY

Goal-setting theory, developed by Locke and Latham (Locke, 1968, 1975, 1997; Locke et al., 1981; Locke & Latham, 1984), provides another way of understanding the effects of compensation on work motivation. According to this theory, fixing goals for individuals increases their motivation and thus their task performance. The initial premise is that individuals have goals that they consciously try to reach of their own initiative. The theory does not, however, try to explain the workings of the psychological process that links these goals to motivation. It rather tries to explain *how* or under which circumstances goals may affect individual behaviors. The theory's general proposition is that setting goals for individuals motivates them and improves their performance when five conditions are fulfilled:

1. The individual thinks he or she is capable of reaching the goals
2. Feedback is built into the system
3. Rewards are given when goals are reached
4. Management supports and keeps to the goals
5. The individual accepts the goals to which he or she is assigned

Three more propositions are defined concerning the qualities of a motivating goal. When setting goals, it is important to make sure that these have: (a) content, (b) intensity and precision, and (c) attributes. The content of the goals supposes that precise and full instructions are given as to the expected results and the process by which these results may be attained. Each party must fully understand the goals to be attained. The intensity and precision of the goals supposes that the expected level of performance be made explicit, as well as the rhythm and amount of working time to be devoted to attaining the goal within a precise pre-established time frame. Finally, the attributes related to motivating goals are their level of difficulty, their specific characteristics, and the feeling of self-efficacy they generate. A goal must be difficult enough to be challenging while remaining reachable; it must therefore be stimulating. It must also be representative of the specific job occupied by the employee and thus be coherent with his or her activity and role. Finally, it must arouse feelings of confidence in one's own capacity to grow and master the situation.

Goal-setting theory assigns great importance to monetary rewards (e.g., Erez, Gopher, & Arazi, 1990; Guthrie & Hollensbeck, 2004; Locke, 1968; Locke & Latham, 1984; Riedel, Nebeker, & Cooper, 1988). Certain empirical studies have shown that some of the negative effects of compensation could be explained by the lack of precision or suitability of the goals to be attained (e.g., Gerhart & Rynes, 2003; Locke et al., 1981). For example, when goals are perceived as too difficult or even inaccessible, a feeling of unfairness can result in reduced effort and performance (Lee, Locke, & Phan, 1997). The difficulty for managers is to set goals that are sufficiently difficult to be challenging, but accessible enough to maintain employee motivation. When this balance is achieved, individual compensation seems to act positively (Riedel et al., 1988; Wright, 1989, 1992). Similarly, group compensation in the form of team bonuses, for example, is effective when the goals set are difficult, stimulating and, coherent with group cohesion if this was previously a characteristic of the team in question (Guthrie & Hollensbeck, 2004; Hollensbeck & Guthrie, 2000; Knight, Duham, & Locke, 2001).

The Contribution of Economic Theories about Pay

The 1970s saw the emergence of economic theories that contributed to spreading the idea among company executives of the importance of performance contingent pay. This mode of thinking was initiated by agency theory (Jensen & Meckling, 1976). Agency theory proposes using compensation as an instrument to control employee behavior with the aim of aligning individual interests to the interest of the organization as a whole. The theories relevant to this research stream (e.g., efficiency wage theory, tournament theory, the fair wage model) suggest that effort is highly sensitive to monetary incentives and that these incentives have a positive effect on motivation and individual performance at work; this performance, obtained either by a cumulative or synergistic effect, in turn acts positively on the performance of the organization. By the end of the 20th century, these theories had contributed to impose the model of incentive pay as an effective managerial practice, notably using systems of pay for performance, merit pay, and stock ownership.

THE CONTRIBUTIONS OF AGENCY THEORY

Agency theory dealt predominantly with the potentially positive effects of incentive rewards on motivation and performance at work (Jensen &

Meckling, 1976). This theory defines the relationship of agency as a contract for which the principal (the shareholders) engages the agent (the CEO) to accomplish a service in their name; this also implies delegating part of the principal's decision-making authority to the agent (Jensen & Meckling, 1976). In the case of companies, this relationship of agency can also be represented by the relationships linking the employer (the principal in the case) with the employee (the agent). Agency theory thus relies on there being a divergence between the personal interests of the principal and those of the agent. According to Jensen and Meckling (1976) this divergence can be explained by the fact that the agent tends to take over some of the company's resources in the form of privileges for his or her own use. As for the CEO in the role of agent, he or she will aim above all to strengthen his or her position as executive at the head of the company. Thus he or she will tend to give preference to the company's social interests (e.g., prefer to buy social peace and avoid conflict by increasing employees' wages) rather than satisfy the interests of shareholders (e.g., distribute dividends). The relationship of agency thus raises the problem of opportunism. More generally, the executive responsible for running the company has privileged information as to how it functions. To maintain his or her power of decision, he or she might be tempted to adopt opportunistic behavior by manipulating this information, communicating only those elements that serve his or her own interests. This results in a situation usually known as "information asymmetry" or unequally shared information. According to Jensen and Meckling, this divergence of interests implies the creation of a new balance in order to satisfy both parties. To do this, the principal (the shareholders) have to set up a system of incentive rewards that push the agent (the CEO) to reveal all information and to make decisions that favor the principal's interests. Next, the principal sets up mechanisms to control the agent (chartered accountants, auditors, monitoring advisors, compensation committee, clauses in case of breach of contract between the agent and the company, internal versus external selection of directors, and so forthto limit the risk of loss brought about by this conflict of interests (Jensen & Meckling, 1976). One of the best ways to motivate the CEO and resolve this conflict of interests is to design reward systems related to performance or to allocate stock options. Agency theory thus considers incentive rewards as one of the most efficient mechanisms for overcoming conflicts of interest and inciting top executives to make decisions that are favorable to shareholders. This contribution of agency theory was subsequently tested by transposing the relationship of agency between chief executive officer (the principal in this case) and employees (the agent). One example is the study by Bitler, Moskowitz, and Vissing-Jorgensen (2005), which attempts to show that giving company shares to employees increases both their personal effort and the company's performance.

Much of the research based on agency theory served to verify efficiency pay or the capacity of rewards to produce positive effects on employees' behaviors and company performance (e.g., Akerlof & Yellen, 1986; Cahuc, & Zylberberg, 1996; Lazear & Oyer, 2004; Lazear & Rosen, 1981; MacDonald & Solow, 1981; Solow, 1979). Other authors, such as Ashton (1991) and Kaplan (1984), also use agency theory to analyze the relationships between managers and their collaborators and add support to the hypotheses regarding the efficiency of systems of variable pay. All this research has encouraged the adoption of incentive pay systems aiming to make the interests of employees and those of the company (represented by the manager) coincide.

We should also note, however, that the analyses carried out by some authors put these results into perspective (Bruce, Buck, & Main, 2005; Lubatkin, Lane, Collin, & Very, 2006). This work highlights the limits of agency theory. First, research has not been able to establish a solid empirical link between top executives' compensation and company performance. Second, agency theory is "under socialized" in the sense that it takes no account of the social context in which the agency relationship occurs. However, according to Gomez-Mejia and Wisman (2007), the principal-agent relationship is above all part of a social context that plays an important role in the definition of the personal interest of each stakeholder, as well as in the conception of effective mechanisms for aligning the interests of principal and agent.

THE CONTRIBUTIONS OF EFFICIENCY WAGE THEORY

One of the essential objectives of incentive rewards is to obtain a high level of effort from employees. Solow's (1979) efficiency wage theory thus tries to highlight the incentive power of the level of base pay by looking at this question for all employees rather than limiting the enquiry to the relationship between shareholder and chief executive officer. This theory proposes to explain the effects of wage level on employees' effort and productivity. Solow (1979) supports the existence of a positive link between the level of wages and level of effort known as the "efficiency relationship," an effect that is supposed to condition employee productivity.

Efficiency wage theory thus predicts that an increase in employee effort and productivity can be directly obtained through increased compensation or high wages, that is, wages higher than the market rate. This hypothesis was tested in econometric studies, such as that of Wadhwani and Wall (1990), undertaken on a panel of companies from different activity sectors. This study confirms the existence of a positive effect of wages level on effort and productivity. These results are based on data gathered between 1972 and 1982 from 219 companies in various sectors of activity in the United Kingdom. They establish a positive relationship between the wage level and motivation then productivity, but also among gainsharing, motivation, and productivity. A study by Giorgiadis (2007) carried out in the United Kingdom in a low-paid activity sector (home nursing) maintains that high wages are necessary to encourage employee motivation. Another study by Raposo and Menezes (2011) in companies in Brazil confirms the predictions of efficiency wage theory. This study shows the existence of a significant positive relationship between effort and wage level. This type of conclusion is widely supported by theorists of the standard economics of incentives who underline the high incentive effect of monetary rewards on motivation at work and employee performance (Brown, Gardner, Oswald, & Qian, 2008; Cahuc & Zylbergberg, 2004; Clark, Masclet, & Villeval, 2006; Gächter & Falk, 2002; Laffont & Martimort, 2002; Lazear, 2004).

THE CONTRIBUTIONS OF THE FAIR WAGE MODEL

In the early 1980's, Akerlof (1982) developed a fair wage model inspired by sociology. In this model, he used what had been learned from social anthropology, maintaining, as Mauss (1923) had already done, that the employment contract is considered as an exchange of "gift/counter-gift." Akerlof and Yellen (1988, 1990) proposed a second model inspired by psychology and based on Adams' (1963, 1965) equity theory. This model holds that employees are envious of each other and are likely to alter their efforts by comparing their wages to a level of reference. Akerlof and Yellen thus put forward a fundamental hypothesis concerning the

definition of the function of employee effort, also known as the "fair-wage hypothesis." According to them, individuals adapt their efforts in such a way as to balance the "fair wage" against the "received wage." According to this proposition, if the real wage is lower than the fair wage, employees will reduce their efforts proportionally in order to maintain the contribution-reward balance. Conversely, if the real wage is superior to the fair wage, this will contribute to increasing employee's level of effort (Akerlof & Yellen, 1990). Nevertheless, the authors insist on the subjective character of what constitutes a fair wage. This fair wage hypothesis was an attempt to improve the basis of Solow's (1979) fair wage model, which relies on the hypothesis of a positive relationship between effort and wage. There is much empirical support for the adoption of an efficiency wage for reasons of fairness and effort at work (Cohn, Fehr, & Götte, 2010; Fehr, Gächter, & Kirchsteiger, 1997; Gneezy, 2002; Gneezy & List, 2006; Kaufman, 1984). This research strongly supported the idea that wage increases incite employees to provide more effort at work. Among these experimental studies, those of Gneezy (2002) or Gneezy and List (2006) confirmed the theoretical considerations of Akerlof's fair wage model. These authors observed that an increase in basic pay has a positive effect on personal commitment and increased performance at work, although this effect remains temporary. The works of Cohn et al. (2010), reveal that wage increases significantly increase employees' performance at work when the employees perceive their basic wage as unfairly low or when they are concerned about fair wages.

THE CONTRIBUTION OF TOURNAMENT THEORY

Tournament theory, developed by Lazear and Rosen (1981), approaches the subject from a different angle by combining incentives with setting employees in competition with each other. The theory studies the conditions of application of an incentive pay system based on merit. In this sense, tournament theory puts forward incentive mechanisms based on competition among employees. The principle of the tournament, according to Lazear and Rosen (1981), consists of rewarding the most deserving employees with a bonus or a promotion on top of their basic wage. Their theory thus uses competition among employees as an instrument of incentive. The underlying idea is that in order to encourage the employee to go beyond the minimum, merely rewarding effort, as proposed by Solow's (1979) efficiency wage theory, is not sufficient. Beyond this, it is necessary to motivate all the employee's colleagues to be in competition as they try to obtain the same reward. According to Lazear and Rosen (1981), making employees compete against each other is an efficient way of stimulating their efforts.

Starting from the contributions of tournament theory, McLaughlin (1988) adds that the structure of an optimal compensation plan depends on the number of employees in competition for the same reward. Indeed, the higher the number of candidates in the running, the less likely the individual is to obtain the reward. This being so, in order to incite employees to make optimal efforts, McLaughlin (1988) suggests that the value of the reward must be proportionate to the number of potential candidates. Lazear and Rosen (1981) similarly hold that when there are only small differences between competitors, the best way to incite them to give their bestis to give the highest reward to the most productive. To stimulate employee effort, tournament theory therefore suggests setting up systems of pay for performance in which the highest reward—bonus or promotion—is attributed to the most productive employee.

In summary, this theory supposes the existence of a positive relationship between wage dispersion, also called wage individualization, and the level of effort made by employees. The underlying idea of tournament theory is thus to reward certain employees significantly more than others because of their individual performances.

This hypothesis was later tested in multiple studies (e.g., Coupé, Smeet, & Warizynski, 2003; Knoeber & Walther, 1994; McLaughlin, 1988). For example, a study carried out in the sporting context of golf by Ehrenberg and Bognanno (1990) was one of the most often cited empirical tests of tournament theory. In this case, the performance of golfers varied both according to the amount of money at stake in the competition and the effort made. Eriksson's (1999) study based on a sample of 2,600 top managers of 210 Danish companies is also cited regularly. The results observe a positive and significant relationship between the productivity of companies and employees' salary dispersion, or individualization. According to Eriksson (1999), this result confirms firstly that greater employee salary dispersion improves companies' economic performance. Secondly, the greater the individualization of employees' salary, the greater the efforts made. However, Erikson (1999) specifies that although employees' cooperation is essential for the

company's success, the rewards attributed according to individual achievements may not necessarily be advantageous for the company. Conversely, in companies where such cooperation is less important, wage discrepancies can improve performance. Finally, regarding the hypothesis that there is a positive relationship between individual effort, the number of participants in the competition, and the amount of the reward at stake, Eriksson's (1999) results show positive correlations between these variables. Another study carried out by Conyon, Peck, and Sadler (2001) examined a database containing information on 532 top executives in 100 British public companies. This study shows firstly that there is a significant relationship between executive pay and the size of the organization, and secondly that the pay discrepancy among these executives is positively correlated to the number of participants in the tournament.

The Paradigm of Motivation through Incentive: Conclusion of Contributions and Limits

To conclude this first part, we can note that the contributions of the main theories relative to motivation and compensation highlight the fact that incentive rewards probably guide employee behavior. All these theories converge to suggest that effort is indeed sensitive to incentive rewards and that these rewards have significant effects on the motivation and performance of employees at work. It is possible to form a paradigm of motivation through incentive because of the convergence of coherent theoretical propositions supported by a set of theories that are influential within their disciplinary fields. In organizational psychology, equity theory (Adams, 1963, 1965), expectancy theory (Nadler & Lawler, 1977; Porter & Lawler, 1968; Vroom, 1964), and goal-setting theory (Locke, 1968, 1975, 1997; Locke et al., 1981; Locke & Latham, 1984) form the basis of this paradigm. In economics, agency theory (Jensen & Meckling, 1976), efficiency wage theory (Solow, 1979), the fair wage model (Akerlof, 1982, 1984; Akerlof & Yellen, 1988, 1990), and tournament theory (Lazear & Rosen, 1981) contribute to consolidate the paradigm and broaden its influence within organizations.

In parallel to the development of these theories, companies have transformed their compensation plans. Throughout a large part of the 20th century, companies and administrations set up fairly egalitarian compensation plans that left little room for the recognition of performance. Thus, job base pay, based on the job, qualifications, and seniority, gradually became a most common mode of compensation, especially from 1945 to 1980. After the great oil and economic crises of 1973 and 1979, issues of productivity, performance, and efficiency took on a new importance, especially in conjunction with the opening of markets, the arrival of new competitors from Asia, and consequently the increase of international competition. Economic theories took off during this period while organizational psychology theories were nearing the end of their development. It can be seen that in the history of organizations, the rapid expansion of these theories converged with the development of new models of compensation that from the 1980s favored the recognition of merit and performance. Merit pay and pay for performance developed considerably. Individual pay increases, bonuses, gainsharing, profit-sharing, and stock ownership became new norms of employee compensation. In this context, all these theories contribute to legitimizing the deployment of such systems.

Finally, these theories, which are both complementary and relatively concurrent, defend a single dominant paradigm that has always relied on the incentive virtues of compensation. However, in the current organizational context, the fragile social balance revealed by successive economic crises raises a certain number of questions to which researchers try to respond. According to our analysis, these questions relate to two major themes: first, the conflict between practices of wage individualization and the quest for cooperation and trust within organizations; and second, the conflict between the practices of performance pay and health and well-being at work. These questions are not developed in this chapter but they serve as starting points for new avenues of research that raise questions about the dominant paradigm of motivation through incentives. This is the subject of the second part of this chapter where we try to respond to the following question: how should the question of motivation through compensation be addressed today?

SDT: An Alternative to the Dominant Paradigm

Since the early 2000s, a set of research in psychology, management, and economics has converged to integrate the contribution of pay-for-performance systems and theories of intrinsic and extrinsic motivation. This effort to integrate two perspectives that until now had opposed each other, aims to reconcile the quest for interest in and pleasure at work (intrinsic motivation) and the need for extrinsic rewards through compensation or other forms of gratification (extrinsic motivation). This reconciliation of incentive theory in economics with intrinsic motivation theory in psychology was made possible through the development of Deci and Ryan's SDT in psychology (Deci & Ryan, 1985; Ryan & Deci, 2000; Deci & Ryan, 2002; Gagné & Deci, 2005). The convergence of several fields of research following this direction is explored in this second part of the chapter.

Reconciling the Incompatible?

The paradigm of motivation through incentive has been regularly criticized. On this subject, one of the first researchers who tried to show the possible inefficiency of compensation on motivation at work was Herzberg. With his collaborators, Herzberg (1957, 1959) distinguishes factors related to intrinsic motivation (relative to the content of the work and the pleasure it procures) from factors related to hygiene or extrinsic motivation (relative to incentives and working conditions). According to Herzberg's two-factor theory, compensation is a hygiene factor with no capacity to motivate people. Herzberg opened up new perspectives for research, taken up by DeCharms (1968), then by Deci (1971, 1972) with cognitive evaluation theory. This proposes to distinguish intrinsic from extrinsic motivation. These authors' propositions aim to show that the effects of compensation follow a vicious circle through the bias of extrinsic motivation. Extrinsic motivation is held to induce a feeling of being controlled and a consequent feeling of loss of autonomy; in the end it appears harmful to individual well-being and performance at work in the medium and long terms. Consequently, compensation used to increase extrinsic motivation would be counter-productive (Deci, 1972, 1975).

This approach was sidelined within research in management, organizational behavior, and organizational psychology. It was regularly criticized both on theoretical and methodological levels (e.g., Pinder, 1984; Salancik, 1975; Scott, 1975; Staw, 1977; Rynes, Gerhart, & Parks, 2005). From a conceptual point of view, few theories converge with the cognitive evaluation theory in support of this type of hypothesis. Most often, the dominant theories accept that compensation is motivating, and refuse to adopt a perspective that seems to oppose intrinsic and extrinsic motivation. Porter and Lawler's model (1968) is a typical illustration of this. It admits that there are intrinsic and extrinsic rewards, but does not separate the analysis of motivation between these two possible forms, as Deci later did. From an empirical point of view, there is a lack of research supporting cognitive evaluation theory in the organizational setting.

Deci and Ryan (1985) developed SDT, which is more consensual and suited to the interests of organizational management (Gagné & Deci, 2005; Sheldon, Turban, Brown, Barrick, & Judge, 2003). This theory opens up new perspectives that arouse much interest today from researchers in management and economics (e.g., Bénabou & Tirole, 2002, 2003; Cameron & Pierce, 1994; Eisenberger & Cameron, 1996; Eisenberger, Pierce, & Cameron, 1999; Tirole, 2008). These new research avenues could constitute a new paradigm based on reconciling different theoretical viewpoints. It is thus necessary to examine how SDT can address the possible effects of compensation on work motivation.

SDT and Compensation

SDT takes a step forward in the sense that conceptually, it accepts the hypothesis of a positive link between compensation and motivation (Deci & Ryan, 2000, 2002). Nevertheless, the theory conceives of this link under highly specific conditions. According to SDT, all individual behaviors can be categorized along a continuum ranging from the absence of autonomy to self-determination. With the exception of amotivation, which reflects a total lack of volition to act, this continuum makes it possible to distinguish "autonomous motivation" from "controlled motivation." Autonomous motivation translates the fact that an individual acts by conviction and/or pleasure. It implies that the individual behaves with a total feeling of free choice (Deci & Ryan, 2008). It supposes that the individual regulates his or her behavior according to an internal locus of causality. Autonomous motivation covers three possible characteristics: intrinsic motivation, integrated regulation, and/or identified regulation, the latter two being forms of extrinsic motivation. Controlled motivation is another type of extrinsic motivation and supposes that the individual regulates his or her behavior according to an external locus of causality. The individual acts under the influence of pressures and requirements linked to a specific productivity goal, specific objective to be attained, or even social expectations (Deci & Ryan, 2008). Controlled motivation covers two possible facets: external regulation and/or introjected regulation. External regulation is typically a form of

motivation particularly conditioned by the attribution of compensation. Introjected regulation implies that the individual pursues a goal in order to feel proud of his or her achievements and/or to avoid a feeling of guilt towards himself or herself and others.

This new conceptualization of motivation constitutes a significant advance relative to Deci's original ideas (1975). Henceforth, incentive is no longer invariably incompatible with personal fulfilment and with autonomous forms of motivation (Gagné & Deci, 2005). These relationships are made possible in SDT by the identification of three basic needs of autonomous motivation: competence, autonomy, and relatedness. Compensation plans that are able to act simultaneously on these three basic needs could promote autonomous work motivation, especially identified regulation and integrated regulation, two of the possible facets of autonomous regulation (Gagné & Deci, 2005; Gagné & Forest, 2008).

The Key Role of Basic Needs as Intermediary Variables between Compensation and Motivation

According to SDT, the existence of three basic psychological needs determines the individual's motivational orientation (controlled or autonomous). SDT theory places feelings of autonomy, relatedness and competence at the heart of the motivational process (Deci & Ryan, 1985, 2002; Ryan & Deci, 2000, 2008). These three motivational factors turn out to be particularly powerful in most social contexts (Deci & Ryan, 2000). Autonomous motivation, including intrinsic motivation, is held to depend on the satisfaction of these three basic needs (Deci & Ryan, 2000, 2008; Gagné & Forest, 2009; Laguardia & Ryan, 2000; Ryan, 1993; Van den Broeck, Vansteenkiste, De Witte, Soenens, & Lens, 2009).

In fact, the literature suggests that the effect of tangible rewards on intrinsic and/or autonomous motivation depends on the true meaning conveyed by these rewards for the satisfaction of basic needs (Deci & Ryan, 1985; Gagné et al., 2008; Ryan, 1980). Individual perceptions of autonomy, competence, and relatedness act as psychological mediators between social factors and motivation (Deci & Ryan, 2000; Gagné & Forest, 2009; Vallerand, 1997; Vallerand & Losier, 1999). These conclusions apply to the possible impact of rewards on the satisfaction of needs for autonomy, competence, and relatedness. According to SDT, the effect of rewards depends on the functional significance that individuals attribute to them. When they are perceived as a means of control, or even pressure, they compromise the need for autonomy and weaken intrinsic motivation; however, when they are perceived as a signal of recognition of competence they increase the feeling of competence and favor intrinsic motivation (Deci & Ryan, 1985; Deci, Koestner, & Ryan, 1999). As an example, performance contingent pay should affect autonomy negatively by changing the locus of causality from internal to external, but it may also have a positive effect on the feelings of competence by providing information on an individual's efficiency (Gagné & Forest, 2008).

These explanations show that SDT considers possible positive and negative influences of tangible rewards on autonomous motivation. The direct relationship remains negative because of the controlling aspect of the rewards, but a positive indirect relationship could be envisioned if, and only if, other basic psychological needs are positively impacted by these rewards. When the rewards are perceived as a signal of competence recognition, not as robbing one of autonomy at work, and/or as enhancing feelings of relatedness to coworkers, they should increase autonomous motivation and even intrinsic motivation. These analyses lead us to suppose that the satisfaction of these three basic needs plays an important role as an intermediary variable between compensation and autonomous motivation.

Compensation, Motivation, and Organizational Justice

According to our analysis, linking compensation and self-determined motivation requires that organizational justice research be taken into account. This proposition is developed in what follows, for the literature makes it possible to first underline the role of justice perceptions in work motivation, and second to suggest the existence of relationships between compensation, organizational justice, and the self-determined motivation.

Research has already shown that individuals are more motivated at work when they perceive themselves to be compensated fairly and equitably (e.g., Adams, 1963, 1965; Folger & Konovsky, 1989; Igalens & Roussel, 1999; Lazear & Rosen, 1981; Scarpello & Jones, 1996; Tremblay & Roussel, 2001). To grasp this question as a whole, research in management and organizational behavior adopts the approach from the angle of organizational justice theory (Bies & Moag, 1986; Greenberg, 1987, 1993). Several empirical studies have shown that organizational justice influences the behavior of employees at work. For example, the meta-analyses of Cohen and Spector (2001), Colquitt et al. (2001), and Konovsky (2000) underlined that the perception of procedural justice increases job satisfaction, confidence toward managers, organizational commitment, productivity, and organizational citizenship behaviors. If we keep to the definition of autonomous motivation, the concepts of job satisfaction, trust, affective commitment, and organizational citizenship behaviors seem very close to the characteristics of autonomous motivation. This leads us to pursue our enquiry: are employees with high perceptions of fairness and justice motivated by autonomous or controlled motivation? How does the nature of motivation relate to fairness and justice? Is the perception of justice truly necessary in order to increase autonomous motivation?

First it seems important to underline that there are very few studies that have examined the effects of organizational justice on intrinsic and/or autonomous motivation (Deci, Reis, Johnston & Smith, 1977; Folger, Rosenfeld, & Hays, 1978; Gagné, Bérubé, & Donia, 2007; Kuvaas, 2006; Tremblay, Senécal, & Rinfret, 2001). The first studies carried out on this subject by Deci et al. (1977) suggested that as far as compensation goes, when employees perceive unfairness, they feel less satisfied and make less effort in their work. Tremblay et al. (2001) also highlighted the contributions of SDT and organizational justice (Bies & Moag, 1986) in a study undertaken with 611 civil servants in Quebec. Their results reveal that the perception of organizational justice has a positive influence on intrinsic motivation at work. A study carried out by Kuvaas (2006) in a Norwegian multinational company also showed that perceptions of justice can affect the satisfaction of autonomous needs and feelings of competence. Other relatively more recent results by Gagné et al. (2007) over a sample of 167 Canadian employees revealed that different forms of justice are positively and significantly correlated with autonomous motivation. These conclusions lead us to suppose that perceptions of organizational justice play an essential role in the relationship between compensation and autonomous motivation.

Compensation and Work Motivation: The Convergence of the Perspectives of Psychology and Economics

Recent research in economics undertaken using the contributions of SDT opens up new theoretical perspectives that could influence companies' compensation policies and human resources management. These studies in economics recognize the crowding-out effect that compensation can create toward intrinsic motivation at work (Baron & Kreps, 1999; Bénabou & Tirole, 2002, 2003; Fehr & Gächter, 2002; Frey & Goette, 1999; Frey & Osterloh, 2005; Gneezy & Rustichini, 2000; Kreps, 1997; Weibel, Rost, & Osterloh, 2007). One of the hypotheses that we can extract from this perspective is that a compensation plan should be designed to avoid employees feeling that they are being controlled. Such a compensation plan should respect the needs of individuals to feel autonomous in their choices, their decisions, and their commitment at work. A compensation plan based on objectives that are the result of consultation between subordinate and superior, or a mechanism of skills-based pay would in our view have the capacity to satisfy this condition. Another hypothesis that could result from this perspective is that a compensation plan should be managed as a tool for recognizing past achievements or performance. A bonus or merit-based pay increase not connected to a specific goal but recognizing a set of contributions over a given period would have the sought-after motivational power. In this particular case, it would be possible to develop pay that is not contingent on performance goals (Deci, 1972; Suvurov & Van de Ven, 2006).

The perspective of a new paradigm based on motivation through compensation that is compatible with SDT could be developed in the light of the convergence of different theoretical perspectives from several disciplines. However, if a number of theories have already converged to support coherent and pertinent propositions concerning the relationship between compensation and motivation, this still remains a work in progress.

THE EFFECT OF COMPENSATION BASED ON THE CONTROL OF INDIVIDUAL PERFORMANCE

SDT demonstrates that resorting to external rewards in exchange for increased performance can, under some conditions, weaken intrinsic motivation. This hypothesis supposes that intrinsic and/or autonomous motivation can decrease after a programme of reinforcement based on reward. Thenceforth, incentive rewards might demotivate the individual if he or she perceives such rewards as a means of controlling his or her activity (Deci et al., 1999). In other words, extrinsic gratifications may erode the intrinsic interest for the job; they may engender a feeling of being controlled

and a reduction of autonomy. The different forms of incentive pay based on performance (bonuses, bonuses for results, objectives, and so forth) are so many means of compensation designed to control behavior (Gerhart, 2000; Gerhart & Rynes, 2003; Milkovich & Newman, 2008; Rynes et al., 2005; Werner & Ward, 2004). These forms of reward, known by certain economists as "ex ante rewards," may produce not only a feeling of being controlled but may also be interpreted by the agent as being characteristic of tasks that are boring and devoid of interest (Bénabou & Tirole, 2003). Bénabou and Tirole (2003) explain this hypothesis by the fact that the introduction of incentives ex ante will be perceived as a means of manipulation and control.

The work of other economists Frey, 1993; Frey & Osterloh, 2005; Weibel et al., 2007 that combine the theoretical perspectives of SDT and agency theory (Jensen & Meckling, 1976) also revealed that the effect of incentive rewards, as supposed in agency theory, result in a crowding-out effect that runs against intrinsic motivation. This hypothesis had already been advanced by studies in cognitive evaluation theory (Deci, 1975; Deci & Ryan, 1985). More recent work has also proposed that not only may these performance-contingent rewards negatively affect autonomy, but may also change the locus of causality from internal to external (Gagné & Deci, 2005). In this situation, instead of making choices freely and feeling unconstrained by their environment, individuals would see their decisions as influenced or even determined by a set of constraints, such as objectives, rewards, or sanctions. Thus, a high level of performance-contingent pay, may well contribute to a significant reduction in intrinsic motivation that in turn may have a negative effect on performance (Weibel et al., 2007). This theoretical perspective raises questions about the widely held belief that money is an efficient and even a necessary means of motivation. It refutes the view of "conditioned behaviour" supported by the behaviorists who put forward that any type of activity would be more easily achieved if it were rewarded.

In conclusion, the literature offers some convergent analyses between the theories of self-determination in psychology and incentive in economics. The literature thus supports the fact that wage increases and bonuses based on previously fixed objectives are contrary to the development of intrinsic and/or autonomous motivation, with all the potentially negative consequences on well-being and performance at work. This proposition runs against the dominant paradigm that, on the contrary, supports the qualities of these compensation plans known as merit pay (Heneman, 1992).

THE EFFECT OF COMPENSATION BASED ON CONTROLLING GROUP PERFORMANCE

We suggested that compensation can act on forms of autonomous motivation, particularly identified regulation and integrated regulation. For this, the compensation must be able to act as a lever on competence needs, autonomous needs, and relatedness needs. If we look more closely at relatedness needs, we might expect a positive link between group compensation and autonomous motivation (Gagné & Forest, 2008). Group compensation plans, such as team bonuses and gainsharing, can potentially act as levers on feelings of competence, relatedness, and autonomy at work. SDT-based research has typically used individual rewards. In principle, any form of incentive reward designed to control individual behavior should produce a feeling of being controlled and reduce autonomy. Group incentive pay allocated according to the achievement of group performance (Arthur & Jelf, 1999; Gerhart & Rynes, 2003; Magnan & Saint-Onge, 2005; Milkovich & Newman, 2008; Milkovich & Wigdor, 1991; Welbourne & Gomez-Mejia, 1995) would also be designed to control individual behavior if we keep to the propositions of SDT (Gagné and Forest, 2008).

Gagné and Forest (2008) explored this proposition. They underline that group compensation plans effectively tend to increase the feeling of relatedness, for these forms of compensation encourage a cooperative culture. However, as certain economists have underlined (Han & Shen, 2007, cited in Gagné & Forest 2008), these modes of group compensation can also be perceived as controlling. In fact, because of the free-rider effect, these forms of reward push employees to control each other. This process of within-team regulation may result in pressure, which possibly reduces the satisfaction of the autonomy need. Surveillance mechanisms are set up within the work groups themselves (also called "mutual incentives" in economics). Consequently, this may result in a reduction in autonomous motivation (Gagné & Forest, 2008). This proposition should apply mainly to group compensation based on previously fixed objectives. With a collection of research derived from game theory and its critics, the economics literature strongly agrees with this analysis (Fitzroy & Kraft, 1987; Kruse, 1992; Weitzman & Kruse, 1990).

THE EFFECT OF SKILL-BASED PAY

The literature on SDT has already revealed that extrinsic incentives may, in certain cases, increase intrinsic motivation through their positive impact on autonomous needs, competence needs, and relatedness needs (Deci & Ryan, 1985, 1999). Analyzing the works of Heider (1958) and DeCharms (1968), Deci (1971) underlined that in order to understand the effects of rewards, it was necessary to consider how individuals interpreted these rewards. Specifically, it was important to take into account the way individuals interpreted these rewards in relation to their own feelings of autonomy, competence, and relatedness. In economics, certain authors even hold that rewards cannot always be negative because any minimal bonus should be a potential incentive for the agent to make an effort.

This would be probable when individuals receive information via the incentive mechanism informing them of their own capacities and competencies (Bénabou & Tirole, 2003). In other words, rewards can incite agents to make efforts when such rewards are perceived as supplying positive information as to employee competence. In this case, rewards should produce positive effects on intrinsic motivation. Conversely, according to Bénabou and Tirole (2003), when employees are not completely sure of their capacities, intrinsic motivation diminishes with the level of reward. These authors conclude that rewards provide positive reinforcement when they convey information on the individual's competencies.

We can observe a convergence among analyses of skill-based pay. Indeed, Weinberg and Gould (2003) held that when individuals received positive information about their competencies, this increased their intrinsic motivation. On this subject, cognitive evaluation theory (Deci, 1975) underlines that any reward contains two facets: a controlling facet and an informational facet. Rewards provide individuals with information on their competence and degree of self-determination. When rewards are perceived as recognition for competence, they increase intrinsic motivation (Deci et al., 1999), probably because they fulfill a psychological need. These observations lead us to suppose that skill-based pay systems (Heneman & Gresham, 1998; Heneman, Ledford, & Gresham, 2000; Klarsfeld, 2001; Lawler, 1990; Lawler, Mohrman, & Ledford, 1998; Lee, Law, & Bobko, 1999; Murray & Gerhart, 1998; Shaw, Gupta, & Delery, 2005; Saint-Onge, Haines, & Klarsfeld, 2004; Saint-Onge & Klarsfeld, 2000) should also be more apt at satisfying basic psychological needs and thus increasing autonomous motivation.

THE EFFECT OF COMPENSATION ON CONTROLLED MOTIVATION

According to SDT, individuals who are motivated by control act under the influence of pressures and demands related to a specific performance goal, objectives, or social expectations perceived as external to themselves (Deci & Ryan, 2008). An individual's actions are controlled only by their consequences, whether theseare positive or negative. Thus pay based on individual or group performance should be a true source of external regulation (Arthur & Jelf, 1999; Gerhart & Rynes, 2003; Magnan & Saint-Onge, 2005; Milkovich & Newman, 2008). In this type of situation, individuals find themselves obliged to act according to an external demand, external to the task itself. Individual bonuses, *ex ante* rewards, bonuses on objectives, group bonuses, and team-based pay are all modes of compensation based on the control of individual or group performance. This proposition thus joins up with the dominant paradigm of motivation through incentive.

THE ECONOMIC PERSPECTIVE OF THE EFFECT OF *EX POST* COMPENSATIONS

Authors of incentive theory have often held that variable rewards would be enough to induce the desired behaviors (Gibbons, 1997; Jensen & Meckling, 1976; Laffont & Martimort, 2002; Lazear, 2000). For the authors of SDT, however, rewards and punishments are often counterproductive because they weaken intrinsic motivation and autonomous motivation (Deci, 1975; Deci et al., 1999; Deci & Ryan, 1985; Gagné & Deci, 2005). Nevertheless, as we have seen, circumstances exist where compensation can be effective. This leads us to pursue our enquiry: why should incentive rewards be appreciated and efficient in certain contexts, but apparently counterproductive in others?

Bénabou and Tirole (2003) analyzed the contribution of SDT in light of incentive theory (Jensen & Meckling, 1976; Laffont & Martimort, 2002) with the aim of reconciling these two theoretical views. Their analysis rests essentially on the control of employee behavior through the mediating effects of rewards. In this perspective they distinguish *ex ante* rewards from *ex post* rewards. As we have seen, managers choose *ex-ante* rewards to encourage efforts or performance. According to these authors, employees interpret such forms of reward partly as a sign of distrust and partly as characteristic of uninspiring and even boring tasks. Such rewards thus create a crowding-out effect on intrinsic motivation. As mentioned previously, the crowding-out hypothesis is supported in several economic studies (Baron & Kreps, 1999; Fehr & Gächter, 2002; Frey & Goette, 1999; Frey & Osterloh, 2005; Gneezy & Rustichini, 2000; Kreps, 1997; Weibel et al., 2007).

On the contrary, *ex post* rewards are not allocated according to the achievement of previously fixed objectives (Suvurov & Van de Ven, 2006). These authors define such rewards as any form of discretionary noncontractual bonus offered by a principal (top executive or manager) who possesses favorable private information about the agent's (collaborator or employee) performance.

According to them, such *expost* rewards are based on a subjective measure of the agent's performance or contribution and do not depend on previously defined performance objective. They are part of the information asymmetry caused by the agency relationship and enable the principal to provide the agent with more credible feedback. This proposition was studied by Suvurov and Van de Ven (2006). Given that the principal's (manager's) aim is to increase the agent's (employee's) performance permanently, relying on a single acknowledgement or verbal feedback would be insufficient or even ineffective. Their proposition relies on the idea that discretionary rewards can be used to ensure the credibility of the response from the principal to the agent. These *ex post* compensations are attributed in recognition of work that the hierarchy values. According to Suvurov and Van de Ven (2006) it is a more credible way to communicate with the agent and incite him or her to work harder. *Ex post* rewards are thus rewards offered by a principal who possesses favorable private information about the agent's performance. According to Bénabou and Tirole (2003) such rewards increase employees' intrinsic motivation. Indeed, according to these authors the fact of offering an *ex post* reward for achieving a difficult task will not lead the employee to consider his or her behavior as being controlled. Quite to the contrary, inasmuch as the employee does not know how to evaluate his or her performance, receiving an *ex post* reward is an indirect measure connecting the employee to his or her own performance. Bénabou and Tirole (2003) thus conclude that a frontier exists between an incentive perceived as "controlling" and thus counterproductive, and that perceived as a signal of the difficulty of the task and thus as recognition of a competence. This perceived recognition is likely to increase intrinsic motivation and more broadly, autonomous motivation.

However, studies in management hold that pay-for-performance may act positively on motivation on the condition that the individual perceives it as fair and equitable (Igalens & Roussel, 1999). This implies that there is a frontier between an *ex post* discretionary compensation that may be perceived as fair, and an *ex post* compensation that may be perceived as arbitrary and unfair. To approach this question from the basis of studies of organizational justice, we suppose that there exist mediator effects between *expost* compensation and autonomous motivation (Kuvaas, 2006; Gagné et al., 2007; Tremblay et al., 2001). The positive perception of distributive, procedural, and interactional justice should ensure effective conditions for *expost* compensation.

Conclusion

Over the past 10 years, mainstream economists have joined up with an often contested research field, that of intrinsic and extrinsic motivation. The dominant research streams in economics and organizational psychology have long shown that performance incentive systems were efficient and satisfied stakeholder expectations by reconciling the interests of the company, shareholders, and employees. This paradigm based on motivation through incentives contributed to the development of compensation mechanisms based on the control of individual performances. However, the hypotheses supported by these theories are today discussed from a new perspective. Deci and Ryan's SDT proposes a set of theoretical advances that enable researchers from different disciplinary fields to converge toward a set of hypotheses that could result in the birth of a new paradigm.

This chapter set out to explore these new research perspectives on the question of motivating employees through compensation. Theoretical propositions were developed in order to sustain new theorization for the relationship between compensation and work motivation. In fact, studies in SDT from economics and management have resulted in two general propositions that could influence organizations' human resources and compensation policies. The first proposition is that any compensation plan should be designed to avoid employees' feeling that they are being controlled. Compensation plans should respond positively to individuals' needs to feel autonomous in their choices, decisions, and commitment at work. The second general proposition is that compensation plans should be managed

as tools of recognition of past achievements or performances. A merit-based bonus or wage increase that is unconnected with a specific *exante* objective, but that recognizes a set of contributions during a given period, will have the sought-after motivational power. More specifically, a compensation plan suited to the development of feelings of autonomy, competence, and relatedness possesses this motivational virtue through the recognition of competencies deployed by the individual through his or her commitment to the organization. These propositions are combined with conditions relative to the positive perception of organizational justice, whether this is distributive, procedural, or interactional.

References

Adams, J. S. (1963). Toward an understanding of inequity. *Journal of Abnormal and Social Psychology, 67*, 422–436.

Adams, J. S. (1965). Inequity in social exchange. In L. Berkowitz (Ed.), *Advances in experimental social psychology* (pp. 267–300). New York: Academic Press.

Akerlof, G. A. (1982). The short-run demand for money: A new look at an old problem. *American Economic Association, 72*(2), 35–39.

Akerlof, G. A. (1984). Gift exchange and efficiency-wage theory: Four views. *American Economic Association, 74*(2), 79–83.

Akerlof, G., & Yellen, J. (1986). *Efficiency wage models of the labour market.* New York: Cambridge University Press.

Akerlof, G., & Yellen J. (1988). Fairness and unemployment. *American Economic Review, Papers and Proceedings, 78*, 44–49.

Akerlof G., & Yellen J. (1990). The fair wage-effort hypothesis and unemployment. *Quarterly Journal of Economics, 105*, 255–283.

Arthur, J. B., & Jelf, G. S. (1999). The effects of gainsharing on grievance rates and absenteeism over time. *Journal of Labor Research, 20*, 133–145.

Ashton, D. (1991). Agency theory and contracts of employment. In D. Ashton, T. Hopper, & R. W. Scapens (Eds.), *Issues in management accounting* (pp. 106–125). New York: Prentice-Hall.

Baron, J. N., & Kreps, D. M. (1999). *Strategic human resources: Frameworks for general managers.* New York: John Wiley and Sons, Inc.

Bénabou, R., & Tirole, J. (2002). Self-confidence and personal motivation. *Quarterly Journal of Economics, 117*, 871–915.

Bénabou, R., & Tirole, J. (2003). Intrinsic and extrinsic motivation. *Review of Economics Studies, 70*, 489–520.

Bies R. J., & Moag, J. S. (1986). Interactional justice: Communication criteria of fairness. In R. J. Lewicki, B. H. Sheppard, & M. H. Bazerman (Eds.), *Research on negotiation in organizations* (pp. 43–55). Greenwich, CT: JAI Press.

Bitler, M., Moskowitz, T., & Vissing-Jorgensen, A. (2005). Testing agency theory with entrepreneur effort and wealth. *Journal of Finance, 60*, 539–576.

Brown, G. D. A., Gardner, J., Oswald, A. J., & Qian, J. (2008). Does wage rank affect employees' well being? *Industrial Relations, 47*, 355–389.

Bruce, A., Buck, T., Main, B. (2005). Top executive compensation: A view from Europe. *Journal of Management Studies, 42*, 1493–1506.

Cahuc, P., & Zylberberg, A. (1996). *Économie du travail: la formation des salaires et les déterminants du chômage*. Paris: De Boeck Université.

Cahuc, P., & Zylberberg, A. (2004). *Labour economics*. London: The MIT Press.

Cameron, J., & Pierce, W. D. (1994). Reinforcement, reward and intrinsic motivation: A meta-analysis. *Review of Educational Research, 64*, 363–423.

Clark, A., Masclet, D., & Villeval, M. C. (2006). Effort, revenu et rang: Approche expérimentale. *Revue Economique, 57*, 635–644.

Cohen, C. Y., & Spector, P. E. (2001). The role of justice in organization: A meta-analysis. *Organisational Behavior and Human Decision Processes, 86*, 278–321.

Cohn, A., Fehr, E., & Götte, L (2010). Fair wages and effort: Evidence from a field experiment. *IEW Working Paper, University of Zurich*. Retrieved from http://www.econ.uzh.ch/faculty/cohn/Discussion%20Paper%20AC.pdf.

Colquitt, J. A., Conlon, D. E., Wesson, M. J., Porter, C. O., & Ng, K. Y. (2001). Justice at the millennium: A meta-analytic review of 25 years of organisational justice research. *Journal of Applied Psychology, 86*, 425–445.

Conyon, M. J., Peck S. I., & Sadler, G (2001). Corporate tournaments and executive compensation: Evidence from the UK. *Strategic Management Journal, 22*, 805–815.

Coupé, T., Smeet, V., & Warizynski, F (2003). Incentives in economic departments: Testing tournaments? *Working paper, Department of Economics Aarhus School of Business*. Retrieved from http://www.hha.dk/nat/wper/03-25_vasfwa.pdf

DeCharms R. (1968). *Personal causation: The internal affective determinants of behavior*. New York: Academic Press.

Deci, E. L. (1971). Effects of externally mediated rewards on intrinsic motivation. *Journal of Personality and Social Psychology, 18*, 105–115.

Deci, E. L. (1972). The effects of contingent and non-contingent rewards and controls on intrinsic motivation. *Organisational Behavior and Human Performance, 8*, 217–229.

Deci, E. L. (1975). *Intrinsic motivation*. New York: Plenum.

Deci, E. L, Koestner, R., & Ryan R. M. (1999). A meta-analytic review of experiments examining the effects of extrinsic rewards on intrinsic motivation. *Psychological Bulletin, 125*, 627–668.

Deci, E. L., Reis, H. T., Johnston, E. J., & Smith, R. (1977). Toward reconciling equity theory and insufficient justification. *Personality and Social Psychology Bulletin, 3*, 224–227.

Deci, E. L, & Ryan R. M. (1985). *Intrinsic motivation and self-determination in human behavior*. New York: Plenum Press.

Deci, E. L., & Ryan, R. M. (2000). The "what" and "why" of goal pursuits: Human needs and the self-determination of behavior. *Psychological Inquiry, 11*, 227–268.

Deci, E. L., & Ryan, R. M. (2002). *Handbook of self-determination research*. New York: The University of Rochester Press.

Deci, E. L., & Ryan, R. M. (2008). Facilitating optimal motivation and psychological well-being across life's domains. *Canadian Psychology, 49*, 14–23.

Ehrenberg, R. G., & Bognanno, M. (1990). The incentive effects of tournaments revisited: Evidence from the European PGA Tour. *Industrial and Labor Relations Review, 43*, 74–88.

Eisenberger, R., & Cameron, J. (1996). Detrimental effects of rewards—Reality or myth? *American Psychologist, 51*, 1153–1166.

Eisenberger, R., Pierce, D. W., & Cameron, J. (1999). Effects of reward on intrinsic motivation-negative, neutral, and positive: Comment on Deci, Koestner, and Ryan. *Psychological Bulletin, 126*, 677–691.

Erez, M., Gopher, D., & Arazi, N. (1990). Effects of self-set goals and monetary rewards on dual task performance. *Organisational Behavior and Human Decision Processes, 47*, 247–269.

Erikson, T. (1999). Executive compensation and tournament theory: Empirical tests on Danish data. *Journal of Labor Economics, 17*, 262–280.

Fehr, E., & Gächter, S. (2002). Do incentive contracts crowd out voluntary cooperation? *Institute for Empirical Research in Economics*. Working Paper No. 34. Retrieved from http://papers.ssrn.com/sol3/papers.cfm?abstract_id=313028

Fehr, E., Gachter, S., & Kirchsteiger, G. (1997). Reciprocity as a contract enforcement device. *Econometrica, 65*, 833–860.

Fitzroy, F., & Kraft, K. (1987). Cooperation, productivity and profit sharing. *Quarterly Journal of Economics, 102*, 23–35.

Folger, R., & Konovsky M. A. (1989). Effects of procedural and distributive justice on reactions to pay raise decisions. *Academy of Management Journal, 32*, 115–130.

Folger, R., Rosenfield, D., & Hays, R. (1978). Equity and intrinsic motivation: The role of choice. *Journal of Personality and Social Psychology, 36*, 557–564.

Frey, B. S. (1993). Does monitoring increase work effort? The rivalry with trust and loyalty. *Economic Inquiry, 31*, 663–670.

Frey B. S., & Goette, L. (1999). Does pay motivate volunteers? *Institute for Empirical Research in Economics, University of Zurich*, Working Paper N° 7. Retrieved from http://www.iew.unizh.ch/wp/iewwp007.pdf

Frey, B. S., & Osterloh, M. (2005). Yes, managers should be paid like bureaucrats. *Journal of Management Inquiry, 14*, 96–111.

Gächter, S., & Falk, A. (2002). Reputation and reciprocity—consequences for the labour relation. *Scandinavian Journal of Economics, 104*, 1–27.

Gagné, M., Bérubé, N., & Donia, M. (2007). *Relationships between different forms of organisational justice and different motivational orientations*. Poster presented at the Society for Industrial and Organisational Psychology, New York, NY.

Gagné, M., & Deci, E. L. (2005). Self-determination theory and work motivation. *Journal of Organisational Behavior, 26*, 331–362.

Gagné, M., & Forest, J. (2008). The study of compensation plans through the lens of self-determination theory: Reconciling 35 years of debate. *Canadian Psychology, 49*, 225–232.

Gagné, M., & Forest, J. (2009). La motivation au travail selon la théorie de l'autodétermination. In J. Rojot, P. Roussel, and C. Vandenberghe (Eds.), *Comportement Organisationnel* (Vol. 3): Théories des organisations, motivation au travail, engagement organisationnel (pp. 215–234). Bruxelles: De Boeck.

Gerhart, B. (2000). Compensation strategy and organization performance. In S. L. Rynes and B. Gerhart (Eds.), *Compensation in organizations* (pp. 151–194). San Francicso: Jossey-Bass.

Gerhart, B., & Milkovich, G. T. (1992). Employee compensation: Research and practice. In M. D. Dunnette, & L. M. Hough (Eds.), *Handbook of industrial and organisational psychology* (Vol. 3, 2nd pp. 481–570). Palo Alto, CA: Consulting Psychologists Press.

Gerhart, B., & Rynes, S. L. (2003). *Compensation: Theory, evidence, and strategic implications*. Thousand Oaks, CA: Sage.

Gibbons, R. (1997). Incentives and careers in organizations. In D. Kreps, and K. Wallis (Eds.), *Advances in economic theory and econometrics* (Vol. II, pp. 1–37). Cambridge, UK: Cambridge University Press.

Giorgiadis, A. (2007). Efficiency wages and the economic effects of the minimum wage: Evidence from a low-wage labour market. *Centre for Economic Performance. London School of Economics.* Retrieved from http://cep.lse.ac.uk/pubs/download/dp0857.pdf

Gneezy, U. (2002). Does high wage lead to high profits? An experimental study of reciprocity using real effort. *The University of Chicago GSB. October 8, 2002,* Retrieved from http://www.chicagocdr.org/cdrpubs/pdf_index/cdr_519.pdf

Gneezy, U., & List, J. A. (2006). Putting behavioral economics to work: Testing for gift exchange in labor markets using field experiments. *Econometrica, 74,* 1365–1384.

Gneezy U., & Rustichini, A. (2000). Pay enough or don't pay at all. *Quarterly Journal of Economics, 115,* 791–810.

Gomez-Mejia, L. R., & Balkin, D. B. (1992). *Compensation, organisational strategy, and firm performance.* Cincinnati, OH: South Western Publishing Co.

Gomez-Mejia, L. R. Balkin, D. B., & Cardy, R. L. (2001). *Managing human resources. Managing Human Resources.* Englewood Cliffs, NJ: Prentice Hall.

Gomez-Mejia, L. R., & Wiseman, R. M. (2007). Does agency theory have universal relevance: A reply to Lubatkin, Lane, Collin and Very. *Journal of Organisational Behavior, 28,* 81–88.

Greenberg, J. (1987). A taxonomy of organisational justice theories. *Academy of Management Review, 12,* 9–22.

Greenberg, J. (1990). Employee theft as a reaction to underpayment inequity. *Academy of Management Journal, 32,* 174–184.

Greenberg, J. (1993). Stealing in the name of justice: Informational and interpersonal moderators of theft reactions to underpayment inequity. *Organisational Behavior and Human Decision Processes, 54,* 81–103.

Gupta, N., & Mitra, A. (1998). The value of financial incentives. *ACA Journal, Autumn, 7*(3), 58–66.

Guthrie, J. P., & Hollensbeck, E. C. (2004). Group incentives and performance: A study of spontaneous goal setting, goal choice and commitment. *Journal of Management, 30,* 263–284.

Heider, F. (1958). *The psychology of interpersonal relations.* New York: John Wiley.

Heneman, R. L. (1992). *Merit pay: Linking pay increases to performance ratings.* Reading, MA: Addison-Wesley.

Heneman, R. L., & Gresham, M. T. (1998). Linking appraisals to compensation and incentives. In J. W. Smither (Ed.), *Performance appraisal: State-of-the art methods for performance management* (pp. 496–536). San Francisco: Jossey-Bass Publishers.

Heneman, R. L., Ledford, G. E., Jr., & Gresham, M. T. (2000). The changing nature of work and its effects on compensation design and delivery. In S. Rynes & B. Gerhert (Eds.), *Compensation in organizations* (pp. 35–73). San Francisco, CA: Jossey-Bass.

Herzberg, F., Mausner, B., Peterson, R. O., & Capwell, D. F. (1957). *Job attitudes: Review of research and opinion.* Pittsburgh, PA: Psychological Service of Pittsburgh.

Herzberg, F., Mausner, B., & Snyderman, B. B. (1959). *The motivation to work.* New York: John Wiley and Son.

Hollensbeck, E. C., & Guthrie, J. P. (2000). Group pay-for-performance plans: The role of spontaneous goal setting. *Academy of Management Review, 25,* 864–872.

Igalens, J., & Roussel, P. (1999). A study of the relationships between compensation package, work motivation and job satisfaction. *Journal of Organisational Behavior, 20,* 1003–1025.

Jensen, M. C., & Meckling, W. H. (1976). Theory of the firm: managerial behavior, agency costs, and ownership structure. *Journal of Financial Economics, 3,* 305–360.

Kanfer, R. (1990). Motivation theory and industrial and organisational psychology. In M. D. Dunnette and L. M. Hough (Eds.), *Handbook of industrial and organisational psychology* (Vol. 1, p. 75–170). Palo Alto, CA: Consulting Psychologists Press.

Kaplan, R. S. (1984). The evolution of management accounting. *The Accounting Review, 59,* 390–418.

Kaufman, R. T. (1984). On wage stickiness in Britain's competitive sector. *British Journal of Industrial Relations, 22,* 101–112.

Klarsfeld, A. (2001). Peut-on rémunérer explicitement les compétences? *Comportamento Organizacional et Gestao, 7,* 319–334.

Knight, D., Durham, C. C., & Locke, E. A. (2001). The relationship of team goals, incentives, and efficacy to strategic risk, tactical implementation, and performance. *Academy of Management Journal, 44,* 326–338.

Knoeber, C. R., & Thurman, W. N. (1994). Testing the theory of tournaments: An empirical analysis of broiler production. *Journal of Labor Economics, 12,* 155–179.

Kohn, A. (1993). *Punished by rewards.* Boston: Houghton Mifflin.

Konovsky, M. A. (2000). Understanding procedural justice and its impact on business organizations. *Journal of Management, 26,* 489–511.

Kreps, D. M. (1997). Intrinsic motivation and extrinsic incentives. *The American Economic Review, 87,* 359–364.

Kruse, D. (1992). Profit sharing and productivity: Microeconomic evidence from the United States. *Economic Journal, 102,* 24–37.

Kuvaas, B. (2006). Work performance and affective commitment, and work motivation: The roles of pay administration and pay level. *Journal of Organisational Behavior, 27,* 365–385.

Laffont, J.-J., & Martimort, D. (2002). *The theory of incentives: The principal-agent model.* Princeton, NJ: Princeton University Press.

Laguardia, J. G., & Ryan, R. M. (2000). Buts personnels, besoins psychologiques fondamentaux, et bien-être: théorie de l'autodétermination et applications. *Revue Québécoise de Psychologie, 21,* 283–306.

Lawler E. E. (1971). *Pay and organisational effectiveness: A psychological view.* New York: MacGraw-Hill.

Lawler, E. E. (1981). *Pay and organization development.* Reading, MA: Addison-Wesley.

Lawler, E. E. (1990). *Strategic pay: Aligning organisational strategies and pay systems.* San Francisco: Jossey Bass.

Lawler, E. E., Mohrman, S. A., & Ledford, G. E., Jr. (1998). *Strategies for high performance organizations.* San Francisco: Jossey-Bass.

Lazear, E. P. (2000). Performance, pay and productivity. *American Economic Review, 90,* 1346–1361.

Lazear, E. P. (2004). Salaire à la performance: incitation ou sélection? *Economie et prévision, 164,* 17–25.

Lazear, E., & Oyer, P. (2004). The structure of wages and internal mobility. *American Economic Review, 94,* 212–216.

Lazear, E. P., & Rosen, S. (1981). Rank-order tournaments as optimum labor contracts. *Journal of Political Economics, 89,* 841–864.

Lee, C., Law, K. S., & Bobko, P. (1999). The importance of justice perceptions on pay effectiveness: A two-year study of a skill-based pay plan. *Journal of Management, 25,* 851–873.

Lee, T. W., Locke, E. A., & Phan, S. H. (1997). Explaining the assigned goal-incentive interaction: The role of self-efficacy and personal goals. *Journal of Management, 23,* 541–559.

Lewin, K. (1938). *The conceptual representation and the measurement of psychological forces. Contributions to psychological theory.* Durham: Duke University Press.

Locke, E. A. (1968). Toward a theory of task motivation and incentives. *Organisational Behavior and Human Performance, 3,* 157–189.

Locke, E. A. (1975). Personnel attitudes and motivation. *Annual Review of Psychology, 26,* 457–480.

Locke, E. A. (1997). The motivation to work: What we know. *Advances in Motivation and Achievement, 10,* 375–412.

Locke, E. A., & Latham, G. (1984). *Goal setting, a motivational technique that works!* Englewood-Cliffs, NJ: Prentice-Hall.

Locke, E. A., Shaw, K. N., Saari, L. M., & Latham, G. P. (1981). Goal setting and task performance: 1969-1980. *Psychological Bulletin, 90,* 125–152.

Lubatkin, M., Lane, P. J., Collin, S., & Very, P. (2006). An embeddedness framing of governance and opportunism: Towards a cross-nationally accommodating theory of agency. *Journal of Organisational Behavior, 28,* 43–58.

MacDonald, I. M., & Solow, R. M. (1981). Wage bargaining and employment. *American Economic Review, 71,* 896–908.

Magnan, M., & Saint-Onge, S. (2005). The impact of profit sharing on the performance of financial services. *Journal of Management Studies, 42,* 4761–4791.

Mauss, M. (1923–1924). Essai sur le don. Forme et raison de l'échange dans les sociétés primitives. *L'Année Sociologique, Seconde Série, 1923-1924.*

McLaughlin, K. (1988). Aspects of tournaments models: A survey. *Journal of Labor Economics, 15,* 403–430.

Milkovich, G. T., & Newman, J. M. (2008). *Compensation* (9th ed). New York: McGraw-Hill Ryerson.

Milkovich, G. T., & Wigdor, A. K. (1991). *Pay for performance.* Washington National Academic Press.

Mitchell, T. R. (1974). Expectancy models of job satisfaction, methodological, and empirical appraisal. *Psychological Bulletin, 81,* 1053–1077.

Murray B., & Gerhart B. (1998). An Empirical Analysis of a Skill-Based Pay Program and Plant performance Outcomes. *Academy of Management Journal, 41,* 68–78.

Nadler, D. A., & Lawler, E. (1977). Motivation: A diagnostic approach. In J. R. Hackman, E. Lawler, and L. W. Porter (Eds.), *Perspectives on behavior in organizations* (pp. 26–38). New York: McGraw-Hill.

Peak, H. (1955). Attitude and motivation. In M. R. Jones (Ed.), *Nebraska symposium on motivation* (pp. 149–188). Lincoln, NE: University of Nebraska Press.

Pinder, C. C. (1984). *Work motivation/theory, issues, and applications.* Glenview, ILScott, Foresman.

Porter, L. W., & Lawler, E. E. (1968). *Managerial attitudes and performance.* Home-Wood, I11: Richard D. Irwin.

Raposo, I., & Menezes, T. (2011). Wage differentials by firm size: The efficiency wage test in a developing country. *ERSA conference papers.* Retrieved from http://www-sre.wu.ac.at/ersa/ersaconfs/ersa11/e110830aFinal01465.pdf

Riedel, J., Nebeker, D., & Cooper, B. (1988). The influence of monetary incentives on goal choice, goal commitment,

and task performance. *Organisational Behavior and Human Decision Processes, 42,* 155–180.

Rotter, J. B. (1955). *The role of the psychological situation in determining the direction of human behavior.* In M. R. Jones (Ed.), *Nebraska symposium on motivation* (pp. 245–268). Lincoln, NE: University of Nebraska Press.

Ryan, E. D. (1980). Attribution, intrinsic motivation, and athletics: A replication and extension. In C. H. Nadeau, W. R. Halliwell, K. M. Newell, and G. C. Roberts (Eds.), *Psychology of motor behavior and sport-1979* (pp. 19–26). Champaign, IL: Human Kinetics Press.

Ryan, R. M. (1993). Agency and organization: Intrinsic motivation, autonomy and the self in psychological development. In J. Jacobs (Ed.), *Nebraska symposium on motivation: Developmental perspectives on motivation* (Vol. 40, pp. 1–56). Lincoln, NE: University Of Nebraska Press.

Ryan, R. M., & Deci, E. L. (2000). Self-determination theory and the facilitation of intrinsic motivation, social development, and well-being. *American Psychologist, 55,* 68–78.

Ryan, R. M., & Deci, E. L. (2008). Self-determination theory and the role of basic psychological needs in personality and the organization of behavior. In O. P. John, R. W. Robbins, & L. A. Pervin (Eds.), *Handbook of personality: Theory and research* (pp. 654–678). New York: The Guilford Press.

Rynes, S., Gerhart, B., & Parks, L. (2005). Performance evaluation and pay for performance. *Annual Review of Psychology, 56,* 571–600.

Saint-Onge, S., Haines, V., & Klarsfeld, A. (2004). La rémunération basée sur les compétences: Déterminants et incidences, *Relations Industrielles, 59,* 651–680.

Saint-Onge, S., & Klarsfeld, A. (2000). La rémunération des compétences: théorie et pratique. In J. M. Peretti, and P. Roussel (Eds.), *Les rémunérations: Politiques et pratiques pour les années 2000* (pp. 65–80). Paris (France): Vuibert.

Saint-Onge, S., & Thériault, R. (2006). *Gestion de la rémunération: Théorie et pratique,* Montréal: Gaëtan Morin éditeur.

Salancik, G. R. (1975). Interaction effects of performance and money on self-perception of intrinsic motivation. *Organisational Behavior and Human Performance, 13,* 339–351.

Scarpello, V., & Jones, F. F. (1996). Why justice matters in compensation decision making. *Journal of Organisational Behavior, 17,* 285–299.

Scott, W. E., Jr. (1975). The effects of extrinsic rewards on "intrinsic motivation": A critique. *Organisational Behavior and Human Performance, 15,* 117–129.

Shaw, J. C., Wild, R. E., & Colquitt, J. A. (2003). To justify or excuse? A meta-analysis of the effects of explanations. *Journal of Applied Psychology, 88,* 444–458.

Shaw, J. D., Gupta, N., & Delery, J. E. (2005). Alternative conceptualizations of the relationship between voluntary turnover and organisational performance. *Academy of Management Journal, 48,* 50–68.

Sheldon, K. M., Turban, D. B., Brown, K. G., Barrick, M. R., & Judge, T. A. (2003). Applying self-determination theory to organisational research. In J. J. Martocchio, and G. R. Ferris (Eds.), *Research in personnel and human resources management* (pp. 357–393). Elsevier Ltd. Thousand Oaks, CA: JAI Press.

Simon, H. A. (1957). The compensation of executives. *Sociometry, 20,* 32–35.

Skarlicki, D. P., & Folger, R. (1997). Retaliation in the workplace: The role of distributive, procedural and interactional justice. *Journal of Applied Psychology, 82,* 434–443.

Solow, R. (1979). Another possible source of wage stickiness. *Journal of Macroeconomics, 1*, 79–82.

Staw, B. M. (1977). Motivation in organizations: Toward synthesis and redirection. In B. M. Staw, and G. R. Salancik (Eds.), *New directions in organisational behavior* (pp. 55–95). Chicago: St. Clair Press.

Suvurov, A., & Van de Ven, J. (2006). Discretionary bonus as a feedback mechanism. Working paper w0088, *Center for Economic and Financial Research (CEFIR)*. Retrieved from http://www1.fee.uva.nl/pp/bin/574fulltext.pdf

Tirole, J. (2008). Motivation intrinsèque, intentions et normes sociales. Revue Economique, Rubrique conférences des congrès de l'AFSE—Association Française de Science Economique—Paris Sorbonne.

Tolman, E. C. (1959). Principles of purposive behavior. In S. Koch (Ed.), *Psychology: A study of a science* (Vol. 2, pp. 92–157). New York: McGraw-Hill.

Tremblay, E., Senécal, C., & Rinfret, N. (2001). Survivre à la décroissance de son organisation: Une question de justice organisationnelle et de motivation. *Psychologie du Travail et des Organisations, 7*, 127–147.

Tremblay, M., & Roussel, P. (2001). Modelling the role of organisational justice: Effects on satisfaction and unionization propensity of Canadian managers. *International Journal of Human Resource Management, 12*, 717–737.

Vallerand, R. J. (1997). Toward a hierarchical model of intrinsic and extrinsic motivation. In M. P. Zanna (Ed.), *Advances in experimental social psychology* (pp. 271–360). San Diego, CA: Academic Press.

Vallerand, R. J., & Losier, G. F. (1999). An integrative analysis of intrinsic and extrinsic motivation in sport. *Journal of Applied Sport Psychology, 11*, 142–169.

Van den Broeck, A., Vansteenkiste, M., De Witte, H., Soenens, B., & Lens, W. (2009). Capturing autonomy, competence, and relatedness at work: Construction and initial validation of the Work-Related Basic Need Satisfaction Scale. *Journal of Occupational and Organisational Psychology, 83*, 981–1002.

Vroom, V. H. (1964). *Work and motivation*. New York, John Wiley.

Wadhwani, S., & Wall, M. (1990). The effects of profit-sharing on employment, wages, stock returns and productivity: Evidence from UK micro data. *The Economic Journal, 100*, 1–17.

Weibel, A., Rost, K., & Osterloh, M. (2007). *Crowding-out of intrinsic motivation: Opening the black box*. Unpublished manuscript, IOU Institute for Organisational and Administrative Science, University of Zurich. Retrieved from http://www.isnie.org/assets/files/papers2007/rost.pdf

Weinberg, R., & Gould, D. (2003). *Foundations of sport and exercise psychology*. Champaign, IL. Human Kinetics Press.

Weitzman, A., & Kruse, D. (1990). Profit sharing and productivity. In A. Blinder (Ed.), *Paying for productivity: A look at the evidence* (pp. 95–140). Washington, DC: Brookings Institute.

Welbourne, T. M., & Gomez-Mejia, L. (1995). Gainsharing: A critical review and a future research agenda. *Journal of Management, 21*, 559–609.

Werner, S., & Ward, S. G. (2004). Recent compensation research: An eclectic review. *Human Resource Management Review, 14*, 201–227.

Wright, P. M. (1989). Test of the mediating role of goals in the incentive-performance relationship. *Journal of Applied Psychology, 74*, 699–705.

Wright, P. M. (1992). An examination of the relationships among monetary incentives, goal level, goal commitment, and performance. *Journal of Management, 18*, 677–695.

CHAPTER
13

Self-Determination Theory and Workplace Training and Development

Anders Dysvik *and* Bård Kuvaas

Abstract

This chapter contributes to the emerging field of self-determination theory (SDT) research in the domain of work by reviewing current studies relating workplace training and development (TAD) and SDT and suggesting possible avenues for future research. First, we briefly present the development of research on TAD and underpin why theories of work motivation have become increasingly relevant for understanding the impact of TAD on employee outcomes. Next, we present SDT within the context of training and development and then elaborate on the available research findings and identify areas of particular interest for future research. Finally, with respect to practical implications, we provide specific advice for organizations and managers interested in developing their training and development practices and aligning them more fully with the recommendations of SDT.

Key Words: workplace training and development, self-determination theory, employee outcomes, transfer of training, training effectiveness

Employee training and development (TAD), a systematic approach to learning and development to improve individual, team, and organizational effectiveness (Kraiger & Ford, 2007, p. 281), is one of the most widespread human resource (HR) practices (Boselie, Dietz, & Boon, 2005). In 2008, companies in the United States alone spent an estimated $134 billion on TAD (Noe, Tews, & McConnell Dachner, 2010). TAD programs now range in terms of content and scope from basic skill acquisition programs to more complex contents, such as diversity training and leadership development (Kraiger & Ford, 2007).

The literature on TAD is substantial and supportive of several of beneficial outcomes following training participation, including individual knowledge and skill acquisition (Arthur, Bennett, Edens, & Bell, 2003; Collins & Holton III, 2004; Colquitt, LePine, & Noe, 2000), increased individual performance (Hall, 1996), and organizational

productivity and performance (Jacobs & Washington, 2003; Maurer, Weiss, & Barbeite, 2003; Tharenou, Saks, & Moore, 2007). In light of the vast amount of research on TAD, a lot is already known. This is fortunate for practitioners who rely on an evidence-based approach (Briner & Rousseau, 2011), but challenging for researchers who aim to make novel contributions to the field. In that respect, this chapter makes a contribution to the field of TAD, and the emerging field of self-determination theory (SDT) research in the domain of work, by reviewing TAD research using SDT as a theoretical framework. To help clarify and structure the content, the chapter is divided into different sections. First, we briefly present the development of TAD from training to learning, and underpin why theories of work motivation have become increasingly relevant for understanding how TAD impacts employee attitudes, motivation, and behaviors. Next, we present SDT within the context of TAD research and argue why SDT is a particularly suited framework for understanding and integrating empirical research on TAD. In this section, we also point to avenues for future research linking SDT and TAD. Finally, we provide specific advice for organizations and managers interested in improving their TAD practices by aligning these with the recommendations offered by SDT.

From Training to Learning

Historically, TAD researchers focused dominantly on antecedents for and outcomes from specific TAD activities (e.g., needs assessment, training objectives, evaluation criteria, and training transfer) through the lens of the traditional instructional design model (Gagné, Briggs, & Wager, 1992). However, as recently noted by Noe et al. (2010), although this string of research has unveiled important aspects of training interventions, it is predominantly technical and instructor-focused. More importantly, the employees or trainees have typically held passive roles. In the last decades, the nature of work has changed in that jobs are more cognitively based, work outcomes more complex and diffuse, and both research and practice concerning the process of training and learning at work have consequently shifted from supervisors and training professionals to the employees' themselves (Kraiger & Ford, 2007). Accordingly, to grasp more fully what actually goes on during training, we need to consider the more active role of employees during training (Bell & Kozlowski, 2008). In addition, we need to integrate training into the wider equation of work because events prior to, during, and after training most likely influence the outcomes of training interventions (Blume, Ford, Baldwin, & Huang, 2010). Finally, whereas early research on the relationship between training and employee knowledge, skills, and performance reported strong direct effects (Tyler, 1969), later research that took the employees more into account suggested a far more complex relationship and employee outcomes. For instance, we now know that the direct relationship between trainee reactions and work performance is marginal. In a meta-analysis by Colquitt et al. (2000), the estimated correlation between training reactions and work performance was .04. This finding, along with those of others (e.g., Arthur et al., 2003), suggests that the impact of training depends on several factors, including those of motivational origin.

Motivation in the context of training has traditionally been conceptualized as training motivation, formally defined as the direction, intensity, and persistence of learning-directed behavior in training contexts (Colquitt et al., 2000). Whereas training motivation is clearly important, such a conceptualization of motivation falls short of incorporating motivation to *use* learning to improve performance in the wider equation of work. In addition, it ignores broader potential implications of TAD, such as intrinsic and prosocial motivation stemming from the perception of being invested in, and that work itself may become more meaningful and interesting when individuals' knowledge and skills increase. Addressing these shortcomings, Noe et al. (2010) recently argued that psychological engagement theory could provide "a valuable new perspective for expanding our understanding by building a stronger theory of learner motivation and workplace learning." (p. 282). To a large extent we agree, because psychological engagement theory considers the more active role of employees when at work, and consequently, attending TAD initiatives. Still, the direction, intensity, and persistence among trainees may stem from different motivational sources. And, because psychological engagement represents a relatively unitary concept of work motivation, it fails to capture extrinsic or controlling motivational sources for engaging in learning behaviors at work.

George (2011) recently argued that the work engagement literature needs to also consider the extrinsic element of work motivation to a greater extent, rather than solely focusing on how work engagement provides intrinsic rewards for employees. Because SDT acknowledges and incorporates different forms of autonomous and controlled motivation within a unifying framework, we believe that SDT is well suited to increase the understanding of how TAD influences employee outcomes. By specifying autonomous and controlled forms of extrinsic motivation, this may be the key to better understand what affects training outcomes. In the following sections, we elaborate more fully on the relevance of SDT and review established findings from the TAD literature within the SDT framework.

The Relevance of SDT for Workplace TAD

Recent reviews of the training literature have pointed to the need for more research on how motivation affects willingness to learn and how perceptions of training relevancy affect motivation (e.g., Chen & Klimoski, 2007; Kraiger & Ford, 2007). In line with a more active perspective of employees participating in TAD

(Bell & Kozlowski, 2008), SDT rests on the premise that all individuals are inherently motivated to develop their interests and skills, to connect and to contribute to other people, and to develop toward enabling their fullest potential (Sheldon, Turban, Brown, Barrick, & Judge, 2003). SDT makes a general distinction between amotivation, or a lack of intention to act, and motivation that is intentional (Gagné & Deci, 2005).

SDT distinguishes between autonomous and controlled motivation (Deci & Ryan, 2000). The former describes acting based on perceived volition and choice, and overlaps considerably with the conceptualization of psychological engagement (Meyer & Gagné, 2008). Furthermore, and in contrast to the confusion about whether the opposite of psychological engagement is lack of engagement, disengagement, or strain (Cooper, Dewe, & O'Driscoll, 2001; Crawford, LePine, & Rich, 2010; Meyer & Gagné, 2008), SDT describes more clearly acting based on perceived pressure, and having to engage in actions as controlled motivation, and recognizes that individuals may also be alienated and mechanized, or passive and disaffected (Deci & Ryan, 2008). Controlled motivation therefore reflects a desire to gain rewards or avoid punishment, or avoid feelings of guilt. Autonomous motivation is regarded to be of higher quality and lead to more favorable outcomes than controlled motivation (Gagné & Deci, 2005). Autonomous motivation can be more external, reflecting the attainment of a valued personal goal, expressing one's sense of self, or it can be fully internal in the form of intrinsic motivation (Deci & Ryan, 2000). Individuals who are intrinsically motivated work on tasks because they find them enjoyable and interesting, and that participation is its own reward (Deci, Connell, & Ryan, 1989). This state reflects an inherent tendency to seek out novelty and challenges, to extend and exercise one's capacities, to explore, and to learn (Ryan & Deci, 2000). With respect to TAD, employees' training motivation may be both autonomous (i.e., the training content is experienced as interesting in itself, or important and of significance to learn) and more controlled (i.e., the rationale for participating in training is more based on acquiring a formal diploma, getting a pay raise, or other external reasons). Even so, with a lack of needs assessment and concern for the individual needs of the employees, TAD may also lead to amotivation and/or resignation. Accordingly, rather than treating training motivation as a unitary construct, through the lens of SDT, training motivation may be separated along three different dimensions with different implications for training outcomes.

In sum, SDT represents a relevant theoretical framework for future TAD research that focuses on the more active role of the learner *and* acknowledges the influence of motivation from sources that are more autonomous or more controlling.

The Importance of Trainee's Reactions to and Perceptions of TAD

There is emerging consensus that trainee reactions are important for our understanding of the relationship between TAD and employee outcomes. For instance, Sitzmann, Brown, Casper, Ely, and Zimmerman (2008) showed in their meta-analysis that trainee reactions were positively associated with affective learning outcomes, declarative knowledge, and procedural knowledge. Dysvik and Kuvaas found that it is the *perception* of having TAD opportunities (Dysvik & Kuvaas, 2008) and the *perception* of being invested in, and having developmental opportunities (Kuvaas & Dysvik, 2009a, 2009b, 2010b, 2011) that are associated with higher levels of task performance, organizational citizenship behavior, and lower levels of turnover intention. Similarly, positive associations between being invested in and having developmental opportunities, and both affective commitment and job satisfaction, have also been established (Lee & Bruvold, 2003). In a cross-level study, Nishii, Lepak, and Schneider (2008) theorized that employees' attributions for *why* the HR practices exist are crucial. In order for HR practices to accentuate individual and in turn organizational performance, they should be experienced as commitment-focused rather than control-focused. In support of their hypotheses, Nishii et al. (2008) found that only commitment-focused HR practices were associated with employees' commitment, satisfaction, unit-level helping behaviors, and unit-level customer satisfaction. Because employee perceptions of HR practices may be significantly different from those of management and/or those responsible for HR in the organization (Edgar & Geare, 2005; Khilji & Wang, 2006), it is the employees who should be asked how they experience TAD to understand its impact on employees, and in turn, organizational outcomes (Arthur & Boyles, 2007). As discussed next, for TAD to satisfy basic psychological needs, the mere presence of TAD is not sufficient; the employees need to perceive TAD as more relevant and satisfying.

TAD and Basic Need Satisfaction

With respect to the relationship between training and basic need satisfaction, having training opportunities should nurture the needs for autonomy, relatedness, and competence. More specifically, when employees experience training as an opportunity, or when they are convinced of the relevance of training, this should satisfy the need for autonomy by increasing feelings of internal control (Dysvik & Kuvaas, 2008; Suazo, Martínez, & Sandoval, 2009). The need for competence could be satisfied when individuals are encouraged to seek challenges relative to their capacities and to attempt persistent maintenance of skills (Dysvik & Kuvaas, 2008; Stone, Deci, & Ryan, 2009). Furthermore, provided that TAD opportunities signal that employees are valued, and that their employer is willing to commit to a long-term relationship with them, TAD opportunities should satisfy the need for relatedness (Dysvik & Kuvaas, 2008; Suazo et al., 2009).

With respect to empirical evidence, available research remains limited. Among the few studies conducted, Marescaux, De Winne, and Sels (2010) found positive associations between perceived training alignment and the needs for autonomy and relatedness, but not for the need for competence. Marescaux et al. (2010) suggested that this contraintuitive result may result from training alignment could be seen as a sign of incompetence, thus thwarting their competence satisfaction. An alternative but related explanation is restrictions of range because most respondents reported high levels of satisfaction of the need for competence and therefore less need for training. Accordingly, when designing TAD opportunities, careful attention to training content and level of difficulty versus individual competence levels seems warranted. In one of our recent studies, we found that the need for competence is only related to intrinsic motivation under the condition of high levels of the need for autonomy, so that workers are intrinsically motivated only when they experienced both satisfaction of the needs for autonomy and competence (Dysvik, Kuvaas, & Gagné, in press). Consequently, and as noted by Deci and Ryan (2000, p. 235), "Perceived competence tends to enhance intrinsic motivation, although people must feel responsible for the competent performance in order for perceived competence to have positive effects on intrinsic motivation." Given the apparent lack of studies on

TAD and need satisfaction in the domain of work, future research attention is warranted to increase knowledge of the role of the need for competence in TAD activities.

In addition, future research attention is needed to unveil conditions under which training opportunities not only subserve the needs for autonomy and relatedness, but also the need for competence. For instance, recent research on developmental support suggests that the impact of developmental initiatives on employee outcomes is contingent on perceived career opportunities. More specifically, development support positively relates to job performance, but only when perceived career opportunity within the organization is high (Kraimer, Seibert, Wayne, Liden, & Bravo, 2011). In addition, recent research on perceived competence mobilization (Lai & Kapstad, 2009) underpins the importance of providing employees with opportunities to use their previously and newly acquired competencies in meaningful and challenging ways. This line of research suggests that there needs to be a match between job requirements and perceived competencies as well as perceived competence mobilization when accepting the job. When such match is lacking, this may result in less intrinsically motivated employees with lower levels of affective organizational commitment and higher turnover intentions (Lai, 2011). As such, both perceived career opportunities and perceived competence mobilization represent interesting frameworks for providing increased insights into the relationship between TAD and the need for competence.

Training and Autonomous Versus Controlled Motivation

Providing TAD may create motivational effects, but which kind of motivation depends on why employees want them, and how and why they are offered (Stone et al., 2009). Like managers, trainers need to support employees' psychological needs if internalization is to take place (Gagné, 2009). If training is provided primarily as coveted external rewards, or is enforced mandatorily with less concern for the say of employees, controlled motivation is the most probable outcome. Although extrinsic rewards and higher levels of controlled motivation could increase training effort and short-term persistence, it may result in poorer training outcomes, as evidenced by longitudinal research in educational settings (Becker, McElvany, & Kortenbruck, 2010). Employees could also feel guilty for not setting aside time to participate in training when faced with other work-related expectations, which could lead to higher levels of introjected motivation. In contrast, if training is experienced as useful for employees in learning new skills, that they clearly see the meaning and purpose of the training intervention, and that training participation is based on volition, and training content is acquired through collaborating with others, then higher levels of identified motivation and/or intrinsic motivation should be expected. Higher levels of autonomous motivation should, in turn, predict higher levels of effort and persistence in training, more knowledge acquisition, higher levels of training transfer, and elevated individual performance. Finally, if employees experience a lack of available resources and/or support for applying knowledge and skills acquired through training in their everyday work setting, training could in extreme cases lead to amotivation.

So what research evidence is available? With respect to the domain of work, we found that the amount and frequency of training participation is unrelated to intrinsic motivation, but that satisfaction with training and the sufficiency of training received is strongly positively related to intrinsic motivation (Dysvik & Kuvaas, 2008). Our observations suggest that providing TAD opportunities is not enough to subserve autonomous motivation, but what matters is how training is offered and experienced by employees. In addition, the general perception of being invested in (including informal arrangements, such as mentoring programs and job rotation, in addition to training opportunities) was also strongly positively related to intrinsic motivation (Kuvaas & Dysvik, 2009a), as was the case for trainees' perceptions of trainee programs (Dysvik, Kuvaas, & Buch, 2010).

TAD may also increase employees' prosocial motivation, or wanting to do good for their organization (Batson, 1987) provided that TAD signals that the employees are important, valuable, and appreciated (Pfeffer, 1998). Within the SDT framework, prosocial motivation is regarded as a subtype of autonomous motivation: identified regulation (Gagné & Deci, 2005). Based on the norm of reciprocity (Blau, 1964; Gouldner, 1960), investing in employee development may foster a climate characterized by trust, cooperation, socioemotional attachment, and long-term orientation (e.g., Bowen & Ostroff, 2004; Collins & Smith, 2006; Shore & Barksdale, 1998; Tsui, Pearce, Porter, & Tripoli, 1997). In turn, employees respond by contributing with behaviors at work beneficial not only for themselves, but for the organization as a whole (Shore, Tetrick, Lynch, & Barksdale, 2006). We are unaware of studies that focus on the relationship between TAD and identified regulation directly in the domain of work, but expect that similar patterns as those found for prosocial and intrinsic motivation would occur. In addition, although studies indicate that a lack of support and/or resources at work for applying training content inhibits training transfer (Blume et al., 2010), there is a lack of studies investigating the mediating role of amotivation. Accordingly, future studies would benefit from investigating the associations between training reactions and the full range of motivational regulations proposed by SDT.

Autonomy-Supportive Leaders and Trainers

With respect to instructional style, Mesmer-Magnus & Viswesvaran (2010) recently meta-analyzed 159 pretraining intervention studies. They found that providing attentional advice, or information, independent of performance content, about the process or strategy that can be used to achieve an optimal learning outcome during training (Cannon-Bowers, Rhodenizer, Salas, & Bowers, 1998) was a salient pretraining influence of learning acquisition. Attentional advice supports individual learning processes through gaining trainee attention and setting appropriate expectancies, advising individuals of learning objectives, and prompting the activation of their relevant existing knowledge. This observation aligns well with a central tenet of SDT, namely providing autonomy support. Autonomy support refers to what one person says and does to enhance another's internal locus of causality, autonomy, and perceived choice during the action (Reeve, 2002). In sport psychology, studies have shown that supportive coaching styles influence athletes' motivation (Mageau & Vallerand, 2003). In the domain of education, Black and Deci (2000) showed that students who experienced autonomy-supportive organic chemistry instructors increased both their autonomous motivation toward chemistry and final grades. Studies on intervention programs designed to support autonomy were recently summarized in a meta-analysis (Su & Reeve, 2011). The results suggest that these interventions are highly effective (measured primarily in terms of self- or other-rated autonomy support). Subsequent moderator analyses revealed that the programs were more effective when focusing on multiple elements of autonomy support, specific skill-based activities, and when conducted in laboratory settings.

Clearly, there is a need for further unveiling the role of autonomy-support with respect to TAD, not only in terms of conducting training, but also with respect to needs assessment prior to training, and transfer of training following training. For instance, it could be that leaders that are perceived as autonomy-supportive are more sensitive toward identifying the individual needs of trainers. Also, such leaders should be able to facilitate training transfer among employees to a larger extent than those who are less autonomy-supportive.

Outcomes from Autonomous Versus Controlled Motivation in TAD Settings

Both proximal and distal outcomes may be expected from TAD activities. The former is often operationalized by way of declarative and procedural knowledge, skills, and affective outcomes, such as self-efficacy, (e.g., Colquitt et al., 2000). The latter may be operationalized in terms of behaviors and attitudes, such as work performance, helping behaviors, turnover intention, and knowledge sharing (e.g., Colquitt et al., 2000; Gagné, 2009; Paré & Tremblay, 2007).

With respect to proximal outcomes from autonomous versus controlled motivation in training settings, there is a paucity of studies in the domain of work using the SDT framework. A vast number of studies have been conducted applying social learning theory (Bandura, 1986). Social learning theory basically proposes that individuals tend to be motivated to perform specific tasks when they perceive they have the ability to do so, or when they feel efficacious (Bandura, 1986). Compelling evidence suggests self-efficacy is both a predictor of training motivation, and a proximal outcome of training interventions (Colquitt et al., 2000). A shortcoming of this perspective, however, is the emphasis on self-assessments of competence while being less concerned whether efficacious behaviors are autonomous versus controlled (Deci & Ryan, 2000). Given the importance of perceived autonomy and control derived from such areas as stress research (e.g., Karasek, 1979), and the compelling meta-analytic evidence pointing to the vital role of autonomy as a central predictor for a range of employee outcomes (Humphrey, Nahrgang, & Morgeson, 2007), it seems that theories attempting to relate training and employee outcomes should address the importance of autonomy more directly. Furthermore, a recent meta-analysis by Judge, Jackson, Shaw, Scott, and Rich (2007) found that self-efficacy predicted performance in jobs or tasks of low complexity, but not in those of medium or high complexity. In addition, Callahan et al. (2003) found that after controlling for the variance attributable to intrinsic motivation, the relationship between self-efficacy and performance failed to attain statistical significance. A possible explanation for this finding is that self-efficacy serves the role of antecedent to intrinsic motivation, rather than being directly related to individual outcomes (Prabhu, Sutton, & Sauser, 2008). As such, highly efficacious individuals may gradually find the tasks they master to be more interesting (Sansone & Thoman, 2005). This may in turn lead to higher levels of autonomous motivation in cases where employees' perceptions of autonomy are not thwarted (Deci & Ryan, 2000). In order to further clarify under which conditions competence perception may lead to beneficial outcomes following training, future research attention is needed.

Findings from the educational domain clearly suggest that autonomous motivation is associated with far more beneficial learning outcomes than that of controlled motivation. Research summarized by Reeve (2002) shows that autonomously motivated students thrive in educational settings compared with control-motivated students in terms of higher academic achievement, more positive emotionality, greater creativity, and higher rates of retention. These observations do not imply that students need to be intrinsically motivated at all times, but that the more internalized the extrinsic motivation in the form of identified regulation (i.e., recognizing the importance of acquiring the learning content) and/or the more intrinsically motivated, the more beneficial the outcomes, as opposed to controlled motivation. In support of this, a recent longitudinal study on reading literacy development among 740 students from 54 classes showed that the more extrinsic their reading motivation was in fourth grade, the lower their reading literacy was in sixth grade. In contrast, the more intrinsic their reading motivation was in fourth grade, the more their reading amount was, and in turn the higher their reading literacy was in sixth grade (Becker et al., 2010).

Because meta-analytic evidence suggests a positive influence of controlled motivation on simpler tasks with less inherent motivational potential (Jenkins, Mitra, Gupta, & Shaw, 1998; Weibel, Rost, & Osterloh, 2010), it may be that controlled motivation should have less detrimental consequences for similar training contents. Overall, however, we would expect autonomous motivation to be associated with more positive outcomes than controlled motivation.

With respect to the more distal outcomes of training, our research suggests that having training opportunities influences task performance, organizational citizenship behavior, and turnover intentions, which can be explained through increased intrinsic motivation (Dysvik & Kuvaas, 2008). We have found similar patterns for the mere generic experience of investments in employee development (Kuvaas & Dysvik, 2009a), and among trainees enrolled in formal trainee programs (Dysvik et al., 2010). It therefore seems that intrinsic motivation may explain why employees' reactions to TAD relate to essential outcomes at the individual level. Beyond measuring the full motivational continuum of SDT, we believe future studies should benefit from including autonomy-supportive leadership. In contemporary organizations, line managers often implement TAD activities on behalf of HR or top management. Because autonomy support has been found to be essential for training outcomes in educational and sport settings (Su & Reeve, 2011), these findings could be replicated and extended to the work domain. Finally, we encourage the pursuit of multilevel designs, because it is now established firmly at the individual level that the autonomous motivation is a predictor of in-role performance, contextual performance, and turnover intention (e.g., Kuvaas, 2006; Kuvaas & Dysvik, 2009a; Piccolo & Colquitt, 2006; Vansteenkiste et al., 2007; Zapata-Phelan, Colquitt, Scott, & Livingston, 2009). These findings could be extended to the work unit level, to investigate whether TAD could collectively accentuate performance through autonomous motivation as well.

Transfer of Training

An important subfield of TAD is that of training transfer. Training transfer is defined as the extent to which the knowledge and skills acquired in a learning setting are applied to different settings, people, and/or situations from those trained, and the extent to which changes that result from a learning experience persist over time (Blume et al., 2010). Meta-analytic evidence on training transfer demonstrates that perceptions of mastery, voluntarily participation, and a supportive work environment are among the most salient predictors for transfer intention and actual transfer (Blume et al., 2010). These observations align well with SDT in emphasizing the importance of need fulfillment and consequent motivational regulation in the workplace. There is limited research on the role of SDT in training transfer available, but Roca and Gagné (2008)

found that employees participating in e-learning training programs were more willing to continue using IT when they felt autonomous and competent, and, in turn, more intrinsically motivated. It therefore seems that need satisfaction and/or motivational regulation is a relevant theoretical framework for increasing the understanding of how and under which conditions training transfer will most likely occur. Although much research has examined relations between need satisfaction and well-being (e.g., Johnston & Finney, 2010), studies examining relations between need satisfaction and autonomous motivation in the domain of work remain relatively rare (Greguras & Diefendorff, 2009). To test the detailed propositions of SDT within a training transfer framework, studies should therefore include need satisfaction, motivational regulations, and autonomy support in order to capture the broad range of influences on training transfer.

Individual Differences

Although SDT emphasizes the more universal aspect of basic psychological needs, it also recognizes the existence of individual differences, first and foremost with respect to autonomy orientation. Autonomy is one of the most fundamental psychological needs (Sheldon, Elliot, Kim, & Kasser, 2001) and individual differences in autonomy orientation can in part explain why people react differently to external interventions, such as training. Autonomy orientation refers to a disposition to attend to environmental cues that signal personal interest and options for free choice behavior (Lee, Sheldon, & Turban, 2003). Research on autonomy orientation suggests that individuals with a strong autonomy orientation are more likely to set mastery goals for themselves (Lee et al., 2003), which in turn lead to more beneficial outcomes (Gagné & Deci, 2005). With respect to TAD in particular, Su and Reeve (2011) found stronger effects for autonomy-supportive training interventions among individuals high in autonomy orientation. This implies that individual attention is needed when tailoring TAD interventions to facilitate a conceptual change among employees with a more controlling orientation.

Second, recent studies suggest that intrinsic motivation may moderate the relationship between perceptions of TAD and outcomes. The argument for a moderating role of intrinsic motivation is found in a recent study on the relationship between person-environment fit and need satisfaction (Greguras & Diefendorff, 2009). Greguras and Diefendorff's study shows that when a match between employer and employee occurs in terms of higher levels of person-environment fit, the employees are more likely to experience need satisfaction. Furthermore, Grant (2008) suggests that inducements, such as TAD opportunities, and investment in employee development, may foster prosocial motivation, in that employees want to do good by reciprocating the favor provided. Such reciprocation, however, should be more salient when it is pleasure-based rather than pressure-based. Therefore, the combination of prosocial and intrinsic motivation should produce more beneficial outcomes than the combination of prosocial and controlled motivation. In support of Grant's propositions, we found that intrinsic motivation moderated the relationship between perceived training opportunities and helping behaviors (Dysvik & Kuvaas, 2008), and between perceptions of trainee programs and work performance (Dysvik et al., 2010).

In contrast, inducing "learning pressure" in the form of perceived training intensity, or employees' perceptions of organizational demands for, expectations toward, and frequency and duration of participation in formal and informal TAD activities may lead to outcomes other than those for training opportunities or investment in employee development. We recently found positive associations between perceived training intensity and knowledge sharing only for employees low in intrinsic motivation, whereas employees high in intrinsic motivation reported higher levels of knowledge sharing regardless of their perceptions of training intensity (Kuvaas, Buch, & Dysvik, 2012). Accordingly, the impact of inducing "learning pressure" in organizations may vary depending on employees' intrinsic motivation. Similar observations with intrinsic motivation as a moderator have been derived from studies on multiple "best-practice" HR activities (Kuvaas & Dysvik, 2010a) and job autonomy (Dysvik & Kuvaas, 2011).

We are unaware of studies investigating whether controlled motivation may moderate the relationship between TAD and individual outcomes. One suggestion for future research is to investigate whether a lack of person-environment fit and, in turn, more controlled motivation, may attenuate the impact of training for more complex training content.

Concluding Remarks and Practical Implications

In their review of the training literature, Kraiger and Ford (2007) noted that "I-O psychology's most significant contributions are most likely to come from research and theories that address issues such as how motivation affects a willingness to learn, how perceptions of training relevancy affects motivation to transfer, or how the probability of transfer is affected by individual perceptions of transfer climate" (p. 302). Throughout this chapter, we present how SDT may serve as a theory for explaining all of these important areas within TAD research. SDT research in organizational settings is growing, but our review of the literature shows that there are still gaps that need future research attention.

Perhaps equally important, what do the findings presented here mean for organizations? How should they manage and run their HR practices in general, and TAD in particular? First, the available findings point to the presence of TAD as necessary but insufficient in terms of obtaining vital employee outcomes. In order for such a relationship to occur, it seems that employees must experience satisfaction and relevance with the training provided. When experienced as more relevant and satisfactory, a positive relationship with autonomous (i.e., intrinsic) motivation is found. But in daily work life, it is important to keep in mind that autonomous and controlled motivation may emanate from other sources than from experiences with TAD. For instance, research on procedural justice (Zapata-Phelan et al., 2009), job characteristics (Gagné, Senecal, & Koestner, 1997), and transformational leadership (Piccolo & Colquitt, 2006) show how all these factors at work influence employees' intrinsic motivation. These findings point to the importance of regarding TAD as an integrated part of the wider workplace equation. In the strategic HRM literature, such alignment is referred to as internally consistent HR, and meta-analytic evidence suggest even stronger relationships between commitment-based HR and organizational performance when HR activities are aligned and internally consistent (Combs, Liu, Hall, & Ketchen, 2006).

Based on these arguments and observations, we conclude with specific advice for managers and training advocates interested in aligning their TAD activities with the available research. The first and foremost advice is to focus on providing TAD opportunities of high quality and structure as perceived by employees. Provide employees with the opportunity to train and develop at work, and work actively for employees to see the training measures as relevant and adequate for their continued development in their jobs (Dysvik & Kuvaas, 2008).

Prior to training participation, efforts should be made to align the content and delivery form to each of the individuals attending training. Clearly show the employees that they are important to the organization by investing time and resources in their personal development, through courses and in daily work through actions like mentor schemes, job rotation, and regular feedback on jobs performed. When these important aspects are considered thoroughly, this should increase the probability of improved learning processes and outcomes for employees.

Second, offer autonomy support during training by providing trainees with a meaningful rationale for why the task/lesson/way of behaving is important and relevant, establishing an interpersonal relationship that emphasizes choice and flexibility as opposed to control and pressure (Reeve, 2002). Providing information and a rationale for why the training is taking place, and helping each trainee relate the content to his or her prior knowledge and relevance for work, should not only increase the learning outcomes of employees (Mesmer-Magnus & Viswesvaran, 2010), but also perceptions of autonomy support and autonomous motivation (Black & Deci, 2000; Reeve, 2002).

Third, when implementing TAD, regard the organization's HR activities as complementary and as a whole. This means that other influences on autonomous motivation, in addition to TAD, should be aligned so that their combination may help increase the employees' perception of autonomy, competence, and relatedness. Because such alignment has been found to be beneficial for the performance of the organization (Combs et al., 2006), it seems profitable to do so. A beneficial "side-effect" is that employees will more likely thrive at work as well.

References

Arthur, J. B., & Boyles, T. (2007). Validating the human resource system structure: A levels-based strategic HRM approach. *Human Resource Management Review, 17*, 77–92.

Arthur, W., Bennett, W., Edens, P. S., & Bell, S. T. (2003). Effectiveness of training in organizations: A meta-analysis of design and evaluation features. *Journal of Applied Psychology, 88*(2), 234–245.

Bandura, A. (1986). *Social foundations of thought and action: A social cognitive theory.* Englewood Cliffs, NJ: Prentice-Hall.

Batson, C. D. (1987). Prosocial motivation: Is it ever truly altruistic? In L. Berkowitz (Ed.), *Advances in experimental social psychology* (Vol. 20, pp. 65–122). New York: Academic Press.

Becker, M., McElvany, N., & Kortenbruck, M. (2010). Intrinsic and extrinsic reading motivation as predictors of reading literacy: A longitudinal study. *Journal of Educational Psychology, 102*(4), 773–785. doi:10.1037/a0020084

Bell, B. S., & Kozlowski, S. W. J. (2008). Active learning: Effects of core training design elements on self-regulatory processes, learning and adaptability. *Journal of Applied Psychology, 93*(2), 296–316.

Black, A. E., & Deci, E. L. (2000). The effects of instructors' autonomy support and students' autonomous motivation on learning organic chemistry: A self-determination theory perspective. *Science Education, 84*(6), 740–756.

Blau, P. M. (1964). *Exchange and power in social life.* New York: Wiley.

Blume, B. D., Ford, J. K., Baldwin, T. T., & Huang, J. L. (2010). Transfer of training: A meta-analytic review. *Journal of Management, 36*(4), 1065–1105. doi:10.1177/0149206309352880

Boselie, P., Dietz, G., & Boon, C. (2005). Commonalities and contradictions in HRM and performance research. *Human Resource Management Journal, 15*(3), 67–94.

Bowen, D. E., & Ostroff, C. (2004). Understanding HRM-firm performance linkages: The role of the "strength" of the HRM system. *Academy of Management Review, 29*(2), 203–221.

Briner, R. B., & Rousseau, D. M. (2011). Evidence-based I–O Psychology: Not there yet. *Industrial and Organizational Psychology, 4*(1), 3–22. doi:10.1111/j.1754-9434.2010.01287.x

Callahan, J. S., Brownlee, A. L., Brtek, M. D., & Tosi, H. L. (2003). Examining the unique effects of multiple motivational sources on task performance. *Journal of Applied Social Psychology, 33*(12), 2515–2535.

Cannon-Bowers, J. A., Rhodenizer, L., Salas, E., & Bowers, C. (1998). A framework for understanding pre-practice conditions and their impact on learning. *Personnel Psychology, 51*, 291–320.

Chen, G., & Klimoski, R. J. (2007). Training and development of human resources at work: Is the state of our science strong? *Human Resource Management Review, 17*, 180–190.

Collins, C. J., & Smith, K. G. (2006). Knowledge exchange and combination: The role of human resource practices in the performance of high-technology firms. *Academy of Management Journal, 49*(3), 544–560.

Collins, D. B., & Holton III, E. F. (2004). The effectiveness of managerial leadership developmental programs: A meta-analysis of studies from 1982 to 2001. *Human Resource Development International, 15*(2), 217–248.

Colquitt, J. A., LePine, J. A., & Noe, R. A. (2000). Toward an integrative theory of training motivation: A meta-analytic path analysis of 20 years of research. *Journal of Applied Psychology, 85*(5), 678–707.

Combs, J., Liu, Y., Hall, A., & Ketchen, D. (2006). How much do high-performance work practices matter? A meta-analysis of their effects on organizational performance. *Personnel Psychology, 59*, 501–528.

Cooper, C. L., Dewe, P. J., & O'Driscoll, M. P. (2001). *Organizational stress: A review and critique of theory, research and applications.* Thousand Oaks, CA: Sage.

Crawford, E. R., LePine, J. A., & Rich, B. L. (2010). Linking job demands and resources to employee engagement and burnout: A theoretical extension and meta-analytic test. *Journal of Applied Psychology, 95*(5), 834–848. doi:10.1037/a0019364

Deci, E. L., Connell, J. P., & Ryan, R. M. (1989). Self-determination in a work organization. *Journal of Applied Psychology, 74*(4), 580–590. doi:10.1037/0021-9010.74.4.580

Deci, E. L., & Ryan, R. M. (2000). The "what" and "why" of goal pursuits: Human needs and the self-determination of behavior. *Psychological Inquiry*, *11*(4), 227–268. doi:10.1207/S15327965PLI1104_01

Deci, E. L., & Ryan, R. M. (2008). Facilitating optimal motivation and psychological well-being across life's domains. *Canadian Psychology*, *49*(1), 14–23. doi:10.1037/0708-5591.49.1.14

Dysvik, A., & Kuvaas, B. (2008). The relationship between perceived training opportunities, work motivation and employee outcomes. *International Journal of Training and Development*, *12*(3), 138–157. doi:10.1111/j.1468-2419.2008.00301.x

Dysvik, A., & Kuvaas, B. (2011). Intrinsic motivation as a moderator on the relationship between perceived job autonomy and work performance. *European Journal of Work and Organizational Psychology*, *20*(3), 367–387. doi:10.1080/13594321003590630

Dysvik, A., Kuvaas, B., & Buch, R. (2010). Trainee programme reactions and work performance: The moderating role of intrinsic motivation. *Human Resource Development International*, *13*(4), 409–423. doi:10.1080/13678868.2010.501962

Dysvik, A., Kuvaas, B., & Gagné, M. (in press). An exploration of the unique, synergistic, and balanced relationships between basic psychological needs and intrinsic motivation. *Journal of Applied Social Psychology*.

Edgar, F., & Geare, A. (2005). HRM practice and employee attitudes: Different measures—different results. *Personnel Review*, *34*(5), 534–549.

Gagné, M. (2009). A model of knowledge-sharing motivation. *Human Resource Management*, *48*(4), 571–589.

Gagné, M., & Deci, E. L. (2005). Self-determination theory and work motivation. *Journal of Organizational Behavior*, *26*(4), 331–362. doi:10.1002/job.322

Gagné, M., Senecal, C. B., & Koestner, R. (1997). Proximal job characteristics, feelings of empowerment, and intrinsic motivation: A multidimensional model. *Journal of Applied Social Psychology*, *27*, 1222–1240. doi:10.1111/j.1559-1816.1997.tb01803.x

Gagné, R. M., Briggs, L.-J., & Wager, W. W. (1992). *Principles of instructional design*. Fort Worth, TX: Harcourt Brace Jovanovich.

George, J. M. (2011). The wider context, costs, and benefits of work engagement. *European Journal of Work and Organizational Psychology*, *20*(1), 53–59.

Gouldner, A. W. (1960). The norm of reciprocity. *American Sociological Review*, *25*, 165–167.

Grant, A. M. (2008). Does intrinsic motivation fuel the prosocial fire? Motivational synergy in predicting persistence, performance, and productivity. *Journal of Applied Psychology*, *93*(1), 48–58.

Greguras, G. J., & Diefendorff, J. M. (2009). Different fits satisfy different needs: Linking person-environment fit to employee commitment and performance using self-determination theory. *Journal of Applied Psychology*, *94*(2), 465–477. doi:10.1037/a0014068

Hall, D. T. (1996). Protean careers of the 21st century. *Academy of Management Executive*, *10*(4), 9–16.

Humphrey, S. E., Nahrgang, J. D., & Morgeson, F. P. (2007). Integrating motivational, social and contextual work design features: A meta-analytic summary and theoretical extension of the work design literature. *Journal of Applied Psychology*, *92*(5), 1332–1356. doi:10.1037/0021-9010.92.5.1332

Jacobs, R. L., & Washington, C. (2003). Employee development and organizational performance: A review of literature and directions for future research. *Human Resource Development International*, *6*(3), 343–354.

Jenkins, G. D., Mitra, A., Gupta, N., & Shaw, J. D. (1998). Are financial incentives related to performance? A meta-analytic review of empirical research. *Journal of Applied Psychology*, *83*(5), 777–787.

Johnston, M., & Finney, S. J. (2010). Measuring basic needs satisfaction: Evaluating previous research and conducting new psychometric evaluations of the Basic Needs Satisfaction in General Scale. *Contemporary Educational Psychology*, *35*, 280–296. doi:10.1016/j.cedpsych.2010.04.003

Judge, T. A., Jackson, C. L., Shaw, J. C., Scott, B. A., & Rich, B. L. (2007). Self-efficacy and work-related performance: The integral role of individual differences. *Journal of Applied Psychology*, *92*(1), 107–127.

Karasek, R. A. (1979). Job demands, job decision latitude and mental strain. Implications for job redesign. *Administrative Science Quarterly*, *24*, 285–308.

Khilji, S. E., & Wang, X. (2006). "Intended" and "implemented" HRM: The missing linchpin in strategic human resource management research. *International Journal of Human Resource Management*, *17*(7), 1171–1189.

Kraiger, K., & Ford, J. K. (2007). The expanding role of workplace training: Themes and trends influencing training research and practice. In L. L. Koppes (Ed.), *Historical perspectives in industrial and organizational psychology* (pp. 281–309). Mahwah, NJ: Lawrence Erlbaum Associates.

Kraimer, M. L., Seibert, S. E., Wayne, S. J., Liden, R. C., & Bravo, J. (2011). Antecedents and outcomes of organizational support for development: The critical role of career opportunities. *Journal of Applied Psychology*, *96*(3), 485–500. doi:10.1037/a0021452

Kuvaas, B. (2006). Work performance, affective commitment, and work motivation: The roles of pay administration and pay level. *Journal of Organizational Behavior*, *27*(3), 365–385. doi:10.1002/job.377

Kuvaas, B., Buch, R., & Dysvik, A. (2012). Perceived training intensity and knowledge sharing: Sharing for intrinsic and prosocial reasons. *Human Resource Management*, *51*(2), 167–187. doi:10.1002/hrm.21464

Kuvaas, B., & Dysvik, A. (2009a). Perceived investment in employee development, intrinsic motivation and work performance. *Human Resource Management Journal*, *19*(3), 217–236. doi:10.1111/j.1748-8583.2009.00103.x

Kuvaas, B., & Dysvik, A. (2009b). Perceived investment in permanent employee development and social and economic exchange perceptions among temporary employees. *Journal of Applied Social Psychology*, *39*(10), 2499–2524. doi:10.1111/j.1559-1816.2009.00535.x

Kuvaas, B., & Dysvik, A. (2010a). Does best practice HRM only work for intrinsically motivated employees? *International Journal Human of Resource Management*, *21*(13), 2339–2357. doi:10.1080/09585192.2010.516589

Kuvaas, B., & Dysvik, A. (2010b). Exploring alternative relationships between perceived investment in employee development, perceived supervisor support and employee outcomes. *Human Resource Management Journal*, *20*(2), 138–156. doi:10.1111/j.1748-8583.2009.00120.x

Kuvaas, B., & Dysvik, A. (2011). Permanent employee investment and social exchange and psychological cooperative climate among temporary employees. *Economic and Industrial Democracy, 32*(2), 261–284. doi:10.1177/0143831x10371990

Lai, L. (2011). Employees' perceptions of the opportunities to utilize their competences: Exploring the role of perceived competence mobilization. *International Journal of Training and Development, 15*(2), 1360–1376.

Lai, L., & Kapstad, J. C. (2009). Perceived competence mobilization: An explorative study of predictors and impact on turnover intentions. *The International Journal of Human Resource Management, 20*(9), 1985–1998. doi:10.1080/09585190903142423

Lee, C. H., & Bruvold, N. T. (2003). Creating value for employees: Investment in employee development. *International Journal of Human Resource Management, 14*(6), 981–1000.

Lee, F. K., Sheldon, K. M., & Turban, D. B. (2003). Personality and the goal-striving process: The influence of achievement goal patterns, goal level, and mental focus on performance and enjoyment. *Journal of Applied Psychology, 88*(2), 256–265.

Mageau, G. A., & Vallerand, R. J. (2003). The coach-athlete relationship: A motivational model. *Journal of Sports Sciences, 21*(11), 883–904.

Marescaux, E., De Winne, S., & Sels, L. (2010, August). *HRM practices and employee attitudes: The role of basic need satisfaction*. Paper presented at the Academy of Management Annual Meeting, Montreal, Canada.

Maurer, T. J., Weiss, E. M., & Barbeite, F. G. (2003). A model of involvement in work-related learning and development activity: The effects of individual, situational, motivational, and age variables. *Journal of Applied Psychology, 88*(4), 707–724.

Mesmer-Magnus, J., & Viswesvaran, C. (2010). The role of pre-interventions in learning: A meta-analysis and integrative review. *Human Resource Management Review, 20*, 261–282.

Meyer, J. P., & Gagné, M. (2008). Employee engagement from a self-determination theory perspective. *Industrial and Organizational Psychology, 1*, 60–62.

Nishii, L. H., Lepak, D. P., & Schneider, B. (2008). Employee attributions of the "why" of HR practices: Their effects on employee attitudes and behaviors, and customer satisfaction. *Personnel Psychology, 61*, 503–545.

Noe, R. A., Tews, M. J., & McConnell Dachner, A. (2010). Learner engagement: A new perspective for enhancing our understanding of learner motivation and workplace learning. *The Academy of Management Annals, 4*, 279–315.

Paré, G., & Tremblay, M. (2007). The influence of high-involvement human resource practices, procedural justice, organizational commitment, and citizenship behaviors on information technology professionals' turnover intentions. *Group & Organization Management, 32*(3), 326–357.

Pfeffer, J. (1998). Seven practices of successful organizations. *California Management Review, 40*(2), 96–124.

Piccolo, R. F., & Colquitt, J. A. (2006). Transformational leadership and job behaviors: The mediating role of core job characteristics. *Academy of Management Journal, 49*(2), 327–340.

Prabhu, V., Sutton, C., & Sauser, W. (2008). Creativity and certain personality traits: Understanding the mediating effect of intrinsic motivation. *Creativity Research Journal, 20*(1), 53–66.

Reeve, J. (2002). Self-Determination Theory Applied to Educational Settings. In E. L. Deci, & R. M. Ryan (Eds.), *Handbook of self-determination research* (pp. 183–203). Rochester, NY: The University of Rochester Press.

Roca, J. C., & Gagné, M. (2008). Understanding e-learning continuance intention in the workplace: A self-determination

theory perspective. *Computers in Human Behavior, 24*, 1585–1604.

Ryan, R. M., & Deci, E. L. (2000). Self-determination theory and the facilitation of intrinsic motivation, social development, and well-being. *American Psychologist, 55*(1), 68–78. doi:10.1037/0003-066X.55.1.68

Sansone, C., & Thoman, D. B. (2005). Interest as the missing motivator in self-regulation. *European Psychologist, 10*(3), 175–186.

Sheldon, K. M., Elliot, A. J., Kim, Y., & Kasser, T. (2001). What is satisfying by satisfying events? Testing 10 candidate psychological needs. *Journal of Personality and Social Psychology, 80*, 325–339. doi:10.1037/0022-3514.80.2.325

Sheldon, K. M., Turban, D. B., Brown, K. G., Barrick, M. R., & Judge, T. A. (2003). Applying self-determination theory to organizational research. In J. J. Martocchio, & G. R. Ferris (Eds.), *Research in personnel and human resource management* (Vol. 22, pp. 357–393). Elsevier.

Shore, L. M., & Barksdale, K. (1998). Examining the degree of balance and level of obligation in the employment relationship: A social exchange approach. *Journal of Organizational Behavior, 19*, 731–744.

Shore, L. M., Tetrick, L. E., Lynch, P., & Barksdale, K. (2006). Social and economic exchange: Construct development and validation. *Journal of Applied Social Psychology, 36*(4), 837–867.

Sitzmann, T., Brown, K. G., Casper, W., Ely, K., & Zimmerman, R. D. (2008). A review and meta-analysis of the nomological network of trainee reactions. *Journal of Applied Psychology, 93*(2), 280–295.

Stone, D. N., Deci, E. L., & Ryan, R. M. (2009). Beyond talk: Creating autonomous motivation through self-determination theory. *Journal of General Management, 34*(3), 75–91.

Su, Y.-L., & Reeve, J. (2011). A meta-analysis of the effectiveness of intervention programs designed to support autonomy. *Educational Psychology Review, 23*, 159–188.

Suazo, M. M., Martínez, P. G., & Sandoval, R. (2009). Creating psychological and legal contracts through human resource practices: A signaling theory perspective. *Human Resource Management Review, 19*(2), 154–166.

Tharenou, P., Saks, A. M., & Moore, C. (2007). A review and critique of research on training and organization level outcomes. *Human Resource Management Review, 17*(3), 251–273.

Tsui, A. S., Pearce, J. L., Porter, L. W., & Tripoli, A. M. (1997). Alternative approaches to the employee-organization relationship: Does investment in employees pay off? *Academy of Management Journal, 40*(5), 1089–1121.

Tyler, R. W. (1969). *Basic principles of curriculum and intstruction*. Chicago: University of Chicago Press.

Vansteenkiste, M., Neyrinck, B., Niemiec, C., Soenens, B., De Witte, H., & Van den Broeck, A. (2007). On the relations among work value orientations, psychological need satisfaction and job outcomes: A self-determination theory approach *Journal of Occupational and Organizational Psychology, 80*(2), 251–277. doi:10.1348/096317906X111024

Weibel, A., Rost, K., & Osterloh, M. (2010). Pay for performance in the public sector-benefits and (hidden) costs. *Journal of Public Administration Research and Theory, 20*(2), 387–412. doi:10.1093/jopart/mup009

Zapata-Phelan, C. P., Colquitt, J. A., Scott, B. A., & Livingston, B. (2009). Procedural justice, interactional justice, and task performance: The mediating role of intrinsic motivation. *Organizational Behavior and Human Decision Processes, 108*(1), 93–105.

PART 4

Outcomes of Work Motivation

CHAPTER
14

Self-Determination and Job Stress

Claude Fernet *and* Stéphanie Austin

Abstract

In this chapter, we present a motivational model of job stress that accounts for certain widely acknowledged stress factors. Drawing on self-determination theory, we identify three key processes behind employee motivation: autonomous motivation, controlled motivation, and amotivation. We then show how job stressors, motivation, strain, and diminished well-being are connected. We suggest that motivational processes play a pivotal, multifunctional role in how employees adapt to the workplace and react to job stressors. We also propose that managers' interpersonal styles wield an indirect effect on these motivational processes through employees' perceptions of job stressors. We conclude with some directions for future research.

Key Words: job stressors, work motivation, strain reactions, well-being, self-determination theory

---

Introduction

Most theoretical models of job stress hypothesize that stress arises from an inadequate fit between the individual and the work environment (see Ganster & Perrewé, 2011; Kahn & Byosiere, 1992). Based primarily on the premise that employee perceptions of the environment are determined by their psychological experience, it is generally held that workplace demands that exceed the individual's capacity (or resources) to adapt lead to stress. Prolonged exposure to such conditions can be costly for individuals and their employers.

To date, several models have synthesized the correlates of job stress. However, they appear to be somewhat limited for understanding the psychological processes involved when individuals cannot adapt to the workplace environment. Nor do they fully explain the resultant stress reactions. In this chapter we suggest *employee motivation* as a promising research avenue—one that has been understudied. Based on self-determination theory

(SDT; Deci & Ryan, 1985a, 2002), we propose and support a motivational model of job stress. We begin with an overview of the main antecedents and consequences of job stress. We then present SDT premises that underlie our conceptual model: the self-determination model of job stress. After presenting the model and some preliminary empirical support from the literature, we offer some directions for future research.

Job Stress

Stress is an increasingly worrisome problem for organizations (see Tetrick & Quick, 2011). It generates substantial negative consequences for the well-being of individuals and the performance of the organizations that employ them. In individuals, stress is evidenced mainly in such symptoms as burnout, psychological strain, and health problems (e.g., somatization, heart problems, musculoskeletal disorders). In organizations, the costs of job stress—including lower productivity as well as higher rates of accident, absenteeism, and turnover—are largely related to employees' counterproductive behaviors. Other less apparent consequences of stress are equally costful for organizations. For instance, workplace conflicts, psychological harassment, and lower employee motivation can translate into psychological withdrawal, job dissatisfaction, cynicism, and intentions to quit.

Job Stressors

Our understanding of job stress is based mainly on studies of organizational antecedents (job stressors) and their consequences (strain or stress reactions; see Kahn & Byosiere, 1992). The daunting challenge for researchers is to identify the environmental factors in the workplace that are responsible for the stress that workers perceive or experience, and to determine how these affect their health and well-being. Although hardly an exhaustive list, the most commonly investigated environmental factors are *job demands* and *lack of resources* (Demerouti, Bakker, Nachreiner, & Schaufeli, 2001; Frese & Zapf, 1994; Lee & Ashforth, 1996). Generally, even though the nature and expression of demands and resources vary across jobs (and work environments), these broad categories are a part of any job. *Job demands* refer to diverse physical, psychosocial, and organizational aspects that are inherent to the job (Demerouti et al., 2001). These demands are stressors, and are considered hindrances insofar as they prevent workers from accomplishing tasks, and more particularly, insofar as they impose a cognitive, physical, or emotional burden on workers (Cavanaugh, Boswell, Roehling, & Boudreau, 2000; LePine, LePine, & Jackson, 2004). Examples of such hindrances are role-related problems (e.g., overload, ambiguity), interpersonal conflicts, and organizational policies.

Demands can also be considered challenges that unleash positive aspects of the stress experience when they act as stimulants rather than threats (Crawford, LePine, & Rich, 2010; LePine, Podsakoff, & Lepine, 2005). For example, workers may be required to multitask or to perform complex tasks under time constraints—albeit manageable—and to be accountable for the results. Nevertheless, by reducing the available energy that employees have to perform their tasks, such demands can engender physical and psychological costs. In their recent meta-analysis, Crawford et al. (2010) found that job burnout—an indicator of ill-being—was positively related to job challenges and job hindrances, whereas work engagement—an indicator of well-being—was positively related to job challenges and negatively to job hindrances. They also demonstrated that job resources were positively related to engagement and negatively to burnout.

Job resources refer to various physical, psychosocial, and organizational factors that provide support to individuals as they perform their tasks (Demerouti et al., 2001). Like demands, resources have different natures (emotional, cognitive, or physical). They are evidenced in the form of social support, job control, and skill discretion, among others. These resources help individuals perform their tasks, and by the same token, they help reduce job demands (Karasek, 1979) by making the work more interesting or by contributing to individual development and well-being (Bakker & Demerouti, 2007; Schaufeli & Bakker, 2004). However, as suggested by Crawford et al. (2010; see also Lee & Ashforth, 1996), lack of job resources can lead to stress reactions.

In addition to exploring the organizational antecedents of stress, the research has revealed that environmental factors in the workplace affect workers differently. Each worker feels, thinks, and behaves in a unique way, which means that they also react differently to job demands and the stress they produce (Parkes, 1994; Spector, 2002). Accordingly, studies have attempted to evaluate how individual differences can explain the vulnerability and resistance thresholds of workers coping with job stressors and health-related problems at work. Thus, the degree of vulnerability to job stressors and strain can be explained by a multitude of factors: locus of control, self-esteem, self-efficacy, and self-determined motivation; or by a combination of individual characteristics, such as capital resources, which include optimism, hope, self-efficacy, and resilience (Luthans, Youssef, & Avolio, 2007). High internal locus of control (Daniels & Guppy, 1994), self-esteem (Rosse, Boss, Johnson, & Crown, 1991), self-efficacy (Schaubroeck, Jones, & Xie, 2001), and self-determined motivation (Fernet, Guay, & Senécal, 2004) are generally associated with low strain.

Stress Reactions

What are the consequences of a harmful work environment and the resultant stress? This question has generated (and continues to generate) an impressive amount of research. The interest is to evaluate the effects of job stressors on the behaviors, well-being, and health of workers and on overall organizational functioning. Stress reactions take different forms, depending on the individual. They can be affective (e.g., anxiety or depressive symptoms), cognitive (e.g., memory lapses), physical (e.g., back pain, headaches), or behavioral (e.g., impulsivity, lifestyle). These reactions do not affect just the worker. They also have ramifications for interpersonal relations (e.g., hostility toward coworkers) and organizational outcomes (e.g., lower productivity). It goes without saying that the intensity and frequency of job stressors are determinant for individual reactions to stress. Over time, benign affective reactions (e.g., fatigue or irritability) can progress toward more serious health conditions (e.g., cardiovascular, musculoskeletal, or digestive dysfunction). From a psychological standpoint, the burnout syndrome is used to capture the psychological experience of an individual subjected to prolonged exposure to a harmful work environment. Although the burnout syndrome has been clinically validated and recognized in countries, such as the Netherlands and Sweden, researchers generally use it to refer to a persistent work-related state of mind resulting from prolonged work stress (Maslach, Schaufeli, & Leiter, 2001; Schaufeli & Enzmann, 1998). Job burnout refers to a psychological syndrome of emotional exhaustion, depersonalization (or cynicism), and diminished personal accomplishment (or professional efficacy) attributable to the job (Maslach, 1982; Maslach et al., 2001). Whereas burnout is tantamount to a depletion of emotional resources, depersonalization is an attitude of detachment and indifference toward the job and the associated people (e.g., colleagues, clients). Diminished personal accomplishment refers to a feeling of being less competent and productive at work.

It is noteworthy that, in addition to negative outcomes (e.g., burnout, strain, somatization), stress reactions can lead to depleted psychological, physical, and social well-being (Quick, Macik-Frey, & Cooper, 2007; World Health Organization, 1958). In other words, without necessarily producing full-blown symptoms or health problems, job stressors can sap employees' energy, vitality, enthusiasm, positive affect, and interest—all of which are indicators of psychological well-being. The concept of work engagement, characterized by vigor, dedication, and absorption, was recently proposed and empirically supported to capture this positive, work-related state of mind (see Bakker, Albrecht, & Leiter, 2011).

Self-Determination Theory

SDT (Deci & Ryan, 1985a, 2002) is a widely held theory of motivation that explains psychological functioning and well-being (see Vansteenkiste, Niemiec, & Soenens, 2010 for a recent review). This theory provides an overarching framework for understanding job stress. Essentially, SDT addresses the socioenvironmental conditions that influence motivational processes as well as adaptive and maladaptive psychological functioning. To appraise the utility of SDT for understanding job stress, we briefly discuss four theoretical postulates that encapsulate (1) the nature of motivation, (2) the satisfaction of basic psychological needs, (3) the role of the social environment, and (4) the role of individual differences. The aim is to lay the groundwork for the presentation of a conceptual model that integrates the correlates of stress as reported in the literature. For a detailed discussion of the theoretical rationale for SDT, the reader is referred to Chapter 1.

The Nature of Motivation

SDT makes an important distinction concerning the nature of human motivation. It proposes that people may not only invest in an activity to varied degrees (a quantifiable aspect) but that they do so for various reasons (a qualitative aspect). Specifically, three categories of motivation (or motivational processes)—autonomous motivation, controlled motivation, and amotivation—may differentially impact employee functioning (see Deci & Ryan, 2000; Vallerand, 1997, for reviews). *Autonomous motivation* refers to acting with volition, as when employees engage in their job for the inherent pleasure and satisfaction they experience (intrinsic motivation) and/or because they personally endorse the importance or value of their tasks (identified regulation). *Controlled motivation* refers to behaviors that are enacted under internal or external pressure, as when employees perform their job to gain a sense of self-worth or to avoid feelings of anxiety and guilt (introjected regulation) and/or because they are pressured by demands, threats, or rewards by an external agent (external regulation). *Amotivation* is a relative lack of both intrinsic and extrinsic motivation. Amotivation occurs when employees do not perceive an adequate fit between their actions and the consequences, and therefore feel incapable of achieving their goals.

Three methodological approaches are generally used to examine motivational processes in employees. Some researchers look at the effect of each motivation type (intrinsic motivation; identified, introjected, and external regulation; and amotivation) on work-related outcomes (e.g., Lin, Tsai, & Chiu, 2009). Others use the two categories that address the quality of motivation: *autonomous motivation*, which encompasses intrinsic motivation, integrated and identified regulation, and *controlled motivation*, which includes introjected and external regulation (e.g., Van den Broeck et al., 2011). Third, in light of the self-determination continuum, some researchers have combined the motivation types to obtain a single score (e.g., Bono & Judge, 2003; Fernet, Gagné, & Austin, 2010). More specifically, the more autonomous motivations (intrinsic, identified) are weighted positively and the more negative motivations (introjected, external) are weighted negatively to create a relative autonomy index. Irrespective of the approach used, the empirical results generally support the postulate that autonomous motivations are positively related to desirable outcomes, and inversely, that controlled motivations and amotivation are associated with undesirable outcomes (for reviews, see Deci & Ryan, 2000, 2008; Vallerand, 1997).

In addition, the research to date has provided support for three mechanisms by which motivation affects employees' psychological functioning and well-being. It may act as a direct antecedent, as an indirect antecedent (i.e., a mediator), or as a moderator between certain environmental factors and employee outcomes. These effects have been determined with various positive and negative indicators, such as the attitudes, behaviors, and well-being of people at work and in life in general. Detailed empirical results in support of these mechanisms are provided in the section on developing the conceptual model of job stress.

Satisfaction of Basic Psychological Needs

According to SDT, autonomous motivation (the most productive type) can flourish only when three basic psychological needs have been satisfied. These needs are *autonomy* (required for initiating and regulating one's behavior; deCharms, 1968; Deci, 1975), *competence* (acting efficaciously to achieve objectives; White, 1959), and *relatedness* (feeling connected, or belonging to a social milieu; Baumeister & Leary, 1995). These basic needs represent sources of energy that are indispensable for high-quality motivation and optimal functioning (Deci & Ryan, 2000).

Many studies conducted in diverse life spheres, such as education, health, and sports, support

this proposition, confirming that the satisfaction of these basic needs is positively associated with autonomous motivation (e.g., Guay & Vallerand, 1997; Lonsdale, Hodge, & Rose, 2009; Sarrazin, Vallerand, Guillet, Pelletier, & Curry, 2002; Vallerand, Fortier, & Guay, 1997), and with diverse positive indicators of well-being, such as positive affect (e.g., Mouratidis, Vansteenkiste, Lens, & Sideridis, 2008), vitality (e.g., Adie, Duda, & Ntoumanis, 2008; Reinboth & Duda, 2006), and emotional well-being (e.g., Reis, Sheldon, Gable, Roscoe, & Ryan, 2000). Other studies indicate that *unsatisfied* needs are related to negative indicators of well-being, such as emotional and physical exhaustion (e.g., Bartholomew, Ntoumanis, Ryan, & Thøgersen-Ntoumani, 2011; Hodge, Lonsdale, & Ng, 2008; Quested & Duda, 2011). In a workplace study, Van den Broeck, Vansteenkiste, De Witt, Soenens, and Lens (2010) corroborated that the satisfaction of psychological needs was positively associated with autonomous motivation and positive indicators of employee functioning, including vigor, satisfaction, and performance, and negatively with burnout.

It is noteworthy that some job stress models (e.g., the job demands–control [JD-C] model, the job demands–resources [JD-R] model) consider either the direct or indirect contribution of the three psychological needs to explain stress and/or well-being in employees. For example, in the JD-C model (Karasek, 1979), *control* is a central dimension of the work organization, and it enables employees to adapt to job demands. Two components make up this dimension: decisional latitude and skill discretion. In a revised version of the model, Karasek and Theorell (1990) added *social support* as a further significant factor for employee adaptation to job demands. Although situated in work organization, these dimensions echo the need for autonomy (possibilities for choosing and deciding), competence (possibilities for applying one's skills), and relatedness (possibilities for feeling connected, listened to, and helped). The JD-R model (Demerouti et al., 2001; Schaufeli & Bakker, 2004) more specifically recognizes the contribution of psychological needs satisfaction, proposed as the mechanism that relates job resources and employee engagement. In support of this proposition, Van den Broeck, Vansteenkiste, De Witte, and Lens (2008) found that needs satisfaction plays a partial mediating role between resources (e.g., job control, decision latitude, social support) and engagement (i.e., vigor). Furthermore, they showed that needs satisfaction acts as a partial mediator between demands (e.g., overload, emotional and physical demands) and burnout (i.e., emotional exhaustion), and as a complete mediator between resources and exhaustion. Similarly, Fernet, Austin, Trépanier, and Dussault (2013) found that different demands (role overload and ambiguity) and resources (decision latitude and social support) predicted dimensions of burnout through the unsatisfied psychological needs of employees. Although the satisfaction of needs may directly mediate the relationship between job stressors and strain or well-being, it could be more informative to examine motivational processes as mechanisms to explain how employees channel their energy to cope with job stressors. Although job stressors can diminish the enjoyment and interest of employees (autonomous motivation), they can also contribute to controlled motivation through psychological accommodations (e.g., internal pressure to meet external demands; Deci & Ryan, 2000) and amotivation. Therefore, strain may be exacerbated not only by unmet psychological needs, but more particularly because when needs are unsatisfied, employees tend to channel their energy in unproductive ways—entailing greater psychological costs.

Social Environment

Unlike theoretical models that expressly address workplace factors or work organization, SDT focuses on the social environment—particularly management styles—and its impact on employee motivation and well-being. More specifically, a manager's interpersonal style can be described as autonomy-supportive or controlling (Deci, Connell, & Ryan, 1989). Managers can provide an autonomy-supportive atmosphere for employees by considering their perspectives, giving them relevant information, and offering them possibilities for exercising choice and making decisions (Baard, Deci, & Ryan, 2004; Deci, Eghrari, Patrick, & Leone, 1994). In contrast, controlling managers adopt coercive behaviors, which are likely to foster stress reactions and strain. They use maximum control and oversight, threaten employees, and make them feel guilty. They generally give critical feedback without acknowledging the employee's perspective. Research has recognized that management styles can influence employee motivation by either facilitating or hindering the motivational processes (e.g., Bono & Judge, 2003). Empirical studies that support this proposition are presented in the section on the self-determination model of job stress.

The autonomy-supportive style shares some features with other commonly studied management styles, including transformational leadership (Bass, 1985) and empowering leadership (Conger & Kanungo, 1988). Transformational leadership refers to management behaviors that aim to transform employees' standards and values and to inspire them to exceed normal expectations (Yukl, 1989). To do this, leaders must delegate responsibility, allow employees to take initiative, promote cooperation and teamwork, and foster constructive conflict resolution (Bass, 1985). Empowering leadership means to allow employees to develop autonomy by granting decisional latitude and by sharing power, responsibilities, and information (Srivastava, Bartol, & Locke, 2006). Although the mechanisms by which leaders can influence subordinates' motivation and well-being have been largely ignored (Avolio, Zhu, Koh, & Bhatia, 2004; see also Gilbert and Kelloway [Chapter 11]), these leadership styles appear to have in common a will to promote their followers' sense of self-determination. Bono and Judge (2003) suggest that transformational leadership behaviors help employees perceive their work as self-congruent—a perception that is critical for developing and sustaining autonomous motivation. Through autonomy-supportive, transformational, or empowering behaviors, managers can therefore help employees achieve their objectives. However, the motivational effect of management styles and the impact on employees' strain and well-being have yet to be examined. For example, management styles could help minimize obstacles (e.g., clarify the mandate, provide a meaningful rationale) and provide access to a broader range of job resources.

Individual Differences

SDT research highlights the environmental variables that are liable for affecting motivation and psychological functioning. Nevertheless, it has been proposed that motivational orientation in turn influences how people perceive or react to their environment. According to Deci and Ryan (1985b), people with an autonomy orientation tend to seek opportunities to interact with the environment on the basis of their interests and self-endorsed values, and to interpret events as being autonomy-supportive. This reinforces their sense of autonomy and facilitates the internalization process, whereby a behavior that was initially regulated by external factors, such as rewards or punishments, becomes internally regulated (Ryan, 1995). In contrast, control-oriented people tend to feel constrained by external and internal contingencies. They tend to interpret events as pressures, which reinforces their "dependence" on such contingencies. As for impersonal-oriented people, they tend to feel incapable of, or inept at, exerting any influence over their environment, and they interpret events as unpredictable or beyond their control. This reinforces their passivity and amotivation.

Deci and Ryan (1985b) developed the General Causality Orientations Scale, a global measure to assess individual motivational orientations, or how people understand, perceive, interpret, and react to their environment. The research shows that the general autonomy orientation is associated with desirable outcomes (e.g., self-actualization, self-esteem), whereas the controlled and impersonal orientations are associated with stress-related problems, such as a Type A behavior pattern, defensive functioning, self-derogation, and depressive symptoms (for a review, see Gagné & Deci, 2005). Without denying the importance of these individual differences in orientation, we prefer to address motivational orientation on the job as such, or work motivation. It is reasonable to assume that a person's general orientation is directly linked to that person's orientations in a variety of life spheres (see Vallerand, 1997). Nevertheless, based on the extensive literature on the specificity of constructs (e.g., Marsh & Yeung, 1998), we believe that it is more informative to examine the specific environment in which the motivational processes operate in order to explain individual differences in the perceptions of workers. Although less related to general orientation, which appears to be more of a personality trait, work motivation is relatively stable. For example, Blais, Brière, Lachance, Riddle, and Vallerand (1993) showed that coefficients of temporal stability varied from .54 to .67 over an 18-month period for autonomous and controlled motivation and amotivation. Our data indicate similar stability coefficients over a 3-year period (.54–.62). Albeit fragmentary, these data suggest that work motivation, as captured by SDT, can constitute a relatively stable individual characteristic that is nonetheless malleable and subject to change and development. This stability–malleability duality is particularly relevant in examinations of stress. It raises the idea that employee motivation is not determined solely by environmental factors, and that it can also contribute to shape and redefine employee perceptions, and even influence how employees adapt to job stressors and respond to the resultant strain.

The Self-Determination Model of Job Stress

The model (Figure 14.1) emphasizes the motivational processes that employees use to adapt to the work environment, and their responses to job stressors. Drawing on SDT, it integrates the postulates of prominent models in job stress research, notably the correlates and mechanisms by which the variables exert their effects. However, it represents a departure in that it accounts for the psychological energy sources for behaviors (energization and direction), and the nature of the regulations responsible for adapting to the workplace and responding to stressors. The aim is to better understand the sequence in which environmental factors act on employees' stress reactions and well-being. In the next section, we describe three propositions that underpin the motivational model.

Proposition 1: Job Stressors Lead to Strain (and diminished well-being) Through Work Motivation

A work environment that contains many stressors would considerably hinder employee motivation and result in physical and psychological costs. As discussed previously, the research on job stress has identified diverse types of job stressors that can affect employee health and well-being. Recently, under the JD-R model, Demerouti et al. (2001) classified them into two overarching categories: demands and resources. Many studies have supported the notion that job demands constitute a major determinant of strain and ill-being (see Demerouti & Bakker,

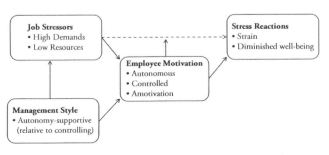

Fig. 14.1. Self-determination model of job stress.

2011; Hakanen & Roodt, 2010). Other studies have shown that a lack of job resources can be detrimental for well-being and can contribute to ill-being (see Crawford et al., 2010). However, research has yet to examine the motivational processes by which job stressors influence strain and well-being.

Whether physical, cognitive, or emotional in nature, all job stressors share a common feature: they place external pressure on the individual (Selye, 1982). They act on employees' psychological energy by influencing the quality of their motivation, a key determinant of both adaptive and maladaptive functioning. In other words, job stressors have the potential to constrain individual behaviors and cause people to feel that they are no longer the authors of their own actions (deCharms, 1968; Deci, 1975). To illustrate, let us take the example of a nurse who routinely makes a three-mile commute to and from work (physical demands), has to solve problems quickly (cognitive demands), and must control her emotions (emotional demands). On top of all this, she is frequently asked to do overtime (overload). How would these demands affect her motivation? Even if, at one point, the nurse might value the outcomes of her work and feel that she is contributing to the collective good, it is highly plausible that with time and the accumulation of these demands she would begin to lose interest and find less satisfaction in performing her job (diminished autonomous motivation). She might also come to feel that some, if not most, of her tasks were obligatory (increased controlled motivation). These job demands could also culminate in amotivation. This type of situation involves job hindrances. However, it is equally possible to suppose that a lack of job resources would have a similarly detrimental effect on motivation. A nurse who is charged with less onerous tasks than the previously mentioned one could still be exposed to strain. She might be required to use technical equipment that is inadequate to handle the physical aspects of her job (physical resource); have little latitude, such as deciding when to take a break when her task requires intense concentration (cognitive resource); or have little peer support, either emotional or informational (emotional resource). In this respect, our model hypothesizes that both the presence of job demands and the lack of job resources affect employee health and well-being, because both are liable to diminish autonomous motivation and increase controlled motivation as well as amotivation.

Although few studies to date have examined this sequence in its totality (i.e., that job stressors lead to strain and diminished well-being through employee motivation), some studies have supported this proposition. However, it is largely held that in both the workplace and in other areas of life, qualitatively different motivations are distinctly associated with individual psychological functioning and well-being. Although autonomous motivation is negatively associated with a number of indicators of strain, such as psychological distress, powerlessness, and somatization, it is positively associated with indicators of well-being, such as life satisfaction, job satisfaction, a sense of accomplishment and efficacy at work, and psychological well-being (e.g., Blais et al., 1993; Fernet, Senécal, Guay, Marsh, & Dowson, 2008; Gagné et al., 2010; Tremblay, Blanchard, Taylor, Pelletier, & Villeneuve, 2009). Generally, controlled motivation and amotivation are inversely associated with these manifestations of strain and well-being (see Blais et al., 1993; Fernet, 2011). However, some studies support specific associations between job stressors and employees' motivational processes. For example, Pelletier, Séguin-Lévesque, and Legault (2002) found that teachers' perceptions of job demands that were stipulated by school authorities (e.g., comply with a curriculum, with colleagues, and with performance standards) and demands concerning students (e.g., poorly motivated students) negatively predicted autonomous motivation compared with controlled motivation. In addition, Fernet, Guay, Senécal, and Austin's (2012) study of teachers supports this proposition: results showed that increased perceptions of work overload and students' disruptive behaviors during a school year led to diminished autonomous motivation relative to controlled motivation in teachers, which in turn predicted increased burnout. These results were obtained taking into consideration the teachers' feelings of self-efficacy. Furthermore, in a study of school principals over a 9-month school year, Fernet, Austin, and Vallerand (2012) found that job resources (job control, recognition, and quality of relationships with school staff) had a positive unidirectional effect on autonomous motivation, but a negative effect on controlled motivation. Taking into account the cross-lagged effects of job resources on emotional exhaustion and occupational commitment, the results also showed that autonomous motivation had a negative effect on exhaustion but a positive effect on commitment, whereas controlled motivation had a positive effect on exhaustion. In summary, these findings provide preliminary evidence that work motivation acts as a mediator between job stressors and strain or diminished well-being.

Proposition 2: Work Motivation Buffers the Relationship between Job Stressors and Strain (including diminished well-being)

More specifically, autonomous motivation mitigates the relationship between job stressors and strain, whereas controlled motivation and amotivation intensify these relationships. As mentioned previously, the research is rather sparse on individual differences in employee motivation. However, by its very nature, employee motivation can strengthen (or weaken) the effects of job stressors on strain and well-being. Because autonomously motivated employees tend to identify with the values of their job and integrate them into their sense of self (Deci & Ryan, 2000), they would be expected to show initiative and to tend to seek opportunities in their environment that concur with and support their interests and values, and which enable them to achieve their objectives. This would result in not only less susceptibility to the effect of environmental contingencies (Fernet et al., 2010), but also a better use of their resources to adjust to job stressors (Fernet et al., 2004). However, control-motivated employees would be more sensitive to environmental factors, which even when partially internalized are essentially external regulators of behavior. These employees would therefore be more vulnerable to job stressors liable to affect their well-being, as well as the associated external and internal contingencies, such as self-esteem and self-worth. Faced with job demands, they could be more apt to perceive them as obstacles, and be more "dependent" on resources in the environment. The rigidity of their motivation could also lead them to invest in their work compulsively, which carries the risk of exhaustion (Van den Broeck, Schreurs, et al., 2011). Finally, the effect of job stressors on strain and diminished well-being would be even more amplified for amotivated employees. These employees would feel relatively powerless before job stressors. They would tend to perceive these demands as neither challenges nor obstacles, but rather insurmountable burdens. Furthermore, they would judge resources as inadequate and insufficient to remedy the situation, which would be perceived as beyond their control. Amotivation at work has been associated with substantial psychological and physical costs, such as psychological strain (depressive symptoms, anxiety, irritability, and cognitive problems), somatization, and burnout (e.g., Blais et al., 1993).

The research to date on individual differences has focused mainly on the buffering role of work motivation. More particularly, these studies have aimed to examine whether employee motivation (autonomous relative to controlled) fosters adaptation to the work environment, and whether it does so by mitigating the negative effects of job stressors on psychological health and well-being. Instead of investigating whether employee motivation affects perceptions of environmental factors, these studies have attempted to determine whether motivation affects stress reactions that stem from this perception. For example, in a two-sample study, Trépanier, Fernet, and Austin (2013) showed that autonomous motivation (relative to controlled motivation) diminished the negative effect of three sources of stress (role overload, ambiguity, and conflict) on psychological distress (depression and anxiety symptoms, irritability, and cognitive problems). Specifically, the results revealed significant interaction effects, suggesting that the effect of stressors on psychological strain is attenuated when employees have a higher degree of autonomous motivation. Similarly, Fernet et al. (2010) examined whether employee motivation buffered the relationship between social resources and job burnout. The results of this prospective 2-year study showed that low-quality relationships with coworkers contributed significantly to burnout, but only for employees with low autonomous motivation. This suggests that these employees are more vulnerable to certain environmental factors at work, and that social resources are crucial for maintaining psychological well-being. Furthermore, some studies have suggested that employees having a higher degree of autonomous motivation are more inclined to make good use of job resources. To illustrate, a two-sample study by Dysvik and Kuvaas (2011) showed that job control fostered the performance of employees who evidenced high intrinsic motivation (relative to low intrinsic motivation).

Other studies have described the complexity of the buffering role of motivation in individual adaptation to the work environment. In a study inspired by the JD-C model (Karasek, 1979), Fernet et al. (2004) examined whether motivation at work buffered the demands–control relationship in order to predict job burnout. The results showed that job control acted to minimize the negative effect of job demands on burnout, but only for employees who exhibited a high degree of autonomous motivation. These results suggest that autonomous employees can make better use of certain resources to cope with demands. Similar results were found by Parker, Jimmieson, and Amiot (2010), who looked at autonomous and controlled motivation separately and in connection with other psychological manifestations (work engagement, health complaints, and anxiety-depression symptoms). In a representative sample of Dutch employees, Van den Broeck, Van Ruysseveldt, Smulders, and De Witte (2011) also found that job control attenuated the effect of job demands on burnout (i.e., emotional exhaustion), but only in employees who showed an intrinsic work value orientation (relative to extrinsic). Finally, in a 2-year longitudinal study, Ten Brummelhuis, Ter Hoeven, Bakker, and Peper (2011) determined that employee motivation explained the extent to which burnout culminated in loss of job resources (job control, social support) and greater job demands (overload, longer work hours). Their results showed that a high degree of intrinsic motivation (relative to a low degree) attenuated the process of diminishing resources, whereas a high degree of external regulation (relative to a low degree) increased the accumulation of job demands.

Essentially, these studies show that motivational processes play a key role in how employees adapt to their environment and their consequent stress reactions. Employees having a high degree of autonomous motivation are less affected by environmental demands, perhaps because they have more energy—or better energy sources—to adapt to these demands, which are perceived as less stressful, or else because they can make better use of the resources at their disposal to cope with demands. In contrast, employees having a controlled orientation appear to be more sensitive and vulnerable to environmental factors, particularly self-worth contingencies, such as coworkers' opinions and superiors' approval. This less flexible orientation means that the pressure of these demands (introjection) could sap the energy needed to identify, mobilize, and use the resources required for optimal adaptation to job stressors. It is noteworthy that even though amotivation appears to be the most stress-enhancing type of motivation, to our knowledge no studies have attempted to explore its effect.

Proposition 3: Management Styles Influence Employee Perceptions of Job Stressors, Which in Turn Lead to Strain (and diminished well-being) Through Work Motivation

The research on autonomy-supportive management reveals that this interpersonal style affects employee motivation as well as their well-being in a variety of ways (Gagné & Deci, 2005). For example, Deci et al. (1989) showed that employees of supervisors who reportedly adopted autonomy-supportive behaviors presented much greater trust in the organization, felt less pressure, and expressed greater satisfaction with their job. This pattern of results was corroborated in studies that examined support as *perceived* by employees. For instance, Lévesque, Blais, and Hess (2004) found that the more teachers perceived that their superiors granted them autonomy, the higher was their autonomous motivation (relative to controlled motivation). In turn, autonomous motivation was positively related to work attitude and psychological well-being. Similar results were found by Blais and Brière (2002) in a study that examined autonomy-supportive and controlling styles separately.

In addition to fostering work motivation, management style would be expected to influence employee perceptions of job stressors. By nature and through their actions, managers tend to shape their employees' perceptions, given that they can define and design the reality in which their employees must work (Smircich & Morgan, 1982). Managers who adopt an autonomy-supportive style can help lighten the burden of employees' tasks. This can be done in many ways. For example, they can provide employees with a meaningful rationale for the purpose or desirability of the task (Arnold, Turner, Barling, Kelloway, & McKee, 2007). They can make themselves available to provide information, clarify ambiguities related to their role or tasks, respond to questions, and offer assistance or guidance as needed. Managers can also foster a positive perception of resources by creating an autonomy-conducive environment, sharing information, and acknowledging employees' contributions. However, controlling managers can make tasks more burdensome. They can exacerbate the psychological demands associated with tasks, for example, by scrutinizing employees' slightest actions, belittling the quantity or quality of their work, or setting excessively tough goals and deadlines. Controlling managers can also misdirect the perception of resources by creating a competitive, individual-oriented environment. In addition, managers can damage employees' perceptions of their job beyond the performance of prescribed tasks. For example, the study by Piccolo and Colquitt (2006) proposes link between management style and employees' perceptions of job characteristics. Their results showed that employees' perceptions of their superior's transformational leadership influenced how they viewed the characteristics of their job (variety, identity, significance, autonomy, and feedback), which in turn predicted their performance and organizational citizenship behaviors through motivational mechanisms (intrinsic motivation and goal commitment). Our recent study (Fernet, Trépanier, Austin, Gagné, & Forest, 2014) provides empirical evidence for the motivational effect of transformational leaderships in connection with job stressors, strain, and well-being. In two occupational settings (nurses and school principals), we found that transformational leadership is simultaneously related to employees' perceptions of job demands and resources, which differently predict employee motivation (autonomous and controlled motivation). In addition, employee motivation differentially predicts job strain (burnout and psychological distress), attitudes (occupational commitment and turnover intention), and performance (self-reported individual and objective organizational performance). Although preliminary, these findings support the proposition that managers can influence employees' perceptions of their work environment as well as resultant stress reactions.

Future Directions

In this chapter, we support the idea that employee motivation furthers the understanding of the psychological processes by which people do or do not adapt to their work environment and helps explain how stress reactions manifest themselves. Although the self-determination and job stress model arises from a series of propositions that are supported by empirical evidence, further studies are needed to establish its full validity. Accordingly, we suggest four avenues for exploration.

First, because stress leads individuals to disengage from their jobs, it is important to pay particular attention to the temporal dimension. Although the model presented in this chapter suggests a specific temporal sequence, whereby environmental factors act on employees' motivational processes, which in turn translate into strain or diminished well-being, this sequence could actually be more complex. Longitudinal studies that include measures over time would thereby be informative. As suggested by Zapf, Dormann, and Frese (1996), they would enable identifying the role or mechanism of the variables (direct, indirect, or buffering), the time frame required for the effects to appear (short- and long-term), and the sequence in which the variables exert their influence (normal, reversed, or reciprocal). With respect to the proposed model, it is highly probable that the variables involved are mutually influential. Further studies could gather data on various occupational groups of workers and at different time intervals to deepen the understanding of this issue.

A second useful research avenue is to examine newly hired employees. Among others, this would allow verifying how environmental factors in the workplace and employees' motivational processes interact, and how strain and diminished well-being *emerge* from this interplay. It would also be helpful to examine the internalization process during organizational socialization. Many studies have shown that this process can explain how individuals manage to assimilate the values and behaviors that are required or sought by social agents (e.g., parents, teachers, and physicians). Nevertheless, there is currently little understanding of how workers internalize environmental factors, particularly stressors. As mentioned, managers can contribute to this process. For instance, they can provide a valid rationale for certain demands that employees may perceive as unreasonable or unrealistic. It is equally possible that, over time, employees can assimilate environmental factors and transpose them into their motivation and psychological experience. Future studies could examine the interplay among motivational processes and their complementary roles (e.g., autonomous and controlled motivation and amotivation) in order to better understand the tendency to assimilate environmental representations, especially when they are related to stressors. It is arguable that the more an individual internalizes environmental factors in an optimal manner (e.g., integrated regulation), the stronger the effect of the internalization on that individual's emotional and psychological experience.

Third, although it is implicit in the proposed model, it would be relevant to examine the independent contribution of the satisfaction and frustration of needs in relation to employee motivation and psychological functioning. To date, the research in the workplace has concentrated almost exclusively on the role of needs satisfaction. Needs satisfaction has been negatively associated with job demands (Fernet et al., 2013) and its nonadaptive consequences (e.g., burnout), and positively associated with autonomous motivation and its adaptive consequences (e.g., job satisfaction, vigor, performance; Van den Broeck et al., 2010). However, compared to needs satisfaction, the frustration of needs would reasonably lead to controlled motivation and greater strain. For example, an employee might strive for a promotion at all costs (external regulation), entailing even heavier psychological and physical consequences (Ryan & Deci, 2000). Beyond these conceptual differences, it would seem reasonable to suggest that employees who feel totally incompetent or rejected by coworkers would have more trouble adjusting than employees who feel that they cannot apply their skills optimally, or who feel detached from their coworkers. Recent studies in sports have pointed in this direction, in that needs frustration in athletes predicts burnout over and above the satisfaction of psychological needs (Bartholomew et al., 2011).

Fourth, although the proposed model addresses job stressors, it integrates both the organizational and individual dimensions. This allows for an understanding of optimal functioning, well-being, and health in employees. Against the background principle that the quality of motivation is critical for employees' psychological experience and perceptions, it is reasonable to suggest that environmental factors (e.g., management style and work organization) affect employee motivation, and therefore influence their development, growth, and well-being. A management style that facilitates the employee's work by providing the appropriate resources, minimizing the presence of hindrance demands, and fostering manageable and suitably challenging demands would promote autonomous motivation. This would not only help prevent stress and the associated adverse reactions, it would also contribute to well-being on the job. Although some environmental factors may be more determining than others in explaining employees' emotional, physical, or behavioral manifestations, we believe that the effects of these factors are essentially equivalent on positive (vitality and well-being) and negative manifestations (strain and ill-being), because they stem from the same motivational processes. Nevertheless, future studies could seek a deeper understanding of how autonomous and controlled motivation can coexist in a same employee, and explore how strain and well-being can operate simultaneously.

Conclusion

This chapter proposes and supports a motivational model of job stress. Drawing on SDT, we identify three motivational processes: (1) autonomous motivation, (2) controlled motivation, and (3) amotivation. We explain the nature of the relationships between job stressors and manifestations of strain and diminished well-being. We propose that motivational processes can play a pivotal, multifunctional role in how employees adapt to

their work environment and their resultant stress reactions. In addition, we propose that managers' interpersonal styles exert an indirect effect on the motivational processes through perceptions of job stressors.

Although the contribution of motivational processes to job stress has not yet been fully determined, we believe that a close examination of employee motivation will procure a deeper, more detailed understanding of workplace issues. The proposed model allows targeting not only the processes responsible for employee inadaptation, but also the processes that enable adaptation to the workplace as well as positive outcomes in terms of behaviors, health, and well-being. In this sense, interventions designed to promote and support high-quality motivation could be doubly beneficial, in that they could prevent strain and foster well-being in employees, and contribute to positive organizational functioning.

References

Adie, J. W., Duda, J. L., & Ntoumanis, N. (2008). Autonomy support, basic need satisfaction and the optimal functioning of adult male and female sport participants: A test of basic needs theory. *Motivation and Emotion*, *32*(3), 189–199.

Arnold, K. A., Turner, N., Barling, J., Kelloway, E. K., & McKee, M. C. (2007). Transformational leadership and psychological well-being: The mediating role of meaningful work. *Journal of Occupational Health Psychology*, *12*, 193–203.

Avolio, B. J., Zhu, W., Koh, W., & Bhatia, P. (2004). Transformational leadership and organizational commitment: Mediating role of psychological empowerment and moderating role of structural distance. *Journal of Organizational Behavior*, *25*(8), 951–968.

Baard, P. P., Deci, E. L., & Ryan, R. M. (2004). Intrinsic need satisfaction: a motivational basis of performance and well-being in two work settings. *Journal of Applied Social Psychology*, *34*(10), 2045–2068.

Bakker, A. B., Albrecht, S. L., & Leiter, M. P. (2011). Key questions regarding work engagement. *European Journal of Work and Organizational Psychology*, *20*(1), 4–28.

Bakker, A. B., & Demerouti, E. (2007). The Job Demands-Resources model: State of the art. *Journal of Managerial Psychology*, *22*(3), 309–328.

Bartholomew, K. J., Ntoumanis, N., Ryan, R. M., & Thøgersen-Ntoumani, C. (2011). Psychological need thwarting in the sport context: Assessing the darker side of athletic experience. *Journal of Sport & Exercise Psychology*, *33*(1), 75–102.

Bass, B. M. (1985). *Leadership and performance beyond expectations*. New York: Free Press.

Baumeister, R. F., & Leary, M. R. (1995). The need to belong: Desire for interpersonal attachments as a fundamental human motivation. *Psychological Bulletin*, *117*(3), 497–529.

Blais, M. R., & Brière, N. M. (2002). *On the mediational role of feelings of self-determination in the workplace: Further evidence and generalization*. Cirano Working Papers, 2002s-39.

Blais, M. R., Brière, N. M., Lachance, L., Riddle, A. S., & Vallerand, R. J. (1993). L'inventaire des motivations au travail de Blais [The Blais Work Motivation Inventory]. *Revue Québécoise de Psychologie, 14*, 185–215.

Bono, J. E., & Judge, T. A. (2003). Self-concordance at work: Toward understanding the motivational effects of transformational leaders. *Academy of Management Journal, 46*(5), 554–571.

Cavanaugh, M. A., Boswell, W. R., Roehling, M. V., & Boudreau, J. W. (2000). An empirical examination of self-reported work stress among U.S. managers. *Journal of Applied Psychology, 85*(1), 65–74.

Conger, J. A., & Kanungo, R. N. (1988). The empowerment process: Integrating theory and practice. *Academy of Management Review, 13*(3), 471–482.

Crawford, E. R., LePine, J. A., & Rich, B. L. (2010). Linking job demands and resources to employee engagement and burnout: A theoretical extension and meta-analytic test. *Journal of Applied Psychology, 95*(5), 834–848.

Daniels, K., & Guppy, A. (1994). Occupational stress, social support, job control, and psychological well-being. *Human Relations, 47*(12), 1523–1544.

deCharms, R. (1968). *Personal causation*. New York: Academic Press.

Deci, E. L. (1975). *Intrinsic motivation*. New York: Plenum Press.

Deci, E. L., Connell, J. P., & Ryan, R. M. (1989). Self-determination in a work organization. *Journal of Applied Psychology, 74*(4), 580–590.

Deci, E. L., Eghrari, H., Patrick, B. C., & Leone, D. R. (1994). Facilitating internalization: The self-determination theory perspective. *Journal of Personality, 62*(1), 119–142.

Deci, E. L., & Ryan, R. M. (1985a). *Intrinsic motivation and self-determination in human behavior*. New York: Platinum Press.

Deci, E. L., & Ryan, R. M. (1985b). The general causality orientations scale: Self-determination in personality. *Journal of Research in Personality, 19*(2), 109–134.

Deci, E. L., & Ryan, R. M. (2000). The "what" and "why" of goal pursuits: Human needs and the self-determination of behavior. *Psychological Inquiry, 11*(4), 227–268.

Deci, E. L., & Ryan, R. M. (2002). *Handbook of self-determination research*. Rochester, NY: University of Rochester Press.

Deci, E. L., & Ryan, R. M. (2008). Self-determination theory: A macrotheory of human motivation, development, and health. *Canadian Psychology/Psychologie Canadienne, 49*(3), 182–185.

Demerouti, E., & Bakker, A. B. (2011). The Job Demands–Resources model: Challenges for future research. *South African Journal of Industrial Psychology, 37*, 1–9.

Demerouti, E., Bakker, A. B., Nachreiner, F., & Schaufeli, W. B. (2001). The Job Demands-Resources model of burnout. *Journal of Applied Psychology, 86*(3), 499–512.

Dysvik, A., & Kuvaas, B. (2011). Intrinsic motivation as a moderator on the relationship between perceived job autonomy and work performance. *European Journal of Work and Organizational Psychology, 20*(3), 367–387.

Fernet, C. (2011). Development and validation of the Work Role Motivation Scale for School Principals (WRMS-SP). *Educational Administration Quarterly, 47*(2), 307–331.

Fernet, C., Austin, S., Trépanier, S. G., & Dussault, M. (2013). How do job characteristics contribute to burnout? Examining the distinct mediating role of perceived autonomy, competence, and relatedness. *European Journal of Work and Organizational Psychology, 22*(2), 123–137.

Fernet, C., Austin, S., & Vallerand, R. J. (2012). The effects of work motivation on employee exhaustion and commitment: An extension of the JD-R model. *Work & Stress, 26*(3), 213–229

Fernet, C., Gagné, M., & Austin, S. (2010). When does quality of relationships with coworkers predict burnout over time? The moderating role of work motivation. *Journal of Organizational Behavior, 31*(8), 1163–1180.

Fernet, C., Guay, F., & Senécal, C. (2004). Adjusting to job demands: The role of work self-determination and job control in predicting burnout. *Journal of Vocational Behavior, 65*(1), 39–56.

Fernet, C., Guay, F., Senécal, C., & Austin, S. (2012). Predicting intraindividual changes in teacher burnout: The role of perceived school environment and motivational factors. *Teaching and Teacher Education, 28*, 514–525.

Fernet, C., Senécal, C., Guay, F., Marsh, H., & Dowson, M. (2008). The Work Tasks Motivation Scale for Teachers (WTMST). *Journal of Career Assessment, 16*(2), 256–279.

Fernet, C., Trépanier, S. G., Austin, S., Gagné, M., & Forest, J. (2014). *Transformational leadership and optimal functioning at work: On the mediating role of employees' perceived job characteristics and motivation*. Submitted for publication.

Frese, M., & Zapf, D. (1994). Methodological issues in the study of work stress: Objective vs subjective measurement of work stress and the question of longitudinal studies. In C. L. Cooper, & R. Payne (Eds.), *Causes, coping and consequences of stress at work* (pp. 375–411). Oxford, England: John Wiley & Sons.

Gagné, M., & Deci, E. L. (2005). Self-determination theory and work motivation. *Journal of Organizational Behavior, 26*(4), 331–362.

Gagné, M., Forest, J., Gilbert, M.-H., Aubé, C., Morin, E., & Malorni, A. (2010). The Motivation at Work Scale: Validation evidence in two languages. *Educational and Psychological Measurement, 70*(4), 628–646.

Ganster, D. C., & Perrewé, P. L. (2011). Theories of occupational stress. In J. C. Quick, & L. E. Tetrick (Eds.), *Handbook of occupational health psychology* (2nd ed., pp. 37–53). Washington, DC: American Psychological Association.

Guay, F., & Vallerand, R. (1997). Social context, students' motivation, and academic achievement: Toward a process model. *Social Psychology of Education, 1*, 211–233.

Hakanen, J. J., & Roodt, G. (2010). Using the Job Demands-Resources model to predict engagement: Analysing a conceptual model. In A. B. Bakker, & M. P. Leiter (Eds.), *Work engagement: A handbook of essential theory and research* (pp. 85–101). New York: Psychology Press.

Hodge, K., Lonsdale, C., & Ng, J. Y. Y. (2008). Burnout in elite rugby: Relationships with basic psychological needs fulfilment. *Journal of Sports Sciences, 26*, 835–844.

Kahn, R. L., & Byosiere, P. (1992). Stress in organizations. In M. D. Dunnette & L. M. Hough (Eds.), *Handbook of industrial and organizational psychology* (2nd ed., Vol. 3, pp. 571–650). Palo Alto, CA: Consulting Psychologists Press.

Karasek, R. A. (1979). Job demands, job decision latitude, and mental strain: Implications for job redesign. *Administrative Science Quarterly, 24*(2), 285–308.

Karasek, R. A., & Theorell, T. (1990). *Healthy work: Stress, productivity, and the reconstruction of working life*. New York: Basic Books.

Lee, R. T., & Ashforth, B. E. (1996). A meta-analytic examination of the correlates of the three dimensions of job burnout. *Journal of Applied Psychology, 81*(2), 123–133.

LePine, J. A., LePine, M. A., & Jackson, C. L. (2004). Challenge and hindrance stress: Relationships with exhaustion, motivation to learn, and learning performance. *Journal of Applied Psychology, 89*(5), 883–891.

LePine, J. A., Podsakoff, N. P., & LePine, M. A. (2005). A meta-analytic test of the challenge stressor-hindrance stressor framework: An explanation for inconsistent relationships among stressors and performance. *Academy of Management Journal, 48*(5), 764–775.

Lévesque, M., Blais, M. R., & Hess, U. (2004). Motivation, comportements organisationnels discrétionnaires et bien-être en milieu Africain: Quand le devoir oblige? [Motivation, discretionary organizational behaviors, and wellbeing in an African setting: When is it a duty?] *Canadian Journal of Behavioural Science/Revue Canadienne des Sciences du Comportement, 36*(4), 321–332.

Lin, C.-P., Tsai, Y. H., & Chiu, C.-K. (2009). Modeling customer loyalty from an integrative perspective of self-determination theory and expectation–confirmation theory. *Journal of Business and Psychology, 24*(3), 315–326.

Lonsdale, C., Hodge, K., & Rose, E. (2009). Athlete burnout in elite sport: A self-determination perspective. *Journal of Sports Sciences, 27*(8), 785–795.

Luthans, F., Youssef, C. M., & Avolio, B. J. (2007). *Psychological capital: Developing the human competitive edge.* New York: Oxford University Press.

Marsh, H. W., & Yeung, A. S. (1998). Top-down, bottom-up, and horizontal models: The direction of causality in multidimensional, hierarchical self-concept models. *Journal of Personality and Social Psychology, 75*(2), 509–527.

Maslach, C. (1982). *Burnout: The cost of caring.* Englewood Cliffs, NJ: Prentice-Hall.

Maslach, C., Schaufeli, W. B., & Leiter, M. P. (2001). Job burnout. *Annual Review of Psychology, 52*, 397–422.

Mouratidis, A., Vansteenkiste, M., Lens, W., & Sideridis, G. (2008). The motivating role of positive feedback in sport and physical education: Evidence for a motivational model. *Journal of Sport & Exercise Psychology, 30*, 240–268.

Parker, S. L., Jimmieson, N. L., & Amiot, C. E. (2010). Self-determination as a moderator of demands and control: Implications for employee strain and engagement. *Journal of Vocational Behavior, 76*(1), 52–67.

Parkes, K. R. (1994). Personality and coping as moderators of work stress processes: Models, methods and measures. *Work & Stress, 8*(2), 110–129.

Pelletier, L. G., Séguin-Lévesque, C., & Legault, L. (2002). Pressure from above and pressure from below as determinants of teachers' motivation and teaching behaviors. *Journal of Educational Psychology, 94*(1), 186–196.

Piccolo, R. F., & Colquitt, J. A. (2006). Transformational leadership and job behaviors: The mediating role of core job characteristics. *Academy of Management Journal, 49*(2), 327–340.

Quested, E., & Duda, J. L. (2011). Antecedents of burnout among elite dancers: A longitudinal test of basic needs theory. *Psychology of Sport and Exercise, 12*(2), 159–167.

Quick, J. C., Macik-Frey, M., & Cooper, C. L. (2007). Managerial dimensions of organizational health: The healthy leader at work. *Journal of Management Studies, 44*(2), 189–205.

Reinboth, M., & Duda, J. L. (2006). Perceived motivational climate, need satisfaction and indices of well-being in team sports: A longitudinal perspective. *Psychology of Sport and Exercise, 7*(3), 269–286.

Reis, H. T., Sheldon, K. M., Gable, S. L., Roscoe, J., & Ryan, R. M. (2000). Daily well-being: The role of autonomy, competence, and relatedness. *Personality and Social Psychology Bulletin, 26*(4), 419–435.

Rosse, J. G., Boss, R. W., Johnson, A. E., & Crown, D. F. (1991). Conceptualizing the role of self-esteem in the burnout process. *Group & Organization Studies, 16*(4), 428–451.

Ryan, R. M. (1995). Psychological needs and the facilitation of integrative processes. *Journal of Personality, 63*(3), 398–427.

Ryan, R. M., & Deci, E. L. (2000). Self-determination theory and the facilitation of intrinsic motivation, social development, and well-being. *American Psychologist, 55*(1), 68–78.

Sarrazin, P., Vallerand, R., Guillet, E., Pelletier, L., & Cury, F. (2002). Motivation and dropout in female handballers: A 21-month prospective study. *European Journal of Social Psychology, 32*(3), 395–418.

Schaubroeck, J., Jones, J. R., & Xie, J. L. (2001). Individual differences in utilizing control to cope with job demands: Effects on susceptibility to infectious disease. *Journal of Applied Psychology, 86*(2), 265–278.

Schaufeli, W. B., & Bakker, A. B. (2004). Job demands, job resources, and their relationship with burnout and engagement: A multi-sample study. *Journal of Organizational Behavior, 25*, 293–315.

Schaufeli, W. B., & Enzmann, D. (1998). *The burnout companion to study and practice: A critical analysis.* London: Taylor & Francis.

Selye, H. (1982). History and present status of the stress concept. In L. Goldberger, & S. Breznitz (Eds.), *Handbook of stress: Theoretical and clinical aspects* (pp. 1–17). New York: The Free Press.

Smircich, L., & Morgan, G. (1982). Leadership: The management of meaning. *Journal of Applied Behavioral Science, 18*(3), 257–273.

Spector, P. E. (2002). Employee control and occupational stress. *Current Directions in Psychological Science, 11*(4), 133–136.

Srivastava, A., Bartol, K. M., & Locke, E. A. (2006). Empowering leadership in management teams: Effects on knowledge sharing, efficacy, and performance. *Academy of Management Journal, 49*(6), 1239–1251.

Ten Brummelhuis, L. L., Ter Hoeven, C. L., Bakker, A. B., & Peper, B. (2011). Breaking through the loss cycle of burnout: The role of motivation. *Journal of Occupational and Organizational Psychology, 84*(2), 268–287.

Tetrick, L. E., & Quick, J. C. (2011). Overview of occupational health psychology: Public health in occupational settings. In J. C. Quick, & L. E. Tetrick (Eds.), *Handbook of occupational health psychology* (2nd ed., pp. 3–20). Washington, DC: American Psychological Association.

Tremblay, M. A., Blanchard, C. M., Taylor, S., Pelletier, L. G., & Villeneuve, M. (2009). Work Extrinsic and Intrinsic Motivation Scale: Its value for organizational research. *Canadian Journal of Behavioural Science, 41*(4), 213–226.

Trépanier, S. G., Fernet, C., & Austin, S. (2013). The moderating role of autonomous motivation in the job demands-strain relation: A two sample study. *Motivation and Emotion. 37*(1), 93–105.

Vallerand, R. J. (1997). Toward a hierarchical model of intrinsic and extrinsic motivation. In M. P. Zanna (Ed.), *Advances in experimental social psychology* (Vol. 29, pp. 271–360). San Diego, CA: Academic Press.

Vallerand, R. J., Fortier, M. S., & Guay, F. (1997). Self-determination and persistence in a real-life setting: Toward a motivational model of high school dropout. *Journal of Personality and Social Psychology, 72*(5), 1161–1176.

Van den Broeck, A., Schreurs, B., De Witte, H., Vansteenkiste, M., Germeys, F., & Schaufeli, W. B. (2011). Understanding workaholics' motivations: A self-determination perspective. *Applied Psychology: An International Review, 60*(4), 600–621.

Van den Broeck, A., Van Ruysseveldt, J., Smulders, P., & De Witte, H. (2011). Does an intrinsic work value orientation strengthen the impact of job resources? A perspective from the Job Demands–Resources Model. *European Journal of Work and Organizational Psychology, 20*(5), 581–609.

Van den Broeck, A., Vansteenkiste, M., De Witte, H., & Lens, W. (2008). Explaining the relationships between job characteristics, burnout, and engagement: The role of basic psychological need satisfaction. *Work & Stress, 22*(3), 277–294.

Van den Broeck, A., Vansteenkiste, M., De Witte, H., Soenens, B., & Lens, W. (2010). Capturing autonomy, competence, and relatedness at work: Construction and initial validation of the Work-Related Basic Need Satisfaction Scale. *Journal of Occupational and Organizational Psychology, 83*(4), 981–1002.

Vansteenkiste, M., Niemiec, C. P., & Soenens, B. (2010). The development of the five mini-theories of self-determination theory: An historical overview, emerging trends, and future directions. In T. Urdan, & S. Karabenick (Eds.), *Advances in motivation and achievement* (Vol. 16, pp. 105–166). Bingley, UK: Emerald Publishing.

White, R. W. (1959). Motivation reconsidered: The concept of competence. *Psychological Review, 66*(5), 297–333.

World Health Organization. (1958). *The first ten years of the World Health Organization.* Geneva: World Health Organization.

Yukl, G. (1989). Managerial leadership: A review of theory and research. *Journal of Management, 15*(2), 251–289.

Zapf, D., Dormann, C., & Frese, M. (1996). Longitudinal studies in organizational stress research: A review of the literature with reference to methodological issues. *Journal of Occupational Health Psychology, 1*(2), 145–169.

CHAPTER
15

Self-Determination as a Nutriment for Thriving: Building an Integrative Model of Human Growth at Work

Gretchen M. Spreitzer *and* Christine Porath

Abstract

Thriving may be defined as the joint experience of vitality and learning. It is a marker of individual growth and forward progress. As a result, thriving can serve as a kind of internal gauge that individuals can use to assess how they are doing in terms of their well-being at work. We review findings regarding thriving including key outcomes and antecedent conditions. Given the focus of this volume on self-determination theory, we articulate how thriving may be nurtured from the nutriments of autonomous motivation. All three nutriments of autonomous motivation—a sense of autonomy, competence, and relatedness—facilitate more thriving at work. To this end, by linking autonomous motivation and thriving, we can build a more integrative model of human growth at work.

Key Words: thriving, self-determination, autonomous motivation, vitality, learning, energy, growth

---

Introduction

As is true for all living creatures, after an organism stops growing, it begins the process of dying. Growth is an essential human process for life. To truly feel alive, individuals need to be growing psychologically as well as physically. Unfortunately, although much is known about how human beings grow physically over the lifespan, less is known about how they grow psychologically. In this chapter, we articulate how self-determination theory (SDT) and thriving together contribute to building an integrative model of human growth. For purposes of this handbook, we focus our attention on growth in a work context. The thriving construct reflects two key markers or indicators of human growth at work: vitality and learning. The two indicators help us to identify how we would know psychological growth when we see it (akin to how more inches or pounds are indicative of physical growth). SDT, in contrast, identifies key nutriments (or psychological antecedents) for human growth more generally. SDT specifies the importance of satisfying three psychological needs for growth to occur: (1) autonomy, (2) competence, and (3) relatedness. In this way, we suggest that SDT specifies three important nutriments for human thriving.

In this chapter, we further develop the interplay between SDT and thriving to begin to build an integrative model of human growth in a work context. We first provide an overview of thriving and distinguish it from related constructs and growth theories. Then, we use SDT to articulate how the satisfaction of the three psychological needs can serve as nutriments to thriving. We also identify other possible nutriments to the process of human growth at work. We draw on empirical research where available to support this integrative model of human growth in a work context. Finally, we

245

offer directions for future research as well as practical implications of the integrative model of human growth at work.[1]

What is Thriving?

The notion of thriving has been embedded in a number of literatures. In medicine, failure to thrive is a diagnosis pertaining to infants and the frail elderly indicated by an acute lack of physical growth—manifest in listlessness, immobility, apathy, and no appetite (Bakwin, 1949; Bergland & Kirkevold, 2001; Verderey, 1995). In psychology, thriving is more about psychological growth than physical growth. When psychologically thriving, individuals are not merely surviving (Saakvitne, Tennen, & Affleck, 1998) or getting by (Benson & Scales, 2009), but they are growing (Calhoun & Tedeschi, 1998; Joseph & Linley, 2008)—on an upward trajectory (Hall et al., 2009; Thomas & Hall, 2008). Although some emphasize thriving more specifically as growth in response to trauma (i.e., resilience; Carver, 1998; Ickovics & Park, 1998), others see thriving as an everyday experience regarding how people interact with their environment (Blankenship, 1998). Although people can indeed thrive amidst a crisis, thriving is more than a rare event experienced only in a crisis or trauma. Indeed, in a series of interviews, Sonenshein, Dutton, Grant, Spreitzer, and Sutcliffe (2005) provided preliminary evidence that thriving can occur at work during everyday moments. Employees in a wide range of jobs across three companies were able to provide at least one narrative of their own experience of thriving at work.

In empirical research in other disciplines, thriving is defined broadly with little consensus (Benson & Scales, 2009; Campa, Bradshaw, Eckenrode, & Zielinski, 2008; Haight, Barba, Tesh, & Courts, 2002; King et al., 2005; Theokas et al., 2005; Walker & Sterling, 2007). However, many of these definitions are specific to the narrow contexts in which these studies were conducted, including the progress of adolescents in school, the recovery of women dealing with domestic abuse, or the health of nursing home residents. For example, in a study of delinquent adolescents (Campa et al., 2008), thriving was conceptualized as being employed, civically engaged, and completing high school. In a study of women recovering from abuse, thriving included a woman's energy, individual resources, and the nature of the relationship with adversity (Poorman, 2002). Although informative in understanding the broad applicability and multidisciplinary foundations of thriving, these definitions are less pertinent to an employment setting.

To this end, we draw on the prior, interdisciplinary literature to help provide evidence for the definition and underlying two dimensions of thriving at work advanced by Spreitzer, Sutcliffe, Dutton, Sonenshein, and Grant (2005): a feeling of vitality at work, and a sense that one is learning or getting better at work. Here we draw on the foundational paper articulating the theory development of thriving by Spreitzer et al. (2005). They define thriving as the psychological experience of growth in a positive capacity. This experience is captured from excerpts from two narratives they collected from employees' stories of thriving at work:

> One social worker described thriving as: "I know thriving as I feel it. It is like going forward. It is not staying in place. It is not stagnant. You are moving forward; not necessarily in job titles or positions, but just being able to move forward thinking and in the activities that you are engaged in and in your mindset, all of those things."
>
> A mid-level manager in a large metropolitan non profit described thriving as "being energized, feeling valued, and that what you do is valued . . . Thriving is being productive . . . being open to the challenges presented and to learn and grow and having those opportunities to grow." (p. 538)

In both of these examples, employees express thriving as the development of some form of enhanced capacity that they experience as an upward movement or progression associated with heightened energy. This definition of thriving is consistent with Ryff's (1989) and Rogers' (1961) perspectives on personal growth. Ryff suggests that when individuals grow, they consider themselves to be expanding in ways that reflect enhanced self-knowledge and effectiveness (Ryff, 1989). Thriving reflects "continually developing and becoming, rather than achieving a fixed state wherein one is fully developed" (Ryff, 1989, p. 1071). Individuals have a sense of realizing their own potential and seeing improvement in the self and their behaviors over time (Ryff, 1989). In short, thriving involves active, intentional engagement in the process of personal growth (Robitschek, 1998).

Like biomarkers in medicine (that is, specific indicators used to measure the effects or progress of a condition) vitality and learning are markers of thriving (Spreitzer et al., 2005, p. 538), acting as an indication of the extent to which a person is thriving at any point in time. Vitality indicates the sense that one is energized (Nix, Ryan, Manly, & Deci, 1999) and has a zest for life (Miller & Stiver, 1997), while learning signifies acquisition and application of knowledge and skills to build capability (Edmondson, 1999). Why vitality and learning as the markers of thriving? The two encompass both the affective (vitality) and cognitive (learning) dimensions of the psychological experience of personal growth. Ryff (1989), for example, suggests that when individuals grow, they consider themselves to be expanding in ways that reflect enhanced self-knowledge and effectiveness. Likewise, Carver (1998) conceives of thriving as the psychological experience of growth in a positive capacity (i.e., a constructive or forward direction) that energizes and enlivens. Thus, prior research in psychology has highlighted both the affective and cognitive foundations of human growth.

Further, building on Spreitzer and colleagues' (2005) conceptualization, thriving is viewed as a state rather than as a personality disposition. Individual differences can be differentiated between distal, trait-like constructs and proximal, state-like constructs (Chen, Gully, Whiteman, & Kilcullen, 2000). Trait-like constructs are more stable over time (Ackerman & Humphreys, 1990). In contrast, state-like individual differences are more malleable over time and influenced by the situation or task in which one is embedded. In Spreitzer et al.'s (2005) model, thriving is "socially embedded"—that is, depending on the specific situation or circumstances a person finds themselves in, he or she may be more or less thriving at any given point in time. For example, certain roles and responsibilities, reporting relationships, or task constraints may be conducive to learning and facilitate vitality or may deplete them. At a more macro level, in a downsizing context when resources are scarce, there may be many demands on people that may deplete energy and reduce resources for learning. But in a context of fast growth, employees may feel more energized and find more opportunities for learning. This social embeddedness may represent the antecedents to feelings of autonomous motivation, which in turn predict thriving.

Consistent with this, thriving is conceptualized as a continuum where people are more or less thriving at any point in time. There may be personality traits that predispose individuals to experience more or less thriving at work. For example, Porath, Spreitzer, Gibson, and Garnett (2012) found thriving to be related to a more proactive personality, more of a learning orientation, and more positive core self-evaluations.

Thriving is a desirable subjective experience (Warr, 1990), helping individuals to understand what and how they are doing, and whether it is increasing their individual functioning and adaptability at work. In this way, thriving can be an internally derived explanatory mechanism for self-regulation, serving as a type of gauge for individuals to sense well-being and progress in their self-regulatory process (Spreitzer et al., 2005). As markers of thriving, we theorize and have found that vitality and learning combine in an additive manner to indicate one's level of thriving. Although each can signify progress toward growth and personal development, more of both markers indicate optimal levels of thriving. If one is learning, but feels depleted, thriving suffers. Conversely, if one feels energized and alive in their work, but finds personal learning to be stagnant, limited thriving is experienced. Thriving, then, is indicated by the joint experience of a sense of vitality and learning.

Recently a measure of thriving has been developed and validated (Porath et al., 2012) across five different samples. The researchers collected data from respondents and their managers across a variety of samples ranging from young adults to well-seasoned executives; from students (i.e., undergraduates and executive MBAs) in academic settings to companies in a range of industries; and those who work in blue collar jobs to those who hold top executive positions in professional firms. The 10 items in Table 15.1 were validated to measure the two dimensions of thriving. The five items measuring each dimension load appropriately on each first order factor and then the two first order factors load onto a thriving higher order factor. The five items measuring vitality are adapted from Ryan and Fredrick (1997)—they have also been shown to be valid and reliable in prior research. The overall thriving scale also has strong item reliability.

Distinguishing Thriving from Related Growth Constructs

As articulated in Spreitzer et al. (2005), thriving can be distinguished from related constructs pertinent to human growth including psychological well-being, self-actualization, and engagement. First, Ryff's (1989) theory of psychological well-being identifies six core dimensions of well-being. Her dimension of personal growth—defined as a sense of continued growth and development as a person—is similar but different to our definition of thriving. Thriving differs from Ryff's psychological well-being because rather than treating all of these

Table 15.1 Items measuring the two dimensions of thriving at work.

Learning items
• I find myself learning often
• I continue to learn more as time goes by
• I see myself continually improving
• I am not learning (reverse code)
• I am developing a lot as a person

Vitality items
• I feel alive and vital
• I have energy and spirit
• I do not feel very energetic (reverse code)
• I feel alert and awake
• I am looking forward to each new day

components as indicators of well-being, as Ryff does, the learning dimension of thriving is consistent with her personal growth component and articulates how the other components are nutriments of growth (consistent with SDT). For example, positive relations with others are similar to a sense of relatedness. Environmental mastery, the capacity to manage one's life and surrounding world, is similar to a sense of competence. Finally, her construct of autonomy is directly analogous to a sense of autonomy. Her other components do not explicitly capture the vitality dimension of thriving.

Second, self-actualization may be defined as the desire for self-fulfillment and the tendency to become, in actuality, everything that one is capable of becoming (Maslow, 1943). Thriving is a state and may be an indicator that one is on the path to self-actualization. We share with Maslow the belief in the potency of work organizations as sites for human growth.

Third, thriving is distinct from work engagement, which is defined as a positive state of mind characterized by vigor, dedication, and absorption (Schaufeli, Bakker, & Salanova, 2006). Engagement and thriving are complementary in their common dimension of energy—called vigor in conceptualizations of engagement and vitality in our conceptualization of thriving. The two also have differences as reflected in the additional dedication/absorption dimensions for engagement and learning for thriving (Spreitzer, Lam, and Fritz, 2010). It is possible

for a person to be engaged at work and not thriving—or thriving and not engaged. For example, an employee can feel engaged at work—energized, dedicated to the purpose of their work, and highly absorbed (maybe even in flow)—but may not necessarily be learning and growing. This might be the case for individuals in a long-term job where they feel a real sense of purpose and involvement as well as experience a high level of competence and efficacy. They may still feel rather stagnant in their opportunities for learning and personal growth. Conversely, one can be thriving but not necessarily engaged. Such individuals might be growing and developing in ways that reduce their dedication to their current job as they explore new avenues for their personal or career development, their work, or even new positions. These may be those people seeking significant career changes (Ibarra, 2002).

Finally, thriving is distinct from the personality trait of growth-need-strength (Hackman & Oldham, 1980), which is an individual difference highlighting one's need to grow. Growth-need-strength is more stable and less malleable by changes in the work environment. The contrasting assumption underlying thriving is that all individuals have a propensity to grow.

Why Care About Thriving?

Thriving can serve as a gauge for people to sense progress in their growth and development. This gauge helps people understand whether what they are doing and how they are doing is increasing their short-term individual functioning and long-term resourcefulness to become more effective at work. Like a thermometer, a thriving gauge helps individuals understand if they are overheating (with a propensity for burning out) or too cold (indicating stagnation and depletion).

This stands in contrast to the traditional use of external cues, largely feedback from others, in self-regulation and assessments of personal effectiveness. Prior research has typically focused on how individuals assess their progress toward goal attainment and effectiveness using feedback from their supervisor, customers, coworkers, or even the job itself (e.g., Tsui & Ashford, 1994; Kluger & DeNisi, 1996). Individuals integrate this information regarding their progress toward goal attainment and regulate their behavioral choices and efforts accordingly (Klein, 1991). Even in social cognitive theory, which offers a more empowered view of volitional regulation, the external information gathered from others through active feedback seeking is used to assess one's progress and make subsequent adjustments (Porath et al., 2012).

Through our articulation of thriving, we are learning more about how people use internally generated cues, such as how they feel (e.g., their affect), in assessing forward progress or growth. In current self-regulatory models, affect is theorized as an outcome of goal attainment, such as the pride that results from achieving one's goals, or as the disappointment that is generated through externally provided negative feedback that motivates corrective changes. However, internal cues can also serve as potential gauges for self-regulation. Paying attention to how one feels is particularly important for self-regulating well-being and burnout as well as personal progress.

For example, one consultant we know checks in with herself multiple times a day to see how she is feeling in terms of her vitality and learning and makes adjustments accordingly. If she feels like she is dragging, she takes a quick power nap (if possible), takes a break and a brief walk outside, and/or grabs a snack and breather. She also tries to schedule the work that is most important during her high-energy periods of the day (typically early morning), and retain other, less crucial professional and personal tasks for periods when she knows she is not typically as energetic or likely to be thriving. A top executive we know uses similar strategies over longer term periods. If he senses that he is in danger of burning out after too many long days and stressful events, he is sure to schedule golf into his weekly schedule. Similarly, he restrains himself from checking work email during much of each weekend. He finds he is far fresher and more productive when he uses these self-regulatory routines to monitor his thriving. While more difficult, even an employee with little autonomy can find ways to enhance vitality and learning. For example, a factory employee on the production line could increase learning by seeking new ways to work more efficiently and safely. By sharing those innovations with coworkers, the factory worker is also likely to increase his or her feelings of vitality.

In these and other ways, people may use their sense of thriving in their work as a gauge to assess progress, in addition to the exogenous feedback received from others about how they are doing. If individuals pay attention to their vitality and learning as they do their work, they can better self-regulate for sustained performance over time, minimizing the potential for burnout. Indeed, consistent with the ideas of thriving as a self-regulatory gauge, as we describe later, thriving has been found to be related to both performance and well-being outcomes across studies (Porath, et al., 2012).

Thriving and Performance

Individuals who report higher levels of thriving in their work are found to have higher levels of job performance. In a sample of blue collar employees in the plant operations section of a large public university, those employees reporting higher levels of thriving were rated by their bosses as performing significantly higher than those reporting lower levels of thriving (Porath et al., 2012). Similarly, in a sample of white collar employees across six organizations, employees who rated themselves with higher levels of thriving were assessed by their bosses as performing at a higher level (Porath et al., 2012). In this study of six firms, employees just one standard deviation (less than one on a seven-point scale) above the mean performed more than 14% better than those one standard deviation below the mean. Additionally, they were 32% more committed to the organization, 46% more satisfied with their job, and 125% less burned out! Thriving has also been found to be related to more career development initiative, suggesting that thriving employees are more proactive in seeking out opportunities to learn and grow (Porath, et al., 2012), which may also contribute to their enhanced performance at work.

Thriving has been found to be particularly important for the effectiveness of leaders. In a sample of executives cutting across a variety of industries, thriving executives were rated substantially higher by their subordinates as more effective than executives who report lower levels of thriving (Porath et al., 2012). The subordinates of thriving leaders describe them as role models of how work can be done, who seek opportunities to take initiative, and who enable others to act. Thriving leaders are apt to enable thriving followers.

Thriving, Extra-Role Performance, and Relationship Building

The theoretical model advanced by Spreitzer et al. (2005) suggests when people are thriving, they heedfully interrelate with others—that is, they look out for the needs of others with whom they work. Our findings suggest that this is the case—those reporting higher levels of thriving developed more supportive relationships from colleagues (after 3 months) than those reporting lower levels of thriving.

Because they also look outside the formal task requirements as a way of learning new things (Spreitzer, et al., 2005), individuals who report more thriving are also likely to see ways to contribute to their work beyond that specified by their formal roles. They see opportunities to engage in affiliative behaviors, such as helping others, sharing, and cooperating. An individual must be able to identify the opportunities for organizational citizenship behaviors (have the focused intention and engage in accumulation of knowledge) and then exert the energy to go beyond the call of duty. In a study of six firms, we have found that those who experience more thriving engage in more organizational citizenship behaviors, as rated by their bosses.

Thriving and Well-being

Across industries, executives who see themselves as thriving report themselves to be healthier with fewer physical or somatic complaints. In another study, professionals across six firms in diverse industries also report feeling less burned out. The better health and reduced propensity to burn out may be what enables employees to sustain their thriving over time. In this way, thriving can enable effective self-regulation for better well-being over time.

Vitality and Learning Dimensions Are Both Important

We should also note that the most positive outcomes of thriving come when both levels of both learning and vitality are high. Just learning or just vitality by itself is not enough. Learning and vitality help regulate sustained performance. For example, those with higher levels of learning and vitality have performance scores that are 15% higher (as rated by their bosses) than when their levels of either or both learning and vitality are low. We have learned that, in particular, when people engage in high levels of learning over time without accompanying high levels of vitality, performance and health may wane. Too much learning focus can contribute to overload and diminishing returns.

These series of findings regarding thriving suggests that thriving matters for individuals and the organizations of which they are a part. Thriving individuals not only perform better, but they go above and beyond the call of duty in helping others. They tend to be healthier and less burned out. We turn now to how to enhance individuals' propensity to thrive in their work.

What Can Be Done to Enable More Thriving at Work?

By drawing on SDT, we can better understand what enables people's inherent growth tendencies.

Bringing SDT and thriving together, we can begin to flesh out a more integrative model of human growth at work. SDT assumes that every human being has an innate tendency toward psychological growth and development. As a whole, individuals strive to master ongoing challenges and to integrate their experiences into a coherent sense of self (Gagné & Deci, 2005). SDT is concerned with the motivation behind the choices that people make without any external influence or control (Deci, Connell, & Ryan, 1989). It focuses on the degree to which an individual's behavior is self-motivated and self-determined.

Empirical research suggests that when individuals are intrinsically motivated (i.e., doing something for its own enjoyment rather than compelled for instrumental reasons), behaviors are less effortful and vitality increases (Nix et al., 1999). Consistent with the vitality dimension of thriving, Deci and Ryan (2000) define vitality as energy available to the self, either directly or indirectly, from meeting basic psychological needs. Subjective vitality captures a sense of enthusiasm, aliveness, and positive energy available to the self (Ryan & Deci, 2008).

The assumption that vitality or energy can be renewed stands in contrast to self-regulation theorists (e.g., Baumeister, Bratlavsky, Muraven, & Tice, 1998) who have posited that self-regulation activity depletes energy. A key assumption of SDT is that energy can be maintained and even enhanced, not just depleted or expended. Whereas self-regulation theory and conservation of resources theory (Hobfoll, 1989) focus on how energy is depleted (through self-control activities), SDT focuses on the forces that may catalyze or generate energy. SDT assumes that although efforts to control the self (such as emotional regulation) can drain energy (Baumeister & Vohs, 2007), autonomous self-regulation is substantially less draining (Muraven, Gagné, & Rosman, 2008; Ryan & Deci, 2008). According to SDT, when individuals have choice and their efforts are volitional, energy is depleted at a slower rate than when activity is imposed (Ryan & Deci, 2008). SDT researchers offer an alternative perspective: whereas controlled regulation depletes energy, autonomous regulation can actually be vitalizing. At its core, SDT proposes that when individuals are intrinsically motivated (i.e., doing something for its own enjoyment or interest rather than being compelled for instrumental reasons) behaviors are less effortful and less depleting.

More specifically, SDT posits that the larger social context can contribute to feelings of vitality

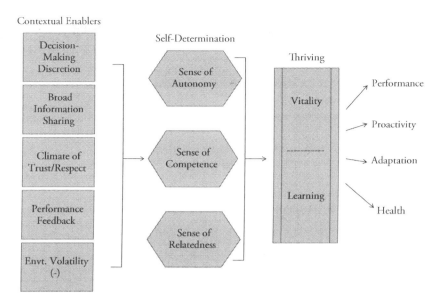

Fig. 15.1. An integrative model of human growth at work.

by satisfying individual psychological needs for relatedness (i.e., feeling connected), competence (i.e., feeling capable), and autonomy (i.e., feeling volitional). Ryan and Deci (2000) suggest that these three dimensions provide the essential psychological nutriments for agentic behavior and ultimately for psychological growth and development. In each case, the three components of autonomous motivation are the key mechanisms explaining how context affects behavior (Figure 15.1). Conceptual work has suggested that these same needs are important for thriving (Spreitzer et al., 2005). In the sections that follow, we address how the SDT components promote greater vitality, learning, and thriving.

A study using an experience-sampling method with college students showed that autonomy, competence, and relatedness were associated with greater vitality (Reis, Sheldon, Gable, Roscoe, & Ryan, 2000). In longitudinal research of elite female gymnasts, support was again shown for the vitality-increasing effects of autonomy, competence, and relatedness, even when they had engaged in physically demanding and calorie-draining activities (Gagné, Ryan, & Bargmann, 2003).

Research on subjective vitality in organizational settings also has begun to emerge. For example, Quinn and Dutton (2005) have theorized how energy can be created in a conversation by enhancing one's feelings of autonomy, competence, and relatedness. A diary study found that people had more subjective vitality when they experienced more autonomous motivation in their daily work experiences (Ryan, Bernstein, & Brown, 2010). Interestingly, they also found that vitality was higher on weekends when there were more opportunities for autonomy and relatedness activities.

Of the three psychological needs, autonomy is the strongest predictor of energy. Autonomy is defined as the self-endorsement of one's actions, or the extent to which one feels a sense of choice concerning one's behaviors (Ryan & Deci, 2008, p. 707). When behavior is autonomous, the assumption is that it requires less inhibition, creates less conflict, and thus is most energizing. Recently, Muravan et al. (2008) sought to integrate SDT with ego-depletion ideas by designing a research study that examined autonomy as a moderator in determining how depleting a self-control activity would be. Drawing from SDT, they hypothesized that more autonomous support of the self-control activity would reduce the magnitude of depletion. In a series of three studies, they found support for the idea that "why" someone exerts self-control may influence how depleting the activity will be. Individuals whose self-control behavior was perceived more as autonomous performed better on subsequent self-control activities than individuals who felt pressured to engage in self-control activities. In fact, they found an increase in vitality following autonomous self-control, which helped replenish lost ego-strength. This supports the idea that positive experiences help negate the effects of depletion (Tice, Baumeister, Shmueli, Muravan, 2007). Consistent with this, autonomous individuals performed better on subsequent self-control activities than individuals whose behavior was controlled by external forces, even when controlling for anxiety, stress, unpleasantness, or reduced motivation (Muravan et al., 2008). Finally, autonomy (along with competence and relatedness) has been found to reduce feelings of burnout (Fernet, Austin, Trépanier, & Dussault, 2012).

Competence involves a sense of efficacy in dealing with the environment (Bandura, 1977) and making effective use of surrounding resources (Ryff, 1989). Feelings of competence have been tied to vitality and cognitive engagement. For instance, Vansteenkiste et al. (2007) found that intrinsic motivation is related to vitality via competency. Other research suggests that competency increases cognitive engagement in work tasks, particularly those that require novel thinking (Vinarski-Peretz, Binyamin, & Carmeli, 2011). Thus, competency should lead to greater thriving because it is related to vitality and learning (e.g., cognitive engagement on useful and novel tasks).

Finally, relatedness refers to feeling connected to others and having a sense of belongingness (Bowlby, 1979). Feelings of relatedness are also likely to increase thriving at work. Feeling connected to others increases affective (Carlson, Charlin, & Miller, 1988) and physiological (Brown, Nesse, Vinokur, & Smith, 2003) energy. People who have a network they feel connected with are likely to feel a greater sense of enthusiasm for the work they are doing within an organization (Gerbasi, Parker, Ballinger, & Cross 2011). The broaden-and-build model suggests that the positive affect developed through a sense of relatedness with people at work broadens thoughts and encourages exploration of people, objects, and situations (Frederickson, 2001), which also enhances the learning component of thriving. Relatedness also promotes psychological safety, in which one feels safe to take risks and explore new approaches (Edmondson, 1999). In doing so, relatedness enables learning (Edmondson, 1999) and subsequently, a sense of thriving.

A key insight from the SDT stream is that when one's context enables autonomy, competence, and relatedness, one is more likely to experience vitality (we should note that the SDT literature does not make any explicit link to the learning dimension of thriving; nevertheless, some of the logic does

link nicely to notions of growth and development, which implies at least some learning). SDT is at the center of our rationale for how context affects thriving because it describes how individuals pursue conditions that foster their own growth and development (Deci & Ryan, 2000). People do not thrive at work simply because they are exhorted to do so by a boss or forced to do so by the organizational system. Rather, when people act with volition, they are more likely to be oriented toward growth and experience vitality (Ryan & Deci, 2000). Empirically, we have tested how need satisfaction is related to thriving in our sample of six organizations (n=335) (Porath, Gibson, & Spreitzer, 2012). We found that the three dimensions of SDT (autonomy, competence, and relatedness) explained an extraordinary amount of variance in thriving—54%. Each of the SDT dimensions was a significant predictor of thriving. Moreover, each of these SDT dimensions significantly predicted both the vitality (affective) and learning (cognitive) dimensions of thriving.

In the sections that follow, we draw on Spreitzer et al.'s (2005) thriving model to articulate key antecedents in a work context that enable more thriving through enhanced autonomous motivation (see also Figure 15.1). We also go beyond Spreitzer et al. (2005) to offer two additional antecedents: performance feedback and environmental volatility. Although prior research has established a link between SDT and the vitality dimension of thriving, in the next sections we also make the case for the link to the learning dimension of thriving and find strong empirical support for it.

Decision-making Discretion

When individuals are exposed to work contexts that foster decision-making discretion, their feelings of *autonomy* are strengthened. Decision-making discretion creates an opportunity for individuals to feel more in control of their work, and to exercise choices about what to do and how to do it (Ryan & Deci, 2000). Decision-making discretion provides individuals with freedom and choices about how to do their work rather than being externally controlled, regulated, or pressured. Individuals who perceive that they have little autonomy to act volitionally by choosing work strategies or influencing working conditions—or who have doubts about their capabilities—prematurely slacken their task focus particularly when faced with challenges (Wood & Bandura, 1989). In contrast, as SDT theory indicates, when people feel autonomous, they are more likely to feel vital (Deci & Ryan, 2000).

Decision-making discretion is also likely to enhance the learning dimension of thriving through the SDT dimensions of competence and relatedness. When individuals can exercise choice about what to do and how to do it, they are more likely to feel *competent* to seek out new directions for doing their work (Amabile, 1993). Being part of organizational decisions helps individuals build new skills and feelings of competence, which leads them to feel more comfortable taking risks and exploring new opportunities (Spreitzer, 1996). Work contexts that support discretion can also strengthen *relatedness* beliefs (Ryan & Deci, 2000). Being part of organizational decisions contributes to a sense of connectedness with others, which encourages individuals to relate heedfully (Spreitzer et al., 2005).

Broad Information Sharing

Information sharing also fuels more thriving at work through enhanced autonomous motivation.[2] Having access to a broad array of information increases the likelihood that individuals will have the requisite knowledge to make good decisions (Spreitzer, 1996). As a result of this knowledge, individuals can feel more *competent* to perform their work. The sharing of information also increases individuals' competence because it increases their abilities to quickly uncover problems as they arise, and to integrate and coordinate actions. Accordingly, this increased capacity to respond effectively in unfamiliar or challenging situations fuels learning new behaviors (Bunderson & Sutcliffe, 2002). When information is disseminated broadly, individuals can increase their understanding of how the system works so they can feel more *autonomous* (Weick & Sutcliffe, 2001).

Climate of Trust and Respect

A climate of trust and respect also promotes more thriving through increased need satisfaction. When individuals are situated in climates of trust and respect they are likely to feel more *competent*, efficacious, and capable of mastering challenges in their environment (Spreitzer, 1995). When individuals feel that they can trust each other, they are more willing to take risks (Edmondson, 1999; Mayer, Davis, & Schoorman, 1995). Moreover, a climate of trust and respect also facilitates learning and experimentation with new behaviors (Bunderson & Sutcliffe, 2002; Spreitzer, 1995), in part because individuals feel safe to experiment. Finally, when individuals are exposed to a climate of trust and respect, they are more likely to believe that

they are worthy and valued organizational members. This fosters a sense of *relatedness*, because individuals are likely to feel much more connected to others (Rhoades & Eisenberger, 2002). This sense of relatedness may also spark feelings of positive emotion, and unleash the broaden-and-build model (Frederickson, 2001), which leads to increased vitality and openness to learning.

Feedback

Access to feedback is also likely to be related to autonomous motivation, particularly the *competence* component. Whereas broad information sharing gives employees access to general organizational knowledge, feedback provides specific information about their current job performance or personal progress on goals and objectives to date (Ashford, 1986). Studies have consistently revealed that feedback increases affective outcomes (cf. Ammons, 1956; Vroom, 1964). Feedback provides knowledge about one's competence. By resolving feelings of uncertainty (e.g., about personal accomplishments and superiors' expectations), feedback allows individuals to more accurately and easily appraise themselves, enabling them to see progress, and reducing individual stress (Ashford & Cummings, 1983). Because feedback keeps people's work-related activities directed toward desired personal and organizational goals (Locke & Latham, 1990), feedback is likely to increase thriving. Feedback provides information regarding the relative importance of various goals to an individual's own progress (Ashford & Cummings, 1983), allowing them to make adjustments in order to maximize the use of their time toward personal growth and improvement.

Environmental Turbulence

In addition to these four enablers, prior research also suggests that levels of thriving suffer amidst substantial upheaval and change in the work context. Environmental turbulence is likely to reduce feelings of autonomous motivation, particularly the competence and autonomy components. More dynamic and unpredictable environments require organizations to spend greater resources for monitoring external conditions and responding to them (Sutcliffe, 1994; 2005). Here, we suggest that environmental volatility creates more uncertainty for employees (Dess & Beard, 1984; Mathieu, Marks, & Zacccaro 2001), defined as the extent to which it is possible to forecast and manage challenges (Waller, 1999). One's feelings of *competence* may be questioned, particularly as uncertainty drains cognitive and affective resources. Individuals possess a limited pool of cognitive resources that are allocated to and withdrawn from various activities (e.g., Kahneman, 1973). Prior research has shown that task performance is dependent on the extent to which this limited attentional capacity is devoted to that specific task (Kahneman, 1973; Porath & Erez, 2007). Environmental turbulence challenges people's ability to focus on the task, versus thinking about how changes may affect them, for example. With less attention and cognitive resources devoted to work performance, it will likely reduce feelings of *competence* in one's ability to be effective at work. In addition, Quy (2002) found that affective processes suffer during times of organizational upheaval, which can contribute to feelings of lack of control and reduced *autonomy*. Thus, in just appraising and making sense of the ever-changing environment, employees are likely to drain scarce resources that would otherwise contribute to learning and vitality, in much the same way that additional processing demands distract employees from the task at hand, reducing task-focused cognitive resources (Montgomery, Kane, & Vance, 2004).

Empirical research provides support for these antecedents of thriving at work in a study of professionals, managers, and executives across six organizations in diverse industries. Porath, Gibson, and Spreitzer (2012) found decision-making discretion and information sharing to be the most powerful antecedents with performance feedback, a climate of trust/respect and environmental turbulence to predict thriving as well. These four antecedents (not including environmental turbulence) explained 42% of the variance in thriving across the six organizations. In sum, a person may be eager to grow and develop, but the work context may enable or squash this capacity.

Directions for Future Research

Here we outline many of the opportunities that abound for further fleshing out an integrative model of human growth at work. First, researchers should strive to learn more about how people use thriving effectively as a gauge. This might involve studying thriving at work over shorter periods of time in an effort to better understand the microdynamics of thriving, particularly how it ebbs and flows over the course of the day or week or work activities, using experience sampling or a diary method to capture assessments of thriving over time (for an example, see Niessen, Sonnentag, & Sach, 2010). Future research should use longitudinal data to tease out

the causal direction of the relationships and better address the reciprocal relationships that are posited in the original theoretical work on thriving. Research investigating thriving over the course of intense projects or transition periods would provide a better understanding of what causes variability in thriving over time and across contexts. It may be that asking people to pause at various times to assess their current level of thriving could be a kind of intervention to self-regulate their thriving to avoid burn out. SDT may be at the heart of explaining how people successfully navigate and thrive through the workday or work week as well as challenging times.

Second, recent research has found thriving to be associated with a range of benefits for employees and organizations. However, much remains to be learned about the longer-term benefits of thriving, and how the generative nature of thriving can create (not just deplete) resources to facilitate subsequent thriving and lead to sustained benefits including more innovation. For example, do thriving employees co-create their work environments for enhanced subsequent thriving? Recent research suggests that when individuals spend more time outside, they feel more vitalized (Ryan, Weinstein, et al., 2010). Are there other ways through specific work activities like microbreaks and helping others that individuals might self-generate higher levels of thriving over time (Fritz, Lam, & Spreitzer, 2011)? In addition, little is known about the potential costs of thriving. For example, could thriving lead to unreasonable expectations that work must always be energizing? Of course, every job has ups and downs.

Third, there is also much to be learned about how thriving at work and outside of work may interrelate. Research by Porath et al. (2012) revealed that thriving at work and in nonwork activities are related, but separate. Using SDT, research might explore how thriving at work or in nonwork activities might be used to catapult more thriving in the other area. Perhaps thriving at work fuels people with positive feelings, energy, and self-efficacy that, consequently, sparks thriving outside of work, carrying over to nonwork activities in meaningful (and perhaps unconscious) ways. However, maybe the competence and relatedness driving thriving at work pulls people into wanting to do more work, tipping the balance heavily in favor of energy and focus in work activities. Longitudinal research might provide greater insight into how people can thrive within and outside of work to achieve the best personal and professional outcomes.

Finally, it may be that some people are better at gauging their thriving. These individuals may have more self-awareness. Mindfulness, whether as a trait or as a mindset induced through meditation (Shapiro, Brown, Thorensen, & Plant, 2011), may be an important variable in helping people better gauge their vitality and learning.

Practical Implications

Based on our findings, the dimensions of autonomy, competence, and relatedness are powerful facilitators of thriving. Thriving, in turn, predicts an impressive range of outcomes for people and organizations, including performance, organizational citizenship behaviors, health outcomes, burnout, career initiative, and positive adaptation. If individuals or organizations want to promote thriving, then thinking about ways to enhance autonomy, competence, and relatedness is a great start. For individuals, it seems important that people who seek to experience more thriving should put themselves in contexts where they have a reasonable amount of decision-making discretion, feel competent in their role, and feel a sense of community or relatedness among their colleagues. Given the enormous role that these contextual factors play in one's ability to thrive, they should play a role in deciding on person-job and person-organization fit. Too often external factors may influence job choices and other project related choices.

A great example of this is the notion of job crafting. Individuals job craft when they make proactive changes to the content and boundaries of their jobs (Wrzesniewski & Dutton, 2001). Job crafters may engage in three types of crafting: (1) *cognitive crafting*, which involves changing task-related boundaries and mindsets; (2) *task crafting*, which involves changing the content of work—the number, scope, and type of job responsibilities; and (3) *relational crafting*, which involves changing the quality and amount of our interaction with others while working. Job crafting offers strategies individuals can use to enhance their autonomous motivation and subsequently their thriving at work.

For organizations, leaders can do much to design jobs to increase decision-making discretion, share information, create a culture of trust/respect, and provide performance feedback. In addition, they can try to mitigate the volatility inherent in organization change. Through these levers, leaders can enhance the three components of autonomous motivation and ultimately thriving. The research suggests that *autonomy* may be especially potent in the workplace. For example, more organizations offer flexible work arrangements, including more discretion over the hours worked, and where the work is completed. Some organizations, including Best Buy, have seen productivity skyrocket and retention as a result (Business Week, 2006).

Reinforcement for work well done rather than face time at the office is likely to garner much appreciation, greater confidence, and increased thriving. Managers and peers are powerful sources for igniting feelings of *competence* (Daniels, 2000). Small comments and compliments go a long way in developing employee competence for greater thriving. Many companies, such as Medtronic, share compliments and ideas from customers as a way to build efficacy and motivation.

Finally, organizations should pay greater attention to their culture because it is critical for building feelings of *relatedness*, in particular. Leaders who are able to craft environments where employees feel a sense of community benefit. Southwest Airlines and other organizations celebrate employee birthdays and other events on a regular basis. Caiman Consulting holds nights out like Taco Tuesdays on a regular basis in addition to various contests and annual company culture-building trips to fabulous destinations. The point is that many of the top, award winning cultures (and Fortune 100 Best Places to Work) started with very small programs to build a sense of community. Some firms have found that volunteering can also provide a real sense of relatedness. Orion Associates, for example, was founded to serve others and has a rich history of encouraging employees to volunteer in the community. Their efforts, as evidenced in their "River of Hope" project (established after Hurricane Katrina to assist New Orleans), have increased a sense of relatedness and pride, and greater employee thriving. All in all, greater attention by employees and their organizations to the SDT dimensions, and factors shown to facilitate employee thriving at work, seem like a great investment given the known benefits of thriving at work.

Conclusion

In this chapter we flesh out the beginnings of an integrative model of human growth at work. The model identifies how the three nutrients of autonomous motivation (autonomy, competence, and relatedness) mediate the relationship between key elements of the social context (including decision-making discretion, broad information sharing, a climate of trust and respect, and performance feedback) and thriving at work. By understanding the social embeddedness of self-determination and thriving, one can understand how organizations can enable more positive work and greater employee performance, well-being, and sustainability.

Notes

1. The authors thank their thriving research collaborators (especially Cristina Gibson and Flannery Garnett) for helping to provide empirical evidence for how and why thriving matters.
2. Indeed, Gagne (2009) also suggests that enhanced self-determination can increase one's motivation to share knowledge with others.

References

Ackerman, P., & Humphreys, L. G. (1990). Individual differences theory in industrial and organizational psychology. In M. D. Dunnette, & L. M. Hough (Eds.), *Handbook of industrial and organizational psychology* (Vol. 1, pp. 223–282). Palo Alto, CA: Consulting Psychologists Press.

Amabile, T. M. (1993). Motivational synergy: Toward new conceptualizations of intrinsic and extrinsic motivation in the workplace. *Human Resource Management Review, 3*, 185–201.

Ammons, R. B. (1956). Effects of knowledge of performance: A survey and tentative theoretical formulation. *Journal of General Psychology, 54*, 279–299.

Ashford, S. J. (1986). Feedback-seeking in individual adaptation: A resource perspective. *Academy of Management Journal, 29*(2), 465–487.

Ashford, S. J., & Cummings, L. L. (1983). Feedback as an individual resource: Personal strategies of creating information. *Organizational Behavior and Human Performance, 32*(3), 370–398.

Bakwin, H. (1949). Emotional deprivation in infants. *Journal of Pediatrics, 35*, 512–521.

Bandura, A. (1977). *Social learning theory.* Englewood Cliffs, NJ: Prentice-Hall Inc.

Baumeister, R. F., Bratslavsky, E., Muraven, M., & Tice, D. M. (1998). Ego depletion: Is the active self a limited resource? *Personality processes and individual differences, 74*, 1252–1265.

Baumeister, R. F., & Vohs, K. (2007). Self-regulation, ego depletion, and motivation. *Social and Personality Psychology Compass, 1*, 115–125.

Benson, P., & Scales, P. (2009). The definition and preliminary measurement of thriving in adolescence. *The Journal of Positive Psychology, 4*(1), 85–104.

Bergland, A., & Kirkevold, M. (2001). Thriving—a useful theoretical perspective to capture the experience of well-being among frail elderly in nursing homes? *Journal of Advanced Nursing, 36*, 426–432.

Blankenship, K. (1998). A race, class, and gender analysis of thriving. *Journal of Social Issues, 54*(2), 393–404.

Bowlby, J. (1979). *The making and breaking of affectional bonds.* London: Tavistock.

Brown, S. L., Nesse, R. M., Vinokur, A. D., & Smith, D. M. (2003). Providing social support may be more beneficial than receiving it: Results from a prospective study of mortality. *Psychological Science, 14*(4), 320–327.

Bunderson, J. S., & Sutcliffe, K. M. (2002). Why some teams emphasize learning more than others: Evidence from business unit management teams. In M. Neal, E. Mannix, & H. Sondak (Eds.), *Research on managing groups and teams* (Vol. 4, pp. 49–84). New York: Elsevier Science.

Business Week (2006, December 1). Smashing the clock: No schedule, no mandatory meetings.

Calhoun, L., & Tedeschi, R. (1998). Beyond recovery from trauma: Implications for clinical practice and research. *Journal of Social Issues, 54*(2), 357–371.

Campa, M., Bradshaw, C., Eckenrode, J., & Zielinski, D. (2008). Patterns of problem behavior in relation to thriving and precocious behavior in late adolescence. *Journal of Youth Adolescence, 37*, 627–640.

Carlson, M., Charlin, V., & Miller, N. (1988). Positive mood and helping behavior: A test of six hypotheses. *Journal of Personality and Social Psychology, 55*, 211–229.

Carver, C. S. (1998). Resilience and thriving: Issues, models, and linkages. *Journal of Social Issues, 54*, 245–266.

Chen, G., Gully, S. M., Whiteman, J. A., & Killacullen, R. N. (2000). Examination of relationships among trait-like individual differences, state-like individual differences, and learning performance. *Journal of Applied Psychology, 85*, 835–847.

Daniels, A. C. (2000). *Bringing out the best in people: How to apply the astonishing power of positive reinforcement.* New York: McGraw-Hill, Inc.

Deci, E. L., Connell, J. P., & Ryan, R. M. (1989). Self-determination in a work organization. *Journal of Applied Psychology, 74*, 580–590.

Deci, E. L., & Ryan, R. M. (2000). The what and why of goal pursuits: Human needs and the self-determination of behavior. *Psychological Inquiry, 11*, 227–268.

Dess, G. G., & Beard, D. W. (1984). Dimensions of organizational task environment. *Administrative Science Quarterly, 28*, 274–291.

Edmondson, A. (1999). Psychological safety and learning behavior in work teams. *Administrative Science Quarterly, 44*, 350–383.

Fernet, C., Austin, S., Trepanier, S. G., & Dussault, M. (2012). How do job characteristics contribute to burnout? Exploring the distinct mediating roles of perceived autonomy, competence, and relatedness. *European Journal of Work and Organizational Psychology, 22*(2), 123–137.

Fredrickson, B. (2001). The role of positive emotions in positive psychology: The broaden and build theory of positive emotions. *American Psychologist, 56*, 218–226.

Fritz, C., Lam, C. F., & Spreitzer, G. M. (2011). It's the little things that matter: An examination of knowledge workers' energy management. *Academy of Management Perspectives, 25*(3), 28–39.

Gagne, M. (2009). A model of knowledge-sharing motivation. *Human Resource Management, 48*(4), 571–589.

Gagne, M., & Deci, E. (2005). Self-determination theory and work motivation. *Journal of Organizational Behavior, 26*, 331–362.

Gagné, M., Ryan, R. M., & Bargmann, K. (2003). The effects of parent and coach autonomy support on the need satisfaction and well being of gymnasts. *Journal of Applied Sport Psychology, 15*, 372–390.

Gerbasi, A., Parker, A., Ballinger, G., & Cross, R. (2011). *The influence of instrumental and affective network ties on voluntary and involuntary turnover* (working paper). Grenoble Ecole de Management, Grenoble, France.

Hackman, J. R., & Oldham, G. (1980). *Work redesign.* Reading, MA: Addison-Wesley.

Haight, B., Barba, B., Tesh, A., & Courts, N. (2002). Thriving: A life span theory. *Journal of Gerontological Nursing, 28*(3), 14–22.

Hall, J., Roman, M. W., Thomas, S. P., Brown Travi, C., Powell, J., Tennison, C., & McArthur, P. M. (2009). Thriving as becoming resolute in narrative of women surviving childhood maltreatment. *American Journal of Orthopsychiatry, 79*(3), 375–386.

Hobfoll, S. E. (1989). Conservation of resources: A new attempt at conceptualizing stress. *American Psychologist, 44*, 513–524.

Ibarra, H. (2002). *Working identity.* Cambridge: Harvard Business School Press.

Ickovics, J., & Park, C. (1998). Paradigm shift: Why a focus on health is important. *Journal of Social Issues, 54*(2), 237–244.

Joseph, S., & Linley, A. (2008). *Trauma, recovery and growth: Positive psychological perspectives on posttraumatic stress.* Hoboken, NJ: John Wiley and Sons.

Kahneman, D. (1973). *Attention and effort.* Englewood Cliffs, NJ: Prentice Hall.

King, P. E., Dowling, E. M., Mueller, R. A., White, K., Schultz, W., Osborn, P., & Scales, P. C. (2005). Thriving in adolescence: The voices of youth-serving practitioners, parents, and early and later adolescents. *Journal of Early Adolescence, 25*, 94–112.

Klein, H. J. (1991). Control theory and understanding motivated behavior: A different conclusion. *Motivation and Emotion, 15*, 29–44.

Kluger, A. N., & DeNisi, A. (1996). The effects of feedback interventions on performance: A historical review, a meta-analysis, and a preliminary feedback intervention theory. *Psychological Bulletin, 119*(2), 254–284.

Locke, E. A., & Latham, G. P. (1990). *A theory of goal setting and task performance.* Englewood Cliffs, NJ: Prentice-Hall.

Maslow, A. (1943). A theory of human motivation. *Psychological Review, 40*, 370–396.

Mathieu, J. E., Marks, M. S., & Zaccaro, S. J. (2001). Multi-team systems. In. N. Anderson, D. Ones, H. K. Sinangil, & C. Viswesvaran (Eds.), *International handbook of work and organizational psychology* (pp. 289–313). London: Sage.

Mayer, R. C., Davis, J. H., & Schoorman, F. D. (1995). An integrative model of organizational trust. *Academy of Management Review, 20*, 709–734.

Miller, J. B., & Stiver, I. P. (1997). *The healing connection: How women form relationships in therapy and in life.* Boston: Beacon Press.

Montgomery, K., Kane, K., & Vance C. M. (2004). Accounting for differences in norms of respect: A study of assessments of incivility through the lenses of race and gender. *Group and Organization Management, 29*, 248–268.

Muraven, M., Gagne, M., & Rosman, H. (2008). Helpful self-control: Autonomy support vitality, and depletion. *Journal of Experimental Social Psychology, 44*, 573–585.

Niessen, C., Sonnentag, S., & Sach, F. (2010). *Thriving at work: A diary study* (working paper). University of Konstanz. *Journal of Organizational Behavior, 33*(4), 468–487.

Nix, G., Ryan, R. M., Manly, J. B., & Deci, E. L. (1999). Revitalization through self-regulation: The effects of autonomous and controlled motivation on happiness and vitality. *Journal of Experimental Social Psychology, 25*, 266–284.

Poorman, P. (2002). Perceptions of thriving by women who have experiences abuse or status-related oppression. *Psychology of Women Quarterly, 26*, 51–62.

Porath, C. L., & Erez, A. (2007). Does rudeness really matter? The effects of rudeness on task performance and helpfulness. *Academy of Management Journal, 50*(5), 1181–1197.

Porath, C., Gibson, C., & Spreitzer, G. (2012). *Thriving at work: An explanation for why organizational mechanisms for self-determination matter for job performance* (working paper). Georgetown University in Washington D.C.: University of Southern California.

Porath, C., Spreitzer, G., Gibson, C., & Garnett, F. (2012). Thriving at work: Toward its measurement, construct validation, and theoretical refinement. *Journal of Organizational Behavior, 33*, 250–271.

Quinn, R., & Dutton, J. E. (2005). Coordination as energy-in-conversation: A process theory of organizing. *Academy of Management Review, 30*, 36–57.

Quy, H. (2002). Emotional balancing of organizational continuity and radical change: The contribution of middle managers. *Administrative Science Quarterly, 47*(1), 31–69.

Reis, H. T., Sheldon, K. M., Gable, S. L., Roscoe, J., & Ryan, R. M. (2000). Daily well-being: The role of autonomy, competence, and relatedness. *Personality and Social Psychology Bulletin, 26*, 419–435.

Rhoades, L., & Eisenberger, R. (2002). Perceived organizational support: A review of the literature. *Journal of Applied Psychology, 87*, 698–714.

Robischek, C. (1998). Personal growth initiative: The construct and its measure. *Measurement and Evaluation in Counseling and Development, 30*, 183–198.

Rogers, C. (1961). *On becoming a person: A therapist's view off psychotherapy.* London: Constable.

Ryan, R. M., Bernstein, J., & Brown, K. W. (2010). Weekends, work, and well-being: Psychological need satisfactions and day of the week effects on mood, vitality, and physical symptoms. *Journal of Social and Clinical Psychology, 29*, 95–122.

Ryan, R. M., & Deci, E. L. (2000). Self-determination theory and the facilitation of intrinsic motivation, social development, and well-being. *American Psychologist, 55*, 68–78.

Ryan, R. M., & Deci, E. L. (2008). From ego depletion to vitality: Theory and findings concerning the facilitation of energy available to the self. *Social and Personality Psychology Compass, 2*(2), 702–717.

Ryan, R. M., & Frederick, C. M. (1997). On energy, personality and health: Subjective vitality as a dynamic reflection of well-being. *Journal of Personality, 65*, 529–565.

Ryan, R. M., Weinstein, N., Bernstein, J., Brown, K., Mistretta, L., & Gagne, M. (2010). Vitalizing effects of being outdoors and in nature. *Journal of Environmental Psychology, 30*, 159–168.

Ryff, C. D. (1989). Happiness is everything, or is it? Explorations on the meaning of psychological well-being. *Journal of Personality and Social Psychology, 57*, 1069–1081.

Saakvitne, K., Teenen, H., & Affleck, G. (1998). Exploring thriving in the context of clinical trauma theory: Constructivist self-development theory. *Journal of Social Issues, 54*(2), 279–299.

Schlaufeli, W., Bakker, A., & Salanova, M. (2006). The measurement of work engagement in a short questionnaire. *Educational and Psychological Measurement, 66*, 701–716.

Shapiro, S., Brown, K., Thorensen, C., & Plante, T. (2011). The moderation of mindfulness-based stress reduction effects by mindfulness. *Journal of Clinical Psychology, 67*, 267–277.

Sonenshein, S., Dutton, J., Grant, A., Spreitzer, G., & Sutcliffe, K. (2005). Narratives of thriving. Presented in a symposium entitled "Narratives of Life in Organizations: Bringing Organizations to Life in and Through Stories." Academy of Management Meetings, August 7–10, Hawaii.

Spreitzer, G. M. (1995). Psychological empowerment in the workplace: Dimensions, measurement, and validation. *Academy of Management Journal, 38*, 1442–1465.

Spreitzer, G. M. (1996). Social structural levers to individual empowerment in the workplace. *Academy of Management Journal, 39*, 483–504.

Spreitzer, G., Sutcliffe, K., Dutton, J., Sonenshein, S., & Grant, A. (2005). A socially embedded model of thriving at work. *Organization Science, 16*(5), 537–549.

Spreitzer, G. M., Lam, C. F., & Fritz, C. (2010). Engagement and human thriving: complementary perspectives on energy and connections to work. In A. Bakker, & Leiter (Eds.) *Work engagement: A handbook of essential theory and research* (pp. 132–146). New York: Psychology Press.

Sutcliffe, K. M. (1994). What executives notice: Accurate perceptions in top management teams. *Academy of Management Journal, 37*, 1360–1378.

Sutcliffe, K. M. (2005). Information handling challenges in complex systems. *International Public Management Journal, 8*(3), 417–424.

Theokas, C., Almerigi, J., Lerner, R. M., Dowling, E. M., Benson, P. L., & Scales, P. C. (2005). Conceptualizing and modeling individual and ecological asset components of thriving in early adolescence. *The Journal of Early Adolescence, 25*, 113–143.

Thomas, S. P., & Hall, J. (2008). Life trajectories of female child abuse survivors thriving in adulthood. *Qualitative Health Research, 18*, 149–166.

Tice, D. M., Baumeister, R. F., Shmeuli, D., & Muraven, M. (2007). Restoring the self: Positive affect helps improve self-regulation following ego depletion. *Journal of Experimental Social Psychology, 43*, 379–384.

Tsui, A. S., & Ashford, S. J. (1994). Adaptive self-regulation: A process view of managerial effectiveness. *Journal of Management, 20*, 93–121.

Vansteenkiste, M., Neyrinck, B., Niemiec, C., Soenens, B., De Witte, H., Van Den Broeck, A. (2007). On the relations among work value orientations, psychological need satisfaction and job outcomes: A self-determination theory approach. *Journal of Occupational & Organizational Psychology, 80*(2), 251–277.

Verderey, R. (1995). Failure to thrive in the elderly. *Clinics in Geriatric Medicine, 11*, 653–659.

Vinarski-Peretz, H., Binyamin, G., & Carmeli, A. (2011). Subjective relational experiences and employee innovative behaviors in the workplace. *Journal of Vocational Behavior, 78*(2), 290.

Vroom, V. H. (1964). *Work motivation.* New York: Wiley.

Walker, L., & Sterling, B. (2007). The structure of thriving/distress among low-income women at 3 months after giving birth. *Family and Community Health, 30*(18), S95–S103.

Waller, M. J. (1999). The timing of adaptive responses to non-routine events. *Academy of Management Journal, 42*, 127–137.

Warr, P. (1990). The measurement of well-being and other aspects of mental health. *Journal of Occupational Psychology, 63*, 193–210.

Weick, K. E., & Sutcliffe, K. M. (2001). *Managing the unexpected: Assuring high performance in an age of complexity.* San Francisco: Jossey Bass.

Wood, R., & Bandura, A. (1989). Social cognitive theory of organizational management. *Academy of Management Review, 14*, 361–384.

Wrzesniewski, A., & Dutton, J. E. (2001). Crafting a job: Revisioning employees as active crafters of their work. *Academy of Management Review, 26*(2), 179–201.

CHAPTER
16

Emotional Labor through the Lens of Self-Determination Theory

Michel Cossette

> ### Abstract
>
> For many jobs, interacting with others is a major part of the job requirement. Because interactions can become emotional, many organizations prescribe what emotions their employees must and must not display to facilitate the achievement of organizational goals. Hence, employees must regulate their emotions in accordance with these expectations. Findings suggest that emotional labor has important individual and organizational outcomes. However, only recently have scholars turned their focus on the motivational mechanism that leads employees to regulate their emotions. Building on previous work, this chapter presents a motivational model of emotional labor based on self-determination theory to better understand "how" employees regulate their emotions at work and, more particularly, "why" they adopt certain strategies. The chapter presents the emotional labor notion, proposes a motivational model of the emotional labor process, and proposes avenues to guide future research.
>
> **Key Words:** emotions, emotional labor, emotion regulation, motivation, self-determination theory, task motivation, psychological well-being, job attitudes

Emotions are part of daily life; they prepare us for behavioral responses, influence our decision-making, and facilitate (or complicate) our interpersonal interactions (see Gross & Thompson, 2007). Given that emotions are shared by all humans, researchers and practitioners place a greater emphasis on emotions at work to better understand employee attitudes, well-being, and job performance. For instance, customer service representatives, waiters, and flight attendants must display positive emotions vis-à-vis their clientele (e.g., enthusiasm, optimism, cheerfulness). However, bill collectors, bouncers, and riot squads need to express a certain level of hostility. Finally, nurses, physicians, and paramedics need to suppress their disgust or sadness when facing injured patients (see Rafaeli & Sutton, 1987). Hence, although cognitively based skills, such as technical knowledge, cognitive ability, and manual abilities, remain important, emotionally

based skills (Salovey & Meyer, 1990) are indispensable for many jobs. Examples of organizationally relevant emotional skills include the capacity to create a positive service experience for the customer, the ability to regulate one's emotions, and the ability to recognize customers' emotions and one's own (Brotheridge, 2006).

Organizations are increasingly emphasizing the importance of emotional skills because jobs require sustained social interactions (Mann, 1999; Tschan, Rochat, & Zapf, 2005). Hence, mastering these competencies is crucial for job applicants who want to be hired as customer service agents (Fox & Spector, 2000). However, competencies alone are not sufficient: employees need to be motivated to use those competencies while interacting with others.

Thus, developing and mobilizing employees' emotional skills have become critical organizational issues (Ashkanasy & Daus, 2002). For example, customers' attitudes and behaviors are related to employees' emotional displays. More specifically, positive emotions displayed by employees lead to a more positive service evaluation from both the supervisor and the customer (Grandey, 2003; Hülsheger & Schewe, 2011; Pugh, 2001; Rafaeli & Sutton, 1987; Sutton & Rafaeli, 1988; Totterdell & Holman, 2003; Tsai, 2001).

Jobs or organizational demands that dictate the expression or suppression of emotions at work have a downside, however (Hess, 2003; Hülsheger & Schewe, 2011; Rubin, Tardino, Daus, & Munz, 2005): employees may be expressing emotions that are discrepant with their inner feelings. This gap between what they truly feel and what they manifest as prescribed emotions has been labeled emotional dissonance or emotion-rule dissonance (Hülsheger & Schewe, 2011; Rubin et al., 2005). Emotional dissonance has several important negative consequences for employees, such as impaired well-being, job dissatisfaction, and lower job performance (see meta-analyses from Bono & Vey, 2005, and Hülsheger & Schewe, 2011).

In order to reduce emotional dissonance, employees can use different strategies to align what they feel and/or express with what is expected from them (Hülsheger & Schewe, 2011; Rubin et al., 2005). In Gross's terms (1998), they try to "influence which emotions they have, when they have them, and how they experience and express these emotions" (p. 275). By doing so, employees perform what has been called emotional labor (Grandey, 2000; Hochschild, 1983) or, in other words, they are regulating their emotions (Gross, 1998; Gross & Thompson, 2007). Although research on the topic of emotional labor is rapidly expanding, with findings appearing to support several predictive models, other interesting questions are simultaneously emerging.

Antecedents of emotional labor have received much less attention compared with its consequences (Bono & Vey, 2005). Although it is imperative to understand "how" employees perform emotional labor, it is equally important to understand "why" they adopt certain strategies in order to better understand the emotional labor process and develop organizational practices that optimize positive consequences and diminish negative ones associated with emotional labor. We believe that motivation is one possible answer explaining "why" employees perform emotional labor, and self-determination theory (SDT) provides a relevant framework to better understand the emotional labor process

(Cossette, Blais, & Hess, 2006; Cossette & Hess, 2009, 2010, 2012; Kim, Deci, & Zuckerman, 2002; Lépine & Cossette, 2010).

In this chapter, building on previous models (Grandey, 2000; Rubin et al., 2005), a motivational framework grounded in SDT is presented to elucidate not only "how" employees regulate their emotions but also "why" they adopt certain strategies. The notion of emotional labor is discussed first, along with existing models that explain how employees regulate their emotions. Second, an exposé on SDT is proffered to better understand why employees regulate their emotions at work. Third, the consequences and the antecedents of emotional labor having received attention from researchers are reviewed and integrated into a novel motivational process model. Finally, the chapter concludes with suggestions for future research.

Emotional Labor: Regulating Emotions at Work

Emotional labor relies on the tenets of job performance. In the same way that many occupations require mastering physical or mental abilities, many occupations require the ability to express or suppress emotions (Brotheridge, 2006; Brotheridge & Grandey, 2002). More specifically, emotion regulation is a task requirement in jobs or occupations where employees interact with others (Hochschild, 1983; Mann, 1999; Tschan et al., 2005). In this context, emotional labor can be a primary or a secondary task that aims at enhancing the quality of interaction between employees and "clients" of various types (e.g., customers, students, patients) while achieving its organizational goals (Zapf, 2002). For example, emotion work is necessary for sales representatives because the customer experience relies not only on the satisfaction of needs, but also on the affective experience felt during interactions with employees (i.e., the overall quality of the interactions; Grandey, 2003; Sutton & Rafaeli, 1988; Tsai, 2001). In contrast, to increase their effectiveness at collecting overdue accounts, bill collectors must convey a sense of urgency by displaying a hint of irritation to debtors (Sutton, 1991).

Hence, organizations and managers demand that employees express certain emotions during their interactions. Hochschild (1983) labeled such organizational demands "feeling rules." Her early contribution was to explicitly address the fact that organizations count on employee emotions to perform designated roles. It is now widely understood that organizations have either formal or informal display rules (Ekman, 1973) that employees must follow using emotion-regulation strategies. The following section describes what emotion regulation is, and the different emotional labor strategies that employees use to comply with such display rules.

The Emotion Regulation Process

People must comply with rules during social interactions (Goffman, 1959) of which are included emotion display rules (Ekman, 1973). In order to positively influence the customer, many companies incorporate rules in their culture, in their job descriptions, or in their formal performance appraisals about how employees ought to act when interacting with customers. However, to understand the emotion regulation strategies that help employees comply with display rules, one needs to consider the emotion regulation process. James Gross (1998) formalized a theory on emotion regulation that influenced Grandey's (2000) emotional labor model.

Gross's emotion regulation model relies on the following premises: an emotion (1) occurs when an individual is in a situation that is relevant to his or her goals, (2) has many dimensions (i.e., subjective experience, physiological response, and behavioral and expressive components), and (3) consists of response tendencies that can be modulated (Gross & Thompson, 2007). It is this third premise of emotion that makes emotion regulation possible as employees can act on different aspects of their emotions. Although emotions can interrupt what we are doing, emotions often compete with other responses that are shaped by social norms. In an organizational context, social norms originate from both the display rules and the expectations that managers have of employees (Hochschild, 1983).

These three features of emotion regulation constitute the modal model of emotion defined as "a person-situation transaction that compels attention, has particular meaning to individual, and gives rise to a coordinated yet flexible multisystem response to the ongoing person-situation transaction" (Gross & Thompson, 2007, p. 5). Hence, people can select the situation they want to be in, act on the situation in which the emotion emerges, focus their attention on different aspects of the situation or interaction, interpret the situation in a manner to facilitate emotional expression, and act on the emotional responses that can be apparent. Moreover, Gross and Thompson (2007) suggested that regulatory processes may be controlled or automatic, and ranging on a continuum "from conscious, effortful,

and controlled regulation to unconscious, effortless, and automatic regulation" (p. 8). Strategies may have their effects on one or multiple points in the emotion-generative process. A person can reduce, intensify, or maintain an emotion depending on his or her goal.

Based on the focal points of regulation, Gross's model distinguishes between antecedent-focused and response-focused emotion regulation strategies (Gross & Thompson, 2007). Situation selection, situation modification, attentional deployment, and cognitive change are all considered "*antecedent-focused* in that they occur before appraisals give rise to full-blown emotional response tendencies" (p. 10). In contrast, regulation strategies that aim at modulating the physiological, behavioral, and facial responses constitute the *response-focused* strategies. Based on Gross's (1998) distinction between antecedent-focused and response-focused strategies, Grandey (2000) proposed an integrative model of emotional labor.

Research prior to Grandey's work (2000) defined emotional labor based on either the characteristics of the job (Morris & Feldman, 1996, 1997), the concept of emotional dissonance (Kruml & Geddes, 2000), or on the actual act of displaying whatever emotion was deemed necessary (Ashforth & Humphrey, 1993). Essentially, Grandey pointed out that Morris and Feldman's (1996, 1997) emotional labor dimensions—frequency of interaction, attentiveness (i.e., intensity of emotions, duration of interaction), and variety of emotions required—referred to organizational expectations toward employees in their interactions with customers. As such, these dimensions represented antecedents of emotional labor. Moreover, Morris and Feldman (1996, 1997) conceived emotional dissonance as another emotional labor dimension (for a similar operationalization, see Kruml and Geddes, 2000). As Grandey (2000) argued, both conceptions, namely characteristics of the job and emotional dissonance, cannot adequately reflect emotional labor as a process by which employees express the prescribed emotions at work. Ashforth and Humphrey's conception focused on the act of displaying the prescribed emotions, and were more concerned about the observable behavior rather than the internal processes underlying the regulation of emotions. Grandey also looked at similarities between studies. One underlying theme that she unearthed across the studies was that "individuals can regulate their emotional expressions at work. Emotional labor, then, is the process of regulating both feelings and expressions for the organizational goals" (Grandey, 2000, p. 97). Hence, the main contributions of Grandey's (2000) article was to integrate different perspectives and to propose emotion regulation theory (Gross, 1998) as a guiding theory for investigating the emotional labor process. The next paragraphs explain the different emotion-regulation strategies.

Emotional Labor Strategies

When interacting with others, employees are likely to react to different events or situations (Weiss & Cropanzano, 1996). For example, customer service representatives interact with customers who can escalate a discussion and become impolite, sarcastic, or even aggressive towards them (Grandey, Dickter, & Sin, 2004); police officers frequently deal with interpersonal violence, confrontational interactions, or intense emotions from victims of crime (Berking, Meier, & Wupperman, 2010); nurses are regularly confronted with severe patient illness, suffering, and even death (Bakker, & Heuven, 2006). Because employees must act in accordance with emotion display rules, their inner feelings may not always correspond to the organizationally prescribed emotions. Hence, when employees' feelings are not consistent with the expected emotions, they find themselves in a dissonance state (Abraham, 1998, 1999a, 1999b; Rubin et al., 2005).

Emotional dissonance is a form of person-role conflict, and is a known source of stress for employees (Abraham, 1998, 1999b; Adelmann, 1995). Hence, Rubin et al. (2005) argued that one way to deal with dissonance is by performing emotional labor. Indeed, an emotional state triggered by dissonance should influence employees' behaviors (i.e., their regulation strategies). Emotional labor arises whenever employees perceive a gap between what they genuinely feel in a given moment and the specific emotion that is required of them to display. This perceived dissonance drives employees to reduce the discomfort associated with it and thus leads employees to regulate their emotions either by using an antecedent-focused or a response-focused strategy. In other words, emotional labor is a motivated behavioral response to perceived dissonance (Rubin et al., 2005).

Two main strategies have been discussed that deal with dissonance in the literature on emotional labor. Researchers define *surface acting* as the modification of the observable aspects of emotions, either by suppressing, faking, or amplifying the emotion displayed (Allen, Pugh, Grandey, & Groth, 2010; Brotheridge & Lee, 2003; Diefendorff, Croyle, & Gosserand, 2005; Grandey, 2000; Grandey et al., 2004; Hochschild, 1983). These strategies correspond to the response-focused emotion regulation strategies mentioned previously (Gross, 1998; Gross & Thompson, 2007).

When employees use *deep acting*, however, they try to consciously change how they feel in order to express the prescribed emotions; in other words, employees are making concerted efforts to align their inner feelings with the displayed emotions (Allen et al., 2010; Ashforth & Humphrey, 1993; Brotheridge & Lee, 2002; Diefendorff et al., 2005; Grandey, 2000; Hochschild, 1983). Deep acting is an antecedent-focused emotion regulation strategy (Grandey, 2000) and is a more authentic strategy than surface acting (Brotheridge & Lee, 2002; Diefendorff et al., 2005).

Nearly 20 years ago, Ashforth and Humphrey (1993) mentioned that employees not only use deep and surface acting strategies in their designated jobs, but also that they spontaneously express the prescribed emotions. However, it is only recently that naturally felt emotions have received more empirical attention. This strategy is a distinct one from other strategies (Cossette & Hess, 2010, 2012; Diefendorff et al., 2005). For Rubin et al. (2005), automatic responses, such as genuine expressions of emotion, are not considered as an emotional labor strategy. Others have argued that naturally felt emotions require employees to continuously monitor their emotional responses in order to comply with the display rules (Cossette & Hess, 2010, 2012; Diefendorff et al., 2005; Diefendorff & Gosserand, 2003; Gross & Thompson, 2007). Still, expressing the naturally felt emotions should be negatively associated with emotional dissonance. Because employees must be attentive to display rules and must continuously monitor their affective displays and compare them with the display norms (Diefendorff & Gosserand, 2003), expressing naturally felt emotions can be considered as an emotional labor strategy.

Deep acting and naturally felt emotions are strategies that are beneficial to individuals, in contrast to surface acting (Bono & Vey, 2005; Cossette et al., 2006; Cossette & Hess, 2010, 2012; Diefendorff et al., 2005; Gross & John, 2003; Gross & Thompson, 2007; Hülsheger & Schewe, 2011; John & Gross, 2004). Emotional labor outcomes differ because strategies used by employees deal more or less adequately with emotional dissonance, whereas response-focused strategies involve high levels of dissonance and antecedent-focused strategies aim at aligning inner feelings with the emotions displayed. Hence, these strategies lead to a more authentic stance from employees. It is important to note that some contexts might require the use of surface acting without compromising employee well-being. For example, a person controlling tickets at the cinema may use the surface acting strategy to express a short-lived but nonetheless polite smile (see Morris & Feldman, 1996; and Zapf, 2002). Even so, considering the fact that dissonance generally has a detrimental effect on individuals and organizational outcomes (Hülsheger & Schewe, 2011), it is important to understand what can predict this dissonance in order to prevent it from occurring. One factor that emerged in recent years is the motivation to perform emotional labor, a notion that is explored in greater depth in the next section.

Motivation to Perform Emotional Labor

So far, we have discussed two main ideas. First, employees have emotional reactions while interacting with others, which can be seen as an "internal" message. Second, an "external" message is sent by the organization and/or the customers regarding which emotions must be expressed in a particular situation. The result of these seemingly distinct messages is that they sometimes conflict with one another. Whenever they do, the employee experiences emotional stress and a desire (or motive) to resolve or reduce the conflict (i.e., emotional dissonance) one way or another (Rubin et al., 2005). To comply with the display rules, employees must behave in a way that is consistent with the prescribed emotions. Although it is only recently that authors have begun to formally discuss the motivational mechanism leading employees to perform emotional labor, some ideas reflecting the notion of motivation were proposed almost two decades ago. The next sections discuss these ideas.

Emotional Labor and Role Internalization

Ashforth and Humphrey (1993) agreed that emotional dissonance is stressful for employees. However, these authors have argued that stress is not inevitable; it depends on the employees' perception of the situation, which fluctuates according to the extent to which employees identify with their role. These authors suggested that when employees identify with their role, fulfilling task requirements such as regulating emotions has a positive impact, notably on psychological well-being. Therefore, emotional labor gives employees the opportunity to express their social identity and, more precisely, their professional identity. Hence, emotional labor will lead to positive outcomes if it is consistent with the employees' salient and valued professional identity. Contrarily, if emotional labor is inconsistent with their professional identity, emotional dissonance is more likely to occur and, consequently, employees will not feel authentic when interacting with others (see Ashforth & Humphrey, 1993).

Role internalization refers to the degree to which employees identify with their job or job values (Ashforth & Humphrey, 1993; Rubin et al., 2005), and it is considered to be an outcome of emotional labor (Ashforth & Humphrey, 1993). More specifically, Ashforth and Humphrey (1993) asserted that longer interactions would lead to greater internalization of role expectations, which would in turn make emotional labor less effortful. Their suggestions were, in fact, confirmed empirically. First, debt collectors, members of a military recruiting battalion, and members of a state nursing association completed a survey designed to assess how job characteristics, role internalization, and emotional dissonance were related. It seems that longer interactions lead to more internalization, which was negatively related to emotional dissonance (Morris & Feldman, 1997). Second, greater role identification led to less surface acting but more deep acting in a sample of employees working in jobs requiring interactions with customers, such as sales clerks, restaurant waiting staff, healthcare professionals, and office employees (Brotheridge & Lee, 2002). These results suggest that, in the long term, employees who identify more intensively with their role perform emotional labor using strategies that require less effort.

In their theoretical paper, Rubin et al. (2005) proposed that role internalization impacts emotional labor by reducing emotional dissonance. The authors suggested that employees who have internalized their roles should experience less dissonance because expressing prescribed emotions had become second nature to them. An earlier qualitative study lent support to this assertion:

> . . . role internalization leads to an experience of deep authenticity whereby one's emotional expression

COSSETTE | 263

or display is consistent with the display rules of a specific identity that one has internalized (or want to internalize) as a reflection of self-*regardless of whether the expression genuinely reflects one's current feeling* (Ashforth & Tomiuk, 2000, p. 195).

Rubin et al. (2005) also indicated that deep authenticity should lead to lower levels of emotional dissonance. Hence, role internalization should buffer the effect of situational demands as well as directly impact-perceived dissonance, leading to less dissonance.

Role internalization contributed to our understanding of "why" employees regulate their emotions. When employees identify with their job and its underlying values, they suffer less from emotional dissonance and regulate their emotions in a healthier way (i.e., more use of deep acting and less use of surface acting). However, this conception and the empirical results that followed do not allow for any firm conclusions to be made about the directional effect. Role internalization is an outcome of compliance with display rules over time (Ashforth & Humphrey, 1993). It is also entirely possible that compliance with the display rules is the outcome of role internalization. Although Morris and Feldman (1997) confirmed Ashforth and Humphrey's (1993) assertion, the cross-sectional design of their study was limited in its ability to infer causality.

On a conceptual level, a given job generally includes many roles and responsibilities, yet the notion of role internalization does not permit the distinction between different facets of that job. In this context, compliance with display rules is only one aspect of a job (Zapf, 2002). Hence, to better understand why employees regulate their emotions, we need to understand how they perceive the display rules.

Commitment to Display Rules: An Expectancy Approach to Emotional Labor

Diefendorff and his colleagues conceptualized display rules as goals that employees must achieve (Diefendorff & Croyle, 2008; Diefendorff et al., 2005; Diefendorff & Gosserand, 2003; Gosserand & Diefendorff, 2005). Hence, as Diefendorff and Croyle (2008) mentioned, an implicit tenet in emotional labor research is that employees make efforts to display the adequate emotion when they encounter display rules. However, not all employees make the necessary efforts to regulate their emotions even if they realize that their expressions are not consistent with organizational norms. In this sense, some employees may lack the necessary motivation to perform emotional labor.

Recently, Diefendorff and his colleagues proposed a motivational mechanism to explain why employees perform emotional labor. Diefendroff and Gosserand (2003) incorporated motivation as a mechanism to explain why some employees follow the display rules, whereas others do not. Indeed, simply perceiving display rules is not sufficient; employees must also be committed to the display rules that are conceived of as goal performance (Diefendorff & Gosserand, 2003). Commitment is essential for employees to become more willing to comply with display rules and to regulate their emotions in a consistent manner to achieve this goal. Being committed to display rules signifies "a person's intention to extend effort toward displaying organizationally desired emotions, persist in displaying these emotions over time, and not abandon the display rules under difficult conditions" (Gosserand & Diefendorff, 2005, p. 1257). This confirms the importance of ascribing motivational factors, because more committed employees are engaged more intensively in regulation activities. Specifically, committed employees who are performing "people work" (e.g., service and sales; professional, technical, and managerial; clerical; education; health care) use more surface acting and deep acting to comply with the display rules compared with employees who are less committed to the display rules (Gosserand & Diefendorff, 2005).

Diefendorff and Croyle (2008) further extend the motivational process by using Vroom's (1964) expectancy theory of motivation. They asked participants working in customer service jobs that require expressing positive emotions to describe, in detail, two interactions beginning with the first moment of the encounter to the end of the interaction. In the first interaction, participants noted a typical interaction after which they completed a questionnaire. Participants were then asked to think of the aforementioned customer service interaction, but to imagine that the customer was being particularly tough and rude. Following their description of this second scenario, they completed the same questionnaire. Results showed that the kind of interaction that employees had with customers impacted their motivation to express positive emotions, because both expectancy theory variables (expectations [E], confidence that an employee has about displaying an emotion; valence [V], employee's anticipated satisfaction or value of expressing an emotion; and the motivational force [E*V], reflects the overall motivation) and commitment variables all received higher scores in the typical customer interaction compared with the one in the incivility condition. Diefendorff and Croyle (2008) also found that extraversion positively explained commitment to display rules in both contexts, whereas agreeableness positively predicted commitment to display rules only in the typical interaction. Neuroticism negatively predicted commitment to display rules in the context of the incivility interaction. Hence, interacting with difficult customers reduces employees' motivation to express positive emotions and it seems that some personality traits act as a motivational disposition to perform emotional labor, at least in certain contexts.

By proposing and testing whether emotional labor is explained by a motivational mechanism, Diefendorff and colleagues made significant contributions to the emotional labor literature. Most research has been focused on emotional labor outcomes and much less on antecedents (except for emotional characteristics mentioned previously). This clearly demonstrates that the presence of display rules alone is insufficient; employees must be committed to the display rules for their behavior to be impacted. Still, other research questions arise in the process of analyzing the extant body of research.

Self-Determined Motivation to Regulate Emotions

In an emotional labor context, one should ask the following question: are employees committed to display rules because they are obliged to do so (controlled motivation) or because it constitutes part of their identity (autonomous motivation)? As mentioned, it seems that the more employees identify with their job role, the more willing they are to regulate their emotions (Ashforth & Humphrey, 1993). SDT (Deci & Ryan, 1985, 2000; Ryan & Deci, 2001) provides an interesting framework that simultaneously considers the type of motivation (controlled vs. autonomous) and the notion of identification. Hence, by adopting an SDT perspective, motivation to perform emotional labor is not only a matter of quantity of motivation (e.g., expectancy theory) but also a matter of quality of the motivation (see Gagné & Deci, 2005).

SDT distinguishes between two classes of intentional behavior: autonomous and controlled (Deci & Ryan, 1985, 2000; Deci & Ryan, 2008; Gagné & Deci, 2005; Ryan & Connell, 1989; Ryan & Deci, 2001). Because emotional labor is considered an intentional act (Rubin et al., 2005),

this distinction can help us to delve further as to why employees adopt certain emotion-regulation strategies. Moreover, this framework enables us to build on Asfhorth and Humphrey's (1993) social identity framework regarding the internalization of job roles. More specifically, SDT posits that employees perform emotional labor because they feel an external or internal pressure to do so, or because they endorse the requirement to regulate one's emotions. Although Chapter 1 provided an overview of the basic SDT concepts, the following paragraphs illustrate how we can apply them to emotion regulation.

SDT posits that there exist different types of motivation aligned on a continuum, which distinguishes autonomous motivation from controlled forms of motivation (Deci & Ryan, 1985, 2000; Gagné & Deci, 2005). At one end of the continuum, there is amotivation (Deci & Ryan, 1985, 2000; Gagné & Deci, 2005). Amotivated employees are those who should regulate emotions without volition and with resignation. They might not regulate their emotions at all and, if they do, they do not feel that they have control over their emotional displays.

SDT posits that there are different forms of extrinsic motivation that vary in the degree to which they are controlled or autonomous, depending on the internalization of the activity to be performed (Gagné & Deci, 2005). First, whenever employees perform emotional labor to obtain a reward or to avoid punishment, this behavior is said to be externally regulated and the locus is purely external (Deci & Ryan, 1985, 2000; Gagné & Deci, 2005). For example, employees who are externally motivated to regulate their emotions do so because they either wish to receive a good performance appraisal by their supervisor or because they want to avoid irritating their customers.

The other forms of extrinsic motivation can be distinguished from their level of internalization. Introjection describes a form of motivation in which individuals act to feel worthy and to preserve their self-esteem. Whereas performing emotional labor when adopting an external motivation is due to external pressure, introjection implies a pressure that comes from within the person. In the context of emotion regulation, introjected motivation occurs whenever employees regulate their emotions to feel pride or to avoid feeling shame or guilt.

Identified motivation occurs whenever an employee recognizes and accepts the value of a behavior (Deci & Ryan, 1985, 2000; Gagné & Deci, 2005), such as regulating one's emotions at work.

By endorsing the emotional labor requirement, individuals internalize its value and the behavior is more likely to occur (although it remains externally motivated). Hence, employees for whom interacting with others, such as customers, is an endorsed challenge regulate their emotions more easily.

Integrated motivation is the most autonomous form of extrinsic motivation. Although it is not performed because of the pleasure associated with it, as is the case with intrinsic motivation, there is still a feeling of choice (Deci & Ryan, 1985, 2000; Gagné & Deci, 2005). Hence, the emotional labor requirements are completely endorsed by the person who is more likely to regulate his or her emotions. In that case, individuals performing emotional labor according to an integrated form of motivation should feel that regulating their emotions is an integral part of who they are as people. Therefore, they are more likely to behave in a way that is consistent with their identity.

At the other end, intrinsic motivation occurs whenever employees regulate their emotions for the sole pleasure of regulating them. In other words, there is no contingency or rewards linked with the behavior, and individuals act for the interest, challenge, or sheer pleasure of regulating emotions. In the context of emotional labor, expressing an authentic smile can be easily seen as an intrinsically motivated act, but it is more difficult to see how employees could be intrinsically motivated to suppress their negative emotions.

At this point, one could ask whether these different forms of motivation represent adequately the underlying reasons for performing emotional labor. It is important to keep in mind that employees regulate their emotions in order to satisfy an organizational demand, which by definition gives an external focus for performing the task at hand. Hence, intrinsic motivation may not be the most relevant form of motivation for understanding why and how employees perform emotional labor. However, individuals can select their own goals and pursue them in an autonomous fashion. As such, emotional display rules are either goals set by the organization or are implicit in some job descriptions (see Diefendorff & Gosserand, 2003). This organizational demand also reflects an organizational value, an example of which is serving the customer with positive emotions and without negative emotions. If employees' values also focus on serving the customer with the prescribed emotions, then organizational demands become congruent with each employee's sense of self.

This emphasis on autonomous forms of motivation for explaining human behavior is discussed in other domains using SDT. For instance, voting behavior is an important social demand on members of a community, but individuals vary greatly in their interest for following political campaigns. A series of studies focused on political motivation during different campaigns and demonstrated that identified motivation was systematically more important for individuals than intrinsic motivation (Koestner, Losier, Vallerand, & Carducci, 1996; Losier & Koestner, 1999; Losier, Perreault, Koestner, & Vallerand, 2001); moreover, this form of motivation better predicted voting behavior than intrinsic motivation (Losier & Koestner, 1999). In the domain of health-promoting behavior, intrinsic motivation is rarely measured because "intrinsic motivation applies to situations in which behaviors are performed because they are interesting and enjoyable and most people do not find health-promoting behaviors to be interesting and enjoyable" (Lévesque et al., 2007, p. 693). Still, individuals might value the importance of an activity (e.g., tobacco cessation, exercising, dieting, voting) and hence perform the activity for autonomous reasons. In the context of emotional labor, employees may find that regulating their emotions is neither fun, nor pleasant, nor enjoyable, especially when negative emotions are involved. However, to the degree to which employees endorse the organizational demands imposed on them, their motivation can still be self-determined.

Besides these theoretical reasons, there is also an empirical justification for not considering intrinsic motivation in the study of emotional labor. First, there is indirect evidence for the usefulness of the SDT framework for explaining motivation to regulate emotions at work. Sutton (2004) found that some of the interviewed teachers regulated their emotions because it was part of their job and because it kept them professional. These reasons correspond to an idealized emotion self image. Using SDT terms, it can be said that these teachers *fully endorsed* emotion regulation. By contrast, other teachers reported that they felt ashamed of showing their anger in the presence of students. Based on the definitions discussed previously, this emotion regulation seems to be introjected. Other teachers wanted to serve as role models for their students, whereas others admitted that they did not know why they regulated their emotions. In these latter cases, we can see both external motivation and amotivation being manifested. Hence, these reasons reflect SDT's different types of motivation, but no reason seems to represent an intrinsic motive for regulating emotions.

Another study, focused more on SDT and dealing with everyday life, provides support for the usefulness of this framework in understanding the motives underlying emotion regulation. Kim et al.'s (2002) research was based on evidence that emotion expression was related to indices of health and that individuals differed in their ways of expressing or regulating emotions. To help clarify the link between the tendency to express negative emotions and the ambivalence of expressing negative emotions due to social norms, they developed scales that reflected reasons to withhold negative emotions in everyday life. First, their scales assessed and confirmed the presence of extrinsic forms of motivation to withhold negative emotions. Second, Kim et al. (2002) found that self-determined motivation to withhold negative emotions was positively associated with psychological well-being and with coping styles, again demonstrating the importance of considering extrinsic reasons for regulating one's emotions.

Third, based on existing measures of self-determined motivation (e.g., Gagné et al., 2010; Vallerand, Fortier, & Guay, 1997; Vallerand et al., 1992, 1993), Lépine and Cossette (2010) focused on jobs in which "service with a smile" is an important requirement and developed parallel measures of self-determined motivation to express positive emotions and to suppress negative ones. Students working in part-time jobs involving customer service interactions were invited to participate in a study in which they were asked why they chose to regulate their emotions at work. A total of 223 students volunteered to participate. All participants were working in a job that required to express positive emotions and to suppress negative emotions. Participants were asked to respond to a series of items representing one of six forms of motivation (amotivation, external, introjected, identified, integrated, or intrinsic motivation). For each reason, participants needed to assess whether they (a) expressed positive emotions, and (b) suppressed negative emotions, either "exactly for this reason" (7) or "not at all for this reason" (1). In other words, for each reason, participants provided two answers, one for expressing positive emotions, and one for suppressing negative emotions. Results supported the factorial structure of the questionnaire, but only when intrinsic motivation was excluded from the analysis. Stated otherwise,

intrinsic motivation prevented good fit from occurring (Lépine & Cossette, 2010).

Hence, it seems that intrinsic motivation is not a relevant dimension for studying motivation to perform emotional labor and that this assumption is supported empirically. Nevertheless, much work needs to be done on this measurement issue. The next section concludes the discussion about the underlying motives for regulating emotions at work.

Self-Determined Motivation and Emotional Labor Strategies

Extrinsic forms of motivation seem most relevant in the study of "why" employees are performing emotional labor, and extend beyond expectancy theory, which is mostly concerned with the amount of motivation than the quality of motivation (see Gagné & Deci, 2005). In this section, the focus is on the link between the motives for regulating emotions and the different strategies employees may use to comply with display rules.

As mentioned, display rules are goals that employees strive to achieve (Diefendorff & Gosserand, 2003). From an SDT perspective, goals that are internalized by individuals contribute to an optimal functioning of individuals and to their well-being (see Ryan & Deci, 2001). More specifically, when goals are self-concordant (i.e., when they are aligned with one's true self) and when those complying with the display rules are well-internalized, self-determined motivation is more likely to occur, resulting in a person's enhanced well-being; in contrast, nonconcordant goals underlie non–self-determined forms of motivation and impair an individual's well-being (Sheldon, Ryan, Rawsthorne, & Ilardi, 1997). Being true to one's self refers to the notion of authenticity (Heppner et al., 2008; Kernis & Goldman, 2006; Lakey, Kernis, Heppner, & Lance, 2008).

Authenticity occurs when individuals possess self-knowledge concerning themselves, such as their motives and their personal standards; process information without distorting, denying or ignoring internal or external sources; engage freely and naturally in behavior because of their values and beliefs; and desire that close others know who they really are (Lakey et al., 2008). High authenticity relates to healthy psychological and interpersonal functioning (see Kernis & Goldman, 2006). Because emotion regulation is also concerned about interpersonal functioning, authenticity becomes a relevant notion for understanding how emotional labor is performed.

As mentioned, when employees endorse the importance of regulating their emotions at work, it should become less effortful for them to be more authentic in their interactions with others and to spontaneously regulate emotions that are in line with their job demands (Ashforth & Humphrey, 1993; Ashforth & Tomiuk, 2000). Evidence exists to support this rationale. Brotheridge and Lee (2002) found that authentic employees were those who identified more strongly with their role, and who regulated their emotions by using deep acting strategies rather than surface acting strategies.

Hence, based on Brotheridge and Lee's (2002) results, authentic employees should value the importance of regulating their emotions. By valuing this task requirement, they should adopt emotion-regulation strategies that aim at aligning felt and expressed emotions (antecedent-focused strategies, such as deep acting) and express their felt emotions naturally. In contrast, less authentic employees should use response-focused emotion regulation strategies, because these strategies aim at modifying the observable aspects of emotion only; as was previously mentioned, these strategies involve a high degree of discrepancy between felt and expressed emotions. By focusing on observable displays, these employees are possibly thinking more about how customers or their supervisor will appraise their behaviors rather than the importance of regulating their emotions. In this context, employees have an external focus over their behavior and regulation should become more effortful. As mentioned, the strategy that requires more effort is surface acting, which is considered faking in bad faith because employees do not endorse the display rules (Allen et al., 2010; Ashforth & Humphrey, 1993; Diefendorff et al., 2005; Zapf, 2002).

Based on these arguments, self-determined motivation to perform emotional labor is expected to be positively related to deep acting and negatively related to surface acting. These hypotheses were tested in two studies involving students working in customer service jobs. If self-determined motivation to perform emotional labor predicted, as expected, the use of deep acting in both studies (ß = .24 and ß = .16), only the second study found a significant and negative correlation between self-determined motivation to perform emotional labor and surface acting (ß = .03 and ß = −.16) (Cossette, et al., 2006; Cossette & Hess, 2012). A possible explanation for these discrepant findings is that the first study (Cossette et al., 2006) focused on motivation to suppress negative emotions, whereas the second

(Cossette & Hess, 2012) focused on motivation to express positive emotions. When focusing on the expression of positive emotions, the suppression of negative emotions may become a more salient strategy for employees. In order to display positive emotions, no observable responses should be apparent for others. However, when participants focus on suppressing their emotions, they might try harder to align their inner feelings with their expressed emotions. This hypothesis is supported and represented by the beta weights shown above. Motivation was more strongly related to deep acting when the focus was on the suppression of negative emotions than when the focus was on the expression of positive emotions. Hence, the emotion valence (positive vs. negative) seems to be crucial when investigating the motivational process of regulating emotions. Although emotional labor refers to the regulation of emotions, authors rarely consider which emotions are regulated.

Emotional Labor as a Mechanism Relating Self-Determined Motivation and Job Outcomes

Many peer-reviewed articles address the issue of emotional labor outcomes (Bono & Vey, 2005; Hülsheger & Schewe, 2011; Zapf, 2002). In the following sections, we present an overview of these consequences, some of which were investigated using an SDT framework. Hence, we propose that emotional labor acts as an intermediate variable between employees' motivation to perform emotional labor and their well-being.

EMOTIONAL LABOR AND EMPLOYEE WELL-BEING

In her seminal work on emotional labor, Hochschild (1983) mentioned that performing emotional labor, regardless of the strategy used, led to alienation and strain. Hochschild's work inspired subsequent researchers to address the links between emotional labor and employee well-being. There is now budding evidence that shows how the link between emotional labor and well-being is much more nuanced in that it depends on both the strategy used by employees and the dimension of well-being under scrutiny. Different indicators of well-being are used in emotional labor research, such as burnout and job satisfaction (see Hülsheger & Schewe, 2011).

Burnout is a syndrome that comprises three sequential dimensions (Maslach, Leiter, & Schaufeli, 2009). The first is emotional exhaustion, described as a lack of energy and fatigue. The second dimension, called depersonalization, is characterized by negative or inappropriate attitudes toward others, irritability, and withdrawal. It is a detachment from the job. The third dimension is the lack or diminished sense of accomplishment. As for job satisfaction, this concept refers to the extent to which employees evaluate their jobs in a positive or negative way (Weiss, 2002).

Two meta-analyses have shown that surface acting has a consistent impact on different indicators of well-being (Bono & Vey, 2005; Hülsheger & Schewe, 2011). Specifically, the strategy impacts employee burnout by increasing their emotional exhaustion and depersonalization, and decreasing their sense of accomplishment and job satisfaction. Surface acting depletes individual resources (Hobfoll, 1989), such as self-authenticity and rewarding social relationships (Brotheridge & Lee, 2002), as well as satisfaction with clients (Martinez-Inigo, Totterdell, Alcover, & Holman, 2007). In contrast, deep acting is not significantly related to emotional exhaustion, depersonalization and job satisfaction, but instead increases personal accomplishment (Hülsheger & Schewe, 2011). This strategy requires effort although much less than surface acting, and has been shown to promote resource gains (Brotheridge & Grandey, 2002; Brotheridge & Lee, 2002). More specifically, deep acting creates a sense of authenticity, an important resource protecting against burnout symptoms (Brotheridge & Lee, 2002). Hence, when performing emotional labor employees consume more or less resources depending on the strategy used.

SDT is concerned with optimal human functioning (Deci & Ryan, 2000; Ryan & Deci, 2001). To ensure this optimality, SDT recommends that individuals must fulfill three basic psychological needs. First, individuals need to feel autonomous in their actions. Second, they must feel competent in their work. Third, they must feel related with others (see Chapter 1 of this book). To the extent that social contexts facilitate the fulfillment of these needs, motivation becomes increasingly more autonomous thereby positively impacting individuals' psychological well-being (Deci & Ryan, 2000; Gagné & Deci, 2005; Ryan & Deci 2001). Self-determined forms of motivation have been found to decrease burnout symptoms and increase job satisfaction among employees (Blais, Brière, Lachance, Riddle, & Vallerand, 1993).

Because self-determined motivation and emotional labor both impact employee well-being,

emotion regulation strategies could act as mediating variables between the motivation to perform emotional labor and employee well-being. In a test of the mediation model proposed in Figure 16.1, deep acting mediated the impact of self-determined motivation to perform emotional labor on job satisfaction (Cossette & Hess, 2012) and emotional exhaustion (Cossette et al., 2006). More specifically, self-determined motivation was shown to have a positive impact on the use of deep acting strategies among students working in customer service jobs. In turn, deep acting strategies reduced burnout symptoms (Cossette, et al., 2006) and increased levels of job satisfaction (Cossette & Hess, 2012). However, in both studies, surface acting did not significantly impact outcomes (Cossette et al., 2006; Cossette & Hess, 2012). It seems that surface acting was not related to outcomes because it depended on whether this strategy was used alone or in combination with other strategies (Cossette & Hess, 2010). Another explanation for this absence of association between surface acting and indicators of employee well-being may be the nature of the jobs themselves. Participants from both studies were students working in part-time jobs. First, these jobs typically require short scripted interactions with customers (e.g., cashier at a coffee shop). Second, because these jobs are performed solely on a part-time basis, the resources depleted from using surface acting strategies (Brotheridge & Grandey, 2002; Brotheridge & Lee, 2002) may have been compensated with the students' other "professional" activity, namely studying and other school-related work.

JOB PERFORMANCE

Organizations expect their employees to treat customers courteously and empathically. In other words, customers expect an emotional performance from employees (Grandey, 2003). Despite the importance of emotional labor in several jobs, it is somewhat surprising that employee job performance in relation to displaying positive emotions and suppressing negative ones has received much less attention from researchers (see Hülsheger & Schewe, 2011). This may be due to the complexity of defining and measuring performance (i.e., multiple meanings, such as overall task performance, emotional performance, or customer appreciation). Moreover, this difficulty may explain results from Hülsheger and Schewe's (2011) meta-analysis, which demonstrates little consistency between studies. Overall, it seems that surface acting and deep acting are not related to global task performance;

whereas surface acting leads to lower emotional performance and customer satisfaction, deep acting positively impacts both performance dimensions. The absence of a relationship between emotional labor and global performance might be explained by the fact that global task performance requires other skills to perform adequately, such as cognitive skills and technical product knowledge.

SDT research also has important implications for understanding job performance. Gagné and Deci's (2005) review suggested that self-determined motivation should have a positive impact on performance, particularly if the task requires creativity, cognitive flexibility, and conceptual understanding, which should be the case in emotional performance (e.g., employees must understand others' emotions and situation, relate others' problems/needs with organizational products or services, and find adequate solutions to a problem/need). Future research should investigate whether performance, and more particularly service performance, can be predicted by the motivational process proposed in Figure 16.1.

TURNOVER

Many researchers suggested that withdrawal behaviors, such as turnover (or voluntary intention to quit), constitute outcomes of emotional labor strategies (Grandey, 2000; Rubin et al., 2005). Earlier work by Abraham (1998) demonstrated that employee emotional dissonance led to heightened intentions to quit. More recent work focusing specifically on emotion regulation strategies has generated some interesting findings. For example, surface acting was found to directly influence turnover intentions (Côté & Morgan, 2002) and turnover (Goodwin, Groth, & Frenkel, 2011). Others have found that surface acting influences turnover intentions via emotional exhaustion (Chau, Dahling, Levy, & Diefendorff, 2009). As for deep acting, Chau et al. (2009) found that this strategy reduces turnover intentions, whereas Goodwin et al. (2011) found a nonsignificant effect on turnover.

SDT was also used to investigate employee turnover intentions. More specifically, researchers tested the following SDT assumptions: social contexts influence the forms of motivation; and the forms of motivation subsequently impact individual outcomes. As predicted, social contexts that supported employee autonomy (Otis & Pelletier, 2005), competence (Otis & Pelletier, 2005; Richer, Blanchard, & Vallerand, 2002), and feelings of relatedness (Otis & Pelletier, 2005) led to the adoption of a more self-determined motivation at work. This self-determined motivation then helped decrease employee turnover intentions (Otis & Pelletier, 2005; Richer et al., 2002). Considering previous findings on the link between emotional labor and job performance on one hand and emotional labor and turnover on the other, future research should investigate whether emotional labor strategies act as a mediator between motivation to regulate one's emotions and turnover intentions. A motivation profile that is more self-determined should lead to the use of deep acting, which positively impacts performance and facilitate employee retention. In

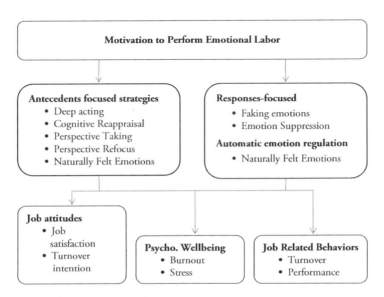

Fig. 16.1. Motivational process of emotional labor and its consequences.

contrast, less self-determined motivation to perform emotional labor should lead to greater use of surface acting, which, in turn increases turnover intentions.

Future Directions

The motivational process of emotional labor proposed in this chapter demonstrates solid potential to explain "why" and "how" employees regulate their emotions at work. Moreover, emotional labor strategies should act as mediating variables between the motivation to perform emotional labor and such outcomes as employee well-being, job attitudes, turnover, and job performance. Overall, self-determined motivation to perform emotional labor should lead to the adoption of different emotion regulation strategies. More specifically, self-determined forms of motivation should lead to the adoption of more antecedent-focused regulation strategies and the expression of naturally felt emotions because these strategies reflect greater authenticity on the part of employees. In contrast, less self-determined motivation should lead to increased use of surface acting. Although findings support most of these predictions, several issues need to be resolved. The following paragraphs therefore discuss what should constitute the next steps in the study of the motivational process of performing emotional labor.

First, the process "motivation → emotional labor strategies → employee well-being" needs to be replicated in more homogenous samples. So far, the work of Cossette and colleagues has focused on jobs requiring "serving customers with a smile." Although their findings support the proposed model, contextual factor should also be considered in order to get a better picture of when motivation should impact emotion regulation strategies. As mentioned by some scholars, when employees are interacting with customers for short periods of time and in scripted ways, their motivation may not have the same impact as in the case when longer interactions take place and in which autonomy is more prevalent. Hence, research on our proposed model should test for contextual factors that may moderate the impact between motivation and emotional labor.

Second, motivation to perform emotional labor has been tested according to the two display rules that have generally garnered the most attention in emotional labor research, namely expressing positive emotions and suppressing negative ones (e.g., Diefendorff, Erickson, Grandey, & Dahling, 2011). As mentioned, different results were found such that when employees focused on their positive emotions they were likely paying more attention to the observable aspects of the emotional display. However, when they focused on suppressing their negative emotions, they might have attended more carefully to their inner feelings and to situational cues as a means of mitigating this affective negativity. Moreover, they might also have been more attentive to the person with whom they interacted (i.e., by taking the other's perspective), thus facilitating the alignment of their inner feelings with the emotional displays (Gross, 1998). At present, these interpretations remain speculative. Therefore, future theory and research should attempt to explain why divergent findings occurred depending on the valence of the emotions regulated.

A third issue, albeit related to the second, concerns the fact that other display rules exist. As highlighted in the introduction, debt collectors and police officers must convey a certain level of hostility to debtors and criminals, respectively (see Rafaeli & Sutton, 1987). In such contexts, one should ask how employees are regulating their emotions and how motivation is related to these strategies. Hence, future research should not only address whether motivation to perform emotional labor can be adapted to different display rules, but also how motivation impacts emotional labor strategies depending on the display rule concerned. In other words, can self-determined motivation to regulate emotions be applied to different display rules? If the answer is yes, another question looms: can the predictions made here concerning the impact of motivation on emotion regulation strategies be applied to different work settings? If yes, then this will suggest that a similar motivational process leading to emotion regulation strategies and the distinction between the display rules should not be made. However, if the distinctions are relevant, then this will lead to different interventions dedicated to optimizing how employees regulate their emotions. To answer this question adequately, a critical issue is to have a questionnaire measuring the different forms of motivation and the same items measuring different display rules. So far, preliminary results are encouraging (Lépine & Cossette, 2010), but much needed research has to be done to properly validate these measures.

The fourth issue raised in the proposed model concerns the relative effect of individual antecedents and organizational antecedents on motivation. On one hand, motivation to perform emotional labor can be conceived of as an individual difference (see Kim et al., 2002). If this is the case, then personality traits related to emotional labor strategies (see Diefendorff et al., 2005) and to emotion display rules (see Diefendorff & Croyle, 2008) may act as antecedents of motivation to perform emotional labor. On the other hand, many studies in work settings within the SDT framework suggest that work motivation is fostered by the social contexts in which employees navigate (Fernet, Guay, & Senécal, 2004; Gagné & Deci, 2005). In other words, the question now becomes: Is the motivation to perform emotional labor an individual predisposition or is it a task motivation? If it is the former, then employees should be selected according this predisposition and social context should remain unrelated to motivation. The working conditions should not influence whether the motivation is self-determined or not. On the other side, if it is the latter, then the working context should exert a strong influence on employee motivation. Still, a third possibility is that both sets of antecedents (individual and organizational) impact motivation to perform emotional labor strategies. Considering the fact that emotions are individuals' reactions to internal and external stimuli (Gross & Thompson, 2007), this third possibility is highly probable. In this case, SDT has much more to offer in the investigation of the emotional labor process; for example, one may wish to also explore need satisfaction and to test the entire theoretical constituency of SDT (see Van den Broeck, Vansteenkiste, De Witte, & Lens, 2008; Van den Broeck, Vansteenkiste, De Witte, Soenens, & Lens, 2010; Vansteenkiste et al., 2007). Other examples include adding job characteristics, such as feedback from others and task significance (Gagné, Senécal, & Koestner, 1997; Millette & Gagné, 2008) or even skill utilization and social support (Van den Broeck et al., 2010) to investigate whether they positively impact self-determined motivation to perform emotional labor.

Conclusion

SDT provides a promising framework to better understand how and why employees are performing emotional labor. The strong basis of this framework allowed us to propose a motivational process of emotional labor. This model is interesting from a theoretical and empirical point of view because we could extend SDT to the emotion regulation domain. In this sense, this framework should help researchers and practitioners alike in their understanding of "why" (i.e., underlying or distal motives) and "how" (i.e., specific or proximal processes) employees regulate their emotions at work.

References

Abraham, R. (1998). Emotional dissonance in organizations: Antecedents, consequences, and moderators. *Genetic, Social, and General Psychology Monographs, 124*(2), 229–246.

Abraham, R. (1999a). The impact of emotional dissonance on organizational commitment and intention to turnover. *Journal of Psychology: Interdisciplinary and Applied, 133*(4), 441–455.

Abraham, R. (1999b). Negative affectivity: Moderator or confound in emotional dissonance-outcome relationships? *Journal of Psychology: Interdisciplinary and Applied, 133*(1), 61–72. doi:10.1080/00223989909599722

Adelmann, P. K. (1995). Emotional labor as a potential source of job stress. In S. L. Sauter & L. R. Murphy (Eds.), *Organizational risk factors for job stress* (pp. 371–381). Washington, DC: American Psychological Association. doi:10.1037/10173-023

Allen, J., Pugh, S., Grandey, A., & Groth, M. (2010). Following display rules in good or bad faith?: Customer orientation as a moderator of the display rule-emotional labor relationship. *Human Performance, 23*(2), 101–115. doi:10.1080/08959281003621695

Ashforth, B. E., & Humphrey, R. H. (1993). Emotional labor in service roles: The influence of identity. *Academy of Management Review, 18*(1), 88–115. doi:10.2307/258824

Ashforth, B. E., & Tomiuk, M. A. (2000). Emotional labour and authenticity: Views from service agents. In S. Fineman (Ed.), *Emotion in organizations* (pp. 184–203). London: Sage.

Ashkanasy, N. M., & Daus, C. S. (2002). Emotion in the workplace: The new challenge for managers. *Academy of Management Executive, 16*(1), 76–86. doi:10.5465/AME.2002.6640191

Bakker, A. B., & Heuven, E. (2006). Emotional dissonance, burnout, and in-role performance among nurses and police officers. *International Journal of Stress Management, 13*(4), 423–440. doi:10.1037/1072-5245.13.4.423

Berking, M., Meier, C., & Wupperman, P. (2010). Enhancing emotion-regulation skills in police officers: Results of a pilot controlled study. *Behavior Therapy, 41*(3), 329–339. doi:10.1016/j.beth.2009.08.001

Blais, M. R., Brière, N. M., Lachance, L., Riddle, A. S., & Vallerand, R. J. (1993). The Blais Inventory of Work Motivation/L'Inventaire des Motivations au Travail de Blais. *Revue Québécoise De Psychologie, 14*(3), 185–215.

Bono, J. E., & Vey, M. A. (2005). Toward understanding emotional management at work: A quantitative review of emotional labor research. In C. E. Härtel, W. J. Zerbe, & N. M. Ashkanasy (Eds.), *Emotions in organizational behavior* (pp. 213–233). Mahwah, NJ: Lawrence Erlbaum Associates Publishers.

Brotheridge, C. M. (2006). The role of emotional intelligence and other individual difference variables in predicting emotional labor relative to situational demands. *Psicothema, 18*, 139–144.

Brotheridge, C. M., & Grandey, A. A. (2002). Emotional labor and burnout: Comparing two perspectives of "people work." *Journal of Vocational Behavior, 60*, 17–39. doi:10.1006/jvbe.2001.1815

Brotheridge, C. M., & Lee, R. T. (2002). Testing a conservation of resources model of the dynamics of emotional labor. *Journal of Occupational Health Psychology, 7*(1), 57–67. doi:10.1037/1076-8998.7.1.57

Brotheridge, C. M., & Lee, R. T. (2003). Development and validation of the Emotional Labour Scale. *Journal of Occupational and Organizational Psychology, 76,* 365. doi:10.1348/096317903769647229

Chau, S. L., Dahling, J. J., Levy, P. E., & Diefendorff, J. M. (2009). A predictive study of emotional labor and turnover. *Journal of Organizational Behavior, 30*(8), 1151–1163. doi:10.1002/job.617

Cossette, M., Blais, M. R., & Hess, U. (2006, July 7-10). *Motivation au travail émotionnel, styles de service à la clientèle et épuisement professionnel.* Paper presented at the AIPTLF, Hammamet, Tunisie.

Cossette, M., & Hess, U. (2009, June 6-9). *How organizational factors impact emotional labour strategies.* Paper presented at the Conference of the Administrative Sciences Association of Canada, Niagara Falls.

Cossette, M., & Hess, U. (2010, August 6-10). *How is emotional labor performed by customer service employees?* A matter of style. Paper presented at the Academy of Management Annual Meeting, Montréal.

Cossette, M., & Hess, U. (2012). Emotion regulation strategies among customer service employees: A motivational approach. In N. M. Ashkanasy, C. E. Härtel, & W. J. Zerbe (Eds.), *Research on emotion in organizations* (Vol. 8, pp. 331–354). Bingley, UK: Emerald Publishing Group. doi:10.1108/S1746-9791(2012)0000008017

Côté, S., & Morgan, L. M. (2002). A longitudinal analysis of the association between emotion regulation, job satisfaction, and intentions to quit. *Journal of Organizational Behavior, 23*(8), 947–962. doi:10.1002/job.174

Deci, E. L., & Ryan, R. M. (1985). *Intrinsic motivation and self-determination in human behavior.* New York: Plenum Press.

Deci, E. L., & Ryan, R. M. (2000). The "what" and "why" of goal pursuits: Human needs and self-determination of behavior. *Psychological Inquiry, 11*(4), 227–268. doi:10.1207/S15327965PLI1104_01

Deci, E. L., & Ryan, R. M. (2008). Facilitating optimal motivation and psychological well-being across life's domains. *Canadian Psychology/Psychologie canadienne, 49*(1), 14–23. doi:10.1037/0708-5591.49.1.14

Diefendorff, J. M., & Croyle, M. H. (2008). Antecedents of emotional display rule commitment. *Human Performance, 21*(3), 310–332. doi:10.1080/08959280802137911

Diefendorff, J. M., Croyle, M. H., & Gosserand, R. H. (2005). The dimensionality and antecedents of emotional labor strategies. *Journal of Vocational Behavior, 66*(2), 339. doi:10.1016/j.jvb.2004.02.001

Diefendorff, J. M., Erickson, R. J., Grandey, A. A., & Dahling, J. J. (2011). Emotional display rules as work unit norms: A multilevel analysis of emotional labor among nurses. *Journal of Occupational Health Psychology, 16*(2), 170–186. doi:10.1037/a0021725

Diefendorff, J. M., & Gosserand, R. H. (2003). Understanding the emotional labor process: A control theory perspective. *Journal of Organizational Behavior, 24*(8), 945–959. doi:10.1002/job.230

Ekman, P. (Ed.). (1973). *Darwin and facial expression: A century of research in review.* Oxford, England: Academic Press.

Fernet, C., Guay, F., & Senécal, C. (2004). Adjusting to job demands: The role of work self-determination and job control in predicting burnout. *Journal of Vocational Behavior, 65*(1), 39–56. doi:10.1016/s0001-8791(03)00098-8

Fox, S., & Spector, P. E. (2000). Relations of emotional intelligence, practical intelligence, general intelligence, and trait affectivity with interview outcomes: It's not all just "G". *Journal of Organizational Behavior. Special Issue: Emotions in organizations, 21*(Spec Issue), 203–220. doi:10.1002/(SICI)1099-1379(200003)21:2

Gagné, M., & Deci, E. L. (2005). Self-determination theory and work motivation. *Journal of Organizational Behavior, 26*(4), 331–362. doi:10.1002/job.322

Gagné, M., Forest, J., Gilbert, M.-H., Aubé, C., Morin, E., & Malorni, A. (2010). The Motivation at Work Scale: Validation evidence in two languages. *Educational and Psychological Measurement, 70*(4), 628–646. doi:10.1177/0013164409355698

Gagné, M., Senécal, C. B., & Koestner, R. (1997). Proximal job characteristics, feelings of empowerment, and intrinsic motivation: A multidimensional model. *Journal of Applied Social Psychology, 27*(14), 1222–1240. doi:10.1111/j.1559-1816.1997.tb01803.x

Goffman, E. (1959). *Presentation of self in everyday life.* New York: Overlook Press.

Goodwin, R. E., Groth, M., & Frenkel, S. J. (2011). Relationships between emotional labor, job performance, and turnover. *Journal of Vocational Behavior, 79*(2), 538–548. doi:10.1016/j.jvb.2011.03.001

Gosserand, R. H., & Diefendorff, J. M. (2005). Emotional display rules and emotional labor: The moderating role of commitment. *Journal of Applied Psychology, 90*(6), 1256–1264. doi:10.1037/0021-9010.90.6.1256

Grandey, A. A. (2000). Emotional regulation in the workplace: A new way to conceptualize emotional labor. *Journal of Occupational Health Psychology, 5*(1), 95–110. doi:10.1037/1076-8998.5.1.95

Grandey, A. A. (2003). When "the show must go on": Surface acting and deep acting as determinants of emotional exhaustion and peer-rated service delivery. *Academy of Management Journal, 46*(1), 86–96. doi:10.2307/30040678

Grandey, A. A., Dickter, D. N., & Sin, H.-P. (2004). The customer is not always right: Customer aggression and emotion regulation of service employees. *Journal of Organizational Behavior, 25*(3), 397–418. doi:10.1002/job.252

Gross, J. J. (1998). The emerging field of emotion regulation: An integrative review. *Review of General Psychology. Special Issue: New directions in research on emotion, 2*(3), 271–299. doi:10.1037/1089-2680.2.3.271

Gross, J. J., & John, O. P. (2003). Individual differences in two emotion regulation processes: Implications for affect, relationships, and well-being. *Journal of Personality and Social Psychology, 85*(2), 348–362. doi:10.1037/0022-3514.85.2.348

Gross, J. J., & Thompson, R. A. (2007). Emotion regulation: Conceptual foundations. In J. J. Gross (Ed.), *The handbook of emotion regulation* (pp. 3–24). New York: The Guilford Press.

Heppner, W. L., Kernis, M. H., Nezlek, J. B., Foster, J., Lakey, C. E., & Goldman, B. M. (2008). Within-person relationships among daily self-esteem, need satisfaction, and authenticity. *Psychological Science, 19*(11), 1140–1145. doi:10.1111/j.1467-9280.2008.02215.x

Hess, U. (2003). Les émotions au travail. *Rapport bourgogne*. Retrieved from http://www.cirano.qc.ca/pdf/publication/2003RB-04.pdf

Hobfoll, S. E. (1989). Conservation of resources: A new attempt at conceptualizing stress. *American Psychologist*, 44(3), 513–524. doi:10.1037/0003-066x.44.3.513

Hochschild, A. R. (1983). *The managed heart: Commercialization of human feeling*. Berkeley and Los Angeles: University of California Press.

Hülsheger, U. R., & Schewe, A. F. (2011). On the costs and benefits of emotional labor: A meta-analysis of three decades of research. *Journal of Occupational Health Psychology*, 16(3), 361–389. doi:10.1037/a0022876

John, O. P., & Gross, J. J. (2004). Healthy and unhealthy emotion regulation: Personality processes, individual differences, and life span development. *Journal of Personality*, 72(6), 1301–1333. doi:10.1111/j.1467-6494.2004.00298.x

Kernis, M. H., & Goldman, B. M. (2006). *A multicomponent conceptualization of authenticity: Theory and research Advances in experimental social psychology, Vol 38*. San Diego, CA: Elsevier Academic Press. doi:10.1016/S0065-2601(06)38006-9

Kim, Y., Deci, E. L., & Zuckerman, M. (2002). The development of the Self-Regulation of Withholding Negative Emotions Questionnaire. *Educational and Psychological Measurement*, 62(2), 316–336. doi:10.1177/0013164402062002008

Koestner, R., Losier, G. F., Vallerand, R. J., & Carducci, D. (1996). Identified and introjected forms of political internalization: Extending self-determination theory. *Journal of Personality and Social Psychology*, 70(5), 1025–1036. doi:10.1037/0022-3514.70.5.1025

Kruml, S. M., & Geddes, D. (2000). Exploring the dimensions of emotional labor. *Management Communication Quarterly: McQ*, 14(1), 8–49.

Lakey, C. E., Kernis, M. H., Heppner, W. L., & Lance, C. E. (2008). Individual differences in authenticity and mindfulness as predictors of verbal defensiveness. *Journal of Research in Personality*, 42(1), 230–238. doi:10.1016/j.jrp.2007.05.002

Lépine, M.-C., & Cossette, M. (2010). "Servir les clients avec le sourire": un cadre motivationnel pour mieux prédire les stratégies de régulation émotionnelle *Série cahier scientifiques*. Retrieved from http://www.cirano.qc.ca/pdf/publication/2010s-39.pdf

Levesque, C. S., Williams, G. C., Elliot, D., Pickering, M. A., Bodenhamer, B., & Finley, P. J. (2007). Validating the theoretical structure of the Treatment Self-Regulation Questionnaire (TRSQ) across three different health behaviors. *Health Education Research*, 22(5), 691–702. doi:10.1093/her/cyl148

Losier, G. F., & Koestner, R. (1999). Intrinsic versus identified regulation in distinct political campaigns: The consequences of following politics for pleasure versus personal meaningfulness. *Personality and Social Psychology Bulletin*, 25(3), 287–298. doi:10.1177/0146167299025003002

Losier, G. F., Perreault, S., Koestner, R., & Vallerand, R. J. (2001). Examining individual differences in the internalization of political values: Validation of the Self-Determination Scale of Political Motivation. *Journal of Research in Personality*, 35(1), 41–61. doi:10.1006/jrpe.2000.2300

Mann, S. (1999). Emotion at work: To what extent are we expressing, suppressing, or faking it? *European Journal of Work and Organizational Psychology*, 8(3), 347–369. doi:10.1080/135943299398221

Martinez-Inigo, D., Totterdell, P., Alcover, C. M., & Holman, D. (2007). Emotional labour and emotional exhaustion: Interpersonal and intrapersonal mechanisms. *Work & Stress*, 21(1), 30–47. doi:10.1080/02678370701234274

Maslach, C., Leiter, M. P., & Schaufeli, W. B. (2009). Measuring burnout. In C. L. Cooper, & S. Cartwright (Eds.), *The Oxford handbook of organizational well-being* (pp. 86–108). Oxford, UK: Oxford University Press.

Millette, V., & Gagné, M. (2008). Designing volunteers' tasks to maximize motivation, satisfaction and performance: The impact of job characteristics on volunteer engagement. *Motivation and Emotion*, 32(1), 11–22. doi:10.1007/s11031-007-9079-4

Morris, J. A., & Feldman, D. C. (1996). The dimensions, antecedents, and consequences of emotional labor. *Academy of Management Review*, 21(4), 986–1010. doi:10.2307/259161

Morris, J. A., & Feldman, D. C. (1997). Managing emotions in the workplace. *Journal of Managerial Issues*, 9(3), 257–274.

Otis, N., & Pelletier, L. G. (2005). A motivational model of daily hassles, physical symptoms, and future work intentions among police officers. *Journal of Applied Social Psychology*, 35(10), 2193–2214. doi:10.1111/j.1559-1816.2005.tb02215.x

Pugh, S. D. (2001). Service with a smile: Emotional contagion in the service encounter. *Academy of Management Journal*, 44(5), 1018–1027. doi:10.2307/3069445

Rafaeli, A., & Sutton, R. I. (1987). Expression of emotion as part of the work role. *Academy of Management Review*, 12(1), 23–37. doi:10.2307/257991

Richer, S. F., Blanchard, C., & Vallerand, R. J. (2002). A motivational model of work turnover. *Journal of Applied Social Psychology*, 32(10), 2089–2113. doi:10.1111/j.1559-1816.2002.tb02065.x

Rubin, R. S., Tardino, V. M. S., Daus, C. S., & Munz, D. C. (2005). A reconceptualization of the emotional labor construct: On the development of an integrated theory of perceived emotional dissonance and emotional labor. In C. E. Härtel, W. J. Zerbe, & N. M. Ashkanasy (Eds.), *Emotions in organizational behavior* (pp. 189–211). Mahwah, NJ: Lawrence Erlbaum Associates Publishers.

Ryan, R. M., & Connell, J. P. (1989). Perceived locus of causality and internalization: Examining reasons for acting in two domains. *Journal of Personality and Social Psychology*, 57(5), 749–761. doi:10.1037/0022-3514.57.5.749

Ryan, R. M., & Deci, E. L. (2001). On happiness and human potentials: A review of research on hedonic and eudaimonic well-being. *Annual Review of Psychology*, 52(1), 141–166. doi:10.1146/annurev.psych.52.1.141

Salovey, P., & Mayer, J. D. (1990). Emotional intelligence. *Imagination, Cognition, and Personality*, 9, 185–211.

Sheldon, K. M., Ryan, R. M., Rawsthorne, L. J., & Ilardi, B. (1997). Trait self and true self: Cross-role variation in the big-five personality traits and its relations with psychological authenticity and subjective well-being. *Journal of Personality and Social Psychology*, 73(6), 1380–1393. doi:10.1037/0022-3514.73.6.1380

Sutton, R. E. (2004). Emotional regulation goals and strategies of teachers. *Social Psychology of Education*, 7(4), 379–398. doi:10.1007/s11218-004-4229-y

Sutton, R. I. (1991). Maintaining norms about expressed emotions: The case of bill collectors. *Administrative Science Quarterly*, 36(2), 245–268. doi:10.2307/2393355

Sutton, R. I., & Rafaeli, A. (1988). Untangling the relationship between displayed emotions and organizational sales: The case of convenience stores. *Academy of Management Journal*, *31*(3), 461–487. doi:10.2307/256456

Totterdell, P., & Holman, D. (2003). Emotion regulation in customer service roles: Testing a model of emotional labor. *Journal of Occupational Health Psychology*, *8*(1), 55–73. doi:10.1037/1076-8998.8.1.55

Tsai, W.-C. (2001). Determinants and consequences of employee displayed positive emotions. *Journal of Management*, *27*(4), 497–512. doi:10.1177/014920630102700406

Tschan, F., Rochat, S., & Zapf, D. (2005). It's not only clients: Studying emotion work with clients and co-workers with an event-sampling approach. *Journal of Occupational and Organizational Psychology*, *78*(2), 195–220. doi:10.1348/096317905X39666

Vallerand, R. J., Fortier, M. S., & Guay, F. (1997). Self-determination and persistence in a real-life setting: Toward a motivational model of high school dropout. *Journal of Personality and Social Psychology*, *72*(5), 1161–1176. doi:10.1037/0022-3514.72.5.1161

Vallerand, R. J., Pelletier, L. G., Blais, M. R., Brière, N. M., Senecal, C., & Vallières, E. F. (1992). The Academic Motivation Scale: A measure of intrinsic, extrinsic, and amotivation in education. *Educational and Psychological Measurement*, *52*(4), 1003–1017. doi:10.1177/0013164492052004025

Vallerand, R. J., Pelletier, L. G., Blais, M. R., Brière, N. M., Senecal, C., & Vallières, E. F. (1993). On the assessment of intrinsic, extrinsic, and amotivation in education: Evidence on the concurrent and construct validity of the Academic Motivation Scale. *Educational and Psychological Measurement*, *53*(1), 159–172. doi:10.1177/0013164493053001018

Van den Broeck, A., Vansteenkiste, M., De Witte, H., & Lens, W. (2008). Explaining the relationships between job

characteristics, burnout, and engagement: The role of basic psychological need satisfaction. *Work & Stress*, *22*(3), 277–294. doi:10.1080/02678370802393672

Van den Broeck, A., Vansteenkiste, M., De Witte, H., Soenens, B., & Lens, W. (2010). Capturing autonomy, competence, and relatedness at work: Construction and initial validation of the Work-Related Basic Need Satisfaction Scale. *Journal of Occupational and Organizational Psychology*, *83*(4), 981–1002. doi:10.1348/096317909x481382

Vansteenkiste, M., Neyrinck, B., Niemiec, C. P., Soenens, B., De Witte, H., & Van den Broeck, A. (2007). On the relations among work value orientations, psychological need satisfaction and job outcomes: A self-determination theory approach. *Journal of Occupational and Organizational Psychology*, *80*(2), 251–277. doi:10.1348/096317906x111024

Vroom, V. H. (1964). *Work and motivation*. Oxford, England: Wiley.

Weiss, H. M. (2002). Deconstructing job satisfaction: Separating evaluations, beliefs and affective experiences. *Human Resource Management Review*, *12*(2), 173–194. doi:10.1016/s1053-4822(02)00045-1

Weiss, H. M., & Cropanzano, R. (1996). Affective events theory: A theoretical discussion of the structure, causes and consequences of affective experiences at work. In B. M. Staw, & L. L. Cummings (Eds.), *Research in organizational behavior: An annual series of analytical essays and critical reviews* (Vol. 18, pp. 1–74). Greenwich: Elsevier Science/JAI Press.

Zapf, D. (2002). Emotion work and psychological well-being. A review of the literature and some conceptual considerations. *Human Resource Management Review*, *12*, 237–268. doi:10.1016/S1053-4822(02)00048-7

CHAPTER

17

Understanding Why Employees Behave Safely from a Self-Determination Theory Perspective

Natasha Scott, Mark Fleming, *and* E. Kevin Kelloway

Abstract

Attention to the part that human behavior plays in occupational safety has increased in recent years. As a result, safety improvement strategies now commonly target employee safety motivation and behavior. This chapter reviews the current employee safety motivation and behavior literature and outlines ways in which the principles of self-determination theory (SDT) can be applied to advance this body of research. In this chapter we argue that SDT provides a theoretical framework that explains how two competing approaches to safety improvement (i.e., behavior-based safety and safety culture/climate) can both be effective at motivating employees to work safely, something that has been missing from much of the literature up until this point. We also present information on the recently developed self-determined safety motivation scale, including initial results of the scale's psychometric properties. This information, along with a detailed future research agenda, is presented to encourage more SDT-based occupational safety research.

Key Words: safety motivation, self-determination theory, safety behaviors, behavior-based safety, safety culture/climate

---

Introduction

According to a recent study, nonfatal workplace injuries cost the United States an average of 1 billion dollars per week in worker compensation costs (Liberty Mutual, 2010). Coupled with the financial cost of workplace injuries, is of course the cost to human life. In just the year 2012 alone, the United States recorded 905,700 nonfatal workplace injuries and illnesses involving missed work days and an additional 4,383 workers lost their lives to injuries stemming from the workplace (Bureau of Labor Statistics, 2012). This issue is not unique to the United States. Within Canada, there were more than 245,000 recorded workplace injuries and 977 deaths in 2012 (Association of Workers' Compensation Boards of Canada, 2012). Similarly, within the United Kingdom it is estimated in 2012 approximately 5.2 million days of lost work occurred due to workplace injuries and an

additional 148 were killed at work (HSE, 2012/13). These workplace injury and fatality statistics highlight the significant consequences of overlooking workplace safety.

The focus over the past 150 years has been on the technical aspects of engineering systems to improve safety. These efforts have been very successful. Large improvements in safety have been achieved through better hardware and design, and through upgraded safety management systems and procedures. This success can be seen in the low accident rates in most safety-critical industries, but it does appear that they have reached a plateau (Lee, 1998). Since the frequency of technological failures in industry has diminished, the role of human behavior has become more apparent. Safety experts estimate that 80–90% of all industrial accidents are attributable to "human factors" (Hoyos, 1995). It seems likely that the most effective way to reduce accident rates even further and improve hazard management is to address the social and organizational factors that impact on safety (Lee, 1995).

Effective hazard management involves designing and implementing control measures that prevent workplace hazards (e.g., noxious fumes) from causing harm. These control measures are often referred to as barriers or defenses. Given the multiple ways that people can be harmed by a hazard, organizations are required to develop complex systems to control hazards. In addition, to reduce the risk of harm to a reasonable level, organizations need to have multiple layers of defenses (e.g., engineering, management systems, behavioral) that protect against the different factors that contribute to workplace injuries and accidents (Reason, 2008). The causes of safety incidents can be categorized as organizational (e.g., management decisions), workgroup (e.g., supervisory practices), and individual failures (e.g., not following safety rules). The behavior of employees at all levels within the organization is crucial for effective management. Many safety programs focus on the behavior of frontline employees, because they are the last line of defense in preventing a safety incident. Properly trained and skilled employees who perform their work according to company policies, rules, and procedures, and who take an active role in the organizations safety program can act as a barrier, to prevent incidents due to breakdowns at other organizational levels (Reason, 1990, 2008).

In addition to there being a defense mechanism for preventing workplace injuries and accidents, frontline employees can also contribute to the occurrence of workplace accidents by performing unsafe acts. When employees behave *un*safely by disregarding safety policies and procedures, or by not being mindful of safety, they can themselves become a contributing factor in a safety incident resulting in injury. Employees performing unsafe acts represent breakdowns in the human line of defense protecting against safety incidents (Reason, 2008). Therefore, employee behavior is a large component of workplace safety.

There is good research evidence that employee self-reported safety behaviors are associated with fewer injuries and accidents (Clarke, 2006; Neal & Griffin, 2006; Probst & Brubaker, 2001; Sinclair, Martin, & Sears, 2010). Furthermore, there is a growing body of literature demonstrating that employee safety behaviors are largely influenced by their motivation to work safely (Christian, Bradley, Wallace, & Burke, 2009; Griffin & Neal, 2000;

Neal & Griffin, 2006; Neal, Griffin, & Hart, 2000). Therefore, an important component of addressing the social and organizational factors that influence workplace safety includes understanding why employees are motivated to work safely.

The goal of this chapter is twofold. First, to review the safety motivation research conducted to date, and second to describe how self-determination theory (Deci & Ryan, 1985) can help advance this line of research. Following the general theme of this book, applying self-determination theory to work and management issues, this chapter concentrates on how self-determination theory can be used to enhance the understanding of what influences employees to work safely, and how the principles of this theory can be used to design effective workplace safety strategies. There is currently limited occupational safety research using the framework of self-determination theory. A study conducted by Burstyn, Jonasi, and Wild (2010) is the only published study we were able to identify. Therefore, we will also describe the research we have been conducting in this area and present some of preliminary results. Finally, it is our belief that self-determination theory has tremendous potential to advance many aspects of the occupational safety literature. For instance, Burstyn et al. (2010) provide evidence of the importance of safety inspectors using an autonomy-supportive approach (i.e., a leadership style described in self-determination theory) to motivate companies to comply with safety regulations. Thus, we conclude this chapter by outlining an agenda for future occupational safety research based on the application of self-determination theory in the hope of inspiring more use of this theory to help explain how organizational, situational, and individual factors influence safety outcomes.

Previous Safety Motivation Research

Although the importance of employee safety motivation has been recognized since the beginning of the 20th century (Heinrich, 1931), it has only been recently that researchers have begun to systematically study employee safety motivation. Table 17.1 provides a description of the research studies that have investigated the topic of employee safety motivation. One of the first studies to examine what motivates employees to work safely was conducted in the late 1970s (Andriessen, 1978). Andriessen concluded that employee safety motivation is largely influenced by the extent to which leaders demonstrate the importance of safety through actions, coworkers and group cohesion, and by the number

Table 17.1 Summary of previous safety motivation research.

Study	Design	Participants	Predictor Constructs	Criterion Constructs	Key Findings
Andriessen (1978)	Cross-sectional	270 Construction employees	SM	Carelessness, self-initiative	Expectations of supervision and accident reduction influenced careful behaviors; expectations of supervision and coworker reactions influenced self-initiative
Griffin & Neal (2000)	Multistudy; cross-sectional	N1 = 1,264; N2 = 326 Manufacturing and mining employees	SC, SK, compliance and participation motivation	SCB, SPB	SC influences compliance and participation motivation and SK; both motivations and SK mediate relationship between SC and behavior
Neal, Griffin, & Hart (2000)	Cross-sectional	525 Healthcare employees	Organizational climate, SC, SK, SM	SCB, SPB	SM influences both SCB and SPB; SM-SCB relationship stronger than SM-SPB; SM partially mediates relationship between SC and both safety behaviors
Probst & Brubaker (2001)	Multistudy; cross-sectional; Longitudinal	N1 = 92; N2 = 76 Food processing plant employees	Job insecurity, job satisfaction, SK, SM	SCB, self-reported injuries and accidents	Job satisfaction influences future SM; SM influences SCB across time
Neal & Griffin (2006)	Longitudinal	N1 = 434; N2 = 490; N3 = 301 Healthcare employees	SC, SM, negative affectivity	SCB, SPB, injuries	Found lagged effect of SC on SM after controlling for prior levels of SM; high levels of SM in T2 associated with increases in SPB in T3; found reciprocal relationship between SPB and SM
Newnam, Griffin, & Mason (2008)	Cross-sectional	385 Government employees, 88 supervisors	Org. and managerial safety values, rule violation and speeding attitudes, self-efficacy, SM	Self-reported accidents	SM predicts self-reported crashes; SM higher when perceptions of managers and supervisors safety values are high; safety attitudes and self-efficacy related to SM
Larsson, Pousette, & Torner (2008)	Cross-sectional	189 Construction employees	SC, SK, SM	Personal, interactive, and structural behaviors	SC influences SK and SM; SM influences personal and interactive behaviors; SC influences structural behaviors

(continued)

Table 17.1 Continued

Study	Design	Participants	Predictor Constructs	Criterion Constructs	Key Findings
Christian, Bradley, Wallace, & Burke (2009)	Meta-analysis	N/A	SC, leadership, personality, job attitudes, SM, SK	SCB, SPB, injuries and accidents	SC moderately related to safety behaviors; found stronger effect of SC and leadership for SPB than SCB; SC more strongly related to SM than SK; Conscientiousness related to SM; SM related to SCB and SPB, SCB and SPB decreases accidents and injuries
Vinodkumar & Bhasi (2010)	Cross-sectional	1,566 Chemical factory employees	Safety management practices, SK, SM	SCB, SPB	Safety training influenced SM; SK and SM influenced SCB and SPB; different safety management practices predicted SCB than SPB
Sinclair, Martin, & Sears (2010)	Cross-sectional	535 Unionized retail employees	Perceived stakeholders safety values, perceived hazards, safety training, SK, SM	SCB, SPB, self-report injuries and near misses	Employees who perceived supervisors and union valued safety reported higher levels of SM; employees with higher levels of SM reported more SCB and SPB; SPB increased reported near misses; SCB but not SPB related to decreased injuries

Note. SC = safety climate; SCB = safety compliance behavior; SK = safety knowledge; SM = safety motivation; SPB = safety participation behaviors.

of hindrances experienced while trying to work safely. However, as can be seen in Table 17.1, most safety motivation research has been published after the year 2000. During this time, employee safety motivation has been conceptualized as the level of motivation. In other words, the focus has been on the overall amount of motivation for working safely. For example, Neal and Griffin (2006) define safety motivation as "an individual's willingness to exert effort to enact safety behaviors and the valence associated with those behaviors" (p. 947). This body of research has concentrated on linking the level of employee safety motivation to their safety behaviors in a variety of different industries, including manufacturing and processing (Griffin & Neal, 2000; Probst & Brubaker, 2001; Vinodkumar & Bhasi, 2010), mining (Griffin & Neal, 2000), health care (Neal et al., 2000; Neal & Griffin, 2006), construction (Larsson, Pousette, & Torner, 2008), and retail (Sinclair et al., 2010).

Much of the current safety motivation research has stemmed from Griffin and Neal's (2000) model of workplace safety. This model proposes that employee safety motivation is a proximal determinant of two main types of employee safety behaviors (i.e., compliance and participation), and distal factors (e.g., organizational and situational factors) have an indirect effect on employee safety behaviors by influencing employees' safety motivation (Griffin & Neal, 2000; Neal & Griffin, 2002, 2003). Employee safety behaviors play an important role in maintaining a safe work environment and have been previously shown to be associated with workplace injuries (Clarke, 2006; Christian et al., 2009; Neal & Griffin, 2006).

Safety compliance behaviors are the core of safety activities required by formal work procedures in order to maintain a minimum level of safety (Griffin & Neal, 2000; Neal & Griffin, 2002).

Examples of safety compliance behaviors include following safety rules and procedures, and complying with occupational safety regulations. Alternatively, safety participation behaviors are voluntary activities that support a company's safety program and help develop an environment that supports and encourages a safe working environment (Neal & Griffin, 2002). Safety compliance behaviors include helping coworkers with safety issues, voicing safety concerns, keeping informed about safety issues, and initiating safety-related changes (Hofmann, Morgeson, & Gerras, 2003). Research consistently concludes that employees who report higher levels of safety motivation also report engaging in more safety compliance and participation behaviors (Christian et al., 2009; Neal & Griffin, 2006; Neal et al., 2000; Sinclair et al., 2010; Vinodkumar & Bhasi, 2010).

There are two dominant psychological approaches to safety improvement: behavior-based safety, and the promotion of a safety culture or climate (Dejoy, 2005). These two approaches are different from each other, and in many ways have opposing views about how to motivate employees to work safely. Although these two approaches propose very different strategies for organizations to enhance safety, there is evidence supporting the effectiveness of both behavior-based (McAfee & Winn, 1989) and safety culture (Guldenmund, 2010) interventions.

Behavior-based safety is founded on behavior modification theory (Skinner, 1938), which has extensive evidence of efficacy in a wide range of settings. Behavior-based safety proposes that employee behavior is dependent on contingencies and that behavior can be controlled by altering these contingencies (Dejoy, 2005). Thus, behavior-based safety aims to control employee behavior by introducing specific consequences in order to motivate employees to adopt safe behaviors. Typically behavior-based safety interventions involve the following five stages: (1) identifying critical safety behaviors, (2) observing employee behavior, (3) identifying the consequences that are reinforcing both the safe and unsafe behaviors, (4) altering the consequences to promote safe behaviors, and (5) assessing behavioral change. Typically, safe behaviors are reinforced by introducing positive feedback to employees (Fleming & Lardner, 2000). This feedback is either provided by peers or by supervisors.

Safety culture improvement interventions target the shared values within the organization in order to enhance the value placed on safety (Dejoy, 2005). Safety culture interventions focus on leader behavior, specifically leader behaviors demonstrating commitment to safety and encouraging subordinates to value safety above other competing goals (e.g., production targets). For example, Mullen and Kelloway (2009) demonstrated that safety leadership training produces changes in subordinate perceptions about the relative priority of safety (i.e., safety culture). Furthermore, Zohar (2002) has also demonstrated that promoting specific supervisory leadership behaviors can reduce injury rates.

Research conducted to date highlights the importance of considering the influence of employee safety motivation on occupational safety outcomes, and demonstrates that organizations can influence employee safety behaviors both directly and indirectly by influencing employees' motivation to work safely (Christian et al., 2009; Neal & Griffin, 2006). However, one of the shortfalls of this research is that it solely focuses on the level of employees' safety motivation. Evidence of the effectiveness of both behavior-based and safety culture strategies for motivating employees to work safely supports the argument that there are different types of safety motivation, one driven by external reward (or punishment) and a second based on the relative value employees place on safety. In moving the safety motivation research forward, it is therefore also important to investigate the reasons why people are motivated to work safely so that we can better understand the mechanisms that drive behavior change. Self-determination theory (Deci & Ryan, 1985) is particularly relevant to this new way of thinking about employee safety motivation.

In addition to providing a theoretical structure to base the investigation of different reasons why employees are motivated to work safely, occupational safety research can also benefit from applying self-determination theory to gaining a better understanding of the mechanisms behind many of the established relationships between factors that influence workplace safety outcomes. For example, although there is good evidence demonstrating the relationships between organizational approaches to safety (e.g., safety culture), employee safety motivation, and self-reported safety behaviors, there is considerably less knowledge regarding the mechanisms behind all of these relationships. Self-determination theory can help explain the context in which these relationships exist.

Self-Determination Theory

Self-determination theory asserts that individuals are motivated to perform behaviors for a variety of reasons and classifies different types of motivation according to these reasons. Specifically, self-determination theory distinguishes between amotivation (i.e., a lack of motivation) and five categories of motivation (external, introjected, identified, integrated, and intrinsic; Deci & Ryan, 1985). The type of motivation varies in the extent to which it is internalized (Deci & Ryan, 1985, 2000, 2002). Internalized motivation results in self-directed (i.e., autonomous) behavior (Deci & Ryan, 1985, 2000, 2002; Gagné & Deci, 2005). Therefore, self-determination theory views motivation as a multidimensional construct and takes into account both the *level* and the *type* of motivation when determining individual behavior (Ryan & Deci, 2002). An extensive review of self-determination theory is beyond the scope of this chapter; however, we systematically address each type of motivation next in describing a more comprehensive framework of employee safety motivation than has been used to date by applying self-determination theory to the construct of safety motivation. Interested readers seeking a more thorough description of self-determination theory should consult the first chapter of this book. Deci and Ryan (2000) and Gagné and Deci (2005) provide excellent overviews of the theory as well.

A Self-Determined Perspective of Employee Safety Motivation

Self-determination theory (Deci & Ryan, 1985) builds upon Porter and Lawler's (1968) work in which they classify the reasons for work behaviors as either extrinsic or intrinsic. Extrinsic reasons for behavior include receiving an outcome that is contingent upon the performance of the behavior. Conversely, intrinsic reasons for behavior include experiencing enjoyment and pleasure from performing the behavior. Within the context of occupational safety, this distinction between extrinsic and intrinsic motivation may not be particularly useful in determining why employees behave safely because most safety activities are not designed to be fun or enjoyable, but rather are designed to keep employees safe.

For example, employees typically do not enjoy wearing their personal protective equipment. In fact, employees often complain that personal protective equipment is uncomfortable and irritating to wear, that it slows them down, and gets in the way of doing their job. Therefore, if we only considered whether employees were extrinsically or intrinsically motivated to work safely we would likely conclude

that employees are generally extrinsically motivated to work safely and that they only engage in safety behaviors that are contingent upon receiving a positive or negative consequence. Following this logic, we would also conclude that the most successful way to change employees' safety behaviors is to reward safe behaviors and to provide negative consequences for risky or unsafe behaviors. We know from behavior-based safety approaches that this method can be successful (Dejoy, 2005; McAfee & Winn, 1989); however, given the equally positive results of alternative approaches to safety (e.g., safety culture and leadership approaches), there is likely more to being motivated to work safely than just receiving rewards and avoiding negative consequences for unsafe behavior.

Self-determination theory (Deci & Ryan, 1985, 2000; Ryan & Deci, 2002) goes beyond categorizing employee safety motivation as either extrinsic or intrinsic and further argues that employees can experience extrinsic motivation as controlling or autonomous depending on the extent to which employees internalize the extrinsic reason or goal of the safety behavior. Controlled safety motivation results in contingent-based behavior, whereas autonomous safety motivation results in self-directed safety behavior. Therefore, instead of focusing on whether extrinsic or intrinsic reasons motivate employee safety behaviors, self-determination theory argues that the focus should be on distinguishing between controlled and autonomous forms of safety motivation, and on the extent to which employee safety behaviors are self-directed.

Figure 17.1 illustrates employee safety motivation in accordance with self-determination theory (Deci & Ryan, 1985, 2000, 2002). As depicted in Figure 17.1, it is possible for employees to be amotivated to work safely, meaning that employees have no reason for working safely and therefore lack motivation to perform safety behaviors and activities. When employees are motivated to work safely, their safety motivation can vary in the extent to which it is perceived as controlling or autonomous.

Controlled Safety Motivation

Controlled motivation represents feelings of *having* to do something (e.g., work safely) or feelings that you *should* do something (e.g., work safely) (Gagné & Deci, 2005). When employee safety motivation is controlled, safety behaviors and activities are performed because the employee feels pressured to do so. In other words, employees feel coerced or obligated to perform certain safety activities. The

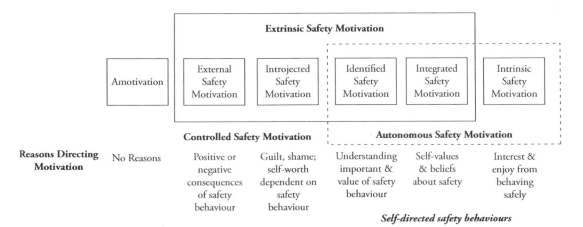

Fig. 17.1. Self-determined safety motivation framework.

pressure to perform safety behaviors can come from another person (e.g., supervisor, coworker), a group (e.g., the organization), society (e.g., the occupational health and safety act), or from the individuals themselves. Therefore, controlled safety motivation can be classified as external pressure (i.e., external safety motivation) or as internal pressure (i.e., introjected safety motivation) to behave safely.

EXTERNAL SAFETY MOTIVATION

External motivation represents the most controlling form of motivation (Deci & Ryan, 1985, 2000). It is what people most commonly envision when they think about extrinsic motivation. Safety behaviors that are externally motivated require the presence of a stimulus in order for the behaviors to occur. The stimulus is typically in the form of a reward for performing work safely or a negative consequence when work is not performed safely. Examples of external reasons for performing safety behaviors include working safely because a safety bonus is contingent on good safety performance, or because one has witnessed other employees being laid off due to unsafe behavior. In addition, there may be pressure from external agencies, such as regulators or professional associations, to work in a safe manner. For example, some provincial governments in Canada have recently introduced administrative penalty legislation that enables health and safety inspectors to fine employees if they are observed breaking safety regulations.

INTROJECTED SAFETY MOTIVATION

Classified as slightly less controlling than external motivation, introjected motivation still entails performing activities because there is pressure to do so; however, the pressure comes from within the employee as opposed to from another person or group (Gagné & Deci, 2005). Introjected safety motivation represents internal pressure to behave safely, most likely experienced as the avoidance of guilt or shame for working safely. For example, an employee may be motivated to wear and attach their safety harness when they work at height, not because they will receive a reward or praise for doing so, but because the employee would feel guilty and ashamed if they did not wear the safety harness. In addition, internal pressure that produces introjected motivation can come from employees' work-related self-esteem or self-worth being contingent on being a good worker (Gagné & Deci, 2005). Employees may be motivated to perform safety activities because their self-worth is contingent on being a safety-conscious worker.

Autonomous Safety Motivation

Autonomous safety motivation can result from both extrinsic and intrinsic reasons for working safely. Employees who are autonomously motivated to work safely take ownership over performing safety activities because they view these activities as being consistent with their own personal values and interests. As a result, autonomously motivated safety behaviors are self-directed and therefore should be performed consistently. As illustrated in Figure 17.1, employees can have different forms of autonomous safety motivation.

IDENTIFIED SAFETY MOTIVATION

Identified safety motivation represents employees who are motivated to engage in safety activities because they believe a safe work environment is important and accept that performing safety activities are necessary to achieve that goal. Take for instance a group of employees who show up to a new worksite and immediately begin conducting a hazard assessment before starting the new job. They do this not because they feel they have too (i.e., controlled motivation), or because this is an interesting and fun work task (i.e., intrinsic motivation), but rather because they believe hazard assessments can provide useful information that can help make the worksite safer, and because the workers value having the information this task provides. Because the safety behavior (i.e., conducting a hazard assessment) is performed to obtain an outcome (i.e., the information it provides), the employees would be classified as being extrinsically motivated; however, because that outcome is valued, the behavior is self-directed.

INTEGRATED SAFETY MOTIVATION

Integrated motivation is the most autonomous form of extrinsic motivation (Ryan & Deci, 2002). As the name suggests, not only do employees value activities and the outcomes of those activities, but they also assimilate the value into other aspects of their self so that they become part of their self-identity (Gagné & Deci, 2005). Workplace safety rules, policies, procedures, and activities become internal convictions in employees with integrated safety motivation. Because employees have incorporated the value of safety behaviors into their sense of self, they should also perform these safety behaviors in non–work-related contexts (e.g., home maintenance and repair activities). Safety culture approaches to motivating employees to work safely, in which leaders attempt to create a shared value of safety throughout the organization, focus on increasing employee's autonomous safety motivation (identified and integrated).

INTRINSIC SAFETY MOTIVATION

Intrinsic safety motivation is characterized as performing safety activities (e.g., volunteering for the joint occupational health and safety committee; following rules and procedures) because the employee finds these activities pleasurable, satisfying, or interesting. Intrinsic safety motivation represents the fullest form of autonomous safety motivation, because the reason for engaging in the safety activity is completely volitional. Although self-determination theory (Deci & Ryan, 1985) clearly distinguishes between integrated and intrinsic types of motivation, this distinction

has been much harder to demonstrate empirically (Gagné et al., 2010).

This theoretical framework provides a more comprehensive explanation of employee safety motivation than currently exists in the literature. Viewing safety motivation as a multidimensional construct provides a better understanding of the different reasons why employees are motivated to work safely. For example, employees motivated by controlling factors (i.e., external and introjected motivation) will likely comply with the organization's safety standards, whereas employees who have internalized the value of working safely will likely not only comply with the mandatory safety standards, but also engage in extra-role safety behaviors (i.e., safety participation behaviors), such as promoting best practices for working safely within the organization, voicing safety concerns, and making recommendations for how to do a job in a safer way. A more comprehensive framework of employee safety motivation can also help to explain how organizational practices influence employee safety motivation. In describing safety motivation both in controlled and autonomous terms, self-determination theory provides a theoretical framework to explain the mechanisms through which two competing views of how best to motivate employees to work safely can both have positive effects. Because behavior-based safety programs aim to change behavior by changing the consequences of behavior, they are likely to increase levels of controlled motivation. Safety culture interventions operate by promoting the importance of safety and therefore are likely to increase levels of autonomous motivation.

Developing a Self-Determination Theory Safety Motivation Scale

Employee safety motivation has not previously been viewed from the perspective of self-determination theory. Therefore, no validated scales that measure the different types of safety motivation outlined in the theory exist. As with any new stream of research, the first step should be to develop valid and reliable measures of the construct. Therefore, to promote this stream of research, we have developed a multidimensional measure of safety motivation based on the motivational framework outlined in the previous section. The process we undertook to develop the Self-Determined Safety Motivation (SDSM) scale and the results from our initial evaluation of this measure are presented next.

SDSM Scale Development Process

We developed a scale to assess all six types of safety motivation as shown in Figure 17.1. In creating items for the SDSM scale, we followed similar practices to others who have developed motivation scales using the framework of self-determination theory (e.g., Gagné et al., 2010). Specifically, based on the idea that motivation is a reflection of reasons for behaving (Ryan & Connell, 1989; Gagné et al., 2010), we developed items that reflect the possible reasons why an employee would work safely. We used the stem "*Why do you work safely?*" as the basis for all items. To develop items, we consulted the definitions of each of the six different types of motivation proposed by self-determination theory (Deci & Ryan, 1985; Gagné & Deci, 2005). In addition, when possible, we adapted items from previously developed scales from other domains (e.g., education, Ryan & Connell, 1989; health care, Ryan, Plant, & O'Malley, 1995).

From the initial item writing stage, we developed a total of 44 items. Next, four individuals with expertise in scale development and who were familiar with self-determination theory were given the six definitions of motivation, the list of 44 initial items, and were asked to sort these 44 items into the six types of motivation. The four individuals initially completed the item-sorting task independently, then discussed their responses and came to an agreement when there were differences in responses. Items that were interpreted as belonging to multiple types of motivation or that were identified as being poorly worded were deleted. Based on the results of the item-sorting task, 10 items were deleted to create the final version of the scale.

Preliminary Testing of the SDSM Scale

We administered the SDSM scale to a sample of young workers. Mullen, Kelloway, and Teed (2011) directly compared safety experiences of young workers with those of an adult full-time employed sample. They found that the same processes (i.e., predictors of safety experiences) emerged in both samples. They concluded that the use of a sample of young workers does not impugn the generalizability of the findings to the traditional workforce. We also collected responses to several outcomes that have previously been studied in the safety motivation literature to establish the predictive validity of the SDSM scale (i.e., safety compliance and participation behaviors). We hypothesized that all types of safety motivation, except amotivation, should

be positively related to employee safety compliance behaviors. Because complying with safety rules and procedures is mandatory, employees may feel pressure to perform these behaviors and therefore we expected controlled forms of safety motivation (i.e., external and introjected motivation) to be predictive of employee compliance behaviors. In addition, employees who value safety and believe that safety is an important issue (i.e., identified, integrated motivation), or who have an interest in workplace safety (i.e., intrinsic motivation), should also perform safety compliance behaviors. Therefore, we also expected autonomous forms of safety motivation to be predictive of employee compliance behaviors.

In addition, we hypothesized a priori that only autonomous forms of safety motivation (i.e., identified, integrated, and intrinsic) would be positively related to, and predictive of, safety participation behaviors. Given that safety participation behaviors are voluntary, it is not expected that controlled forms of safety motivation would be predictive of these types of safety behaviors. Finally, we expected that amotivation would be negatively associated with both safety compliance and safety participation behaviors because amotivation represents employees who are not motivated to work safely.

PARTICIPANTS

Data were collected from a sample of 312 employed students (220 females, 89 males, and 3 individuals did not report their gender). Participants were recruited from the Saint Mary's University psychology department's research participation bonus system. Participants received one point toward their final grade in a psychology class for their decision to participate in this research. Participants worked in a variety of occupational settings, including retail and customer service (36.5%), food and beverage establishments (16.7%), office settings (9.6%), manual labor (5.6%), and homecare (3.5%). Participants worked an average of 19.4 hours per week (SD = 10.0) and were employed at their current job for an average of 1.8 years (SD = 18.9).

MEASURES

SDSM was measured using the final 34-item SDSM scale described previously. Participants used a 7-point scale (1 = not at all true; 7 = very true) to indicate whether each of the 34 items were a reason why they work safely. Safety behaviors were assessed using a scale developed by Neal et al. (2000). Respondents used a 5-point scale (1 = strongly disagree; 5 = strongly agree) to indicate if they engaged in safety compliance behaviors and safety participation behaviors. Three items assessed participant's safety compliance behaviors (e.g., "*I use the correct safety procedures for carrying out my job*") and three items assessed safety participation behaviors (e.g., "*I promote the safety program within the organization*").

Statistical Analysis Approach

Our goal with the initial testing of the SDSM scale was to reduce the total number of items and to find a core subgroup of items that measured each type of safety motivation. Following data collection, we conducted a series of item analyses, deleting items that did not contribute to the reliability of the subscales, were redundant with other items, or displayed other unacceptable psychometric properties. The goal of the item analyses was to develop short subscales of each of the types of motivation. The final scale comprised 18 items, with 3 items per subscale.

To examine the extent to which each item represented the type of motivation it was intended to represent we conducted an exploratory structural equation modeling analysis (Asparouhov & Muthén, 2009; Marsh et al., 2010; Marsh et al., 2009) using maximum likelihood estimation in MPLUS 6.11 (Muthén & Muthén, 1998-2011). Exploratory structural equation modeling combines features of both confirmatory and exploratory factor analysis. In essence, the researcher can specify the number of factors but does not constrain the items to load on only one factor, as is the case for the typical application of confirmatory factor analysis. Our choice to conduct this analysis was based on the recognition that we had a well-developed theory supporting the number and nature of subscales, but we were unwilling to impose unrealistic constraints (e.g., no cross-loadings) at the initial phase of scale development.

We followed the recommendation of Meyers, Gamst, and Guarino (2006) to use the comparative fit index (CFI) and the root mean square error of approximation (RMSEA) to assess model fit. CFI values of .95 and above indicate acceptable model fit (Meyers et al., 2006). Conversely, lower values on the RMSEA represent better fit, with values of less than .08 indicating good fit and close fit is indicated by an RMSEA that does not significantly differ from .05 (Meyers et al., 2006). We also examined the Tucker Lewis Index (TLI) and the p of Close Fit (PCLOSE) values when assessing the model fit. The validity of the SDSM scale was examined by inspecting the correlations between the motivational subscales. In addition, we evaluated the extent to which the SDSM scale predicted employee safety behaviors (i.e., compliance and participation) by conducting multiple regression analyses in which we first controlled for job characteristics and demographics before assessing the combined and unique effect of each type of safety motivation.

Results

FACTOR STRUCTURE

We began by estimating a six-factor structure based on the six types of motivation described in self-determination theory. Consistent with an exploratory structural equation modeling approach, each item was allowed to load on each of the six factors. Each loading or parameter estimate was assessed for statistical significance. The six-factor structure provided a good fit to the data (χ^2 [60] = 106.22, p < .001; CFI = .98; TLI = .96; RMSEA = .05 [confidence interval = .03–.07, PCLOSE = .49]). We also tested several plausible alternative models to determine if the theoretical six-factor model was the best-fitting safety motivation model. Specifically, we tested a five-factor model based on previous literature that reports integrated motivation often does not hold as an independent factor (Gagné et al., 2010), a four-factor model in which all types of partially or fully internalized safety motivation form one factor (i.e., introjected, identified, and integrated), and a three-factor model in which safety motivation is broken down into amotivation, controlled (i.e., external and introjected), and autonomous (i.e., identified, integrated, and intrinsic). Results of each model fit are presented in Table 17.2. Although models 1 and 2 both demonstrated acceptable fit, the χ2 difference test and AIC values support the theorized six-factor model.

Standardized parameter estimates for the six-factor model are presented in Table 17.3. As shown, although there were some significant cross-loadings, each item significantly loaded on its intended factor.

SUBSCALE RELIABILITIES AND CORRELATIONS

Correlations between the subscales and subscale reliabilities are presented in Table 17.4. Each subscale achieved a Cronbach's alpha of at least .70 and there was no indication of scale redundancy based on the corrected correlations. Self-determination theory proposes that the six different types of motivation fall along a continuum representing the extent to which the motivation has been internalized (Deci & Ryan, 2000; Ryan & Deci, 2002). Therefore, subscales representing the different types

Table 17.2 Fit statistics for six-factor SDSM scale.

Model and description	χ^2	df	Sig.	CFI	TLI	RMSEA	RMSEA 90% CI	SRMR	AIC	χ^2 diff test
Model 1: six factors (amotivation, external, introjected, identified, integrated, intrinsic)	106.22	60	.000	.98	.96	.05	.03–.07	.02	18719.76	
Model 2: five factors (amotivation, external, introjected, identified, intrinsic)	183.17	73	.000	.96	.92	.07	.06–.08	.02	18770.71	M1 vs. M2 χ^2 (13) = 76.95*
Model 3: four factors (amotivation, external, internalized, intrinsic)	297.73	87	.000	.93	.88	.09	.08–.10	.03	18857.27	M1 vs. M3 χ^2 (27) = 191.51*
Model 4: three factors (amotivation, controlled, autonomous)	444.26	102	.000	.89	.83	.10	.09–.11	.05	18973.80	M1 vs. M4 χ^2 (42) = 338.04*

Note. AIC = Akaike information criterion; CFI = comparative fit index; CI = confidence interval; RMSEA = root mean square error of approximation; SRMR = Standardized Root Mean Square Residual; TLI = Tucker Lewis Index.
*$p < .001$.

of safety motivation should form a simplex pattern whereby subscales of types of safety motivation that are theoretically similar and adjacent to one another along the continuum should have stronger correlations than to nonadjacent subscales (Gagné et al., 2010). Furthermore, because amotivation presents a lack of motivation, it should be negatively related to the remaining subscales, which all represent a form of safety motivation. As shown in Table 17.2, there is general support for the simplex-like pattern with a few exceptions. First, external safety motivation is not significantly related to any other motivational subscale (amotivation, $r = .14$, *ns*; introjected, $r = .09$, *ns*; identified, $r = .11$, *ns*; integrated, $r = .14$, *ns*; intrinsic, $r = .18$, *ns*). Furthermore, introjected safety motivation is more strongly related to integrated ($r = .61$; $p < .01$) and intrinsic ($r = .46$; $p < .01$) safety motivation than would be expected (because the correlation between introjected and identified safety motivation is only $r = .23$; $p < .01$).

PREDICTING SAFETY BEHAVIORS

Results from the regression analyses in which the six types of safety motivation were regressed on both safety compliance behaviors and safety participation behaviors after controlling for job characteristics and demographics (i.e., occupational setting, tenure, hours worked per week, and gender) are presented in Table 17.5. Employee safety motivation predicted

both safety compliance ($R^2 = .43$; $p < .001$) and safety participation behaviors ($R^2 = .31$; $p < .05$). Several types of safety motivation were unique predictors of employee safety compliance behaviors. Specifically, intrinsic ($\beta = .15$; $p < .05$), identified ($\beta = .39$; $p < .001$), and introjected ($\beta = .13$; $p < .05$) safety motivation were all unique significant predictors of safety compliance behaviors, whereas only intrinsic safety motivation was a unique significant predictor of employee participation behaviors ($\beta = .38$; $p < .001$).

Discussion

The results from the initial test of the SDSM scale provide evidence that items from the SDSM scale generally reflect the six types of safety motivation that they were intended to measure. Seven of the items did cross-load on another factor. However, all of the items did load on their intended factor and most of the cross-loaded items loaded on the next closest factor. The two exceptions to this pattern were one introjected and one identified item, both of which negatively loaded onto amotivation. Furthermore, of the seven cross-loaded items, only two items loaded more highly on the opposing factor than the intended factor. Specifically, the item *"It makes me feel good"* had a stronger loading on the integrated factor than on the intrinsic factor, and the item *"Working safely corresponds to my true*

Table 17.3 Results from the exploratory structural equation model.

	Amotivation	External	Introjected	Identified	Integrated	Intrinsic
Item						
Why do you work safely?						
It makes me feel good					.48	**.32**
It makes me happy						**.96**
For the enjoyment it brings to the work day						**.85**
In order to fulfill my personal goals					**.84**	
Striving to work safely is part of who I am					**.71**	
Working safely corresponds to my true nature				.48	**.29**	
I personally value safety				**.55**	.35	
I value a safe working environment	−.19			**.50**		
Safety is important to me				**.76**		
I feel a moral obligation to work safely			.54	**.29**		
I would be ashamed if I didn't work safely	−.11		**.95**			
I would feel bad if I didn't work safely			**.49**		.26	
In order to get a pay raise		**.68**				
In order to get a promotion		**.98**				
Because I want my coworkers to admire me		**.27**				
Although it doesn't make a difference whether I work safely or not	**.76**					
I work safely even though I think it's pointless	**.63**					
I work safely even though I don't have a good reason to	**.60**					

Note. All parameters $p < .01$; nonsignificant parameters are not shown. Loadings corresponding to hypothesis are in bold.

nature" loaded more strongly on the identified factor than on the integrated factor.

As expected, both controlled and autonomous forms of employee safety motivation were predictive of employee safety compliance behaviors. Specifically, three forms of safety motivation influenced compliance behavior. Identified safety motivation was the strongest predictor of safety compliance behavior, suggesting that employees are more likely to comply with safety rules and procedures when they understand and identify with the importance of these rules or procedures. In addition, employees are also more likely to comply with safety rules and procedures when they put internal pressure on themselves (i.e., introjected safety motivation). Interestingly, external motivation was not a significant predictor of safety compliance behaviors. It may be that external motivation only influences employee safety compliance behaviors when there is consistent monitoring of behaviors.[1]

Table 17.4 Factor intercorrelations and scale reliabilities.

	1	2	3	4	5	6
1. Amotivation	(.70)					
2. External	.14	(.73)				
3. Introjected	−.17	.09	(.85)			
4. Identified	−.26*	.11	.23*	(.83)		
5. Integrated	−.17	.14	.61*	.48*	(.76)	
6. Intrinsic	−.11	.18	.46*	.39*	.75*	(.89)

Note. Cronbach's alpha for each scale presented in parenthesis along the diagonal.
*$p < .01$.

The results from this initial study do contradict our original statement regarding employees viewing safety behaviors and activities as uninteresting or not enjoyable, as intrinsic safety motivation was a significant predictor of both safety compliance behaviors and safety participation behaviors. In fact, intrinsic safety motivation was the only unique significant predictor of safety participation behaviors.

Thus, the results partially support our hypothesis that safety participation behaviors are extra-role behaviors and were therefore only influenced by autonomous forms of safety motivation.

A few things should be noted about this study and the results. First, this study should be considered as just the first step in the scale development process. Although, the results of this study are promising,

Table 17.5 Relationship between types of safety motivation and safety behaviors.

	Compliance Behaviors		Participation Behaviors	
	β	ΔR^2	β	ΔR^2
Step 1: Controls		.04*		.05**
Occupational setting	−.05		.02	
Tenure	.06		.13*	
Hrs worked/week	−.05		.02	
Gender	.18**		.19***	
Step 2: Safety Motivation Types		.38***		.26***
Intrinsic safety motivation	.15*		.38***	
Integrated safety motivation	.03		−.02	
Identified safety motivation	.39***		.09	
Introjected safety motivation	.13*		.11	
External safety motivation	.08		−.05	
Amotivation	−.07		−.02	
Total *R^2*		**.42*****		**.31*****

*$p < .05$.
**$p < .01$.
***$p < .001$.

more scale development and refinement is needed. Further scale refinement may benefit from drawing more closely on recent successful measure development in the broader work motivation literature (e.g., Gagné et al., 2010). These refinements should also be tested and confirmed using much larger and more diverse samples before firm conclusions can be drawn about the reliability and validity of the scale. That being said, the 18-item SDSM scale as shown here provides a solid basis for future scale development.

One of our main goals in writing this chapter was to illustrate how self-determination theory can be used to bring together competing perspectives in the occupational safety literature on how to motivate employees to work safely under one theoretical framework. Self-determination theory guided the SDSM scale development process and results from the initial evaluation of this scale support our proposition that employees are motivate to work safely for a variety of reasons, and that there are different types of safety motivation that influence employees' safety behaviors. More generally, the results presented above also demonstrate that the field of occupational safety can benefit from viewing employee safety motivation and behavior from a self-determination theory perspective. Thus, much more research involving the application of self-determination theory to understand and solve occupational safety issues is warranted. What has been described thus far is just one of the many potential ways in which self-determination theory can contribute to the field of occupational safety. In the remainder of this chapter, we build on this work by discussing the implications of these results for safety practitioners and by identifying a number of potential future research avenues that can be undertaken to further explore the contributions that self-determination theory can make to occupational safety research.

Practical Implications

These results provide evidence that viewing safety motivation from a self-determination theory perspective is valuable. Specifically, safety practitioners need to consider the type, not just the level, of employee safety motivation. Many practices used by organizations to increase employee safety motivation involve the provision of rewards for working safely (e.g., safety bonuses) or participating in safety activities (e.g., prizes for those who identify and fix hazards). These practices are likely to promote controlled rather than autonomous motivation, and based on our findings, they are likely to be of limited value. Organizations should focus on promoting autonomous motivation, by enhancing employees' sense of competence, autonomy, and relatedness around safety. Safety training programs should recognize the safety expertise of employees rather than focus on their lack of knowledge. Employees should be given the opportunity to become experts in some aspect of safety (e.g., chemical hazards) that they are interested in, rather than just focusing on knowledge of rules and procedures designed by others. By increasing employee competence, employees can understand the purpose of the rules based on a deeper understanding rather than just blind compliance. With this additional competence, employees may have a greater sense of autonomy, because they will know when and why it is important to comply with specific rules.

These results support the argument that practitioners should design interventions to encourage employees to value and enjoy safety. Most organizations and safety professionals give the impressions that safety management is a necessary evil, which is uninteresting and unpleasant. Given the importance of intrinsic motivation in predicting participation in safety, this may be counterproductive. Organizations should focus on the intellectual challenge involved in managing occupational hazards, and the value of this activity. Organizations should focus on promoting the shared value of the importance of safety to enhance autonomous motivation. Safety culture interventions are likely to be effective in promoting autonomous motivation. For example, transformational safety leadership interventions may be effective in promoting autonomous motivation.

Future Directions

Despite the popularity of self-determination theory in many different domains including health care (Williams, McGregor, King, Nelson, & Glasgow, 2005), education (Deci, Vallerand, Pelletier, & Ryan, 1991), sports and exercise (Wilson, & Rodgers, 2002), and most recently the workplace (Gagne & Deci, 2005; Parker, Jimmieson, & Amiot, 2010; Ryan, Bernstein, & Brown, 2010), it has seldom been used in occupational safety research. The results presented above demonstrate the usefulness of self-determination theory as a framework for understanding what motivates different types of employee safety behaviors. This research is one of the first to apply self-determination theory to the area of occupational safety. Therefore, our predominant suggestion is for more research using self-determination theory to explain why employees work safely (or unsafely), and how organizational factors influence different types of employee safety motivation. Next, we specify a series of future research directions that demonstrate a wide array of applications of self-determination theory to occupational safety.

Research Question 1: Do Controlled and Autonomous Forms of Safety Motivation Influence Safety Compliance and Safety Participation Behaviors to the Same Degree?

Self-determination theory posits that autonomous forms of motivation produce more consistent and higher-quality behavior than controlled forms of motivation (Ryan & Deci, 2002). Although this proposition has been confirmed in several different settings (e.g., education, Black & Deci, 2000; exercise, Duncan, Hall, Wilson, & Jenny, 2010), it has yet to be tested within an occupational safety context. Workplace safety provides a unique context to test this particular proposition stemming from self-determination theory because unlike many of the behaviors examined thus far with self-determination theory (e.g., health and exercise, academic, and so forth), workplace safety behaviors are more strongly regulated through occupational health and safety legislation. The controlling nature of occupational health and safety regulation may or may not have an effect on the type of safety motivation. Moreover, researchers can have the greatest impact on industry and organizational safety practices by providing clear evidence that autonomous safety motivation is not only associated with improved employee safety behaviors, but is also associated with reductions in time-loss injuries, workplace accidents, and workers' compensation premiums. This evidence is only possible through longitudinal data. This is another worthwhile objective of future research.

Research Question 2: What Motivates Employees to Work Unsafely?

Throughout this chapter, we have focused on using self-determination theory to understand what motivates employees to work safely. Understanding the different reasons why employees are motivated to engage in safety compliance and safety participation behaviors can help develop safety initiatives targeted toward these specific forms of motivation. However, it is equally important to understand what motivates employees to work unsafely, to deliberately break safety rules and procedures, and engage in generally risky behaviors. It is certainly plausible to think about situations where employees feel external pressure to work unsafely. Production pressure, in which employees are under high demands to work faster and cut corners, is a component of an unsafe work environment (Flin, Mearns, O'Connor, & Bryden, 2000), and is often cited as a contributing factor to many occupational accidents (Fleming & Scott, 2012a). The existence of social pressure from coworkers is often present in workplaces. For example, Mullen (2004) found that being teased and harassed by coworkers (and to a lesser extent by supervisors) was a major factor motivating employees to behave unsafely. Although occurrences of controlled forms of motivation to work unsafely can be found in the occupational literature, to date there has been limited focus on employee motivation to work unsafely. Building on these examples of controlled motivation to work unsafely, a particularly interesting area for future research to explore would be if employees are ever autonomously motivated to engage in unsafe behaviors.

Research Question 3: Do Employee's Perceptions of Autonomy, Competence, and Relatedness Influence Their Safety Motivation?

Self-determination theory posits that safety motivation will be influenced by three individual factors: (1) perceived autonomy, (2) competence, and (3) how connected individuals feel to others in the workplace (Deci & Ryan, 1985, 2000). Specifically, self-determination theory hypothesizes that in order for employees to be motivated at all to work safely, they need to feel capable to perform the intended safety activities, and that perceptions of autonomy and being related to other individuals will help facilitate autonomous safety motivation (Ryan & Deci, 2002). Within the occupational safety literature, the effect of social relationships within the work environment (e.g., supervisors, coworkers) has received the most attention out of these three factors (Burt, Sepie, & McFadden, 2008; Mullen, 2004). Moreover, in investigating the relationship between various work characteristics (i.e., job autonomy, role stressors, supervision, training, job security, and communication) and self-reported safe working behaviors, Parker, Axtell, and Turner (2001) concluded that having autonomy over one's job was associated with an increase in self-reported safe working over a year later. However, to date no study has examined the combined effect of autonomy, competence, and relatedness on employee safety motivation, or the combined effect these three factors have on safety outcomes (e.g., injuries, accidents). Given the evidence for the relationship between these three factors (i.e., autonomy, competence, and relatedness) and individual motivation in the self-determination theory literature, this is a worthy area for future occupational safety research.

Research Question 4: Does Supervisor's Safety Motivation Influence Employee's Safety Motivation?

It is currently unknown whether supervisor's safety motivation has any effect on their subordinate's safety motivation. Within an educational setting, Wild, Enzle, Nix, and Deci (1997) found that individuals learning a skill from a teacher who had a controlled form of teaching motivation reported less interest in learning the skill than individuals who learned the skill from an autonomously motivated teacher. The results from this study support the argument that autonomously motivated leaders (e.g., teachers, supervisors) encourage subordinates to be more intrinsically motivated (i.e., interest) than leaders with controlled motivation. Therefore, investigating if and how supervisor's safety motivation influences employee safety motivation and subsequent safety behaviors is another valuable stream of research.

To date, the relationship between employee safety motivation and safety behaviors has only been examined using frontline employees. Supervisors are also expected to engage in similar safety behaviors, in addition to engaging in safety leadership behaviors. The extent to which supervisors are motived to engage in safety leadership behaviors, and what motivates supervisors to be good safety leaders, has received little attention in the occupational safety literature. Self-determination theory provides a theoretical framework to explore these questions in future research. This research would be practically significant because the results could be used to design supervisor safety training programs that promote autonomously motivated supervisors, and could be used to guide selection decisions for supervisory positions.

Research Question 5: Do Safety Management Practices have an Effect on the Type of Employee Safety Motivation?

Safety management practices not only influence safety outcomes (e.g., injuries and accidents) by controlling hazards and improving the physical working conditions, but they can also influence employees' attitudes and perceptions about safety (Vinodkumar & Bhasi, 2010). Although there is no agreed on list of practices that encompass a safety management system, several common themes have emerged across different literatures. The literatures on high-reliability organizations (Weick & Sutcliffe, 2001), low-accident organizations, (Cleveland, Cohen, Smith, & Cohen, 1979), and high-performance work systems (Zacharatos, Barling, & Iverson, 2005) all identify similar components of effective safety management practices. Examples of commonly identified safety management practices include effective safety training, two-way communication, workforce involvement, and safety performance evaluation and feedback (Fleming & Scott, 2012b; Vindkumar & Bhasi, 2010).

These safety management practices may promote autonomous forms of employee safety motivation as opposed to controlled forms of safety motivation. Furthermore, safety management practices may indirectly influence employee's safety motivation by increasing employee autonomy, competence, and the extent that they are viewed as an important part of the work group. For example, receiving effective safety training likely increases employees' level of competence for dealing with workplace hazards, and practices designed to involve employees in safety decisions should increase employee autonomy and their sense of being an important part of the organization.

Research Question 6: Does a Positive Safety Climate Increase Employees' Autonomous Safety Motivation?

There is good evidence indicating that a positive safety climate increases the amount of employees' safety motivation (Neal & Griffin, 2006); however, there is less evidence about what type of safety motivation is associated with a positive safety climate. Safety climate is defined as employees' shared perceptions of *enacted* safety policies and procedures (Zohar, 2003). In other words, safety climate is a reflection of supervisors' demonstrated safety values and behaviors. Maierhofer, Griffin, and Sheehan (2000) investigated the relationships between managers' safety values and behaviors and their subordinates' safety values and behaviors. The authors concluded that managers' safety behaviors directly influenced their subordinates' safety behaviors through a behavioral modeling process.

Subordinates modeled the managers' safety behaviors to impress the manager, or to receive some type of reward. However, Maierhofer et al. found that managers' safety values also influenced subordinates' safety behaviors. Specifically, employees internalized the managers' safety values, which were reflected in subordinates' safety behaviors.

Both processes found by Maierhofer et al. (2000) are possible explanations for how safety climate influences employee behavior, and would suggest that safety climate may promote both controlled safety motivation (through a behavior modeling process) and autonomous safety motivation (through a value internalization process). There is a need for more research like the study by Maierhofer et al., which explains the processes through which organizational factors influence employee safety motivation and behavior.

Conclusion

Despite the fact that self-determination theory is a popular theory of work motivation and employee well-being, there has been relatively few applications in occupational safety research. Self-determination theory can advance our understanding of the relationship between employee safety motivation and safety behaviors by specifying different types of safety motivation. In addition, self-determination theory can be a particularly useful theoretical framework for explaining how organizational factors influence employee safety motivation and subsequent safety outcomes (e.g., behavior, injuries). Because occupational safety research is often criticized for lacking a theoretical basis, more occupational safety research applying the principles of self-determination theory is strongly encouraged.

Note

1. The authors thank the editor for this suggestion.

References

Andriessen, J. H. T. H. (1978). Safe behavior and safety motivation. *Journal of Occupational Accidents, 1,* 363–376.

Asparouhov, T., & Muthén, B. (2009). Exploratory structural equation modeling. *Structural Equation Modeling, 16,* 397–438.

Association of Workers' Compensation Boards of Canada (AWCBC). (2012). *Number of accepted time-loss injuries, by jurisdiction,* 1993-2012. Retrieved from: http://www.awcbc.org/common/assets/nwisptables/all_tables.pdf

Black, A. E., & Deci, E. L. (2000). The effects of instructors' autonomy support and students' autonomous motivation on learning organic chemistry: A self-determination theory perspective. *Science Education, 84,* 740–756.

Bureau of Labor Statistics. (2012). *Workplace injuries and illnesses.* Retrieved from: http://www.bls.gov/iif/

Burstyn, I., Jonasi, L., & Wild, C. (2010). Obtaining compliance with occupational health and safety regulations: A multilevel study using self-determination theory. *International Journal of Environmental Health Research, 20,* 271–287.

Burt, C. D. B., Sepie, B., & McFadden, G. (2008). The development of a considerate and responsible safety attitude in work teams. *Safety Science, 46,* 79–91.

Christian, M. S., Bradley, J. C., Wallace, J. C., & Burke, M. J. (2009). Workplace safety: A meta-analysis of the roles of person and situation factors. *Journal of Applied Psychology, 94,* 1103–1127.

Clarke, S. (2006). The relationship between safety climate and safety performance: A meta-analytic review. *Journal of Occupational Health Psychology, 11,* 315–327.

Cleveland, R., Cohen, R. C., Smith, M., & Cohen, A. (1979). *Safety program practices in record-holding plants.* DHEW (NIOSH) Publication No. 79–136, National Institute for Occupational Safety and Health, Cincinnati, Ohio 45226.

Deci, E. L., & Ryan, R. M. (1985). *Intrinsic motivation and self-determination in human behavior.* New York: Plenum.

Deci, E. L., & Ryan, R. M. (2000). The "what" and "why" of goal pursuits: Human needs and the self-determination of behavior. *Psychological Inquiry, 11,* 227–268.

Deci, E. L., & Ryan, R. M. (2002). *Handbook of self-determination research.* Rochester, NY: The University of Rochester Press.

Deci, E. L., Vallerand, R. J., Pelletier, L. G., & Ryan, R. M. (1991). Motivation and education: The self-determination perspective. *The Educational Psychologist, 26,* 325–346.

Dejoy, D. M. (2005). Behavior change versus culture change: Divergent approaches to managing workplace safety. *Safety Science, 43,* 105–129.

Duncan, L., Hall, C. R., Wilson, P., & Jenny, O. (2010). Exercise motivation: A cross-sectional analysis examining its relationships with frequency, intensity, and duration of exercise. *International Journal of Behavioral Nutrition and Physical Activity, 7:7,* doi:10.1186/1479-5868-7-7

Fleming, M., & Lardner, R. (2000). *Behaviour modification programmes: Establishing best practice.* Suffolk: HSE Books

Fleming, M., & Scott, N. (2012a). Cultural disasters: Learning from yesterday's failures to be safe tomorrow. *Oil and Gas Facilities, 1*(3), 24–26.

Fleming, M., & Scott, N. (2012b). Beyond hard hats and harnesses: How small construction companies manage safety effectively. In E. K. Kelloway, & C. L. Cooper (Eds.), *Occupational health and safety in small and medium sized enterprises* (pp. 26–47). London: Elgar.

Flin, R., Mearns, K., O'Connor, P., & Bryden, R. (2000). Measuring safety climate: Identifying the common features. *Safety Science, 34,* 177–192.

Gagné, M., & Deci, E. L. (2005). Self-determination theory and work motivation. *Journal of Organizational Behavior, 26,* 331–362.

Gagné, M., Forest, J., Gilbert, M. H., Aubé, C., Morin, E., & Malorni, A. (2010). The motivation at work scale: Validation evidence in two languages. *Educational and Psychological Measurement, 70,* 628–646.

Griffin, M. A., & Neal, A. (2000). Perceptions of safety at work: A framework for linking safety climate to safety performance, knowledge, and motivation. *Journal of Occupational Health Psychology, 5,* 347–358.

Guldenmund, F. W. (2010). Understanding and exploring safety culture. Uitgeverij BOX Press.

Heinrich, H. (1931). *Industrial accident prevention: A scientific approach* (1st ed.). London: McGraw-Hill Publishing Co. Ltd.

Hofmann, D. A., Morgeson, F. P., & Gerras, S. J. (2003). Climate as a moderator of the relationship between leader–member exchange and content specific citizenship: Safety climate as an exemplar. *Journal of Applied Psychology, 88*, 170–178.

Hoyos, C. G. (1995). Occupational safety: Progress in understanding the basic aspects of safe and unsafe behaviours. *Applied Psychology: An International Review, 44*, 233–250.

HSE (2012/13). *The health and safety executive annual statistics report for Great Britain 2012/13.* Retrieved from: http://www.hse.gov.uk/statistics/overall/hssh1213.pdf.

Larsson, S., Pousette, A., & Törner, M. (2008). Psychological climate and safety in the construction industry: Mediated influence on safety behavior. *Safety Science, 46*, 405–412.

Lee, T. R. (1995). *The role of attitudes in the safety culture and how to change them.* Paper presented at the Conference on "Understanding Risk Perception". Aberdeen: Offshore Management Centre, The Robert Gordon University.

Lee, T. (1998). Assessment of safety culture at a nuclear reprocessing plant. *Work and Stress, 12*, 217–237.

Liberty Mutual Research Institute for Safety (2010). *2010 Liberty Mutual Workplace Safety Index.* Retrieved from: www.libertymutualgroup.com/researchinstitute.

Maierhofer, N. I., Griffin, M. A., & Sheehan, M. (2000). Linking manager values and behavior with employee values and behavior: A study of values and safety in the hairdressing industry. *Journal of Occupational Health Psychology, 5*, 417–427.

Marsh, H. W., Lüdtke, O., Muthén, B., Asparouhov, T., Morin, A. J. S., Trautwein, U. & Nagengast, B. (2010). A new look at the big-five factor structure through exploratory structural equation modeling. *Psychological Assessment, 22*, 471–491.

Marsh, H. W., Muthén, B., Asparouhov, A., Lüdtke, O., Robitzsch, A., Morin, A. J. S., & Trautwein, U. (2009). Exploratory structural equation modeling, integrating CFA and EFA: Application to students' evaluations of university teaching. *Structural Equation Modeling, 16*, 439–476.

McAfee, R. B., & Winn, A. R. (1989). The use of incentives/feedback to enhance workplace safety: A critique of the literature. *Journal of Safety Research, 20*, 7–19.

Meyers, L. S., Gamst, G., & Guarino, A. J. (2006). *Applied multivariate research: Design and interpretation.* Thousand Oaks, CA: Sage Publications.

Mullen, J. (2004). Investigating factors that influence individual safety behavior at work. *Journal of Safety Research, 35*, 275–285.

Mullen, J., & Kelloway, E. K. (2009). Safety leadership: A longitudinal study of the effects of transformational leadership on safety outcomes. *Journal of Occupational and Organizational Psychology, 20*, 253–272.

Mullen, J., Kelloway, E. K., & Teed, M. (2011). Inconsistent leadership as a predictor of safety behavior. *Work & Stress, 25*, 41–54.

Muthén, L. K., & Muthén, B. O. (1998-2011). *Mplus user's guide* (6th ed.) Los Angeles, CA: Muthén & Muthén.

Neal, A., & Griffin, M. A. (2002). Safety climate and safety behavior. *Australian Journal of Management, 27*, 67–75.

Neal, A., & Griffin, M. A. (2003). Safety climate and safety at work. In J. Barling, & M. Frone (Eds.), *The psychology of workplace safety.* Washington, DC: American Psychological Association.

Neal, A., & Griffin, M. A. (2006). A study of the lagged relationships among safety climate, safety motivation, safety behavior, and accidents at the individual and group levels. *Journal of Applied Psychology, 91*, 946–953.

Neal, A., Griffin, M. A., & Hart, P. M. (2000). The impact of organizational climate on safety climate and individual behavior. *Safety Science, 34*, 99–109.

Newnam, S., Griffin, M. A., Mason, C. (2008). Safety in work vehicles: A multilevel study linking safety values and individual predictors to work-related driving crashes. *Journal of Applied Psychology, 93*, 632–644.

Parker, S. K., Axtell, C. M., & Turner, N. (2001). Designing a safer workplace: Importance of job autonomy, communication quality, and supportive supervisors. *Journal of Occupational Health Psychology, 6*, 211–228.

Parker, S. L., Jimmieson, N. L., & Amiot, C. E. (2010). Self-determination as a moderator of demands and control: Implications for employee strain and engagement. *Journal of Vocational Behavior, 76*, 52–67.

Porter, L. W. & Lawler, E. E. (1968). *Managerial attitudes and performance.* Homewood, IL: Richard D. Irwin, Inc.

Probst, T. M., & Brubaker, T. L. (2001). The effects of job insecurity on employee safety outcomes: Cross-sectional and longitudinal explorations. *Journal of Occupational Health Psychology, 6*, 139–159.

Reason, J. (1990). *Human error.* Cambridge, MA: Cambridge University Press.

Reason, J. (2008). *The human contribution: Unsafe acts, accidents and heroic recoveries.* Surrey, England, Ashgate.

Ryan, R. M., Bernstein, J. H., & Brown, K. W. (2010). Weekends, work, and well-being: Psychological need satisfactions and day of the week effects on mood, vitality, and physical symptoms. *Journal of Social and Clinical Psychology, 29*, 95–122.

Ryan, R. M., & Connell, J. P. (1989). Perceived locus of causality and internalization: Examining reasons for acting in two domains. *Journal of Personality and Social Psychology, 57*, 749–761.

Ryan, R. M., & Deci, E. L. (2002). An overview of self-determination theory: An organismic-dialectical perspective. In E. L. Deci, & R. M. Ryan (Eds.), *Handbook of self-determination research* (pp. 3–36). Rochester, NY: The University of Rochester Press.

Ryan, R. M., Plant, R. W., & O'Malley, S. (1995). Initial motivations for alcohol treatment: Relations with patient characteristics, treatment involvement and dropout. *Addictive Behaviors, 20*, 279–297.

Sinclair, R. R., Martin, J. E., & Sears, L. E. (2010). Labor unions and safety climate: Perceived union safety values and retail employee safety outcomes. *Accident Analysis and Prevention, 42*, 1477–1487.

Skinner, B. F. (1938). *The behavior of organisms: an experimental analysis.* Oxford, England: Appleton-Century.

Vinodkumar, M. N., & Bhasi, M. (2010). Safety management practices and safety behavior: Assessing the mediating role of safety knowledge and motivation. *Accident Analysis and Prevention, 42*, 2082–2093.

Weick, K. E., & Sutcliffe, K. M. (2001). *Managing the unexpected.* San Francisco, CA: Jossey-Bass.

Wild, T. C., Enzle, M. E., Nix, G., & Deci, E. L. (1997). Perceived others as intrinsically or extrinsically motivated: Effects on expectancy formation and task engagement. *Personality and Social Psychology Bulletin, 23*, 837–848.

Williams, G. C., McGregor, H. A., King, D. K., Nelson, C. C., & Glasgow, R. E. (2005). Variation in perceived competence, glycemic control, and patient satisfaction: Relationship to autonomy support form physicians. *Patient Education and Counseling, 57*, 39–45.

Wilson, P. M., & Rodgers, W. M. (2002). The relationship between exercise motives and physical self-esteem in female exercise participants: An application of self-determination theory. *Journal of Applied Biobehavioral Research, 7*, 30–43.

Zacharatos, A., Barling, J., & Iverson, R. D. (2005). High performance work systems and occupational safety. *Journal of Applied Psychology, 90*, 77–93.

Zohar, D. (2002). Modifying supervisory practices to improve subunit safety: A leadership-based intervention model. *Journal of Applied Psychology, 87*, 156–163.

Zohar, D. (2003). The influence of leadership and climate on occupational health and safety. In: Hofmann, D. A., & Tetrick, L. E. (Eds.), *Health and safety in organizations, a multilevel perspective* (pp. 201–230). New York: John Wiley & Sons, Inc.

CHAPTER

18

Understanding Workplace Violence: The Contribution of Self-Determination Theory

Véronique Dagenais-Desmarais *and* François Courcy

Abstract

This chapter aims at a better understanding of the emergence and maintenance of workplace violence through the lens of self-determination theory (SDT), an innovative perspective that has until now been granted little attention from the scientific community. First, what is and what is not workplace violence is defined. Then, classical and modern theories of violence are presented and compared with SDT. Next, empirical evidence linking workplace violence directly or indirectly with components of SDT, including autonomy support and psychological control, general causality orientations, needs fulfillment and thwarting, and various forms of motivation at work, are documented. The chapter concludes with a research agenda and some recommendations for interventions based on workplace violence and SDT literature.

Key Words: workplace violence, self-determination theory, workplace motivation, basic psychological needs, victims, aggressors

Introduction

Violence in the workplace is certainly not a new or emerging concern.[1] It is apparent in the daily lives of workers around the world, in all economic sectors, in all professions, and at all occupational levels (Chappell & Di Martino, 2006). Despite the attention given to this endemic problem in recent decades, several concerns remain. In addition, although focus to date has been on the most severe forms of violence, including homicide, physical assault, and harassment, more insidious acts are now receiving greater attention (Greenberg, 2010). Individual motivations to explain the emergence and maintenance of these harmful behaviors, however, remain to be clarified, and promising avenues for interventions regarding these motivations are only slowly being validated. Although the work of many leading researchers provides compelling answers to several aspects of these fundamental issues, the social statistics on the prevalence and

detrimental effects of these acts suggest the need to look at new explanatory and preventive avenues.

Several institutions and organizations monitor these behaviors and inform the public about the prevalence of workplace violence and its specific forms (e.g., Occupational Safety and Health Organization, National Institute for Occupational Safety and Health, International Labor Organization), and the statistics available on workplace violence and similar behaviors are now varied and abundant. Some also widely available statistics compare this prevalence by segmenting it into various contexts (e.g., economic sector, prior or inexistent relationship between actors), geographical areas (e.g., countries, continents), forms of behavior (e.g., harassment, bullying), or impacts (e.g., monetary, physical, or psychological). Indeed, such misconduct is not without consequences for victims, organizations, and society as a whole. Calculating the cost of the various forms of workplace violence

295

takes into account such negative effects as loss of motivation, rise in absenteeism, higher turnover, health and rehabilitation costs, loss of efficiency, lower revenue, and, ultimately, decline in productivity. For example, in the United States, the annual cost of workplace violence is estimated at $4.1 billion (Chappell & Di Martino, 2006).

In terms of prevalence, studies by the International Labor Organization (Chappell & Di Martino, 2006) describe workplace violence as a global problem affecting all countries to varying degrees. For example, according to the US Occupational Safety and Health Administration (2002), about two million workers a year are victims of some form of violence. However, according to the British Crime Survey (see Packham, 2010), the risk of being a victim of severe aggression or of being threatened with violence at work, in terms of probability, remains low; the results of this survey indicate that 1.4% of working adults are victims of one or more violent incidents at work. In numbers, approximately 318,000 workers in England and Wales have experienced at least one incident of assault or threat in 2009–2010, in comparison with 327,000 workers in 2008–2009. According to the 2009–2010 British Crime Survey, an estimated 677,000 incidents of violence at work occurred in that period, representing 310,000 assaults and 366,000 threats, with the highest-risk age groups being 25–34 for men (2.2%), whereas it is 16–24 (2.0%) and 45–54 (1.8%) for women (Packham, 2010).

The prevalence of more insidious forms of violence, however, reflects a quite different picture. In an in-depth analysis of 148 organizations worldwide, Hodson, Roscigno, and Lopez (2006) revealed that 49% of the analyzed workplaces showed evidence of bullying on a relatively routine basis. Studies in the United States also suggest alarming prevalence rates for this specific form of workplace violence. A 2010 survey by the Workplace Bullying Institute indicated that 35% of workers had been bullied (26% over their career, 9% at the time of the survey), corresponding to 53.5 million US workers (Namie, 2010). The European Survey of Enterprises on New and Emerging Risks (2005) reported a wide variation among European countries in terms of prevalence of risk of victimization, ranging from 2% in Italy and Bulgaria, to 12% in Holland, and to as much as 17% in Finland. According to the authors of the study, such differences are more likely to reflect different degrees of sensitivity or cultural awareness of violence than its actual prevalence (Milczarek, 2010).

Other agencies report the prevalence of sexual violence in the workplace. In 2007, the US Equal Employment Opportunity Commission received more than 12,000 complaints of sexual harassment (cited in Sung, 2008). In India, according to a recent survey on sexual harassment against women employees, 88% of female workers said they had experienced sexual harassment in their jobs (Sharma, 2010). In half of the reported incidents, female workers described the harassment as extreme, including abusive language, physical contact, and requests for sexual favors, and supervisors committed 72% of these acts. Most (91%) of victims did not denounce the aggressor because of fear of reprisals. In 2008, in Singapore, according to a survey by the Association of Women for Action and Research (2011), 54% of respondents reported experiencing some form of sexual harassment. Among them, 12% had received threats of termination if they did not comply with the requests of the harasser.

Beyond its alarming prevalence, workplace violence is a concern because of the damage it causes in the workplace. Statistics on workplace violence and similar behaviors primarily emphasize the incidence of these behaviors and their impact on victims and social systems, such as organizations. The effects of workplace violence are multiple for victims; numerous reports, scientific studies, and testimonials emphasize the physical and psychological consequences of workplace violence. For example, victims of violence at work are more likely than victims of violence outside of work to declare that it is difficult for them to go about their daily activities because of violence (25% vs. 14%; de Léséleuc, 2004). Each year in Sweden, bullying is responsible for 10–15% of suicides (Priest, 2006). Finally, a joint study by several international agencies indicates that in the health community, including that of developing countries and transitional economies, workplace violence causes health workers to abandon their professions (World Health Organization, 2002). In summary, workplace violence remains a topical subject that, although not a new phenomenon, still deserves efforts to better understand it in order to better prevent it.

What is Workplace Violence?

Workplace violence includes a multiplicity of interpersonal deviant behaviors taking different forms and names. The terms harassment, bullying, mobbing, assault, emotional abuse, and incivility are often substituted for or associated with one another, or are concepts related to workplace violence. These various similar concepts, however, refer to different realities (Caponecchia & Wyatt, 2011; Neuman & Keasly, 2010). This section clarifies such distinctions.

Deviant Behavior and Workplace Violence

Workplace violence is defined as hostile behavior toward another person (Kelloway, Barling, & Hurrell, 2006). It is part of a wider range of harmful behaviors called workplace antisocial behaviors, a concept defined as a set of deviant or delinquent behaviors of an individual member of an organization toward the organization or its members (Giacalone & Greenberg, 1997). Sometimes defined as a universe of deviant (Robinson & Bennett, 1995), or counterproductive (Fox & Spector, 1999), behaviors, they include actions both against persons, such as workplace violence, and against the organization (Griffin & Lopez, 2005), such as sabotage or work slowdown. As Robinson and Bennett (1995) specify, workplace violence is seen as antisocial workplace behavior of an interpersonal nature. Such actions are aimed at individuals, their physical or psychological integrity, their property, or their performance (Rioux, Roberge, Brunet, Savoie, & Courcy, 2005). The forms of these actions vary, ranging from acts of serious physical aggression to more insidious acts. This chapter thus focuses solely on workplace violence and excludes antisocial behavior aimed at the organization.

Forms of Violence in the Workplace

Four types of violence in the workplace have been identified based on who the perpetrators are and what their relationship is with the victims: criminal violence, occupational violence, domestic violence, and workplace violence per se (Merchant & Lundell, 2001; LeBlanc & Barling, 2005).

Criminal violence (also called Type I) is an act committed by a person outside the organization who attacks an employee of the organization (Merchant & Lundell, 2001). The victim knows little or nothing about the aggressor. Examples include robberies of banks or taxis, and terrorist attacks. *Occupational violence* (Type II) involves violent behavior committed by a client or service user of an organization toward one or more members of the organization in the course of the latter's work. Bus drivers, police officers, nurses, correctional agents, customer service personnel, and teachers are at risk for this second category of violence (Merchant & Lundell, 2001). *Domestic violence* (Type IV) is an aggression committed by a person maintaining or having maintained a personal relationship with a member of the organization but not necessarily working for the same company. The most frequently conveyed image of this category of violence is the ex-husband who appears at his ex-wife's workplace and assaults her. Finally, *workplace violence* (Type III) is a behavior of a member or ex-member of an organization in violation of the norms of that organization and seeking to harm or coerce another member (Courcy, Savoie, & Brunet, 2009).

Workplace violence is in itself a broad concept associated with several other more specific concepts sometimes used interchangeably. For example, *bullying* and *harassment* are specific forms of violence characterized by the notion of "repetition" or "chain" of assaults against one or several victims, and by the asymmetry of power between the "bully" and the "victim" (Neuman & Keashly, 2010; Rayner, Hoel, & Cooper, 2002). In turn, *mobbing* is a "social interaction through which one individual is attacked by one or more individuals almost on a daily basis and for periods of many months, bringing the person into an almost helpless position with potentially high risk of expulsion" (Leymann, 1996, p. 168). *Emotional abuse* corresponds to "hostile verbal and nonverbal behaviors (excluding physical contact) by one or more persons towards another that are aimed at undermining the other to ensure compliance" (Keashly, Trott, & McClean, 1994, p. 342). This misconduct involves specific forms of workplace violence and a deliberate attempt to inflict psychological and emotional harm on the victim in order to achieve a goal (Koonin & Green, 2004). Finally, *workplace incivility* involves "low-intensity deviant behavior with ambiguous intent to harm the target, in violation of workplace norms for mutual respect" (Andersson & Pearson, 1999, p. 457). These behaviors are characterized mainly by ambiguity of intent and low intensity of action (Blau & Andersson, 2005). These conceptual distinctions are useful for understanding the severity of the actions discussed in the literature, but should also be articulated around a typology of observable behavior in order to provide a better understanding of the ramifications of these manifestations (Griffin & Lopez, 2005). Figure 18.1 illustrates the relationships between the concepts associated with workplace violence that are the subject of this chapter.

Taxonomies and Typologies of Workplace Violence

Models of violence traditionally operate around two perspectives: intentionality and

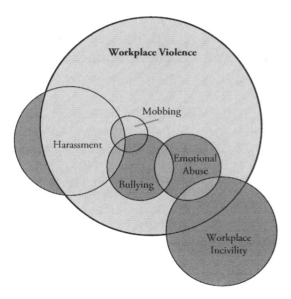

Fig. 18.1. Graphical representation of workplace violence.

manifested forms. The typology of Feshbach (1964) has influenced several proposed models. Essentially, according to this theorist, aggressive acts are of two kinds. *Hostile* (or *reactive*) *aggression* is when the aggressor commits an assault following an external stimulus deemed to be aversive (Feshbach, 1964). However, the same act can be committed to achieve a goal without the triggering presence of an aversive stimulus. In this second type of aggression, the behavior becomes the instrument for achieving a goal. This strategy is called *instrumental aggression*.

Buss's (1961) classic taxonomy of violence manifestations follows three axes: (1) direct-indirect, (2) active-passive, and (3) verbal-physical. Some violent acts are clearly committed in the presence of the victim (*direct* violence). Other acts are subtler and may be committed without the victim knowing or being present (*indirect* violence). Furthermore, although most violence is based on an observable emission of behavior (*active* violence), some acts of violence may derive from an omission of expected behavior involving serious consequences (*passive* violence). Finally, the means used to attack others operates along the third axis, physical-verbal, in which the use of words, gestures, and symbols (*verbal* violence) is differentiated from acts using the body or objects (*physical* abuse; Buss, 1961; Neuman & Baron, 1998).

Explanatory Theories of Violence

Beyond descriptive models, several theories have been developed to explain the appearance and maintenance of violence. This section presents the main theoretical currents on aggression to better understand the theoretical framework underpinning most studies on the subject. Because such behavior usually occurs in the context of social interaction and is often preceded by social determinants, the presentation focuses on violence from a social perspective. It should, however, be noted that other theoretical proposals and models have been developed but are not described in detail here. Instead, the aim of this section is to focus on classical theories to help familiarize the reader with a broad interdisciplinary perspective. Theories developed from this point of view can be grouped into four main perspectives, depending on whether aggression is considered principally a function of instinct, drive, learning, or cognition.

Instinct Theories of Aggression

The first theoretical approach of aggression considers aggressive behavior as instinctive or innate. In this perspective, two main theoretical approaches have been developed: psychoanalytic and evolutionary. According to the psychoanalytic approach of Freud (1920), the death instinct, called *thanatos*, is part of the human makeup and guides behavior toward destruction and death. The other major instinct, *eros*, guides human behavior toward the preservation of life, and, in so doing, is in perpetual conflict with thanatos. This conflict results in thanatos energy being redirected to other people in the form of aggression. In a manner similar to catharsis, the expression of aggression subsequently reduces the death and destruction instinct. This perspective has received much criticism and has not gained wide acceptance (Baron & Richardson, 1994).

The evolutionary perspective formulated by Lorenz (1966, 1974) suggests that the principle of natural selection predisposes human beings to aggression. The ethological approach argues that humans have a "functional" aggressive instinct serving three main functions: (1) dispersing members of a same species over a wide geographical area, therefore maximizing resources; (2) favoring continuous improvement of the species by ensuring that only the strongest reproduce; and (3) protecting offspring (Baron & Richardson, 1994). This approach has received much criticism due to lack of proof for the theory and because it does not consider such factors as the "behavioral flexibility" of humans (Baldwin & Baldwin, 1981; Gould, 1978; Zillmann, 1979).

Frustration-Aggression Hypothesis

In 1939, a group of five authors (Dollard, Doob, Miller, Mowrer, & Sears) published a now-classic book, *Frustration and Aggression*. According to their theory, frustration, defined as an interference with or threat to attaining a goal, produces an aggressive impulse (drive). Two main basic assumptions support this explanation: aggression always presupposes the presence of frustration, and the presence of frustration always leads to a form of aggression. The aggressive response, however, may be temporarily inhibited and shifted to another source because of a fear of punishment. The intensity of aggression resulting from frustration is proportional to the strength of the frustration and the importance granted by the subject to the desired goal. In addition, the authors consider that prior or simultaneous frustration can have a cumulative effect, which subsides after the aggressive behavior is emitted. This theory has stimulated numerous studies and several research programs. The results of these studies, however, provide only partial support to the theory in its original version (Geen, 1991).

The assumptions of the frustration-aggression theory that all aggression is preceded by frustration and that all frustration leads to aggression have raised criticisms (Geen, 1991), and have led to several attempts at extending, refining, and delimiting the theory. First, the work of Berkowitz (1965, 1969) was based on a revision entitled *aggressive-cue theory*. According to this author, an aversive stimulus, such as frustration, predisposes a person to aggression. However, for the aggression to be manifested, a *cue* must be present in the environment (e.g., a firearm). These triggers are environmental stimuli associated with anger and aggression through a process similar to classical conditioning. Second, Zillmann (1983a; 1983b) formulated the *excitation-transfer theory*. According to Zillmann (1971), aggression is the result of an observable and measurable state of *arousal*. This state derives from a physiological response to stimuli from various sources. Unlike in the original frustration-aggression hypothesis, the arousal produced by one source can be transferred to another target while altering the strength of the produced response (Zillmann, 1983a).

In short, drive-related theories explain aggression as the effect of a frustrating environmental stimulus, whether aversive or arousal producing. This assertion thus shifts aggression from an instinctual response to an attempt at reducing sources of irritation. Despite some criticism (e.g., Felson, 2006), these theories have been the source of many influential studies on aggression and are still quite relevant (Kelloway et al., 2006).

Social Learning Theory

Social learning theory considers aggression essentially as an acquired and retained behavior, without ignoring the importance of biological determinants (Bandura, 1973). The most important factors triggering aggression are prior learning, models, and contingencies resulting from the behavior (reinforcement and punishment), and self-regulation mechanisms as learning retention factors (Baron & Richardson, 1994). In addition to these determinants, cognitive mediation (e.g., attention, motivation, and the ability to learn and reproduce actions), and neutralizing strategies (e.g., justifying aggression, and guilt) are also conditions that instigate such behavior (Zillmann, 1988). This approach has raised awareness among researchers about the influence of the social environment in predicting aggressive behavior, and has influenced many intervention programs aimed at reducing aggressive behavior (Hershcovis & Barling, 2006).

Cognitive Theories

Several theories previously described have neglected the importance of cognitive processes in explaining aggression. In a revision of his excitation-transfer theory, Zillmann (1988) suggests that cognitions can by themselves reduce or increase arousal levels. Individuals confronted with a potentially provocative behavior generally attempt to understand what may have caused this behavior. Such attributions play an important role in structuring their response. If individuals attribute this behavior to external causes (e.g., accidents), they are more likely to respond in a less aggressive way than if they believed the behavior to have internal causes (e.g., intentional behavior). It is important to note, however, that a high arousal level may interfere with cognitions and lead to impulsive reactions (Geen, 1991).

A second cognitive model, the *cognitive-neoassociation theory of aggression*, is a revision of Berkowitz's frustration-aggression hypothesis (1983, 1988, 1989). In this model, the emphasis is on the *unpleasant* nature, or the negative affect, generated by an event, which hinders the attainment of a goal. Negative affect (the result of cognition) here becomes an indispensable mediator between frustration and aggression. Whatever the true nature of the frustration, the response is modulated by one's interpretation of the obstacles preventing attainment of the goal. When one is faced with frustration, two tendencies arise—*flight* or *fight*—depending on one's interpretation of the negative affect. The *fight* response, expressing aggression, can reduce the negative affect (Berkowitz, 1993). In their models, Berkowitz (1983) and Zillmann (1988) recognize the role of cognitions and emotions in triggering aggression. They also recognize, however, that strong emotions can lead to impulsive reactions against which cognitive interventions are ineffective.

Theoretical Models Specific to the Workplace

In industrial and organizational psychology and organizational behavior, the classical and contemporary theories of aggression presented above have greatly influenced the conception of theoretical models explaining workplace misconduct (see Fox & Spector, 1999; LeBlanc & Kelloway, 2002; Martinko & Zellars, 1996). The models specific to the workplace have in common to propose combining one or more theories with various other theories of psychology and organizational behavior to predict deviant behaviors, including workplace violence. Particular attention is also given to better understand the interactions between individuals (cognitions, emotions, and personality) and the environment (interactions, controls, and opportunities). These models have suggested diverse mechanisms in explaining violence and misconduct, and have rigorously tested their assumptions and hypotheses in organizational settings. These models have also pursued the common objective to understand the motivation of perpetrators for behaving violently. However, few of these theoretical or heuristic models incorporate key elements of motivational theories to better understand violent behavior (Neuman & Keashly, 2010; Vardi & Wiemer, 1996). One important motivational theory, self-determination theory (SDT), may address this gap in the literature specific to workplace violence and thus make an original and relevant contribution to understanding the mechanisms that operate in triggering and maintaining workplace violence.

Toward a Paradigm Shift? Violence from a Humanistic Perspective

The phenomenon of workplace violence is still studied as a dysfunctional or pathological facet of organizations that must be "treated." We observe that little has been done to develop more *optimistic* models of workplace violence. It is in this innovative perspective that SDT has begun to be considered by some authors as a useful explanatory avenue for violence in different life domains. As a motivational theory, SDT is based on a humanistic vision of human beings. Although, at first glance, studying workplace violence from the angle of SDT may seem counterintuitive, this confrontation of paradigms may in fact help broaden current knowledge about the contexts in which violence emerges and is maintained, and about the impact of violence on individuals and organizations. To date, little has been done to establish links between SDT and workplace violence. However, several promising avenues deserve consideration to form a body of knowledge from several fields of research and from which a promising research agenda can be identified.

Overview of SDT

SDT provides a theoretical model of human motivation according to which humans are active beings oriented toward personal growth, inclined to include these psychic elements in their identity, and to integrate themselves into a larger social structure (Deci & Ryan, 2000). Achievement of these goals is based on satisfying three fundamental and universal psychological needs: (1) autonomy, (2) relatedness, and (3) competence. Several studies have empirically demonstrated that the more individuals feel autonomous, competent, and affiliated with others, the more they develop *autonomous motivation* and tend to freely engage in activities. However, when individuals act through constraint, their three fundamental needs are thwarted (or frustrated), and they tend to develop a *controlled motivation* to perform given tasks (Gagné & Deci, 2005). Autonomous motivation, fueled by fulfillment of the three needs, is associated with various benefits (e.g., perseverance in a task, job performance, job satisfaction, work-related positive attitudes, organizational citizenship behaviors, psychological adjustment, and well-being; see Gagné & Deci, 2005 for a review). However, controlled motivation leads to negative consequences (e.g., more psychological distress and burnout, less concentration at work, more psychosomatic disorders, less mutual aid and sharing of information, greater intention to leave the organization, and more absenteeism; see Forest, Crevier-Braud, & Gagné, 2009).

Within organizations, various drivers lead to the fulfillment or thwarting of the three psychological needs, which in turn determine the form of motivation adopted by workers. First, *leadership* and *interpersonal relationships* can help or hinder satisfaction of these basic needs (e.g., Baard, Deci, & Ryan, 2004). According to SDT, supervisors are among the social agents most likely to affect fulfillment of employees' fundamental needs (Gagné & Forest, 2009). As such, according to SDT, management practices can be classified into two motivational styles: autonomy-supportive or controlling (Deci & Ryan, 1987). *Autonomy support* is defined as the action of a person in a position of authority that considers the feelings and points of view of others, provides them with meaningful and useful information about rules and expectations, offers them opportunities to make choices and take initiative, and gives positive and constructive feedback (Black & Deci, 2000; Mageau & Vallerand, 2003). An influential person adopting practices that are autonomy-supportive has a positive impact on the satisfaction of these basic needs and promotes more self-determined motivation (Gagné & Deci, 2005). *Psychological control*, in turn, is defined as the motivational style of "an authority who pressures others to behave in particular ways, either through coercive or seductive techniques that generally include implicit or explicit rewards or punishments" (Black & Deci, 2000, p. 742). This interpersonal style is characterized by such behaviors as giving orders, threatening, making others feel guilty, punishing, and manipulating by offering rewards (Mageau & Vallerand, 2003). When individuals operate in a controlling environment, or with significant others who adopt a controlling interpersonal style, their fundamental needs are thwarted.

In organizational settings, *job design* can also help fulfill the three basic needs of employees and affect their motivation (Gagné & Forest, 2009). Improved job design (based, for example, on the model first proposed by Hackman & Oldham, 1975) is associated with more autonomous motivation among workers (Gagné, Senecal, & Koestner, 1997) and volunteers (Millette & Gagné, 2008). Finally, *compensation* can influence need satisfaction (Gagné & Forest, 2009). Contrary to organizational practices that consider compensation as a source of motivation, the effect of monetary rewards can be a double-edged sword hindering autonomous motivation (Deci, Koestner, & Ryan, 1999; Gagné & Forest, 2008). Indeed, compensation is motivating for simple tasks (Weibel, Rost, & Osterloh, 2007), but potentially detrimental to motivation to perform complex tasks that are intrinsically motivating (Gagné & Deci, 2005).

In addition to environmental variables, SDT posits that a personality variable may be determinative in the type of motivation adopted by an individual. *General causality orientation* refers to a relatively stable personality orientation concerning the initiation and regulation of behavior (Deci & Ryan, 1985). Akin to the locus of causality, causality orientation can take three forms: (1) autonomy orientation, (2) control orientation, or (3) impersonal orientation. *Autonomy orientation* is the tendency to perceive one's behavior as freely chosen, whereas *control orientation* is the tendency to perceive that one's behavior is controlled by external constraints, such as punishments and rewards. *Impersonal orientation* is the tendency to believe that achieving desired results is outside one's control and is primarily a question of luck or fate (Moller & Deci, 2010).

How Does SDT Relate to Classical Theories of Violence?

Classical theories of aggression emphasize human biological factors, such emotions as anger and frustration, cognitive processes, and environmental conditions in explaining violent behavior. In comparison with the classical theories presented previously, SDT has the potential to bring a new and complementary point of view in understanding the etiology of workplace violence. First, SDT encompasses many of the components suggested by classical theories, including frustration, cognitive processes, and external determinants. For example, SDT postulates that environmental and relational contexts can facilitate or hinder the fulfillment of basic human psychological needs, and shares with some classical theories the focus on nonfulfillment/frustration (in this case, of fundamental needs) as a source of unfavorable consequences. According to Spector (1978), frustration can be conceived as the presence of obstacles preventing individuals from reaching their objectives, and creating aversive conditions that lead to violence as solution-seeking behavior (Felson, 2006). SDT can also help explain an issue left unresolved by classical theories of violence: why some people act violently when frustrated, whereas others do not. Indeed, this theoretical framework offers an explanatory avenue linking external influences and intraindividual processes by suggesting a self-determination process. As discussed previously, basic need frustration leads to controlled motivation, which in turn leads to negative consequences, such as workplace violence. Finally, SDT can contribute to broadening our understanding of workplace violence by considering the positive expressions of the fulfillment and/or absence of frustration of the three basic needs.

Workplace Violence: A Self-Determination Perspective

The next section focuses on describing the relationship between workplace violence and SDT. As will be seen, violence can be postulated as both a determinant and as a result of the various environmental, relational, and individual configurations proposed by SDT. At this point, however, a word of caution is in order: the state of knowledge about the relationships between SDT and workplace violence is, at most, embryonic. This section connects the dots by deriving a series of hypotheses based on the literature from various research fields and theoretical frameworks. It is hoped that this exercise will be fruitful in two ways: first, to clearly identify gaps in the literature; and second, to contribute to establishing the foundations of a research agenda.

Effect of SDT Components on Violence

As postulated by SDT and demonstrated empirically in different settings, (lack of) self-determination has many consequences for individuals and organizations. Among these consequences is violence in its multiple forms.

EFFECT OF LEADERSHIP STYLE AND INTERPERSONAL RELATIONSHIPS

As mentioned, one of the main sources of autonomy support lies in management, where supervisors appear to play a role of primary importance. With regard to workplace violence, Van Fleet and Griffin (2006) argue: "Since leaders are an important determinant of organizational culture, [. . .] they therefore play an important role in motivating dysfunctional work behaviors" (p. 706). Although not adopting an SDT framework, Hoel, Glasø, Hetland, Cooper, and Einarsen (2010) have recently shown that certain management styles are associated with more frequent episodes of workplace bullying. In particular, autocratic or *tyrannical leadership* behavior is associated with a higher frequency of bullying episodes (Hoel & Cooper, 2000; O'Moore, 2000; Vartia, 1996). Although this hypothesis has not yet been tested, we postulate that autocratic leaders, because of their directive and coercive style (Hoel et al., 2010), adopt more controlling management practices. This may trigger a "domino effect," in which psychological control by managers affects the fundamental needs of their employees, creating greater controlled motivation among the employees, which in turn creates fertile ground for the emergence of occupational violence, as discussed later.

In addition, some dimensions of transactional leadership are related to bullying. *Noncontingent punishment*, "an unpredictable style of leadership, where punishment is meted out or delivered on leaders' own terms, independent of the behavior of subordinates" (Hoel et al., 2010, p. 453), emerges as a strong predictor of employees' perception of being bullied at work. These findings may be explained through the lens of SDT: by making the work environment unpredictable, managers do not contribute to employees' self-determination or sense of control over their environment. As we shall see, the thwarting of fundamental needs is associated with an increased risk of anger and aggressive behaviors or attitudes.

Passive leadership is also a vector of workplace violence. *Laissez-faire leadership*, in which leaders offer a physical presence but do not carry out their duties, is a determinant of bullying (Hoel et al., 2010). A similar result was also obtained by Vartia (1996) with regard to mobbing: an "almost helpless or uninterested management" characterizes environments where bullying is more present. Although this link has not yet been empirically established, we postulate that such a leadership style does not fulfill employees' needs of competence, relatedness, and autonomy. Indeed, although employees have some latitude in the way they act with a laissez-faire leader, this type of "autonomy" is actually harmful because it offers no real autonomy *support* from immediate superiors, in addition to leaving room for deviant behaviors.

Other inappropriate management practices may contribute to workplace violence. A recent study showed that *abusive supervision* (e.g., ridiculing and humiliating subordinates publicly, improperly blaming subordinates, and invading subordinates' privacy; see Tepper, 2000) leads to more organizational deviance, and this relationship is mediated by lower employee need satisfaction (Lian, Lance Ferris, & Brown, 2012). Although not tested empirically by the authors, abusive supervision involves, by definition, psychological control over employees. However, whether or not these results can be generalized to workplace violence specifically (i.e., to interpersonal forms of workplace deviance) remains to be tested.

Beyond management style, the quality of relationship between superiors and their employees also appears crucial in terms of workplace violence. Some studies show that experiencing low-quality leader-member relationships increases the risk of committing deviant behavior directed at other individuals at work, including rumor spreading, verbal abuse, harassment, and stealing from coworkers (Chullen, Dunford, Angermeier, Boss, & Boss, 2010). Although it remains to be tested empirically, we can hypothesize from these results that poor leader-member relations affect the fulfillment of employees' need for relatedness at the very least. This can potentially result in antisocial behaviors of various kinds.

In conclusion, management practices and leadership styles involving more authoritarian approaches or withdrawal behaviors are associated with more workplace violence. Although until now no research adopting a SDT framework is available to validate such a hypothesis in the workplace, it seems theoretically reasonable to postulate that one of the processes by which this relationship exists involves the thwarting of employees' basic psychological needs, but this remains to be tested.

Beyond the immediate supervisor, *peer support* is another source of autonomy support according to SDT. Hence, it seems reasonable to postulate that support from colleagues can reduce the risk of workplace violence. In a study providing indirect evidence on this issue, Fitzgerald, Haythornthwaite, Suchday, and Ewart (2003) showed that social support acts as a moderator between a job offering low control and autonomy, and the expression of anger. Thus, extrapolating these results to the expression of violent behaviors from an SDT perspective, we hypothesize that, especially in the absence of an autonomy-supportive work environment, peer support may act as a buffer in the emergence of workplace violence. Informal groups and friendly relations at work may indeed support members by fulfilling some of their needs (Brunet & Savoie, 2003), thereby altering the accumulation of frustration or allowing the expression of anger in a more socially acceptable manner.

Although no research evidence allows confirming or refuting SDT predictions about workplace violence, the inevitable question arises: Why (from a theoretical perspective) do control and lack of autonomy support lead to increased violence in organizations? A useful avenue for explaining the link between support or control and the appearance and maintenance of workplace violence has recently emerged. A process called *dehumanization*, (i.e., the denial of humanness to others; Moller & Deci, 2010), seems to be involved at the perpetrator-level in several forms of violence and is a potentially useful moderator. This hypothesis was tested empirically: Moller & Deci (2010) showed

that psychological control tends to increase violence via some form of dehumanization, and that conversely, autonomy support leads to less violence and dehumanization. This seems to be a useful explanatory avenue and a worthwhile variable to consider in explaining workplace violence.

EFFECT OF THE WORK ENVIRONMENT ON WORKPLACE VIOLENCE

Beyond interpersonal relationships, SDT acknowledges that the work environment can also be autonomy-supportive or controlling. Based on the literature on bullying, we postulate that control or autonomy-support may be related to workplace violence. Indeed, "organizational cultures may contribute to [. . .] dysfunctional behavior in a variety of ways" (Van Fleet & Griffin, 2006, p. 706). With regard to bullying specifically, it was reported that workers who perceived low organizational support also observed more bullying in their workplace (Djurkovic, McCormack, & Casimir, 2008). According to a review of the literature by Salin (2003), job design characteristics, including a heavy workload, a hectic work environment, organizational constraints, a lack of control or autonomy over one's job, a lack of clear objectives, and a presence of role conflict or role ambiguity, along with a poor social climate, lead to bullying. According to Wheeler, Halbesleben, and Shanine (2010), bullying is a response to an unsupportive work environment. For example, an organizational structure or organizational processes that reward a "win-at-all-costs" mentality specific to highly competitive cultures, or a lack of accountability regarding bullying at work, foster the emergence of bullies (Wheeler et al., 2010). Although the relationships between autonomy-support and workplace violence remains to be tested within a SDT framework, this environmental parameter appears to be a potentially useful lever to prevent bullying and perhaps other forms of workplace violence.

A third environmental variable influencing motivation and need satisfaction, according to SDT, is compensation (Gagné & Forest, 2009). To our knowledge, no study has demonstrated the effect of compensation on workplace violence. However, following the theoretical premises of SDT, some compensation practices may contribute indirectly to increased psychological control in that they are associated with the nonsatisfaction and thwarting of the three basic needs and with more controlled motivation. All these concepts are linked to workplace violence. One may postulate that some rewards, by eliciting a more controlled form of motivation (e.g., pay-for-performance incentive systems), may encourage undesirable behaviors, such as instrumental aggression (e.g., intimidating a competitive colleague). This is a worthwhile avenue to explore further in order to investigate the nature and strength of such links.

In sum, the effect of a controlling work environment on workplace violence, through its influence on need frustration and controlled motivation, has not been empirically demonstrated. However, SDT has shown that, whether through work organization, or reward systems, a controlling work environment (Gagné & Forest, 2009) potentially hinders employees' basic needs, which when left unfulfilled, contribute to the emergence of violence (discussed later). It seems therefore legitimate to suggest that the work environment, through its effect on other psychological variables, may have an indirect effect on the emergence of workplace violence.

EFFECT OF CAUSALITY ORIENTATION ON WORKPLACE VIOLENCE

Although causality orientation has not been studied in connection with violence in organizational settings, some evidence suggests that this personality variable studied within SDT is relevant in explaining the phenomenon. Several studies have helped to establish a relationship between the various causality orientations and correlates of violence.

With regard to *autonomy orientation*, individuals with this orientation tend to commit fewer acts of aggression, interpersonal harm, and aggressive driving, and display more prosocial behavior (see Moller & Deci, 2010 for a literature review). These individuals also report less self-derogation and hostility (Deci & Ryan, 1985), and experience less domestic violence (Hove, Parkhill, Neighbors, McConchie, & Fossos, 2010). Not only do highly autonomy-oriented individuals display less violence and aggression, but they also experience more open, honest, and positive interactions (Hodgins, Koestner, & Duncan, 1996). Parallel to this first causality orientation, individuals with a *control orientation* experience more problematic use of alcohol, more acts of domestic violence (Hove et al., 2010), more self-aggression, more driving anger and aggression (Knee, Neighbors, & Vietor, 2001), and more antisocial behavior (Moller & Deci, 2010, p. 43, see studies cited), and have a greater tendency for lying and "saving face" (Hodgins, Liebeskind, & Schwartz, 1996). Thus, it seems that autonomy orientation is a personality variable that

reduces the risk of engaging in violent, or at least aggressive behavior, whereas the opposite seems to be true for individuals adopting a control orientation. These findings may potentially apply to workplace violence, but further investigation should be devoted to the question.

EFFECT OF BASIC NEEDS ON WORKPLACE VIOLENCE

Most studies making the connection between violence and the frustration of basic needs were not conducted in work settings; however, these studies lead to several interesting observations for research in organizational settings. For example, children whose developmental needs are hampered tend to have a more deviant development (Rossman & Rosenberg, 1991). Additionally, in school, unsatisfied needs of children were found to be associated with more bullying behaviors (Schwamb, 2005).

Some findings suggest the relevance of need frustration in the emergence of violence. For example, when people believe their autonomy is thwarted, they respond by acting in a less civilized and more antisocial manner (see Moller & Deci, 2010 for a review). Furthermore, Aquino, Grover, Bradfield, and Allen (1999) have shown that individuals experiencing a sense of control over their environment are more empowered in terms of avoiding mistreatment or modifying interpersonal interactions in order to be less vulnerable to the aggressions of others. Similarly, difficult interpersonal relationships at work can increase the risk of violence. For example, Hauge, Skogstad, and Einarsen (2009) have shown that interpersonal conflicts explain a small amount of variance for being a perpetrator of bullying. One can interpret these results in light of SDT and assert that a frustrated need for relatedness increases the likelihood of adopting inappropriate conduct at work. The presence of interpersonal conflict is also a trigger of workplace bullying, as confirmed by Wheeler et al. (2010, p. 556), who state that "Bullying emerges from environments where interpersonal conflict regularly occurs, where employees feel pressure to perform in an environment lacking support, where employees feel over-worked, and where employees feel a lack of control over their job and work environment." These findings illustrate that the need for relatedness, autonomy, and competence, when unfulfilled, or perhaps even thwarted, are determinants in the emergence of this type of workplace violence. More investigations based specifically on SDT in relation to workplace bullying and other forms of workplace violence, however, should be conducted to further clarify knowledge within this theoretical framework.

EFFECT OF MOTIVATION TYPE ON WORKPLACE VIOLENCE

Proponents of SDT have not yet investigated the role of various forms of motivation in the emergence of violence at work. However, knowledge derived from other settings may provide an interesting perspective on the relationship between motivation and workplace violence. In sports teams, Ntoumanis and Standage (2009) found that autonomous motivation was associated with more sportsmanship and less antisocial moral attitudes, whereas controlled motivation led to less sportsmanship and more antisocial moral attitudes. Some indirect evidence specific to the workplace also suggests the important role of motivation type in the emergence of violent behavior. Intrinsic motivation, a form of self-determined motivation, appears to play an important role in reducing the likelihood of deviant behavior (Chullen et al., 2010). The impact of other less self-determined forms of motivation on the emergence of workplace violence, however, still remains to be studied.

Effect of Violence on SDT Components

In studying the relationships between workplace violence and SDT, it is intuitive to consider violence as one of the many consequences of autonomy support or psychological control, need satisfaction or thwarting, or an individual's form of motivation. Indeed, we have seen up to now that a certain lack of self-determination at work may be at the root of workplace violence. Although less intuitive, the directionality of SDT-violence relationships can be seen as a chicken-and-egg situation. Indeed, although not abundant, some empirical and theoretical evidence suggests that violence may also have a real impact on individuals' self-determination and motivation, suggesting a feedback loop. In an effort to better understand the dynamic processes that may be involved in workplace violence, we focus in this section on presenting the effects of workplace violence on practices supporting autonomy, fulfillment of basic needs, and motivation of individuals.

EFFECT OF WORKPLACE VIOLENCE ON THE WORK ENVIRONMENT

Although the impact of workplace violence on autonomy-supportive or controlling practices has been little studied within SDT, we know that when confronted with violence, we tend to restrict the individual freedoms of the offenders (Moller & Deci, 2010). We therefore assume that authority figures, such has managers, will tend to control more closely the behavior of persons acting violently in order to minimize their impact on the work environment. Other indirect evidence suggests the negative impact of workplace violence: one study empirically showed that interpersonal conflicts on the job are related to low social support and low decision latitude among young adults (Fitzgerald, Kolodner, & Ewart, 2003).

EFFECT OF WORKPLACE VIOLENCE ON BASIC NEEDS

The detrimental effect of violence on the fulfillment of basic needs was observed in a variety of settings and among diverse populations, such as refugees exposed to civil war and violence (Zuniga, 2002), children exposed to domestic violence or psychological maltreatment (Rossman & Rosenberg, 1991, 1997), and children living in violent communities (Akande, 2001). Specific to the workplace, some indirect evidence suggests that violence affects all three basic psychological needs proposed by SDT, although this research question remains to be addressed. Regarding the need for relatedness, it was observed that bullying involves social isolation, social stigmatization, and social maladaptation for the victims (Leymann, 1990, 1996), which are all elements impeding good interpersonal relationships. Workplace violence may also affect fulfillment of the need for autonomy. For example, it is known in this regard that in environments where interpersonal conflicts (an important correlate of workplace violence) are ubiquitous, workers report less job control (Fitzgerald, Haythornthwaite, et al., 2003). Furthermore, violence may affect the need for competence: a study by Deans (2004) showed that occupational violence had a negative impact on perceived sense of competence, especially when perceived organizational support was low. Another study revealed that exposure to bullying diminishes self-esteem among nurses (Randle, 2003). Generally speaking, workplace bullying impacts negatively on self-esteem and self-confidence (see Einarsen, 2000 for a summary).

EFFECT OF WORKPLACE VIOLENCE ON MOTIVATION

In addition to impeding the satisfaction of basic needs, workplace violence may affect the motivation of individuals exposed to it. Indeed, it has been shown in several studies that nurses who are victims of workplace psychological violence have, among many other consequences, low motivation at work (Einarsen, 2000; Yildirim, 2009). In addition, Gagné and Schabram (2011) demonstrated that autonomous, but not controlled, motivation is directly impacted by physical and psychological violence in the workplace. Little is known about how various forms of motivation are affected by workplace violence, but this would be an interesting avenue for further investigation.

Where Do We Go From Here?
State of Knowledge

The literature review has shown links between violence and the main concepts of SDT in the work environment. Although most studies have not specifically focused on components of SDT in relation to violence *at work*, this chapter allows linking SDT with violence in other life domains, as well as associating SDT-related concepts to various forms of workplace violence. Furthermore, we may suggest from the literature review that SDT components and violence have, for the most part, bidirectional relationships. Figure 18.2 summarizes SDT-violence relationships identified to date.

As the reader can see in Figure 18.2, only one relationship between workplace violence and some SDT components (in this case, autonomous motivation) is supported through what we call *direct evidence* (represented by the *black arrow*), findings that (1) have been tested empirically, (2) are obtained within an organizational setting, and (3) derive from an SDT framework and the operationalization of SDT variables.

The vast majority of the relationships identified in this literature review are supported through *indirect evidence* (represented by the *grey arrow*), empirical demonstrations relying on *either* an SDT framework and the operationalization of SDT variables, but in a life domain other than work (e.g., violence in marital relationship) or the investigation of violence in the workplace specifically, but are not supported by any SDT theoretical foundations. In either case, conclusions relying on indirect evidence should be further validated as to their generalizability to workplace violence and its relationship with key SDT concepts.

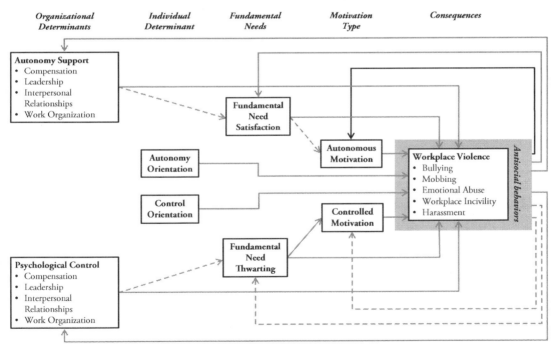

Fig. 18.2. Summary of empirical links documented and postulated between SDT key components and workplace violence.

Finally, some direct and indirect (mediation) effects appeared to be theoretically coherent with SDT assumptions, but we did not find empirical findings to support such effects. Hence, we hypothesize their existence (see *dashed grey arrows*), but these links remain to be tested in the context of workplace violence.

Some Future Research Avenues

Based on the literature from various research fields and theoretical frameworks, the empirical results discussed above can be considered as preliminary evidence showing how SDT could be used in future research on violence to help understand this problem and develop interventions. To better understand the phenomenon of workplace violence through the innovative lens of SDT, several avenues of research may be considered. A necessary first step is to validate, in an organizational context, all components of the SDT-violence model proposed in Figure 18.2. Indeed, the few studies available to date either measure SDT components in contexts of violence outside of work, or measure proxies of SDT concepts related to various forms of workplace violence or its correlates. A more systematic empirical investigation would help validate the postulated links beyond the indirect evidence allowing us to suggest their existence. For example, the link between motivation and violence at work has only been studied once within the framework of SDT (Gagné & Schabram, 2011), where various forms of motivation (from controlled to self-determined) were shown to lead to quite different consequences. In addition, it is possible to integrate recent refinements of SDT in the study of workplace violence. In particular, some authors (e.g., Bartholomew, Ntoumanis, Ryan, & Thøgersen-Ntoumani, 2011) have suggested that *thwarting* of the three psychological needs does not equal an absence of their *satisfaction*. Consequently, the intrapsychic processes involved in the emergence of phenomena, such as workplace violence, may be affected differentially, and this is a promising avenue for further investigation.

Second, most of the studies reviewed in this chapter examine direct relationships between the concepts, but there is reason to believe that, in addition to these direct links, there are several mediation effects that may contribute to explaining the phenomenon. For example, several researchers in SDT have proposed the sequence "autonomy support → basic needs satisfaction → autonomous motivation → positive consequences." We hypothesize that this process, mainly used until now to predict positive results, can also apply to negative results, such as workplace violence. Another avenue of research, therefore, would be to investigate the process by which violence occurs at work according to the full process of self-determination.

In terms of a dynamic process, the preliminary evidence identified in this chapter suggests that SDT components and violence may mutually influence one another through a feedback loop, as seen in Figure 18.2. Although the concept of violence as the result of exogenous factors has been a subject of great interest in the literature, this observation does not refute the possibility that violence is also a determinant of certain aspects of SDT, including work motivation, satisfaction/frustration of basic psychological needs, and psychological control in the work environment. Given the correlational research design of the surveyed studies, we cannot conclude, beyond conceptual foundations, that the phenomenon of workplace violence relies on a unidirectional relationship alone. In the absence of more extensive literature on the process by which SDT components influence violence and vice versa, we are faced with a chicken-and-egg situation, which merits further empirical investigation. To this end, the "causality" of the postulated relationships may be examined using longitudinal research designs and quasiexperimental studies to better document the process connecting SDT and workplace violence.

The study of workplace violence in itself raises interesting research avenues when considering the issue from an SDT perspective. For example, are the consequences of workplace violence on need satisfaction and work motivation different for perpetrators, victims, and witnesses? Do some working conditions or interpersonal parameters at work, by their various effects on employees' basic psychological needs, lead to the emergence of different types of workplace violence? Do different forms of violent manifestations in the workplace have differential effects on the victims or witnesses? Do other undesirable behaviors that cannot be classified as workplace violence but are nevertheless aggressive (e.g., counterproductive behaviors toward the organization) have an effect on motivation or need satisfaction of the victims or witnesses? It is too early to suggest formal hypotheses on such issues, but there are vast opportunities to investigate the relationships between the various components of SDT and workplace violence.

In sum, in light of the current state of knowledge, much remains to be done to investigate the

SDT-workplace violence relationship. In the coming years, the current effervescence of research on workplace violence would therefore benefit from considering more closely the importance of the sociocognitive mechanisms suggested by SDT to better understand the factors involved in the emergence and maintenance of violence and its impact on individuals and organizations. These future studies may eventually be an opportunity to test the effectiveness of intervention mechanisms based on SDT, because the central goal of this research field remains to provide helpful knowledge on preventing and promptly correcting such misconduct.

Overview of Interventions to Prevent Workplace Violence

Many countries, nations, and workers' rights organizations defend, by various means, the right for employees to work in a supportive environment that is protective of their health and safety. All organizations have the responsibility to prevent and counter negative behavior, such as violence, which threatens this right. To this end, much documentation deals with best practices for preventing and controlling violence in organizations. This section summarizes the contributions of these generally accepted practices, and suggests avenues for intervention that can be implemented in light of current knowledge on the links between SDT and violence.

Best Practices in Violence Prevention

The responsibility for preventing and managing violence in the workplace lies especially with managers, who must strive to take all necessary means to prevent and effectively manage violent situations (Balicco, 2001; Wheeler et al., 2010). It is generally accepted that to do so, managers themselves must often overcome two barriers: denial (e.g., "harassment does not exist here") and fear of the consequences of an intervention (e.g., reprisals, departure of a strategic member of the organization). The first step involves recognizing the significance of the problem and the need for *all* personnel to be accountable in this regard, particularly those responsible for these actions (Tengilimoğlu, Mansur, & Dziegielewski, 2010). Such a commitment becomes an essential condition for success in order to send a clear message about the importance of this issue and to clarify expectations regarding conduct for each and every one (Wheeler et al., 2010). This commitment may be reflected, in particular, by adopting normative codes of conduct, such as antiharassment policies (Baillien, De Cuyper, & De White,

2009; Chappell & Di Martino, 2006; Harvey & Courcy, 2005).

Operationally, it is recommended to translate this normative framework into mechanisms of reporting (i.e., complaint filing), prevention, and rapid intervention by immediate supervisors or heads of specialized departments (see Chappell & Di Martino, 2006 for a detailed review). Establishing a supportive work environment, providing adequate resources to reduce job-related stress, adopting "zero-tolerance anti-bullying" policies, and ensuring that perpetrators are accountable for their actions, also appear to be best practices for reducing bullying and violence (Wheeler et al., 2010). According to Baillien and De Witte (2009), companies must address job-related stress issues by reducing job-based role overload, ambiguity, and conflict, to reduce workplace violence. Fox and Stallworth (2009) specifically recommend such practices as training managers in mediation. Keashly and Neuman (2008) also recommend that companies use mentoring or coaching programs. Mentoring and coaching are used in this context as a mechanism to identify employee problems, such as bullying. If employees trust their mentors or coaches, they will likely report workplace bullying behaviors to them as soon as these behaviors are experienced or witnessed.

These recommendations stress the important role of managers and their management practices in the conduct of team members. Employees need to feel the support of their managers (Tuckett, Parker, Eley, & Hegney, 2009). As such, one way to reduce aggression is for managers to provide a reasonable and complete explanation for decisions affecting employees, in order to increase the latter's sense of organizational fairness. Such explanation should include adequate information and data to support the decisions (e.g., employee evaluations and expectations). The manner in which these explanations are communicated is equally important. When managers encourage participation in decision processes that affect employees, they also communicate to employees that they respect and value their input (Hershcovis & Barling, 2006). Overall, these recommendations are not inconsistent with the practical implications of SDT.

Preventing Violence through a Self-Determination Approach

SDT can also provide a framework for reflection as well as useful avenues for interventions that connect with and expand on traditional recommendations for the prevention of workplace violence.

308 | UNDERSTANDING WORKPLACE VIOLENCE

Again, when confronted with violence, we generally tend to restrict the individual freedoms of the offenders (Moller & Deci, 2010). Accordingly, by adopting practices identified in the previous section—from termination, to disciplinary measures, and even to legal action—figures of authority would have more control over the behavior of aggressors. However, such practices may have adverse consequences and create a vicious circle in which the presence of workplace violence leads to increased psychological control, which in turn leads to more violence and incivility. In such a context, therefore, workplace violence appears to be a spiraling process, in which many different factors interact (Salin, 2003). In this sense, based on knowledge derived from SDT and the preliminary empirical evidence surveyed in this chapter, it is possible to schematize this process of (de)constructing violence through the lens of SDT as a downward spiral combining the behaviors of various actors in the workplace (Figure 18.3).

This theoretical heuristic quickly and eloquently enables practitioners and managers to understand the additive effects of measures for preventing and managing workplace violence. It is of course important to properly weigh the seriousness of violent acts against the effects of psychological control on aggressors before excluding all repressive measures, but this model helps demonstrate that if caught quickly, workplace violence can be reduced while avoiding undue psychological control of the perpetrators. That said, before suggesting such a model scientifically, further investigation must be conducted. Nonetheless, in light of the empirical findings identified above, several avenues of interventions may be suggested.

Fig. 18.3. Proposed model for the downward spiral of workplace violence, as seen from the perspective of SDT.

EVIDENCE-BASED RECOMMENDATIONS

In light of the literature review, it is possible to identify practices specifically based on SDT that are likely to have a positive impact on the prevalence and intensity of violent behavior at work. Although the intrapersonal influence of causality orientation cannot be easily modified in an organizational context directly, acting at the level of the work environment may offer the most effectiveness in this regard. Thus, SDT is consistent with traditional approaches of responding to violence, in that managers play a role of primary importance for employees; by adopting a management style supportive of employees and promoting a high-quality manager-subordinate relationship, managers ensure that the psychological needs of their employees are met, thereby reducing the risks of violence at work. Moreover, autonomy support seems to be "contagious": in one study, autonomy support by physicians supervising medical residents led the latter to adopt autonomy-supportive behaviors toward patients (Williams & Deci, 1996). Peers also have a role to play in promoting a climate of social support, which can be reinforced or encouraged by immediate supervisors and line managers. Although enlightening, these conclusions are not based on validated interventions but on the results of predictive studies; it is important, therefore, to bear in mind that these practices are related to a decrease in violence, but a causal relationship cannot be postulated.

INTERVENTIONS BASED ON SDT

To our knowledge, no interventions aimed at preventing or reducing violence using SDT have been developed or tested scientifically. Furthermore, studies have shown that management practices supporting self-determination, including those that seem to help reduce workplace violence, can be taught. Although only a few studies exist on the topic, it has been empirically shown that these practices can be taught in training programs with different populations (Deci, Connell, & Ryan, 1989; Reeve, 1998; Reeve, Jang, Carrell, Jeon, & Barch, 2004; Tessier, 2006). This opens the possibility for managers trained in autonomy support to become agents of workplace violence prevention. Through their management practices supporting autonomy and avoiding undue psychological control, they may act as multipliers in organizations.

Beyond training, it is difficult to identify with certitude the best methods and practices for effectively preventing the emergence of violent behavior at work. Certainly, control and suppression should be considered as a last resort because, although they neutralize the aggressors in the short term, these measures create in the medium and long term an interpersonal and social climate conducive to the re-emergence and maintenance of workplace violence. In this sense, both traditional approaches to violence prevention and SDT concur on the central role of managers and, more broadly, the work environment, in reducing these behaviors, which have serious consequences for organizations.

A Comparison of Traditional Workplace Violence Interventions and SDT-Derived Applications

Similarly to classical approaches of workplace violence prevention, SDT aims to reduce sources of frustration and enhance sources of satisfaction in the workplace. Classical approaches aim to define acceptable and unacceptable behaviors, and in most cases, these norms constitute a basis for prevention and corrective intervention. However, SDT brings an important nuance to these interventions by raising awareness about the possible negative side effects of controlling approaches on perpetrators. Based on SDT principles, both peers and supervisors should rely more heavily on preventive actions and early intervention when manifestations of violence first occur, and on fostering relationships and an environment that are strongly supportive. In such a perspective, dissuasion and sanctions would be last resorts for intervening in cases of workplace violence, for these appear to be short-term solutions to controlling the problem.

Conclusion

Even if one considers, a priori, that research on workplace violence stems from a scientific culture that is distinct from, even foreign to research on SDT, the links established to date between these two areas of research lead to several observations. The first is the need to better understand the determinants of human behavior to better grasp how harmful behavior, such as workplace violence, is adopted and maintained, in order to prevent it more effectively. Consequently, theoretical models and empirical studies to date suggest the relevance of further investigating the contribution of SDT in explaining violent behavior at work. These investigations would help better define the role of SDT in predicting such behavior, but also identify mechanisms of prevention, such as promoting self-determination, and assess their effectiveness. Both the scientific

community and professionals who, for now, are all too often confined to normative and coercive measures, would certainly welcome such contributions.

Note

1. Preparation of this presentation was made possible by a grant to the first author from the Université de Sherbrooke. The authors thank Roxanne Gingras for her assistance on the preparation of this chapter, and Jeffrey Freedman for linguistic revision.

References

Akande, A. (2001). A way of being: A program for aggression control of male children. *Early Child Development and Care*, *167*, 127–148.

Andersson, L. M., & Pearson, C. M. (1999). Tit for tat? The spiraling effect of incivility in the workplace. *Academy of Management Review*, *24*(3), 452–471.

Aquino, K., Grover, S. L., Bradfield, M., & Allen, D. G. (1999). The effects of negative affectivity, hierarchical status, and self-determination on workplace victimization. *Academy of Management Journal*, *42*(3), 260–272.

Association of Women for Action and Research (2011). Workplace sexual harassment. Retrieved from http://www.aware.org.sg/ati/wsh-site/14-statistics/

Baard, P. P., Deci, E. L., & Ryan, R. M. (2004). Intrinsic need satisfaction: A motivational basis of performance and well-being in two work settings. *Journal of Applied Psychology*, *34*(10), 2045–2068.

Baillien, E., De Cuyper, N., & De White, H. (2009). Job autonomy and workload as antecedents of workplace bullying: A two-wave test of Karasek's Job Demand Control Model for targets and perpetrators. *Journal of occupational and organizational psychology*, *84*, 191–208.

Baillien, E., & De Witte, H. (2009). Why is organizational change related to workplace bullying? Role conflict and job insecurity as mediators. *Economic and Industrial Democracy*, *30*, 348–371.

Baldwin, J. D., & Baldwin, J. I. (1981). *Beyond sociobiology*. New York: Elsevier.

Balicco, C. (2001). *Pour en finir avec le harcèlement psychologique [To end psychological harassment]*. Paris: Éditions d'organisation.

Bandura, A. (1973). *Aggression: A social learning analysis*. Englewood Cliffs, NJ: Prentice-Hall.

Baron, R. A., & Richardson, D. R. (1994). *Human aggression*. New York: Plenum Press.

Bartholomew, K. J., Ntoumanis, N., Ryan, R. M., & Thøgersen-Ntoumani, C. (2011). Psychological need thwarting in the sport context: Assessing the darker side of athletic experience. *Journal of Sport & Exercise Psychology*, *33*, 75–102.

Berkowitz, L. (1965). The concept of aggressive drive: Some additional considerations. In L. Berkowitz (Ed.), *Advances in experimental social psychology* (vol. 2, pp. 301–329). New York: Academic Press.

Berkowitz, L. (1969). The frustration-aggression hypothesis revisited. In L. Berkowitz (Ed.), *Roots of aggression* (pp. 1–28). New York: Atherton Press.

Berkowitz, L. (1983). The experience of anger as a parallel process in the display of impulsive, "angry" aggression. In R. G. Geen, & E. I. Donnerstein (Eds.), *Aggression: Theoretical and empirical reviews* (vol. 1, pp. 103–133). Orlando, FL: Academic Press.

Berkowitz, L. (1988). Frustrations, appraisals, and aversively stimulated aggression. *Aggressive Behavior, 14*(1), 3–11.

Berkowitz, L. (1989). Frustration-aggression hypothesis: Examination and reformulation. *Psychological Bulletin, 106*(1), 59–73.

Berkowitz, L. (1993). *Aggression: Its causes, consequences and control.* Philadelphia, PA: Temple University Press.

Black, A. E., & Deci, E. L. (2000). The effects of instructors' autonomy support and students' autonomous motivation on learning organic chemistry: A self-determination theory perspective. *Science Education, 84*(6), 740–756.

Blau, G., & Andersson, L. (2005). Testing a measure of instigated workplace incivility. *Journal of Occupational and Organizational Psychology, 78*, 595–614.

Brunet, L., & Savoie, A. (2003). *La face cachée de l'organisation: Groupes, cliques et clans. [The hidden face of organizations: Groups, cliques, and clans].* Montréal, Canada: Les Presses de l'Université de Montréal.

Buss, A. H. (1961). *The psychology of aggression.* New York: John Wiley & Sons.

Caponecchia, C., & Wyatt, A. (2011). *Preventing workplace bullying: An evidence-based guide for managers and employees.* New York: Routledge.

Chappell, D., & Di Martino, V. (2006). *Violence at work* (3rd ed.). Geneva, Switzerland: International Labour Office.

Chullen, C. L., Dunford, B. B., Angermeier, I., Boss, R. W., & Boss, A. D. (2010). Minimizing deviant behavior in healthcare organizations: The effects of supportive leadership and job design. *Journal of Healthcare Management, 55*(6), 381–397.

Courcy, F., Savoie, A., & Brunet, L. (2009). *Violences au travail: diagnostic et prévention [Violences at work: Diagnostic & prevention].* Montréal, Canada: Les Presses de l'Université de Montréal.

Deans, C. (2004). Nurses and occupational violence: The role of organisational support in moderating professional competence. *The Australian Journal of Advanced Nursing: A Quarterly Publication of the Royal Australian Nursing Federation, 22*(2), 14–18.

Deci, E. L., Connell, J. P., & Ryan, R. M. (1989). Self-determination in a work organization. *Journal of Applied Psychology, 74*(4), 580–590.

Deci, E. L., Koestner, R., & Ryan, R. M. (1999). A meta-analytic review of experiments examining the effects of extrinsic rewards on intrinsic motivation. *Psychological Bulletin, 125*(6), 627–668.

Deci, E. L., & Ryan, R. M. (1985). The general causality orientations scale: Self-determination in personality. *Journal of Research in Personality, 19*(2), 109–134.

Deci, E. L. & Ryan, R. M. (1987). The support of autonomy and the control of behavior. *Journal of Personality & Social Psychology, 53*, 1024–1037.

Deci, E. L., & Ryan, R. M. (2000). The "what" and "why" of goal pursuits: Human needs and the self-determination of behavior. *Psychological Inquiry, 11*(4), 227–268.

De Léséleuc, S. (2004). *Criminal victimization in the workplace (Report No. 85F0033MIF).* Ottawa, Canada: Statistics Canada.

Djurkovic, N., McCormack, D., & Casimir, G. (2008). Workplace bullying and intention to leave: The moderating effect of perceived organisational support. *Human Resource Management Journal, 18*(4), 405–422.

Dollard, J., Doob, L., Miller, N., Mowrer, O. H., & Sears, R. R. (1939). *Frustration and aggression.* New Haven, CT: Yale University Press.

Einarsen, S. (2000). Harassment and bullying at work: A review of the Scandinavian approach. *Aggression and Violent Behavior, 5*(4), 379–401.

European Agency for Safety and Health at Work (2005). *European Survey of Enterprises on New and Emerging Risks: Managing safety and health at work.* Bilbao, Spain: European Agency for Safety and Health at Work.

Felson, R. B. (2006). Violence as instrumental behavior. In E. K. Kelloway, J. Barling, & J. Hurrell, Jr. (Eds). *Handbook of workplace violence.* Thousand Oaks, CA: Sage.

Feshbach, S. (1964). The function of aggression and the regulation of aggressive drive. *Psychological Review, 71*, 257–272.

Fitzgerald, S. T., Haythornthwaite, J. A., Suchday, S., & Ewart, C. K. (2003). Anger in young black and white workers: Effects of job control, dissatisfaction, and support. *Journal of Behavioral Medicine, 26*(4), 283–296.

Fitzgerald, S. T., Kolodner, K. B., & Ewart, C. K. (2003). *Adolescent personality characteristics: Predictors of markers of job stress.* Washington, DC: American Psychological Association, Public Interest Directorate.

Forest, J., Crevier-Braud, L., Gagné, M. (2009). Mieux comprendre la motivation au travail [Understanding workplace motivation]. *Effectif, 12*(3), 23–27.

Fox, S., & Spector, P. E. (1999). A model of work frustration-aggression. *Journal of Organizational Behavior, 20*, 915–931.

Fox, S., & Stallworth, L. (2009). Building a framework for two internal organizational approaches to resolving and preventing workplace bullying: Alternative dispute resolution and training. *Consulting Psychology Journal: Practice and Research, 61*, 220–241.

Freud, S. (1920). *A general introduction to psycho-analysis.* New-York: Boni & Liveright.

Gagné, M., & Deci, E. L. (2005). Self-determination theory and work motivation. *Journal of Organizational Behavior, 26*(4), 331–362.

Gagné, M., & Forest, J. (2008). The study of compensation systems through the lens of self-determination theory: Reconciling 35 years of debate. *Canadian Psychology, 49*, 225–232.

Gagné, M., & Forest, J. (2009). La motivation au travail selon la théorie de l'autodétermination [Workplace motivation according to self-determination theory]. In J. Rojot, C. Vandenberghe, & P. Roussel (Eds.), *Théories des organisations, motivation au travail, engagement dans l'organisation* (3rd ed.). Belgique: De Boeck.

Gagné, M., & Schabram, K. (2011). Relations between perceptions of workplace violence and psychological health: A motivational look. Paper presented at the 27th Annual Conference of the Society for Industrial and Organizational Psychology, San Diego, CA.

Gagné, M., Senecal, C., & Koestner, R. (1997). Proximal job characteristics, feelings of empowerment, and intrinsic motivation: A multidimensional model. *Journal of Applied Social Psychology, 27*, 1222–1240.

Geen, R. G. (1991). *Human aggression.* Pacific Grove, CA: Brooks/Cole.

Giacalone, R. A., & Greenberg, J. (1997). *Antisocial behavior in organizations.* Thousand Oaks, CA: Sage Publications.

Gould, S. J. (1978). Biological potential versus biological determinism. In A. L. Caplan (Ed.), *The sociobiology debate* (pp. 343–354). New York: Harper & Row.

Greenberg, J. (2010). *Insidious workplace behavior*. New York: Routledge.

Griffin, R. W., & Lopez, Y. P. (2005). "Bad behavior" in organizations: A review and typology for future research. *Journal of Management, 31*, 988–1005.

Hackman, J. R., & Oldham, G. R. (1975). Development of the Job Diagnostic Survey. *Journal of Applied Psychology, 60*, 159–170.

Harvey, S., & Courcy, F. (2005). Psychological hostility in the workplace: Seeking change through human resource policies and organizational culture. *International Journal of Business Research, 2*(1), 42–48.

Hauge, L. J., Skogstad, A., & Einarsen, S. (2009). Individual and situational predictors of workplace bullying: Why do perpetrators engage in the bullying of others? *Work & Stress, 23*(4), 349–358.

Hershcovis, M. S., & Barling, J. (2006). Preventing insider-initiated workplace violence. In E. K. Kelloway, J. Barling, & J. J. J. Hurrell (Eds.), *Handbook of workplace violence* (pp. 617–621). Thousand Oaks, CA: Sage Publications.

Hodgins, H. S., Koestner, R., & Duncan, N. (1996). On the compatibility of autonomy and relatedness. *Personality and Social Psychology Bulletin, 22*, 227–237.

Hodgins, H. S., Liebeskind, E., & Schwartz, W. (1996). Getting out of hot water: Facework in social predicaments. *Journal of Personality and Social Psychology, 71*, 300–314.

Hodson, R., Roscigno, V. J., & Lopez, S. H. (2006). Chaos and the abuse of power: Workplace bullying in organizational and interactional context. *Work and Occupations, 33*(4), 382–416.

Hoel, H., & Cooper, C. (2000). *Destructive conflict and bullying at work*. Manchester, UK: University of Manchester, Institute of Science and Technology.

Hoel, H., Glasø, L., Hetland, J., Cooper, C. L., & Einarsen, S. (2010). Leadership styles as predictors of self-reported and observed workplace bullying. *British Journal of Management, 21*(2), 453–468.

Hove, M. C., Parkhill, M. R., Neighbors, C., McConchie, J. M., & Fossos, N. (2010). Alcohol consumption and intimate partner violence perpetration among college students: The role of self-determination. *Journal of Studies on Alcohol and Drugs, 71*(1), 78–85.

Keashly, L., & Neuman, J. H. (2008). *Final report: Workplace behaviour (bullying) project survey*. Mankato, MN: Minnesota State University-Mankato.

Keashly, L., Trott, V., & MacLean, L. M. (1994). Abusive behavior in the workplace: A preliminary investigation. *Violence and Victims, 9*, 341–357

Kelloway, W. K., Barling, J., & Hurrel, J. H. Jr. (2006). *Handbook of workplace violence*. Thousand Oaks, CA: Sage Publications.

Knee, C. R., Neighbors, C., & Vietor, N. A. (2001). Self-determination theory as a framework for understanding road rage. *Journal of Applied Social Psychology, 31*(5), 889–904.

Koonin, M., & Green, T. M. (2004). The emotionally abusive workplace. *Journal of Emotional Abuse, 4*, 71–79.

Leblanc, M. M., & Barling, J. (2005). Understanding the many faces of violence. In S. Fox & P. E. Spector (Eds.), *Counterproductive work behavior: Investigations of actors and targets* (pp. 41–63). Washington, DC: American Psychological Association.

LeBlanc, M. M., & Kelloway, K. E. (2002). Predictors and outcomes of workplace violence and aggression. *Journal of Applied Psychology, 87*, 444–453.

Leymann, H. (1990). Mobbing and psychological terror at workplaces. *Violence and Victims, 5*(2), 119–126.

Leymann, H. (1996). The content and development of mobbing at work. *European Journal of Work and Organizational Psychology, 5*(2), 165–184.

Lian, H., Lance Ferris, D., & Brown, D. J. (2012). Does taking the good with the bad make things worse? How abusive supervision and leader-member exchange interact to impact need satisfaction and organizational deviance. *Organizational Behavior and Human Decision Processes, 117*(1), 41–52.

Lorenz, K. (1966). *On aggression*. New York: Bantam.

Lorenz, K. (1974). *Civilized man's eight deadly sins*. New York: Harcourt Brace Javanovich.

Mageau, G. A., & Vallerand, R. J. (2003). The coach-athlete relationship: A motivational model. *Journal of Sports Sciences, 21*, 883–904.

Martinko, M. J., & Zellars, K. L. (1996). Toward a theory of workplace violence and aggression: A cognitive appraisal perspective. In R. A. Giacalone, & J. Greenberg (Eds), *Antisocial behavior in organizations* (pp. 1–42). Thousand Oaks, CA: Sage Publications.

Merchant, J. A., & Lundell, J. A. (2001). Workplace violence intervention research workshop, April 5-7, 2000, Washington, DC: Background, rationale, and summary. *American Journal of Preventive Medicine, 20*, 135–140.

Milczarek, M. (2010). Workplace violence and harassment: A European picture. Luxembourg: Publications Office of the European Union. Retrieved from: http://osha.europa.eu/en/publications/reports/violence-harassment-TERO09010ENC

Millette, V., & Gagné, M. (2008). Designing volunteers' tasks to maximize motivation, satisfaction and performance: The impact of job characteristics on volunteer engagement. *Motivation and Emotion, 32*, 11–22.

Moller, A. C., & Deci, E. L. (2010). Interpersonal control, dehumanization, and violence: A self-determination theory perspective. *Group Processes & Intergroup Relations, 13*(1), 41–53.

Namie, G. (2010). The WBI U.S. Workplace Bullying Survey. Retrieved from http://workplacebullying.org/docs/WBI_2010_Natl_Survey.pdf

Neuman, J. H., & Baron, R. A. (1998). Workplace violence and workplace aggression: Evidence concerning specific forms, potential causes, and preferred targets. *Journal of Management, 24*(3), 391–419.

Neuman, J. H., & Keashly, L. (2010). Means, motive, opportunity, and aggressive workplace behavior. In J. Greenberg (Ed.), *Insidious workplace behavior* (pp. 31–76). New York: Routledge.

Ntoumanis, N., & Standage, M. (2009). Morality in sport: A self-determination theory perspective. *Journal of Applied Sport Psychology, 21*(4), 365–380.

O'Moore, M. (2000). *National survey on bullying in the workplace*. Dublin: Trinity College.

Packham, C. (2010). *Violence at work: Findings from the 2009/2010 British crime survey*. London, Great Britain: Health and Safety Executive.

Priest, A. (2006). Taming the beast: A look at the many forms and guises of workplace violence. *World of Work, 56*, 23–26.

Randle, J. (2003). Bullying in the nursing profession. *Journal of Advanced Nursing, 43*(4), 395–401.

Rayner, C., Hoel, H., & Cooper, C. L. (2002). *Workplace bullying: What we know, who is to blame, and what can we do?* London, England: Taylor & Francis.

Reeve, J. (1998). Autonomy support as an interpersonal motivating style: Is it teachable? *Contemporary Educational Psychology, 23*, 321–330.

Reeve, J., Jang, H., Carrell, D., Jeon, S., & Barch, J. (2004). Enhancing students' engagement by increasing teachers' autonomy support. *Motivation and Emotion, 28*, 147–168.

Rioux, P., Roberge, M.-E., Brunet, L., Savoie, A., & Courcy, F. (2005). Établissement d'une nouvelle classification des comportements antisociaux au travail [Development of a new classification of antisocial workplace behaviors]. *Interactions, 9*, 85–115.

Robinson, S. L., & Bennett, R. J. (1995). A typology of deviant workplace behaviors: A multidimensional scaling study. *Academy of Management Journal, 38*, 555–572.

Rossman, B. B. R., & Rosenberg, M. S. (1991, June). *Current research & future directions on children in abusive families.* Paper presented at the American Psychological Association Annual Convention, San Francisco, CA.

Rossman, B. B. R., & Rosenberg, M. S. (1997). Psychological maltreatment: A needs analysis & application for children in violent families. In R. Geffner, S. B. Sorenson, & P. K. Lundberg-Love (Eds.), *Violence & sexual abuse at home: Current issues in spousal battering & child maltreatment* (pp. 245–262). Binghamton, NY: Haworth Press.

Salin, D. (2003). Ways of explaining workplace bullying: A review of enabling, motivating and precipitating structures and processes in the work environment. *Human Relations, 56*(10), 1213–1232.

Schwamb, J. (2005). *Exploring the school experience of students who bully: a look inside the classroom.* Dissertation Abstracts International Section A, 66, Retrieved from EBSCOhost.

Sharma, P. (2010, November). *India's first "Workplace Sexual Harassment Survey" reveals startling revelations.* Retrieved from http://www.release-news.com/index.php/society/47708-indias-first-workplace-sexual-harassment-survey-reveals-startling-revelations.html

Spector, P. E. (1978). Organizational frustration: A model and review of the literature. *Personnel Psychology, 31*, 815–829.

Sung, S. (2008). *Handling sexual harassment in the workplace.* Unpublished manuscript, Trinity Western University at Langley, BC, Canada.

Tengilimoğlu, D., Mansur, F. A., & Dziegielewski, S. F. (2010). The effect of the mobbing on organizational commitment in the hospital setting: A field study. *Journal of Social Service Research, 36*(2), 128–141.

Tepper, B. J. (2000). Consequences of abusive supervision. *Academy of Management Journal, 43*, 178–190.

Tessier, D. (2006). *Le climat motivationnel en éducation physique et sportive: Étude des antécédents des comportements contrôlants de l'enseignant et formation au soutien des besoins psychologiques des élèves* [The motivational climate in physical and sport education: A study of antecedents of teacher's controlling

behaviors and training for students' psychological need support]. (Unpublished doctoral dissertation). Université Joseph Fourier, Grenoble, France.

Tuckett, A., Parker, D., Eley, R. M., & Hegney, D. (2009). "I love nursing, but. . ."—Qualitative findings from Australian aged-care nurses about their intrinsic, extrinsic and social work values. *International Journal of Older People Nursing, 4*(4), 307–317.

U.S. Occupational Safety and Health Administration. (2002). OSHA fact sheet. Retrieved from http://www.osha.gov/OshDoc/data_General_Facts/factsheet-workplace-violence.pdf

Van Fleet, D. D., & Griffin, R. W. (2006). Dysfunctional organization culture: The role of leadership in motivating dysfunctional work behaviors. *Journal of Managerial Psychology, 21*(8), 698–708.

Vardi, Y., & Wiener, Y. (1996). Misbehavior in organizations: A motivational framework. *Organizational Science, 7*, 151–165.

Vartia, M. (1996). The sources of bullying—Psychological work environment and organizational climate. *European Journal of Work and Organizational Psychology, 5*(2), 203–214.

Weibel, A. A., Rost, K., & Osterloh, M. (2007). *Crowding-out of intrinsic motivation: Opening the black box.* Retrieved from http://ssrn.com/abstract=957770

Wheeler, A. R., Halbesleben, J. R. B., & Shanine, K. (2010). Eating their cake and everyone else's cake, too: Resources as the main ingredient to workplace bullying. *Business Horizons, 53*(6), 553–560.

Williams, G. C., & Deci, E. L. (1996). Internalization of biopsychosocial values by medical students: A test of self-determination theory. *Journal of Personality and Social Psychology, 70*, 767–779.

World Health Organization. (2002). *New research shows workplace violence threatens health services.* Retrieved from www.who.int/mediacentre/news/releases/release37/en/index.html

Yildirim, D. (2009). Bullying among nurses and its effects. *International Nursing Review, 56*(4), 504–511.

Zillmann, D. (1971). Excitation transfer in communication-mediated aggressive behavior. *Journal of Experimental Social Psychology, 7*, 419–434.

Zillmann, D. (1979). *Hostility and aggression.* Hillsdale, NJ: Erlbaum.

Zillmann, D. (1983a). Arousal and aggression. In R. G. Geen, & E. I. Donnerstein (Eds.), *Aggression: Theoretical and empirical reviews* (vol. 1, pp. 75–101). New York: Academic Press.

Zillmann, D. (1983b). Transfer of excitation in emotional behavior. In T. J. Cacciopo, & R. E. Petty (Eds.), *Social psychophysiology* (pp. 215–240). New York: Guilford Press.

Zillmann, D. (1988). Cognitive-excitation interdependencies in aggressive behavior. *Aggressive Behavior, 14*, 51–64.

Zuniga, M. E. (2002). Latino immigrants: Patterns of survival. *Journal of Human Behavior in the Social Environment, 5*(3–4), 137.

CHAPTER
19

Encouraging Environmental Actions in Employees and in the Working Environment: A Self-Determination Theory Perspective

Luc G. Pelletier *and* Nicole M. Aitken

Abstract

Many organizations have begun implementing a variety of programs and practices to diminish their environmental impact, including the adoption of environmental management systems to comply with new governmental policies, and specific initiatives, such as green purchasing, the design of products more friendly to the environment, recycling, and energy conservation practices. To improve their environmental performance, operations, products, services, and public image, organizations are increasingly interested in finding ways to encourage employees to take environmental action. In this chapter, using self-determination theory as a framework and recent research on proenvironmental behaviors, we increase the understanding of engagement in proenvironmental behaviors at work and explain the processes that facilitate such behavior at the employee level. In addition, we suggest tangible ways in which businesses, entrepreneurs, and managers can meaningfully foster autonomous motivation in their employees. Finally, we highlight future directions for research in the business and organization world.

Key Words: organization's environmental sustainability, employees' proenvironmental behavior, communication of information, working environment

---

Introduction

Industrialization over the last century has had a substantial negative impact on the natural environment due to extensive economic growth and increased quality of life in developed countries. In addition to the localized problems of air pollution, surface-water degradation, and toxic wastes in groundwater, we can now observe global scale effects, such as ozone depletion, climate change, and the worldwide destruction of such resources as ocean fisheries (World Resources Institute, 2004; United Nations, 2004). Environmental sustainability is becoming an important issue as increasing human consumption patterns, increasing population, and increasing industrializations are having a larger and larger impact on the exploitation of the earth's resources and quality of life (Swim, et al., 2009). The long-term economic impact of

these effects will be quite substantial as most of the world's economic output is dependent on the viability of natural systems (Costanza et al., 1997).

Environmental Sustainability and Economic Growth

Interest in environmental sustainability represents a significant shift in how people view the relationship between environmental problems, economic growth, and humanity's well-being. The current international scientific consensus is that human activities and the exploitation of natural resources are changing the climate at a planetary level, and that further effects are inevitable because both socioeconomic growth in developing countries and population growth are inevitable (Intergovernmental Panel on Climate Change, 2007). The United Nations Population Fund (2009) reported that, after growing very slowly for most of human history, the world's population has reached 6 billion in late 1999. In October 2011, the world population reached 7 billion, and it is expected to reach a total of 9.1 billion in 2050. The population increase expected in the next 40 years is close to the total world population in 1950. This dramatic growth in population will increase the number of inhabitants competing for the world's finite resources. If present patterns of exploitation continue, then the human activities needed to reach a high quality of life in both developed and developing countries will inevitably lead to an increase in climate change.

This serves to illustrate the complexity of the problem of sustainable development, and how closely tied it is to human activity and industrialization. In fact, many other environmental problems—such as the rise of air pollution, the reduction of clean water supplies, the depletion of the Earth's ozone layer, and the clearing of tropical rain forests—are the direct result of human activities that were initially designed to improve humanity's well-being, generate economic growth, and correct socioeconomic disparities like low quality of life (Gardner & Stern, 2002; Hopwood, Mellor, & O'Brien, 2005).

The process of bringing together environmental issues, economic growth, and humanity's well-being is the central idea encapsulated in the Brundtland Report's definition of environmental sustainability—as meeting the needs of the present without compromising the ability of future generations to meet their needs (World Commission on Economic Development, 1987). Although it is increasingly clear that human activities cause climate change, the solutions that have thus far been proposed simply involve trade-offs between environmental, economical, and social concerns. For instance, is it acceptable to cause large-scale pollution when one's country is using tar sands in order to produce energy, stimulate the economy, and increase growth? Or is the loss of jobs in the car industry acceptable for cleaner air? In other words, the proposed strategies ignore the fact that a sustainable future can only be achieved through a substantial shift in the values, attitudes, and behaviors of the individuals and institutions that caused the harm to the environment (McKenzie-Mohr & Oskamp, 1995). The current environmental situation has made many people and entrepreneurs realize that sustainable development needs to be a central goal of society and its institutions. The achievement of this goal is extremely difficult and complex because it is intertwined with competing socioeconomic and well-being goals.

The Role of the Corporate World

The role of the corporate world and entrepreneurship in dealing with the problems of environmental sustainability has been the subject of some debate over the last 20 years. For some entrepreneurs the relationship between environmental practices and corporate performance is quite simple: pursuing environmental goals is inversely related to sound business strategy. Conventional wisdom held that any investment in improved environmental performance would increase lead times, reduce quality, or increase costs, all of which would lead to reduced profits and decreased returns to stakeholders. Some would go as far as saying that the economic system motivates environmentally degrading behaviors for the purpose of creating economic growth and it prevents entrepreneurial action from resolving environmental problems (Tietenberg, 2000).

In contrast, opportunities for entrepreneurial action have been created due to individuals in the marketplace who desire the cessation of environmentally degrading products and are willing to pay. This type of entrepreneurial action can lead to an enhancement of environmental sustainability (Schaltegger & Synnestvedt, 2002). Compared with an entrepreneurship driven only by profits, a sustainable entrepreneurship seeks to reduce environmental degradation and even to achieve environmental sustainability through the exploitation of potentially profitable opportunities (Dean & McMullen, 2005).

Since the beginning of the 21st century more and more entrepreneurs are seeing the possibility that profitability and environmental responsibility are not mutually exclusive goals. As more corporations now embrace the goal of sustainable development, they commit to policies of environmental protection and they devote substantial time and resources to environmental management, either through the application of quality environmental management processes or through the design of products and manufacturing technologies. As a result, increasingly proenvironmental corporations are searching for ways to encourage employees to take actions that reduce their ecological footprint, and improve the environmental impact of company operations, products, and services. Although it is not always apparent to managers how to encourage creative environmental ideas, to help their business move toward this goal of sustainable development, they believe that different forms of environmental interventions are necessary to transform business into sustainable enterprises (Ramus, 2002).

There are many ways to create proenvironmental change, to build a more sustainable future for business and the world. Companies themselves can create change by investing in greener technology, developing sustainable business practices, or doing business in one of the emerging environmental domains (e.g., build electric cars, recycling materials to create new products). A second way to create proenvironmental change is through individual behavior change. Individual proenvironmental behavior (PEB), in this case employee behavior, can have a large positive impact on the environment (Statistics Canada, 2011).

In other words, there are different ways that businesses impact the environment, ranging from the type of business to the type of employee behavior. Some businesses can improve the environmental situation while making a profit from protecting the environment (e.g., solar panel production, sustainable lumber, recycled carpet). Although not all businesses can derive their profit from protecting the earth, they can still have a positive impact on the environment through the behaviors of employees. Businesses and companies are an important place to target personal PEB change, regardless of the type of business, because many consume a large amount of energy, they produce large amounts of waste, and sometimes they exploit large amounts of natural resources. In sum, they have very significant ecological footprints that can effectively be reduced with employee PEB.

Why Do Business and Companies Adopt Environmental Practices?

Understanding why and how firms adopt beyond-compliance environmental practices is a critically important question to understand the type of organizational support necessary to encourage environmental actions. Participation in a voluntary environmental program may provide financial savings (Maxwell & Decker, 2006) or competitive advantage (Arora & Cason, 1996), enable access to technical assistance (Khanna, 2001; Delmas & Keller, 2005), help firms weaken regulations (Segerson & Miceli, 1998; Lyon & Maxwell, 2002; Johnston, 2006), or shape future regulations (Delmas & Terlaak, 2001). Further, participation may create an image of environmental friendliness for customers, suppliers, employees, or the public (Khanna, 2001; Potoski & Prakash, 2002), and demonstrate a firm's responsiveness to community and employee concerns (Henriques & Sadorsky, 1996; Blackman & Bannister, 1998; Gunningham, Thornton, & Kagan,

2005). These reasons, however, may be contingent on several factors including the firm's competitive environment; exposure to regulatory or technological change; and the actions or demands of customers, investors, and community groups (Arora & Cason, 1996; Reinhardt, 2000; Vogel, 2005).

Missing from much of this work on the reasons for environmental practice is a theoretical approach grounded in the literature on motivation. Without a theoretical framework, we are left with at best a partial sense of where a particular environmental management style comes from, why one style is distinct from another, and whether a particular style will lead to changes that endure over time (Howard-Grenville, 2005). Indeed, without refinement and theoretical understanding of the reasons for adopting environmental practices, constructs like management style or motivation for PEB risk becoming catch-all categories.

In this chapter we suggest that the success of corporate environmental initiatives depends not just on government intervention and environment policy regulation, or on environmental management systems and technological innovations, but also on the willingness of individual employees to engage in PEBs that preserve or restore the quality of the natural environment (Boiral, 2009; Daily, Bishop, & Govindarajulu, 2009). In order to make progress toward sustainable development, we argue that a central target is the motivation of individual people, whether they are private citizens, managers, heads of industries, or leaders of governments. Using self-determination theory (SDT; Deci & Ryan, 1985, 2000, 2008) as a framework, we seek to increase the understanding of engagement in PEB at work and explain the processes that facilitate such behavior at the employee level. SDT provides a useful framework for organizing and understanding society's response to environmental sustainability, and most importantly for promoting PEB. This motivation theory can inform organizational practice by focusing on the role that environmental policies within an organization and supportive supervisory behaviors can have on the employees' motivation to engage in PEB and to attempt environmental initiatives. Also, SDT can inform us about the psychological processes that are needed for individuals to learn new environmentally responsible behaviors, adopt these behaviors, and more importantly, maintain them and integrate them into their lifestyles.

SDT and the Motivation for PEB

As was outlined in Chapter 1 of this book, SDT (Deci & Ryan, 1985, 2000, 2008) represents a theoretical perspective of human motivation that has received a great deal of attention from researchers over the last 20 years. SDT is particularly focused on the processes through which a person acquires different forms of motivation and the consequences that these forms of motivation have for the initiation and maintenance of new behaviors. SDT proposes that a sense of autonomy, competence, and relatedness are critical to the processes through which a person comes to self-regulate and sustain behaviors over time. Thus, contexts that afford autonomy and support confidence are likely to enhance the initiation of behavior, the maintenance of behavior, as well as the outcomes that people derive from doing these behaviors. A sense of relatedness is equally important for these processes to take place; a person is more likely to adopt values and behaviors promoted by those to whom they feel connected and in whom they trust.

Several behaviors that people do everyday are not necessarily inherently enjoyable activities (e.g., exercising, working, doing PEBs). Thus, if such behaviors are to be successfully performed and maintained over time, then people must come to value the behaviors and personally endorse their importance. These behaviors must somehow be regulated. Unfortunately, many people engage in behavior only because of controlled motivation.

As illustrated previously in this book, one common form of controlled motivation is external regulation, in which a person acts only to get an external reward or avoid a punishment. Another form of controlled motivation is introjection in which a person might act to receive approval or praise, or to avoid disapproval or feelings of guilt. Both forms of controlled motivation (external and introjected regulations) lead to less interest for a behavior, less well-being, and they are not related to long-term maintenance (Deci & Ryan, 2000).

In contrast, behavior initiation and behavior change can be a function of autonomous motivation. Because many PEBs are not enjoyable in and of themselves (i.e., intrinsically motivated) research has explored ways to motivate these instrumental behaviors. One form of autonomous motivation is identified regulation in which a person endorses or identifies with the value or importance of a behavior. Research shows that identification is facilitated when significant persons in our environment provide relevant information and meaningful rationales for a behavior (and that they do not apply external pressures or sources of control). A second form of autonomous motivation is integrated regulation, in which a person values a behavior and has also oriented this behavior with other central behaviors that are valued and part of a lifestyle pattern. The more autonomous the motivation the more a person behaves with positive freedom. The behavior originates with the self and the actions are "up to you." Conversely, controlled motivation involves behaving due to the experience of pressure or demands that are external to the self (i.e., nonautonomous). The actions are no longer truly "up to you."

Although the determinants of autonomous motivation have not been studied extensively, Deci and Ryan (2000) have proposed that this form of motivation can be facilitated by supporting people as they explore barriers to behavior change and maintenance of behavior, and by helping them to identify ways to reconcile behaviors that lead to goals that are in conflict. Both forms of autonomous behavior regulations (identified and integrated regulations) are associated with enhanced maintenance and well-being (Deci & Ryan, 2000).

Along with a sense of autonomy, autonomous motivation requires that a person experience the confidence and the competence to adopt and maintain a behavior. Support for competence is afforded by providing information on the efficacy of behaviors to achieve a significant or personally relevant goal and by providing feedback that informs individuals on the extent to which actions were efficacious to achieving a desired goal. This way a person is afforded the skills and tools for doing a behavior and is informed when these skills and tools are effective or when barriers emerge.

A social context that involves a supervisor-supervisee relationship is an important medium for change. In the working environment this is especially so, because employees often look for technical expertise, input, and guidance from their supervisor to determine how a behavior should be performed, why it should be performed, and which behavior is valued. In this process, a sense of being understood and respected by their supervisor or their employer can significantly enhance employees' openness to information, likelihood of following instructions, as well as their adherence to recommendations and proposed goals.

Several studies have documented the advantages of autonomous motivation, relative to controlled motivation, when it comes to persistence, maintenance of behavior, information processing, and well-being (Deci & Ryan, 2008); the domain of the environment is no exception. More specifically, SDT holds the potential to significantly contribute to our understanding of the issues related to environmentally responsible behaviors for several reasons. First, it presents clear hypotheses regarding the social, contextual, and interpersonal conditions that should hinder or facilitate individuals' motivation to adopt a new environmentally responsible behavior. Second, it distinguishes between different types of motivation that can have a distinct impact on the maintenance and integration of behaviors. Third, SDT addresses the issue of internalization, the process by which changes that were initially reinforced by external sources (e.g., incentives or a significant other) become integrated within the individual to form a permanent part of his or her character. Fourth, it provides the mechanics for the process by which people, and more specifically for the purpose of the present discussion, employees, could internalize PEB and even resolve conflicts that could result from pursuing different goals.

Also, SDT has been very useful in explaining why some environmental strategies are problematic or ineffective in motivating PEB, and why some people may be motivated at first to do PEB, but do not maintain the behavior over time. Among others, the strategies used so far to motivate people have relied on monetary incentives; external forms of pressures, such as laws and regulations; a sense of guilt; information that emphasizes the importance of doing something to achieve extrinsic goals (e.g., to save money, to fit in); or information that emphasizes only the importance of doing something without educating people about what they need to do and how they should do a behavior. As a result, research shows that most of the strategies used so far can lead to the initiation of PEB, but long-term maintenance of these behaviors remains a serious problem (Bamberg & Möser, 2007). People seem to react positively to the strategies initially, but their behavior declines over time, and, more importantly, behavior returns to baseline if the source of "motivation" is withdrawn (Lehman & Geller, 2004).

There are several reviews of proenvironmental promotion research (Osbaldiston, 2004; Pelletier, 2002; Pelletier, Baxter, & Huta, 2011; Pelletier, Lavergne, & Sharp, 2008; Pelletier & Sharp, 2008) that have focused on the different ways SDT can contribute to our understanding of the motivation for PEB and the factors that could affect motivation. This chapter looks at the research related to these contributions and applies the findings to the context of the workplace and motivating employee PEB change.

Participating in PEB

Following the development of a scale designed to measure proenvironmental motivation (Pelletier, Green-Demers, & Béland, 1997; Pelletier, Tuson, Green-Demers, Noels, & Beaton, 1998), recent studies have supported the existence of the different types of motivation proposed by SDT (i.e., intrinsic motivation; integrated, identified, introjected, and external regulation of extrinsic motivation; amotivation) in the environmental context (Osbaldiston & Sheldon, 2003; Pelletier, 2002; Villacorta, Koestner, & Lekes, 2003). Consistent with research on SDT in other life domains, several studies have shown that different types of motivation were related to several PEBs (such as recycling, conserving energy, purchasing specific products, and others; Pelletier, et al., 1998; Villacorta, et al., 2003) and environmental activism (Séguin, Pelletier, & Hunsley, 1998). The more that people report being autonomous for PEB, more specifically having higher levels of integrated and identified regulation, not necessarily more intrinsic motivation, as compared with being controlled, the more likely they are to report a higher frequency of PEB. Pelletier and Sharp (2007) have also reported that higher levels of self-determined motivation for PEB were associated with higher maintenance of behavior over time (e.g., sustained recycling over 2 months), along with behavioral patterns consistent with adopting not only one behavior, but several behaviors (e.g., recycling, conserving energy, conserving water, and buying biodegradable products) that are indicative of becoming somebody that cares about the environment.

Some environmental strategies aim at making an activity more accessible (e.g., a curbside recycling program) and therefore easier to achieve. Recently, researchers have examined how self-determination relates to behaviors that have been made more easily accessible, behaviors for which barriers have been removed, and behaviors with different levels of difficulty.

In a first study, Green-Demers, Pelletier, and Ménard (1997) examined the impact of the perceived level of difficulty of environmental behaviors on the magnitude of the relationship between environmental self-determination and the occurrence of three types of PEB with an increasing level of difficulty (recycling, purchasing environmentally friendly products, and educating oneself about what can be done for the environment). The results showed (1) that frequency of behaviors was higher when self-determination was higher, and lower when behavioral difficulty was higher; (2) that the decrease in the frequency of self-reported PEB caused by the behavior's difficulty was less pronounced when people were self-determined; and (3) that the positive relationship between self-determination and frequencies of PEB was greater for more difficult PEB. In sum, participants reported doing easier PEB whatever their level of self-determined motivation; however, only self-determined people were more likely to do more difficult PEB.

In a second study, Pelletier and Sharp (2007) used a quasi experimental design and randomly selected residents of three municipalities to participate in a survey on motivation for PEB. The researchers recorded the household recycling of the residents and the frequency of other PEB. In one of the municipalities, residents had access to a curbside recycling program (easy recycling); in the second municipality, residents had access to a recycling program, but had to bring their recyclables to one of the available local municipal depots (moderate recycling); in the third municipality, residents did not have access to a local municipal recycling program, but could dispose of their recyclables by driving 20 minutes to the next municipality that had a local recycling program (difficult recycling). Thus, it was possible to isolate differences in the level of difficulty for the same behavior by examining the impact of the degree of self-determination and three levels of difficulty for recycling behavior on the amount of recycling. For the easy recycling condition, the quantity of recycling was not significantly different for self-determined and non–self-determined individuals. However, for the moderate condition, the amount of recycling for self-determined and non–self-determined individuals became significantly different, although both groups recycled less than participants in the easy condition. This trend held true for the difficult recycling condition as well, indicating that self-determined people recycled even when it was difficult.

In addition, analyses revealed that the ease of access to recycling had no relationship with the frequency of other PEB but frequency of PEB other than recycling was positively related to people's degree of self-determination. Apparently, the benefits of making recycling easier or accessible did not transfer to other PEB domains, whereas the benefits of self-determination did generalize to other PEB domains. The investigators also examined the effects of self-determination and difficulty on the residents' perceived satisfaction with local environmental conditions, satisfaction with government environmental policy, and the perceived importance of the environment. Self-determined residents were less satisfied with current environmental conditions, government environmental policy, and considered the ecological situation more important than non–self-determined individuals. However, these perceptions did not differ significantly as a function of the level of difficulty of recycling behaviors. In sum, making recycling more accessible and easier had some effect on recycling behavior but did not have any effect on frequency of other PEB and it did not impact the residents' perceptions of environmental conditions.

In a third study, Aitken, Pelletier, and Baxter (2010) measured students' frequency of PEBs and perceived difficulty of those PEBs in two contexts—at home and at university residence. Results indicated once again that higher self-determined motivation was associated with more frequent difficult PEB. For PEB perceived as being easy, autonomous motivation had no influence on behavior frequency. This pattern was consistent at home and at students' school residence. Furthermore, a mediation analysis showed that feeling competent regarding PEB had a positive indirect relationship with frequency of difficult PEB (via autonomous motivation), whereas the effect of feeling competent on difficult behaviors (via controlled motivation) was not significant. In sum, this study suggests that a sense of competence and self-determined motivation regarding PEB are particularly effective at encouraging difficult PEB, potentially leading to a larger environmental impact.

Altogether, these studies suggest that PEBs *could* be encouraged in the workplace by making them easier (e.g., providing compost in the lunchroom, automatic power down during the night) but this strategy has some limitations. First, the behavior is less likely to be maintained if the behavior ceases to be easy; second, this strategy does not seem to generalize to other PEBs; and third, this strategy does not affect people's attitudes and perceptions regarding the environment. Studies regarding SDT and PEB suggest that PEBs performed for self-determined reasons have a better chance of becoming more frequent and being maintained once initiated because as PEBs become more integrated into the person's self-system and lifestyle, the negative impact of the behavior's perceived difficulty diminishes. A business can use both strategies to improve the overall impact on the environment. By removing barriers to PEB for employees and by fostering self-determined motivation in employees, a business can create a culture of sustainability.

The Processing of Information about the Environment and About Health Risks

Information that describes justifications for doing versus not doing PEB appears to be an important predictor of PEB (an aspect examined in more detail later). More specifically, the effect of information on the perception of health risks has been the object of much attention. Although the perception of information on health risks can be a determinant of motivation, it could also be a consequence of motivation because people who become more and more motivated to do something about the environment also become more interested to find out which environmental conditions could present risks for their health. In this section we suggest that industry should pay attention to research on the way people with different motivational orientations perceive health risks because several businesses and industries are perceived as a threat to the environment and to people's health. Government and industry tend to emphasize a different aspect of risk than does the general public. Whereas the general public is more prone to perceive risk, government and industry may be more prone to discount risk (Kasperson et al., 1988; Renn, Burns, Kasperson, Kasperson, & Slovic, 1992). These differences can lead the public to view the desire of government and industry to protect the environment as untrustworthy and driven only by financial factors, not as a genuine endeavor.

Individuals' perceptions of risks from ecological issues can be affected by the specific information they obtain from different sources, such as the media, governments agencies, activist organizations, public groups, or scientists, and the sources of information could either amplify or attenuate the perceptions of environmental health risks of ecological issues and consequently lead to more or less PEB (Kasperson et al., 1988; Renn et al., 1992). Séguin et al. (1998) tested a model of PEB and environmental activism in which the combined contribution of self-determined motivation and perceptions of various environmental health risks were examined. It was reasoned that the more people perceive health risks in the environment and the more confidence they have in a particular source of environmental information, the more they should try to correct a situation by becoming actively involved. Participants received environmental information from different sources (e.g., university scientists, medical doctors, environmental groups, government officials, and the industries) and then completed measures of perceived problems in the local

environment, perceptions of health risks related to environmental conditions, perceptions of the level of responsibility of specific organization to prevent health risks (e.g., the government, private industry), and their personal level of environmental activism (e.g., participation in events organized by ecological groups, financial support to these groups, circulation of petitions, writing letters to industries that manufacture harmful products). Overall, results showed that the more individuals were self-determined, the more they paid attention to information about health risks, to problems in their local environment, and to the responsibility of different organizations to prevent health risks. Finally, the more individuals perceived health risks in their environment, the more they engaged in PEB and environmental activism.

In a second study, Séguin, Pelletier, and Hunsley (1999) examined more closely the relationship between self-determination and environmental health risks by asking participants to report their perceptions of current environmental health risks, the extent to which they were seeking information on health risks from different sources, their level of confidence in these sources, their motivation, and their frequency of PEB. The sources of information on health risks included federal government agencies, the government itself, public interest groups, environmental groups, the media, scientists, and industry. The results showed that self-determination was associated with the amount of information individuals sought from various sources of information on health risks, which led to more confidence in these sources of information. In turn, the level of confidence in the different sources of information (not the amount of information) was a significant predictor of individuals' perceptions of environmental health risks, and these perceptions were predictors of PEB. It is noteworthy that self-determination toward the environment was a direct and strong predictor of PEB over and above the perceptions of health risks, even after controlling for the effect of motivation on the search for information on health risks.

In sum, the research reviewed so far suggests that people are not only engaging in environmentally responsible behaviors for different reasons, but these reasons are related to important consequences. In agreement with SDT, the greater people's autonomous motivation toward the environment, the more they engage in PEB, the more they engage in difficult PEB, and the more they seek out information about health risks. Some of the research also suggests that higher levels of autonomous motivation for PEB are associated with higher maintenance of behavior over time and consistency across contexts, with the adoption of multiple PEB indicative of being an eco-citizen.

Although prior to the 1990s there were few publications on sustainable development, entrepreneurship, and employees' behavior (Hall, Daneke, & Lenox, 2010), some research has started to examine more specifically employee PEB in the workplace (Andersson & Bateman, 2000; Bansal, 2003; Bansal & Gao, 2006; Barrett, Lee, & McPeak, 2005; Korhonen, von Malmborg, Strachan, & Ehrenfeld, 2004; Stark & Marcus, 2000). To our knowledge, no research to date has examined how autonomous and controlled motivations relate specifically to employees' PEB. Future research could pay attention to several types of employee behaviors that have been examined in prior studies and rely on SDT to guide research activities. These could include typical PEB that employees do at home and at work, such as recycling, use of environmentally friendly forms of transportation like car-pooling, turning off lights when the employee is not in his or her office, buying biodegradable products, water conservation, composting organic waste, buying recycled products, buying or using products that are less harmful to the environment, reusing plastic containers, avoiding littering, help support financially an ecological group, questioning practices that hurt the environment, and encouraging others to consider the environment. Quasiexperimental designs like those used in Pelletier and Sharp (2007) can be used in the workplace to test similar hypotheses about the relationship between behavior difficulty and self-determined motivation. Employees' PEBs may differ in the degree to which they are cognitively simple or complex, easy or difficult. Also, they could be actions taken by employees that improve the environmental performance of the company. In practice, these actions could fall within three categories: (1) those that decrease the environmental impact of the company (e.g., recycling, pollution prevention), (2) those that solve an environmental problem for a company (e.g., reducing the need for hazardous waste disposal, eliminating chemicals that are harmful to worker health/natural environment), and (3) those that develop a more ecoefficient product or service (e.g., increasing resource efficiency by producing a less energy-intensive product, the redesign of a system to eliminate the use of products harmful to environment or that use large amount of energy, the development of a cleaner product for sale on the consumer market). By relying on SDT to guide research, researchers interested in the work environment could then examine more specifically whether or not the reasons for adopting PEB in the workplace lead to more or less persistence and to a transfer of the PEB adopted at work to life domains outside of work (e.g., at home or when away on vacation).

Determinants of Self-Determined Motivation for PEB

Given the positive consequences associated with a more self-determined profile of motivation, it becomes important to investigate possible factors that could either enhance or impair motivational orientation. In this section, we turn our attention to studies that have examined the determinants of environmental motivation.

According to SDT, people are inherently motivated to integrate the regulation of activities that are useful for functioning in society, even if the activities are not necessarily interesting (i.e., intrinsically motivated). Most people are now aware that the environment has important implications for the economy, our health, and the quality of our lives. Therefore, people's desire to be effective in dealing with the challenges posed by the ecological situation should prompt them to take in the regulation of PEB and gradually to transform socially valued behaviors into personally endorsed activities. As discussed earlier, SDT proposes that social contexts that support the satisfaction of innate psychological needs for competence, autonomy, and relatedness should promote the internalization of autonomous regulation or functional forms of regulation, and well-being (Deci & Ryan, 2000). Although in principle, internalization of behavior should be facilitated by significant people in a relatively close social environment (e.g., a spouse, friends, children, educators, and supervisors) that could represent a daily source of influence on motivation, we think that the impact of broader sources could be influential as well (e.g., the government, the media, managers of industries, and public role models).

As indicated previously, informative actions from closer and broader sources of influence (i.e., sources that point the way to being more effective) that support autonomy (i.e., sources that provide a good rationale for PEB, that let people freely choose among different options) foster the development of autonomous motivation (Deci & Ryan, 2000, 2008). In contrast, actions that pressure people toward specific outcomes or that represent attempts to control behaviors, such as financial incentives, punishments, or imposed rules, may produce temporary compliance but do not lead to lasting commitment or personal investment. Finally, situations where no rationale for acting is provided, where no guidance is provided about a solution to the perceived problem, and where people perceive solutions to be out of their reach create a sense of helplessness that leads individuals to disengage from a behavior (Pelletier, Dion, Tuson, & Green-Demers, 1999).

With respect to the environment, we feel that the same factors that have been shown to affect motivation in different life domains should also have an impact on the motivation for PEB. However, we feel that some social-contextual factors should be particularly promising for industries and business: the extent to which employees are exposed to the outdoors or to natural environments and the way policies about environmental programs target PEB are implemented.

Exposure to the Outdoors and the Natural Environment

The physical environment we live in and work in could have a significant impact on our mood and our well-being. One aspect of the physical environment that has been the object of more attention lately is the extent to which we feel connected to the outdoors, to the natural environment or to conditions that make us think about our natural environment. Contact with nature has several positive benefits, such as the ability to restore attentional resources, improve concentration, speed recovery from illness, and reduce stress (e.g., Herzog, Black, Fountaine, & Knotts, 1997; Plante, Cage, Clements, & Stover, 2006), as well as increasing productivity at work (Smith, Tucker, & Pitt, 2011). People feel less frustrated and more patient, find their job more challenging, have greater enthusiasm for their job, and report higher life satisfaction as well as overall health (Bringslimark, Hartig, & Patil, 2009). It seems that having plants indoors can be beneficial to the individual due to increased well-being and reduced stress, in the workplace due to increased productivity, and for the planet due to increased nature relatedness leading to more participation in PEB. But can exposure to the outdoors or to natural environments influence individuals' motivational orientation toward environmentally sustainable attitudes and behavior? Recent research suggests that it can.

Ryan et al. (2010) examined whether being outdoors and in nature had an impact on the experience of vitality. Across five studies using varied strategies (including surveys, vignettes, experimental manipulations that involved walking outdoors versus indoors, and diary methods that assessed the extent to which people were outdoors), results suggest that being outdoors and around natural elements had a positive impact on subjective vitality above and beyond the effects of physical activities or social interactions that can take place in natural settings. Nisbet and Zelenski (2011) reported similar results with participants that took outdoor walks compared with indoor walks. Interestingly, the participants made affective forecasting errors, such as underestimating the effect that nature would have on their mood. In reality, once exposed to nature, participants felt a stronger sense of connection to nature than anticipated (a concept strongly associated with concern for the environment and PEB).

Finally, Weinstein, Przybylski, and Ryan (2009) examined whether immersion in nature would increase the value of intrinsic aspirations and decrease the value of extrinsic aspirations, compared with immersion in nonnatural environments. To test this hypothesis, participants in three studies were exposed to images of either natural or nonnatural environments while listening to a guided imagery script. They reported on aspirations both before and after image presentations. In a fourth study, the presence or absence of plants was manipulated. All studies showed that participants exposed to nature valued intrinsic goals more and extrinsic goals less than they had before exposure. Moderation analyses in all studies showed that individuals more immersed in their environments reported increases in intrinsic aspirations and decreases in extrinsic ones. Interestingly, higher immersion in nature predicted higher nature relatedness and autonomy. In turn, higher nature relatedness and autonomy had an effect on decision-making indicative of valuing intrinsic aspirations (i.e., altruism) over extrinsic aspirations. For instance, participants immersed in natural settings were generous in sharing the money gained in a previous task, and they showed more willingness to promote others' interest.

Together these findings suggest that contact with nature can have positive effects on vitality and well-being, and it can make people more aware of the environmental conditions. Also, it can have humanizing effects, fostering greater authenticity and connectedness and, in turn, fostering other-orientations that enhance valuing of, and generosity toward others. Businesses can incorporate more use of indoor greenspaces and help facilitate access to outdoor natural environments (e.g., place picnic tables outside for breaks in green space, organize nature walks, encourage walking and bike riding to work, management retreats in nature rather than downtown) to take advantage of the benefits to employees and the overall workplace.

The Influence of Policies

Fresh insights for corporate environmental governance can be gained from research related to public government (Benz & Frey, 2007). Although people assign an important role to their government in the pursuit of environmental sustainability, little attention has been paid to the impact of the government's approach toward environmental policy on the environmental behaviors of individuals. Understanding this is important, because government environmental programs and policies are universally applied and, therefore, they have the potential to exert a systemic influence on every citizen and on every enterprise. Governments at a community through to a national level are responsible for providing the infrastructure for several large-scale PEBs, such as curbside recycling programs or energy conservation, and they are responsible for the development and the implementation of several programs and policies aimed at motivating individuals to engage in PEB (e.g., advertisements, transit pass tax credits, rebates for programmable thermostats, discounts on insurance of hybrid vehicles).

The effects of the government's approach toward introduction and implementation of such programs and policies on the motivation for PEB are not well researched. A few studies show that policies are perceived as coercive (e.g., policies that involve inducements for changing or threats of punishment for not changing) but they can motivate change in the short term. However, policies have been shown to be relatively ineffective over the long run in creating stable behavior change. That is, the targeted behaviors tend not to be maintained over time or to transfer when contexts change. When policy makers rely on the use of external controls to promote change, they essentially create a long-term process of using contingencies and policing people's behavior to administer the consequences to those who fail to comply. Examples of policies that use external, coercive methods are laws intended to control toxic waste or contamination of ground water. These laws are reasonably effective, but the contingencies and policing of the behavior need to remain indefinitely, making such methods enormously expensive and, thus, difficult to apply to change PEB. These regulations can even

end up having the exact opposite effect (Cardenas, Stranlund, & Willis, 2000; Frey & Oberholzer-Gee, 1997; Livernois & McKenna, 1999). Several policies also rely on controlling methods, such as the use of incentives. When contingencies involve controlling incentives (e.g., refunds for recycling aluminum cans), the incentives tend to lose their appeal over time, making them inadequate for instilling lasting change even when the contingencies are still in effect (DeYoung, 1993; Geller, Winnett, & Everett, 1982; Katzev & Johnson, 1984; Pelletier, 2002; see Fall and Roussel [Chapter 12], this volume, for an overview of research related to compensation in the workplace).

Therefore, there is a need to examine if and how government environmental regulation affects the motivation for PEB. There is also a need to examine what individuals perceive to be the most efficient ways to motivate people to act in times of crisis or when there is need to consider contexts that affect the population in general (e.g., use of natural resources like water or the choice of more or less risky sources of energy like nuclear energy, coal, or tar sands). That is, if the protection of the environment and climate change are perceived as real threats, and there is a sense of urgency to do something about it, how do individuals believe the government should proceed to motivate people to act?

Most environmental laws and policies are a form of control and should lead to a controlled form of motivation and low levels of PEB integration in one's lifestyle if they are not implemented with an understanding of human needs and psychological functioning, as SDT predicts (Deci & Ryan, 1987). In one study, Lavergne, Sharp, Pelletier, and Holtby (2010) tested a motivational model of PEB that used perception of government style in the implementation of environmental programs and policies as a predictor of motivation for PEB. In agreement with previous studies, autonomous motivation predicted a higher frequency of PEB, controlled motivation did not predict frequency of PEB, and amotivation predicted lower frequency of PEB. Also, the perception of the government as autonomy-supportive (e.g., the extent to which a rationale for action was provided, and citizens had some form of choice) contributed to higher levels of self-determination, which was evidenced by a direct positive effect on autonomous motivation and a direct negative effect on amotivation. Perception of the government as controlling (e.g., the government relies on incentives and punishment) did not support participants' self-determination; instead, it had a strong direct positive effect on both controlled motivation and amotivation. In short, the way that the government is perceived by the individual has a significant impact on that person's PEB, either in a positive direction if government is seen as autonomy-supportive, or in a negative direction if government is perceived as controlling. Because autonomous motivation is much more closely associated with PEB, the most valuable form of government is one that is autonomy-supportive, to foster the type of motivation necessary to encourage members of a society to become eco-citizens. These finding can be directly applied to the business world even if there is no direct research available. Controlling environmental policies in the workplace will likely have a negative impact on long-term employee participation of PEB. Employees who perceive the workplace to be autonomy-supportive will develop more self-determined motivation toward the environment and will likely participate in PEB.

In another study, Lavergne and Pelletier (2011) examined the possibility that individuals may turn toward government control when they experience psychological threat for environmental issues of different psychological distance (i.e., water conservation is more concrete and proximal; climate change is more abstract and distal). As hypothesized, climate change was rated as more distal and associated with a greater preference for a controlling (but not autonomy-supportive) government style, compared with water conservation. Furthermore, autonomous motivation toward the environment predicted preferences for a more controlling and less autonomy-supportive government style for both issues (i.e., global warming and water conservation), especially as perceived psychological distance *increased*. Controlled motivation predicted a preference for a controlling (but not an autonomy-supportive) style for water conservation (i.e., proximal issue) but did not predict preferences for climate change (i.e., distal issue); and amotivation predicted preferences for an autonomy-supportive (but not a controlling) government style for both climate change and water conservation. This research highlights the "motivated preference for control paradox," that is, individuals who are more self-determined and who consider taking care of the environment as a priority seem to prefer a government that imposes rules and regulations about the environment to force individuals who are less self-determined and amotivated to change their behavior. To the extent that preferences for government style are indicative of voting intentions and behavior, the most highly motivated environmentalists may in fact be creating a political climate that undermines environmental motivation, especially for far-reaching environmental issues.

In sum, research on the influence of government policies suggests that people may see the benefit of an autonomy-supportive approach when it is time to implement a policy. However, they may prefer a controlling approach because they believe that it is urgent to do something to protect the environment and because they believe that most people either are not motivated or are extrinsically motivated to adopt PEB. As a result they may be encouraging a government to adopt an approach that creates low levels of motivation or controlled motivation that is conducive to low levels of PEB (Pelletier & Vallerand, 1996). This same process is likely to be happening within the business context where customers are requesting a company to make immediate and controlling changes to the company's policies, although more research is needed to test how much of these findings can be generalized to the business world.

The Influence of Information on Environmental Issues

An alternative to policies is providing meaningful information that lets people engage in mindful consideration of what is right for them. As such, the communication of information does not require the same level of external monitoring and enforcing by agencies that is required by an externally controlling approach, and thus it tends to be less expensive. Furthermore, the quality of the resulting autonomous choices is a direct function of the quality and type of information available.

One type of communication strategy consists of providing extensive information about different ecological threats (e.g., global climate change, toxic pollution of air and water supplies), urging individuals to prevent further deterioration of the environment, and stressing the necessity of having individuals directly participate in PEB to address current environmental degradation. These messages tend to focus on those behaviors that people do not perform on a regular basis but that are known to effect positive changes in the environment (e.g., walk to work, shut down electronics when not in use). Describing the nature and severity of an ecological problem could make people more conscious of the situation. It can also make them aware that there is a discrepancy between the importance they attribute to the environmental situation and their level of activity to correct that situation. As a consequence, this may create discomfort or cognitive dissonance.

In this section, we first examine how providing knowledge about the seriousness of the situation can create discomfort or cognitive dissonance, but it can also lead to paradoxical effects in people with different motivational orientations. Second, we examine how information campaigns on the environment could take advantage of recent principles of persuasive communication strategies, principles of behavior change, and principles derived from SDT to make people aware of the importance of environmental conditions and lead them to change their behavior.

THE REDUCTION OF COGNITIVE DISSONANCE FOLLOWING THE PROCESS OF CONFLICTING MESSAGES

As discussed at the beginning of this chapter, it is increasingly clear that human activities cause several environmental problems and the solutions to this problem involve trade-offs among environmental, economical, and social well-being. These trade-offs may be a source of psychological discomfort (i.e., negative affect) induced by the presence of a conflict (i.e., dissonance) between a cognition and a behavior. This conflict has been shown to motivate individuals to adopt a strategy to reduce the dissonance. Discomfort occurs when individuals face a dilemma, such as the presence of large-scale pollution when one's country is using tar sands to produce energy and stimulate the economy, or the loss of jobs as a result of ocean fisheries protection. The cognitive dissonance that results from trade-offs or conflicts is an aversive state, and an alleviation of this psychological discomfort is the motivation underlying dissonance-induced attitude change (Higgins, Rhodewalt, & Zanna, 1979; Losch & Cacioppo, 1990; Zanna, Higgins, & Taves, 1976). However, according to Harmon-Jones (2000), when a person becomes aware of a discrepancy between their belief that environmental degradation has occurred and their lack of action to reduce that degradation, they may well choose to downplay the seriousness of the environmental situation rather than changing their behavior. This may occur because changing one's attitude or perception is perceived as being easier than changing one's behavior.

This analysis reinforces the importance of company leadership having a clear strategy when a message is communicated to employees and the public (for more information about the role of leadership see Gilbert and Kelloway [Chapter 11], this volume). Simply alarming people about the seriousness of an environmental situation, without giving them clear and accessible means to solve the situation, or providing the psychological support needed to move toward the solution, may create cognitive dissonance and a change of attitude toward the seriousness of the environmental situation, rather than motivation to adopt environmentally responsible behaviors.

Recently, Lavergne, Pelletier, and Aitken (2010) explored this issue by examining whether people's level of self-determined motivation plays a role in the amount of dissonance people experience and in how they decide to reduce (or not reduce) this dissonance. In an initial study, people's reactions were assessed after they were made aware of dissonance between their perception of the importance of environmental sustainability and their participation in PEB. Four types of reactions were identified: (1) doing nothing, (2) deflecting (i.e., thinking that environmental problems are not their responsibility, or hoping nobody notices their lack of action), (3) self-bolstering (i.e., reminding themselves that they try the best they can but sometimes make mistakes), or (4) using self-monitoring and bringing their behavior more in line with their beliefs (i.e., reminding themselves to pay more attention in the future, or planning to do more PEB). In a second study, these four types of reactions were related to self-determined motivation and dissonance. The results revealed that controlled motivation predicted a tendency to react to dissonance by inaction or deflection, whereas autonomous motivation predicted a tendency to use self-bolstering and especially self-monitoring and planning behavior change to address dissonance. In agreement with SDT, it appears that when autonomous people experience dissonance regarding an issue that is important to them, they reduce the dissonance by acting consistently with their values. In contrast, inducing dissonance in people with a controlled motivation seems to backfire, pushing them in the opposite direction of the goal intended by the message. Studies are needed to examine what happens when employees face conflicting messages that constantly remind them that their job may cause damage to the environment but that protecting the environment may lead them to lose their job.

THE STRATEGIC USE OF MESSAGE TAILORING AND MESSAGE FRAMING

Recently, Pelletier and Sharp (2008) proposed a theory-based understanding of how information should be provided to people so that it motivates people to act and, more importantly, leads to the integration of PEB into people's lifestyles. These authors proposed combining two approaches for effectively communicating information. The first approach proposes the strategic use of persuasive communication by tailoring and framing messages to influence behaviors and to shape how people construe behaviors (Rothman & Salovey, 2007). The second approach, based on SDT (Deci & Ryan, 2000, 2008), distinguishes the effect that message framing in terms if intrinsic/extrinsic goals can have on the implementation of a targeted behavior, its regulation, and its integration into a person's lifestyle.

According to the first approach, a message is truly effective when it is guided by the processes people use to manage and change their behavior (Rothman & Salovey, 2007; Rothman, Stark, & Salovey, 2006). The communication of information leads people not only to attend to the messages, but also to process them in a manner that optimizes their impact on how people think about the information (Petty & Wagener, 1998). This suggests that a message should be tailored to the decision-making processes people rely on when they are in a specific phase of behavior change (Rothman, Kelly, Hertel, & Salovey, 2003), and the information should be communicated in a manner that is relevant to a person's thoughts when in a specific phase, in order to have an impact on behavior, and behavior internalization (Petty & Cacioppo, 1986).

Accumulated research provides considerable support for three stages of behavior change (detection phase, decision phase, and implementation phase; Burkholder & Evers, 2002; Rosen, 2000; Rothman & Salovey, 2007). It is likely that different messages have different impacts depending on the stage of change a person is in. During the *detection phase*, people are more sensitive to messages that help them gather and interpret information and determine whether there is a problem. Once people have detected the presence of a problem, and see this problem as important, they reach a *decision phase*. During this phase, people become more sensitive to messages that help them decide whether to take action and choose a course of action. Once people have decided to act, they become more sensitive to messages that provide them with information about how to *implement behavior*, and how they can maintain the behavior by integrating it into their lifestyle (Rothman & Salovey, 2007). Gollwitzer (1999) suggested that forming a goal

intention induces a sense of commitment that motivates the individual to realize the goal. Simply listing one's goals is not sufficient to ensure that the goals will be accomplished (Sheeran, Webb, & Gollwitzer, 2005) because people may not be motivated for the activity that they need to perform to achieve the goal, or they fail to develop action plans for how they are going to implement the actions that will lead to the goal. Recent research suggests that conceptualizing implementation intentions separately from goal intentions helps specify where, when, and how specific responses will lead to goal attainment (Gollwitzer, 1999; Gollwitzer & Schaal, 1998; Sheeran et al., 2005). Implementation intentions greatly ease the self-regulatory demands of goal pursuit because the mental representation of what one wants to achieve becomes highly activated and easily accessible. Koestner (2008) suggested that these effects can be further enhanced by combining implementation intentions and self-determined goals because they complement one another: self-determined motivation to achieve a goal leads to goal progress and greater progress can be achieved when it is combined with implementation intentions.

According to the second approach, PEB could be further facilitated by the way different goals for the targeted behaviors are framed, and the way the information about different activities is implemented. According to SDT, goal framing has an important influence on motivation because it defines what is valued within a specific context, what people attend to, what knowledge and attitudes become cognitively accessible, and what behaviors are being considered (Vansteenkiste, Lens, & Deci, 2006; Vansteenkiste et al., 2004). Vansteenkiste and colleagues (2004) have proposed that people pursue qualitatively different types of goals: intrinsic goals (e.g., PEB can contribute to a clean and healthy environment) and extrinsic goals (e.g., PEB can save money), and these goals lead to considerably different outcomes. These authors showed that when college students were learning about reusing and recycling as part of a class, they learned more and persisted with the behavior longer if the relevant material was said to be instrumental to an intrinsic value (helping save the environment) rather than an extrinsic value (helping save money). Furthermore, introducing the topic and learning material in an autonomy-supportive way rather than a controlling way also significantly improved learning and persistence. Thus, this study showed that both intrinsic message framing and autonomy-supportive communication styles are effective means of promoting actions and new choices over the long-term.

In sum, Pelletier and Sharp (2008) proposed three types of message. The first type of message (i.e., detection phase) should serve the important purpose of providing people with a rationale for the actions. Once people are aware of an issue, the second type of messages should serve the purpose of identifying the specific behaviors or solutions that are effective in meeting the challenges introduced in the first phase. Finally, once people have decided to take action, they should be more interested by information about when, where, and how a specific behavior could be implemented (i.e., the implementation phase). For example, in a company that wants to reduce overall energy consumption, the initial message should provide information about energy consumption rates of the company and why this is an issue (e.g., our energy use affects the climate). A second set of messaging should target how employees can help by turning off electronics and lights at the end of the day. The third set of message would provide specific details on how to perform the targeted behavior, like providing information about energy saving features of specific equipment. Information about how to implement an action represents an important step because it helps individuals set the conditions that will determine when they get started and how they stay on track. Pelletier and Sharp (2008) also proposed that motivation could be further facilitated by messages that emphasize intrinsic as opposed to extrinsic goal framing. For example, framing messages targeting energy reduction in terms of the benefits for future generations (i.e., intrinsic) rather than the cost saving benefits for the company or how it will improve the image of the company (i.e., extrinsic). This is especially important because research on motivation suggests that people's goals for changing their behavior are not all equally effective. More specifically, it is important to pay attention to the type of motives used when a goal is framed because this influences what people attend to, what knowledge and attitudes become cognitively accessible, and what behaviors are being considered. As a consequence, when a goal is framed as a function of intrinsic motives, relative to extrinsic motives, it should lead to more engagement in an activity, more persistence over time, and its effects should generalize to other PEB.

It is important to emphasize some future research pertaining to the influence of information on PEB and the propositions described in the previous sections. The test of these proposed principles should shed some light on the role that motivation plays in the perception and the processing of persuasive messages, when individuals form judgments about risk, how they evaluate potential solutions, and when they decide to implement a new behavior. Finally, research in this area should also help determine if the different reasons for changing behavior are equally effective.

Ways to Encourage Employees to Take Environmental Actions

So far we have seen that people's motivational orientation matters. More specifically, the distinction between autonomous and controlled motivation, as proposed by SDT, is useful to predict different levels of engagement in PEB, whether these behaviors involve processing information about the environment or actually doing easy and difficult PEB. We have also seen that the extent to which people are connected to nature, the way environmental policies are proposed and implemented, and the way the information is tailored (in terms of stage of change) and framed (in terms of extrinsic compared to extrinsic goals) could have a positive impact of people's motivational orientation. However, paradoxical effects can be created by both the way information about the environment is presented and the way environmental policies could be implemented. When information about the environment scares people, it may create cognitive dissonance that could lead some people, especially less self-determined people, to apathy and deciding the environmental situation is not that bad after all. We saw that these people are more likely not to participate in PEB because behavior change is too difficult compared with changing their attitude about the current state of the environment. People, especially more autonomous and environmentally engaged people, are inclined to favor controlling environmental policies because it may force others who are less autonomously motivated toward the environment to do PEB, although implementing policies in a controlling way may ironically create controlled motivation and lead people to become even less engaged toward the environment.

We believe that this research is useful to understand people's motivation for PEB and can be applied to understand employees' PEB as well. Employees' PEB encompasses a broad set of environmentally conscious activities including following established environmental rules, performing required environmental tasks, recycling, reusing, conserving energy, learning more about the environment, finding more environmentally friendly ways of working, developing and applying ideas for reducing the company's environmental impact, developing green processes and products, questioning practices that hurt the environment, and encouraging others to consider the environment. More importantly, research on the determinants of motivation for PEB will be useful to understand how employee motivation is affected by conditions in the employees' environment and managers' initiatives. In this section we examine how an organization's mission, environmental policies, and supervisory behaviors could be implemented to have the most important and significant impact on employee motivation to initiate, engage, and hopefully maintain environmental actions.

Organization's Mission and Environmental Policies

Some companies or organizations decide to implement policies that meet the minimal compulsory changes to comply with regulations, whereas others take voluntary measures above and beyond the minimum to reduce their impact on the natural environment. We believe that this distinction between a reactive and a proactive approach to environmental management practices should affect the relative strength of the signal from the organization and from management regarding protection of the natural environment, and therefore should have a direct impact on the willingness of employees to engage in environmental initiatives.

We propose that one way for businesses and organizations to be proactive and to send a strong signal when they decide to implement environmental and sustainability policies is to include the protection of the environment and to further environmental sustainability in their mission. Including the protection of the environment and environmental sustainability in a business' mission, and having environmental policies, shows managers and employees that their organization expects and is willing to support environmental initiatives and actions. It also serves the purpose of encouraging managers to promote and support employee creativity, environmental initiatives, and individual PEB. The environmental policies and supervisors' support could target specific behaviors and encourage new initiatives from employees. These initiatives could aim at finding more environmentally friendly ways of working, developing, and applying ideas for reducing the company's environmental impact, developing green processes and products, questioning practices that

hurt the environment, or encouraging others to consider the environment.

In line with research on goal framing, an organization's mission statement on environmental sustainability, its environmental policies, and its managers' actions should be framed in terms of intrinsic goals (e.g., the quality of the environment itself, the health and well-being of individuals and employees) as opposed to extrinsic goals (e.g., to make or save money, to make a profit, to promote a good public image, to comply with the public's expectations). Ironically, as the research on goal framing suggests, the promotion of intrinsic goals could lead to more positive outcomes, more engagement, more persistence, and therefore could be more profitable for a business or organization than the promotion of PEB to achieve extrinsic goals.

An organization's environmental policies could cover a wide variety of behaviors and activities, such as environmental purchasing; a system for implementing, monitoring, and evaluating goals related to environmental activities; environmental training and education; or policies that aim specifically at reducing specific activities (e.g., the use of fossil fuel, the use of toxic chemical, or the use of products that are not sustainable). Finally, all these behaviors could be encouraged at home, in the working environment, and abroad (e.g., when visiting a client).

Supervisors' Interpersonal Behaviors

The organization's written mission statement and environmental policies can send a strong signal and can act as a guide for employees. However, statements and policies, in themselves, do not make a company environmentally sustainable. Supervisors' interpersonal behaviors that demonstrate environmental support for environmental actions also provide an important message to employees—that the organization's environmental policies are meaningful. In agreement with SDT (Deci & Ryan, 2008), the internalization of PEB and motivation should be optimal when supervisors provide a good rationale for PEB, outline effective ways in meetings challenges, communicate that employees can freely choose among different options, and suggest that goals for these PEB are intrinsic. By contrast, supervisors can hinder internalization when they do not supply any rationale for acting, pressure employees toward specific extrinsic goals, provide no information about the solution to the perceived problem, or provide no solution about how employees could implement behavior in their lifestyle (Pelletier et al., 1999).

More specifically, employees' autonomous motivation for PEB could be facilitated by supervisors' interpersonal behaviors that create an autonomy-supportive work climate. As indicated throughout this book, focusing on how to change the environment to promote autonomous motivation, as well as intrinsic motivation, is a fruitful approach to organizational commitment. Research on SDT proposes several behaviors that could help fulfill the core psychological needs of employees and their motivation for work (Gagné & Deci, 2005; Stone, Deci, & Ryan, 2009). These behaviors can foster employees' motivation for PEB as well.

• *Asking open questions and inviting participation in solving problems regarding the environment.* This approach invites exploration of an employee's perception of an environmental problem and their proposed solutions. In contrast, closed questions place the manager in the expert role and imply the need for passive compliance from employees. Open questions raise problems without implying a preferred manager solution.

• *Active listening, including acknowledging the employee's point of view on an environmental issue.* Open questions are best followed by active listening that includes explicit acknowledgment of employees' perceptions of a problem. Summarizing is another effective active listening technique that consists of briefly restating employees' ideas or proposed solutions. Such summaries may begin with statements that invite clarification of misunderstandings or misperceptions. Statements of affirmation are also critical to active listening. Affirmations are sincere expressions of thanks or appreciation that may include acknowledging difficulties already encountered.

• *Offering choices within structure, including the clarification of responsibilities.* Offer a menu of possible actions that take into consideration the other goals of the organization and that follows from a dialogue based on open questions and active listening. Clarifying employees' responsibilities and contributions is also integral to an SDT approach. For example, methods for acknowledging employees' perspective while clarifying their responsibilities involve providing a meaningful rationale for PEB and acknowledging the employees' feelings of dislike or disinterest in an initiative, or possible conflicts with other goals pursued by an organization.

• *Providing sincere, positive, nonjudgmental feedback that acknowledges initiative.* Pointing out an employee's behavior that is damaging for the environment along with open questions and active listening invites mutual exploration of the full range of possibilities for addressing the problem. This allows employees to learn from their less-successful endeavors. Following the exploration of possibilities, feedback on the solutions proposed and praise for insightful initiatives and suggestions can motivate, if it supports competence and autonomy, and demotivate if it is perceived as controlling. Effective praise is sincere and specific; it acknowledges unique and unusual contributions and initiatives. Praise that acknowledges mere compliance (e.g., "good, you did just as told you to do") tends to feel controlling; in contrast, praise that acknowledges proactive engagement and initiative supports people's competence and autonomy.

• *Develop and share knowledge to enhance competence and autonomy for PEB.* Employees may value educational opportunities primarily as opportunities for increasing autonomy, and learning new skills (i.e., competence), as opposed to opportunities for external rewards. Offering environmental educational opportunities as a means for personal and professional development creates positive motivational effects. In addition, similar beneficial effects are created by increasing awareness of learning and advancement opportunities to help meet core intrinsic goals stated in environmental policies. Managers should avoid using educational opportunities as external rewards to prevent employees from feeling controlled, which in turn has a negative impact on their motivation for PEB.

• *Minimizing coercive controls and maximizing the use autonomy-supportive behaviors.* Many organizations still hold a perspective that money is the only relevant consideration in rewarding employees for PEB. SDT offers a constructive alternative approach. The SDT approach seeks to minimize the salience of monetary rewards as a motivational strategy because they do not promote autonomous motivation. Some organizations also use competition-based compensation schemes that pit employees against one another. These strategies are counterproductive because they do not promote fulfillment of the basic psychological needs.

• *Be mindful of stages of change (detection, decision, and implementation).* Tailor interventions to the stage where the employee is currently located. Aim to facilitate movement through the current stage and transition to the next stage of change by providing information about the environmental problem, while simultaneously providing concrete steps for arriving at a solution, and by providing step-by-step procedures (i.e., implementation goals and implementation intentions) as a means of tracking progress and providing feedback.

To create a culture of environmentalism among employees, management needs to be supportive of the employees' autonomy and they need to lead by example. Management involvement is perceived to be the most important facilitator to encourage and support employees to be "green" (Zibarras & Woods, 2010). When there is backing from management for proenvironmental initiatives (e.g., car pool program), best practices for environmental business polices (e.g., green procurement policy), and just everyday PEB (e.g., recycling old reports), then employees feel supported in making a change toward integrating environmentally responsible behaviors. It is not surprising that lack of management commitment and support is seen as the most significant barrier to employee PEB (Zibarras & Woods, 2010). When there is little support from management the employees do not feel responsible to participate in environmental initiatives or do not develop initiatives based on an anticipated denial from management. When management dictates environmental policy but does not show proenvironmental leadership, employees can view this as a form of controlled support, which leads to controlled motivation rather than autonomous motivation. In sum, creating a proenvironmental culture in a workplace only develops if there is participation from all levels of the organization, top down and bottom up. Autonomously supportive management can foster workplace participation in PEB and the development of a proenvironmental culture. In turn, a proenvironmental culture at work could facilitate the internalization of proenvironmental values and attitudes, and foster eco-citizenship in the wider society.

Conclusion

Employees' PEBs are critical to the success of organizational environmental initiatives. Increasingly, businesses, companies, and organizations are interested in findings ways to encourage employees to engage in environmental actions that could improve the environmental performance of organizational operations, their products, and the

services they offer. Recent research on SDT mainly drawn from the environmental domain provides practical information that companies and organizations could use to transform their current operations if they wish to strengthen their employees' autonomous motivation and their environmental programs. In this chapter we focus our attention on the difference that the quality of motivation makes when individuals deal with more or less difficult PEB, as well as the proactive role that autonomous motivation plays when individuals search for and process information. We also examine how government policies could be implemented to affect positively motivation, we introduce new research on the positive and negative strategies people use to reduce their cognitive dissonance regarding PEB, and we examine how tailoring and framing messages could guide individuals and help them become more self-determined.

Future Directions

We offer a few avenues for future research. Although the studies described in this chapter are informative for organizations that aim to encourage employees to engage in positive environmental actions, more research is necessary to test the proposed principles in the work environment. We also need more research that assesses behavioral indicators of employees' PEB. That is, regardless of the type of business, we need to examine whether employee autonomous motivation can lead to less consumption of energy, more consumption of "greener" sources of energy, reduction of waste including more recycling, and the development of products and services that could have a positive impact on the environment. In sum, we need to examine if it is possible to reduce the ecological footprints of organizations by increasing employees' autonomous motivation and individual PEB.

Participation in environmental programs may provide financial savings and competitive advantage; enable access to technical assistance; help firms weaken regulations or shape future regulations; or create an image of environmental friendliness for customers, suppliers, employees, or the public. It also may demonstrate a firm's responsiveness to governmental policies, as well as to community and employee concerns. These reasons may be contingent on several factors, such as the firm's competitive environment; exposure to regulatory or technological change; or the actions and demands of customers, investors, and community groups. However, close to nothing is known about how these reasons or motives affect an organization's participation in environmental programs, how they relate to an organization's mission and vision, or how these motives could affect managers' behaviors. We think that all these factors could represent pressures from above (e.g., the ways government policies are implemented) or pressure from below (e.g., demands from customers, low motivation of employees) that could affect managers' or supervisors' motivation and interpersonal behaviors, and in turn the employees' motivational orientation (Pelletier, Séguin, & Legault, 2002; Pelletier & Sharp, 2009). In other words, we think that understanding why and how firms adopt beyond-compliance environmental practices is an important question to determine the quality and the type of organizational support that will be provided to encourage environmental actions at all levels.

Also, very little is known about the effect that corporate social responsibility policies targeting the environment have on managers' interpersonal behaviors and the employees' motivation and PEB. It is becoming more frequent now for large organizations to have a corporate social responsibility policy, to value the environment, or have some other sustainability program (if not in the mission statement itself). Future research should examine how specific organization policies or mission statements that benefit the environment affect members of an organization and their motivation to engage in PEB.

Recent research (Nisbet & Zelinski, 2011; Weinstein et al., 2009) has examined how contact with nature (e.g., adding plants to environments, using images depicting natural environments, or encouraging employees to engage in outdoor activities during the day) can make people more aware of environmental conditions, which can have positive effects on vitality and well-being, can have humanizing effects, and can foster other-orientations that enhance valuing of, and generosity toward, others. It is important to replicate these studies in a work environment and to examine more specifically if increasing contact with nature affects employee motivation and levels of engagement in PEB.

We also propose other avenues for fostering managers' autonomy-supportive behaviors and employees' autonomous motivation for PEB, such as including the protection of the environment and the promotion of sustainability in the mission of the organization, and adopting and communicating environmental policies. A mission statement and environmental policies could play an important role because they make employees sensitive to the signals coming from different levels of management.

Although no empirical work has been done to test the effect that a mission statement could have on the protection of the environment and environmental policies, these steps could represent organizational factors that could have an impact on managers' interpersonal behaviors, employees' motivation, and employees' PEB and initiatives.

It is a challenging task to motivate employees to change behaviors that are harmful to the environment and lead them to adopt new PEB. Almost no SDT research has examined the relationship between environmental sustainability, business environmental engagement, and performance but our review suggests that research, grounded in SDT and the motivation for PEB in the general population, could have important implications for the business world. It is time to take the lead in new research, because the degradation of the environment represents an opportunity to advance our knowledge of people's motivation to change, and thereby reduce environmentally degrading behaviors in the business and organization world.

References

Aitken, N. M., Pelletier, L. G., & Baxter, D. (2010, May). *Doing the hard stuff: Influence of self-determined motivation toward the environment on pro-environmental behaviours.* Paper presented at the Fourth International Self-Determination Theory Conference, Ghent, Belgium.

Andersson, L. M., & Bateman, T. S. (2000). Individual environmental initiative: Championing natural environmental issues in U.S. business organizations. *Academy of Management Journal, 43,* 548–570.

Arora, S., & Cason, T. (1996). Why do firms volunteer to exceed environmental regulations? Understanding participation in EPA's 33/50 program. *Land Economics, 72,* 413–432.

Bamberg, S., & Möser, G. (2007). Twenty years after Hines, Hungerford, and Tomera: A new meta-analysis of psycho-social determinants of pro-environmental behavior. *Journal of Environmental Psychology, 27,* 14–25.

Bansal, P. (2003). From issues to actions: The importance of individual concerns and organizational values in responding to natural environmental issues. *Organization Science, 14,* 510–527.

Bansal, P., & Gao, J. (2006). Building the future by looking to the past: Examining research published on organizations and environment. *Organization & Environment, 19,* 458–478.

Barrett, C. B., Lee, D. R., & McPeak, J. G. (2005). Institutional arrangements for rural poverty reduction and resource conservation. *World Development, 33, 2,* 193–197.

Benz, M., & Frey, B. S. (2007). Corporate governance: What can we learn from public governance? *Academy of Management Review, 32,* 92–104. doi:10.5465/AMR.2007.23463860

Blackman, A., & Bannister, G. J. (1998). Community pressure and clean technology in the informal sector: An econometric analysis of the adoption of propane by traditional Mexican brickmakers. *Journal of Environmental Economics and Management, 35,* 1–21.

Boiral, O. (2009). Greening the corporation through organizational citizenship behaviors. *Journal of Business Ethics, 87,* 221–236.

Bringslimark, T., Hartig, T., & Patil, G. G. (2009). The psychological benefits of indoor plants: A critical review of the experimental literature. *Journal of Environmental Psychology, 29,* 422–433. doi:10.1016/j.jenvp.2009.05.001

Burkholder, G. J., Evers, K. E. (2002). Application of the transtheoretical model to several problem behaviors. In P. M. Burbank, & D. Riebe (Eds.), *Promoting exercise and behavior change in older adults: Interventions with the transtheoretical model* (pp. 85–145). New York: Springer.

Cardenas, J. C., Stranlund, J., & Willis, C. (2000). Local environmental control and institutional crowding-out. *World Development, 28,* 1719–1733. doi:10.1016/S0305-750X(00)00055-3

Costanza, R., d'Arge, R., de Groot, R., Farber, S., Hanson, B., Limburg, K.,...Paruelo, J. (1997). The value of the world's ecosystem services and natural capital. *Nature, 387,* 253–260.

Daily, B. F., Bishop, J. W., & Govindarajulu, N. (2009). A conceptual model for organizational citizenship behavior directed toward the environment. *Business & Society, 48,* 243–256.

Dean, T. J., & McMullen, J. S. (2005). Toward a theory of sustainable entrepreneurship: Reducing environmental degradation through entrepreneurial action. *Journal of Business Venturing, 22,* 50–76.

Deci, E. L., & Ryan, R. M. (1985). *Intrinsic motivation and self-determination in human behavior.* New York: Plenum Press.

Deci, E. L., & Ryan, R. M. (1987). The support of autonomy and the control of behavior. *Journal of Personality and Social Psychology, 53,* 1024–1037.

Deci, E. L., & Ryan, R. M. (2000). The "what" and "why" of goal pursuits: Human needs and self-determination of behavior. *Psychological Inquiry, 11,* 227–268.

Deci, E. L., & Ryan, R. M. (2008). Facilitating optimal motivation and well-being across life's domains. *Canadian Psychology, 49,* 14–23.

Delmas, M., & Keller, A. (2005). Free riding in voluntary environmental programs: The case of the U.S. EPA wastewise program. *Policy Sciences, 38,* 91–106.

Delmas, M., & Terlaak, A. (2001). A framework for analyzing environmental voluntary agreements. *California Management Review, 43,* 44–63.

DeYoung, R. (1993). Changing behavior and making it stick: The conceptualization and management of conservation behavior. *Environment and Behavior, 25,* 485–505.

Frey, B. S., & Oberholzer-Gee, F. (1997). The cost of price incentives: An empirical analysis of motivation crowding-out. *American Economic Review, 87,* 746–755.

Gagné, M., & Deci, E. L. (2005). Self-determination theory and work motivation. *Journal of Organizational Behavior, 26,* 331–362.

Gardner, G. T., & Stern, P. C. (2002). *Environmental problems and human behavior* (2nd ed.). Boston: Pearson Custom Publishing.

Geller, E. S., Winett, R. A., & Everett, P. B. (1982). *Preserving the environment: New strategies for behavior change.* Elmsford, NY: Pergamon.

Gollwitzer, P. M. (1999). Implementation intentions: Strong effects of simple plans. *American Psychologist, 54,* 493–503.

Gollwitzer, P. M., & Schaal, B. (1998). Meta-cognition in action: The importance of implementation intentions. *Personality and Social Psychology Review, 2,* 124–136.

Green-Demers, I., Pelletier, L. G., & Ménard, S. (1997). The impact of behavioral difficulty on the saliency of the association between self-determined motivation and environmental behaviors. *Canadian Journal of Behavioral Sciences, 29,* 157–166.

Gunningham, N., Thornton, D., & Kagan, R. (2005). Motivating management: Corporate compliance in environmental protection. *Law & Policy, 27,* 289–316.

Hall, J. K., Daneke, G. A., Lenox, M. J. (2010). Sustainable development and entrepreneurship: Past contributions and future directions. *Journal of Business Venturing, 25,* 439–448.

Harmon-Jones, E. (2000). An update on cognitive dissonance theory, with a focus on the self. In A. Tesser, R. B. Felson, & J. M. Suls (Eds.) *Psychological perspectives on self and identity* (pp. 119–144). Washington, DC: American Psychological Association.

Henriques, I., & Sadorsky, P. (1996). The determinants of an environmentally responsible firm: An empirical approach. *Journal of Environmental Economics and Management, 30,* 381–395.

Herzog, T. R., Black, A. M., Fountaine, K. A., & Knotts, D. J. (1997). Reflection and attentional recovery as distinctive benefits of restorative environments. *Journal of Environmental Psychology, 17,* 165–170.

Higgins, E. T., Rhodewalt, F., & Zanna, M. P. (1979). Dissonance motivation: Its nature, persistence, and reinstatement. *Journal of Experimental Social Psychology, 15,* 16–34.

Hopwood, B., Mellor, M., & O'Brien, G. (2005). Sustainable development: Mapping different approaches. *Sustainable Development, 13,* 38–52.

Howard-Grenville, J. (2005). Explaining shades of green: Why do companies act differently on similar environmental issues?. *Law & Social Inquiry, 30,* 551–581.

Intergovernmental Panel on Climate Change. (2007). Summary for policymakers. In S. Solomon, D. Qin, M. Manning, Z. Chen, M. Marquis, K. B. Averyt,...H. L. Miller (Eds.). *Climate change 2007: The physical science basis. Contribution of Working Group I to the Fourth Assessment Report of the Intergovernmental Panel on Climate Change.* Cambridge, UK and New York: Cambridge University Press. Retrieved from http://www.ipcc-wg2.org/

Johnston, J. S. (2006). The promise and limits of voluntary management-based regulatory reform: An analysis of EPA's strategic goals program. In C. Coglianese, & J. Nash (Eds.), *Leveraging the private sector: Management-based strategies for improving environmental performance.* Washington, DC: Resources for the Future Press.

Kasperson, R. E., Renn, O., Slovic, P., Brown, H. S., Emel, J., Goble, R.,...Ratick, S. (1988). The social amplification of risk: A conceptual framework. *Risk Analysis, 8,* 177–187.

Katzev R. D., & Johnson, T. (1984). Comparing the effects of monetary incentives and foot-in-the-door strategies in promoting residential electricity conservation. *Journal of Applied Social Psychology, 14,* 12–27.

Khanna, M. (2001). Non-mandatory approaches to environmental protection. *Journal of Economic Surveys, 15,* 291–324.

Koestner, R. (2008). Reaching one's personal goals: A motivational analysis focusing on autonomy. *Canadian Psychology, 49,* 60–67.

Korhonen, J., von Malmborg, F., Strachan, P. A., Ehrenfeld, J. R. (2004). Management and policy aspects of industrial ecology: An emerging research agenda. *Business Strategy and the Environment, 13*, 289–305. doi:10.1002/bse.415

Lavergne, K. J., & Pelletier, L. G. (2011). *Preferences for a controlling government implementation style for environmental strategies: A matter of autonomous motivation, controlled motivation, and psychological distance.* Poster presented at the 9th Biennial Conference on Environmental Psychology, Eindhoven, Netherlands.

Lavergne, K. J., Pelletier, L. G., & Aitken, N. (2010, May). *The role of self-determined motivation in the dissonance process: An exploratory study.* Paper presented at the Fourth International Self-Determination Theory Conference, Ghent, Belgium.

Lavergne, K. J., Sharp, E. C., Pelletier, L. G., & Holtby, A. (2010). The role of perceived government style in the facilitation of self-determined and non self-determined pro-environmental behavior. *Journal of Environmental Psychology, 30*, 169–177.

Lehman, P. K., & Geller, E. S. (2004). Behavioral analysis and environmental protection: Accomplishments and potential for more. *Behavioral and Social Issues, 13*, 13–24.

Livernois, J., & McKenna, C. J. (1999). Truth or consequences: Enforcing pollution standards with self-reporting. *Journal of Public Economics, 71*, 415–440.

Losch, M. E., & Cacioppo, J. T. (1990). Cognitive dissonance may enhance sympathetic tonus, but attitudes are changed to reduce negative affect rather than arousal. *Journal of Experimental Social Psychology, 26*, 289–304.

Lyon, T., & Maxwell, J. (2002). "Voluntary" approaches to environmental regulation. In M. Franzini, & A. Nicita (Eds.), *Economics institutions and environmental policy* (pp. 75–120). Brookfield, VT: Ashgate Publishing.

Maxwell, J. W., & Decker, C. S. (2006). Voluntary environmental investment and responsive regulation. *Environment and Resource Economics, 33*, 425–443.

McKenzie-Morh, D., & Oskamp, S. (1995). Psychology and sustain capacity: An introduction. *Journal of Social Issues, 51*, 1–14.

National Research Council. (2010). *America's climate choices: Panel on adapting to the impacts of climate change; Adapting to the Impacts of Climate Change.* Washington, DC: The National Academies Press.

Nisbet, E. K., & Zelenski, J. M. (2011). Underestimating nearby nature: Affective forecasting errors obscure the happy path to sustainability. *Psychological Science, 22*, 1101–1106. doi:10.1177/0956797611418527.

Osbaldiston, R. (2004). *Meta-Analysis of the responsible environmental literature.* Unpublished Doctoral Dissertation, University of Missouri-Columbia.

Osbaldiston, R., & Sheldon, K. M. (2003). Promoting internalized motivation for environmental responsible behavior: A prospective study of environmental goals. *Journal of Environmental Psychology, 23*, 349–357.

Pelletier, L. G. (2002). A motivational analysis of self-determination for pro-environmental behaviors. In E. L. Deci, & R. M. Ryan (Eds.), *The handbook of self-determination research* (pp. 205–232). Rochester, NY: University of Rochester Press.

Pelletier, L. G., Baxter, D., & Huta, V. (2011). Personal autonomy and environmental sustainability. In V. Chirkov, R. Ryan, & K. Sheldon (Eds.), *Personal autonomy in cultural contexts: Global perspectives on the psychology of agency,* *freedom, and people's well-being* (pp. 257–278). New York, NY: Springer.

Pelletier, L. G., Dion, S., Tuson, K. M., & Green-Demers, I. (1999). Why do people fail to adopt environmental behaviors? Towards a taxonomy of environmental amotivation. *Journal of Applied Social Psychology, 29*, 2481–2504.

Pelletier, L. G., Green-Demers, I., & Béland, A. (1997). Pourquoi effectuez-vous des comportements écologiques? Validation en langue française de l'échelle de motivation vis-à-vis les comportements écologiques. *Revue Canadienne des Sciences du Comportement, 29*, 145–156.

Pelletier, L. G., Lavergne, K. J., & Sharp, E. C. (2008). Environmental psychology and sustainability: Comments on topics important for our future. *Canadian Psychology, 49*, 304–308.

Pelletier, L. G., Séguin, C., & Legault, L. (2002). Pressure from above and pressure from below as determinants of teachers' motivation and teaching behaviors. *Journal of Educational Psychology, 94*, 186–196.

Pelletier, L. G., & Sharp, E. C. (2007, June). *From the promotion of pro-environmental behaviors to the development of an eco-citizen: The self-determination theory perspective.* Paper presented at The Annual Conference of the Canadian Psychological Association, Ottawa, Ontario.

Pelletier, L. G., & Sharp, E. C. (2008). Persuasive communication and pro-environmental behaviors: How message tailoring and message framing can improve the integration of behaviours through self-determined motivation. *Canadian Psychology, 49*, 210–217.

Pelletier, L. G., & Sharp, E. C. (2009). Educational pressures from above and teachers interpersonal behaviors. *Theory and Research in Education, 7*, 175–184.

Pelletier, L. G., Tuson, K. M., Green-Demers, I., Noels, K., & Beaton, A. M. (1998). Why are you doing things for the environment? The motivation toward the environmental scale (MTES). *Journal of Applied Social Psychology, 28*, 437–468.

Pelletier, L. G., & Vallerand, R. J. (1996). Supervisors' beliefs and subordinates' intrinsic motivation: A behavioral confirmation analysis. *Journal of Personality and Social Psychology, 71*, 331–340.

Petty, R. E., & Cacioppo, J. T. (1986). The elaboration likelihood model of persuasion. In L. Berkowitz (Ed.), *Advances in experimental social psychology* (pp. 124–194). New York: Academic Press.

Petty, R. E., & Wegener, D. T. (1998). Attitude change: Multitude roles for persuasion variables. In D. Gilbert, S. Fiske, & G. Lindzey (Eds.), *The handbook of social psychology* (4th ed., Vol. 1, pp. 323–390). New York: McGraw-Hill.

Plante, T. G., Cage, C., Clements, S., & Stover, A. (2006). Psychological benefits of exercise paired with virtual reality: Outdoor exercise energizes while indoor virtual exercise relaxes. *International Journal of Stress Management, 13*, 108–117.

Potoski, M., & Prakash, A. (2002). Protecting the environment: Voluntary regulations in environmental governance. *Policy Currents, 11*, 9–14.

Ramus, C. A. (2002). Encouraging innovative environmental actions: What companies and managers must do. *Journal of World Business, 37*, 151–164. doi:10.1016/S1090-9516(02)00074-3

Reinhardt, F. (2000). *Down to earth: Applying business principles to environmental management*. Boston: Harvard University Press.

Renn, O., Burns, W. J., Kasperson, J. X., Kasperson, R. E., & Slovic, P. (1992). The social amplification of risk: Theoretical foundations and empirical applications. *Journal of Social Issues, 48*, 137–160.

Rosen, C. S. (2000). Is the sequencing of change processes by stage consistent by health problems? A meta-analysis. *Health Psychology, 19*, 593–604.

Rothman, A. J., Kelly, K. M., Hertel, A., & Salovey, P. (2003). Message frames and illness representations: Implications for interventions to promote and sustain healthy behavior. In L. D. Cameron, & H. Leventhal (Eds.), *The self-regulation of health and illness behavior* (pp. 278–296). London: Routledge.

Rothman, A. J., & Salovey, P. (2007). The reciprocal relation between principles and practice. In A. Kruglanski, & E. T. Higgins (Eds.), *Social psychology: Handbook of basic principle* (2nd ed., pp. 826–849). New York: Guilford Press.

Rothman, A. J., Stark, E., & Salovey, P. (2006). Using message framing to promote healthy behavior: A guide to best practices. In J. Trafton (Ed.), *Best practices in the behavioral management of chronic diseases* (Vol. 3, pp. 31–48). Los Altos, CA: Institute for Disease Management.

Ryan, R. M., Weinstein, N., Bernstein, J. H., Brown, K. W., Mistretta, L., & Gagné, M. (2010). Vitalizing effects of being outdoors and in nature. *Journal of Environmental Psychology, 30*, 159–168.

Schaltegger, S., & Synnestvedt, T. (2002). The link between "green" and economic success: Environmental management as the crucial trigger between environmental and economic performance. *Journal of Environmental Management, 65*, 339–346.

Segerson, K., & Miceli, T. (1998). Voluntary environmental agreements: Good or bad news for environmental protection?. *Journal of Environmental Economics and Management, 36*, 109–130.

Séguin, C., Pelletier, L. G., & Hunsley, J. (1998). Toward a model of environmental activism. *Environment and Behavior, 30*, 628–652.

Séguin, C., Pelletier, L. G., & Hunsley, J. (1999). Predicting environmental behaviors: The influence of self-determination and information about environmental health risks. *Journal of Applied Social Psychology, 29*, 1582–1600.

Sheeran, P., Webb, T. L., & Gollwitzer, P. M. (2005). The interplay between goal intentions and implementation intentions. *Personality and Social Psychology Bulletin, 31*, 87–98.

Smith, A., Tucker, M., & Pitt, M. (2011). Healthy, productive workplaces: Towards a case for interior plantscaping. *Facilities, 29*(5/6), 209–223. doi:10.1108/02632771111120529

Stark, M., & Marcus, A. A. (2000). Introduction to the special forum on the management of organizations in the natural environment: A field emerging from multiple paths, with many challenges ahead. *Academy of Management Journal, 43*, 4, 539–546.

Statistics Canada. (2011). *Human activity and the environment: Economy and the environment (Catalog no. 16-201-X)*. Ottawa, ON: Statistics Canada.

Stone, D., Deci, E. L., & Ryan, R. M. (2009). Beyond talk: Creating autonomous motivation through self-determination theory. *Journal of General Management, 34*, 75–91.

Swim, J., Clayton, S., Doherty, T., Gifford, R., Howard, G., Reser, J., ... Weber, E. (2009). *Psychology and global climate change: Addressing a multi-faceted phenomenon and set of challenges*. A Report by the American Psychological Association's Task Force on the Interface Between Psychology and Global Climate Change. Washington, DC: American Psychological Association.

Tietenberg, T. (2000). *Environmental and natural resource economics*. New York: Addison Wesley.

United Nations. (2004). *UNEP 2004*. Annual report. Retrieved from http://www.un.org/publications/wpp2004/pressrelease.pdf.

United Nations Population Fund. (2009). *World population to exceed 9 billion by 2050*. Retrieved from http://www.un.org/esa/population/publications/wpp2008/pressrelease.pdf.

Vansteenkiste, M., Lens, W., Deci, E. L. (2006). Intrinsic versus extrinsic goal contents in self-determination theory: Another look at the quality of motivation. *Educational Psychologist, 41*, 19–31.

Vansteenkiste, M., Simons, J., Lens, W., Soenens, B., Matos, L., & Lacante, M. (2004). "Less is sometimes more": Goal-content matters. *Journal of Educational Psychology, 96*, 755–764.

Villacorta, M., Koestner, R., & Lekes, N. (2003). Further validation of the motivation toward the environment scale. *Environment and Behavior, 35*, 486–505.

Vogel, D. (2005). *The market for virtue: The potential and limits of corporate social responsibility*. Washington, DC: Brookings Institution Press.

Weinstein, N., Przybylski, A. K., & Ryan, R. M. (2009). Can nature make us more caring? Effects of immersion in nature on intrinsic aspirations and generosity. *Personality and Social Psychology Bulletin, 35*, 1315–1329.

World Commission on Economic Development. (1987). *Our common future*. New York: Oxford University Press.

World Resources Institutes. (2004). *World resources 2002-2004*. Washington, DC: World Resources Institutes.

Zanna, M. P., Higgins, T. E., & Taves, P. A. (1976). Is dissonance phenomenologically aversive? *Journal of Experimental Social Psychology, 12*, 530–538.

Zibarras, L. D., & Woods, S. A. (2010). A survey of UK selection practices across different organizations sizes and industry sectors. *Journal of Occupational and Organizational Psychology, 83*, 499–511.

CHAPTER

20

Translating Research Results in Economic Terms: An Application of Economic Utility Analysis Using SDT-Based Interventions

Jacques Forest, Marie-Hélène Gilbert, Geneviève Beaulieu, Philippe LeBrock, *and* Marylène Gagné

Abstract

This article demonstrates the economic utility of self-determined motivation and translates research results into economic terms, by using the cost-procedures-processes-outcomes-analysis, in order to reduce the scientist-practitioner gap. These economic utility analyses demonstrate how organizations can increase their profits and lessen their expenses by stimulating self-determined work motivation. We show how each dollar invested can generate $3.19 in return. It thus seems that being able to translate research results in economic terms is one way of reducing the scientist-practitioner gap because it uses a language understood by, namely money. Previous research results have shown the positive effect of having self-determined types of motivation but never were they translated into the language of money. Using economic utility analyses to translate research results in terms of money can efficiently help reduce the research-practitioner divide.

Key Words: motivation, self-determination theory, mental health, economic utility, return on investment

The Economic Utility of Self-Determined Motivation

In the last few years, a vertiginous increase in psychological problems related to work has been observed (Schott, 1999), so much so that these problems now represent a multibillion dollar bill for corporations and societies around the globe. Mental health problems related to work can bring deleterious consequences, such as lost productivity, increased healthcare cost, poor relationships, diminished innovative capacity, errors and accidents, and even legal actions (Conference Board of Canada, 2005). In Canada, these problems cost between $14 billion (Stephens & Joubert, 2001) and $33 billion yearly (Global Business and Economic Roundtable on Addiction and Mental Health, 2004) depending on the estimation. In the United States, direct and indirect costs of mental health problems at work average around $150 billion (Danna &

Griffin, 1999). This estimation goes up to $300 billion according to the American Institute of Stress (Stambor, 2006). At the international level, mental health problems associated with work are so important and widespread that some authors even argue that they can affect the economic competitiveness of a country by absorbing 3–4% of its gross national product (Liimatainen & Gabriel, 2000).

One possible cause of psychological problems at work is the type of motivational orientation an individual has toward working. Reasons why people work can vary from just earning a paycheck, to gaining some self-esteem and self-worth, to making this world a better place, to living or doing something interesting. These reasons can lead to differential outcomes. The goal of this article is to demonstrate the economic utility of self-determined motivation and to translate research results in economic terms by using concepts taken from economic utility techniques.[1]

335

Self-Determination Theory

One theory that covers a wide spectrum of human motivation and its different consequences in various life settings (including work) is self-determination theory (SDT; Deci & Ryan, 1985, 2000, 2001, 2008; Ryan & Deci, 2000, 2001). SDT (Deci & Ryan, 2008) posits that underlying reasons to perform an activity (such as work) vary along a continuum that goes from intrinsic (i.e., I work because of my interest and enjoyment of the tasks) to extrinsic (i.e., I work for an instrumental reason) to amotivation (the absence of motivation). SDT also proposes that extrinsic motivation can vary in terms of how internalized the motivation is, yielding three different types of extrinsic motivation. At one end of the self-determination continuum (Deci & Ryan, 2008), intrinsic motivation refers to the most self-determined type of motivation. When intrinsically motivated, an individual feels that his or her actions are freely experienced and self-endorsed. Actions are done for the sake of the enjoyment and the inherent satisfaction they bring. The first form of extrinsic motivation is termed *identified regulation*, which represents doing something because it is personally meaningful or judged to be important (Ryan & Deci, 2001). As an example of identified motivation behavior, Gagné and Deci (2005) give the example of a nurse who strongly values her patient's comfort and well-being. If a nurse understands the importance of doing her part of more unpleasant tasks, she might feel relatively autonomous in doing tasks such as taking care of the patients' personal hygiene, even though these activities are not inherently motivating. Next is *introjected regulation* (Deci & Ryan, 1985, 2001), which represents doing something out of inner pressures, whether it is obtaining internal rewards (e.g., boosting one's self-worth) or avoiding internal punishments (e.g., avoiding guilt). The least self-determined type of motivation is *extrinsic motivation* (Deci & Ryan, 1985, 2001). This is when behaviors are controlled by external factors, such as obtaining something positive (e.g., money or an award) or avoiding negative consequences (e.g., losing one's job). On the other end of the self-determination continuum stands *amotivation*, which is the absence of motivation or, in lay person's term, demotivation. These different types of motivation can be measured in the realm of work (e.g., Gagné et al., 2010) and its structure is invariant across different languages and culture (e.g., Gagné et al., 2014). We can regroup motivation types into two categories: autonomous motivation (comprising intrinsic motivation and identified regulation) and controlled motivation (comprising extrinsic and introjected regulation). These categories are sometimes used instead of the four distinct types of motivation (Sheldon, Turban, Brown, Barrick, & Judge, 2003).

For the last 30 years, SDT has received widespread attention in the domains of education, health care, and sports. In research examining these different realms of life, autonomous motivation has been linked to various positive consequences, such as enhanced creativity (Amabile, 1983), self-esteem (Deci, Schwartz, Sheinman, & Ryan, 1981), and general well-being (Langer & Rodin, 1976) just to name a few. Recent robust empirical findings support SDT as an integrative, coherent, and solid theory of work motivation as it is now establishing itself as a well-recognized theory of work motivation (Deci, Connell, & Ryan, 1989; Gagné & Deci, 2005; Gagné & Forest, 2009; Sheldon et al., 2003) to study important organizational topics, such as commitment (Gagné, Chemolli, Forest, & Koestner, 2008; Meyer, Becker, & Vandenberghe, 2004; Meyer & Gagné, 2008), performance and success (Baard, 2002; Baard, Deci, & Ryan, 2004; Burton, Lydon, D'Allessandro, & Koestner, 2006; Kuvaas, 2006a, 2007, 2009; Lee, Sheldon, & Turban, 2003), compensation (Gagné & Forest, 2008), leadership (Bono & Judge, 2003), acceptance of organizational change (Gagné, Koestner, & Zuckerman, 2000), turnover (Richer, Blanchard, & Vallerand, 2002), work-family conflict (Senécal, Vallerand, & Guay, 2001), work conditions in different countries (Deci et al., 2001), training (Dysvik & Kuvaas, 2008), job characteristics (Gagné, Senécal, & Koestner, 1997; Millette & Gagné, 2008), and career choice and management (Guay, 2005; Guay, Ratelle, Senécal, Larose, & Deschênes, 2006; Guay, Senécal, Gauthier, & Fernet, 2003; Vansteenkiste, Duriez, Simons, & Soenens, 2006; Vansteenkiste, Lens, De Witte, De Witte, & Deci, 2004; Vansteenkiste, Lens, De Witte, & Feather, 2005; Waterman, 2004, 2005; Waterman et al., 2003).

Finally, SDT has also been linked to mental health. Numerous researchers agree that mental health problems are costly and that they can have harmful effects on individual and organizational outcomes (Driskell & Salas, 1996; Kahn & Langlieb, 2002; Motowidlo, Manning, & Packard, 1986; Quick, Murphy, & Hurrel, 1992; Quick, Quick, Nelson, & Hurrel, 1997; Quick & Tetrick, 2003). The existing literature on mental health makes it possible to emphasize the fact that mental health is not simply the absence of disease or distress (e.g., Achille 2003a, 2003b; Keyes, 2003; Lent, 2004) but is characterized both by a nonexistent or low level of negative aspects and a fairly frequent occurrence of positive aspects (e.g., Achille, 2003a, 2003b; Bruchon-Schweitzer, 2002; Massé et al., 1998). Research linking SDT and mental health (e.g., Lévesque, Blais, & Hess, 2004a, 2004b; Lynch, Plant, & Ryan, 2005; Van den Broeck, Vansteenkiste, De Witte, & Lens, 2008; Vansteenkiste et al., 2007) has followed this general idea by using positive indicators, such as satisfaction (Ilardi, Leone, Kasser, & Ryan, 1993), adjustment (Kasser, Davey, & Ryan, 1992), and affective commitment (Kuvaas, 2006b), and negative indicators, such as burnout (Fernet, Guay, & Senécal, 2004) and physical symptoms (Otis & Pelletier, 2005).

Translating Research Results in Economic Terms

To go beyond theoretical evidence, organizations and managers often want to know if theories in organizational behavior and human resources management can help them increase the effectiveness and efficiency of their organization. One problem with organizational behavior and organizational psychology research results is that they can sometimes be difficult to understand for managers because it is in a language with which they are not familiar. Even though they would entirely comprehend the link between the variables we study (such as the link between self-determined motivation and mental health), it is often problematic for researchers to translate these results into an understandable business language (e.g., return on investment). One possible solution to find a commonly understood language between researchers and managers could be to use economic terms to express research results, which is precisely the purpose of economic utility analyses.

Overview of Economic Utility Analyses

Economic utility analysis is a general term used for methods and strategies aimed at putting an economic value on things that are not straightforwardly quantifiable. This kind of analysis has been successfully applied and well-accepted in such domains as psychiatry (Hoch & Dewa, 2005), behavioral medicine (Kaplan & Groessl, 2002), environmental medicine (Goetzel et al., 2004; Stave, Muchmore, & Gardner, 2003), and marital therapy (Fals-Stewart, Yates, & Klostermann, 2005). Fields closer to the organizational behavior literature where economic

utility analysis has been accepted and used include employee selection systems (Boudreau & Rynes, 1985; Boudreau, Sturman, & Judge, 1994; Burke & Doran, 1989; Cronshaw & Alexander, 1985; Hunter, Schmidt, & Coggin, 1988; Judiesch, Schmidt, & Hunter, 1993), performance evaluation (Hunter, Schmidt, & Judiesch, 1990; Judiesch, Schmidt, & Mount, 1992; Schmidt & Hunter, 1983), human resource intervention programs (Law, 1995; Rauschenberger & Schmidt, 1987), and general human resources management (Boudreau, 1991, 1996; Boudreau & Ramstad, 2003; Cascio & Boudreau, 2008; Huselid, 1995, 1996; Le Louarn & Daoust, 2008a, 2008b; Le Louarn & Wils, 2001; Macan & Highhouse, 1994; Saks, 2000). Specific research topics where it has been applied include mental health (Yates, 1996) and healthcare services (Drummond, Sculpher, Torrance, O'Brien, & Stoddart, 1997), psychological control (Falk & Kosfeld, 2006), employee absenteeism (Harrison & Martocchio, 1998), work-life balance (Duxbury, Higgins, & Johnson, 1999), training (Cascio, 1989; Mathieu & Leonard, 1987; Morrow, Jarrett, & Rupinski, 1997; Phillips, 1997, 2003), engagement (Xanthopoulou, Bakker, Demerouti, & Schaufeli, 2009), health and wellness programs (Aldana, 2001; Aldana, Merrill, Price, Hardy, & Hager, 2005; Chapman, 2003; DeRango & Franzini, 2002; Parks & Steelman, 2008), and stress management programs (Elo, Ervasti, Kuosma, & Mattila, 2008; Richardson & Rothstein, 2008), as well as high-performance workplaces (Lloyd & Foster, 2006).

Reasons why economic utility analysis is not more prevalent in organizational behavior research are understandable. We agree with authors, such as Kaplan and Groessl (2002), who say that economic utility analysis can seem unemotional, cold, and even offensive. Putting a dollar sign, monetizing, or quantifying mental distress or human suffering is not a natural reflex in organizational research where the human experience is valued over the monetary cost it can eventually prompt. Although this argument is understandable, this must not prevent organizational psychology or management researchers to collect economic data and/or to use notions from economic utility analysis. Economic utility calculations are very important because such information as returns on investment or costs/benefit ratio are often the only one that a manager or a CEO wishes to obtain from an organizational psychology consultant or researcher. For example, influential international governing bodies, such as the World Health

Organization, identify cost-effectiveness analysis as a topic of interest to which researchers should devote more energy (Murray, Evans, Acharya, & Baltussen, 2000; World Health Organization, 2000). Economic utility calculations can also convince organizations of their social responsibility toward their workers. Although it may sound ironic to rely on extrinsic incentives (i.e., money) to motivate managers to pay attention to this issue, demonstrating to them the economic benefits of good practices also educates them about the importance of promoting health at work (Conference Board of Canada, 2002). Finally, economic utility analyses applied to research results could be an efficient way to translate research results into intelligible terms to practitioners and managers (Shapiro, Kirkman, & Courtney, 2007), which would subsequently help disseminate research results to a wider public (rather than to scientific journal readers only; see Sommer, 2006) and diminish the research-practitioner divide as is emphasized by professional organizations, such as Society for Industrial and Organizational Psychology (Latham, 2009), specific journals, such as the *Journal of Occupational and Organizational Psychology* (Gelade, 2006; Hodgkinson, 2006; Symon, 2006; Wall, 2006), and researchers alike (Cascio, 2008; Cascio & Aguinis, 2008; Deadrick, & Gibson, 2009; Rynes, 2007a, 2007b; Rynes, Bartunek, & Daft, 2001).

Far from reducing the worker's experience to a dollar sign, notions from economic utility analysis have the advantage of exposing and explaining important research results in a financial and economic language that is understood by a wider range of people working in organizations. Moreover, this enhanced understanding of research results could increase the likelihood that managers listen to our recommendations and also the probability that they will participate in future studies and use research results.

However, the costs/benefit ratio and return on investment methods are often too simple for detecting and explaining the nuances and subtleties of the impact of our interventions. A more complete and sensible method exists to calculate the economic utility of interventions: the cost-procedures-processes-outcomes-analysis (CPPOA) technique (Yates, 1996).[2] To better understand how economic utility analyses can be used in organizational behavior research, the CPPOA technique is applied next to previously published research results on SDT (Deci et al., 1989).

Economic Utility Analysis Applied to SDT

By using the intervention presented in Deci and colleagues (1989), we use the CPPOA method to show the economic utility of interventions aimed at increasing self-determined motivation at work. More precisely, we show—by extrapolating on these research results—that each dollar invested in a training session to increase the frequency of managers' autonomy-supportive behaviors (intended to enhance the degree of self-determined motivation in employees) can generate $3.19 in profit for the organization after 1 year. The interventions were done over a little more than a 12-month period and in five different locations, and a delayed-treatment study was used in order to evaluate the efficacy of a training session aimed at coaching managers to support their subordinates' self-determined motivation. More precisely, three main themes were covered through group workshops and discussions: (1) maximizing the opportunity to take initiatives by subordinates; (2) improving the quantity and quality of informational feedback given to subordinates; and (3) helping managers accept, acknowledge, and recognize their subordinates' perspective (see the article by Deci and colleagues [1989] for full details of interventions). Deci and colleagues (1989) found that enhancing the interpersonal skills of managers through training produced increases in subordinates' trust in supervisors and the organization, feeling less pressured, satisfaction with quality of feedback, opportunity for inputs, security, higher perception of potential for advancement, and general satisfaction. We can also suppose that another positive consequence to add to this list is mental health. Apart from the psychological benefits of enhancing the managers' capacity to support their subordinates' self-determined motivation, organizations are also interested in knowing the economic impact of the programs by asking: "How much does each dollar invested generate in savings/profits?"

Take the example of an organization with 68 employees (one CEO, two employees within human resources and five managers, each one having 12 employees under their supervision) in which we would apply the training regimen described in Deci and colleagues (1989). This company would have a wage bill[3] of $3,750,000. It is generally recognized that problems associated with work (e.g., absence, disease, burnout) represent, at the very least, an expenditure equivalent to 5% of the wage bill (e.g., Mercer Human Resources, 2006), which translates into $187,500 for the current example. In order to actually use the CPPOA method, we first have to calculate the cost[4] of the training session. This is what is shown in Table 20.1.

By combining notions from CPPOA (Yates, 1996) and human resources calculation (Le Louarn & Wils, 2001, pp. 110–113), we are able to say that at Time 1 (i.e., before the training session), and in light of the normal distribution curve, 17% of employees costs 1.5 times more than the normal cost to the organization in terms of expenses related to absence (e.g., leave of absence due to burnout), that 66% of employees have a normal cost (i.e., 5% of their salary) to the organization, and that 17% are costing half the normal cost to their company (e.g., they are less absent and/or are not using employee assistance program services as frequently). At Time 2, after training managers, we can generally assume that this will have a positive impact on employees' self-determined motivation. To calculate this impact on mental health and costs, we need to observe what happens when people change cost category. In the example, some people will change categories resulting in less people in the most expensive category (four people less in

the 1.5 times the normal cost), there will be more people in the least expensive category (four people more in the half times the normal cost), and the same number of people in the middle category. This results in a $12,500 savings from Time 1 to Time 2 (Table 20.2).

The same logic can be applied to increased employee performance. On the left hand side of Table 20.3, we can see that there is a normal distribution of employees by output categories: 10 employees have a 90% output (0.9 x $100,000 in output), 40 have a normal output (i.e., $100,000), and 10 have a higher output than[5] (1.1 x $100,000). Again, following managers' training, four employees will switch from the 90% output category to the normal output category and four employees of this middle category will reach the 110% category, resulting in a $80,000 increase in employee output (right hand side of Table 20.3).

In order to calculate how much each invested dollar yields at the end of the year, it is necessary to add the savings made on the expenses related with mental health and disability ($12,500) and the rise in profits ($80,000), and then divide the total by

Table 20.1 Costs estimation for the training session to enhance the support of managers.

Cost per hour	Training development	Transportation/room/food	Training	Equipment/material/training facilities	Follow-up	TOTAL
Consultant ($300/hr)	16 hr × $300/hr = $4,800	500 × $0.35/km = $175 $150/night × 3 = $50 $25/(meal) × 8 days = 200$	16 hr × $300/hr = $4,800	$2,000	1.5 hr × $300/hr = $450	$12,875
Junior consultant ($150/hr)	16 hr × $150/hr = $2,400	$150/night x 3 = $450 $25/(meal) × 8 days = $200	16 hr × $150/hr = $2,400	——	1.5 hr × $150/hr = $225	$5,675
Managers ($75/hr)	0.25 hr × $75/hr × 5 managers = $93.75	500 × .35/km = $175 $150/night × 2 = $300 $25/(meal) × 6 days = $150 $625 × 5 managers = $3,125	16 hr × $75/hr × 5 managers = $6,000	—	1.5 hr × $75/hr × 5 managers = $562.50	1956.25 × 5 managers = $9781.25
Human resources ($75/hr)	2 hr × $75/hr = $150					
Employees ($20/hr)	0.25 hr × $20/hr × 50 = $250				0.25 hr × $20/hr × 50 = $250	
	$7,693.75	$4,600	$13,200	$2,000	$1,487.50	$28,981.25

Table 20.2 Reduction of organizational expenditures related to psychological problems following the training of managers.

Pretraining (Time 1)				Posttraining (Time 2)				Economies made in 1 year after training (Time 1— Time 2)
10 persons × (1.5 × $3,125)	40 persons × $3,125	10 persons × (0.5 × $3,125)	Total of expenses at Time 1	6 persons × (1.5 × $3,125)	40 persons × $3,125	14 persons × (0.5 × $3,125)	Total of expenses at Time 2	187,500 −175,000
$46,875	$125,000	$15,625	$187,500	$28,125	$125,000	$21,875	$175,000	= $12,500

the cost of training ($28,981.25). On the basis of this calculation, it is possible to advance that each dollar invested in a training session generates, after 1 year, $3.19 for the organization. This value in profit for each dollar invested in our example is similar to what was found in other interventions. For example, Lloyd and Foster (2006) presented three organizational interventions (two in business organizations and one in a city administration) where each dollar invested generated, a year later, $1.42, $3.40, and $3.60, respectively.

General Discussion

Researchers and consultants can learn from this exercise that far from reducing the worker to a simple dollar sign, the CPPOA method makes it possible to check the economic utility and the financial effectiveness of psychological interventions with more nuance and subtlety than the simple cost/benefit ratio or return on investment. More specifically, the CPPOA method enables the explanation of mechanisms or mediating variables on which the interventions have an effect (Table 20.4). This experience can afterward be quantified in terms of savings and/or profits. It is our belief that the use of economic-utility analyses in research can help reduce the scientist-practitioner gap, which is in line with numerous recent calls for action in this direction (Cascio, 2008; Deadrick, & Gibson, 2009; Gelade, 2006; Hodgkinson, 2006; Latham, 2009; Rynes, 2007a, 2007b; Rynes et al., 2001; Shapiro et al., 2007; Sommer, 2006; Symon, 2006; Wall, 2006). The CPPOA method makes it possible to express worker outcomes in terms that managers understand and care about: money. To have an impact, researchers and consultants in organizations should thus more systematically use the CPPOA method (Yates, 1996) or other economic utility analyses in order to demonstrate the economic utility of their interventions. Recognized international governing bodies, such as World Health Organization (Murray et al., 2000; World Health Organization, 2000), insist on the importance of systematically using simple and useful economic utility estimations in health studies. This will allow for more effective publicity of the impact and the effectiveness of our work with an economic and financial language understood by a wide range of people in work organizations.

Table 20.3 Increase in employee performance following the training of managers.

Pretraining (Time 1)				Posttraining (Time 2)				Increase in profits from Time 1 to Time 2 (Time 2— Time 1)
10 persons × (0.9 × $100,000)	40 persons × $100,000	10 persons × (1.1 x $100,000)	Profits at Time 1	6 persons × (0.9 x $100,000)	40 persons × $100,000	14 persons × (1.1 × $100,000)	Profits at Time 2	$6,080,000 −$6,000,000
$900,000	$4,000,000	$1,100,000	$6,000,000	$540,000	$4,000,000	$1,540,000	$6,080,000	$80,000

Table 20.4 Complete representation of the CPPOA method.

Costs		Procedures		Processes		Outcomes
Costs of the training session as presented in Table 20.1	→	Training managers to increase and support their subordinates' self-determined motivation support	→	Displacement of the self-determination index toward more self-determined motivation	→	More mental health (more well-being and less distress) More output per employee

Conclusion

The goal of this article is to demonstrate the economic utility of promoting self-determined motivation in work organizations. To fulfill this goal, the CPPOA method (Yates, 1996) is used to demonstrate how organizations can turn psychological benefits for their employees into monetary value. As shown in a simulated example, each dollar invested in managerial training was able to produce $3.19 in return. This value in a theoretical example is comparable with what was found in previous organizational interventions (e.g., Lloyd & Foster, 2006). Although they are not immune to critics (e.g., Latham & Whyte, 1994; Whyte & Latham, 1997), the simplicity and usefulness of economic utility analysis in general and the CPPOA method in particular should encourage use by researchers and practitioners alike. Future research should thus aim at including economic utility analyses, such as CPPOA, in addition to the usual effect sizes currently used. This would help industrial-organizational psychology, management, and other administrative sciences get more recognition in the business community.

Because mental health problems constitute a multibillion dollar problem for organizations, and SDT has been identified as a useful model to understand and promote mental health, future research on the relation between types of motivation and health outcomes seems warranted. In this vein, the present article is just a small step to a complete understanding of how, when, and under what circumstances the different types of motivation have a proximal impact on workers' health and a distal impact on the economy. If it is systematically applied, economic utility analyses usage in research can contribute to recent research movements, such as the study of well-being/happiness as an economic advantage (e.g., Diener, Kesebir, & Lucas, 2008; Diener, Lucas, Schimmack, & Helliwell, 2008; Diener & Seligman, 2004; Frey & Stutzer, 2007), as a tool to enhance the quality of life of entire nations (e.g., Blustein, 2008; Cummins, Lau, Mellor, & Stokes, 2009; Dolan & White, 2007; Keyes, 2006, 2007), and to attain a sustainable future for mankind (O'Brien, 2008). Great research challenges thus lie ahead, but it is all worth it if we want healthy workers in a thriving economy.

Future Directions

One option to reduce the scientific-practitioner gap is for journal editors and granting agencies to request economic-utility analyses as a research output in articles and grant proposals. This could be a grassroots' approach in order to increase the diffusion and adoption of these analyses. To educate the scientific community on economic utility analyses, a journal editorial could be written to present pitfalls, challenges, and errors to avoid as well as best practices and good examples of use of these analyses.

In published articles where economic utility analyses are used, authors should be prudent in their monetary estimations and thoroughly explain the significance of this monetary increased output and/or reduction in costs. In other words, researchers should not use economic utility analyses if the monetary translation is poorly done. The thing to avoid is the development of patterns or habits in the production of numbers that would be meaningless. In other words, good monetary translation is the goal, not monetary number production.

Notes

1. The research and the writing of this article was facilitated through a doctoral fellowship from the Fonds Québécois de Recherche sur la Société et la Culture to the second author, and preparation of the article was facilitated through a postdoctoral fellowship from the Institut de Recherche Robert-Sauvé en Santé et Sécurité au Travail to the first author. Any information concerning this chapter may be addressed to Jacques Forest, UQAM—School of Management Science, ORH Department, C.P. 8888, Downtown Station, Montréal, Québec, Canada, H3C 3P8. Email: forest.jacques@uqam.ca.
2. Economic utility analyses can be separated into three categories (e.g., DeRango & Franzini, 2002, p. 418), which differ by their measurement of consequences. There is cost-effectiveness (where physical units, such as life years gained, are used as a consequence), cost-utility (where utility-weighted health outcomes, such as quality-adjusted

life years, are used as a consequence), and cost-benefit (where dollars are used as a consequence). The CPPOA method could thus be considered as a hybrid between cost-benefit and cost-effectiveness because it translates in dollars (cost-benefit) psychological consequences (cost-effectiveness). For the sake of simplicity, we just present the CPPOA method to raise awareness of researchers on economic utility analyses rather than explain the different categories of economic utility analyses.

3. Details of the wage bill are not important for understanding the logic of economic utility analysis but readers interested in it can contact the first author.

4. Costs for the training session were derived from the authors' experience as consultants.

5. We voluntarily exaggerated the differences between categories of cost and diminished the variation in output categories in order to be as conservative as possible. Readers should note that output values, just as in the example, are hypothetical and presented in order to illustrate the CPPOA method. This is in accordance with research on utility analysis, which suggests that conservative estimates or ranges of value should be used (e.g., Sturman, 2000). It is also suggested to regularly make assumption reviews as to what the numbers are really "saying" in order to prevent wrong decisions or interpretations.

References

Achille, M. (2003a). Définir la santé au travail. I. La base conceptuelle d'un modèle de la santé au travail [Defining health at work. I. The conceptual basis of a health at work model]. In R. Foucher, A. Savoie, L. Brunet. (Eds.), *Concilier performance organisationnelle et santé psychologique au travail [Reconciling performance and mental health at work]* (pp. 65–89). Montréal: Éditions Nouvelles AMS.

Achille, M. (2003b). Définir la santé au travail. II. Un modèle multidimensionnel des indicateurs de la santé au travail [Defining health at work. II. A multidimensional model with health at work indicators]. In R. Foucher, A. Savoie, L. Brunet. (Eds.), *Concilier performance organisationnelle et santé psychologique au travail [Reconciling performance and mental health at work]* (pp. 91–109). Montréal: Éditions Nouvelles AMS.

Aldana, S. G. (2001). Financial impact of health promotion programs: A comprehensive review of the literature. *American Journal of Health Promotion, 15,* 296–320.

Aldana, S. G., Merrill, R. M., Price, K., Hardy, A., & Hager, R. (2005). Financial impact of a comprehensive multisite workplace health promotion program. *Preventive Medecine, 4,* 31–37.

Amabile, T. M. (1983). *The social psychology of creativity.* New York: Springer-Verlag.

Baard, P. P. (2002). Intrinsic need satisfaction in organizations: A motivational basis of success in for-profit and not-for-profit settings. In E. L. Deci, & R. M. Ryan (Eds.), *Handbook of self-determination research* (pp. 255–275). Rochester, NY: University of Rochester Press.

Baard, P. P., Deci, E. L., & Ryan, R. M. (2004). Intrinsic need satisfaction: A motivational basis of performance and well-being in two work settings. *Journal of Applied Social Psychology, 34,* 2045–2068.

Blustein, D. L. (2008). The role of work in psychological health and well-being: A conceptual, historical, and public policy perspective. *American Psychologist, 63,* 228–240.

Bono, J. E., & Judge, T. A. (2003). Self-concordance at work: Toward understanding the motivational effects of transformational leaders. *Academy of Management Journal, 46,* 554–571.

Boudreau, J. W. (1991). Utility analysis for decisions in human resource management. In M. D. Dunnette, & L. M. Lough (Eds.), *Handbook of industrial and organizational psychology* (Vol. 2, 2nd ed., pp. 621–745). Palo Alto, CA: Consulting Psychologists Press.

Boudreau, J. W. (1996). The motivational impact of utility analysis and HR measurement. *Journal of Human Resource Costing and Accountancy, 1,* 73–84.

Boudreau, J. W., & Ramstad, P. M. (2003). Strategic I/O psychology and the role of utility analysis models. In W. Borman, D. Ilgen, & R. Klimoski (Eds.), *Handbook of psychology—industrial and organizational psychology* (Vol. 12, pp. 193–221). New York: Wiley.

Boudreau, J. W., & Rynes, S. L. (1985). Role of recruitment and staffing utility analysis. *Journal of Applied Psychology, 70,* 354–366.

Boudreau, J. W., Sturman, M., & Judge, T. (1994). Utility analysis: What are the "black boxes", and do they affect decisions. In N. Anderson, & P. Herriot (Eds.), *International Handbook of selection and assessment* (pp. 77–96). London: John Wiley & Sons.

Bruchon-Schwetzer, M. (2002). *Psychologie de la santé: Modèles, concepts et methods [Psychology of health: Models, concepts, and methods].* Paris: Dunod.

Burke, M. J., & Doran, L. I. (1989). A note on the economic utility of generalized validity coefficients in personnel selection. *Journal of Applied Psychology, 74,* 171–175.

Burton, K. D., Lydon, J. E., D'Allessandro, D. U., & Koestner, R. (2006). The differential effects of intrinsic and identified motivation on well-being and performance: Prospective, experimental, and implicit approaches to self-determination theory. *Journal of Personality and Social Psychology, 91,* 750–762.

Cascio, W. F. (1989). Using utility analysis to assess training outcomes. In I. L. Goldstein (Ed.), *Training and development in organizations* (pp. 63–88). San Francisco, CA: Jossey-Bass

Cascio, W. F. (2008). To prosper, organizational psychology should . . . bridge application and scholarship. *Journal of Organizational Behavior, 29,* 455–469.

Cascio, W. F., & Aguinis, H. (2008). Research in industrial and organizational psychology from 1963 to 2007: Changes, choices, and trends. *Journal of Applied Psychology, 93,* 1062–1081.

Cascio, W. F., & Boudreau, J. W. (2008). *Investing in people: Financial impact of human resources initiatives.* Upper Saddle River, NJ: Pearson.

Chapman, L. S. (2003). Meta-evaluation of worksite health promotion economic return studies. *American Journal of Health Promotion, 6,* 1–10.

Conference Board of Canada (2002). *Health promotion programs at work: A frivolous cost or a sound investment?* Ottawa: Conference Board of Canada.

Conference Board of Canada (2005). *What you need to know about mental health at work: A tool for managers.* Ottawa: Conference Board of Canada.

Cronshaw, S. F., & Alexander, R. A. (1985). One answer to the demand for accountability: Selection utility analysis as an investment decision. *Organizational Behavior and Human Performance, 35,* 102–118.

Cummins, R. A., Lau, A. L. D., Mellor, D., & Stokes, M. A. (2009). Encouraging governments to enhance the happiness of their nation: Step 1: Understand subjective well-being. *Social Indicators Research, 91*, 23–36.

Danna, K., & Griffin, R. W. (1999). Health and well-being in the workplace: A review and synthesis of the literature. *Journal of Management, 25*, 357–384.

Deadrick, D. L., & Gibson, P. A. (2009). Revisiting the research-practice gap in HR: A longitudinal analysis. *Human Resource Management Review, 19*, 144–153.

Deci, E. L., Connell, J. P., & Ryan, R. M. (1989). Self-determination in a work organization. *Journal of Applied Psychology, 74*, 580–590.

Deci, E. L., & Ryan, R. M. (1985). *Intrinsic motivation and self-determination in human behavior.* New York: Plenum Press.

Deci, E. L., & Ryan, R. M. (2000). The "what" and "why" of goal pursuits: Human needs and the self-determination of behavior. *Psychological Inquiry, 11*, 227–268.

Deci, E. L., & Ryan, R. M. (2001). *Handbook of self-determination research.* New York: University of Rochester Press.

Deci, E. L., & Ryan, R. M. (2008). Facilitating optimal motivation and psychological well-being across life's domains. *Canadian Psychology, 49*, 14–23.

Deci, E. L., Ryan, R. M., Gagné, M., Leone, D. R., Usunov, J., & Kornazheva, B. P. (2001). Need satisfaction, motivation, and well-being in the work organizations of a former eastern bloc country: A cross-cultural study of self-determination. *Personality and Social Psychology Bulletin, 27*, 930–942.

Deci, E. L., Schwartz, A. J., Sheinman, L., & Ryan, R. M. (1981). An instrument to assess adults' orientations toward control versus autonomy with children: Reflections on intrinsic motivation and perceived competence. *Journal of Educational Psychology, 73*, 642–650.

DeRango, K., & Franzini, L. (2002). Economic evaluations of workplace health interventions: Theory and literature review. In J. C. Quick, & L. E. Tetrick (Eds.), *Handbook of occupational health psychology* (pp. 417–430). Washington, DC: American Psychological Association.

Diener, E., Kesebir, P., & Lucas, R. (2008). Benefits of accounts of well-being—For societies and for psychological science. *Applied Psychology: An International Review, 57*, 37–53.

Diener, E., Lucas, R., Schimmack, U., & Helliwell, J. (2008). *Accounts of well-being for policy use.* Oxford: Oxford University Press.

Diener, E., & Seligman, M. E. P. (2004). Beyond money: Toward an economy of well-being. *Psychological Science in the Public Interest, 5*, 1–31.

Dolan, P., & White, M. P. (2007). How can measures of subjective well-being be used to inform public policy? *Perspectives on Psychological Science, 2*, 71–85.

Driskell, J. E., & Salas, E. (1996). *Stress and human performance.* Mahwah, New Jersey: Lawrence Erlbaum Associates.

Drummond, M. F., Sculpher, M. J., Torrance, G. W., O'Brien, B. J., & Stoddart, G. L. (1997). *Methods for the economic evaluation of health care programmes* (3rd ed.). New York: Oxford Medical Publications, Oxford University Press.

Duxbury, L., Higgins, C., & Johnson, K. (1999). *Un examen des répercussions et des coûts du conflit travail-famille au Canada [An examination of the costs of work-family conflict in Canada].* Ottawa: Santé Canada.

Dysvik, A., & Kuvaas, B. (2008). The relationship between perceived training opportunities, work motivation and employee outcomes. *International Journal of Training and Development, 12*, 138–157.

Elo, A.-L., & Ervasti, J., Kuosma, E., & Mattila, P. (2008). Evaluation of an organizational stress management program in a municipal public works organization. *Journal of Occupational Health Psychology, 13*, 10–23.

Falk, A., & Kosfeld, M. (2006). The hidden cost of control. *The American Economic Review, 96*, 1611–1630.

Fals-Stewart, W., Yates, B. T., & Klostermann, K. (2005). Assessing the costs, benefits, cost-benefit ratio, and cost-effectiveness of marital and family treatments: Why we should and how we can. *Journal of Family Psychology, 19*, 28–39.

Fernet, C., Guay, F., & Senécal, C. (2004). Adjusting to job demands: The role of work self-determination and job control in predicting burnout. *Journal of Vocational Behavior, 65*, 39–56.

Frey, B. S., & Stutzer, A. (2007). *Economics and psychology: A promising new cross-disciplinary field.* Cambridge, MA: The MIT Press

Gagné, M., Chemolli, E., Forest, J., & Koestner, R. (2008). A temporal analysis of the relation between organisational commitment and work motivation. *Psychologica Belgica, 48*, 219–241.

Gagné, M., & Deci, E. L. (2005). Self-determination theory and work motivation. *Journal of Organizational Behavior, 26*, 331–362.

Gagné, M., & Forest, J. (2008). The study of compensation systems through the lens of self-determination theory: Reconciling 35 years of debate. *Canadian Psychology, 49*, 225–232.

Gagné, M., & Forest, J. (2009). La motivation au travail selon la théorie de l'autodétermination [Motivation at work according to Self-Determination Theory]. In J. Rojot, C. Vandenberghe, & P. Roussel (Eds.), *Comportement organisationnel—Volume 3: Théorie des organisations, motivation au travail, engagement dans l'organisation [Organizational behavior—Volume 3: Organizational theory, motivation at work, commitment in organization]* (pp. 215–234). Brussels, Belgium: De Boeck.

Gagné, M., Forest, J., Gilbert, M.-H., Aubé, C., Morin, E. M., & Malorni, A. (2010). The Motivation at Work Scale: Validation evidence in two languages. *Educational and Psychological Measurement, 70*, 628–646.

Gagné, M., Forest, J., Vansteenkiste, M., Crevier-Braud, L., Van den Broeck, A., Aspeli, A. K.,…Westbye, C. (2014). The Multidimensional Work Motivation Scale: Validation evidence in seven Languages and nine countries. *European Journal of Work and Organizational Psychology.*

Gagné, M., Koester, R., & Zuckerman, M. (2000). Facilitating acceptance of organizational change: The importance of self-determination. *Journal of Applied Social Psychology, 30*, 1843–1852.

Gagné, M., Senécal, C., & Koestner, R. (1997). Proximal job characteristics, feelings or empowerment, and intrinsic motivation: A multidimensional model. *Journal of Applied Social Psychology, 27*, 1222–1240.

Gelade, G. A. (2006). But what does it mean in practice? The *Journal of Occupational and Organizational Psychology* from a practitioner perspective. *Journal of Occupational and Organizational Psychology, 79*, 153–160.

Global Business and Economic Roundtable on Addiction and Mental Health (2004). *CEO survey on mental health.*

Retrieved from http://www.mentalhealthroundtable.ca/apr_2004/CEO_survey_march_2004.pdf

Goetzel, R. Z., Long, S. R., Ozminkowski, R. J., Hawkins, K., Wang, S., & Lynch, W. (2004). Health, absence, disability, and presenteeism cost estimates of certain physical and mental health conditions affecting U.S. employers. *Journal of Occupational and Environmental Medicine, 46,* 398–412.

Guay, F. (2005). Motivations underlying career decision-making activities: The Career Decision-Making Autonomy Scale (CDMAS). *Journal of Career Assessment, 13,* 77–97.

Guay, F., Ratelle, C. F., Senécal, C., Larose, S., & Deschênes, A. (2006). Distinguishing developmental from chronic career indecision: Self-efficacy, autonomy, and social support. *Journal of Career Assessment, 14,* 235–255.

Guay, F., Senécal, C., Gauthier, L., & Fernet, C. (2003). Predicting career indecision: A self-determination theory perspective. *Journal of Counseling Psychology, 50,* 165–177.

Harrison, D. A., & Martocchio, J. J. (1998). Time for absenteeism: A 20-year review of origins, offshoots, and outcomes. *Journal of Management, 24,* 305–350.

Hoch, J. S., & Dewa, C. S. (2005). An introduction to economic evaluation: What's in a name? *Canadian Journal of Psychiatry, 50,* 159–166.

Hodgkinson, G. P. (2006). The role of JOOP (and other scientific journals) in bridging the practitioner-researcher divide in industrial, work and organizational (IWO) psychology. *Journal of Occupational and Organizational Psychology, 79,* 173–178.

Hunter, J. E., Schmidt, F. L., & Coggin, T. D. (1988). Problems and pitfalls in using capital budgeting and financial accounting techniques in assessing the utility of personnel programs. *Journal of Applied Psychology, 73,* 522–528.

Hunter, J. E., Schmidt, F. L., & Judiesch, M. K. (1990). Individual differences in output variability as a function of job complexity. *Journal of Applied Psychology, 75,* 28–42.

Huselid, M. A. (1995). The impact of human resource management practices on turnover, productivity, and corporate financial performance. *Academy of Management Journal, 38,* 635–672.

Huselid, M. A. (1996). Methodological issues in cross-sectional and panel estimates of the human resource-firm performance link. *Industrial Relations, 35,* 400–422.

Ilardi, B. C., Leone, D., Kasser, R., & Ryan, R. M. (1993). Employee and supervisor ratings of motivation: Main effects and discrepancies associated with job satisfaction and adjustment in a factory setting. *Journal of Applied Social Psychology, 23,* 1789–1805.

Judiesch, M. K., Schmidt, F. L., & Hunter, J. E. (1993). Has the problem of judgement in utility analysis been solved? *Journal of Applied Psychology, 78,* 903–911.

Judiesch, M. K., Schmidt, F. L., & Mount, J. E. (1992). Estimates of the dollar value of employee output in utility analyses: An empirical test of two theories. *Journal of Applied Psychology, 77,* 234–250.

Kahn, J. P., & Langlieb, A. M. (2002). *Mental health and productivity in the workplace: A handbook for organizations and clinicians.* San Francisco, CA: Jossey-Bass.

Kaplan, R. M., & Groessl, E. J. (2002). Applications of cost-effectiveness methodologies in behavioral medicine. *Journal of Consulting and Clinical Psychology, 70,* 482–493.

Kasser, T., Davey, J., & Ryan, R. M. (1992). Motivation, dependability, and employee-supervisor discrepancies in psychiatric

vocational rehabilitation settings. *Rehabilitation Psychology, 37,* 175–187.

Keyes, C. L. M. (2003). Complete mental health: An agenda for the 21st century. In C. L. M. Keyes, & J. Haidt (Eds.), *Flourishing: Positive psychology and the life well-lived* (pp. 293–312). Washington, DC: American Psychological Association.

Keyes, C. L. M. (2006). Subjective well-being in mental health and human development research worldwide: An introduction. *Social Indicators Research, 77,* 1–10.

Keyes, C. L. M. (2007). Promoting and protecting mental health as flourishing: A complementary strategy for improving national mental health. *American Psychologist, 62,* 95–108.

Kuvaas, B. (2006a). Work performance, affective commitment, and work motivation: The roles of pay administration and pay level. *Journal of Organizational Behavior, 27,* 365–385.

Kuvaas, B. (2006b). Performance appraisal satisfaction and employee outcomes: Mediating and moderating roles of motivation. *The International Journal of Human Resource Management, 17,* 504–522.

Kuvaas, B. (2007). Different relationships between perceptions of developmental performance appraisal and work performance. *Personnel Review, 36,* 378–397.

Kuvaas, B. (2009). A test of hypothesis derived from Self-Determination Theory among public sector employees. *Employee Relations, 31,* 39–56.

Langer, E. J., & Rodin, J. (1976). The effects of choice and personal responsibility for the aged: A field experiment in an institutional setting. *Journal of Personality and Social Psychology, 34,* 191–198.

Latham, G. P. (2009). Bridging the scientist-practitioner gap. *The Industrial Psychologist, 46,* 7–9.

Latham, G. P., & Whyte, G. (1994). The futility of utility analysis. *Personnel Psychology, 47,* 31–46.

Law, K. S. (1995). Estimating the dollar value contribution of human resources intervention programs: Some comments on the Brogden utility equation. *Australian Journal of Management, 20,* 197–206.

Lee, F. K., Sheldon, K. M., & Turban, D. B. (2003). Personality and the goal-striving process: The influence of achievement goal patterns, goal level, and mental focus on performance and enjoyment. *Journal of Applied Psychology, 88,* 256–265.

Le Louarn, J.-Y., & Daoust, J. (2008a). Finance et ressources humaines: La grande séduction! [Finance and human resources: The great seduction!]. *Gestion, Revue Internationale de Gestion, 32,* 72–78.

Le Louarn, J.-Y., & Daoust, J. (2008b). Les ratios financiers liés aux ressources humaines: Une application au secteur bancaire Canadien [Financial ratios related to human resources: An application to the Canadian banking industry]. *Gestion, Revue Internationale de Gestion, 32,* 79–87.

Le Louarn, J.-Y., & Wils, T. (2001). *L'évaluation de la gestion des ressources humaines [Evaluation of human resources management].* Paris: Liaisons.

Lent, R. W. (2004). Toward a unifying theoretical and practical perspective on well-being and psychological adjustment. *Journal of Counseling Psychology, 51,* 482–509.

Lévesque, M., Blais, M. R., & Hess, U. (2004a). Dynamique motivationnelle de l'épuisement et du bien-être chez des enseignants africains [Motivational dynamic of exhaustion and well-being of African teachers]. *Canadian Journal of Behavioural Science, 36,* 190–201.

Lévesque, M., Blais, M. R., & Hess, U. (2004b). Motivation, comportements organisationnels discrétionnaires et bien-être en milieu Africain: Quand le devoir oblige? [Motivation, discretionary organizational behaviors and well-being in Africa: When duty calls?] *Canadian Journal of Behavioural Science, 36,* 321–332.

Liimatainen, M., & Gabriel, P. (2000). *Mental health in the workplace. Situation analysis: United Kingdom.* Geneva: International Labour Office.

Lloyd, P. J., & Foster, S. L. (2006). Creating healthy, high-performance workplaces: Strategies from health and sports psychology. *Consulting Psychology Journal: Practice and Research, 58,* 23–39.

Lynch, M., Plant, R., & Ryan, R. M. (2005). Psychological needs and threat to safety: Implications for staff and patients in a psychiatric hospital for youth. *Professional Psychology—Research and Practice, 36,* 415–425.

Macan, T. H., & Highhouse, S. (1994). Communicating the utility of human resource activities: A survey of I/O and HR professionals. *Journal of Business and Psychology, 8,* 425–436.

Massé, R., Poulin, C., Lambert, J., Dassa, C., Lambert, J., Bélair, S., & Battaglini, A. (1998). The structure of mental health: Higher-order confirmatory factor analyses of psychological distress and well-being measures. *Social Indicators Research, 45,* 475–504.

Mathieu, J. E., & Leonard, R. L. (1987). Applying utility concepts to a training program in supervisory skills: A time-based approach. *Academy of Management Journal, 30,* 316–335.

Mercer Human Resources (2006). *Mercer/Marsh survey on health, productivity and absence management programs.* New York: Mercer HR.

Meyer, J. P., Becker, T. E., & Vandenberghe, C. (2004). Employee commitment and motivation: A conceptual analysis and integrative model. *Journal of Applied Psychology, 89,* 991–1007.

Meyer, J. P., & Gagné, M. (2008). Employee engagement from a self-determination theory perspective. *Industrial and Organizational Perspectives, 1,* 60–62.

Millette, V., & Gagné, M. (2008). Designing volunteers' tasks to maximize motivation, satisfaction and performance: The impact of job characteristics on the outcomes of volunteer involvement. *Motivation and Emotion, 32,* 11–22.

Morrow, C. C., Jarrett, M. Q., & Rupinski, M. T. (1997). An investigation of the effect and economic utility of corporate-wide training. *Personnel Psychology, 50,* 91–119.

Motowidlo, S. J., Manning, M. R., & Packard, J. S. (1986). Occupational stress: Its causes and consequences for job performance. *Journal of Applied Psychology, 71,* 618–629.

Murray, C. J. L., Evans, D. B., Acharya, A., Baltussen, R. M. P. M. (2000). Development of WHO guidelines on generalized cost-effectiveness analysis. *Health Economics, 9,* 235–251.

O'Brien, C. (2008). Sustainable happiness: How happiness studies can contribute to a more sustainable future. *Canadian Psychology, 49,* 289–295.

Otis, N., & Pelletier, L. G. (2005). A motivational of daily hassles, physical symptoms, and future work intentions among police officers. *Journal of Applied Social Psychology, 35,* 2193–2214.

Parks, K. M., & Steelman, L. A. (2008). Organizational wellness programs: A meta-analysis. *Journal of Occupational Health Psychology, 13,* 56–68.

Phillips, J. J. (1997). *Handbook of training evaluation and measurement methods.* Boston, MA: Gulf Professional Publishing.

Phillips, J. J. (2003). *Return on investment in training and performance improvement* (2nd ed.). Amsterdam: Elsevier.

Quick, J. C., Murphy, L. R., & Hurrel, J. J. (1992). *Stress and well-being at work: Assessments and interventions for occupational mental health.* Washington, DC: American Psychological Association.

Quick, J. C., Quick, J. D., Nelson, D. L., & Hurrell, J. J. (1997). *Preventive stress management in organizations.* Washington, DC: American Psychological Association.

Quick, J. C., & Tetrick, L. E. (2003). *Handbook of occupational health psychology.* Washington, DC: American Psychological Association.

Rauschenberger, J. M., & Schmidt, F. L. (1987). Measuring the economic impact of human resource programs. *Journal of Business and Psychology, 2,* 50–59.

Richardson, K. M., & Rothstein, H. R. (2008). Effects of occupational stress management intervention programs: A meta-analysis. *Journal of Occupational Health Psychology, 13,* 69–93.

Richer, S. F., Blanchard, C., & Vallerand, R. J. (2002). A motivational model of work turnover. *Journal of Applied Social Psychology, 32,* 2089–2113.

Ryan, R. M., & Deci, E. L. (2000). The darker and brighter sides of human existence: Basic psychological needs as a unifying concept. *Psychological Inquiry, 11,* 319–338.

Ryan, R. M., & Deci, E. L. (2001). On happiness and human potentials: A review of research on hedonic and eudaimonic well-being. In Fiske S. (Ed.), *Annual Review of Psychology, 52,* 141–166.

Rynes, S. L. (2007a). Tackling the "great divide" between research production and dissemination in human resource management. *Academy of Management Journal, 50,* 985–986.

Rynes, S. L. (2007b). Let's create a tipping point: What academics and practitioners can do, alone and together. *Academy of Management Journal, 50,* 1046–1054.

Rynes, S. L., Bartunek, J. M., & Daft, R. L. (2001). Across the great divide: Knowledge creation and transfer between practitioners and academics. *Academy of Management Journal, 44,* 340–355.

Saks, A. M. (2000). *Research, measurement, and evaluation of human resources.* Toronto: Nelson Thompson Learning.

Schmidt, F. L., & Hunter, J. E. (1983). Individual differences in productivity: An empirical test of estimates derived from studies of selection procedure utility. *Journal of Applied Psychology, 68,* 407–414.

Schott, R. L. (1999). Managers and mental health: Mental illness and the workplace. *Public Personnel Management, 28,* 161–183.

Senécal, C., Vallerand, R. J., & Guay, F. (2001). Antecedents and outcomes of work-family conflict: Toward a motivational model. *Personality and Social Psychology Bulletin, 27,* 176–186.

Shapiro, D. L., Kirkman, B. L., & Courtney, H. G. (2007). Perceived causes and solutions of the translation problem in management research. *Academy of Management Journal, 50,* 249–266.

Sheldon, K. M., Turban, D. V., Brown, K., Barrick, M., & Judge, T. (2003). Applying self-determination theory to organizational research. *Research in Personnel and Human Resources Management, 22,* 357–394. Amsterdam: Elsevier.

Sommer, R. (2006). Dual dissemination: Writing for colleagues and the public. *American Psychologist, 61,* 955–958.

Stambor, Z. (2006). Employees: A company's best asset. *Monitor on Psychology, 37,* 28–30.

Stave, G. M., Muchmore, L., & Gardner, H. (2003). Quantifiable impact of the contract for health and wellness: Health behaviors, health care costs, disability, and workers' compensation. *Journal of Occupational and Environmental Medicine, 45,* 109–117.

Stephens, T., & Joubert, N. (2001). Le fardeau économique des problèmes de santé mentale au Canada [The economic burden of mental health problems in Canada]. *In Maladies Chroniques au Canada, 22,* 18–23.

Sturman, M. C. (2000). Implications of utility analysis adjustments for estimates of human resource intervention value. *Journal of Management, 26,* 281–299.

Symon, G. (2006). Academics, practitioners and the journal of occupational and organizational psychology: Reflecting on the issues. *Journal of Occupational and Organizational Psychology, 79,* 167–171.

Van den Broeck, A., Vansteenkiste, M., De Witte, H., & Lens, W. (2008). The role of basic need satisfaction in explaining the relationship between job demands, job resources, burnout and engagement. *Work & Stress, 22,* 277–294.

Vansteenkiste, M., Duriez, B., Simons, J., & Soenens, B. (2006). Materialistic values and well-being among business students: Further evidence for their detrimental effect. *Journal of Applied Social Psychology, 36,* 2892–2908.

Vansteenkiste, M., Lens, W., De Witte, S., De Witte, H., & Deci, E. L. (2004). The "why" and "why not" of job search behaviour: Their relation to searching, unemployment experience, and well-being. *European Journal of Social Psychology, 34,* 345–363.

Vansteenkiste, M., Lens, W., De Witte, H., & Feather, N. T. (2005). Understanding unemployed people's search behavior, unemployment experience and well-being: A comparison of expectancy-value theory and self-determination theory. *British Journal of Social Psychology, 44,* 269–287.

Vansteenkiste, M., Neyrinck, B., Niemiec, C., Soenens, B., De Witte, H., & Van den Broeck, A. (2007). On the relations among work value orientations, psychological need satisfaction and job outcomes: A self-determination theory approach. *Journal of Occupational and Organizational Psychology, 80,* 251–277.

Wall, T. (2006). Is JOOP only of academic interest? *Journal of Occupational and Organizational Psychology, 79,* 161–165.

Waterman, A. S. (2004). Finding someone to be: Studies on the role of intrinsic motivation in identity formation. *Identity: An International Journal of Theory and Research, 4,* 208–228.

Waterman, A. S. (2005). When effort is enjoyed: Two studies of intrinsic motivation for personally salient activities. *Motivation and Emotion, 29,* 165–188.

Waterman, A. S., Schwartz, S. J., Goldbacher, E., Green, H., Miller, C., & Philip, S. (2003). Predicting the subjective experience of intrinsic motivation: The roles of self-determination, the balance of challenges and skills, and self-realization values. *Personality and Social Psychology Bulletin, 29,* 1447–1458.

Whyte, G., & Latham, G. (1997). The futility of utility analysis revisited: When even an expert fails. *Personnel Psychology, 50,* 601–610.

World Health Organization (2000). *Considerations in evaluating the cost-effectiveness of environmental health interventions.* Retrieved from http://www.who.int/quantifying_ehimpacts/publications/en/wsh00-10.pdf

Xanthopoulou, D., Bakker, A. B., Demerouti, E., & Schaufeli, W. B. (2009). Work engagement and financial returns: A diary study on the role of job and personal resources. *Journal of Occupational and Orgnizational Psychology, 82,* 183–200.

Yates, B. T. (1996). *Analyzing costs, procedures, processes, and outcomes in human services.* London: Sage.

PART 5

Domains of Application

CHAPTER 21

Teacher Motivation

Johnmarshall Reeve *and* Yu-Lan Su

Abstract

Teacher motivation involves the desire to teach and one's interpersonal style toward students while doing so. A teacher's own personal motivation revolves around the extent of psychological need satisfaction experienced during the act of teaching, and it manifests itself in terms of teacher enthusiasm and job satisfaction. A teacher's motivating style toward students revolves around what teachers say and do during instruction to motivate students to engage in learning activities, and it manifests itself in terms of autonomy-supportive versus controlling teaching. Because there are meaningful benefits to both students and teachers when teachers give autonomy support, we first identify what autonomy-supportive teachers uniquely say and do during instruction, and second explain how teachers can purposively become more autonomy supportive toward students. The chapter concludes by addressing the practical question of whether autonomy support is realistic and easy-to-implement and by offering directions for future research on teacher motivation.

Key Words: autonomy support, autonomy-supportive teaching, motivating style, structure, teacher motivation, teaching efficacy, teacher enthusiasm, teachers' psychological need satisfaction

Introduction

To understand teacher motivation, two stories need to be told. The first concerns the teacher's own motivation. This half of the story begins with an analysis of the reasons why someone might want to become a teacher, revolves around teachers' day-to-day experiences while delivering instruction, and concludes with a consideration of how well versus how poorly teachers function in terms of enthusiasm and satisfaction versus exhaustion and frustration. The second concerns teachers' interpersonal motivating style toward students. This half of the story begins with an analysis of autonomy-supportive versus controlling teaching, revolves around whether teachers take their students' perspectives and support their initiatives (autonomy-supportive teaching) or neglect their students' perspectives and prescribe what their students should think and do

(controlling teaching), and concludes with a consideration of students' and teachers' flourishing with autonomy support but suffering from psychological and behavioral control.

The present chapter tells both of these stories. The greater emphasis, however, is on teachers' motivating styles, and this is so for two reasons. First, our 15-year-old program of research has sought a deep understanding of what motivating style is; where it comes from; why it matters; how it is expressed in teachers' words and actions; how it affects students' motivation and functioning; whether it can be developed or changed; and how it is informed by personality, context, and culture. Now that this research literature has matured, we would like to pass along what we have learned. Second, a focus on teachers' motivating styles affords this chapter with an opportunity to connect with the other chapters in this Handbook, because an analysis of teachers' motivating styles serves as a template to understand the motivating style of any supervisor, including the workplace manager, CEO, entrepreneur, parent, coach, therapist, doctor, or dentist.[1]

A Teacher's Own Motivation
Why Become a Teacher? Intrinsic versus Extrinsic Goals

Why become a teacher? While some preservice teachers say that they forged the goal during childhood, most preservice teachers say that they are still working through this career decision (Schutz, Crowder, & White, 2001). The goal to become a teacher typically arises from one of the following antecedents: a desire to work specifically with children or adolescents; a belief that one possesses the abilities required of teachers; the sheer joy one experiences while teaching; the desire to contribute constructively to the next generation; a desire to do what one can to reverse social inequalities; the seeking of job security; the appeal of a profession that allows time for personal projects and for one's family; an initial spark from a critical incident in which one successfully enacted the role of a teacher (e.g., tutoring, teaching religious school); a past teacher who was especially admired—to the point of emulation; and the suggestion, recommendation, or encouragement of family and friends (Alexander, Chant, & Cox, 1994; Chivore, 1988; Moran, Kilpatrick, Abbott, Dallatt, & McClune, 2001; Richardson & Watt, 2005, 2006; Schutz et al., 2001). Once under consideration, the goal-setting and decision-making process is then filtered through social-cultural factors, such as the status and pay of the profession, as well as its demands, circumstances, conditions, and lifestyle. In communities and countries in which teachers invariably enjoy high social status (e.g., Asian and African nations), this decision-making process often starts with (rather than is modified by) a consideration of these sorts of contextual factors—even to the point that social-contextual factors, rather than personal preferences, give rise to the goal to become a teacher.

From a self-determination theory (SDT) perspective, *why* one adopts the goal of becoming a teacher matters. This is because engagement and well-being are not so much the product of *what* one is striving for as they are *why* one is striving for it (Vansteenkiste, Lens, & Deci, 2006). To make the distinction between the *what* versus the *why* within any goal pursuit, SDT researchers distinguish between intrinsic goals and extrinsic goals (Kasser, 2002; Vansteenkiste et al., 2006). Commonly cited reasons to become a teacher that represent intrinsic goals include enjoying teaching for its own sake, personal satisfaction from contributing to one's community, a desire to help others, and the pursuit of one's own personal growth. Commonly cited reasons to become a teacher that represent extrinsic goals include seeking a high salary, job security, career status, social respect, or a means to a more desired end (e.g., to have one's summers off).

People who pursue a goal for intrinsic reasons, compared to those who pursue that same goal for extrinsic reasons, experience more favorable levels of adjustment, learning, performance, and well-being (Vansteenkiste, Simons, Soenens, & Lens, 2004; Vansteenkiste, Simons, Lens, Sheldon, & Deci, 2004). The reason for these differences is that the pursuit of intrinsic goals engenders an inward orientation that affords frequently recurring opportunities for psychological need satisfaction (of autonomy, competence, and relatedness), whereas the pursuit of extrinsic goals engenders an outward orientation that distracts one away from intrinsic need satisfactions (Vansteenkiste, Niemiec, & Soenens, 2010). Research on the different reasons that people decide to become a teacher generally confirms that intrinsic reasons to teach predict relatively better levels of instructional effort and persistence (e.g., how much teachers prepare for class, how long they stay in the profession) and professional development (e.g., how open they are to new instructional methods and in-service training opportunities; Watt & Richardson, 2008). Intrinsic goals to teach also lead teachers to adopt a greater mastery-oriented approach in their professional practice (Malmberg, 2008). When teachers make progress in realizing these intrinsic goals—when they enjoy teaching, when they relate well to students and to colleagues, and when they see personal growth in their students and in themselves—they report high levels of teaching enthusiasm and satisfaction (Dinham & Scott, 1998; Scott, Stone, & Dinham, 2001). This research is important because it shows that the pursuit of intrinsic goals predisposes the teacher to experience a higher quality of motivation to teach.

Are You Good at Teaching? Teaching Efficacy

Teaching efficacy is a future-oriented, competency-based expectation a teacher holds in reference to his or her capacity to bring desired outcomes to fruition (e.g., enhance students' engagement, learning, achievement). This expectation is a balanced judgment that integrates the teacher's perceived capacity to carry out particular acts of instruction on the one hand and the perceived demands, circumstances, constraints, and obstacles within the teaching situation on the other hand. The model of teaching efficacy offered by Tschannen-Moran and colleagues (1998, 2001) suggests that teaching efficacy reflects the integration of (1) a teacher's appraisal of whether a specific teaching task will be easy or difficult, simple or complex; (2) a self-assessment of one's personal teaching capabilities specific to that specific teaching task; and (3) a self-assessment of one's personal teaching vulnerabilities and limitations specific to that specific teaching task (e.g., when teaching students new vocabulary words, teaching efficacy reflects the difficulty, complexity, and environmental constraints of the lesson to be taught; how resourceful the teacher feels in delivering the day's learning activities; and how unprepared or overwhelmed the teacher feels in delivering the particular lesson).

Teaching efficacy is important to a teacher's motivation for many reasons. It predicts teacher enthusiasm (Allinder, 1994; Guskey, 1984) as well as its conceptual opposite—teacher burnout (Fernet, Guay, Senecal, & Austin, 2012; Skaalvik & Skaalvik, 2007). Teaching efficacy also predicts commitment to teaching (Coladarci, 1992), and it predicts extent of job satisfaction (Caprara, Barbaranelli, Borgogni, & Steca, 2003; Caprara, Barbaranelli, Steca, & Malone, 2006; Klassen & Chiu, 2010; Tschannen-Moran & Woolfolk Hoy, 2001; Wolters & Daugherty, 2007). Teaching efficacy also predicts teachers' in-class functioning in terms of their effort and persistence devoted to the delivery of instruction and also to its planning (Allinder, 1994). Teaching efficacy further predicts teachers' persistence in the face of setbacks, and it predicts teachers' constructive (rather than critical) reaction to the errors their students make (Ashton & Webb, 1986), as well as their general optimism versus pessimism about student learning (Ngidi, 2012). A strong and resilient sense of teaching efficacy, once formed and tested through the trials of teaching, predicts how long teachers stay in the profession (Bruinsma & Jansen, 2010), presumably because highly efficacious teachers are able to do what less efficacious teachers are unable to do: produce gains in the quality of their students' thinking (Anderson, Greene, & Loewen, 1988), motivation (Midgley, Feldlaufer, & Eccles, 1989), and achievement (Ashton & Webb, 1986; Ross, 1992).

Rather than thinking of teachers' goals and sense of efficacy as stable and enduring characteristics, both are better conceptualized as developmentally fragile (Alexander, 2008). Constantly, the teaching profession communicates new goals and requirements for teachers to pursue, and many of these profession-imposed goals are extrinsic goals. Similarly, the teaching profession gives rise to new challenges, obstacles, constraints, and difficulties for teachers to cope with. For these reasons, the profession is stressful (Malmberg, 2008). The profession also places an emotionally taxing and heavy workload on teachers that is paired with a relatively low salary. As a classroom teacher, one has responsibilities for the learning of others; for dealing with a multitude of imposed external demands; and for orchestrating the behaviors of a motivationally, cognitively, and socioculturally diverse students (Alexander, 2008). That is, there are plenty of occasions within day-to-day teaching to doubt one's teaching efficacy.

A mismatch between teachers' initial expectations versus their actually-experienced rewards and demands may lead to early attrition. Schools typically lose 40% of their new K-12 teachings in their first five years of the profession, and this is true in the United States (Budig, 2006; Roness, 2011) as well as the United Kingdom (Kyriacou & Kunc, 2006). These are bleak statistics for anyone reflecting on teacher motivation. But, many teachers do find their way to greater passion, enthusiasm, and satisfaction (Carbonneau, Vallerand, Fernet, & Guay, 2008; Maskit, 2011). But, it is important to note that gains in teaching efficacy are not enough to provide a strong sense of professional satisfaction; teaching itself needs to be enjoyable (Fernet et al., 2012; Moe, Pazzaglia, & Ronconi, 2010).

Is Teaching Fun? Teachers' Psychological Need Satisfaction

What makes a task (or job) interesting and enjoyable is an intriguing question. In an SDT analysis, the answer to this question is that interest and enjoyment emerge out of the experience of psychological need satisfaction (in terms of autonomy, competence, and relatedness) during activity engagement (Deci, 1992; Krapp, 2002; Tsai, Kunter, Lüdtke, Trautwein, & Ryan, 2008). Whether teaching is fun or not—whether teachers experience autonomy, competence, and relatedness need satisfaction while teaching and interacting with students, colleagues, principals, and parents—depends a great deal on the sociocontextual classroom and schooling environments. One framework used to understand teachers' psychological need satisfaction versus frustration is to consider teachers' extent of professional support versus pressure from above, from within, and from below (Pelletier, Seguin-Levesque, & Legault, 2002; Reeve, 2009; Soenens, Sierens, Vansteenkiste, Dochy, & Goossens, 2012). Support versus pressure from above refers to how constructive versus coercive teachers experience interactions with administrators and parents, how heavy educational policies and societal expectations force on teachers the twin burdens of responsibility and accountability to produce students' learning, performance, and targeted behavior. Support versus pressure from within refers to teachers' own autonomous versus controlled motivations to teach and to the autonomy- and control-oriented beliefs and personality dispositions they harbor. Support versus pressure from below refers to teachers' day-to-day perceptions about how motivated and engaged their students are (or are not) and to their beliefs about the nature of student motivation.

The more teachers experience pressuring constraints and coercions from above and from within, the more they tend toward emotional exhaustion, depersonalization of students, and a controlling motivating style during instruction (Soenens et al., 2012). Furthermore, the more teachers perceive pressures from below, the less likely they are to use autonomy-supportive instructional strategies and the more likely they are to use controlling ones (Sarrazin, Tessier, Pelletier, Trouilloud, & Chanel, 2006; Taylor & Ntoumanis, 2007). Similarly, when teachers see their principals promoting intrinsic goals for teaching that encourage them to find challenge, meaning, and a sense of purpose in their teaching, the more teachers experience high autonomy and low burnout; but when teachers see their principals promoting extrinsic goals for teaching that use contingent rewards to motivate their compliance with rules and policies, the more teachers experience high burnout and low autonomy (Eyal & Roth, 2011). Overall, a teacher's experience of psychological need satisfaction is affected—for better or for worse—by a wide range of job-related conditions, and how much psychological need satisfaction teachers experience foreshadows their enactment of an autonomy-supportive classroom motivating style (Taylor, Ntoumanis, & Standage, 2008), which leads us into the second half of the story about teacher motivation.

A Teacher's Motivating Style toward Students

A teacher's motivating style manifests itself during instruction as the tone of his or her sentiment and behavior while trying to motivate and engage students during learning activities (Deci, Schwartz, Sheinman, & Ryan, 1981; Reeve, 2009). For instance, a teacher might try to encourage a student to read a book, follow a rule, or improve performance. Motivating style captures the quality of the teacher's sentiment (the tone of interaction) and behavior (what the teacher says and does) while trying to spark, encourage, and sustain students' initiative and active involvement in the activity. It can be conceptualized along a bipolar continuum that ranges from a highly controlling style on one end of the continuum through a somewhat neutral style to a highly autonomy-supportive style on the other end of the continuum (Deci, Schwartz, et al., 1981).

Autonomy support is whatever the teacher does to vitalize and support students' classroom experience of autonomy. (Autonomy is the inner endorsement of one's actions—the sense that one's goals, plans, thoughts, emotions, and actions emanate from oneself and are one's own [Deci & Ryan, 1985; Ryan & Deci, 2000]). More specifically, it is the interpersonal sentiment and behavior teachers provide during instruction to identify, vitalize, nurture, and develop students' inner motivational resources (Assor, Kaplan, & Roth, 2002; Reeve, 2009). For instance, in practice, a teacher who relies on an autonomy-supportive style at the beginning of a lesson would first anticipate and assess students' interest in the upcoming lesson. The teacher would then seek to vitalize that interest by offering an instructional opportunity capable of sparking situational interest (e.g., offering a challenge, piquing curiosity). Once vitalized, the teacher would then work to nurture and grow that interest—throughout the lesson, but also developmentally as in the cultivation of an enduring individual interest in the topic.

The opposite of autonomy support is a controlling style, which is the interpersonal sentiment and behavior teachers provide during instruction to pressure students to think, feel, or behave in a specific teacher-defined way (Assor, Kaplan, Kanat-Maymon, & Roth, 2005; Reeve, 2009; Reeve, Deci, & Ryan, 2004; Soenens et al., 2012). In practice, controlling teachers discount, neglect, or outright thwart students' inner motivational resources (especially autonomy need satisfaction) and, instead, motivate and engage by (1) telling or prescribing what students are to think, feel, or do and (2) applying subtle or not-so-subtle pressure until students forego their own preferences (their own inner motivational resources) to adopt the teacher's prescribed way of thinking, feeling, or acting. For instance, the controlling teacher would prescribe a course of action (e.g., "revise your paper," "follow the rule," "try harder," "participate more") and add a twist of compliance-pushing pressure until the student did indeed enact the prescribed action (e.g., by invoking an urgent deadline, by uttering pressuring language).

Benefits from Receiving and Giving Autonomy Support

In many respects, students' perceived autonomy is only a latent potential. This is true not only of students' perceived autonomy but also of all inner motivational resources, including their interest, curiosity, preference for optimal challenge, and so on. For student autonomy to actualize itself to the point that it energizes and directs students' classroom activity, its latent potential needs to be vitalized and, once vitalized, supported. This is what autonomy-supportive teachers do so well—they identify students' inner motivational resources, vitalize them during instructional activities, support their flourishing, and developmentally strengthen them to the point that the student gains a greater capacity to motivate himself or herself. Another way of saying this is that autonomy-supportive teachers provide students with an interpersonal relationship that affords them with opportunities to experience learning activities within a motivational climate of personal autonomy.

Students benefit when teachers support their autonomy (Assor et al., 2002; Deci & Ryan, 1985; Reeve, 2009; Reeve & Jang, 2006; Ryan & Deci, 2000). Students taught by autonomy-supportive teachers, compared with students taught by neutral or controlling teachers, experience and display more constructive *motivation* (e.g., perceived autonomy, intrinsic motivation, curiosity, internalized valuing; Deci et al., 1981; Reeve, Jang, Hardré, & Omura, 2002; Reeve, Nix, & Hamm, 2003), greater classroom *engagement* (e.g., behavioral engagement, class attendance; Assor et al., 2002; Assor et al., 2005; Black & Deci, 2000; Reeve, Jang, Carrell, Barch, & Jeon, 2004; Vallerand, Fortier, & Guay, 1997), healthier

development (e.g., creativity, self-worth, preference for optimal challenge; Deci, Nezlak, & Sheinman, 1981; Deci, Schwartz, et al., 1981; Koestner, Ryan, Bernieri, & Holt, 1984; Shapira, 1976), enhanced *learning* (e.g., conceptual understanding, deep information processing, self-regulation strategies; Benware & Deci, 1984; McGraw & McCullers, 1979; Vansteenkiste, Simons, Lens, et al., 2004; Vansteenkiste, Zhou, Lens, & Soenens, 2005), improved *performance* (e.g., grades, standardized test scores; Black & Deci, 2000; deCharms, 1976; Grolnick & Ryan, 1987; Soenens & Vansteenkiste, 2005; Vansteenkiste, Simons, Lens, Soenens, & Matos, 2005), and greater *well-being* (e.g., psychological well-being, vitality, biological well-being; Chirkov & Ryan, 2001; Levesque, Zuehlke, Stanek, & Ryan, 2004; Nix, Ryan, Manly, & Deci, 1999; Reeve & Tseng, 2011). These benefits occur for students in preschool (Koestner et al., 1984), elementary school (Deci, Schwartz, et al., 1981), middle school (Vansteenkiste, Simons, et al., 2005), and high school (Reeve, Jang, et al., 2004), as well as for undergraduate (Black & Deci, 2000) and graduate (Sheldon & Krieger, 2004) students, and for students with special needs (Deci, Hodges, Peirson, & Tomassone, 1992), in after-school programs (Grolnick, Farkas, Sohmer, Michaels, & Valsiner, 2007), and for those in classrooms around the globe (outside of North American and Europe), including those situated in China (Vansteenkiste, Zhou, et al., 2005), Singapore (Hagger et al., 2007; Lim & Wang, 2009), Korea (Cheon, Reeve, & Moon, 2012; Jang, Reeve, Ryan, & Kim, 2009), Taiwan (Hardré et al., 2006), Israel (Assor et al., 2005), Brazil (Chirkov, Ryan, & Willness, 2005), and Russia (Chirkov & Ryan, 2001).

Teacher-provided autonomy support benefits more than just students. Teacher-provided autonomy support further benefits the teachers who give it. When teachers give autonomy support, they experience greater personal accomplishment and lesser emotional exhaustion from their teaching, compared with their relatively controlling counterparts (Roth, Assor, Kanat-Maymon, & Kaplan, 2007). They also experience greater psychological need satisfaction while teaching, feel more efficacious while teaching, and report greater job satisfaction (Cheon, Reeve, Yu, & Jang, 2014). Some research even shows that when asking who benefits more—the person receiving autonomy support or the person giving it—the answer is actually the latter (Deci, La Guardia, Moller, Scheiner, & Ryan, 2006)!

Autonomy Support: What It Is, How to Practice It

What one autonomy-supportive teacher says and does during instruction varies widely from what another will say and do. Still, autonomy-supportive teachers all tend to share three fundamentals: (1) adopt the students' perspective and frame of reference during instruction; (2) invite, welcome, and incorporate students' thoughts, feelings, suggestions, and behaviors into the flow of the lesson; and (3) enact some constellation of the following five instructional behaviors discussed in the paragraphs below. Here, it is important to point out that these five acts of instruction have been empirically validated as autonomy (Reeve & Jang, 2006) and engagement (Reeve, Jang, et al., 2004; Reeve & Jang, 2006) supports and therefore can function as recommended practice to support student autonomy.

Before detailing what autonomy-supportive teachers say and do during instruction, it is important to emphasize that any instructional effort to support students' autonomy involves prerequisite perspective taking and acknowledging. Such perspective taking is reflective mental work in which teachers proactively take, appreciate, and ask about their students' perspective on the forthcoming classwork. For instance, they would develop their lesson plans in response to such questions as, "Will students find this interesting? Is this lesson relevant and useful to my students' goals and aspirations? If I asked students how they might improve the lesson, what would they likely say—would they want to revise the lesson in some way?" At the start of instruction, autonomy-supportive teachers often openly solicit and integrate students' ideas, suggestions, and contributions. This might be as simple as "Any suggestions?," but it might also be as involved as an open discussion about the lesson or about the class more generally. It may take the form of a formative assessment. Throughout the lesson, autonomy-supportive teachers monitor students' engagement signals so that they can take in information about how well their instructional strategies are tapping into and involving their students' motivational resources, because the more teachers respond to students' engagement signals the more likely they are to become in synch with their students (Lee & Reeve, 2012).

VITALIZE INNER MOTIVATIONAL RESOURCES

Students walk into any classroom possessing a host of latent motivational resources, including their inherent psychological needs (for autonomy, competence, and relatedness), intrinsic motivation, intrinsic goals, self-endorsed (internalized) values, individual interests, curiosity, and a preference for optimal challenge (see Reeve, Deci, & Ryan, 2004). (Of course, they also walk into classrooms with smartphones, an intention to update their Facebook page, a desire to talk with their friends, the strategy to hide and listen only when the teacher says "this will be on the test," and the goal to do as little work as possible.) Vitalizing inner motivational resources means adapting instruction so that it taps into and involves students' inner resources to the point that students' classroom activity is initiated and regulated by these inner resources. That is, the reason why students begin working on a lesson and the reason why they continue to do so because it is satisfying (enjoyable), meaningful (important), goal-relevant, curiosity-piquing, challenge inviting, and so forth, and not because they have to obey a directive, fulfill a request, or prepare for Friday's test. It is a particularly useful ingredient within a teacher's repertoire when introducing a learning activity and seeking initial engagement. For instance, when designed to vitalize inner motivational resources, the first moment of instruction might begin with a curiosity-inducing question, such as when a language teacher asks, "In which country are more people trying to learn the English language—the United States or China?" Such a question might pique (i.e., "vitalize") curiosity because, surprisingly, there are five times as many people in China trying to learn English. Or, a mathematics teacher might use the first moment of instruction to offer an optimal challenge, "Here is a question/problem for you; let's see if you can figure it out. . ." Similarly, an English teacher might begin the day's lesson by promoting an intrinsic goal for writing, "Today we are going to read a passage by the writer Philip Roth. As you read, notice how good the writing is. Ask yourself what makes this such good writing, and use your answer to discover how to become a better writer yourself." The idea is that students' naturally want to do what is curiosity-arousing, optimally challenging, and relevant to their personal goals. In contrast, controlling instruction ignores or by-passes such opportunities to vitalize inner resources and, instead, relies on artificial or pressuring sources of motivation to try to manufacture student engagement.

PROVIDE EXPLANATORY RATIONALES

A rationale is a verbal explanation as to why putting forth effort during a learning activity might be a useful thing to do (Reeve et al., 2002). Providing rationales means communicating to students the usefulness of an activity or a recommended course of action. Explanatory rationales are particularly engagement-fostering when the personal utility of the request or activity is unknown to students. For instance, as students face a learning activity that they initially find to be unappealing (e.g., "Do we really have to do this?"), teachers can help support students' otherwise fragile motivation by providing explanatory rationales, such as "The reason I'm asking you to do this is because. . ." It is a particularly useful motivational support when teachers ask students to engage in an activity, procedure, or rule that is, from their point of view, uninteresting, unappealing, or simply "not worth doing." The idea is that honest, valid, and satisfying rationales afford students an opportunity to internalize the value of what others (e.g., teacher, community) find worthwhile. If internalized and accepted as one's own and if the teacher-provided rationale is believed to be useful enough to justify the students' attention and effort, then the now self-endorsed reason becomes capable of acting as an inner motivational resource for that student (i.e., as a self-endorsed value). In contrast, when students do not understand why the teacher is making a request of them, they often view the request as arbitrary, imposed, or simply meaningless busywork.

Together, vitalizing inner resources and providing explanatory rationales afford classroom teachers with a one-two punch in how to introduce a learning activity or a teacher request: when the task is potentially interesting then focus on vitalizing an inner motivational resource, but when the task is expected to be unappealing to students then focus on providing explanatory rationales.

RELY ON NONCONTROLLING, INFORMATIONAL LANGUAGE

Noncontrolling, informational language is teacher-provided communication that is non-evaluative, flexible, diagnostic, and constructive. Noncontrolling means avoiding messages that communicate external evaluation and pressure ("you should . . . you have to . . . you must. . ."); informational means offering insight that students can use to understand, diagnose, and solve a problem (e.g., poor performance, disengagement, disrespectful behavior). For instance, when a teacher relies on noncontrolling and informational language, he or she would begin a discussion of students' poor performance or irresponsible behavior by asking the student about it, "I've noticed that you made a surprisingly low score on the test. Do you know why that might be?" Such language is a particularly useful to supporting students' motivation when communicating requirements and responsibilities, when offering feedback, and when addressing motivational and behavioral problems. The idea is to address the problem yet still preserve the student's sense of ownership and responsibility (i.e., perceived autonomy) for regulating their own behavior and for diagnosing and solving their own problems. The teacher essentially takes on the role of an ally who helps the student make progress in improving his or her adjustment, citizenship, and development. In contrast, controlling language would verbally push and pressure the student toward a teacher-specified behavior or solution without enlisting the students' problem-solving effort (e.g., "you must improve your grades").

DISPLAY PATIENCE TO ALLOW TIME FOR SELF-PACED LEARNING

Time constraints, high-stakes testing, and panic-laced telephone calls from parents make it easy to understand why teachers are sometimes not patient, but the reason to be patient (motivationally speaking) comes from a deep valuing for the student's autonomy and an understanding that learning processes, such as conceptual change, and the building and revising of sophisticated knowledge structures take time. Displaying patience means that students need both time and space to explore and manipulate learning materials, formulate and try out hypotheses, set goals and make plans, make mistakes and start over, monitor and revise their work, and alter their problem-solving strategies. Displaying patience as students struggle to understand a concept or adjust their behavior is a particularly useful motivational support when students involve themselves in learning activities that are unfamiliar, complex, or involve new skills, new ways of thinking, and new ways of behaving. In practice, patience involves postponing advice or intervention until understanding and appreciating the student's perspective and goals. It also means timing teacher support until it is requested or clearly needed (e.g., hints when students seem stuck). In contrast, controlling instruction impatiently rushes in to show or tell students the answer or solution according to the teacher's perspective and timetable (i.e., "Here, let me show you how to do it."), thereby by-passing the learning opportunity. Teacher patience facilitates student autonomy and learning; teacher impatience pushes pressure and compliance (e.g., get the right answer, enact a targeted behavior).

ACKNOWLEDGE AND ACCEPT EXPRESSIONS OF NEGATIVE AFFECT

As students struggle through motivational conflicts and behavioral problems, they often experience negative emotion that leads them to complain, resist, protest, sulk, and display a "bad attitude." Acknowledging and accepting such negative emotionality means taking it to heart and even welcoming such expressions as potentially valid reactions to unexplained rules, confusing assignments, unwelcomed requests, unrealistic expectations, unreasonable demands, or imposed structures. Acknowledging and accepting negative affect is a particularly useful motivational support when students work through conflicts that pit what teachers want students to do (e.g., read a book, revise a paper) against what students want students to do (e.g., something different, something less demanding). For instance, sensing a rising tide of negative affect, an autonomy-supportive teacher might acknowledge a motivational problem (e.g., "I see that you all are not very interested in today's lesson."), accept the negative emotionality (e.g., "Yes, we have practiced this same skill many times before, haven't we?"), and welcome suggestions as to how to resolve the problem (e.g., "Let's see; what might we do differently—any suggestions?"). The idea is that students' motivational problems and negative feelings, if unaddressed, interfere with their engagement and learning. Soothing negative feelings therefore becomes a prerequisite to motivationally readying students to accept the forthcoming lesson and to learn and really benefit from it. In contrast, controlling instruction does not see students' resistance as valid ("You're immature; you're irresponsible.") and, hence, it counters or tries to change students' negative emotionality into something more acceptable to the teacher (e.g., "Quit your complaining; grow up; get to work.").

Becoming More Autonomy Supportive

On average, most teachers are not autonomy supportive during instruction (Jang, Reeve, & Deci, 2010; Reeve, Jang, et al., 2004; Sarrazin et al., 2006; Tessier, Sarrazin, & Ntoumanis, 2008, 2010). Rather, most teachers need to learn how to be autonomy supportive. Fortunately, intervention-based research in which teachers participate in informational and mentoring sessions on how to support students' autonomy shows that teachers can learn to become significantly more autonomy supportive toward their students (Cheon et al., 2012; Cheon & Reeve, 2013; Su & Reeve, 2011). This positive training effect has been shown to occur for both preservice (Reeve, 1998) and veteran teachers, including both middle-school (Cheon et al., 2012; deCharms, 1976) and high-school (Reeve, Jang et al., 2004) teachers.

In their meta-analysis of the teacher training literature on how to become more autonomy supportive, Su and Reeve (2011) located 20 empirical investigations in which the research team initiated an intervention program designed specifically to help teachers and others (e.g., workplace managers) learn how to be more autonomy supportive. In general, these studies first invited classroom teachers to participate in a training intervention that was based on SDT principles and provided skill-based training of how to enact the earlier-discussed autonomy-supportive instructional behaviors and then assessed the course-specific outcomes experienced by the students of the trained teachers. The two general findings have been that trained teachers do generally learn how to be more autonomy supportive during instruction, and the students of trained teachers show meaningful and substantial gains in terms of their motivation and indices of positive classroom functioning, such as engagement. The average training effect size for all studies was $d = 0.63$ (95% confidence interval, 0.43–0.83), and it was $d = 1.33$ (95% confidence interval, 1.18–1.49) for those interventions judged to employ particularly well-designed interventions.

Some of interventions were more effective than others. According to Su and Reeve (2011), the relatively more effective interventions tended to include most of the following: (1) a training experience that featured the full range of the autonomy-supportive instructional behaviors; (2) a brief (2 hours) initial training experience; (3) an intervention that focused more on skill (how to be autonomy supportive) than on content (what autonomy support is); (4) a group discussion component where teachers could express their concerns and share ideas; (5) a reliance on both electronic media and supplemental reading materials to deliver the intervention; (6) an explicit effort to address participants' pretraining beliefs, values, and personality dispositions that would otherwise conflict with the training message; (7) supplemental follow-up activities to serve as a booster effect to the original training session; and (8) a continuing flow of support throughout the intervention's implementation, as through the availability of an on-going mutual support group. These characteristics identify best-practices training programs.

Autonomy Support and Structure

The starting point of autonomy-supportive teaching is to appreciate, value, and take the students' perspective during instruction. Such an approach to instruction does not, however, downplay the importance and necessity of appreciating, valuing, and taking the perspective of the teacher and the larger perspective of the school, parents, state, or culture. The principal way that teachers communicate their (or the school's) expectations, standards, requirements, priorities, goals, plans, and needs is to provide students with a highly structured classroom experience, (Jang et al., 2010; Reeve, 2006). For instance, to make their perspective and priorities salient, teachers communicate what they expect students to do, define their standards as to what does and does not constitute good work, set goals for students to pursue, provide directions for students to follow, scaffold students' learning and motivation, provide feedback, analyze strengths and weaknesses, and so on.

Teachers generally do a good job of communicating and promoting the needs and preferences of the school and its curriculum (Jang et al., 2010). However, the problem with structure is that it can, potentially, overscript learning and therefore undermine students' perceived autonomy, sense of personal responsibility, or what Richard deCharms' (1976) called "personal causation." But structure's opposite—permissiveness—is no better than is overscripted structure, and it is potentially even worse (Hickey, 1997). A key classroom challenge autonomy-supportive teachers routinely face, motivationally speaking, is therefore how to introduce students to school-valued expected outcomes, goals, priorities, communications, rules, rewards, feedback, and other structure-enhancing elements in autonomy-supportive, rather than in controlling, ways.

A teacher's plans, priorities, and goals (i.e., perspective) can be expressed in autonomy-supportive ways. Furthermore, when trained raters observe teachers they consistently find that autonomy-supportive teachers are *more* likely, not less likely, to offer their students a highly structured learning environment (Jang et al., 2010; Sierens, Vansteenkiste, Goossens, Soenens, & Dochy, 2009). That is, the same teachers who clearly communicate their expectations, set high standards,

introduce classroom goals for students to pursue, and show strong classroom guidance are the ones who are more, not less, likely to vitalize students' inner motivational resources, provide explanatory rationales, rely on noncontrolling language, display patience, and acknowledge and accept negative affect. This means, in practice, that teachers do not need to overhaul what they do in the classroom to become more autonomy supportive. Rather, what it means is that teachers need to adapt what they already do (provide structure as they implement their lessons plans) so that they support autonomy rather than control behavior.

From this perspective, autonomy support need not be a stand-alone approach to instruction. It can be integrated into a highly structured approach to motivating and engaging students to the point that the teacher's decision is not to enact autonomy support or structure but, rather, it is how to provide students with high levels of both autonomy support and structure (Jang et al., 2010). This dualistic perspective on a teacher's motivating style (provide both autonomy support and structure) is becoming a popular and effective approach to provide students with optimal classroom instruction (Ntoumanis & Standage, 2009; Standage, Duda, & Ntoumanis, 2003; Taylor & Ntoumanis, 2007).

C'mon, Get Real: Autonomy Support Is Unrealistic and Too Difficult!

We have conducted about 12 large-scaled interventions with teachers over the last decade to help them become more autonomy supportive toward students (e.g., Reeve, 1998; Reeve, Jang, et al., 2004; Cheon et al., 2012; Cheon & Reeve, 2013, 2014). Prior to the intervention experience, teachers tend to believe that autonomy support is a bit unrealistic and too difficult to implement, given the demands and reality of the classroom situation (Reeve et al., 2014; Turner, Warzon, & Christensen, 2011). Because autonomy-supportive teaching is often believed to be difficult to implement, we typically find it necessary to conduct these teacher intervention programs in three phases, as follows.

PHASE I: INTRODUCE AUTONOMY SUPPORT

We begin each teaching training program with a conversation and PowerPoint presentation to define autonomy support, introduce empirical evidence on its benefits, and model examples of the five categories of autonomy-supportive instructional behavior. As we present this information, teachers' typical stream of consciousness goes something like this: Autonomy support—what is that? Oh no, you can't just let students do whatever they want. C'mon, get real: This sounds like a lot of work! Okay, this might work for highly motivated students, but good luck trying this with some of my students!

PHASE 2: IT IS "AUTONOMY SUPPORT AND STRUCTURE, NOT AUTONOMY SUPPORT OR STRUCTURE" PRECEDED AND FOLLOWED BY GROUP DISCUSSION

After teachers have had a chance to digest the concept of supporting students' autonomy and to discuss its feasibility in their own classrooms, we introduce the concept of teacher-provided structure, acknowledge its role in effective instruction and in motivating and engaging students, endorse the instructional goal of high structure with high autonomy support, and provide modeled examples of how teachers might provide classroom structure in highly autonomy-supportive ways. As we present this information, teachers' typical stream of consciousness goes something like this: Okay, structure sounds good. I see that you are not trying to totally change my motivating style, but rather trying to overlay autonomy support onto what I already do. This still sounds like too much work though; I don't have time to do all of this—it sounds kind of nice, but it's naïve, it's unrealistic. We then invite teachers to participate in a group discussion in which they voice their concerns; identify potential obstacles; and share, suggest, and critique possible autonomy-supportive acts of instruction. These discussions quickly gain momentum as teachers hear creative ideas and instructional strategies from their fellow teachers. We then ask teachers to try out one or more of the previously mentioned autonomy-supportive instructional behaviors and ask them to return for one more group discussion.

PHASE 3: GROUP DISCUSSION AFTER EXPERIMENTING WITH AUTONOMY-SUPPORTIVE CLASSROOM INSTRUCTION

After teachers sample autonomy support within the context of their own instruction (e.g., provide an explanatory rationale for a request, acknowledge and accept a student's complaint, prepare a lesson to spark students' interest and curiosity), they invariably have an experience—or series of experiences—in which students respond with immediate spikes of engagement. Teachers themselves report experiencing at least an occasional surge of enthusiasm accompanied by a healthy dose of

psychological need satisfaction. In this second group discussion, teachers again voice their concerns; identify obstacles; and share, suggest, and critique autonomy-supportive acts of instruction. But the sense of autonomy support as being unrealistic is typically gone.

A FOURTH PHASE

In one study, we continued the teaching intervention into a fourth phase by following-up teachers who participated a year earlier in a teacher intervention program (Cheon & Reeve, 2013). The goal of the study was to ask whether teachers were still autonomy supportive toward students and whether they continued to experience benefits, such as psychological need satisfaction, teacher enthusiasm, teaching efficacy, and job satisfaction. Specifically, we asked teachers: Compared with a year ago, are you now more autonomy-supportive, less autonomy-supportive, or about the same as last year? Every teacher (physical education teachers in Korean middle schools) reported being more autonomy supportive. When we asked them why, some explained that they were more autonomy supportive because their students were now so much more engaged than before (i.e., because of student benefits), whereas others explained that their teaching was now so much more enjoyable and effective than before (i.e., because of teacher benefits). Some teachers volunteered that they had no interest in returning back to their pretraining (controlling) motivating style; their reasoning was that it was much easier, less conflictual, and a greater joy to teach a class of highly engaged students than it was to teach a class of highly unengaged students.

What these trained and highly accomplished teachers told us was that, once learned, autonomy support was actually easier and more realistic than was controlling teaching. It is a reliable and replicated finding that one primary reason why teachers are controlling during instruction is because their students are unmotivated and misbehaving (Sarrazin et al., 2006). That is, when unmotivated, listless, and disengaged, students "pull" a controlling style out of the teacher's repertoire (Pelletier et al., 2002). But, autonomy-supportive teacher training programs act as opportunities for teachers to build a more autonomy-supportive style into their instructional repertoire. What autonomy-supportive teaching does is promote students' autonomy and engagement during instruction (Cheon et al., 2012; Reeve, Jang, et al., 2004). Once students become autonomously motivated and highly engaged, the pull for a controlling style evaporates. When students are highly motivated and engaged, teacher control seems out of place—even inappropriate. Under these conditions, teachers no longer believe that autonomy-supportive teaching is either unrealistic or too difficult.

Conclusion

"How can I motivate others?" Perhaps you read this chapter to find a constructive, practical, and satisfying answer to this question. As pointed out by Deci (1995), however, the question itself is stated in a problematic way because "motivating others" implies taking charge and doing something to them, such as persuading, modeling, inspiring, or just plain yelling at students. A constructive way to rephrase this question, as pointed out by Deci (1995), is as follows: "How can I create the conditions under which people can motivate themselves?" This paraphrase guides practitioners toward an autonomy-supportive style, because it presumes that others are fully capable of motivating themselves. What others need from you is some support in vitalizing their otherwise latent inner motivational resources. The practical purpose of the present chapter is to provide the rationale and classroom practice behind this recommendation. Overall, our suggestion is to deeply appreciate the students' perspective, welcome their thoughts and suggestions into the flow of instruction, and find or create new ways to vitalize students' inner motivational resources, explain your requests and instructional activities, communicate with noncontrolling and informational language, be patient, and acknowledge and accept students' negative emotionality as they work through the process of creating the conditions under which they can motivate and engage themselves.

Future Directions

1. What predicts and explains teacher motivation? Teacher motivation is a multifaceted construct, consisting of the positive faces of enthusiasm, efficacy, satisfaction, and well-being, as well as the negative faces of burnout, inefficacy, dissatisfaction, and ill-being. These aspects of teacher motivation are affected by contextual factors; personal beliefs and values; and relationships with colleagues, administrators, parents, and students. It would be a welcome advance to create a framework that integrated this complexity into a full understanding of teacher motivation and its fruits (e.g., skill development, professional retention).

2. How reciprocal is a teacher's motivating style on the one hand and students' motivation, engagement, and behavior on the other hand? Most investigations in the teacher motivation literature use a cross-sectional, survey-based research design. These studies have generated a preliminary understanding of how teachers affect students and how students affect teachers. But teacher-student relations are reciprocal, dynamic, and developmental. This literature now needs longitudinally designed investigations that can tap into and model the complex interrelations that occur within teacher-student relationships.

3. Is teacher-provided autonomy support the opposite of teacher control, or do autonomy support and control represent two distinct aspects of a teacher's motivating style. The question here is whether being autonomy supportive necessarily means that one cannot be controlling, or whether teachers can be both autonomy supportive and controlling, even during a single teacher-student interaction.

4. Do teachers benefit from giving autonomy support? It is clear that students benefit from receiving a teacher's autonomy support. It is beginning to look like teachers too benefit not only from receiving autonomy support (as from principals) but from giving it as well. This research is quite new, and it is a promising new area of investigation that holds the potential to contribute important findings to teacher motivation.

Note

1. This research was supported by the World Class University Program funded by the Korean Ministry of Education, Science and Technology, consigned to the Korea Science and Engineering Foundation (Grant no. R32-2008-000-20023-0).

References

Alexander, D., Chant, D., & Cox, B. (1994). What motivates people to become teachers? *Australian Journal of Teacher Education, 19*, 40–49.

Alexander, P. A. (2008). Charting the course for the teaching profession: The energizing and sustaining role of motivational forces. *Learning and Instruction, 18*, 483–491.

Allinder, R. M. (1994). The relationship between efficacy and the instructional practices of special education teachers and consultants. *Teacher Education and Special Education, 17*, 86–95.

Anderson, R., Greene, M., & Loewen, P. (1988). Relationships among teachers' and students' thinking skills, sense of efficacy, and student achievement. *Alberta Journal of Educational Research, 34*, 148–165.

Ashton, P. T., & Webb, R. B. (1986). *Making a difference: Teacher's sense of efficacy and student achievement.* New York: Longman.

Assor, A., Kaplan, H., Kanat-Maymon, Y., & Roth, G. (2005). Directly controlling teacher behaviors as predictors of poor motivation and engagement in girls and boys: The role of anger and anxiety. *Learning and Instruction*, *15*, 397–413.

Assor, A., Kaplan, H., & Roth, G. (2002). Choice is good, but relevance is excellent: Autonomy-enhancing and suppressing teaching behaviors predicting students' engagement in schoolwork. *British Journal of Educational Psychology*, *27*, 261–278.

Benware, C., & Deci, E. L. (1984). The quality of learning with an active versus passive motivational set. *American Educational Research Journal*, *21*, 755–765.

Black, A. E., & Deci, E. L. (2000). The effects of instructors' autonomy support and students' autonomous motivation on learning organic chemistry: A self-determination theory perspective. *Science Education*, *84*, 740–756.

Bruinsma, M., & Jansen, E. P. W. A. (2010). Is the motivation to become a teacher related to pre-service teachers' intentions to remain in the profession? *European Journal of Teacher Education*, *33*, 185–200.

Budig, G. A. (2006). A perfect storm. *Phi Delta Kappan*, *88*, 114–116.

Caprara, G. V., Barbaranelli, C., Borgogni, L., & Steca, P. (2003). Efficacy beliefs as determinants of teachers' job satisfaction. *Journal of Educational Psychology*, *5*, 821–832.

Caprara, G. V., Barbaranelli, C., Steca, P., & Malone, P. S. (2006). Teachers' self-efficacy beliefs as determinants of job satisfaction and students' academic achievement: A study at the school level. *Journal of School Psychology*, *44*, 473–490.

Carbonneau, N., Vallerand, R. J., Fernet, C., & Guay, F. (2008). The role of passion for teaching in intrapersonal and interpersonal outcomes. *Journal of Educational Psychology*, *100*, 977–987.

Cheon, S. H., & Reeve, J. (2013). Do the benefits of autonomy-supportive PE teacher training endure? A one-year follow up investigation. *Psychology of Sport and Exercise*, *14*, 508–518.

Cheon, S. H., Reeve, J., Yu, T. H., & Jang, H. R. (2014). *Teacher benefits from giving students autonomy support during physical education instruction*. Manuscript under review.

Cheon, S. H., Reeve, J., & Moon, I. S. (2012). Experimentally based, longitudinally designed, teacher-focused intervention to help physical education teachers be more autonomy supportive toward their students. *Journal of Sport & Exercise Psychology*, *34*, 365–396.

Chirkov, V. I., & Ryan, R. M. (2001). Parent and teacher autonomy-support in Russian and U.S. adolescents: Common effects on well-being and academic motivation. *Journal of Cross-Cultural Psychology*, *32*, 618–635.

Chirkov, V. I., Ryan, R. M., & Willness, C. (2005). Cultural context and psychological needs in Canada and Brazil: Testing a self-determination approach to internalization of cultural practices, identify, and well-being. *Journal of Cross-Cultural Psychology*, *36*, 425–443.

Chivore, B. S. R. (1988). A review of factors that determine the attractiveness of teaching profession in Zimbabwe. *International Review of Education*, *34*, 59–77.

Coladarci, T. (1992). Teachers' sense of efficacy and commitment to teaching. *Journal of Experimental Education*, *60*, 323–337.

deCharms, R. (1976). *Enhancing motivation: Change in the classroom*. New York: Irvington.

Deci, E. L. (1992). The relation of interest to the motivation of behavior: A self-determination theory perspective. In K. A. Renninger, S. Hidi, & A. Krapp (Eds.), *The role of interest in learning and development* (pp. 43–60). Hillsdale, NJ: Erlbaum.

Deci, E. L. (1995). *Why we do what we do: Understanding self-motivation*. New York: Penguin Books.

Deci, E. L., Hodges, R., Pierson, L., & Tomassone, J. (1992). Autonomy and competence as motivational factors in students with learning disabilities and emotional handicaps. *Journal of Learning Disabilities*, *25*, 457–471.

Deci, E. L., La Guardia, J. G., Moller, A. C., Scheiner, M. J., & Ryan, R. M. (2006). On the benefits of giving as well as receiving autonomy support: Mutuality in close friendships. *Personality and Social Psychology Bulletin*, *32*, 313–327.

Deci, E. L., Nezlak, J., & Sheinman, L. (1981). Characteristics of the rewarder and intrinsic motivation of the rewardee. *Journal of Personality and Social Psychology*, *40*, 1–10.

Deci, E. L., & Ryan, R. M. (1985). *Intrinsic motivation and self-determination in human behavior*. New York: Plenum.

Deci, E. L., Schwartz, A., Sheinman, L., & Ryan, R. M. (1981). An instrument to assess adult's orientations toward control versus autonomy in children: Reflections on intrinsic motivation and perceived competence. *Journal of Educational Psychology*, *73*, 642–650.

Dinham, S., & Scott, C. (1998). A three domain model of teacher and school executive career satisfaction. *Journal of Educational Administration*, *36*, 362–378.

Eyal, O., & Roth, G. (2011). Principals' leadership and teachers' motivation: Self-determination theory analysis. *Journal of Educational Administration*, *49*, 256–275.

Fernet, C., Guay, F., Senecal, C., & Austin, S. (2012). Predicting intraindividual changes in teacher burnout: The role of perceived school environment and motivational factors. *Teaching and Teacher Education*, *28*, 514–525.

Grolnick, W. S., Farkas, M. S., Sohmer, R., Michaels, S., & Valsiner, J. (2007). Facilitating motivation in young adolescents: Effect of an after-school program. *Journal of Applied Developmental Psychology*, *28*, 332–344.

Grolnick, W. S., & Ryan, R. M. (1987). Autonomy in children's learning: An experimental and individual difference investigation. *Journal of Personality and Social Psychology*, *52*, 890–898.

Guskey, T. R. (1984). The influence of change in instructional effectiveness upon the affective characteristics of teachers. *American Educational Research Journal*, *21*, 245–259.

Hagger, M. S., Chatzisarantis, N. L. D., Hein, V., Pihu, M., Soos, I., & Karsai, I. (2007). The perceived autonomy support scale for exercise settings (PASSES): Development, validity, and cross-cultural invariance in young people. *Psychology of Sport and Exercise*, *8*, 632–653.

Hardré, P. L., Chen, C., Huang, S., Chiang, C., Jen, F., & Warden, L. (2006). Factors affecting high school students' academic motivation in Taiwan. *Asia Pacific Journal of Education*, *26*, 198–207.

Hickey, D. T. (1997). Motivation and contemporary socio-constructivist instructional perspectives. *Educational Psychologist*, *32*, 175–193.

Jang, H., Reeve, J., & Deci, E. L. (2010). Engaging students in learning activities: It is not autonomy support or structure but autonomy support and structure. *Journal of Educational Psychology*, *102*, 588–600.

Jang, H., Reeve, J., Ryan, R. M., & Kim, A. (2009). Can self-determination theory explain what underlies the productive, satisfying learning experiences of collectivistically-oriented

Korean adolescents? *Journal of Educational Psychology, 101*, 644–661.

Kasser, T. (2002). *The high price of materialism*. Cambridge, MA: MIT Press.

Klassen, R. M., & Chiu, M. M. (2010). Effects of teachers' self-efficacy and job satisfaction: Teacher gender, years of experience, and job stress. *Journal of Educational Psychology, 102*, 741–756.

Koestner, R., Ryan, R. M., Bernieri, F., & Holt, K. (1984). Setting limits on children's behavior: The differential effects of controlling versus informational styles on intrinsic motivation and creativity. *Journal of Personality, 52*, 233–248.

Krapp, A. (2002). An educational-psychological theory of interest and its relation to SDT. In E. L. Deci, & R. M. Ryan (Eds.), *Handbook of self-determination research* (pp. 405–427). Rochester, NY: University of Rochester Press.

Kyriacou, C., & Kunc, R. (2006). Beginning teachers' expectations of teaching. *Teaching and Teacher Education, 23*, 1246–1257.

Lee, W., & Reeve, J. (2012). Teachers' estimates of their students' motivation and engagement: Being in synch with students. *Educational Psychology, 32*, 727–747.

Levesque, C., Zuehlke, A. N., Stanek, L. R., & Ryan, R. M. (2004). Autonomy and competence in German and American University students: Comparative study based on self-determination theory. *Journal of Educational Psychology, 96*, 68–84.

Lim, B. S. C., & Wang, C. K. J. (2009). Perceived autonomy support, behavioural regulations in physical education and physical activity intention. *Psychology for Sport and Exercise, 10*, 52–60.

Malmberg, L.-E. (2008). Student teachers' achievement goal orientations during teacher studies: Antecedents, correlates and outcomes. *Learning and Instruction, 18*, 438–452.

Maskit, D. (2011). Teachers' attitudes toward pedagogical changes during various stages of professional development. *Teaching and Teacher Education, 27*, 851–860.

McGraw K. O., & McCullers J. C. (1979). Evidence of a detrimental effect of extrinsic incentives on breaking a mental set. *Journal of Experimental Social Psychology, 15*, 285–294.

Midgley, C., Feldlaufer, H., & Eccles, J. (1989). Change in teacher efficacy and student self—and task-related beliefs in mathematics during the transition to junior high school. *Journal of Educational Psychology, 81*, 247–258.

Moe, A., Pazzaglia, F., & Ronconi, L. (2010). When being able is not enough: The combined value of positive affect and self-efficacy for job satisfaction in teaching. *Teaching and Teacher Education, 26*, 1145–1153.

Moran, A., Kilpatrick, R., Abbott, L., Dallat, J., & McClune, B. (2001). Training to teach: Motivating factors and implications for recruitment. *Education & Research in Education, 15*, 17–32.

Ngidi, D. P. (2012). Academic optimism: an individual teacher belief. *Educational Studies, 38*(2), 139–150. doi:10.1080/03 055698.2011.567830

Nix, G. A., Ryan, R. M., Manly, J. B., & Deci, E. L. (1999). Revitalization through self-regulation: The effects of autonomous and controlled motivation on happiness and vitality. *Journal of Experimental Social Psychology, 35*, 266–284.

Ntoumanis, N., & Standage, M. (2009). Motivation in physical education classes: A self-determination theory perspective. *Theory and Research in Education, 7*, 194–202.

Pelletier, L. G., Seguin-Levesque, C., & Legault, L. (2002). Pressures from above and pressures from below as determinants of teachers' motivation and teaching behavior. *Journal of Educational Psychology, 94*, 186–196.

Reeve, J. (1998). Autonomy support as an interpersonal motivating style: Is it teachable? *Contemporary Educational Psychology, 23*, 312–330.

Reeve, J. (2006). Extrinsic rewards and inner motivations. In C. Weinstein, & T. L. Good (Eds.), *Handbook of classroom management: Research, practice, and Contemporary issues* (pp. 645–664). Hillsdale, NJ: Lawrence Erlbaum.

Reeve, J. (2009). Why teachers adopt a controlling motivating style toward students and how they can become more autonomy supportive. *Educational Psychologist, 44*, 159–175.

Reeve, J., Deci, E. L., & Ryan, R. M. (2004). Self-determination theory: A dialectical framework for understanding the sociocultural influences on student motivation. In D. McInerney, & S. Van Etten (Eds.), *Research on sociocultural influences on motivation and learning: Big theories revisited* (Vol. 4, pp. 31–59). Greenwich, CT: Information Age Press.

Reeve, J., & Jang, H. (2006). What teachers say and do to support students' autonomy during a learning activity. *Journal of Educational Psychology, 98*, 209–218.

Reeve, J., Jang, H., Carrell, D., Barch, J., & Jeon, S. (2004). Enhancing high school students' engagement by increasing their teachers' autonomy support. *Motivation and Emotion, 28*, 147–169.

Reeve, J., Jang, H., Hardré, P., & Omura, M. (2002). Providing a rationale in an autonomy-supportive way as a strategy to motivate others during an uninteresting activity. *Motivation and Emotion, 26*, 183–207.

Reeve, J., Nix, G., & Hamm, D. (2003). Testing models of the experience of self-determination in intrinsic motivation and the conundrum of choice. *Journal of Educational Psychology, 95*, 375–392.

Reeve, J. & Tseng, C.-M. (2011). Cortisol reactivity to a teacher's motivating style: The biology of being controlled versus supporting autonomy. *Motivation and Emotion, 35*, 63–74.

Reeve, J., Vansteenkiste, M., Ahmad, I., Assor, A., Cheon, S. H., Jang, H.,…Wang, C. K. J. (2014). The beliefs that underlie autonomy-supportive and controlling teaching: A multinational investigation. *Motivation and Emotion, 38*, 93–110.

Richardson, P. W., & Watt, H. M. G. (2005). "I've decided to become a teacher": Influences on career change. *Teaching and Teacher Education, 21*, 475–489.

Richardson, P. W., & Watt, H. M. G. (2006). Who chooses teaching and why? Profiling characteristics and motivations across three Australian universities. *The Asia-Pacific Journal of Teacher Education, 34*, 27–56.

Roness, D. (2011). Still motivated? The motivation for teaching during the second year in the profession. *Teaching and Teacher Education, 27*, 628–638.

Ross, J. A. (1992). Teacher efficacy and the effect of coaching on student achievement. *Canadian Journal of Education, 17*, 51–65.

Roth, G., Assor, A., Kanat-Maymon, Y., & Kaplan, H. (2007). Autonomous motivation for teaching: How self-determined teaching may lead to self-determined learning. *Journal of Educational Psychology, 99*, 761–774.

Ryan, R. M., & Deci, E. L. (2000). Self-determination theory and the facilitation of intrinsic motivation, social development, and well-being. *American Psychologist, 55*, 68–78.

Sarrazin, P. G., Tessier, D. P., Pelletier, L. G., Trouilloud, D. O., & Chanal, J. P. (2006). The effects of teachers' expectations about students' motivation and teachers' autonomy-supportive and controlling behaviors. *International Journal of Sport and Exercise Psychology, 4*, 283–301

Schutz, P. A., Crowder, K. C., & White, V. E. (2001). The development of a goal to become a teacher. *Journal of Educational Psychology, 93*, 299–308.

Scott, C., Stone, B., & Dinham, S. (2001). "I love teaching but. . ." International patterns of teaching discontent. *Education Policy Analysis Archives, 9*(28), 1–18. Available at http://epaa.asu.edu/epaa/v9n28.html.

Shapira, Z. (1976). Expectancy determinants of intrinsically motivated behavior. *Journal of Personality and Social Psychology, 34*, 1235–1244.

Sheldon, K. M., & Krieger, L. (2004). Does law school undermine law students? Examining change in goals, values, and well-being. *Behavioral Sciences and the Law, 22*, 261–286.

Sierens, E., Vansteenkiste, M., Goossens, L., Soenens, B., & Dochy, F. (2009). The synergistic relationship of perceived autonomy support and structure in the prediction of self-regulated learning. *British Journal of Educational Psychology, 79*, 57–68.

Skaalvik, E. M., & Skaalvik, S. (2007). Dimensions of teacher self-efficacy and relations with strain factors, perceived collective teacher efficacy, and teacher burnout. *Journal of Educational Psychology, 99*, 611–625.

Soenens, B., Sierens, E., Vansteenkiste, M., Dochy, F., & Goossens, L. (2012). Psychologically controlling teaching: Examining outcomes, antecedents, and mediators. *Journal of Educational Psychology, 104*, 108–120.

Soenens, B., & Vansteenkiste, M. (2005). Antecedents and outcomes of self-determination in three life domains: The role of parents' and teachers' autonomy support. *Journal of Youth and Adolescence, 34*, 589–604.

Standage, M., Duda, J. L., & Ntoumanis, N. (2003). A model of contextual motivation in physical education: Using constructs and tenets from self-determination and goal perspective theories to predict leisure-time exercise intentions. *Journal of Educational Psychology, 95*, 97–110.

Su, Y.-L., & Reeve, J. (2011). A meta-analysis of the effectiveness of intervention programs designed to support autonomy. *Educational Psychology Review, 23*, 159–188.

Taylor, I. M., & Ntoumanis, N. (2007). Teacher motivational strategies and student self-determination in physical education. *Journal of Educational Psychology, 99*, 747–760.

Taylor, I. M., Ntoumanis, N., & Standage, M. (2008). A self-determination theory approach to understanding antecedents to teachers' motivational strategies in physical education. *Journal of Sport and Exercise Psychology, 30*, 75–94.

Tessier, D., Sarrazin, P., & Ntoumanis, N. (2008). The effects of an experimental programme to support students' autonomy on the overt behaviours of physical education teachers. *European Journal of Psychology of Education, 23*, 239–253.

Tessier, D., Sarrazin, P., & Ntoumanis, N. (2010). The effect of an intervention to improve newly qualified teachers' interpersonal style, students' motivation and psychological need satisfaction in sport-based physical education. *Contemporary Educational Psychology, 35*, 242–253.

Tsai, Y., Kunter, M., Lüdtke, O., Trautwein, U., & Ryan, R. M. (2008). What makes lessons interesting? The role of situational and individual factors in three school subjects. *Journal of Educational Psychology, 100*, 460–472.

Tschannen-Moran, M., & Woolfolk Hoy, A. (2001). Teacher efficacy: Capturing an elusive construct. *Teaching and Teacher Education, 17*, 783–805.

Tschannen-Moran, M., Woolfolk Hoy, A., & Hoy, W. K. (1998). Teacher efficacy: Its meaning and measure. *Review of Educational Research, 68*, 202–248.

Turner, J. C., Warzon, K. B., & Christensen, A. (2011). Motivating mathematics learning: Changes in teachers' practices and beliefs during a nine-month collaboration. *American Educational Research Journal, 48*, 718–762.

Vallerand, R. J., Fortier, M. S., & Guay, F. (1997). Self-determination and persistence in a real life setting: Toward a motivational model of high school dropout. *Journal of Personality and Social Psychology, 72*, 1161–1176.

Vansteenkiste, M., Lens, W., & Deci, E. L. (2006). Intrinsic versus extrinsic goal contents in self-determination theory: Another look at the quality of academic motivation. *Educational Psychologist, 41*, 19–31.

Vansteenkiste, M., Niemiec, C., & Soenens, B. (2010). The development of the five mini-theories of self-determination theory: An historical overview, emerging trends, and future directions. In T. Urdan, & S. Karabenick, (Eds.), *Advances in motivation and achievement: The decade ahead* (Vol. 16, pp. 105–166). Bingley, UK: Emerald Publishing.

Vansteenkiste, M., Simons, J., Lens, W., Sheldon, K. M., & Deci, E. L. (2004). Motivating learning, performance, and persistence: The synergistic role of intrinsic goals and autonomy-support. *Journal of Personality and Social Psychology, 87*, 246–260.

Vansteenkiste, M., Simons, J., Lens, W., Soenens, B., & Matos, L., (2005). Examining the impact of extrinsic versus intrinsic goal framing and internally controlling versus autonomy-supportive communication style upon early adolescents' academic achievement. *Child Development, 76*, 483–501.

Vansteenkiste, M., Simons, J., Soenens, B., & Lens, W. (2004). How to become a persevering exerciser? Providing a clear, future intrinsic goal in an autonomy supportive way. *Journal of Sport and Exercise Psychology, 26*, 232–249.

Vansteenkiste, M., Zhou, M., Lens, W., & Soenens, B. (2005). Experiences of autonomy and control among Chinese learners: Vitalizing or immobilizing? *Journal of Educational Psychology, 97*, 468–483.

Watt, H. M. G., & Richardson, P. W. (2008). Motivations, perceptions, and aspirations concerning teaching as a career for different types of beginning teachers. *Learning and Instruction, 18*, 408–428.

Wolters, C. A., & Daugherty, S. G. (2007). Goal structures and teachers' sense of efficacy: Their relation and association to teaching experience and academic level. *Journal of Educational Psychology, 99*, 181–193.

CHAPTER
22

At the Interface of Work and Health: A Consideration of the Health Gradient using Self-Determination Theory

Maynor G. González, Christopher P. Niemiec, *and* Geoffrey C. Williams

Abstract

A considerable body of research has pointed toward an association between occupational status and health outcomes, such that employees in lower-status occupations experience poorer health outcomes and shorter life expectancies than those in higher-status occupations. These differences in health across incremental levels of occupational status are referred to as the health gradient and have been linked to social, psychological, and economic factors that distinguish various levels of the employment hierarchy. However, a theoretical framework that may explain the psychosocial mechanisms that underlie these associations has not been adequately established. In this chapter we discuss research on the health gradient and several of its psychosocial determinants, describe research from self-determination theory on the promotion of physical and psychological health, present an application of self-determination theory to understanding the mechanisms that account for the health gradient, and call for future research on this topic.

Key Words: basic psychological needs, health gradient, occupational health, occupational status, psychosocial determinants of health, self-determination theory, Whitehall studies

In recent decades, the nature of work in industrialized nations has undergone a dramatic change from being physically demanding to more sedentary and psychologically demanding. Such a shift in the nature of work, coupled with consumption of calorically dense foods, has contributed to a variety of health epidemics, such as obesity, hypertension, and hyperlipidemia (Lundberg & Cooper, 2011). Each of these epidemics is a risk factor for the development of chronic health conditions, including cardiovascular disease, cancer, and diabetes, which account for 70% of all deaths in the United States (Centers for Disease Control and Prevention, n.d.). Accordingly, it is important to consider how work-related factors affect employee health and wellness.

A considerable body of research has pointed toward an association between occupational status and health outcomes, such that employees in

lower-status occupations experience poorer health outcomes and shorter life expectancies than those in higher-status occupations (Hertzman & Siddiqi, 2009; Siegrist & Marmot, 2006; van Rossum, Shipley, van de Mheen, Grobbee, & Marmot, 2000). This association has been found to be monotonic, such that differences in health emerge across incremental levels of occupational status, and is referred to as the *health gradient* (Marmot, 2006). At the same time, emerging research has established a link between the experience of stress at work and employee health and wellness. Workplace stress is known to contribute to the development of chronic health conditions in two ways (DeSteno, Gross, & Kubzansky, in press). First, stress is associated with unpleasant emotions that accelerate the process of atherosclerosis and inhibit immune system functioning. Second, stress is associated with use of alcohol and tobacco to mitigate the experience of those emotions. Workplace stress has psychological and behavioral costs as well, including depressive symptoms, somatic symptom burden, emotional exhaustion, turnover intention, and absenteeism (Krasner et al., 2009; Williams et al., 2012).

There is general consensus that occupational status within the employment hierarchy, as well as the nature and demands of contemporary work conditions, are important predictors of health outcomes. Yet research is only beginning to develop a theoretical framework that may explain the psychosocial mechanisms that underlie these associations, which in turn can be linked to pathophysiological causes of disease. In this chapter, we discuss evidence from self-determination theory (SDT) on the factors that are associated with physical and psychological health. In doing so, we hope to lay initial groundwork for an application of SDT to understanding the mechanisms that may underlie the health gradient and its associated health outcomes. To elucidate these ideas, this chapter is divided into three sections. In the first, we discuss research on the health gradient and several of its psychosocial determinants, namely, perceptions of control, reciprocity, social support, and stress. In the second, we describe research from SDT on the promotion of physical and psychological health. In the third, we present an application of SDT to understanding the mechanisms that account for the health gradient, and call for future research on this topic.

The Health Gradient

In their groundbreaking work with British civil servants, Michael Marmot and colleagues showed that morbidity and mortality rates differ across various levels of occupational status. The first longitudinal study on the health gradient (Marmot, Rose, Shipley, & Hamilton, 1978) was conducted during the 1960s and examined the incidence of coronary heart disease among 17,530 working individuals. Marmot et al. found that civil servants in lower-status occupations were more likely to die prematurely from coronary heart disease compared with those in higher-status occupations. Results also showed that several key risk factors for coronary heart disease, such as tobacco use, an imbalance in plasma glucose levels, blood pressure, and physical inactivity, were not evenly distributed across levels of occupational status. Rather, these risk factors were more prevalent among those in lower-status occupations. It is important to note as well that research has shown evidence of the health gradient in a variety of countries,

including India, Sri Lanka, Costa Rica, the United Kingdom, and the United States (McDonough, Duncan, Williams, & House, 1997; Smith, 1999; Tarlov, 2000).

On the Determinants of the Health Gradient

One of the major challenges for those who study the health gradient is to understand the factors that determine the uneven distribution of health, morbidity, and mortality across the employment hierarchy. The health gradient is thought to arise from an array of biological, social, psychological, and economic factors that distinguish various levels of the employment hierarchy (Wilkinson, 2001, 2005). Yet the specificity and relative impact of these factors are widely debated topics (Major, Mendes, & Dovidio, in press). With respect to the level of specificity, some have identified economic and social circumstances as the major determinants of health disparities among individuals and groups (Lynch, Smith, Kaplan, & House, 2000; Ross et al., 2006), whereas others have suggested that broader assessments of socioeconomic status are more useful to consider (Graham, 2007; Lynch, Kaplan, & Salonen, 1997). Likewise with respect to their relative impact on the health gradient, some have found better predictive utility with income and education, relative to occupation (Geyer & Peter, 2000), whereas others have reported the opposite pattern of results (Davey Smith et al., 1998). It is clear, therefore, that additional theory and research is needed to sort out the multitude of complex factors that affect the health gradient.

Although the factors that underlie the health gradient are still debated, researchers have given increased attention to the *psychosocial* determinants of health. Indeed, comprehensive studies have suggested that these factors play a significant role in explaining differences in health across the employment hierarchy (Dunn, Veenstra, & Ross, 2006; Marmot, 2006; Marmot, Bosma, Hemingway, Brunner, & Stansfeld, 1997; Marmot & Wilkinson, 2001). Such a focus may also offer insight into what appears to be a paradox within the health gradient literature, namely, that differences in health are observed even among individuals who are not in poverty and who are not exposed to workplace hazards. That is, the health gradient also exists among those in higher-status occupations (Marmot et al., 1991). The importance of considering the psychosocial determinants of the health gradient is, therefore, readily apparent.

Following their earlier research, Marmot et al. (1991) conducted a second study—known as Whitehall II—to examine the psychosocial determinants of health disparities. Their results replicated those of Marmot et al. (1978) and showed that psychological stressors contribute to the health gradient. For instance, working conditions marked by high demand and low control were found to be associated with higher levels of physical illness. To explain this finding, Marmot et al. (1991) suggested that those in lower-status occupations had less control at work and thus were less able to react effectively in highly demanding situations. Indeed, research has shown that the amount of control that individuals have at work accounts for about half of the association between the health gradient and cardiovascular disease (Bosma et al., 1997; Marmot, Bosma, Hemingway, Brunner, & Stansfeld, 1997). Interestingly, the adverse consequences of an imbalance between demands and control include workplace stress (Karasek & Theorell, 1990), which may accelerate the rate at which cholesterol builds up in the artery walls (i.e., atherosclerosis) and yield higher incidences of myocardial infarctions, strokes, aneurysms, and sudden death (Karasek, Baker, Marxer, Ahlbom, & Theorell, 1981). Therefore, one psychosocial factor that appears to influence the health gradient is employees' perceptions of control over outcomes at work.

Two other psychosocial determinants of the health gradient are employees' perceptions of reciprocity and social support at work. The criteria for reciprocity are derived from the underlying employment contract between employer and employee, which defines responsibilities at work and the compensation that can be expected to be received on successful completion of those responsibilities. Indeed, employee wellness can be jeopardized when fair compensation for effort at work is not received (Siegrist, 1996). For instance, working conditions marked by high effort and low reward were found to be associated with symptoms of physical and psychological ill-being, including high blood pressure, myocardial infarction, anxiety, psychological distress, and depression (Siegrist & Marmot, 2004; Stansfeld & Candy, 2006). Social support at work has been found to mitigate the adverse consequences associated with low perceptions of control among employees, specifically for their cardiovascular disease risk (Johnson & Hall, 1994). Such findings point toward an association between the social context at work and employee health and wellness.

An additional psychosocial determinant of the health gradient, indeed one under which perceptions of control, reciprocity, and social support may be subsumed, is perceived stress at work. There is ample evidence suggesting that experiences of prolonged and acute stress in the workplace can suppress immune system functioning, thereby undermining psychological health and leaving employees at a higher risk for various health problems. For instance, experiences of stress at work were found to be associated with coronary heart disease, musculoskeletal disorders, cancer, diabetes, and infections (Brunner & Marmot, 2006; DeSteno et al., in press; Marmot et al., 1991), as well as with anxiety and depressive symptoms (Gentry, Benson, & de Wolff, 1985; Marmot, Siegrist, Theorell, & Feeney, 1999). Beyond their direct relations to physical and psychological health outcomes, experiences of stress at work are associated with engagement in risky health behaviors, such as use of tobacco, alcohol, and drugs, as well as over-eating (Siegrist & Rödel, 2006; Wardle et al., 1999). It bears noting that the adverse consequences associated with engagement in risky health behaviors accumulate over time and are synergistic in their detrimental impact on health, ultimately increasing the risk of premature morbidity and mortality. Importantly, many of these health-related factors and outcomes are associated with occupational status.

A Summary and Segue

To summarize this brief review of the health gradient literature, there is ample evidence to suggest that work-related factors affect employee wellness. Yet it seems unlikely that the health gradient is solely a function of uneven distribution of income across the employment hierarchy and/or differential exposure to adverse material and workplace conditions, because health differences are evident even among those in higher-status occupations (Marmot et al., 1991). One important challenge, therefore, is to understand the mechanisms that may explain the association between occupational status and health outcomes across the health gradient. This knowledge may provide a more refined understanding of how experiences in the workplace affect the physical and psychological health of employees. Additional theory and research is needed (Marks, Murray, Evans, & Estacio, 2011), and to bridge this gap we turn to a consideration of SDT, which provides a theoretical framework that may be useful for understanding the health gradient and its psychosocial determinants.

Self-Determination Theory

Self-determination theory (SDT; Deci & Ryan, 2008; Niemiec, Ryan, & Deci, 2010) is an approach to human motivation, emotion, and personality in social contexts with applications to the domains of work (Gagné & Deci, 2005) and health care (Williams, 2002), among others. With its philosophical roots grounded in organismic theory (Ryan & Deci, 2002), SDT assumes that humans are proactive by nature and are oriented toward healthy development, which is marked by integration at the psychological (autonomy) and interpersonal (homonomy) levels (Angyal, 1965). Yet SDT also recognizes that humans are vulnerable to passivity, psychological fragmentation, and interpersonal disharmony, especially when the social surround is not supportive of their inherent growth tendencies. Such a dynamic gives rise to an organismic-dialectic meta-theory that is used to guide subsequent theorizing.

At the core of SDT is the proposal of three basic psychological needs for (1) autonomy, (2) competence, and (3) relatedness. Satisfaction of these three needs is necessary for psychological growth and internalization of ambient values, beliefs, and practices into the self (Deci & Ryan, 2000). The need for autonomy (de Charms, 1968) refers to the experience that behavior is enacted with a sense of choice, volition, and reflective endorsement. The opposite of autonomy is heteronomy, or the experience of pressure and control to think, feel, and behave in particular ways (Ryan & Deci, 2006). The need for competence (White, 1959) refers to the experience of effectance in interacting with the physical and social environment. The need for relatedness (Baumeister & Leary, 1995; Ryan, 1995) refers to the experience of warm, caring, and mutual connections with others. It is important to note that within SDT, psychological needs do not refer to desires or values, but rather "needs specify *innate psychological nutriments that are essential for ongoing psychological growth, integrity, and well-being*" (Deci & Ryan, 2000, p. 229, italics in original). Thus, satisfaction of the basic psychological needs for autonomy, competence, and relatedness is expected to promote optimal physical, psychological, and social functioning, and adverse consequences are predicted to follow when needs are not supported or are actively thwarted.

As alluded to previously, social-contextual support for satisfaction of the basic psychological needs is theorized to facilitate internalization, or the natural, active process of coming to endorse the value of a behavior that was originally prompted by external sources (Ryan, 1993). Through the process of internalization, the value of and requisite skills for important (yet nonintrinsically motivated) behaviors are brought into coherence with other aspects of the self and are regulated with a sense of volition. SDT specifies a continuum of internalization along which behavioral regulations vary in the extent to which they are experienced as controlled versus autonomous. To illustrate, an employee is said to be controlled if she or he completes tasks on time so as to obtain a letter of commendation or to avoid reprimand. Indeed, the experiences of pressure and coercion that underlie controlled forms of behavioral regulation can also originate from inside the person, as when an employee completes tasks on time so as to gain a sense of pride or to avoid feelings of guilt and shame. In contrast, an employee is said to be autonomous if she or he completes tasks on time because the value of doing so is self-endorsed and aligned with other deeply held values. The relative autonomy with which behavior is regulated has been shown to be associated with full functioning and organismic wellness across a variety of life's domains (for a review, see Deci & Ryan, 2008).

More specific to our focus, Gagné and Deci (2005) reviewed a considerable amount of empirical evidence on the importance of need support, need satisfaction, and internalization for optimal functioning in organizational contexts. This evidence provides some initial support for an application of SDT to the health gradient, because Gagné and Deci's (2005) review underscores the importance of autonomy in the work domain. To provide additional support for an application of SDT to the health gradient, herein we briefly review empirical evidence on the importance of need support, need satisfaction, and internalization in the health-care domain. Such a review is warranted given the elevation of support for patient autonomy in biomedical ethics (Beauchamp & Childress, 2001, 2009) and patient autonomy in medical professionalism (American Board of Internal Medicine Foundation et al., 2002) as outcomes that are equivalent in importance to enhancing patient well-being. Respect for autonomy involves helping the patient to make a clear and informed decision about whether and how to attempt health-behavior change and its maintenance (Williams & Niemiec, 2012; Williams et al., 2011). The opposite of respect for autonomy is to pressure or coerce the patient into health-behavior change, or to leave the patient with ambivalence about whether she or he would want to attempt such change. This review, in turn, paves the way for our consideration of the health gradient using SDT.

On the Promotion of Physical and Psychological Health

Much research using SDT has examined the relations of need support, need satisfaction, and internalization to physical and psychological health. Rather than provide a full discussion of this large corpus of findings, we describe results from a recently completed systematic review of the SDT literature on health and wellness (Ng et al., 2012). In total, 184 data sets met the criteria for inclusion in a meta-analysis, and results provided strong support for SDT. Provision of need support related positively to physical and psychological health, and negatively to ill-being. In a similar way, need satisfaction and autonomous self-regulation related positively to physical and psychological health, and negatively to ill-being. Controlled regulation, in contrast, related negatively to psychological health and positively to ill-being. It is interesting to note that most, but not all, of the associations between controlled regulation and physical health were negative, although they were not always significantly different from zero. Taken together, these results show that need support, need satisfaction, and internalization relate consistently and positively to physical and psychological health. In a subsequent analysis, Ng et al. found confirmation for a model in which (1) need support related positively to autonomous self-regulation and perceived competence; (2) autonomous self-regulation related positively to perceived competence, physical health, and psychological health; and (3) perceived competence related positively to physical and psychological health. This set of associations is consistent with the SDT model of health-behavior change (Ryan, Patrick, Deci, & Williams, 2008; Williams et al., 2002).

Overall, the results of Ng et al.'s (2012) meta-analysis underscore the importance of need support, need satisfaction, and internalization for physical and psychological health, especially given that data were obtained from a large number of studies, investigators, domains, and cultures. Yet a critical limitation is the correlational nature of the data used in the analysis, which precludes a conclusion of causality for these associations. Fortunately, several randomized clinical trials have been conducted using SDT to assess whether physical and psychological health is improved when interventions provide support for basic psychological need satisfaction in the context of treatment. This research has demonstrated the efficacy of SDT-based interventions for such behaviors as tobacco dependence (Williams, McGregor, Sharp, Levesque, et al., 2006), cholesterol (Williams, McGregor, Sharp, Kouides, et al., 2006), weight loss maintenance (Teixeira et al., 2009), physical activity (Fortier, Sweet, O'Sullivan, & Williams, 2007), dental hygiene (Münster Halvari & Halvari, 2006), and diabetes care (Williams, Lynch, & Glasgow, 2007). Together, the trials have shown that autonomous self-regulation and perceived competence are facilitated in healthcare climates that provide support for basic psychological needs, and that autonomous self-regulation and perceived competence are the psychological mechanisms by which maintenance of health-behavior change occurs (Ryan et al., 2008).

Although more work is needed to garner additional evidence in support of this theoretical model among other cultures and behaviors, this body of research offers causal evidence for the beneficial impact that need-supportive healthcare climates have on initiation and maintenance of health-behavior change. Therefore, it is useful to consider how healthcare practitioners can provide support for their patients' basic psychological needs. In the healthcare domain, support for autonomy involves eliciting and acknowledging the patient's ideas and perspectives, taking interest in and accepting the patient's feelings, exploring how the patient's values relate to health-behavior change, providing clinical recommendations with a rationale for how they may improve health, offering a menu of effective options for treatment, supporting the patient's self-initiation of change, and minimizing use of controlling language (should, must, ought, have to). Support for competence involves ensuring that the patient is fully volitional with regard to the treatment being offered, remaining positive that the patient can succeed, identifying possible barriers to change, and assisting the patient in developing skills and techniques for problem solving. Support for relatedness involves being warm, empathic, and nonjudgmental so that the patient can succeed in achieving her or his goals (see Williams et al., 2011).

On the Importance of Need-Supportive Social Contexts

These correlational and experimental findings from the healthcare domain suggest that provision of need support and the experience of need satisfaction are associated with higher levels of autonomous self-regulation and perceived competence, which in turn predict physical and psychological health. Indeed, the dynamics of need support (or lack thereof) extend beyond the therapeutic encounter and describe a general interpersonal style that is relevant in a variety of domains and types of social interactions. To illustrate this, we describe additional evidence for the importance of need-supportive social contexts for internalization and psychological health in the domain of medical education.

Williams and Deci (1996) found that medical students who perceived more provision of need support from instructors reported higher levels of autonomous self-regulation, perceived competence, and interest in medical interviewing. It is also important to note that at a 2-year follow-up, those with higher levels of autonomous self-regulation were rated as more autonomy supportive by standardized patients. Other evidence suggests that need-supportive social contexts affect medical students' career choice. Williams, Saizow, Ross, and Deci (1997; also Williams, Wiener, Markakis, Reeve, & Deci, 1994) found that medical students' likelihood of selecting either internal medicine or surgery as their specialty was predicted by their perceptions of need support from the instructors of the corresponding third-year clerkships, and this association was mediated by perceived competence and interest in those medical specialties. Still other evidence suggests that need-supportive social contexts affect clinicians' actual therapeutic practice. Williams, Levesque, Zeldman, Wright, and Deci (2003) recruited healthcare practitioners to attend a smoking cessation workshop that was intended to support their autonomy, competence, and interest in counseling. Results showed that practitioners who perceived more provision of need support from leaders reported higher levels of autonomous self-regulation and perceived competence for tobacco counseling. Furthermore, autonomous self-regulation predicted increases in the amount of time spent counseling and the use of clinical guidelines over 3 months.

The results of these studies highlight the importance of providing support for autonomy, competence, and relatedness in the domains of health care and medical education. Need-supportive social contexts have been shown to facilitate autonomous self-regulation, perceived competence, and interest, which are associated with higher levels of well-being and lower levels of burnout among physicians (Shanafelt, Sloan, & Habermann, 2003). With the experience of need support, medical students and physicians may be better able to integrate their emotional responses to the overwhelming demands on their time (Yarnall, Pollak, Ostbye, Krause, & Michener, 2003), and in turn make the decision to use effective interventions in clinical practice.

The Case of Somatization (At the Interface of Work and Health)

Thus far, we have reviewed empirical evidence on the importance of need support, need satisfaction, and internalization in the healthcare domain, and have only made passing reference to research using SDT in the work domain (again, we refer the interested reader to [Gagné and Deci's (2005)] comprehensive review of the topic). At this point, however, it is important to consider the interface of work and health from the perspective of SDT, which may offer several important directions for future research on the health gradient. One point of intersection between the domains of work and health is somatization, or the manifestation of psychosocial distress as physical symptoms that are unexplained by physical illness (Lipowski, 1988). Somatization is of particular interest to both employers and healthcare practitioners, because when employees experience somatic symptoms they often miss work and seek medical care and/or testing (Kroenke, 2007). Indeed, somatic symptoms account for at least 50% of all outpatient medical encounters in the United States (Katon, Ries, & Kleinman, 1984; Schappert, 1993), as well as an estimated $256 billion per year in healthcare utilization and lost job productivity (Barsky, Orav, & Bates, 2005).

To explain part of the etiology of somatization, Williams et al. (2012) collected data from 287 employees of four leading Nordic companies. Results showed that employees who perceived more provision of need support from managers reported higher levels of autonomous self-regulation at work, and autonomous self-regulation predicted lower levels of somatic symptoms. This inverse association is important to note given that somatic symptoms related positively to emotional exhaustion, turnover intention, and absenteeism. Such findings provide a motivational model based on SDT that explains important outcomes at the intersection of work and health. Related to this line of research, Vaananen et al. (2005) collected data from 13,795 employees of a globally operating corporation in Canada, China, Finland, France, and Sweden. Results showed that employees who had more job autonomy reported lower levels of functional incapacity and, interestingly, this association was most pronounced in China. These studies underscore the importance of need support and autonomy in the domains of work and health in various cultures.

Given that need satisfaction has been shown to affect physical and psychological health in the workplace, it is important to consider whether managers can learn to provide support for their employees' basic psychological needs. One of the potential benefits for managers is that in need-supportive climates employees may attend work more regularly, be more productive, and experience less stress. Deci, Connell, and Ryan (1989) found that employees who perceived more provision of need support from managers reported higher levels of satisfaction with their jobs and trust in top management, and lower levels of pressure. Also, managers who received an organizational development intervention that focused on the concept of supporting employees' autonomy became more need supportive toward their employees. Other evidence suggests employees who perceive managers as need supportive experience more well-being, better job performance, and less anxiety at work (Baard, 2002; Baard, Deci, & Ryan, 2004). Therefore, the importance of managers' creating need-supportive contexts for the promotion of employees' physical and psychological health at work is readily apparent.

A Consideration of the Health Gradient using SDT

In the introduction of this chapter we noted that the nature of work has been transformed over a relatively brief period of time. Such dramatic changes carry with them benefits and risks, and one important challenge at the interface of work and health is to understand how work-related factors affect employee health and wellness. A considerable body of research points toward the existence of health disparities across various levels of occupational status, yet there is no clear theoretical framework that may explain the psychosocial mechanisms that underlie these associations. Of course, a focus on psychosocial determinants does not invalidate the social factors that contribute to health disparities, such as income inequality, unemployment, poor housing, and malnourishment. Indeed, it is useful to incorporate both social and psychological factors into a theoretical framework to provide a more complete understanding of prevention and health promotion. Our focus in this chapter is to introduce SDT as a framework that can be used to guide future research on the health gradient and its psychosocial determinants.

From the perspective of SDT, the basic psychological needs for autonomy, competence, and relatedness are universal requirements for full functioning and wellness (Niemiec & Ryan, 2013). In other words, regardless of their gender, age, ethnicity, level of income, amount of education, occupational status, or any other delimiting factor, all individuals require support for basic psychological need satisfaction for the promotion of optimal physical, psychological, and social wellness. It follows from this postulate that the etiology of physical disease and psychological illness can be traced, at least in part, to an individual's not having her or his basic psychological needs supported (or actively thwarted) by the social context. To depict these concepts, Figure 22.1 presents a preliminary sketch of SDT dynamics that may be relevant and useful for understanding the health gradient and its psychosocial determinants. We suggest that occupational status and other aspects of the social hierarchy (gender, age, ethnicity, level of income, amount of education) may be associated with provision of need support (or lack thereof) in the workplace, although additional research is needed to examine this. Employees' perceptions of need support have been shown to predict their satisfaction of basic psychological needs (Gagné & Deci, 2005), which in turn has been shown to predict autonomous self-regulation and perceived competence for healthy behavior. Such motivation has been shown to predict physical and psychological health (Ng et al., 2012). Accordingly, we propose that the dynamics of need support (or lack thereof), need satisfaction (or lack thereof), and internalization are important to consider in developing an explanation of how the health gradient and its psychosocial determinants relate to physical and psychological health. Indeed, González (2012) has shown that perceptions of basic psychological need satisfaction at work explain part of the association between occupational status and general health among employees, thereby providing initial support for this set of associations.

This proposal offers a framework for investigating the emergence of differences in health across various levels of occupational status. For instance, health maladies, such as cardiovascular disease and their associated risk factors, are not evenly distributed across levels of occupational status (Marmot et al., 1978). Future research, therefore, might examine whether perceptions of need support, experiences of need satisfaction, and levels of internalization are similarly skewed across the employment hierarchy.

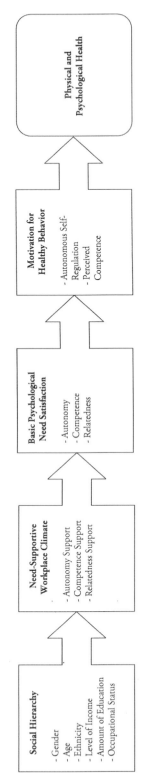

Fig. 22.1. A preliminary sketch of SDT dynamics that may be relevant and useful for understanding the health gradient and its psychosocial determinants.

Such uneven distributions, if found, may explain at least part of the association between occupational status and health.

SDT may also provide a deeper understanding of the psychosocial determinants of health, because theories of workplace stress tend to be limited in their exclusive focus on the psychological imbalances associated with perceptions of high demand, low control, low reciprocity, and low social support (see Karasek & Theorell, 1990). For instance, employees who have low levels of control over outcomes at work may experience frustration of their needs for autonomy and competence. In a similar way, employees who perceive low reciprocity and social support at work may experience frustration of their need for relatedness. Indeed, as we believe that perceptions of control, reciprocity, and social support may be subsumed under the general category of stress, employees who experience high levels of stress at work may experience frustration of each of the basic psychological needs.

In closing, it is worthwhile to note that SDT examines the interface between the person and the social context to understand the factors that predict health and wellness. Knowledge of such factors and how they relate to motivation for healthy behavior may assist employers in addressing occupational health problems and may provide a better understanding of the uneven distribution of health, morbidity, and mortality across the employment hierarchy. Of course, more research on the health gradient and its psychosocial determinants is needed to examine these dynamics more thoroughly and systematically. Such research may not only have theoretical importance, but may also have implications for policy matters related to employment and health.

References

American Board of Internal Medicine Foundation, American Board of Internal Medicine, ACP-ASIM Foundation, American College of Physicians, American Society of Internal Medicine, & European Federation of Internal Medicine. (2002). Medical professionalism in the new millennium: A physician charter. *Annals of Internal Medicine, 136*, 243–246.

Angyal, A. (1965). *Neurosis and treatment: A holistic theory.* New York: Wiley.

Baard, P. P. (2002). Intrinsic need satisfaction in organizations: A motivational basis of success in for-profit and not-for-profit settings. In E. L. Deci, & R. M. Ryan (Eds.), *Handbook of self-determination research* (pp. 255–275). Rochester, NY: University of Rochester Press.

Baard, P. P., Deci, E. L., & Ryan, R. M. (2004). Intrinsic need satisfaction: A motivational basis of performance and well-being in two work settings. *Journal of Applied Social Psychology, 34*, 2045–2068.

Barsky, A. J., Orav, E. J., & Bates, D. W. (2005). Somatization increases medical utilization and costs independent of psychiatric and medical comorbidity. *Archives of General Psychiatry, 62*, 903–910.

Baumeister, R. F., & Leary, M. R. (1995). The need to belong: Desire for interpersonal attachments as a fundamental human motivation. *Psychological Bulletin, 117*, 497–529.

Beauchamp, T. L., & Childress, J. F. (2001). *Principles of biomedical ethics* (5th ed.). New York: Oxford University Press, Inc.

Beauchamp, T. L., & Childress, J. F. (2009). *Principles of biomedical ethics* (6th ed.). New York: Oxford University Press, Inc.

Bosma, H., Marmot, M. G., Hemingway, H., Nicholson, A., Brunner, E. J., & Stansfeld, S. (1997). Low job control and risk of coronary heart disease in the Whitehall II (prospective cohort) study. *British Medical Journal, 314*, 558–565.

Brunner, E., & Marmot, M. G. (2006). Social organization, stress, and health. In M. G. Marmot, & R. G. Wilkinson (Eds.), *Social determinants of health* (2nd ed., pp. 6–30). Oxford: Oxford University Press.

Centers for Disease Control and Prevention. (n.d.) *Chronic disease prevention and health promotion.* Retrieved from http://www.cdc.gov/chronicdisease/index.htm

Davey Smith, G., Hart, C., Hole, D., MacKinnon, P., Gillis, C., Watt, G., Blane, D., Hawthorne, V. (1998). Education and occupational social class: Which is the more important indicator of mortality risk? *Journal of Epidemiology and Community Health, 52*, 153–160.

de Charms, R. (1968). *Personal causation.* New York: Academic Press.

Deci, E. L., Connell, J. P., & Ryan, R. M. (1989). Self-determination in a work organization. *Journal of Applied Psychology, 74*, 580–590.

Deci, E. L., & Ryan, R. M. (2000). The "what" and "why" of goal pursuits: Human needs and the self-determination of behavior. *Psychological Inquiry, 11*, 227–268.

Deci, E. L., & Ryan, R. M. (2008). Facilitating optimal motivation and psychological well-being across life's domains. *Canadian Psychology, 49*, 14–23.

DeSteno, D., Gross, J. J., & Kubzansky, L. (2013). Affective science and health: The importance of emotion and emotion regulation. *Health Psychology, 32*, 474–486.

Dunn, J. R., Veenstra, G., & Ross, N. (2006). Psychosocial and neo-material dimensions of SES and health revisited: Predictors of self-rated health in a Canadian national survey. *Social Science and Medicine, 62*, 1465–1473.

Fortier, M. S., Sweet, S. N., O'Sullivan, T. L., & Williams, G. C. (2007). A self-determination process model of physical activity adoption in the context of a radomized controlled trial. *Psychology of Sport and Exercise, 8*, 741–757.

Gagné, M., & Deci, E. L. (2005). Self-determination theory and work motivation. *Journal of Organizational Behavior, 26*, 331–362.

Gentry, W. D., Benson, H., & de Wolff, C. J. (1985). *Behavioral medicine: Work, stress, and health.* Dordrecht: Nijhoff.

Geyer, S., & Peter, R. (2000). Income, occupational position, qualification and health inequalities--competing risks? (Comparing indicators of social status). *Journal of Epidemiology and Community Health, 54*, 299–305.

González, M. G. (2012). *Self-determination theory and the health gradient in the workplace: Exploring psychological pathways to improving health* (Doctoral dissertation). Available from

ProQuest Dissertations and Theses database. (Accession Order No. AAT 10195)

Graham, H. (2007). *Unequal lives: Health and socioeconomic inequalities.* New York: Open University Press.

Hertzman, C., & Siddiqi, A. (2009). Population health and the dynamics of collective development. In P. A. Hall, & M. Lamont (Eds.), *Successful societies: How institutions and culture affect health* (pp. 23–52). New York: Cambridge University Press.

Johnson, J., & Hall, E. (1994). Social support in the work environment and cardiovascular disease. In A. S. Shumaker, & M. S. Czajkowski (Eds.), *Social support and cardiovascular disease* (pp. 145–166). New York: Plenum Press.

Karasek, R., Baker, D., Marxer, F., Ahlbom, A., & Theorell, T. (1981). Job decision latitude, job demands, and cardiovascular disease: A prospective study of Swedish men. *American Journal of Public Health, 71*, 694–705.

Karasek, R., & Theorell, T. (1990). *Healthy work: Stress, productivity, and the reconstruction of working life.* New York: Basic Books.

Katon, W., Ries, R. K., & Kleinman, A. (1984). The prevalence of somatization in primary care. *Comprehensive Psychiatry, 25*, 208–215.

Krasner, M. S., Epstein, R. M., Beckman, H., Suchman, A. L., Chapman, B., Mooney, C. J., Quill, T. E. (2009). Association of an educational program in mindful communication with burnout, empathy, and attitudes among primary care physicians. *Journal of the American Medical Association, 302*, 1284–1293.

Kroenke, K. (2007). Efficacy of treatment for somatoform disorders: A review of randomized controlled trials. *Psychosomatic Medicine, 69*, 881–888.

Lipowski, Z. J. (1988). Somatization: The concept and its clinical application. *American Journal of Psychiatry, 145*, 1358–1368.

Lundberg, U., & Cooper, C. L. (2011). *The science of occupational health: Stress, psychobiology and the new world of work.* Oxford: Wiley-Blackwell.

Lynch, J. W., Kaplan, G. A., & Salonen, J. T. (1997). Why do poor people behave poorly? Variation in adult health behaviours and psychosocial characteristics by stages of the socioeconomic lifecourse. *Social Science and Medicine, 44*, 809–819.

Lynch, J. W., Smith, G. D., Kaplan, G. A., & House, J. S. (2000). Income inequality and mortality: Importance to health of individual income, psychosocial environment, or material conditions. *British Medical Journal, 320*, 1200–1204.

Major, B., Mendes, W. B., & Dovidio, J. (2013). Intergroup relations and health disparities: A social psychological perspective. *Health Psychology, 32*, 514–524.

Marks, D. F., Murray, M., Evans, B., & Estacio, E. (2011). *Health psychology: Theory, research and practice* (3rd ed.). London: SAGE Publications Ltd.

Marmot, M. G. (2006). Status syndrome: A challenge to medicine. *Journal of the American Medical Association, 295*, 1304–1307.

Marmot, M. G., Bosma, H., Hemingway, H., Brunner, E., & Stansfeld, S. (1997). Contribution of job control and other risk factors to social variations in coronary heart disease incidence. *Lancet, 350*, 235–239.

Marmot, M. G., Rose, G., Shipley, M., & Hamilton, P. J. (1978). Employment grade and coronary heart disease in British civil servants. *Journal of Epidemiology and Community Health, 32*, 244–249.

Marmot, M. G., Siegrist, J., Theorell, T., & Feeney, A. (1999). Health and the psychosocial environment at work. In M. G. Marmot, & R. G. Wilkinson (Eds.), *Social determinants of health* (pp. 105–131). New York: Oxford University Press.

Marmot, M. G., Smith, G. D., Stansfeld, S., Patel, C., North, F., Head, J., White, I., Brunner, E., Feeney, A. (1991). Health inequalities among British civil servants: The Whitehall II study. *Lancet, 337*, 1387–1393.

Marmot, M. G., & Wilkinson, R. G. (2001). Psychosocial and material pathways in the relation between income and health: A response to Lynch et al. *British Medical Journal, 322*, 1233–1236.

McDonough, P., Duncan, G. J., Williams, D., & House, J. (1997). Income dynamics and adult mortality in the United States, 1972 through 1989. *American Journal of Public Health, 87*, 1476–1483.

Münster Halvari, A. E., & Halvari, H. (2006). Motivational predictors of change in oral health: An experimental test of self-determination theory. *Motivation and Emotion, 30*, 295–306.

Ng, J. Y. Y., Ntoumanis, N., Thøgersen-Ntoumani, C., Deci, E. L., Ryan, R. M., Duda, J. L., & Williams, G. C. (2012). Self-determination theory applied to health contexts: A meta-analysis. *Perspectives on Psychological Science, 7*, 325–340.

Niemiec, C. P., & Ryan, R. M. (2013). What makes for a life well lived?: Autonomy and its relation to full functioning and organismic wellness. In S. A. David, I. Boniwell, & A. C. Ayers (Eds.), *Oxford handbook of happiness* (pp. 214–226). Oxford: Oxford University Press.

Niemiec, C. P., Ryan, R. M., & Deci, E. L. (2010). Self-determination theory and the relation of autonomy to self-regulatory processes and personality development. In R. H. Hoyle (Ed.), *Handbook of personality and self-regulation* (pp. 169–191). Malden, MA: Blackwell Publishing.

Ross, N., Wolfson, M., Kaplan, G. A., Dunn, J. R., Lynch, J. W., & Sanmartin, C. (2006). Income inequality as a determinant of health. In J. Heymann, C. Hertzman, M. L. Barer, & R. G. Evans (Eds.), *Healthier societies: From analysis to action* (pp. 202–236). New York: Oxford University Press.

Ryan, R. M. (1993). Agency and organization: Intrinsic motivation, autonomy and the self in psychological development. In J. Jacobs (Ed.), *Nebraska symposium on motivation: Developmental perspectives on motivation* (Vol. 40, pp. 1–56). Lincoln, NE: University of Nebraska Press.

Ryan, R. M. (1995). Psychological needs and the facilitation of integrative processes. *Journal of Personality, 63*, 397–427.

Ryan, R. M., & Deci, E. L. (2002). Overview of self-determination theory: An organismic dialectical perspective. In E. L. Deci, & R. M. Ryan (Eds.), *Handbook of self-determination research* (pp. 3–33). Rochester, NY: University of Rochester Press.

Ryan, R. M., & Deci, E. L. (2006). Self-regulation and the problem of human autonomy: Does psychology need choice, self-determination, and will? *Journal of Personality, 74*, 1557–1585.

Ryan, R. M., Patrick, H., Deci, E. L., & Williams, G. C. (2008). Facilitating health behaviour change and its maintenance: Interventions based on self-determination theory. *The European Health Psychologist, 10*, 2–5.

Schappert, S. M. (1993). National Ambulatory Medical Care Survey: 1991 Summary. *Advance Data, 230*, 1–16.

Shanafelt, T. D., Sloan, J. A., & Habermann, T. M. (2003). The well-being of physicians. *American Journal of Medicine, 114*, 513–519.

Siegrist, J. (1996). Adverse health effects of high-effort/low-reward conditions. *Journal of Occupational Health Psychology, 1*, 27–41.

Siegrist, J., & Marmot, M. (2004). Health inequalities and the psychosocial environment--two scientific challenges. *Social Science and Medicine, 58*, 1463–1473.

Siegrist, J., & Marmot, M. (2006). *Social inequalities in health: New evidence and policy implications.* New York: Oxford University Press.

Siegrist, J., & Rödel, A. (2006). Work stress and health risk behavior. *Scandinavian Journal of Work, Environment and Health, 32*, 473–481.

Smith, J. P. (1999). Healthy bodies and thick wallets: The dual relation between health and economic status. *Journal of Economic Perspectives, 13*, 145–166.

Stansfeld, S., & Candy, B. (2006). Psychosocial work environment and mental health--a meta-analytic review. *Scandinavian Journal of Work, Environment and Health, 32*, 443–462.

Tarlov, A. R. (2000). Coburn's thesis: Plausible, but we need more evidence and better measures. *Social Science and Medicine, 51*, 993–995.

Teixeira, P. J., Silva, M. N., Coutinho, S. R., Palmeira, A. L., Mata, J., Vieira, P. N., Carraca, E. V., Santos, T. C., Sardinha, L. B. (2009). Mediators of weight loss and weight loss maintenance in middle-aged women. *Obesity, 18*, 725–735.

Vaananen, A., Pahkin, K., Huuhtanen, P., Kivimaki, M., Vahtera, J., Theorell, T., Kalimo, R. (2005). Are intrinsic motivational factors of work associated with functional incapacity similarly regardless of the country? *Journal of Epidemiology and Community Health, 59*, 858–863.

van Rossum, C. T., Shipley, M. J., van de Mheen, H., Grobbee, D. E., & Marmot, M. G. (2000). Employment grade differences in cause specific mortality: A 25 year follow up of civil servants from the first Whitehall study. *Journal of Epidemiology and Community Health, 54*, 178–184.

Wardle, J., Farrell, M., Hillsdon, M., Jarvis, M., Sutton, S., & Thorogood, M. (1999). Smoking, drinking, physical activity and screening uptake and health inequalities. In D. Gordon, M. Shaw, D. Dorling, & G. Davey Smith (Eds.), *Inequalities in health: The evidence presented to the Independent Inquiry into Inequalities in Health, chaired by Sir Donald Acheson* (pp. 213–239). Bristol, UK: Policy Press.

White, R. W. (1959). Motivation reconsidered: The concept of competence. *Psychological Review, 66*, 297–333.

Wilkinson, R. G. (2001). *Mind the gap: Hierarchies, health and human evolution.* New Haven, CT: Yale University Press.

Wilkinson, R. G. (2005). *The impact of inequality: How to make sick societies healthier.* New York: The New Press.

Williams, G. C. (2002). Improving patients' health through supporting the autonomy of patients and providers. In E. L.

Deci, & R. M. Ryan (Eds.), *Handbook of self-determination research* (pp. 233–254). Rochester, NY: University of Rochester Press.

Williams, G. C., & Deci, E. L. (1996). Internalization of biopsychosocial values by medical students: A test of self-determination theory. *Journal of Personality and Social Psychology, 70*, 767–779.

Williams, G. C., Halvari, H., Niemiec, C. P., Sorebo, O., Olafsen, A., & Westbye, C. (2012). *A self-determination theory perspective on the social-contextual and motivational origins of somatic symptom burden and its work-related correlates.* Unpublished manuscript, University of Rochester, Rochester, NY.

Williams, G. C., Levesque, C., Zeldman, A., Wright, S., & Deci, E. L. (2003). Health care practitioners' motivation for tobacco-dependence counseling. *Health Education Research, 18*, 538–553.

Williams, G. C., Lynch, M., & Glasgow, R. E. (2007). Computer-assisted intervention improves patient-centered diabetes care by increasing autonomy support. *Health Psychology, 26*, 728–734.

Williams, G. C., McGregor, H., Sharp, D., Kouides, R. W., Lévesque, C. S., Ryan, R. M., Deci, E. L. (2006). A self-determination multiple risk interention trial to improve smokers' health. *Journal of General Internal Medicine, 21*, 1288–1294.

Williams, G. C., McGregor, H. A., Sharp, D., Levesque, C., Kouides, R. W., Ryan, R. M., Deci, E. L. (2006). Testing a self-determination theory intervention for motivating tobacco cessation: Supporting autonomy and competence in a clinical trial. *Health Psychology, 25*, 91–101.

Williams, G. C., Minicucci, D. S., Kouides, R. W., Levesque, C. S., Chirkov, V. I., Ryan, R. M., Deci, E. L. (2002). Self-determination, smoking, diet and health. *Health Education Research, 17*, 512–521.

Williams, G. C., & Niemiec, C. P. (2012). Positive affect and self-affirmation are beneficial, but do they facilitate maintenance of health-behavior change? A self-determination theory perspective. *Archives of Internal Medicine, 172*, 327–328.

Williams, G. C., Patrick, H., Niemiec, C. P., Ryan, R. M., Deci, E. L., & Lavigne, H. M. (2011). The Smoker's Health Project: A self-determination theory intervention to facilitate maintenance of tobacco abstinence. *Contemporary Clinical Trials, 32*, 535–543.

Williams, G. C., Saizow, R., Ross, L., & Deci, E. L. (1997). Motivation underlying career choice for internal medicine and surgery. *Social Science and Medicine, 45*, 1705–1713.

Williams, G. C., Wiener, M. W., Markakis, K. M., Reeve, J., & Deci, E. L. (1994). Medical students' motivation for internal medicine. *Journal of General Internal Medicine, 9*, 327–333.

Yarnall, K. S., Pollak, K. I., Østbye, T., Krause, K. M., & Michener, J. L. (2003). Primary care: Is there enough time for prevention? *American Journal of Public Health, 93*, 635–641.

CHAPTER 23

What is a Functional Relationship to Money and Possessions?

Dan Stone

Abstract

Considerable research and investigation articulates the nature and consequences of a dysfunctional relationship to money and material possessions. But in technology-based, capitalistic societies, core human needs include a *functional* relationship to money and possessions. This chapter builds on previous work that extends self-determination theory and Kinder's model of money maturity to propose the attributes of a functional relationship to money and possessions. Evidence supports cross-cultural commonality in three core financial needs that extend self-determination theory's core psychological needs to the financial domain: (1) financial autonomy, (2) financial competence, and (3) financial relationships. In contrast, evidence suggests that financial values are culturally embedded. The proposed pyramid-shaped model includes a scaffolding relationship among the three, previously mentioned, tiers. It radically differs from the dominant self-centered view of financial functionality in its inclusion of transcendent financial motivation and embeds a paradox: a functional relationship to money is *nonmaterialist*, financial resources are merely a means to achieving nonfinancial, transcendent goals.

Key Words: financial motivation, self-determination theory, George Kinder, positive psychology, financial self-efficacy, financial materialism

---

Introduction

An important impetus for studying accounting as an undergraduate, and eventually becoming a CPA and accounting professor, was an early epiphany that neither I, nor anyone whom I knew well, had a functional relationship to money and material possessions. A later, more jolting realization was that, although most accounting and finance professionals and academics have (perhaps more than) sufficient financial resources, they also lacked a functional relationship to money. Sadly, my undergraduate and masters' degrees in accountancy provided fewer insights into creating a functional relationship to money than I sought. Now, 40 years into this quest, and guided by the insights of self-determination theory (SDT) and George Kinder's (1999) model of money maturity (KMMM), I offer a nascent understanding of these

relations. But much investigation and articulation remains if the brief sketch that I offer is to become the rich, true portrait of a functional human relation to money that I first sought more than 40 years ago.

This chapter proceeds as follows. This introduction is followed by a brief review of literature investigating human relations to money and possessions. Following this, consideration is given to the synthesizing model, and the evidence (or lack thereof) supporting its elements and aspects. Practical implications and research possibilities are followed by a summation of the meaning, importance, and deficiencies of the model.[1]

Money, Possessions, and Human Functioning

Although a relatively recent focus of scholarship, psychology-based investigation of human relations to money and material possessions has proceeded consistent with the more general development of the psychological literature. Specifically, following Freud's lead that "money is dirty" (Herbert, 2002), psychological research investigating money and material possessions is dominated by research investigating the nature and consequences of a *dysfunctional* relationship to money and material possessions (e.g., Burroughs & Rindfleisch, 2002; Kasser, 2002; Kasser & Kanner, 2004; Tang, 2007). Particularly strange is the near complete neglect of issues of personal finance and human relations to money in the finance and accounting literature. Although these scholarly domains seem to be likely focal points for such research, their neglect likely results from these literatures' near-complete focus on financing and reporting issues in corporations rather than individuals. Although corporations may be, according to the common interpretation of a recent decree of the Supreme Court of the United States (Citizens United v. Federal Election Commission 2009) "people too," apparently, as George Orwell might have put it in *Animal Farm* (1945), to accounting and finance scholars, some people (i.e., corporations) are more equal than other people (i.e., human beings). More accurately, "corporate people" are worthy objects of study, research, and acclaim, whereas "individual people" are not. One suspects in this regard that the power of corporate financial influence is not restricted to politicians and political candidates but may also extend to accounting, finance, and economic scholars whose professional lives are given to, in some cases, the sympathetic study of corporations who fund their grants (and research). Is it possible that the "orphan" status of the research areas of personal finance and human relations to money results, ironically, from the uninvestigated and unexamined personal financial motivations of researchers?

The Prefinancial Competence Literature: Financial Incentives and Motivation

A vast body of scholarly endeavor, extending across over 60 years and many disciplines, attempts to prove the validity of the central assumption of economics that Adam Smith eloquently articulated in *The Wealth of Nations*: that money motivates humans through a simple, stimulus-response mechanism. The necessity of obtaining evidence supporting this relation to ease the work of economists—be they Marxist or libertarian, Keynesian or Friedmanites—is evident. If financial motivation is other than a simple drive mechanism, if it is

complex, contingent, and multidimensional, then economists must expend scarce resources (i.e., their professional careers) understanding and articulating these complex relations. For a couple of hundred years, it was far easier to assume that Adam Smith got it right in his intuitive, simplistic sketch and to get on with the business of plotting simple demand and supply curves and crafting models that embedded the "more-money-is-always-better" assumption and ethic. Hence, in mainstream neoclassical microeconomics the assumption that human financial motivation is, for example, more simplistic than the average tribe of bonobos' motivations for food (Hare & Kwetuenda, 2010) and would exclude as inexplicable, play, which research indicates is critical to, and considered fun among, vertebrates (Chick, 1998; Lewis 1982) including, but not limited to, *homo sapiens*—or at least among those lucky *homo sapiens* who have eschewed graduate degrees in economics, finance, and accounting.

Assuming a simpler-than-other-mammal financial drive response motivation also greatly simplifies the work of scholars investigating and designing management and accounting control systems, for example, in the large literature that applies agency theory to organizational issues (e.g., Kunz & Pfaff, 2002). Simplistic human financial motivation means such systems may ignore, for example, individual and cultural differences in motivation. Such simplistic assumptions partly explain the otherwise inexplicable madness of such systems, where the insanity is best documented in comics (e.g., Dilbert) and in television comedies (e.g., on "The Office") rather than in the far less entertaining scholarly literature about such systems.

The alternative (i.e., that human financial motivation is complex and contingent) is now well-established in research and well-known among practicing managers (cf. Gagné & Deci, 2005; Moller, Ryan, & Deci, 2006; Stone, Deci, & Ryan, 2009), but is less commonly in evidence in the work of economic, accounting, and finance scholars. For example, in top accounting journals it still seems to be a "politically incorrect" impossibility to say a single discouraging word about the power and majesty of financial incentives. Hence, the publication of papers in top accounting journals (e.g., Sprinkle, 2000) that say nothing other than the old time religion—perhaps stated first in Genesis, "By the sweat of your brow will you have food to eat. . ." (Genesis 3:19—New Living translation; Group Publishing & Tyndale House Publishers 2008;

i.e., given an unpleasant task, people work harder with an external motivator).

That entire careers and literatures now rest on a largely fallacious portrait of a simplistic and mechanical human financial motivation is a certainty. The possibilities for replacing the now-known-to-be-nonsensical simple drive motivation for financial incentives with a more accurate description likely necessitates the accumulation of sufficient obituaries, or retirements, among the faith-based believers (e.g., see Kuhn, 1970) of this doctrine to permit acceptance of a more accurate description of motivation. The emerging literature of behavioral finance and behavioral accounting offers possibilities for a more complex portrait of financial motivations (Stone, Bryant, & Wier 2010). But sadly these have, to date, remained close to the literatures that preceded them in largely assuming "economically rational" (Rubenstein 2001), meaning unrealistically simplistic and mechanical, stimulus-response human financial motivations.

Toward a Model of Functional Financial Relations

To paraphrase William of Ockham (Duffy, 1994; Duncan, 1957) and Albert Einstein (Quote Investigator, 2011), theories should be as simple as possible but not too simple—and the line was clearly crossed from simplicity to simplistic with economists' and others need to view human financial motivation as linear and simplistic. Efforts to complicate the portrait of human motivation include, among many other important and worthy contributions, multidimensional measures of human perceptions of money (e.g., Mitchell & Mickel, 1999), investigations of the motivators for saving (Furnham, 1985) and explorations of the meaning and nature of frugality and thrift (e.g., Kasser, 2005; Lastovicka, Bettencourt, Hughner, & Kuntze, 1999). But comprehensive, holistic models of functional relations to money are less in evidence. Herein, I adapt and extend two holistic approaches to articulate a functional human relationship to money: SDT and KMMM.

The Precompetent, Financial Childhood: Financial Innocence, Pain, and Suffering

No one emerges from the womb knowing about credit cards, ATMs, money transfers, investments, or retirement accounts. Yet, unless one disavows a material life (as in a few roles within the Christian [St. Scholastica Monastery, 2012] or Buddhist monastery [Yang, 1950]), knowing about such technologies is essential to financial well-being in modern culture. In addition, there is evidence that cultural norms for primary goals of financial materialism decrease happiness (Kasser & Ryan, 1993). Hence, the starting point for many individuals relationship to money could be called financial childhood and "financial suffering." Given that most previous research related to human relationships to money focuses, in some form, on this "cycle of suffering," it is worth noting that the starting point for financial wisdom is often financial suffering. Figure 23.1 illustrates Kinder's (1999) application of the Buddhist Wheel of Life to financial relations (see also Kasser, 2009), in showing two stages to financial suffering: financial innocence and financial pain. Hence, Figure 23.1 illustrates "financial childhood," which for many adults is the endpoint of development, meaning that many adults remain Peter Pan-like in perpetual childhood in their financial lives. Furthermore, some argue that the consumerist culture is a powerful impediment to individuals' efforts to advance beyond financial childhood (e.g., see Kasser 2002; Kasser & Kanner 2004).

According to Kinder, financial innocence can include an absence of knowledge about one's own wants (versus needs) (e.g., see Tatzel, 2003), one's financial resources, and the financial technologies articulated in the previous paragraph. The financially innocent may also be inappropriately trusting, as is evident, for example, in victims' descriptions of their relationship to Bernie Madoff and his Ponzi scheme (Henriques, 2011). Madoff victims' financial innocence seemed to center around an inability to grasp a fundamental truth of investing: abnormally high

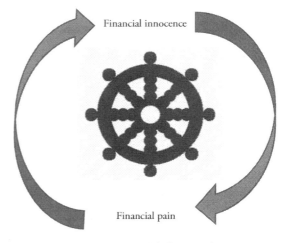

Fig. 23.1. A precompetence model of money relations. Adapted from Kinder (1999).

investment returns cannot be sustained indefinitely, despite Madoff's promises (i.e., lies) to the contrary (Henriques, 2011).

For those fortunate individuals who advance beyond the perpetual suffering of "financial childhood," financial adulthood (stage 2) and financial awakening (stage 3) follow (Table 23.1). Viewed from the perspective of the healthy ego, financial pain is a "call to awaken" to the greater financial insight and knowledge (Kinder, 1999) that is found in the adult (second) stage of financial maturity. By extending SDT to the financial domain, it is possible to trace the path of development of this financial awakening using SDT constructs. SDT is a macrotheory of human motivation that seeks to explain the interrelations of human needs with environmental circumstances (Deci, Eghrari, Patrick, & Leone, 1994; Ryan & Deci, 2000). SDT includes the capacity to inform efforts to understand when behaviors and actions may, versus may not, contribute to optimal human functioning. For example,

Table 23.1 Kinder's seven-stage model of money maturity.

Childhood

1. Innocence: The childhood state we are born in, devoid of any concept of money

2. Pain: The discovery that we have more money than some and less than others, and that work is necessary to make a living

Adulthood

1. Knowledge: The intellectual task of learning financial techniques, such as saving, budgeting, and investing

2. Understanding: The emotional work done in coming to terms with feelings around money, such as greed, envy, and resentment (which are rooted in Pain)

3. Vigor: The energy (physical, emotional, and spiritual) that must be expended to reach financial goals

Awakening (Transcendence)

1. Vision: The direction of Vigor outward toward the health and welfare of communities, with or without profit motive

2. Aloha: The compassionate goodwill that allows one to use money to perform acts of kindness without expecting a "return" (i.e., reciprocity)

materialistic values include the belief that pursuing financial success, obtaining desirable possessions, projecting a desirable image, and achieving high status are primary human goals (Kasser & Kanner, 2004). The insights of SDT were critical to articulating the failure of financially materialist values and behaviors to contribute to human well-being (Kasser, 2002). Specifically, materialist values fail to contribute to the three core human psychological needs articulated by SDT: (1) autonomy, that is volitional agency in relation to one's circumstances; (2) relatedness, that is functional and supportive relationships with others; and (3) competence, that is an accurate perception that one is or can build confidence in relation to critical areas of one's needs and environment (Kasser, 2002).

But do functional financial values exist, and if so, what are they? Stone et al. (2010) extend SDT by positing four financial need belief constructs, and applying them in a model predicting that core financial need beliefs influence financial values which, in turn, influence subjective well-being (SWB; i.e., "hedonic" utility or happiness; Figure 23.2). The four financial need belief constructs are (1) financial self-efficacy, the belief that one is capable of successfully managing financial events; (2) financial autonomy, the belief that one's financial decisions are volitional choices; (3) financial community-trust, the belief that significant others can be trusted and relied on to help with one's financial issues and problems; and (4) financial community-support, the belief that financial resources can contribute to supporting communities and interpersonal relationships (Table 23.2 *Panel A*).

In addition, two measured forms of financial values, i.e., altruistic and materialistic (Table 23.2 *Panel B*), differentially impacted SWB. Altruistic financial values are a desire to use financial resources to enhance one's community or interpersonal relationships. Materialistic financial values were measured using Richins and Dawson (1992) possession-defined success metric, which is a desire for financial wealth, economic luxury, and economically based expansion of individual power, for example through enhanced mating opportunities or improved social position or rank.[2]

The results largely support the validity of constructs, and the relations among constructs, in the financial domain that extend the core human needs posited by SDT. Specifically (1) the core financial need beliefs form cohesive constructs; (2) financial values partially mediate the effects of financial need beliefs on SWB; and, (3) financial altruism

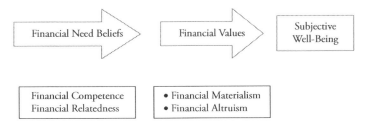

Fig. 23.2. Extension of SDT to financial beliefs and values. Adapted from Stone, Bryant, & Wier (2010).

Table 23.2 Constructs and instruments from Stone et al. (2010).

Panel A: Financial Need Beliefs

Financial Self-Efficacy

Definition: The belief that one is capable of successfully managing the financial events in one's life.

1. I am good at managing my money.
2. I am satisfied with my ability to manage my money.
3. Compared to other people, I think I do pretty well at making financial decisions.
4. I am pretty skilled at making financial decisions.
5. I budget my money very well.
6. I use my money very carefully.

Financial Autonomy (reverse scored)

Definition: The belief that one's financial decisions are volitional choices that reflect one's interests and beliefs.

1. My financial life is out of control.
2. I don't have a choice about making money decisions.
3. I make financial decisions because I have to, not because I want to.
4. In making financial decisions, I feel pushed, forced, and pressured.

Financial Community-Trust

Definition: The belief that significant others can be trusted, and relied upon, to help with one's financial issues and problems.

1. I can rely on other people to help me when I am in financial need.
2. I can depend on other people for help with money problems.
3. I trust that the people I care most about will keep their financial commitments to me.

Financial Community-Support

Definition: The belief that financial resources can contribute to supporting communities and interpersonal relationships.

Table 23.2 Continued

1. I am willing to help the people I care most about financially if they need it.
2. I feel that I can talk about money problems with my close friends and loved ones.
3. Money is valuable because it can help you support the people that you love.
4. The people I care most about are willing to help me financially if I need it.

Panel B: Financial Values

Financial Materialism: Possession-Defined Success
(source: Richins & Dawson 1992)

Definition: A desire for financial wealth, economic luxury and economically-based expansion of individual power, for example, through enhanced mating opportunities, or greater social position or rank.

1. I admire people who own expensive homes, cars, and clothes.
2. Some of the important achievements in life include acquiring material possessions.
3. The things I own say a lot about how well I'm doing in life.
4. I like to own things that impress people.

Financial Altruism

Definition: A desire to use financial resources to enhance one's community or interpersonal relationships.

1. Donating money to charity is a waste of money. (reversed)
2. Either now or in the future, I intend to donate money to causes that I care about.
3. Money can be used for acts of kindness.
4. Money is useful because it can help make the world a better place.
5. Money, wisely used, can help build communities.

(continued)

positively, whereas financial materialism negatively, predicted SWB. Hence, the results suggest that SDT's core needs extend to the financial domain, and provide evidence that the fulfillment of financial needs can contribute to SWB. However, the sample of the study is US college students.

Recent investigation (Guo et al., 2013) using data from six countries suggests high levels of cross-cultural consistency in the four financial *need* belief constructs from Stone et al. (2010). Specifically, confirmatory factor analysis suggests cross-cultural measurement equivalence (i.e., stability) in model of financial *need* beliefs in student samples drawn from China, Taiwan, and the United States, and in nonstudent samples drawn from Brazil, China, Russia, Tunisia, and the United States. In contrast, less support obtains for cross-cultural convergence in the financial *value* constructs investigated in Stone et al. (2010). These results suggest stronger cross-culture invariance (i.e., stability) in the financial need belief model than in the financial value model. Hence, the results provide some support for extending SDT's arguments of the universality of three core human needs (autonomy, competence, and relatedness) to the domain of financial needs. But the results also suggest greater cross-cultural variability in the constructs of financial altruism and financial materialism, which are not, according to SDT, core psychological human needs. Therefore, the results both support SDT, and, because differing results obtain across constructs, suggest that the results are not easily attributed to monomethod or monomeasurement biases.

Financial Adulthood: Financial Knowledge and Self-Efficacy

Pondering the nature of financial functionality for the previous 40 years leads me to the incautious enterprise of proposing a model of financial functionality. This model is incomplete. It benefits considerably from, and attempts to integrate, the insights of SDT and the KMMM. Some aspects of the model are supported by large sample data (e.g., the financial need belief constructs); other aspects are speculative and based on self and other observation (i.e., a regrettably small sample) and intuition.

Figure 23.3 presents the proposed model of functional financial achievement; it contains a scaffolding relationship among elements in a pyramid shape, meaning that one begins with the foundational element of the model, followed by the second tier of the model, followed by, at least for some advanced individuals, the pyramidal apex or peak. Following from the KMMM, its foundational element is financial knowledge, which

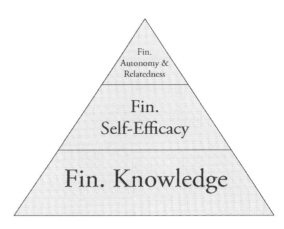

Fig. 23.3. A scaffolding model of functional financial achievement.

is the initial path out of the cycle of suffering of financial innocence and financial pain. Financial knowledge as a core element of functional financial ability derives from the KMMM, whereas knowledge is found only implicitly in SDT (i.e., embedded in the construct of "competence"). The required foundational financial knowledge includes declarative and procedural components. One must, for example, know both what a savings account is (i.e., descriptive knowledge) and how to use one (i.e., procedural knowledge) to advance to a functional level of financial knowledge. Several organizations, including Jump$tart (Mandell & Jump$tart, 2002), and several US states have articulated core financial knowledge that is needed for functionality in a modern capitalist country.

To illustrate such standards, Table 23.3 presents the six core financial literacy standards adopted by the State of Indiana (Indiana Department of Education, 2011). These standards guide learning objectives at the middle and high school levels for achieving financial literacy. Indiana's and most other such standards include knowledge related to financial planning; saving and investment strategies; risk management strategies, including understanding multiple types of insurance; concepts related to income, expenses, and taxation; and career and continuing education decisions and resources. Many nonaccountants expect that accounting education includes training and education in these topics; regrettably, however, most accounting curriculums cover only the topic of taxation. Hence, to the extent that accountants learn the principles of financial literacy they do so through self-education or nonaccounting elective courses.

Financial self-efficacy, the second level of the pyramidal structure, follows and builds on foundational financial knowledge. Financial self-efficacy roughly

Table 23.3 Indiana Department of Education: Core standards—personal financial responsibility.

Domain	Standard
1. Financial responsibility and decision making	Students demonstrate management of individual and family finances by applying reliable information and systematic decision making
2. Relating income and careers	Students analyze how education, income, career, and life choices relate to achieving financial goals
3. Planning and managing money	Students manage money effectively by developing financial goals and budgets
4. Managing credit and debt	Students manage credit and debt to remain both creditworthy and financially secure
5. Risk management and insurance	Students analyze the features of insurance, its role in balancing risk and benefit in financial planning
6. Saving and investing	Students analyze saving and investing to build long-term financial security and wealth

Adapted from Indiana Department of Education (2011). Financial literacy education—Content standards. Retrieved from http://www.doe.in.gov/achievement/career-education/financial-literacy-education.

equates to the SDT construct of *competence*. Both are self-perception, domain-specific constructs of individual capability. For example, within SDT, validated measures of competence measure individuals' competence in managing their diabetes (Williams et al., 2009), and expected competence in learning the content of a specific domain (e.g., chemistry; Black, & Deci, 2000). The tier of financial self-efficacy can be related to the KMMM through Kinder's (1999) constructs of "understanding" (i.e., patience and peace) and "vigor" (i.e., directed energy and enthusiasm), which together with "knowledge" constitute Kinder's adult (second) level of financial maturity. Financial self-efficacy promotes and is integral to developing understanding in that both are concerned with increasing self-awareness of one's feelings, capability, and limitations around money and material possessions. Financial self-efficacy promotes and is integral to the KMMM's construct of vigor because without financial self-efficacy one lacks the resilience and perseverance to manage material resources in the face of " . . . the slings and arrows of outrageous (financial) fortune" (Hamlet, Act III). Together, financial knowledge and financial self-efficacy provide the knowledge, understanding, and vigor that enable movement to a higher, transcendent (i.e., beyond self-interest) relationship to money and material resources.

Financial Transcendence: Financial Autonomy and Relatedness

The apex of the pyramidal model of functional functionality is financial autonomy and relatedness.

Financial autonomy is the perception that one makes volitional choices with respect to one's financial and material resources. Financial autonomy builds on financial knowledge and self-efficacy, because one surely cannot accurately perceive self-volition without both financial self-efficacy and financial knowledge. In addition, although the previous elements of the model (i.e., financial knowledge, self-efficacy, and autonomy) are primary self-focused, financial relatedness extends one's capabilities and competences beyond the individual to the community and world. Specifically, the construct of financial community-trust is the belief that significant others can be trusted, and relied on, to help with one's financial issues and problems. Of course, the development of financial community-trust requires creating and nurturing trusting financial relationships within which one can realistically trust others (versus, for example, the financial deceptions created by Bernie Madoff). In addition, the construct of financial community-support is concerned with the belief that financial resources are critical to building and supporting communities and interpersonal relationships.

Such constructs can be placed within the KMMM in the third or transcendent level of financial maturity, called "awakening," which is "vision" joined with "aloha." In the KMMM, individuals in the third stage of money maturity evidence two attributes: "vision" (i.e., the directing of financial vigor toward the creation and nurturing of community) and "aloha" (i.e., compassionate goodwill within which financial resources are means to acts of kindness without concern with payback or reciprocity).[3] In contrast, SDT makes no distinction of levels or stages in relation to the three core human psychological needs (competence, autonomy, and relatedness). Hence, the proposed model uses adapted SDT constructs within the framework of the hierarchical KMMM.

Implications and Limitations of the Model
One World versus Two World Financial Motivation

The model of financial functionality presented herein is radically at odds with the common model of financial functionality derived from neoclassical economics. The principle point of division between the model proposed herein and that found in neoclassical economics is whether one believes in a *One World*, or *Two World*, model of financial functionality. The One World (i.e., economic) model of financial functionality posits that the exclusive motivation of the self is a stimulus-drive relation to money and material resources. Historically, the common operationalization of this model in neoclassical microeconomics posited a (cardinal) utility function that often, for simplicity, focused on money; hence, money, to economists, became synonymous with happiness (e.g., see Bruni, 2006). This One World model (i.e., money = happiness), which dominates economic discourse and education, may explain why economics majors have been found to be less cooperative (i.e., more self-interested) than are other collegiate majors (Frank, Gilovich, & Regan, 1993; Yezer, Goldfarb, & Poppen, 1996; see also Grouzet [Chapter 24] in this volume). Although speculative, it is possible that the One World (i.e., self-centered) model of financial functionality may contribute to rising levels of narcissism among college students (cf. Joubert, 1992; Wink, 1991). The One World model of financial functionality also dominates academic discourse in decision sciences and several business disciplines (e.g., accounting and finance).

The Two World model of financial functionality includes a two-parameter utility function: self-interested and other-interested. Hence, the dividing line between neoclassical economics, versus the model proposed herein, is that the model shown in Figure 23.3 includes a transcendent, meaning beyond-the-self, highest level of financial functioning. Therefore, the Two World model allows for the possibility that the "cost" of money, in terms of individual autonomy and relatedness,

may exceed its value. But whereas social science, and most specifically economics, have been reluctant to allow more complex models of human relations to financial resources, neuroeconomic research is beginning to suggest that dual-process models of brain functioning hold great promise in explaining human attitudes and behaviors in relation to money and financial resources (Loewenstein, Rick, & Cohen, 2008; Stone, 2011; see also Murayama, Matsumoto, Izuma, & Matsumoto, 2010). The remaining resistance to Two World models of financial functionality would seem to derive from their greater complexity, relative to the neoclassical model of human financial motivation, and their apparent "fuzziness" or "softness" (e.g., see Rubenstein's [2001] argument that so-called "irrational" investor behavior should be considered only as a "last resort when all else has failed"). However, the great irony of the state of research on human motivation is that developing realistic models of human financial motivation functioning requires that social scientists and economists reconcile themselves to what was previously considered "unscientific" in the study of human motivation (i.e., transcendent, nonmaterial motivations); one hopes that more than 200 years of unrealistically simplistic (economic) portraits of human financial motivation are enough.

Unresolved Issues and Research Opportunities

The validity of the proposed model—conceptual and empirical—is unresolved and largely untested. There is some evidence that hierarchical models of motivation, such as that proposed by Maslow, result in greater intuitive appeal than empirical support (Wahba & Bridwell, 1976). However, one important distinction between Maslow's and the model suggested herein is that whereas Maslow's is a model of human needs, the model proposed herein is of human capabilities. In fact, scaffolding models of capabilities are now widely accepted in psychology and education (e.g., Erikson's [1977] developmental models).

In addition, the model advanced herein has parallels to "The Evolving Self" model of Robert Kegan (1982, 1994), which adapts Piagetian principles to propose six stages of adult social and interpersonal development. Interestingly, although Kegan's theory is an important influence on the practice of coaching executives, the few tests of its descriptive veracity are mixed (McCauley, Drath, Palus, O'Connor, & Baker, 2006), suggesting that theories of motivation need not necessarily be true, or at least empirically verifiable, to be useful. It would be unsurprising if similar results obtained for the stage theory advanced herein. At the same time, it seems reasonable and feasible to consider empirical tests of aspects of the model proposed herein, such as assessing whether levels of social and emotional development (perhaps measured as emotional intelligence [Goleman, 1995]) predict financial behaviors, assessed according to their functionality (e.g., opening a savings account) versus dysfunctionality (e.g., drinking away one's paycheck at a local bar after work).

At the same time, a number of vexing issues remain to investigate, as a part of more completely articulating the nature of financially functional relations to money. For example, data that I and my coauthors (unpublished) and others (Helliwell & Putnam, 2004) have collected suggest that those who are trusting, including trusting regarding finances, are, on average, happier. But this is, of course, only true if those who are more financially trusting have not recently had that trust abused, for example, as is evident in Bernie Madoff's financial frauds. Hence, financial trust brings greater happiness only when it is knowledgeable and informed, rather than innocent and naive, financial trust. Therefore, the valence of financial trust itself seems to depend on whether it is well-placed or results from financial naiveté, as is implied in Figures 23.1 and 23.3.

The construct of financial mindfulness, proposed and discussed in Stone (2011) and Brown & Ryan (2003), holds promise as a means for advancing from financial childhood through financial awakening (see also Kinder, 1999). Financial mindfulness is openness and attention to, and awareness of, present financial events and experiences. Financial mindfulness can be argued to incorporate several aspects of Kinder's financial virtues, including vigor, understanding, vision, and aloha. Despite its extensive investigation in medicine, education, and psychotherapy, very few studies consider or investigate money mindfulness, although a recent book (Gonzalez, 2010) proposes mindfulness as an important mindset for investors riding out market turbulence (i.e., normal market behavior). One important contribution of such investigation may be the discovery of a viable path for advancing through some stages of financial maturity (e.g., see Kasser, 2009; Stone, 2011). The achievement of financial mindfulness, which would likely lead to moving beyond the cycle of financial pain illustrated in Figure 23.1, likely depends on achieving a state of broader, nonjudgmental awareness, from which it is possible to integrate one's financial with other spheres of one's life. Short "financial meditations," such as those suggested in Kinder's book (1999), may be one means of achieving such integration.

Economists will argue that my characterization of the One World view is overly simplistic—a caricature—of the depth and breadth of the academic construct of a utility function. This complaint is valid with respect to the academic literature on utility, which is astounding in its depth and complexity. However, this complaint fails with respect to the policies and politics advocated by neoclassical economists. When neoclassical economists leave the ivory tower and (perhaps foolishly) march into the realm of political and social policy, they seem to go armed with them the caricatured view of the academic utility function that I articulate in the One World model. For example, the neoconservative policies advocated by neoclassical economists (e.g., Milton Friedman's work) incorporate the money-asking One World view, as do their policies and prescriptions for education reform (i.e., figure out how to pay teachers "the right way").

One suggestion that derives from considering the scientific literature related to the model is the futility of more experiments investigating whether financial incentives motivate human behavior. Over 30 years of investigations with human participants, and the insights of SDT, offer a clear answer to this question: yes, but financial motivations are complicated by, and often conjoined with, motivations for autonomy, competence, and relatedness. In fact, asking whether humans desire financial incentives—in isolated experiments that lack context—is an overly simplistic research question that is motivated by the flawed portrait of human motivation that emerged from neoclassical economics and its stepchild, behaviorist psychology. Relevant questions in relation to the emerging, more complex portrait of financial motivation include the following:

1. In specific contexts and settings, do extrinsic, introjected, integrated, and intrinsic financial motivations follow the simplex relations found with respect to nonfinancial motivation in SDT research? Does this relation hold across cultures (e.g., individualist versus collectivist) and levels of wealth (i.e., among richer and poorer)?

2. How do people trade off specific financial versus nonfinancial motivations in specific contexts? For example, when and how are motivations for

financial gain traded off against motivations for autonomy, competence, and relatedness?

3. What is the scope and breadth of functional financial motivations? Are some cultures more adept at achieving functional financial motivations than others? Are functional financial motivations tied to, and dependent on, socioeconomic variables? Are wealthy people really greedier (Miller, 2012)?

4. Is the highest level of financial functioning too complex to be operationalized? Is the sample size of individuals functioning at the highest level of financial ability too small to enable large sample research?

Summary and Conclusion

Tolstoy begins his novel *Anna Karenina* with the observation that, "happy families are all alike but unhappy families are each unique in their unhappiness" (Tolstoy, 1889, p. 1). The portrait of financial functionality offered herein accords with Tolstoy's observations to this extent: I sketch the outline, and some key components, of a functional relationship to money that are likely near-universals in functional financial relationships within technology-based capitalist countries. This model integrates evidence suggesting that financial needs are near invariants across cultures. But the specifics, and mechanics, of how functional humans save, spend, borrow, and give are sure to exhibit considerable differences between individuals and cultures. In addition, financial values, including the nature and meaning of altruism and materialism, are closely tied to cultural values, with, for example, the nature and meaning of these constructs varying considerably between East (e.g., China) and West (e.g., United States). Finally, there is likely to be greater variability in dysfunctional than in functional financial behaviors, because, for example, financial frauds often rely on deception and deliberate misdirection.

The model proposed herein is radically at odds with the implicit model of financial functionality that dominates in academic business and economics in its rejection of a One World (i.e., self-centered) perspective. In fact, some of the financial materialism of Western, and increasingly Eastern, civilization may derive from the propagation of economists', and their many acolytes, One (self-centered) World view. Ironically, given what we now know about these relations, the incorporation of nonmaterialist, transcendent elements in economic models of utility functions and financial relations, while strongly

resisted among economic, finance, and accounting scholars, would seem to be essential if these disciplines are to regain their status as scientific, rather than increasingly faith-based, disciplines. In addition, the final paradox of the model is that, a functional relationship to money is nonmaterialist and transcendent.

Notes

1. The author thanks the Gatton College of Business and the Von Allmen School of Accountancy for financial support of this research, and Marylène Gagné, Zhe Ni Wang, and Mike Larsen for insightful comments on earlier drafts of this chapter.

2. Although some would speculate that altruism and materialism are opposing or contrasting financial values, data presented in Stone et al. (2010) indicate a weak, positive correlation among these constructs ($r = .09$; $p < .05$).

3. The author thanks Marylène Gagné for noting the similarity of Kinder's construct of "aloha" to Erikson's concept of "generativity" (Mcadams & Destaubin, 1992).

References

Black, A. E., & Deci, E. L. (2000). The effects of instructors' autonomy support and students' autonomous motivation on learning organic chemistry: A self-determination theory perspective. *Science Education, 84,* 740–756.

Brown, K. W., & Ryan, R. M. (2003). The benefits of being present: Mindfulness and its role in psychological well-being. *Journal of Personality & Social Psychology, 84,* 822–848. doi:10.1037/0022-3514.84.4.822

Bruni, L. (2006). *Civil happiness: Economics and human flourishing in historical perspective.* London: Routledge.

Burroughs, J. E., & Rindfleisch, A. (2002). Materialism and well-being: A conflicting values perspective. *Journal of Consumer Research, 29,* 348–370. doi:10.1086/344429

Chick, G. (1998). *What is play for? Sexual selection and the evolution of play.* Keynote address at the Association for the Study of Play, St. Petersburg, FL. Retrieved from http://www.personal.psu.edu/gec7/PlayFor.pdf.

Citizens United v. Federal Election Commission (2009) (Docket No. 08-205). Cornell University School of Law. Retrieved from http://topics.law.cornell.edu/supct/cert/08-205.

Deci, E. L., Egharri, H., Patrick, B. C., & Leone, D. R. (1994). Facilitating internalization—the self-determination theory perspective. *Journal of Personality, 62*(1), 119–142. doi:10.1111/j.1467-6494.1994.tb00797.x

Duffy, M. (1994). *Occam's razor.* London: Flamingo.

Duncan, D. (1957). *Occam's razor.* New York: Ballantine Books.

Erikson, E. H. (1977). *Toys and reasons: Stages in the ritualization of experience.* New York: Norton.

Frank, R. H., Gilovich, T., & Regan, D. T. (1993). Does studying economics inhibit cooperation? *Journal of Economic Perspectives, 7*(2), 159–171.

Furnham, A. (1985). Why do people save? Attitudes to, and habits of saving money in Britain. *Journal of Applied Social Psychology, 15*(5), 354–373. doi:10.1111/j.1559-1816.1985.tb00912.x

Gagné, M., & Deci, E. L. (2005). Self-determination theory and work motivation. *Journal of Organizational Behavior, 26*(4), 331–362. doi:10.1002/Job.322.

Goleman, D. (1995). *Emotional intelligence*. New York: Bantam Books.

Gonzalez, M. (2010). *The mindful investor: How a calm mind can bring you inner peace and financial security*. Mississauga, Ontario: John Wiley & Sons.

Group Publishing, & Tyndale House Publishers. (2008). *Live: Holy Bible: New living translation* (2nd ed.). Loveland, CO: Group Pub.; Tyndale House Publishers.

Guo, L., Stone, D., Bryant, S., Wier, B., Nikitkov, A., Ren, C.,...Zhang, L. (2012). Are consumers' financial needs and values common across cultures? Evidence from Six Countries, *International Journal of Consumer Studies*, *37*, 675–688, doi:10.1111/ijcs.12047.

Hare, B., Kwetuenda, S. (2010). Bonobos voluntarily share their own food with others. *Current Biology*, *20* (5), R230–R231. doi:10.1016/j.cub.2009.12.038.

Helliwell, J. F., & Putnam, R. D. (2004). The social context of well–being. *Philosophical Transactions of the Royal Society of London. Series B: Biological Sciences*, *359*(1449), 1435–1446. doi:10.1098/rstb.2004.1522

Henriques, D. B. (2011). *The wizard of lies: Bernie Madoff and the death of trust* (1st ed.). New York: Times Books/Henry Holt.

Herbert, C. (2002). Filthy lucre: Victorian ideas of money. *Victorian Studies*, *44*(2), 185–213.

Indiana Department of Education. (2011). Financial literacy education—content standards, Retrieved from http://www.doe.in.gov/achievement/career-education/financial-literacy-education.

Joubert, C. E. (1992). Antecedents of narcissism and psychological reactance as indicated by college students' retrospective reports of their parents' behaviors. *Psychological Reports*, *70*, 1111–1115. doi:10.2466/pr0.1992.70.3c.1111

Kasser, T. (2002). *The high price of materialism*. Cambridge, MA: MIT Press.

Kasser, T. (2005). Frugality, generosity, and materialism in children and adolescents. In K. A. Moore, & L. H. Lippman (Eds.), *What do children need to flourish? conceptualizing and measuring indicators of positive development* (pp. 357–373). New York: Springer Science.

Kasser, T. (2009). Can Buddhism and consumerism harmonize? A review of the psychological evidence. *Journal of Religion and Culture*, *2*, 167–193.

Kasser, T., & Kanner, A. D. (2004). *Psychology and consumer culture: The struggle for a good life in a materialistic world*. Washington, DC: American Psychological Association.

Kasser, T., & Ryan, R. M. (1993). A dark side of the American dream: Correlates of financial success as a central life aspiration. *Journal of Personality and Social Psychology*, *65*, 410–422. doi:10.1037/0022-3514.65.2.410.

Kegan, R. (1982). *The evolving self: Problem and process in human development*. Cambridge, MA: Harvard University Press.

Kegan, R. (1994). *In over our heads: The mental demands of modern life*. Cambridge, MA: Harvard University Press.

Kinder, G. (1999). *The seven stages of money maturity: Understanding the spirit and value of money in your life*. New York: Delacorte Press.

Kuhn, T. S. (1970). *The structure of scientific revolution* (2nd ed.). Chicago: University of Chicago Press.

Kunz, A. H., & Pfaff, D. (2002). Agency theory, performance evaluation, and the hypothetical construct of intrinsic motivation. *Accounting, Organizations and Society*, *27*, 275–295. doi:10.1016/S0361-3682(01)00031-9

Lastovicka, J. L., Bettencourt, L. A., Hughner, R. S., & Kuntze, R. J. (1999). Lifestyle of the tight and frugal: Theory and measurement. *Journal of Consumer Research*, *26*, 85–98. doi:10.1086/209552

Lewis, M. (1982). Play as whimsy. *Behavioral and Brain Sciences*, *5*, 166–166. doi:10.1017/S0140525X00011067.

Loewenstein, G., Rick, S., & Cohen, J. D. (2008). Neuroeconomics. *Annual Review of Psychology*, *59*, 647–672. doi:10.1146/annurev.psych.59.103006.093710

Mandell, L., & Jump$tart. (2002). *Financial literacy: A growing problem*. Washington, DC: Jump$tart.

Mcadams, D. P., & Destaubin, E. (1992). A theory of generativity and its assessment through self-report, behavioral acts, and narrative themes in autobiography. *Journal of Personality and Social Psychology*, *62*(6), 1003–1015.

McCauley, C. D., Drath, W. H., Palus, C. J., O'Connor, P. M. G., & Baker, B. A. (2006). The use of constructive-developmental theory to advance the understanding of leadership. *Leadership Quarterly*, *17*(6), 634–653. doi:10.1016/j.leaqua.2006.10.006

Miller, L. (2012). The money-empathy gap, *New York Magazine*. Retrieved from http://nymag.com/news/features/money-brain-2012-7/.

Mitchell, T. R., & Mickel, A. E. (1999). The meaning of money: An individual-difference perspective. *Academy of Management Review*, *24*(3), 568–578.

Moller, A. C., Ryan, R. M., & Deci, E. L. (2006). Self-determination theory and public policy: Improving the quality of consumer decisions without using coercion. *Journal of Public Policy & Marketing*, *25*(1), 104–116

Murayama, K., Matsumoto, M., Izuma, K., & Matsumoto, K. (2010). Neural basis of the undermining effect of monetary reward on intrinsic motivation. *Proceedings of the National Academy of Sciences of the United States of America*, *107*, 20911–20916. doi:10.1073/pnas.1013305107

Orwell, G. (1945). *Animal farm; a fairy story*. London: Secker & Warburg.

Quote Investigator. (2011). Everything should be made as simple as possible, but not simpler. Retrieved from http://quoteinvestigator.com/2011/05/13/einstein-simple/.

Richins, M. L., & Dawson, S. (1992). A consumer values orientation for materialism and its measurement: Scale development and validation. *Journal of Consumer Research*, *19*(3), 303–316.

Rubinstein, M. (2001). Rational markets: Yes or no? the affirmative case. *Financial Analysts Journal*, *57*(3), 15–29. doi:10.2139/ssrn.242259

Ryan, R. M., & Deci, E. L. (2000). Self-determination theory and the facilitation of intrinsic motivation, social development, and well-being. *American Psychologist*, *55*, 68–78. doi:10.1037/0003-066X.55.1.68

Sprinkle, G. B. (2000). The effect of incentive contracts on learning and performance. *The Accounting Review*, *75*(3), 475–502.

St. Scholastica Monastery. (2012). Join us. Retrieved from http://www.duluthbenedictines.org/join-us/.

Stone, D. (2011). Cultivating financial mindfulness: A dual-processing theory. In D. J. Lamdin (Ed.), *Consumer knowledge and financial decisions: Lifespan perspectives* (pp. 15–27). New York: Springer.

Stone, D. N., Bryant, S. M., & Wier, B. (2010). Why are financial incentive effects unreliable? An extension of self-determination theory. *Behavioral Research in Accounting, 22*(2), 105–132. doi:10.2308/bria.2010.22.2.105

Stone, D., Deci, E., & Ryan, R. (2009). Beyond talk: Creating autonomous motivation through self-determination theory. *Journal of General Management, 34*(3), 75–91.

Tang, T. L. P. (2007). Income and quality of life: Does the love of money make a difference? *Journal of Business Ethics, 72*(4), 375–393. doi:10.1007/s10551-006-9176-4

Tatzel, M. (2003). The art of buying: Coming to terms with money and materialism. *Journal of Happiness Studies, 4*, 405–435. doi:10.1023/B:JOHS.0000005770.92248.77

Tolstoy, L. (1889). *Anna Karenina*. New York: T. Y. Crowell & co.

Wahba, M. A., & Bridwell, L. G. (1976). Maslow reconsidered: A review of research on the need hierarchy theory. *Organizational Behavior and Human Performance, 15*(2), 212–240. doi:10.1016/0030-5073(76)90038-6.

Williams, G. C., Patrick, H., Niemiec, C. P., Williams, L. K., Divine, G., Lafata, J. E.,... Pladevall M. (2009). Reducing the health risks of diabetes: How self-determination theory may help improve medication adherence and quality of life. *The Diabetes Educator, 35*, 484–492.

Wink, P. (1991). Two faces of narcissism. *Journal of Personality & Social Psychology, 61*(4), 590–597.

Yang, L. (1950). Buddhist monasteries and four money-raising institutions in Chinese history. *Harvard Journal of Asiatic Studies, 13*(1/2), 174–191.

Yezer, A. M., Goldfarb, R. S., & Poppen, P. J. (1996). Does studying economics discourage cooperation? Watch what we do, not what we say or how we play. *Journal of Economic Perspectives, 10*(1), 177–186.

CHAPTER 24

Development, Changes and Consolidation of Values and Goals in Business and Law Schools: The Dual Valuing Process Model

Frederick M. E. Grouzet

Abstract

Education in some professions, such as business and law, seems to inculcate certain work and life values that have been shown to negatively affect people's well-being and could possibly have more pervasive effects on ethical thinking and decision-making. However, because of pre-existing values and goals students may also select and persist in such careers despite the cost on ethics and well-being. In order to explain both phenomena, the dual valuing process model (Grouzet, 2013) is proposed as a theoretical framework.

Key Words: values, intrinsic and extrinsic goals, valuing process, professional education, socialization

---

Introduction

From 2002 to 2004 Léger Marketing published reports on the degree of trust that Canadians associate with various professions. Lawyers were constantly at the bottom of the list and the percentage of Canadians who trust them decreased every year, from 54% in 2002 to 44% in 2004. In the United States, the percentage was as low as 25%, sharing the same level of trust with CEOs of large corporations (i.e., 23%; Gallup Poll 2002). Forty percent of Americans rated the honesty and ethical standards of lawyers and business executives as low or very low (Gallup Poll 2009). Business people and lawyers are often described as cold persons simply interested in profits or success. These perceptions seem to originate from scandals in the business world (e.g., WorldCom and Enron scandals). High levels of depression and suicide have also been reported in legal professions (e.g., Eaton, Anthony, Mandel, & Garrison, 1990). When people want to explain these findings, two main hypotheses are proposed: (1) individuals with low ethical standards and love of money are attracted by business

and law professions; and (2) business people and lawyers have received a professional education that has shaped their ethics and values. Although the second hypothesis has received some support from research on business and law students' values, ethics, and well-being, one may wonder why young adults would choose careers with such low levels of public trust.

In this chapter, I start by drawing a general overview of the ethical and mental health issues that have been identified in business and legal professions, as well as among students who aspire to these professions. Then, I use *self-determination theory* (SDT) and the concept of *valuing* to explain the role of professional education in selecting and shaping future managers' and leaders' ethical standards and values. The concept of *valuing* includes both a process and its outcome. As Rohan (2000) summarized, "used as a verb, *value* refers to the process of ascertaining the merit of an entity with reference to an abstract value system structure. Used as a noun, *value* refers to the result of this process" (p. 258). Values are defined as "desirable transsituational goals" (Schwartz, 1994) and have been found to be important predictors of social judgments, attitudes, behaviors, and more recently well-being. This predicting power of values and goals resides principally in the circumplex structure. In the second section of this chapter, I show how the nature and the structure of what individuals or professional cultures value (i.e., personal value and goal systems) explain ethical and mental health issues that are prevalent in business and law schools (and professions). In the third section, I present the dual valuing process model (Grouzet, 2013) that can serve as a framework to understand the origin of students' values and goals. More specifically, I contrast the socialization and self-selection (or attraction-selection-attrition-success [ASAS]) models. In conclusion, I propose some suggestions for future research and applications.[1]

What's Going Wrong with Business and Law Students?
Ethical and Moral Reasoning

The bad reputation of the business world has a long history and highly publicized ethical scandals (e.g., WorldCom, Enron, Siemens, and Parmalat scandals) have engendered considerable distrust and cynicism among the general population. Many scholars and executives have questioned the role of business education and MBA programs to explain questionable management practices and problems in moral and ethical reasoning (e.g., Ghoshal, 2005; Merritt, 2002; Mittroff, 2004; *The Economist*, 2004). One approach has been to investigate business students' ethics and other related behaviors in comparison with other students. For instance, researchers have found that business students were more willing to engage into corruption than psychology students (Tang, Chen, & Sutarso, 2008) and tended to make ethically questionable choices when competitive pressure increased (Nill, Schibrowsky, & Peltier, 2004).

Other unethical behaviors, like cheating, have also been observed among business students. Research showed that business students tended to cheat more than their nonbusiness peers (e.g., Caruana, Ramaseshan, & Ewing, 2000; McCabe, Butterfield, & Treviño, 2006). At the college level, business students were among the most dishonest, showing the highest cheating rate (87%) when compared with engineering, science, and humanities students who averaged 68% (Meade, 1992 as cited in Caruana et al., 2000; see also Smyth & Davis, 2004). McNeel (1994) observed

that business students showed less growth in principled reasoning than students in other disciplines (e.g., psychology, social work). At the interpersonal level, business students scored lower on an emotional empathy test than social sciences students (Myyry & Helkama, 2001).

Lawyers and law students have, unfortunately, nothing to pride themselves in relative to business people. Jokes and negative stereotypes cast lawyers as dishonest, liars, and morally biased. Beyond the fact that business is sometimes intimately related to law, including in the professional education curriculum (e.g., business law programs), the moral reasoning of lawyers and law students has been questioned and investigated by researchers (for a review see Schiltz, 1998). At the interpersonal level, recent research showed that law students were less altruistic than medical students, or even business students (Coulter, Wilkes, & Der-Martirosian, 2007). Law students have also showed higher levels of Machiavellianism, scoring lower on measures of positive view of human nature and presenting a more highly cynical view of human nature than psychology students.

Mental Health and Well-Being

Among various possible careers, some seem to be more stressful and more associated with mental health issues (e.g., depression, suicide) than others. Among them, the legal professions (e.g., attorney and lawyers) have received particular attention during the last 20 years. From anecdotal reports to extensive empirical research, mental health issues have been identified as pandemic among lawyers. For example, in a widely cited study conducted by Eaton and his colleagues at Johns Hopkins University (Eaton et al., 1990), lawyers have been found to be 3.6 times more likely than any of the other 103 sampled occupational groups to suffer from major depressive disorder. Male lawyers were reported to commit suicide "at twice the expected rate of the general population" (Gatland, 1997). Other mental health problems have also been identified as prevalent among lawyers, such as alcoholism and substance use (e.g., Benjamin, Kaszniak, Sales, & Shanfield, 1986; Drogin, 1991; Schiltz, 1999; Seligman, Verkuil, & Kang, 2005), obsessive-compulsive disorders, general anxiety and phobic anxiety, paranoid ideation, social alienation, and isolation (Beck, Sales, & Benjamin, 1996). In addition, divorce and suicide rates tend to be higher in lawyers than in nonlawyers (Schiltz, 1999; Sheldon & Krieger, 2004). In a study conducted by the North Carolina Bar Association (1991), it was found that 11% of lawyers had experienced suicidal ideations at least once a month in the previous year. These findings have been replicated in other parts of the world, such as in Australia (Priest, 2007) where 15% of lawyers and 10% of accountants had moderate to severe depression symptoms.

Unfortunately, research with law students parallels findings in the legal profession. Therefore, legal education has been identified as the possible starting point of lawyers' mental health problems. In 1986, Benjamin and his colleagues found that on entering law school, students exhibited depression to the same extent as did the general population. However, by late spring of their first year, 32% of these students were characterized as depressed. Furthermore, by the spring of their third year, the rate of depression in these students had risen to 40%. Two years after law school, 17% of them reported being still depressed. In an extensive review, Dammeyer and Nunez (1999) have noted that students in law reported higher levels of anxiety and depression than control groups, including medical students, and in some cases the mean level of anxiety was similar to psychiatric populations. Other research noted that law students had declining physical and psychological states, with depression and negative affect increasing in students following their first year of law school (Pritchard & McIntosh, 2003).

It is interesting to note that Schiltz (1999) made a direct link between ethical, mental health issues, and values, proposing some "big picture" advice: "Don't get sucked into the game. Don't let money become the most important thing in your life. Don't fall into the trap of measuring your worth as an attorney—or as a human being—by how much money you make" (p. 921). In other words, "don't value money more than everything else."

Values and Goal Contents
Two-Dimensional Structures and Circumplex Models

Since Rokeach's (1968, 1979) seminal work on values, researchers have made substantial progress toward understanding the basic aims toward which people strive, as well as the way in which values are organized in people's psyches. In an attempt to understand the basic types of strivings and values about which people generally care, Shalom Schwartz and his colleagues proposed a circumplex model (Schwartz & Bilsky, 1987, 1990), which has since been refined both methodologically and conceptually over the course of many studies conducted

in multiple cross-cultural samples (e.g., Schwartz, 1992; Schwartz & Bardi, 2001; Schwartz & Boehnke, 2004; Schwartz et al., 2001; Schwartz & Sagie, 2000; Schwartz & Sagiv, 1995). More recently, using an approach similar to Schwartz's, my colleagues and I (Grouzet et al., 2005) have examined the organization of the life goals that people typically value. Like Schwartz, our analyses showed that life goals were organized in a very similar circumplex fashion across 15 different cultures (Figure 24.1), because some goals were relatively consistent with each other, whereas other goals were in conflict with each other. Specifically, we found that goals can be differentiated along a horizontal axis: *intrinsic* goals (i.e., physical health, personal growth, affiliation, and community feelings) versus *extrinsic* goals (i.e., amassing wealth, gaining adulation, presenting an attractive image, and conforming to societal standards). A second orthogonal axis organized intrinsic and extrinsic goals along a continuum from the *physical* and *intrapersonal* self (i.e., physical health and self-acceptance vs. financial success) to an *interpersonal* self (i.e., affiliation vs. popularity and image), to *self-transcendence* (i.e., community feelings vs. conformity). In addition, two goals have been found to be prototypical of the physical self (i.e., hedonism) and self-transcendence (i.e., spirituality).

Although values and goals are distinct constructs, they naturally share the same quasi-circumplex structure. Indeed, after rotating Schwartz's model, the same types of values and goals juxtapose or oppose each other. For example, the intrinsic versus extrinsic distinction can thus be discerned among values in Schwartz's model, in which universalism and benevolence (akin to the intrinsic goals of community feeling and affiliation) oppose power and achievement (which are akin to extrinsic goals; see Kasser & Ahuvia, 2002). According to SDT (Deci & Ryan, 2000), the distinction between intrinsic and extrinsic goals possesses an important explanatory and predictive value. As I describe below, SDT offers a theoretical framework that explains the relationships between certain types of values and goals and ethical and personal judgments, behaviors, and well-being (see also Kasser, 2002; Kasser, Kanner, & Ryan, 2003).

Guides for Ethical and Healthy Lifestyle

SDT proposes that intrinsic goals, such as developing a sense of agency and personal growth, having close and fulfilling relationships, and contributing

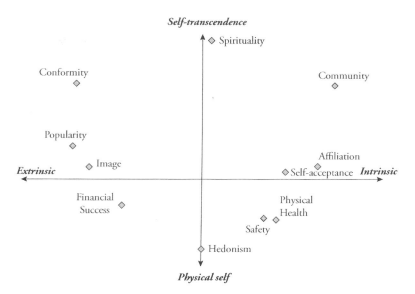

Fig. 24.1. The circumplex model of goal content. Copyright 2005 by the American Psychological Association. Reproduced with permission. The official citation that should be used in referencing this material is Grouzet, F.M.E., et al. (2005). The structure of goal contents across 15 cultures. *Journal of Personality and Social Psychology, 89*, 800–816. The use of APA information does not imply endorsement by APA.

to making the world a better place to live, are inherently satisfying because they are congruent with the fundamental psychological needs experienced by all individuals (Deci & Ryan, 2000; Kasser, 2002). Pursuing and valuing intrinsic goals leads to fulfillment of relatedness, autonomy, and competence needs, which in turn fosters personal well-being. In contrast, extrinsic goals, such as amassing wealth, gaining adulation, presenting an attractive image, and conforming to societal standards, are primarily concerned with obtaining some reward or social praise. Because they are typically means to some other ends, they are less likely to be inherently satisfying (see Kasser, 2002). Therefore, an emphasis on extrinsic goals distracts people away from intrinsic goals and the fulfillment of psychological needs. Furthermore, the pursuit of extrinsic goals is associated with a perpetual striving for the transient valuation and validation of others, which makes individuals more likely to be influenced by social comparisons, contingent self-esteem, and self-objectification, which in turn undermines their need satisfaction. Although direct evidence of the link between goals and need satisfaction is limited (e.g., Rijavec, Brdar, & Miljikovic, 2006), indirect and conceptual evidence has been shown (for an extensive review see Vansteenkiste, Soenens, & Duriez, 2008).

More than 30 years of SDT research has provided strong supports for the positive relationship between psychological need satisfaction and happiness, human potential, and mental health (see Ryan & Deci, 2001 and Ryan, Deci, Grolnick, & La Guardia, 2006 for extensive reviews). By fostering (vs. thwarting) psychological need satisfaction, intrinsic (vs. extrinsic) goals and values are consequently associated with subjective and psychological well-being (see Kasser, 2002 for a review). In SDT, the satisfaction of the basic psychological needs is considered the main mediational mechanism that explains the impact of goals on well-being (see Vansteenkiste et al., 2008). For example, Vansteenkiste and his colleagues (2007) examined the relations among work value orientations, psychological need satisfaction, and job outcomes. They found evidence for the mediating role of psychological needs in the influence of holding an extrinsic (relative to an intrinsic) work value orientation on employee's dedication, job satisfaction, emotional exhaustion, and turnover intentions.

Life goals and values are also associated with forms of interpersonal relationships that could lead to ethical or unethical behaviors. In an attempt to understand the role of values and goals on human relationships, I (Grouzet, 2009) drew a parallel between the intrinsic-extrinsic dimension and Triandis's (1995) horizontality-verticality distinction and Hofstede's (2001) power distance dimension (low vs. high). Horizontality refers to an emphasis on an egalitarian approach to relationships, considering people on the same level. In contrast, verticality corresponds to a hierarchical view of people and groups, with some being superior to others, as well as a detachment from others, which could lead to an instrumentalization of people and mechanistic dehumanization (Haslam, 2006). As shown next, empirical research supports the idea that a focus on extrinsic goals and values can lead to hierarchical and abusive relationships, which are commonly associated with problematic ethical behavior.

First, values and goals have been found to be related to different views of personal and social relationships. For example, research has shown that extrinsic values and goals are associated with a social dominance orientation (i.e., a generalized support for group-based inequality and dominance; Sidanius & Pratto, 1999), right-wing authoritarianism, and prejudice (e.g., Duriez, Vansteenkiste, Soenens, & De Witte, 2007; Feather & McKee, 2008; McKee & Feather, 2008). In contrast, intrinsic values, such as universalism, were associated with high levels of moral reasoning among MBA students (Lan, Growing, Rieger, McMahon, & King, 2010). Second, to attain extrinsic goals, such as material affluence and financial success, individuals consider other people as instrumental for their own desires, or a means to an end (Kasser, 2002). For example, holding extrinsic goals and materialistic values has been associated with engaging in more antisocial activities (e.g., Cohen & Cohen, 1996; Kasser & Ryan, 1993), being more manipulative and Machiavellian (McHoskey, 1999), more competitive (vs. cooperative) behaviors (Sheldon, Sheldon, & Osbaldiston, 2000), and vengeance attitudes and preferences for capital punishment (McKee & Feather, 2008). In contrast, holding intrinsic values and goals has been associated with empathy (Myyry & Helkama, 2001; Sheldon & Kasser, 1995).

To sum up, the type of values and goals that people prioritize influence their thoughts, social judgment, personal relationships, and well-being. Therefore, a closer examination of students' values and goals can explain the prevalence of problematic ethical and mental health issues.

Students' Values and Goals: Business, Law, and Other Fields of Study

An extensive literature in social psychology of education documents the difference of attitudes, beliefs, and values across fields of study (Pascarella & Terenzini, 1991, 2005). Among the various comparisons that can be made between majors, the contrast between "power professions" (i.e., business, law, and related fields; as defined by Sidanius, Pratto, Martin, & Stallworth, 1991) and "liberal" programs (i.e., social sciences and humanities) received particular attention. This attention was directed to differences regarding (1) worldviews and sociopolitical beliefs and values, and (2) ethical and materialistic values and goals.

First, worldviews and sociopolitical values correspond to people's beliefs about the way the world is or should be. Research showed that students enrolled in social sciences and humanities tended to hold relatively liberal, progressive, or leftist views, whereas students in business, public administration, law, and related fields tended to hold relatively conservative and hierarchical views (see Bereiter & Freedman, 1962; Guimond, 1998; Hastie, 2007a; Sidanius et al., 1991). This preference for the status-quo has been observed in students' legitimization of hierarchies through intergroup attitudes. For example, business and law students have reported higher levels of "consensual racism" and prejudice against immigrants (Guimond, Dambrun, Michinov, & Duarte, 2003; Guimond & Palmer, 1996; Sidanius et al., 1991; Van Laar, Sidanius, Rabinowitz, & Sinclair, 1999), more negative attitudes toward socialists and labor unions, and more positive attitudes toward capitalists (Guimond & Palmer, 1996) than students in other fields of study. Guimond and his colleagues (2003) evidenced that students' social dominance orientation is a mediator that explained the observed difference between law and psychology student groups. Similarly, Guimond and Palmer (1996) observed that, in comparison with students in social sciences, students attending business programs were more likely to attribute poverty and unemployment to internal dispositions (person-blaming) rather than systemic factors (system-blaming), which is also an indication of preference for status quo in hierarchical relations and structure (see also Hastie, 2007b). Furthermore, research using Schwartz's value types showed that business students value more conservatism, but less universalism and benevolence, than students of the humanities and social sciences (Lindeman & Verkasalo, 2005; Myyry & Helkama, 2001; Verkasalo, Daun, & Niit, 1994). Also, Myyry (2008) found that social science students tend to associate social justice with an ideal value, while only 7% of business students make such association.

Second, business and law students have also been found to espouse higher competitive value orientation (Killeen & McCarrey, 1986) and love-of-money orientation (Cunningham, Frauman, Ivy, & Perry, 2004; Tang et al., 2008), as well as have a much higher probability to face issues regarding unethical behavior than psychology students (Tang et al., 2008). Business students tend to prioritize power and achievement more than students in social sciences (Myyry & Helkama, 2001). In the same vein, social science students seem to associate the value "ambitious" to intrinsic goals (e.g., pursuing maturity, personal development, self-esteem, and integrity), whereas business students associate the same value to extrinsic goals (e.g., pursuing money, career, degree, and other's respect; Myyry, 2008). Vansteenkiste, Duriez, Simons, and Soenens (2006) also found that business students place higher importance for extrinsic goals, such as financial success, image, and popularity, but lower importance for intrinsic goals, such as personal growth, affiliation, and community feelings, than future school teachers.

To sum up, between-field-of-study comparisons tend to support the idea that business and law students hold extrinsic values, such as conservatism, power, and material affluence. Considering that extrinsic values and goals were found to be associated with unethical behaviors and lower well-being, it is possible to conclude that business and law students' ethical and mental health issues are the results of valuing extrinsic goals (Kasser & Ahuvia, 2002).

Valuing Processes in Business and Law Schools

Values and life goals that business and law students hold are quite different from those held by other students. This difference seems to impact students' ethical reasoning and well-being, not only during their education but also later as professionals. This has led researchers to wonder if business and law schools could be the source of the problem; through a socialization process, business and law schools may shape students' identities, including their value and goal systems. In order to understand the effect of professional education on students' development, I propose to use the dual valuing processes model (Grouzet, 2013) as a framework. Then, I contrast the socialization model with alternative hypotheses that suggest a self-selection effect.

The Dual Valuing Process Model

The dual valuing process model (Grouzet, 2013) provides an account of how valuing can occur in two different (but concurrent) ways. The dual valuing process model takes its origin from two approaches in psychology: humanistic psychology and social psychology (for a more theoretical overview see Grouzet, 2013). In this model, I proposed the existence of two valuing processes that operate at the same time: the organismic valuing process (OVP) and the sociocognitive valuing process (SVP).

THE ORGANISMIC VALUING PROCESS

The concept of OVP was first described by humanistic psychologist Carl Rogers (1951). Congruent with the main postulate of humanistic psychology suggesting that human beings are intrinsically "good," Rogers proposed that people are intrinsically motivated to value what is good for (or fosters) the growth of the organism. Like plants seek light, humans seek psychological nutrients to grow. Therefore, people would naturally prioritize values and goals that allow them to fulfill their organismic needs, such as the psychological needs for autonomy, competence, and relatedness (see also Deci & Ryan, 2000; Sheldon, Arndt, & Houser-Marko, 2003). Because intrinsic values and goals are associated with the fulfillment of these psychological needs, people would systematically select intrinsic over extrinsic values and goals.

Ken Sheldon contributed greatly to the empirical test of the existence of an OVP. For example, in a series of three studies, Sheldon and his colleagues (2003) showed that people tended to move toward intrinsic goals and away from extrinsic goals over periods ranging from 20 minutes to 6 weeks. The changes remained significant after controlling for social desirability. Interestingly, the OVP seemed to operate out of participants' consciousness. Indeed, participants were asked to remember the importance they placed on intrinsic and extrinsic goals 6 weeks before. The findings showed that the remembered importance for intrinsic goals was higher than the former ratings, but equal to the revised importance ratings. This memory bias was also observed within a period of 20 minutes. This move toward intrinsic goals was also observed at the life-span level. In a university sample Sheldon (2005) evidenced a significant decrease from freshman to senior year in the importance placed on extrinsic goals and a nearly significant increase of intrinsic goal importance. Further evidence for the OVP was also provided through negative relations between chronological age and extrinsic goal importance (e.g., Kasser & Ryan, 1996; Lyons, Duxbury, & Higgins, 2007; Sheldon & Kasser, 2001).

Rogers (1964) viewed the OVP as adaptive but also added a condition for its activation: "a growth-promoting climate." In SDT terms, the OVP can be activated and operates when the environment supports psychological needs. This would explain the relationship between need support and preference for intrinsic goals. For example, in a 26-year longitudinal study, Kasser, Koestner, and Lekes (2002) found that 31-year-old adults were more likely to hold extrinsic values (e.g., conformity) if their parents had reported a restrictive parenting style when they were 5 years old. Conversely, if their parents had demonstrated a warm parenting style, the kids valued more intrinsic goals (e.g., self-direction) 26 years later. Similar evidence for the relation between parental need support and intrinsic goal orientation was found in other longitudinal studies (e.g., Cohen & Cohen, 1996; Kasser, Ryan, Zax, & Sameroff, 1995; Williams, Cox, Hedberg, & Deci, 2000). As part of the dual valuing process model, I also propose the existence of other ways to activate the OVP, such as wake-up calls and organismic calls (for a review see Grouzet, 2013), but they are less relevant in the context of professional education.

THE SOCIOCOGNITIVE VALUING PROCESS

Although the OVP implies that the person "knows" what is good for the organism and pursues values and goals that can foster organismic growth, the SVP places the person in a position of informational dependence on others (Kelley & Thibaut, 1969) to discover what is "good" and/or "appropriate." Social psychology and developmental psychology propose that people's values and goals are shaped and influenced by the various "socialization agents" or "significant others" with whom they are in frequent contact. Influential theories of persuasion and social influence have proposed processes to explain the development and changes in values and goals. The distinction between normative and informational influences (Deutsch & Gerard, 1955) has been central in explaining the social and cognitive process involved in valuing. *Normative influence* is when a social group that the person belongs to (e.g., other law students) or aspires to belong to (e.g., lawyers) conveys the socially expected values, thereby influencing the person's valuing process. *Informational influence* refers to the cognitive process of information and argumentation that is used to form the person's knowledge and value system.

More recently, Kruglanski and his colleagues (2005) proposed that the concept of "epistemic authority" is central in explaining how individuals process both the information (social norms or arguments) and its source (social groups or experts). The concept of "epistemic authority" was first introduced in 1989 by Kruglanski and refers to the process of relying on and accepting a source's information, which could be persons (e.g., teachers, peers) or objects (e.g., textbooks, media). The degree of epistemic authority that is associated with a source determines the influence that the source has on the individual. Whereas children assign epistemic authority only to the primary caregivers and indistinguishably for all knowledge domains, with age individuals assign epistemic authorities to different sources (e.g., peers, teachers) for different knowledge domains (including values) (e.g., Raviv, Bar-Tal, Raviv, & Houminer, 1990). In contrast to dual-mode theories (i.e., elaboration likelihood model, Petty & Cacioppo, 1986; heuristic-systematic model, Chaiken et al., 1989) but in congruence with the parametric unimodel (Kruglanski & Thompson, 1999), Kruglanki and his colleagues proposed that people use both the peripheral (or heuristic) cues that are associated with social groups or experts (e.g., "if belongs to the group, then correct" or "if expert, then correct") and the "message argument" to assign an "epistemic authority" to a group, a person, or an argument. As I describe later, the concept of epistemic authority has been used and empirically tested in the context of socialization in college.

Kruglanski and his colleagues (2005) also proposed that the self may also be assigned degrees of epistemic authority in different knowledge domains. Resulting from personal development, individuals may rely more on their own experience and expertise than on external sources. The self-ascription of epistemic authority allows the person to develop informational independence from others. The SVP operates as a result of negotiation between internal and external epistemic authorities that direct the individual to prioritize intrinsic and/or extrinsic values and goals.

To sum up, the dual valuing process model (Grouzet, 2013) proposes that the OVP and SVP can explain how people prioritize, develop, and change their values and goals. When activated, the OVP leads people to move toward intrinsic values and goals. However, people's informational dependence on others places them under the influence of epistemic authorities that may make them moving toward intrinsic or extrinsic values and goals through SVP. This influence is reduced while the individual begins to assign epistemic authority to oneself. In sum, pending the information transmitted by the epistemic authorities (i.e., promoting intrinsic vs. extrinsic values and goals), the OVP and SVP may "work" together toward the development of an intrinsic orientation or conflict with one another. In other words, the SVP may reinforce the OVP if congruent in promoting an intrinsic goal orientation or thwart it by promoting an extrinsic goal orientation.

The Dual Valuing Process Model in Business and Law Schools

Educational researchers, sociologists, and social psychologists have developed various theories and models to explain value differences among fields of study that I reviewed previously. Two main groups of theories emerged: *socialization theories*, which focus on the effect of field of study on values and goals; and *attraction-selection-attrition-success theories*, which imply that students' values and goals create the majors as we see them. In this section, I review the empirical evidence that supports these theories. Then, I show how the dual valuing process model can integrate these two opposite models.

SOCIALIZATION

The popular notion that colleges and universities shape students' identity, values, goals, and beliefs, which will direct their actions and life choices during their adult life, has been largely documented and supported by socialization theories (Pascarella & Terenzini, 1991, 2005). The main proposition is that through interactions with professors and fellow students, ideas and arguments bring changes in students' values and goals. The ideology that is promoted in a particular field of study and the associated theories that are taught create differences among majoring students. The "impressionable" population of students ascribes high degrees of epistemic authority to their professors, their peers, but also to their course manuals (Guimond, 1999), which in turn make them receptive to the "hidden curriculum." For example, Mittroff (2004) suggested that "the theories of business that [are] developed and therefore [taught] are based upon the narrowest and the basest of human motives. For instance, two of the most prominent theories of business—Transaction Cost Analysis and Agency Theory—assume that at their core, humans are completely and entirely ruthless, motivated solely by greed, opportunistic, purely selfish, and it should come as no surprise, totally out for themselves and

no one else" (p. 185). Findings from longitudinal studies support this idea. For example, MBA students reported lower importance for intrinsic values, like being helpful, and higher importance for extrinsic values, like a comfortable life, after 2 years in the program (Krishman, 2008).

Serge Guimond has made important empirical contributions to understand the socialization of sociopolitical worldviews within fields of study. In a first series of cross-sectional and longitudinal studies, Guimond and Palmer (1990, 1996) observed that, whereas no significant difference was observed among first-year students, 1 year and 3 years later, business students showed a more conservative orientation (e.g., blaming the person to explain poverty, being in favor of capitalism and less in favor of labor unions), and social science students a more liberal orientation (e.g., system-blaming). Similarly, Guimond and his colleagues (2003) found that third-year law students' social dominance orientation was higher than first-year law students', and higher than first- and third-year psychology students'. To distinguish normative and informative influences, Guimond and Palmer (1996) examined the epistemic authority that students ascribed to their peers, professors, and courses. They found that a higher degree of epistemic authority ascribed to professors and course contents was associated with greater increases in business students' conservatism. By contrast, social science students for whom professors and courses represents epistemic authority tended over time to engage less in system justification, or to attribute unemployment to the person.

Based on the evidence above, it is clear that the socialization theories tend to rely on SVP to explain the differential effect of the field of study. However, OVP could also explain this effect. Indeed, because OVP needs a growth-promoting climate to be activated, a school that supports students' psychological needs may foster OVP and consequently the development of intrinsic goals. Empirical support for this hypothesis is rare. Senécal, Pelletier, and Vallerand (1992) found that psychology students perceived higher autonomy support from their program than business students, which could explain why the OVP cannot operate in business schools. However, as I mentioned in the previous section, some business and law schools are doing better than others. For example, Sheldon and Krieger (2007) compared two law schools and noticed differences in the perceived support of psychological needs. Other evidence for OVP can be found in Johnson

(2002) where the importance that college students placed on financial success decreased over time. Similarly, Biddle and his colleagues (1990) found that social science students showed higher value on community feelings than business students, but this difference was reduced one semester later; business students valued more community feelings over time. However, this last finding may challenge the socialization hypothesis because differences among fields of study were observed as soon as in the first semester.

ATTRACTION-SELECTION-ATTRITION-SUCCESS

Compelling critiques have been made regarding the socialization effect. The alternative hypothesis is known as "self-selection effect" but hides a large spectrum of mechanisms through which people "make the place" (Schneider, 1987) rather than being influenced by the place. For example, Schneider (1987) proposed three interrelated mechanisms that could support the alternative hypothesis: (1) the attraction, (2) the selection, and (3) the attrition effects. First, students are differentially *attracted* to a field of study based on its perceived ideology, or the perceived values of professors and fellow students. Then, schools *select* those who are most compatible. Finally, if during the program "incompatibilities" are detected, student *attrition* occurs. In a similar vein, Haley and Sidanius (2005) proposed four different processes. On one side, self-selection and institutional selection processes corresponds to "attraction" and "selection," which occur before any exposure to the field of study. The other two processes, differential success and differential attrition, occur during the program and provide an important distinction within the "attrition" mechanism. Overall, the four mechanisms are attraction-selection-attrition-success (ASAS).

The *attraction (or self-selection) process* suggests that students evaluate academic majors and select those that could help them attain their goals and that share similar values and worldviews to their own (e.g., Astin, 1993). According to Bourdieu (1979, 1984) most student socialization occurs prior to starting higher education, as "students generally tend to choose the institution [. . .] that requires and inculcates the (aesthetic, ethical, and political) dispositions most similar to those inculcated by their family." Work by Sidanius and his colleagues support this idea by showing that students who held conservative attitudes and a social dominance orientation tended to prefer "hierarchy-enhancing" majors and careers (e.g., business and law; Sidanius,

Sinclair, & Pratto, 2006; Sidanius, van Laar, Levin, & Sinclair, 2003). Schools also contribute to attracting students using specific values. Reedy and Learmonth (2009) suggested that "in competing to attract students, business schools frequently stress that lucrative careers and personal success can be achieved through [. . .] the competitive and individualistic pursuit of wealth, status and power [. . .]" (p. 241).

The *selection process* implies that schools would differentially select students based on their values, goals, and sociopolitical orientation. Although, the selection that operates in business and law schools is principally based on grades and standardized tests, such as the LSAT, some schools and MBA programs may engage in screening, evaluation, and selection practices that allow them to accept students who already possess the desired value system (e.g., Vaara & Faÿ, 2011). In a series of experimental studies, Pratto and her colleagues (Pratto & Espinoza, 2001; Pratto, Stallworth, Sidanius, & Siers, 1997) found that students who were asked to recruit employees for fictive work positions tended to select candidates who demonstrated attitudes that fit to the perceived company's ideology. The combination of self-selection and institutional selection creates the ideal condition to observe differences among fields of study before socialization starts.

The *attrition process* explains why students may decide to change their academic major and drop out of school. The lack of congruence between their expectations and what the school offers might not be reduced via socialization, which may create dissatisfaction, stress, lack of motivation, and finally dropping out. Research in personnel psychology showed that employees who perceived a mismatch between their ethical values and the organization's ethical climate were more susceptible to turnover (e.g., Schwepker, 1999; Sims & Kroeck, 1994). Similar findings have been found with other types of values, which supports the relation between perceived person-organization fit and well-being (see Edwards, 2008, for a review). The attrition process (or lack of person-environment fit) may explain mental health issues and the cynism that law students experience (Granfield, 1986).

Attrition could also be initiated by the school itself through the evaluation of students, which in turn leads to their *success* or failure. What is called the "hidden curriculum" (i.e., norms, values, and practices) is not only transmitted through decisions about curricular inclusion and exclusion, but also reinforced during evaluations. Therefore, students who have already integrated the promoted values have a higher chance of success. Empirical evidence supports the positive relationship between student-major fit and GPA (e.g., Sidanius et al., 2003; Tracey & Robbins, 2006; van Laar et al., 1999).

To sum up, the ASAS model offers an important challenge to the socialization model. On one hand, the attraction-selection processes suggest that business and law students' values and goals exist before entering the program. On the other hand, the attrition-success processes suggest that business and law students who end up in the program (by error) will leave the program and will not appear in the statistics of the school.

PUTTING IT ALL TOGETHER

The debate between socialization theorists and ASAS supporters has received a lot of attention in organizational psychology and higher education. Empirical evidence has been presented to support, with more or less success, one or the other position. For example, the absence of significant differences among first-year students while a differentiation occurs years later has been used to support the socialization hypothesis. However, an absence of significant differences does not mean that there are no differences; it simply means that the difference has not been detected by the measures and in the sample under study. Similarly, the socialization hypothesis cannot be rejected because significant differences were observed among first year students. As Bourdieu suggested, a primary socialization (childhood) precedes a secondary socialization (education). Therefore, values and goals developed through a primary socialization may lead students to select or be selected by a field of study. In turn, these values and goals may be reinforced (through success), changed (through secondary socialization), or rejected (through attrition).

As discussed above, the dual valuing process model (Grouzet, 2013) can enhance our understanding of socialization effects by suggesting that a growth-promoting climate and/or epistemic authority's intrinsic orientation is associated with students' move toward intrinsic values and goals, whereas a need-thwarting climate and/or epistemic authority's extrinsic orientation may be associated with students' move toward extrinsic values and goals. Similarly, the dual valuing process model can shed light on the ASAS model. First, the OVP suggests that students should be attracted by majors and careers that can fulfill their organismic needs through intrinsic values and goals. The SVP (through primary socialization) may, however, direct them to majors and careers that promote the extrinsic values and goals that were promoted by epistemic authorities (e.g., parents, peers). The schools then select students based on their expressed values and goals. Second, resulting from a maturing process (or OVP) students in business or law may tend to move toward intrinsic values and goals (e.g., Biddle et al., 1990). It is possible to hypothesize that the incongruence between intrinsic values due to OVP and extrinsic values due to SVP in business or law cultures will generate anxiety and stress, which may ultimately result in attrition. However, SVP might be so strong that students' pre-existing extrinsic values and goals may be reinforced by success and graduation. As discussed previously in this chapter, business people and lawyers may pay the cost of this success through ethical and mental health issues.

Conclusion and Hope for the Future

Business and law professions are currently facing challenges related to ethical and mental health issues. Professional associations and scholars in these academic fields question the source of these problems and search for possible remedies. Among potential suspects, professional education has received a great deal of attention. Indeed, business and law students seem to have similar ethical and mental health problems. Based on research on values and goals, and more specifically using Grouzet et al.'s (2005) circumplex model of goal content, it is possible to explain why business and law students' extrinsic value orientations are associated with unethical thinking and poor well-being. The dual valuing process model (Grouzet, 2013) sheds light on how such extrinsic value orientation could be developed through SVP and against OVP. The dual valuing process model also explains how students' extrinsic value orientation may lead them to choose and succeed in business or law careers, but also experience incongruence between their organismic needs and work values, and drop out.

However, it might be premature to generalize the above findings to all business and law students. First, comparisons among fields of study were generally conducted within specific universities and colleges. Other researchers have failed to find differences between business and nonbusiness students in other universities (e.g., Neubaum, Pagell, Drexler Jr., McKee-Ryan, & Larson, 2009). Second, differences between two business/law schools in two different countries and within the same country have been found. For example, in a cross-cultural study comparing Canadian and Chinese business students, Bu and McKeen (2001) found that Chinese students exhibited a weaker concern for a balanced life but a stronger interest in intrinsic rewards, simplicity, and moral congruence. Other cross-cultural research has shown that American business students reported being more concerned by ethics than East-Asian business students (Chung, Eichenseher, & Taniguchi, 2008), but less concerned by environmental issues than Chilean students (Cordano, Welcomer, Scherer, Pradenas, & Parada, 2010). Within the United States, Sheldon and Krieger (2007) found differences between two different law schools regarding the satisfaction of psychological needs. Some schools are doing better than others, and business and law schools are becoming more aware of ethical and mental issues that their students are facing. This is what made Schiltz (1999) say in a letter to law students:

> *I have good news and bad news. The bad news is that the profession that you are about to enter is one of the most unhappy and unhealthy on the face of the earth— and, in the view of many, one of the most unethical. The good news is that you can join this profession and still be happy, healthy, and ethical* (p. 872).

Therefore, this chapter also includes hope for business and law students. A better understanding of OVP and the importance of supporting and activating it should provide professional educators with some solutions to enhance ethical reasoning and mental health in schools and for future professionals. For example, Sheldon and Krieger's work clearly showed that some law schools were able to reverse the tendencies and support psychological needs, which in turn can foster OVP. In addition, SVP should be considered as an important process. Indeed, professors and textbooks are important sources of epistemic authority. Several scholars and deans have actually initiated changes by proposing new approaches and new orientations for their schools (e.g., Grey, 2004). One example is the inclusion of social responsibility and sustainability as a pillar in business education.

Future research on OVP and SVP is needed in order to better understand how students' values and goals develop and change over time. Longitudinal studies have always been privileged to study socialization effects and distinguish them from ASAS effects. Therefore, one direction of future research could be longitudinal research where students' values and goals are assessed periodically from selection into the program (e.g., in high school) to graduation and even several years later. Need support and social influence processes could then be examined to explain changes across time. A second direction is the experimental tests of the dual valuing process model (Grouzet, 2013) and more specifically of the interaction between OVP and SVP. These research efforts would contribute to the advancement of knowledge in organizational psychology and would enable professional educators to offer strategies to form the future leaders of the world.

Note

1. The author gratefully acknowledges the operating grant support he has received from the Social Sciences and Humanities Research Council. He also thanks Richard Koestner and Marylène Gagné for their precious comments on a previous version of the chapter, and Elliott Lee for his assistance in organizing and formatting references for this chapter.

References

Astin, A. W. (1993). *What matters in college: Four critical years revisited.* San Francisco: Jossey-Bass.

Beck, C. J. A., Sales, B. D., & Benjamin, G. A. H. (1996). Lawyer distress: Alcohol-related problems and other psychological concerns among a sample of practicing lawyers. *Journal of Law & Health, 10,* 1–60.

Benjamin, G. A. H., Kaszniak, A., Sales, B., & Shanfield, S. B. (1986). The role of legal education in producing psychological distress among law students and lawyers. *American Bar Foundation Research Journal, 11,* 225–252.

Bereiter, C., & Freedman, M. B. (1962). Fields of study and the people in them. In N. Sanford (Ed.), *The American college* (pp. 563–596). New York: Wiley.

Biddle, B. J., Bank, B. J., & Slavings, R. L. (1990). Modality of thought, campus experiences, and the development of values. *Journal of Educational Psychology, 82,* 671–682.

Bourdieu, P. (1979). *La distinction: critique sociale du jugement [Distinction: A social critique of the judgement of taste].* Paris: Les Editions de Minuit.

Bourdieu, P. (1984). *Homo academicus.* Paris: Les Editions de Minuit.

Bu, N., & McKeen, C. A. (2001). Work goals among male and female business students in Canada and China: The effects of culture and gender. *The International Journal of Human Resource Management, 12,* 166–183.

Caruana, A., Ramaseshan, B., & Ewing, M. T. (2000). The effect of anomie on academic dishonesty among university students. *The International Journal of Educational Management, 14,* 23–29.

Chaiken, S., Liberman, A., & Eagly, A. H. (1989). Heuristic and systematic processing within and beyond the persuasion context. In J. S. Uleman, & J. A. Bargh (Eds.), *Unintended thought* (pp. 212–252). New York: Guilford.

Chung, K., Eichenseher, J. W., & Taniguchi, T. (2008). Ethical perceptions of business students: Differences between East Asia and the USA and among "Confucian" cultures. *Journal of Business Ethics, 79,* 121–132.

Cohen, P., & Cohen, J. (1996). *Life values and adolescent mental health*. Mahwah, NJ: Erlbaum.

Cordano, M., Welcomer, S., Scherer, R., Pradenas, L., & Parada, V. (2010). Understanding cultural differences in the antecedents of pro-environmental behavior: A comparative analysis of business students in the United States and Chile. *Journal of Environmental Education, 41*, 224–238.

Coulter, I. D., Wilkes, M., & Der-Martirosian, C. (2007). Altruism revisited: A comparison of medical, law and business students' altruistic attitudes. *Medical Education, 41*, 341–345.

Cunningham, P. H., Frauman, E., Ivy, M. I., & Perry, T. L. (2004). The value of money and leisure and college students' choice of major. *SCHOLE: A Journal of Leisure Studies and Recreation Education, 19*, 65–72.

Dammeyer, M. M., & Nunez, N. (1999). Anxiety and depression among law students: Current knowledge and future directions. *Law and Human Behavior, 23*, 55–72.

Deci, E. L., & Ryan, R. M. (2000). The "what" and "why" of goal pursuits: Human needs and the self-determination of behavior. *Psychological Inquiry, 11*, 227–268.

Deutsch, M., & Gerard, H. B. (1955). A study of normative and informational social influences upon individual judgment. *Journal of Abnormal and Social Psychology, 51*, 629–636.

Drogin, E. (1991). Alcoholism in the legal profession: Psychological and legal perspectives and interventions. *Law & Psychology Review, 15*, 117–127.

Duriez, B., Vansteenkiste, M., Soenens, B., & De Witte, H. (2007). The social costs of extrinsic relative to intrinsic goal pursuits: Their relation with social dominance and racial and ethnic prejudice. *Journal of Personality, 75*, 757–782.

Eaton, W., Anthony, J., Mandel, W., & Garrison, R. (1990). Occupations and the prevalence of major depressive disorder. *Journal of Occupational Medicine, 32*, 1079–1087.

Edwards, J. R. (2008). Person-environment fit in organizations: An assessment of theoretical progress. *The Academy of Management Annals, 2*, 167–230.

Feather, N. T., & McKee, I. R. (2008). Values and prejudice: Predictors of attitudes towards Australian Aborigines. *Australian Journal of Psychology, 60*, 80–90.

Gatland, L. (1997). Dangerous dedication. *American Bar Association Journal, 83*, 28.

Ghoshal, S. (2005). Bad management theories are destroying good management practices. *Academy of Management Learning and Education, 4*, 75–91.

Granfield, R. (1986). Legal education as corporate ideology: Student adjustment to the law school experience. *Sociological Forum, 1*, 514–523.

Grey, C. (2004). Reinventing business schools: The contribution of critical management education. *Academy of Management Learning & Education, 3*, 178–186.

Grouzet, F. M. E. (2009). Values and relationships. In H. T. Reis, & S. K. Sprecher (Eds.), *Encyclopedia of human relationships* (pp. 1668–1671). Thousand Oaks, CA: Sage.

Grouzet, F. M. E. (2013). Self-regulation and autonomy: The dialectic between organismic and sociocognitive valuing processes. In B. Sokol, F. M. E. Grouzet, & U. Mueller (Eds.). *Self-regulation and autonomy: Social and developmental dimensions of human conduct* (pp. 47–77). New York: Cambridge University Press.

Grouzet, F. M. E., Kasser, T., Ahuvia, A., Dols, J., Kim, Y., Lau, S.,…Sheldon, K. M. (2005). The structure of goal contents across 15 cultures. *Journal of Personality and Social Psychology, 89*, 800–816.

Guimond, S. (1998). Processus de socialisation dans l'enseignement superieur: le pouvoir de la connaissance [Socialization processes in higher education: The power of knowledge]. In J.-L. Beauvois, R. V. Joule, & J.-M. Monteil (Eds.), *20 ans de psychologie sociale expérimentale francophone [Twenty years of francophone experimental social psychology]* (pp. 231–272). Grenoble, France: Presses Universitaires de Grenoble.

Guimond, S. (1999). Attitude change during college: Normative or informational social influence? *Social Psychology of Education, 2*, 237–261.

Guimond, S., Dambrun, M., Michinov, N., & Duarte, S. (2003). Does social dominance generate prejudice? Integrating individual and contextual determinants of intergroup cognitions. *Journal of Personality and Social Psychology, 84*, 697–721.

Guimond, S., & Palmer, D. L. (1990). Type of academic training and causal attributions for social problems. *European Journal of Social Psychology, 20*, 61–75.

Guimond, S., & Palmer, D. L. (1996). The political socialization of commerce and social science students: Epistemic authority and attitude change. *Journal of Applied Social Psychology, 26*, 1985–2013.

Haley, H., & Sidanius, J. (2005). Person-organization congruence and the maintenance of group-based social hierarchy: A social dominance perspective. *Group Processes & Intergroup Relations, 8*, 187–203.

Haslam, N. (2006). Dehumanization: An integrative review. *Personality and Social Psychology Review, 10*, 252–264.

Hastie, B. (2007a). Cold hearts and bleeding hearts: Disciplinary differences in university students' sociopolitical orientations. *Journal of Social Psychology, 147*, 211–241.

Hastie, B. (2007b). Higher education and sociopolitical orientation: The role of social influence in the liberalisation of students. *European Journal of Psychology of Education, 22*, 259–274.

Hofstede, G. (2001). *Culture's consequences, comparing values, behaviors, institutions, and organizations across nations.* Thousand Oaks, CA: Sage.

Johnson, M. K. (2002). Social origins, adolescent experiences, and work value trajectories during the transition to adulthood. *Social Forces, 80*, 1307–1340.

Kasser, T. (2002). Sketches for a self-determination theory of values. In E. L. Deci & R. M. Ryan (Eds.), *Handbook of self-determination research* (pp. 123–140). Rochester, NY: University of Rochester Press.

Kasser, T., & Ahuvia, A. (2002). Materialistic values and well-being in business students. *European Journal of Social Psychology, 32*, 137–146.

Kasser, T., & Kanner, A. (2003). *Psychology and consumer culture: The struggle for a good life in a materialistic society.* Washington, DC: American Psychological Association.

Kasser, T., Koestner, R., & Lekes, N. (2002). Early family experiences and adult values: A 26-year, prospective longitudinal study. *Personality and Social Psychology Bulletin, 28*, 826–835.

Kasser, T., & Ryan, R. M. (1993). A dark side of the American dream: Correlates of financial success as a central life aspiration. *Journal of Personality and Social Psychology, 65*, 410–422.

Kasser, T., & Ryan, R. M. (1996). Further examining the American dream: Differential correlates of intrinsic and extrinsic goals. *Personality and Social Psychology Bulletin, 22*, 280–287.

Kasser, T., Ryan, R. M., Zax, M., & Sameroff, A. J. (1995). The relations of maternal and social environments to late adolescents' materialistic and prosocial values. *Developmental Psychology, 31*, 907–914.

Kelley, H. H., & Thibaut, J. W. (1969). Group problem solving. In G. Lindzey, & E. Aronson (Eds.), *The handbook of social psychology* (Vol. 4, pp. 1–101). Reading, MA: Addison-Wesley.

Killeen, J., & McCarrey, M. (1986). Relations of altruistic versus competitive values, course of study, and behavioral intentions to help or compete. *Psychological Reports, 59*, 895–898.

Krishnan, V. R. (2008). Impact of MBA education on students' values: Two longitudinal studies. *Journal of Business Ethics, 83*, 233–246.

Kruglanski, A. W. (1989). *Lay epistemics and human knowledge: Cognitive and motivational bases.* New York: Plenum.

Kruglanski, A. W., Raviv, A., Bar-Tal, D., Raviv, A., Sharvit, K., Ellis, S.,…Mannetti, L. (2005). Says who? Epistemic authority effects in social judgment. In M. P. Zanna (Ed.), *Advances in experimental social psychology* (vol. 37, pp. 345–392). New York: Academic Press.

Kruglanski, A. W., & Thompson, E. P. (1999). Persuasion by a single route: A view from the unimodel. *Psychological Inquiry, 10*, 83–109.

Lan, G., Gowing, M., Rieger, F., McMahon, S., & King, N. (2010). Values, value types and moral reasoning of MBA students. *Business Ethics: A European Review, 19*, 183–198.

Lindeman, M., & Verkasalo, M. (2005). Measuring values with the short Schwartz's value survey. *Journal of Personality Assessment, 85*, 170–178.

Lyons, S. T., Duxbury, L., & Higgins, C. (2007). An empirical assessment of generational differences in basic human values. *Psychological Reports, 101*, 339–352.

McCabe, D. L., Butterfield, K. D., & Treviño, L. K. (2006). Academic dishonesty in graduate business programs: Prevalence, causes, and proposed action. *Academy of Management Learning & Education, 5*, 294–305.

McHoskey, J. W. (1999). Machiavellianism, intrinsic versus extrinsic goals, and social interest: A self-determination theory analysis. *Motivation and Emotion, 23*, 267–283.

McKee, I. R., & Feather, N. T. (2008). Revenge, retribution, and values: Social attitudes and punitive sentencing. *Social Justice Research, 21*, 138–163.

McNeel, S. P. (1994). College teaching and student moral development. In J. R. Rest, & D. Narváez (Eds.), *Moral development in the professions: Psychology and applied ethics* (pp. 27–49). Hillsdale, NJ: Lawrence Erlbaum Associates.

Meade, J. (1992). Cheating: Is academic dishonesty par for the course? *ASEE Prism, 1*(7), 30–32.

Merritt, J. (2002). The best B-schools. *Business Week, 42*, 85–100.

Mitroff, I. I. (2004). An open letter to the deans and faculties of American business schools. *Journal of Business Ethics, 54*, 185–189.

Myyry, L. (2008). The diversity of value meanings among university students. *Scandinavian Journal of Educational Research, 52*, 549–564.

Myyry, L., & Helkama, K. (2001). University students' value priorities and emotional empathy. *Educational Psychology, 21*, 25–40.

Neubaum, D. O., Pagell, M., Drexler Jr., J. A., McKee-Ryan, F. M., & Larson, E. (2009). Business education and its relationship to student personal moral philosophies and attitudes toward profits: An empirical response to critics. *Academy of Management Learning & Education, 8*, 9–24.

Nill, A., Schibrowsky, J. A., & Peltier, J. W. (2004). The impact of competitive pressure on students' ethical decision-making in a global setting. *Marketing Education Review, 14*, 1–73.

North Carolina Bar Association. (1991). *Report of the Quality of Life Task Force and recommendations.* Raleigh, NC: Author.

Pascarella, E. T., & Terenzini, P. T. (1991). *How college affects students (Vol. 1): Findings and insights from twenty years of research.* San Francisco, CA: Jossey-Bass.

Pascarella, E. T., & Terenzini, P. T. (2005). *How college affects students (Vol. 2): A third decade of research.* San Francisco, CA: Jossey-Bass.

Petty, R. E., & Cacioppo, J. T. (1986). The elaboration likelihood model of persuasion. In L. Berkowitz (Ed.), *Advances in experimental social psychology* (Vol. 19, pp. 123–205). San Diego, CA: Academic Press.

Pratto, F., & Espinoza, P. (2001). Gender, race, and power. *Journal of Social Issues, 57*, 763–780.

Pratto, F., Stallworth, L., Sidanius, J., & Siers, B. (1997). The gender gap in occupational role attainment: A social dominance approach. *Journal of Personality and Social Psychology, 72*, 37–53.

Priest, M. (2007, April 22). Pressure-cooker lives push lawyers into depression. *Australasian Business Intelligence*, COMTEX News Network, Inc. 2007.

Pritchard, M. E., & McIntosh, D. N. (2003). What predicts adjustment among law students? A longitudinal panel study. *The Journal of Social Psychology, 14*, 727–745.

Raviv, A., Bar-Tal, D., Raviv, A., & Houminer, D. (1990). Development in children's perceptions of epistemic authorities. *British Journal of Developmental Psychology, 8*, 157–169.

Reedy, P., & Learmonth, M. (2009). Other possibilities? The contribution to management education of alternative organizations. *Management Learning, 40*, 241–258.

Rijavec, M., Brdar, I., Miljković, D. (2006). Extrinsic vs. intrinsic life goals, psychological needs, and well-being. In A. Delle Fave (Ed.), *Dimensions of well-being* (pp. 91–103). Milano: Franco Ageli.

Rogers, C. R. (1951). *Client-centered therapy.* Oxford, England: Houghton Mifflin.

Rogers, C. R. (1964). Toward a modern approach to values: The valuing process in the mature person. *The Journal of Abnormal and Social Psychology, 68*, 160–167.

Rohan, M. J. (2000). A rose by any name? The values construct. *Personality and Social Psychology Review, 4*, 255–277.

Rokeach, M. (1968). *Beliefs, attitudes, and values: A theory of organizational change.* San Francisco: Jossey-Bass.

Rokeach, M. (1979). *Understanding human values: Individual and societal.* New York: The Free Press.

Ryan, R. M., & Deci, E. L. (2001). On happiness and human potentials: A review of research on hedonic and eudaimonic well-being. *Annual Review of Psychology, 52*, 141–166.

Ryan, R. M., Deci, E. L., Grolnick, W. S., & La Guardia, J. G. (2006). The significance of autonomy and autonomy support in psychological development and psychopathology. In D. Cicchetti & D. J. Cohen (Eds.), *Developmental psychopathology, Vol. 1: Theory and method* (2nd ed., pp. 795–849). Hoboken, NJ US: John Wiley & Sons.

Schiltz, P. J. (1998). On being a happy, healthy, and ethical member of an unhappy, unhealthy, and unethical profession. *Vanderbilt Law Review, 52*, 871–952.

Schiltz, P. J. (1999). Legal ethics in decline: The elite law firm, the elite law school, and the moral formation of the novice attorney. *Minnesota Law Review, 82*, 705–792.

Schneider, B. (1987). The people make the place. *Personnel Psychology, 40*, 437–453.

Schwartz, S. H. (1992). Universals in the content and structure of values: Theoretical advances and empirical tests in 20 countries. In M. P. Zanna (Ed.), *Advances in experimental social psychology* (vol. 25, pp. 1–65). San Diego: Academic Press.

Schwartz, S. H. (1994). Are there universal aspects in the structure and contents of human values? *Journal of Social Issues, 50*, 19–45.

Schwartz, S. H., & Bardi, A. (2001). Value hierarchies across cultures: Taking a similarities perspective. *Journal of Cross-Cultural Psychology, 32*, 268–290.

Schwartz, S. H., & Bilsky, W. (1987). Toward a universal psychological structure of human values. *Journal of Personality and Social Psychology, 53*, 550–562.

Schwartz, S. H., & Bilsky, W. (1990). Toward a theory of the universal content and structure of values: Extensions and cross-cultural replications. *Journal of Personality and Social Psychology, 58*, 878–891.

Schwartz, S. H., & Boehnke, K. (2004). Evaluating the structure of human values with confirmatory factor analysis. *Journal of Research in Personality, 38*, 230–255.

Schwartz, S. H., Melech, G., Lehmann, A., Burgess, S., & Harris, M. (2001). Extending the cross-cultural validity of the theory of basic human values with a different method of measurement. *Journal of Cross Cultural Psychology, 32*, 519–542.

Schwartz, S. H., & Sagie, G. (2000). Value consensus and importance: A cross-national study. *Journal of Cross-Cultural Psychology, 31*, 465–497.

Schwartz, S. H., & Sagiv, L. (1995). Identifying culture-specifics in the content and structure of values. *Journal of Cross-Cultural Psychology, 26*, 92–116.

Schwepker, C. (1999). Research note: The relationship between ethical conflict, organizational commitment and turnover intentions in the sales force. *Journal of Personal Selling & Sales Management, 19*, 43–49.

Seligman, M. E. P., Verkuil, P. R., Kang, T. H. (2005). Why lawyers are unhappy? *Deakin Law Review, 10*, 49–66.

Senécal, C. B., Pelletier, L. G., & Vallerand, R. J. (1992). Type de programme universitaire et sexe de l'étudiant: Effets sur la perception du climat et sur la motivation. *Revue des sciences de l'éducation, 18*, 375–388.

Sheldon, K. M. (2005). Positive value change during college: Normative trends and individual differences. *Journal of Research in Personality, 39*, 209–223.

Sheldon, K. M., Arndt, J., & Houser-Marko, L. (2003). In search of the organismic valuing process: The human tendency to move towards beneficial goal choices. *Journal of Personality, 71*, 835–869.

Sheldon, K. M., & Kasser, T. (1995). Coherence and congruence: Two aspects of personality integration. *Journal of Personality and Social Psychology, 68*, 531–543.

Sheldon, K. M., & Kasser, T. (2001). Getting older, getting better? Personal strivings and psychological maturity across the life span. *Developmental Psychology, 37*, 491–501.

Sheldon, K. M., & Krieger, L. S. (2004). Does law school undermine law students? Examining changes in goals, values, and well-being. *Behavioral Sciences and the Law, 22*, 261–286.

Sheldon, K. M., & Krieger, L. S. (2007). Understanding the negative effects of legal education on law students: A longitudinal test of self-determination theory. *Personality and Social Psychology Bulletin, 33*, 883–897.

Sheldon, K. M., Sheldon, M., & Osbaldiston, R. (2000). Prosocial values and group assortation within an N-person prisoner's dilemma game. *Human Nature, 11*, 387–404.

Sidanius, J., & Pratto, F. (1999). *Social dominance: An intergroup theory of social hierarchy and oppression.* New York: Cambridge University Press.

Sidanius, J., Pratto, F., Martin, M., & Stallworth, L. M. (1991). Consensual racism and career track: Some implications of social dominance theory. *Political Psychology, 12*, 691–721.

Sidanius, J., Sinclair, S., & Pratto, F. (2006). Social dominance orientation, gender, and increasing educational exposure. *Journal of Applied Social Psychology, 36*, 1640–1653.

Sidanius, J., van Laar, C., Levin, S., & Sinclair, S. (2003). Social hierarchy maintenance and assortment into social roles: A social dominance perspective. *Group Processes & Intergroup Relations, 6*, 333–352.

Sims, R., & Kroeck, K. G. (1994). The influence of ethical fit on employee satisfaction, commitment and turnover. *Journal of Business Ethics, 13*, 939–947.

Smyth, M. L., & Davis, J. R. (2004). Perceptions of dishonesty among two-year college students: Academic versus business situations. *Journal of Business Ethics, 51*, 63–73.

Tang, T., Chen, Y., & Sutarso, T. (2008). Bad apples in bad (business) barrels: The love of money, machiavellianism, risk tolerance, and unethical behavior. *Management Decision, 46*, 243–263.

The Economist (2004, May). 'But can you teach it?' *The Economist, 371(8376)*, 61–63.

Tracey, T. J. G., & Robbins, S. B. (2006). The interest–major congruence and college success relation: A longitudinal study. *Journal of Vocational Behavior, 69*, 64–89.

Triandis, H. C. (1995). *Individualism and collectivism.* Boulder, CO: Westview Press.

Vaara, E., & Faÿ, E. (2011). How can a Bourdieusian perspective aid analysis of MBA education? *Academy of Management Learning & Education, 10*, 27–39.

van Laar, C., Sidanius, J., Rabinowitz, J., & Sinclair, S. (1999). The three R's of academic achievement: Reading, 'riting, and racism. *Personality and Social Psychology Bulletin, 25*, 139–151.

Vansteenkiste, M., Duriez, B., Simons, J., & Soenens, B. (2006). Materialistic values and well-being among business students: Further evidence of their detrimental effect. *Journal of Applied Social Psychology, 36*, 2892–2908.

Vansteenkiste, M., Neyrinck, B., Niemiec, C. P., Soenens, B., De Witte, H., & Van den Broeck, A. (2007). On the relations among work value orientations, psychological need satisfaction and job outcomes: A self-determination theory approach. *Journal of Occupational and Organizational Psychology, 80*, 251–277.

Vansteenkiste, M., Soenens, B., & Duriez, B. (2008). Presenting a positive alternative to materialistic strivings and the thin-ideal: Understanding the effects of extrinsic relative to intrinsic goal pursuits. In S. J. Lopez (Ed.), *Positive psychology (Vol. 4): Exploring the best in people* (pp. 57–86). Westport, CT: Greenwood.

Verkasalo, M., Daun, Å., & Niit, T. (1994). Universal values in Estonia, Finland and Sweden. *Ethnologia Europaea, 24*, 101–117.

Williams, G. C., Cox, E. M., Hedberg, V., & Deci, E. L. (2000). Extrinsic life goals and health risk behaviors in adolescents. *Journal of Applied Social Psychology, 30*, 1756–1771.

CHAPTER
25

A Self-Determination Theory Approach to Goals

Richard Koestner *and* Nora Hope

Abstract

Self-determination theory has expanded goal-setting research beyond the question of how best to set personal goals by exploring questions about the meaning of personal goals. In asking why we pursue a goal, researchers can determine the extent to which a goal is truly personal, in the sense that it emanates from one's abiding interests and values. In asking what is the nature of our aspirations, researchers can estimate the extent to which goal pursuit is likely to satisfy intrinsic psychological needs of relatedness, competence, and autonomy. In asking who will support our goal pursuits, researchers can identify the vital role that close others play in our ongoing struggles to reach valued goals. Goal research inspired by self-determination theory has provided evidence that goal strivings are most successful and adaptive when they are based in autonomous motivation; when they are aligned with intrinsic, need-satisfying aspirations; and when they are supported by empathic rather than directive others.

Key Words: goals, motivation, autonomy, autonomy support, intrinsic aspirations

---

One important way that individuals strive to organize and give meaning to their lives is by setting personal goals. Goals refer to end states that one strives to achieve. For example, a college student may decide at the beginning of the school year that she wants to improve her study habits and to begin an exercise program. Making progress at one's goals is associated with improved well-being, whereas failing is linked with diminished well-being (Diener, Suh, Lucas, & Smith, 1999). Unfortunately, prospective studies suggest that failure at personal goals is more common than success (Baumeister & Tierney, 2011). For example, only about 40% of people who make New Year resolutions report being successful 6 months later (Norcross, Ratzin, & Payne, 1989). The prevalence of personal goal setting, combined with the high rates for failure, raises questions about what individuals can do to improve their chance of success at achieving their goals.

How to Set and Pursue Goals Effectively

A great deal of research has examined the question of *how* to effectively set personal goals. A consensus has emerged among organizational and sports psychology researchers that there are five critical factors to consider in effectively setting goals, with the labels of the five factors corresponding to the acronym of SMART goals (Weinberg & Gould, 2007). It is recommended that individuals frame their goals in a highly *specific* manner, ensure that they can *measure* their progress in relation to the goal, be careful to select goals that are *achievable* by their own efforts, guarantee that the level of difficulty of the goals is *realistic* or moderate, and outline a clear *time-frame* to guide their goal pursuit. Research has shown that setting ambiguous goals, failing to systematically monitor one's progress in relation to goals, and miscalculating one's capacity to reach particular goals are all common problems that lead to self-regulatory failure (Baumeister and Heatherton, 1996). Of the five factors listed previously, organizational researchers have highlighted the central importance of setting specific and challenging goals as opposed to an ambiguous goal like "I will try my best" (Locke & Latham, 2002). Specific goals are thought to direct attention and effort toward goal-relevant activities and away from goal-irrelevant activities. Specific and challenging goals have been shown to lead to the exertion of greater effort (Locke & Latham, 2002).

More recently, a great deal of research has examined the question of how to sustain goal-engagement over time in the face of inevitable problems, such as forgetting to keep the goal in mind, being distracted by competing goals, and exhausting one's self regulatory capacities because of the demands of daily life. There is evidence that carefully formulated implementation plans can alleviate such self-regulatory difficulties (Gollwitzer, 1999; Webb & Sheeran, 2004). Implementation plans are mental planning exercises in which goal setters specify when and where they will initiate their goal pursuit and how they will ensure their persistence in the face of distractions and obstacles (Gollwitzer, 1999). For example, an office worker who has the goal of drinking 32 ounces of water per day can develop an implementation plan that specifies when, where, and how he will reach this goal. He may decide to keep a water bottle at his desk, drink while he is in front of his computer, and refill the bottle from an office fountain each time he goes to check his mail. The specific implementation intention (e.g., drink at my desk, refill bottle) is thus placed under the direct control of situational cues (e.g., computer screen, unfilled bottle, passing water fountain) and removed from conscious and effortful control. Implementation intentions promote successful goal striving because they link desired behaviors with certain situations and allow for automatic responding (Gollwitzer & Schaal, 1998). Implementation intentions can also be tied to subjective motivational states (Achtzinger, Gollwitzer, & Sheeran, 2008). A meta-analysis of more than 100 studies confirmed that people who supplemented their goals with implementation intentions had markedly higher rates of success across diverse goal domains (Gollwitzer & Sheeran, 2006). Importantly, the benefits of implementation intentions held true for goals that were difficult and for goals where progress was measured with objective outcomes.

Why Do We Set a Goal?

Research on *how* to set goals has contributed greatly to our understanding of the ways in which individuals can improve their chances of achieving personal goals. However, there are other important questions about personal goals that concern the interplay of human needs and personal goals in psychological health. In an important chapter titled, "All goals are not created equal: An organismic perspective on the nature of goals and their regulation," Ryan, Sheldon, Kasser, and Deci (1996, p. 7) argue that

> While goal theories typically examine how one can efficaciously pursue goals, they typically ignore **why** one pursues particular goals and/or the significance of **what** specific goals are pursued. Yet both of these issues are critical for understanding the effectiveness, persistence, and experiential qualities associated with goal activity, as well as the functional impact of goal activities on personal well-being.

Ryan and colleagues outlined a self-determination theory (SDT) of personal goals that argued that we must consider the role of innate psychological needs when trying to understand the motivation underlying personal goals and whether achieving a personal goal will translate into improved well-being. The outline was elaborated empirically in two largely separate programs of research lead by Ken Sheldon and Tim Kasser. The present chapter briefly reviews SDT and Ryan et al.'s (1996) hypotheses about goal motivation and goal content. We then systematically review the 15 years of goal-related research that was inspired by Ryan et al.'s (1996) seminal contribution. Finally, we suggest that besides exploring the why and what of goal pursuit, one additional critical question remains: "with whom will one pursue this goal?" Nearly all personal goal pursuits require support from important individuals in our lives if they are to be successfully achieved. Whether such support is forthcoming and what form such support takes may have an important influence on goal pursuit.

SDT (Deci & Ryan, 1985, 2000, 2008) uses the concept of innate, universal, psychological needs to understand human motivation. The theory assumes that all humans have the fundamental needs to feel related, competent, and autonomous, and that satisfaction of these basic needs is required in order to develop and function optimally (Deci & Ryan, 2000). Relatedness refers to feeling close and connected to others, whereas competence refers to feelings of mastery over one's environment. Autonomy refers to the experience of freedom in initiating or endorsing behaviors, that is, to authentically concur with the internal or external forces that influence behaviors (Deci & Ryan, 2000; Ryan & Deci, 2000). The need for autonomy is paramount in SDT largely because it has been neglected in other broad theories of human behavior, which focus instead only on competence and relatedness. The need for autonomy should not be confused with the traits of independence, individualism, or selfishness (Deci & Ryan, 2000). Instead, autonomy is about volitional, harmonious, and integrated functioning, in contrast to more pressured, conflicted, or alienated experiences.

The central issue for an SDT perspective on goal setting is whether the way in which individuals select and pursue their goals reflects processes related to autonomy. The theory suggests that whether motivation for a goal is autonomous can be discerned by asking individuals to report on why they are pursuing the goal. Ryan and colleagues (1996, p. 8) noted the following:

> The why question concerns the source or impetus that gives rise to a goal, and its answer has direct implications for how goal pursuit is regulated. More specifically, the answer to why people perform an action illuminates the regulatory process that underlies it and this has a great many experiential and functional consequences. Perhaps most crucial to answering the why question is whether one perceives the goal-directed behavior emanates from one self or, alternatively, is brought about by forces or pressures external to the self.

An individual can have many different reasons for setting a goal, and these reasons vary in the extent to which they represent autonomy. Thus, one person can pursue an exercise goal because it reflects their evolving interests and personal values, whereas another may be prompted to pursue the same exercise goal because of external or internalized pressures. Furthermore, it is possible for the same individual to simultaneously hold both autonomous and controlled motives for pursuing a goal. The importance of autonomous motivation in goal pursuits was first explored by Sheldon and colleagues, who completed a series of short-term prospective studies that examined the extent to which the source of goals influenced their attainment (Sheldon & Elliot, 1999; Sheldon & Houser-Marko, 2001; Sheldon & Kasser, 1998). College students were asked to list several goals that they planned to strive for during the semester and to rate the goals in terms of the source of their motivation. Specifically, they rated each of four possible reasons, which reflected a continuum running from highly controlled to highly autonomous.

Autonomous goals were defined as those that reflected personal interests and values rather than something one feels compelled to do by external or internal pressures. These studies consistently found that autonomous goals were significantly associated with greater goal progress over time than nonautonomous goals. Other researchers obtained the same pattern of results (Downie, Koestner, Horberg, & Haga, 2006; Koestner et al., 2006; Koestner, Lekes, Powers, & Chicoine, 2002). A meta-analysis of prospective studies examining the relation of goal autonomy to goal progress yielded an average r of .20 (Koestner, Otis, Powers, Pelletier, & Gagnon, 2008). Thus, having goals that are tied to personal interests and values was consistently related to greater goal progress.

The question of why we set goals is more complex when one considers goal pursuit in work settings. Because organizations often prescribe goals for their employees, one might think that personal goal setting would not be relevant in work settings. However, there is considerable evidence that the effects of assigned goals are mediated by personal goals that people choose in response to the assignment (Locke & Latham, 2002). Thus, prescribed goals are transformed by individual workers into personal goals, which may vary in the extent to which they are experienced as volitional and autonomous. Allowing workers to participate in setting goals appears to result in better performance than having the supervisor simply assign the goals (Locke & Latham, 2002). Most interestingly, Judge, Bono, Erez, and Locke (2005) tested Sheldon's model of goal autonomy in a prospective study of 251 employees. Their results showed that goal autonomy in the work setting was significantly related to goal progress and job satisfaction. These researchers highlighted the implications of their findings by noting that personal goals may be flexible and sensitive enough to allow organizations to help workers improve their work-life by pursuing more autonomous goals at work, ones that are tied into their intrinsic interests and identified values.

Several studies also examined the specific nature of the relationship between goal autonomy and goal progress. Thus, it was shown that the benefits of having autonomous goals were maintained after controlling for personality traits, such as neuroticism and self-regulatory skill (Sheldon, 2002). Autonomous goals were also associated with greater goal progress even when controlling for other important goal variables, such as importance, commitment, and difficulty level (Koestner et al., 2002). The benefits of autonomy were demonstrated with sophisticated goal attainment scaling methods (Sheldon & Elliot, 1998) and objective measures of goal progress, such as weight loss measured in a laboratory (Koestner et al., 2008). Self-reports of goal autonomy were confirmed by peer reports, and it was shown that the goal progress effects held up over a 6-month time span (Koestner et al., 2006). Finally, the effect of autonomy on progress was shown to be mediated by the capacity to maintain sustained effort (Sheldon & Elliot, 1998, 1999). That is, autonomous goals appear to be protected and maintained in the face of task-irrelevant temptations because they are continually energized. Reduced conflict among personal goals has also been associated with goal autonomy (Downie et al., 2006), reflecting the fact that goals that are tied to one's true self are more likely to be harmonious and synergistic.

Although the association between autonomous motivation and positive goal progress has been reliably demonstrated, there are two problems with this body of research. First, the effect size of the relation between goal autonomy and progress (Pearson $r =.20$), although statistically significant, would be categorized as small. It is the kind of relation that could not be easily recognized by observers. The second problem is that research on autonomy and goals is almost entirely correlational in nature, thus leaving open the possibility that some unmeasured third variable is accounting for both the level of autonomy and the goal progress. For example, one might argue that more psychologically mature individuals (e.g., those high in ego development) are likely to report both greater autonomous motivation and greater well-being, and thus an apparent relation between the latter two variables may simply be due to their association with level of ego development. Experimental evidence in which participants are randomly assigned to conditions designed to enhance autonomous motivation versus a controlled condition are required to demonstrate that increases in autonomous motivation will result in enhanced goal progress over time.

Two attempts to use experimental procedures to enhance autonomy for goals and to measure subsequent goal progress yielded only partially successful results. Koestner et al. (2002) demonstrated that a brief self-reflection exercise, in which participants considered the intrinsic, personally meaningful reasons for pursuing New Year's resolutions, increased their level of autonomy for the goals and that goal autonomy, in turn, was associated with goal progress. The study failed, however, to find a direct effect of the self-reflection condition on goal progress. Sheldon, Kasser, Smith, and Share (2002) assigned college students randomly either to a goal-training program focused on enhancing autonomy or to a control condition. The goal training program was designed to "promote participants' sense of ownership of their listed goals and also their ability to regulate their experiences as they pursued the goals" (Sheldon et al., 2002, p. 8). The intervention consisted of two counseling sessions in which diverse methods were used to present and reinforce strategies for enhancing goal functioning. The results revealed no main effects of program participation on later goal attainment, but a significant interaction effect indicated that participants who were already high in autonomy perceived the program as most useful and benefited the most from the program in terms of goal attainment. Clearly, more experimental studies are required to confirm the causal relation between autonomous motivation and goal progress.

The obtained small effect size between goal autonomy and goal progress may underestimate the importance of autonomy in goal pursuit because autonomy may exert indirect effects on goal pursuit by fostering goal-supporting behaviors. Importantly, there is evidence that individuals with autonomous goals are better prepared to use implementation plans to reach their goals. In a pair of studies, Koestner et al. (2002) examined the combined effect of autonomous goals and implementation plans. It was hypothesized that pursuing goals because of personal interest and meaning would be especially helpful to progress when such autonomous goals were accompanied by implementation plans specifying "How will I get started?" and "How will I stay on task?" The results of both studies revealed significant interaction effects between autonomy and implementations reflecting the fact that autonomy moderated the effect of implementation plans on goal progress, such that implementation plans were associated with relatively greater goal progress when combined with autonomous goals. Two later studies confirmed that implementation intentions are more effective when individuals hold autonomous rather than controlled goals (Koestner et al., 2008). Thus, autonomy may indirectly foster greater goal progress by potentiating the effects of implementation plans.

The special value of linking autonomy and implementation plans was also demonstrated in an experimental study in which implementation plans were given in an autonomy-supportive, controlling, or neutral manner (Koestner et al., 2006, Study 1). Students were asked to list their most important academic and social goals. They were then instructed to take a few minutes to outline their implementation plans, but they were guided in this exercise in either a way that emphasized choice and self-initiation or a way that was pressuring and directive. The results showed that autonomy-supportive implementation plans led participants to feel more autonomous about how they made their plans. That is, they reported that the plans they developed seemed to reflect who they were and in what they believed. At a 1-month follow-up, the autonomy-supportive implementation plans resulted in greater goal progress than the no-implementation condition, whereas the controlling implementation plans had no effect relative to the control condition.

Why does the combination of autonomy and implementation plans yield such positive goal progress? The interactive effects of having autonomous goals along with implementation intentions can be explained in reference to Kuhl and Fuhrmann's (1998) dual-component model of volition. These researchers contend that effective goal pursuit involves maintaining an awareness of aspects of oneself that support the goal while concomitantly developing strategies to maintain the goal in consciousness when competing motivations arise. One can accomplish the former process of self-maintenance by selecting goals that are autonomous, whereas one can facilitate the latter process of goal maintenance by making implementation intentions, which have been shown to facilitate retrieval of goal intentions in memory, heighten accessibility of environmental cues for goal completion, and reduce the number of interruptions while one is in goal pursuit (Gollwitzer, 1999). Both self-maintenance and goal maintenance are viewed as necessary conditions for goal success.

Some recent research suggests that how autonomy is defined and measured in relation to goal progress requires refinement. Goal autonomy has typically been examined with a summary index that subtracts controlled motivation (pressure from others and from introjects) from autonomous motivation (based on intrinsic and identified reasons). The rationale for this method was previous theorizing and evidence that an underlying continuum of self-determination can be identified in the correlations among scales assessing intrinsic, identified, introjected, and external regulation (Ryan & Connell, 1989). Researchers have noted two potential problems in aggregating autonomous and controlled goals to form a summary self-concordance index (Judge et al., 2005). First, autonomy and control are often not significantly negatively related to each other, as one may expect if a difference score was to be calculated with them. Instead, the scales were nonsignificantly positively related. Second, the relations of autonomous and controlled reasons to various goal outcomes were not mirror image opposites. Indeed, in two studies of working adults by Judge et al. (2005), autonomous goals were associated with positive outcomes, whereas controlled goals were unrelated to outcomes (rather than being negatively related to positive outcomes).

The results of three studies indicated that the relation between autonomous goal motivation and controlled goal motivation was surprisingly small, with an average r of only $-.02$ (Koestner et al., 2008). Furthermore, although autonomous motivation was substantially related to goal progress, controlled motivation was unrelated to progress in all three studies. These results suggest that intrinsic motivation and identification may represent the active ingredients that account for the positive relation of autonomous motivation to goal progress. Stated differently, it seems that having external and introjected motivation for pursuing a goal does not reliably *impede* progress; instead, the effects of these controlled motives tend to be null. Practically speaking, what this refinement means is that individuals who reflect on their reasons for choosing a goal should be most concerned with enhancing their level of autonomous motivation rather than struggling to reduce their controlled motivation. Fortunately, there is evidence that intrinsic motivation and identification can be enhanced by various techniques that could be adapted for self-use (Cordova & Lepper, 1996; Green-Demers et al., 1998). For organizations, this research suggests that a focus on promoting intrinsic and identified motivation will be more fruitful than trying to curb or eradicate extrinsic and introjected forms of motivation.

Many of the studies that examined the relation of autonomy to goal progress also included measures of well-being, as reflected in reports of positive emotions, life satisfaction, vitality, and the absence of negative affect. These studies consistently found that achieving goal progress was reliably associated with significant improvements in well-being over time

404 | A SELF-DETERMINATION THEORY APPROACH TO GOALS

(Koestner et al., 2002). Two studies also obtained support for a more fine-grained prediction: that goal progress will especially result in enhanced well-being when the goals were rooted in autonomous rather than controlled motivation. Thus, achieving a fitness goal that was motivated by personal interests and values was more likely to enhance well-being than achieving a similar fitness goal motivated by pressure from others. Finally, a multiwave study by Sheldon and Houser-Marko(2001) showed that there are reciprocal relations among autonomy, goal progress, and well-being such that the enhanced well-being that resulted from students success in one semester was associated with setting more autonomous goals in the subsequent semester, which in turn was associated with greater goal progress and further increases in well-being. The authors suggested that selecting autonomous goals may set in motion a virtuous upward cycle involving goal progress and well-being.

What Goals Do We Choose to Pursue?

The preceding section highlighted how self-determination theorists encouraged a shift in goal research from asking "how can people set goals effectively?" to the question of "why do we set certain goals?" We reviewed research that has explored the experiential and functional effects of choosing relatively more or less autonomous goals. There is now mounting evidence that selecting autonomous goals (i.e., ones that connect with our interests and values) typically results in greater goal progress. This greater progress appears to be due to certain experiential benefits of autonomous goals: they allow individuals to exert more effort, and to experience less conflict as they pursue their goals (Koestner 2008). Autonomous goal motivation also appears to allow individuals to make better use of implementation plans that specify how, when, and where they will enact goal-directed behaviors.

The second unique addition of SDT to goal-setting research is that it has encouraged researchers to look more carefully at the specific content of the goals that individuals strive for. Thus, in their classic chapter in the edited volume *The Psychology of Action: Linking Cognition and Motivation to Behaviour*, Ryan et al. (1996) argued that not all goals are created equal and that there are distinct experiential and functional effects that are tied to whether the content of the goals allows individuals to satisfy their basic psychological needs for autonomy, competence, and relatedness. Although most of the research in this area has been done at the level of the individual, there is a natural bridge between how the content of goals differentially impacts the well-being and motivation of a group of individuals, and how overarching institutional goals (e.g., as expressed by the mission statement and workplace culture) impact employee well-being and motivation.

Tim Kasser and Richard Ryan hypothesized that the pursuit (and attainment) of only certain goals provides direct satisfaction of the basic psychological needs, thereby enhancing well-being (Kasser & Ryan, 1993, 1996). They differentiated between two basic forms of goal striving: the pursuit of extrinsic and intrinsic aspirations. *Intrinsic aspirations* are those that inherently satisfy the core psychological needs (of relatedness, autonomy, and competence), such as striving for personal growth, building intimate relationships, and community contribution. In contrast, *extrinsic aspirations* are those that are contingent on the approval of others or another form of external reward, such as striving for wealth, popularity, and beauty.

Initially the research was particularly interested in how financial and materialistic aspirations impact well-being. Kasser and Ryan observed that there was almost no empirical examination of the effects of materialistic aspirations on well-being, despite an abundance of theorizing on the subject among 20th century humanistic psychologists, such as Abraham Maslow, Carl Rogers, and Erich Fromm (Kasser 2002a). Rogers (1961) theorized that the good life is one in which the person continues to grow throughout life; enjoys every moment rather than seeking means to an end; and acts authentically as oneself rather than conforming to external pressures from others, or presenting a false façade. Fromm (1976) warned that the great promise of mass production and material expansion that grew from the industrial revolution provided false hope and a deleterious path away from achieving well-being and fulfillment in life. He cautioned that being guided by the gain of external rewards, or approval from others, was the route to unhappiness.

In their original study, Kasser and Ryan (1993) hypothesized individuals who set goals on the basis of intrinsic aspirations benefit from enhanced psychological health and well-being in comparison with individuals that set goals on the basis of extrinsic aspirations. The pursuit of extrinsic goals may detract from the fulfillment of basic psychological needs, and thus decrease well-being. In order to test the hypothesis that the specific content of goals can differentially enhance or thwart psychological health, these researchers created the aspirations index, which assesses the centrality of a number of aspirations in an individual. Aspirations are defined as relatively stable beliefs that transcend objects and situations and guide our actions. In the original version of the aspirations index participants rated the importance of aspirations related to financial success, affiliation, self-development, and community contributions. Results of an initial study showed that students who prioritized financial aspirations over intrinsic aspirations reported very low levels of self-actualization, as well as high levels of depression and anxiety (Kasser & Ryan 1993).

In a second study, the centrality of financial aspirations was again shown to be negatively correlated to college students' well-being and mental health (Kasser & Ryan 1993). In a third study that used a clinical interview to assess adjustment in a community sample of youth, the researchers found that financial aspirations were associated with lower global adjustment, lower social productivity, and more behavioral disorders (Kasser & Ryan, 1993). At this time, the aspirations index was revised to include two other common aspirations of capitalistic cultures beyond financial success: the possession of good looks or beauty, and fame or social popularity. Factor analyses of the revised aspiration index showed that individuals who placed great importance on one of the three extrinsic aspirations, such as beauty, tended to place importance on the other two, supporting the validity of a cluster of extrinsic aspirations. The intrinsic aspirations were also shown to cluster together. The initial study with the revised aspirations index revealed that adults who reported the strongest orientation towards extrinsic aspirations relative to intrinsic aspirations tended to report more symptoms of depression, and scored lower on self-actualization and vitality.

The negative correlation between orientation toward extrinsic aspirations and well-being has been replicated in more recent university samples in North America (Sheldon, Ryan, Deci, & Kasser, 2004), as well as extended to Russia (Ryan et al., 1999), Germany, (Schmuck, Kasser, & Ryan, 2000), Singapore (Kasser & Ahuvia, 2002), and South Korea (Kim, Kasser, & Lee, 2003). In addition to the evidence from correlational studies, a longitudinal study by Sheldon and Kasser (1998) found that well-being was significantly enhanced by attaining intrinsic goals, whereas attaining extrinsic goals conferred no significant benefits. A more recent study extended these findings by prospectively following a large group of college graduates

over 1 year, tracking the attainment of both extrinsic and intrinsic goals (Niemiec, Ryan, & Deci, 2009). Results revealed that the attainment of intrinsic goals was positively related to measures of well-being, yet the attainment of extrinsic goals was positively related to measures of *ill-being* (negative affect, anxiety, and physical symptoms). In another recent study, Sheldon and colleagues demonstrated that individuals with a strong orientation toward extrinsic aspirations are vulnerable to making "affective forecasting errors," tending to overestimate the emotional benefits of attaining extrinsic goals (Sheldon, Gunz, Nichols, & Ferguson, 2010). In a correlational study, the researchers found that those with an extrinsic orientation are less happy than those with an intrinsic orientation, but tend to believe that attaining extrinsic goals will bring about happiness.

The research on the benefits of intrinsic versus extrinsic aspirations seems to have implications of goal pursuit in work organizations. Most organizations emphasize salary and benefits as a way to recruit and retain valued employees. Although it is certainly true that workers must feel that their compensation is commensurate with their training, skills, and contribution, these more "extrinsic" aspects may not be as important to workers' motivation and satisfaction as are other less salient aspects of work organizations, such as the larger values of the organization, the work-climate, and the opportunity for cooperation and autonomy in how one pursues one's work goals. It has been noted that the three job qualities that are most strongly associated with job satisfaction are autonomy, complexity, and strong connections between effort and rewards (Gladwell, 2008). Organizations are therefore well advised to balance their emphasis on financial rewards with an emphasis on opportunities to pursue autonomous, complex, and satisfyingly effortful activities.

Do certain environments foster the development of extrinsic aspirations? In an important longitudinal study by Sheldon and Krieger (2004), changes in both aspirations and subjective well-being were investigated in law students from entry into law school to the end of the first year. It was hypothesized that the competitive structure and intense pressure at law school causes students to orient away from intrinsic personal aspirations, toward reward, image, and popularity-based aspirations, causing a steady deterioration of well-being and life satisfaction. The students were found to have begun law school with significantly *higher* levels of subjective well-being than a comparison sample of undergraduates, but their well-being was shown to decline steeply over the course of the year. Importantly, Sheldon and Krieger demonstrated that the law students' drastic change in well-being was linked with marked decreases in intrinsic aspiration orientation relative to extrinsic aspirations over the first year of law school. This pattern of results was replicated over a longer period of time in a second school, showing once again that law students experienced an increase in extrinsic aspirations relative to intrinsic aspirations over time, as well as a simultaneous decline in well-being. Interestingly, Grouzet (Chapter 24 in this Handbook) reviews evidence that business training may have a similar powerful impact on extrinsic aspirations and well-being outcomes.

Although the research that found a relationship between the prioritization of extrinsic over intrinsic aspirations, and decreased well-being, increased anxiety, and depression is striking, causation cannot be inferred from correlational and longitudinal research. That is to say, whereas intrinsic aspiration prioritization in goal setting appears to be linked to well-being, without experimental research, other external factors (e.g., genetics, personality, and family environment) cannot be ruled out. The question of whether intrinsic orientation leads to enhanced well-being can only be answered by directly manipulating aspirations as the independent variable, and examining whether an experimentally controlled change in aspirations leads to a change in well-being.

Recognizing the need for experimental studies on the emergence and consequences of orientation toward extrinsic relative to intrinsic aspirations, researchers began designing experimental studies involving aspirations. In a series of three experimental studies, Sheldon and Kasser (2008) demonstrated that psychological threat increases orientation toward extrinsic, compared with intrinsic goals. Kasser had previously proposed that environmental conditions, or temporary threats, that thwart psychological need satisfaction will provoke orientation toward extrinsic goals as a compensatory strategy (2002b). An exploratory study showed that when individuals are made aware of their own mortality, they are more likely to orient toward extrinsic goals. A second study showed that imagining an economic threat (being unable to find a job and barely scraping by after graduating from college) was associated with displaying a stronger orientation to extrinsic goals relative to intrinsic goals, compared with a control condition (Sheldon & Kasser, 2008). In a final study, Sheldon, Gunz, and colleagues (2010)

designed a longitudinal experimental study in which participants were randomly assigned to pursue three extrinsic goals or three intrinsic goals (e.g., get to know someone beyond the superficial level) over a 4-week period. Results showed that participants in the intrinsic goal pursuit condition (regardless of whether they were intrinsically or extrinsically oriented prior to participation in the study) tended to experience increased well-being following the attainment of intrinsic goals. Participants did not benefit from attaining extrinsic goals, even when they had strong extrinsic aspiration orientations prior to participation in the study (Sheldon, Gunz, et al., 2010).

In another 6-month longitudinal experimental study, participants were randomly assigned to set goals in one of three experimental conditions, all based on enhancing the satisfaction of the three core psychological needs, or one comparison condition (Sheldon, Abad, et al., 2010). Participants in the three treatment conditions were instructed to set four goals to pursue in order to enhance feelings of autonomy, competence, or relatedness in life, whereas participants in the comparison condition were instructed to set goals to change their circumstances (such as changing one's appearance, buying certain products, or moving to a higher income neighborhood) over the next 6 months. Both goal progress and subjective well-being were measured after 2, 4, and 6 months. The authors predicted that there would be a significant interaction between treatment and goal progress, more specifically, that participants in the intrinsic treatment conditions who reported significant progress on their goals would experience increased well-being, whereas those in the comparison condition would not, even if they attained their changing life circumstances goals. The results confirmed this prediction, showing that among participants who reported high levels of goal progress, only those in the three intrinsic treatment conditions reported significant changes in well-being. These experimental studies highlight the potential for using life aspiration manipulations as a pathway for improving well-being.

Most recently, Lekes, Hope, Gouveia, Koestner, and Philippe (2012) explored whether an orientation toward intrinsic aspirations relative to extrinsic aspirations could be increased through a reflection intervention, and whether this increased prioritization of intrinsic aspirations would subsequently lead to an increase in well-being. Although this represented a first attempt to manipulate orientation to intrinsic and extrinsic aspirations, there have been other studies that attempted to intervene on participants' aspirations priorities (e.g., value self-confrontation; Rokeach, 1973; Grube, Mayton, & Ball-Rokeach, 1994).

In the Lekes et al. (2012) study, participants attended an initial laboratory session, and completed follow-up activities by email for the following 4 weeks. In the laboratory session, participants were randomized into the experimental intrinsic aspirations group, or an active control condition in which focused on "life details." Participants in the experimental condition were given information and exercises that outlined the differences between intrinsic and extrinsic aspirations, and provided rationale as well as previous research on why people who prioritize intrinsic over extrinsic aspirations often experience enhanced well-being compared with those who prioritize extrinsic aspirations. Experimental participants completed a series of exercises to demonstrate that they discerned the difference between intrinsic and extrinsic aspirations, followed by a 20-minute written essay in which they reflected on their two most important intrinsic aspirations as selected from a list, outlining why they were important to them, and how these aspirations were incorporated into their life. In the control group, participants were given a parallel set of exercises; however, the topic was "life details" (based on the protocol of Sheldon & Lyubormirsky, 2006) rather than intrinsic aspirations. In alignment with the intrinsic aspirations condition, participants were given text that informed them that they were receiving an intervention designed to increase well-being, because paying attention to life details could be beneficial to psychological health.

In order to maintain the effects of treatment and prompt further reflection, participants were emailed weekly reflection activities and reminded of the intrinsic aspirations (or life details in the case of the control group) about which they had written. The weekly reflection included two quotes reflecting intrinsic aspirations and a new reflection question that participants responded to by email. The researchers found an increase in well-being in the experimental group, demonstrating initial efficacy of the treatment. This change in well-being was mediated by increased orientation toward intrinsic relative to extrinsic aspirations. Furthermore, it was found that those participants who reported high levels of engagement in the weekly intervention activities tended to experience the largest changes in well-being. At the end of the 4-week intervention, the more engaged participants had been in the

reflection exercises, the more they prioritized intrinsic over extrinsic aspirations, and the greater their well-being.

The recent experimental studies conducted by Lekes et al. and Sheldon et al. provide initial support for the idea that holding intrinsic rather than extrinsic life aspirations is *causally* related to enhanced well-being, whereas holding a preponderance of extrinsic aspirations is *causally* related to diminished well-being. It will be interesting to see whether such brief interventions can be successfully used in work and clinical settings.

The What and Why of Goal Pursuit

One consideration to keep in mind when examining the *what* (content) and *why* (motivation) of goal striving, is that there is a significant interplay between the two that cannot be neglected. Skeptics of the self-determination approach to studying life aspirations raised the question, "is an intrinsic aspiration still beneficial to well-being if it is pursued for controlled (non-autonomous) reasons?" For example, an individual could volunteer for a local environmental group involved in cleaning up the community (a seemingly intrinsic aspiration) not because they personally value the activity, but to gain approval from a friend or family member. Carver and Baird (1998) posited that both autonomous and controlled reasons could influence an individual's aspirations, and that this would contribute to the influence of an aspiration on well-being. Carver and Baird tested this prediction and found that an individual's endorsement of autonomous reasons for *either* intrinsic or extrinsic aspirations was positively related to self-actualization, whereas endorsement of controlled reasons for intrinsic or extrinsic aspirations was negatively related to self-actualization.

Self-determination theorists responded to Carver and Baird's concerns, and conducted three studies that examined both aspirations, and autonomous versus controlled motives (Sheldon et al., 2004). However, in contrast to Carver and Baird, these SDT researchers predicted extrinsic versus intrinsic aspirations would contribute "to the prediction of well-being, over and above the influence of autonomous versus controlled motives" (p. 477). In the first of three studies, Sheldon et al. found that participants' self-reported autonomous motivation for a series of aspirations was significant and positively related to well-being independent of goal content. As the researchers predicted, goal content (endorsing intrinsic vs. extrinsic aspirations) was also significantly related to well-being, independent of the participants' motives for pursuing a goal. A second correlational study replicated these findings, whereas a third study used a 1-year prospective longitudinal design to following participants' evolving intrinsic and extrinsic aspirations, as well as the motives behind them. Once again, it was found that motives behind goal pursuit (the *why* of goal pursuit) and goal content (the *what* of goal pursuit) had independent effects of well-being. Autonomous motivation for aspirations had a significantly positive effect on well-being, controlled motivation for aspirations had no effect, and extrinsic relative to intrinsic aspirations had a negative effect on well-being (Sheldon et al., 2004). These studies underscore the importance of considering both content of goals, and the motive behind pursuing those goals in psychological research on goal striving and well-being.

With Whom Are You Pursuing the Goal?

The present review has noted how self-determination theorists have extended goal research to explore whether the reason why people select a goal will influence their progress and whether the content of people's goals (are they related to satisfying basic needs) will influence adaptive outcomes. There is considerable evidence that autonomous motivation is associated with goal progress and that a focus on intrinsic aspirations is associated with well-being. Researchers are currently engaged in confirming that the association of autonomy with goal progress and intrinsic aspirations with well-being are causal in nature.

We suggest that there is one final contribution SDT can make to guide research on personal goals. Specifically, recent research in diverse domains has highlighted the importance of other people in our goal pursuits. Thus, if a middle-aged man has a goal to improve his health by exercising and eating better, the likelihood of him succeeding depends on whether important people in his life (e.g., wife, friends, and children) support him in his goal efforts. Indeed, recent health research attests to the dramatic influence of social networks on whether individuals change maladaptive health behaviors, such as smoking. Social support can take many forms, including emotional, tangible, direct, and indirect. SDT can provide guidance for this research by highlighting the kinds of support that are likely to promote effective and fulfilling goal striving.

The motivational role of other people in relation to goal pursuits has primarily been examined in terms of how healthcare providers help motivate patients to achieve goals, such as losing weight or quitting smoking. The role of both autonomous motivation and autonomy support in relation to health-related goals has been examined extensively by Williams and his colleagues (Williams, Gagné, Ryan, & Deci, 2002; Williams, Grow, Freedman, Ryan, & Deci, 1996; Williams, McGregor, Zeldman, Freedman, & Deci, 2004). These studies assessed autonomy in terms of an individual's reasons for pursuing a specific health goal, with a distinction made between autonomous reasons for goal pursuit ("I plan to stay in this weight loss program because it is important to me personally to succeed in losing weight") versus controlled reasons ("because I'll feel like a failure if I don't"). However, Williams and colleagues also assessed the extent to which individuals perceive healthcare personnel to be supportive of their autonomy as they pursue their health goals ("My doctor listens to how I would like to do things"). Both autonomous motivation and autonomy support appear to play an important role in achieving health-related goals. In one study, autonomous motivation predicted greater weight loss in a sample of obese patients and also predicted better maintenance of that weight loss (Williams et al., 1996). Autonomous motivation for weight loss was, in turn, predicted by perceived autonomy support from the healthcare providers. In a study of diabetes management, autonomy and competence were predicted by perceived autonomy support from providers, and changes in perceptions of autonomy and competence predicted greater glycemic control (Williams et al., 2004). Similar results have been found in studies of smoking cessation and adherence to other medical treatments (Williams, Gagné, et al., 2002; Williams, Minicucci, et al., 2002). Furthermore, this line of research has been extended to examine the role of goal motivation in individuals' efforts in psychotherapy to overcome such problems as depression (Zuroff et al., 2007).

Some research has also explored the role of friends and family in facilitating personal goal pursuit. Social support can facilitate progress on personal goals because it serves to enhance feelings of self-efficacy, transforms the interest level of goal-related activities, and helps individuals generate effective coping strategies (Aspinwall, 2004). SDT research has shown, however, that the effect of other people's motivational support depends on whether it is perceived as autonomy supportive versus controlling (Deci, Koestner, & Ryan, 1999; Downie et al., 2006).

Autonomy support involves taking another's perspective, acknowledging feelings, and encouraging self-initiation and self direction (Koestner, Ryan, Bernieri, & Holt, 1984). Control involves pressuring someone to act, think, or feel in a particular way. Earlier studies showed that motivational effect of rewards, limits, and feedback depended on whether they were delivered in an autonomy-supportive rather than controlling manner (Deci et al., 1999; Joussemet, Koestner, Lekes, & Houlfort, 2004).

The preponderance of research has examined the role of autonomy support from healthcare providers; however, a measure of autonomy support that patients perceived from their "important others" was developed by Williams, et al. (2006). These researchers demonstrated that such support was associated with increases in perceived autonomy and perceived competence, as well as better progress on goals, such as smoking cessation and dietary change. Furthermore, the measure of autonomy support from important others provided variance distinct from a measure of autonomy support from the healthcare providers. When allowed to compete for variance, both sources of support contributed to smoking outcomes, but the important other measure appeared to be the stronger and more consistent predictor of dietary outcomes (Williams et al., 2006). This finding demonstrates the importance of partner support, and suggests that autonomy support from significant others may be even more important than the support of healthcare providers.

Can autonomy support be distinguished from other types of support commonly offered to individuals who are pursuing a goal? A study by Powers, Koestner, and Gorin (2008) compared the influence of autonomy support from family and friends with encouraging directive support on participants' goal motivation and weight-related goal progress over time. Female college students with a specific weight-loss goal reported on the support they received from significant others (and their current goal progress) three times over a month's time. All participants were also given information on healthy weight loss strategies, but this information was conveyed in an autonomy-supportive versus neutral manner. The results showed that participants reported significantly greater weight loss when they perceived their family and friends as supporting their autonomy as they pursued their goal. An example of an item assessing autonomy support was, "I feel that my family and friends understood how I see things with respect to my weight." Autonomy support from family and friends also interacted with the autonomy-supportive instruction to produce higher levels of progress. The effects of autonomy support were distinguished from more directive support from significant others, which did not show similar effects. An example of an item assessing directive support was, "My family and friends consistently called attention to situations where I had to control my behavior." The findings highlight the specific importance of receiving autonomy support as one pursues health-related goals.

A more recent study examined the role of autonomy support versus more directive support in the context of an 18-month randomized control intervention for overweight individuals (Gorin et al, in press). The study distinguished between autonomy-support from one's partner or family member and more directive forms of support, such as encouraging one to eat a healthy diet. The results showed that autonomy support and autonomous motivation assessed at 6 months were significantly positively associated with weight loss at 18 months, whereas the more directive form of support was significantly negatively related to weight loss. These results highlight the uniquely helpful aspects of autonomy support from friends and family as one pursues health-related goals.

Is autonomy support equally important for other kinds of personal goals? A recent investigation further explored the functional significance of receiving autonomous versus directive support from close others as one pursued a range of personal goals (Koestner et al., 2012). Specifically, three studies examined the relations of autonomy support versus directive support to goal progress over 3 months. Autonomy support was defined in terms of empathic, perspective-taking ("my friend understands how I see my goals"), whereas directive support was defined in terms of the provision of positive guidance ("my friend reminds me what I need to be doing"). Study 1 involved male-female romantic partners reporting about goals in four domains; Study 2 included female-friend dyads reporting goals in three domains; and Study 3 involved individuals who reported on a vicarious goal another person held for them. Participants' goal progress, relationship quality, and well-being were followed over 3 months. Factor analyses supported the distinction between autonomous and directive forms of support. Results from Study 1 revealed that autonomy support was significantly positively related to goal progress over 3 months, and that the beneficial effect of autonomy support was mediated by enhanced autonomous goal motivation. Study 2 extended the goal progress results to include both self-reports and reports by peers. Study 3 showed that autonomy support similarly promoted progress at vicarious goals. Across all three studies, autonomy support was significantly associated with improved dyadic functioning and personal well-being. Directive support was not associated with goal progress across the three studies and was unrelated to relationship quality or well-being. The pattern of results points to the importance of distinguishing autonomy support from other forms of encouraging support that are commonly offered as we pursue our personal goals, especially in the context of coequal relationships.

The Unique Elements of a Self-Determination Perspective on Personal Goals

The major contribution of SDT to research on goal pursuit is that it has expanded the focus beyond the primarily technical questions of how best to set personal goals to a deeper set of questions about the meaning of our personal goals. In asking why we pursue a goal, researchers can determine the extent to which the goal is truly personal, in the sense that it emanates from one's abiding interests and values rather than from influences outside the self. In asking what is the nature of our life aspirations, researchers can estimate the extent to which goal pursuit is likely to satisfy intrinsic psychological needs of relatedness, competence, and autonomy, and thus foster growth and development. In asking who will support our goal pursuits, researchers can identify the vital supportive role that our close others play in our ongoing struggles to reach valued goals. Goal research inspired by SDT has provided evidence that goal strivings are most successful and adaptive when they are aligned with intrinsic, need-satisfying aspirations; when they are based in autonomous motivation; and when they are supported by empathic rather than directive others.

Future Directions

Future research should explore SDT propositions about goal setting and goal pursuit in work contexts. Here are five questions that merit attention:

1. Why do some workers align their personal goals with organizational goals, whereas others do not? Leadership qualities and interpersonal style of managers no doubt play an important role (Gagné & Deci, 2005).

2. What is the role of intrinsic versus identified motivation for goals in organizational settings? Some previous research has suggested that identified motivation may be more important than intrinsic motivation in domains where participation has compulsory aspects (Koestner & Losier, 2002). Indeed, some researchers have suggested that intrinsic motivation may distract workers from organizational goals (Osterloh & Frey, 2000).

3. Who exerts the greatest influence on worker's goal-setting practices, managers or coworkers? Some interesting recent research suggests that coworkers may have at least as strong of a motivational influence as managers (Moreau & Mageau, 2012).

4. What role do intrinsic and extrinsic aspirations play in the workplace? Will workplaces that emphasize opportunities for personal growth, good relationships, and community concern provide greater opportunities for workers' need satisfaction and well-being.

5. Is it possible to design cost-efficient interventions that encourage workers to self-regulate in a more autonomous manner, to link their goals with intrinsic aspirations, and to provide their coworkers with autonomy-supportive goal supports? The combination of autonomous goal motivation but cooperative work style would seem to be ideal for the complex and creative tasks required by knowledge-based economies.

References

Achtziger, A., Gollwitzer, P. M., & Sheeran, P. (2008). Implementation intentions and shielding goal striving from unwanted thoughts and feelings. *Personality and Social Psychology Bulletin, 34*, 381–393.

Aspinwall, L. G. (2004). Dealing with adversity: Self-regulation, coping, adaptation, and health. In M. B Brewer, and M. Hewstone (Eds.), *Applied social psychology* (pp. 3–27). Malden, MA: Blackwell Publishing.

Baumeister, R. F., & Heatherton, T. F. (1996). Self-regulations failure: An overview. *Psychological Inquiry, 7*, 1–15.

Baumeister, R. F., & Tierney, J. (2011). *Willpower: Rediscovering the greatest human strength*. New York: Penguin Press.

Carver, C. S., & Baird, E. (1998). The American dream revisited: Is it *what* you want or *why* you want it that matters? *Psychological Science, 9*(4), 289.

Cordova, D. I., & Lepper, M. R. (1996). Intrinsic motivation and the process of learning: Beneficial effects of contextualization, personalization, and choice. *Journal of Educational Psychology, 88*, 715–730.

Deci, E. L., & Ryan, R. M. (1985). *Self-Determination*. John Wiley & Sons, Inc.

Deci, E. L., & Ryan, R. M. (2000). The "what" and "why" of goal pursuits: Human needs and the self-determination of behavior. *Psychological Inquiry, 11*, 227–268.

Deci, E. L., & Ryan, R. M. (2008). Self-determination theory: A macrotheory of human motivation, development, and health. *Canadian Psychology/Psychologie Canadienne, 49*(3), 182.

Deci, E. L., Koestner, R., & Ryan, R. M. (1999). A meta-analytic review of experiments examining the effects of extrinsic rewards on intrinsic motivation. *Psychological Bulletin, 125*(6), 627.

Diener, E., Suh, E. M., Lucas, R. E., & Smith, H. L. (1999). Subjective well-being: Three decades of progress. *Psychological Bulletin, 125*, 276–302.

Downie, M., Koestner, R., Horberg, E., & Haga, S. (2006). Exploring the relation of independent and interdependent self-construals to why and how people pursue personal goals. *Journal of Social Psychology, 146*, 517–531.

Downie, M., Chua, S. N., Koestner, R., Barrios, M., Rip, B., & M'Birkou, S. (2007). The relations of parental autonomy support to cultural internalization and well-being of immigrants and sojourners. *Cultural Diversity and Ethnic Minority Psychology, 13*, 241–249.

Fromm, E. (1976). *To have or to be?* New York: Harper& Row.

Gagné, M., & Deci, E. L. (2005). Self-determination theory and work motivation. *Journal of Organizational Behavior, 26*, 331–362.

Gladwell, M. (2008). *Outliers*. New York: Little, Brown & Co.

Gollwitzer, P. M. (1999). Implementation intentions: Strong effects of simple plans. *American Psychologist, 54*, 493–503.

Gollwitzer, P. M., & Schaal, B. (1998). Metacognition in action: The importance of implementation intentions. *Personality and Social Psychology Review, 2*, 124–136.

Gollwitzer, P. M., & Sheeran, P. (2006). Implementation intentions and goal achievement: A meta-analysis of effects and processes. *Advances in Experimental Social Psychology, 38*, 69–119.

Gorin, A. A., Powers, T. A., Koestner, R., Wing, R. R., & Raynor, H. A. (in press). Autonomy support, self-regulation, and weight loss. *Health Psychology*.

Green-Demers, I., Pelletier, L. G., Stewart, D. G., & Gushue, N. R. (1998). Coping with less interesting aspects of training: Toward a model of interest and motivation enhancement in individual sports. *Basic and Applied Social Psychology, 20*, 251–261.

Grube, J. W., Mayton, D. M., & Ball-Rokeach, S. J. (1994). Inducing changes in values, attitudes, and behavior: Belief system theory and the method of value self-confrontation. *Journal of Social Issues, 50*(4), 153–173.

Joussemet, M., Koestner, R., Lekes, N., & Houlfort, N. (2004). Introducing uninteresting tasks to children: A comparison of the effects of rewards and autonomy support. *Journal of Personality, 72*(1), 139–166.

Judge, T. A., Bono, J. E., Erez, A., & Locke, E. A. (2005). Core self-evaluations and job and life satisfaction: The role of self-concordance and goal attainment. *Journal of Applied Psychology, 90*, 257–268.

Kasser, T. (2002a). *The high price of materialism*. Cambridge, MA: MIT Press.

Kasser, T. (2002b). Sketches for a self-determination theory of values. In E. L Deci, & R. M. Ryan (Eds.), *Handbook of self-determination research* (pp. 123–140). Rochester, NY: Rochester Press.

Kasser, T., & Ahuvia, A. (2002). Materialistic values and well-being in business students. *European Journal of Social Psychology, 32*(1), 137–146.

Kasser, T., & Ryan, R. M. (1993). A dark side of the American dream: Correlates of financial success as a central life aspiration. *Journal of Personality and Social Psychology, 65*(2), 410–422.

Kasser, T., & Ryan, R. M. (1996). Further examining the American dream: Differential correlates of intrinsic and extrinsic goals. *Personality and Social Psychology Bulletin, 22*(3), 280–287.

Kim, Y., Kasser, T., & Lee, H. (2003). Self-concept, aspirations, and well-being in South Korea and the United States. *The Journal of Social Psychology, 143*(3), 227–290.

Koestner, R. (2008). Reaching one's personal goals: A motivational perspective focused on autonomy. *Canadian Psychology, 49*, 60–67.

Koestner, R., Lekes, N., Powers, T. A., & Chicoine, E. (2002). Attaining personal goals: Self-concordance plus implementation intentions equals success. *Journal of Personality and Social Psychology, 83*, 231–244.

Koestner, R., & Losier, G. (2002). Distinguishing among three types of highly motivated individuals. In E. L. Deci, & R. M. Ryan (Eds.), *Handbook of self-determination research* (pp. 101–122). Rochester, NY: University of Rochester press.

Koestner, R., Horberg, E. J., Gaudreau, P., Powers, T., DiDio, P., Bryan, C., Jochum, R., Salter, N. (2006). Bolstering implementation plans for long haul: The benefits of simultaneously boosting self-concordance or self-efficacy. *Personality and Social Psychology Bulletin, 32*, 1547–1558.

Koestner, R., Otis, N., Powers, T. A., Pelletier, L. G., & Gagnon, H. (2008). Autonomous motivation, controlled motivation, and goal progress. *Journal of Personality, 76*, 1201–1230.

Koestner, R., Powers, T. A., Carbonneau, N., Milyavskaya, M., & Chua, S. N. (2012). Distinguishing Autonomous and Directive Forms of Goal Support Their Effects on Goal Progress, Relationship Quality, and Subjective Well-Being. *Personality and Social Psychology Builetin, 38*(12), 1609–1620.

Koestner, R., Ryan, R., Bernieri, F., & Holt, K. (1984). The effects of controlling vs informational limit-setting styles on children's intrinsic motivation and creativity. *Journal of Personality, 52*, 233–247.

Kuhl, J., & Fuhrmann, A. (1998). Decomposing self-regulation and self-control: The volitional components inventory. In J. Heckhausen, & C. Dweck (Eds.), *Lifespan perspectives on motivation and control* (pp. 15–49). Hillsdale, NJ: Erlbaum.

Lekes, N., Hope, N. H., Gouveia, L., Koestner, R., & Philippe, F. L. (2012). Influencing value priorities and increasing well-being: The effects of reflecting on intrinsic values. *The Journal of Positive Psychology, 7*(3), 249–261.

Locke, E. A., & Latham, G. P. (2002). Building a practically useful theory of goal setting and task motivation: A 35-year odyssey. *American Psychologist, 57*, 705–717.

Moreau, E., & Mageau, G. A. (2012). The importance of perceived autonomy support for the psychological health and work satisfaction of health professionals: Not only supervisors count, colleagues too!. *Motivation and Emotion, 36*(3), 268–286.

Niemiec, C. P., Ryan, R. M., & Deci, E. L. (2009). The path taken: Consequences of attaining intrinsic and extrinsic aspirations in post-college life. *Journal of Research in Personality, 45*(3), 291–306.

Norcross, J. C., Ratzin, A. C., & Payne, D. (1989). Ringing in the New Year: The change processes and reported outcomes of resolutions. *Addictive Behaviors, 14*, 205–212.

Osterloh, M., & Frey, B. S. (2000). Motivation, knowledge transfer, and organizational forms. *Organization Science, 11*, 538–550.

Powers, T., Koestner, R., Gorin, A. A. (2008). Autonomy support from family and friends and weight loss in college women. *Families, Systems, & Health, 26*, 404–416.

Rogers, C. (1961). *On becoming a person*. Boston: Houghton Mifflin.

Rokeach, M. (1973). *The nature of human values*. New York: Free Press.

Ryan, R. M., Chirkov, V., Little, T. D., Sheldon, K. M., Timoshina, E., & Deci, E. L. (1999). The American dream in Russia: Extrinsic aspirations and well-being in two cultures. *Personality and Social Psychology Bulletin, 25*, 1509–1524.

Ryan, R. M., & Connell, J. P. (1989). Perceived locus of causality and internalization: examining reasons for acting in two domains. *Journal of personality and social psychology, 57*(5), 749.

Ryan, R. M., & Deci, E. L. (2000). Self-determination theory and the facilitation of intrinsic motivation, social development, and well-being. *American Psychologist, 55*, 68–78.

Ryan, R. M., Sheldon, K. M., Kasser, T., & Deci, E. L. (1996). All goals are not created equal: An organismic perspective on the nature of goals and their regulation. In P. M. Gollwitzer, & J. A. Bargh (Eds.), *The psychology of action: Linking cognition and motivation to behavior* (pp. 7–26). New York: Guilford Press.

Schmuck, P., Kasser, T., & Ryan, R. M. (2000). Intrinsic and extrinsic goals: Their structure and relationship to well-being in German and U. S. college students. *Social Indicators Research, 50*(2), 225–241.

Sheldon, K. M. (2002). The self-concordance model of healthy goal striving: When personal goals correctly represent the person. In E. L Deci, & R. M. Ryan (Eds.), *Handbook of self-determination research* (pp. 123–140). Rochester, NY: Rochester Press

Sheldon, K. M., Abad, N., Ferguson, Y., Gunz, A., Houser-Marko, L., Nichols, C. P., & Lyubomirsky, S. (2010). Persistent pursuit of need-satisfying goals leads to increased happiness: A 6-month experimental longitudinal study. *Motivation and Emotion, 34*(1), 39–48.

Sheldon, K. M., & Elliot, A. J. (1999). Goal striving, need-satisfaction, and longitudinal well-being: The self-concordance model. *Journal of Personality and Social Psychology, 76*, 482–497.

Sheldon, K. M., Gunz, A., Nichols, C. P., & Ferguson, Y. (2010). Extrinsic value orientation and affective forecasting: Overestimating the rewards, underestimating the costs. *Journal of Personality, 78*(1), 149–178.

Sheldon, K. M., & Houser-Marko, L. (2001). Self-concordance, goal-attainment, and the pursuit of happiness: Can there be an upward spiral? *Journal of Personality and Social Psychology, 80*, 152–165.

Sheldon, K. M., & Kasser, T. (1998). Pursuing personal goals: Skills enable progress, but not all progress is beneficial. *Personality and Social Psychology Bulletin, 24*, 1319–1331.

Sheldon, K. M., & Kasser, T. (2008). Psychological threat and extrinsic goal striving. *Motivation and Emotion, 31*(1), 37–45.

Sheldon, K. M., Kasser, T., Smith, K., & Share, T. (2002). Personal goals and psychological growth: Testing an intervention to enhance goal-attainment and personality integration. *Journal of Personality, 70*, 5–31.

Sheldon, K. M., & Krieger, L. S. (2004). Does legal education have undermining effects on law students? Evaluating changes in motivation, values, and well-being. *Behavioral Sciences & the Law, 22*(2), 261–286.

Sheldon, K. M., & Lyubomirsky, S. (2006). How to increase and sustain positive emotion: The effects of expressing gratitude and visualizing best possible selves. *The Journal of Positive Psychology, 1*(2), 73–82.

Sheldon, K. M., Ryan, R. M., Deci, E. L., & Kasser, T. (2004). The independent effects of goal contents and motives on well-being: It's both what you pursue and why you pursue it. *Personality and Social Psychology Bulletin, 30*(4), 475–486.

Webb, T. L., & Sheeran, P. (2004). Identifying good opportunities to act: Implementation intentions and cue discrimination. *European Journal of Social Psychology, 34*, 407–419.

Weinberg, R. S., & Gould D. (2007). *Foundations of sport and exercise psychology*. Champaign, IL: Human Kinetics.

Williams, G. C., Gagne, M., Ryan, R. M., & Deci, E. L. (2002). Facilitating autonomous self-regulation for smoking cessation. *Health Psychology, 21*, 40–50.

Williams, G. C., Grow, V. M., Freedman, Z. R., Ryan, R. M., & Deci, E. L. (1996). Motivational predictors of weight loss and weight loss maintenance. *Journal of Personality and Social Psychology, 70*, 115–126.

Williams, G. C., Lynch, M. F., McGregor, H. A., Ryan, R. M., Sharp, D., & Deci, E. L. (2006). Validation of the "important other" climate questionnaire: Assessing autonomy support for health-related change. *Families, Systems, & Health, 24*, 179–194.

Williams, G. C., Minicucci, D. S., Kouides, R. W., Levesque, C. S., Chirkov, V. I., Ryan, R. M., & Deci, E. L. (2002). Self-determination, smoking, diet and health. *Health Education Research, 17*(5), 512–521.

Williams, G. C., McGregor, H. A., Zeldman, A., Freedman, Z. R., & Deci, E. L. (2004). Testing a self-determination process model for promoting glycemic control through diabetes self-management. *Health Psychology, 23*, 58–66.

Zuroff, D. C., Koestner, R., Moskowitz, D. S., McBride, C., Marshall, M., & Bagby, M. R. (2007). Autonomous motivation for therapy: A new common factor in brief treatments for depression. *Psychotherapy Research, 17*(2), 137–147.

CHAPTER

26

Self-Determination Theory in the Work Domain: This is Just the Beginning

Marylène Gagné

Abstract

This Handbook covers a wide range of applications of self-determination theory to the world of work, and offers a multitude of ideas for future research. In this chapter, I reiterate some of the major points raised across the chapters by organizing them into coherent themes. I also cover other areas of application that were not covered in the chapters, but where self-determination theory has left its mark, or where it could potentially make a difference. The themes I uncovered include the concept of psychological needs, practical applications, the darker side of psychology, energy, managing employees, and compensation. The additional areas I added include performance monitoring, time, teams, information technology, knowledge sharing, innovation, career and job choice, and volunteer work.

Key Words: self-determination theory, need satisfaction, autonomous motivation, controlled motivation, work motivation

---

Introduction

Motivation is at the heart of organizational behavior. Whether one studies leadership, teams, job design, performance, strategy, or compensation, motivation is always an important explanatory mechanism. In this Handbook, several authors report on organizational research they and others have conducted using self-determination theory (SDT). Every chapter of this volume eloquently demonstrates the pivotal role that motivation plays across a variety of applications, from how we design jobs to how we compensate workers, and from promoting well-being to promoting safety. All chapters show not only how level, but also how quality of motivation matters, how values differentially predict outcomes, and how a variety of contextual and personal factors influence these processes.

Each chapter of this volume reviews existing evidence and highlights new directions for the study of motivation in organizations using SDT. In this discussion I first extract themes that emerge out of the chapters of this volume. In addition, I want to provide additional examples of SDT applications in organizations that have not been fully covered in these chapters as well as ideas for new applications of the theory to other important organizational phenomena.[1]

The Themes Explored
The Concept of Psychological Needs

Across the chapters of this Handbook, the theme of psychological need satisfaction is omnipresent. This theme constitutes one of the strongest and distinguishing aspects of SDT. The concept of psychological needs plays a pivotal role in explaining and predicting what will lead to the different types of motivation, and it helps us understand how we can design organizations and jobs in a way that promotes optimal outcomes. For the researcher who wants to study how organizational practices and individual characteristics influence the motivation, performance, and well-being of workers, a key issue to consider is how these practices and characteristics are likely to affect feelings of autonomy, competence, and relatedness. Because the concept of needs in organizational psychology has been used in many other theories, the conceptualization of needs in SDT had to be explained and distinguished from these other conceptualizations. Deci and Ryan (Chapter 2) provide this long overdue explanation of the unique way in which SDT uses the concept of needs. To propose three specific psychological needs and to deem them basic and universal is a bold statement to make, but compelling rigorous research makes these strong assumptions credible (Deci & Ryan, 2000, 2012).

Greguras, Diefendorff, Carpenter, and Tröster (Chapter 9) provide an interesting angle from which to understand psychological need satisfaction in organizations by using person-environment fit theory. Their model proposes that different types of fit, such as person-organization fit and person-job fit, fulfil different psychological needs, and that fit should lead to higher levels of autonomous work motivation, because fit increases the likelihood of internalization. The authors also propose the use of social network analysis as a way to examine these processes, which would provide a fresh and powerful method for examining the dynamics of need satisfaction in organizations.

In addition, Stone (Chapter 23) presents a very interesting outlook on the concept of a functional relationship to money that is based on the idea that one's relationship to money can be "nonmaterialistic" if one views money as a means to achieving nonfinancial or more transcendent goals in one's life. He uses the psychological needs to argue that the belief that one is able to manage one's money (competence), that one's financial decisions are volitional (autonomy), that one can rely on others to make good financial decisions (relatedness), and that one's financial resources can be used to achieve community goals (relatedness), leads to higher levels of well-being. This view offers a more nuanced analysis of how valuing money can influence one's well-being, because previous research has shown that holding materialistic values (such as wanting to have lots of money and possessions) negatively affects well-being (Kasser & Ryan, 1993).

Practical Applications of SDT in the Workplace

Many chapters address how to use or transform organizational practices in order to yield maximal returns. For example, Dysvik and Kuvaas (Chapter 13) show how SDT can contribute to transforming trainees from passive recipients into active participants. They discuss three important motivational issues with training programs in organizations: (1) making training programs into a source of need satisfaction and engagement, (2) motivating employees to attend training, and (3) motivating trainees to use what they have learned in their daily work.

Similarly, Fall and Roussel (Chapter 12) discuss the possible motivational effects of compensation systems on work motivation. Weibel, Wiemann, and Osterloh (Chapter 5) also discuss this topic from the point of view of behavioral economics. These chapters challenge common assumptions in the field of human resources that performance must be tied to monetary incentives, which is too often considered the primary source of work motivation. I elaborate on this later in the section on "compensation."

Gagné and Panaccio (Chapter 10) explain how and why the design of jobs can influence need satisfaction and work motivation. Gilbert and Kelloway (Chapter 11) discuss how leadership may influence need satisfaction and work motivation, as well as the role that the motivation to lead may play in influencing leadership styles. Scott, Fleming, and Kelloway (Chapter 17) provide a very interesting review of the occupational safety literature through the lens of SDT. They show that the safety culture approach to promoting safe behaviors in the workplace makes similar assumptions about human motivation and self-regulation to those made in SDT, and that safety programs based on this approach yield better results than behavior-based approaches, which rely on reinforcement theories. The authors also present a promising new safety motivation scale that they have been using to examine how "safety culture approaches" work from a motivational standpoint. Finally, Forest and colleagues (Chapter 20) present a new method to calculate the return on investments derived from SDT-based interventions. This method may provide practitioners who wish to convince organizations of the advantages of using practices and interventions based on SDT principles with a tool to do so.

A methodological note is provided by Meyer (Chapter 3), who addresses the issue of examining commitment mindsets using person-centered approaches. The same thing could be applied to motivation, where instead of focusing on the different types of motivation as variables, one could examine motivational profiles at the person-level.

This approach has recently been used in the domain of sports and work motivation, with interestingly unique results. Gillet, Vallerand, and Rosnet (2009) found that the performance of tennis players who had a less "autonomous" profile, that is, who had a profile that consisted of being moderate on autonomous motivation and high on controlled motivation, was lower than the performance of players with profiles that were higher on autonomous and lower on controlled motivation. However, Van den Broeck, Lens, De Witte, and Van Coillie (2013) found that workers with high levels of autonomous motivation in their profile experienced greater job satisfaction and work engagement, as well as lower strain. They also found that those who had low autonomous combined with high controlled motivation experienced the lowest levels of engagement and the highest levels of strain. It therefore seems that across these two domains, one's level of both autonomous and controlled motivation affects outcomes.

The Darker Side of Psychology

Some chapters discuss issues that would definitely not be considered as part of the positive psychology movement, although SDT is often considered to be a positive psychology theory (Gagné & Vansteenkiste, 2013). For example, Dagenais-Desmarais and Courcy (Chapter 18) develop a model to explain violence at work using SDT. In this model, need satisfaction (or perhaps more accurately need thwarting) plays a crucial role in the downward spiral of workplace violence. Not only do they discuss how violence predicts need thwarting, but also discuss how need thwarting leads to violence. They further discuss how need satisfaction may be the means by which we can prevent and put an end to workplace violence. By exploring the motivation to engage in violent behavior, and by examining the consequences of workplace violence through the lens of SDT, they provide a nice integration between prominent theories of violence and SDT, and argue for a new humanistic perspective on violence. Their chapter is a good example of how SDT can potentially change the way interventions are designed: in this case, it shows that instead of focusing on sanctions, interventions could focus on prevention and support as means to end violence.

Deci and Ryan (Chapter 2) also talk about how controlled, relative to autonomous motivation, can lead to other deviant forms of behavior in the workplace, such as cheating and taking shortcuts. New research on high stakes testing in the education system provides another compelling example of how controlling contexts can lead to unintended consequences (Ryan & Weinstein, 2009). These phenomena have also been examined through the lens of other motivation theories, such as expectancy theory and goal-setting theory, but explanations based on SDT are more compelling because the concept of internalization can more deeply explain how and why these behaviors happen.

Fernet and Austin (Chapter 14) use SDT to better understand how stressors affect workers, and how to mitigate against their effects by using job resources that are likely to affect need satisfaction. They propose different routes by which motivation impacts on strain (direct, mediating, and moderating effects). Ferris (Chapter 8) examines the concept of contingent self-esteem in the work domain, which is strongly related to the understudied regulation of introjection. Not only does he argue that need thwarting may lead to the development of contingent self-esteem, but that contingent self-esteem may hinder a person's ability to subsequently fulfil their psychological needs, thereby creating a vicious cycle.

On Energy

Psychological energy is a concept that is becoming more and more popular in the organizational psychology field, and SDT has provided an important contribution to our understanding of the energy concept. Starting with Ryan and Frederick's (1997) work on subjective vitality, we now know that vitality is affected by need satisfaction and by one's motivational orientation (Nix, Ryan, Manly, & Deci, 1999). What has been called ego-depletion (Muraven & Baumeister, 2000) has also been shown to be affected by one's motivation, as it seems that we only deplete our mental energy when we feel controlled or when we have controlling reasons to engage in an activity (Moller, Deci, & Ryan, 2006; Muraven, Gagné, & Rosman, 2008; Muraven, Rosman, & Gagné, 2007). Spreitzer and Porath's (Chapter 15) concept of thriving at work draws heavily from Ryan and Frederick's subjective vitality concept and from SDT. Gonzalez and colleagues' (Chapter 22) psychosocial model of the health gradient also draws heavily from the idea that need satisfaction differences across incremental levels of occupational health status may be closely linked to differences in health.

Cossette (Chapter 16) discusses how SDT can contribute to our understanding of emotional labor by helping in the evaluation of individual and contextual factors that may help or hinder employees' regulation of their emotions at work. Emotional labor is another good example of how we use our energy at work and of how our self-regulation choices may affect those energy levels. Cossette argues that our reasons (motivation) for engaging in emotional labor may affect the regulatory choices we make (surface vs. deep acting), which has repercussions on our energy levels and on our well-being.

Strauss and Parker (Chapter 4) present a model of workplace proactivity that is a good example of how recent organizational behavior theories are moving away from a reactive view of the worker to a more agentic one. This model draws heavily from SDT to explain people's reason to engage in proactive behavior, as well as whether they feel capable and energized to do so. As mentioned in the chapter, there is an interesting dilemma when it comes to attempting to foster and promote proactive work behavior in organizations. By making proactive behavior part of the job description, and potentially rewarding it, one may actually make it "disappear" so to speak, given that the very definition of proactivity is that it is *self*-initiated. It will therefore be challenging for organizations to find other ways to promote such behavior besides the traditional ones, which usually involve the development of performance management and reward systems that are meant to "direct" employee behavior. Another interesting issue, which I also apply to knowledge sharing behavior later, is to examine what people try to achieve by being proactive, and whether this behavior actually helps or hurts the organization. As such, future research could examine the motivational conditions under which proactive behavior is most helpful.

Vallerand, Houlfort, and Forest (Chapter 6) feature the role that being passionate in one's work plays in generating the energy necessary for high-level performance, and the sorts of repercussions that different types of passion can have on one's well-being. They present the dual model of passion; compare and contrast it with motivation; and show how it has been applied to understanding work-related outcomes, such as concentration, flow, performance, and well-being. Interestingly, they also discuss research that examines how passion develops, including how people select activities, how they come to value them, and how they forge their identity around them.

On Managing Employees

An essential task in an organization is the management of its members' goals and behaviors. This important area of study has not only focused on how to structure organizations in order to get effective performance, but also on how to direct and energize the behavior of employees. Gilbert and Kelloway (Chapter 11) discuss how and why managerial leadership behavior influences subordinate motivation and outcomes, while Reeve and Su (Chapter 21) present research on what motivates teachers, and how this in turn affects their behavior toward students. In addition, Ronen and Mikulincer (Chapter 7) argue that managers can provide a "secure work base" out of which employees can form secure attachments to their organization, which would foster their work engagement. These three chapters provide rich information about how people in one-up positions, such as managers and teachers, can influence people in one-down positions, such as employees and students.

I often hear, during leadership training, managers saying that their employees are not genuinely intrinsically motivated at work, that they want to be told what to do, and certainly do not want to take on more responsibility. These managers often feel compelled to use controlling leadership methods, such as telling people what to do without consulting them, and using threats or rewards to get work out of their employees. They are more than skeptical about the apparent simplicity of transforming their employees into autonomously driven workers. Edward Deci has eloquently discussed this issue in his book *Why we do what we do* (1995, p. 148): "if you control people enough, they may begin to act as if they want to be controlled. As a self-protective strategy, they become focused outward—looking for clues about what the people in one-up positions expect of them, looking for what will keep them out of trouble." If a person has experienced being controlled in this way throughout life, from early school all the way to the workplace, there is reason to believe that he or she will have been transformed into a pawn in the process. He or she does not expect anything more than control from authorities and has lost the energy to truly engage in work.

Some research suggests ways in which this happens. Students working on anagrams under an authoritarian and evaluative teacher have been shown to be less willing to choose subsequent tasks to work on themselves (Haddad, 1982). They fear that their choice will be evaluated negatively by the teacher. Unfortunately, this pushes the authority figure to use more controlling behaviors, because they now feel that control is necessary to get the student or the employee to work. Indeed, teachers who perceive their students not to have autonomous motivation tend to act in a more controlling manner toward them (Pelletier, Séguin-Lévesque, & Legault, 2002; Taylor, Ntoumanis, & Standage, 2008), even when they are wrong or misled about their students' motivation (Pelletier & Vallerand, 1996; Sarrazin, Tessier, Pelletier, Trouilloud, & Chanal, 2006).

These results, which were found in the education domain, are likely to apply to management. One essential thing to focus on when training managers (and teachers) is to carefully explain this vicious cycle and offer alternative means that gradually bring back some spontaneity into employees' behavior. Although this might require more extensive interventions, which might not only require a more autonomy supportive management style, but possibly some work redesign (Clegg & Spencer, 2007), the starting point should be to change managers' mindsets from "how do I motivate my employees" to "how do I get my employees to motivate themselves." Koestner and Hope (Chapter 25) provide some interesting tools that could also be used to achieve this, through a combination of proper goal setting involving deliberation about why one wants to pursue a certain goal, and proper goal implementation. Strauss and Parker's proactivity model (Chapter 4) may also provide useful tips on how to bring about a more proactive mindset in employees.

We often speak of managerial autonomy support and leadership as if they functioned in a vacuum. But managers are also managed, even at the top. CEOs and executives must also answer to stakeholders, who could (and often do) act in a controlling manner. For example, CEO compensation is often heavily contingent on the financial performance of the company. Research has shown that pressure from above can create trickle down effects on motivation throughout the organization. For example, it has been demonstrated that teachers who feel controlled by school administration are in turn more controlling with their own students (Deci, Spiegel, Ryan, Koestner, & Kauffman, 1982; Pelletier et al., 2002), and that this may be explained by the fact that this pressure from above makes them depersonalize their own students (Soenens, Sierens, Vansteenkiste, Dochy, & Goossens, 2012). Reeve (2009) and Reeve and Su (Chapter 21) define controlling behavior as putting pressure on a person to think, feel, and behave in a particular way, and includes such acts as relying on rewards, punishments, and surveillance, failing to provide explanations (e.g., you don't need to know

why, just do it!), displaying impatience, asserting one's power, and demeaning or strategically ignoring the person. Reeve describes three major reasons why teachers may act controllingly toward their students: (1) pressure from above, which may come from high-stakes testing, principals' leadership style, parents, and cultural values in general; (2) student passivity or lack of interest and motivation; and (3) a personality disposition to be controlling and a belief that motivation comes from external sources. It would be very interesting to examine the same factors in managers in order to find the best ways to train them not to act in a controlling way (possibly based on their reason for acting like this in the first place) and to replace the controlling behavior with an autonomy-supportive one.

Gilbert and Kelloway (Chapter 11) also propose that autonomously motivated employees may require less leadership than those who are not. Some research concurs with this observation. For example, Fernet, Gagné, and Austin (2010) found that autonomously motivated teachers seem to be immune to the negative effects of job demands, and thus require less social support from their leaders to buffer against the risk of burnout. The fact that autonomously motivated employees may require less monitoring and less support to sustain their engagement implies that as long as leaders ensure that psychological needs are fulfilled, they may need to monitor and reward employees less in order to get high performance.

It would also be useful to dig deeper into how autonomy support influences changes in motivation. For example, because autonomy support is most often operationalized as offering choice and encouraging initiative, providing rationales for goals and tasks, and being empathic (Deci & Ryan, 2008), it implies that managers must trust their subordinates in order to do these. Therefore, research on trust may be worth examining as a possible mediator. Trust has been defined as one's willingness to make oneself vulnerable to the actions of another party that one cannot control, and is determined by the perception that the other party is competent, benevolent, and has integrity (Mayer, Davis, & Schoorman, 1995). Trust can be studied from different angles. Not only do managers need to learn to trust that their employees "have it in them" to be autonomously motivated, but employees must also trust their manager. In regards to the first angle, research shows that when managers trust subordinates, subordinates feel more autonomous and this in turn enhances their trust toward their manager (Seppala, Lipponen, Pirttila-Backman, & Lipsanen, 2011). In regards to the second, Deci, Connell, and Ryan (1989) showed that managerial autonomy support increases trust in management. Recent research also shows that trust in management is related to the satisfaction of the needs for autonomy, competence, and relatedness (Carpini & Gagné, 2013), and that autonomous motivation mediates the relation between trust in management and employee performance (Gagné, 2009; Kuvaas, Buch, Dysvik, & Haerem, 2012). Alternatively, it is possible that trusting one's management frees up cognitive resources that can be dedicated to tasks instead of monitoring the actions of management, thereby increasing performance (Mayer & Gavin, 2005), so this would need to be taken into account in future research. Other research shows that trust does not have a direct effect on performance. Instead, it might be that trust acts as a moderator between individual motivation and unit performance. In other words, trust would channel one's energy toward reaching organizational goals (Dirks, 1999).

On Compensation

Compensation is inextricably linked to working. Although self-determination scholars have argued, through cognitive evaluation theory, that rewards can undermine intrinsic motivation (Deci, 1971), the mainstream compensation literature advocates linking compensation to performance based on the premises of expectancy theory and agency theory (Rynes, Gerhart, & Parks, 2005). Fall and Roussel (Chapter 12) provide a very good historical review of these opposing views and propose some avenues for research that aims at arriving at a consensus regarding the most efficient use of compensation to motivate workers. Weibel, Wiemann, and Osterloh (Chapter 5) present the relatively new behavioral economics view of incentives, which contrasts with the previously dominant view based on agency theory, and describes how SDT has influenced this movement in economics. Gagné and Forest (2008) have also proposed a model to test the effects of compensation on autonomous versus controlled motivation, which adds elements of need satisfaction and justice into the equation. They argue that it is not efficient to examine elements of a compensation package separately, as most studies have done. For example, many studies examine the effects of commission plan or profit-sharing on changes in organizational performance (rarely do they measure individual performance), without controlling for or evaluating the effects of other elements of the compensation package, such as base pay and benefits (Han & Shen, 2007; Magnan & St-Onge, 2005; Piekkola, 2005). Gagné and Forest (2008) propose to break down the total compensation package into basic characteristics, such as the absolute amount of pay, the ratio of fixed versus variable pay, the basis on which payments are made (e.g., performance evaluation, skills), whether payment is based on individual or group performance, and the perceived equity of the compensation components. Each of these is hypothesized to have effects on need satisfaction and on perceptions of procedural justice, which in turn have effects on work motivation. Moderators are considered as well, such as the climate and culture of the organization. Such a model, if used in empirical research, would help us disentangle the positive and negative effects of different compensation components on work motivation, and would help us understand why these effects are occurring. Such research is critically lacking in the area of compensation.

Two elements of compensation systems are worth expanding on. The first one is the issue of fairness. Emerging research shows that fairness perceptions positively influence need satisfaction and autonomous motivation. For example, it has been shown that both procedural and distributive justice are related to autonomous work motivation, and that this is mediated through need satisfaction (Gagné, Bérubé, & Donia, 2007). Intrinsic motivation has been shown to mediate the effect of procedural justice on task performance (Zapata-Phelan, Colquitt, Scott, & Livingston, 2009), and need satisfaction has been shown to mediate the effect of organizational justice on job satisfaction (Mayer, Bardes, & Piccolo, 2008). In addition, when people are deprived of autonomy satisfaction, they become more sensitive to procedural justice considerations (van Prooijen, 2009). Lastly, perceptions of both distributive and procedural justice around the administration of bonus pay have been positively related to the intrinsic motivation of managers (Hartmann & Slapnicar, 2012).

Secondly, the quality of the feedback matters and affects perceptions of justice. People generally are more intrinsically motivated after they receive positive than negative feedback (Deci, Koestner, & Ryan, 1999). However, whether feedback is given in a controlling or in an informational manner also affects motivation (Ryan, 1982). Research on feedback has also focused on how people react to quantitative versus qualitative feedback. Much research on performance appraisals has focused on giving voice to the ratee, which should indeed be an integral part of any feedback meeting (Levy & Williams, 2004). Giving voice is an important component of procedural justice (Colquitt, Conlon, Wesson, Porter, & Ng, 2001), and is probably an important driver of the relation between justice and autonomous work motivation (Gagné et al., 2007) because it is likely to increase feelings of autonomy. The quality of the relationship between the rater and the ratee is also likely to affect ratee reactions (Levy & Williams, 2004). SDT predicts that a relationship based on satisfying the needs for autonomy, competence, and relatedness would yield the best reactions. As mentioned previously, a relationship based on trust, where the rater is perceived to be competent, benevolent, and high on integrity, is also likely to help.

But most organizations would not rely solely on the manager for performance appraisals. If we strictly follow guidelines based on SDT, the least controlling performance management system would ask employees to rate their own performance. It is possible to obtain self-appraisals that are accurate, honest, and useful, although they do tend to be more positive than ratings by others (Murphy & Cleveland, 1991). If a performance management system supports the psychological needs, people should in principle be honest and accurately assess their own performance. After all, they are the ones with the most information to rate their own performance. If employees perceive that the purpose of the appraisal is to help their development (and thrive; Spreitzer & Porath, Chapter 15), as opposed to using it to make decisions about them (reward, promote, or fire them), they are more likely to be honest in their self-assessment.

There are many other potential applications of SDT in the world of compensation. For example, finance scholars typically conduct research on CEO and executive compensation using agency theory (Jensen & Meckling, 1976), which advocates for the use of contingent compensation (Bartol, 1999). It appears from reading this literature that such compensation systems have failed miserably at yielding the desired behavior from executives, and it almost seems like finance experts are at a loss when trying to explain why this is happening, and what should be done (Kerr, 1995; Pfeffer, 1998). SDT could provide some answers to their questions, so efforts should be made to make the theory known in this field. In contrast to agency theory, which assumes that human beings are inherently averse to effort and egotistical, SDT assumes inherent growth tendencies (which would make human beings seek challenges) and a need for human contact (i.e., relatedness). These different assumptions would yield very different hypotheses regarding the behavior of executives working under different compensation models.

Another topic touched on in Deci and Ryan's chapter that is embedded within compensation is competition. Some theories of compensation argue that organizations should create competitions between workers based on the assumption that they will be motivated to surpass others (see Fall and Roussel, Chapter 12). Tournament theory, in particular, proposes that employees will be motivated to work harder if they are competing for a promotion or for a reward (Lazear & Rosen, 1981). A frequent example in practice is the use of performance appraisals to rank employees and give the top 10% a bonus (and at GE, it was the Jack Welch approach of firing the bottom 10% every year). However, SDT research has shown that competition can be detrimental to intrinsic motivation (Deci, Betley, Kahle, Abrams, & Porac, 1981), especially for the losers of such competitions (and there are generally more losers than winners), because it decreases feelings of competence (Vansteenkiste & Deci, 2003) and feelings of autonomy (Reeve & Deci, 1996). Such systems also discourage cooperation among employees, which could decrease feelings of relatedness (Gagné & Forest, 2008). However, competition can be perceived as providing an interesting challenge for a somewhat boring task, and could provide people with an opportunity to test themselves and improve (Frederick-Recascino & Schuster-Smith, 2003). The sports domain is ripe with examples of how competition can enhance intrinsic motivation. The trick is to find how best to use competition in the workplace to get stimulated, autonomously motivated employees, and once again, SDT can provide a framework from which to build testable hypotheses.

Other Areas of Investigation
Performance Monitoring

Organizations are using technology more and more to monitor the behavior and performance of their employees. The last decades have seen increases in the use of card swipe systems; physiological monitoring equipment (eye and fingerprint detectors); location-sensing technologies, such as global positioning systems; and computer monitoring and the use of cameras to monitor employee behaviors. A 2007 Electronic Monitoring and Surveillance Survey (American Management Association, 2008) revealed that 66% of the surveyed US employers reported using Internet monitoring, 43% reported using email monitoring, 45% reported using telephone monitoring, 48% reported using video surveillance, and 8% reported using global positioning systems to monitor company vehicles.

These technologies are very useful to organizations, not only for surveillance purposes, but also to make retail and marketing decisions. Such technologies often replace human surveillance, as employees now often work from remote office locations, knowledge work is more prevalent and more difficult to monitor, and today's managers are typically overwhelmed with paperwork and meetings, preventing close monitoring of employee behavior. Many organizations also use these technologies to help employees. For example, my university's information technology group is able to enter into my computer to fix things and help me, no matter where I am on the planet (I guess they could also use this to check how I use my computer). Monitoring would appear, through the lens of SDT, to be a very convenient means to control people's behavior, and consequently switching their locus of causality to external. Some research indeed shows that surveillance has detrimental effects on intrinsic motivation and creativity (Amabile, 1979; Enzle & Anderson, 1993; Lepper & Greene, 1975). But the effect of monitoring may depend on what it is used for, what message is conveyed through it, and how it is actually used.

Early research on performance monitoring has shown that it can increase stress levels and lead to health problems (Aiello, 1993; Carayon, 1993; Smith, Carayon, Sanders, Lim, & LeGrande, 1992), whereas other research has shown that it can increase work performance (Komaki, 1986; Komaki, Desselles, & Bowman, 1989; Larson & Callahan, 1990), but not so much on complex tasks (Aiello & Svek, 1993). These effects may be partly due to the effects of monitoring on feelings of autonomy (Carayon, 1994), but research also shows that it is possible to use monitoring without its negative effects (Stone & Stone, 1990). For example, computer-based performance monitoring is less stressful when employees are given more job autonomy (Ball & Wilson, 2000) or feedback (Aiello & Shao, 1993; Griffith, 1993; Wells, Moorman, & Werner, 2007). Ways to restore feelings of autonomy have included allowing employee input into the design of the monitoring system (De Tienne &

Abbott, 1993) and control over the monitoring system, such as the ability to switch it off (Stanton & Barnes-Farrell, 1996). SDT could be used to make sense of all of these findings and to craft a better use of monitoring in a way that will not negatively impact need satisfaction.

Deadlines and Time

Everyone has goals to reach and expectations to meet in their work, and this is usually to be done in a (not always) reasonable amount of time. Most workers have to either produce goods or render services within a specified timeframe, and many of us are faced with deadlines for work projects. Deadlines have been shown to negatively affect intrinsic motivation (Amabile, DeJong, & Lepper, 1976) because they decrease feelings of autonomy. But it is possible to set deadlines in a way that is less controlling. Indeed, when people are allowed to set their own deadlines or to modify existing deadlines, their intrinsic motivation does not seem to suffer as much (Burgess, Enzle, & Schmaltz, 2004). Setting a deadline for a boring task may also help increase task challenge, which may increase intrinsic motivation (Amabile, 1988). More research could be done to evaluate whether giving a deadline with autonomy support (Deci, Eghrari, Patrick, & Leone, 1994) could also prevent its negative effects on work motivation.

Other time effects on motivation could possibly be better understood through the framework of SDT. We know from research on goals that the further away from goal attainment one is, the more goal desirability affects goal choice, whereas with shorter time frames, feasibility concerns become more important (Liberman & Trope, 1998). If we assume that long-term thinking provides more meaning to one's activities than only thinking about short-term results, one could then predict that being future-oriented would be associated with higher levels of autonomous motivation. In fact, de Bilde, Vansteenkiste, and Lens (2011) found that students with a future-time perspective were more likely to be autonomously motivated toward their studies than those with a present-time perspective. It is therefore reasonable to expect that interest and meaning (i.e., intrinsic and identified motivation) for a goal may influence goal choice when the person has plenty of time to reach the goal, but that more "practical" concerns may be more potent when time is of essence. It is difficult at this point to say exactly how "practical concerns" would translate in motivational terms. Would this mean more extrinsic forms of motivation? Schmidt and DeShon (2007) found that incentives pushed people to allocate more time to goals on which progress had been made, but not for goals on which progress was small. So when time is of essence, people may consider more tangible costs and benefits than when they have lots of time. It would therefore be interesting to extend the study of goals through SDT (see Koestner and Hope, Chapter 25) by adding a time dimension.

What time represents may also have interesting effects on the motivation to engage in various activities. DeVoe and Pfeffer (2010) found that when workers need to account for their time at work (e.g., for billing purposes), they are less likely to allocate time to volunteering activities (even when controlling for their attitudes toward volunteering). In essence, people come to view their own time as a compensable factor. Although they have shown that this effect is not attributable to changing intrinsic motivation or feelings of autonomy, they found that holding more extrinsic values (such as valuing money; Grouzet et al., 2005) enhanced the effect. It would be interesting to see if values actually change as a function of having to account for one's time, as professional education has been shown to influence them (Grouzet, Chapter 24).

Teams

Organizations are increasingly using team work, because team work has been shown to be an effective, economical, and stimulating way to organize work. But research on team motivation has used theories of motivation that only account for the level of motivation within a team without regard for its quality (e.g., Chen & Kanfer, 2006). Using SDT to examine team motivation requires one to take into account the level of both autonomous and controlled motivation in the team, and possibly the composition of individual members' motivation (e.g., how many are predominantly autonomously motivated, vs. controllingly motivated). Grenier, Chiocchio, Gagné, and Sarrazin (2013) suggested using SDT in such a group composition perspective. They proposed to study how the composition of team members' individual motivation within a team influences team processes, including team performance and individual member satisfaction. For example, individual members' reasons for pursuing team goals may affect coordinated action (Koestner, Losier, Vallerand, & Carducci, 1996), interpersonal conflict within the team, goal progress, and goal attainment (Sheldon & Elliot, 1998), such that predominantly autonomous teams may be less likely to experience conflict than heterogeneous or predominantly controlled teams. This in turn should influence the need satisfaction of team members and team outcomes. Grenier and colleagues (2013) also propose that the composition of motivation within teams may give rise to a phenomenon of team goal motivation that stands apart from individual-level motivation, something that may be mediated by social identification processes. How needs are supported within teams may influence this process as well. In a first test of these ideas, Grenier, Gagné, and Chiocchio (2013) examined lifeguard teams and found that both individual autonomous motivation and team autonomous motivation (calculated as the average level of autonomous motivation across team members) influenced member's satisfaction with their work on the team. Moreover, an interaction effect was found, whereby team motivation enhanced the relation between individual motivation and satisfaction. These findings tell us that the composition of team motivation does indeed affect individual team members, beyond their individual motivation.

Information Technology Usage

A recent application of SDT is in the field of technology acceptance. This field of research has relied strongly on other motivational theories, especially the theory of planned behavior (Ajzen, 1991), on which the popular technology acceptance model is based (Davis, 1989; Davis, Bagozzi, & Warshaw, 1992). However, Venkatesh and colleagues have found that intrinsic motivation also plays a big part in getting people to accept new technologies and to use them in their work (Venkatesh, 2000; Venkatesh & Johnson, 2002; Venkatesh & Speier, 1999; Venkatesh & Speier, 2000). More recently, SDT has been incorporated into these models to better predict technology acceptance. For example, the three psychological needs have been shown to enhance workers' and teachers' willingness to take online courses (Roca & Gagné, 2008; Sorebo, Halvari, Gulli, & Kristiansen, 2009), and intrinsic motivation to use a new software to book appointments in hospitals has been related to its acceptance and usage (Mitchell, Gagné, Beaudry, & Dyer, 2012). Such research can be very useful when planning new technology implementations.

Knowledge Sharing

Today's organizations rely more and more on the knowledge of employees. The knowledge-based theory of the firm (Grant, 1996) argues that knowledge-sharing firms maximize intangible and tangible asset value and profitability by actively identifying, collecting, storing, and sharing knowledge. Organizations are more and more aware of this fact, and want to encourage the sharing of this knowledge among their members (but not necessarily with outsiders or competitors). The use of team work, as described previously, can constitute a means to increase knowledge sharing, and the use of information technology can also facilitate it. But employees' reasons for sharing or for not sharing knowledge are crucial variables to consider. I suggested a model of knowledge-sharing motivation (Gagné, 2009) in which it is proposed that knowledge sharing is more likely to occur when employees have identified or intrinsic reasons for sharing their knowledge. Such motivation is likely to be influenced by different human resource management practices, such as job design, compensation systems, managerial support, and training, but also by norms about sharing behavior and fit between personal and organizational values. A few studies have found support for this model. Reinholt, Pedersen, and Foss (2011) found that autonomous motivation toward knowledge sharing interacts with one's place in a network, and with organizational resources that enhance knowledge sharing, in affecting the extent to which one gives and receives knowledge with and from colleagues. Foss, Minbaeva, Pedersen, and Reinholt (2009) also found that job characteristics indirectly influence sending and receiving knowledge through intrinsic motivation.

Cockrell and Stone (2010) have pointed out that the 2009 model focuses exclusively on how to increase the sharing of useful knowledge. However, they argue that we must also address the issue of how to stop people from sharing useless knowledge in organizations (what they call pseudoknowledge), which may lead to the loss of other resources, such as time and money. Contributing such worthless knowledge is thought to be done for personal gain, such as to appear knowledgeable or cooperative. Cockrell and Stone found that financial incentives encouraged pseudoknowledge sharing and that autonomous motivation countered it. There is also the issue of why people do not share their knowledge and there may be many reasons for this that would imply using different interventions. For example, people may not share because they do not see the utility of doing so, because they do not feel competent to do so, or because they want to keep the knowledge to themselves as a form of power.

SDT would again be a useful framework to study these issues.

Innovation

Organizations want to harness creativity in order to innovate and to become or remain competitive. Amabile's (1983) model of creativity proposes three important factors: (1) expertise on the topic; (2) intrinsic motivation; and (3) creativity-relevant characteristics, such as openness to experience. Although there are some debates about this (Eisenberger & Shanock, 2003), research on creativity derived from SDT has shown that rewards, evaluations, and deadlines can undermine it (Amabile, 1979; Amabile et al., 1976; Amabile, Hennessey, & Grossman, 1986; Joussemet & Koestner, 1999), whereas autonomy support can enhance it (Koestner, Ryan, Bernieri, & Holt, 1984). However, many jobs require workers to be creative (e.g., research and development, advertising, software development), and depending on how it is presented to employees, it can have differential effects on motivation and creative behavior. For example, perceiving that one's work requires creative performance has been shown to increase creative work behavior (Unsworth, Wall, & Carter, 2005). Amabile, Conti, Coon, Lazenby, and Herron (1996) developed the KEYS scale to measure organizational factors that influence creativity at work. The scale contains subscales to measure support, autonomy, pressure, resources and impediments to creativity in the workplace. Amabile and Conti (1999) demonstrated that changes in each of these organizational factors are associated with changes in creativity in work groups. It would be interesting to evaluate how need satisfaction mediates the effect of each factor on creativity and innovation, and knowing this could help in the development of interventions aimed at improving the organizational context for creativity.

Amabile (1993) also argued that different types of motivations may be needed at different stages of innovation. Innovation has been argued to involve three behavioral steps: (1) idea generation, (2) promotion, and (3) realization (Janssen, 2000). Amabile (1993) argued that intrinsic motivation may be particularly important at the idea-generation stage (where creativity is crucial), but that extrinsic motivation may help for the other stages. We could expect that autonomous forms of extrinsic motivation would yield better outcomes in each of these stages than controlling forms. It might also be worth looking at the strength of motivational effects across these stages, because Axtell et al. (2000) found that individual factors (such as motivation) are stronger predictors of idea generation, whereas organizational factors (such as support) are stronger predictors of idea realization.

Career and Job Choice Behavior

Grouzet (Chapter 24) presents an interesting view of how professional training can influence the development of values in young adults. We could take this discussion further and consider factors that may also affect career and job choices. One's interests, values, abilities, and of course, opportunities influence these choices. In addition, as Guay (2005) has shown, young adults' motivation for choosing a career path has an influence over how this process unfolds. For example, having autonomous reasons for deciding on a career path is related to less career indecision than having controlled reasons. Moreover, the quality of one's relationship with parents and one's self-efficacy have been positively related to having autonomous reasons toward career decision-making activities. In addition, Guay, Ratelle, Senécal, Larose, and Deschênes (2006) found that not feeling self-efficacious and not being autonomously motivated both predict chronic inability to make career-related decisions.

Similar interesting findings have been found in the domain of unemployment. Vansteenkiste, Lens, De Witte, and Feather (2005) found that autonomous reasons to search for a job were related to job search intensity, whereas controlled reasons to search for a job were related to feeling worthless and socially rejected. Some recent interesting research in the domain of job search behavior focuses not only on why people search for jobs, but also on why they do not search for jobs. Beyond looking at autonomous reasons (e.g., because work is personally meaningful to me) and controlled reasons (e.g., because I need money) for searching for a job, Vansteenkiste, Lens, De Witte, De Witte, and Deci (2004) also examined autonomous and controlled reasons *not* to look for a job. Instead of assuming that people who do not actively search for jobs do so out of discouragement or lack of confidence, the authors also examined possible autonomous reasons not to look for a job, such as giving priority to alternative activities (such as hobbies), and possible controlled reasons not to look for a job, such as feeling like a bad person if you do not attend to other tasks (such as raising children). Although autonomous motivation to search for a job was related to intensity of job search behavior, autonomous motivation

not to search was positively related to well-being in this unemployed sample. Unemployed individuals are also more flexible in their job search, that is, willing to accept jobs that deviate from their ideal (in terms of qualifications or conditions) when they have high intrinsic job values and low extrinsic job values (Van den Broeck, Vansteenkiste, Lens, & De Witte, 2010).

Volunteer Work

It is often believed that organizations that rely on volunteers are likely to get highly variable performance, and that the overall performance will tend to be low because the organization cannot rely on monetary incentives or on other forms of controls (e.g., performance appraisals) to motivate their volunteers (Farmer & Fedor, 1999, 2001). Given that most organizations that hire volunteer workers have difficulty recruiting and retaining enough of them, they often cannot afford to be picky and must accept whatever help they can get from them. As explained previously, the view that workers can only be attracted to work (and put in the effort) through incentives and monitoring is a classic example of the agency view of human nature (Jensen & Meckling, 1976). According to this view, human beings are inherently self-interested and lazy, and therefore one must use incentives and controls to ensure that they fulfil organizational goals. This view differs drastically from SDT's view of human nature. SDT assumes that human beings are oriented toward growth and stimulation, have the capacity to internalize behavioral regulation, and might be interested in work activities for their own sake.

Pelletier and Aitken (Chapter 19) have convincingly demonstrated that identified motivation may be a more potent driver of environmental behaviors than intrinsic motivation. This shows how internalization can serve to engage human beings in activities that may be effortful yet not inherently interesting, but that come to be seen as important. The same may apply to volunteer work. Although it is possible for volunteer work to be interesting and enjoyable, many other reasons have been shown to drive people to volunteer (Clary et al., 1998). Among these reasons are to benefit others, to meet new people, to increase one's self-esteem, to reduce one's guilt over one's good fortune, to distract from personal problems, to learn new things, and to build one's career. Some of these reasons could be considered forms of identified motivation (e.g., benefiting others), because they rely on the internalization of values. Volunteers motivated by values commit more to the nonprofit organization they work for, especially if they are satisfied by this work (Bang, Ross, & Reio, 2013). Other reasons, such as furthering one's careers, can be considered more external, and evidence shows that this particular motive for volunteering is related to lower levels of engagement (Farmer & Fedor, 2001). Because many tasks that volunteers do cannot be changed to make them more intrinsically motivating (e.g., cleaning up patients' beds or animal cages, carrying goods for disabled clients, and so forth), organizations must attempt to encourage the internalization of the value of these tedious tasks in order to attract, engage, and retain volunteers (Grube & Piliavin, 2000). This is why SDT is so well-suited to explain volunteer work and to find effective ways to promote it.

Volunteering is, like knowledge sharing, a form of prosocial behavior. Therefore, what has been proposed regarding knowledge sharing in regards to differential engagement based on different forms of motivation (Gagné, 2009) may apply here as well. It could be that people with external reasons for volunteering will show less sustained engagement, whereas introjected people may volunteer only when it can provide an opportunity for self-enhancement (Clary & Snyder, 1999), thus leading to volunteer performance that is less beneficial to the organization or to the intended beneficiaries. Again, we would expect that identified reasons for volunteering may be the most beneficial form, because people would in this case do whatever it takes to ensure that the organization or beneficiaries profit from their work efforts. Some research supports this idea by showing that having self-oriented motives predicts in-role volunteer behavior (doing what one is expected to do), whereas having other-oriented motives predicts extra-role volunteer behavior (going beyond expectations; Cornelis, Van Hiel, & De Cremer, 2013).

Some research has indicated that paid employees are more attracted to socially responsible firms (Turban & Greening, 1997), and that many employees prefer to work for companies that have volunteering programs (Deloitte, 2007). Organizations have been quick to pick up on this and strategically use volunteering programs to attract applicants. But corporate volunteering programs (i.e., allowing employees to volunteer during work hours) can also help employees learn new skills that are useful to the organization, and serve as a way to enhance organizational identity and belongingness, which have positive effects on employee retention

(Bussell & Forbes, 2008; Farmer & Fedor, 2001). Organizations should be aware of a few things that can hinder participation in corporate volunteering programs. One factor is their compensation system. As mentioned previously, it appears that time-contingent pay systems make people see time as a compensable factor, which makes them less willing to volunteer their time. For example, people who bill for their time at work (e.g., accountants, lawyers) or who are paid on an hourly basis, and who hold more extrinsic values, are less willing to volunteer (DeVoe & Pfeffer, 2007, 2010).

A second factor has to do with how volunteers are recognized or praised for their work. SDT research has clearly shown that praise can have detrimental effects on intrinsic motivation if it is perceived to be controlling as opposed to being informational (Ryan, 1982). Therefore, organizations should take care to recognize volunteer work in a noncontrolling and genuine manner (Grant, 2012). A third factor is that organizations should steer away from creating mandatory volunteering programs, because these have been shown to block the internalization of the value of volunteering in high school students (Stukas, Snyder, & Clary, 1999). Organizations should also ensure that they make their employees feel autonomous in their volunteering work, because job characteristics and autonomy support have been shown to enhance the satisfaction, engagement, performance, and retention of volunteers (Gagné, 2003; Millette & Gagné, 2008). Therefore, it may even be better when corporate volunteer programs are initiated and managed by the employees themselves (Grant, 2012). In addition, organizations who "hire" volunteers also need to ensure that volunteer jobs are designed to be motivating (Grant, 2012; Millette & Gagné, 2008).

No research to date has directly examined the role of need satisfaction in attracting, engaging, and retaining volunteer workers. Clary et al. (1998) demonstrated, however, that volunteer work that satisfies one's motives for volunteering is likely to be sustained over time. Grant (2012) takes this idea further by proposing that when paid work is not fulfilling those motives, volunteer work can serve as a compensatory mechanism, a different space where personal motives can be fulfilled. For example, research on volunteer motivation often identifies social reasons for volunteering, such as meeting new people and feeling that one belongs to a group that shares one's values (McDougle, Greenspan, & Handy, 2011; Omoto & Snyder, 1995). We could therefore predict that satisfaction of the need for relatedness may be a particularly salient factor in these predictions, and that this may be a particularly important lever to consider when trying to attract and retain volunteer workers. There is already good evidence for this idea, because Grube and Piliavin (2000) found that the ability to form social networks through volunteering is associated with the number of hours worked by volunteers, whereas another study found that number of blood donations is related to how many friends donate blood (Piliavin & Callero, 1991). Clary and Snyder (1999) also identified "meeting people" as an important motive to start volunteering. To take this argument further, we could argue that working with like-minded people can reinforce one's values, which can enhance internalization for volunteering, hence leading to volunteer retention through two mechanisms: relatedness and autonomy.

Another important motive of volunteers is the perception that one has an impact on beneficiaries (Agostinho & Paco, 2012; Omoto & Snyder, 1995). Task significance has been shown to have particularly strong motivational power in service-oriented jobs, and has been shown to significantly influence job performance in paid workers (Grant, 2007, 2008). This effect may be partly explained by the effects of task significance on feelings of competence and relatedness, which can be enhanced by allowing for direct contact between volunteers and beneficiaries (Grant, 2007; Grant et al., 2007). It may also be stronger when people already have strong identified motivation (i.e., motivated by values and meaning) for their volunteer work.

Given all this, we can argue that volunteering is not only good for the beneficiaries and society in general, but that it also has a direct positive impact on the volunteers themselves. There is evidence that volunteering is good for one's mental health (Harlow & Cantor, 1996) and career advancement (Wilson & Musick, 2003), and that it can also lead to longevity (Musick, Herzog, & House, 1999). We could better understand why these effects are happening by using the concept of need satisfaction from SDT.

Final Personal Reflections

What I hoped to achieve through this Handbook was to inspire readers to conduct research and build organizational practices using SDT in the work domain. I have brought together researchers to talk about how they have applied the theory to their areas of interest. I asked all authors to also talk about what else we could do with the theory in the work

domain that has not yet been done, and they have answered this call by providing plenty of ideas! In this concluding chapter, I discuss additional applications of the theory to give readers an even wider array of what has been done to date, and of what could be done in the future. I hope that researchers, seasoned and neophytes, will pounce on these ideas and turn them into new knowledge. Editing this Handbook has left me amazed by the variety and richness of the applications of the theory, and by the endless new things for which it could be used. SDT has only recently begun to be applied to the work domain. I can only imagine what the future holds for SDT in this domain, and I hope to see it transform tomorrow's organizations.

Note

1. I thank Sharon Parker for providing feedback on a previous draft of this chapter.

References

Agostinho, D., & Paço, A. (2012). Analysis of the motivations, generativity and demographics of the food bank volunteer. *International Journal of Nonprofit and Voluntary Sector Marketing*, *17*(3), 249–261. doi:http://dx.doi.org/10.1002/nvsm.1427

Aiello, J. R. (1993). Computer-based work monitoring: Electronic surveillance and its effects. *Journal of Applied Social Psychology*, *23*, 499–500.

Aiello, J. R., & Shao, Y. (1993). Electronic performance monitoring and stress: The role of feedback and goal setting. In M. J. Smith, & G. Salvendy (Eds.), *Human-computer interaction: Applications and case studies* (pp. 1011–1016). Amsterdam: Elsevier Science Publishers

Aiello, J. R., & Svek, C. M. (1993). Computer monitoring of work performance: Extending the social facilitation framework to electronic presence. *Journal of Applied Social Psychology*, *23*, 537–548.

Ajzen, I. (1991). The theory of planned behavior. *Organizational Behavior and Human Decision Processes*, *50*(2), 179–211. doi:http://dx.doi.org/10.1016/0749-5978%2891%2990020-T

Amabile, T. M. (1979). Effects of external evaluations on artistic creativity. *Journal of Personality and Social Psychology*, *37*, 221–233.

Amabile, T. M. (1983). The social psychology of creativity: A componential conceptualization. *Journal of Personality and Social Psychology*, *45*(2), 357–376. doi:http://dx.doi.org/10.1037/0022-3514.45.2.357

Amabile, T. M. (1988). From individual creativity to organizational innovation. In K. Gronhaug, & G. Kaufmann (Eds.), *Innovation: A cross-disciplinary perspective* (pp. 139–166). Oslo, Norway: Norwegian University Press.

Amabile, T. M. (1993). Motivational synergy: Toward new conceptualizations of intrinsic and extrinsic motivation in the workplace. *Human Resource Management Review*, *3*(3), 185–201.

Amabile, T. M., & Conti, R. (1999). Changes in the work environment for creativity during downsizing. *Academy of Management Journal*, *42*(6), 630–640. doi:http://dx.doi.org/10.2307/256984

Amabile, T. M., Conti, R., Coon, H., Lazenby, J., & Herron, M. (1996). Assessing the work environment for creativity. *Academy of Management Journal, 39*(5), 1154–1184. doi:http://dx.doi.org/10.2307/256995

Amabile, T. M., DeJong, W., & Lepper, M. R. (1976). Effects of externally imposed deadlines on subsequent intrinsic motivation. *Journal of Personality and Social Psychology, 34*, 92–98.

Amabile, T. M., Hennessey, B. A., & Grossman, B. S. (1986). Social influences on creativity: The effects of contracted-for reward. *Journal of Personality and Social Psychology, 50*(1), 14–23. doi:http://dx.doi.org/10.1037/0022-3514.50.1.14

American Management Association (2008). *Electronic monitoring and surveillance survey from the American Management Association and the Epolicy Institute.* New York. http://www.plattgroupllc.com/jun08/2007ElectronicMonitoringSurveillanceSurvey.pdf

Axtell, C. M., Holman, D., Unsworth, K., Wall, T., Waterson, P., & Harrington, E. (2000). Shopfloor innovation: Facilitating the suggestion and implementation of ideas. *Journal of Occupational and Organizational Psychology, 73*(3), 265–285. doi:http://dx.doi.org/10.1348/096317900167029

Ball, K., & Wilson, D. C. (2000). Power, control and computer-based performance monitoring: Repertoires, resistance and subjectivities. *Organization Studies, 21*(3), 539–565. doi:http://dx.doi.org/10.1177/0170840600213003

Bang, H., Ross, S., & Reio, T. G., Jr. (2013). From motivation to organizational commitment of volunteers in non-profit sport organizations: The role of job satisfaction. *Journal of Management Development, 32*(1), 96–112. doi:http://dx.doi.org/10.1108/02621711311287044

Bartol, K. M. (1999). Reframing salesforce compensation systems: An agency theory-based performance management perspective. *Journal of Personal Selling & Sales Management, 19*(3), 1–16.

Burgess, M., Enzle, M. E., & Schmaltz, R. (2004). Defeating the potentially deleterious effects of externally imposed deadlines: Practitioners' rules-of-thumb. *Personality and Social Psychology Bulletin, 30*(7), 868–877. doi:http://dx.doi.org/10.1177/0146167204264089

Bussell, H., & Forbes, D. (2008). How UK universities engage with their local communities: A study of employer supported volunteering. *International Journal of Nonprofit and Voluntary Sector Marketing, 13*(4), 363–378. doi:http://dx.doi.org/10.1002/nvsm.331

Carayon, P. (1993). Effect of electronic performance monitoring on job design and worker stress: Review of the literature and conceptual model. *Human Factors, 35*(3), 385–395.

Carayon, P. (1994). Effects of electronic performance monitoring on job design and worker stress: Results of two studies. *International Journal of Human-Computer Interaction, 6*(2), 177–190. doi:http://dx.doi.org/10.1080/10447319409526089

Carpini, J. A., & Gagné, M. (2013, June). *Leaders' trustworthiness and the mediating role of autonomy in predicting employee performance and turnover intentions.* Paper presented at the 5th International Conference on Self-Determination Theory, Rochester, NY.

Chen, G., & Kanfer, R. (2006). Toward a systems theory of motivated behavior in work teams. *Research in Organizational Behavior, 27*, 223–267. doi:10.1016/S0191-3085(06)27006-0

Clary, E., & Snyder, M. (1999). The motivations to volunteer: Theoretical and practical considerations. *Current Directions in Psychological Science, 8*(5), 156–159. doi:http://dx.doi.org/10.1111/1467-8721.00037

Clary, E., Snyder, M., Ridge, R. D., Copeland, J., Stukas, A. A., Haugen, J., & Miene, P. (1998). Understanding and assessing the motivations of volunteers: A functional approach. *Journal of Personality and Social Psychology, 74*(6), 1516–1530. doi:http://dx.doi.org/10.1037/0022-3514.74.6.1516

Clegg, C., & Spencer, C. (2007). A circular and dynamic model of the process of job design. *Journal of Occupational and Organizational Psychology, 80*(2), 321–339. doi:http://dx.doi.org/10.1348/096317906X113211

Cockrell, R., & Stone, D. N. (2010). Industry culture influences pseudo-knowledge sharing: A multiple mediation analysis. *Journal of Knowledge Management, 14*(6), 841–857. doi:http://dx.doi.org/10.1108/13673271011084899

Colquitt, J. A., Conlon, D. E., Wesson, M. J., Porter, C. O., & Ng, K. (2001). Justice at the millennium: A meta-analytic review of 25 years of organizational justice research. *Journal of Applied Psychology, 86*(3), 425–445. doi:http://dx.doi.org/10.1037/0021-9010.86.3.425

Cornelis, I., Van Hiel, A., & De Cremer, D. (2013). Volunteer work in youth organizations: Predicting distinct aspects of volunteering behavior from self- and other-oriented motives. *Journal of Applied Social Psychology, 43*(2), 456–466. doi:http://dx.doi.org/10.1111/j.1559-1816.2013.01029.x

Davis, F. D. (1989). Perceived usefulness, perceived ease of use, and user acceptance of information technology. *MIS Quarterly, 13*, 319–339.

Davis, F. D., Bagozzi, R. P., & Warshaw, P. R. (1992). Extrinsic and intrinsic motivation to use computers in the workplace. *Journal of Applied Social Psychology, 22*, 1111–1132.

de Bilde, J., Vansteenkiste, M., & Lens, W. (2011). Understanding the association between future time perspective and self-regulated learning through the lens of self-determination theory. *Learning and Instruction, 21*(3), 332–344. doi:http://dx.doi.org/10.1016/j.learninstruc.2010.03.002

De Tienne, K. B., & Abbott, N. T. (1993). Developing an employee-centered electronic monitoring system. *Journal of Systems Management, 44*, 12–13.

Deci, E. L. (1971). Effects of externally mediated rewards on intrinsic motivation. *Journal of Personality and Social Psychology, 18*, 105–115.

Deci, E. L. (1995). *Why we do what we do: The dynamics of personal autonomy.* New York: Putnam.

Deci, E. L., Betley, G., Kahle, J., Abrams, L., & Porac, J. (1981). When trying to win: Competition and intrinsic motivation. *Personality and Social Psychology Bulletin, 7*(1), 79–83. doi:http://dx.doi.org/10.1177/014616728171012

Deci, E. L., Connell, J., & Ryan, R. M. (1989). Self-determination in a work organization. *Journal of Applied Psychology, 74*, 580–590.

Deci, E. L., Eghrari, H., Patrick, B. C., & Leone, D. R. (1994). Facilitating internalization: The self-determination theory perspective. *Journal of Personality, 62*, 119–142.

Deci, E. L., Koestner, R., & Ryan, R. M. (1999). A meta-analytic review of experiments examining the effects of extrinsic rewards on intrinsic motivation. *Psychological Bulletin, 125*, 627–668.

Deci, E. L., & Ryan, R. M. (2000). The "what" and "why" of goal pursuits: Human needs and the self-determination of behavior. *Psychological Inquiry, 11*, 227–268.

Deci, E. L., & Ryan, R. M. (2008). Self-determination theory: A macrotheory of human motivation, development, and health. *Canadian Psychology/Psychologie Canadienne, 49*(3), 182–185. doi:http://dx.doi.org/10.1037/a0012801

Deci, E. L., & Ryan, R. M. (2012). Motivation, personality, and development within embedded social contexts: An overview of self-determination theory. In R. M. Ryan (Ed.), *The Oxford handbook of human motivation* (pp. 85–107). New York: Oxford University Press.

Deci, E. L., Spiegel, N. H., Ryan, R. M., Koestner, R., & Kauffman, M. (1982). Effects of performance standards on teaching styles: Behavior of controlling teachers. *Journal of Educational Psychology, 74*(6), 852–859. doi:http://dx.doi.org/10.1037/0022-0663.74.6.852

Deloitte. (2007). *Executive summary: Volunteer impact survey.* Retrieved from http://www.handsonnetwork.org/files/resources/Deloitte_impact_survey07.pdf

DeVoe, S. E., & Pfeffer, J. (2007). Hourly payment and volunteering: The effect of organizational practices on decisions about time use. *Academy of Management Journal, 50*(4), 783–798. doi:http://dx.doi.org/10.5465/AMJ.2007.26279171

DeVoe, S. E., & Pfeffer, J. (2010). The stingy hour: How accounting for time affects volunteering. *Personality and Social Psychology Bulletin, 36*(4), 470–483. doi:http://dx.doi.org/10.1177/0146167209359699

Dirks, K. T. (1999). The effects of interpersonal trust on work group performance. *Journal of Applied Psychology, 84*(3), 445–455. doi:http://dx.doi.org/10.1037/0021-9010.84.3.445

Eisenberger, R., & Shanock, L. (2003). Rewards, intrinsic motivation, and creativity: A case study of conceptual and methodological isolation. *Creativity Research Journal, 15*(2–3), 121–130. doi:http://dx.doi.org/10.1207/S15326934CRJ152&3_02

Enzle, M. E., & Anderson, S. C. (1993). Surveillant intentions and intrinsic motivation. *Journal of Personality and Social Psychology, 64*(2), 257–266. doi:http://dx.doi.org/10.1037/0022-3514.64.2.257

Farmer, S. M., & Fedor, D. B. (1999). Volunteer participation and withdrawal: A psychological contract perspective on the role of satisfaction, expectations, and organizational support. *Nonprofit Management and Leadership, 9*, 86–99.

Farmer, S. M., & Fedor, D. B. (2001). Changing the focus on volunteering: An investigation of volunteers' multiple contributions to a charitable organization. *Journal of Management, 27*, 191–211.

Fernet, C., Gagné, M., & Austin, S. (2010). When does quality of relationships with coworkers predict burnout over time? The moderating role of work motivation. *Journal of Organizational Behavior, 31*(8), 1163–1180. doi:http://dx.doi.org/10.1002/job.673

Foss, N. J., Minbaeva, D. B., Pedersen, T., & Reinholt, M. (2009). Encouraging knowledge sharing among employees: How job design matters. *Human Resource Management, 48*(6), 871–893. doi:http://dx.doi.org/10.1002/hrm.20320

Frederick-Recascino, C. M., & Schuster-Smith, H. (2003). Competition and intrinsic motivation in physical activity: A comparison of two groups. *Journal of Sport Behavior, 26*(3), 240–254.

Gagné, M. (2003). The role of autonomy support and autonomy orientation in prosocial behavior engagement. *Motivation and Emotion, 27*(3), 199–223.

Gagné, M. (2009). A model of knowledge-sharing motivation. *Human Resource Management, 48*(4), 571–589. doi:http://dx.doi.org/10.1002/hrm.v48:410.1002/hrm.20298

Gagné, M. (2009, June). *The mediating effect of work motivation on the relation between trust and performance.* Paper presented in a symposium (Chair T. Hecht) of the Canadian Psychological Association, Montreal, Canada.

Gagné, M., Bérubé, N., & Donia, M. (2007). *Relationships between different forms of organizational justice and different motivational orientations.* Paper presented at the the Society for Industrial and Organizational Psychology, New York, NY.

Gagné, M., & Forest, J. (2008). The study of compensation systems through the lens of self-determination theory: Reconciling 35 years of debate. *Canadian Psychology/Psychologie Canadienne, 49*(3), 225–232. doi:http://dx.doi.org/10.1037/a0012757

Gagné, M., & Vansteenkiste, M. (2013). Self-determination theory's contribution to positive organizational psychology. In A. B. Bakker (Ed.), *Advances in positive organizational psychology* (Vol. 1, pp. 61–82). Bingley, UK: Emerald.

Gillet, N., Vallerand, R. J., & Rosnet, E. (2009). Motivational clusters and performance in a real-life setting. *Motivation and Emotion, 33*(1), 49–62. doi:http://dx.doi.org/10.1007/s11031-008-9115-z

Grant, A. M. (2007). Relational job design and the motivation to make a prosocial difference. *The Academy of Management Review, 32*(2), 393–417. doi:http://dx.doi.org/10.2307/20159308

Grant, A. M. (2008). The significance of task significance: Job performance effects, relational mechanisms, and boundary conditions. *Journal of Applied Psychology, 93*(1), 108–124. doi:http://dx.doi.org/10.1037/0021-9010.93.1.108

Grant, A. M. (2012). Giving time, time after time: Work design and sustained employee participation in corporate volunteering. *Academy of Management Review, 37*(4), 589–615. doi:http://dx.doi.org/10.5465/amr.2010.0280

Grant, A. M., Campbell, E. M., Chen, G., Cottone, K., Lapedis, D., & Lee, K. (2007). Impact and the art of motivation maintenance: The effects of contact with beneficiaries on persistence behavior. *Organizational Behavior and Human Decision Processes, 103*(1), 53–67. doi:http://dx.doi.org/10.1016/j.obhdp.2006.05.004

Grant, R. M. (1996). Toward a knowledge-based theory of the firm. *Strategic Management Journal, 17*, 109–122.

Grenier, S., Chiocchio, F., Gagné, M., & Sarrazin, L.-P. (2013). *Individual and team motivational process: Multilevel implications of social interactions on self-determined motivation.* Unpublished manuscript, University of Montreal.

Grenier, S., Gagné, M., & Chiocchio, F. (2013). *The motivational composition of work teams: Relations with team member satisfaction.* Unpublished manuscript, University of Montreal.

Griffith, T. L. (1993). Monitoring and performance: A comparison of computer and supervisor monitoring. *Journal of Applied Social Psychology, 23*, 549–572.

Grouzet, F., Kasser, T., Ahuvia, A., Fernandez-Dols, J. M., Kim, Y., Lau, S.,...& Sheldon, K. M. (2005). The structure of goal contents across 15 cultures. *Journal of Personality and Social Psychology, 89*, 800–806.

Grube, J. A., & Piliavin, J. A. (2000). Role identity, organizational experiences and volunteer performance. *Personality and Social Psychology Bulletin, 26*(9), 1108–1119. doi:http://dx.doi.org/10.1177/01461672002611007

Guay, F. (2005). Motivations underlying career decision-making activities: The career decision-making autonomy scale (CDMAS). *Journal of Career Assessment, 13*(1), 77–97. doi:http://dx.doi.org/10.1177/1069072704270297

Guay, F., Ratelle, C. F., Senecal, C., Larose, S., & Deschenes, A. (2006). Distinguishing developmental from chronic career indecision: Self-efficacy, autonomy, and social support. *Journal of Career Assessment*, *14*(2), 235–251. doi:http://dx.doi.org/10.1177/1069072705283975

Haddad, Y. S. (1982). *The effect of informational versus controlling verbal feedback on self-determination and preference for challenge* (Unpublished doctoral dissertation). University of Rochester, Rochester, NY.

Han, T.-S., & Shen, C.-H. (2007). The effects of bonus systems on firm performance in Taiwan's high-tech sector. *Journal of Comparative Economics*, *35*, 235–249.

Harlow, R., & Cantor, N. (1996). Still participating after all these years. *Journal of Personality and Social Psychology*, *71*, 1235–1249.

Hartmann, F., & Slapnicar, S. (2012). Pay fairness and intrinsic motivation: The role of pay transparency. *International Journal of Human Resource Management*, *23*(20), 4283–4300. doi:http://dx.doi.org/10.1080/09585192.2012.664962

Janssen, O. (2000). Job demands, perceptions of effort-reward fairness and innovative work behaviour. *Journal of Occupational and Organizational Psychology*, *73*(3), 287–302. doi:http://dx.doi.org/10.1348/096317900167038

Jensen, M. C., & Meckling, W. H. (1976). Theory of the firm: Managerial behavior, agency costs, and ownership structure. *Journal of Financial Economics*, *3*, 305–360.

Joussemet, M., & Koestner, R. (1999). Effect of expected rewards on children's creativity. *Creativity Research Journal*, *12*(4), 231–239. doi:http://dx.doi.org/10.1207/s15326934crj1204_1

Kasser, T., & Ryan, R. M. (1993). A dark side of the American dream: Correlates of financial success as a central life aspiration. *Journal of Personality and Social Psychology*, *65*, 410–422.

Kerr, S. (1995). On the folly of rewarding A while hoping for B. *Academy of Management Executive*, *9*, 7–14.

Koestner, R., Losier, G. F., Vallerand, R. J., & Carducci, D. (1996). Identified and introjected forms of political internalization: Extending self-determination theory. *Journal of Personality and Social Psychology*, *70*, 1025–1036.

Koestner, R., Ryan, R. M., Bernieri, F., & Holt, K. (1984). Setting limits on children's behavior: The differential effects of controlling vs informational styles on intrinsic motivation and creativity. *Journal of Personality*, *52*, 231–248.

Komaki, J. L. (1986). Toward effective supervision: An operant analysis and comparions of managers at work. *Journal of Applied Psychology*, *71*, 270–279.

Komaki, J. L., Desselles, M. L., & Bowman, E. D. (1989). Definitely not a breeze: Extending an operant model of effective supervision to teams. *Journal of Applied Psychology*, *74*, 522–529.

Kuvaas, B., Buch, R., Dysvik, A., & Haerem, T. (2012). Economic and social leader-member exchange relationships and follower performance. *The Leadership Quarterly*, *23*(5), 756–765. doi:http://dx.doi.org/10.1016/j.leaqua.2011.12.013

Larson, J. R., & Callahan, C. (1990). Performance monitoring: How it affects work productivity. *Journal of Applied Psychology*, *75*(5), 530–538. doi:http://dx.doi.org/10.1037/0021-9010.75.5.530

Lazear, E. P., & Rosen, S. (1981). Rank-order tournaments as optimum labor contracts. *Journal of Political Economics*, *89*, 841–864.

Lepper, M. R., & Greene, D. (1975). Turning play into work: Effects of adult surveillance and extrinsic rewards on children's intrinsic motivation. *Journal of Personality and Social Psychology*, *31*, 479–486.

Levy, P. E., & Williams, J. R. (2004). The social context of performance appraisal: A review and framework for the future. *Journal of Management*, *30*(6), 881–905. doi:http://dx.doi.org/10.1016/j.jm.2004.06.005

Liberman, N., & Trope, Y. (1998). The role of feasibility and desirability considerations in near and distant future decisions: A test of temporal construal theory. *Journal of Personality and Social Psychology*, *75*(1), 5–18. doi:http://dx.doi.org/10.1037/0022-3514.75.1.5

Magnan, M., & St-Onge, S. (2005). The impact of profit sharing on the performance of financial services firms. *Journal of Management Studies*, *42*, 761–791.

Mayer, D. M., Bardes, M., & Piccolo, R. F. (2008). Do servant-leaders help satisfy follower needs? An organizational justice perspective. *European Journal of Work and Organizational Psychology*, *17*(2), 180–197. doi:http://dx.doi.org/10.1080/13594320701743558

Mayer, R. C., Davis, J. H., & Schoorman, F. (1995). An integrative model of organizational trust. *The Academy of Management Review*, *20*(3), 709–734. doi:http://dx.doi.org/10.2307/258792

Mayer, R. C., & Gavin, M. B. (2005). Trust in management and performance: Who minds the shop while the employees watch the boss? *Academy of Management Journal*, *48*(5), 874–888. doi:http://dx.doi.org/10.5465/AMJ.2005.18803928

McDougle, L. M., Greenspan, I., & Handy, F. (2011). Generation green: Understanding the motivations and mechanisms influencing young adults' environmental volunteering. *International Journal of Nonprofit and Voluntary Sector Marketing*, *16*(4), 325–341. doi:http://dx.doi.org/10.1002/nvsm.431

Millette, V., & Gagné, M. (2008). Designing volunteers' tasks to maximize motivation, satisfaction and performance: The impact of job characteristics on volunteer engagement. *Motivation and Emotion*, *32*(1), 11–22. doi:http://dx.doi.org/10.1007/s11031-007-9079-4

Mitchell, J. I., Gagné, M., Beaudry, A., & Dyer, L. (2012). The role of perceived organizational support, distributive justice and motivation in reactions to new information technology. *Computers in Human Behavior*, *28*(2), 729–738. doi:http://dx.doi.org/10.1016/j.chb.2011.11.021

Moller, A. C., Deci, E. L., & Ryan, R. M. (2006). Choice and ego-depletion: The moderating role of autonomy. *Personality and Social Psychology Bulletin*, *32*(8), 1024–1036. doi:http://dx.doi.org/10.1177/0146167206288008

Muraven, M., & Baumeister, R. F. (2000). Self-regulation and depletion of limited resources: Does self-control resemble a muscle? *Psychological Bulletin*, *126*(2), 247–259. doi:http://dx.doi.org/10.1037/0033-2909.126.2.247

Muraven, M., Gagné, M., & Rosman, H. (2008). Helpful self-control: Autonomy support, vitality, and depletion. *Journal of Experimental Social Psychology*, *44*(3), 573–585. doi:10.1016/j.jesp.2007.10.008

Muraven, M., Rosman, H., & Gagné, M. (2007). Lack of autonomy and self-control: Performance contingent rewards lead to greater depletion. *Motivation and Emotion*, *31*, 322–330. doi:10.1007/s11031-007-9073-x

Murphy, K. R., & Cleveland, J. N. (1991). *Performance appraisal: An organizational perspective*. Boston, MA: Allyn & Beacon.

Musick, M. A., Herzog, A. R., & House, J. S. (1999). Volunteering and mortality among older adults: Findings from a national sample. *Journal of Gerontology: Psychological Sciences and Social Sciences, 54*(B), S173-S180.

Nix, G. A., Ryan, R. M., Manly, J. B., & Deci, E. L. (1999). Revitalization through self-regulation: The effects of autonomous and controlled motivation on happiness and vitality. *Journal of Experimental Social Psychology, 35*, 266–284.

Omoto, A. M., & Snyder, M. (1995). Sustained helping without obligation: Motivation, longevity of service, and perceived attitude change among aids volunteers. *Journal of Personality and Social Psychology, 68*(4), 671–686. doi:http://dx.doi.org/10.1037/0022-3514.68.4.671

Pelletier, L. G., Séguin-Lévesque, C., & Legault, L. (2002). Pressure from above and pressure from below as determinants of teachers' motivation and teaching behaviors. *Journal of Educational Psychology, 94*, 186–196.

Pelletier, L. G., & Vallerand, R. J. (1996). Supervisors' beliefs and subordinates' intrinsic motivation: A behavioral confirmation analysis. *Journal of Personality and Social Psychology, 71*(2), 331–340. doi:http://dx.doi.org/10.1037/0022-3514.71.2.331

Pfeffer, J. (1998). Six dangerous myths about pay. *Harvard Business Review*, 108–119.

Piekkola, H. (2005). Performance-related pay and firm performance in Finland. *International Journal of Manpower, 26*, 619–635.

Piliavin, J. A., & Callero, P. L. (1991). *Giving blood: The development of an altruistic identity*. Baltimore, MD: The John Hopkins University Press.

Reeve, J. (2009). Why teachers adopt a controlling motivating style toward students and how they can become more autonomy supportive. *Educational Psychologist, 44*, 159–178.

Reeve, J., & Deci, E. L. (1996). Elements of the competitive situation that affect intrinsic motivation. *Personality and Social Psychology Bulletin, 22*, 24–33.

Reinholt, M., Pedersen, T., & Foss, N. J. (2011). Why a central network position isn't enough: The role of motivation and ability for knowledge sharing in employee networks. *Academy of Management Journal, 54*(6), 1277–1297.

Roca, J. C., & Gagné, M. (2008). Understanding e-learning continuance intention in the workplace: A self-determination theory perspective. *Computers in Human Behavior, 24*(4), 1585–1604. doi:http://dx.doi.org/10.1016/j.chb.2007.06.001

Ryan, R. M. (1982). Control and information if the interpersonal sphere: An extension of cognitive evaluation theory. *Journal of Personality and Social Psychology, 43*, 450–461.

Ryan, R. M., & Frederick, C. (1997). On energy, personality, and health: Subjective vitality as a dynamic reflection of well-being. *Journal of Personality, 65*(3), 529–565. doi:http://dx.doi.org/10.1111/j.1467-6494.1997.tb00326.x

Ryan, R. M., & Weinstein, N. (2009). Undermining quality teaching and learning: A self-determination theory perspective on high-stakes testing. *Theory and Research in Education, 7*(2), 224–233.

Rynes, S. L., Gerhart, B., & Parks, L. (2005). Personnel psychology: Performance evaluation and pay for performance. *Annual Review of Psychology, 56*, 571–600.

Sarrazin, P. G., Tessier, D. P., Pelletier, L. G., Trouilloud, D. O., & Chanal, J. P. (2006). The effects of teachers' expectations about students' motivation on teachers' autonomy-supportive and controlling behaviors. *International Journal of Sport and Exercise Psychology, 4*(3), 283–301.

Schmidt, A. M., & DeShon, R. P. (2007). What to do? The effects of discrepancies, incentives, and time on dynamic goal prioritization. *Journal of Applied Psychology, 92*(4), 928–941. doi:http://dx.doi.org/10.1037/0021-9010.92.4.928

Seppala, T., Lipponen, J., Pirttila-Backman, A.-M., & Lipsanen, J. (2011). Reciprocity of trust in the supervisor-subordinate relationship: The mediating role of autonomy and the sense of power. *European Journal of Work and Organizational Psychology, 20*(6), 755–778. doi:http://dx.doi.org/10.1080/1359432X.2010.507353

Sheldon, K. M., & Elliot, A. J. (1998). Not all personal goals are "personal": Comparing autonomous and controlling goals on effort and attainment. *Personality and Social Psychology Bulletin, 24*, 546–557.

Smith, M. J., Carayon, P., Sanders, K. J., Lim, S., & LeGrande, D. (1992). Employee stress and health complaints in jobs with and without electronic performance monitoring. *Applied Ergonomics, 23*, 17–27. doi:10.1016/0003-6870(92)90006-H

Soenens, B., Sierens, E., Vansteenkiste, M., Dochy, F., & Goossens, L. (2012). Psychologically controlling teaching: Examining outcomes, antecedents, and mediators. *Journal of Educational Psychology, 104*(1), 108–120. doi:http://dx.doi.org/10.1037/a0025742

Sorebo, O., Halvari, H., Gulli, V. F., & Kristiansen, R. (2009). The role of self-determination theory in explaining teachers' motivation to continue to use e-learning technology. *Computers & Education, 53*(4), 1177–1187. doi:http://dx.doi.org/10.1016/j.compedu.2009.06.001

Stanton, J. M., & Barnes-Farrell, J. L. (1996). Effects of electronic performance monitoring on personal control, task satisfaction, and task performance. *Journal of Applied Psychology, 81*(6), 738–745. doi:http://dx.doi.org/10.1037/0021-9010.81.6.738

Stone, E. F., & Stone, D. L. (1990). Privacy in organizations: Theoretical issues, research findings, and protection mechanisms. In G. R. Ferris, & K. M. Rowland (Eds.), *Research in personnel and human resource management* (Vol. 8, pp. 349–411). Greenwich, CT: JAI.

Stukas, A. A., Snyder, M., & Clary, E. G. (1999). The effects of "mandatory volunteerism" on intentions to volunteer. *Psychological Science, 10*, 59–64.

Taylor, I. M., Ntoumanis, N., & Standage, M. (2008). A self-determination theory approach to understanding the antecedents of teachers' motivational strategies in physical education. *Journal of Sport & Exercise Psychology, 30*(1), 75–94.

Turban, D. B., & Greening, D. W. (1997). Corporate social performance and organizational attractiveness to prospective employees. *Academy of Management Journal, 40*(3), 658–672. doi:http://dx.doi.org/10.2307/257057

Unsworth, K. L., Wall, T. D., & Carter, A. (2005). Creative requirement: A neglected construct in the study of employee creativity? *Group & Organization Management, 30*(5), 541–560. doi:http://dx.doi.org/10.1177/1059601104267607

Van den Broeck, A., Lens, W., De Witte, H., & Van Coillie, H. (2013). Unraveling the importance of the quantity and the quality of workers' motivation for well-being: A person-centered perspective. *Journal of Vocational Behavior, 82*(1), 69–78. doi:http://dx.doi.org/10.1016/j.jvb.2012.11.005

Van den Broeck, A., Vansteenkiste, M., Lens, W., & De Witte, H. (2010). Unemployed individuals' work values and job flexibility: An explanation from expectancy-value theory and self-determination theory. *Applied Psychology: An*

International Review, 59(2), 296–317. doi:http://dx.doi.org/10.1111/j.1464-0597.2009.00391.x

van Prooijen, J.-W. (2009). Procedural justice as autonomy regulation. *Journal of Personality and Social Psychology, 96*(6), 1166–1180. doi:http://dx.doi.org/10.1037/a0014153

Vansteenkiste, M., & Deci, E. L. (2003). Competitively contingent rewards and intrinsic motivation: Can losers remain motivated? *Motivation and Emotion, 27*(4), 273–299. doi:http://dx.doi.org/10.1023/A:1026259005264

Vansteenkiste, M., Lens, W., De Witte, H., & Feather, N. (2005). Understanding unemployed people's job search behaviour, unemployment experience and well-being: A comparison of expectancy-value theory and self-determination theory. *British Journal of Social Psychology, 44*(2), 269–287. doi:http://dx.doi.org/10.1348/014466604X17641

Vansteenkiste, M., Lens, W., De Witte, S., De Witte, H., & Deci, E. L. (2004). The "why" and "why not" of job search behaviour: Their relation to searching, unemployment experience, and well-being. *European Journal of Social Psychology, 34*(3), 345–363. doi:http://dx.doi.org/10.1002/ejsp.202

Venkatesh, V. (2000). Determinants of perceived ease of use: Integrating control, intrinsic motivation, and emotion into the technology acceptance model. *Information Systems Research, 11*(4), 342–365. doi:http://dx.doi.org/10.1287/isre.11.4.342.11872

Venkatesh, V., & Johnson, P. (2002). Telecommuting technology implementations: A within- and between-subjects longitudinal field study. *Personnel Psychology, 55*(3), 661–688. doi:http://dx.doi.org/10.1111/j.1744-6570.2002.tb00125.x

Venkatesh, V., & Speier, C. (1999). Computer technology training in the workplace: A longitudinal investigation of the effect of mood. *Organizational Behavior and Human Decision Processes, 79*(1), 1–28. doi:http://dx.doi.org/10.1006/obhd.1999.2837

Venkatesh, V., & Speier, C. (2000). Creating an effective training environment for enhancing telework. *International Journal of Human-Computer Studies, 52*(6), 991–1005. doi:http://dx.doi.org/10.1006/ijhc.1999.0367

Wells, D. L., Moorman, R. H., & Werner, J. M. (2007). The impact of the perceived purpose of electronic performance monitoring on an array of attitudinal variables. *Human Resource Development Quarterly, 18*(1), 121–138. doi:http://dx.doi.org/10.1002/hrdq.1194

Wilson, J., & Musick, M. (2003). Doing well by doing good: Volunteering and occupational achievement among American women. *Sociological Quarterly, 44*, 433–450.

Zapata-Phelan, C. P., Colquitt, J. A., Scott, B. A., & Livingston, B. (2009). Procedural justice, interactional justice, and task performance: The mediating role of intrinsic motivation. *Organizational Behavior and Human Decision Processes, 108*(1), 93–105. doi:http://dx.doi.org/10.1016/j.obhdp.2008.08.001

INDEX

A

Abraham, R., 270
absorption, levels of, 95
abusive supervisor, 150, 302
academic-contingent self-esteem, 132
accidents, 277
accomplishment, diminished sense of, 269
action theory, 52
active violence, 298. *See also* workplace violence
activity engagement, 43
activity selection, 96–97
activity valuation, 97, 98
adult attachment research, 109
affective commitment, 34, 36–37, 39
affiliative behaviors, 54
agency theory, 200, 203–204
aggression, 297–300. *See also* workplace violence
Agnew, T.G., 42
Aitken, N.M., 319, 325
Akelof, G., 200
Akerlof, G.A., 205
Alderfer, C.P., 15
Alderfer's theory, 167–168, 170
Allen, D.G., 304
Allen, J.W., 128
Allen, N.J., 34, 35
Alm, J., 80
altruism, 75
Ambrose, M.L., 5, 28
Amiot, C., 101
Amiot, C.E., 238–239
amotivated, 16
amotivation, 43, 110, 144, 194, 208, 233, 237–238, 265, 324, 336. *See also* motivation
Andriessen, J.H.T.H., 277–279
Anna Karenina (Tolstoy), 383
antecedent-focused strategies, 261
Anthony, D.B., 131
anticipation phase, 52
appearance-contingent self-esteem, 128, 132
Aquino, K., 304

Argyris, C., 26
Arthur, M.B., 188
Arthur, W.A., Jr., 143
Ashford, S.J., 52
Ashforth, B.E., 261, 262
Association of Women for Action and Research, 296
attachment anxiety, 114–115
attachment avoidance, 115–116
attachment security, 116–117, 122
attachment styles, 114–115
attachment theory
    definition of, 109
    relatedness support in workplace, 118–119
    research on concept of, 112–113
    stress regulation and, 113
attachment working models, 113–114
attentional advice, 222
attraction-selection-attrition model, 149
attraction-selection-attrition-success theories, 393, 394–395
attribution theory, 188
attrition, teacher, 351
Austin, S., 235, 237, 238
authenticity, 267–268
authentic leadership, 189–190
autonomous causality orientation, 183
autonomous goals, 402–403
autonomous internalization, 97
autonomously motivated proactivity, 58–59, 66
autonomously regulated proactivity, 61–62, 65–66
autonomous motivation. *See also* motivation
    attachment anxiety and, 115
    attachment avoidance and, 115–116
    attachment security and, 116–117
    compensation and, 208
    complementary fit and, 153
    controlled motivation and, 110–111
    controlled motivation vs., 221–223, 408
    definition of, 16–17, 109, 220, 233–234, 300, 317

    facilitation of, 27
    feedback and, 253
    goal pursuit and, 402, 405–406, 409
    information sharing and, 253
    job design and, 165–166
    job satisfaction and, 17–18
    job stressors and, 238–239
    knowledge sharing and, 422–423
    PE fit and, 152–155
    for proenvironmental behavior, 329–330
    self-reported, 408–409
    supplementary fit and, 153–155
    teachers and, 352–353
    toward environment, 324
    training and, 221–223
    at workplace, 63, 282–283, 416
autonomous self-regulation, 61, 176, 182, 186, 189, 247–250, 299, 367–370, 415
autonomous work group, 173–174
autonomy
    actual, 98
    control vs., 4
    controversy of, 23–24
    definition of, 366, 401–402, 404
    dependence vs., 23
    goal pursuit and, 404
    independence vs., 4, 183
    interference, 121
    job, 171
    job characteristics model and, 169
    need for, 18–19, 144, 182–183
    in organizations, 64
    perceived, 98
    proactivity and, 59–60
    self-determination theory and, 23–24
    student, 353
    support for, 63–64
    supportive of, 19
    thriving and, 251
    well-being and, 23–24, 41
    in the workplace, 121–122
autonomy orientation, 20, 111, 182, 224, 301, 304

433

autonomy support
  definition of, 301
  goal pursuit and, 410–411
  peer, 303
  receiving and giving, 353
  structure and, 357
  for students, 353
  teacher-provided, 353–354, 418–419
autonomy-supportive environments, 150, 184
avoidant attachment, 114
Avolio, B.J., 189

B

Baard, P.P., 21, 44, 59, 182, 194–195
Baillien, E., 308
Baird, E., 22, 408
Bakker, A.B., 58, 153, 174, 239
balanced processing of information, 189
Bamforth, K., 173
Bandura, A., 63
Barling, J., 63
Bar-On Emotional Quotient Inventory, 98–99
Barsoux, J.-L., 58–59
Bartol, K.M., 22
basic psychological needs. *See also* need satisfaction; psychological need satisfaction
  definition of, 111–112
  healthcare practitioners and, 367
  satisfaction of, 366
  workplace violence and, 304–305
  and work-related outcomes, 16–18
Bateman, T.S., 52
Baum, J.R., 86, 95
Baumeister, R., 16
Baxter, D., 319
behavioral economics, 73–75
behavioral engagement, 42–43
behavioral leadership theory, 191–192
behavioral systems, 112
behavior modification theory, 280
behaviors
  controlling, 418
  discretionary, 38–39
  drinking, 133
  health-promoting, 266
  intentional, 265
  interfering, 122
  internalization of, 321
  motivated, 144
  self-esteem effects on, 138
  stages of change, 326–327
Bell, M.P., 151
Bell, S.T., 143
belongingness, 16. *See also* relatedness
Bénabou, R., 77, 210, 212–213
Bernstein, J.H., 18
Bhasi, M., 279
Biddle, B.J., 394
Bies, R.J., 202
Bindl, U.K., 52–53, 57, 61

binge drinking, 133
Black, A.E., 222
Blais, M.R., 236, 239
Blanchard, C., 17, 101
Bognanno, M., 206
Bolino, M.C., 56
Bolle, F., 77
Bon Jovi, John, 85
Bono, J.E., 235, 402
bonuses, 210, 212
Bourdieu, P., 395
Bowlby, J., 112–114
Bradfield, M., 304
Bradley, J.C., 279
Brière, N.M., 150, 236, 239
British Crime Survey, 296
Broaden-and-Build theory, 91
Brotheridge, C.M., 268
Brown, K.G., 220
Brown, K.W., 18
Brubaker, T.L., 278
Bruggeman, A., 60
Bu, N., 396
bullying, 297, 302, 303, 304–305. *See also* workplace violence
Burke, M., 279
Burkhardt, M.E., 156
burnout, 135, 232, 233, 235, 238–239, 268–269, 337
Busch, H., 17
businesses. *See* corporations
business students
  moral reasoning for, 387
  students' values and goals, 390–391
Buss, A.H., 298

C

Caiman Consulting, 255
Callahan, J.S., 223
Campbell, D.J., 54, 173
Campion, M.A., 168–169
can do motivation, 60, 61
Carbonneau, N., 90
Cardon, M.S., 86
Carver, C.S., 22, 408
Casper, W., 220
Cassidy, J., 114
causality
  autonomous, 183
  between commitment and motivational states, 39
  direction of, 45
  locus of, 2
causality orientations, 20, 21, 44, 304
Chakravarthy, S., 23
Chan, D., 56
Chan, K., 194
Chandler, M.M., 181
Charest, J., 92
charismatic leadership theory, 188–189
Chen, Z., 191
Chirkov, V.I., 4, 23
choice, 25–26, 27

Christian, M.S., 279
circumplex model, 388
citizenship behavior, 40
clan culture, 100
Clark, C.B., 133–134
Clark, M.S., 132
Clegg, C.W., 173
coaching, 308
cognitive crafting, 255
cognitive developmental theory, 112
cognitive dissonance, 325
cognitive evaluation theory (CET), 1–2, 5, 28, 76, 207
cognitive neoassociation theory of aggression, 299–300
cognitive processes, 90
Cohen, C.Y., 209
Cohen, S.G., 173
Collins, C.G., 55
Colquitt, J.A., 187, 219, 239–240
commitment
  behavioral implications of, 36–37
  binding nature of, 37
  components of, 34
  consequences of, 36
  definition of, 35–36
  development of, 36, 45–46
  differences across cultures, 46
  discretionary, 36
  to display rules, 264–265
  and employee well-being, 41
  mindsets of, 35
  motivation and, 37–42
  organizational, 34
  person-centered approach to, 415–416
  targets and, 34–35
commitment profile, 37, 40–41
commitment theory, general model of, 34–37
communication of information
  cognitive dissonance and, 325
  conflicting messages, 325
  environmental issues, 324–327
  message framing, 325–327
  message tailoring, 325–327
  noncontrolling, 355
Community Game, 80
compensation. *See also* rewards
  bonuses, 210, 212
  crowding-in effect, 76, 79–81
  crowding-out effect, 76–79, 210
  economic theories about, 203–206
  efficiency wage theory and, 200, 204–205
  equity theory and, 202
  expectancy theory, 201–202
  fair wage model of, 200, 205
  free-rider effect, 211
  goal-setting theory and, 203
  history of, 199–200
  as an incentive, 199, 406
  merit pay, 207
  motivational effects of, 212, 415

need satisfaction and, 301
negative effects of, 203
organizational justice theory and, 202–203
organizational psychology theories, 200–203
pay-for-performance, 72–73, 76–79, 166, 207
performance and, 206–207, 210–211
piece-rate pay, 166
self-determination theory and, 208, 419–420
skill-based pay, 211–212
tournament theory, 200, 205–206
wage dispersion, 206
workplace violence and, 303–304
compensation plans, 211
competence
definition of, 182, 366
environmental turbulence and, 253–254
leadership and, 183
need for, 2, 19
perceived, 221
rewards and, 211
vitality and, 252
well-being and, 41
in the workplace, 120–121
competence motivation, 120
competition, 25, 420
complementary fit, 146–147, 153
Conger, J.A., 188
Connell, J.P., 3, 64, 369
consensual racism, 390
consideration, 191–192, 195
constructs of interest, 130
contamination effect, 27
contingent domains, 128
contingent engagement, 43–44
contingent self-esteem
academic, 132
appearance and body concerns, 132
behavioral effects of, 138
in Chinese populations, 130
contingent domains, 128
definition of, 127–128
domain-specific, 129–130
drinking behavior, 133
internal vs. external, 131
job performance and, 137–138
measures of, 129–131
narcissism and, 133–134
negative relationship events, 133
noncontingent domains, 128
in organizations, 134–137
as overall construct, 130
perfectionism and, 133
relationships and, 132–133
research findings for, 131–134
self-determination theory and, 128–129
self- vs. other-, 131
self-worth, 129
social motivation and, 134
well-being and, 133, 138

on workplace performance, 134–137
continuance commitment, 34, 36–39
controlled, 16
controlled internalization, 97
controlled motivation
autonomous motivation vs., 408–409
definition of, 110–111, 208, 220–222, 233–234, 300, 317
self-control vs., 56
toward environment, 324
well-being and, 22, 237–238
controlled orientation, 20
controlled regulation, 56–57
controlled safety motivation, 281–282
controlling incentives, 323–324
control orientation, 111, 235–236, 301, 304
control systems theory, 112
control vs. autonomy, 4
Conyon, M.J., 206
Cooper, C.L., 302
Corbett, J.M., 173
corporations. *See also* organizations
environmental practices of, 316
environmental sustainability and, 315–316, 323–324
proenvironmental behavior, 315–316
volunteer work and, 425
corruption effect, 73
Cossette, M., 267, 271
cost-procedur es-processes-outcomes-analysis (CPPOA) technique, 338–341
CPPOA technique, 338–341
Crawford, E.R., 232
creativity, 423–424
criminal violence, 297. *See also* workplace violence
Crocker, J., 128–133
crowding-in effect, 76, 79–81
crowding-out effect, 76–79, 210
Croyle, M.H., 264–265
cues, 248–249
Cullen, J.C., 40

D
DA fit. *See* demands-abilities (DA) fit
Dammeyer, M.M., 388
Danner, F.W., 120
Dansereau, F., 190
Das, R., 23
Dawson, S., 377
Day, D.V., 190
death instinct, 298. *See also* workplace violence
DeCharms, R., 1–2, 207, 211, 357
Deci, E.L.
on autonomous motivation at workplace, 23–24, 27, 64, 170, 171, 186, 317, 366
on autonomy-supportive leaders, 222
on compensation, 200, 207, 209, 211
on competence, 60, 120
on contingent self-esteem, 128

on ego-involvement, 2
on engagement, 44
on goal theories, 401–402
on interference, 121
on internalization, 64, 184
on job stress, 239
on locus of causality, 76
on manager training, 338
on motivation, 145, 235–236
on need support, 16–17, 369
self-determination theory, 1, 208
on self-regulation, 368
on work behavior, 110–111, 172
on workplace safety, 291
decision-making discretion, 252–253
decision-making frames, 80
decision phase of behavior change, 326–327
deep acting, 262–263, 269–270
dehumanization, 303
deliberate practice, 95
demands-abilities (DA) fit, 146, 151, 155–156, 157
demotivation. *See* amotivation
depersonalization, 269
Descartes, 86
desires. *See* need strength
detection phase of behavior change, 326–327
deviant behavior, 297, 416
De Winne, S., 221
De Witte, H., 22, 234–235, 239, 308
Diefendorff, J.M., 58, 147–148, 152, 181, 224–225, 264–265
diminished sense of accomplishment, 269
direct evidence, 306
direct fit, 147
direct violence, 298. *See also* workplace violence
discomfort, 325
discretion, 252–253
discretionary behaviors, 38–39
discretionary commitment, 36
discriminant validity, 134–135
disengagement, 42, 43–44
display rules, 264–265, 267, 271
distributive justice, 80, 192, 202
DMP. *See* dualistic model of passion (DMP)
DMP (dualistic model of passion), 86–88
domain-specific contingent self-esteem, 129–130
domestic violence, 297. *See also* workplace violence
Dormann, C., 240
Doverspike, D., 143
Drasgow, F., 194
drinking behaviors, 133
drive theory, 1
dualistic model of passion (DMP), 86–88
dual valuing process model, 391–395
Duriez, B., 391
Dussault, M., 235

Dutton, J.E., 175, 246, 251
Dysvik, A., 171, 220, 238

E
economic growth, 314–315
economics. *See* behavioral economics
economic utility analysis
    applied to SDT, 338–340
    overview of, 337–338
Edwards, J.R., 147
effectance motivation, 1–2, 120
effective goal regulation, 61
efficiency wage theory, 200, 204–205
Eghrari, H., 128, 184
ego-depletion, 416
ego-development, 20
ego-involvement, 2–3
Ehrenberg, R.G., 206
Einarsen, S., 302, 304
e-learning training programs, 224. *See also*
    training and development (TAD)
Electric Monitoring and Surveillance
    Survey, 420–421
electronic monitoring, 420–421
Elliot, A.J., 144, 154
Elsbach, K., 176
Ely, K., 220
Emmons, R.A., 117
emotional abuse, 297. *See also* workplace
    violence
emotional dissonance, 260, 261, 262, 270
emotional exhaustion, 268–269
emotional intelligence, 98–99
emotional labor
    deep acting, 262, 263, 269
    definition of, 260, 261
    display rules and, 264–265
    employee well-being and, 268–269
    integrative model of, 261–262
    job performance and, 269–270
    motivation to perform, 263–271
    naturally felt emotions, 262–263
    negative, 271
    personality traits related to, 271–272
    regulating at workplace, 260–263,
        416–417
    regulation process, 261–262
    role internalization and, 263–264
    self-determination theory and, 265–267
    self-determined motivation and,
        265–269
    strategies, 262–263, 267–268
    surface acting, 262, 263, 269
emotional skills, importance of, 259–260
emotion regulation model, 261–262, 269
employee engagement, 42–45
employee well-being. *See* well-being
energy, 250–252
engagement
    behavioral, 42–43
    categories of, 43–44
    climate for, 44
    definition of, 42–43

    development of, 44–45
    evidence-based model of, 42–45
    model for, 43–45
    proactivity and, 61
    thriving and, 248
    trait, 43
environmental activism, 320
environmental effects on basic psychologi-
    cal needs, 18–21
environmental degradation, 325
environmental governance, 323–324
environmental health risks, 320–321
environmental sustainability
    in a business' mission, 328
    communication strategy, 324–327
    conflicting messages, 325
    corporations and, 315–316
    definition of, 315
    degrading products, 315
    economic growth and, 314–315
    government's approach to, 323–324
    natural, 322–323, 331
    proenvironmental behavior, 315–316
    sustainable development and, 315
environmental turbulence, 253–254
environmental volatility, 253–254
Enzle, M.E., 291
epistemic authority, 392
equity theory, 202
Erez, A., 402
Eriksson, T., 206
eros, 298
ethical leadership, 189
ethics, 386–387
Ethier, N., 128
ethology, 112
European Survey of Enterprises on New
    and Emerging Risks, 296
"The Evolving Self" model, 381–382
ex ante rewards, 210, 212–213
expectancy theory, 201–202
explanatory rationales, 355
exploration drive, 1
exploration systems, 112
ex post rewards, 212–213
external motivation, 53, 282
external regulation, 38, 110, 145, 208, 317
external rewards, 55. *See also* rewards
extrinsic aspirations, 21–22, 405–408
extrinsic goals, 144, 389–390, 407
extrinsic incentives, 77
extrinsic motivation
    compensation and, 207, 208
    definition of, 3, 16, 265, 336
    external regulation and, 145
    leadership and, 193
    management and, 26
    passion and, 88
    proenvironmental behavior, 326
    prosocial behavior and, 75
    for teachers, 350
extrinsic regulation, 51
extrinsic rewards. *See* rewards

F
fairness, 80, 419
fair-wage hypothesis, 205
fair wage model, 200, 205
Fang, Y., 170
Fay, D., 52
feedback, 169, 253
"feeling rules," 260–261
Feeney, B.C., 118–122
Fehr, E., 80
Feld, L., 79–80
Feldman, D.C., 261
felt competence, 120
felt security, 112
Fernet, C., 235, 237, 238
Ferris, D.L., 135
"fight or flight," 113
financial aspirations, 406
financial autonomy, 380–381
financial behaviors, 382
financial beliefs and values, 377–378
financial functionality, 379–383
financial innocence, 376–377
financial knowledge, 379
financial maturity, 380–381
financial mindfulness, 382
financial motivation, 375, 382–383
financial need belief constructions,
    377–379
financial self-efficacy, 378, 379–380
financial suffering, 376
financial values, 377
Fine, S., 42
fit. *See* person-environment (PE) fit
flexible role orientation, 54
flight or fight, 300
flow, 90, 153
Ford, J.K., 225
Forest, J., 80, 92, 99
Fortier, M.S., 150
Foster, S.L., 340
Fox, S., 308
Frederickson, B.L., 93
free-choice period, 2
free-rider effect, 211
Frese, M., 52, 240
Freud, S., 298, 375
Frey, B., 72, 76, 77, 79–80, 210
Frey, D., 80
Fromm, E., 405
frustration-aggression hypothesis, 299
Fuhrmann, A., 404
full engagement, 43–44
Fuller, J.B., 64
Future Work Self, 55, 64

G
Gagné, M.
    on autonomous motivation at work-
        place, 63, 170, 184, 185, 366
    on commitment, 39
    on compensation, 209
    on fairness, 80

on internalization, 64
on motivation, 145, 306
on need satisfaction, 18, 20
on psychological empowerment, 171
on training transfer, 224
Gamst, G., 285
Gardner, W.L., 189
Garnett, F., 247
Gellatly, I.R., 40
general causality orientation, 44, 109, 111, 301
General Causality Orientations Scale, 236
George, J.M., 219
Gerhart, B., 73
Gerstner, C.R., 190
Gibson, C., 247, 254
gift/counter-gift, exchange of, 205
Glasø, L., 302
Gneezy, U., 78
goal attainment, 248–249
goal autonomy, 402, 404
goal differentiation, 117
goal-directed behavioral systems, 112
goal-framing theory, 76–77
goal integration, 117
goal pursuit
autonomous goals, 402–403
extrinsic aspirations, 405–408
extrinsic goals, 407
financial aspirations, 406
implementation intentions, 401, 403–404
intrinsic aspirations, 405–408
intrinsic goals, 407
motivational role of other people, 409–411
motives behind, 408–409, 418
nature of, 401
self-determination theory perspective on, 402, 411
SMART goals, 400–401
social support, 409
in work settings, 402
goal-setting theory, 203
goal-system organization, 117–118
goal training program, 403
Goldman, B.G., 130
Gollwitzer, P.M., 326
Gomez-Mejia, L.R., 204
González, M.G., 369
Gorin, A.A., 410
Gosserand, R.H., 264
Gould, D., 211
Gouveia, L., 407
Graen, G., 190
Grandey, A.A., 261–262
Grant, A.M., 52, 55–56, 60, 62, 172–173, 225, 246
Grant, J.M., 52
Greenberg, J., 202
Green-Demers, I., 318–319
Greguras, G.J., 58, 147–148, 152, 224–225
Griffin, M.A., 278, 279, 291–292

Griffin, R.W., 302
Groessl, E.J., 337
Gross, J.J., 260–261
group cohesion, 119
group compensation, 211. *See also* compensation
Grover, S.L., 304
"growth need strength," 170
Guarino, A.J., 285
Guay, F., 150, 237
Guimond, S., 390, 393
Gunz, A., 407
Gupta, N., 77

H

Hackett, R.D., 191
Hackman, J.R., 15, 151, 169, 171, 185
Haga, W.J., 190
Hahn, V.C., 56
Halbesleben, J.R.B., 303
Hallsten, L., 135
harassment, 297
harmonious passion, 87–88, 90, 93–96, 97
Harmon-Jones, E., 325
Harrison, D., 151
Hart, P.M., 278
Hauge, L.J., 304
Hawthorne effect, 166–167
Hazan, C., 114
hazard management, 277
health and wellness, 363–364, 421
health gradient. *See also* job stress
definition of, 363
determinants of, 364–365
morbidity and mortality rates, 364
occupational status, 364
psychosocial determinants, 369–371, 416
social support at work, 365
using self-determination theory, 369–371
Whitehall studies, 364–365
health-promoting behavior, 266
Hebb, D.O., 1
hedonistic preference, 75
Hegel, 85, 86, 94
Heider, F., 211
Henrich, J., 75
Herscovitch, L., 35, 36–37, 38–39
Herzberg, F., 26, 167–168, 200, 207
Hess, U., 239
Hetland, J., 302
"hidden cost of rewards," 73
Ho, V.T., 95
Hochschild, A.R., 260–261, 268
Hodson, R., 296
Hoel, H., 302
Hofer, J., 17
Hofstede, G., 389–390
Holmas, H., 77
Holmes, J.G., 131
Holtby, A., 323–324
Homo Economicus model, 73–74
Hope, N.H., 407

horizontality-verticality distinction, 389–390
hostile aggression, 298
Houlfort, N., 89, 92, 99–100
House, R.J., 188
Houser-Marko, L., 405
Hu, J., 130
Hull, C.L., 1
Human Relations Movement, 166
Humphrey, R.H., 261, 262
Humphrey, S.E., 27, 172
Hunsley, J., 320
hygiene vs. motivators framework, 167–168

I

identification, 3
identified activity, 154
identified motivation, 265–266, 282–283, 424
identified regulation, 38, 51, 54, 110, 145, 170, 193–194, 317, 336
Ilies, R., 190
ill-being, 92, 406
image motivation, 80
impersonal orientation, 20, 111, 236, 301
implementation intentions, 401, 403–404
implementation phase of behavior change, 326–327
importance of performance to self-esteem (IPSE), 134–137
impression management tactic, 55
incentive pay, 72–73, 76, 199, 211. *See also* compensation
incentive theory, 212–213, 421–422
indebted obligation, 40
independence vs. autonomy, 4
indirect evidence, 306
indirect fit, 147
indirect violence, 298. *See also* workplace violence
individualized consideration, 195
industrialization, 314
informational influence, 392
informational language, 355
information asymmetry, 204
information sharing, 253, 422–423
initiating structure, 191–192
injuries and accidents, 277
innovation, 423–424
in-role behaviors, 54
instrumental aggression, 298
integrated motivation, 54, 283
integrated regulation, 38, 110, 145, 317
integrative model of commitment and motivation, 39–42
integrative model of emotional labor, 261–262
interactional justice, 192, 202
interference, 121–122
interfering behavior, 122
intergoal conflict, 117
internal equity, 202

INDEX | 437

internalization
   autonomous, 97
   autonomous motivation and, 152–153, 174
   of behavior, 321
   definition of, 3, 117, 265, 318, 366
   health gradient and, 369
   proactive goals through, 59, 64–65
   process of, 144, 146
internalization processes, 110
International Labor Organization, 296
interpersonal relationships, 93–94
interpersonal self, 388
interventions
   autonomy support, 357–359
   mental health, 340
   with teachers, 357–359
   workplace violence, 308–310
intrinsic aspirations, 21–22, 405–408
intrinsic goals, 388–390, 407
intrinsic motivation
   compensation and, 207
   competition and, 25
   crowding-in effect, 76, 79–81
   crowding-out effect, 76–79
   deadlines and, 421–422
   definition of, 16, 170
   fit and, 157–158
   job design and, 166
   leadership and, 193
   locus of causality and, 1–2, 3
   management and, 26
   passion and, 88
   positive feedback and, 25
   proactivity and, 53
   proenvironmental behavior, 326
   prosocial behavior and, 75
   rewards and, 24–26
   SDT and, 110
   for teachers, 350
   wages and, 81
introjected motivation, 55, 282
introjected regulation, 38, 54, 110, 208, 336
introjection, 3, 265, 317
intrusive behavior, 121–122
IPSE (importance of performance to self-esteem), 134–137

J
Jackson, C.L., 223
Jackson, P.R., 173
Jago, A.G., 27
JD-C (job demands-control) model, 234
JD-R (job demands-resources) model, 174, 234, 236–238
Jegen, R., 77
Jenkins, D.G., 77
Jensen, M.C., 204
Jimmieson, N.L., 238–239
job autonomy, 171
job characteristics model, 151, 169–173
job choice behavior, 424
job crafting, 175, 255

job demands, 232, 240–241
job demands-control (JD-C) model, 234
job demands-resources (JD-R) model, 174, 234, 236–238
job-demands resources theory, 63
job design
   autonomous motivation and, 165–166, 301
   changing work environment, 175–176
   conceptualization of, 172
   definition of, 165
   early approaches to, 166–168
   job characteristics model, 169–173
   multimethod model, 168–169
   relationship side of, 172–173
   sociotechnical systems approach to, 173–174
   telecommuting, 176
   workplace violence and, 303
Job Diagnostic Survey, 185
job enrichment, 169
job performance, 40–41, 137–138, 269–270
job-related knowledge, 155–156
Jobs, S., 85
job satisfaction, 17–18, 60, 62–63, 145, 149, 151–152, 201–202, 419
job specialization, 166
job stress
   affective, 233
   burnout and, 232, 235, 238–239 (*see also* burnout)
   chronic health conditions and, 363–364 (*see also* health gradient)
   cognitive, 233
   costs of, 231–232
   emotional dissonance and, 262
   physical, 233
   reactions to, 232–233
   resources, lack of, 232
   self-determination model of, 236–240
job stressors, 232, 239–240, 416
Johns, G., 170
Jonas, E., 80
Judge, T.A., 154, 192, 223, 235, 402, 404
justice. *See* organizational justice

K
Kahn, W.A., 42–43
Kanungo, R.N., 135, 188
Kaplan, R.M., 337
Kaplan, U., 4, 23
Karasek, R.A., 174
Kasser, T., 17, 21–22, 66, 392, 401–402, 403, 405, 407
Keashly, L., 308
Kegan, R., 381–382
Kelloway, E.K., 63, 280, 284
Kemp, N.J., 173
Kernis, M.H., 130
KEYS scale, 423
Kiback, R.R., 114
Kim, Y., 4, 23, 267
Kinder, G., 374

Kinder's model of money maturity (KMMM), 374, 379–383
Kinder's seven-stage model of money maturity, 377
Kitayama, S., 23
knowledge sharing, 422–423
Koestner, R., 2, 25, 63, 154, 184, 326, 392, 403, 407, 410
Kraiger, K., 225
Krieger, L.S., 393–394, 396, 406
Kristof-Brown, A.M., 147, 151, 154
Kruglanski, A.W., 392
Kuhl, J., 404
Kulik, C.T., 5, 28
Kuvaas, B., 220, 238

L
Lachance, L., 236
Laissez-faire leadership, 186, 302
Lam, C.F., 86
Larsson, S., 278
Latham, G., 203
Lavergne, K.J., 323–324, 325
Lavigne, G.L., 90, 92
Law, K.S., 191
Lawler, E.E., 26, 171, 201, 207–208
lawyers and law students
   ethical standards for, 386
   moral reasoning for, 387
   social dominance orientation and, 393
   students' values and goals, 390–391
Lazear, E.P., 73, 205–206
leader-member exchange (LMX), 119–120, 149–150, 190–191
leadership. *See also* management/manager
   amotivation and, 194
   authentic, 189–190
   autonomous motivation and, 115–116, 184
   behavioral leadership theory, 191–192, 417
   behaviors, 182–186, 193
   charismatic leadership theory, 188–189
   definition of, 181
   effective, 119
   employee influence, 187
   empowering, 235
   ethical, 189
   Laissez-faire, 186, 302
   leader-member exchange (LMX), 119–120, 149–150, 190–191
   motivation to lead, 192–194, 417
   need for power, 14
   need satisfaction and, 182–186
   participative, 27
   passive, 302
   for proenvironmental initiatives, 330
   role of, 181
   safety training and, 280
   styles, 99–100, 187, 235
   transactional, 99–100, 186
   transformational, 28, 45–46, 99–100, 145, 186–188, 235
   tyrannical, 302
   workplace violence and, 302–303

438 | INDEX

lean production practices, 168–169
Learmonth, M., 394
learning
    definition of, 246–247
    patience and, 355–356
    self-paced, 355–356
    vitality and, 250
learning pressure, 225, 353
Leary, M.R., 16
Ledford, G.E., 173
Lee, R.T., 268
Léger Marketing, 386
leisure, 91
Lekes, N., 392, 407–408
Lemay, E.P., Jr., 132
Lens, W., 22, 234–235
Leone, D.
    on contingent self-esteem, 128
    on internalization, 184
Lépine, M.-C., 267
Levesque, C., 368
Lévesque, M., 239
life goals, 21–22
Likert, R., 167
Lindenberg, S., 76
Liu, D., 94–95
Liu, Y., 130
Lloyd, P.J., 340
LMX (leader-member exchange), 119–120,
    149–150, 190–191
Locke, E.A., 22, 38, 95, 203, 402
locus of causality, 2, 25–26, 76. *See also*
    causality
Lonky, E., 120
Lopez, S.H., 296
Lorenz, K., 298
Losier, G.F., 154
Luhtanen, R.K., 128, 129, 130, 131, 133

M

Macey, W.H., 42
Machiavellianism, 387
Madoff, B., 376–377
Maier, G.W., 80
Maierhofer, N.I., 291–292
Maltin, E.R., 41
management-by-exception, 186
management/manager. *See also* leadership;
    organizations
    abusive supervisor, 150, 302
    authentic leadership, 189–190
    autonomy, 184, 185–186
    charismatic leadership theory, 188–189
    environmental practices of, 316
    job stressors and, 239–240
    motivation and, 26, 194–195, 418
    pay-for-performance and, 72–73
    person-supervisor (PS) fit, 147, 149–150
    for proenvironmental initiatives, 330–331
    self-determination theory and, 5
    styles, 167, 184
    supervisor behavior, 64, 150, 328–330
    supervisor/supervisee relationship, 317

Theory Y approach to, 15
transformational leadership theory,
    186–188
workplace safety, 291–292
Manzoni, J.-F., 58–59
Marescaux, E., 221
Marinova, S.V., 55
market culture, 100
Markus, H.R., 23
Marmot, M., 364
Marsh, H.W., 89
Martin, J.E., 279
Martin, R., 173
Maslow's needs hierarchy theory, 14–16,
    167–168, 381
Mason, C., 278
Masson, R.C., 42
Masterson, S.S., 149
Mauss, M., 205
McClelland, D.C., 14, 168
McGregor, D., 15, 26, 167
McKeen, C.A., 396
McLaughlin, K., 206
McNeel, S.P., 387
Meckling, W.H., 204
mediating processes, 170–171
Ménard, S., 318–319
mental health
    CPPOA technique for, 339
    definition of, 336–337
    in legal profession, 386–388
    organization expenditures related to,
        339–340
    volunteering and, 426
    well-being and, 387–388
    workplace consequences of, 335
mentoring, 308
merit pay, 207
Mesmer-Magnus, J., 222
message framing, 325–327
message tailoring, 325–327
Meyer, J.P., 34, 35–39, 41, 43–45
Meyers, L.S., 285
Mikulincer, M., 114, 117–118
Miller, J.G., 23
Millette, V., 63
Mims, V., 25
mindfulness, 255
Mitra, A., 77
Mittroff, I.I., 393
Moag, J.S., 202
mobbing, 297. *See also* workplace violence
monetary rewards, 25, 203. *See also* rewards
money and material possessions
    dysfunctional relationship to, 375
    financial beliefs and values, 378
    financial incentives and motivation,
        375–376
    functional relationship to, 376–381, 415
    Kinder's seven-stage model of money
        maturity, 377
    precompetence model, 376–377
moral imperative, 40

moral perspective, 189
moral reasoning, 387, 390
morbidity and mortality rates, 364
Morgeson, F.P., 169, 172
Morris, J.A., 261
Morrison, E.W., 155
motivated behavior, 144
motivation. *See also* amotivation
    autonomous forms of (*see* autonomous
        motivation)
    behavioral consequences of, 38–39
    can do, 60, 61
    categories of, 233–234
    classic theory of, 167
    commitment and, 37–42
    with compensation (*see* compensation)
    controlled, 22, 56
    definition of, 37
    effectance, 1
    ego-based, 2–3
    emotional labor strategies and,
        267–268, 270–272
    employee, 19–20
    equity theory and, 202
    expectancy theory and, 201–202
    extrinsic, 3, 265–266
    financial, 375
    forms of, 53, 145
    goal-setting theory and, 203
    hygiene vs. motivators framework, 167–168
    identified, 265–266
    image, 80
    inner resources, 354
    intrinsic, 1–2
    job characteristics model, 169–173
    job satisfaction and, 201–202
    justice perceptions and, 209
    to lead, 192–194
    management and (*see* leadership;
        management/manager)
    as mediating mechanism, 172
    nature of, 38
    need satisfaction and, 19–20
    organizational justice theory and,
        202–203
    in organizations, 5
    proenvironmental behavior and, 318–319
    profiles of, 41–42
    psychological needs of (*see* psychologi-
        cal needs)
    reason to, 61, 62
    to regulate emotions, 265–267
    self-determined, 265–269
    social networks and, 158
    task performance, 38–39
    teacher (*see* teacher/teaching)
    through incentives, 200–207
    time on, effects of, 421–422
    types of, 233–234
    to volunteer, 425–426
    workplace violence and, 305–306
motivational orientation, 235
Motivational Potential Score, 63

INDEX | **439**

motives. *See* motivation; need strength

Mullen, J., 280, 284

Multifactor Leadership Questionnaire, 100

Muraven, M., 56

N

Nadler, D.A., 201

narcissism, 133–134

natural environment, 322–323, 331

naturally felt emotions, 262–263

Neal, A., 278, 279

need satisfaction. *See also* psychological needs
  by authentic leaders, 190
  in banking, 21
  of behavioral leaders, 192
  of charismatic leaders, 189
  compensation and, 301
  concept of, 148
  effective performance and, 17
  employees' motivation and, 19–20, 154–155
  engagement and, 45–46
  intrinsic, 144, 182
  job characteristics model and, 170
  job demands and, 240–241
  by leader-member exchange (LMX), 191
  as mediating mechanism, 234–235
  in a not-for-profit organization, 20
  passion and, 92
  for physical and psychological health, 367–368
  proactive motivation and, 62
  psychological health and, 144
  regression analysis and, 17
  social networks effects on, 156–157
  team members and, 422
  training and development relationship with, 221
  transformational leadership and, 188
  volunteer work and, 425
  well-being and, 154–155
  when not working, 18
  workload and, 63
  in the workplace, 22, 92

needs-supplies (NS) fit, 146, 151

need strength, 14

need substitutes, 15

negative relationship events, 133

Neighbors, C., 133

network diversity argument, 155

Neuman, J.H., 308

Newnam, S., 278

Ng, J.Y.Y., 367

Niemiec, C.P., 16–17, 22

Nisbet, E.K., 322

Nix, G., 291

Noe, R.A., 219

noncontingent domains, 128

noncontingent punishment, 302

nonpassionate workers, 101

nonwork activities, 91, 94

normative commitment, 34, 36–40

normative influence, 392

North Carolina Bar Association, 387–388

NS (needs-supplies) fit, 146, 151

Nunez, N., 388

O

objective fit, 147

obsessive passion, 86–87, 88, 90, 93–96, 97

occupational safety, 289–290, 415

occupational violence, 297. *See also* workplace violence

Ohio Leadership Studies, 191

Oldham, G.R., 151, 169, 171, 185

Önder, Ç., 46

One World model of financial functionality, 381, 382

opportunism, 204

organismic integration theory, 2–3, 366

organismic valuing process (OVP), 391–392, 395

organizational commitment, 145

organizational culture, 99–100

organizational engagement, 43

organizational fairness perceptions, 80

organizational identity, 176

organizational justice, 192, 202–203, 209, 419–420

organizational leadership. *See* leadership

organizational psychology theories, 200–203

organization-based self-esteem, 134

organizations. *See also* corporations; leadership; management/manager
  agency theory, 200, 203–204
  autonomous motivation and, 152–153
  autonomy in, 64
  commitment in, 34
  contingencies in, 138–139
  contingent self-esteem in, 134–137
  culture in, 255
  emotional skills in, importance of, 259–260
  information sharing and, 253, 422–423
  interventions, 340
  learning pressure, 225
  mental health expenditures for, 339–340
  motivation in (*see* motivation)
  need satisfaction in, 20
  proactivity and, 59
  proenvironmental behavior in employees, 327–330
  surveillance mechanisms, 211, 420–421
  sustained proactivity in, 62–65
  teams and, 422
  three-component model (TCM), 34
  training and development (*see* training and development (TAD))
  vitality in, 251

orientations, causality, 20

Orion Associates, 255

Osterloh, M., 210

the Other, 131

Otto, P., 77

outcome simulations, 57

overjustification effect, 73

OVP (organismic valuing process), 391–392, 395

P

Palmer, D.L., 390, 393

Paquet, Y., 92

paradigm of motivation through incentives, 200–207

Park, L.E., 128–129, 132–133

Park, N., 99

Parker, S.K., 52–55, 61, 63–64, 169, 172–173, 175

Parker, S.L., 238–239

participation, 79–80

passion
  activity selection, 96–97
  cognitive processes and, 90
  concept of, 86
  definition of, 86
  determinants of, 96–101
  development of, 96–98
  dualistic model of, 86–88
  emotional intelligence, 98–99
  extrinsic motivation and, 88
  flow and, 90
  harmonious, 87–88, 90
  interpersonal relationships and, 93–94
  intrinsic motivation and, 88
  nonpassionate workers, 101
  obsessive, 86–87, 88, 90
  performance and, 94–96
  personal factors, 98–99
  psychology of, 86–88
  research on concept of, 88–89
  social factors, 99–101
  transference of, 101
  well-being and, 90–93
  in the workplace, 89, 96

Passion Scale, 88–89

passive leadership, 302

passive violence, 298. *See also* workplace violence

Patall, E.A., 27

patience, 355–356

Patrick, B.C., 128, 184

pay-for-performance, 72–73, 76–79, 166, 207

PEB (proenvironmental behavior)
  autonomous motivation for, 329–330
  definition of, 315–316
  employees' motivation for, 329–331
  future directions for, 330–331
  health risks perception, 320–321
  management initiatives, 330
  motivation, 318–319
  participating in, 318–319
  self-determination theory and, 316–321
  self-determined motivation, 321–322
  in the workplace, 319

Peck, S.I., 206

peer support, 303

PE fit. *See* person-environment (PE) fit

Pelletier, L.G., 150, 318–319, 320, 323–327, 393
Peper, B., 239
perceived competence, 221
perfectionism, 133
performance contingent pay, 166, 202, 203, 209
performance contingent rewards, 25, 56, 78, 210, 415
performance contingent self-esteem, 137–138
performance goal orientation, 55
performance monitoring, 420–421
performance-related payment, 72–73
permissiveness, 357
personal causation, 357
personal growth, 246, 247–248
personal initiative, 52, 55–56
person-environment (PE) fit
    autonomous-controlled motivation and, 152–155
    concept of needs, 148
    definition of, 146
    measuring, 147
    psychological need satisfaction and, 148–152
    research on concept of, 143–144
    self-concordance model and, 154–155
    social networks and, 155–157
    types of, 146–148
person-group (PG) fit, 147, 151, 156–157
person-job (PJ) fit, 147, 151–153
person-organization (PO) fit, 146–149
person-supervisor (PS) fit, 147, 149–150
Pertulla, K., 86
Peterson, C., 99
Peterson, S.J., 189
PG (person-group) fit, 147, 151, 156–157
Philippe, F., 91, 92, 93–94, 407
physical environment, 322–323
Piccolo, R.F., 187, 239–240
Pickard, J.D., 133–134
piece-rate pay, 73, 166
PJ (person-job) fit, 147, 151–153
PO (person-organization) fit, 146
Ponzi scheme, 376–377
Porath, C., 247, 254
Porter, L.W., 201, 207–208
positive activated states, 61
positive psychology theory, 416
Pouliakas, K., 78
Pousette, A., 278
Powers, T., 410
Pratto, F., 394
Price, K.H., 151
price-effect, 72–73
primary socialization, 395
principal-agent relationship, 204
proactive behavior, 58
proactive goal regulation, 52–53, 57, 60
proactive personality, 52
proactive work behavior, 52
proactivity
    autonomously motivated, 58–59, 61, 66
    autonomously regulated, 61–62, 65–66

definition of, 50
motivation toward, 53–55
for the organization, 59
outcomes of, 50–51
reflection and, 57
regulation for, 55–62
rewarding behavior, 65
self-determination theory and, 53–55
sustained, 59–61
work behavior, 175
in the workplace, 51–53, 417
Problems at Work Scale, 184–186
Probst, T.M., 278
procedural fairness, 80
procedural justice, 192, 202, 209, 225, 420
process simulations, 57
proenvironmental behavior (PEB)
    autonomous motivation for, 329–330
    definition of, 315–316
    employees' motivation for, 329–331
    future directions for, 330–331
    health risks perception, 320–321
    management initiatives, 330
    motivation, 318–319
    participating in, 318–319
    self-determination theory and, 316–321
    self-determined motivation, 321–322
    in the workplace, 319
prosocial behavior, 75
prosocial motivation, 222
prosocial preference, 75
Przybylski, A.K., 322
PS (person-supervisor) fit, 147, 149–150
psychological control, 301
psychological energy, 416–417
psychological engagement theory, 219
psychological health, 367–368. See also mental health
psychological needs. See also need satisfaction
    Alderfer's theory, 15
    concept of, 414–415
    environmental effects on, 18–21
    higher-order, 15
    lower-order, 15
    in a manufacturing setting, 17
    Maslow's theory, 14–16
    mediating role of, 389
    need strength, 14
    people's life goals and, 21–22
    satisfaction of, 234–235
    satisfaction vs. thwarting of, 16
    social environment and, 18–21
    types of, 4
    as universal necessities, 22–24
    in the workplace, 17–18
psychological need satisfaction. See also need satisfaction
    autonomously motivated proactivity and, 58–59
    concept of, 415
    linking PJ fit to, 151–152
    mediating role of, 152

proactivity for the organization and, 59
sustained proactivity and, 59–61
teachers and, 351–352
psychological problems. See mental health
psychological well-being. See well-being
psychosocial determinants of health, 364–365, 369–371
public goods game, 80

Q

Quinn, R., 251

R

Ratelle, C.F., 42
rationale, definition of, 354–355
Raub, S., 54
reason to motivation, 61, 62
reciprocity, 75, 222
Reedy, P., 394
Reeson, A.F., 80
Reeve, J., 223, 224, 356
reflection, 57
regression analysis, 17
regulatory focus theory, 38
Reid, G., 120
reinforcement, 255
relatedness
    definition of, 4, 182, 366, 401
    leadership and, 183
    proactivity and, 60
    thriving and, 252
    universal need for, 15–16, 19, 22–23, 144
    well-being and, 41
    in the workplace, 118–120
relational crafting, 255
relational transparency, 189
relationships
    building, 249–250
    contingent self-esteem and, 132–133
    interpersonal, 93–94
    negative events, 133
    passion and, 93–94
    quality of, 93–94
Renn, R.W., 170
Rentsch, J.R., 156
response-focused strategies, 261
rewards. See also compensation
    contamination effect, 27
    contingent, 186–187
    effects of, 208–209
    enjoyment and, 2
    ex ante, 210, 212–213
    expectations vs., 351
    external, 42
    extrinsic, 42
    hidden cost of, 73
    intrinsic motivation and, 24–26
    monetary, 25, 203
    negative effect of, 77–78
    punishment and, 185
    self-determination theory and, 26–27
    tangible, 24–26, 208
    workplace violence and, 303–304

INDEX | 441

Rich, B.L., 223
Richer, S.F., 17
Richins, M.L., 377
Riddle, A.S., 236
"River of Hope" project, 255
Robert, C., 54
Roca, J.C., 18, 224
Rockenbach, B., 80
Rogers, C., 246, 391–392, 405
Rohan, M.J., 386–387
role internalization, 263–264
role occupancy, 193
Roscigno, V.J., 296
Rosen, S., 205–206
Rousseau, F.L., 91–92
Royal, M.A., 42
Rubin, R.S., 262, 263–264
Rustichini, A., 78
Ryan, R.M.
   on autonomy, 4, 23, 64, 171, 317
   on compensation, 200
   on competence, 60, 120
   on contingent self-esteem, 128
   on engagement, 44
   on goal theories, 401–402, 405
   on intrinsic motivation, 2, 3
   on life goals, 21–22
   on motivation, 235–236
   on natural environments, 322
   on need satisfaction, 16–18
   on need support, 369
   reward study, 25
   self-determination theory, 1, 208
   on work behavior, 110–111, 172
Ryff, C.D., 246–247
Rynes, S.L., 73

S
Sadler, G., 206
safe haven, 112–113
safety, workplace
   autonomous motivation for, 282–283
   behavior-based, 280
   behaviors, 286
   climate for, 291–292
   compliance behaviors, 279–280
   controlled motivation, 281–282
   external motivation, 282
   hazard management, 277
   identified motivation, 282–283
   improvements in, 276–277
   integrated motivation, 283
   intrinsic motivation, 282–283
   introjected motivation, 282
   leadership training, 280
   model for workplace, 279
   motivation for, 277–280, 281–283,
      290–291, 415
   occupational, 289–290
Saks, A.M., 42
Salin, D., 303
Schabram, K., 306
Schaufeli, W.B., 42–43, 174

Schiltz, P.J., 388
Schneider, B., 42, 149, 394
Schwartz, Shalom, 388
Scott, B.A., 223
Sears, L.E., 279
secondary attachment strategies, 114
secure attachment, 112–113
secure base, 109, 112–113
secure home base, 113–118, 123
secure work base, 118–122, 123
Séguin, C., 320
the Self, 57–58, 100, 131, 392
self-actualization, 248
self-awareness, 189
self-concept theory, 188
self-concordance model, 57, 145, 154–155
self-control, 56, 251–252
self-determination theory (SDT)
   career and job choice behavior, 424
   compensation and, 208, 419–420
   concept of, 110–112
   contingent self-esteem and, 128–129
   contributions made by, 26–27
   definition of, 14, 16, 182
   dominant paradigm and, 207–213
   economic utility analysis and, 338–340
   emotional labor and, 265–267
   employee safety motivation and, 281–
      283 (see also Self-Determined Safety
      Motivation scale (SDSM))
   engagement and, 44–45
   environmental health risks and, 320
   environmental variables, 301
   to financial beliefs and values, 377–378
   history of, 1–5
   information technology usage, 422
   innovation, 423–424
   intentional behavior and, 265
   internalization and, 146
   job stress, 233, 236–240
   leadership and, 184, 193
   management applications of, 5
   manager autonomy support, 183–186
   on managing employees, 417–419
   Maslow's theory and, 15–16
   motivated action and, 144–145
   need satisfaction and, 144
   optimal human functioning and, 269
   overview of, 280–281, 300–301, 336–337,
      366–367, 401–402
   performance monitoring, 420–421
   proactivity and, 53–55
   proenvironmental behavior and, 316–321
   psychological energy and, 416–417
   psychological need satisfaction and,
      58–59, 414–415
   psychosocial determinants of health, 371
   rewards and, 26–27
   somatization, 368–369
   team work and, 422
   thriving and, 250–252
   training and development, 219–220
   volunteer work and, 424–426

in the work domain, 5, 415–416
   workplace violence and, 301–306,
      308–310
self-determined motivation. See also
   motivation
   emotional labor as mechanism to,
      268–269
   emotional labor strategies and, 267–268
   employee turnover and, 270–271
   for proenvironmental behavior, 321–322
   to regulate emotions, 265–267
Self-Determined Safety Motivation scale
   (SDSM)
   development of, 283–284
   fit statistics for, 285–286
   measures of, 284–285
   participative, 284
   results of, 285–289
   safety behaviors, predicting, 286, 288
   scale reliabilities, 288
   statistical analysis approach to, 285
   testing of, 284–285
self-efficacy, 60, 223, 232, 237, 379–380,
   424
self-efficacy theory, 23
self-esteem, 15, 20, 58, 87, 134–137, 232,
   238. See also contingent self-esteem
self-less behavior, 75
self-motivated management style, 167
self-paced learning, 355–356
self-regulation, autonomous, 61, 176, 182,
   186, 189, 247–250, 299, 367–370, 415
self-regulation theory, 52–53, 250
self-regulatory failure, 401
self-regulatory goal process, 56–57,
   248–249
self-reliance, 129
self-selection effect, 394
self-transcendence, 388
self-worth, 129, 135, 238
Seligman, M.E.P., 99
Sels, L., 221
Senécal, C.B., 63, 237, 393
sexual harrassment, 296
Shamir, B., 188
Shanine, K., 303
Share, T., 403
Sharp, E.C., 318–319, 323–327
Shaver. P.R., 114, 117–118
Shaw, J.C., 223
Shaw, J.D., 77
Sheehan, M., 291–292
Sheldon, K.M., 66, 144–145, 154, 393–394,
   396, 401–403, 405–407
Sidanius, J., 394
similarity-attraction hypothesis, 151
simmelian ties, 156–157
Simons, J., 391
simulations, 57
Sinclair, R.R., 40, 279
Sitzmann, T., 220
skill-based pay, 211–212
skill variety, 169

442 INDEX

Skogstad, A., 304
Sliwka, D., 81
SMART goals, 400–401
Smith, A., 375
Smith, K., 403
Smulders, P., 239
social acceptance, 87
social dominance orientation, 390, 393
social environment, basic psychological
  needs and, 18–21
social identities, 129
socialization, 3, 240, 395
socialization theories, 393
social learning theory, 190, 223, 299
socially embedded, 247
social motivation, 134
social networks
  and DA fit, 155–156
  effects on need satisfaction, 156–157
  and PE fit formation, 155, 157
  and PG fit, 156
sociocognitive valuing process (SVP),
  392–393, 395
Soenens, B., 234, 391
Solow, R., 204–205
somatization, 368–369
Somers, M.J., 41
Sommers, S.R., 131
Sonenshein, S., 246
Southwest Airlines, 255
Spector, P.E., 209
Spreitzer, G.M., 173, 246–247, 254
Srivastava, A., 22
Stallworth, L., 308
Stamper, C.L., 149
standard economic theory, 73–74
Steen, t.A., 99
Steg, L., 76
Stogdill, R.M., 191
Stone, D., 377, 379
Strahan, E.J., 128
Streicher, B., 80
stress. *See* job stress
stress regulation, 113
strong reciprocity, 75
structural equation modeling, 20
student autonomy, 353
Su, Y.-L., 224, 356
subordinates, feelings and perspectives of, 27
supervisors. *See* management/manager
supplementary fit, 146–147, 153–155
surface acting, 262, 263, 269–270
surveillance mechanisms, 211, 420–421
sustainable development, 315
sustained enacting, 57
sustained proactivity
  jobs that facilitate, 62–63
  in organizations, 62–65
  psychological need satisfaction and,
    59–61
Sutcliffe, K., 246
Sutton, R.I., 266
Suvurov, A., 212

SVP (sociocognitive valuing process),
  392–393, 395

T

TAD. *See* training and development
  (TAD)
tangible rewards, 24–26, 208. *See also*
  rewards
task clusters, 168–169
task crafting, 255
task identity, 169, 171
task performance, 254
task significance, 169, 172–173
tax morale, 80
Taylorism, 166
teacher/teaching
  attrition and, 351
  autonomy support, 352–359, 418–419
  autonomy-supportive, 357
  controlling style, 352–353
  expectations vs. rewards, 351
  intervention programs, 357–359
  intrinsic vs. extrinsic goals, 350
  motivating style toward students, 352–353
  patience and, 355–356
  psychological need satisfaction, 351–352
  student autonomy and, 353
  support vs. pressure, 352
  teaching efficacy, 350–351
  training, 356
teams, motivation within, 422
Teed, M., 284
telecommuting, 176
Ten Brummelhuis, L.L., 239
Ter Hoeven, C.L., 239
thanatos, 298
Thayer, P.W., 168–169
Theory X management style, 167
Theory Y management style, 15, 167
Thomas, J.P., 52
Thomas, K.W., 63
three-component model (TCM)
  engagement and, 44–45
  formulation of, 33–34
  of organizational commitment, 34
thriving
  benefits of, 254
  definition of, 246–247
  engagement and, 248
  as gauge to progress toward goals,
    248–249
  information sharing and, 253
  job crafting and, 255
  learning dimension of, 246–247, 248
  markers of, 246–247
  in nonwork activities, 254
  performance and, 249
  related growth constructs vs., 247–248
  relatedness and, 252
  relationships and, 249–250
  self-actualization and, 248
  trust and respect, 253
  vitality and, 246–247

well-being and, 250
  at workplace, 250–252, 416
Thrush, R.L., 118, 119, 120, 121–122
Tirole, J., 77, 210, 212–213
Tisdell, J.G., 80
Tolstoy, L., 383
Torgler, B., 79–80
Torner, M., 278
tournament theory, 200, 205–206, 420
training and development (TAD)
  autonomous vs. controlled motivation
    and, 221–223
  autonomy support in, 226
  autonomy-supportive leaders and
    trainers, 222–223
  and basic need satisfaction, 221
  content and delivery forms, 224–225,
    226
  definition of, 218
  employee perception of, 220–221
  learning pressure, 225
  manager, 338–340
  outcomes of, 224–225
  psychological engagement theory, 219
  self-determination theory and, 219–220,
    415–416
  skill-based, 356
  teacher, 356
  trainee's reactions to, 220–221
  from training to learning, 219
  training transfer, 224
  work performance and, 219
training transfer, 224
trait engagement, 43
transactional leadership, 99–100, 186
Transaction Cost Analysis and Agency
  Theory, 393
transformational leadership, 99–100,
  186–190, 192–194, 225, 235
transparency, relational, 189
Tremblay, E., 209
Trépanier, S.G., 235, 238
Triandis, H.C., 389–390
Trist, E., 173
Trump, D., 85
trust, 418–419
Tschannen-Moran, M., 351
Tucker, J.S., 40
turnover, 17–18, 34, 40, 151, 232, 270–271
two-dimensional structures, 388
two-factor theory, 207
Two World model of financial
  functionality, 381
tyrannical leadership, 302

U

United Nations Population Fund, 314–315
universalism, 390
unmotivated management style, 167
U.S. Equal Employment Opportunity
  Commission, 296
U.S. Occupational Safety and Health
  Administration, 296

INDEX | 443

V

Vaananen, A., 368–369
valence-instrumentality-expectancy
  theory, 201
Vallerand, R.J., 17, 86, 88–91, 94, 98–101,
  120, 150, 236–237, 393
value, definition of, 386–387
value congruence, 146, 153–154
Vandenberg, R.J., 170
Van den Broeck, A., 22, 174, 234–235, 239
Van de Ven, J., 212
Van Fleet, D.D., 302
Van Ruysseveldt, J., 239
Vansteenkiste, M., 22, 234–235, 252, 326,
  389, 391
Velthouse, B.A., 63
victimization, 296
Villadio, A.J., 143
Vinodkumar, M.N., 279
Viswesvaran, C., 52, 222
vitality, 61, 246–247, 250–252, 416
volitional dependence, 23
volunteer work, 424–426
Vroom, V.H., 27, 201

W

wage dispersion, 206
wage individualization, 206
wages, 72–73, 81
Wall, T.D., 173
Wallace, J.C., 279
Wall-Street-Game, 80
Walumbwa, F.O., 189
Wang, D., 130, 191
Wang, H., 191
Wasti, S.A., 40, 41, 46
Waugh, C.E., 93
The Wealth of Nations (Smith), 375
Weibel, A., 210
Weinberg, R., 211
Weinstein, N., 322
well-being
  autonomy and, 23–24
  commitment and, 41
  dimensions of, 247–248
  emotional labor and, 268–269
  intrinsic goals and, 406
  mental health and, 387–388
  motivation and, 145, 237
  passion and, 90–93, 95–96
  predictors of, 22
  self-esteem and, 133, 138
  student autonomy and, 353
  sustained thriving and, 250
Wernsing, T.S., 189
Wheeler, A.R., 303
White, R.W., 1–2, 19, 120
Whitehall studies, 364–365
Whitman, D.S., 52
Wild, T.C., 291

Williams, G.C., 368
Wilson, A.E., 128
Wisman, R.M., 204
Wood, J.V., 131
work adjustment theory, 149
Work Climate Survey, 184, 185
work compensation. *See* compensation
work domain, 5. *See also* workplace
work engagement, 61
working models, 113–114
work involvement scale, 135
work motivation. *See* motivation
work performance, 21
workplace
  autonomous motivation at, 63
  autonomous work groups, 173–174
  autonomy support in, 121–122
  behavior, 110
  burnout, 135, 232, 233, 235, 238–239,
    268–269, 337
  changing environment in, 175–176
  compensation (*see* compensation)
  competence support in, 120–121
  contingent self-esteem in, 134
  creativity, 423
  depersonalized work design, 176
  emotional labor at, 260–263, 416–417
  goal pursuit in, 402
  group cohesion, 119
  incentive pay, 72–73
  injuries and accidents, 277
  innovation, 423–424
  job design (*see* job design)
  job-related knowledge, 155–156
  job satisfaction, 17–18, 60, 62–63, 145,
    149
  job stressors, 232
  management (*see* management/
    manager)
  mental health consequences at, 335
  motivation at (*see* motivation)
  natural environment and, 322–323, 331
  nonterritorial, 176
  organizational culture, 99–100
  organizational identity, 176
  participation at, 79–80
  passion in, 89, 96
  proactivity in, 51–53, 417
  proenvironmental behavior in, 319
  psychological needs in, 17–18
  relatedness support in, 118–120
  rewards, 27
  safety (*see* safety, workplace)
  self-determination theory in, 415–416
  somatization, 368–369
  stress, 363–364, 365 (*see also* health
    gradient)
  supervisors (*see* management/manager)
  teams, motivation within, 422
  telecommuting, 176

thriving at, 250–253
training (*see* training and development
  (TAD))
turnover, 17–18, 34, 40, 151, 232,
  270–271
violence in (*see* workplace violence)
Work Climate Survey, 184–186
workplace adjustment, 14, 17–18, 21, 27
workplace-contingent self-esteem, 134
workplace environment, 303–304
workplace incivility, 297
workplace violence
  aggression and, 297–300
  basic psychological needs and, 304–305
  bullying, 297, 302, 303, 304–305
  causality orientation and, 304
  cost of, 295–296
  definition of, 296–298
  dehumanization, 303
  deviant behavior and, 297
  effect of, 305
  environment and, 303–305
  forms of, 297
  from a humanistic perspective, 300
  interventions to prevent, 308–310
  leadership and, 302–303
  models of, 297–298
  motivation and, 305–306
  motivation type and, 305
  prevalence of, 296
  prevention of, 308–310
  self-determination theory and, 301–306,
    416
  sexual harassment and, 296
  study of, 307–308
  taxonomy of, 298
  theories regarding, 298–299
  typology of, 298
work readiness, 17
World Health Organization, 337–338
world population, 314–315
Wright, C., 40
Wright, S., 368
Wrzeniewski, A., 175

X

Xie, L., 170

Y

Yang, Y., 130
Yellen, J., 205
Yellon, J., 200

Z

Zapf, D., 240
Zeigler-Hill, V., 133–134
Zeldman, A., 368
Zelenski, J.M., 322
Zimmerman, R.D., 220
Zuckerman, M., 184

Printed in Great Britain
by Amazon